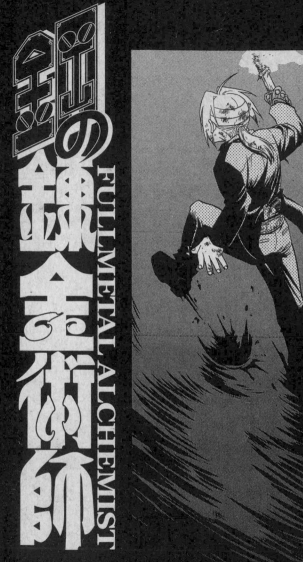

鋼の錬金術師

FULLMETAL ALCHEMIST

HIROMU ARAKAWA

荒川弘

13

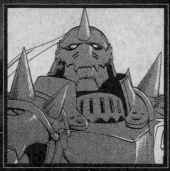

■ アルフォンス・エルリック

Alphonse Elric

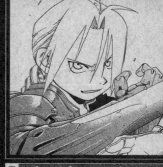

■ エドワード・エルリック

Edward Elric

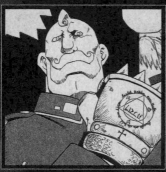

■ アレックス・ルイ・アームストロング

Alex Louis Armstrong

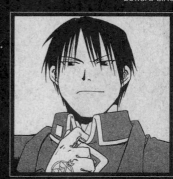

■ ロイ・マスタング

Roy Mustang

OUTLINE
FULLMETAL ALCHEMIST

Using a forbidden alchemical ritual, the Elric Brothers attempted to bring their dead mother back to life. But the ritual went wrong, consuming Edward Elric's leg and Alphonse Elric's entire body. At the cost of his arm, Edward was able to graft his brother's soul into a suit of armor. Equipped with mechanical "auto-mail" to replace his missing limbs, Edward becomes a state alchemist, serving the military on deadly missions. Now, the two brothers roam the world in search of the Philosopher's Stone, the legendary substance with the power to restore what they have lost…

The Elric brothers have redoubled their efforts, and together with Prince Lin of Xing and some help from Roy Mustang, they capture a live homunculus-- Gluttony. But not even the bonds of an alchemist can hold Gluttony when he recognizes the one who killed his best friend Lust. Gluttony escapes, revealing his true monstrous form, just as Envy arrives to provide support. Meanwhile, Roy Mustang races towards his own destiny, returning to Central City military command with a scandalous secret about the Führer-President himself!

鋼の錬金術師
FULLMETAL ALCHEMIST

CHARACTERS
FULLMETAL ALCHEMIST

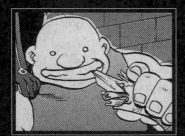

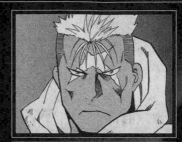

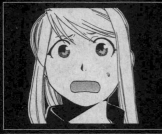

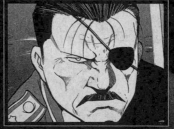

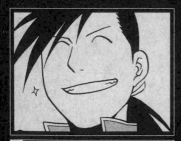

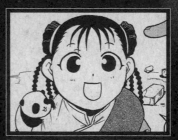

■ ウィンリィ・ロックベル

Winry Rockbell

■ スカー

Scar

■ グラトニー

Gluttony

■ キング・ブラッドレイ

King Bradley

■ リン・ヤオ

Lin Yao

■ メイ・チャン

May Chang

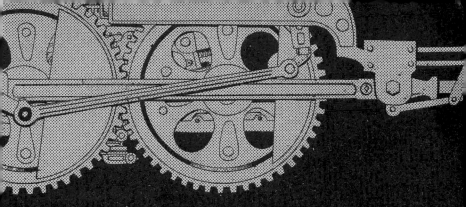

CONTENTS

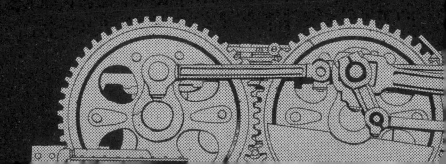

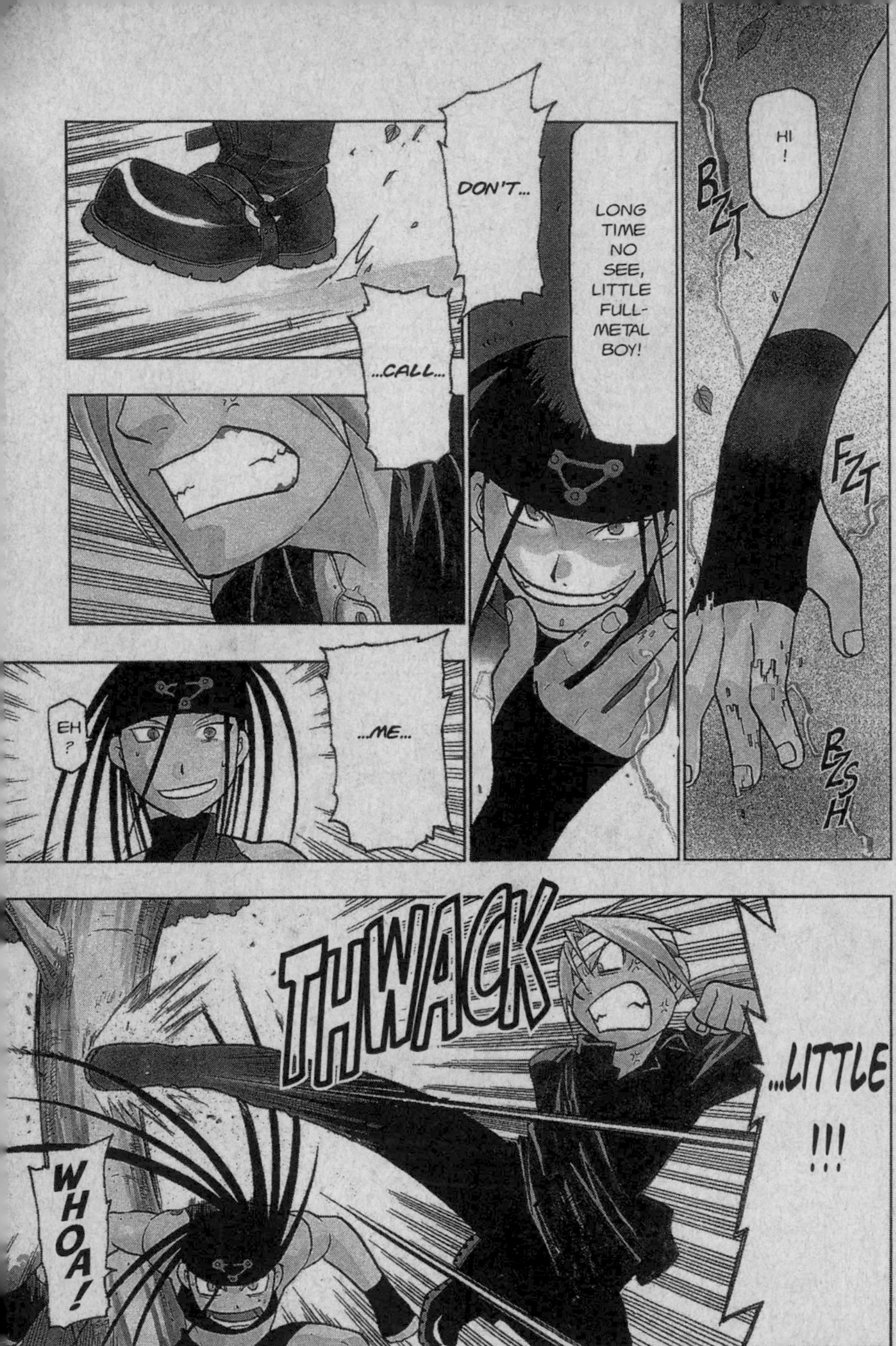
HI!
BZT
FZT
BZSH
LONG TIME NO SEE, LITTLE FULL-METAL BOY!
DON'T...
...CALL...
...ME...
EH?
...LITTLE !!!
THWACK
WHOA!

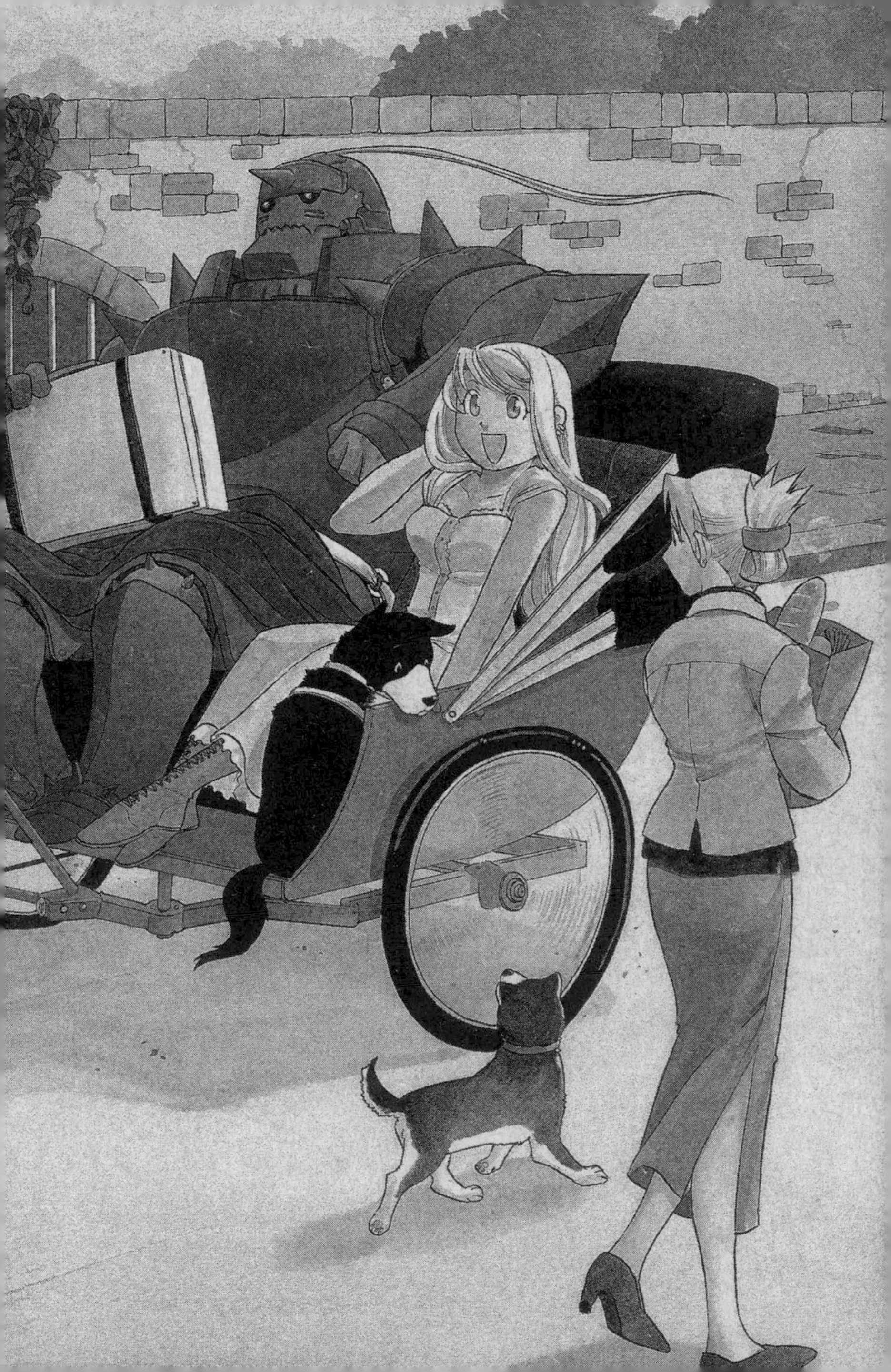

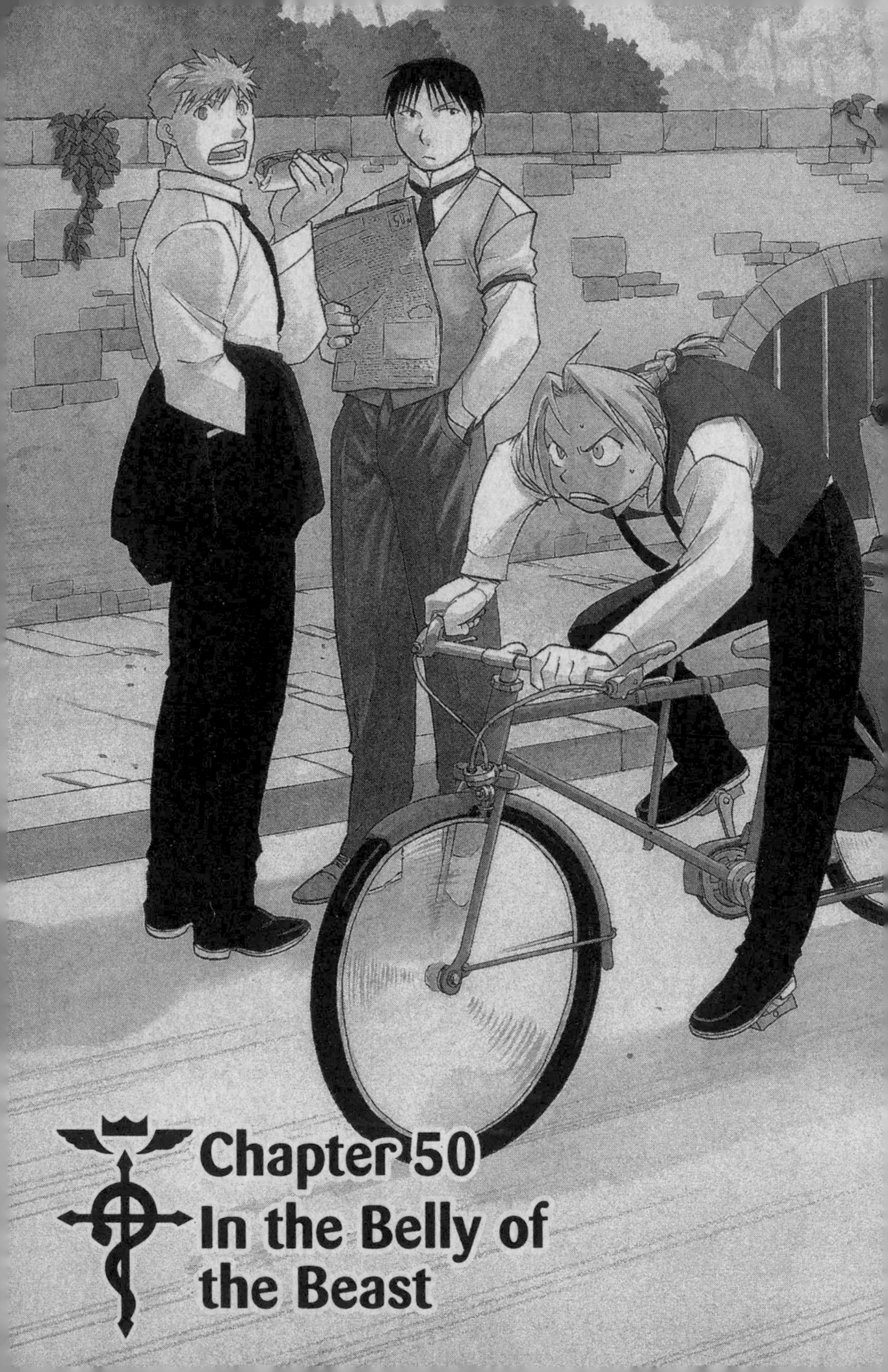

Chapter 50
In the Belly of the Beast

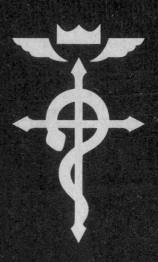

FULLMETAL
ALCHEMIST

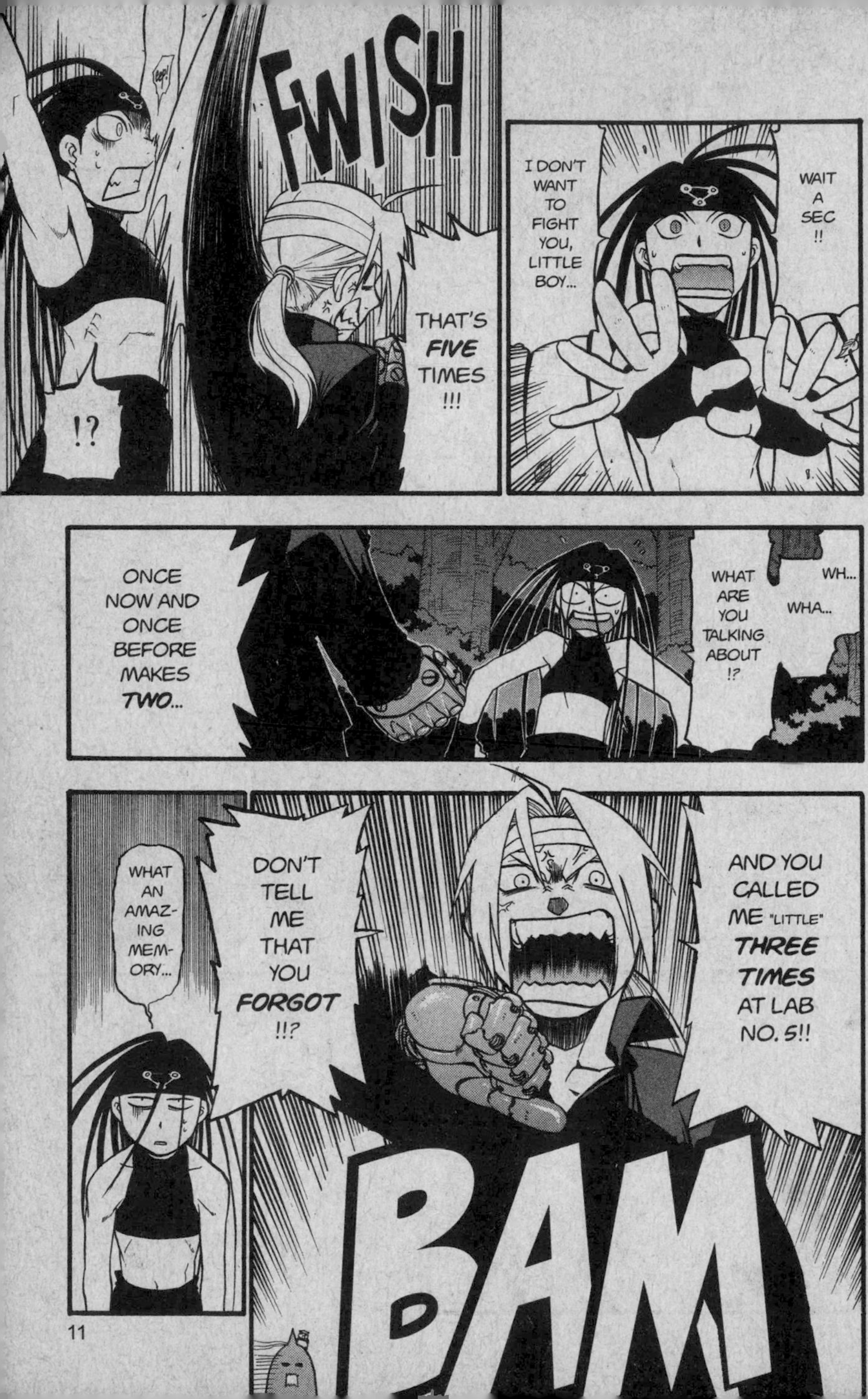
WAIT A SEC!!
I DON'T WANT TO FIGHT YOU, LITTLE BOY...
FWISH
eep!
THAT'S *FIVE* TIMES!!!
!?
WH...
WHA...
WHAT ARE YOU TALKING ABOUT!?
ONCE NOW AND ONCE BEFORE MAKES *TWO*...
AND YOU CALLED ME "LITTLE" *THREE TIMES* AT LAB NO. 5!!
DON'T TELL ME THAT YOU *FORGOT*!!?
BAM
WHAT AN AMAZING MEMORY...

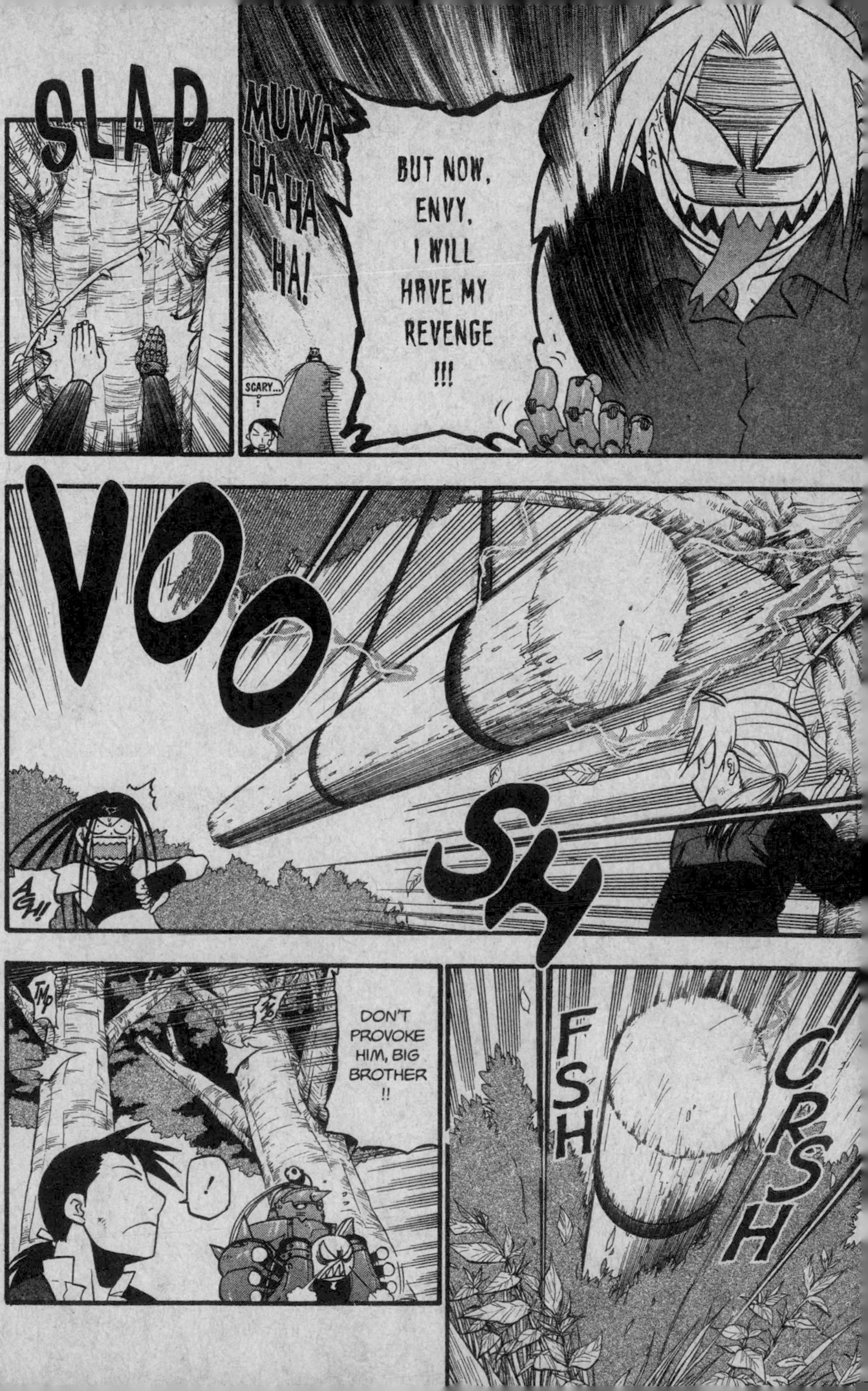
MUWA HA HA HA!
BUT NOW, ENVY, I WILL HAVE MY REVENGE !!!
SCARY...
SLAP
VOOOSH
AGH!!
FSH
CRSH
DON'T PROVOKE HIM, BIG BROTHER !!
!
TMP

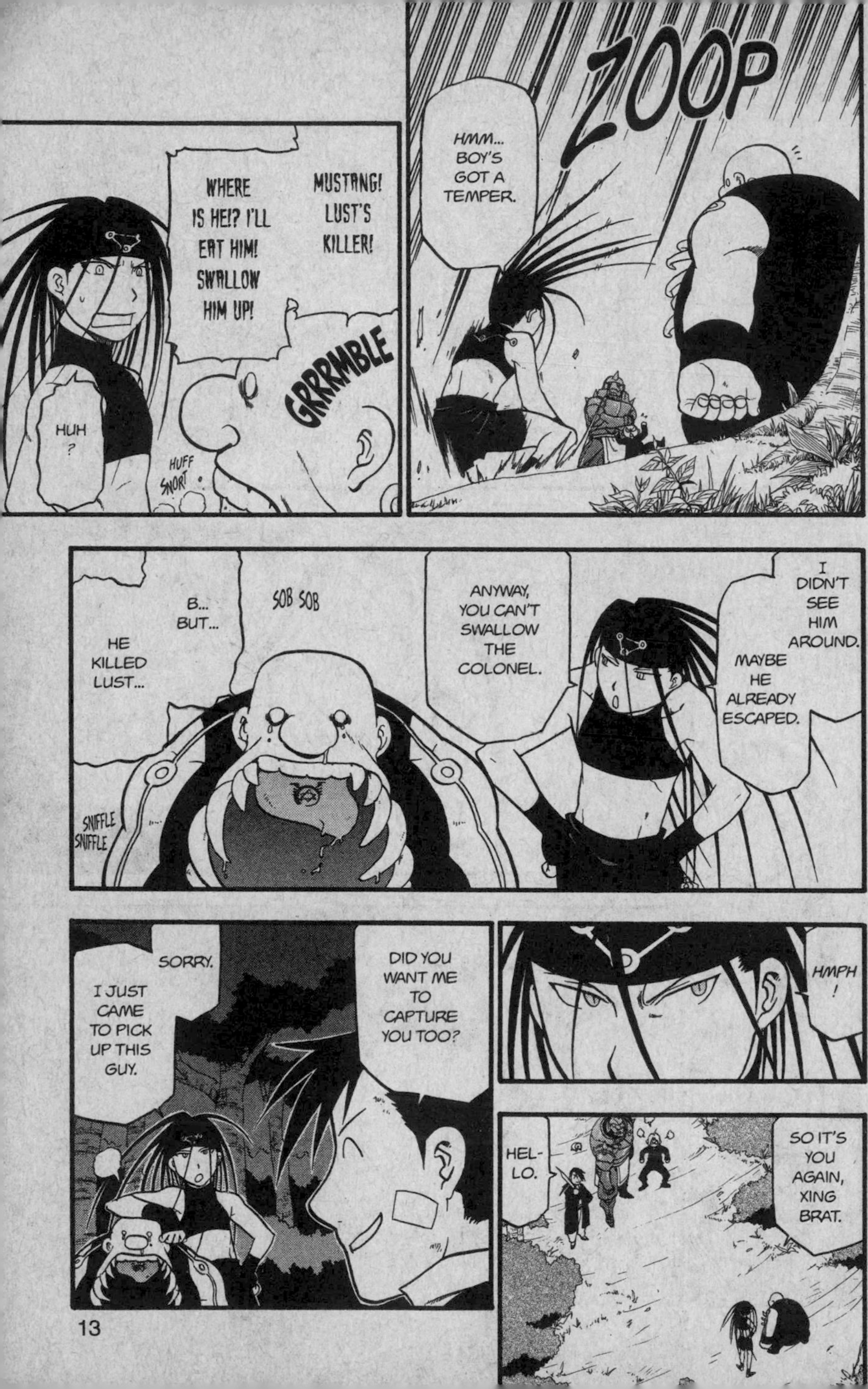
ZOOP
HMM... BOY'S GOT A TEMPER.
MUSTANG! LUST'S KILLER!
WHERE IS HE!? I'LL EAT HIM! SWALLOW HIM UP!
GRRRMBLE
HUH?
HUFF SNORT
I DIDN'T SEE HIM AROUND.
MAYBE HE ALREADY ESCAPED.
ANYWAY, YOU CAN'T SWALLOW THE COLONEL.
SOB SOB
B... BUT...
HE KILLED LUST...
SNIFFLE SNIFFLE
HMPH!
SO IT'S YOU AGAIN, XING BRAT.
HEL-LO.
DID YOU WANT ME TO CAPTURE YOU TOO?
SORRY.
I JUST CAME TO PICK UP THIS GUY.

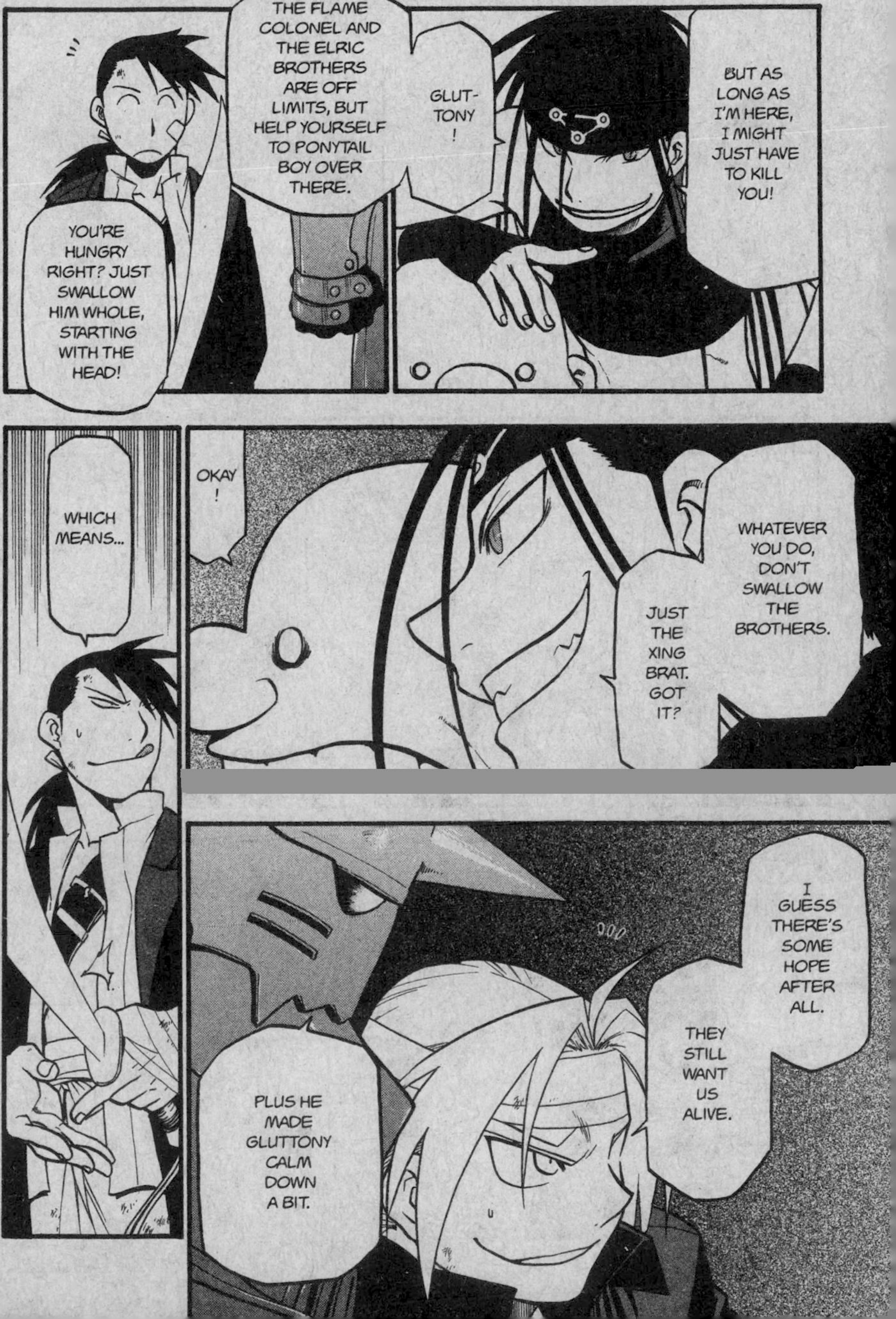
BUT AS LONG AS I'M HERE, I MIGHT JUST HAVE TO KILL YOU!
GLUT-TONY!
THE FLAME COLONEL AND THE ELRIC BROTHERS ARE OFF LIMITS, BUT HELP YOURSELF TO PONYTAIL BOY OVER THERE.
YOU'RE HUNGRY RIGHT? JUST SWALLOW HIM WHOLE, STARTING WITH THE HEAD!
WHATEVER YOU DO, DON'T SWALLOW THE BROTHERS.
JUST THE XING BRAT. GOT IT?
OKAY!
I GUESS THERE'S SOME HOPE AFTER ALL.
THEY STILL WANT US ALIVE.
PLUS HE MADE GLUTTONY CALM DOWN A BIT.
WHICH MEANS...

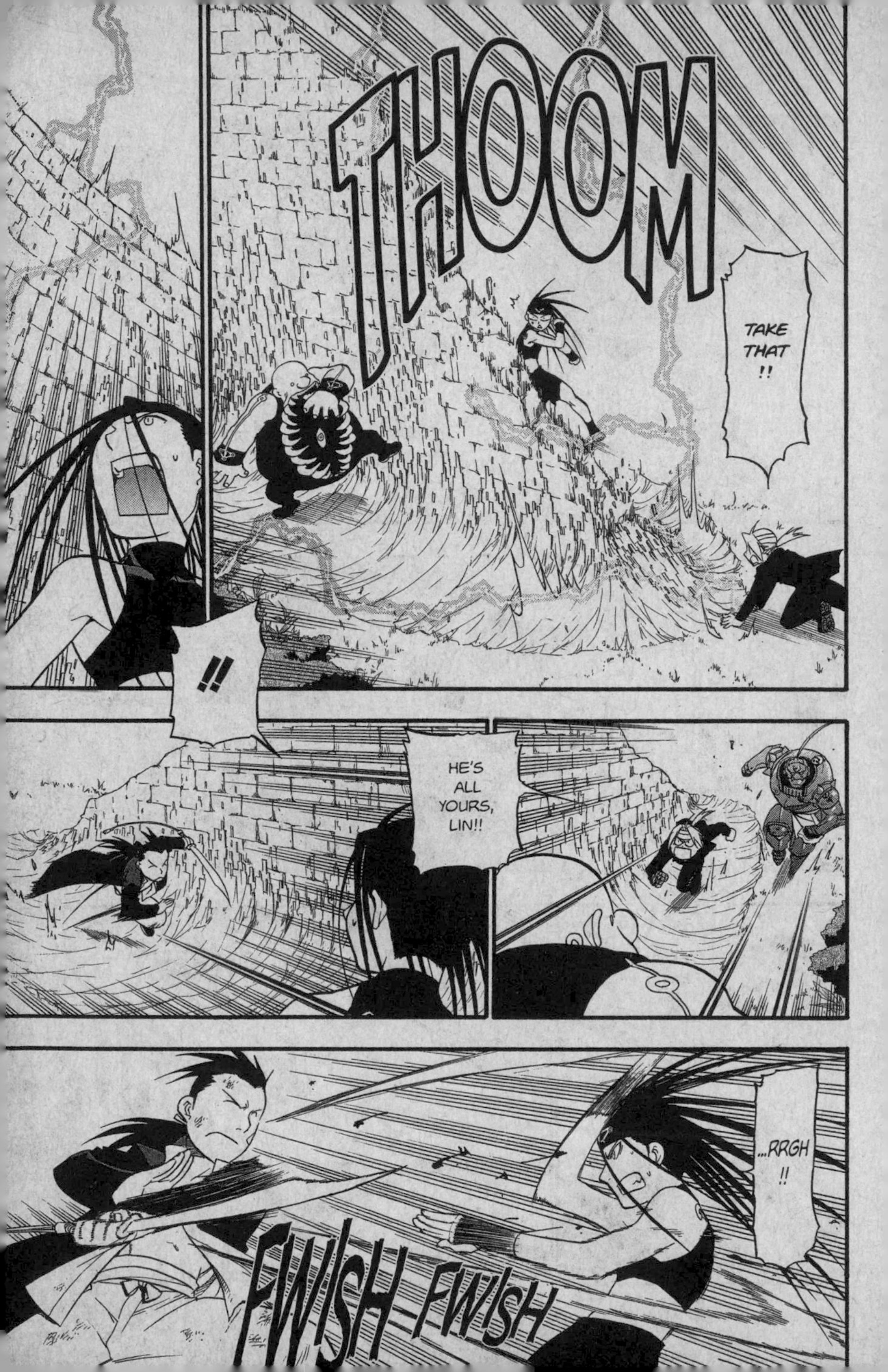
THOOM
TAKE THAT !!
!!
HE'S ALL YOURS, LIN!!
...RRGH !!
FWISH FWISH

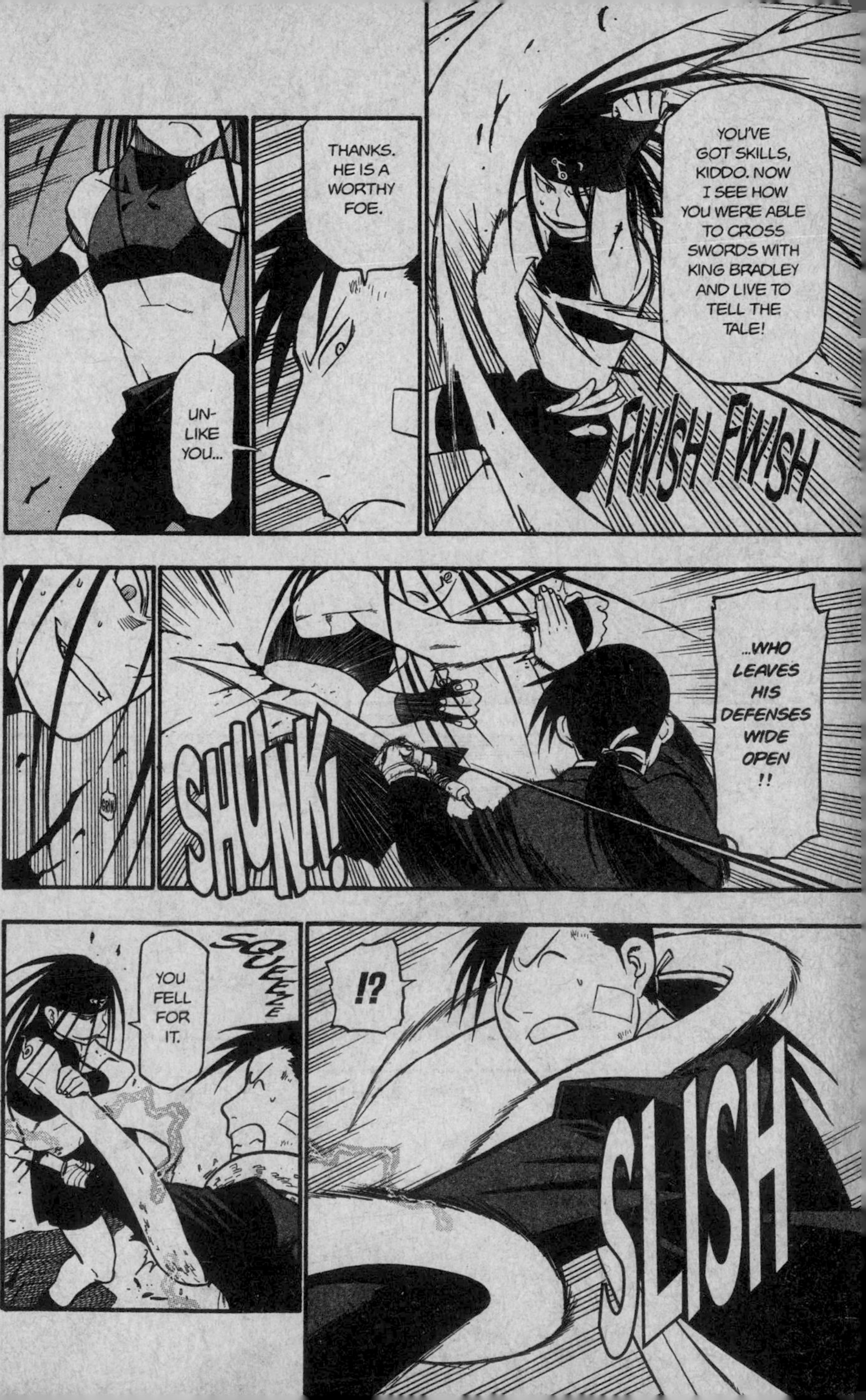
YOU'VE GOT SKILLS, KIDDO. NOW I SEE HOW YOU WERE ABLE TO CROSS SWORDS WITH KING BRADLEY AND LIVE TO TELL THE TALE!
FWISH FWISH
THANKS. HE IS A WORTHY FOE.
UN-LIKE YOU...
...WHO LEAVES HIS DEFENSES WIDE OPEN!!
SHUNK!
!?
SLISH
YOU FELL FOR IT.
SQUEEZE

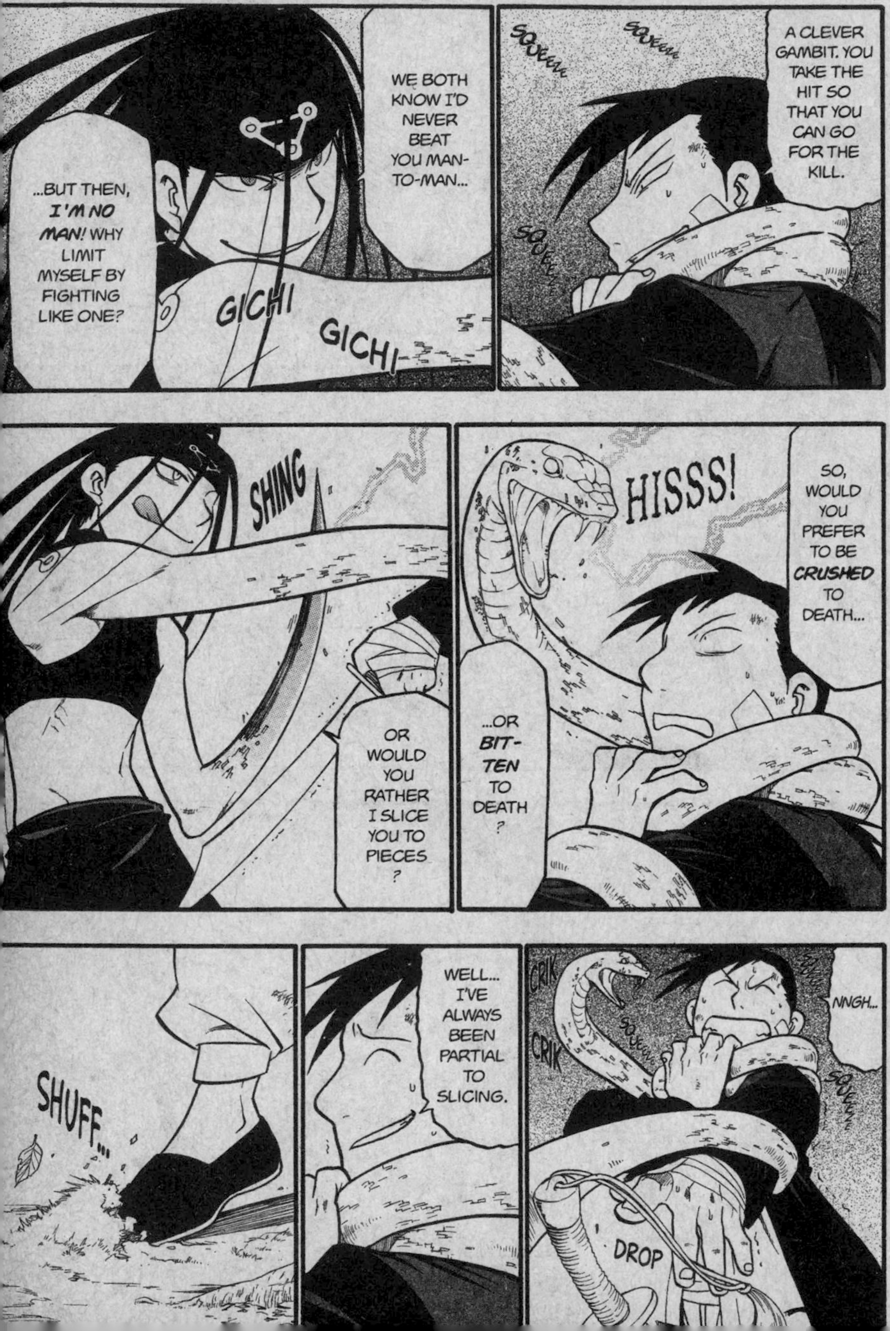
A CLEVER GAMBIT. YOU TAKE THE HIT SO THAT YOU CAN GO FOR THE KILL.
WE BOTH KNOW I'D NEVER BEAT YOU MAN-TO-MAN...
...BUT THEN, **I'M NO MAN!** WHY LIMIT MYSELF BY FIGHTING LIKE ONE?
GICHI
GICHI
HISSS!
SO, WOULD YOU PREFER TO BE **CRUSHED** TO DEATH...
...OR **BITTEN** TO DEATH?
SHING
OR WOULD YOU RATHER I SLICE YOU TO PIECES?
NNGH...
CRIK
CRIK
DROP
WELL... I'VE ALWAYS BEEN PARTIAL TO SLICING.
SHUFF...

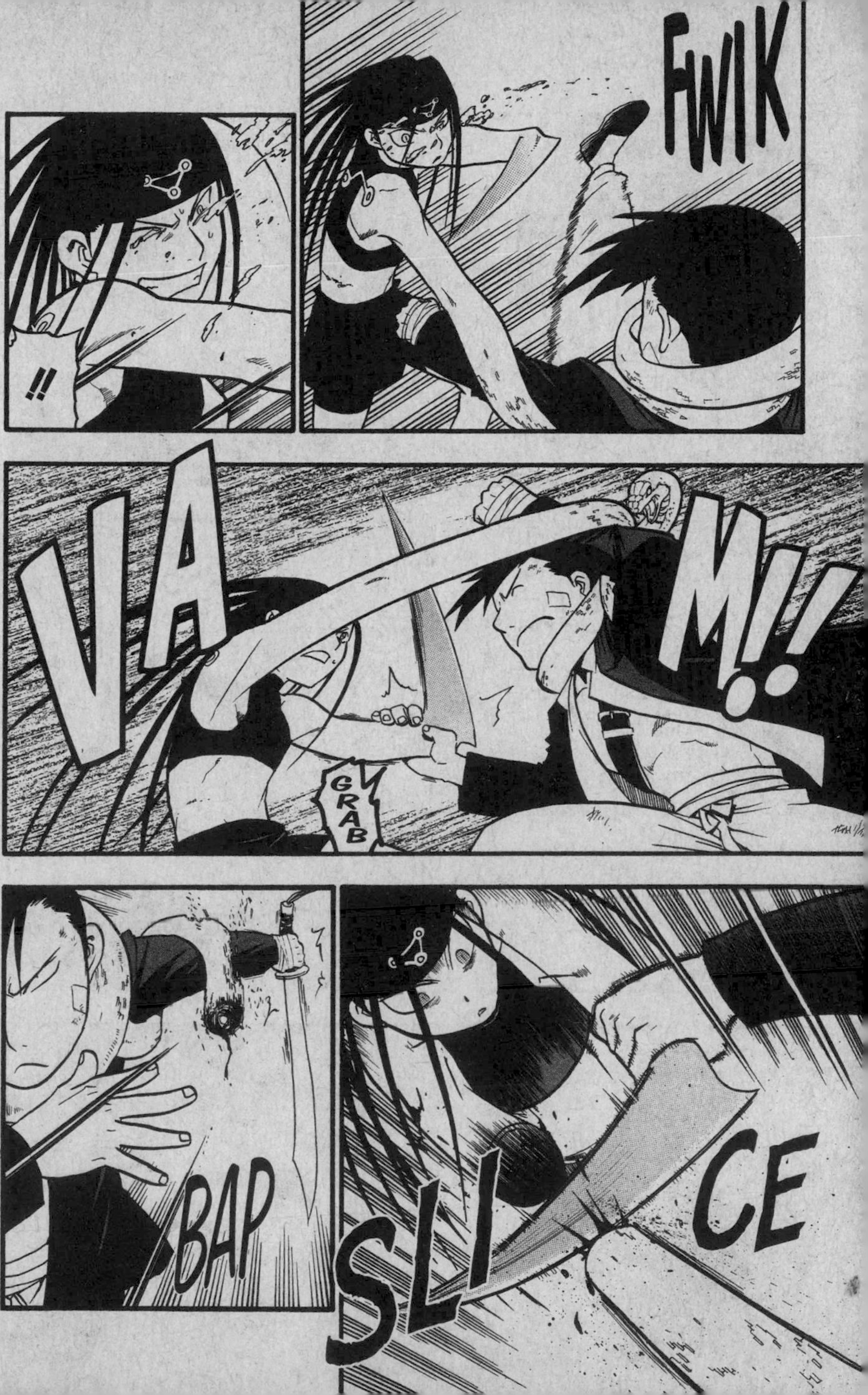
FWIK
!!
VAM!!
GRAB
SLICE
BAP

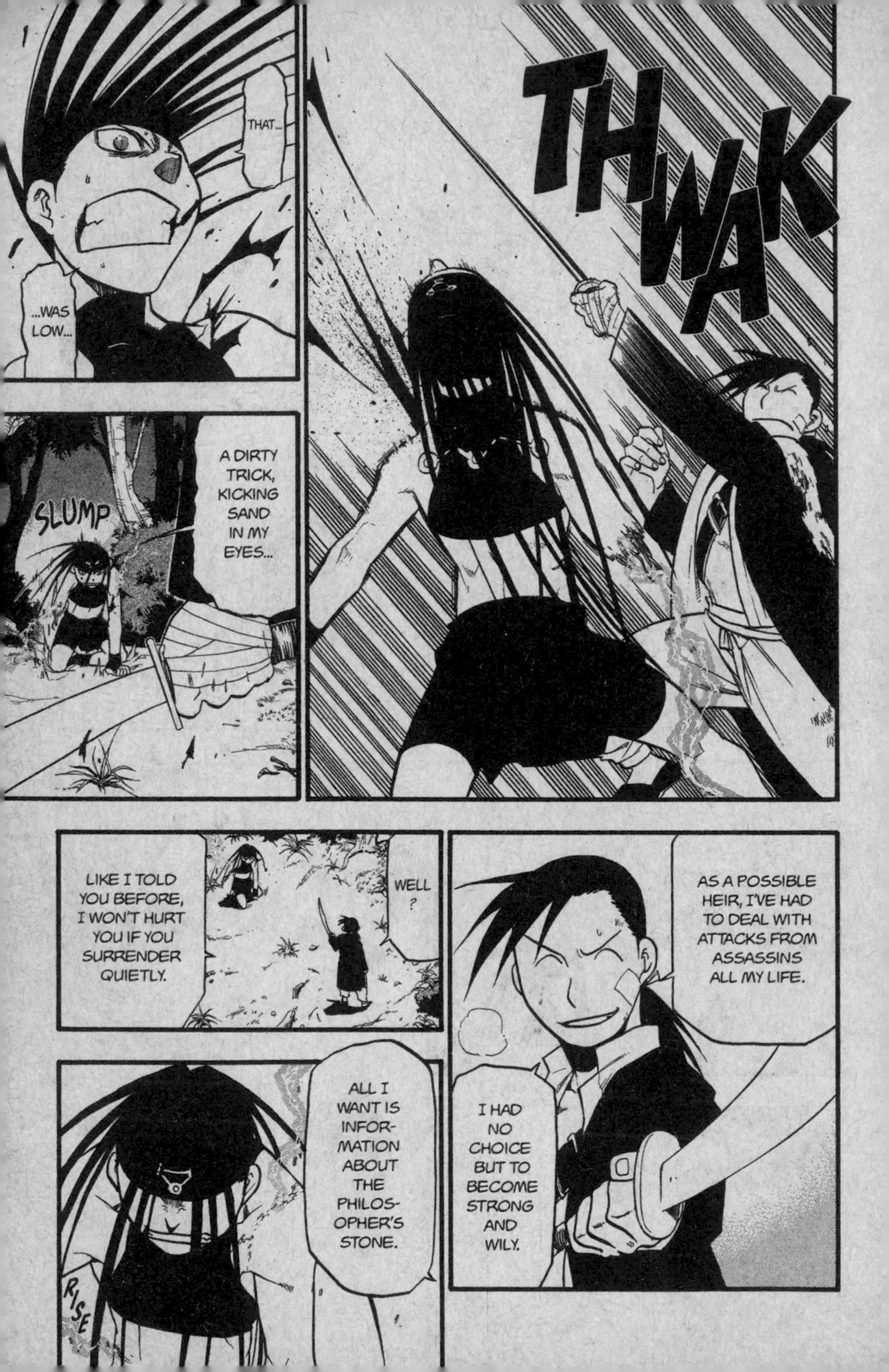
THWAK
THAT...
...WAS LOW...
A DIRTY TRICK, KICKING SAND IN MY EYES...
SLUMP
AS A POSSIBLE HEIR, I'VE HAD TO DEAL WITH ATTACKS FROM ASSASSINS ALL MY LIFE.
I HAD NO CHOICE BUT TO BECOME STRONG AND WILY.
WELL ?
LIKE I TOLD YOU BEFORE, I WON'T HURT YOU IF YOU SURRENDER QUIETLY.
ALL I WANT IS INFOR-MATION ABOUT THE PHILOS-OPHER'S STONE.
RISE

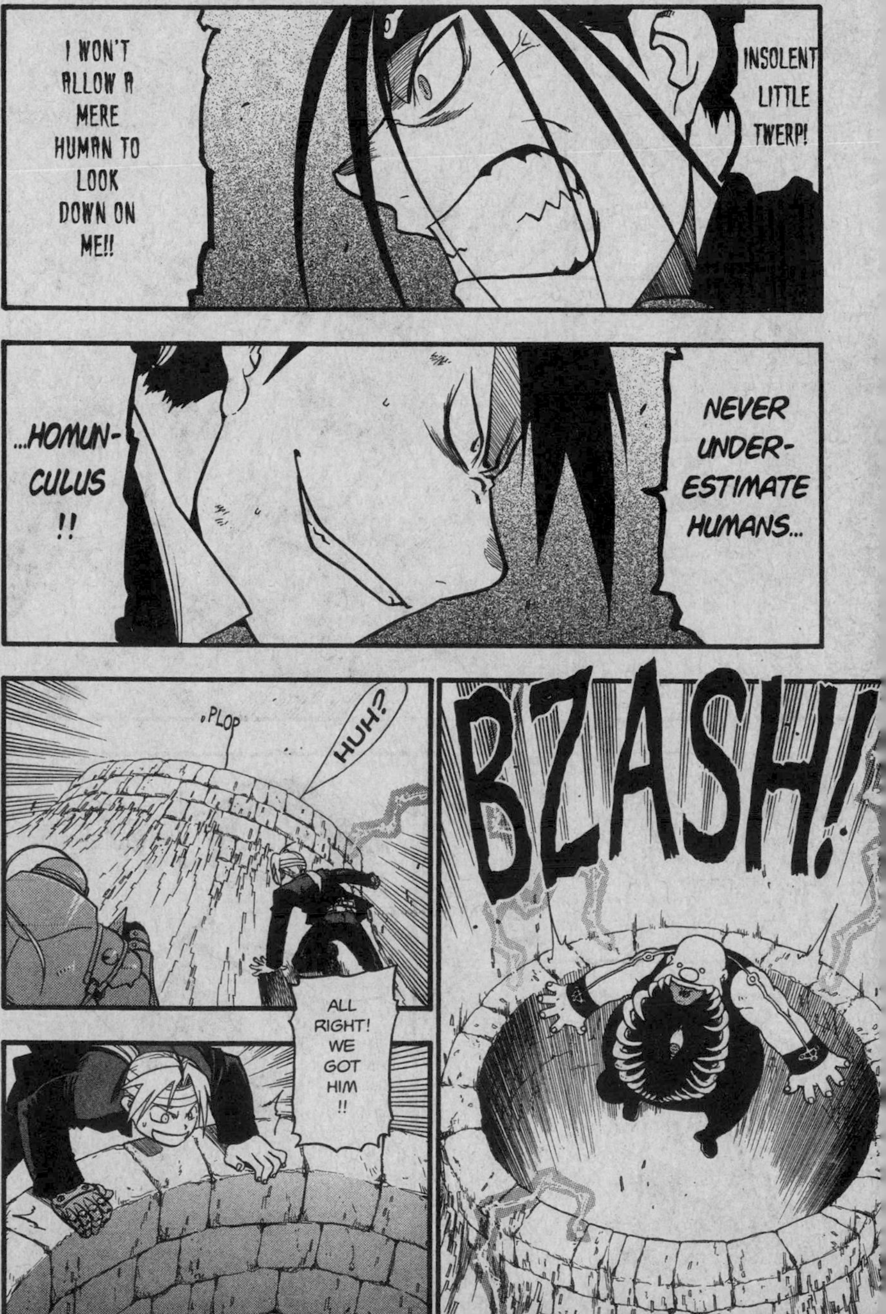
INSOLENT LITTLE TWERP!
I WON'T ALLOW A MERE HUMAN TO LOOK DOWN ON ME!!
NEVER UNDER-ESTIMATE HUMANS...
...HOMUN-CULUS!!
BZASH!
PLOP
HUH?
ALL RIGHT! WE GOT HIM!!

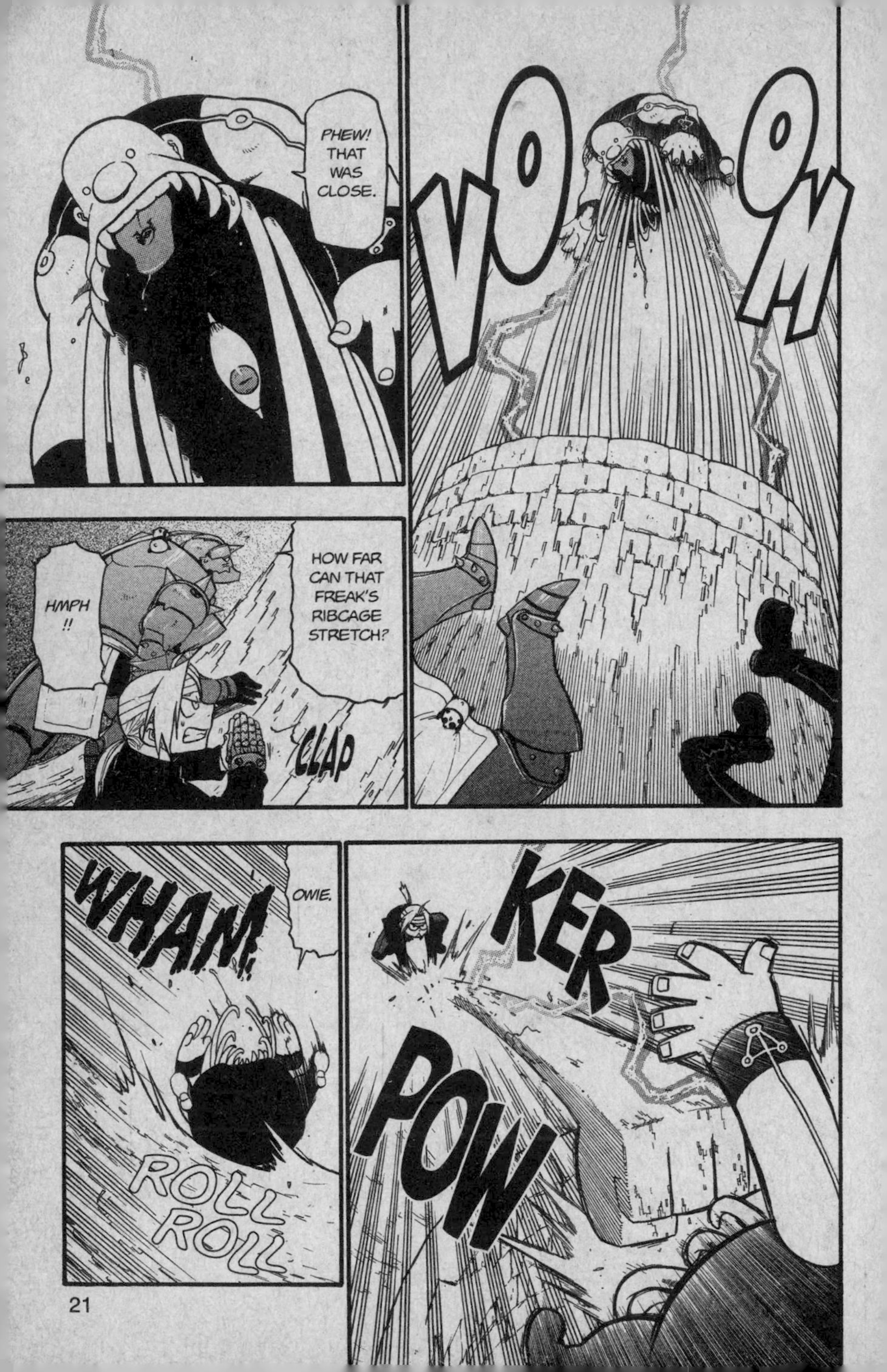
VOOOM
PHEW! THAT WAS CLOSE.
HOW FAR CAN THAT FREAK'S RIBCAGE STRETCH?
HMPH !!
CLAP
KER
POW
OWIE.
WHAM!
ROLL ROLL

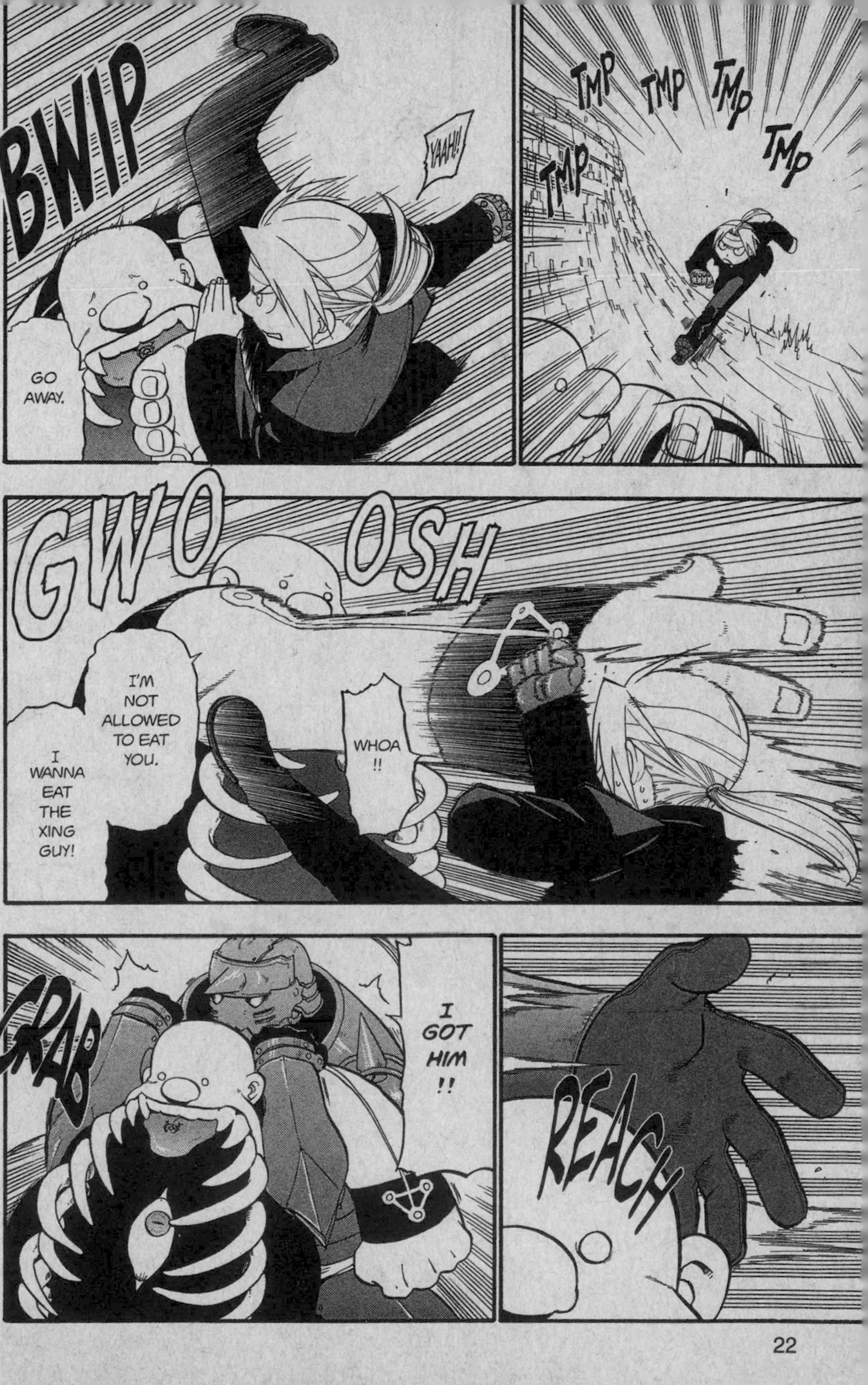
TMP TMP TMP TMP TMP
BWIP
YAAH!!
GO AWAY.
GWO OSH
WHOA !!
I'M NOT ALLOWED TO EAT YOU.
I WANNA EAT THE XING GUY!
REACH
I GOT HIM !!
GRAB

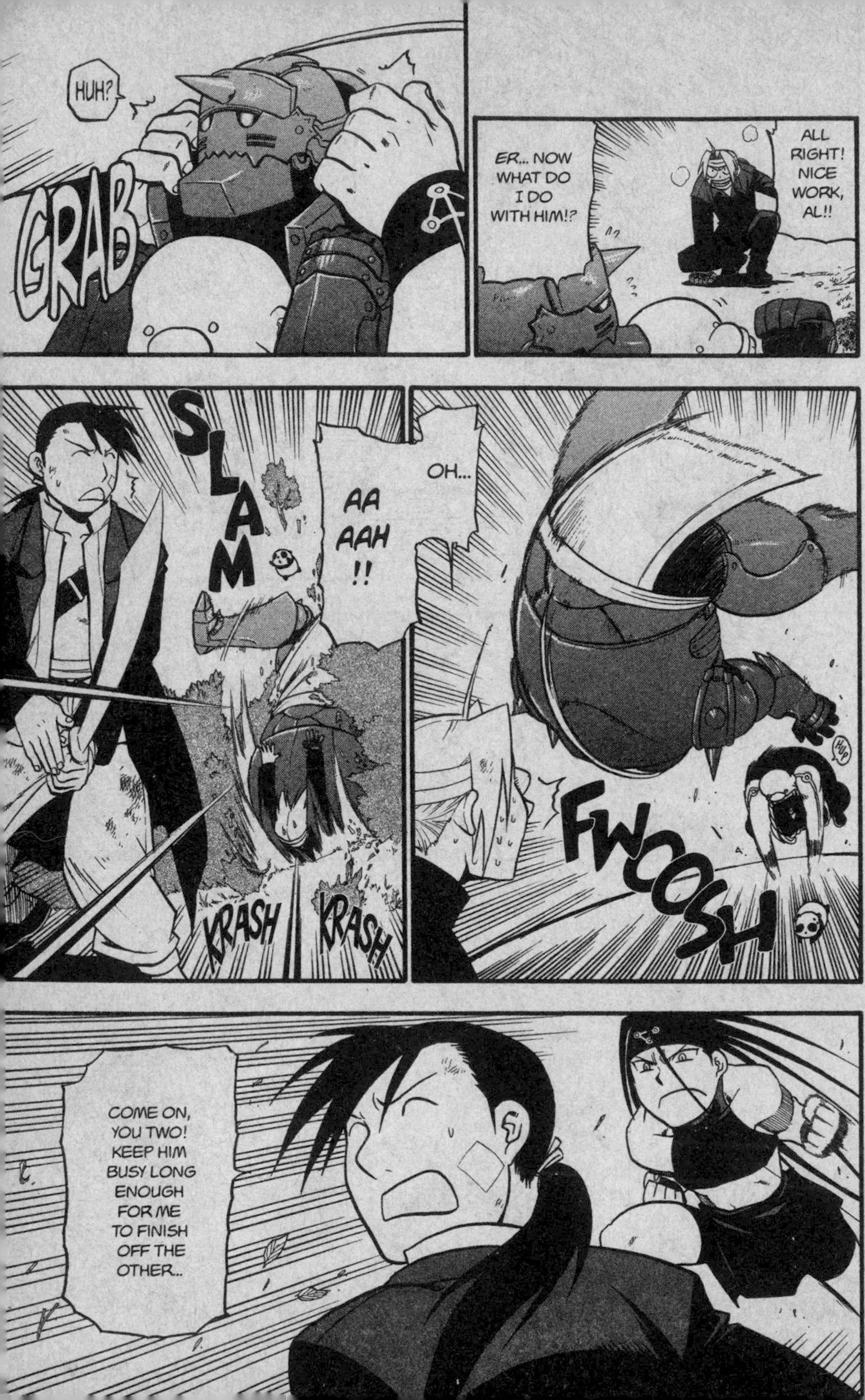
ALL RIGHT! NICE WORK, AL!!
ER... NOW WHAT DO I DO WITH HIM!?
HUH?
GRAB
OH...
HUP
FWOOSH
AA AAH!!
SLAM
KRASH
KRASH
COME ON, YOU TWO! KEEP HIM BUSY LONG ENOUGH FOR ME TO FINISH OFF THE OTHER..

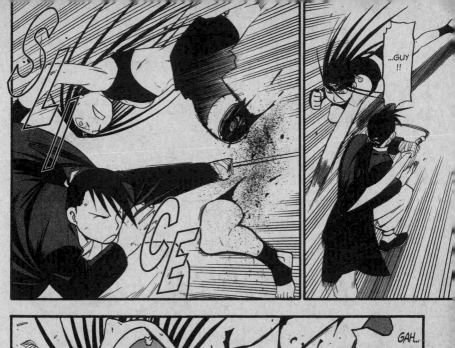

...GUY

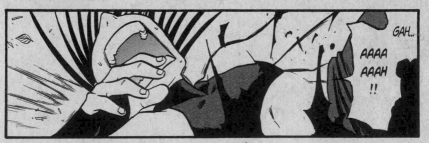

GAH...

AAAA
AAAH
!!

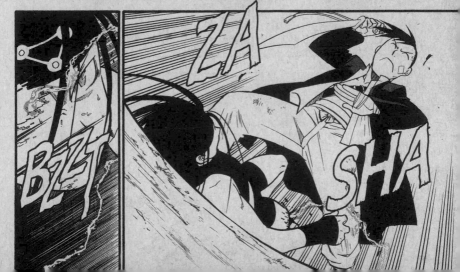

ZA

BZZT

SHA

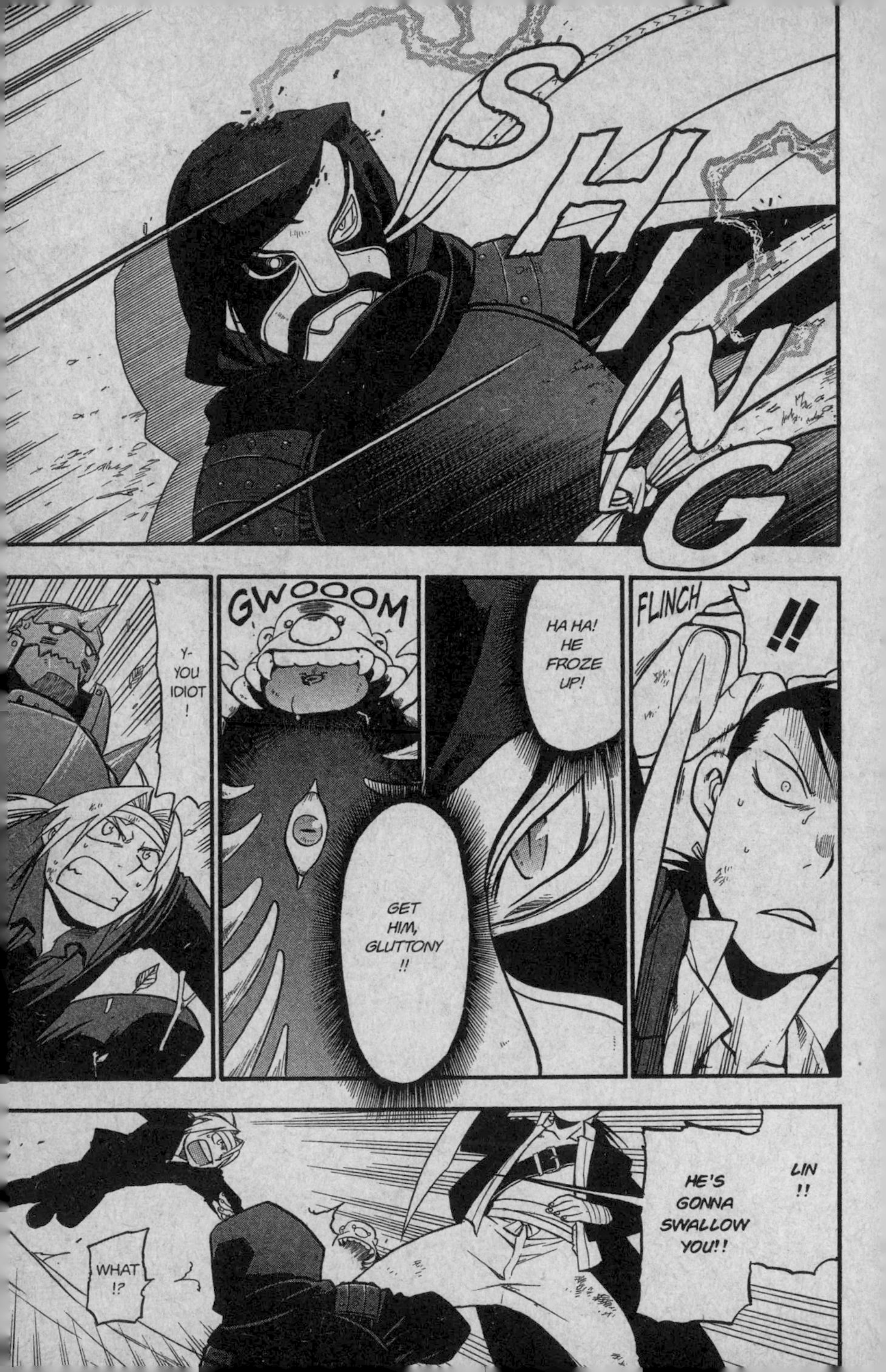
SHING
FLINCH
!!
HA HA! HE FROZE UP!
GWOOOM
GET HIM, GLUTTONY!!
Y-YOU IDIOT!
LIN!!
HE'S GONNA SWALLOW YOU!!
WHAT!?

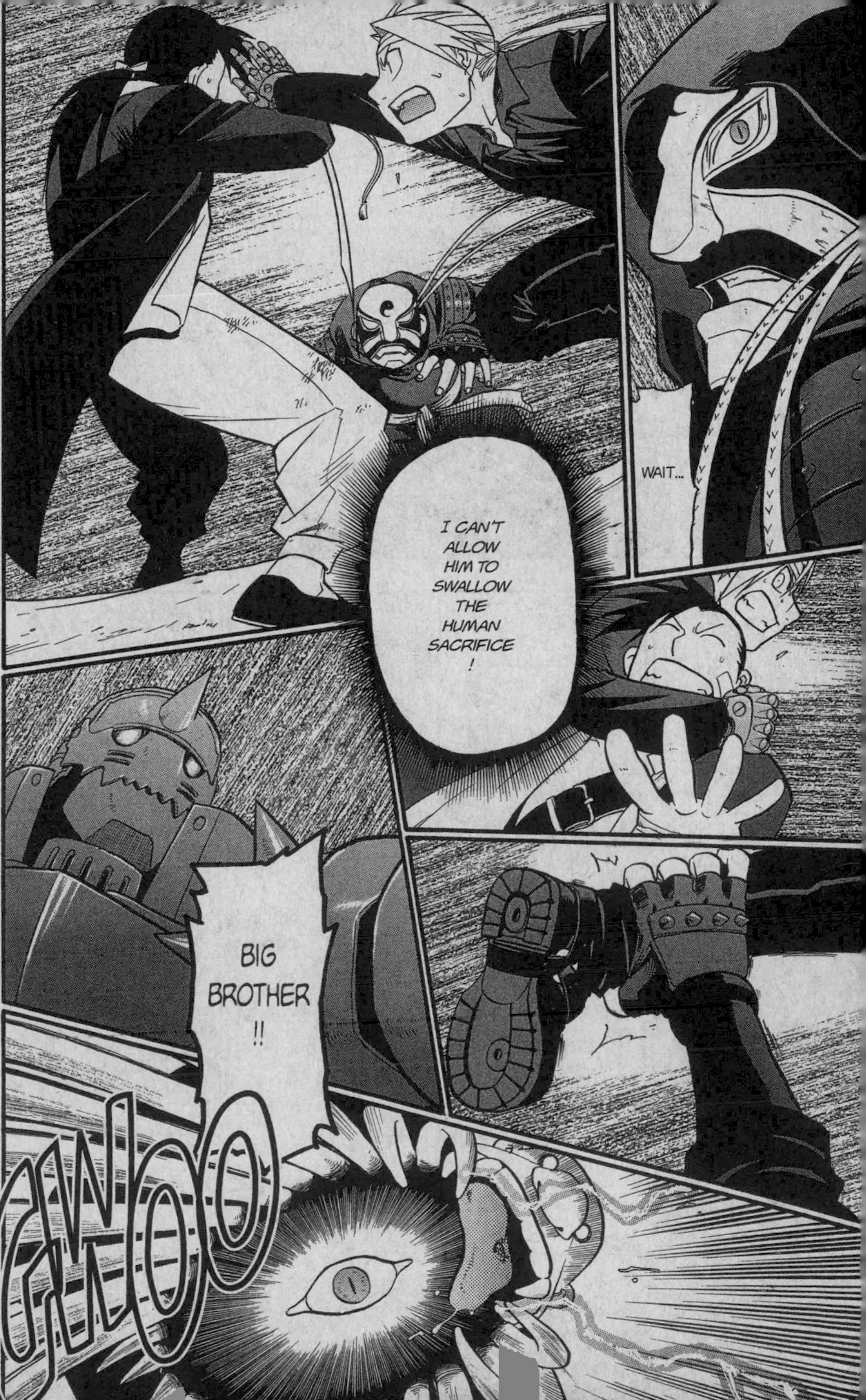
WAIT...
I CAN'T ALLOW HIM TO SWALLOW THE HUMAN SACRIFICE!
BIG BROTHER!!
GWOO

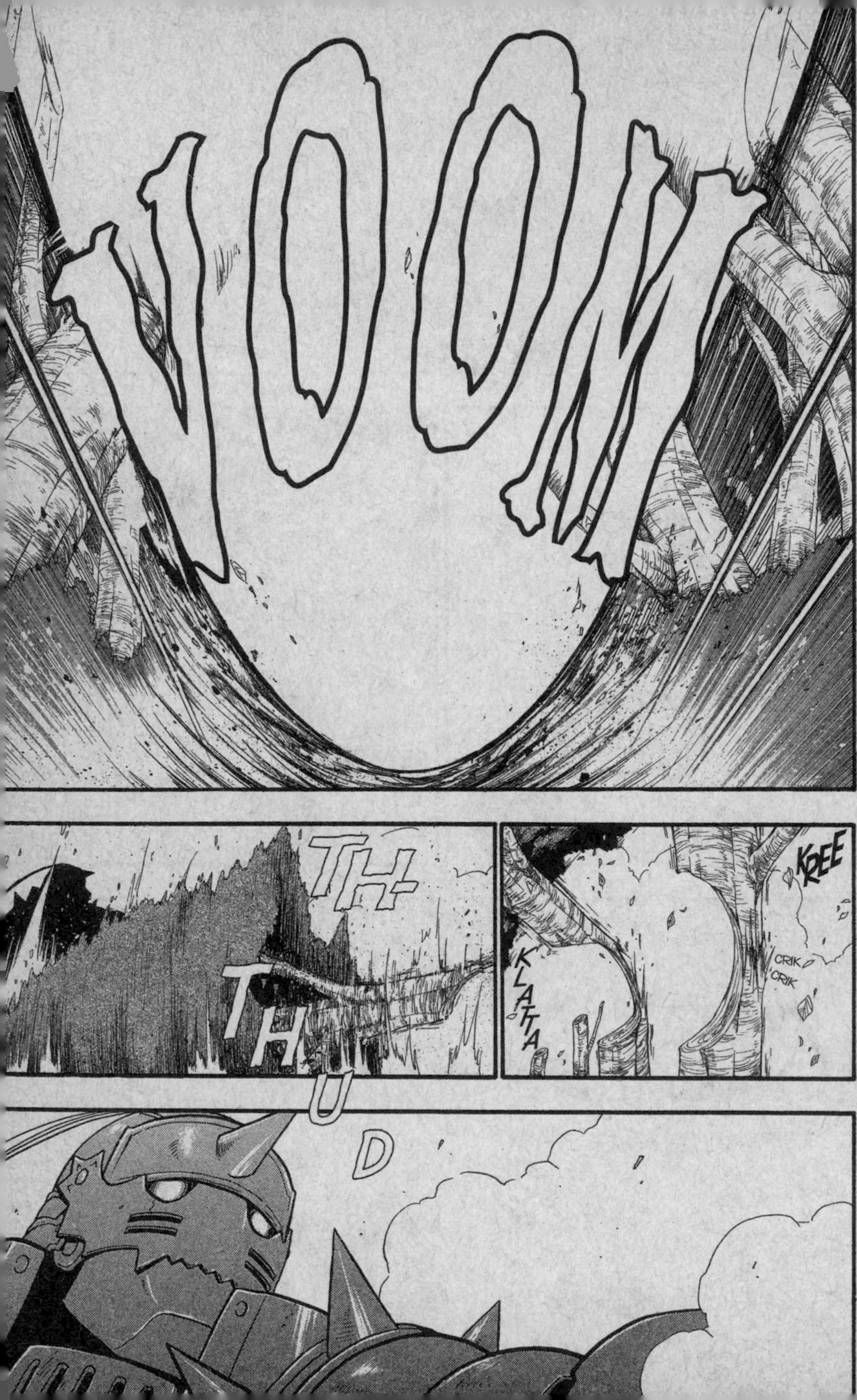
VOOM
KREEE
CRIK
CRIK
KLATTA
TH-
THUD

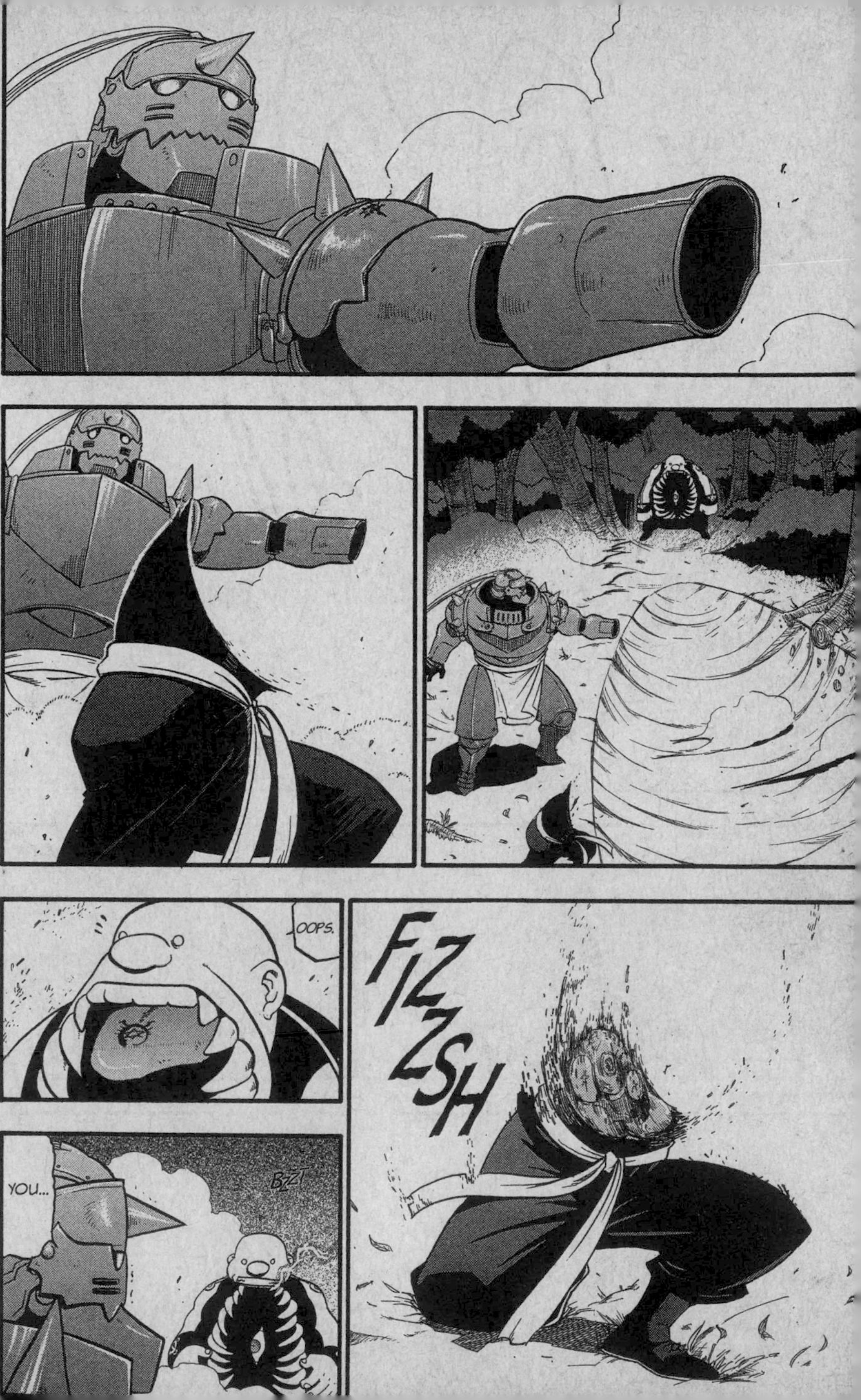
FIZZSH
OOPS.
BZZT
YOU...

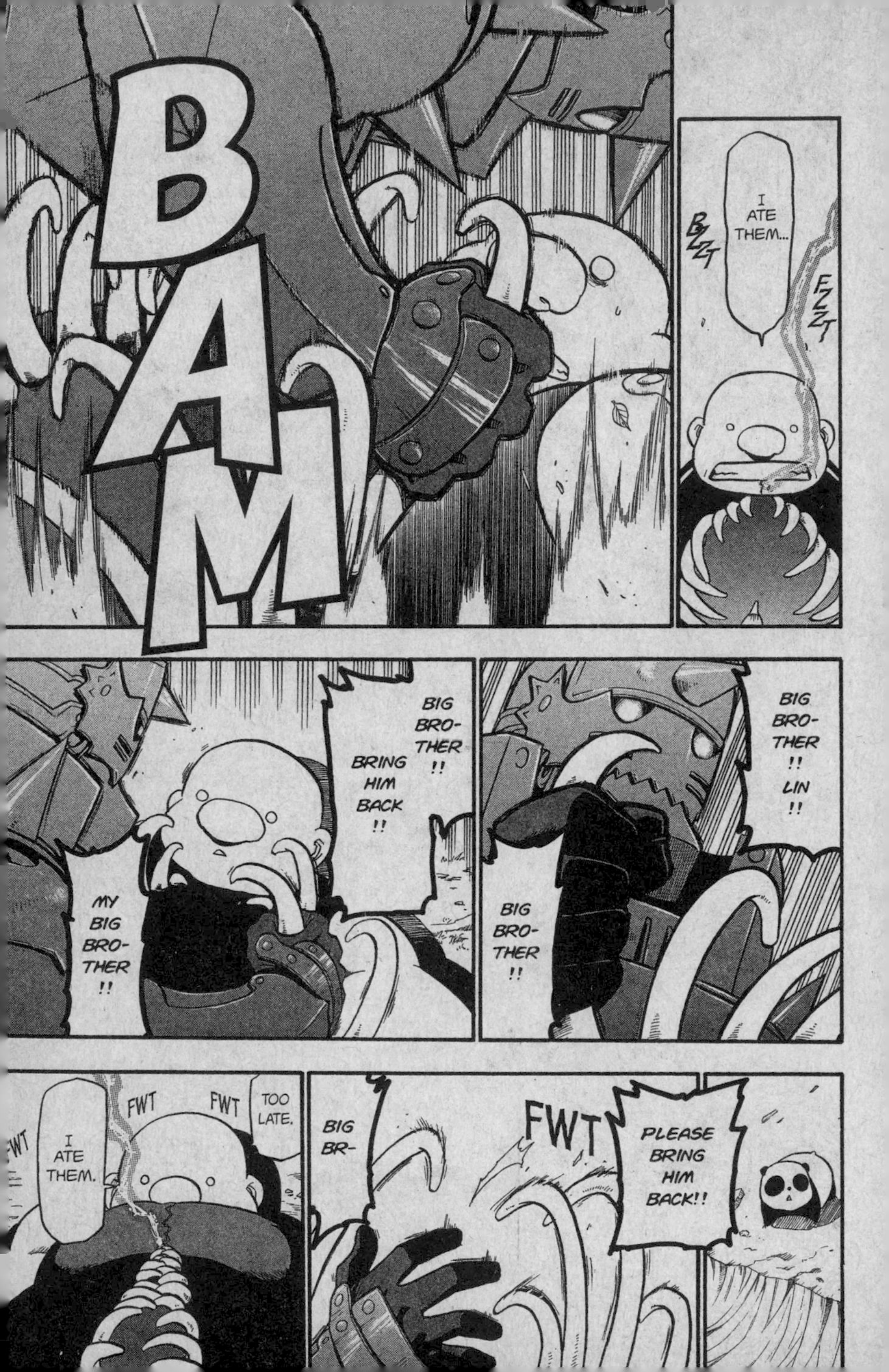
I ATE THEM...
BZZT
FZZT
BAM
BIG BRO-THER!! LIN!!
BIG BRO-THER!!
BIG BRO-THER!!
BRING HIM BACK!!
MY BIG BRO-THER!!
PLEASE BRING HIM BACK!!
FWT
BIG BR-
TOO LATE.
FWT
FWT
I ATE THEM.
FWT

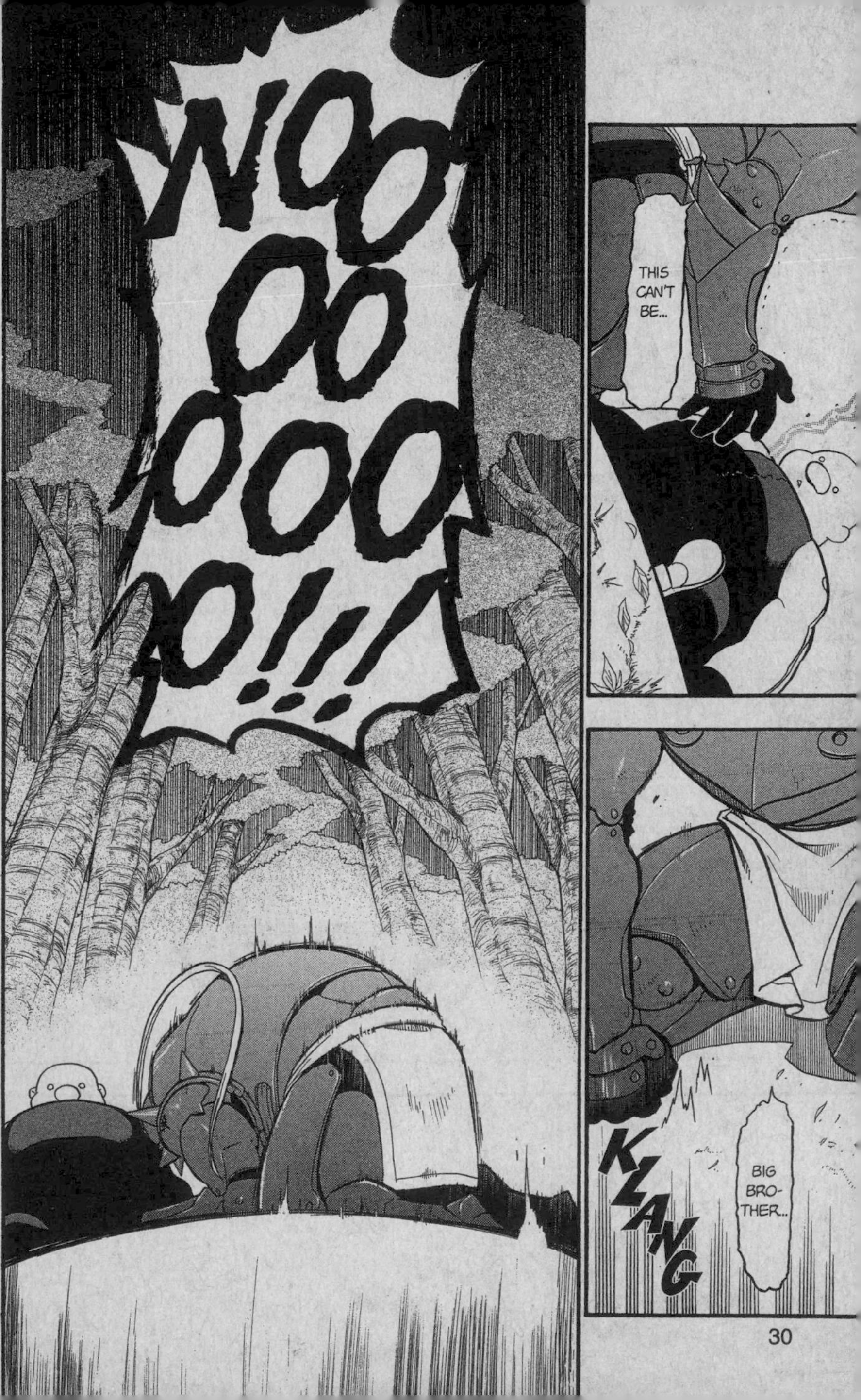
THIS CAN'T BE...
KLANG
BIG BRO-THER...
WOOOOOOOOOOO!!!

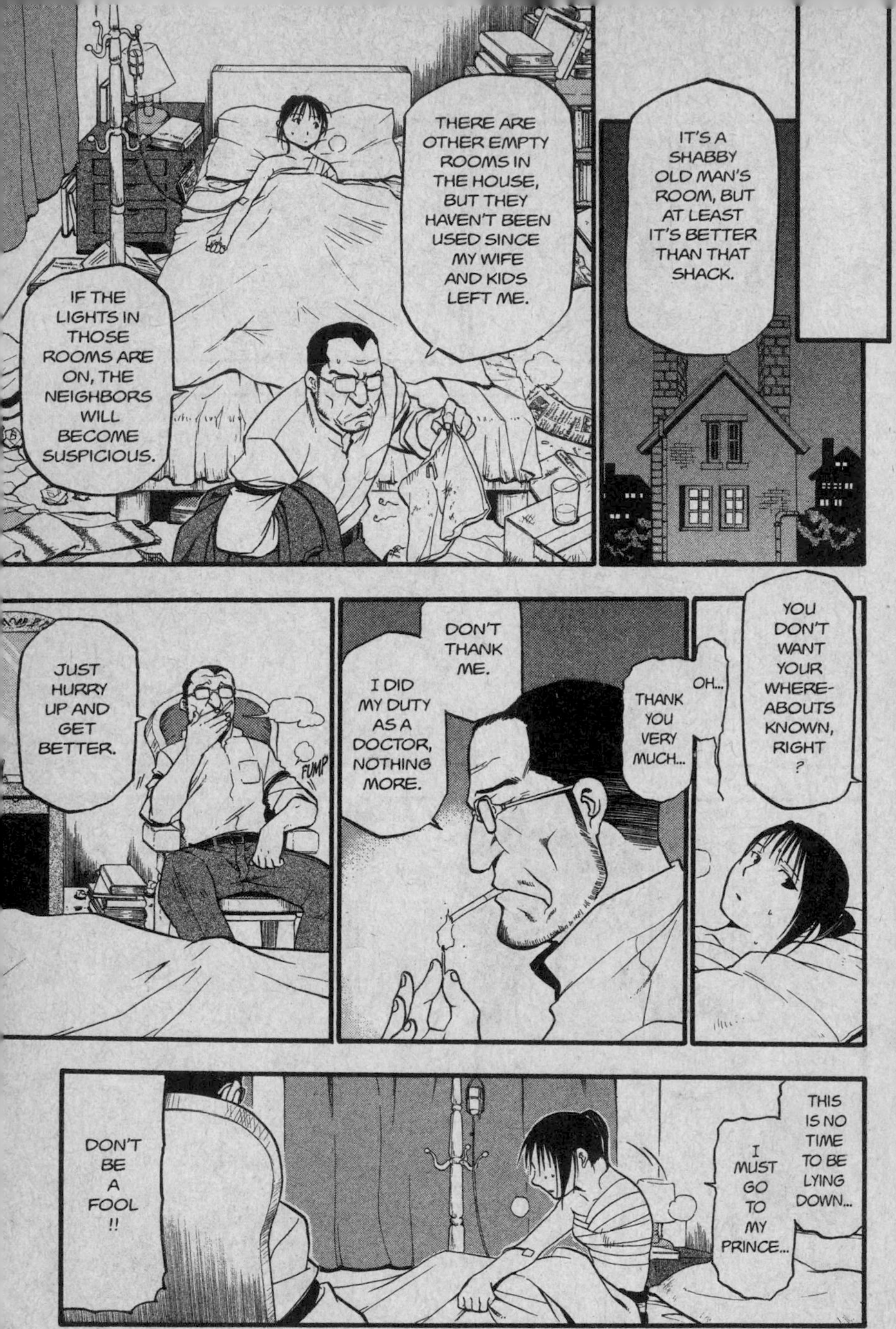
IT'S A SHABBY OLD MAN'S ROOM, BUT AT LEAST IT'S BETTER THAN THAT SHACK.
THERE ARE OTHER EMPTY ROOMS IN THE HOUSE, BUT THEY HAVEN'T BEEN USED SINCE MY WIFE AND KIDS LEFT ME.
IF THE LIGHTS IN THOSE ROOMS ARE ON, THE NEIGHBORS WILL BECOME SUSPICIOUS.
YOU DON'T WANT YOUR WHERE-ABOUTS KNOWN, RIGHT?
OH...
THANK YOU VERY MUCH...
DON'T THANK ME.
I DID MY DUTY AS A DOCTOR, NOTHING MORE.
JUST HURRY UP AND GET BETTER.
FUMP
THIS IS NO TIME TO BE LYING DOWN...
I MUST GO TO MY PRINCE...
DON'T BE A FOOL!!

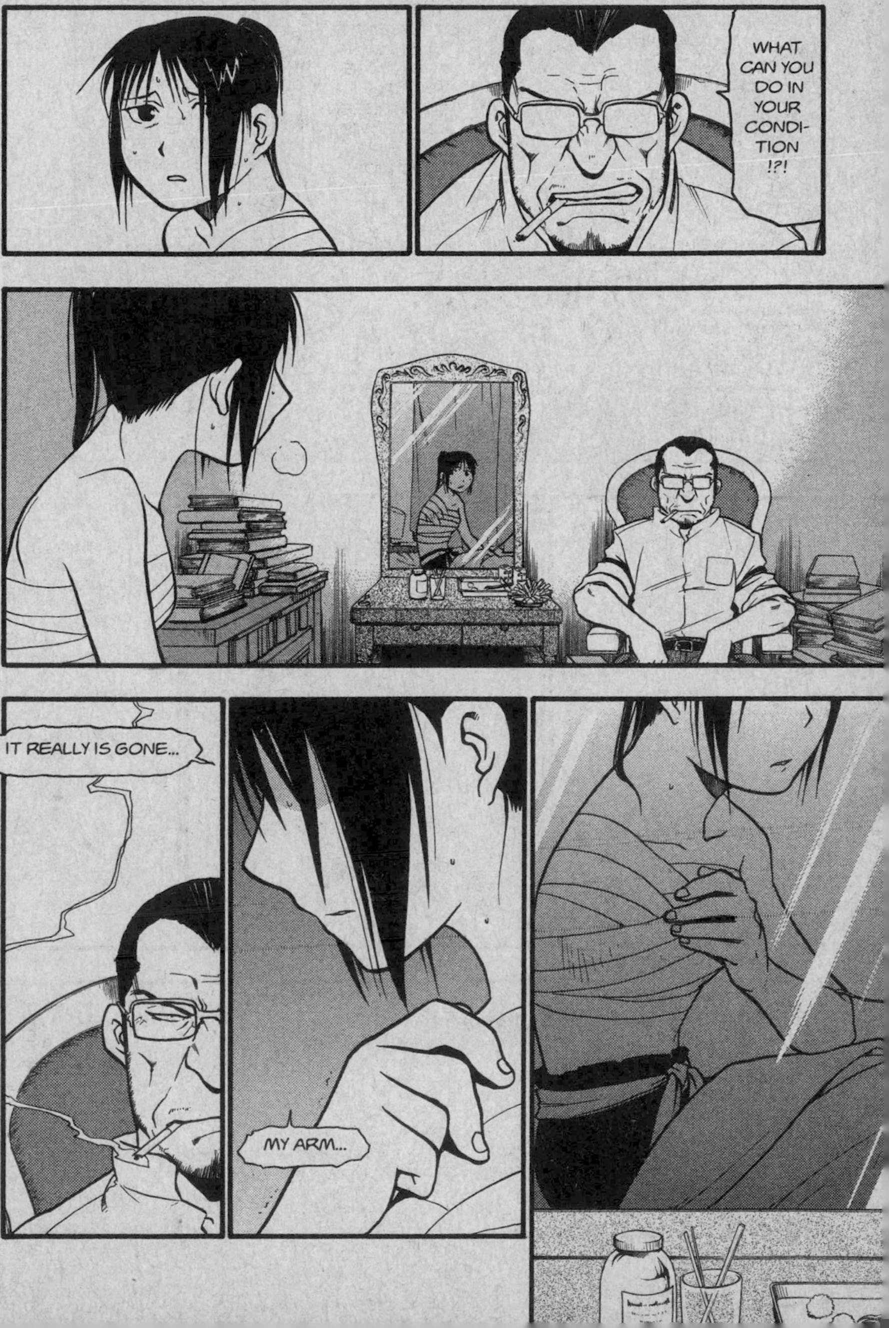
WHAT CAN YOU DO IN YOUR CONDITION !?!
MY ARM...
IT REALLY IS GONE...

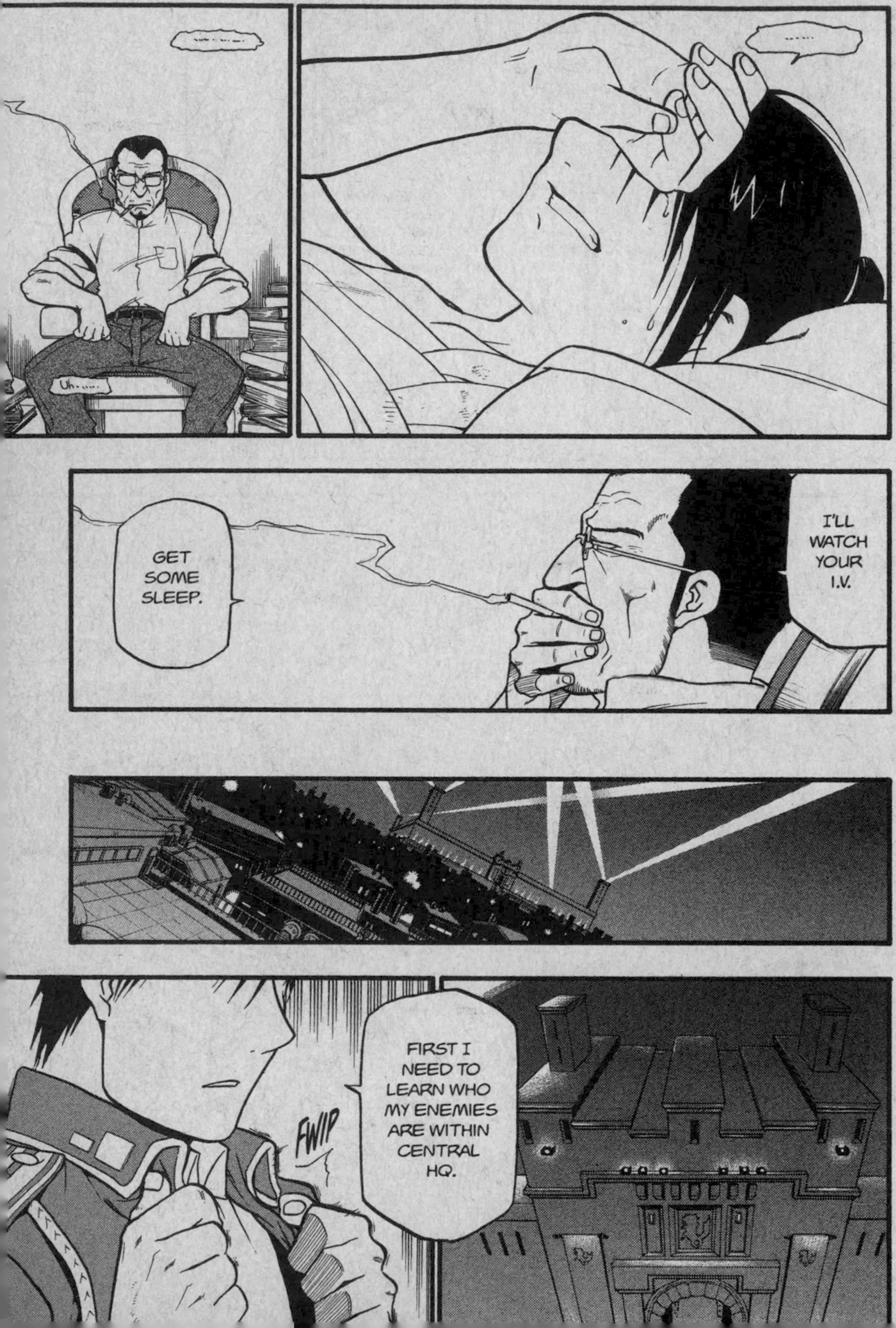
......
......
Uh......
I'LL WATCH YOUR I.V.
GET SOME SLEEP.
FIRST I NEED TO LEARN WHO MY ENEMIES ARE WITHIN CENTRAL HQ.
FWIP

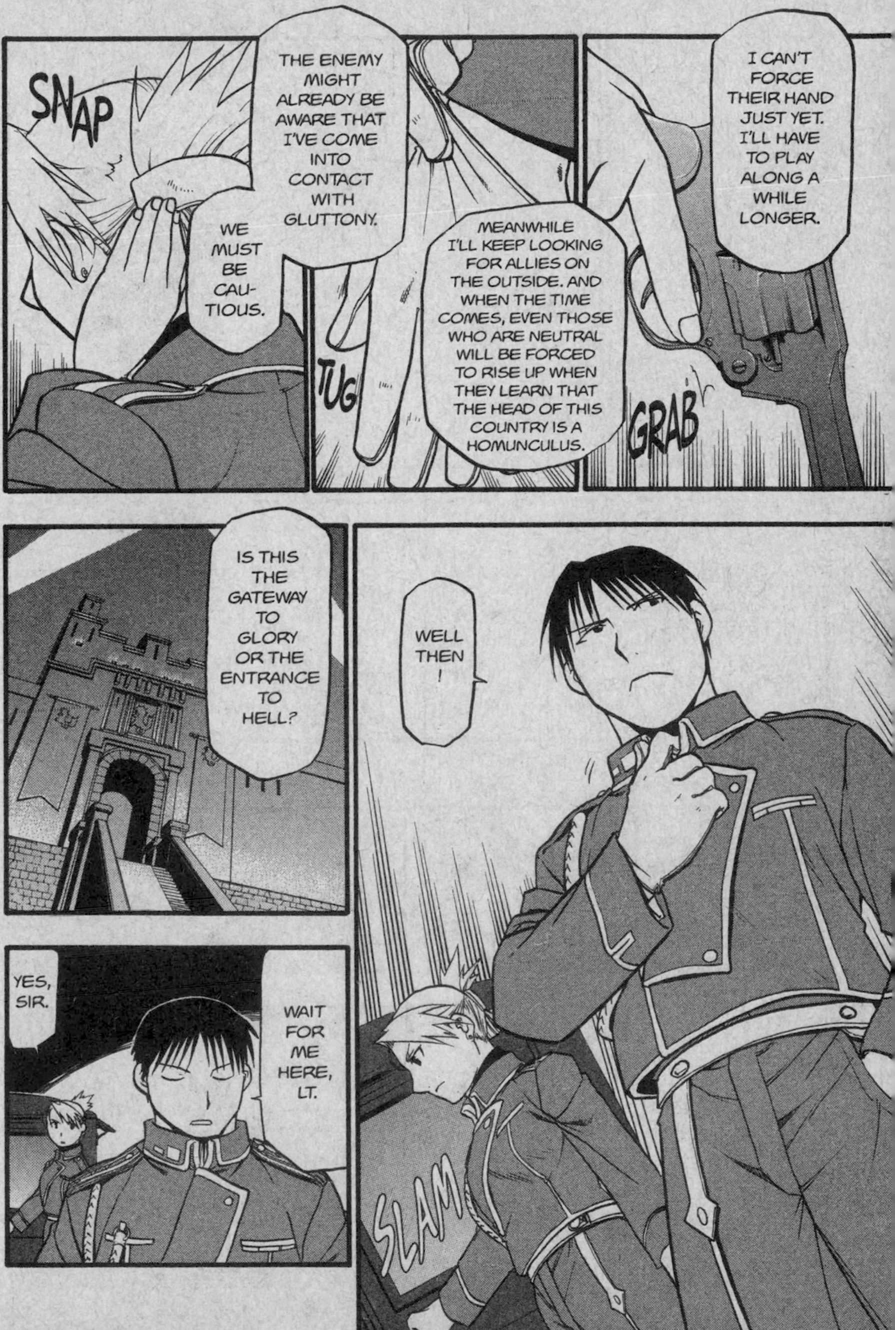
I CAN'T FORCE THEIR HAND JUST YET. I'LL HAVE TO PLAY ALONG A WHILE LONGER.
GRAB
MEANWHILE I'LL KEEP LOOKING FOR ALLIES ON THE OUTSIDE. AND WHEN THE TIME COMES, EVEN THOSE WHO ARE NEUTRAL WILL BE FORCED TO RISE UP WHEN THEY LEARN THAT THE HEAD OF THIS COUNTRY IS A HOMUNCULUS.
TUG
THE ENEMY MIGHT ALREADY BE AWARE THAT I'VE COME INTO CONTACT WITH GLUTTONY.
SNAP
WE MUST BE CAU-TIOUS.
WELL THEN!
SLAM
IS THIS THE GATEWAY TO GLORY OR THE ENTRANCE TO HELL?
WAIT FOR ME HERE, LT.
YES, SIR.

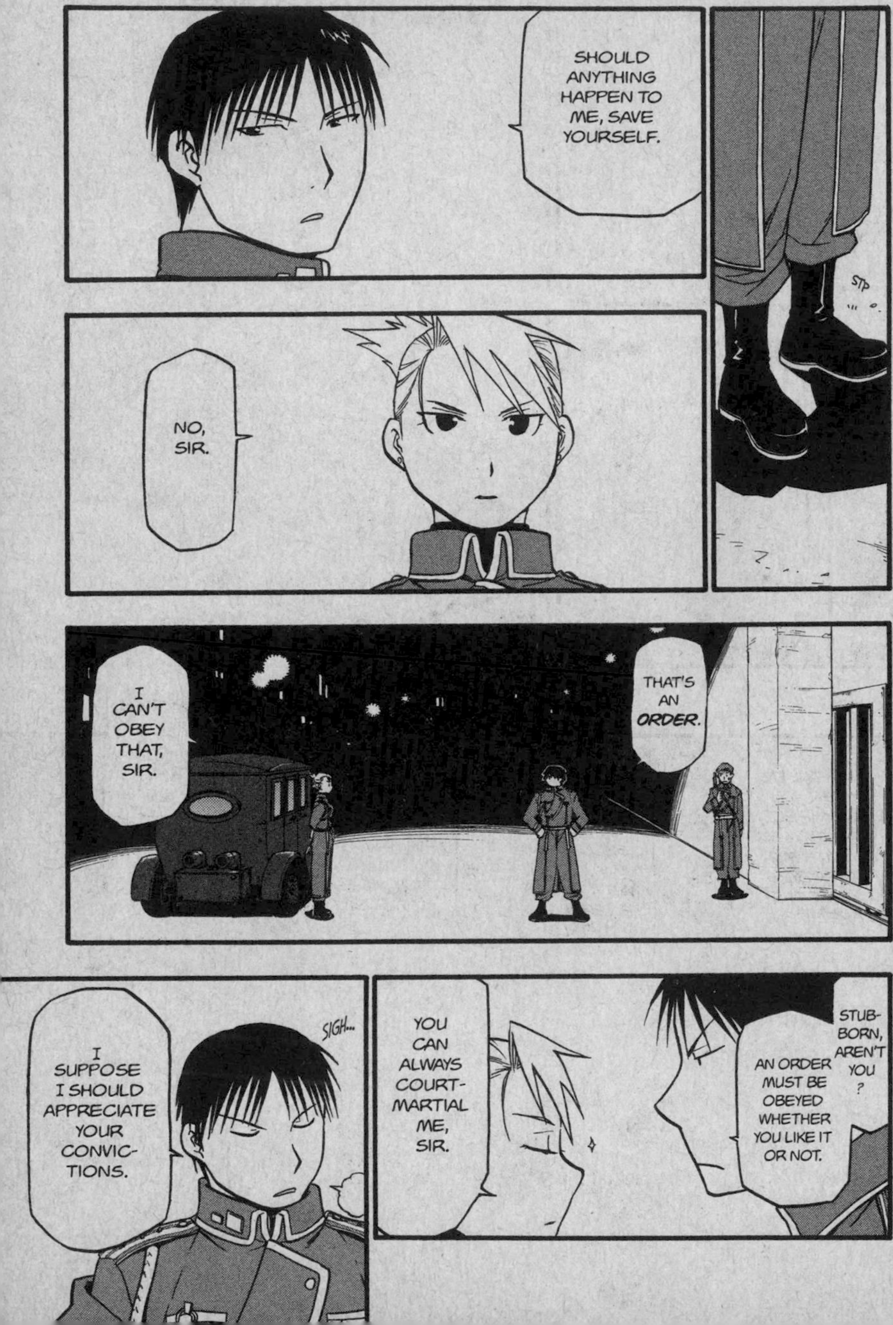
STP
SHOULD ANYTHING HAPPEN TO ME, SAVE YOURSELF.
NO, SIR.
THAT'S AN ORDER.
I CAN'T OBEY THAT, SIR.
STUB-BORN, AREN'T YOU?
AN ORDER MUST BE OBEYED WHETHER YOU LIKE IT OR NOT.
YOU CAN ALWAYS COURT-MARTIAL ME, SIR.
SIGH...
I SUPPOSE I SHOULD APPRECIATE YOUR CONVIC-TIONS.

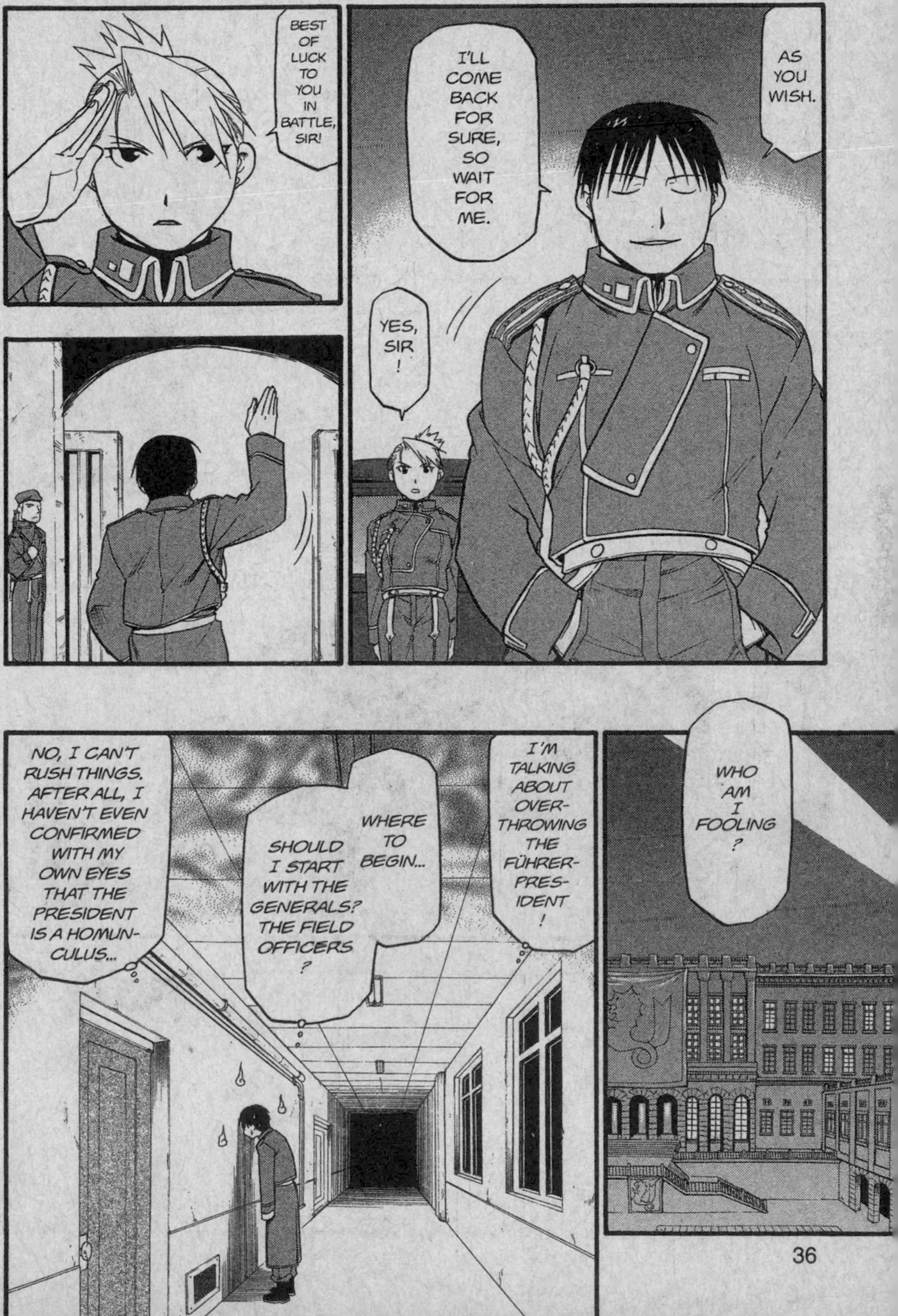
AS YOU WISH.
I'LL COME BACK FOR SURE, SO WAIT FOR ME.
YES, SIR!
BEST OF LUCK TO YOU IN BATTLE, SIR!
WHO AM I FOOLING?
I'M TALKING ABOUT OVERTHROWING THE FÜHRER-PRESIDENT!
WHERE TO BEGIN...
SHOULD I START WITH THE GENERALS? THE FIELD OFFICERS?
NO, I CAN'T RUSH THINGS. AFTER ALL, I HAVEN'T EVEN CONFIRMED WITH MY OWN EYES THAT THE PRESIDENT IS A HOMUNCULUS...

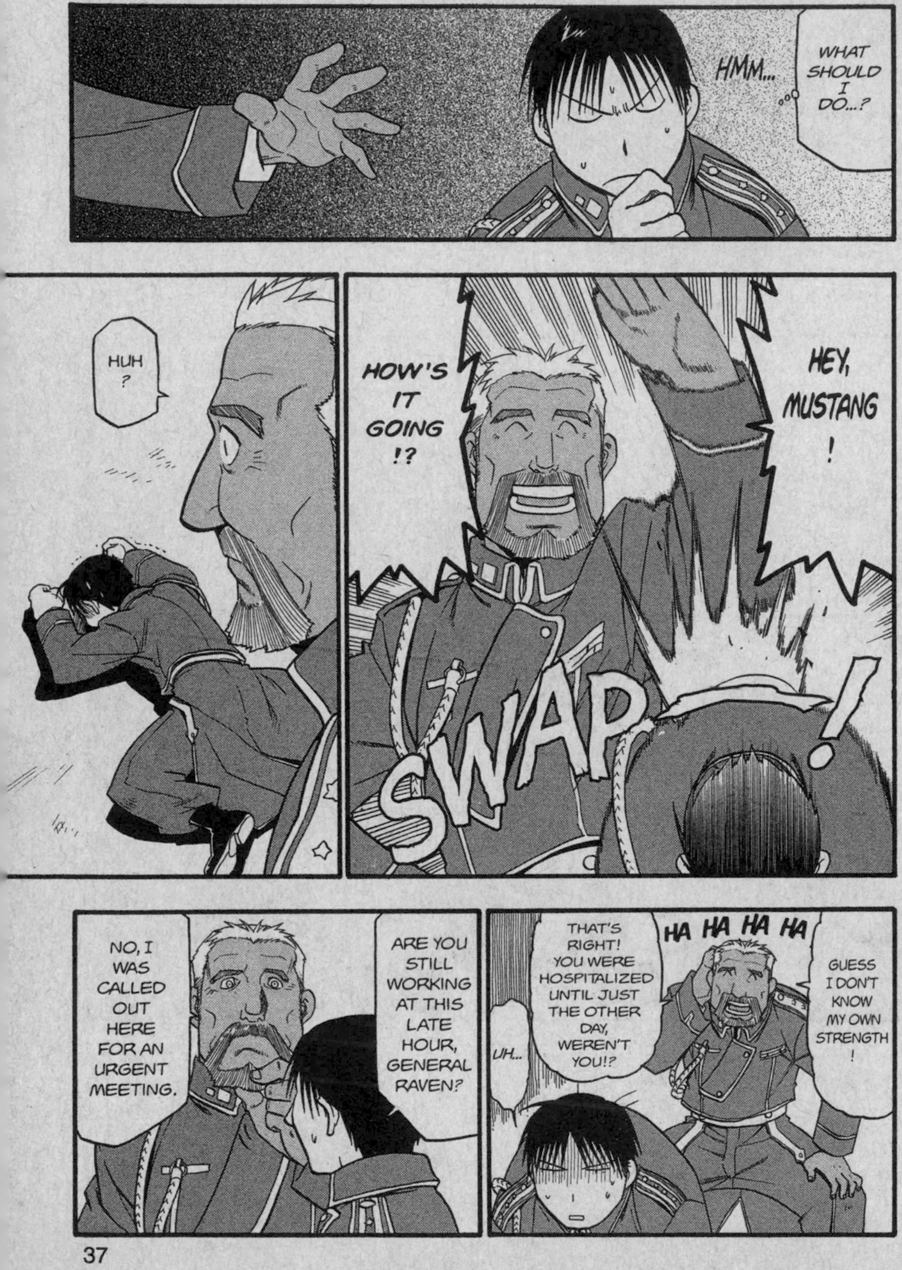
WHAT SHOULD I DO...?
HMM...
HEY, MUSTANG!
HOW'S IT GOING!?
SWAP!
HUH?
GUESS I DON'T KNOW MY OWN STRENGTH!
HA HA HA HA
THAT'S RIGHT! YOU WERE HOSPITALIZED UNTIL JUST THE OTHER DAY, WEREN'T YOU!?
UH...
ARE YOU STILL WORKING AT THIS LATE HOUR, GENERAL RAVEN?
NO, I WAS CALLED OUT HERE FOR AN URGENT MEETING.

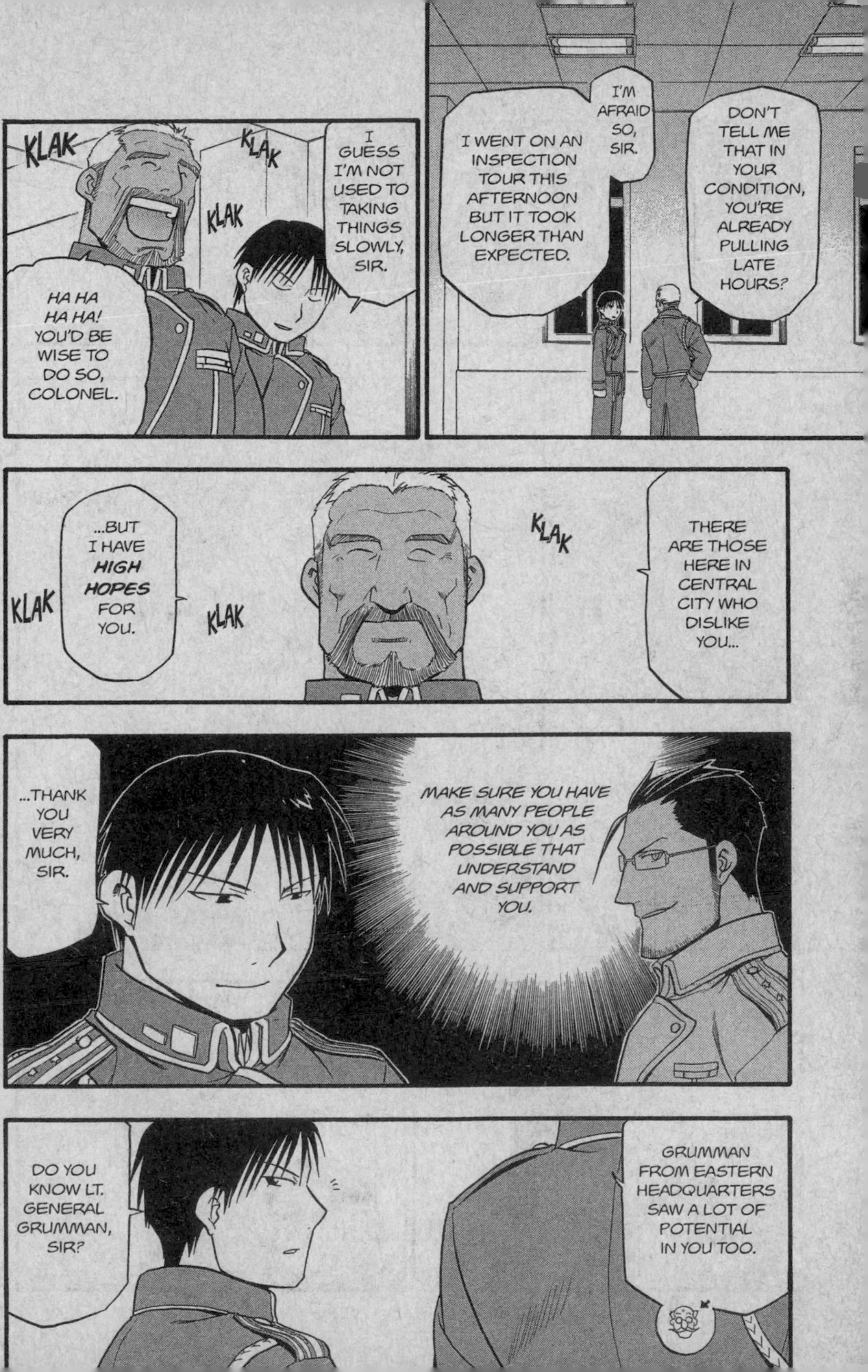
DON'T TELL ME THAT IN YOUR CONDITION, YOU'RE ALREADY PULLING LATE HOURS?
I'M AFRAID SO, SIR.
I WENT ON AN INSPECTION TOUR THIS AFTERNOON BUT IT TOOK LONGER THAN EXPECTED.
I GUESS I'M NOT USED TO TAKING THINGS SLOWLY, SIR.
KLAK
KLAK
KLAK
HA HA HA HA! YOU'D BE WISE TO DO SO, COLONEL.
THERE ARE THOSE HERE IN CENTRAL CITY WHO DISLIKE YOU...
KLAK
...BUT I HAVE HIGH HOPES FOR YOU.
KLAK
KLAK
MAKE SURE YOU HAVE AS MANY PEOPLE AROUND YOU AS POSSIBLE THAT UNDERSTAND AND SUPPORT YOU.
...THANK YOU VERY MUCH, SIR.
GRUMMAN FROM EASTERN HEADQUARTERS SAW A LOT OF POTENTIAL IN YOU TOO.
DO YOU KNOW LT. GENERAL GRUMMAN, SIR?

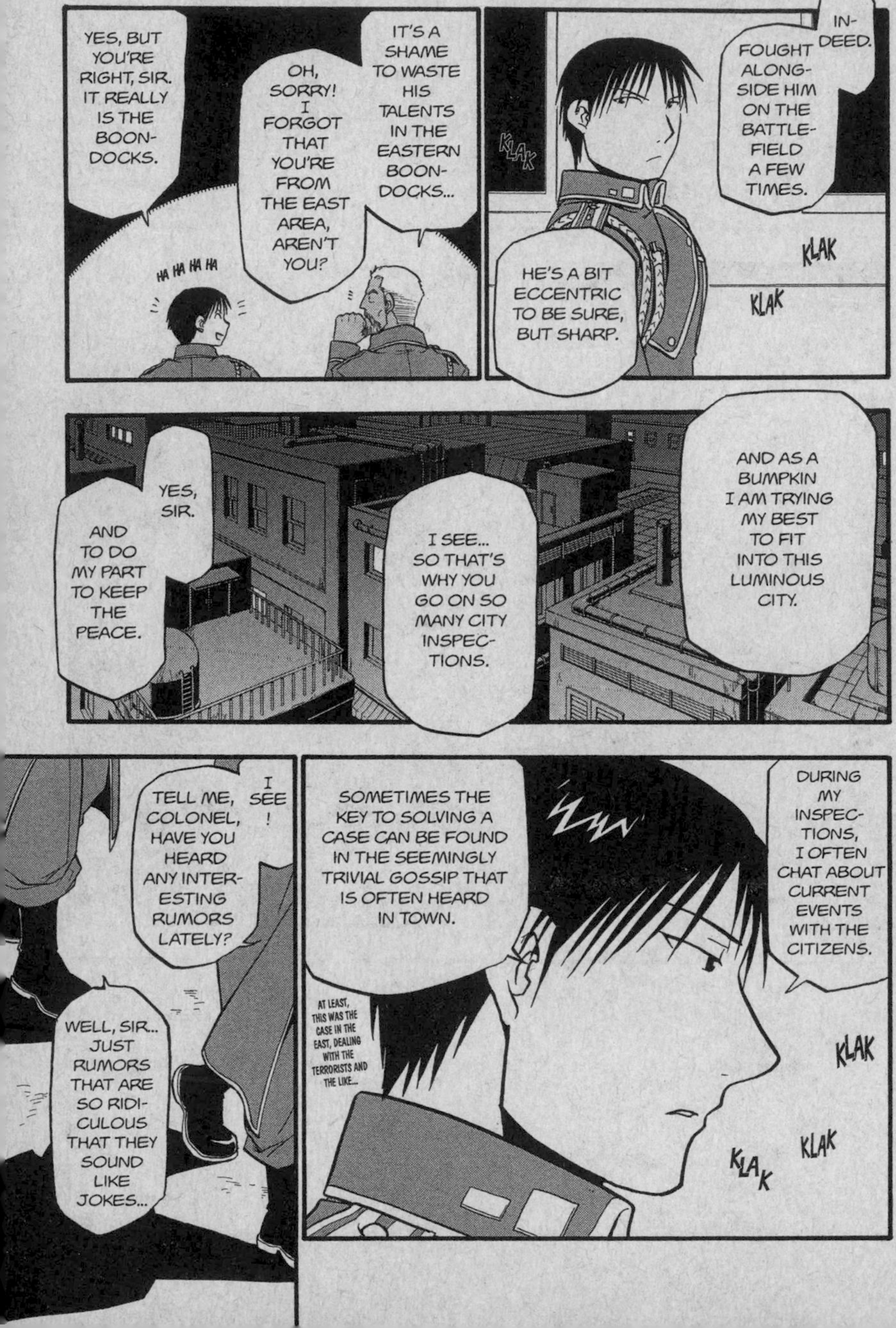
IN-DEED.
FOUGHT ALONG-SIDE HIM ON THE BATTLE-FIELD A FEW TIMES.
KLAK
KLAK
KLAK
HE'S A BIT ECCENTRIC TO BE SURE, BUT SHARP.
IT'S A SHAME TO WASTE HIS TALENTS IN THE EASTERN BOON-DOCKS...
OH, SORRY! I FORGOT THAT YOU'RE FROM THE EAST AREA, AREN'T YOU?
YES, BUT YOU'RE RIGHT, SIR. IT REALLY IS THE BOON-DOCKS.
HA HA HA HA
AND AS A BUMPKIN I AM TRYING MY BEST TO FIT INTO THIS LUMINOUS CITY.
I SEE... SO THAT'S WHY YOU GO ON SO MANY CITY INSPEC-TIONS.
YES, SIR.
AND TO DO MY PART TO KEEP THE PEACE.
DURING MY INSPEC-TIONS, I OFTEN CHAT ABOUT CURRENT EVENTS WITH THE CITIZENS.
SOMETIMES THE KEY TO SOLVING A CASE CAN BE FOUND IN THE SEEMINGLY TRIVIAL GOSSIP THAT IS OFTEN HEARD IN TOWN.
AT LEAST, THIS WAS THE CASE IN THE EAST, DEALING WITH THE TERRORISTS AND THE LIKE...
KLAK
KLAK
KLAK
I SEE!
TELL ME, COLONEL, HAVE YOU HEARD ANY INTER-ESTING RUMORS LATELY?
WELL, SIR... JUST RUMORS THAT ARE SO RIDI-CULOUS THAT THEY SOUND LIKE JOKES...

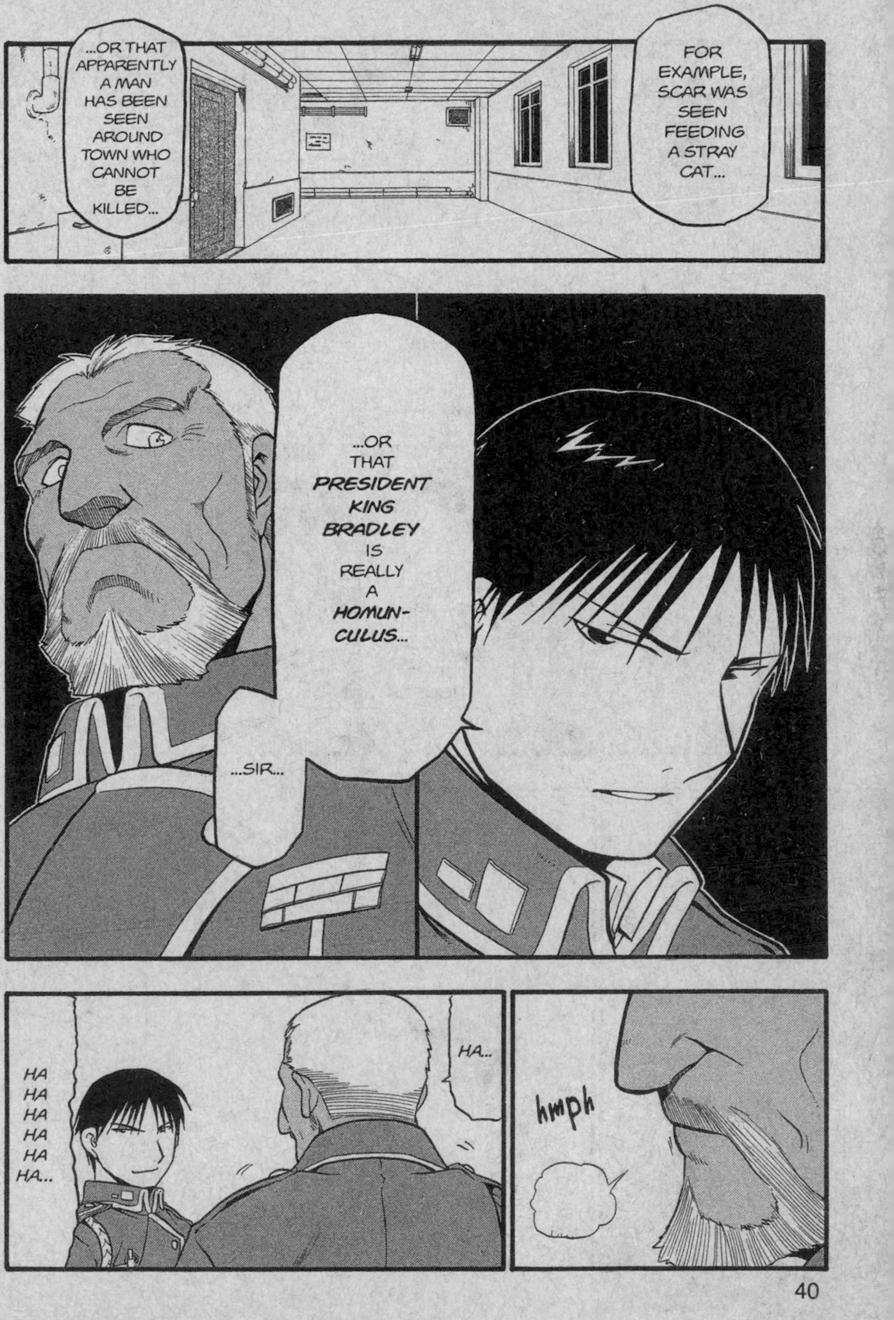
FOR EXAMPLE, SCAR WAS SEEN FEEDING A STRAY CAT...
...OR THAT APPARENTLY A MAN HAS BEEN SEEN AROUND TOWN WHO CANNOT BE KILLED...
...OR THAT PRESIDENT KING BRADLEY IS REALLY A HOMUNCULUS...
...SIR...
hmph
HA...
HA HA HA HA HA HA...

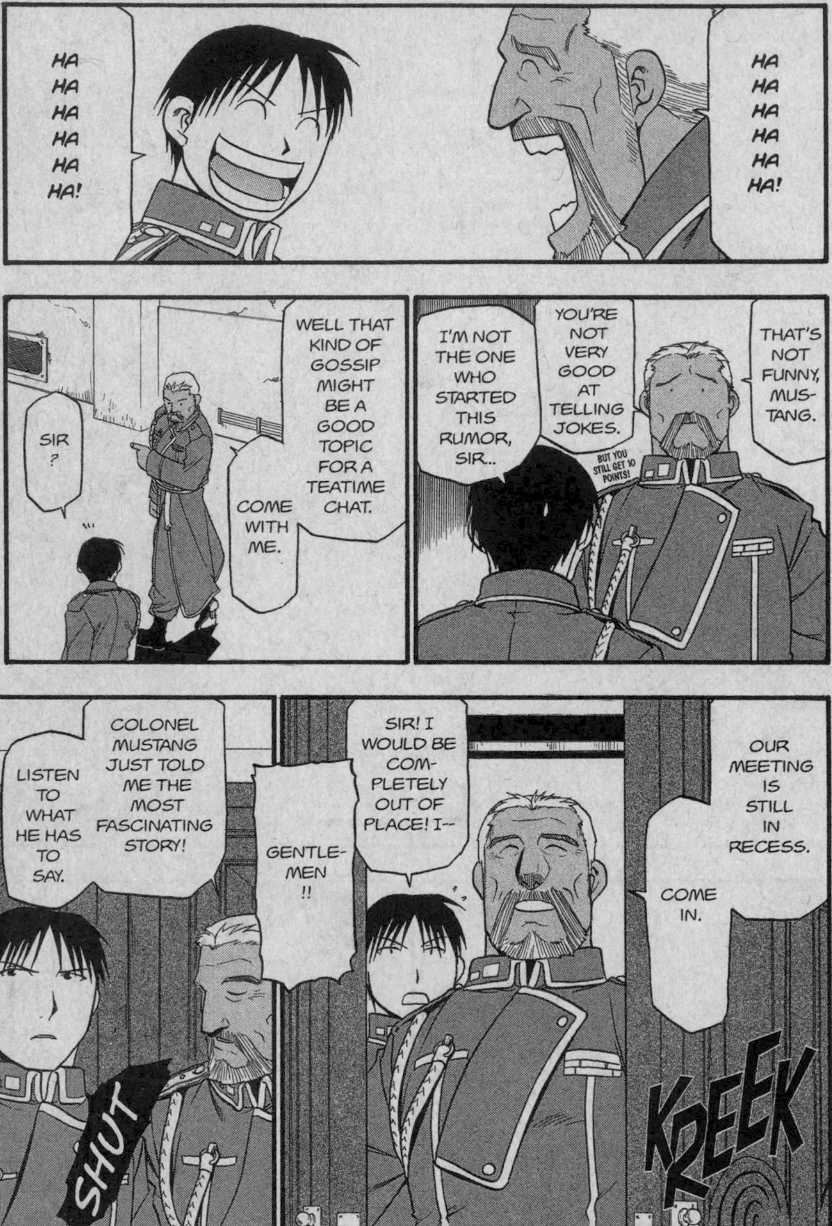
HA HA HA HA HA HA!
HA HA HA HA HA HA!
THAT'S NOT FUNNY, MUS-TANG.
YOU'RE NOT VERY GOOD AT TELLING JOKES.
BUT YOU STILL GET 10 POINTS!
I'M NOT THE ONE WHO STARTED THIS RUMOR, SIR...
WELL THAT KIND OF GOSSIP MIGHT BE A GOOD TOPIC FOR A TEATIME CHAT.
COME WITH ME.
SIR ?
OUR MEETING IS STILL IN RECESS.
COME IN.
KREEK
SIR! I WOULD BE COM-PLETELY OUT OF PLACE! I--
GENTLE-MEN !!
COLONEL MUSTANG JUST TOLD ME THE MOST FASCINATING STORY!
LISTEN TO WHAT HE HAS TO SAY.
SHUT

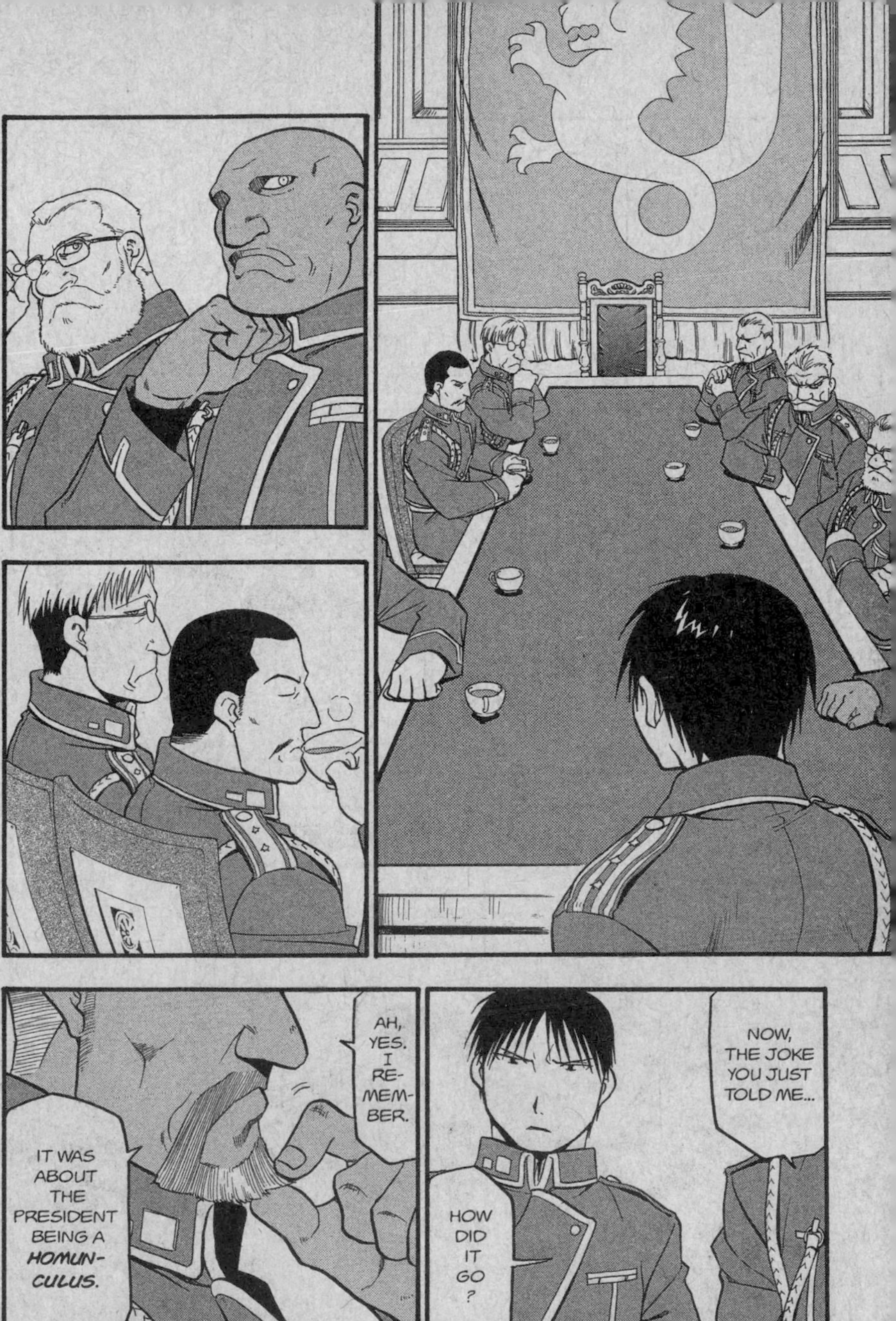
NOW, THE JOKE YOU JUST TOLD ME...
HOW DID IT GO?
AH, YES. I RE-MEMBER.
IT WAS ABOUT THE PRESIDENT BEING A *HOMUNCULUS*.

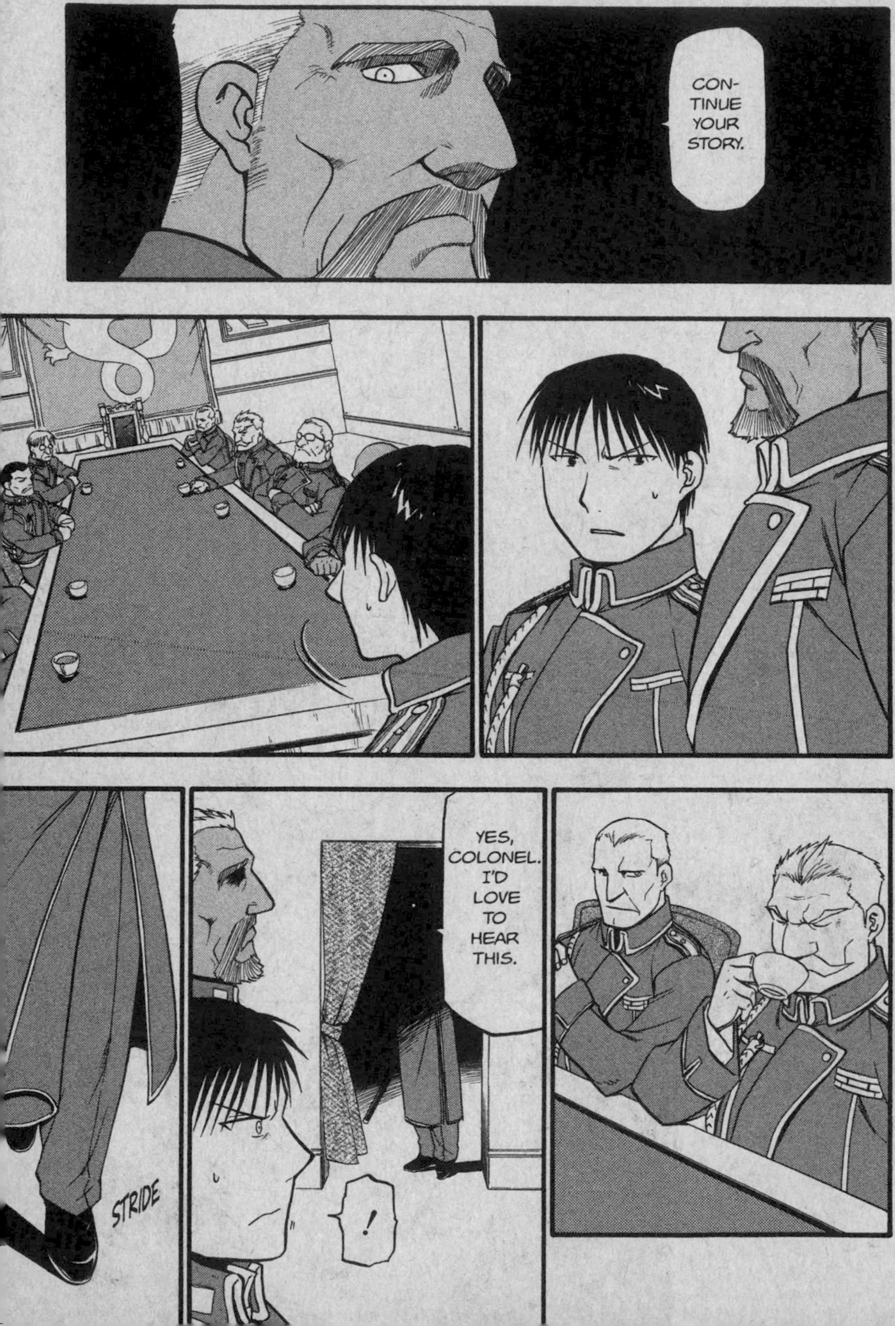
CON-TINUE YOUR STORY.
YES, COLONEL. I'D LOVE TO HEAR THIS.
!
STRIDE

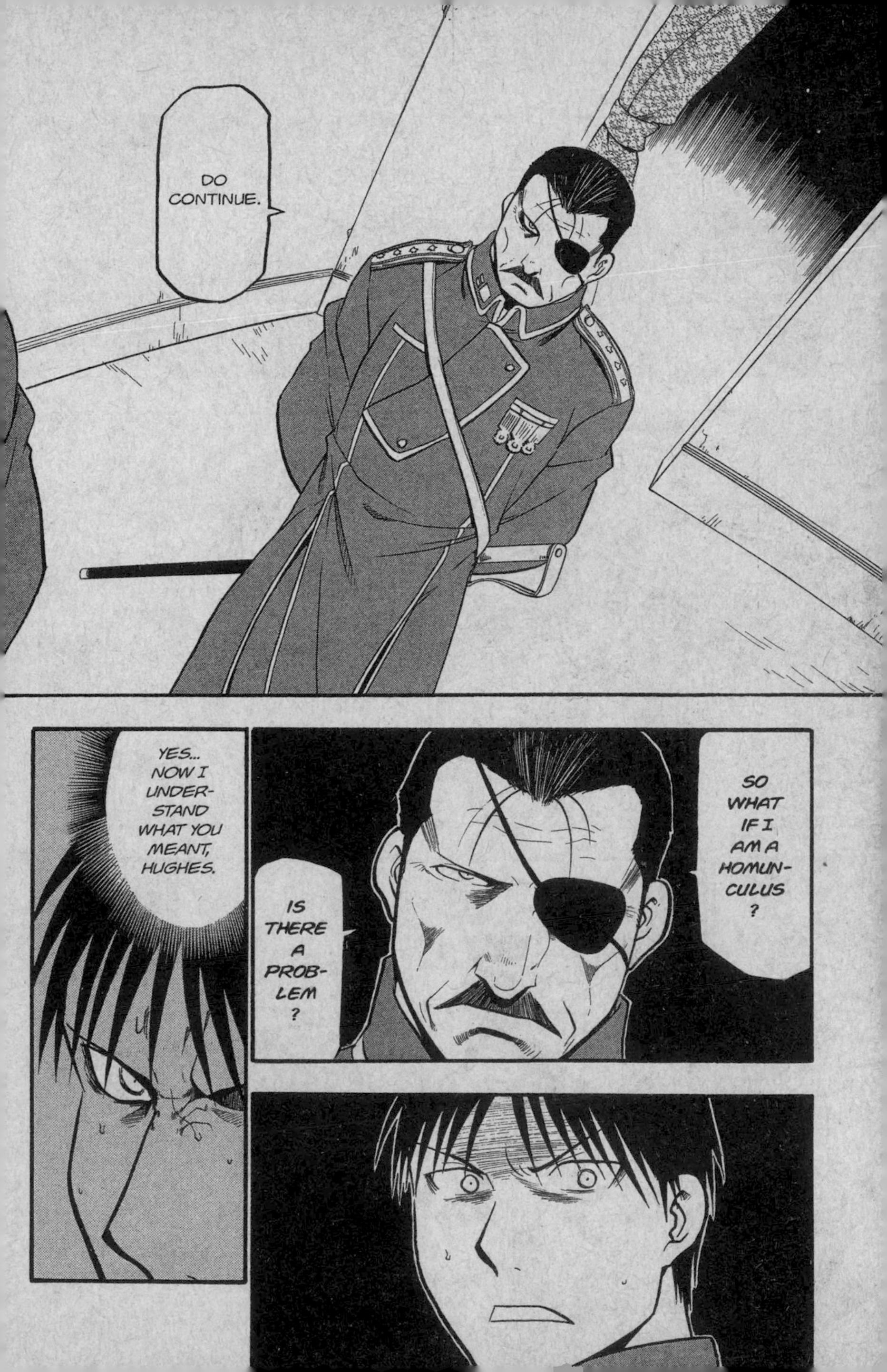
DO CONTINUE.
SO WHAT IF I AM A HOMUNCULUS?
IS THERE A PROBLEM?
YES... NOW I UNDERSTAND WHAT YOU MEANT, HUGHES.

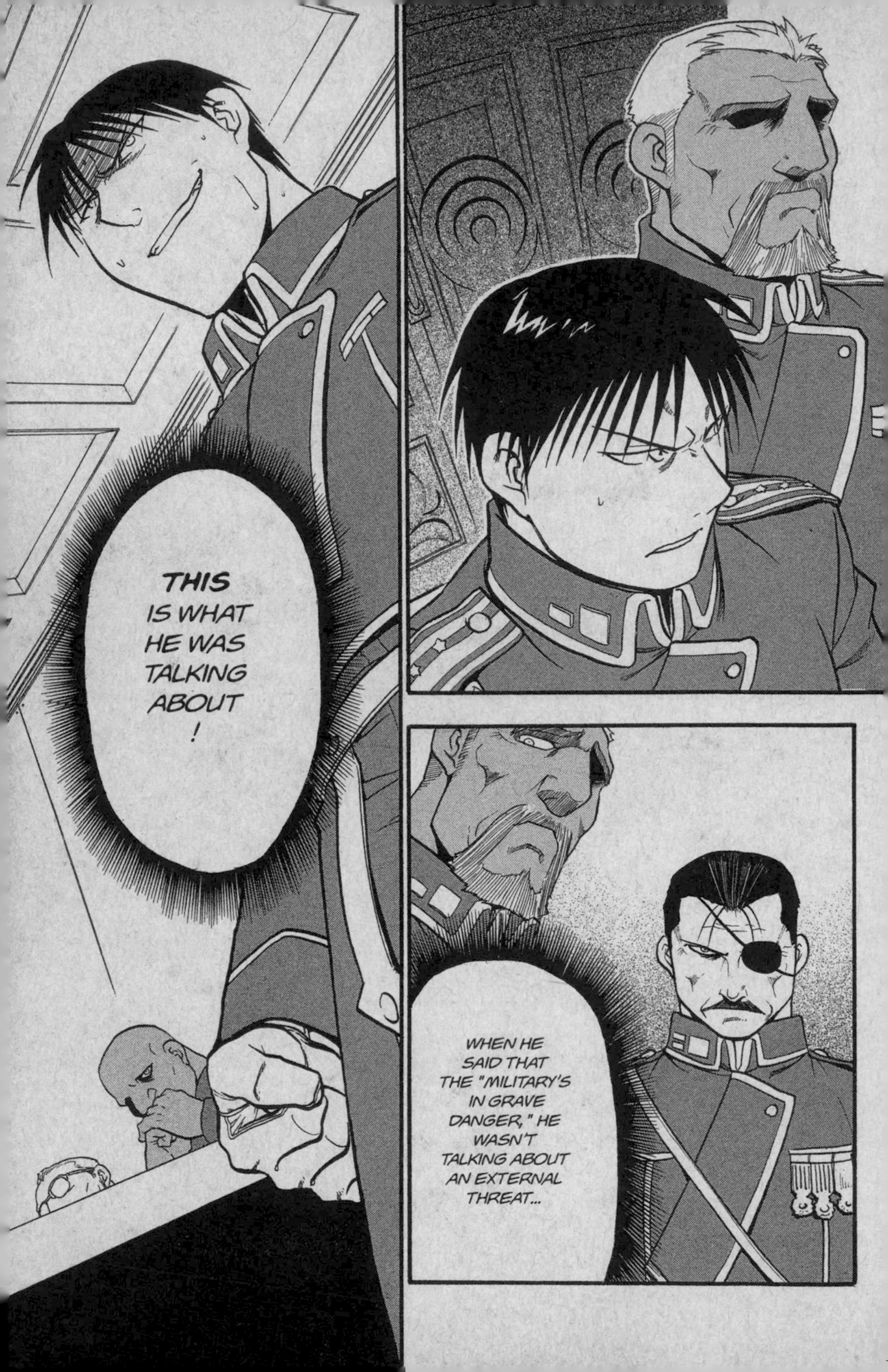
WHEN HE SAID THAT THE "MILITARY'S IN GRAVE DANGER," HE WASN'T TALKING ABOUT AN EXTERNAL THREAT...
THIS IS WHAT HE WAS TALKING ABOUT!

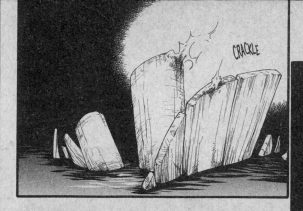

CRACKLE

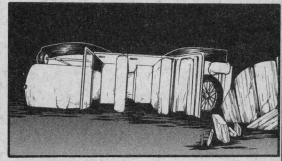

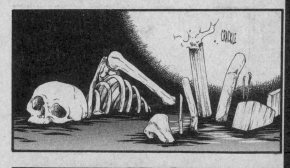

CRACKLE

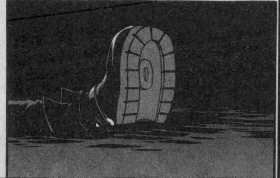

CRACKLE

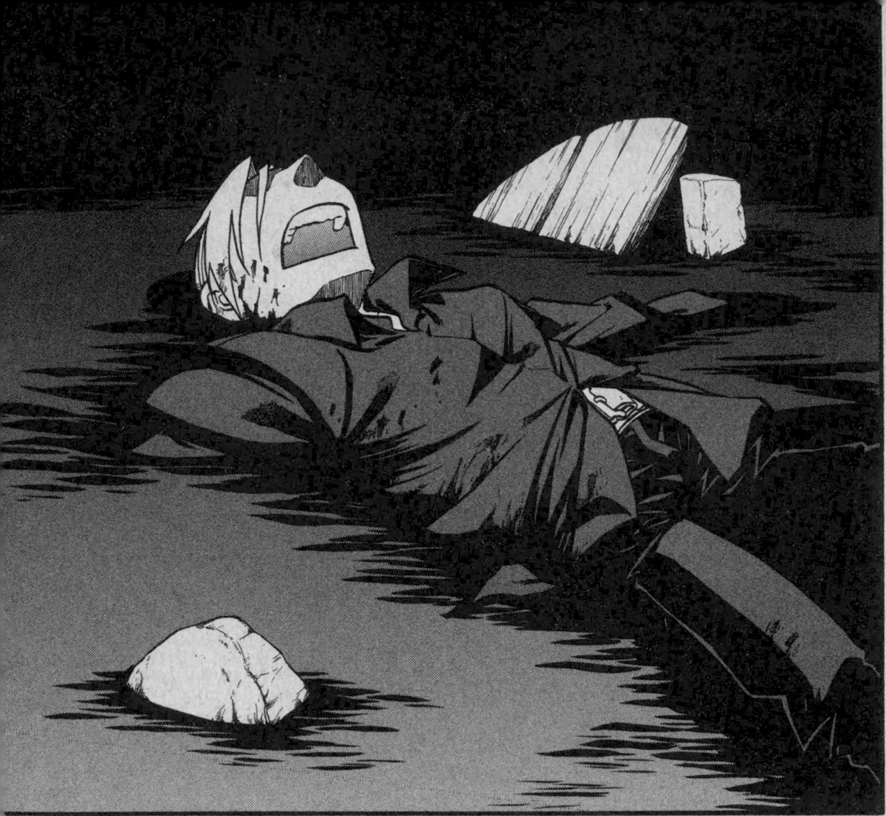
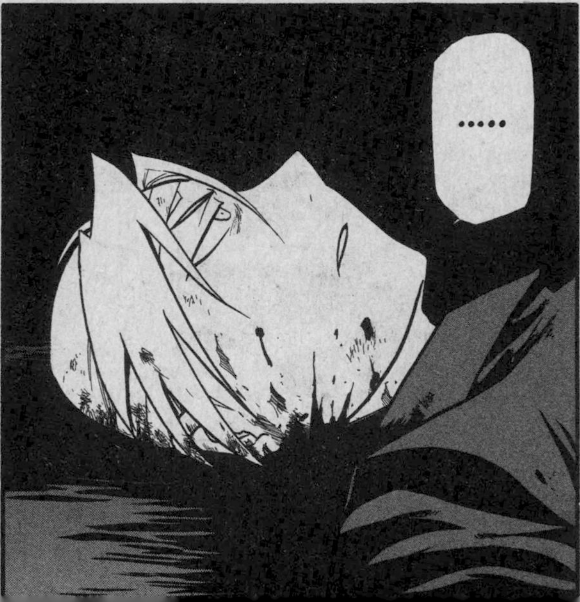
.....
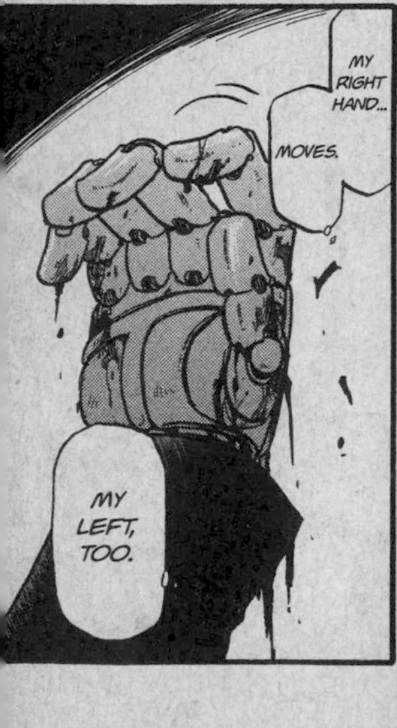
MY RIGHT HAND...
MOVES.
MY LEFT, TOO.

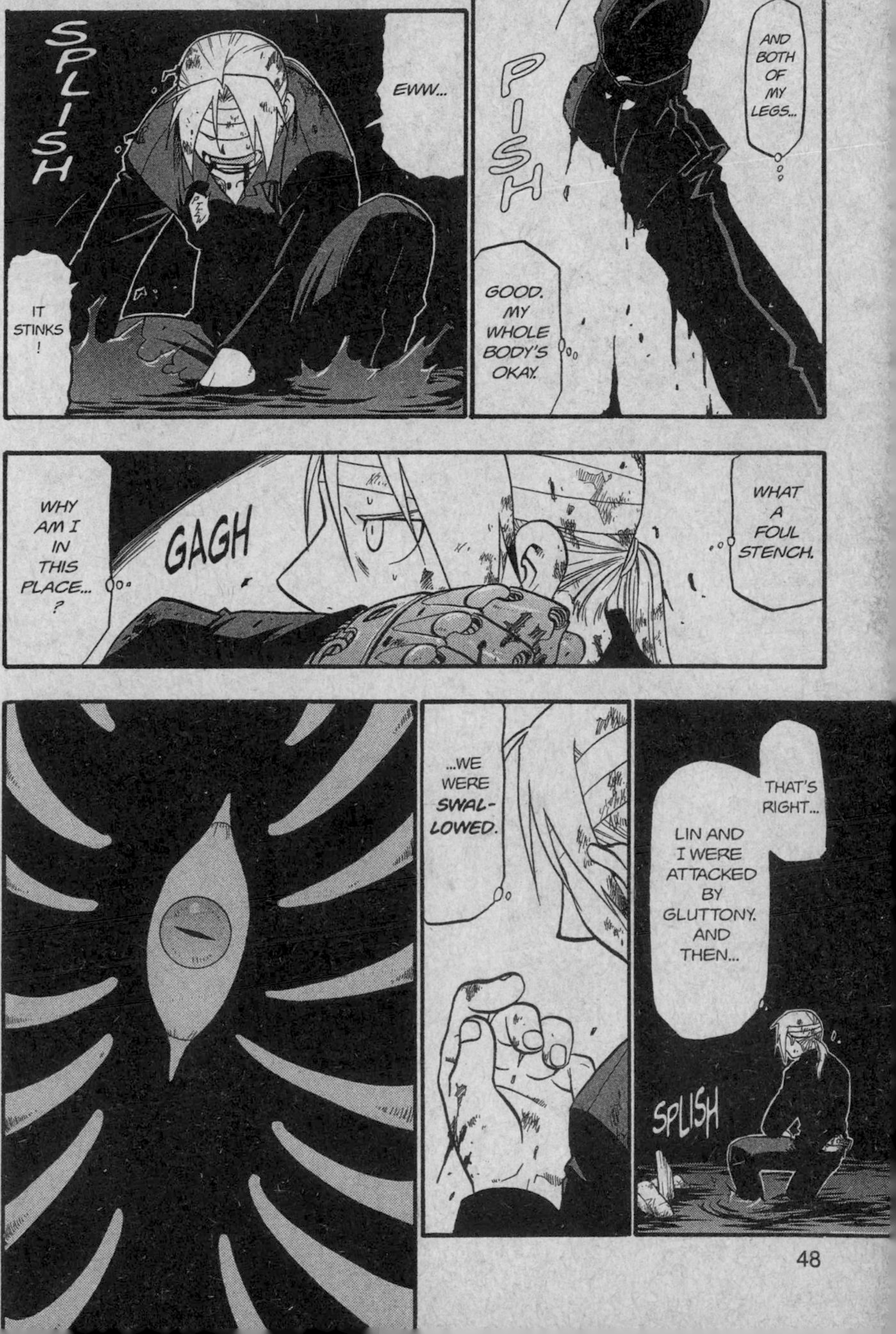
AND BOTH OF MY LEGS...
PISH
GOOD. MY WHOLE BODY'S OKAY.
SPLISH
EWW...
IT STINKS!
WHAT A FOUL STENCH.
GAGH
WHY AM I IN THIS PLACE...?
THAT'S RIGHT...
LIN AND I WERE ATTACKED BY GLUTTONY. AND THEN...
SPLISH
...WE WERE **SWALLOWED**.

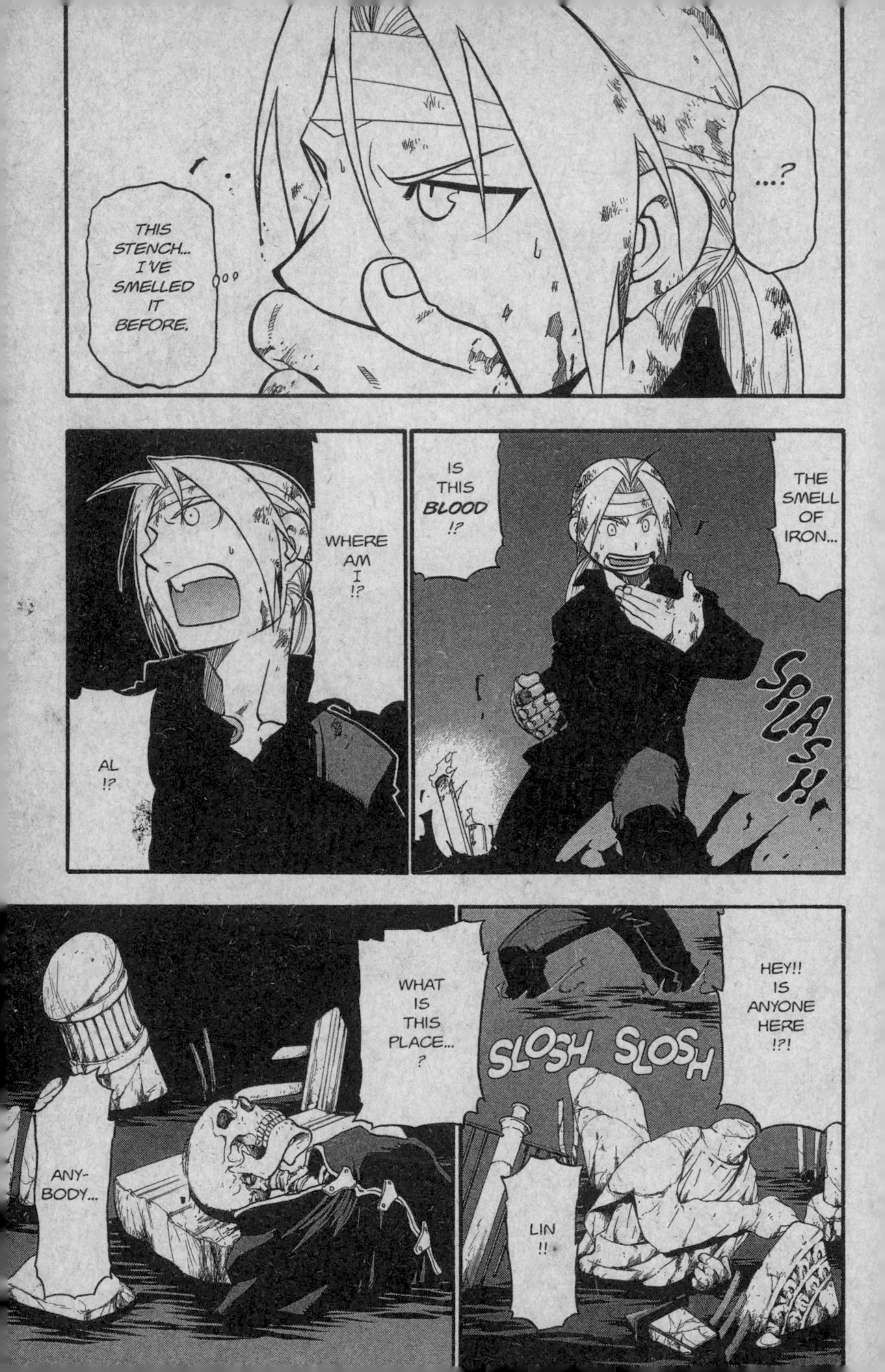
...?
THIS STENCH... I'VE SMELLED IT BEFORE.
THE SMELL OF IRON...
IS THIS BLOOD !?
SPLASH
WHERE AM I !?
AL !?
HEY!! IS ANYONE HERE !?!
SLOSH SLOSH
LIN !!
WHAT IS THIS PLACE... ?
ANY-BODY...

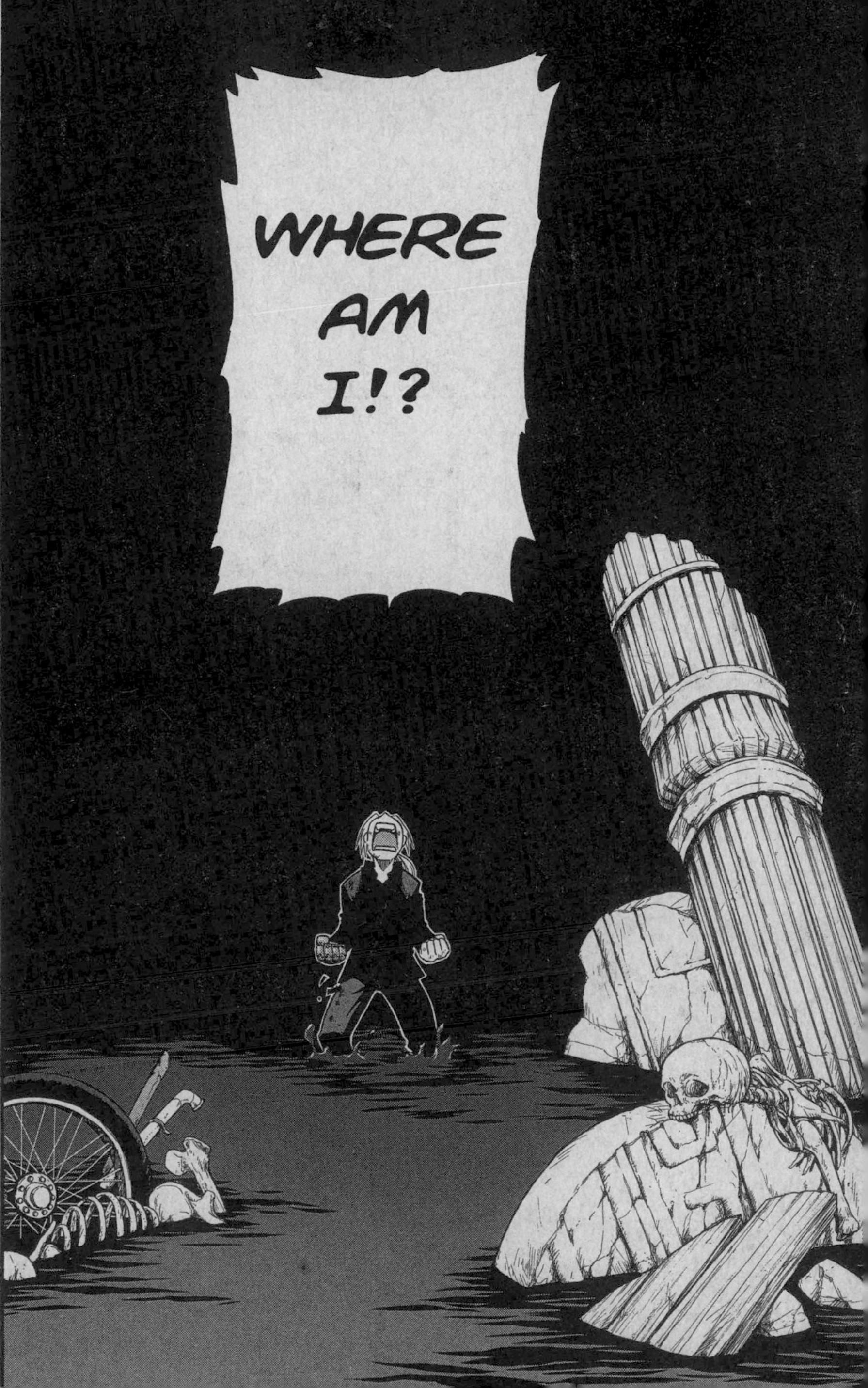
WHERE AM I!?

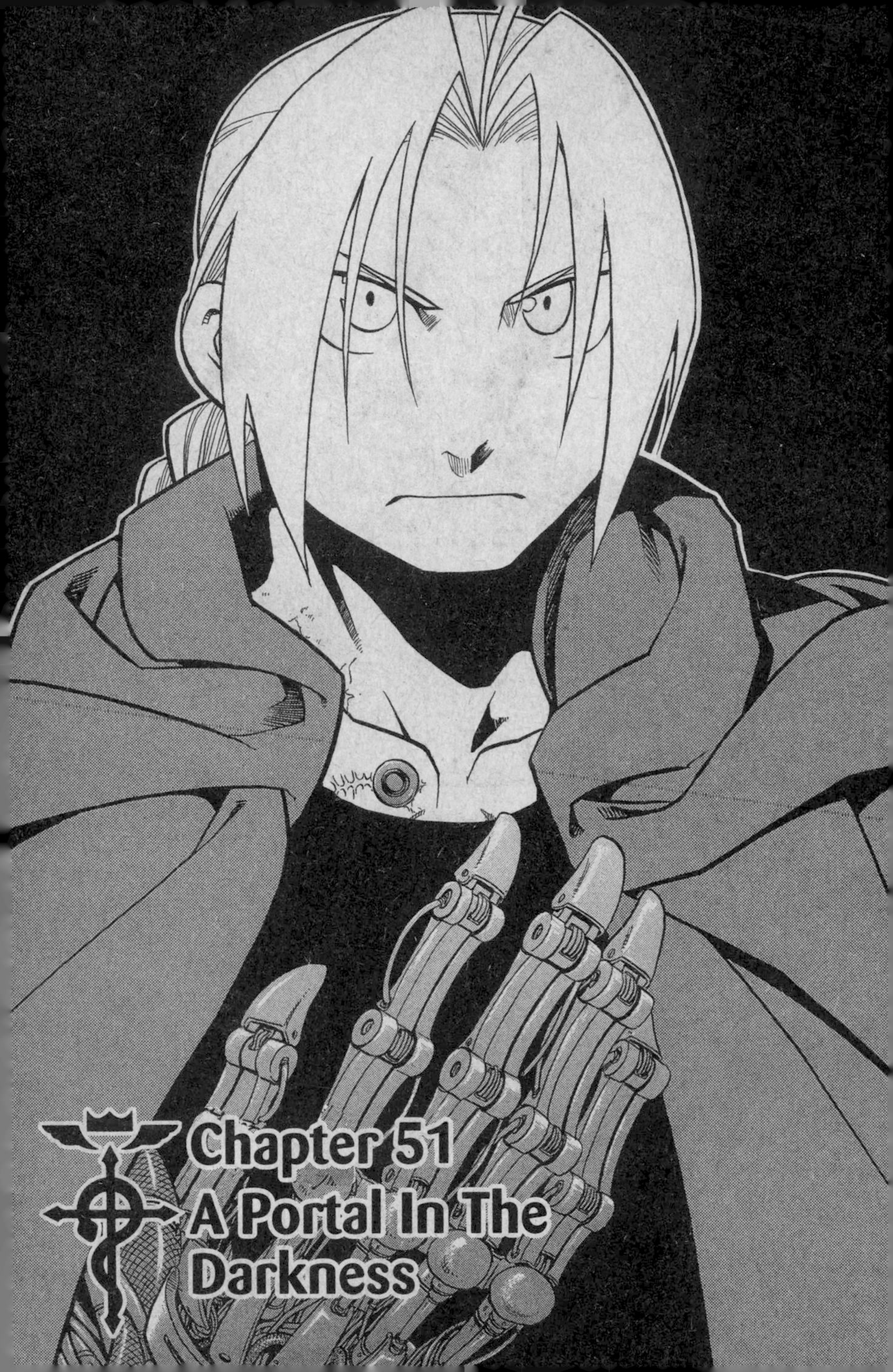
Chapter 51
A Portal In The Darkness

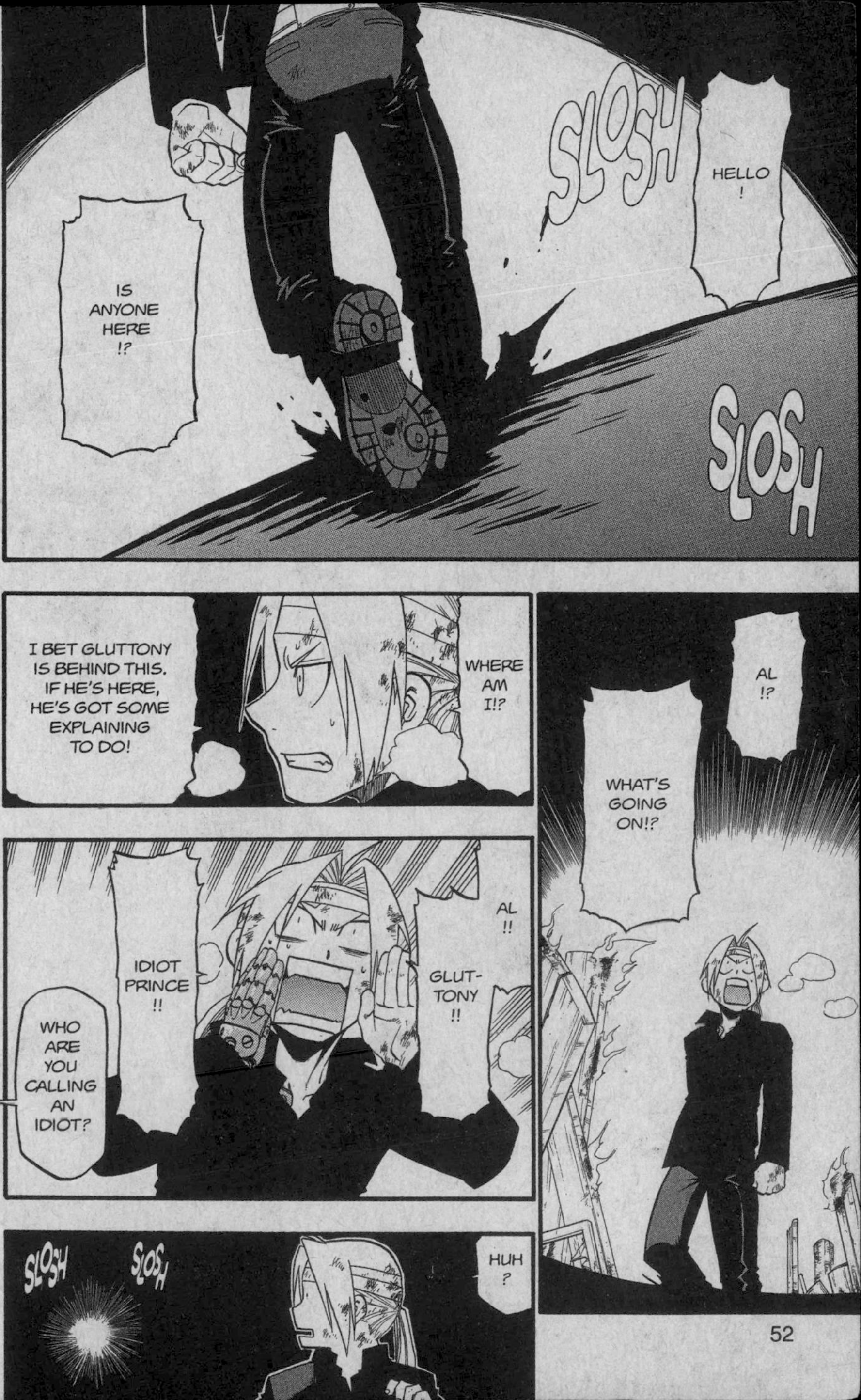
HELLO !
SLOSH
SLOSH
IS ANYONE HERE !?
AL !?
WHAT'S GOING ON!?
WHERE AM I!?
I BET GLUTTONY IS BEHIND THIS. IF HE'S HERE, HE'S GOT SOME EXPLAINING TO DO!
AL !!
GLUT-TONY !!
IDIOT PRINCE !!
WHO ARE YOU CALLING AN IDIOT?
HUH ?
SLOSH
SLOSH

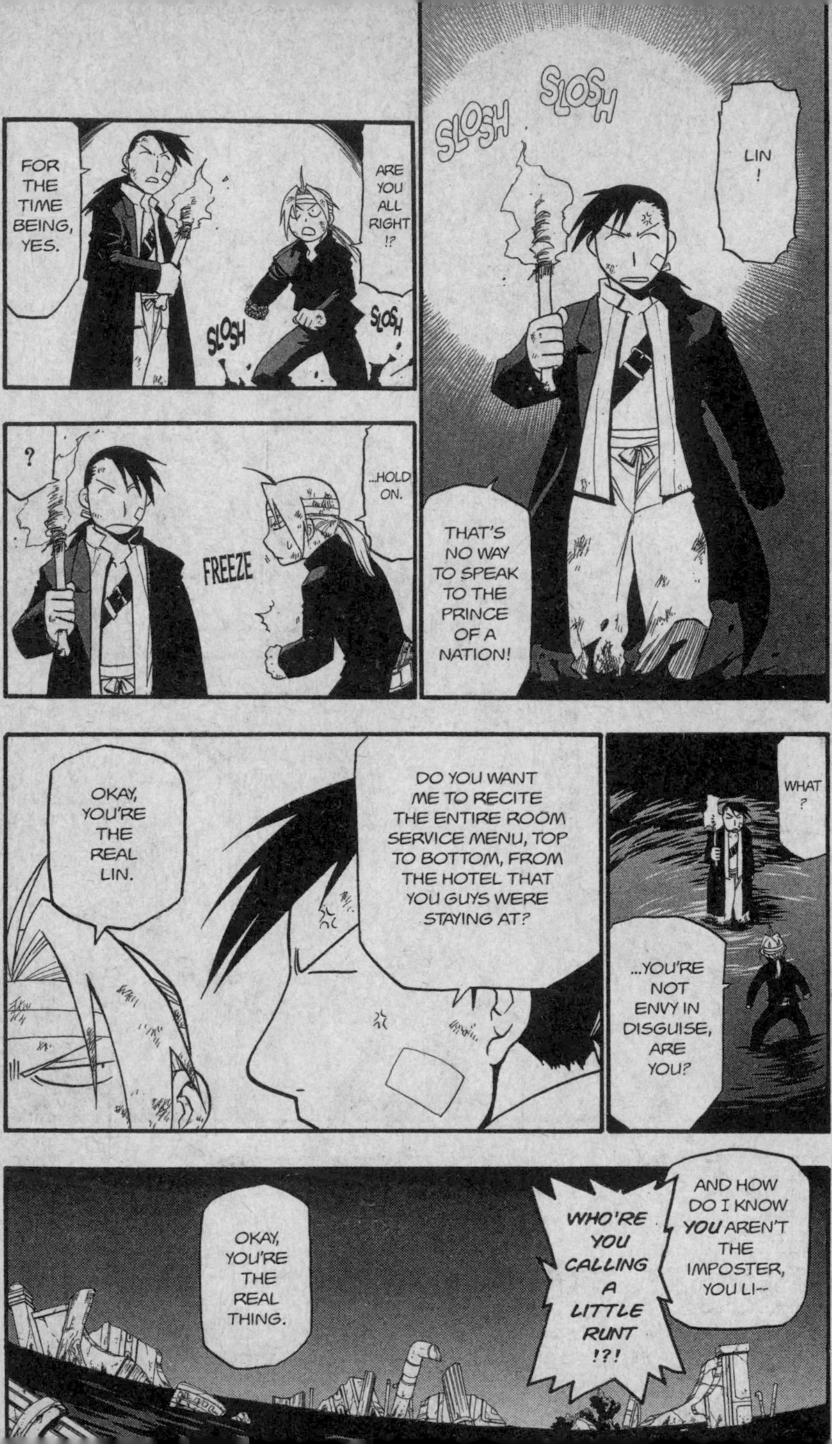
SLOSH
SLOSH
LIN!
THAT'S NO WAY TO SPEAK TO THE PRINCE OF A NATION!
ARE YOU ALL RIGHT!?
FOR THE TIME BEING, YES.
SLOSH
SLOSH
...HOLD ON.
FREEZE
?
WHAT?
...YOU'RE NOT ENVY IN DISGUISE, ARE YOU?
DO YOU WANT ME TO RECITE THE ENTIRE ROOM SERVICE MENU, TOP TO BOTTOM, FROM THE HOTEL THAT YOU GUYS WERE STAYING AT?
OKAY, YOU'RE THE REAL LIN.
AND HOW DO I KNOW YOU AREN'T THE IMPOSTER, YOU LI--
WHO'RE YOU CALLING A LITTLE RUNT!?!
OKAY, YOU'RE THE REAL THING.

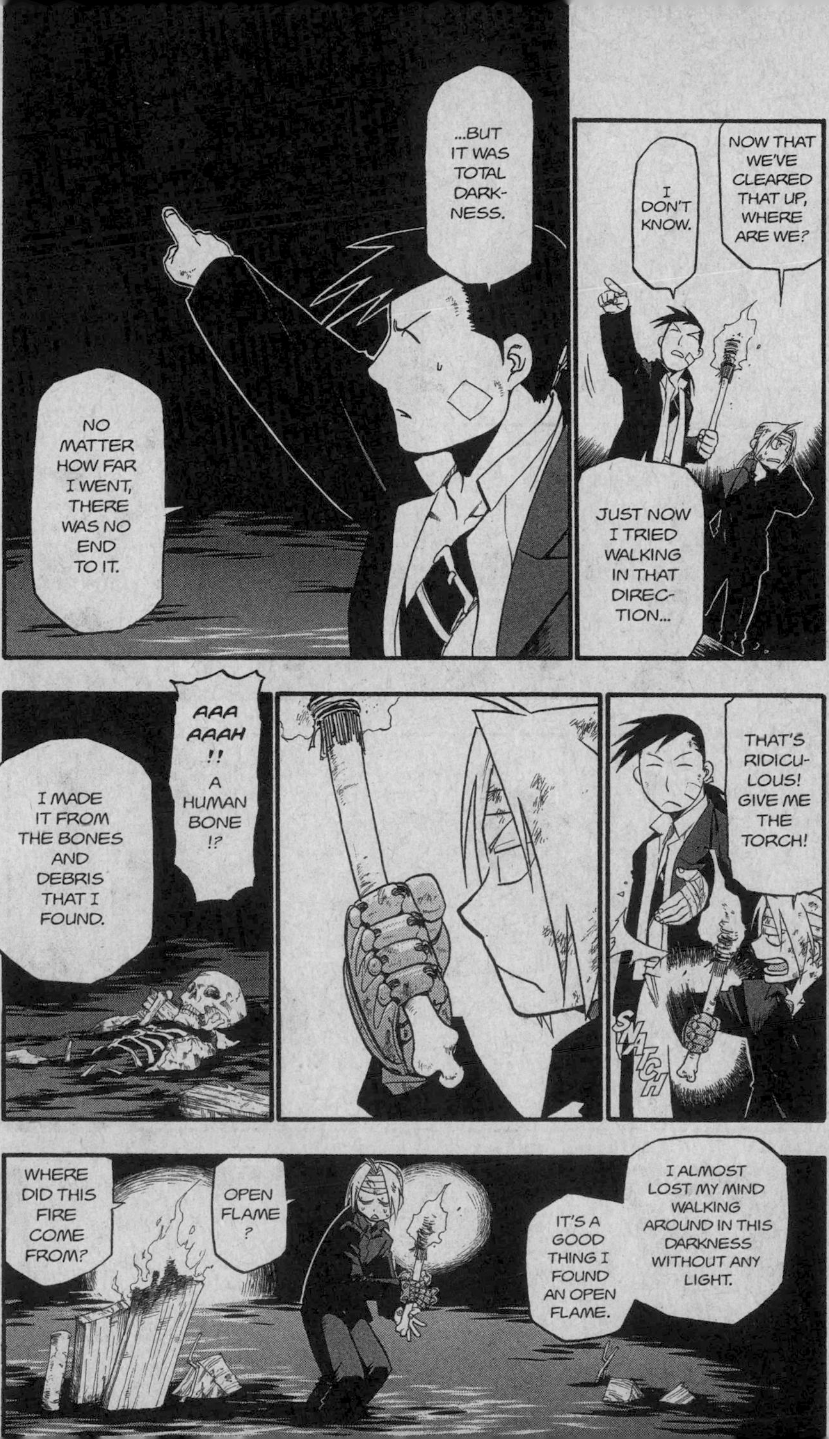
NOW THAT WE'VE CLEARED THAT UP, WHERE ARE WE?
I DON'T KNOW.
JUST NOW I TRIED WALKING IN THAT DIREC-TION...
...BUT IT WAS TOTAL DARK-NESS.
NO MATTER HOW FAR I WENT, THERE WAS NO END TO IT.
THAT'S RIDICU-LOUS! GIVE ME THE TORCH!
SNATCH
AAAAAAH!! A HUMAN BONE!?
I MADE IT FROM THE BONES AND DEBRIS THAT I FOUND.
I ALMOST LOST MY MIND WALKING AROUND IN THIS DARKNESS WITHOUT ANY LIGHT.
IT'S A GOOD THING I FOUND AN OPEN FLAME.
OPEN FLAME?
WHERE DID THIS FIRE COME FROM?

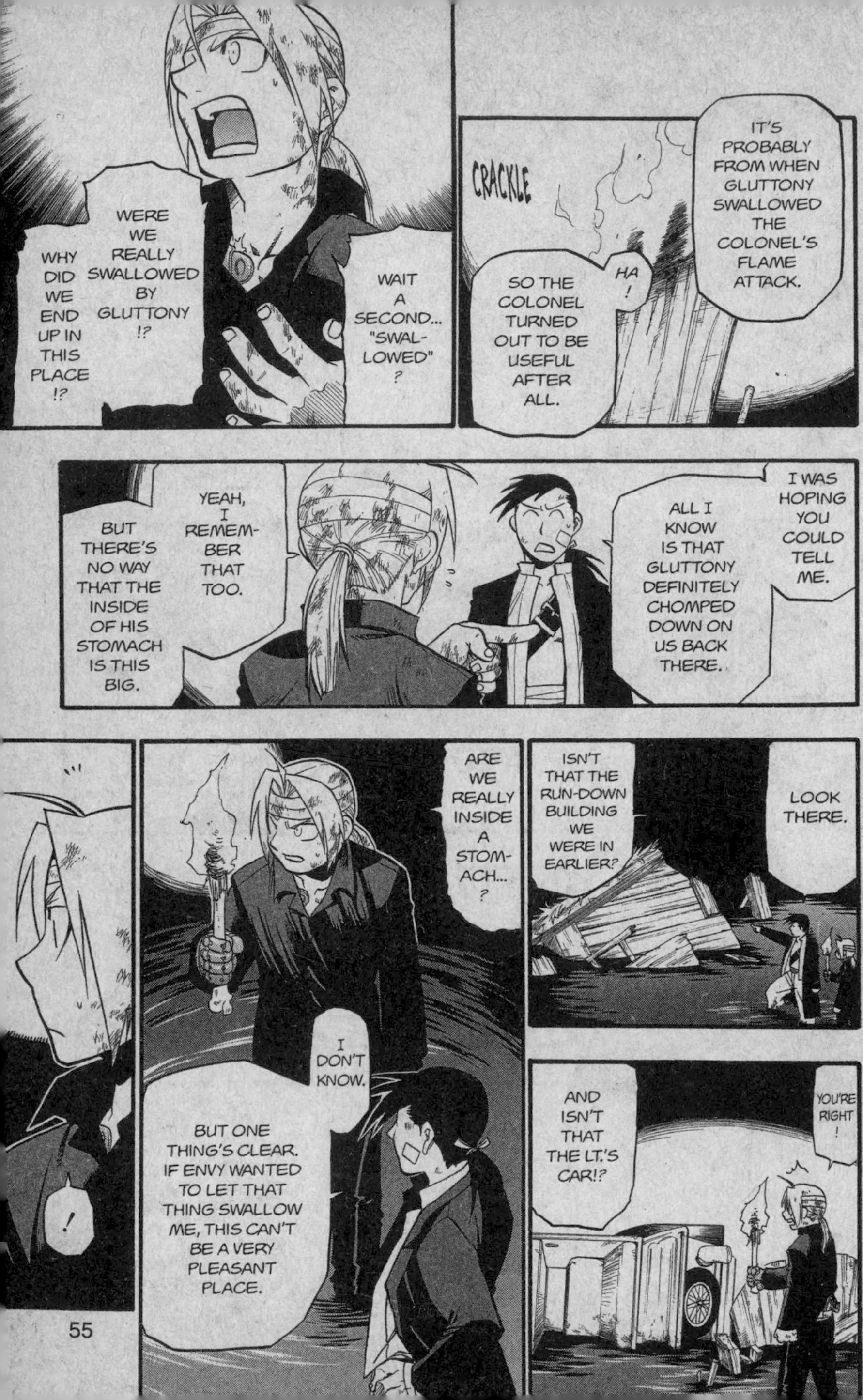

IT'S PROBABLY FROM WHEN GLUTTONY SWALLOWED THE COLONEL'S FLAME ATTACK.
CRACKLE
HA!
SO THE COLONEL TURNED OUT TO BE USEFUL AFTER ALL.
WAIT A SECOND... "SWAL-LOWED"?
WERE WE REALLY SWALLOWED BY GLUTTONY!?
WHY DID WE END UP IN THIS PLACE!?
I WAS HOPING YOU COULD TELL ME.
ALL I KNOW IS THAT GLUTTONY DEFINITELY CHOMPED DOWN ON US BACK THERE.
YEAH, I REMEM-BER THAT TOO.
BUT THERE'S NO WAY THAT THE INSIDE OF HIS STOMACH IS THIS BIG.
LOOK THERE.
ISN'T THAT THE RUN-DOWN BUILDING WE WERE IN EARLIER?
YOU'RE RIGHT!
AND ISN'T THAT THE LT.'S CAR!?
ARE WE REALLY INSIDE A STOM-ACH...?
I DON'T KNOW.
BUT ONE THING'S CLEAR. IF ENVY WANTED TO LET THAT THING SWALLOW ME, THIS CAN'T BE A VERY PLEASANT PLACE.
!

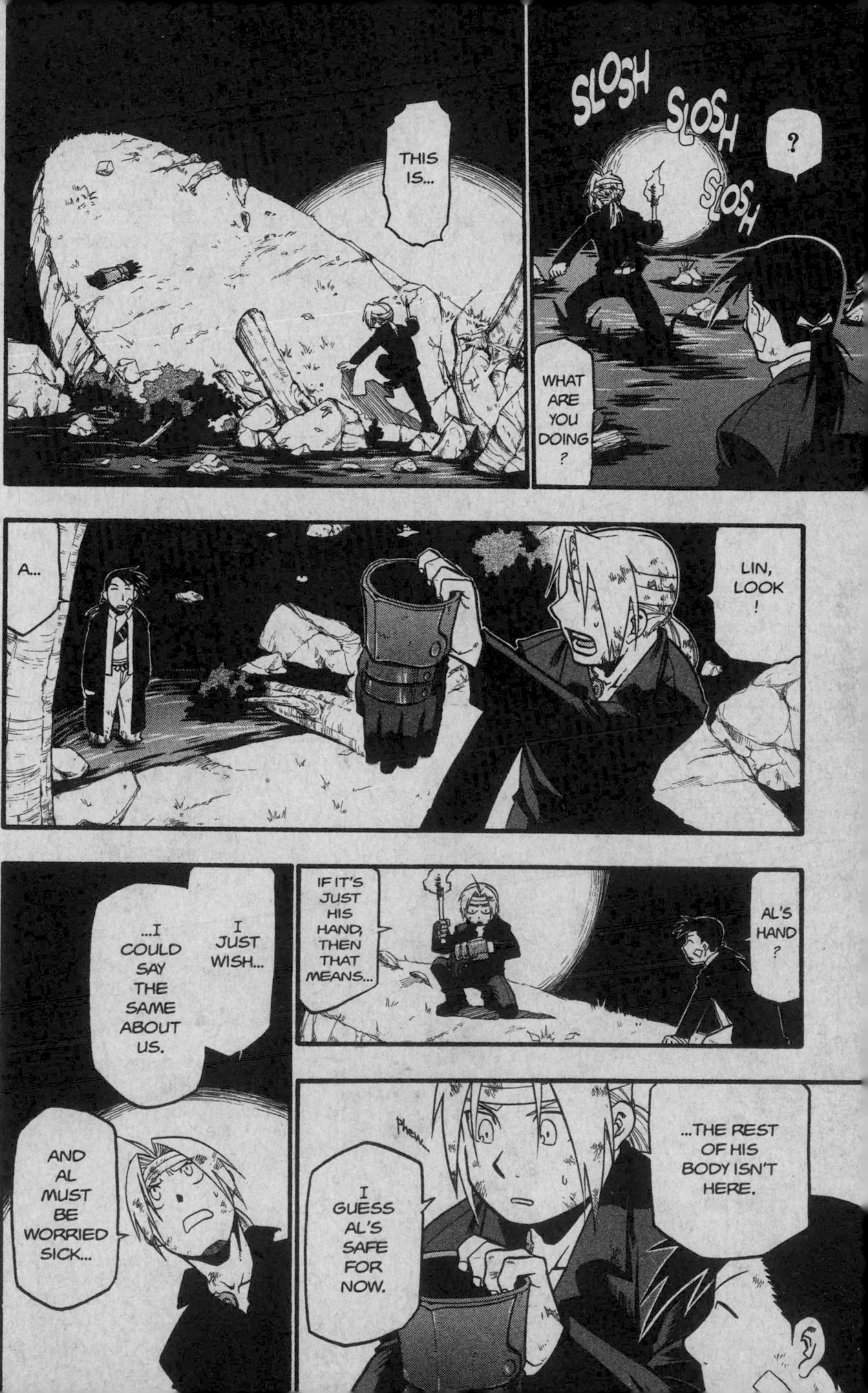
SLOSH
SLOSH
SLOSH
?
WHAT ARE YOU DOING?
THIS IS...
LIN, LOOK!
A...
AL'S HAND?
IF IT'S JUST HIS HAND, THEN THAT MEANS...
...THE REST OF HIS BODY ISN'T HERE.
Phew...
I GUESS AL'S SAFE FOR NOW.
I JUST WISH...
...I COULD SAY THE SAME ABOUT US.
AND AL MUST BE WORRIED SICK...

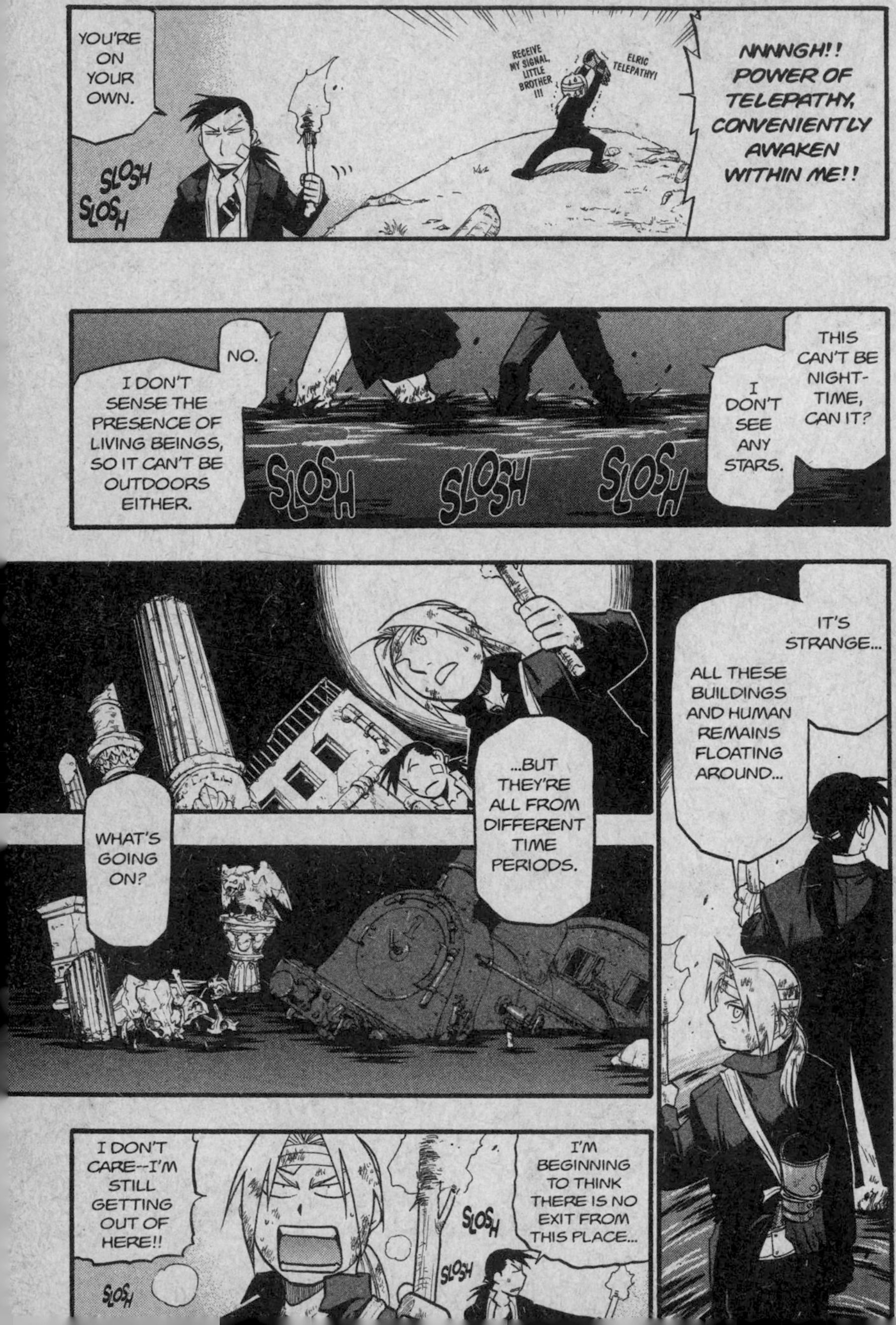
NNNNGH!! POWER OF TELEPATHY, CONVENIENTLY AWAKEN WITHIN ME!!
ELRIC TELEPATHY!
RECEIVE MY SIGNAL, LITTLE BROTHER !!!
SLOSH
SLOSH
YOU'RE ON YOUR OWN.
THIS CAN'T BE NIGHT-TIME, CAN IT?
I DON'T SEE ANY STARS.
SLOSH
SLOSH
SLOSH
NO.
I DON'T SENSE THE PRESENCE OF LIVING BEINGS, SO IT CAN'T BE OUTDOORS EITHER.
IT'S STRANGE...
ALL THESE BUILDINGS AND HUMAN REMAINS FLOATING AROUND...
...BUT THEY'RE ALL FROM DIFFERENT TIME PERIODS.
WHAT'S GOING ON?
I'M BEGINNING TO THINK THERE IS NO EXIT FROM THIS PLACE...
SLOSH
SLOSH
I DON'T CARE--I'M STILL GETTING OUT OF HERE!!
SLOSH

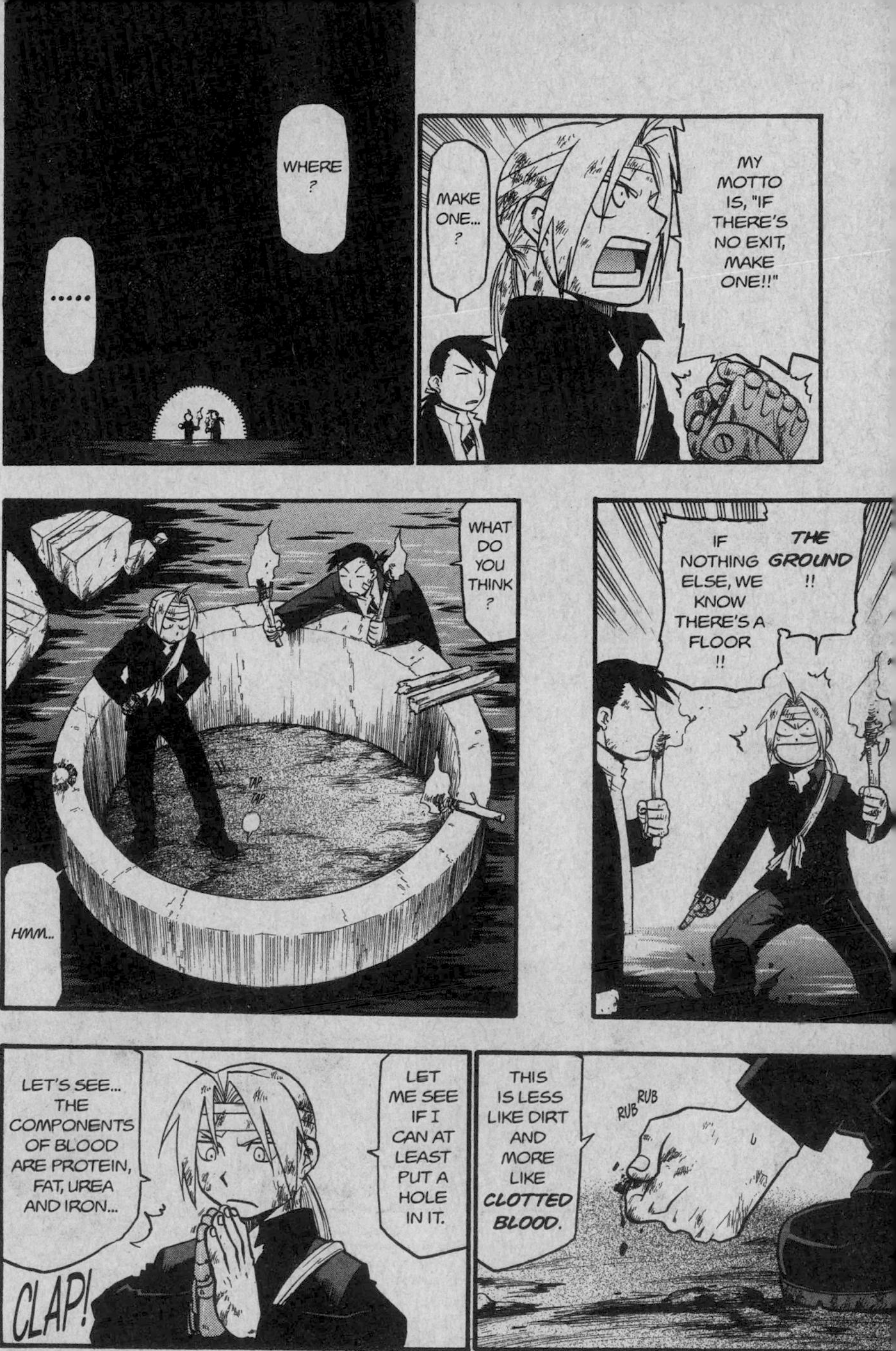
MY MOTTO IS, "IF THERE'S NO EXIT, MAKE ONE!!"
MAKE ONE... ?
WHERE ?
......
IF NOTHING ELSE, WE KNOW THERE'S A FLOOR !!
THE GROUND !!
WHAT DO YOU THINK ?
TAP TAP
HMM..
THIS IS LESS LIKE DIRT AND MORE LIKE CLOTTED BLOOD.
RUB RUB
LET ME SEE IF I CAN AT LEAST PUT A HOLE IN IT.
LET'S SEE... THE COMPONENTS OF BLOOD ARE PROTEIN, FAT, UREA AND IRON...
CLAP!

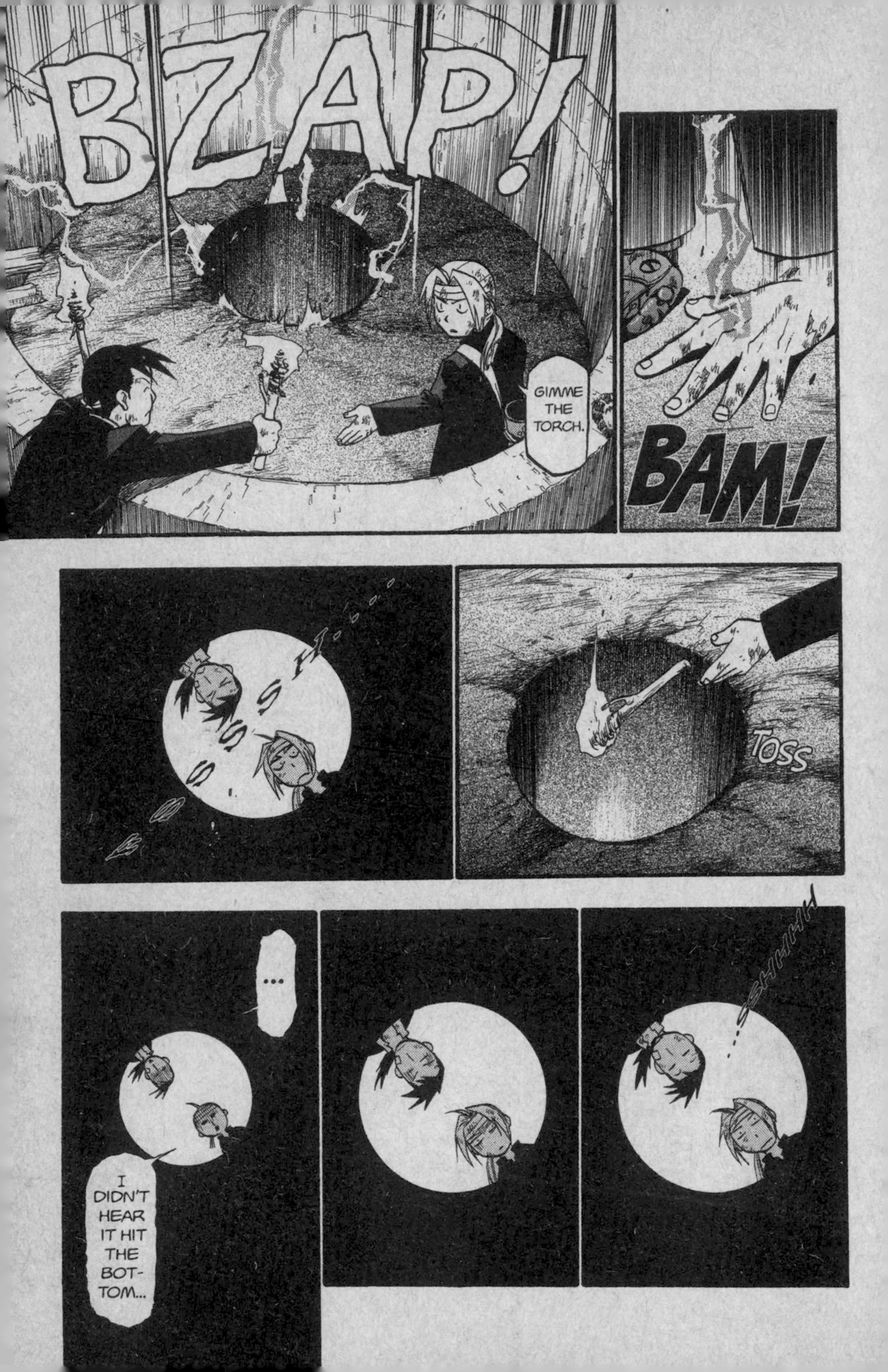
BAM!
BZAP!
GIMME THE TORCH.
TOSS
...
I DIDN'T HEAR IT HIT THE BOT-TOM...

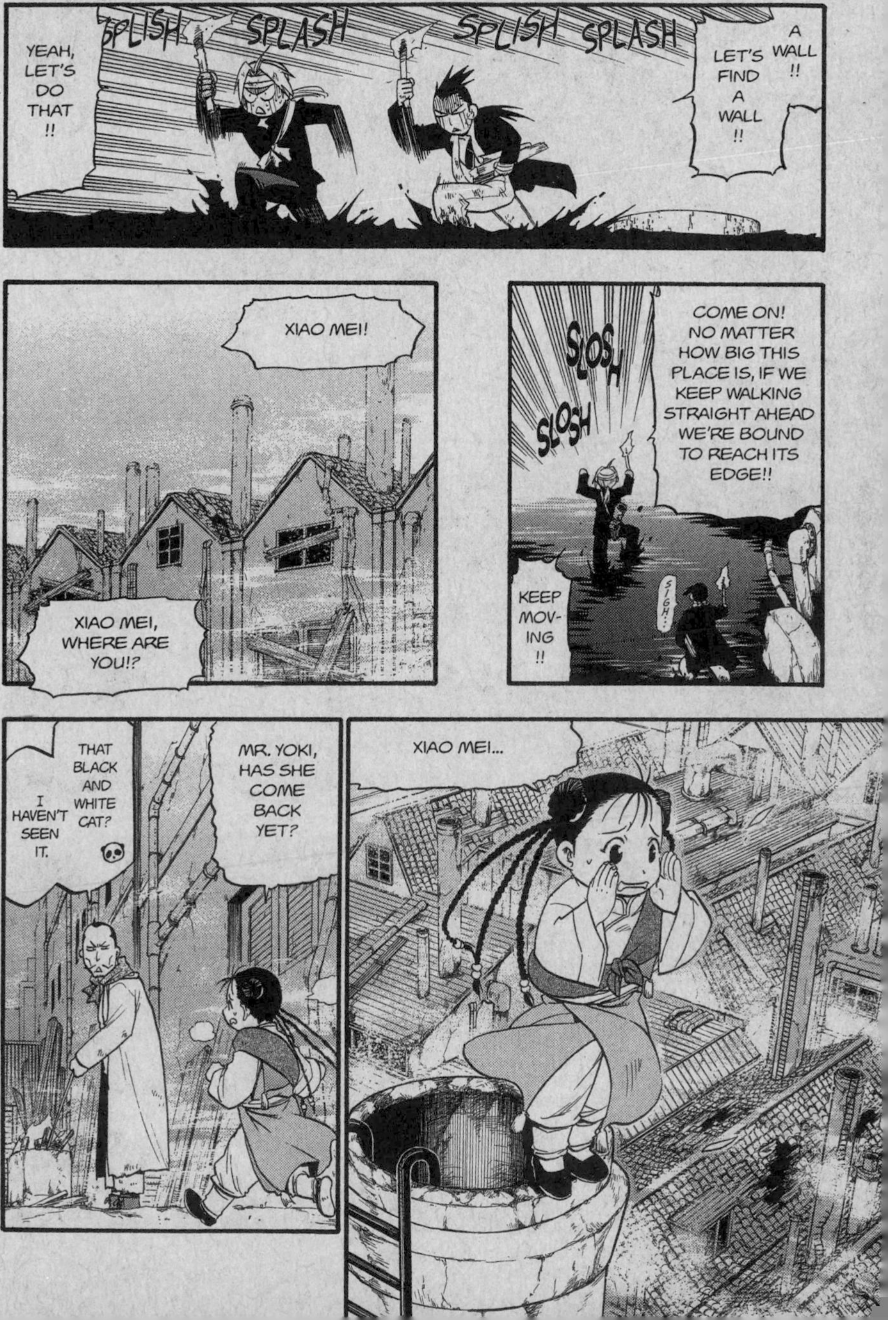
A WALL!!
LET'S FIND A WALL!!
SPLISH SPLASH
SPLISH SPLASH
YEAH, LET'S DO THAT!!
COME ON! NO MATTER HOW BIG THIS PLACE IS, IF WE KEEP WALKING STRAIGHT AHEAD WE'RE BOUND TO REACH ITS EDGE!!
SLOSH
SLOSH
SIGH...
KEEP MOV-ING!!
XIAO MEI!
XIAO MEI, WHERE ARE YOU!?
XIAO MEI...
MR. YOKI, HAS SHE COME BACK YET?
THAT BLACK AND WHITE CAT?
I HAVEN'T SEEN IT.

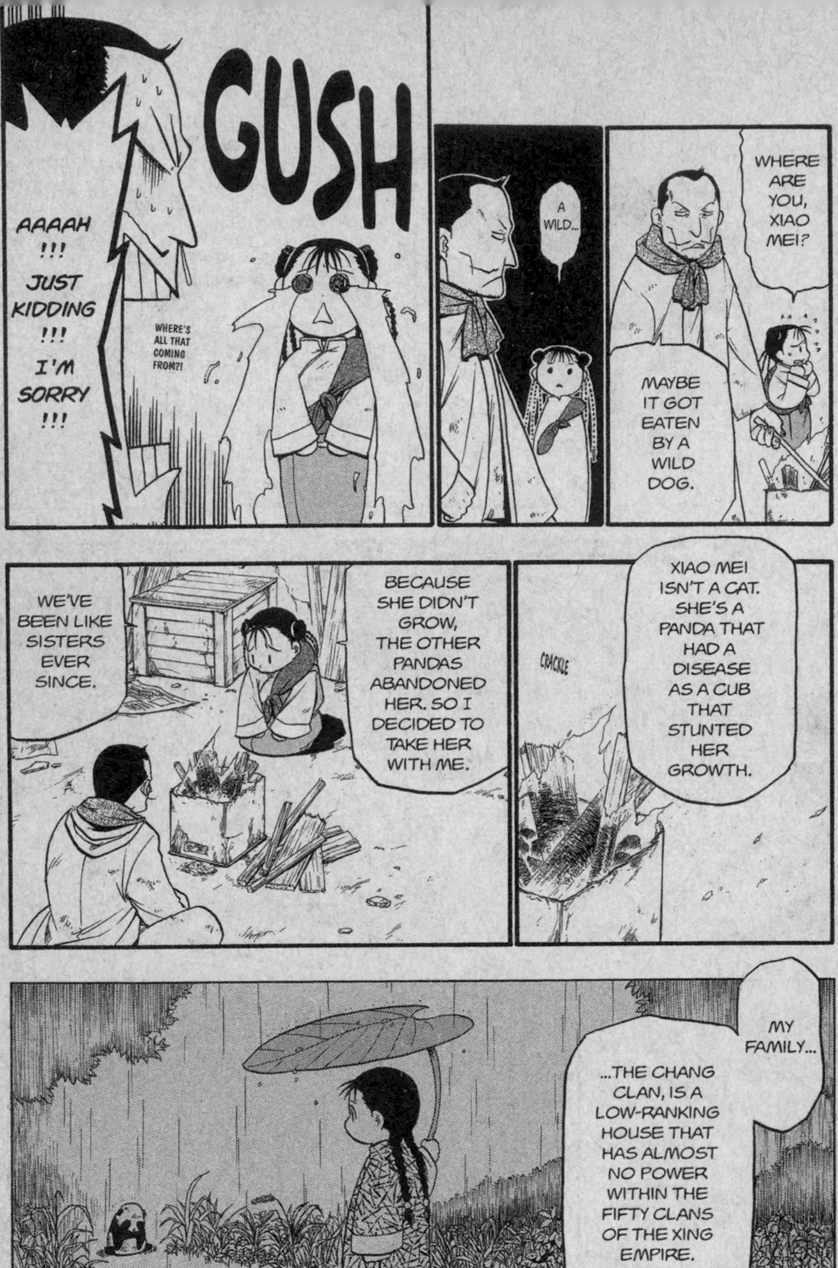
WHERE ARE YOU, XIAO MEI?
MAYBE IT GOT EATEN BY A WILD DOG.
A WILD...
GUSH
AAAAH!!! JUST KIDDING!!! I'M SORRY!!!
WHERE'S ALL THAT COMING FROM?!
CRACKLE
XIAO MEI ISN'T A CAT. SHE'S A PANDA THAT HAD A DISEASE AS A CUB THAT STUNTED HER GROWTH.
BECAUSE SHE DIDN'T GROW, THE OTHER PANDAS ABANDONED HER. SO I DECIDED TO TAKE HER WITH ME.
WE'VE BEEN LIKE SISTERS EVER SINCE.
MY FAMILY...
...THE CHANG CLAN, IS A LOW-RANKING HOUSE THAT HAS ALMOST NO POWER WITHIN THE FIFTY CLANS OF THE XING EMPIRE.

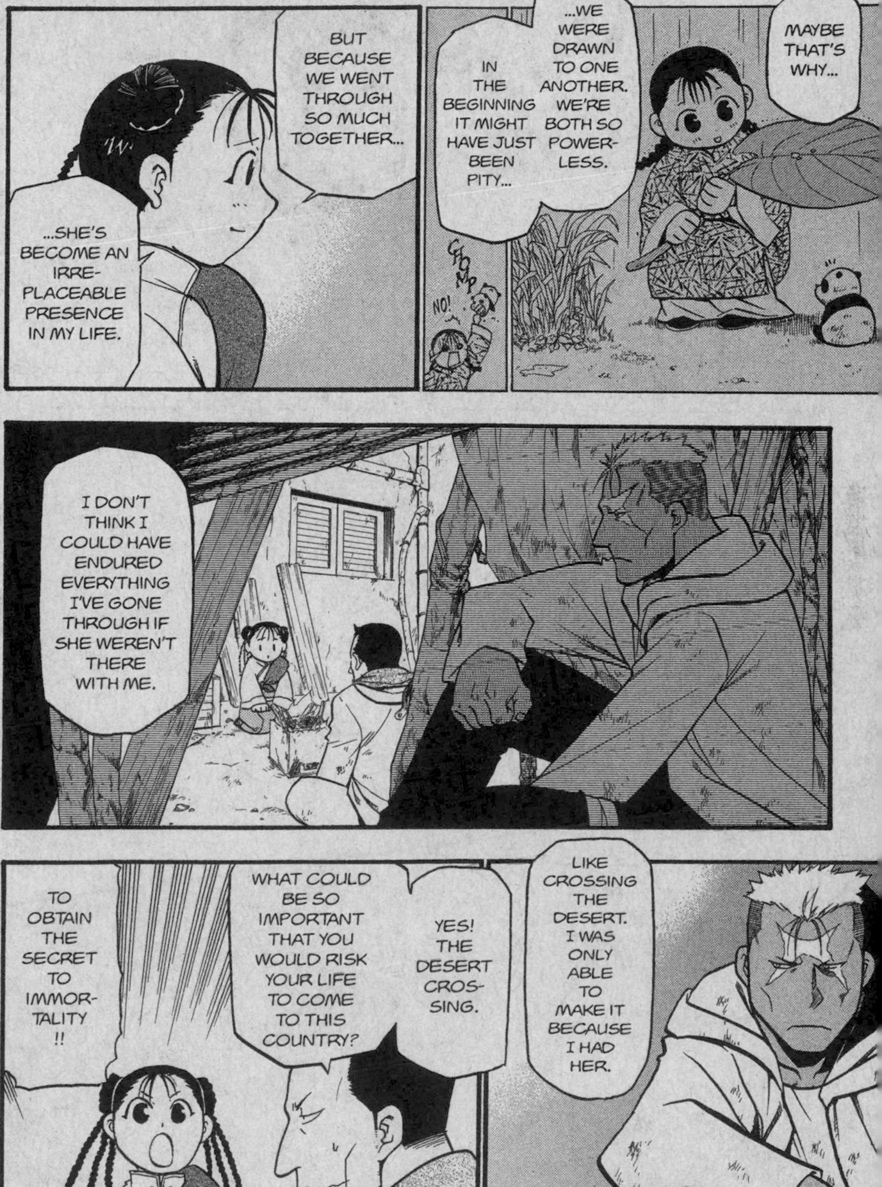
MAYBE THAT'S WHY...
...WE WERE DRAWN TO ONE ANOTHER. WE'RE BOTH SO POWER-LESS.
IN THE BEGINNING IT MIGHT HAVE JUST BEEN PITY...
CHOMP
NO!
BUT BECAUSE WE WENT THROUGH SO MUCH TOGETHER...
...SHE'S BECOME AN IRRE-PLACEABLE PRESENCE IN MY LIFE.
I DON'T THINK I COULD HAVE ENDURED EVERYTHING I'VE GONE THROUGH IF SHE WEREN'T THERE WITH ME.
LIKE CROSSING THE DESERT. I WAS ONLY ABLE TO MAKE IT BECAUSE I HAD HER.
YES! THE DESERT CROS-SING.
WHAT COULD BE SO IMPORTANT THAT YOU WOULD RISK YOUR LIFE TO COME TO THIS COUNTRY?
TO OBTAIN THE SECRET TO IMMOR-TALITY !!

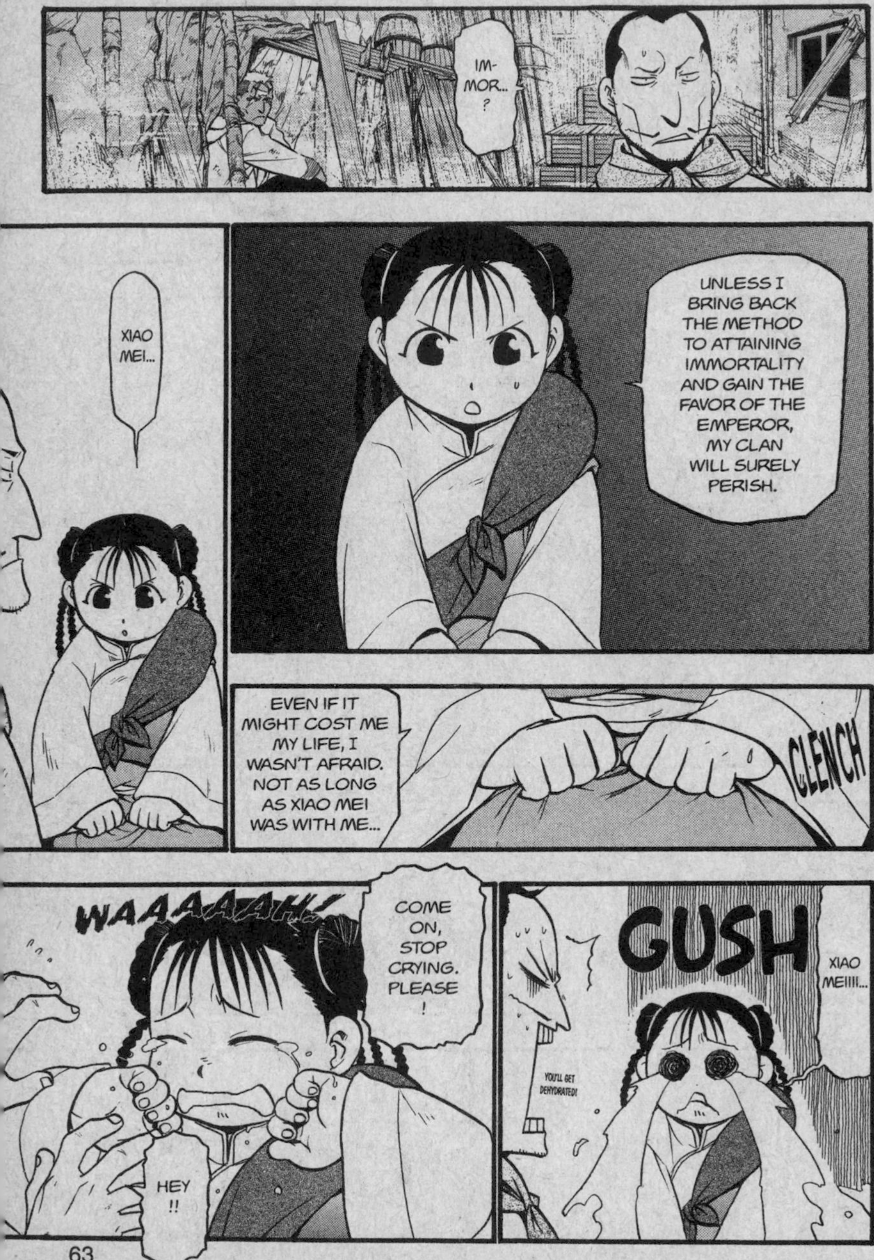
IM-MOR...?
UNLESS I BRING BACK THE METHOD TO ATTAINING IMMORTALITY AND GAIN THE FAVOR OF THE EMPEROR, MY CLAN WILL SURELY PERISH.
EVEN IF IT MIGHT COST ME MY LIFE, I WASN'T AFRAID. NOT AS LONG AS XIAO MEI WAS WITH ME...
CLENCH
XIAO MEI...
XIAO MEIIII...
GUSH
YOU'LL GET DEHYDRATED!
COME ON, STOP CRYING. PLEASE!
WAAAAAH!
HEY!!

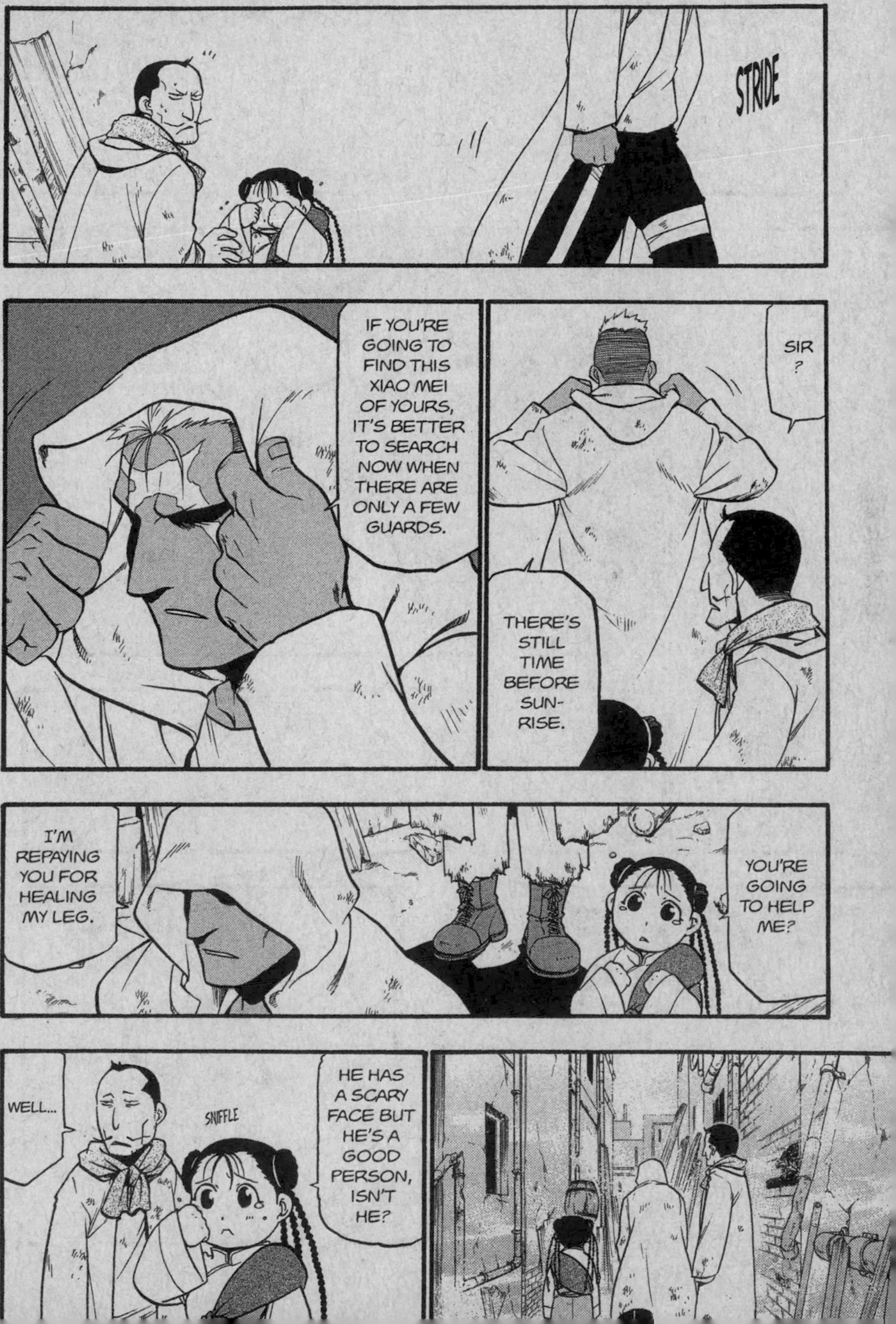
STRIDE
SIR?
THERE'S STILL TIME BEFORE SUNRISE.
IF YOU'RE GOING TO FIND THIS XIAO MEI OF YOURS, IT'S BETTER TO SEARCH NOW WHEN THERE ARE ONLY A FEW GUARDS.
YOU'RE GOING TO HELP ME?
I'M REPAYING YOU FOR HEALING MY LEG.
HE HAS A SCARY FACE BUT HE'S A GOOD PERSON, ISN'T HE?
SNIFFLE
WELL...

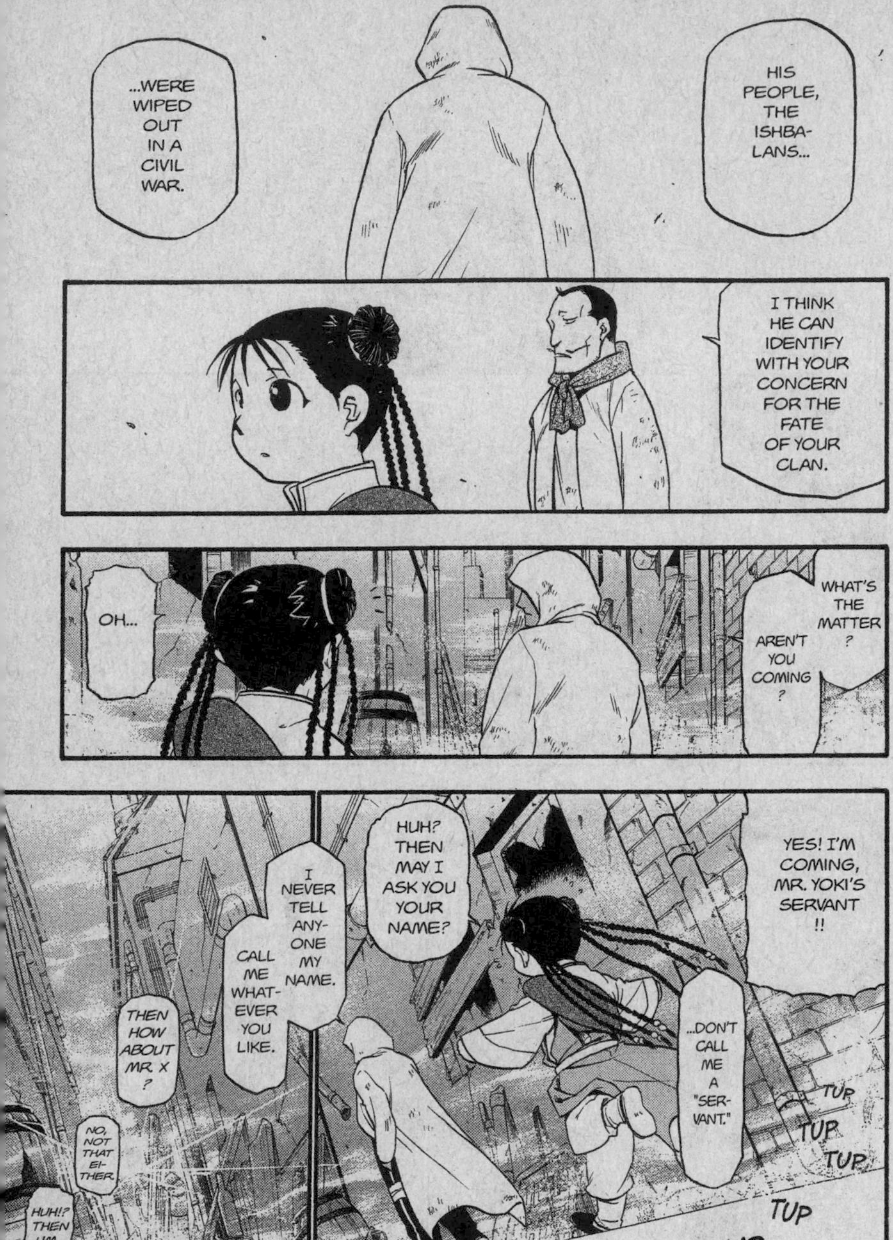
HIS PEOPLE, THE ISHBALANS...
...WERE WIPED OUT IN A CIVIL WAR.
I THINK HE CAN IDENTIFY WITH YOUR CONCERN FOR THE FATE OF YOUR CLAN.
WHAT'S THE MATTER?
AREN'T YOU COMING?
OH...
YES! I'M COMING, MR. YOKI'S SERVANT!!
...DON'T CALL ME A "SERVANT."
TUP
TUP
TUP
TUP
TUP
HUH? THEN MAY I ASK YOU YOUR NAME?
I NEVER TELL ANYONE MY NAME.
CALL ME WHATEVER YOU LIKE.
THEN HOW ABOUT MR. X?
NO, NOT THAT EITHER.
HUH!? THEN UM... UM... UH...

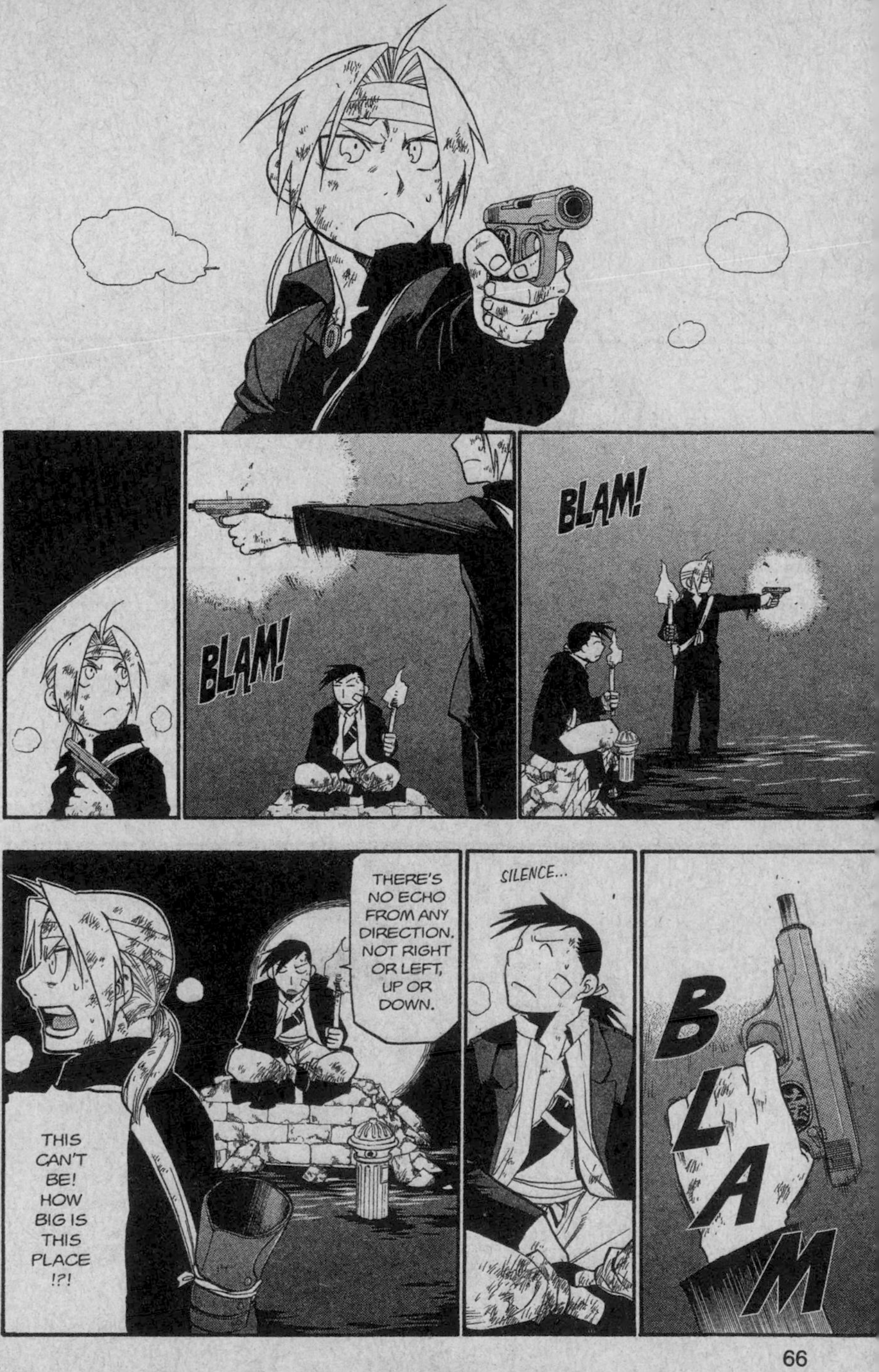
BLAM!
BLAM!
BLAM
SILENCE...
THERE'S NO ECHO FROM ANY DIRECTION. NOT RIGHT OR LEFT, UP OR DOWN.
THIS CAN'T BE! HOW BIG IS THIS PLACE !?!

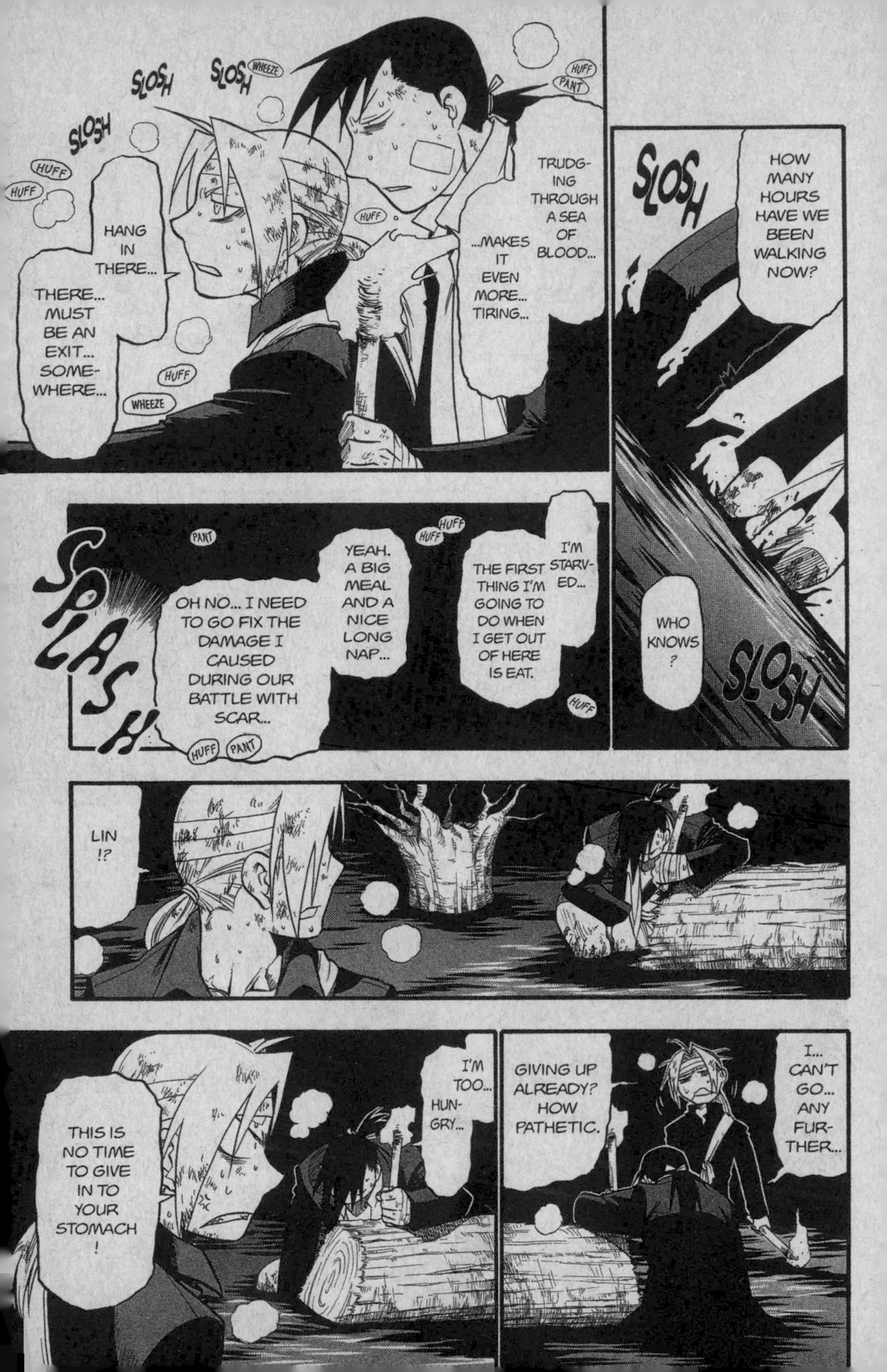
SLOSH
SLOSH
WHEEZE
HUFF
PANT
SLOSH
HUFF
HUFF
TRUDGING THROUGH A SEA OF BLOOD...
...MAKES IT EVEN MORE... TIRING...
HUFF
HANG IN THERE...
THERE... MUST BE AN EXIT... SOMEWHERE...
HUFF
WHEEZE
SLOSH
HOW MANY HOURS HAVE WE BEEN WALKING NOW?
WHO KNOWS?
SLOSH
I'M STARVED...
THE FIRST THING I'M GOING TO DO WHEN I GET OUT OF HERE IS EAT.
HUFF
HUFF
HUFF
YEAH. A BIG MEAL AND A NICE LONG NAP...
PANT
OH NO... I NEED TO GO FIX THE DAMAGE I CAUSED DURING OUR BATTLE WITH SCAR...
HUFF
PANT
SPLASH
LIN!?
I... CAN'T GO... ANY FURTHER...
GIVING UP ALREADY? HOW PATHETIC.
I'M TOO... HUNGRY...
THIS IS NO TIME TO GIVE IN TO YOUR STOMACH!

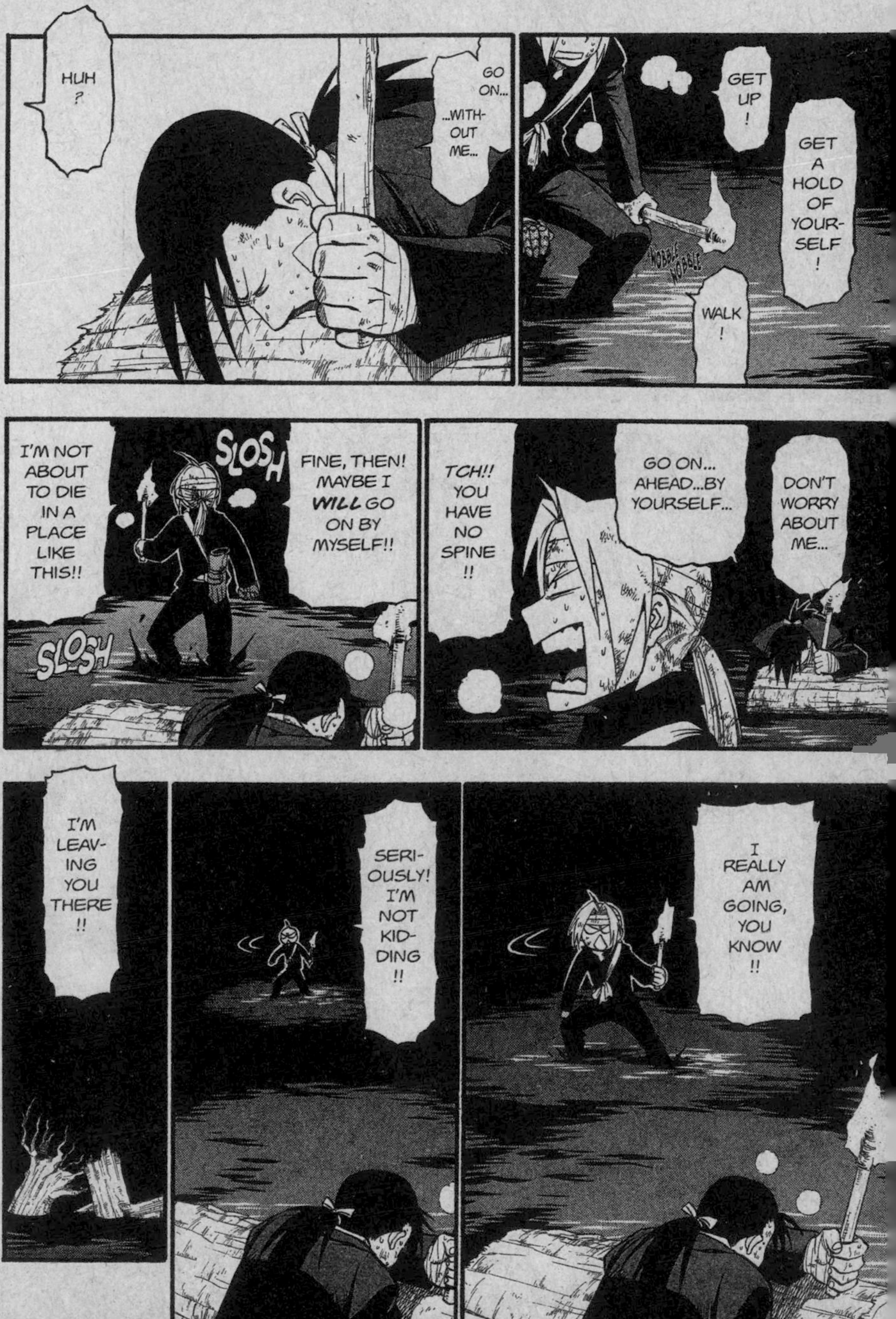
GET UP!
GET A HOLD OF YOURSELF!
WOBBLE WOBBLE
WALK!
GO ON... ...WITHOUT ME...
HUH?
DON'T WORRY ABOUT ME...
GO ON... AHEAD...BY YOURSELF...
TCH!! YOU HAVE NO SPINE!!
FINE, THEN! MAYBE I WILL GO ON BY MYSELF!!
SLOSH
I'M NOT ABOUT TO DIE IN A PLACE LIKE THIS!!
SLOSH
I REALLY AM GOING, YOU KNOW!!
SERIOUSLY! I'M NOT KIDDING!!
I'M LEAVING YOU THERE!!

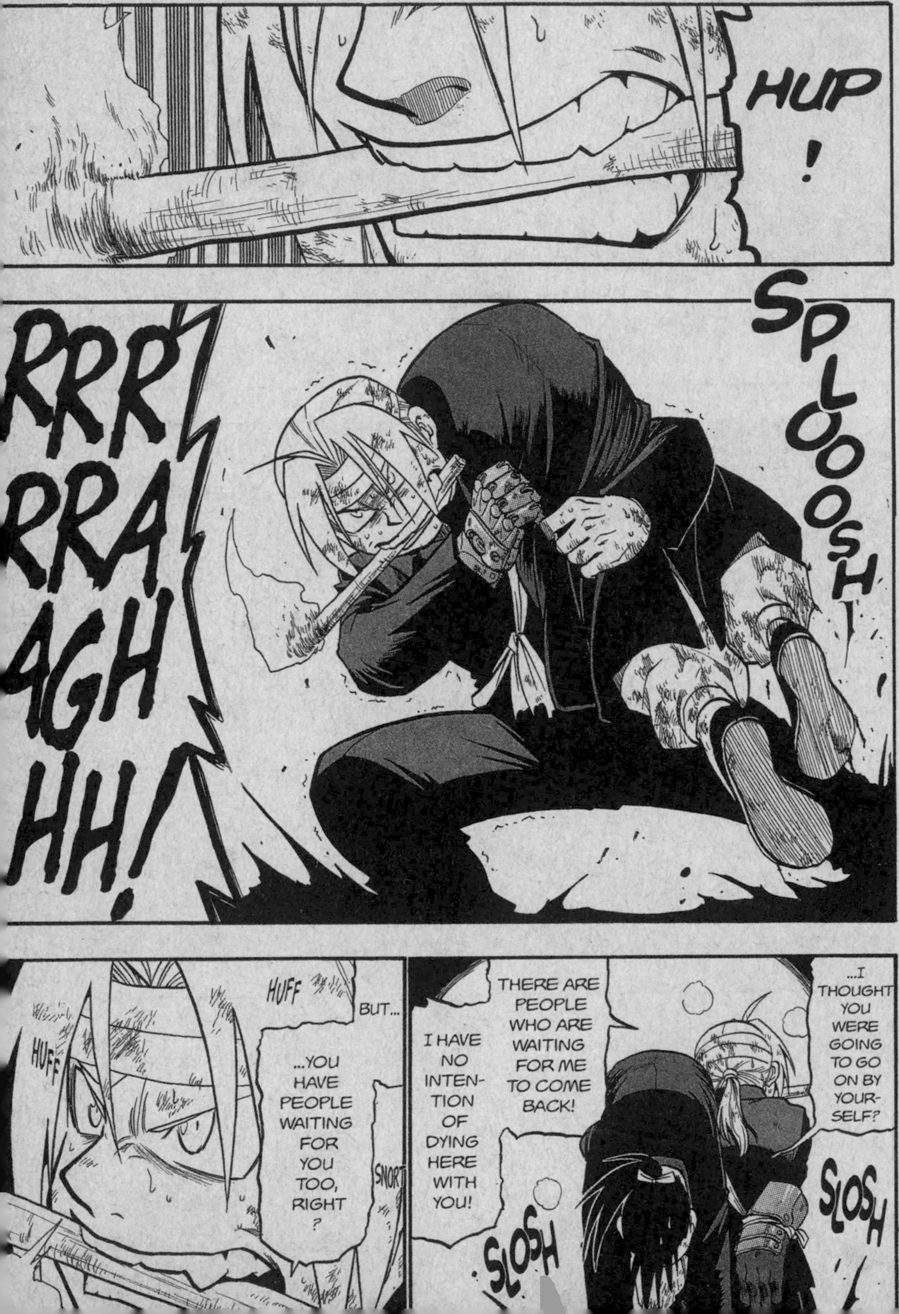
HUP!
SPLOOOOSH!
RRRRRAAGHHH!
...I THOUGHT YOU WERE GOING TO GO ON BY YOURSELF?
THERE ARE PEOPLE WHO ARE WAITING FOR ME TO COME BACK!
I HAVE NO INTENTION OF DYING HERE WITH YOU!
SLOSH
SLOSH
HUFF
BUT...
...YOU HAVE PEOPLE WAITING FOR YOU TOO, RIGHT?
SNORT
HUFF

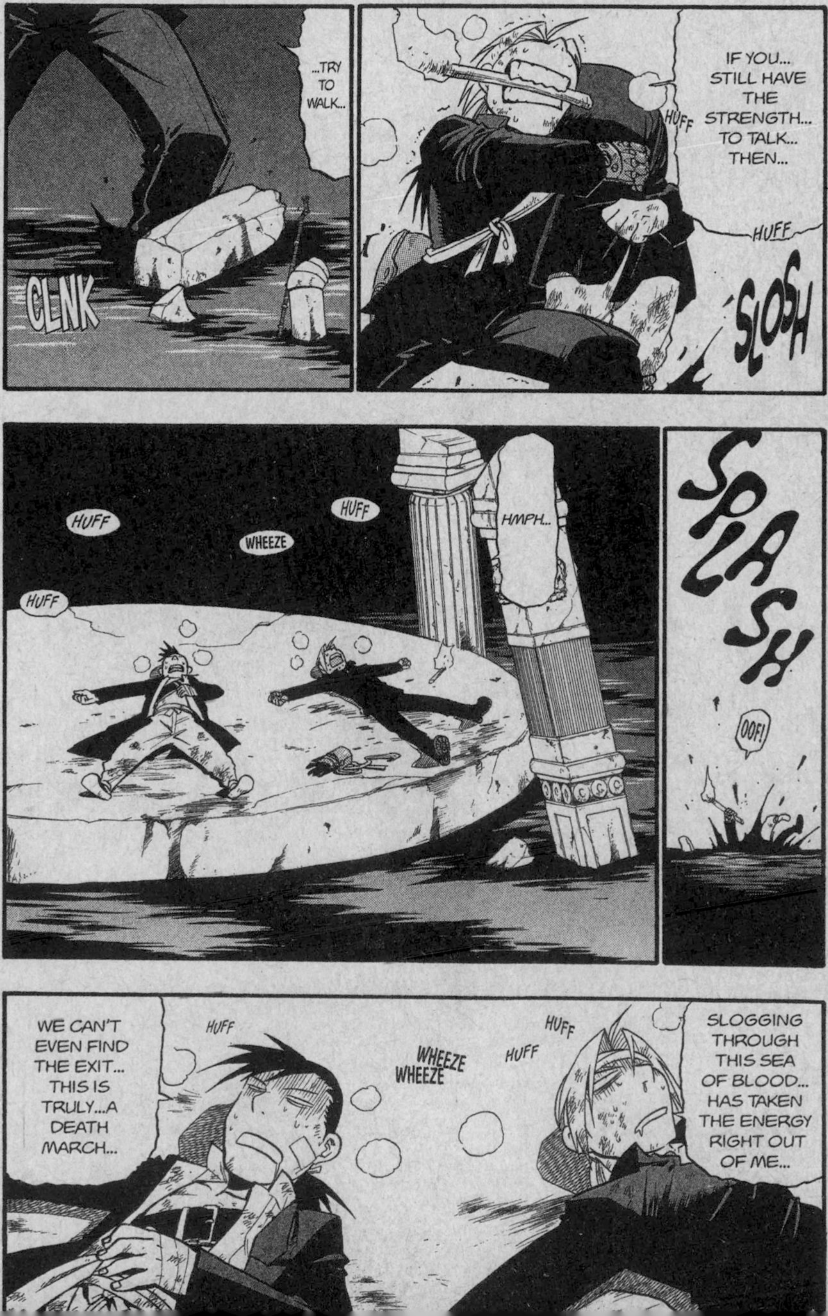
IF YOU... STILL HAVE THE STRENGTH... TO TALK... THEN...
HUFF
HUFF
SLOSH
...TRY TO WALK...
CLNK
SPLASH
OOF!
HMPH...
HUFF
WHEEZE
HUFF
HUFF
SLOGGING THROUGH THIS SEA OF BLOOD... HAS TAKEN THE ENERGY RIGHT OUT OF ME...
HUFF
HUFF
WHEEZE
WHEEZE
HUFF
WE CAN'T EVEN FIND THE EXIT... THIS IS TRULY...A DEATH MARCH...

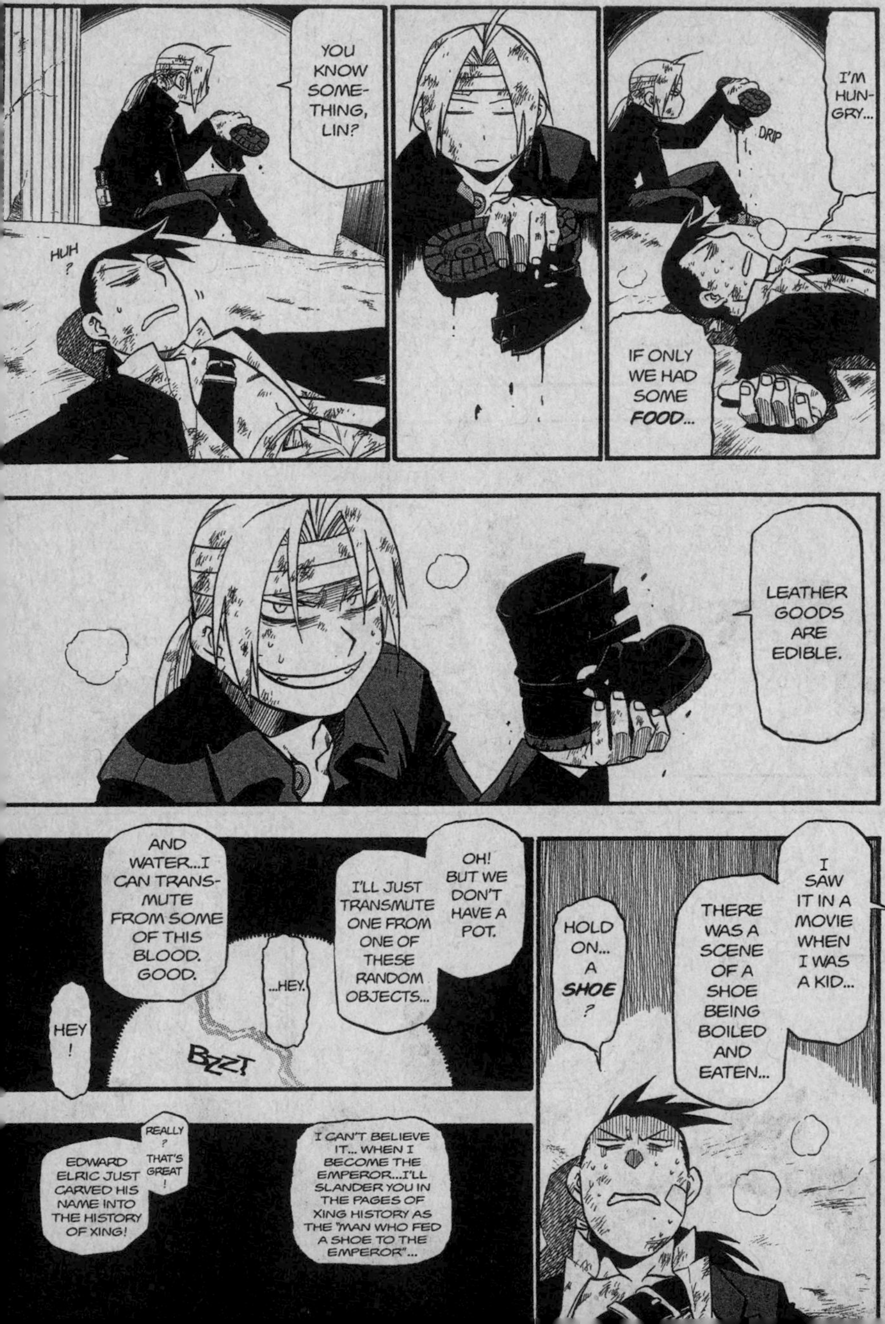
I'M HUNGRY...
DRIP
IF ONLY WE HAD SOME **FOOD**...
YOU KNOW SOMETHING, LIN?
HUH?
LEATHER GOODS ARE EDIBLE.
I SAW IT IN A MOVIE WHEN I WAS A KID...
THERE WAS A SCENE OF A SHOE BEING BOILED AND EATEN...
HOLD ON... A **SHOE**?
OH! BUT WE DON'T HAVE A POT.
I'LL JUST TRANSMUTE ONE FROM ONE OF THESE RANDOM OBJECTS...
AND WATER...I CAN TRANSMUTE FROM SOME OF THIS BLOOD. GOOD.
...HEY.
BZZT
HEY!
I CAN'T BELIEVE IT... WHEN I BECOME THE EMPEROR...I'LL SLANDER YOU IN THE PAGES OF XING HISTORY AS THE "MAN WHO FED A SHOE TO THE EMPEROR"...
REALLY? THAT'S GREAT!
EDWARD ELRIC JUST CARVED HIS NAME INTO THE HISTORY OF XING!

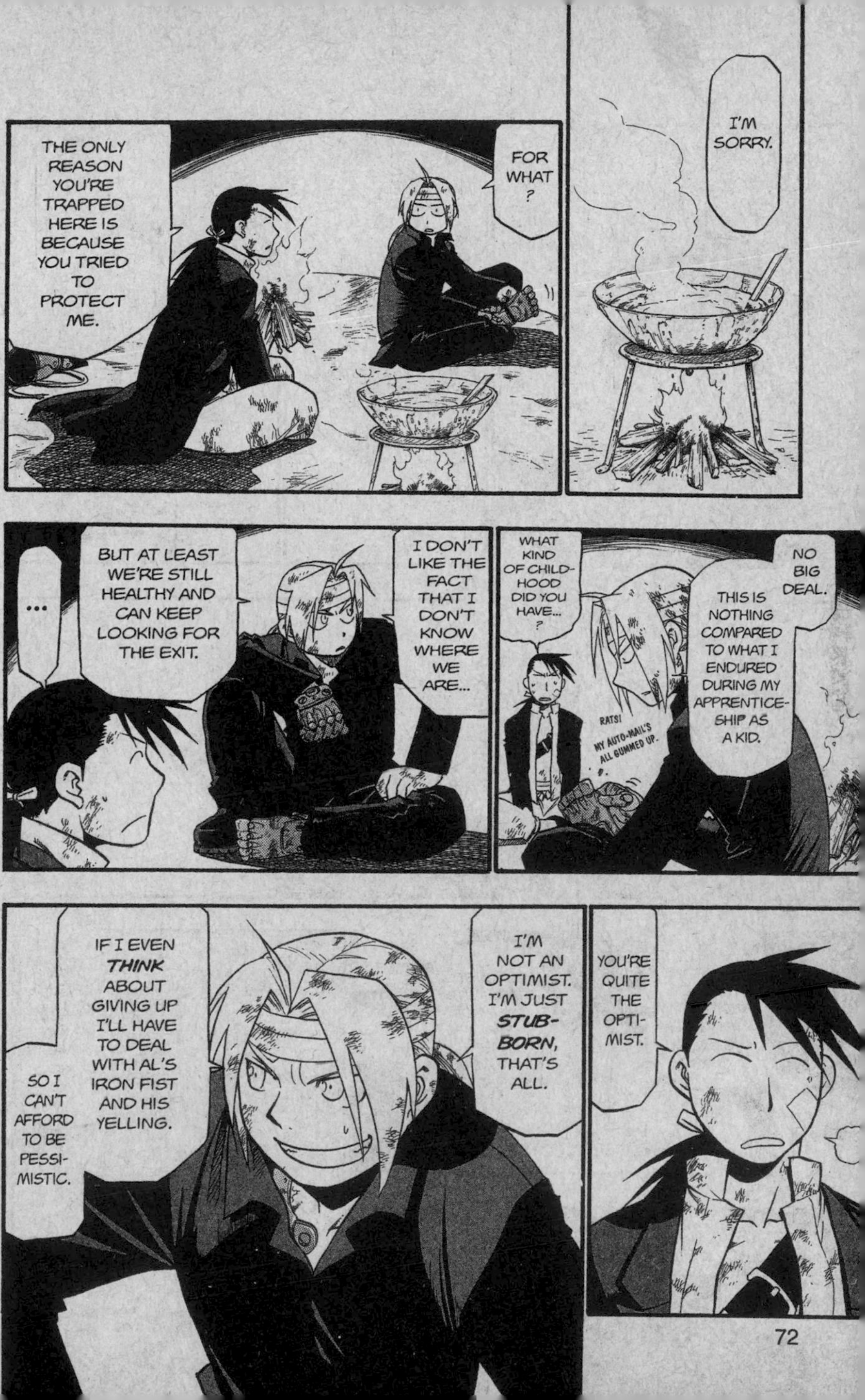
I'M SORRY.
FOR WHAT ?
THE ONLY REASON YOU'RE TRAPPED HERE IS BECAUSE YOU TRIED TO PROTECT ME.
NO BIG DEAL.
THIS IS NOTHING COMPARED TO WHAT I ENDURED DURING MY APPRENTICE-SHIP AS A KID.
WHAT KIND OF CHILD-HOOD DID YOU HAVE... ?
RATS! MY AUTO-MAIL'S ALL GUMMED UP.
I DON'T LIKE THE FACT THAT I DON'T KNOW WHERE WE ARE...
BUT AT LEAST WE'RE STILL HEALTHY AND CAN KEEP LOOKING FOR THE EXIT.
...
YOU'RE QUITE THE OPTI-MIST.
I'M NOT AN OPTIMIST. I'M JUST ***STUB-BORN***, THAT'S ALL.
IF I EVEN ***THINK*** ABOUT GIVING UP I'LL HAVE TO DEAL WITH AL'S IRON FIST AND HIS YELLING.
SO I CAN'T AFFORD TO BE PESSI-MISTIC.

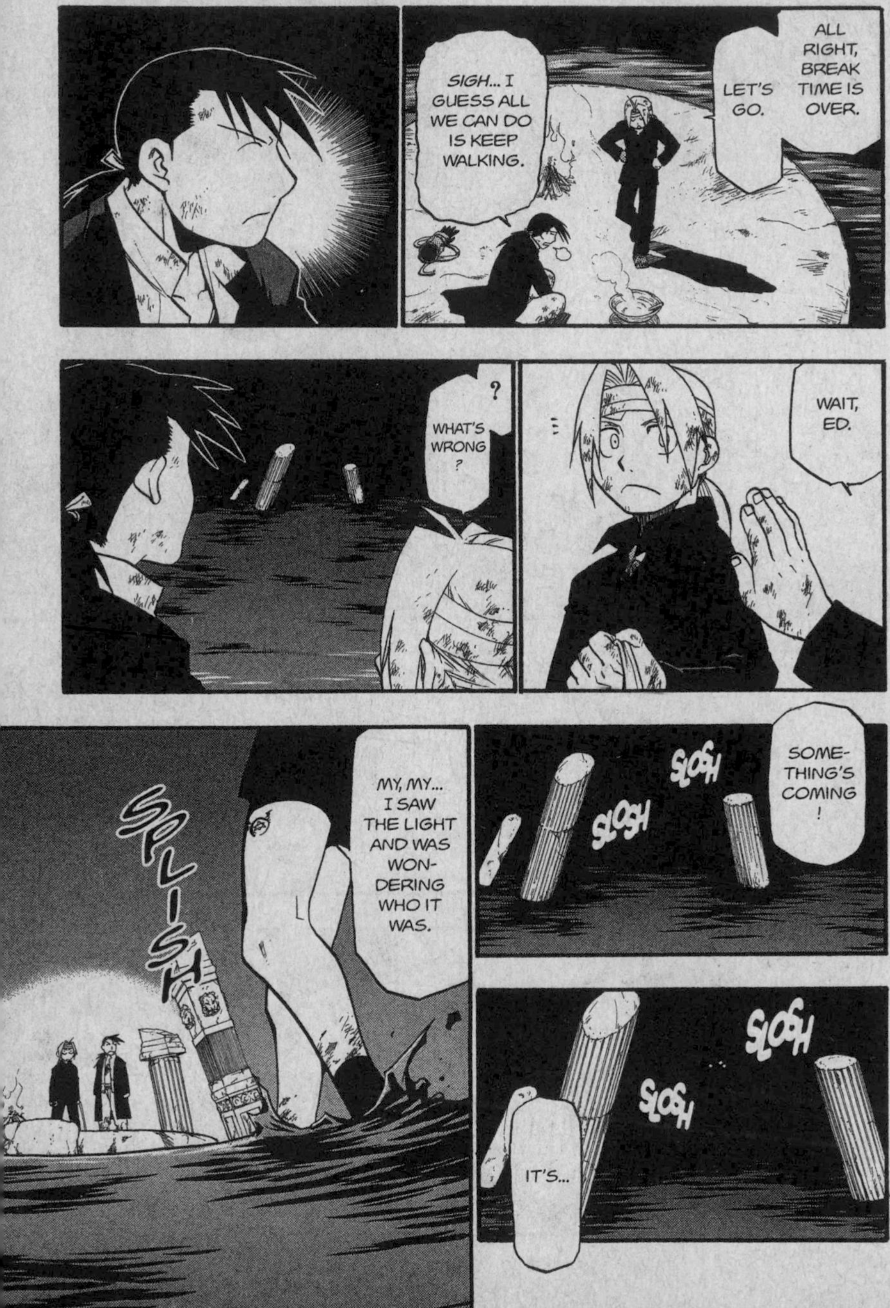
ALL RIGHT, BREAK TIME IS OVER.
LET'S GO.
SIGH... I GUESS ALL WE CAN DO IS KEEP WALKING.
WAIT, ED.
?
WHAT'S WRONG?
SOMETHING'S COMING!
SLOSH
SLOSH
SLOSH
SLOSH
IT'S...
MY, MY... I SAW THE LIGHT AND WAS WONDERING WHO IT WAS.
SPLISH

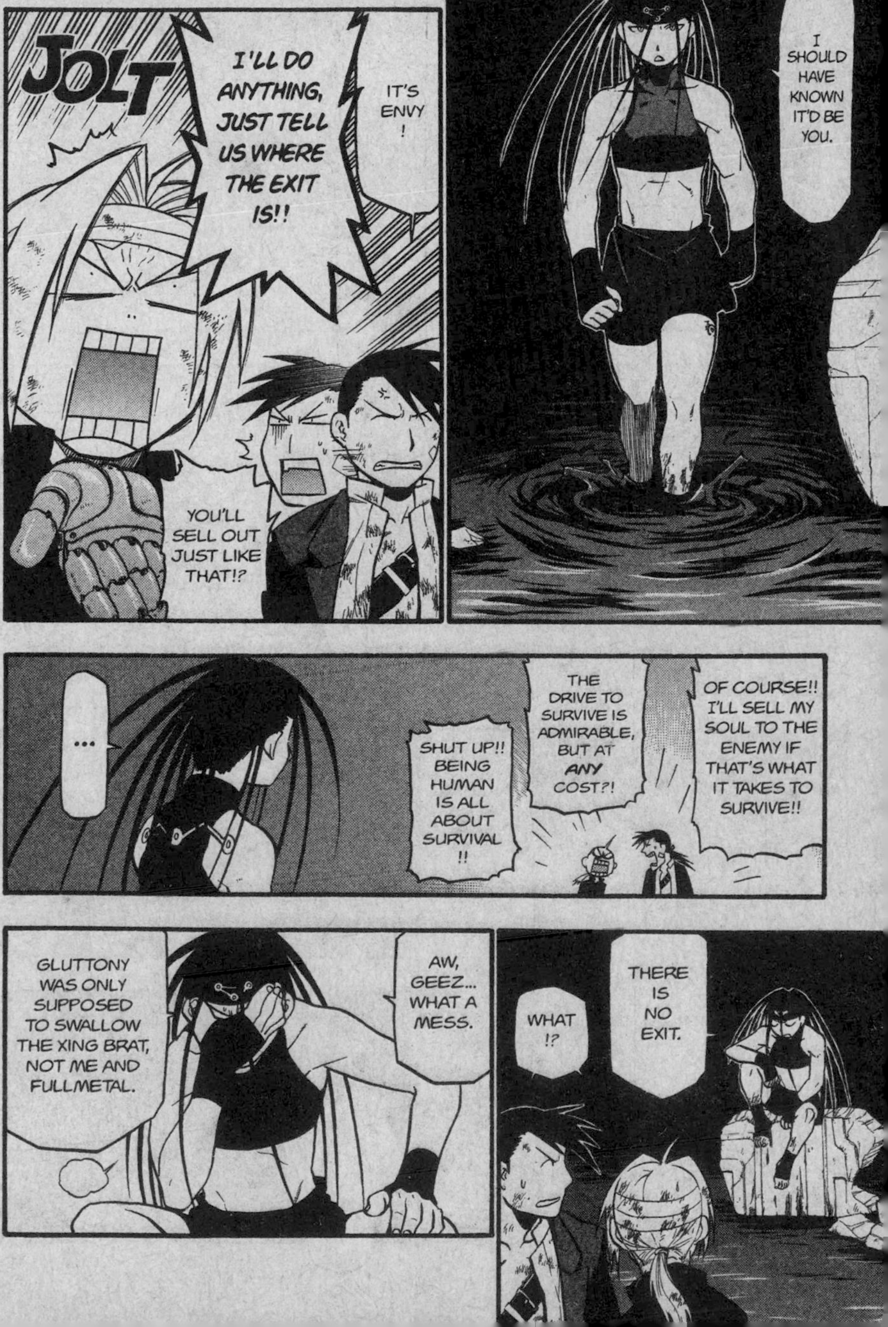
I SHOULD HAVE KNOWN IT'D BE YOU.
IT'S ENVY!
I'LL DO ANYTHING, JUST TELL US WHERE THE EXIT IS!!
JOLT
YOU'LL SELL OUT JUST LIKE THAT!?
OF COURSE!! I'LL SELL MY SOUL TO THE ENEMY IF THAT'S WHAT IT TAKES TO SURVIVE!!
THE DRIVE TO SURVIVE IS ADMIRABLE, BUT AT ANY COST?!
SHUT UP!! BEING HUMAN IS ALL ABOUT SURVIVAL!!
...
THERE IS NO EXIT.
WHAT!?
AW, GEEZ... WHAT A MESS.
GLUTTONY WAS ONLY SUPPOSED TO SWALLOW THE XING BRAT, NOT ME AND FULLMETAL.

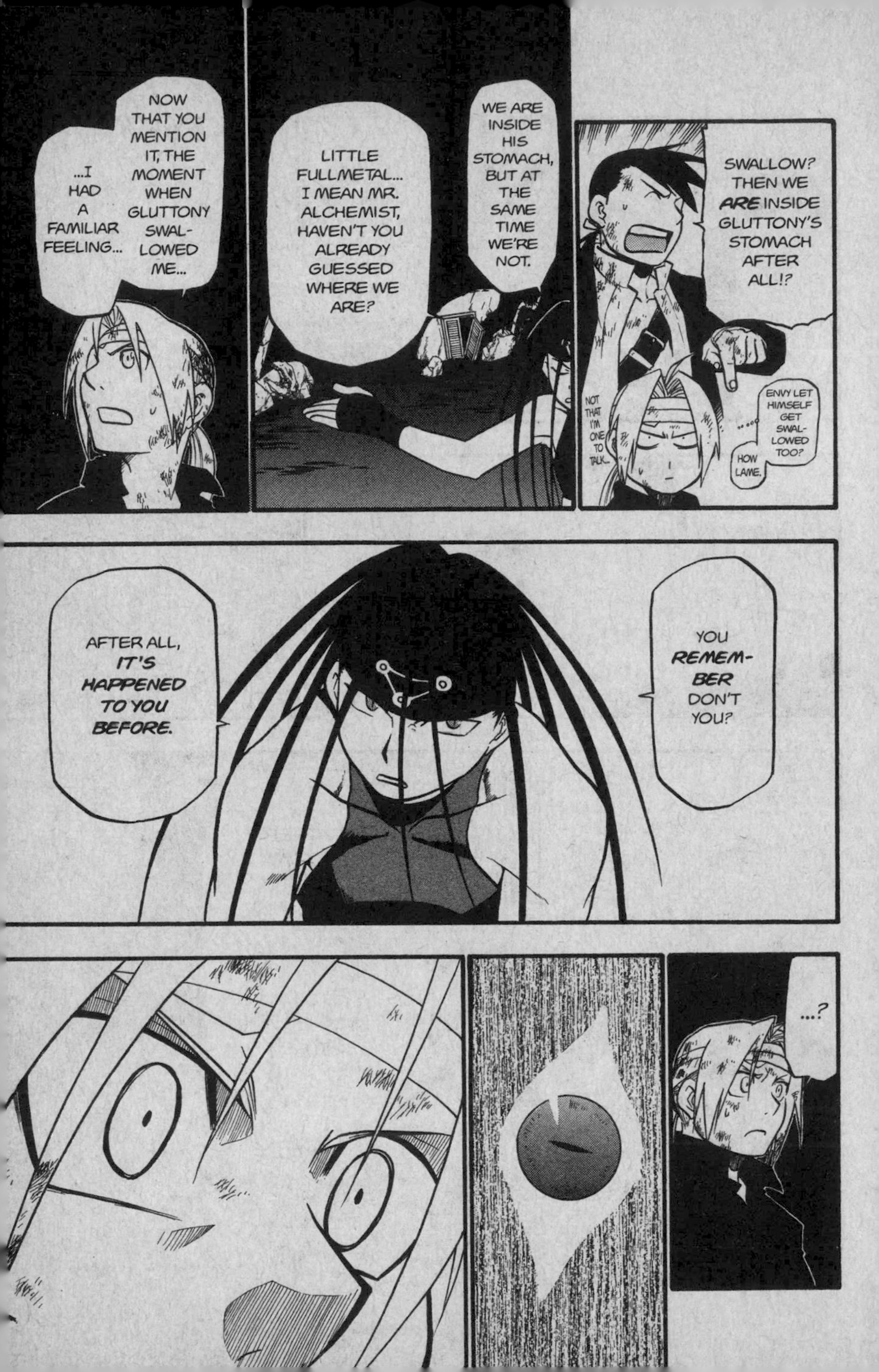
SWALLOW? THEN WE ARE INSIDE GLUTTONY'S STOMACH AFTER ALL!?
...ENVY LET HIMSELF GET SWAL-LOWED TOO?
HOW LAME.
NOT THAT I'M ONE TO TALK...
WE ARE INSIDE HIS STOMACH, BUT AT THE SAME TIME WE'RE NOT.
LITTLE FULLMETAL... I MEAN MR. ALCHEMIST, HAVEN'T YOU ALREADY GUESSED WHERE WE ARE?
NOW THAT YOU MENTION IT, THE MOMENT WHEN GLUTTONY SWAL-LOWED ME...
...I HAD A FAMILIAR FEELING...
YOU REMEM-BER DON'T YOU?
AFTER ALL, IT'S HAPPENED TO YOU BEFORE.
...?

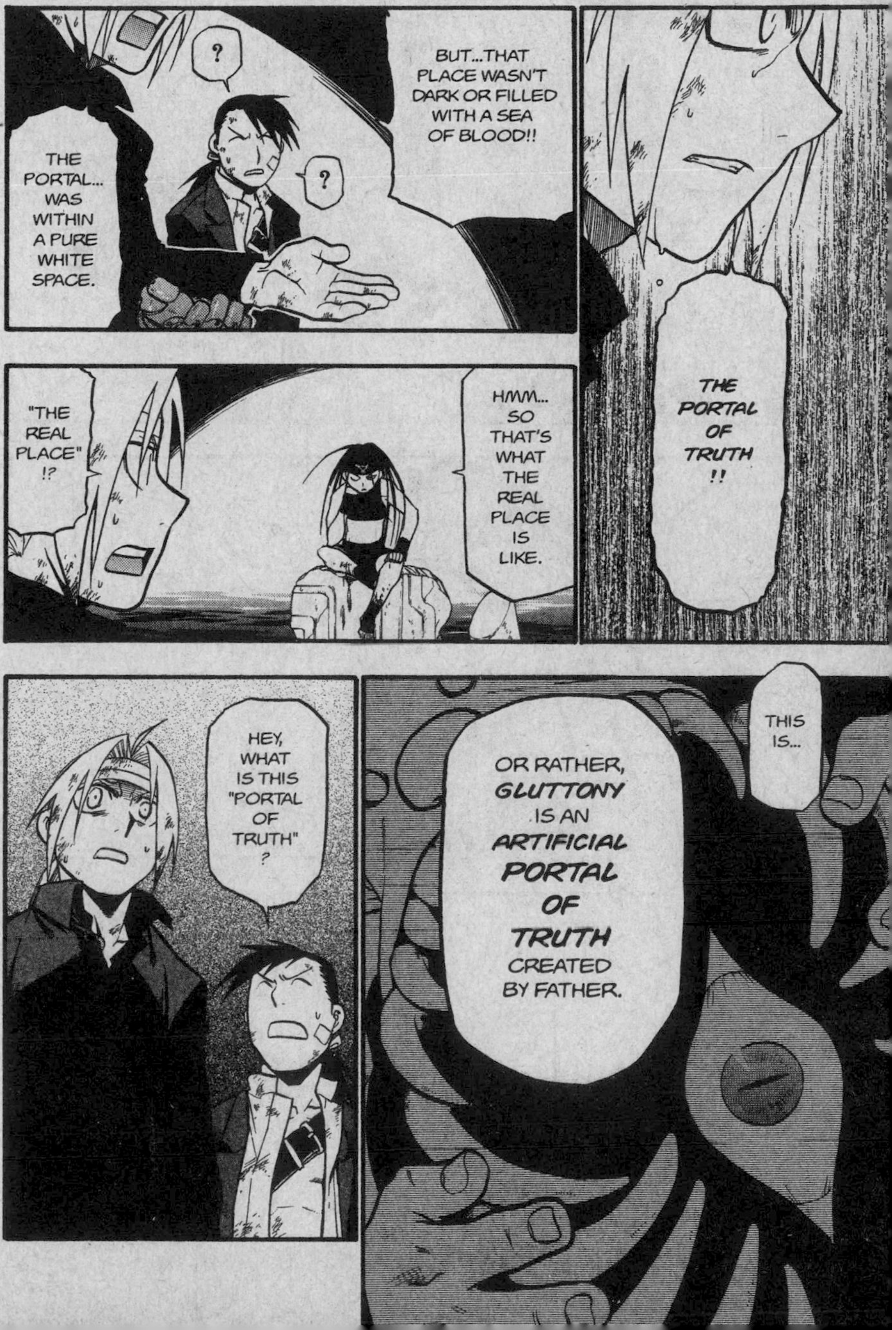
THE PORTAL OF TRUTH!!
BUT...THAT PLACE WASN'T DARK OR FILLED WITH A SEA OF BLOOD!!
?
?
THE PORTAL... WAS WITHIN A PURE WHITE SPACE.
HMM... SO THAT'S WHAT THE REAL PLACE IS LIKE.
"THE REAL PLACE" !?
THIS IS...
OR RATHER, GLUTTONY IS AN ARTIFICIAL PORTAL OF TRUTH CREATED BY FATHER.
HEY, WHAT IS THIS "PORTAL OF TRUTH"?

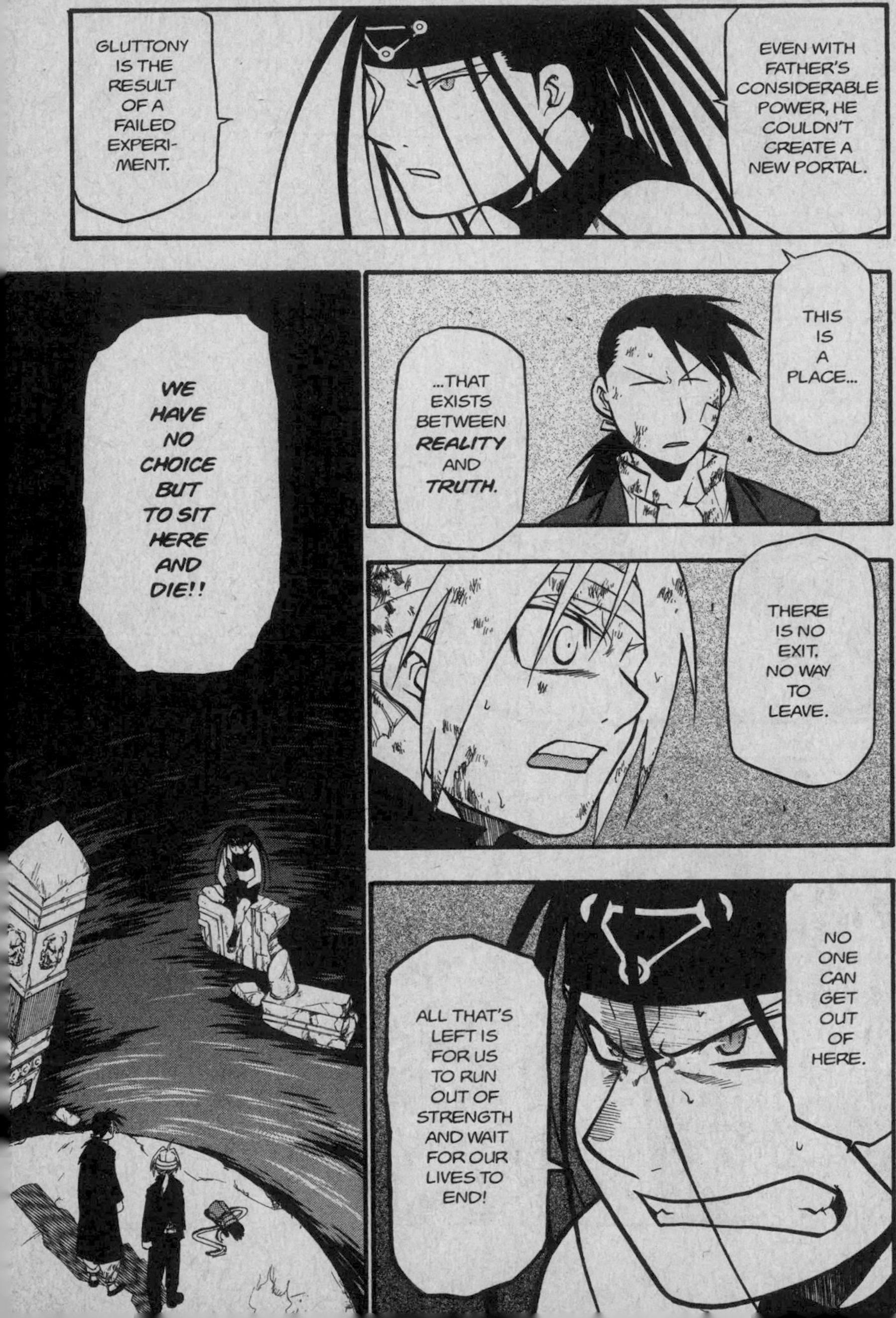
EVEN WITH FATHER'S CONSIDERABLE POWER, HE COULDN'T CREATE A NEW PORTAL.
GLUTTONY IS THE RESULT OF A FAILED EXPERIMENT.
THIS IS A PLACE...
...THAT EXISTS BETWEEN REALITY AND TRUTH.
THERE IS NO EXIT. NO WAY TO LEAVE.
NO ONE CAN GET OUT OF HERE.
ALL THAT'S LEFT IS FOR US TO RUN OUT OF STRENGTH AND WAIT FOR OUR LIVES TO END!
WE HAVE NO CHOICE BUT TO SIT HERE AND DIE!!

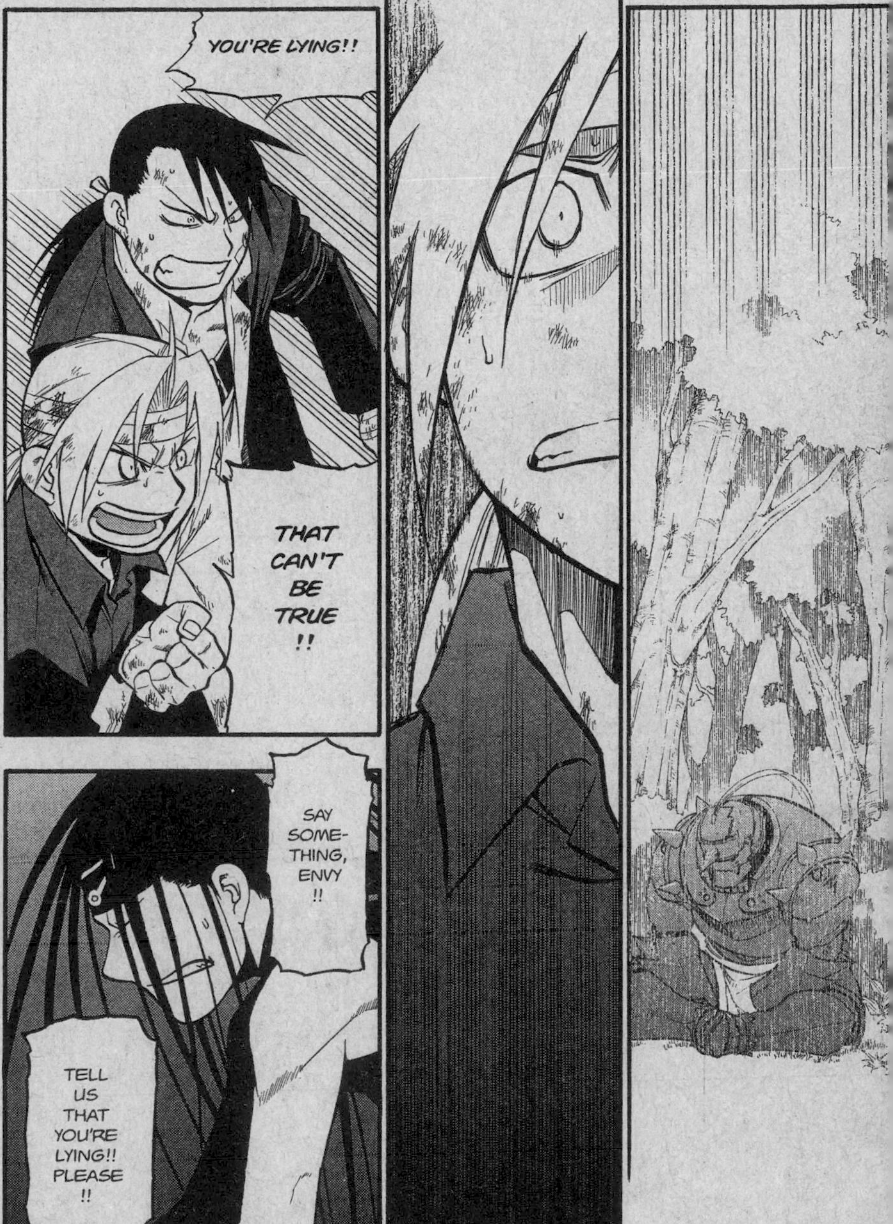
YOU'RE LYING!!
THAT CAN'T BE TRUE!!
SAY SOMETHING, ENVY!!
TELL US THAT YOU'RE LYING!! PLEASE!!

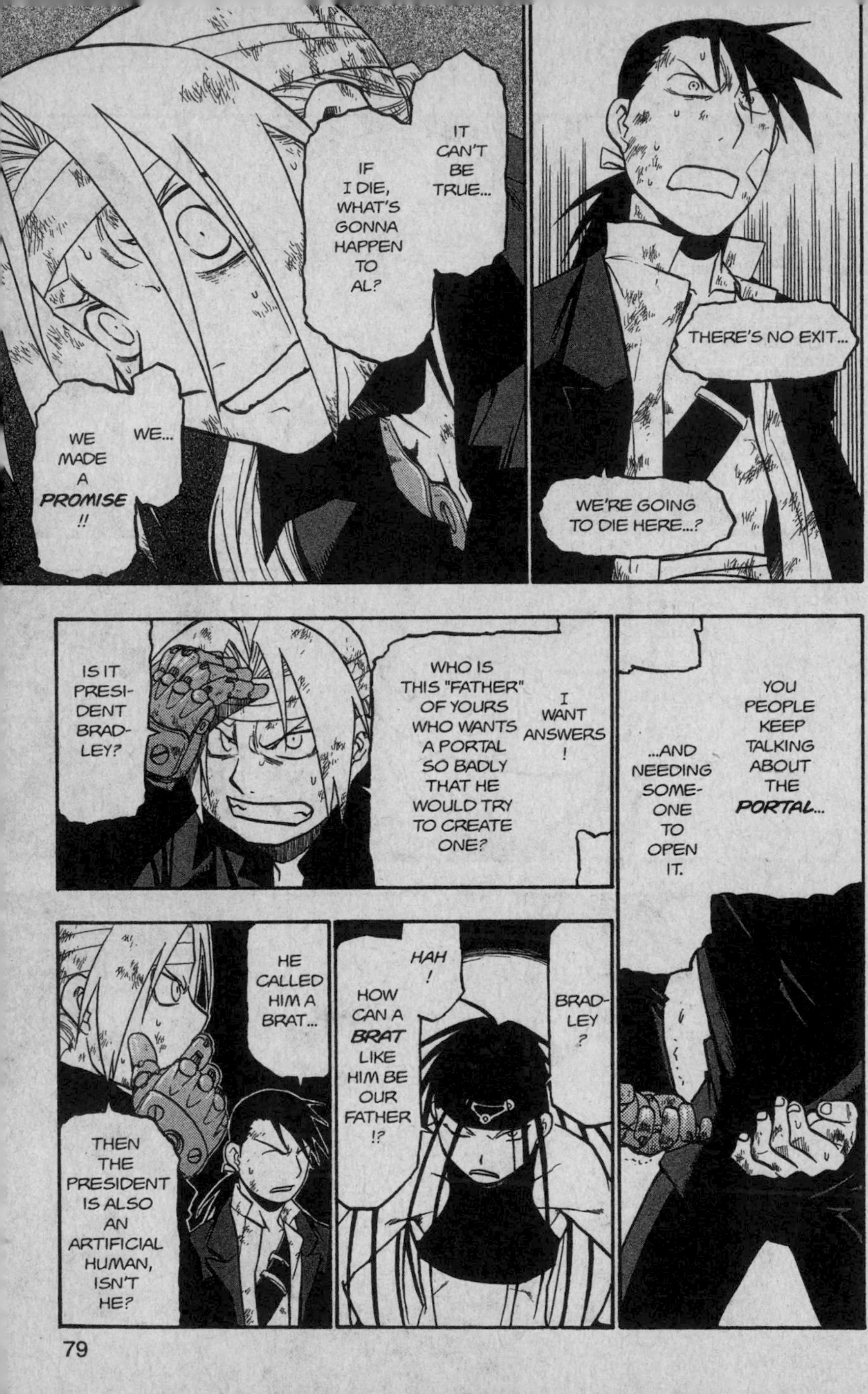

THERE'S NO EXIT...
WE'RE GOING TO DIE HERE...?
IT CAN'T BE TRUE...
IF I DIE, WHAT'S GONNA HAPPEN TO AL?
WE...
WE MADE A PROMISE!!
YOU PEOPLE KEEP TALKING ABOUT THE PORTAL...
...AND NEEDING SOME-ONE TO OPEN IT.
I WANT ANSWERS!
WHO IS THIS "FATHER" OF YOURS WHO WANTS A PORTAL SO BADLY THAT HE WOULD TRY TO CREATE ONE?
IS IT PRESI-DENT BRAD-LEY?
BRAD-LEY?
HAH!
HOW CAN A BRAT LIKE HIM BE OUR FATHER!?
HE CALLED HIM A BRAT...
THEN THE PRESIDENT IS ALSO AN ARTIFICIAL HUMAN, ISN'T HE?

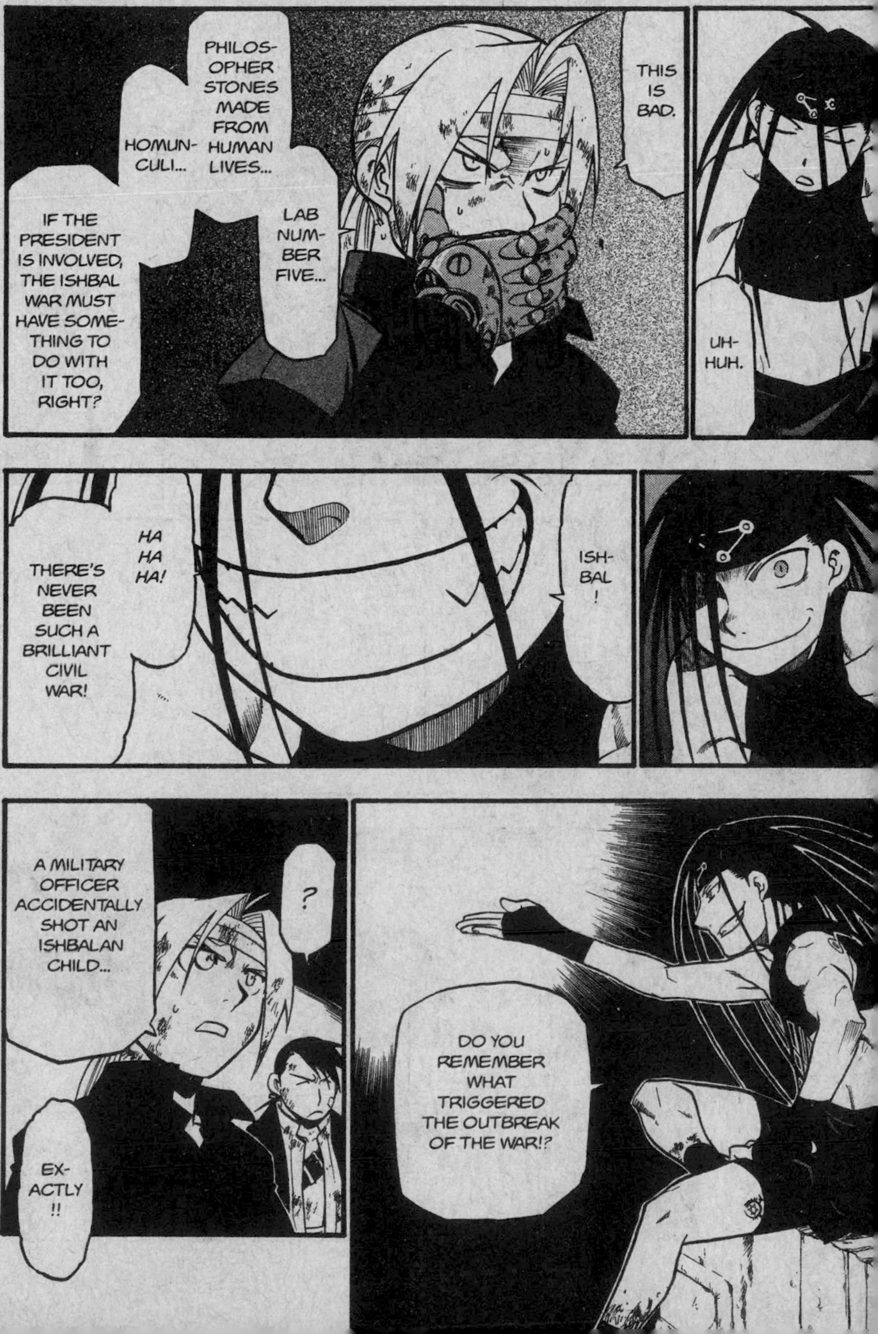
UH-HUH.
THIS IS BAD.
PHILOSOPHER STONES MADE FROM HUMAN LIVES...
HOMUNCULI...
LAB NUMBER FIVE...
IF THE PRESIDENT IS INVOLVED, THE ISHBAL WAR MUST HAVE SOMETHING TO DO WITH IT TOO, RIGHT?
ISHBAL!
HA HA HA!
THERE'S NEVER BEEN SUCH A BRILLIANT CIVIL WAR!
DO YOU REMEMBER WHAT TRIGGERED THE OUTBREAK OF THE WAR!?
?
A MILITARY OFFICER ACCIDENTALLY SHOT AN ISHBALAN CHILD...
EXACTLY!!

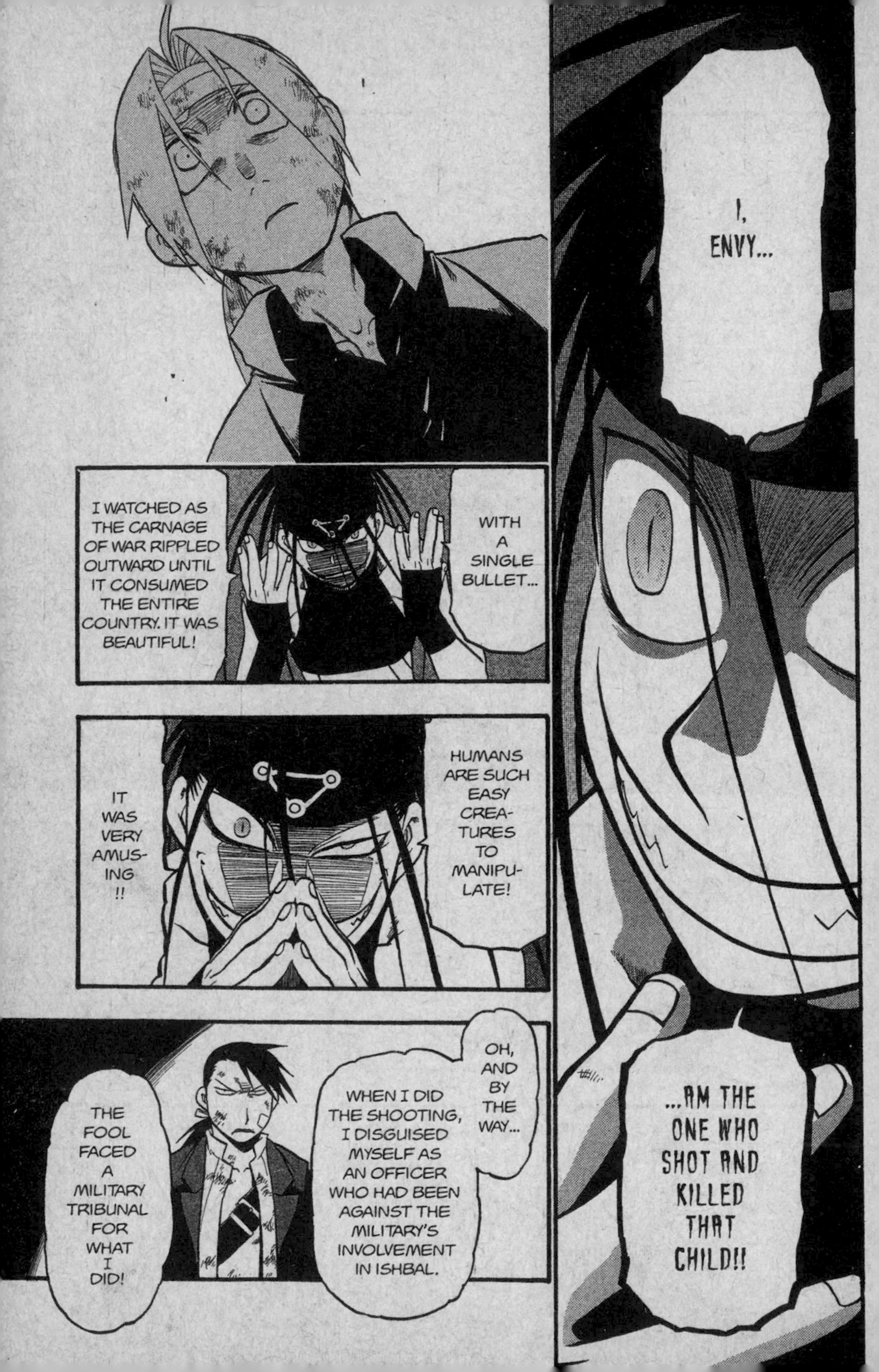
I, ENVY...
...AM THE ONE WHO SHOT AND KILLED THAT CHILD!!
WITH A SINGLE BULLET...
I WATCHED AS THE CARNAGE OF WAR RIPPLED OUTWARD UNTIL IT CONSUMED THE ENTIRE COUNTRY. IT WAS BEAUTIFUL!
HUMANS ARE SUCH EASY CREA-TURES TO MANIPU-LATE!
IT WAS VERY AMUS-ING !!
OH, AND BY THE WAY...
WHEN I DID THE SHOOTING, I DISGUISED MYSELF AS AN OFFICER WHO HAD BEEN AGAINST THE MILITARY'S INVOLVEMENT IN ISHBAL.
THE FOOL FACED A MILITARY TRIBUNAL FOR WHAT I DID!

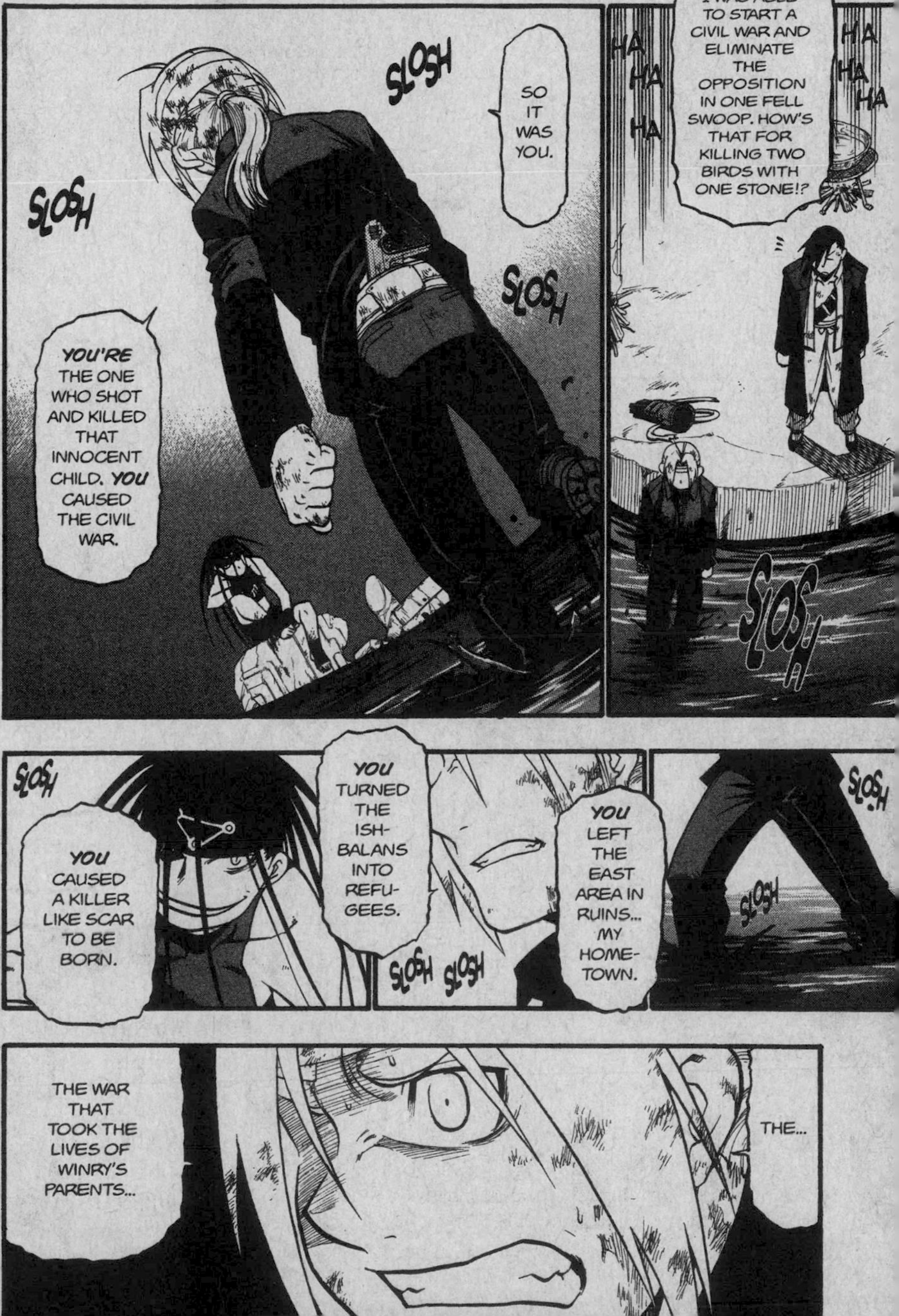
HA HA HA
HA HA HA
I WAS ABLE TO START A CIVIL WAR AND ELIMINATE THE OPPOSITION IN ONE FELL SWOOP. HOW'S THAT FOR KILLING TWO BIRDS WITH ONE STONE!?
SLOSH
SLOSH
SO IT WAS YOU.
SLOSH
SLOSH
YOU'RE THE ONE WHO SHOT AND KILLED THAT INNOCENT CHILD. YOU CAUSED THE CIVIL WAR.
SLOSH
SLOSH
YOU LEFT THE EAST AREA IN RUINS... MY HOME-TOWN.
YOU TURNED THE ISH-BALANS INTO REFU-GEES.
SLOSH SLOSH
SLOSH
YOU CAUSED A KILLER LIKE SCAR TO BE BORN.
THE...
THE WAR THAT TOOK THE LIVES OF WINRY'S PARENTS...

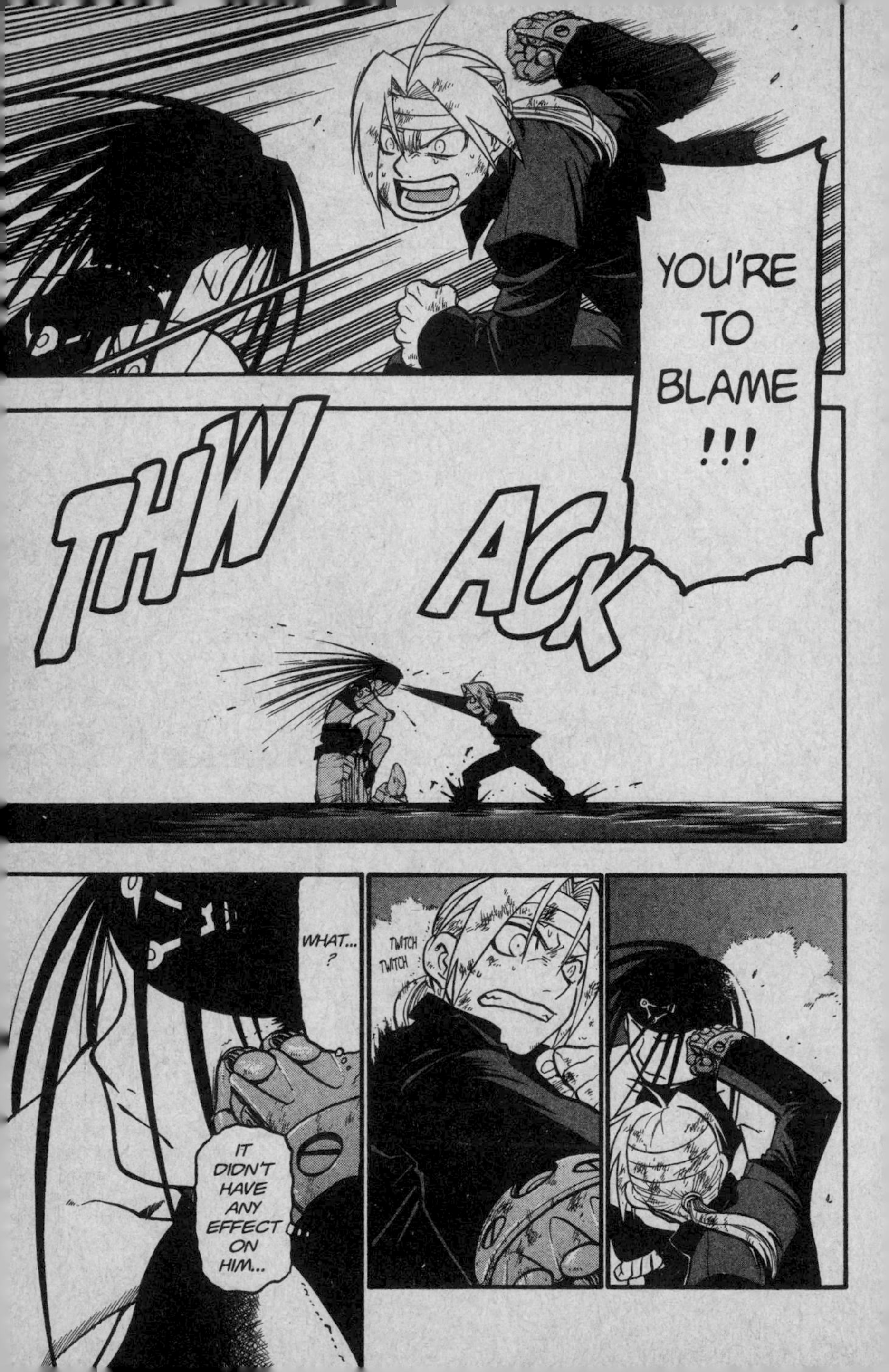
YOU'RE
TO
BLAME
!!!
THWACK
TWITCH
TWITCH
WHAT...
?
IT
DIDN'T
HAVE
ANY
EFFECT
ON
HIM...

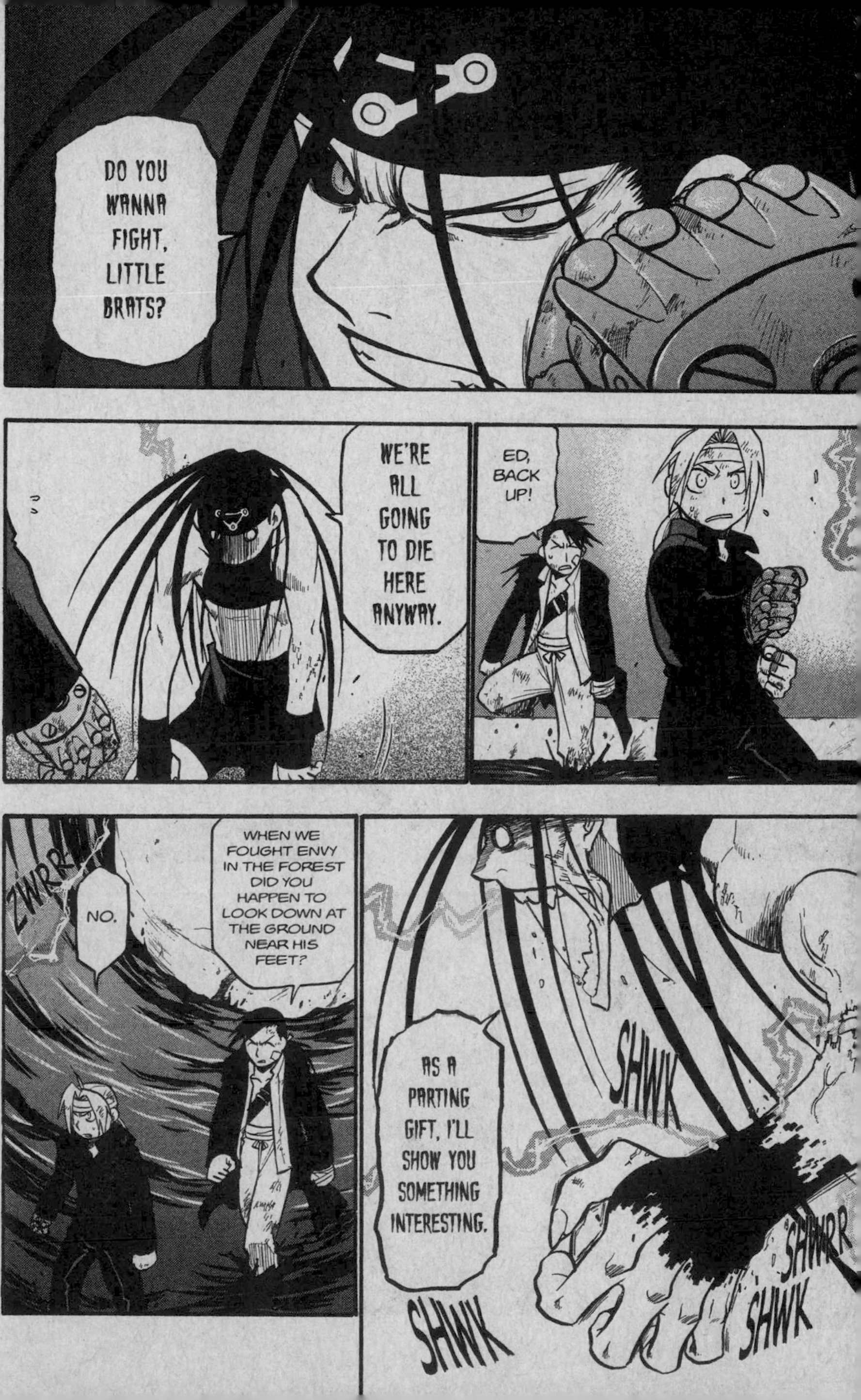
DO YOU WANNA FIGHT, LITTLE BRATS?
ED, BACK UP!
WE'RE ALL GOING TO DIE HERE ANYWAY.
AS A PARTING GIFT, I'LL SHOW YOU SOMETHING INTERESTING.
SHWK
SHWRR
SHWK
SHWK
WHEN WE FOUGHT ENVY IN THE FOREST DID YOU HAPPEN TO LOOK DOWN AT THE GROUND NEAR HIS FEET?
NO.
ZWRR

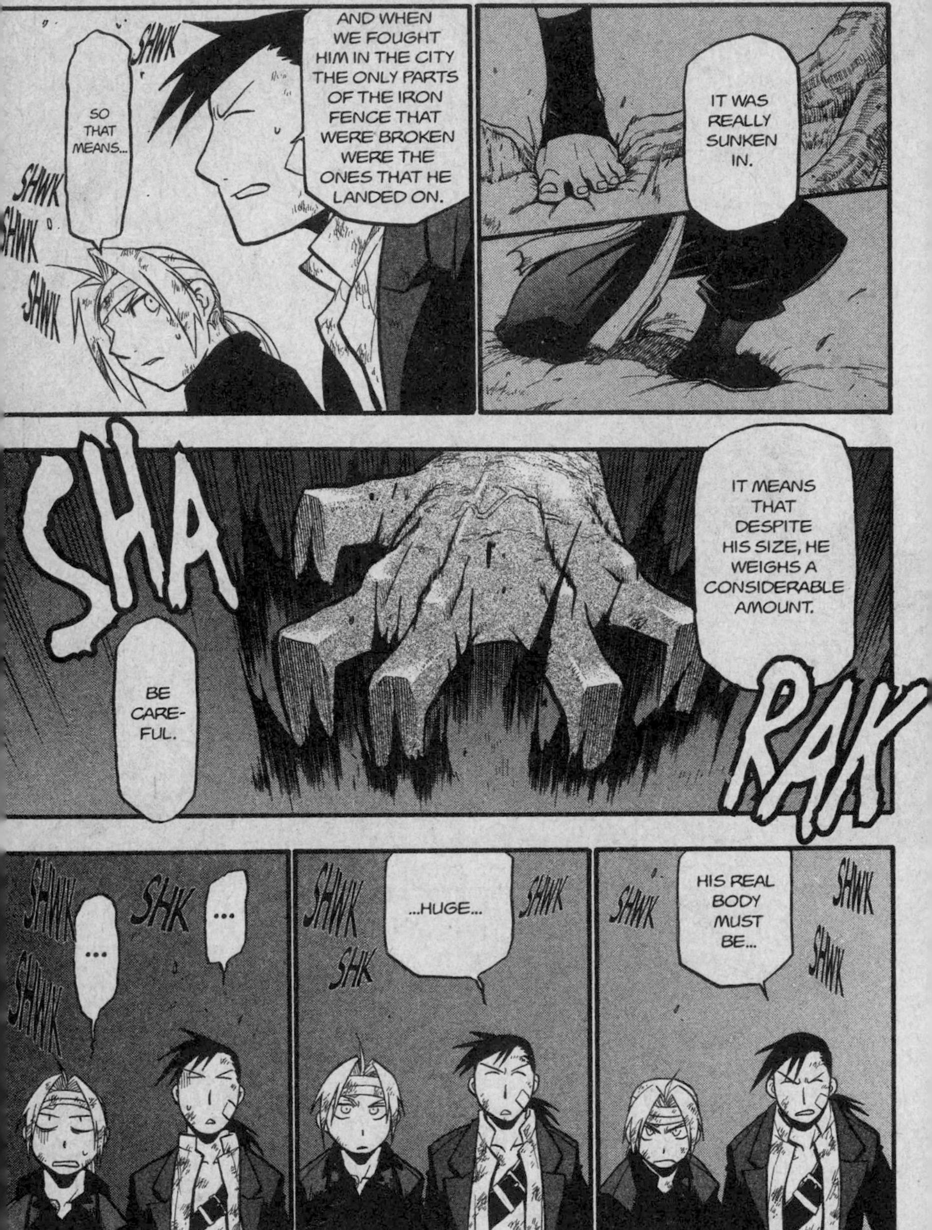
IT WAS REALLY SUNKEN IN.
AND WHEN WE FOUGHT HIM IN THE CITY THE ONLY PARTS OF THE IRON FENCE THAT WERE BROKEN WERE THE ONES THAT HE LANDED ON.
SHWK
SO THAT MEANS...
SHWK
SHWK
SHWK
IT MEANS THAT DESPITE HIS SIZE, HE WEIGHS A CONSIDERABLE AMOUNT.
SHA
RAK
BE CARE-FUL.
SHWK
HIS REAL BODY MUST BE...
SHWK
SHWK
SHWK
...HUGE...
SHWK
SHK
...
SHK
...
SHWK
SHWK

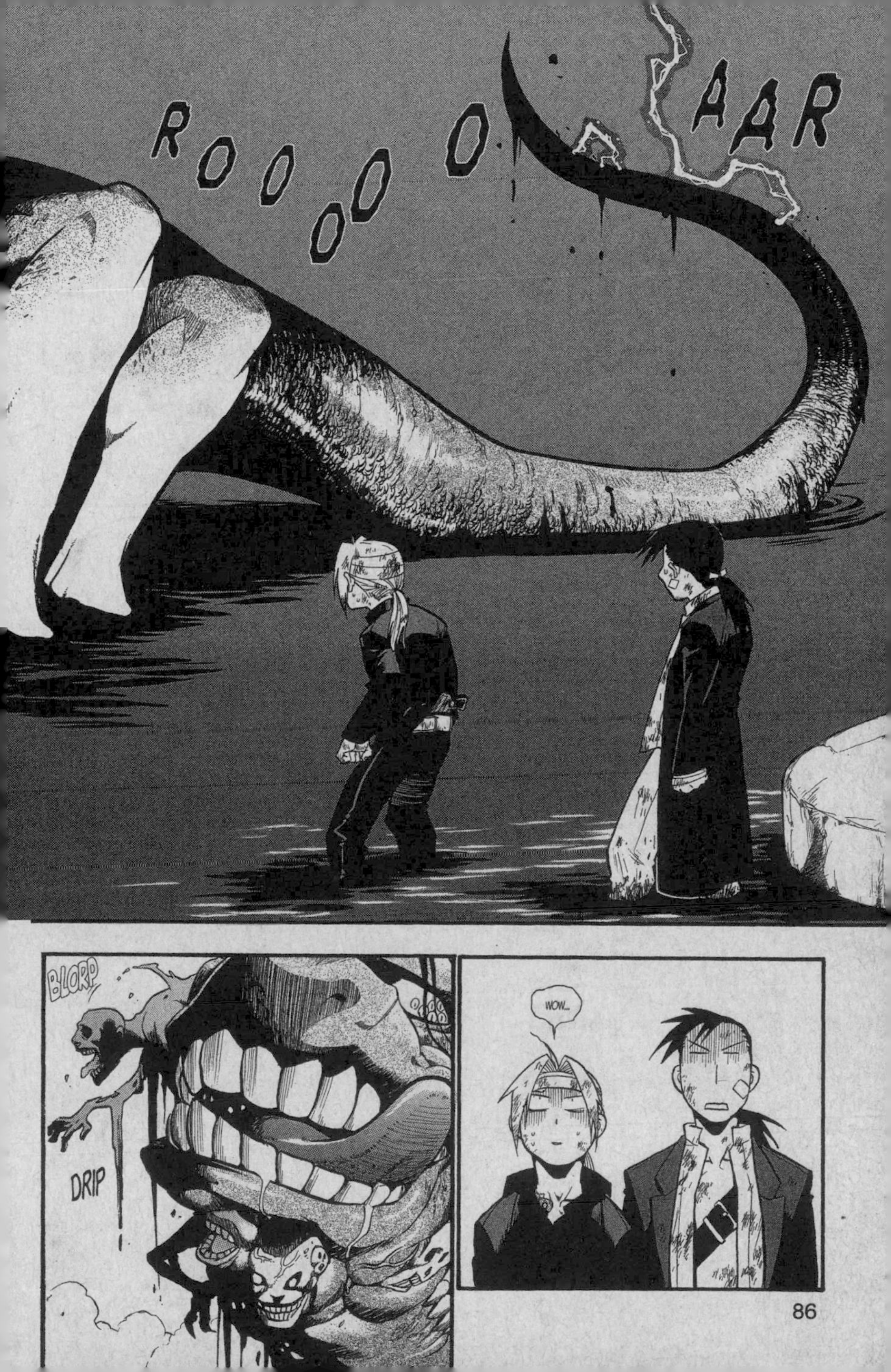
ROOOOOAAR
WOW...
BLORP
DRIP

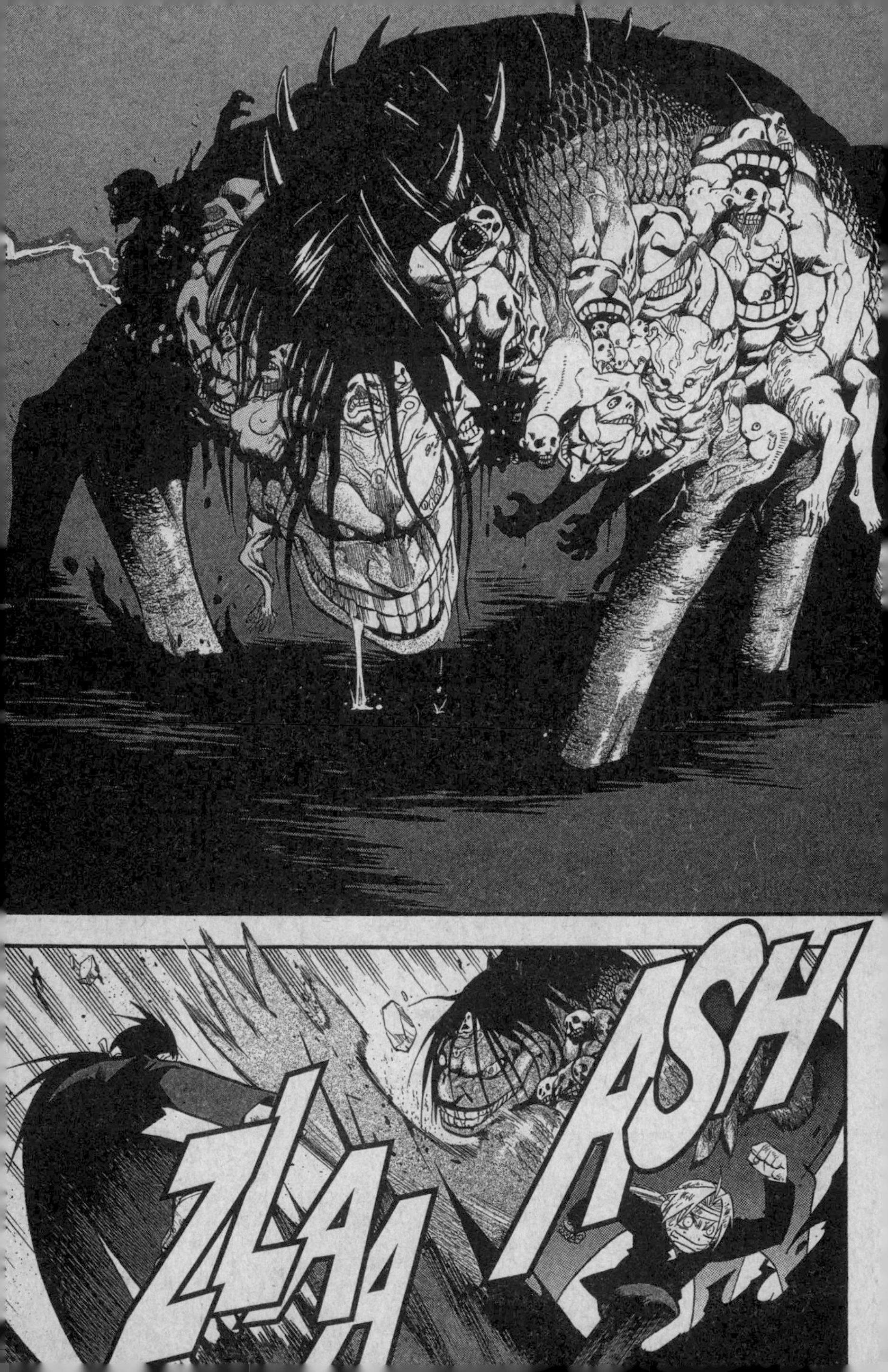
ZLAAASH

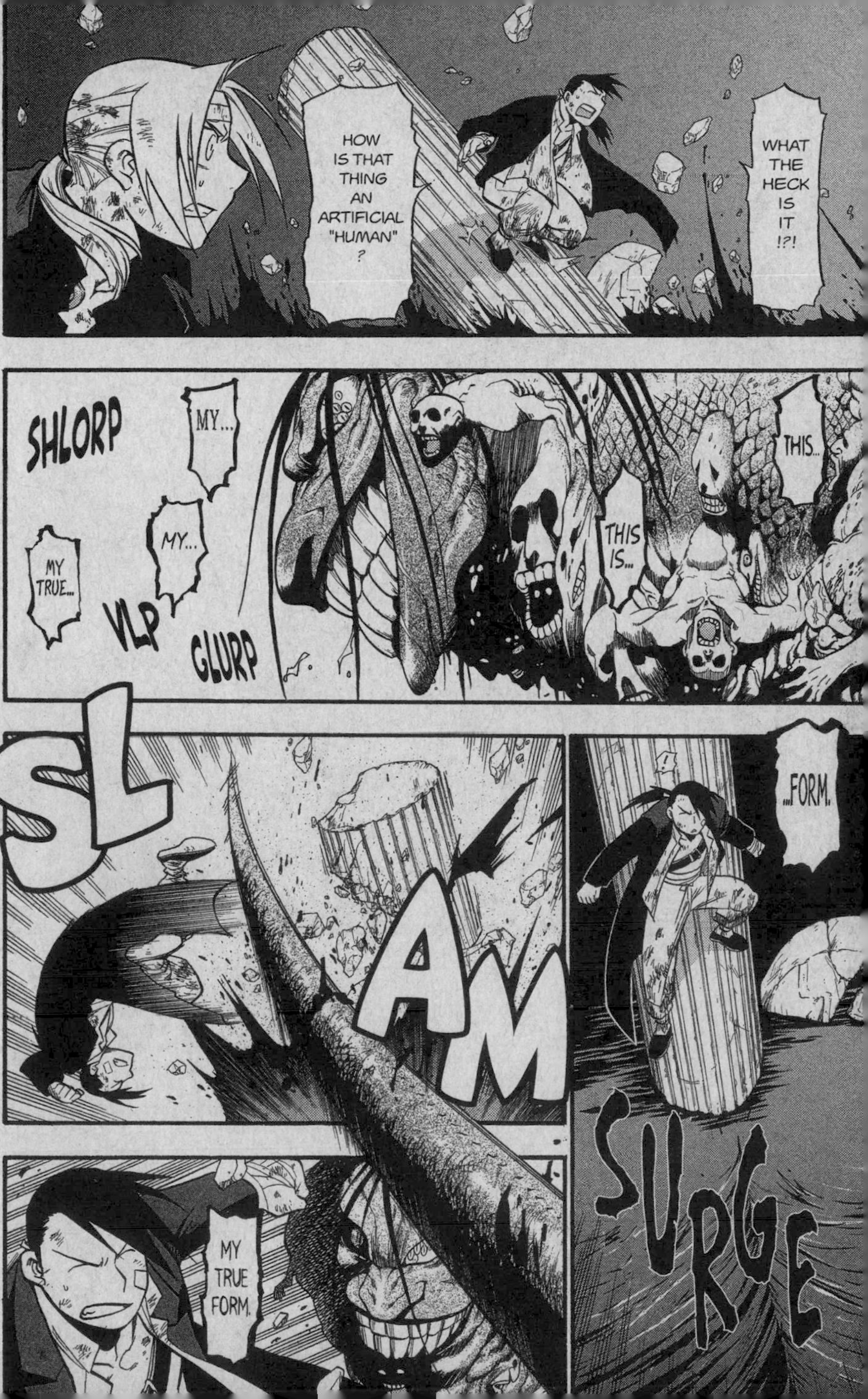
WHAT THE HECK IS IT !?!
HOW IS THAT THING AN ARTIFICIAL "HUMAN"?
THIS...
THIS IS...
MY...
SHLORP
MY...
MY TRUE...
VLP
GLURP
...FORM.
!
SURGE
SLAM
MY TRUE FORM.

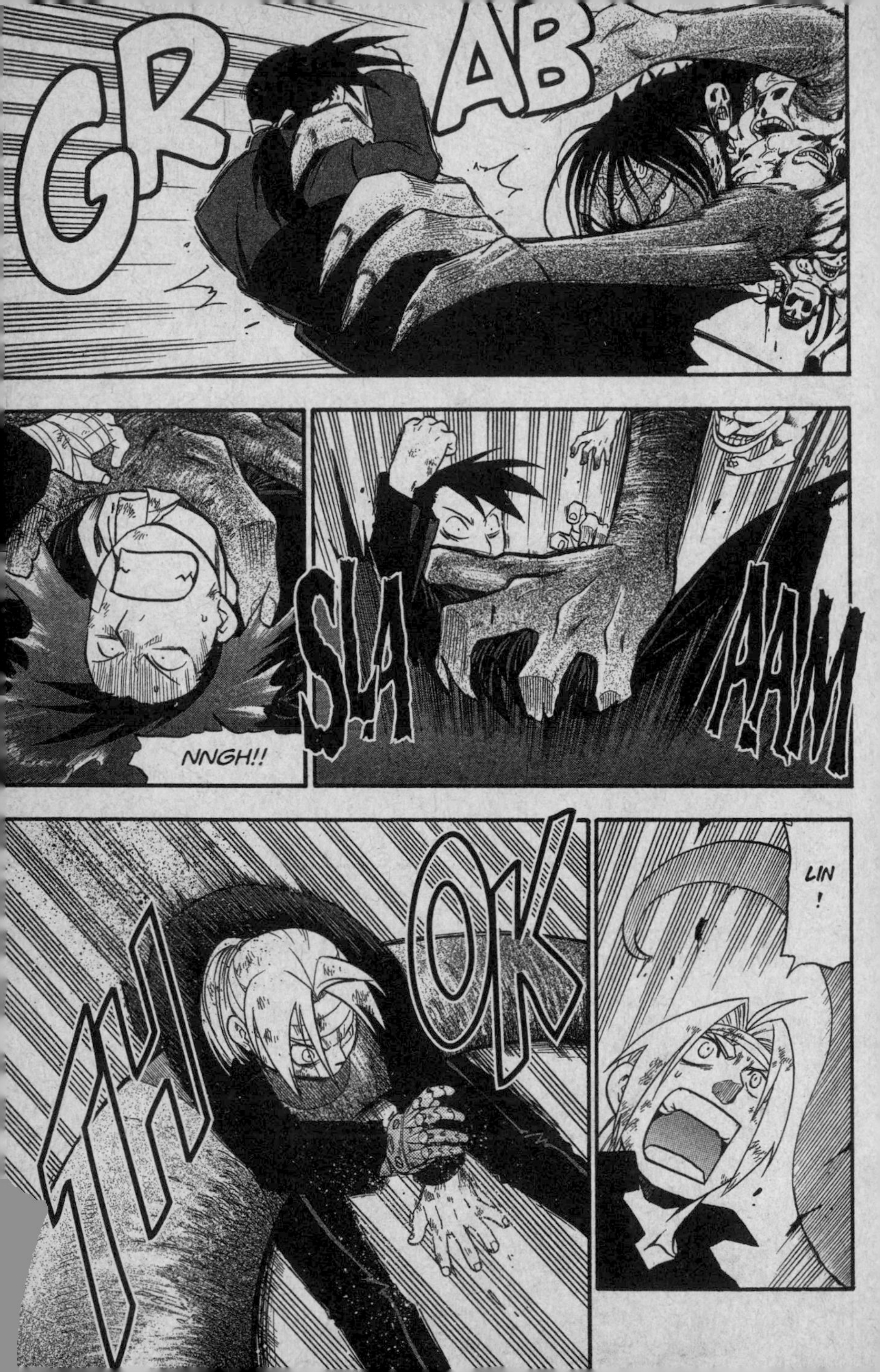
GRAB
SLAAM
NNGH!!
LIN!
THOK

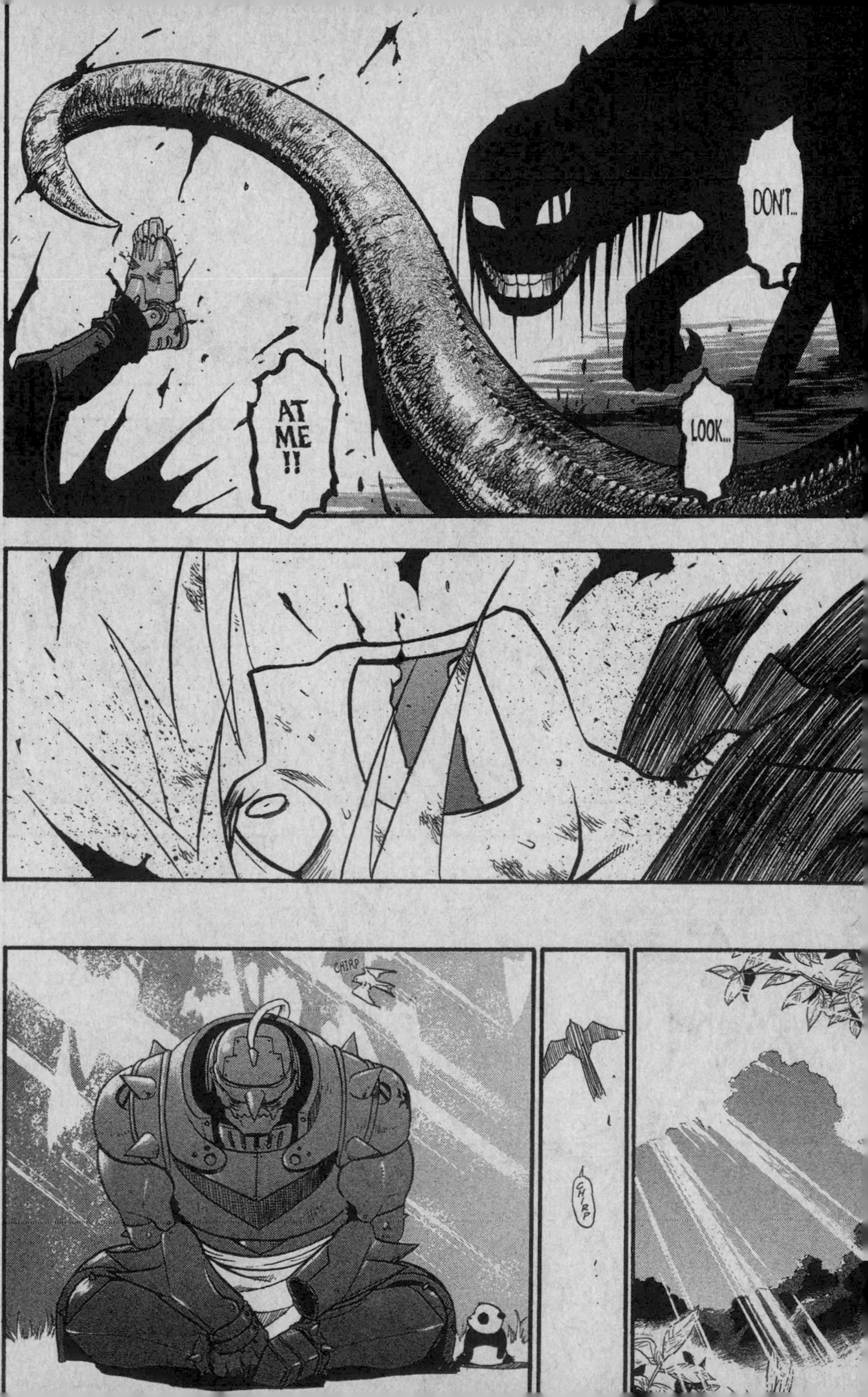
DON'T...
LOOK...
AT ME !!
CHIRP
CHIRP

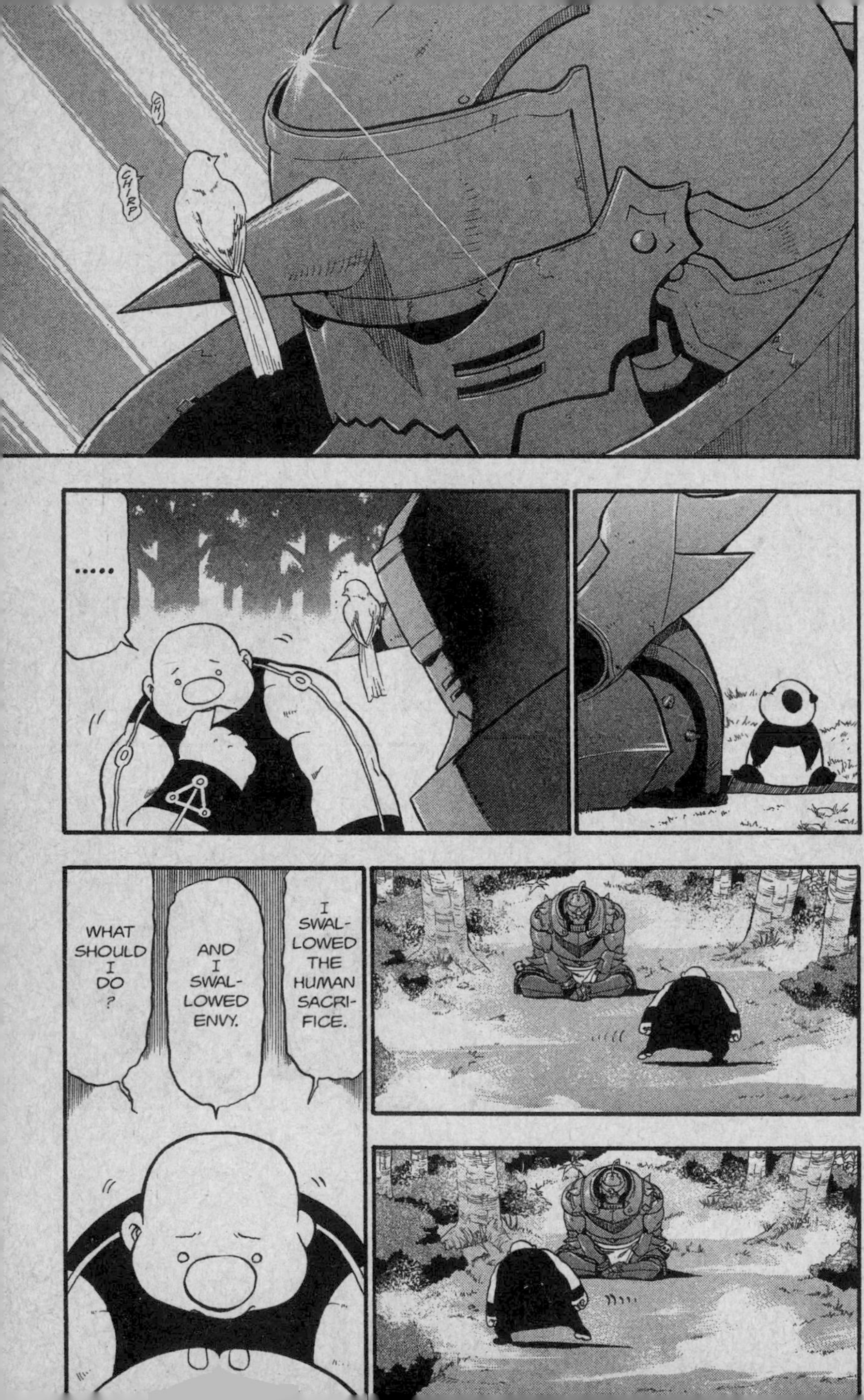
CHI
CHIRP
.....
I SWALLOWED THE HUMAN SACRIFICE.
AND I SWALLOWED ENVY.
WHAT SHOULD I DO?

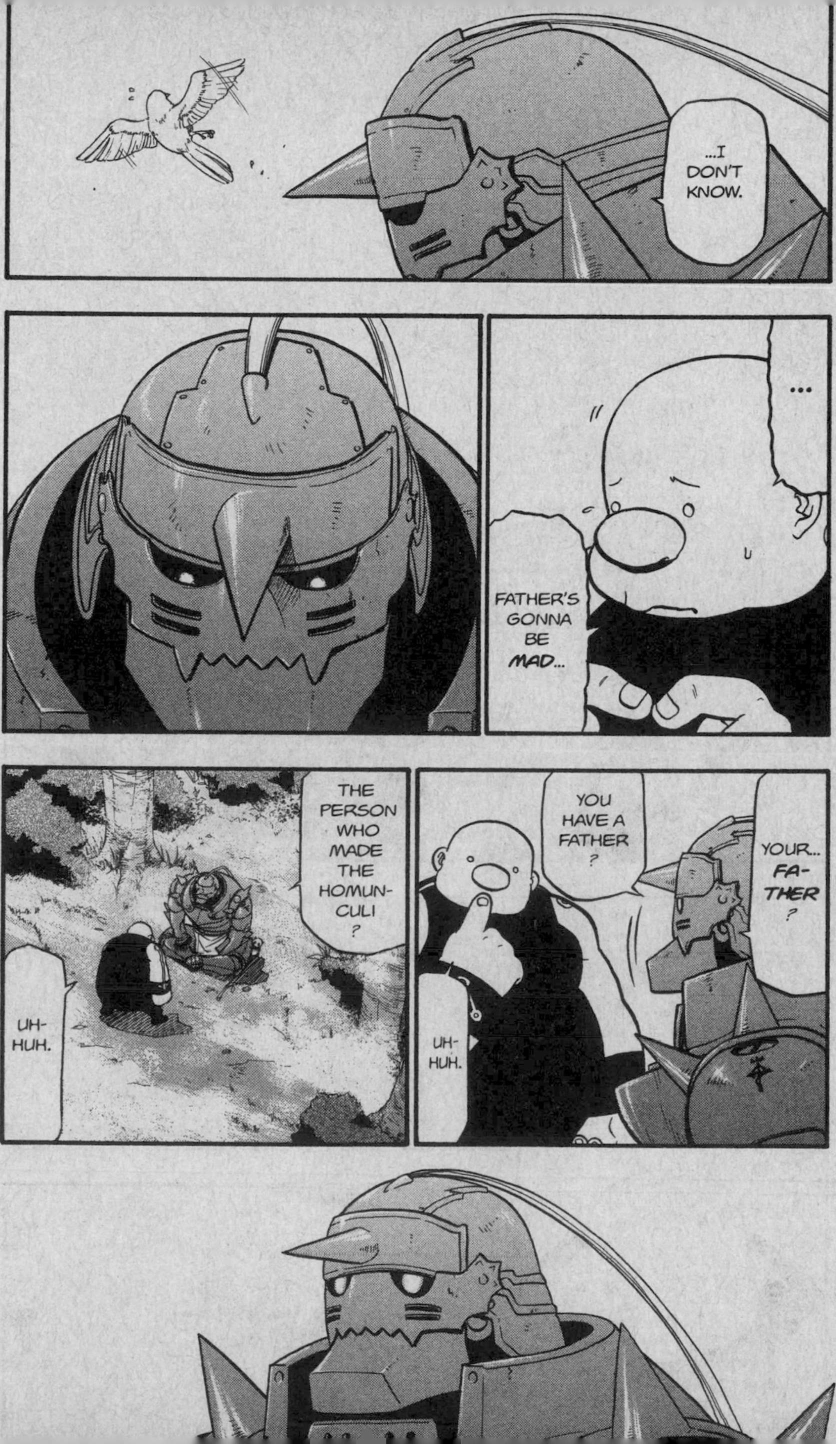
...I DON'T KNOW.
...
FATHER'S GONNA BE *MAD*...
YOUR... *FA-THER*?
YOU HAVE A FATHER?
UH-HUH.
THE PERSON WHO MADE THE HOMUNCULI?
UH-HUH.

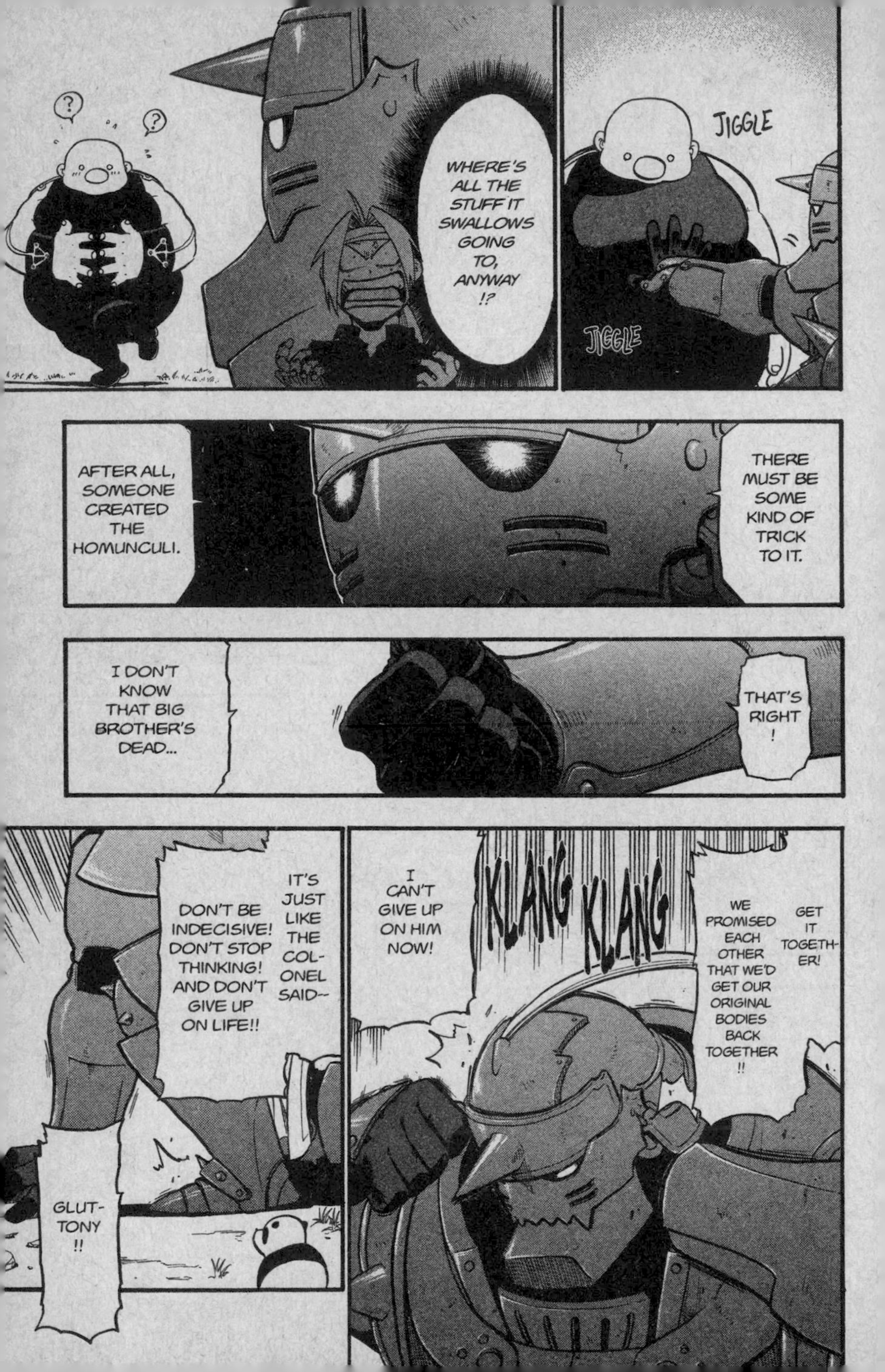
JIGGLE
JIGGLE
WHERE'S ALL THE STUFF IT SWALLOWS GOING TO, ANYWAY !?
?
?
THERE MUST BE SOME KIND OF TRICK TO IT.
AFTER ALL, SOMEONE CREATED THE HOMUNCULI.
THAT'S RIGHT !
I DON'T KNOW THAT BIG BROTHER'S DEAD...
GET IT TOGETH-ER!
WE PROMISED EACH OTHER THAT WE'D GET OUR ORIGINAL BODIES BACK TOGETHER !!
KLANG KLANG
I CAN'T GIVE UP ON HIM NOW!
IT'S JUST LIKE THE COL-ONEL SAID~
DON'T BE INDECISIVE! DON'T STOP THINKING! AND DON'T GIVE UP ON LIFE!!
GLUT-TONY !!

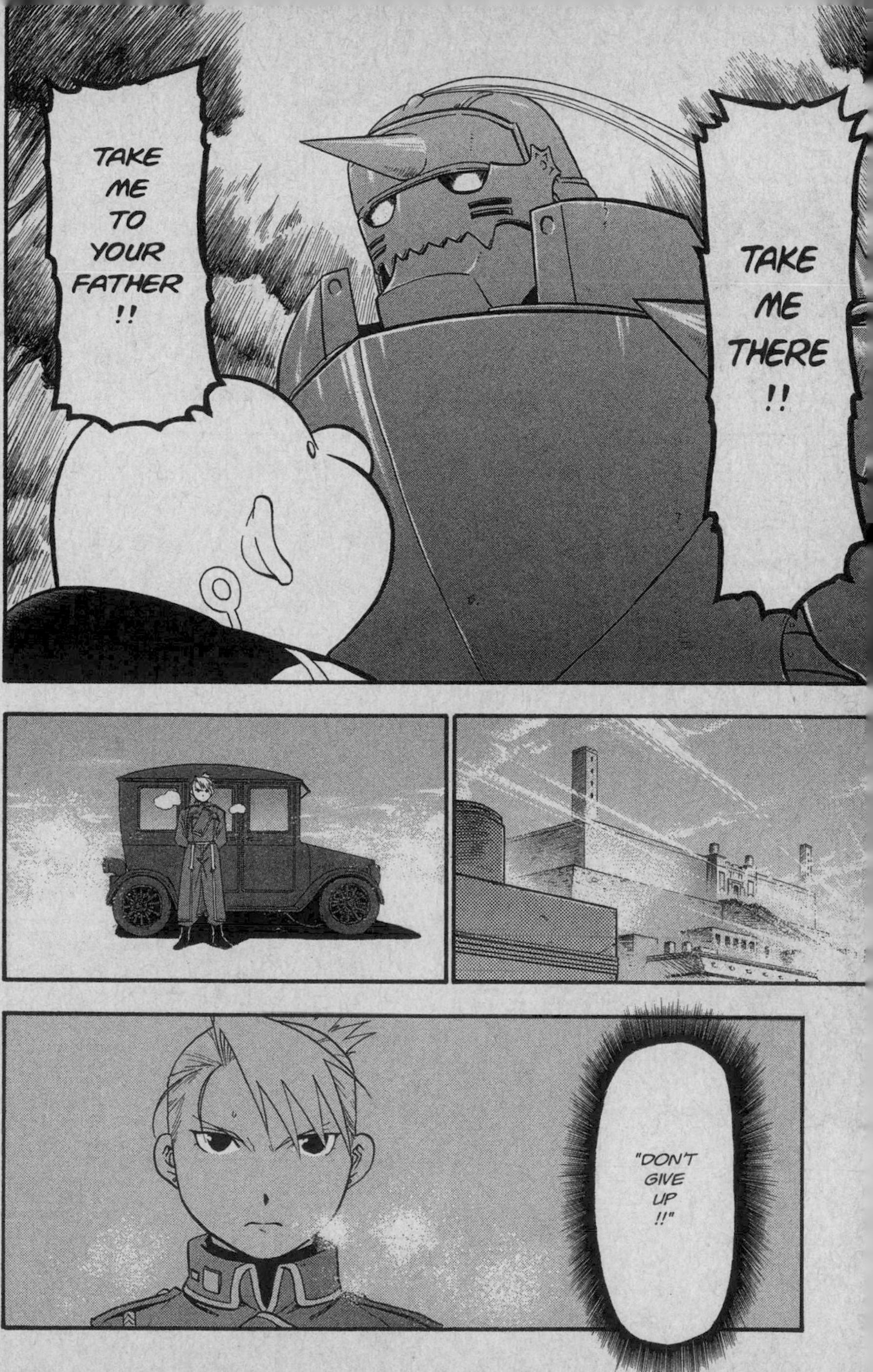
TAKE ME THERE !!
TAKE ME TO YOUR FATHER !!
"DON'T GIVE UP !!"

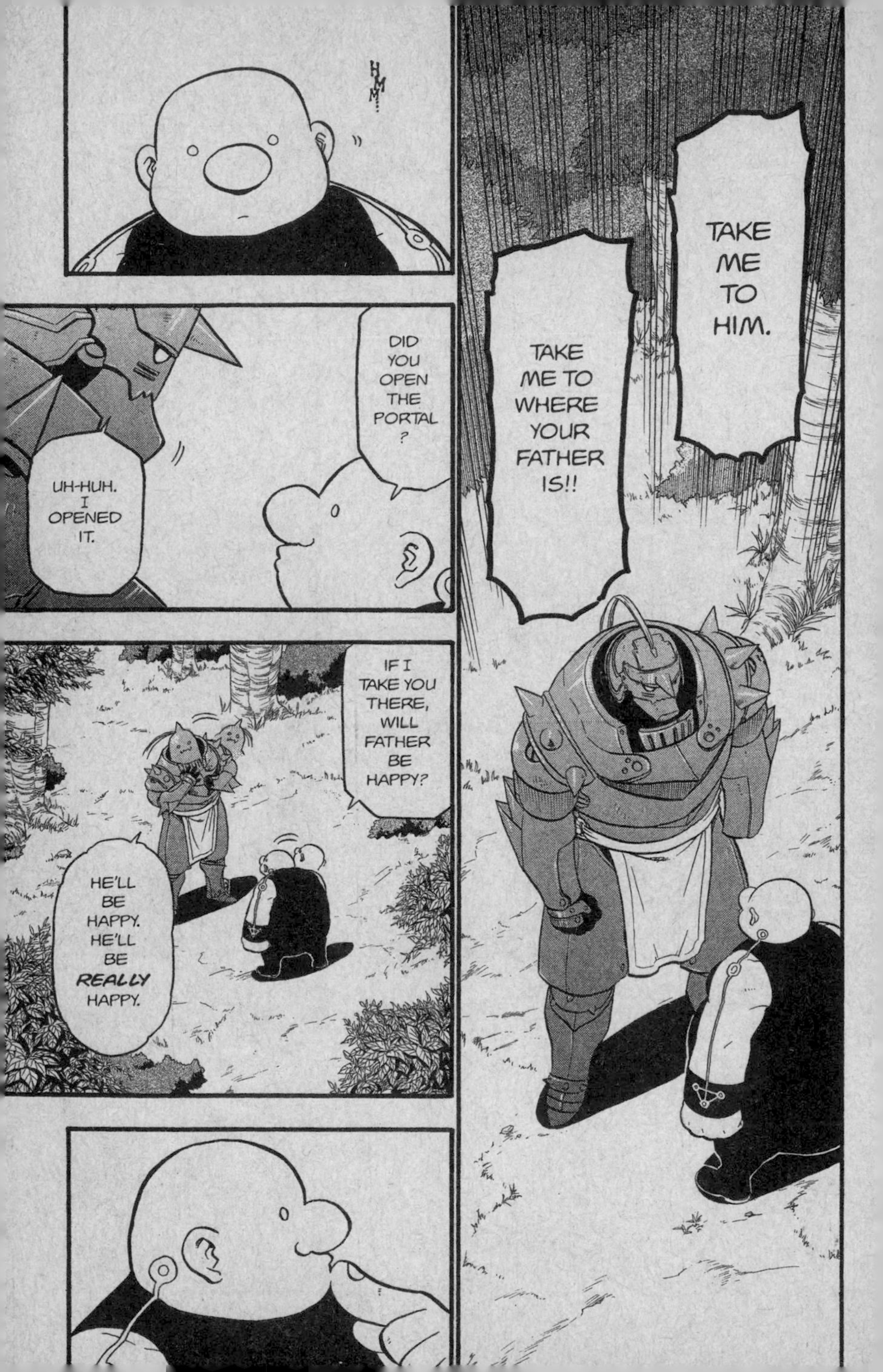
TAKE ME TO HIM.
TAKE ME TO WHERE YOUR FATHER IS!!
HMM...
DID YOU OPEN THE PORTAL?
UH-HUH. I OPENED IT.
IF I TAKE YOU THERE, WILL FATHER BE HAPPY?
HE'LL BE HAPPY. HE'LL BE *REALLY* HAPPY.

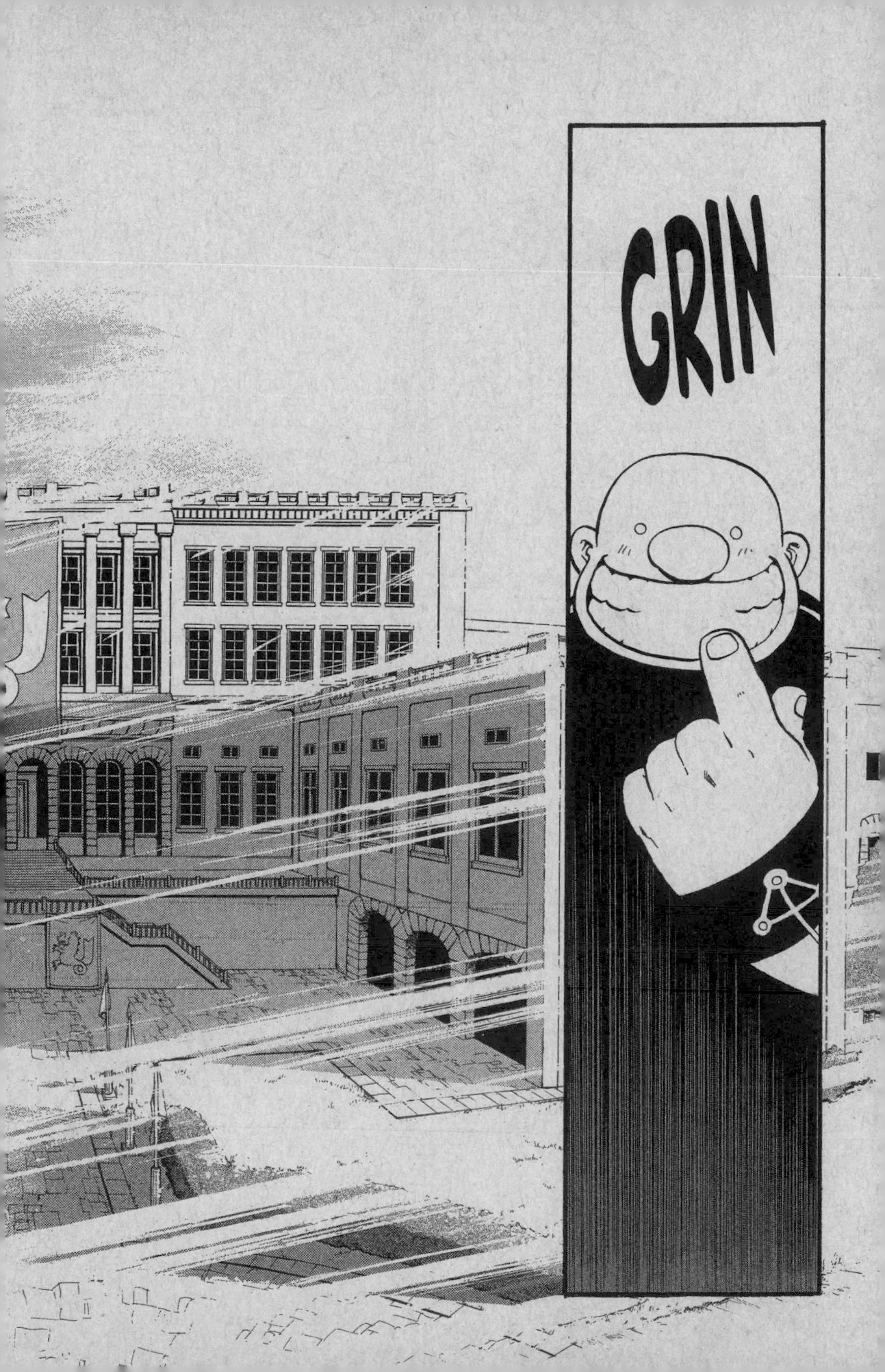
GRIN

Chapter 52 Lord Of The Demon's Lair

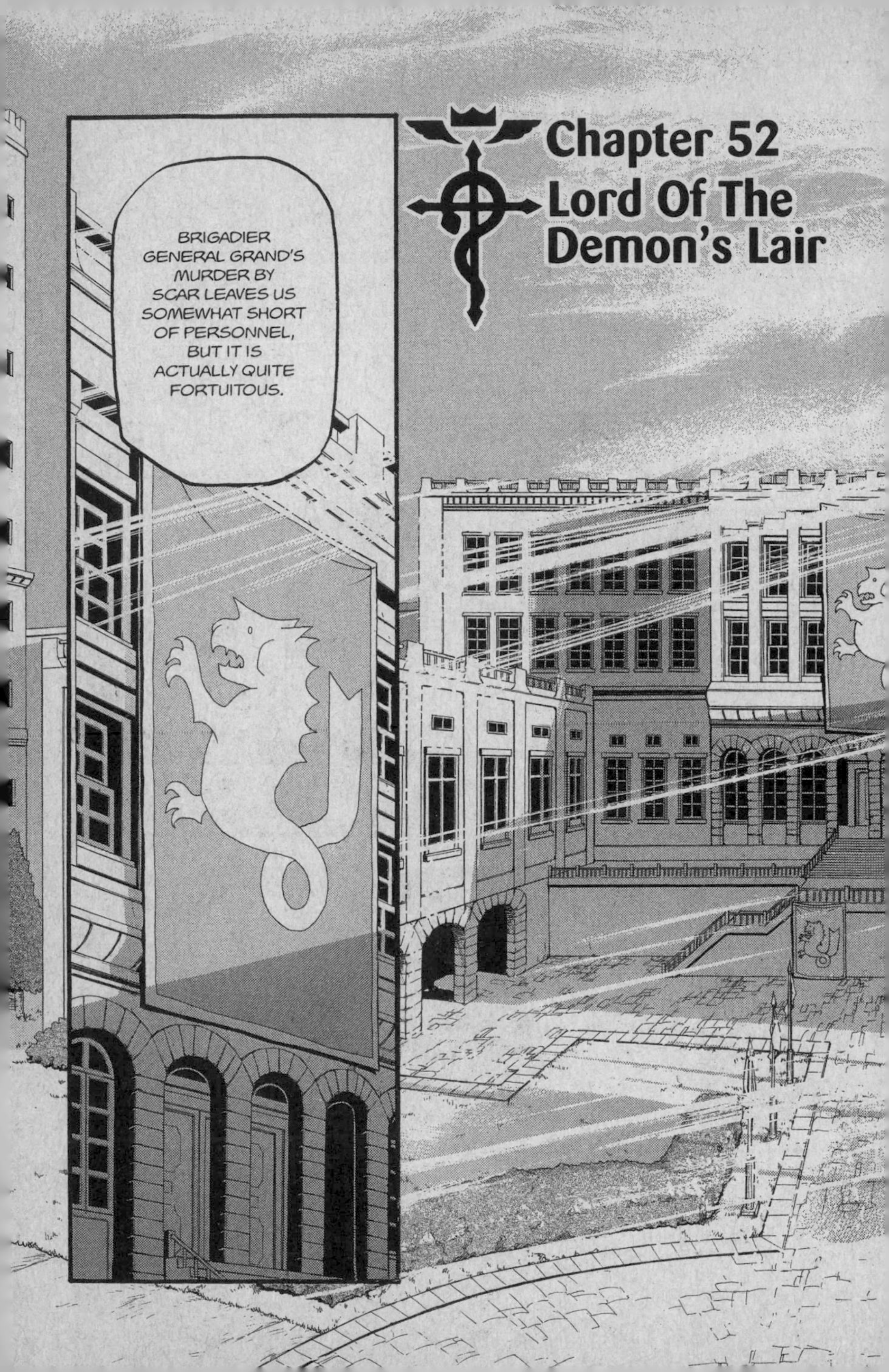
BRIGADIER GENERAL GRAND'S MURDER BY SCAR LEAVES US SOMEWHAT SHORT OF PERSONNEL, BUT IT IS ACTUALLY QUITE FORTUITOUS.

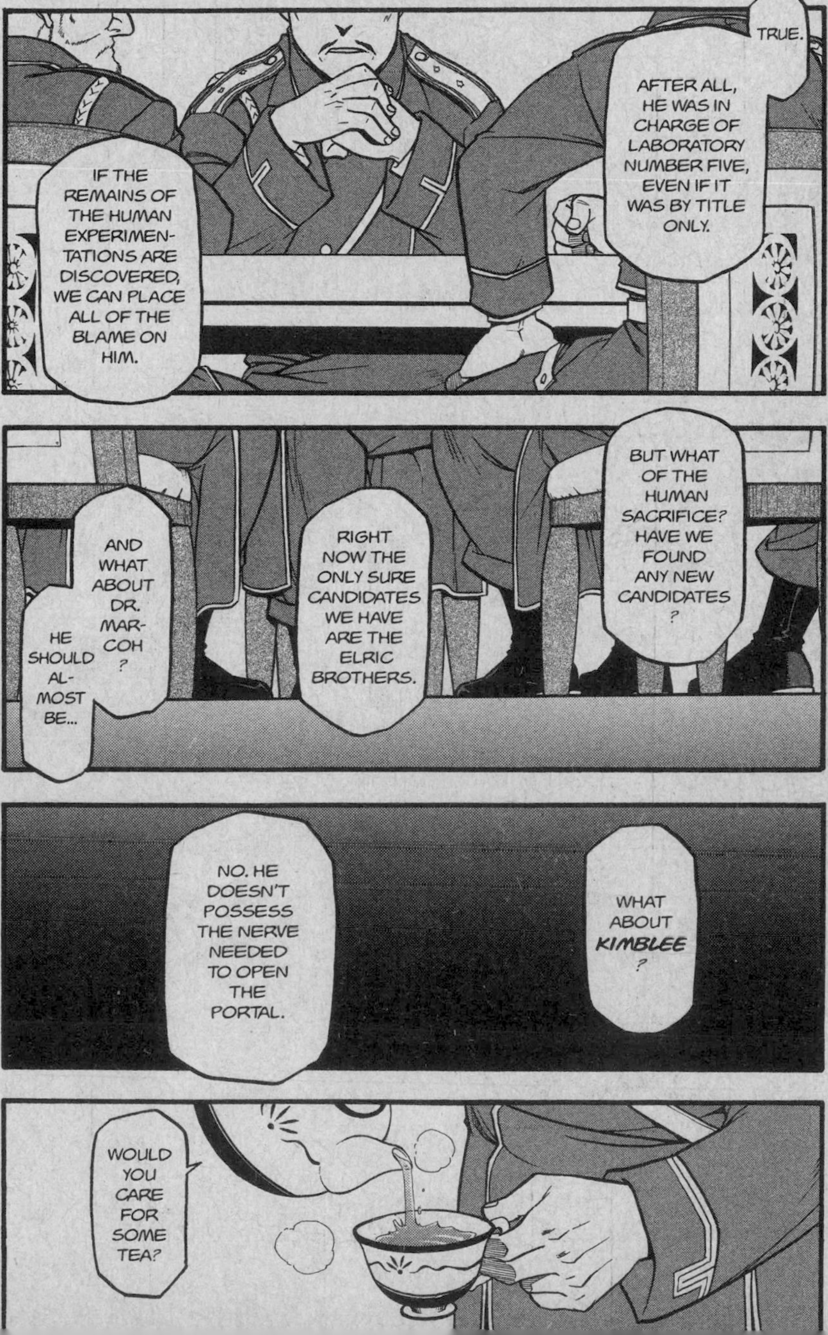
TRUE.
AFTER ALL, HE WAS IN CHARGE OF LABORATORY NUMBER FIVE, EVEN IF IT WAS BY TITLE ONLY.
IF THE REMAINS OF THE HUMAN EXPERIMENTATIONS ARE DISCOVERED, WE CAN PLACE ALL OF THE BLAME ON HIM.
BUT WHAT OF THE HUMAN SACRIFICE? HAVE WE FOUND ANY NEW CANDIDATES?
RIGHT NOW THE ONLY SURE CANDIDATES WE HAVE ARE THE ELRIC BROTHERS.
AND WHAT ABOUT DR. MARCOH?
HE SHOULD ALMOST BE...
WHAT ABOUT *KIMBLEE*?
NO. HE DOESN'T POSSESS THE NERVE NEEDED TO OPEN THE PORTAL.
WOULD YOU CARE FOR SOME TEA?

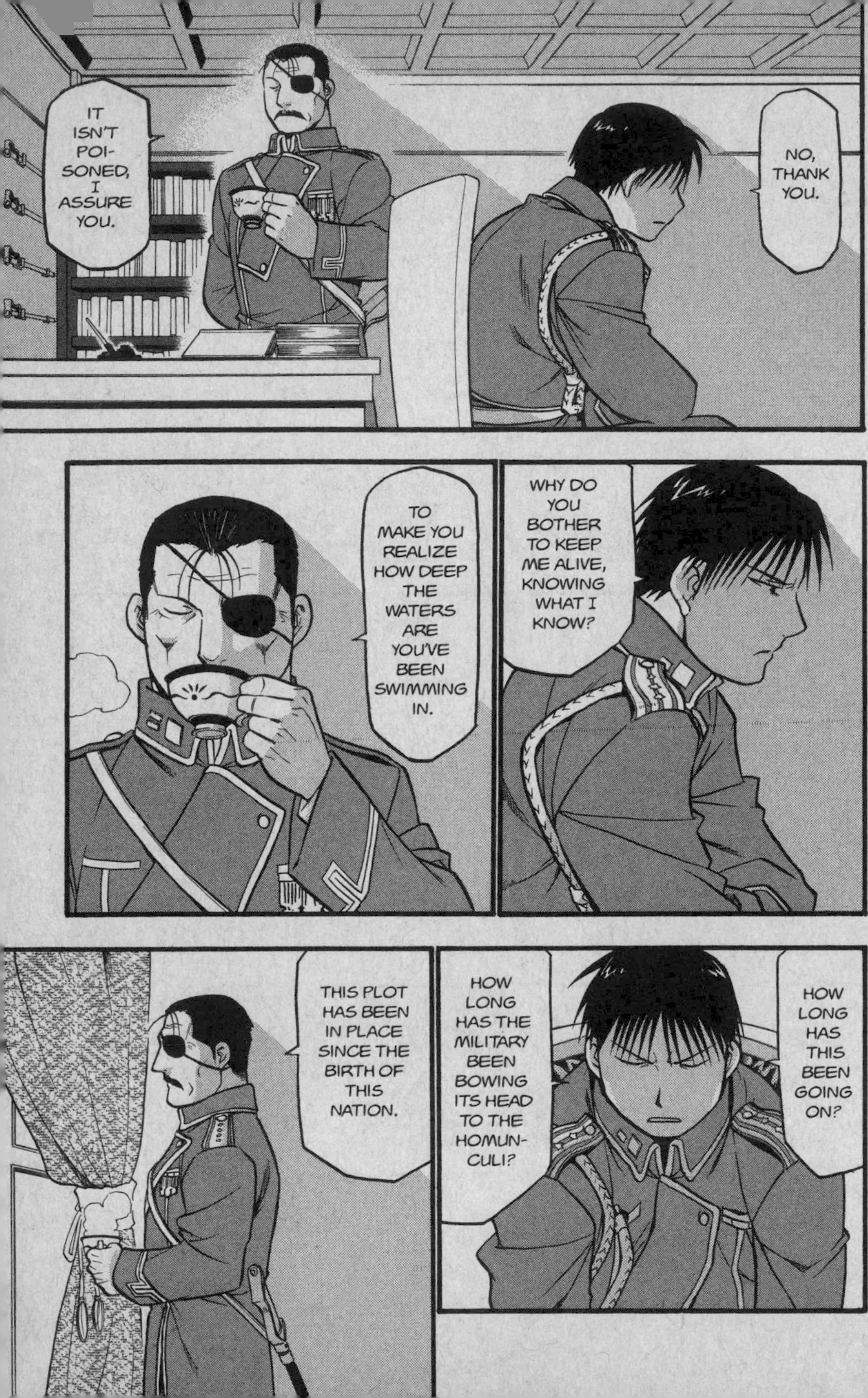
NO, THANK YOU.
IT ISN'T POI-SONED, I ASSURE YOU.
WHY DO YOU BOTHER TO KEEP ME ALIVE, KNOWING WHAT I KNOW?
TO MAKE YOU REALIZE HOW DEEP THE WATERS ARE YOU'VE BEEN SWIMMING IN.
HOW LONG HAS THIS BEEN GOING ON?
HOW LONG HAS THE MILITARY BEEN BOWING ITS HEAD TO THE HOMUN-CULI?
THIS PLOT HAS BEEN IN PLACE SINCE THE BIRTH OF THIS NATION.

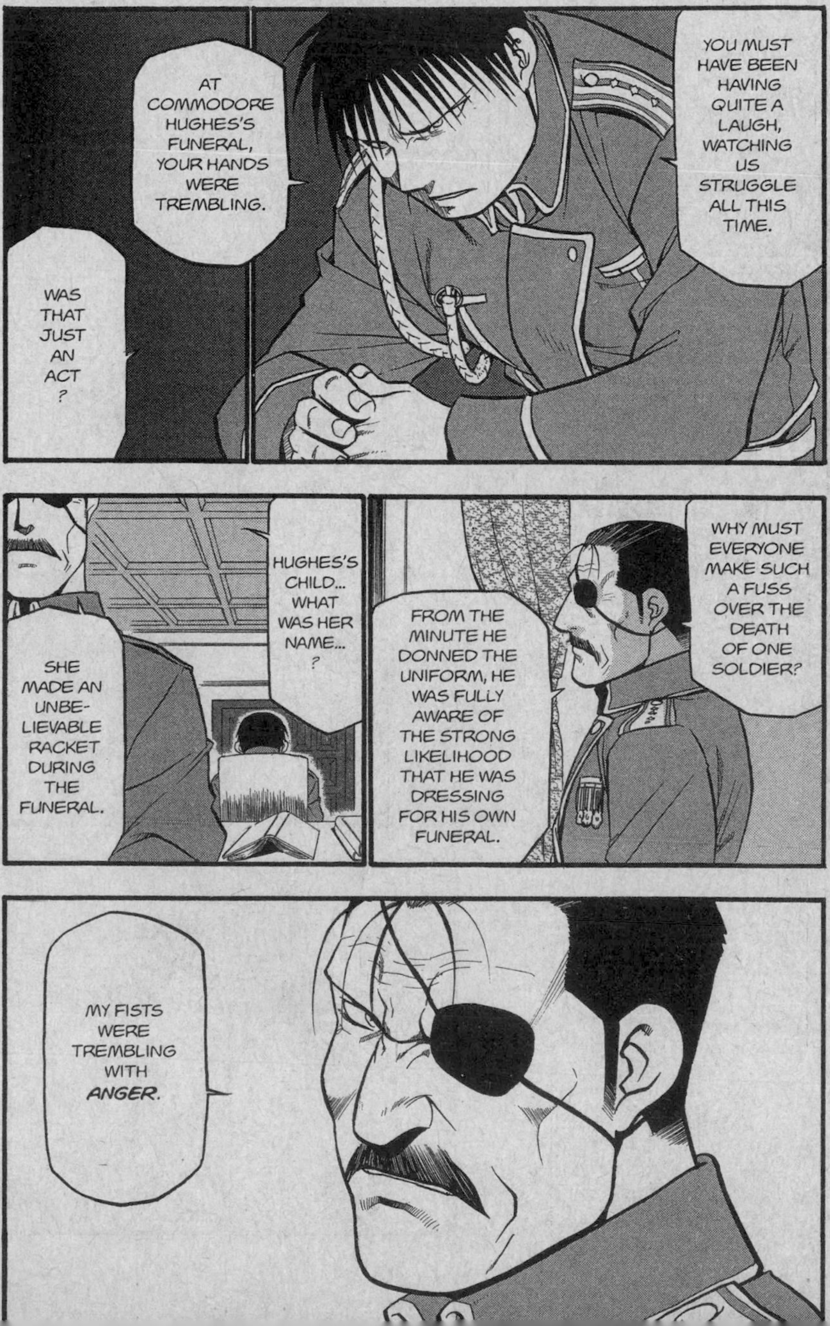
YOU MUST HAVE BEEN HAVING QUITE A LAUGH, WATCHING US STRUGGLE ALL THIS TIME.
AT COMMODORE HUGHES'S FUNERAL, YOUR HANDS WERE TREMBLING.
WAS THAT JUST AN ACT?
WHY MUST EVERYONE MAKE SUCH A FUSS OVER THE DEATH OF ONE SOLDIER?
FROM THE MINUTE HE DONNED THE UNIFORM, HE WAS FULLY AWARE OF THE STRONG LIKELIHOOD THAT HE WAS DRESSING FOR HIS OWN FUNERAL.
HUGHES'S CHILD... WHAT WAS HER NAME...?
SHE MADE AN UNBE-LIEVABLE RACKET DURING THE FUNERAL.
MY FISTS WERE TREMBLING WITH *ANGER*.

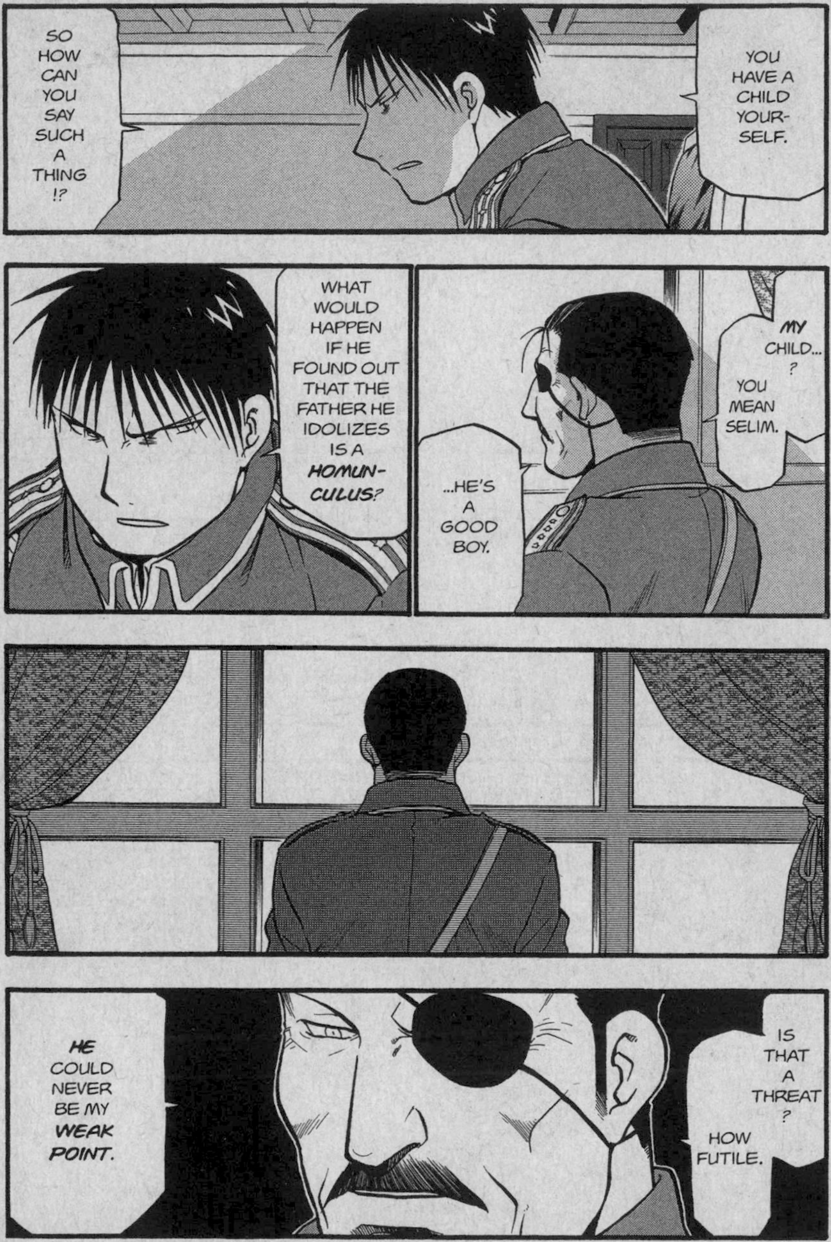
YOU HAVE A CHILD YOURSELF.
SO HOW CAN YOU SAY SUCH A THING!?
MY CHILD...? YOU MEAN SELIM.
...HE'S A GOOD BOY.
WHAT WOULD HAPPEN IF HE FOUND OUT THAT THE FATHER HE IDOLIZES IS A HOMUNCULUS?
IS THAT A THREAT? HOW FUTILE.
HE COULD NEVER BE MY WEAK POINT.

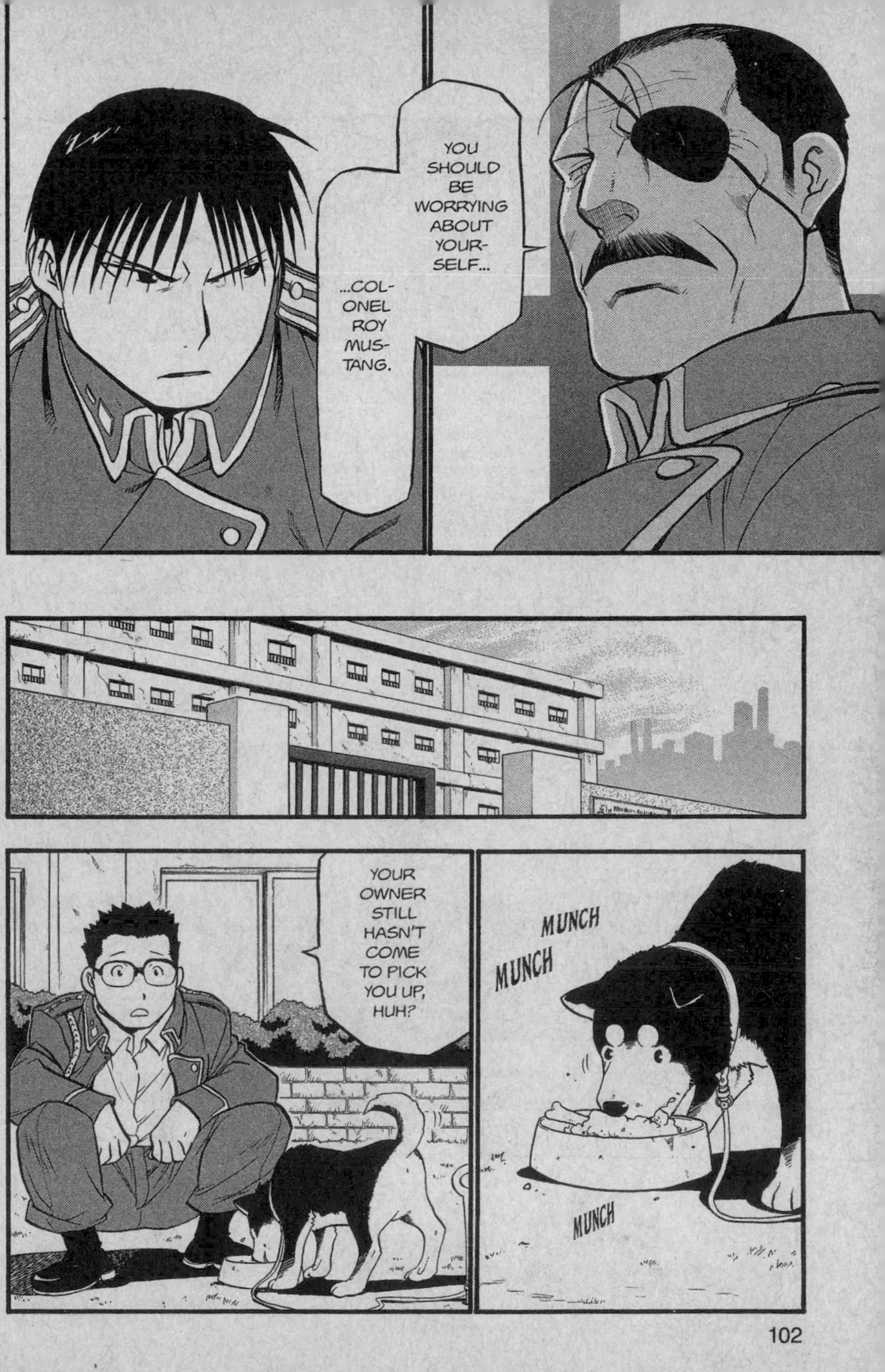
YOU SHOULD BE WORRYING ABOUT YOUR-SELF... ...COL-ONEL ROY MUS-TANG.
MUNCH
MUNCH
MUNCH
YOUR OWNER STILL HASN'T COME TO PICK YOU UP, HUH?

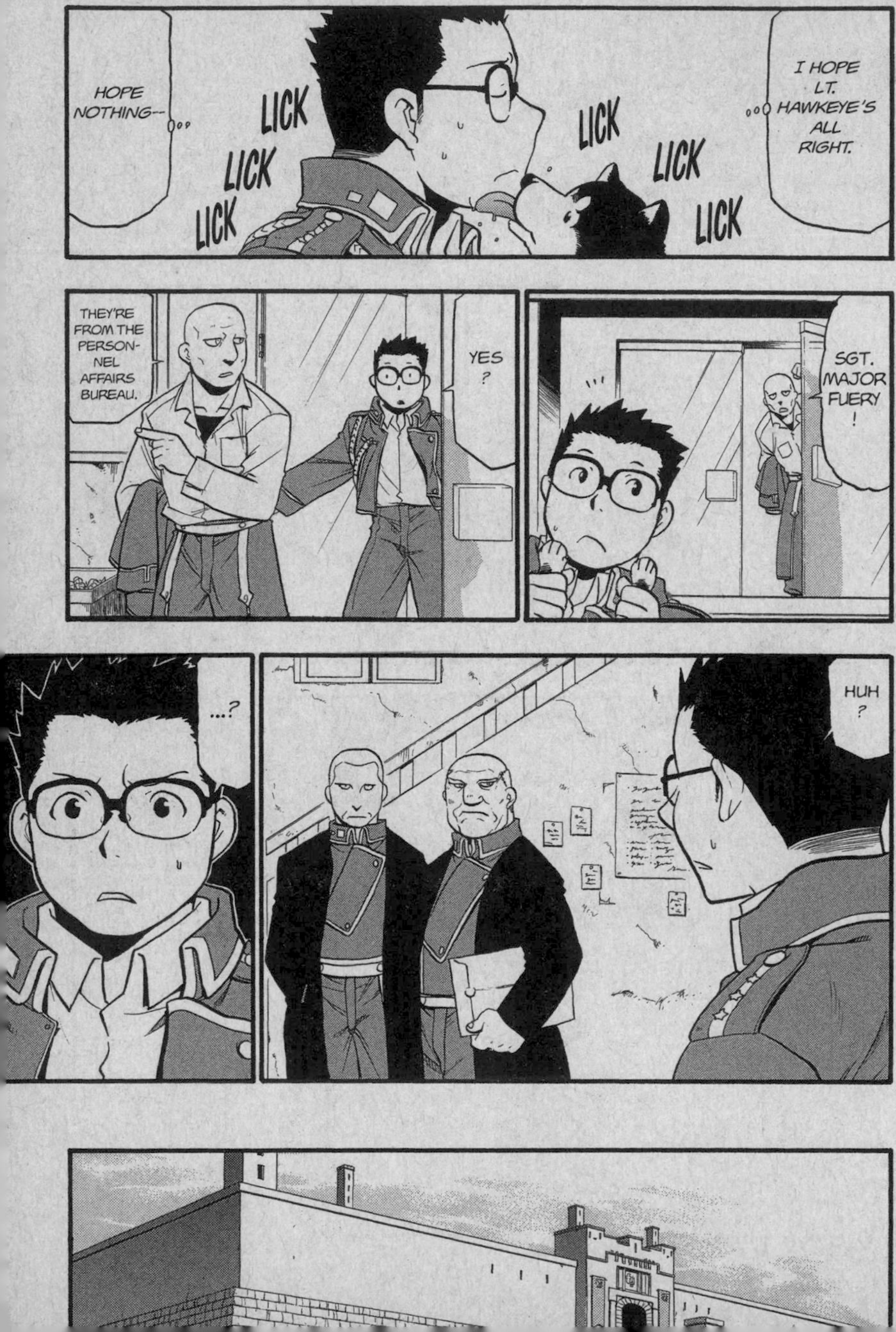
I HOPE LT. HAWKEYE'S ALL RIGHT.
LICK
LICK
LICK
HOPE NOTHING--
LICK
LICK
LICK
SGT. MAJOR FUERY!
YES?
THEY'RE FROM THE PERSON-NEL AFFAIRS BUREAU.
HUH?
...?

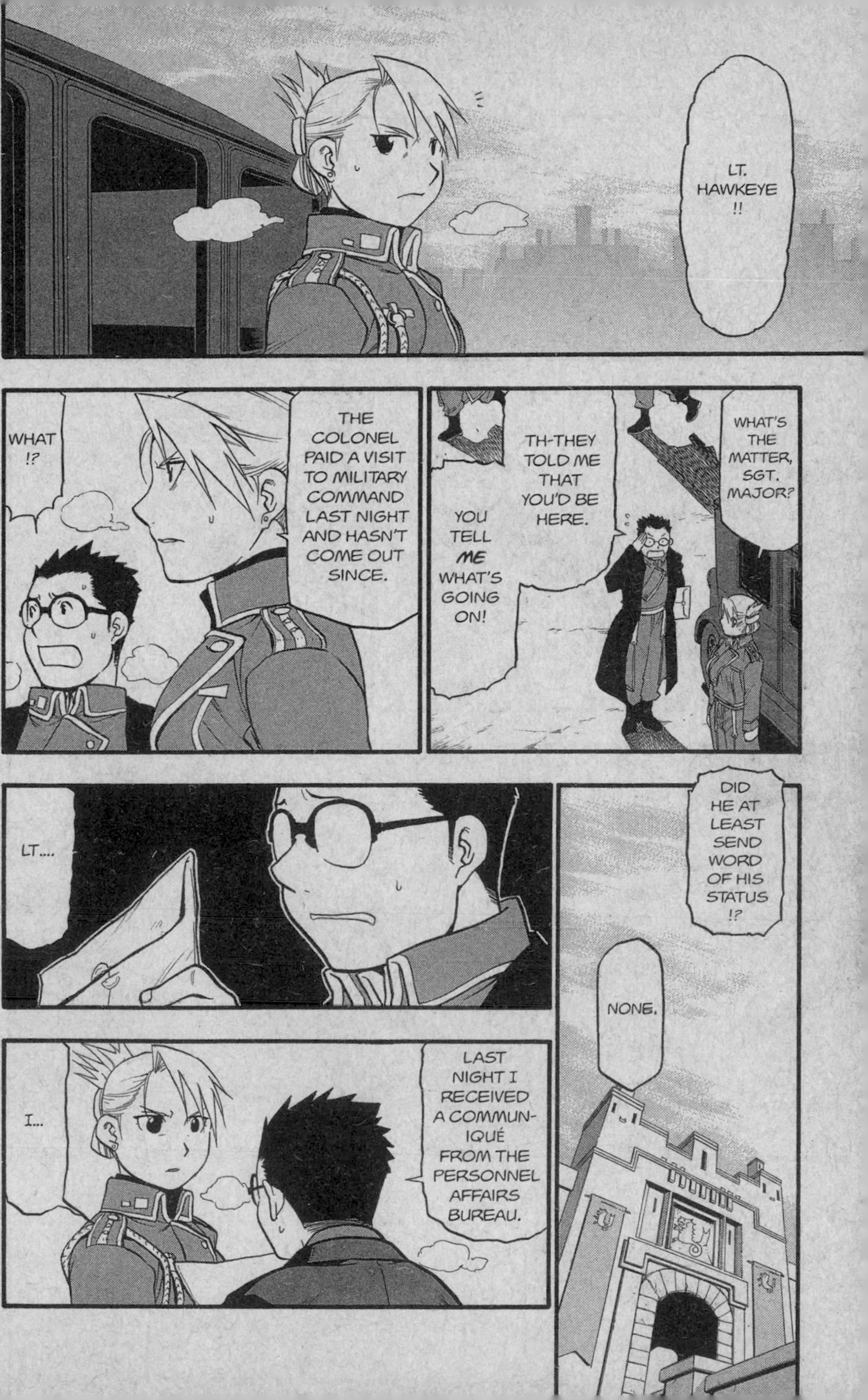
LT. HAWKEYE !!
WHAT'S THE MATTER, SGT. MAJOR?
TH-THEY TOLD ME THAT YOU'D BE HERE.
YOU TELL *ME* WHAT'S GOING ON!
THE COLONEL PAID A VISIT TO MILITARY COMMAND LAST NIGHT AND HASN'T COME OUT SINCE.
WHAT !?
DID HE AT LEAST SEND WORD OF HIS STATUS !?
NONE.
LT....
LAST NIGHT I RECEIVED A COMMUNIQUÉ FROM THE PERSONNEL AFFAIRS BUREAU.
I...

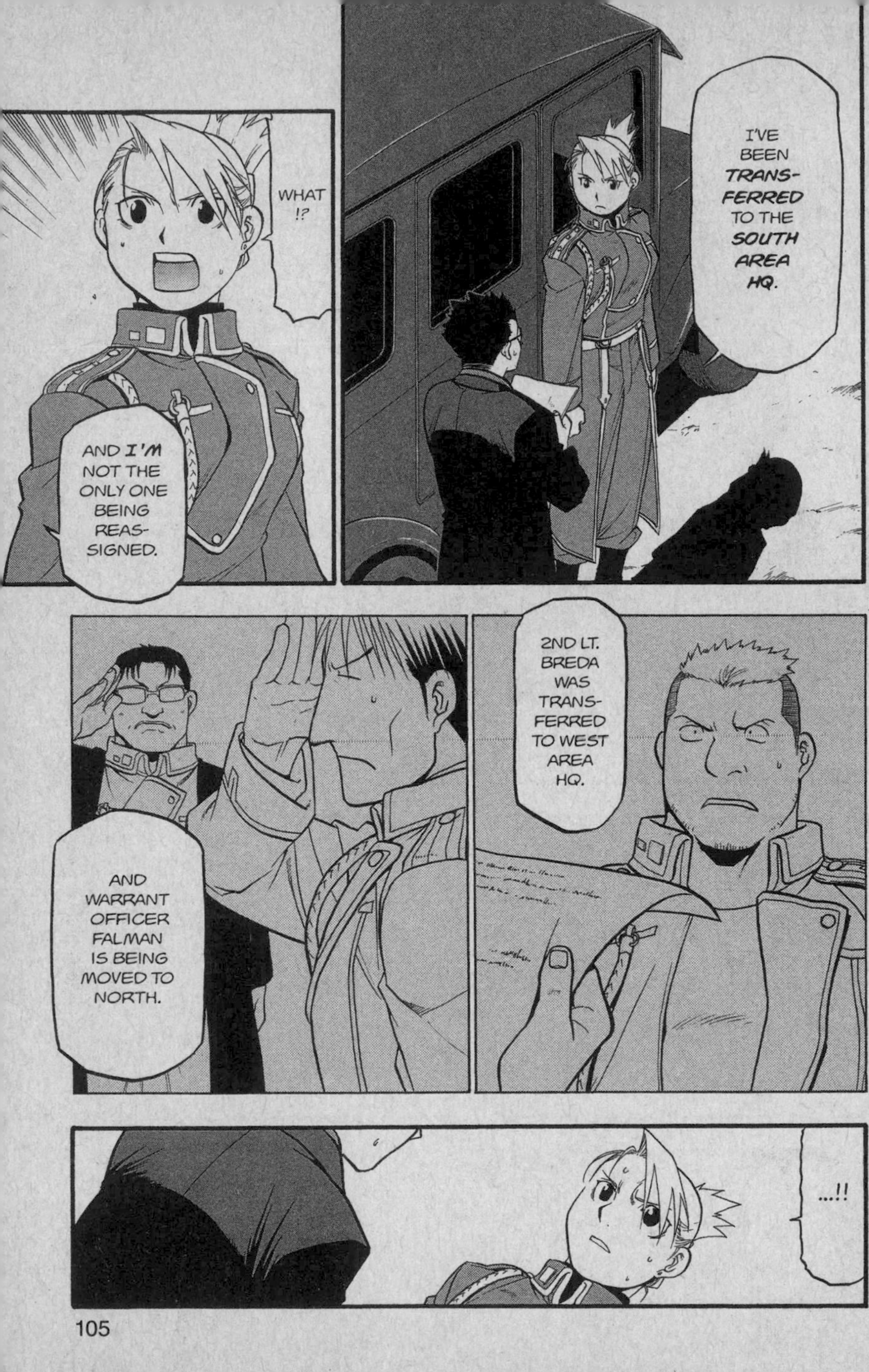
I'VE BEEN TRANSFERRED TO THE SOUTH AREA HQ.
WHAT!?
AND I'M NOT THE ONLY ONE BEING REASSIGNED.
2ND LT. BREDA WAS TRANSFERRED TO WEST AREA HQ.
AND WARRANT OFFICER FALMAN IS BEING MOVED TO NORTH.
...!!

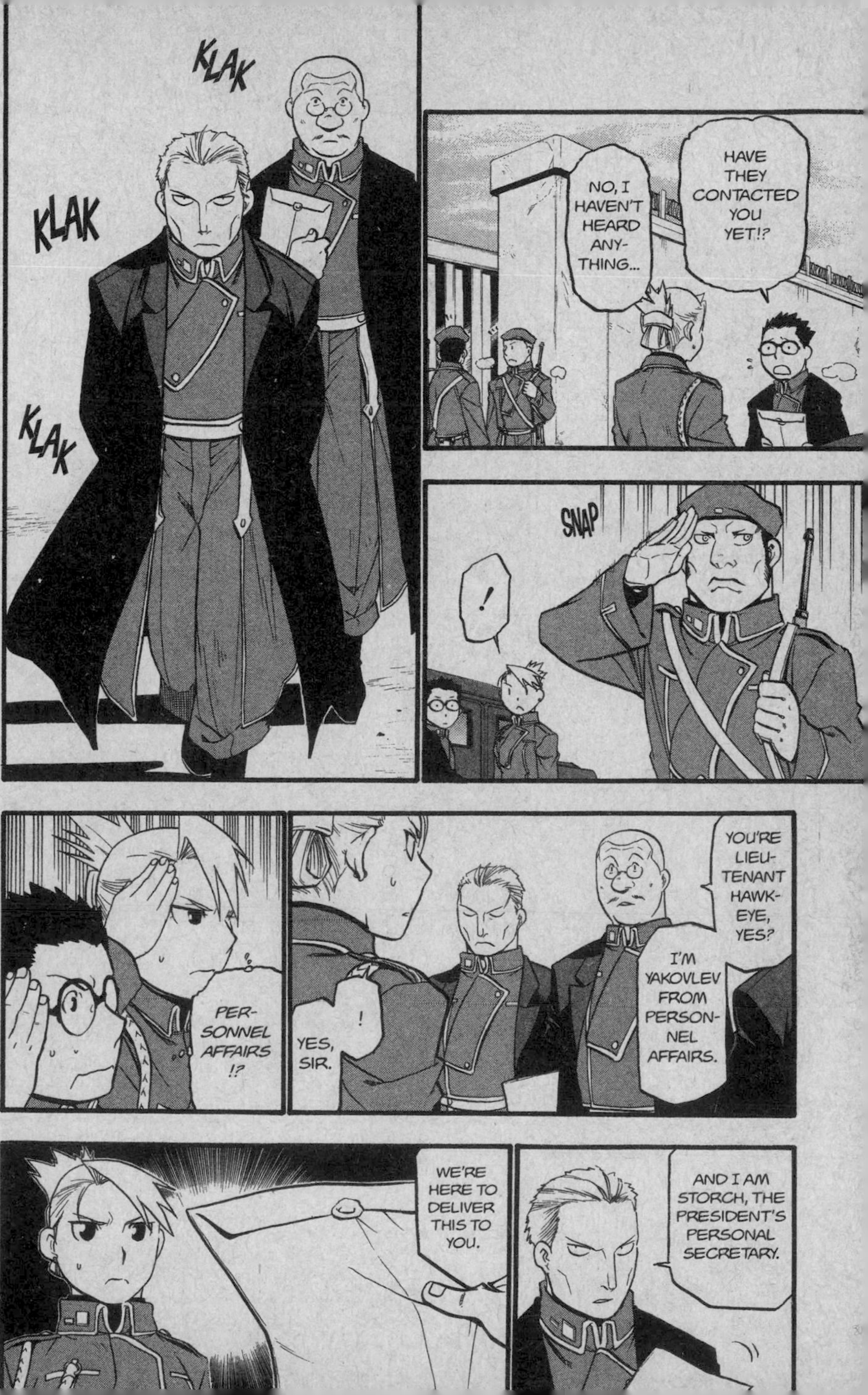
HAVE THEY CONTACTED YOU YET!?
NO, I HAVEN'T HEARD ANYTHING...
SNAP
!
KLAK
KLAK
KLAK
YOU'RE LIEUTENANT HAWKEYE, YES?
I'M YAKOVLEV FROM PERSONNEL AFFAIRS.
!
YES, SIR.
PERSONNEL AFFAIRS!?
AND I AM STORCH, THE PRESIDENT'S PERSONAL SECRETARY.
WE'RE HERE TO DELIVER THIS TO YOU.

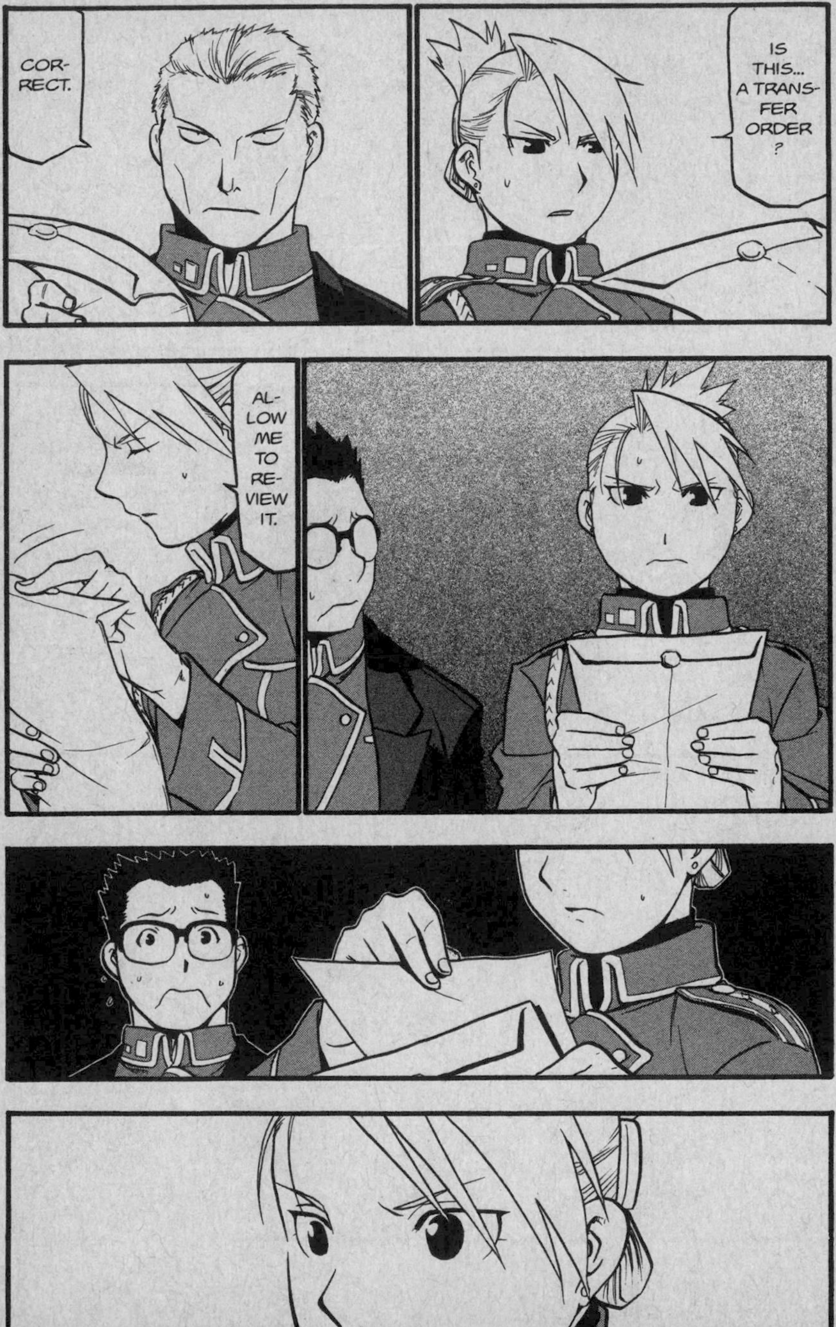
IS THIS... A TRANSFER ORDER?
CORRECT.
ALLOW ME TO REVIEW IT.

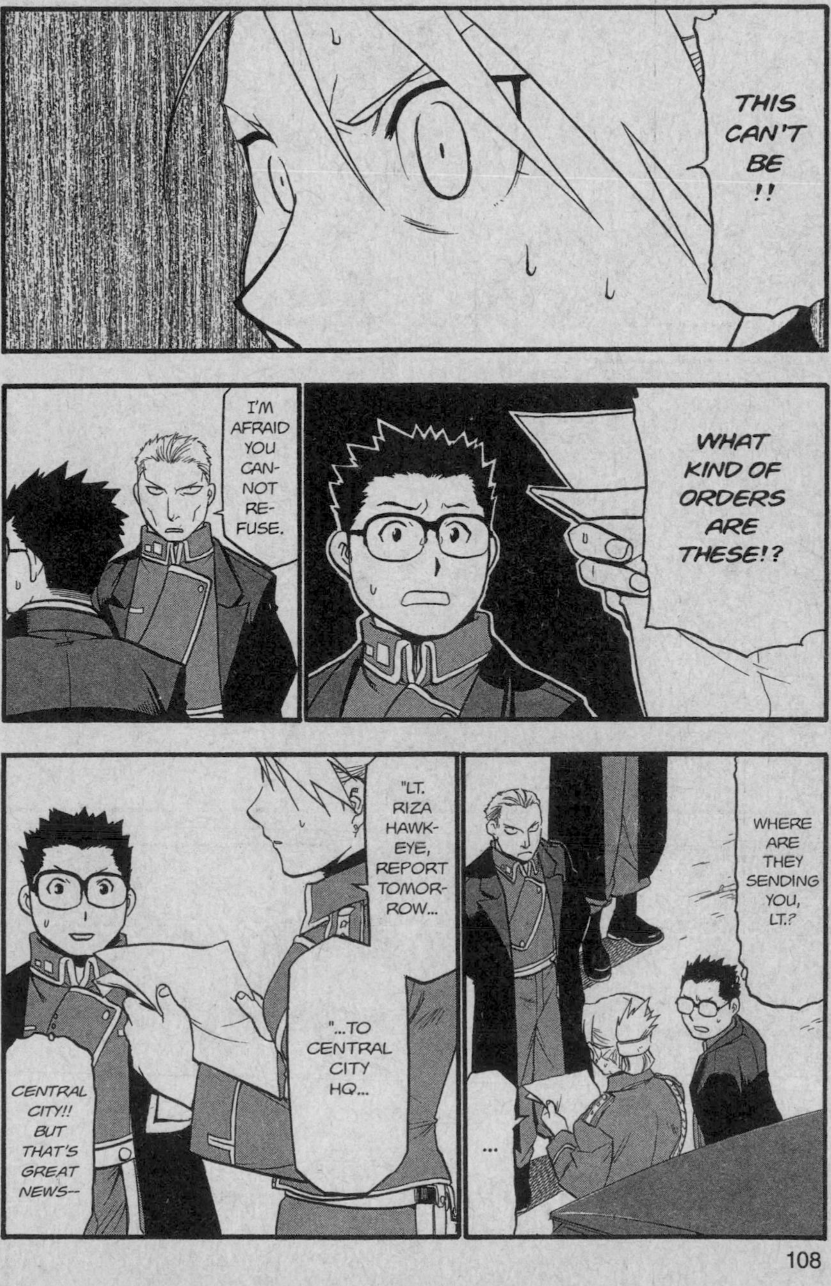
THIS CAN'T BE !!
WHAT KIND OF ORDERS ARE THESE!?
I'M AFRAID YOU CANNOT REFUSE.
WHERE ARE THEY SENDING YOU, LT.?
...
"LT. RIZA HAWKEYE, REPORT TOMORROW...
"...TO CENTRAL CITY HQ...
CENTRAL CITY!! BUT THAT'S GREAT NEWS--

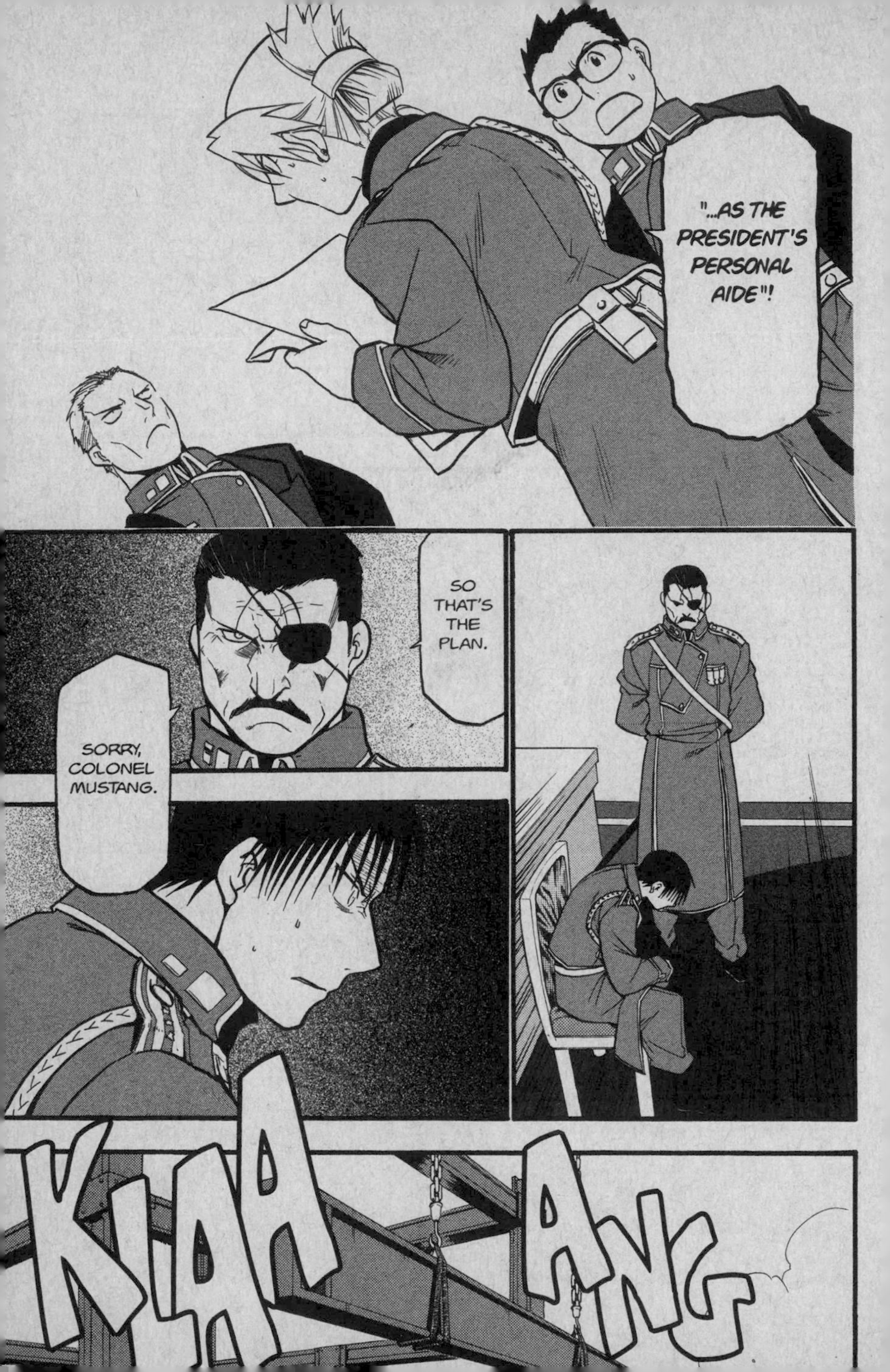
"...AS THE PRESIDENT'S PERSONAL AIDE"!
SO THAT'S THE PLAN.
SORRY, COLONEL MUSTANG.
KIAAANG

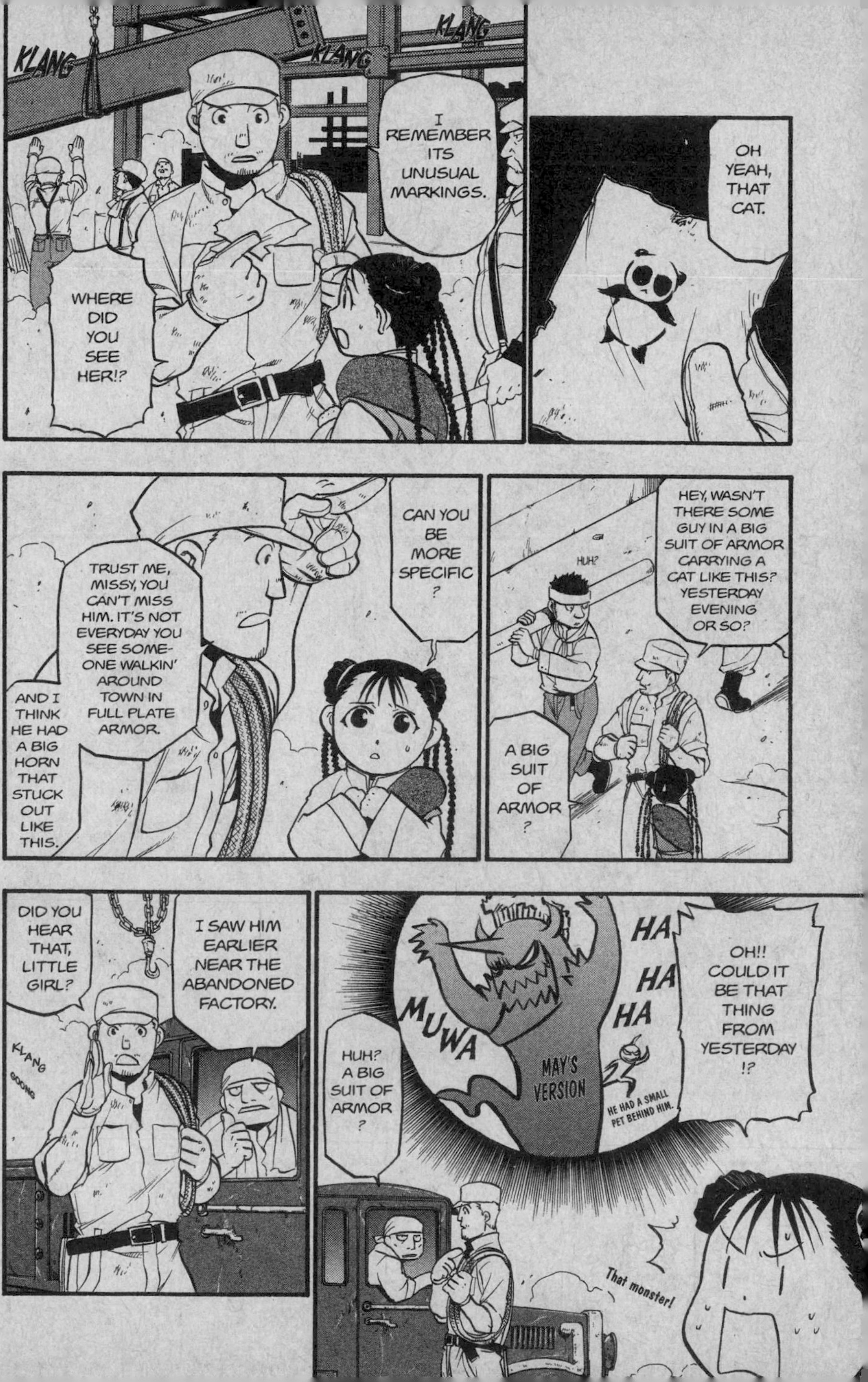
OH YEAH, THAT CAT.
KLANG
KLANG
KLANG
I REMEMBER ITS UNUSUAL MARKINGS.
WHERE DID YOU SEE HER!?
HEY, WASN'T THERE SOME GUY IN A BIG SUIT OF ARMOR CARRYING A CAT LIKE THIS? YESTERDAY EVENING OR SO?
HUH?
A BIG SUIT OF ARMOR?
CAN YOU BE MORE SPECIFIC?
TRUST ME, MISSY, YOU CAN'T MISS HIM. IT'S NOT EVERYDAY YOU SEE SOME-ONE WALKIN' AROUND TOWN IN FULL PLATE ARMOR.
AND I THINK HE HAD A BIG HORN THAT STUCK OUT LIKE THIS.
OH!! COULD IT BE THAT THING FROM YESTERDAY!?
HA
HA
HA
MUWA
MAY'S VERSION
HE HAD A SMALL PET BEHIND HIM.
HUH? A BIG SUIT OF ARMOR?
That monster!
I SAW HIM EARLIER NEAR THE ABANDONED FACTORY.
DID YOU HEAR THAT, LITTLE GIRL?
KLANG
GOONG

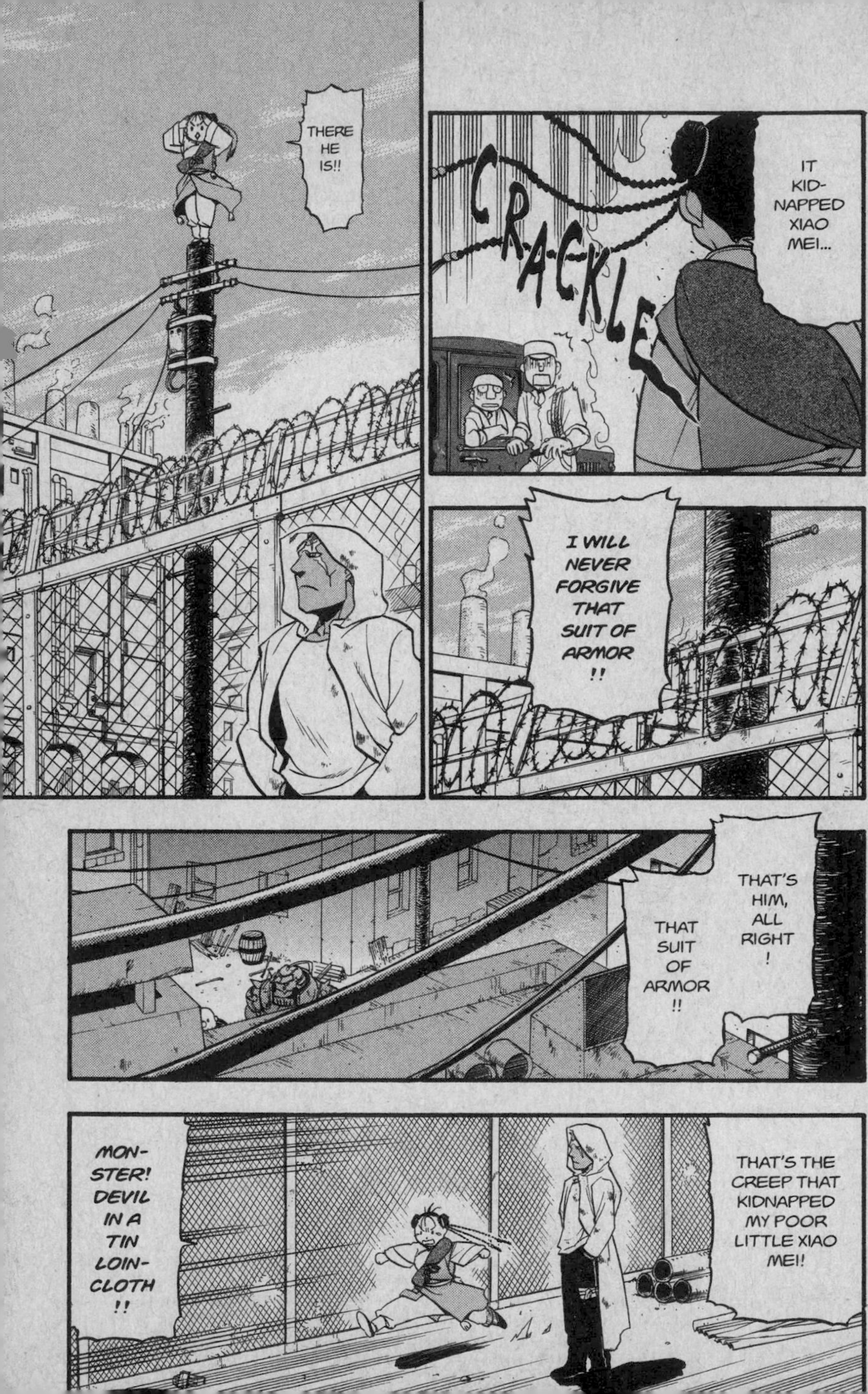
IT KID-NAPPED XIAO MEI...
CRACKLE
I WILL NEVER FORGIVE THAT SUIT OF ARMOR!!
THERE HE IS!!
THAT'S HIM, ALL RIGHT!
THAT SUIT OF ARMOR!!
THAT'S THE CREEP THAT KIDNAPPED MY POOR LITTLE XIAO MEI!
MON-STER! DEVIL IN A TIN LOIN-CLOTH!!

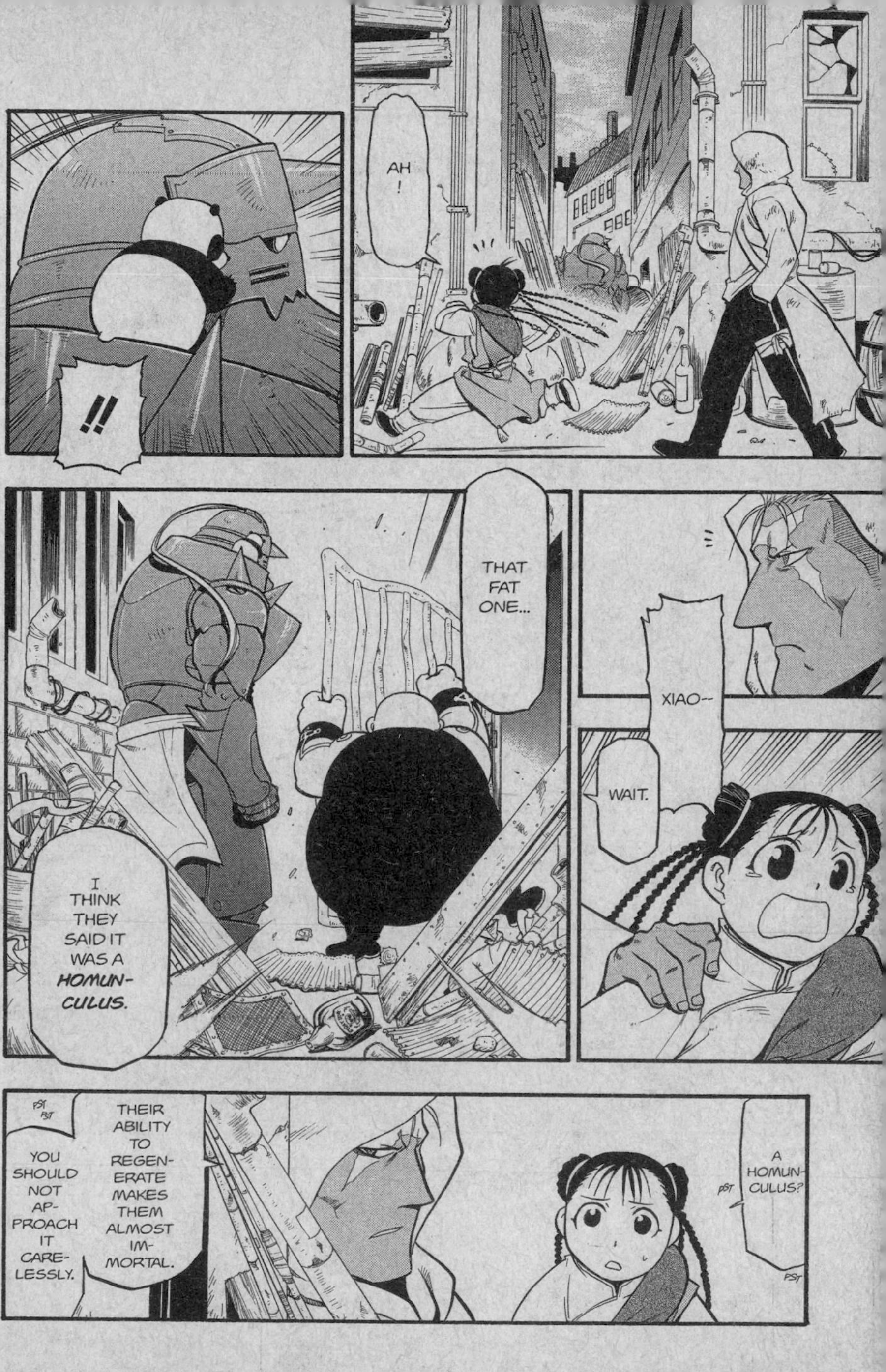
AH!
!!
XIAO--
WAIT.
THAT FAT ONE...
I THINK THEY SAID IT WAS A **HOMUNCULUS**.
A HOMUNCULUS?
PST
PST
THEIR ABILITY TO REGENERATE MAKES THEM ALMOST IMMORTAL.
PST PST
YOU SHOULD NOT APPROACH IT CARELESSLY.

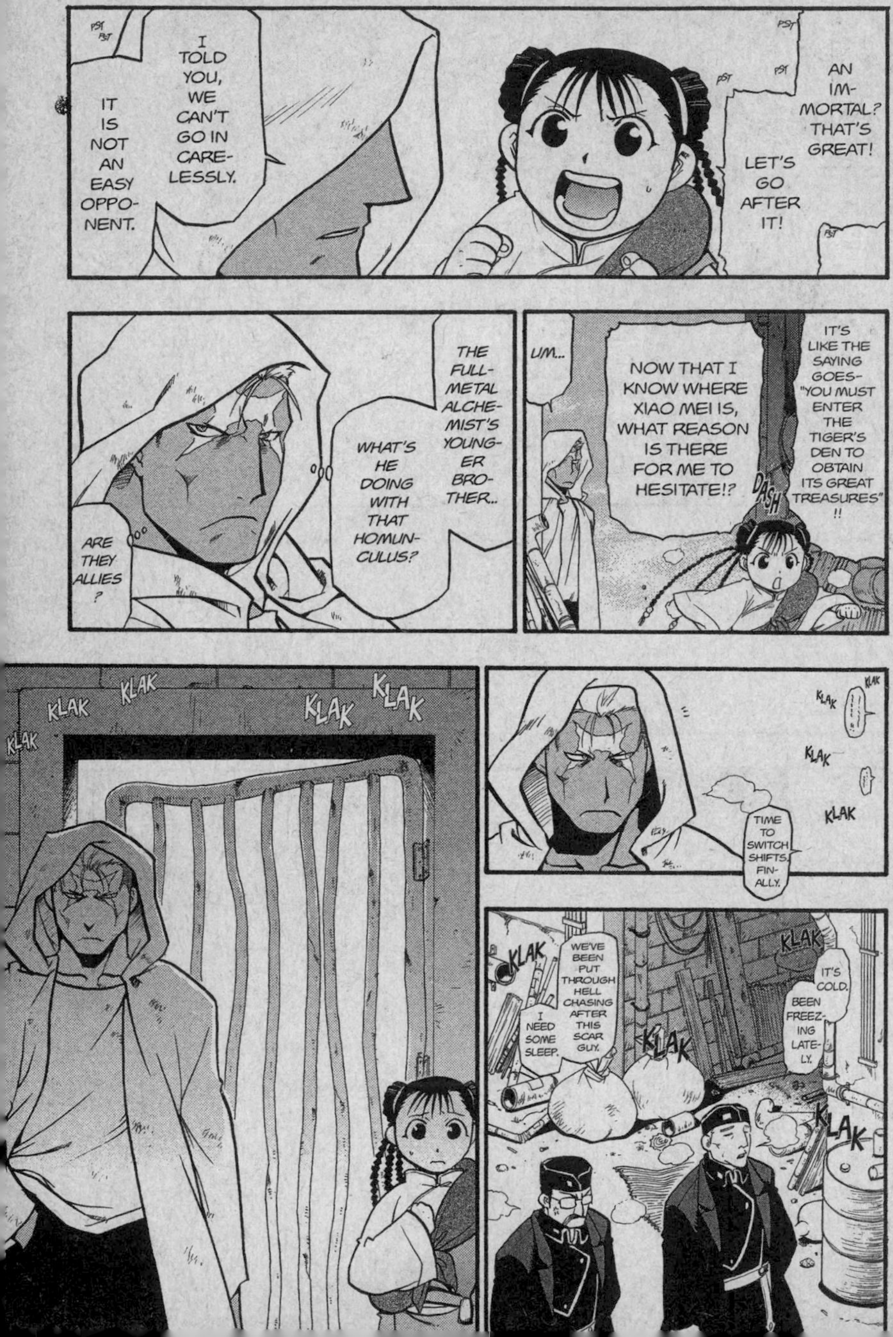
PST
AN IMMORTAL? THAT'S GREAT!
LET'S GO AFTER IT!
PST PST
I TOLD YOU, WE CAN'T GO IN CARELESSLY.
IT IS NOT AN EASY OPPONENT.
IT'S LIKE THE SAYING GOES- "YOU MUST ENTER THE TIGER'S DEN TO OBTAIN ITS GREAT TREASURES"!!
NOW THAT I KNOW WHERE XIAO MEI IS, WHAT REASON IS THERE FOR ME TO HESITATE!?
DASH
UM...
THE FULLMETAL ALCHEMIST'S YOUNGER BROTHER...
WHAT'S HE DOING WITH THAT HOMUNCULUS?
ARE THEY ALLIES?
KLAK
KLAK
KLAK
KLAK
TIME TO SWITCH SHIFTS. FINALLY.
KLAK
IT'S COLD. BEEN FREEZING LATELY.
WE'VE BEEN PUT THROUGH HELL CHASING AFTER THIS SCAR GUY.
KLAK
I NEED SOME SLEEP.
KLAK
KLAK
KLAK
KLAK
KLAK
KLAK
KLAK

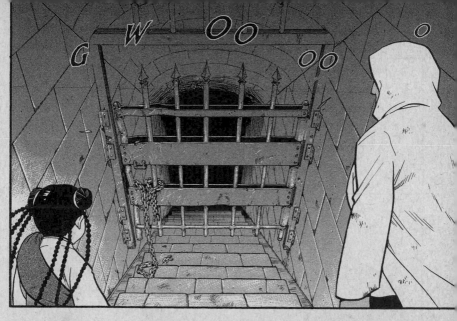

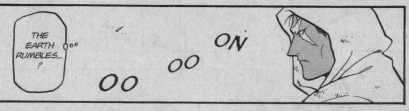

GWOOOOOOO
OOOOON
THE EARTH RUMBLES...?
WHAT IS WRONG?
THIS... PLACE IS... STRANGE...
GWOOOON
EVER SINCE I CAME TO THIS COUNTRY, I'VE HAD A STRANGE FEELING.
A FEELING THAT I HAVEN'T BEEN ABLE TO PUT INTO WORDS...

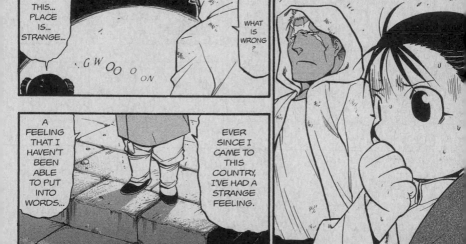

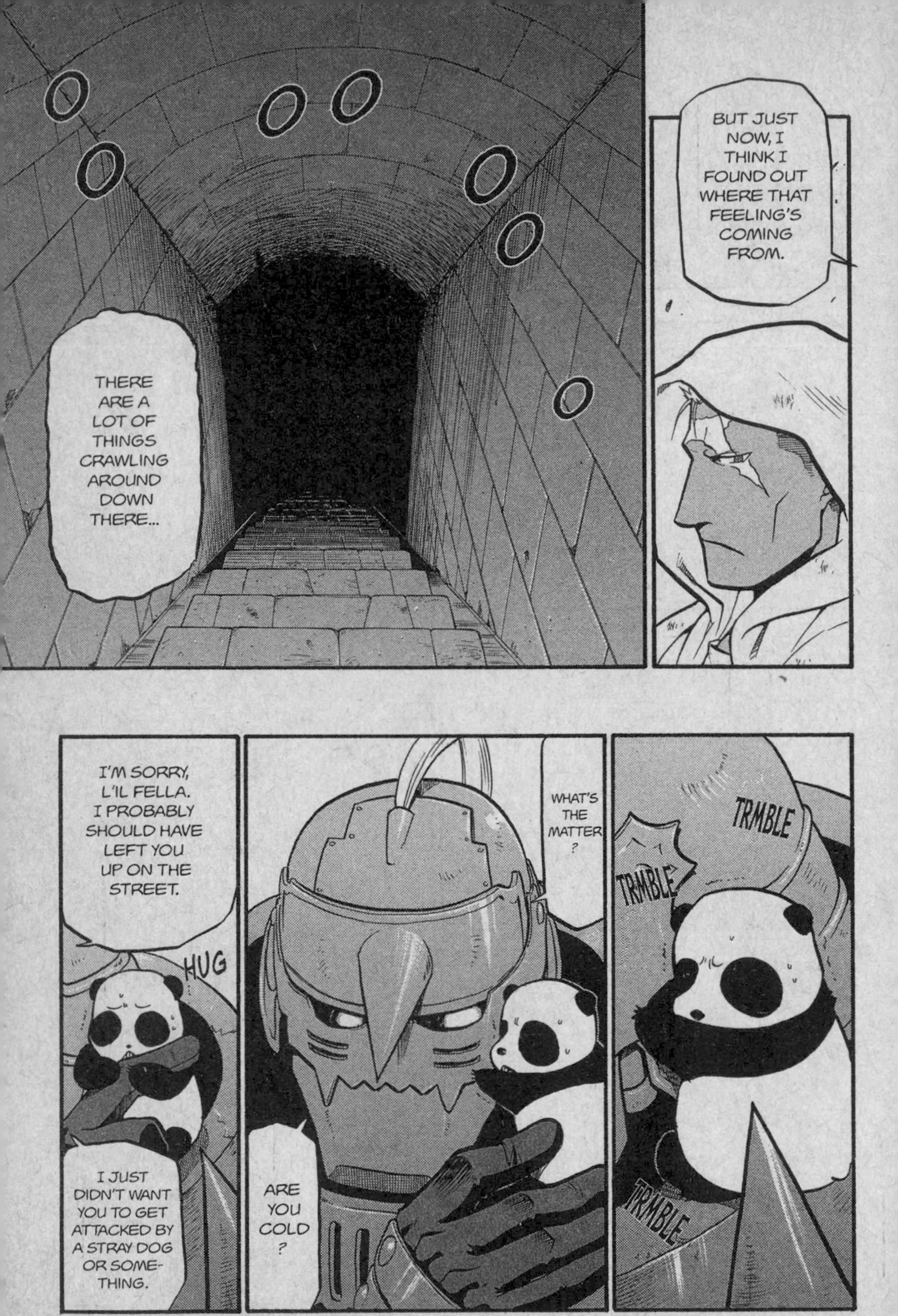
BUT JUST NOW, I THINK I FOUND OUT WHERE THAT FEELING'S COMING FROM.
THERE ARE A LOT OF THINGS CRAWLING AROUND DOWN THERE...
TRMBLE
TRMBLE
TRMBLE
WHAT'S THE MATTER?
ARE YOU COLD?
I'M SORRY, L'IL FELLA. I PROBABLY SHOULD HAVE LEFT YOU UP ON THE STREET.
HUG
I JUST DIDN'T WANT YOU TO GET ATTACKED BY A STRAY DOG OR SOME-THING.

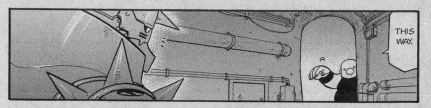

THIS WAY.

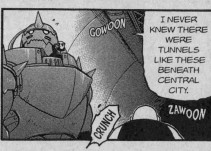

I NEVER KNEW THERE WERE TUNNELS LIKE THESE BENEATH CENTRAL CITY.

GOWOON

CRUNCH

ZAWOON

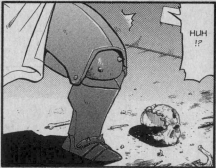

HUH!?

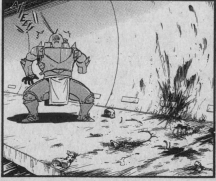

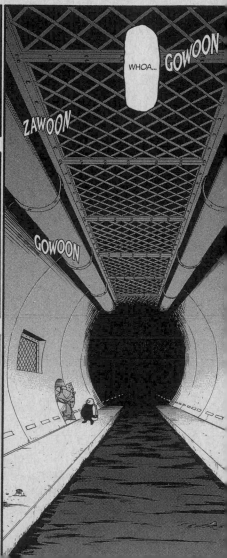

WHOA...

GOWOON

ZAWOON

GOWOON

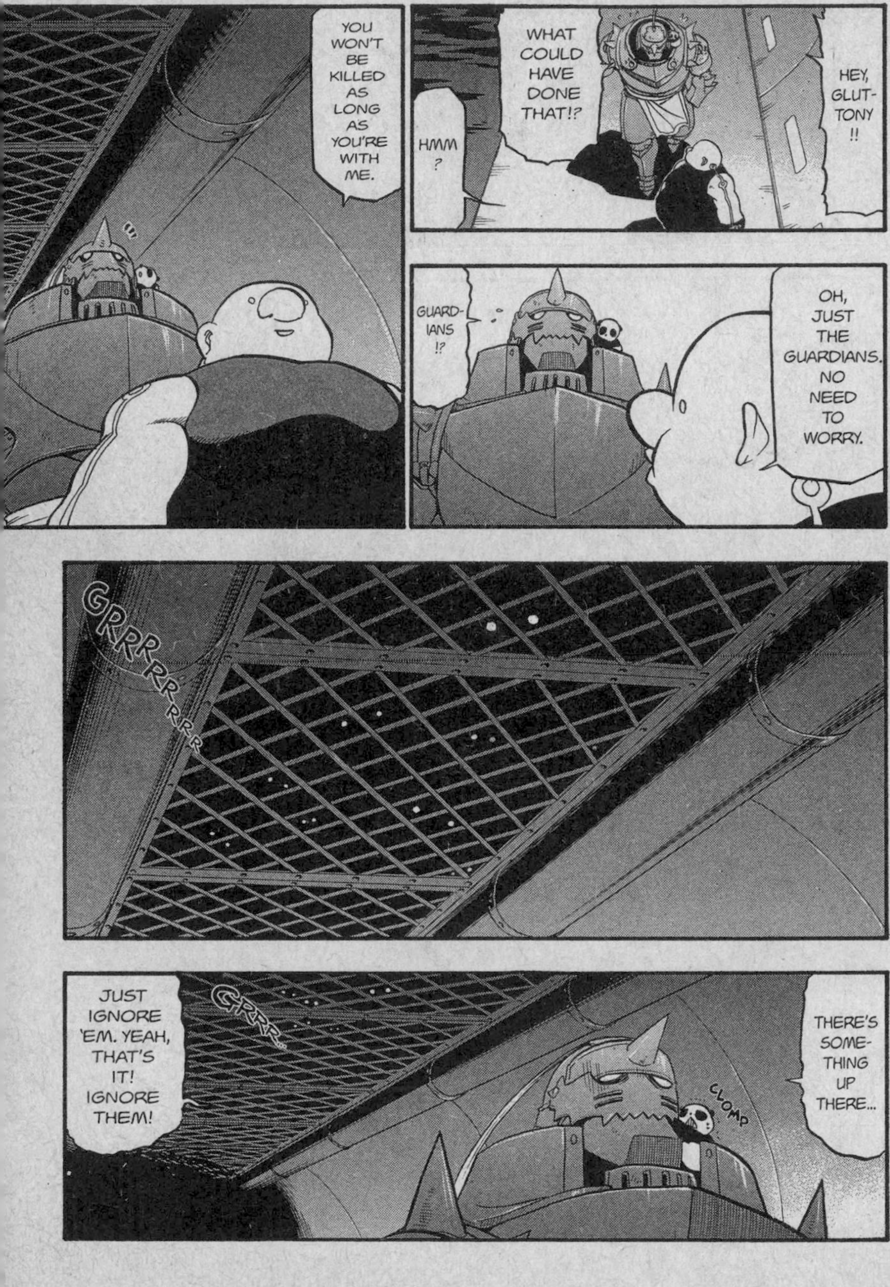
HEY, GLUTTONY!!
WHAT COULD HAVE DONE THAT!?
HMM?
OH, JUST THE GUARDIANS. NO NEED TO WORRY.
GUARDIANS!?
YOU WON'T BE KILLED AS LONG AS YOU'RE WITH ME.
GRRRRRRRRR
THERE'S SOMETHING UP THERE...
CLOMP
GRRR...
JUST IGNORE 'EM. YEAH, THAT'S IT! IGNORE THEM!

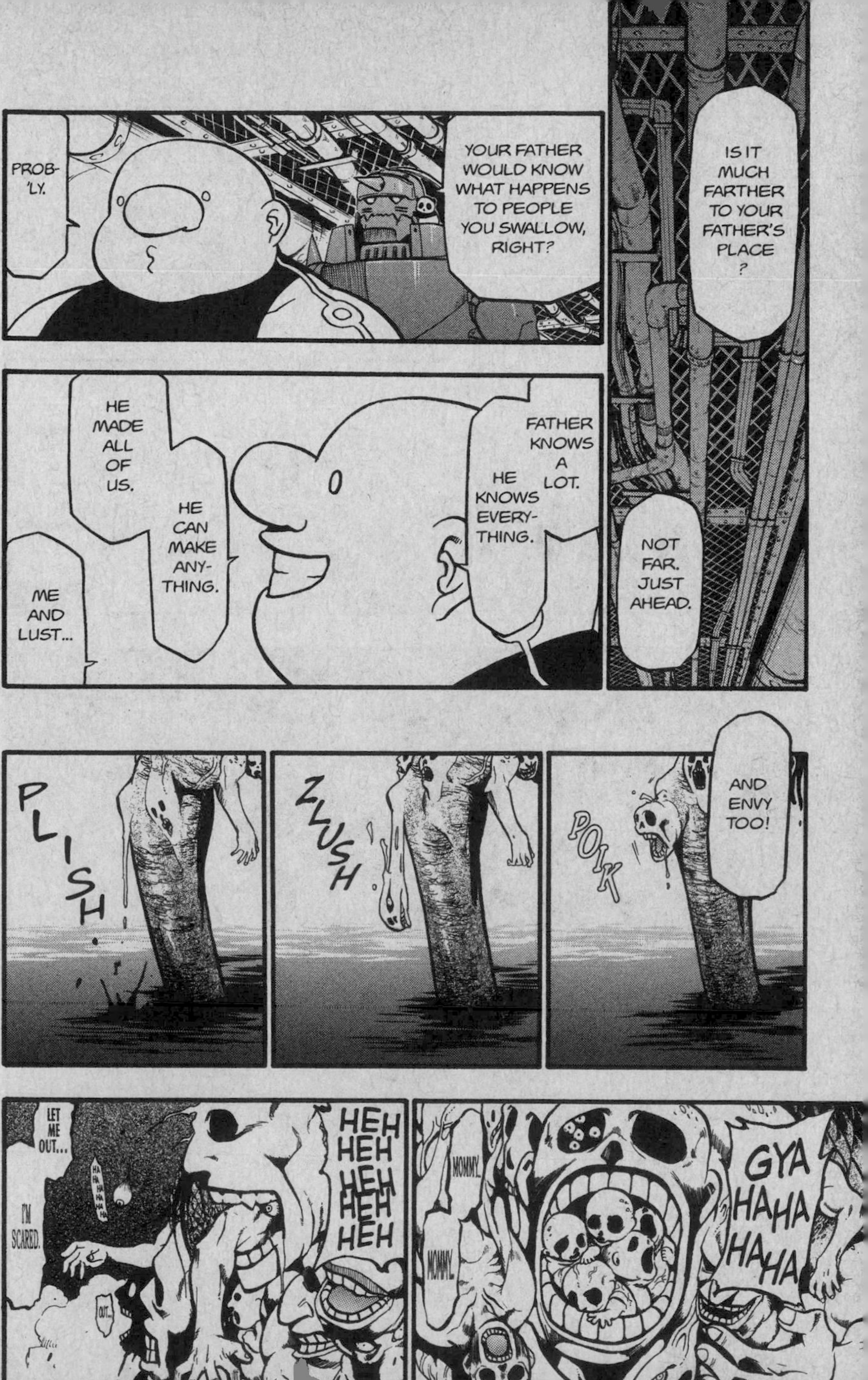
IS IT MUCH FARTHER TO YOUR FATHER'S PLACE?
NOT FAR. JUST AHEAD.
YOUR FATHER WOULD KNOW WHAT HAPPENS TO PEOPLE YOU SWALLOW, RIGHT?
PROB-'LY.
FATHER KNOWS A LOT.
HE KNOWS EVERY-THING.
HE MADE ALL OF US.
HE CAN MAKE ANY-THING.
ME AND LUST...
AND ENVY TOO!
POIK
ZLUSH
PLISH
GYA HAHA HAHA HA
MOMMY.
MOMMY.
HEH HEH HEH HEH HEH HEH
HA HA HA HA HA HA
LET ME OUT...
I'M SCARED.
OUT...

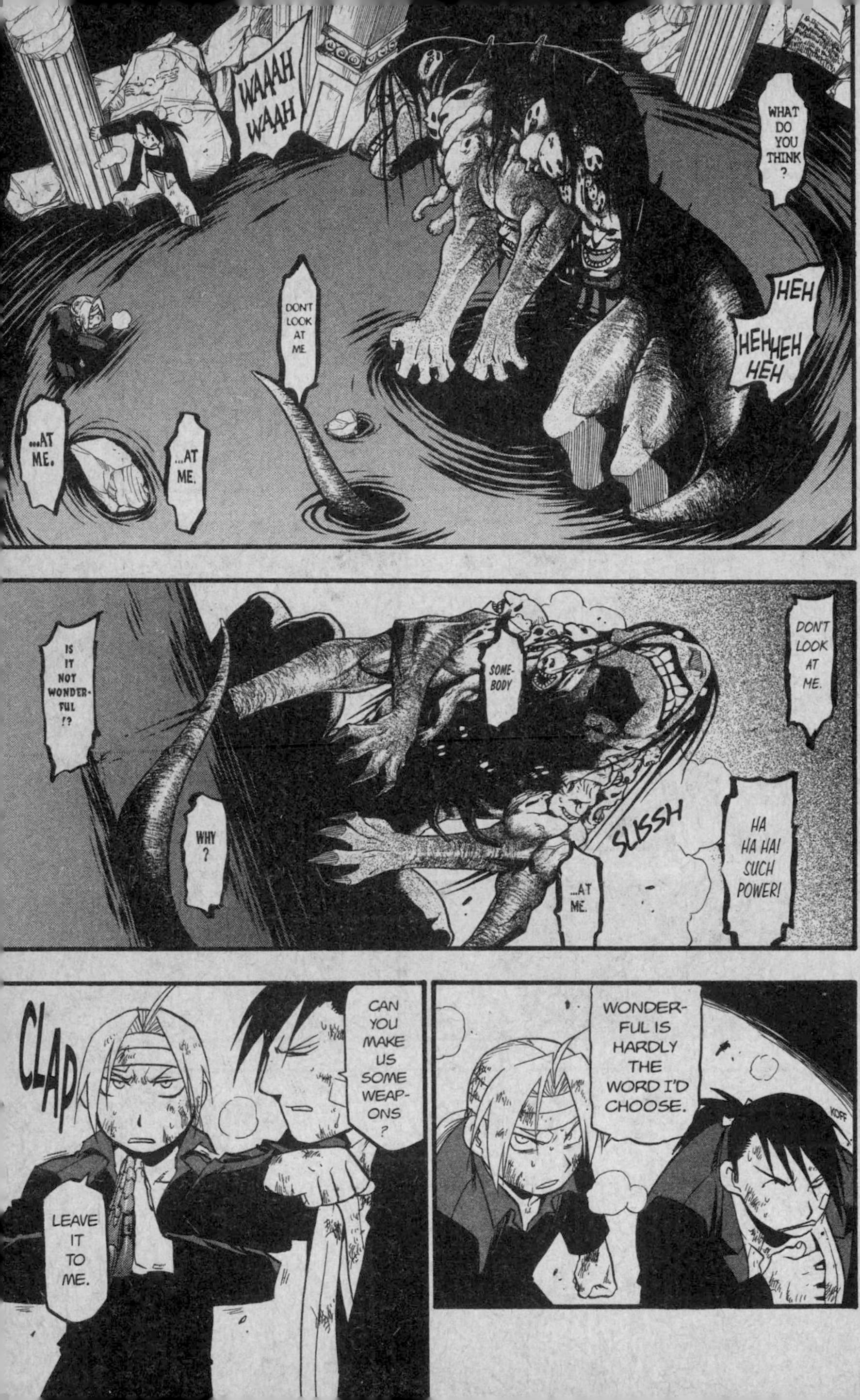
WHAT DO YOU THINK?
HEH HEH HEH HEH
WAAAH WAAH
DON'T LOOK AT ME.
...AT ME.
...AT ME.
DON'T LOOK AT ME.
HA HA HA! SUCH POWER!
SLISSH
...AT ME.
SOME-BODY
IS IT NOT WONDERFUL!?
WHY?
KOFF
WONDERFUL IS HARDLY THE WORD I'D CHOOSE.
CAN YOU MAKE US SOME WEAPONS?
CLAP
LEAVE IT TO ME.

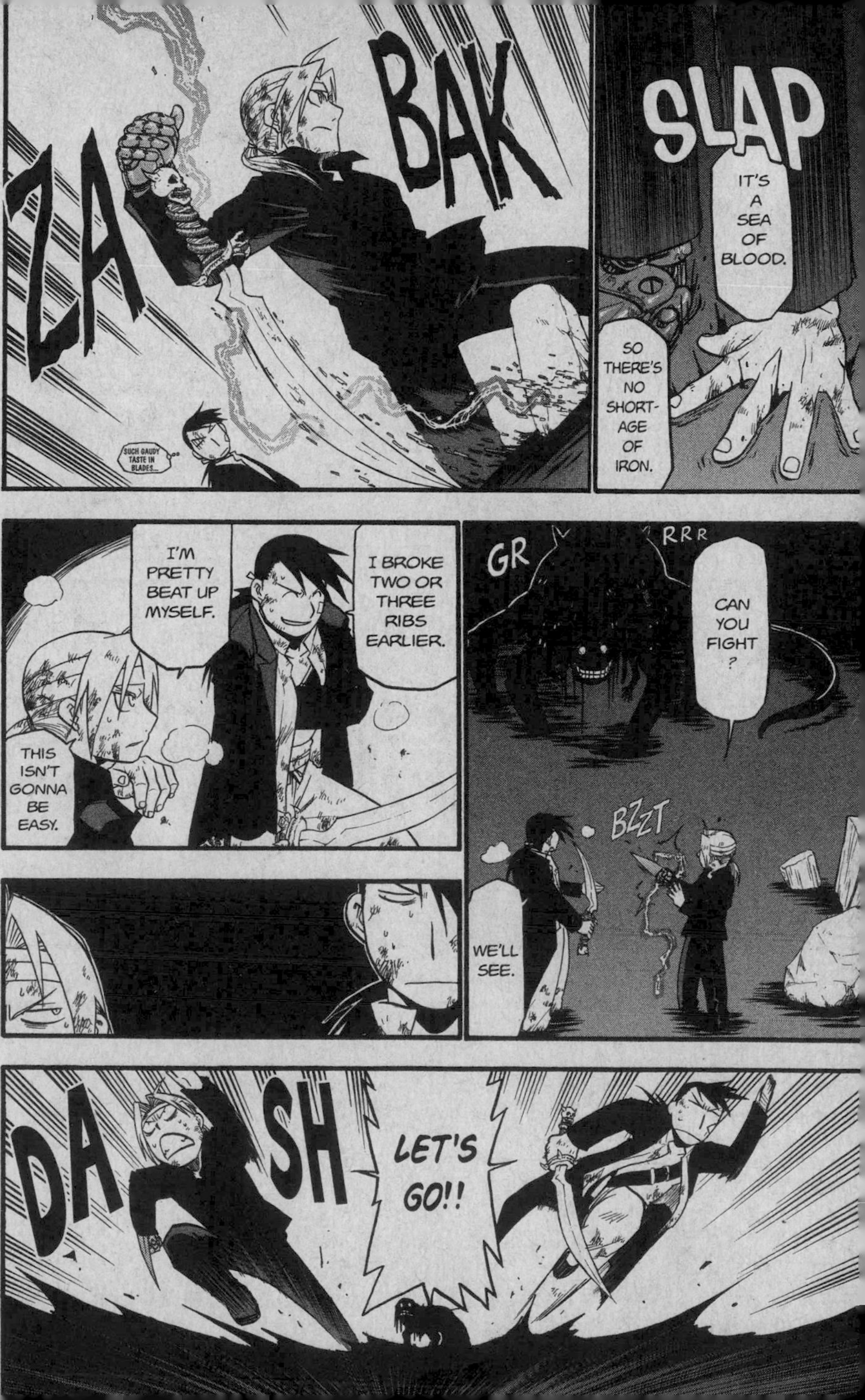
SLAP
IT'S A SEA OF BLOOD.
SO THERE'S NO SHORT-AGE OF IRON.
ZA BAK
SUCH GAUDY TASTE IN BLADES...
GR RRR
CAN YOU FIGHT?
BZZT
WE'LL SEE.
I BROKE TWO OR THREE RIBS EARLIER.
I'M PRETTY BEAT UP MYSELF.
THIS ISN'T GONNA BE EASY.
DA SH
LET'S GO!!

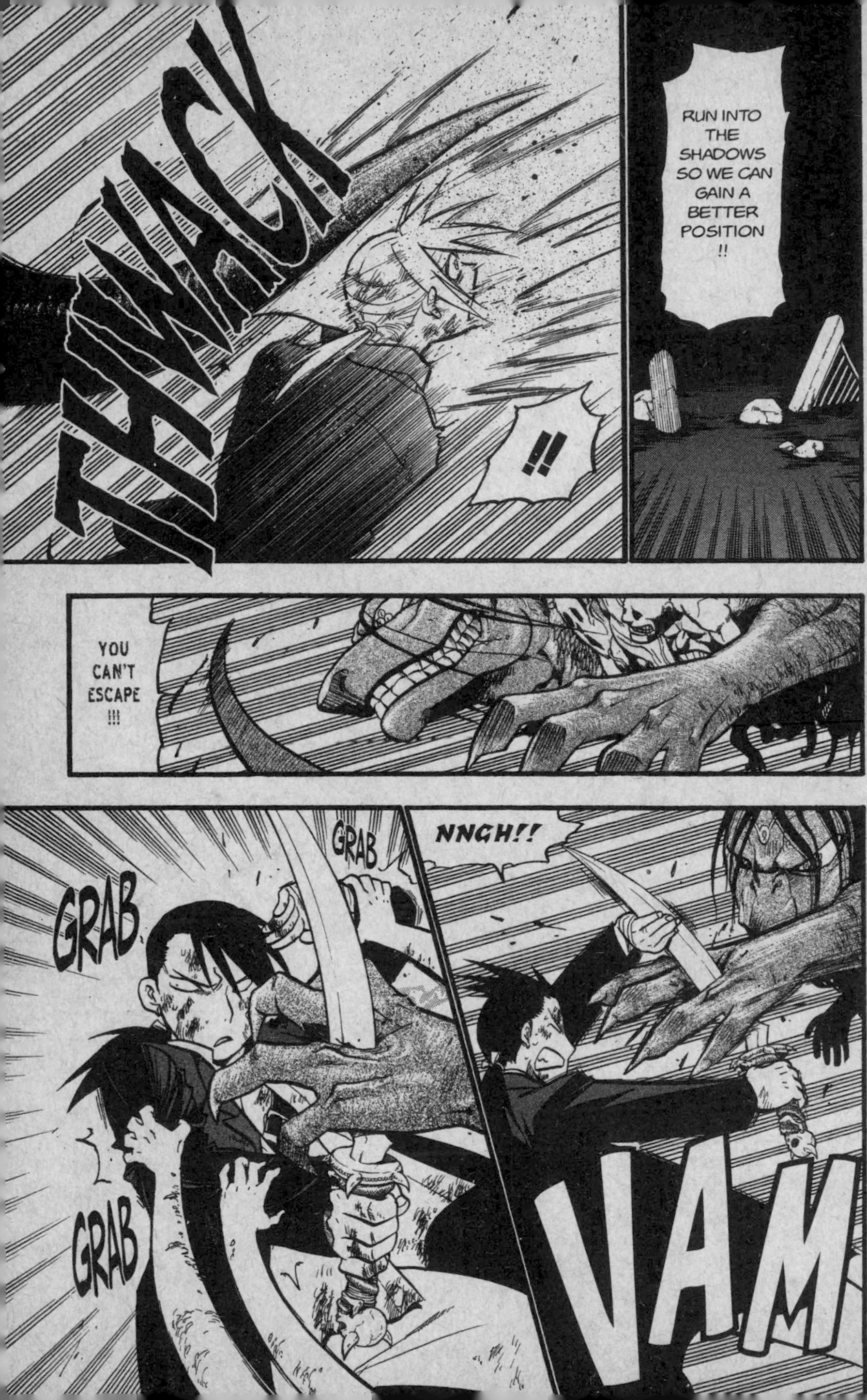
RUN INTO THE SHADOWS SO WE CAN GAIN A BETTER POSITION !!
THWACK
!!
YOU CAN'T ESCAPE !!!
NNGH!!
VAM
GRAB
GRAB
GRAB

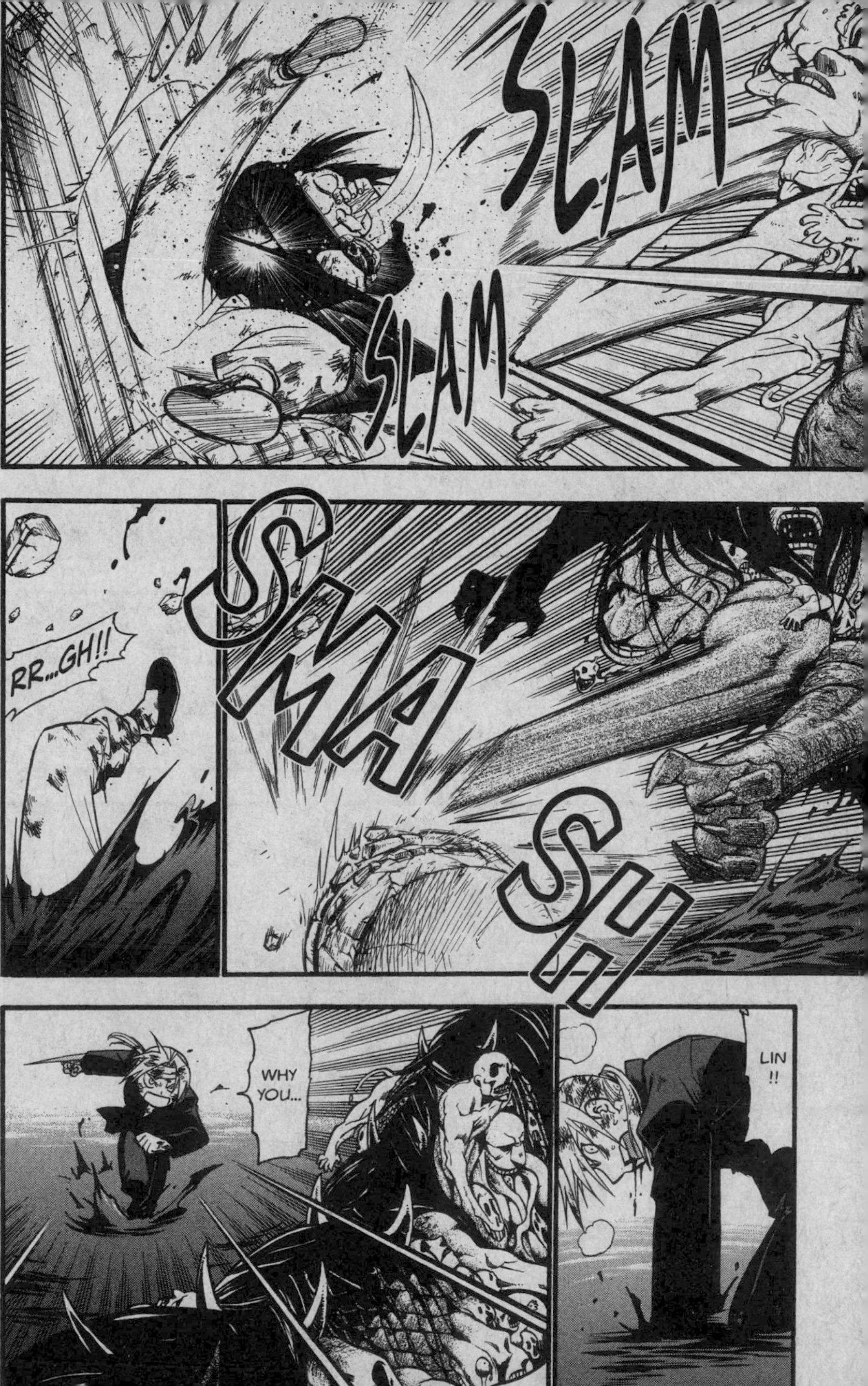
SLAM
SLAM
SMASH
RR...GH!!
LIN !!
WHY YOU...

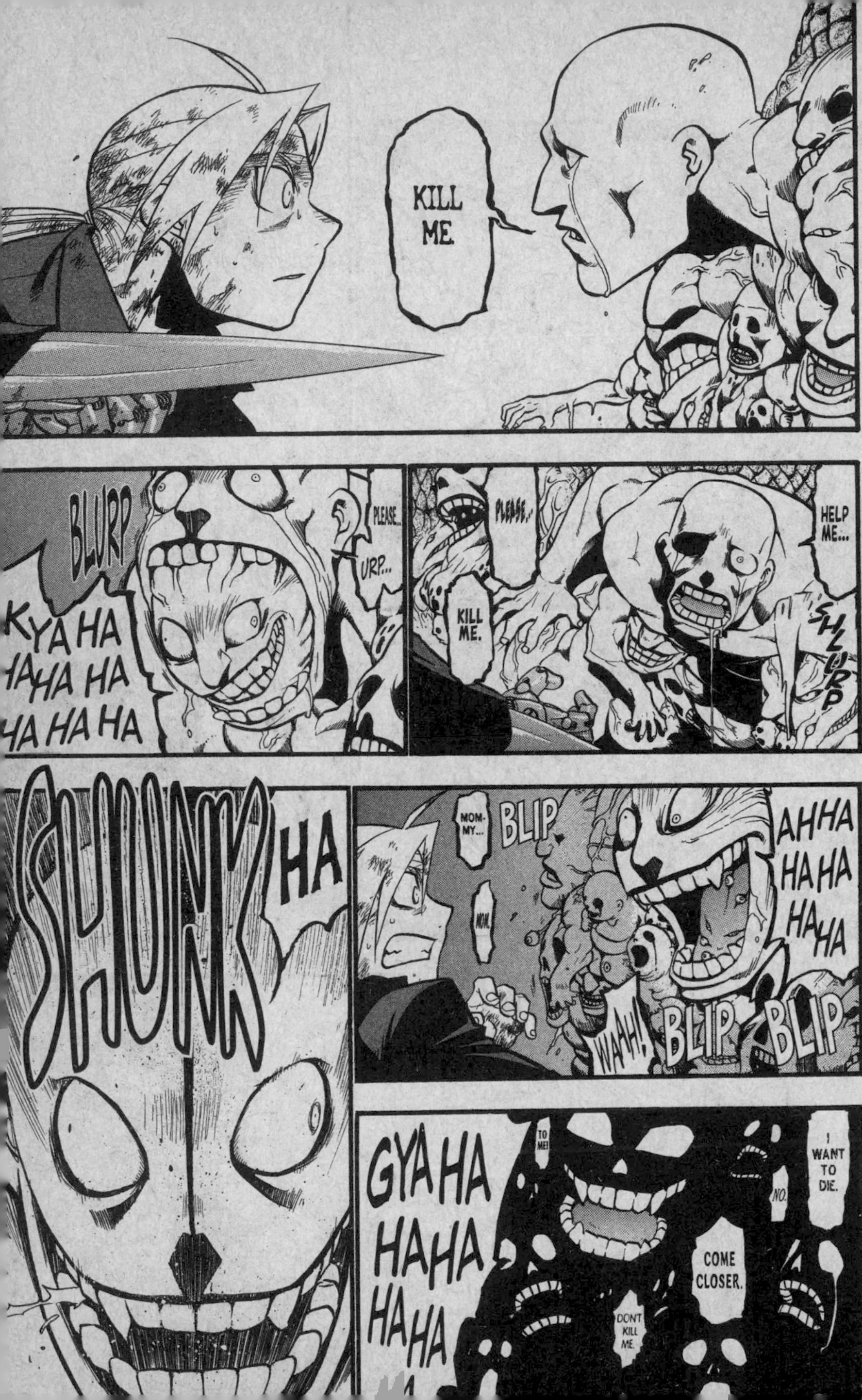
KILL ME.
HELP ME...
PLEASE...
KILL ME.
SHLURP
PLEASE...
URP...
BLURP
KYAHA HAHA HAHA HA HA HA HA
AHHA HAHA HAHA
MOMMY...
BLIP
MOM.
BLIP BLIP
WAAH!
I WANT TO DIE.
NO.
TO ME!
COME CLOSER.
DONT KILL ME.
GYAHA HAHA HAHA HAHA
SHUNK
HA

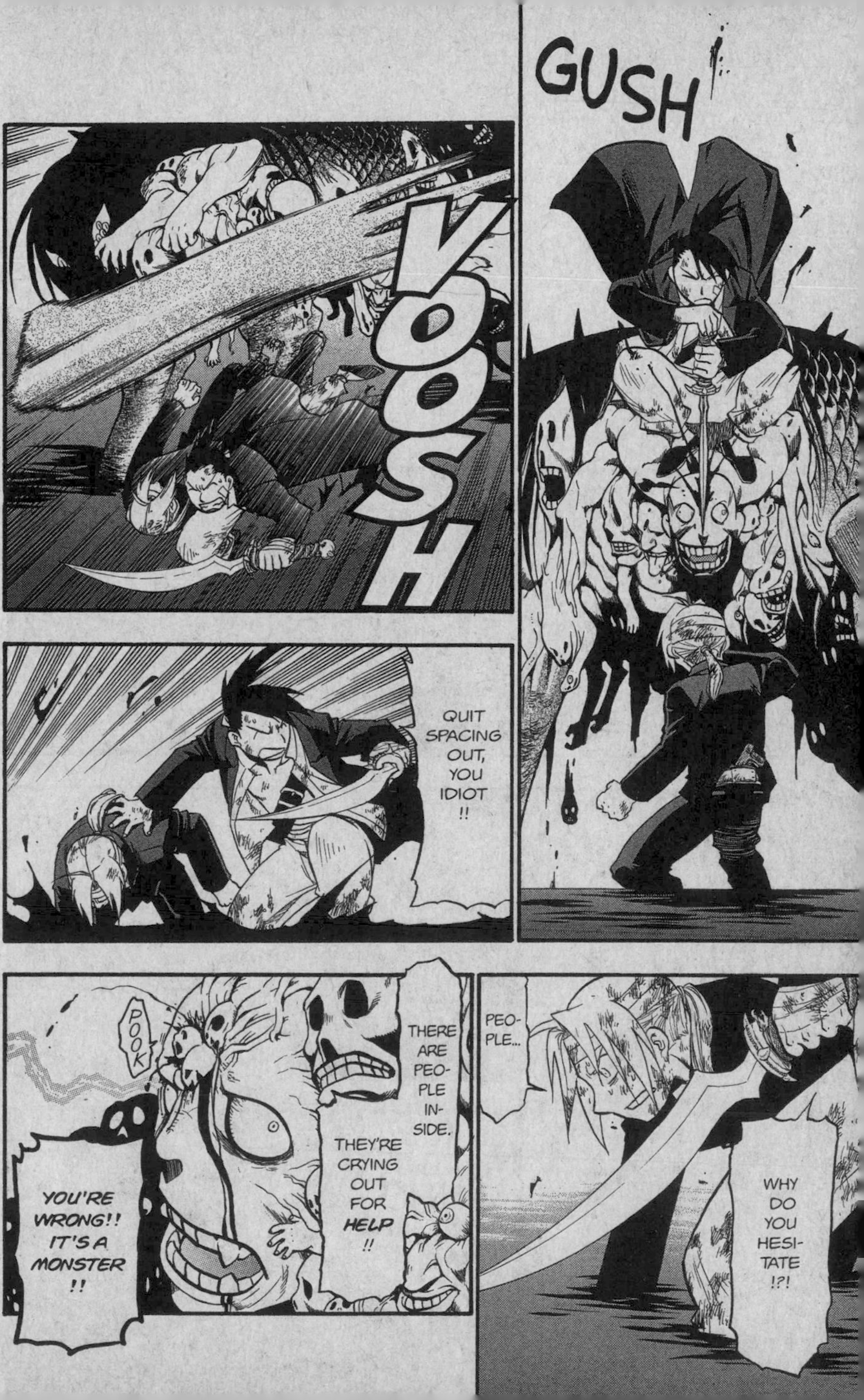
GUSH
VOOSH
QUIT SPACING OUT, YOU IDIOT!!
WHY DO YOU HESITATE!?!
PEOPLE...
THERE ARE PEOPLE INSIDE.
THEY'RE CRYING OUT FOR *HELP*!!
POOK
YOU'RE WRONG!! IT'S A MONSTER!!

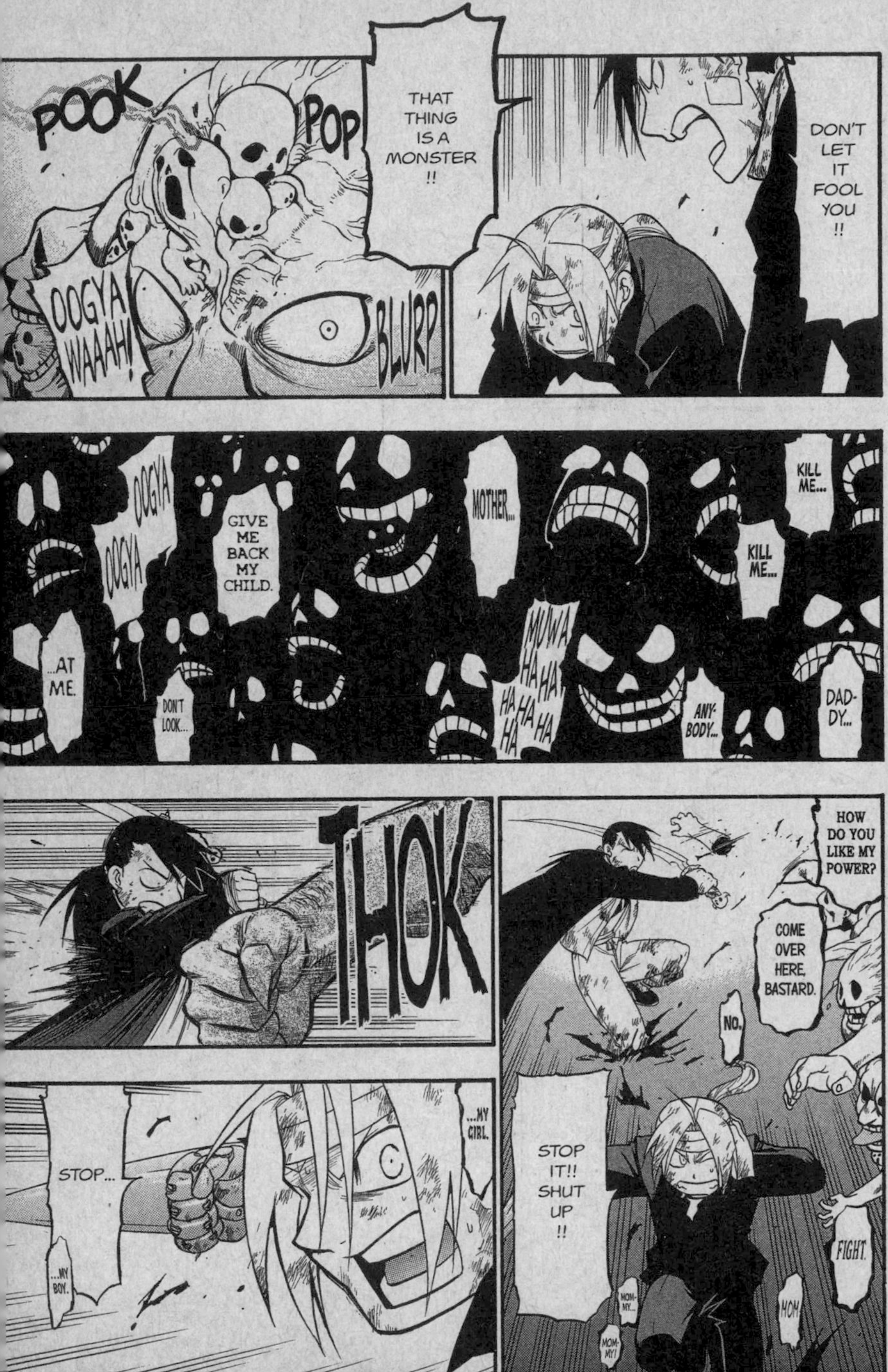
DON'T LET IT FOOL YOU !!
THAT THING IS A MONSTER !!
POP
POOK
BLURP
OOGYA WAAAH!
KILL ME...
KILL ME...
DADDY...
MOTHER...
MUWA HA HA HA HA HA HA HA
ANYBODY...
GIVE ME BACK MY CHILD.
OOGYA
OOGYA
...AT ME.
DON'T LOOK...
HOW DO YOU LIKE MY POWER?
COME OVER HERE, BASTARD.
NO.
STOP IT!! SHUT UP !!
FIGHT.
MOM
MOMMY...
MOMMY!
THOK
...MY GIRL.
STOP...
...MY BOY.

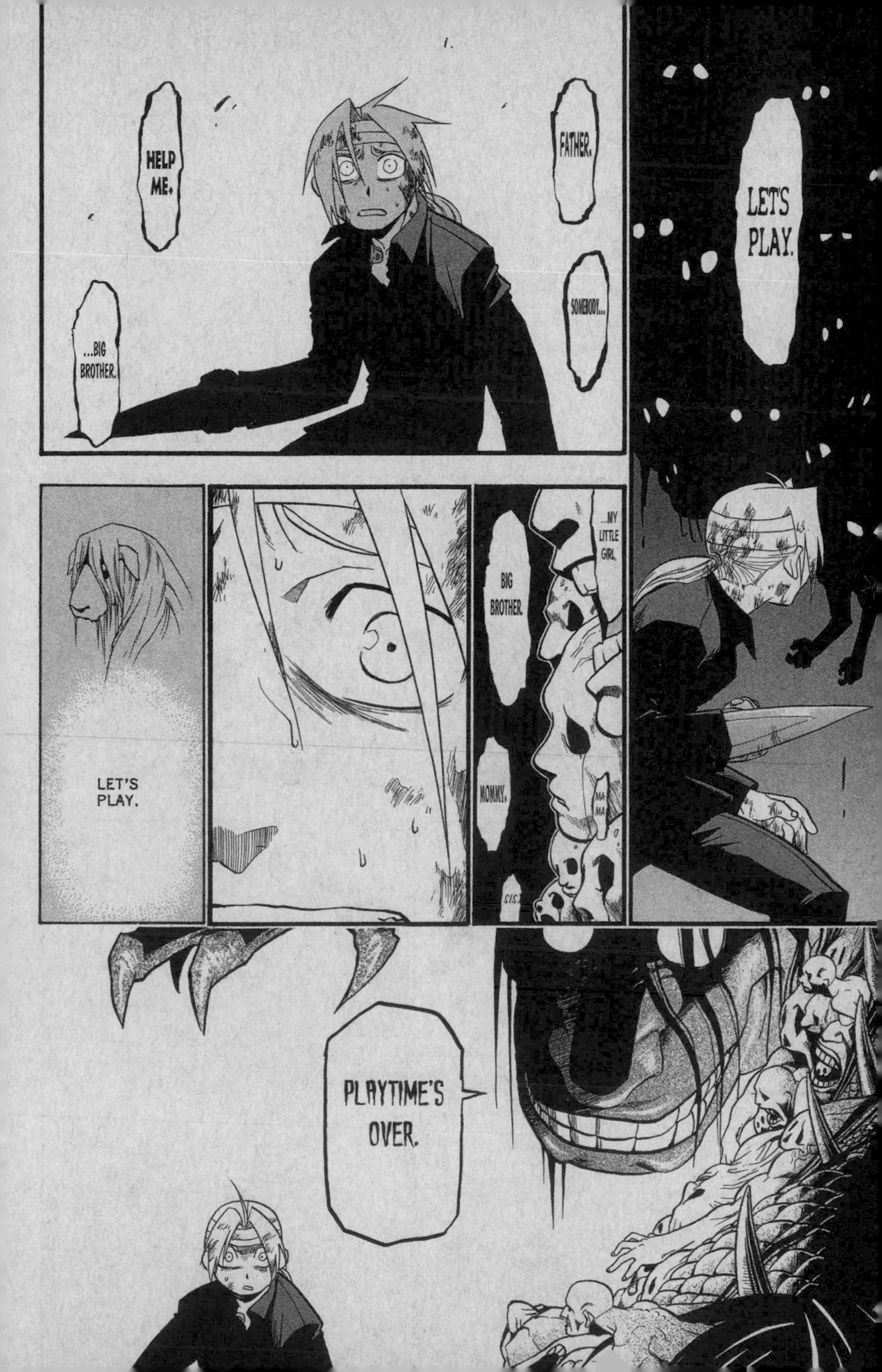

LET'S PLAY.
FATHER.
SOMEBODY...
HELP ME.
...BIG BROTHER.
...MY LITTLE GIRL.
BIG BROTHER.
MAMA
MOMMY.
SIS
LET'S PLAY.
PLAYTIME'S OVER.

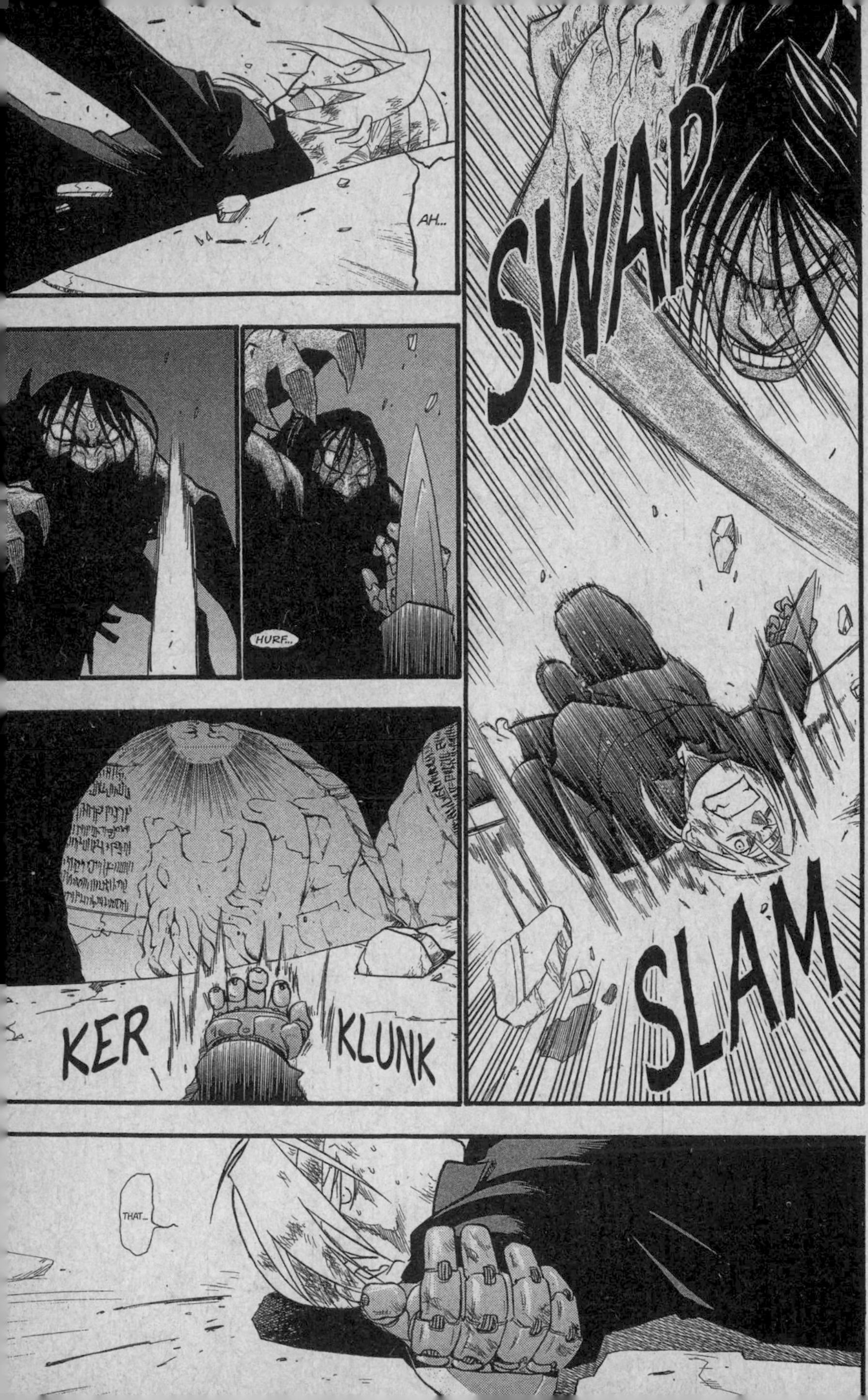
SWAP
SLAM
AH...
HURF...
KER
KLUNK
THAT...

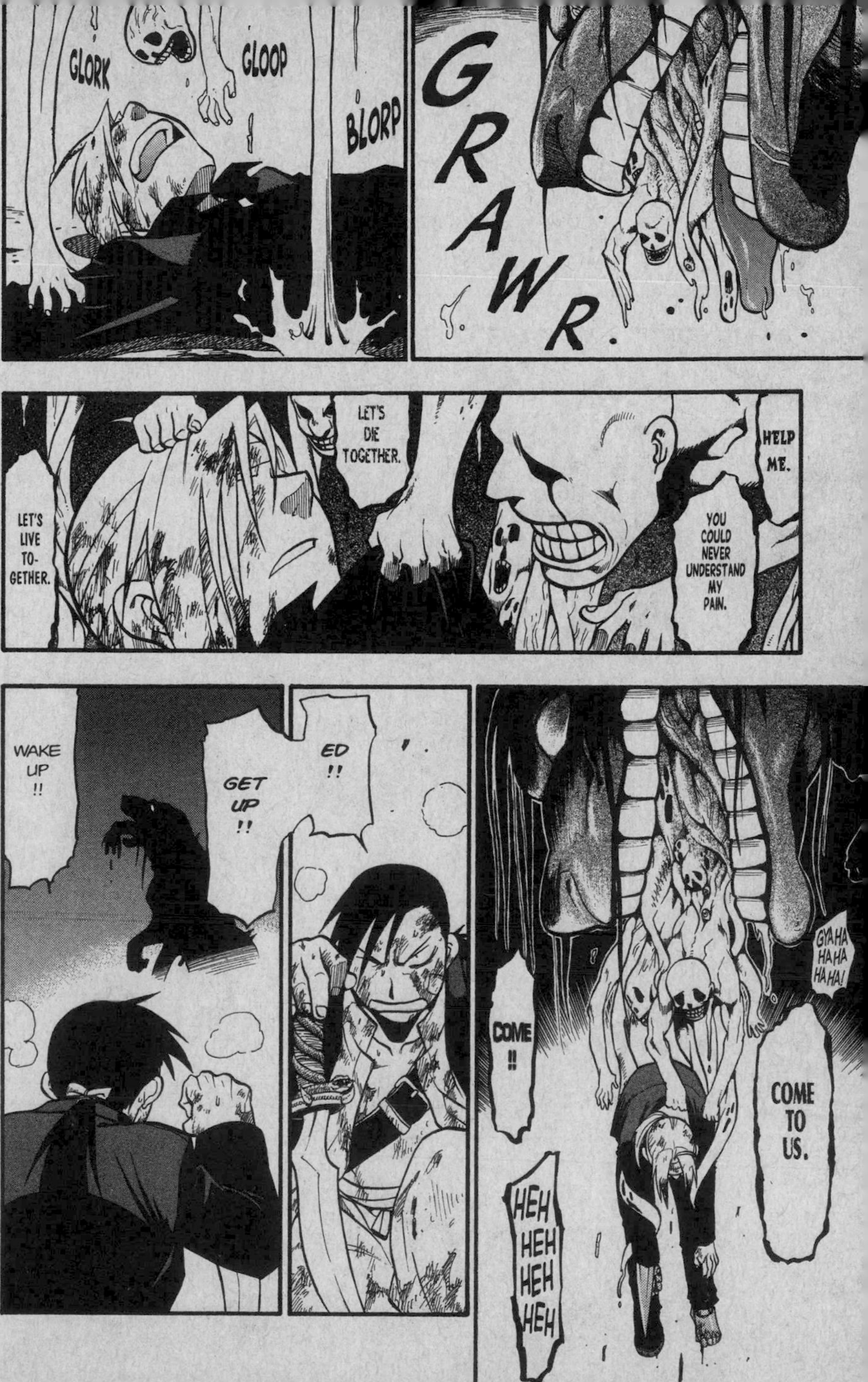
GRAWR
BLORP
GLOOP
GLORK
HELP ME.
YOU COULD NEVER UNDERSTAND MY PAIN.
LET'S DIE TOGETHER.
LET'S LIVE TO-GETHER.
GYAHA HAHA HAHA!
COME TO US.
COME!!
HEH HEH HEH HEH HEH
ED!!
GET UP!!
WAKE UP!!

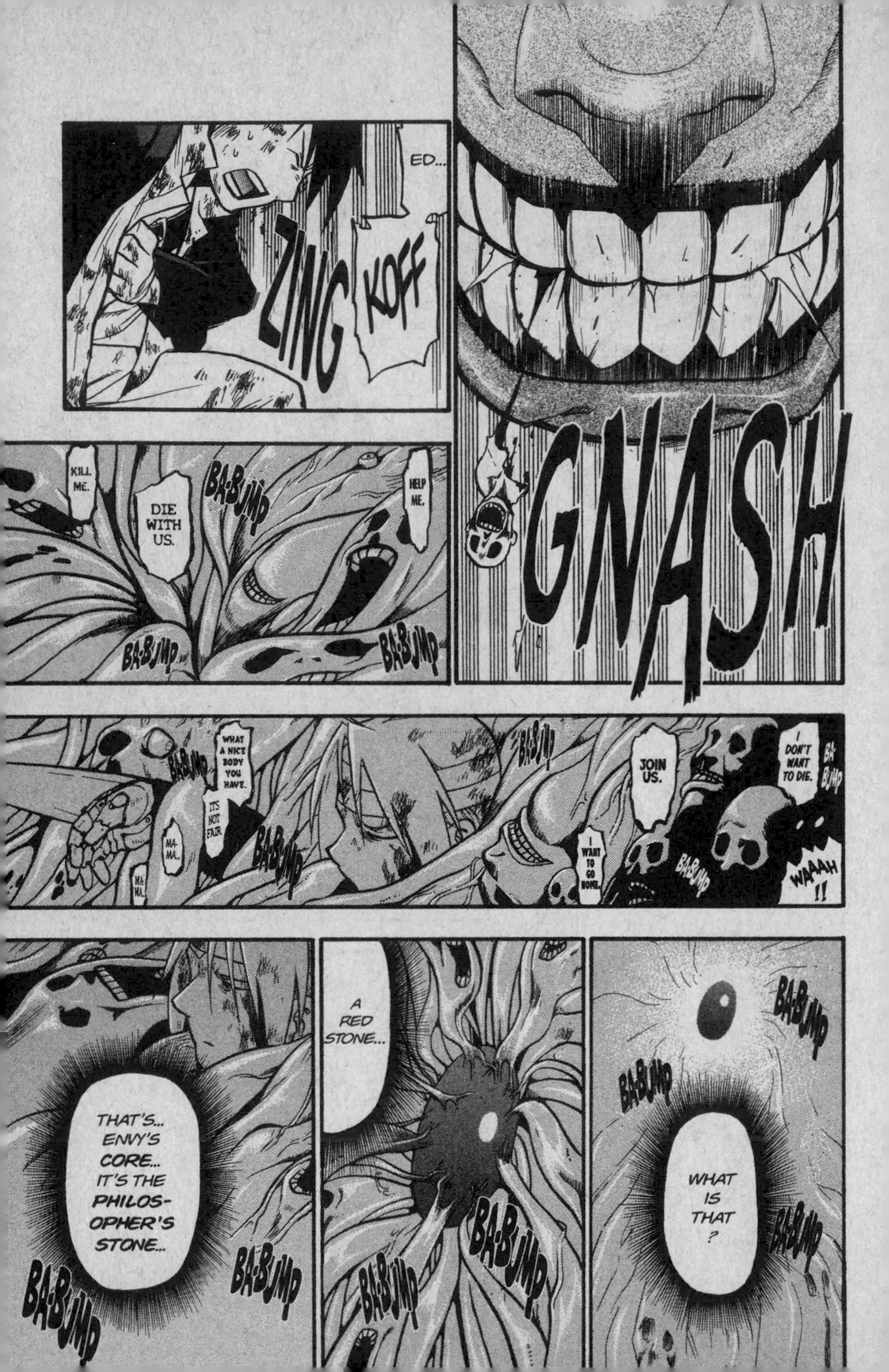
GNASH
ED...
KOFF
ZING
HELP ME.
BA-BUMP
DIE WITH US.
KILL ME.
BA-BUMP
BA-BUMP
BA-BUMP
I DON'T WANT TO DIE.
JOIN US.
WAAAH!!
BA-BUMP
I WANT TO GO HOME.
BA-BUMP
WHAT A NICE BODY YOU HAVE.
BA-BUMP
IT'S NOT FAIR
BA-BUMP
MA-MA...
MA-MA.
BA-BUMP
BA-BUMP
WHAT IS THAT ?
BA-BUMP
A RED STONE...
BA-BUMP
BA-BUMP
THAT'S... ENVY'S CORE... IT'S THE PHILOSOPHER'S STONE...
BA-BUMP
BA-BUMP

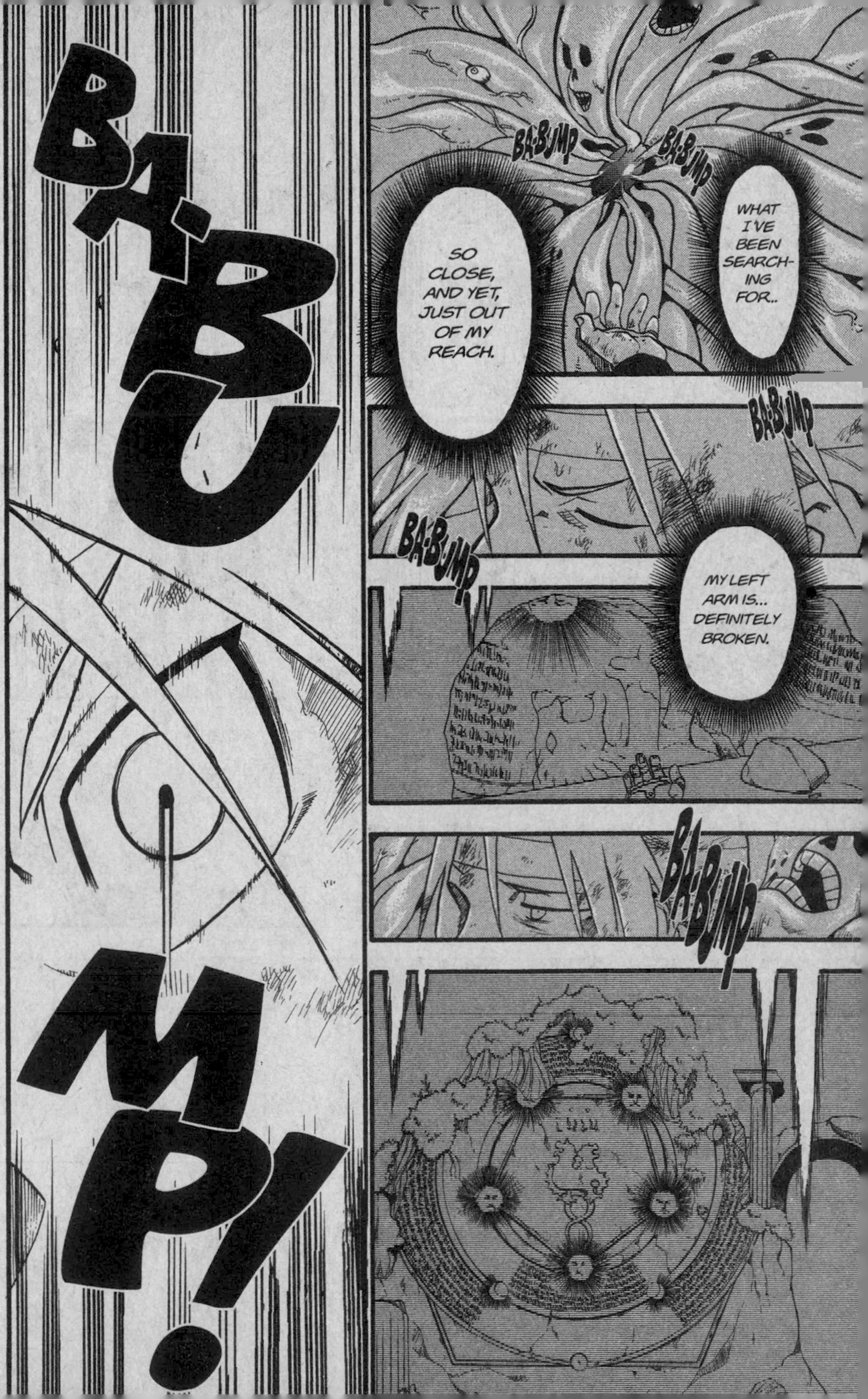
BA-BUMP
BA-BUMP
WHAT I'VE BEEN SEARCHING FOR..
SO CLOSE, AND YET, JUST OUT OF MY REACH.
BA-BUMP
BA-BUMP
MY LEFT ARM IS... DEFINITELY BROKEN.
BA-BUMP
BA-BUMP!

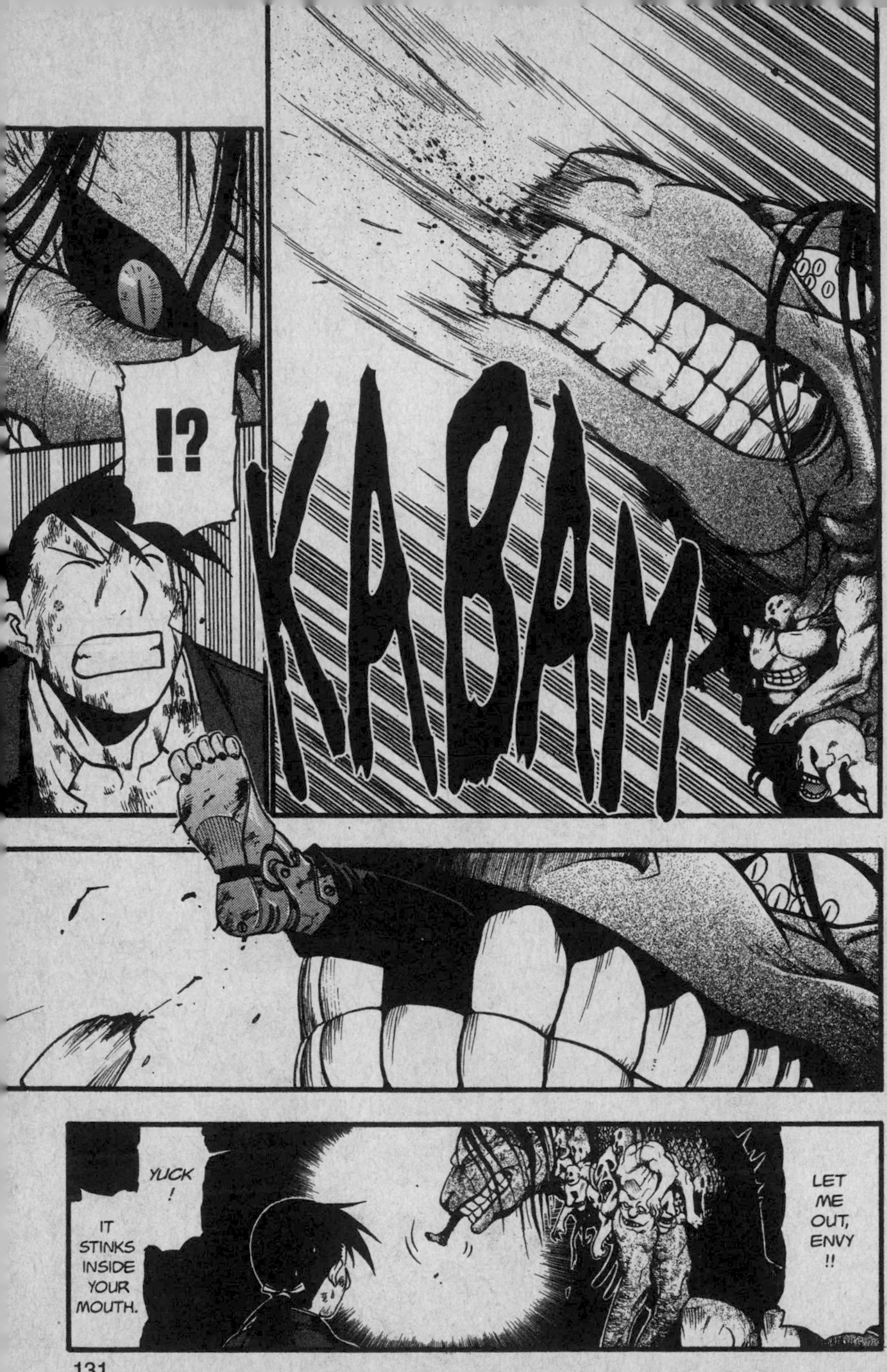
KABAM
!?
LET ME OUT, ENVY!!
YUCK!
IT STINKS INSIDE YOUR MOUTH.

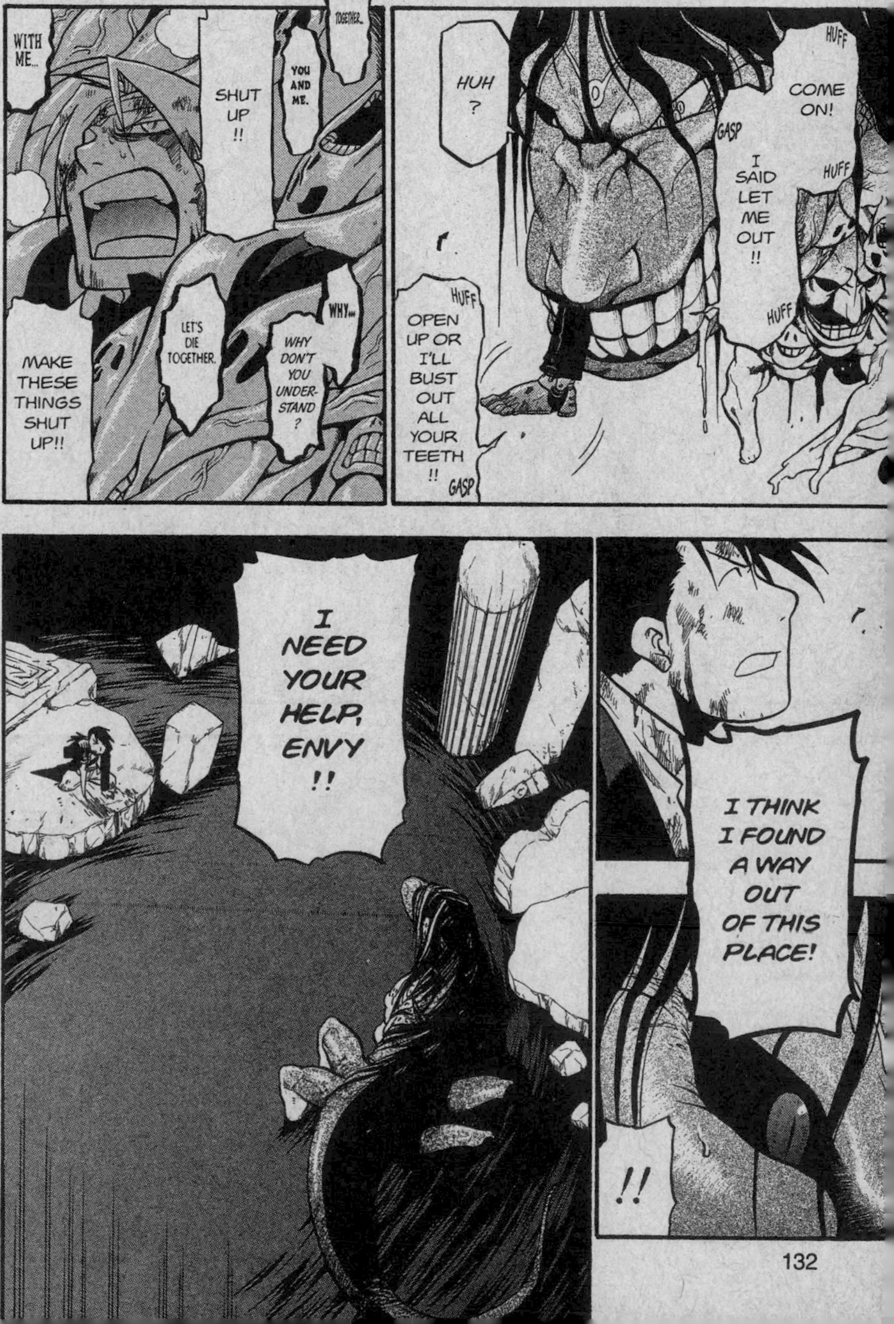
HUFF
COME ON!
GASP
I SAID LET ME OUT!!
HUFF
HUFF
HUH?
HUFF
OPEN UP OR I'LL BUST OUT ALL YOUR TEETH!!
GASP
TOGETHER...
YOU AND ME.
SHUT UP!!
WITH ME...
WHY...
WHY DON'T YOU UNDER-STAND?
LET'S DIE TOGETHER.
MAKE THESE THINGS SHUT UP!!
I THINK I FOUND A WAY OUT OF THIS PLACE!
!!
I NEED YOUR HELP, ENVY!!

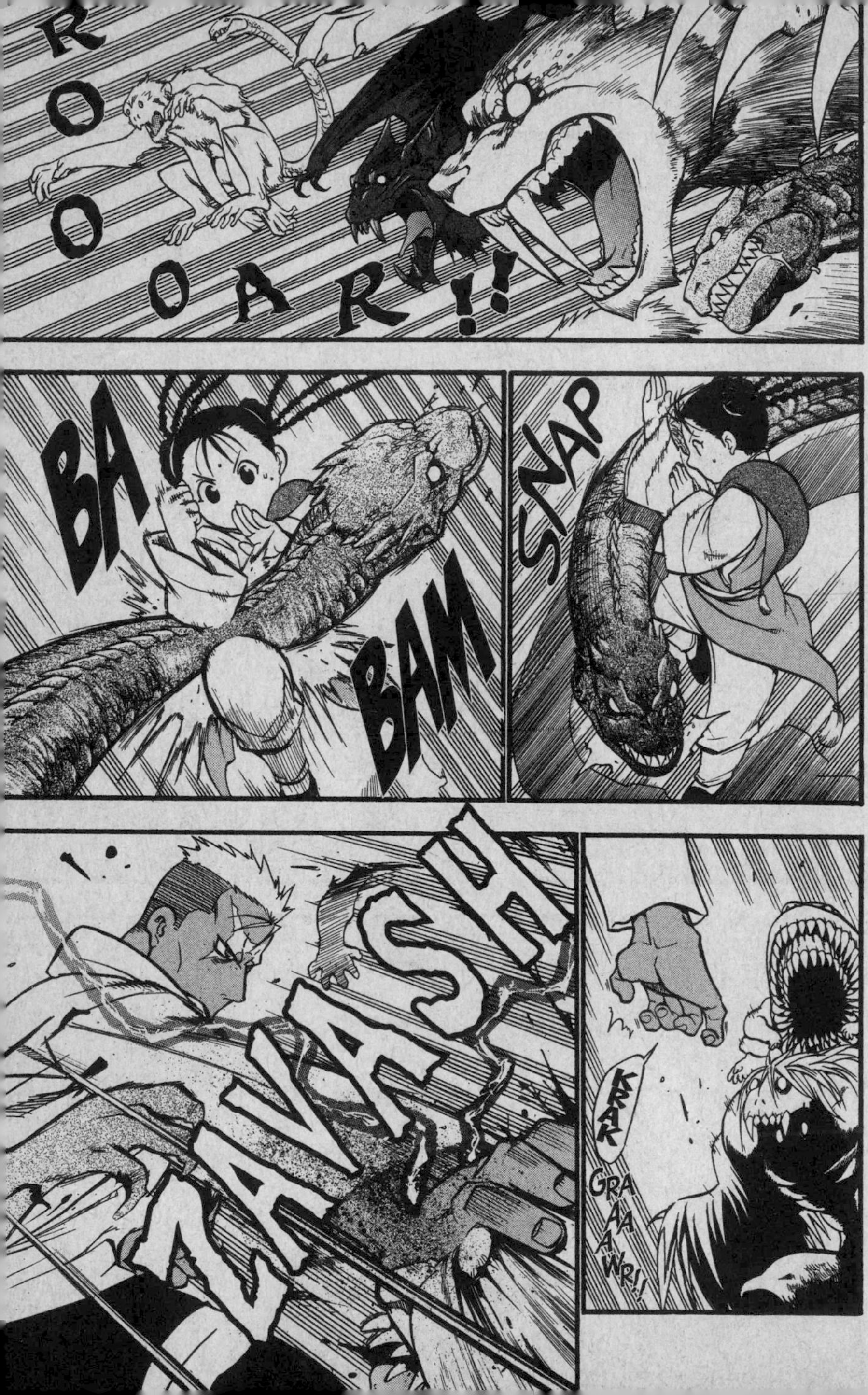
ROOOAR!!
SNAP
BA
BAM
KRAK
GRAAAAWR!!
ZAVASH!!

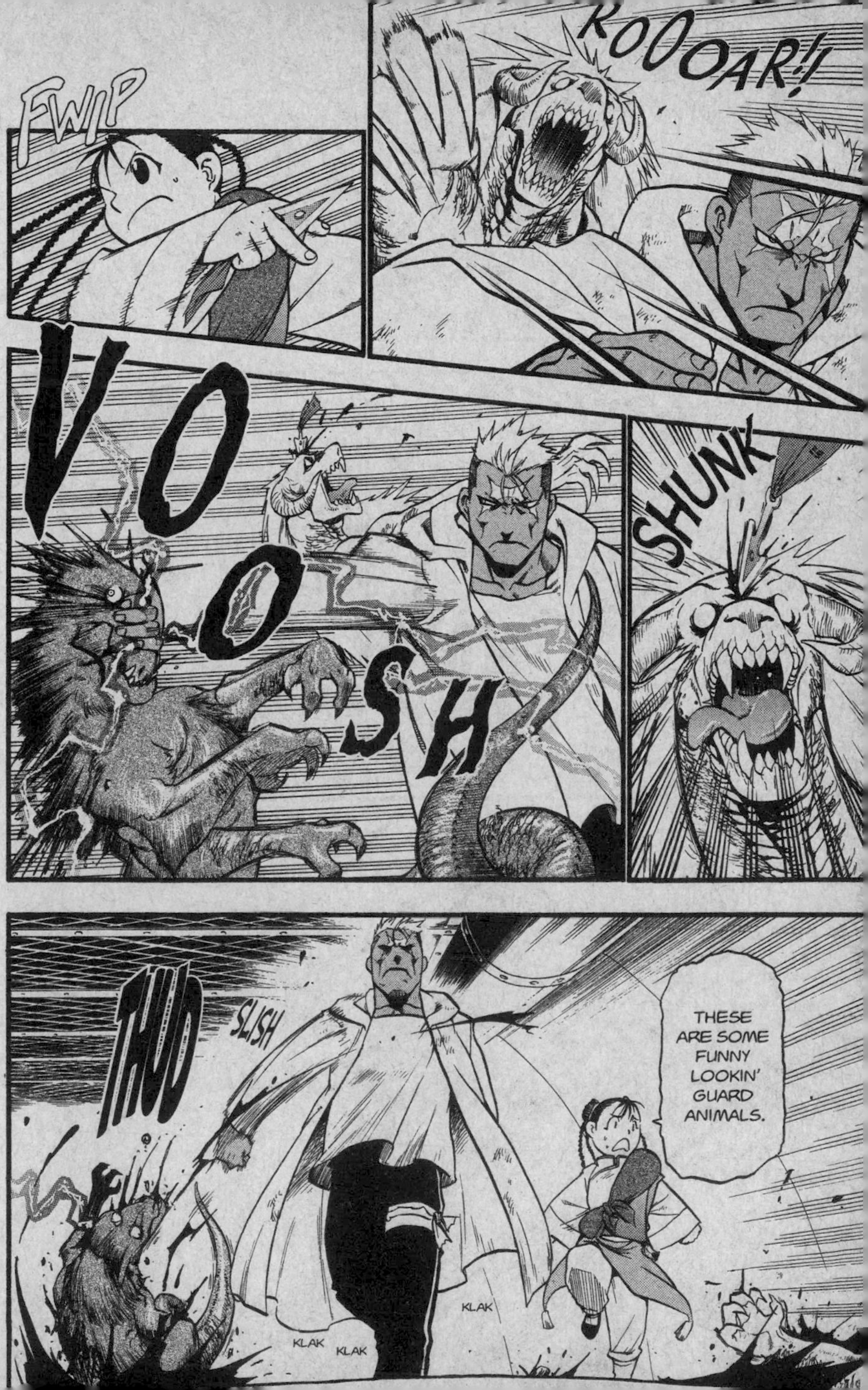
KOOOAR!!
FWIP
SHUNK
VOOSH
THESE ARE SOME FUNNY LOOKIN' GUARD ANIMALS.
SLISH
THUD
KLAK
KLAK
KLAK

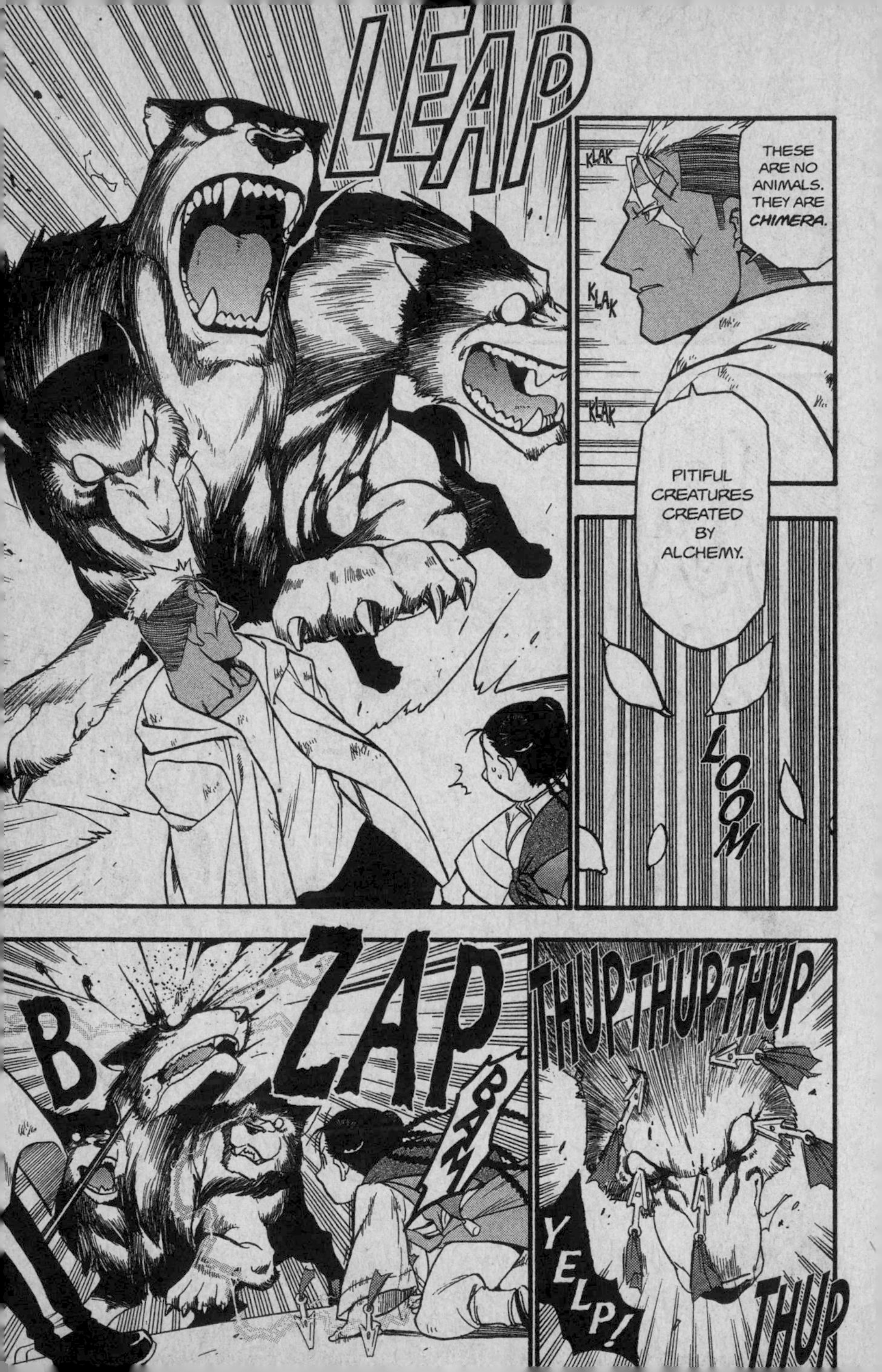

KLAK
THESE ARE NO ANIMALS. THEY ARE *CHIMERA*.
KLAK
KLAK
PITIFUL CREATURES CREATED BY ALCHEMY.
LOOM
LEAP
THUP THUP THUP
YELP!
THUP
B
ZAP
BAM

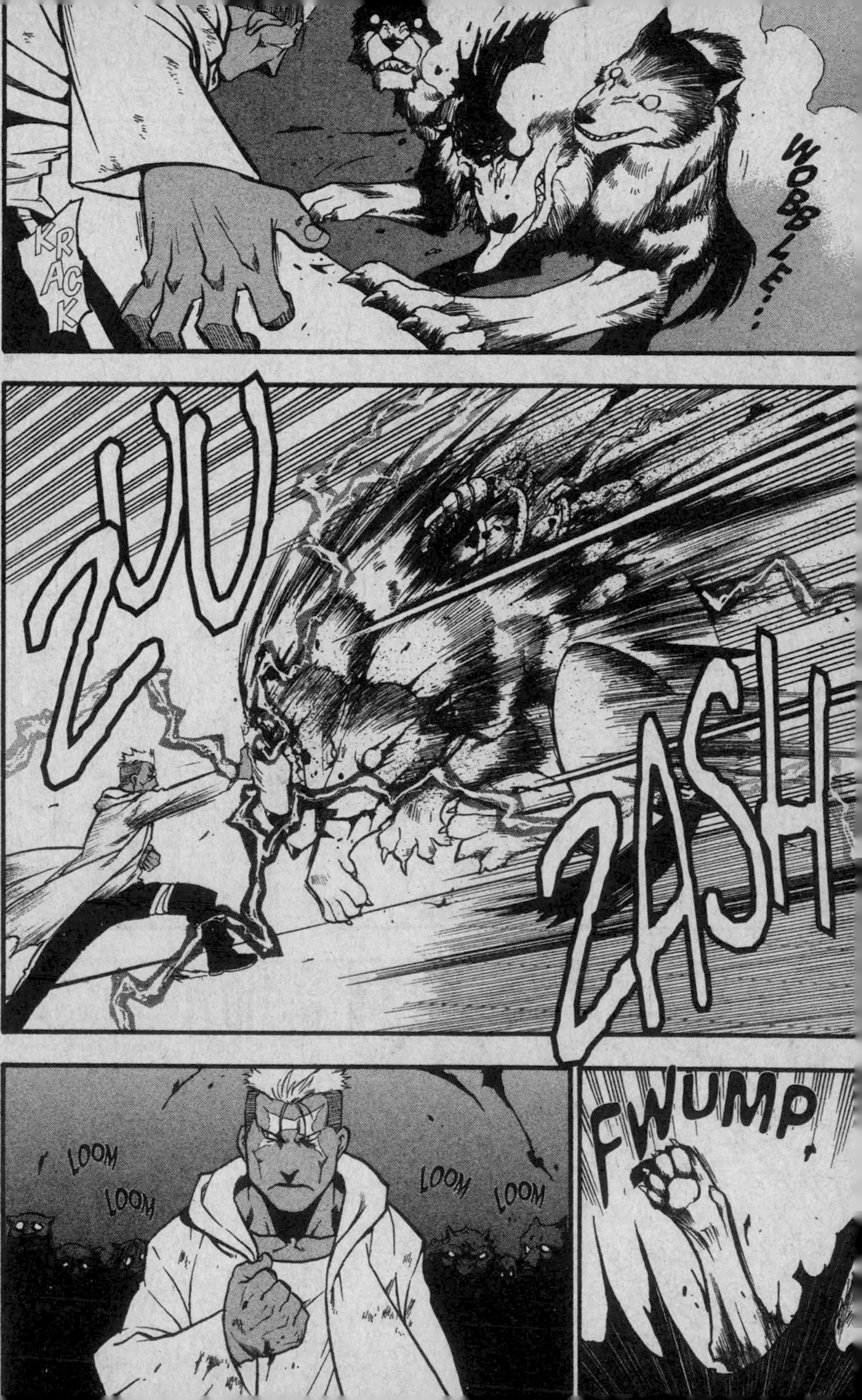
WOBBLE...
KRACK
ZASH
ZUU
FWUMP
LOOM
LOOM
LOOM
LOOM

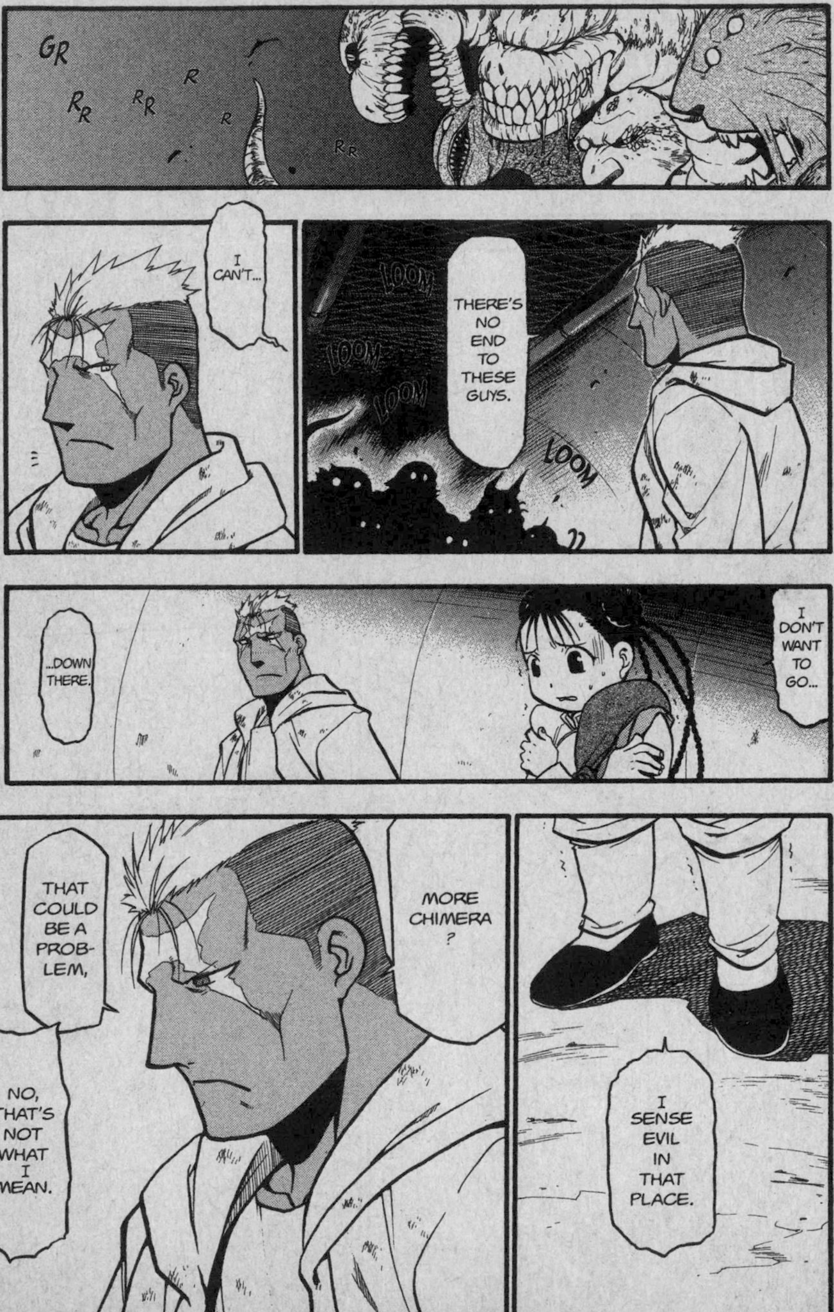
GR
RR
RR
R
R
RR
THERE'S NO END TO THESE GUYS.
LOOM
LOOM
LOOM
LOOM
I CAN'T...
I DON'T WANT TO GO...
...DOWN THERE.
I SENSE EVIL IN THAT PLACE.
MORE CHIMERA?
THAT COULD BE A PROB-LEM,
NO, THAT'S NOT WHAT I MEAN.

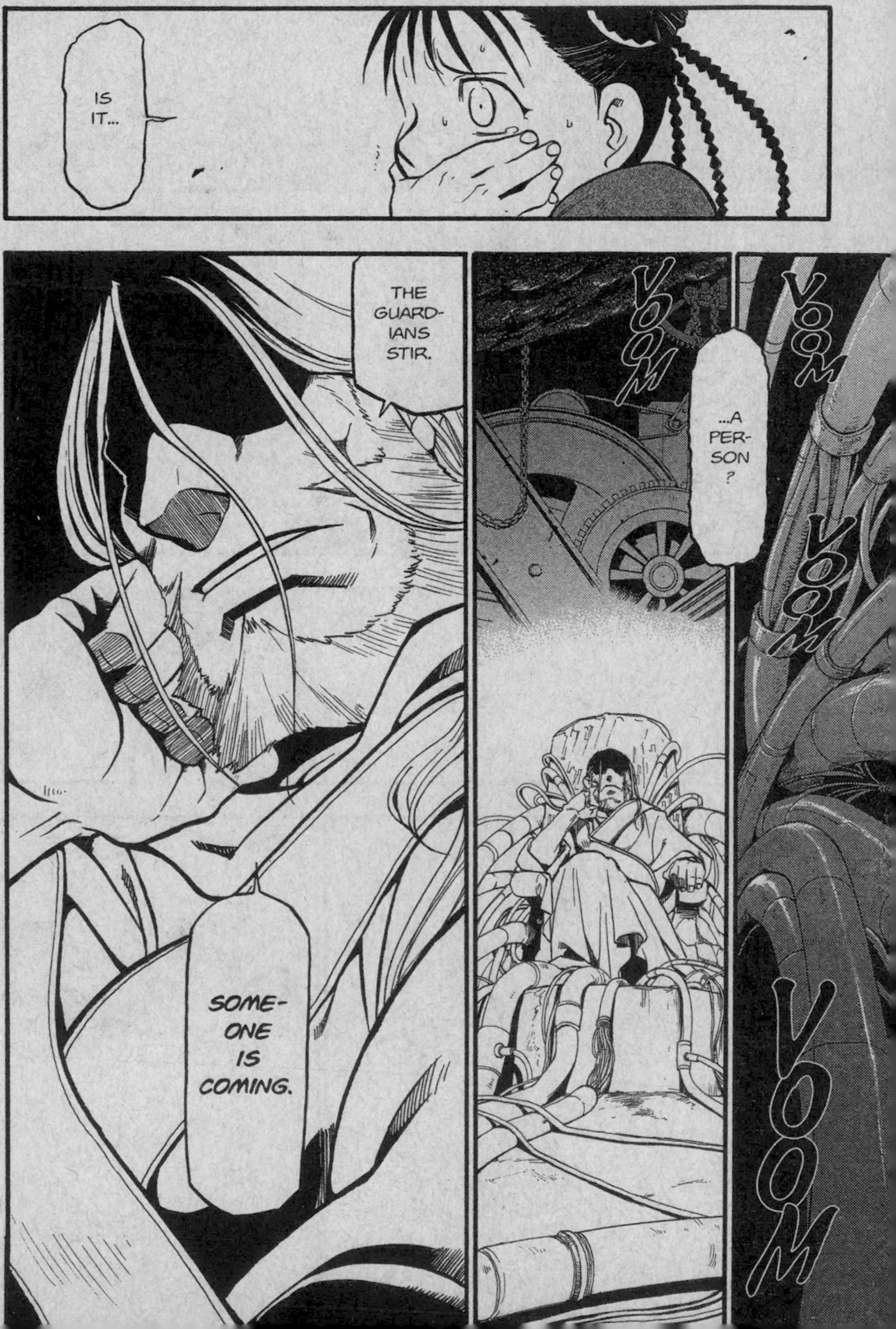
IS IT...
VOOM
VOOM
VOOM
VOOM
...A PER-SON?
THE GUARD-IANS STIR.
SOME-ONE IS COMING.

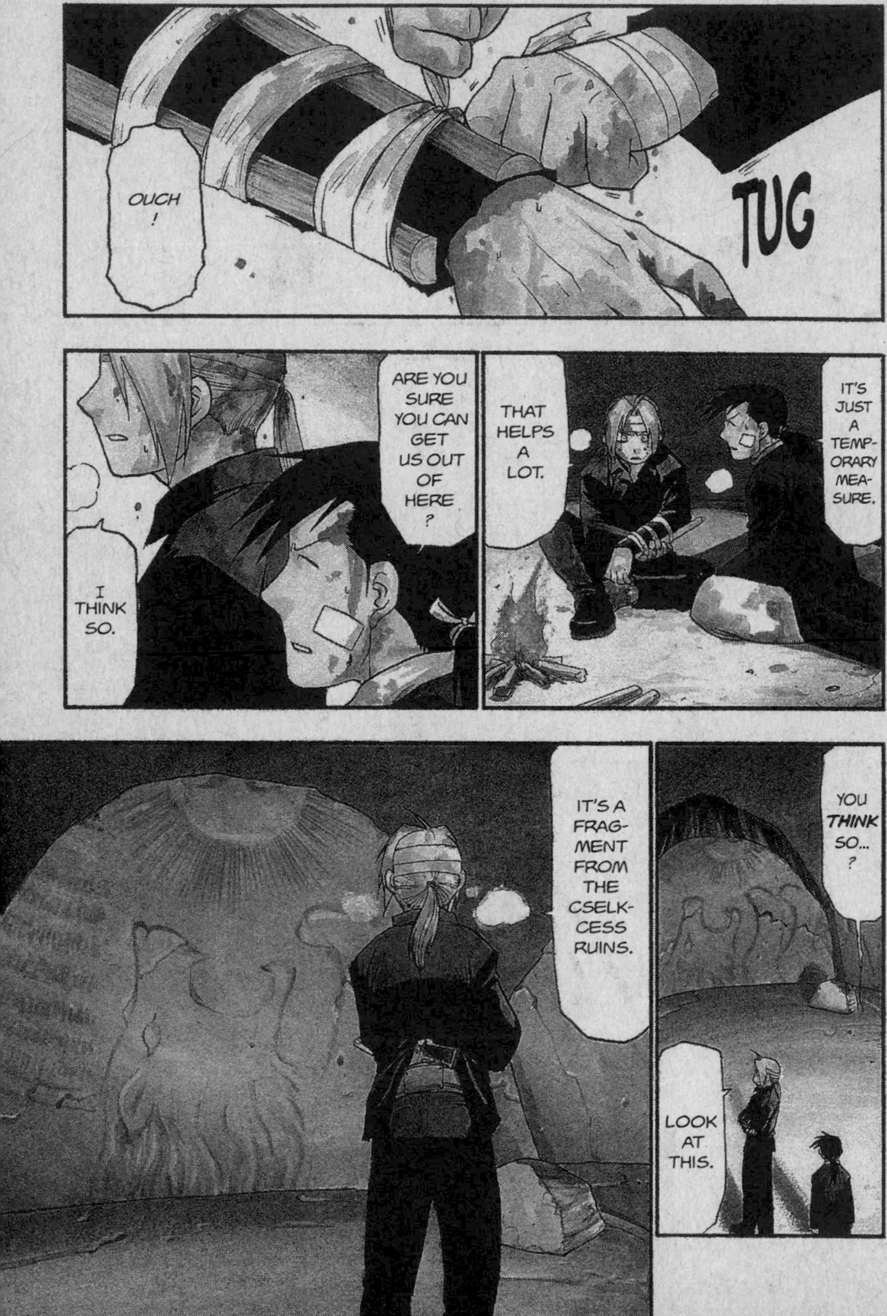
TUG
OUCH!
IT'S JUST A TEMPORARY MEASURE.
THAT HELPS A LOT.
ARE YOU SURE YOU CAN GET US OUT OF HERE?
I THINK SO.
YOU THINK SO...?
LOOK AT THIS.
IT'S A FRAGMENT FROM THE CSELKCESS RUINS.

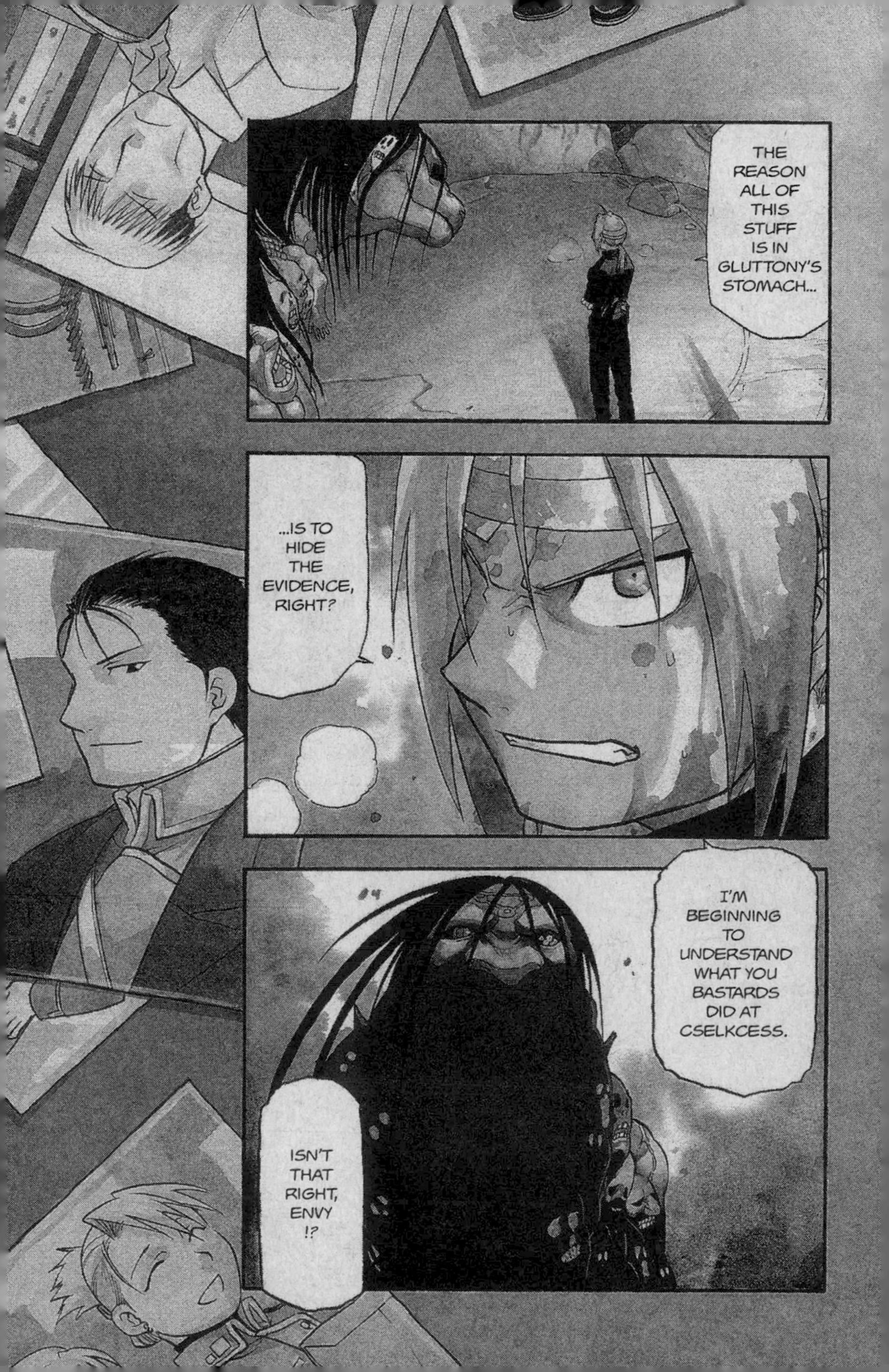
THE REASON ALL OF THIS STUFF IS IN GLUTTONY'S STOMACH...
...IS TO HIDE THE EVIDENCE, RIGHT?
I'M BEGINNING TO UNDERSTAND WHAT YOU BASTARDS DID AT CSELKCESS.
ISN'T THAT RIGHT, ENVY !?

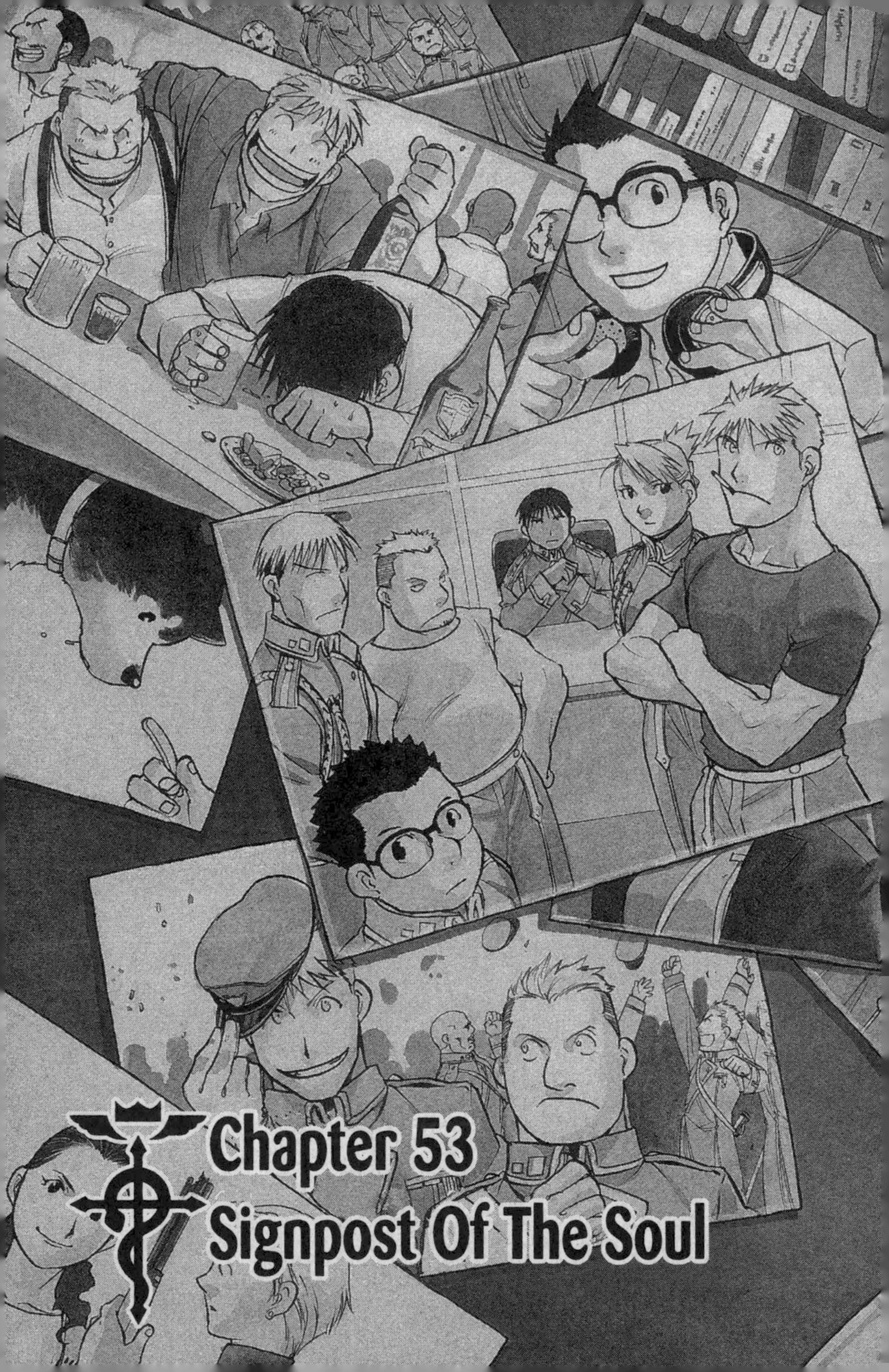
Chapter 53
Signpost Of The Soul

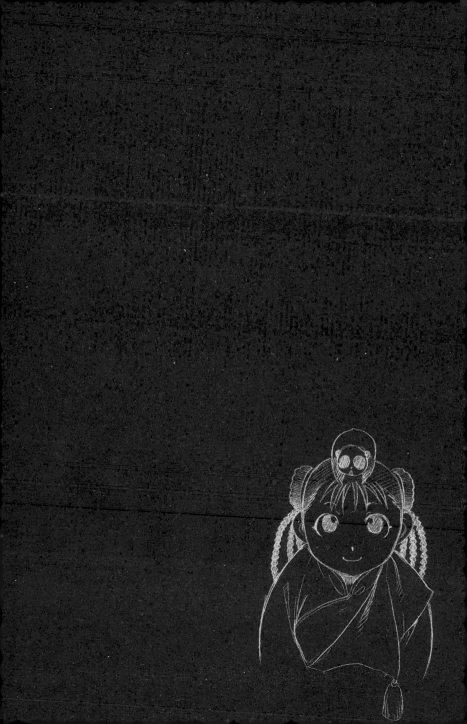

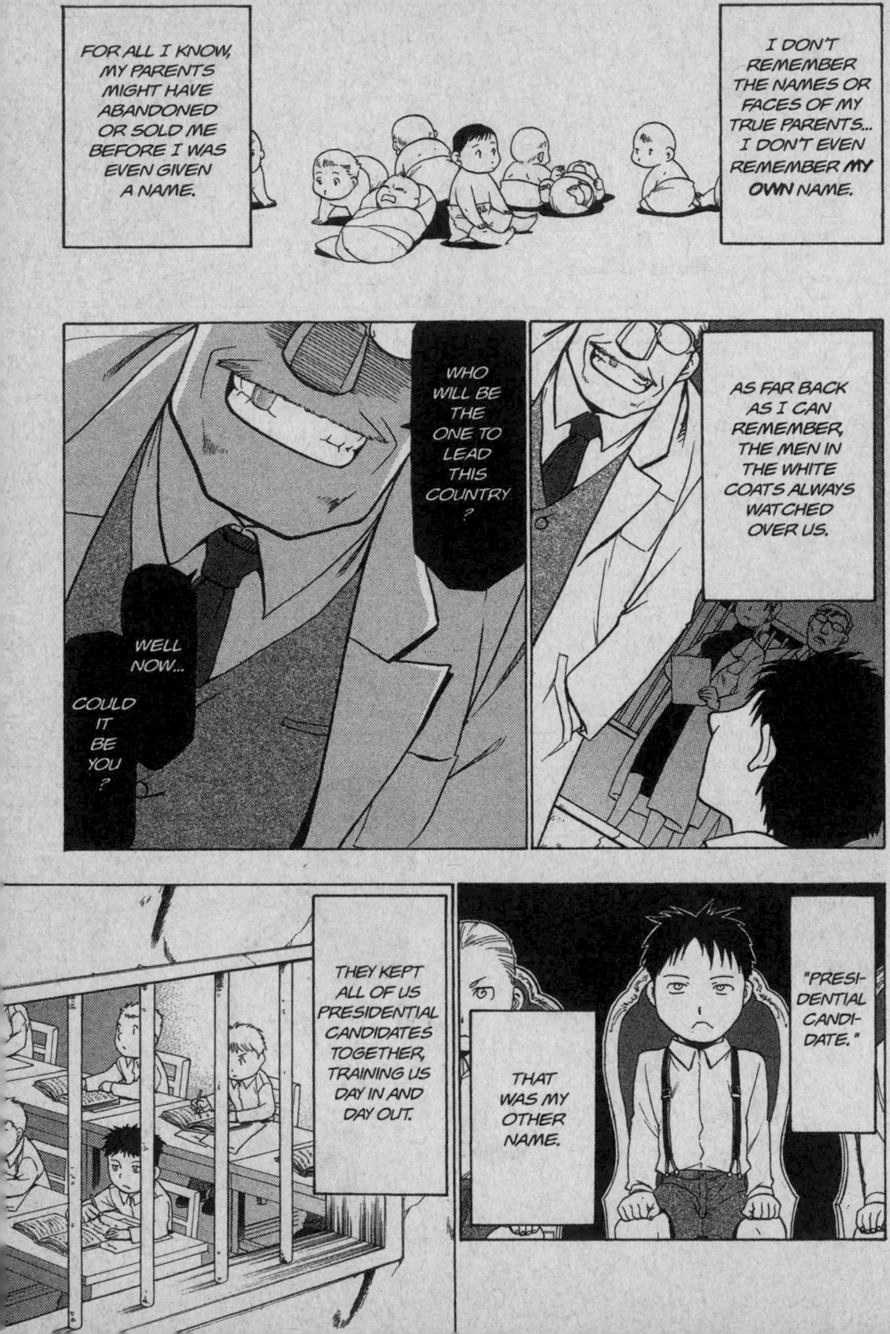
I DON'T REMEMBER THE NAMES OR FACES OF MY TRUE PARENTS... I DON'T EVEN REMEMBER **MY OWN** NAME.
FOR ALL I KNOW, MY PARENTS MIGHT HAVE ABANDONED OR SOLD ME BEFORE I WAS EVEN GIVEN A NAME.
AS FAR BACK AS I CAN REMEMBER, THE MEN IN THE WHITE COATS ALWAYS WATCHED OVER US.
WHO WILL BE THE ONE TO LEAD THIS COUNTRY?
WELL NOW...
COULD IT BE YOU?
"PRESIDENTIAL CANDIDATE."
THAT WAS MY OTHER NAME.
THEY KEPT ALL OF US PRESIDENTIAL CANDIDATES TOGETHER, TRAINING US DAY IN AND DAY OUT.

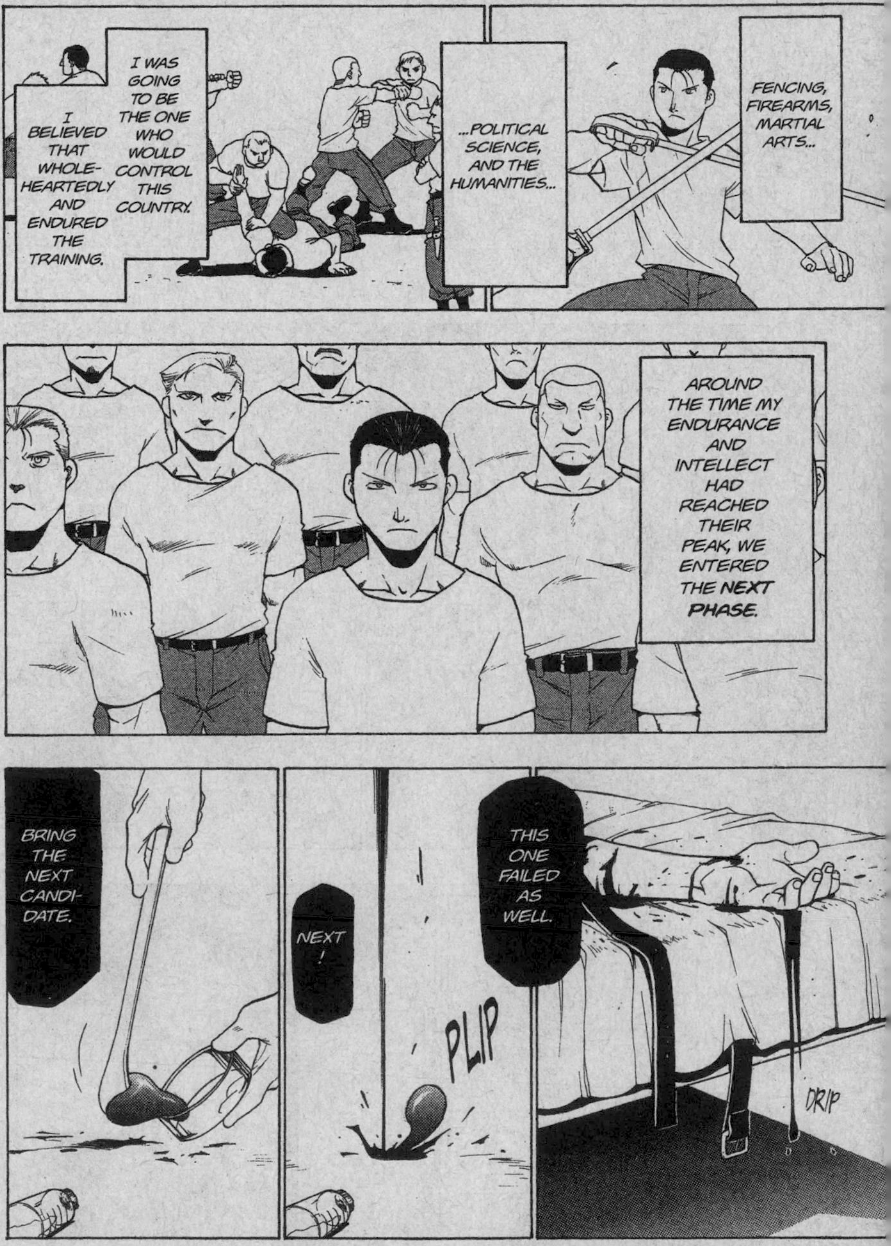

FENCING, FIREARMS, MARTIAL ARTS...
...POLITICAL SCIENCE, AND THE HUMANITIES...
I WAS GOING TO BE THE ONE WHO WOULD CONTROL THIS COUNTRY.
I BELIEVED THAT WHOLE-HEARTEDLY AND ENDURED THE TRAINING.
AROUND THE TIME MY ENDURANCE AND INTELLECT HAD REACHED THEIR PEAK, WE ENTERED THE **NEXT PHASE.**
THIS ONE FAILED AS WELL.
DRIP
NEXT!
PLIP
BRING THE NEXT CANDI-DATE.

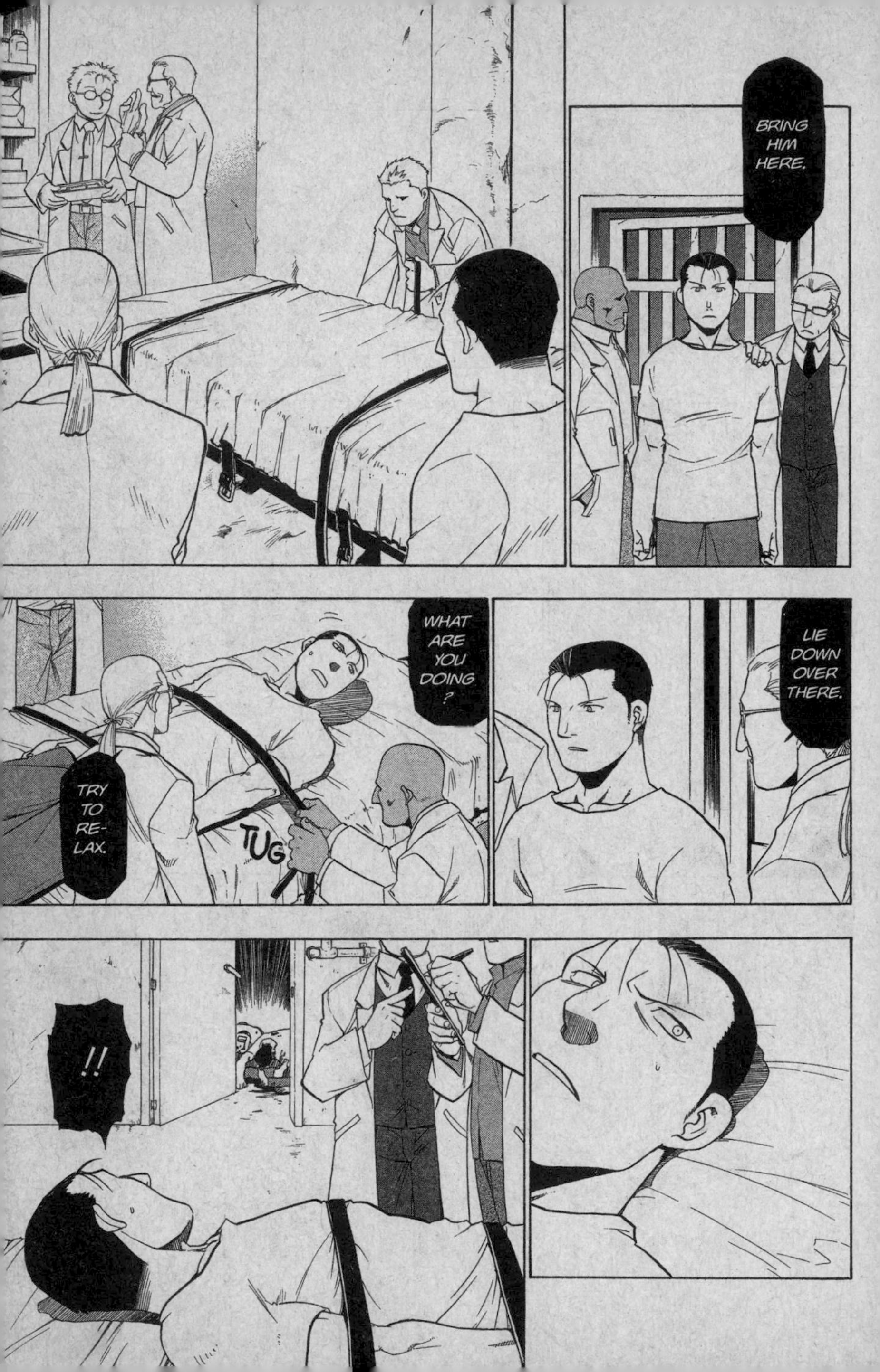
BRING HIM HERE.
LIE DOWN OVER THERE.
WHAT ARE YOU DOING?
TRY TO RE-LAX.
TUG
!!

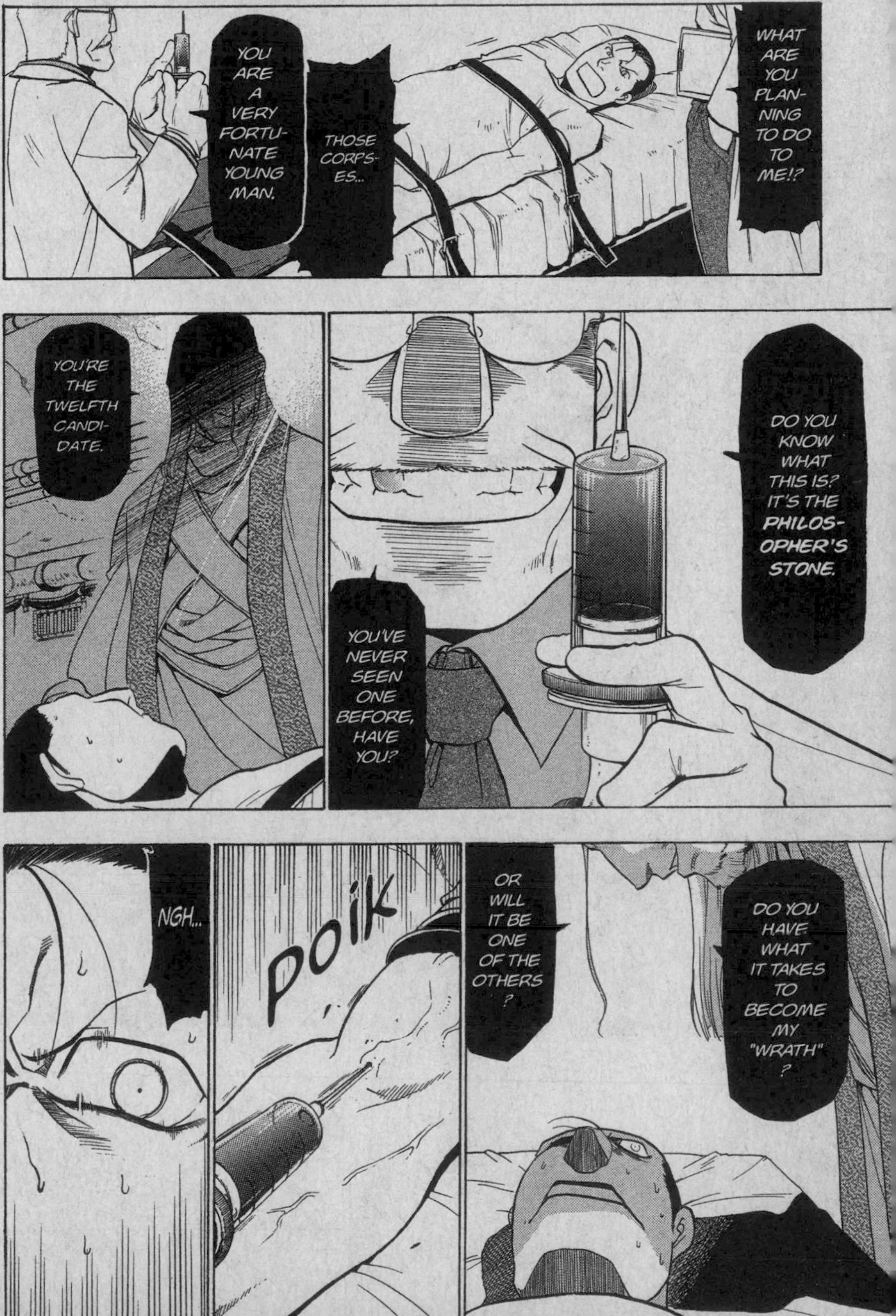
WHAT ARE YOU PLANNING TO DO TO ME!?
THOSE CORPSES...
YOU ARE A VERY FORTUNATE YOUNG MAN.
DO YOU KNOW WHAT THIS IS? IT'S THE **PHILOSOPHER'S STONE.**
YOU'VE NEVER SEEN ONE BEFORE, HAVE YOU?
YOU'RE THE TWELFTH CANDIDATE.
DO YOU HAVE WHAT IT TAKES TO BECOME MY "WRATH"?
OR WILL IT BE ONE OF THE OTHERS?
POiK
NGH...

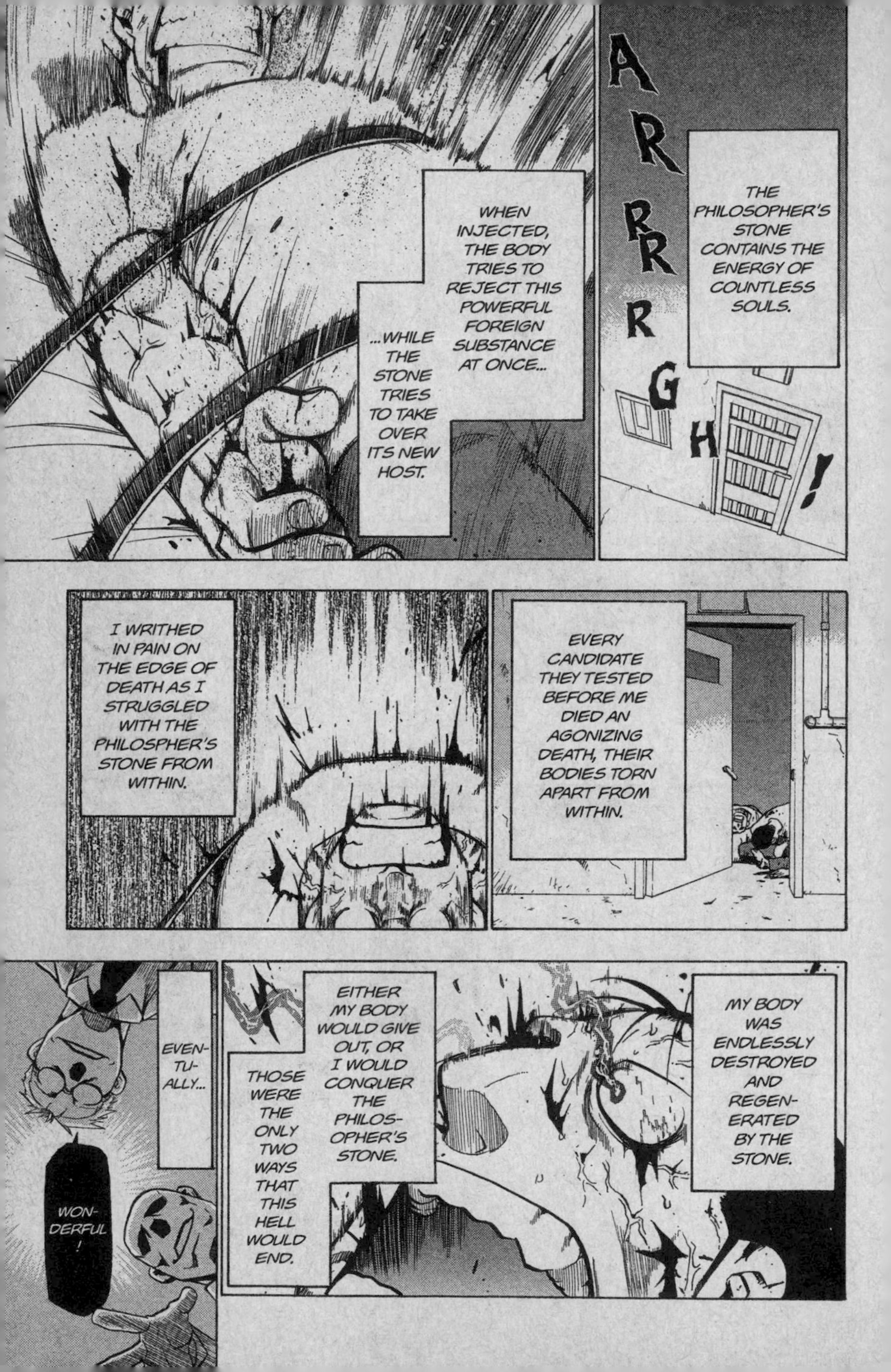
THE PHILOSOPHER'S STONE CONTAINS THE ENERGY OF COUNTLESS SOULS.
ARRRRGH!
WHEN INJECTED, THE BODY TRIES TO REJECT THIS POWERFUL FOREIGN SUBSTANCE AT ONCE...
...WHILE THE STONE TRIES TO TAKE OVER ITS NEW HOST.
EVERY CANDIDATE THEY TESTED BEFORE ME DIED AN AGONIZING DEATH, THEIR BODIES TORN APART FROM WITHIN.
I WRITHED IN PAIN ON THE EDGE OF DEATH AS I STRUGGLED WITH THE PHILOSPHER'S STONE FROM WITHIN.
MY BODY WAS ENDLESSLY DESTROYED AND REGEN-ERATED BY THE STONE.
EITHER MY BODY WOULD GIVE OUT, OR I WOULD CONQUER THE PHILOS-OPHER'S STONE.
THOSE WERE THE ONLY TWO WAYS THAT THIS HELL WOULD END.
EVEN-TU-ALLY...
WON-DERFUL!

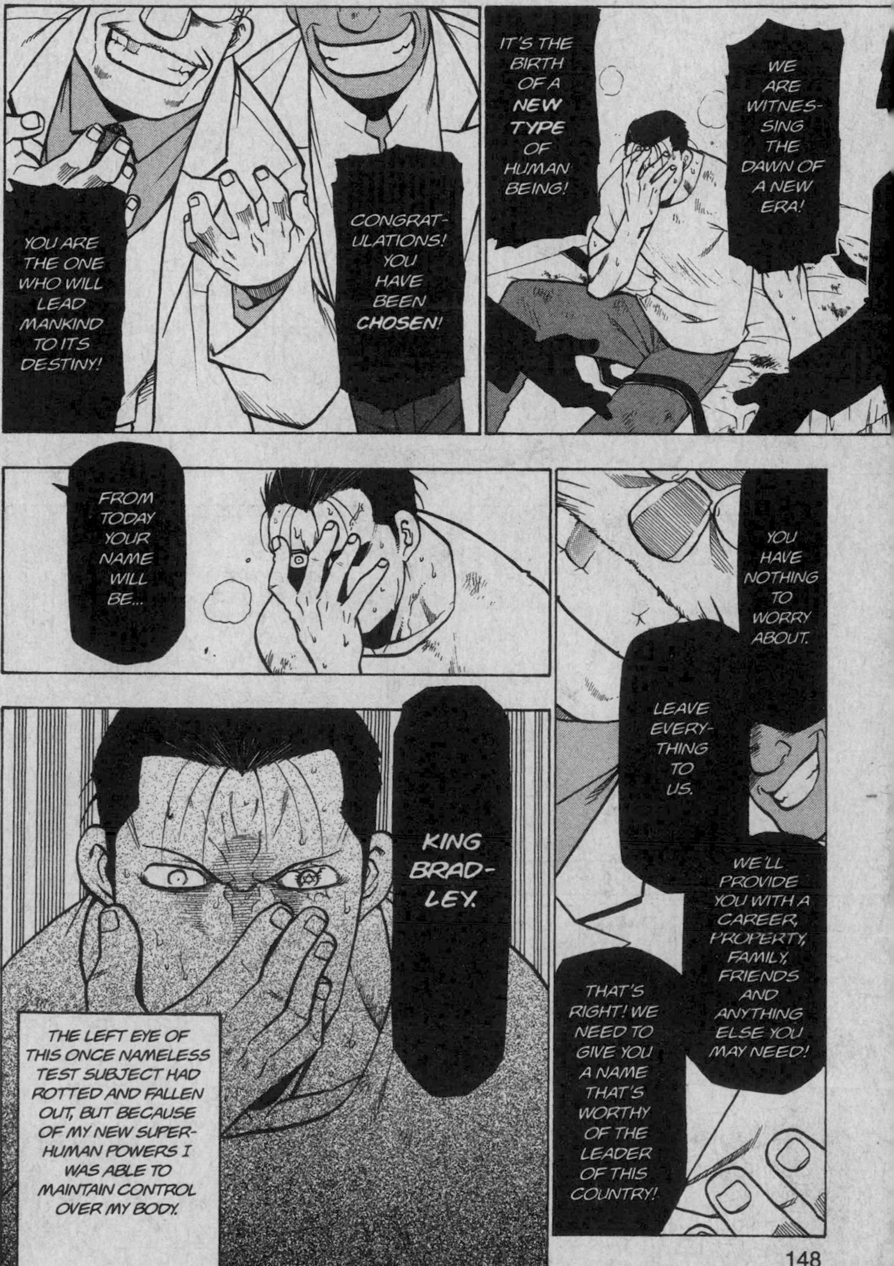
WE ARE WITNESSING THE DAWN OF A NEW ERA!
IT'S THE BIRTH OF A **NEW TYPE** OF HUMAN BEING!
CONGRATULATIONS! YOU HAVE BEEN **CHOSEN**!
YOU ARE THE ONE WHO WILL LEAD MANKIND TO ITS DESTINY!
YOU HAVE NOTHING TO WORRY ABOUT.
LEAVE EVERYTHING TO US.
WE'LL PROVIDE YOU WITH A CAREER, PROPERTY, FAMILY, FRIENDS AND ANYTHING ELSE YOU MAY NEED!
THAT'S RIGHT! WE NEED TO GIVE YOU A NAME THAT'S WORTHY OF THE LEADER OF THIS COUNTRY!
FROM TODAY YOUR NAME WILL BE...
KING BRADLEY.
THE LEFT EYE OF THIS ONCE NAMELESS TEST SUBJECT HAD ROTTED AND FALLEN OUT, BUT BECAUSE OF MY NEW SUPER-HUMAN POWERS I WAS ABLE TO MAINTAIN CONTROL OVER MY BODY.

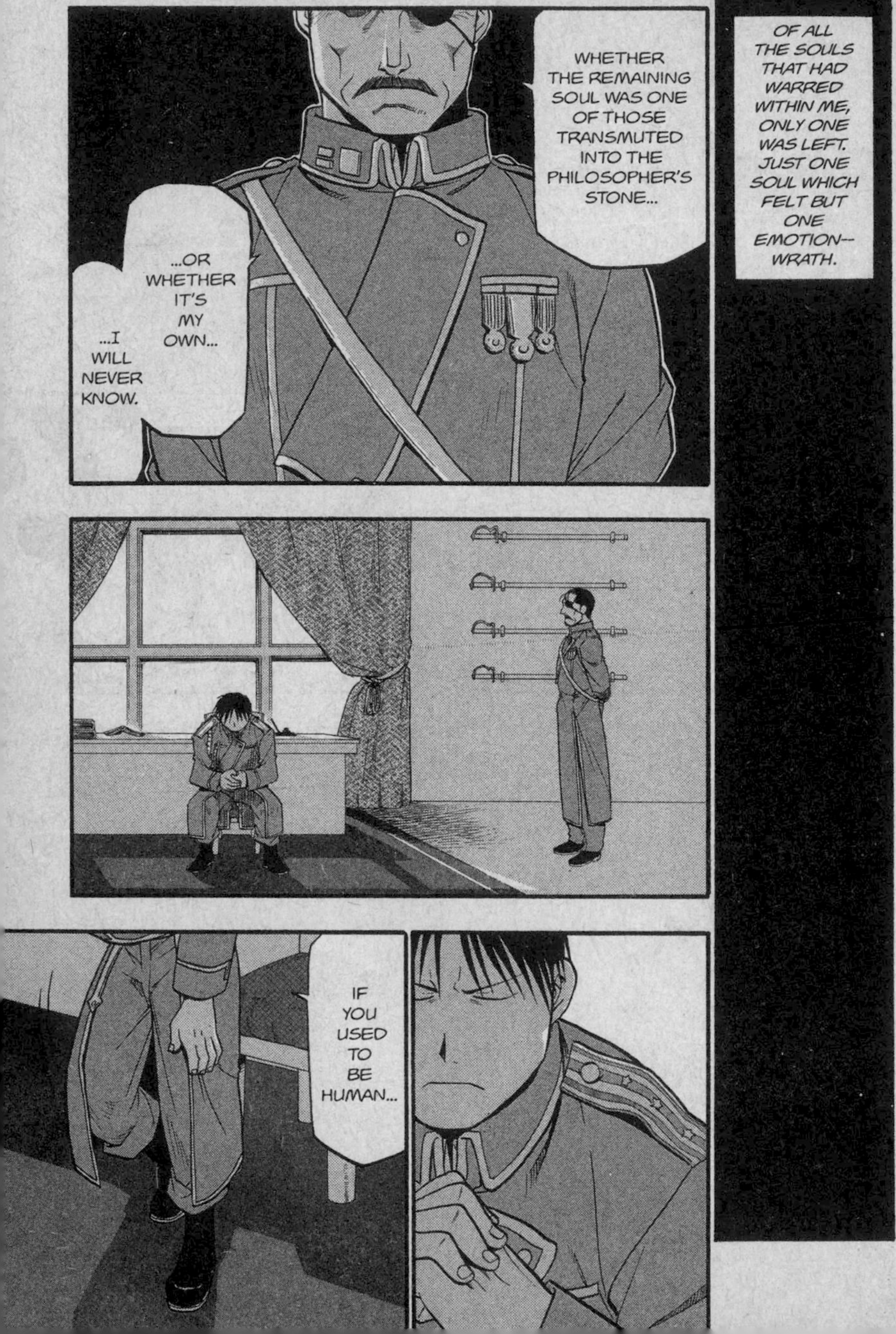
OF ALL THE SOULS THAT HAD WARRED WITHIN ME, ONLY ONE WAS LEFT. JUST ONE SOUL WHICH FELT BUT ONE EMOTION--WRATH.
WHETHER THE REMAINING SOUL WAS ONE OF THOSE TRANSMUTED INTO THE PHILOSOPHER'S STONE...
...OR WHETHER IT'S MY OWN...
...I WILL NEVER KNOW.
IF YOU USED TO BE HUMAN...

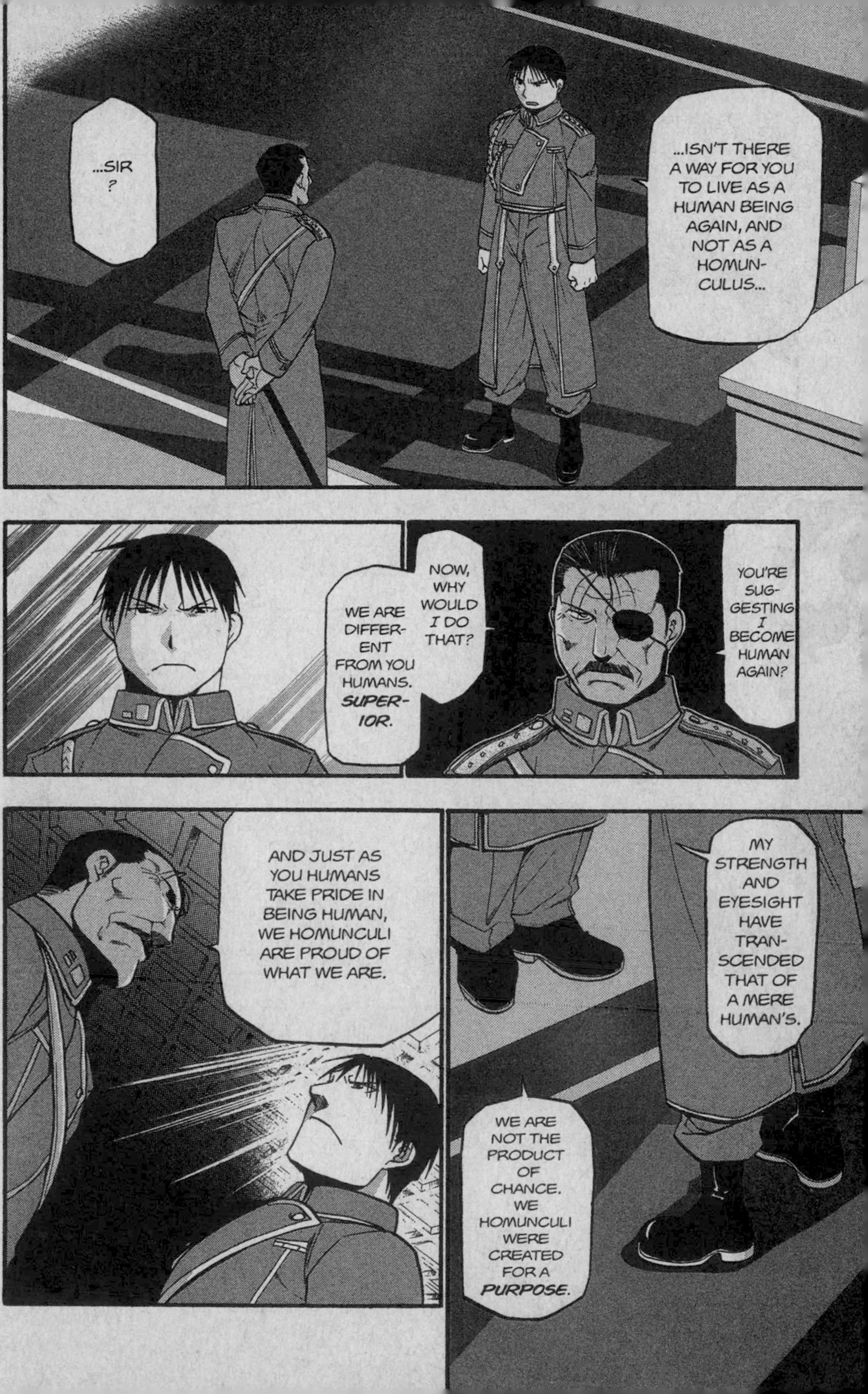
...ISN'T THERE A WAY FOR YOU TO LIVE AS A HUMAN BEING AGAIN, AND NOT AS A HOMUNCULUS...
...SIR?
YOU'RE SUGGESTING I BECOME HUMAN AGAIN?
NOW, WHY WOULD I DO THAT?
WE ARE DIFFERENT FROM YOU HUMANS. SUPERIOR.
MY STRENGTH AND EYESIGHT HAVE TRANSCENDED THAT OF A MERE HUMAN'S.
WE ARE NOT THE PRODUCT OF CHANCE. WE HOMUNCULI WERE CREATED FOR A PURPOSE.
AND JUST AS YOU HUMANS TAKE PRIDE IN BEING HUMAN, WE HOMUNCULI ARE PROUD OF WHAT WE ARE.

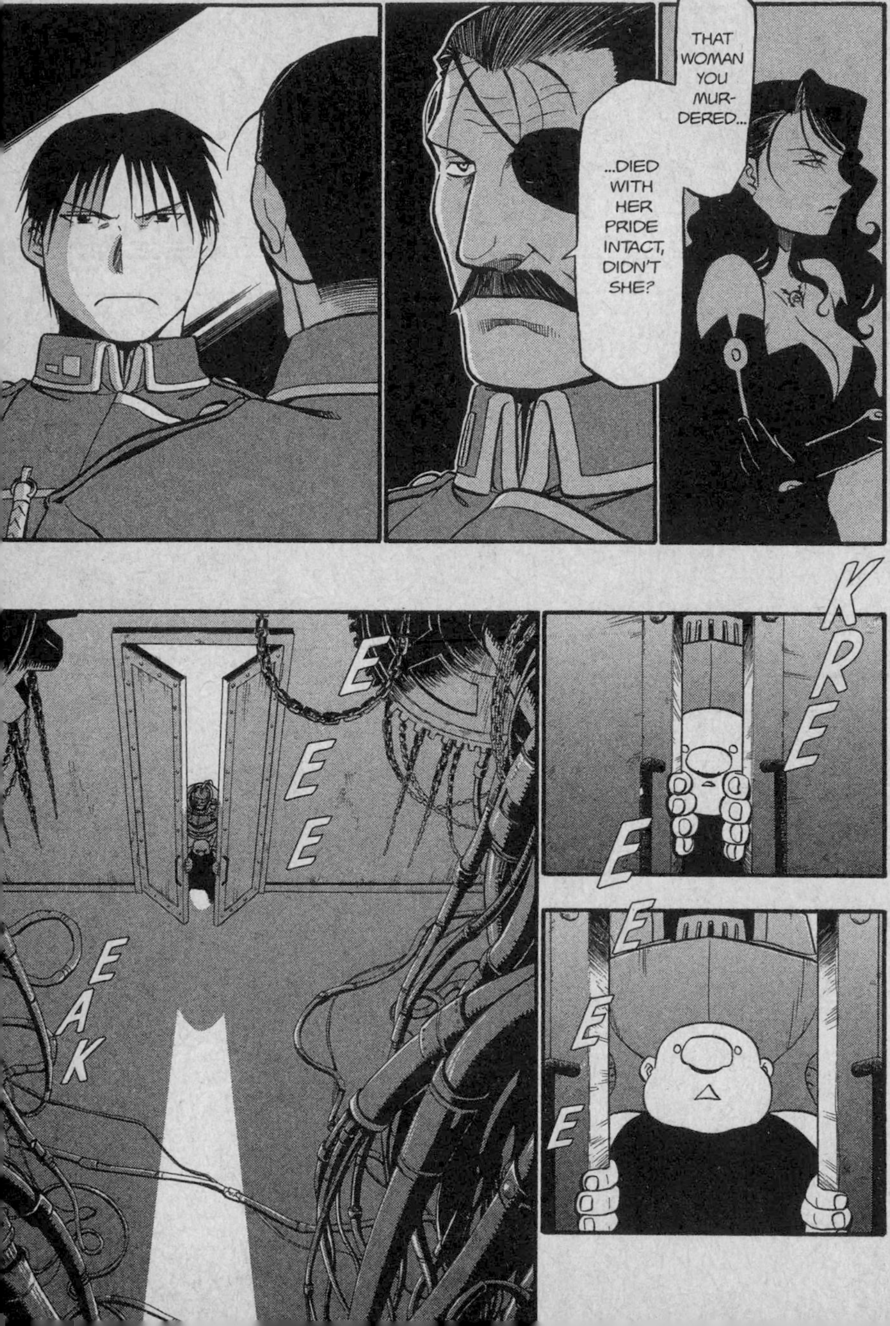
THAT WOMAN YOU MUR-DERED...
...DIED WITH HER PRIDE INTACT, DIDN'T SHE?
KREEEEEEE
EEEEAK

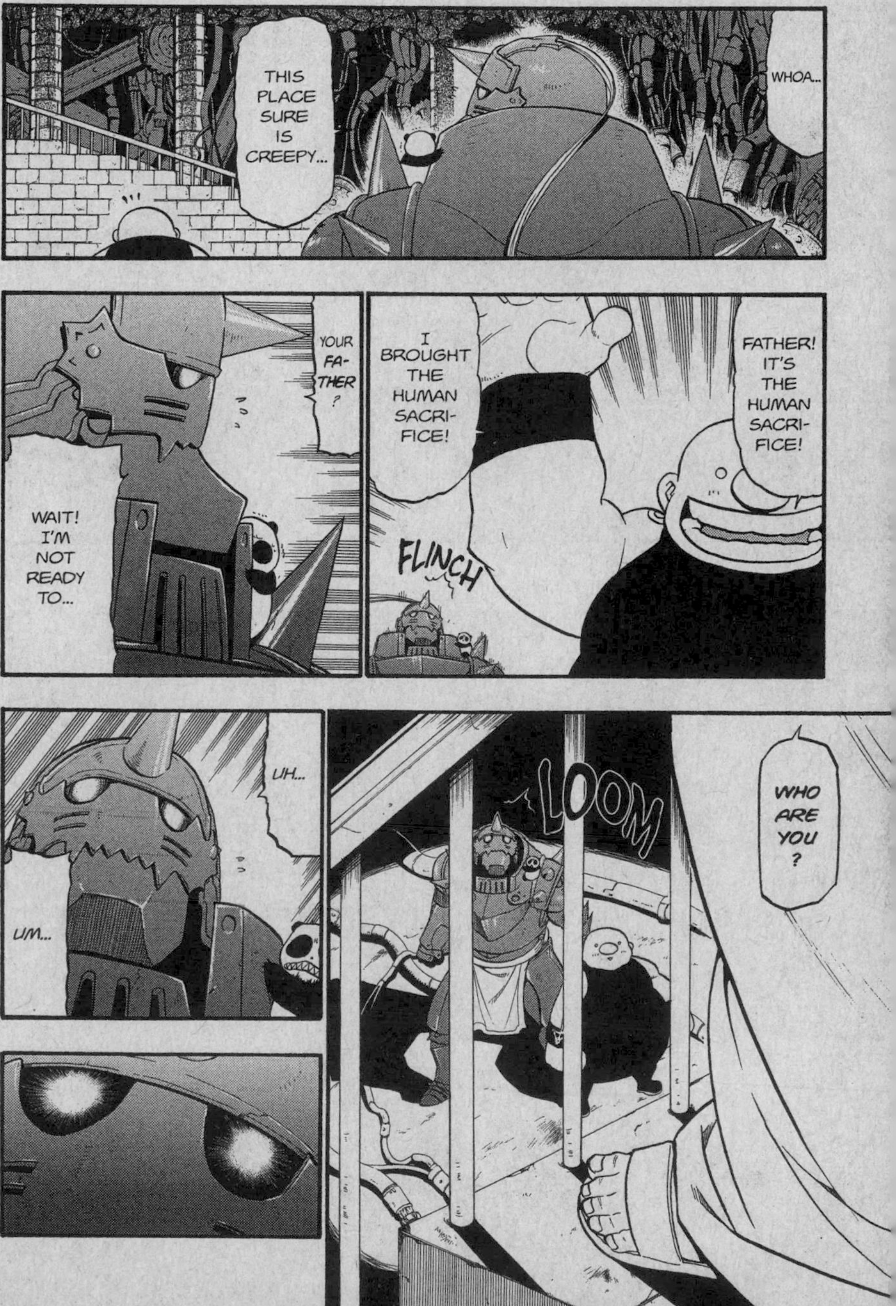
WHOA...
THIS PLACE SURE IS CREEPY...
FATHER! IT'S THE HUMAN SACRIFICE!
I BROUGHT THE HUMAN SACRIFICE!
FLINCH
YOUR FATHER?
WAIT! I'M NOT READY TO...
WHO ARE YOU?
LOOM
UH...
UM...

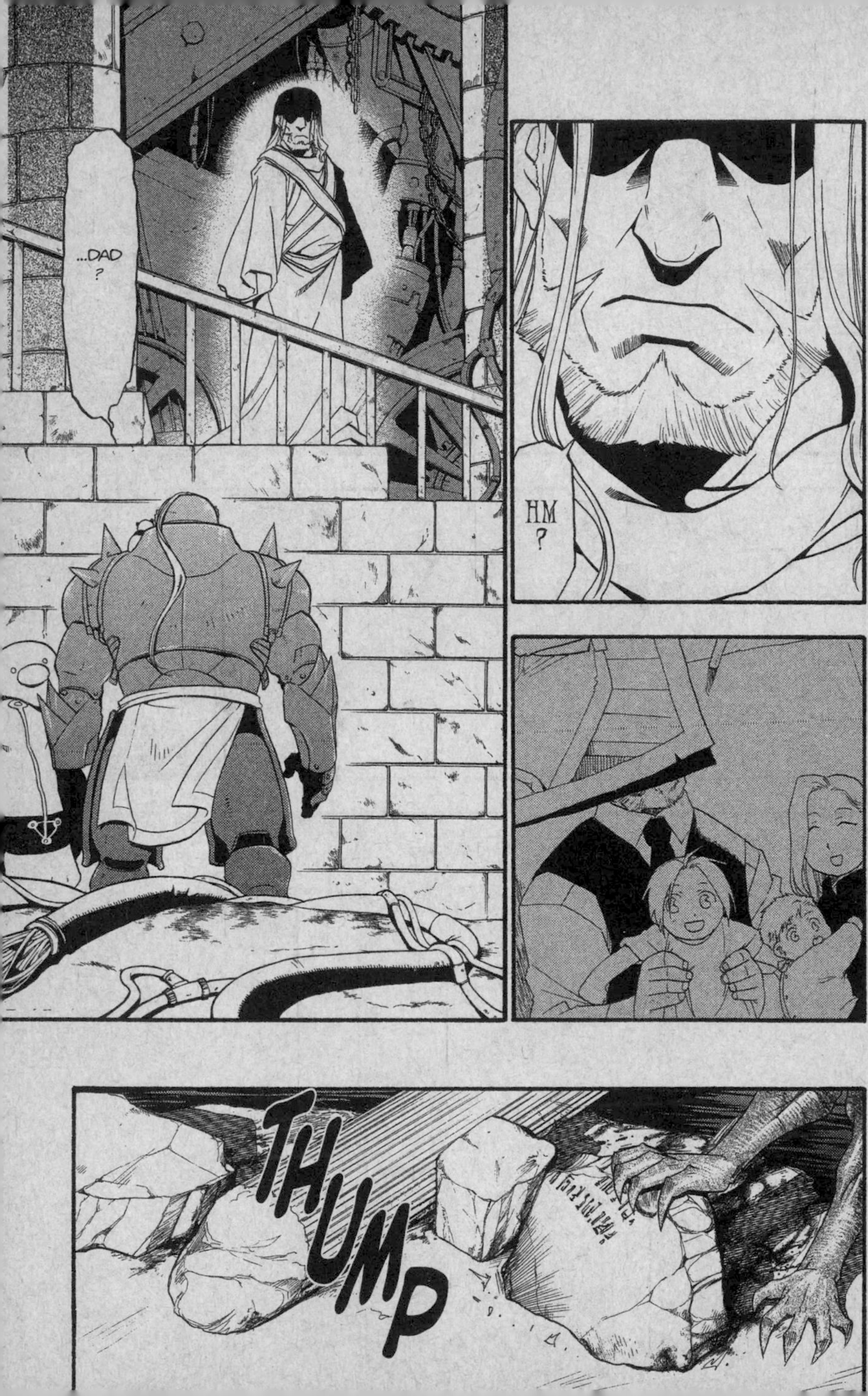
HM?
...DAD?
THUMP

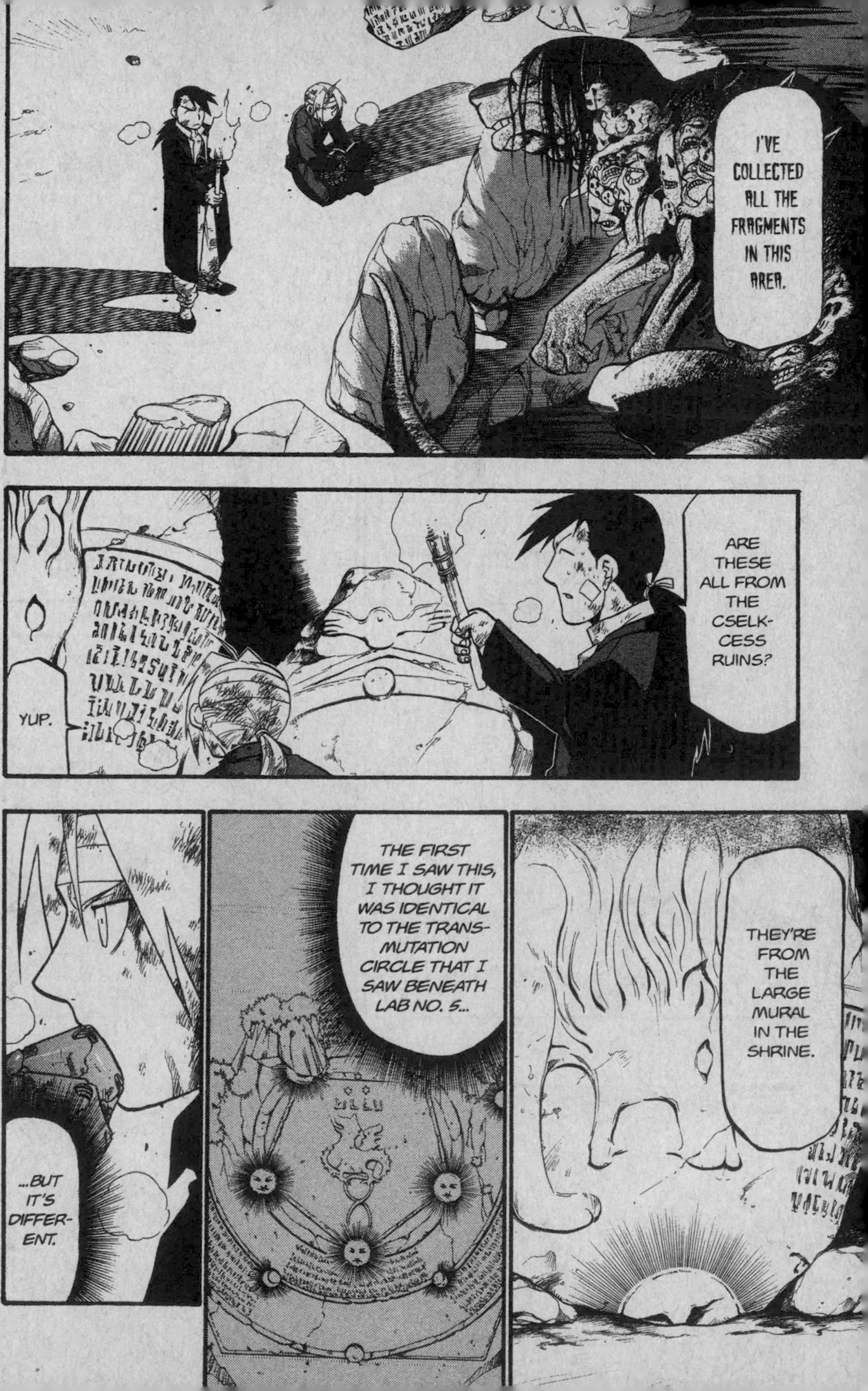
I'VE COLLECTED ALL THE FRAGMENTS IN THIS AREA.
ARE THESE ALL FROM THE CSELKCESS RUINS?
YUP.
THEY'RE FROM THE LARGE MURAL IN THE SHRINE.
THE FIRST TIME I SAW THIS, I THOUGHT IT WAS IDENTICAL TO THE TRANSMUTATION CIRCLE THAT I SAW BENEATH LAB NO. 5...
...BUT IT'S DIFFERENT.

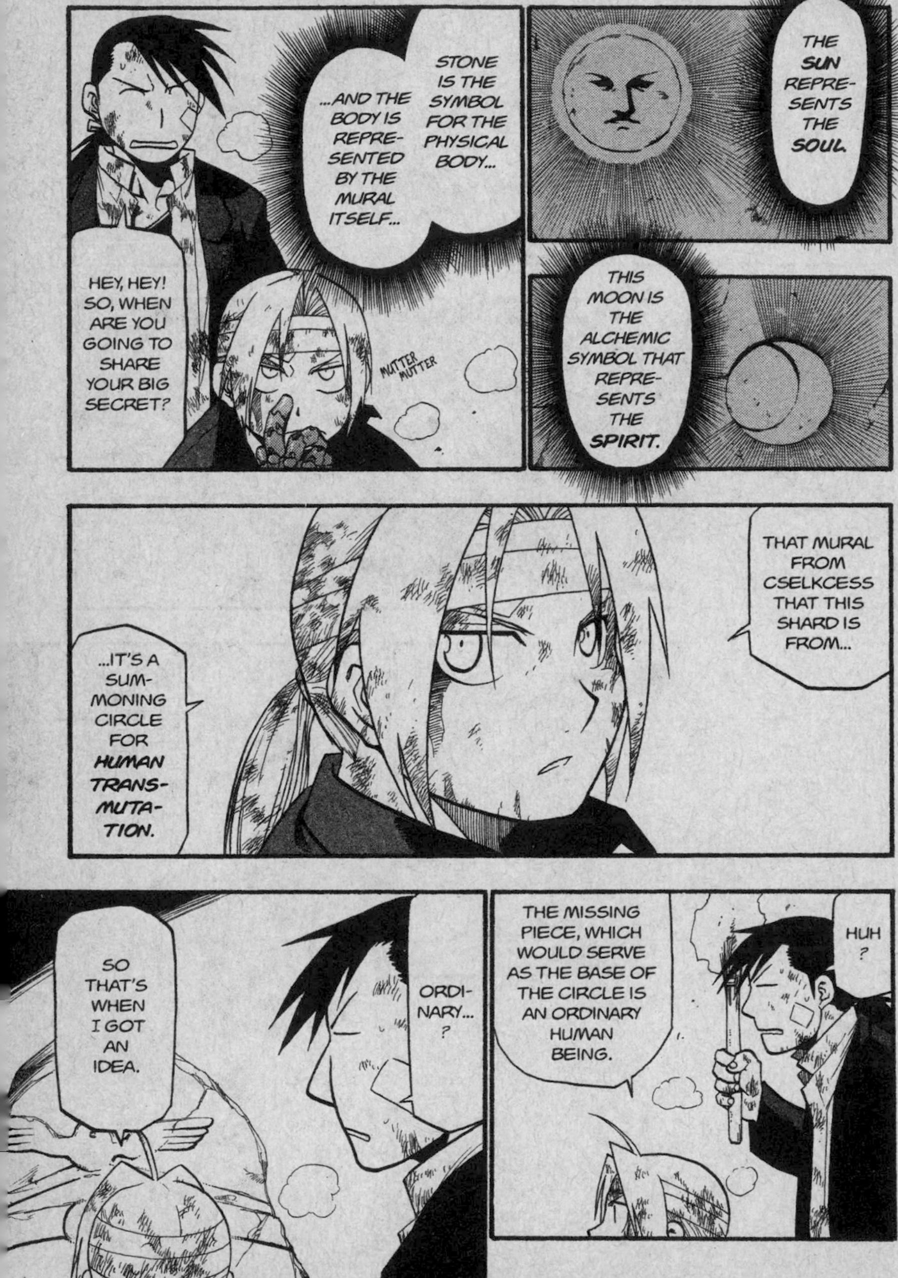
THE SUN REPRESENTS THE SOUL.
THIS MOON IS THE ALCHEMIC SYMBOL THAT REPRESENTS THE SPIRIT.
STONE IS THE SYMBOL FOR THE PHYSICAL BODY...
...AND THE BODY IS REPRESENTED BY THE MURAL ITSELF...
MUTTER MUTTER
HEY, HEY! SO, WHEN ARE YOU GOING TO SHARE YOUR BIG SECRET?
THAT MURAL FROM CSELKCESS THAT THIS SHARD IS FROM...
...IT'S A SUMMONING CIRCLE FOR HUMAN TRANSMUTATION.
HUH?
THE MISSING PIECE, WHICH WOULD SERVE AS THE BASE OF THE CIRCLE IS AN ORDINARY HUMAN BEING.
ORDINARY...?
SO THAT'S WHEN I GOT AN IDEA.

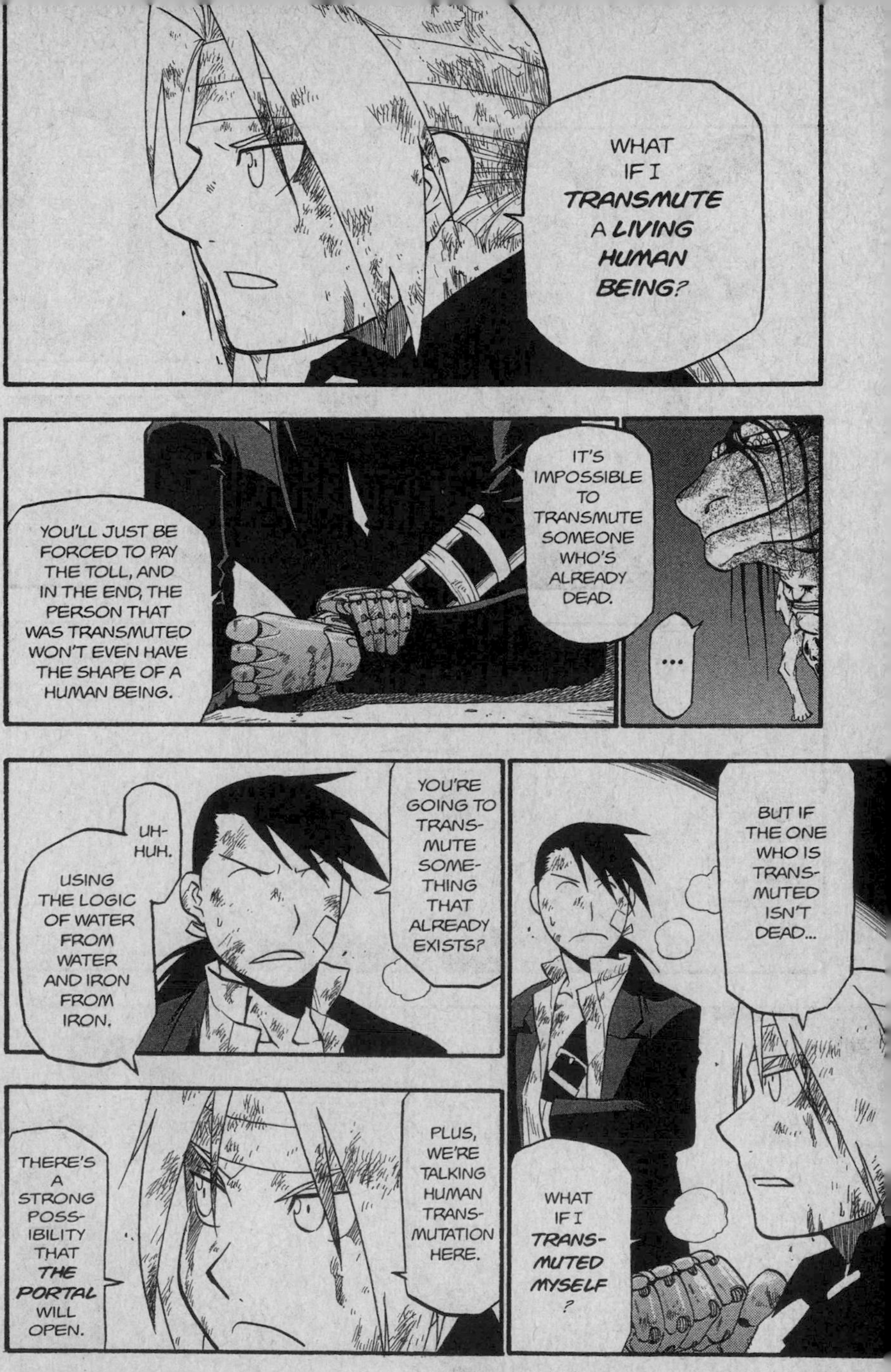
WHAT IF I TRANSMUTE A LIVING HUMAN BEING?
IT'S IMPOSSIBLE TO TRANSMUTE SOMEONE WHO'S ALREADY DEAD.
...
YOU'LL JUST BE FORCED TO PAY THE TOLL, AND IN THE END, THE PERSON THAT WAS TRANSMUTED WON'T EVEN HAVE THE SHAPE OF A HUMAN BEING.
BUT IF THE ONE WHO IS TRANSMUTED ISN'T DEAD...
WHAT IF I TRANSMUTED MYSELF?
YOU'RE GOING TO TRANSMUTE SOMETHING THAT ALREADY EXISTS?
UH-HUH.
USING THE LOGIC OF WATER FROM WATER AND IRON FROM IRON.
PLUS, WE'RE TALKING HUMAN TRANSMUTATION HERE.
THERE'S A STRONG POSSIBILITY THAT THE PORTAL WILL OPEN.

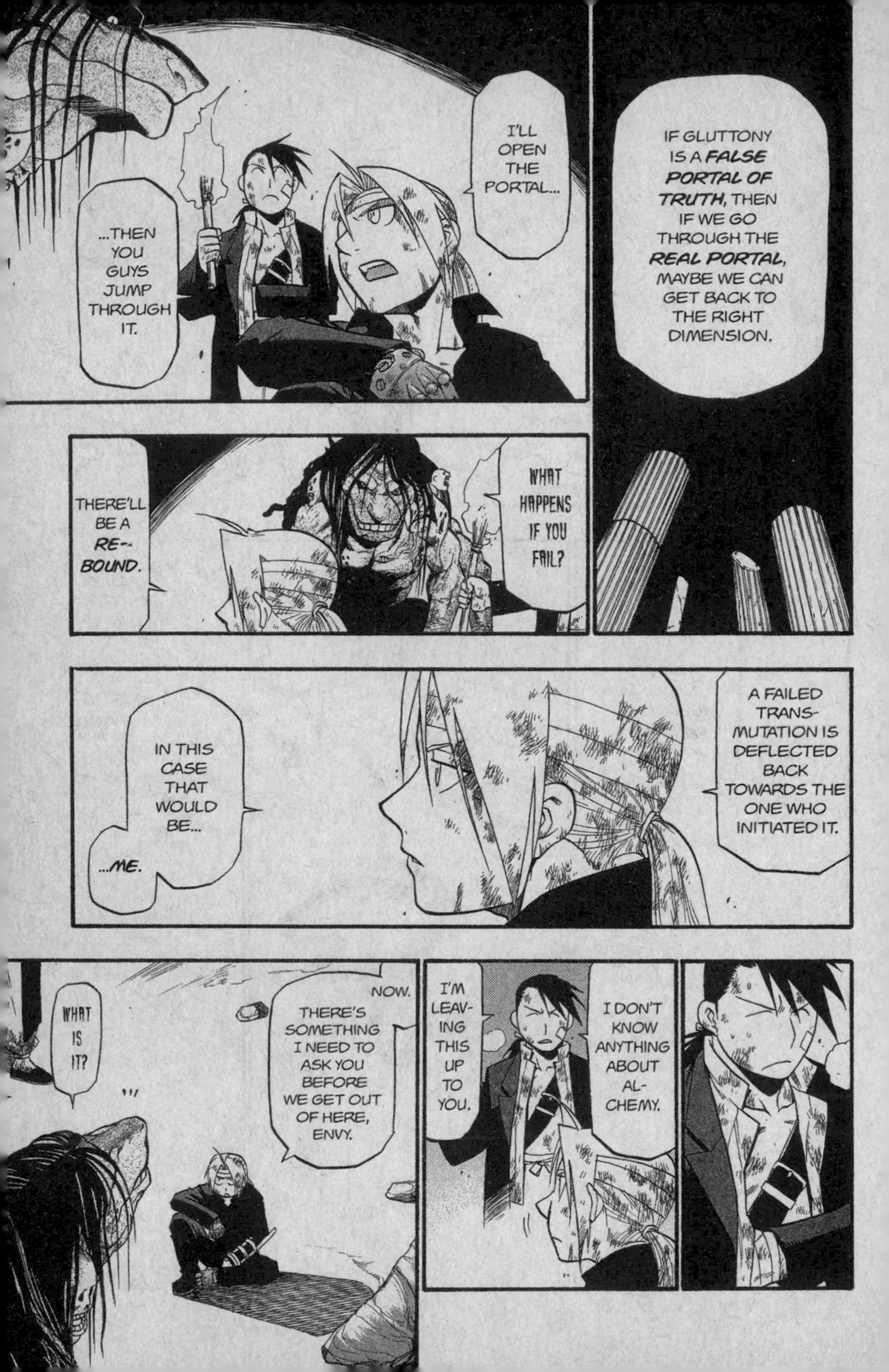
IF GLUTTONY IS A FALSE PORTAL OF TRUTH, THEN IF WE GO THROUGH THE REAL PORTAL, MAYBE WE CAN GET BACK TO THE RIGHT DIMENSION.
I'LL OPEN THE PORTAL...
...THEN YOU GUYS JUMP THROUGH IT.
WHAT HAPPENS IF YOU FAIL?
THERE'LL BE A RE--BOUND.
A FAILED TRANS-MUTATION IS DEFLECTED BACK TOWARDS THE ONE WHO INITIATED IT.
IN THIS CASE THAT WOULD BE...
...ME.
I DON'T KNOW ANYTHING ABOUT AL-CHEMY.
I'M LEAV-ING THIS UP TO YOU.
NOW.
THERE'S SOMETHING I NEED TO ASK YOU BEFORE WE GET OUT OF HERE, ENVY.
WHAT IS IT?

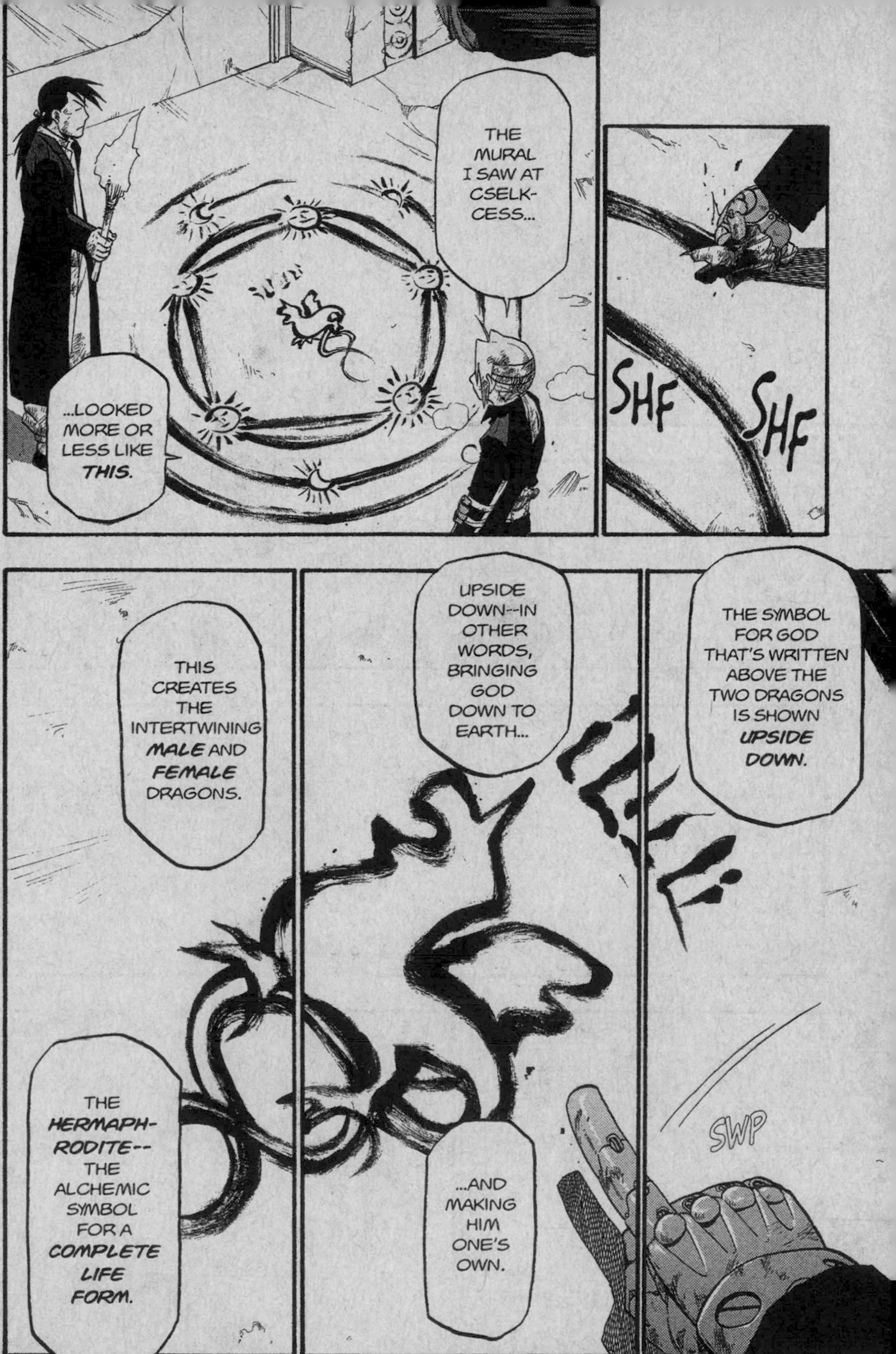
SHF SHF
THE MURAL I SAW AT CSELKCESS...
...LOOKED MORE OR LESS LIKE *THIS*.
THE SYMBOL FOR GOD THAT'S WRITTEN ABOVE THE TWO DRAGONS IS SHOWN ***UPSIDE DOWN***.
SWP
UPSIDE DOWN--IN OTHER WORDS, BRINGING GOD DOWN TO EARTH...
...AND MAKING HIM ONE'S OWN.
THIS CREATES THE INTERTWINING ***MALE*** AND ***FEMALE*** DRAGONS.
THE ***HERMAPHRODITE***--THE ALCHEMIC SYMBOL FOR A ***COMPLETE LIFE FORM***.

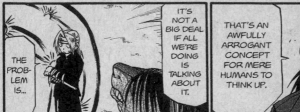

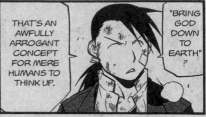

"BRING GOD DOWN TO EARTH" ?
THAT'S AN AWFULLY ARROGANT CONCEPT FOR MERE HUMANS TO THINK UP.
IT'S NOT A BIG DEAL IF ALL WE'RE DOING IS TALKING ABOUT IT.
THE PROBLEM IS...
THIS.
THE MISSING PIECE SHOWS THE SUN BEING SWALLOWED BY THE LION.
IT SYMBOLIZES THE *PHILOSOPHER'S STONE*.
THE PHILOSOPHER'S STONE IS MADE OF LIVING HUMAN BEINGS...
...RIGHT, ENVY ?
THAT'S RIGHT.
MORE ACCURATELY, IT'S A HIGH-ENERGY SUBSTANCE THAT'S CREATED BY EXTRACTING SOULS FROM HUMAN BODIES AND CONDENSING IT.
THE SPIRIT AND THE PHYSICAL BODY ARE NOTHING BUT BY-PRODUCTS.
WHEN I WENT TO THE CSELKCESS RUINS, I COULDN'T BELIEVE THAT A COUNTRY WITH SUCH ADVANCED TECHNOLOGY COULD BE DESTROYED IN ONE NIGHT.
AND THERE'S NOTHING IN THE LEGENDS THAT SAYS THEY EMIGRATED TO A DIFFERENT COUNTRY EITHER.

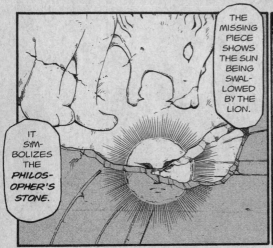

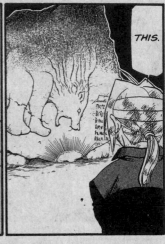

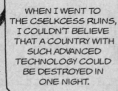

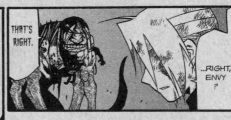

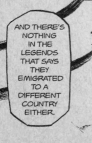

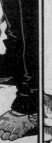

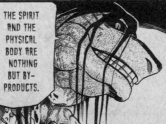

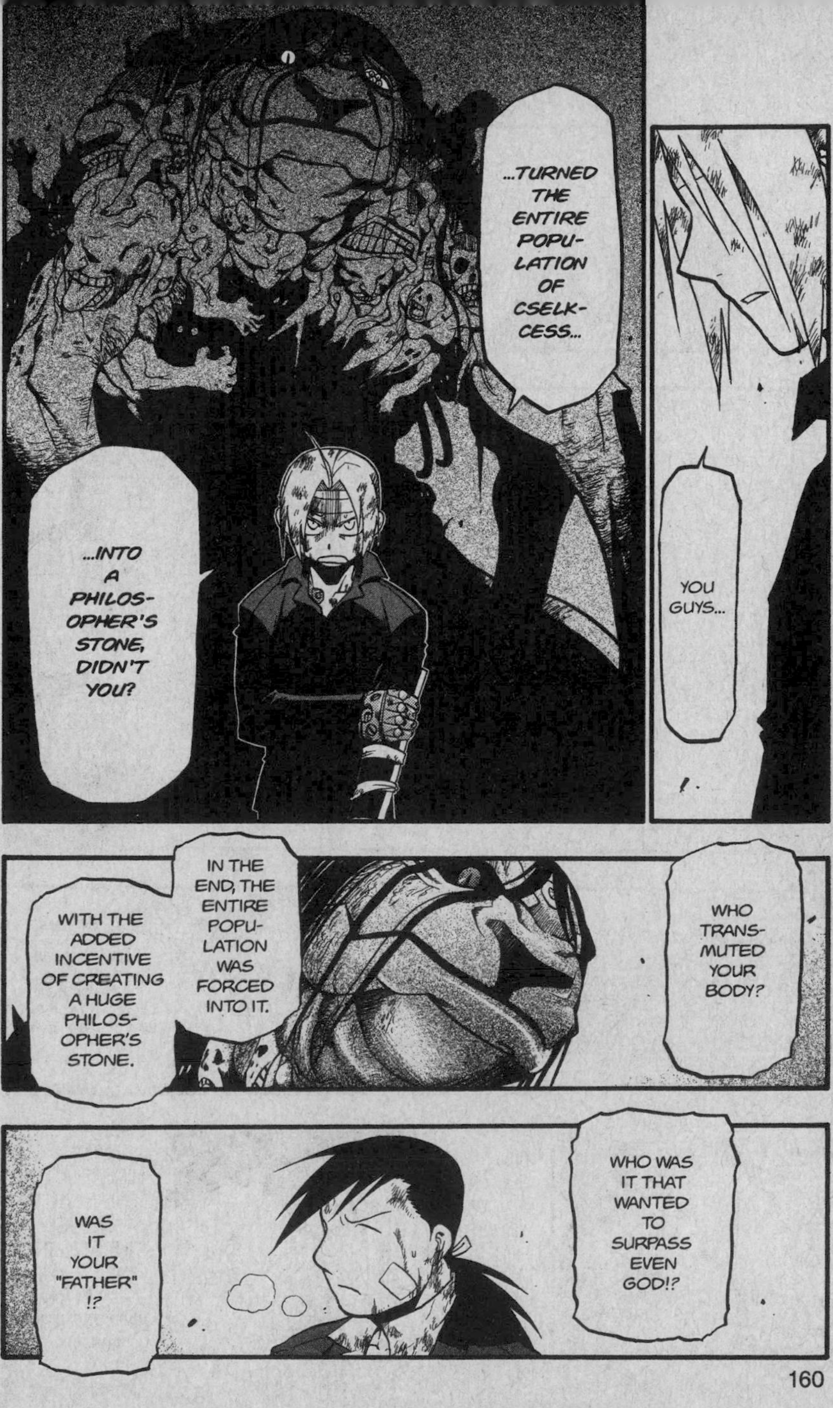
YOU GUYS...
...TURNED THE ENTIRE POPULATION OF CSELKCESS...
...INTO A PHILOSOPHER'S STONE, DIDN'T YOU?
WHO TRANSMUTED YOUR BODY?
IN THE END, THE ENTIRE POPULATION WAS FORCED INTO IT.
WITH THE ADDED INCENTIVE OF CREATING A HUGE PHILOSOPHER'S STONE.
WHO WAS IT THAT WANTED TO SURPASS EVEN GOD!?
WAS IT YOUR "FATHER"!?

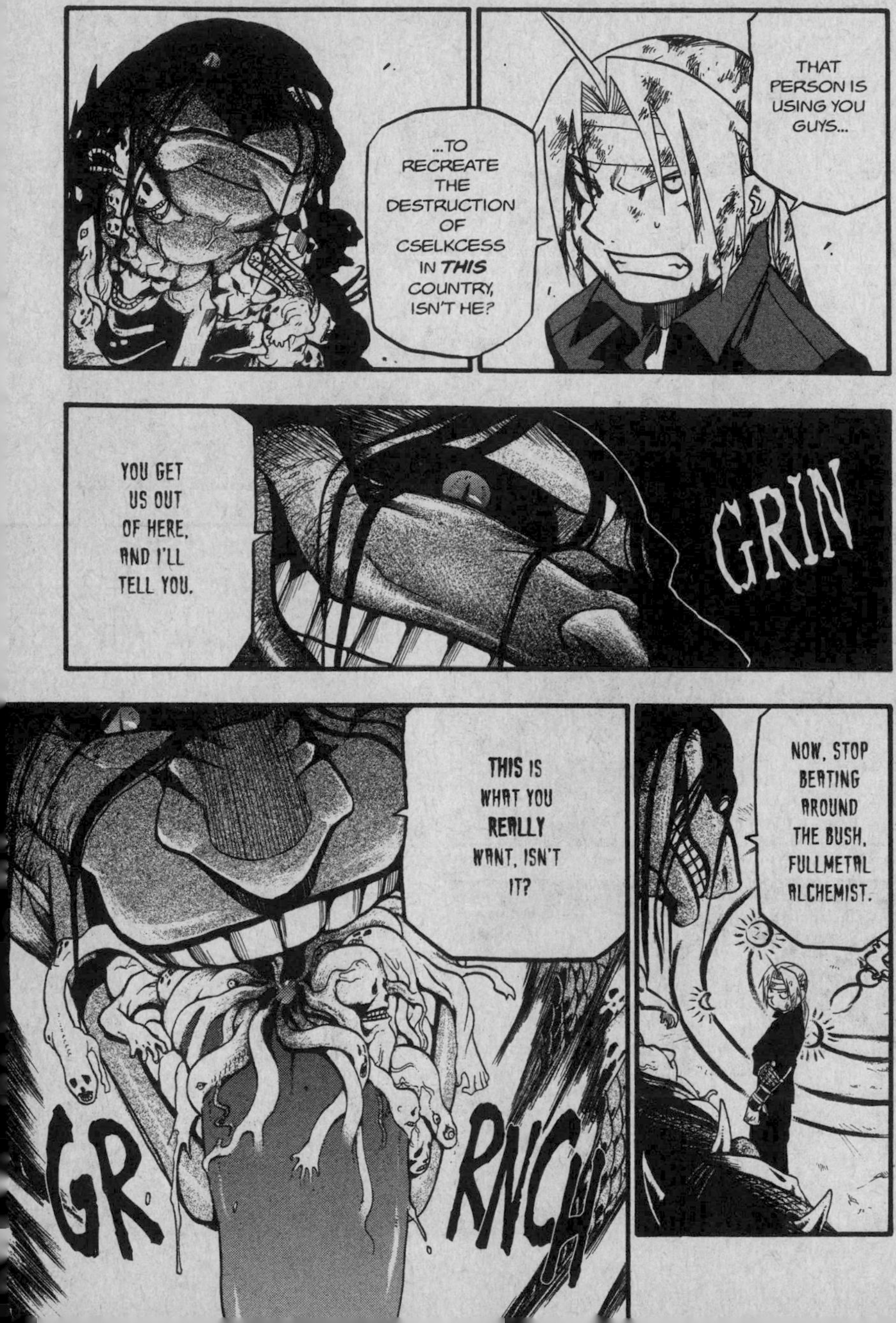
THAT PERSON IS USING YOU GUYS...
...TO RECREATE THE DESTRUCTION OF CSELKCESS IN **THIS** COUNTRY, ISN'T HE?
GRIN
YOU GET US OUT OF HERE, AND I'LL TELL YOU.
NOW, STOP BEATING AROUND THE BUSH, FULLMETAL ALCHEMIST.
THIS IS WHAT YOU REALLY WANT, ISN'T IT?
GR
RNCH

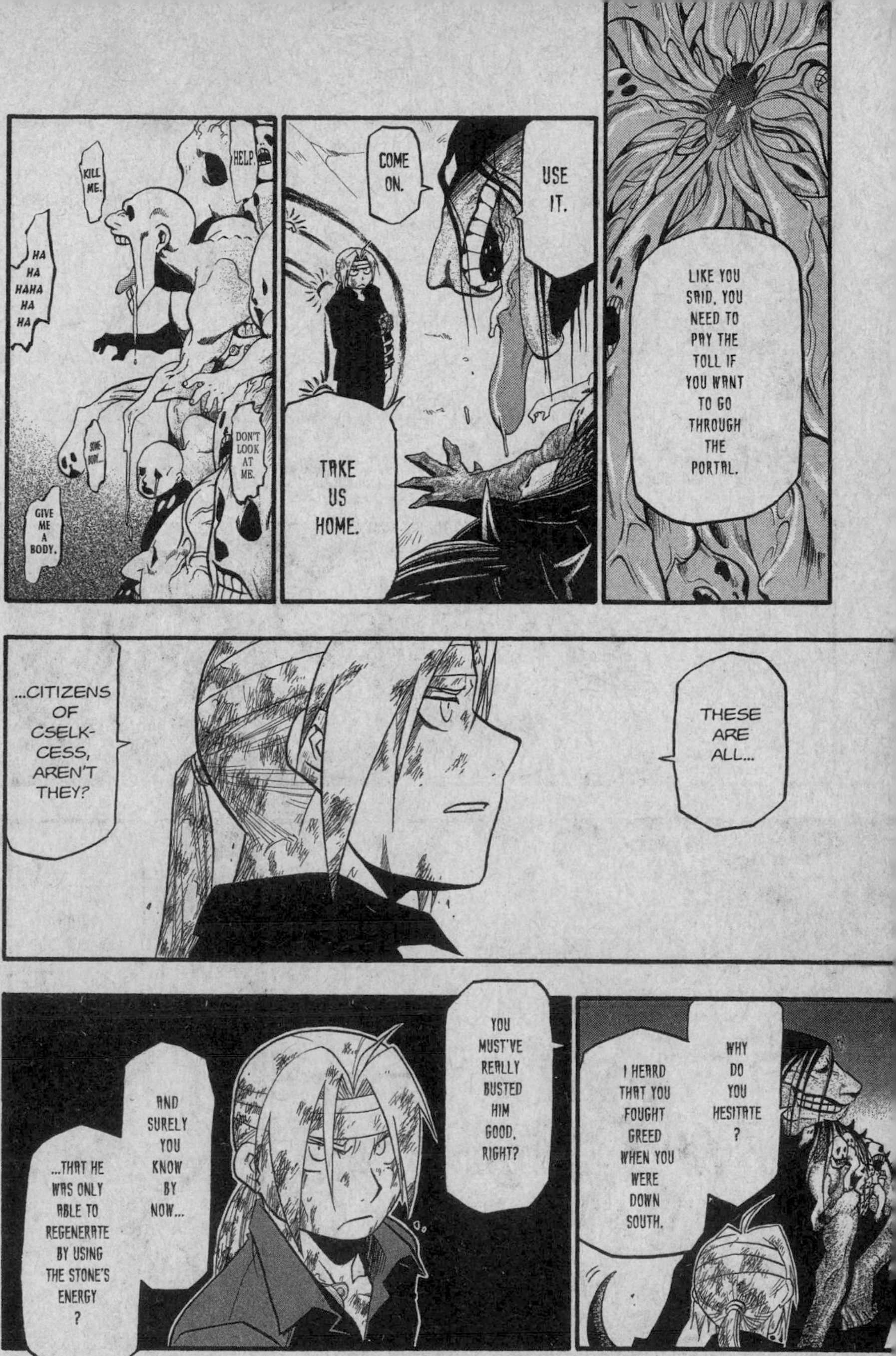
LIKE YOU SAID, YOU NEED TO PAY THE TOLL IF YOU WANT TO GO THROUGH THE PORTAL.
USE IT.
COME ON.
TAKE US HOME.
HELP.
KILL ME.
HA HA HAHA HA HA
DON'T LOOK AT ME.
SOME-BODY...
GIVE ME A BODY.
THESE ARE ALL...
...CITIZENS OF CSELK-CESS, AREN'T THEY?
WHY DO YOU HESITATE?
I HEARD THAT YOU FOUGHT GREED WHEN YOU WERE DOWN SOUTH.
YOU MUST'VE REALLY BUSTED HIM GOOD, RIGHT?
AND SURELY YOU KNOW BY NOW...
...THAT HE WAS ONLY ABLE TO REGENERATE BY USING THE STONE'S ENERGY?

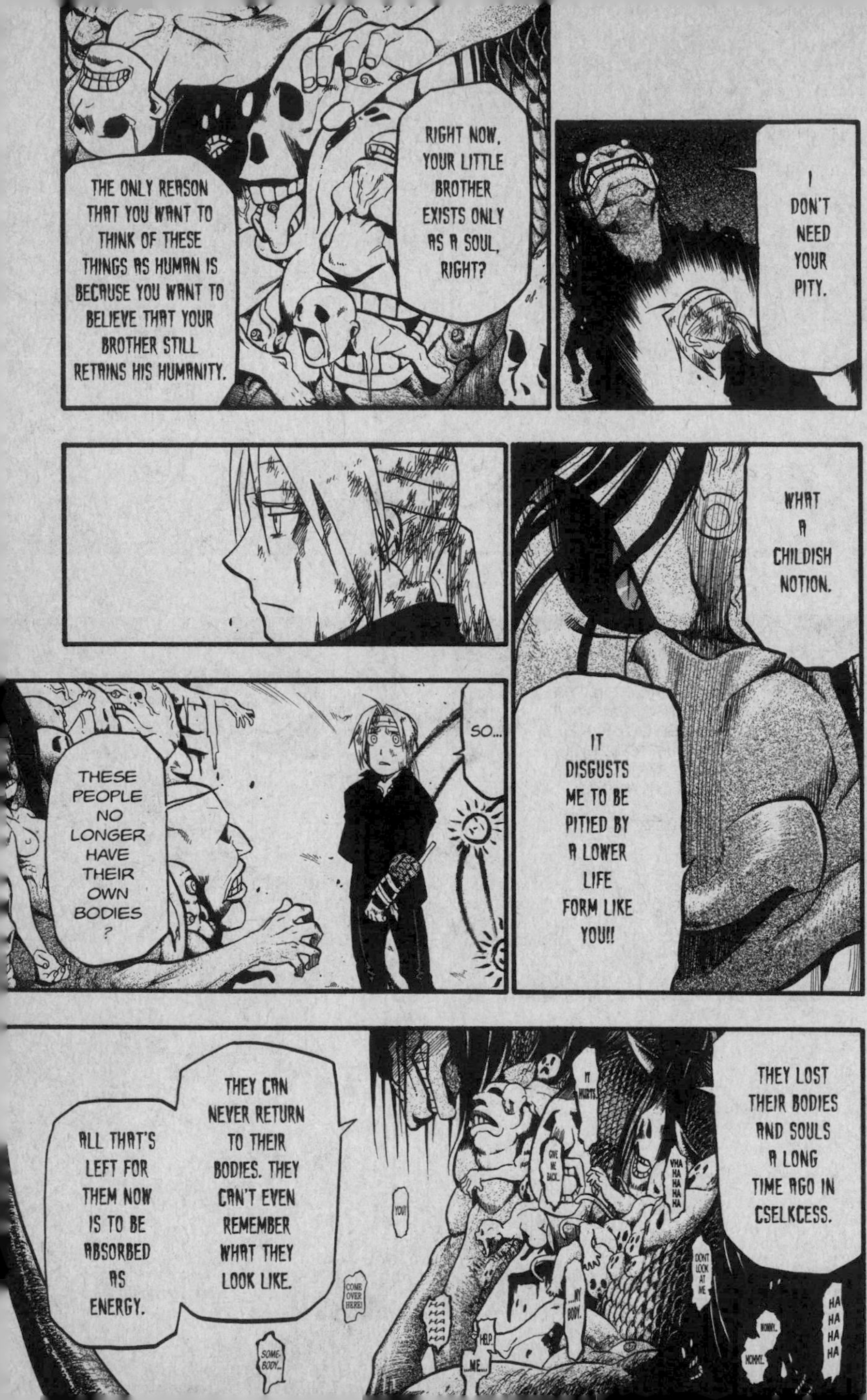
I DON'T NEED YOUR PITY.
RIGHT NOW, YOUR LITTLE BROTHER EXISTS ONLY AS A SOUL, RIGHT?
THE ONLY REASON THAT YOU WANT TO THINK OF THESE THINGS AS HUMAN IS BECAUSE YOU WANT TO BELIEVE THAT YOUR BROTHER STILL RETAINS HIS HUMANITY.
WHAT A CHILDISH NOTION.
IT DISGUSTS ME TO BE PITIED BY A LOWER LIFE FORM LIKE YOU!!
SO...
THESE PEOPLE NO LONGER HAVE THEIR OWN BODIES ?
THEY LOST THEIR BODIES AND SOULS A LONG TIME AGO IN CSELKCESS.
IT HURTS.
GIVE ME BACK.
VHA HA HA HA HA
DONT LOOK AT ME
HA HA HA HA
MOMMY.
MOMMY.
...MY BODY.
HELP.
...ME...
HA HA HA HA HA
YOU!
COME OVER HERE!
SOME-BODY...
THEY CAN NEVER RETURN TO THEIR BODIES. THEY CAN'T EVEN REMEMBER WHAT THEY LOOK LIKE.
ALL THAT'S LEFT FOR THEM NOW IS TO BE ABSORBED AS ENERGY.

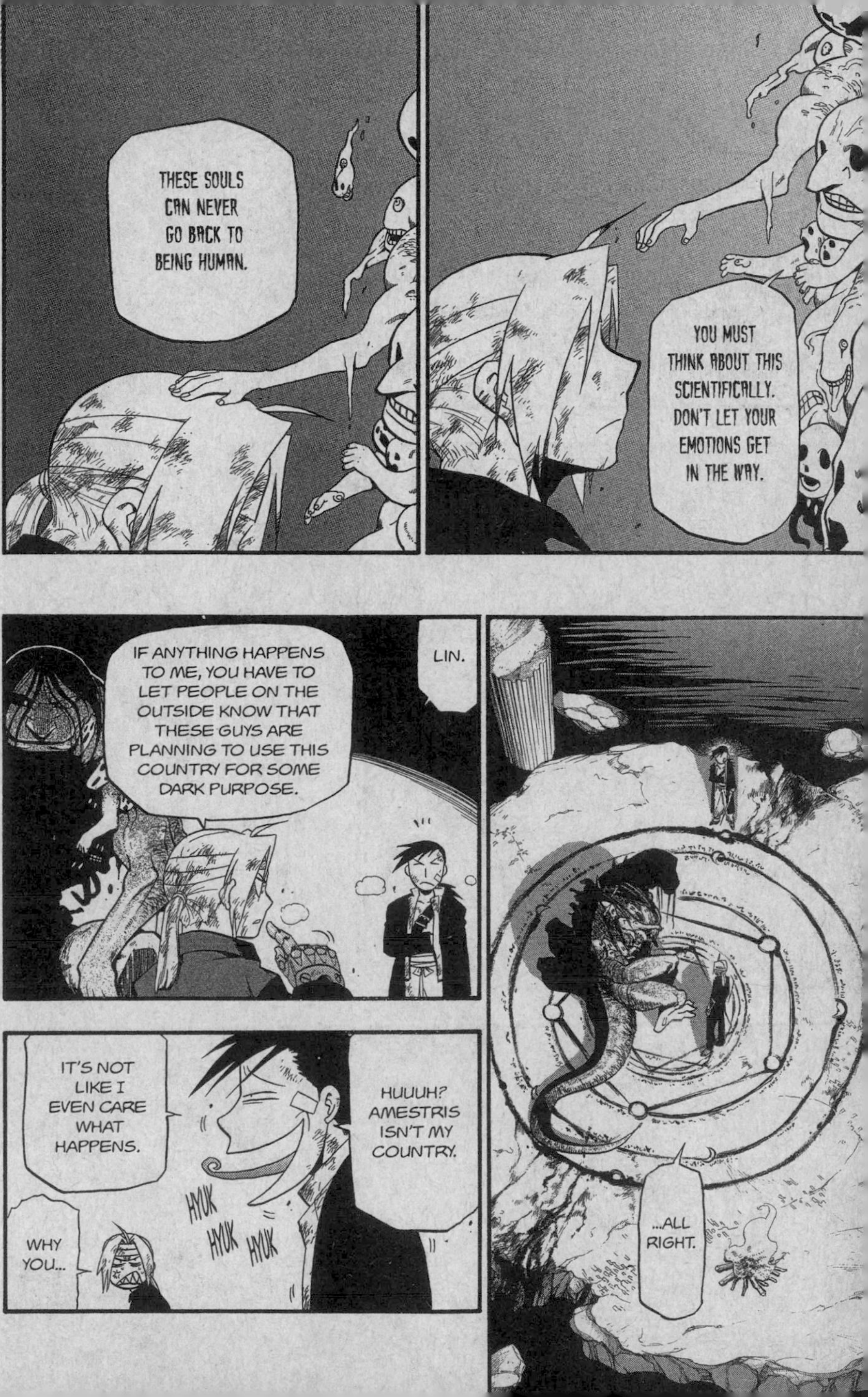
YOU MUST THINK ABOUT THIS SCIENTIFICALLY. DON'T LET YOUR EMOTIONS GET IN THE WAY.
THESE SOULS CAN NEVER GO BACK TO BEING HUMAN.
...ALL RIGHT.
LIN.
IF ANYTHING HAPPENS TO ME, YOU HAVE TO LET PEOPLE ON THE OUTSIDE KNOW THAT THESE GUYS ARE PLANNING TO USE THIS COUNTRY FOR SOME DARK PURPOSE.
HUUUH? AMESTRIS ISN'T MY COUNTRY.
IT'S NOT LIKE I EVEN CARE WHAT HAPPENS.
HYUK HYUK HYUK
WHY YOU...

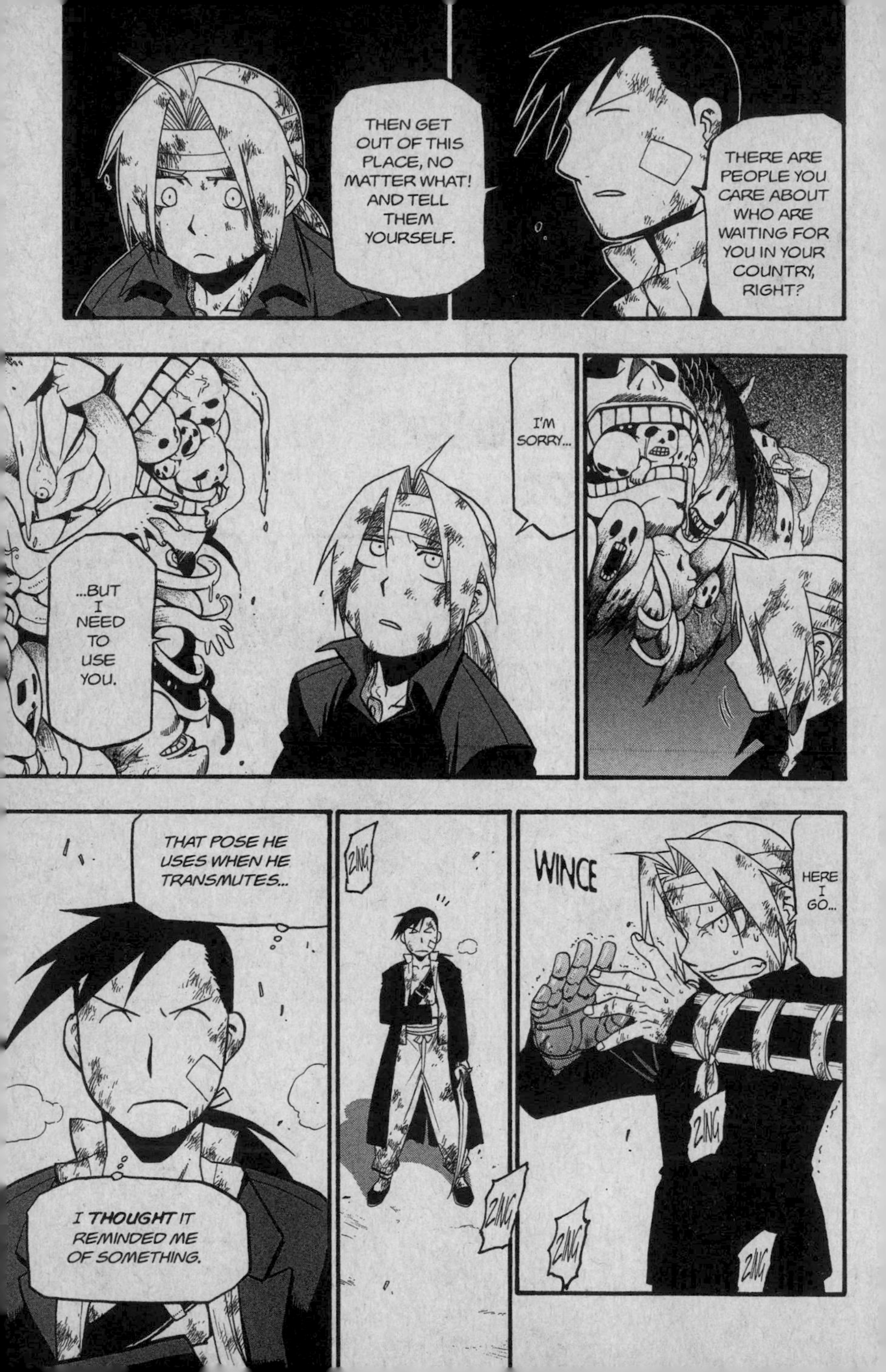
THERE ARE PEOPLE YOU CARE ABOUT WHO ARE WAITING FOR YOU IN YOUR COUNTRY, RIGHT?
THEN GET OUT OF THIS PLACE, NO MATTER WHAT! AND TELL THEM YOURSELF.
I'M SORRY...
...BUT I NEED TO USE YOU.
WINCE
HERE I GO...
ZING
ZING
ZING
ZING
ZING
THAT POSE HE USES WHEN HE TRANSMUTES...
I *THOUGHT* IT REMINDED ME OF SOMETHING.

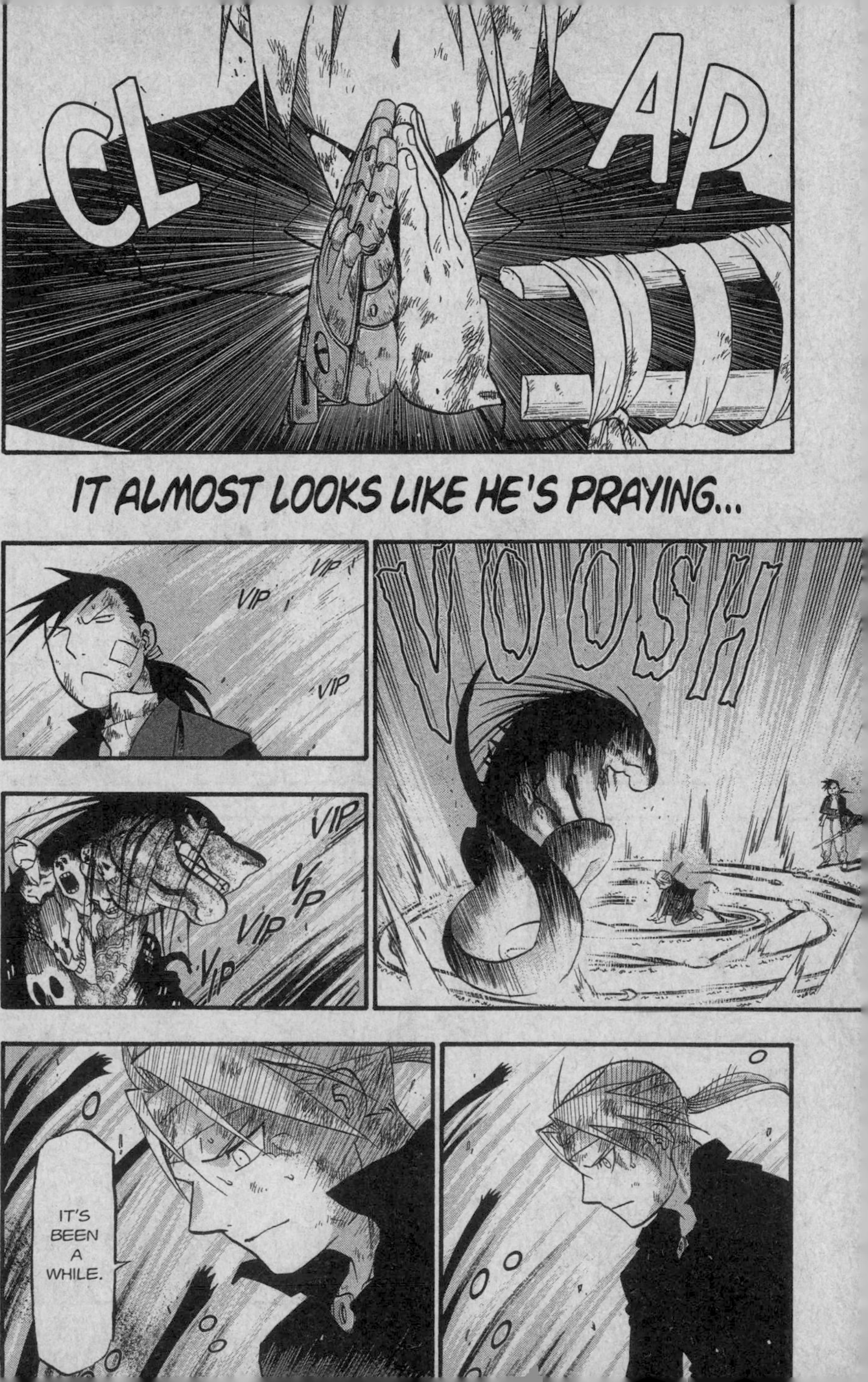
CLAP
IT ALMOST LOOKS LIKE HE'S PRAYING...
VOOSH
VIP
VIP
VIP
VIP
VIP
VIP
VIP
IT'S BEEN A WHILE.

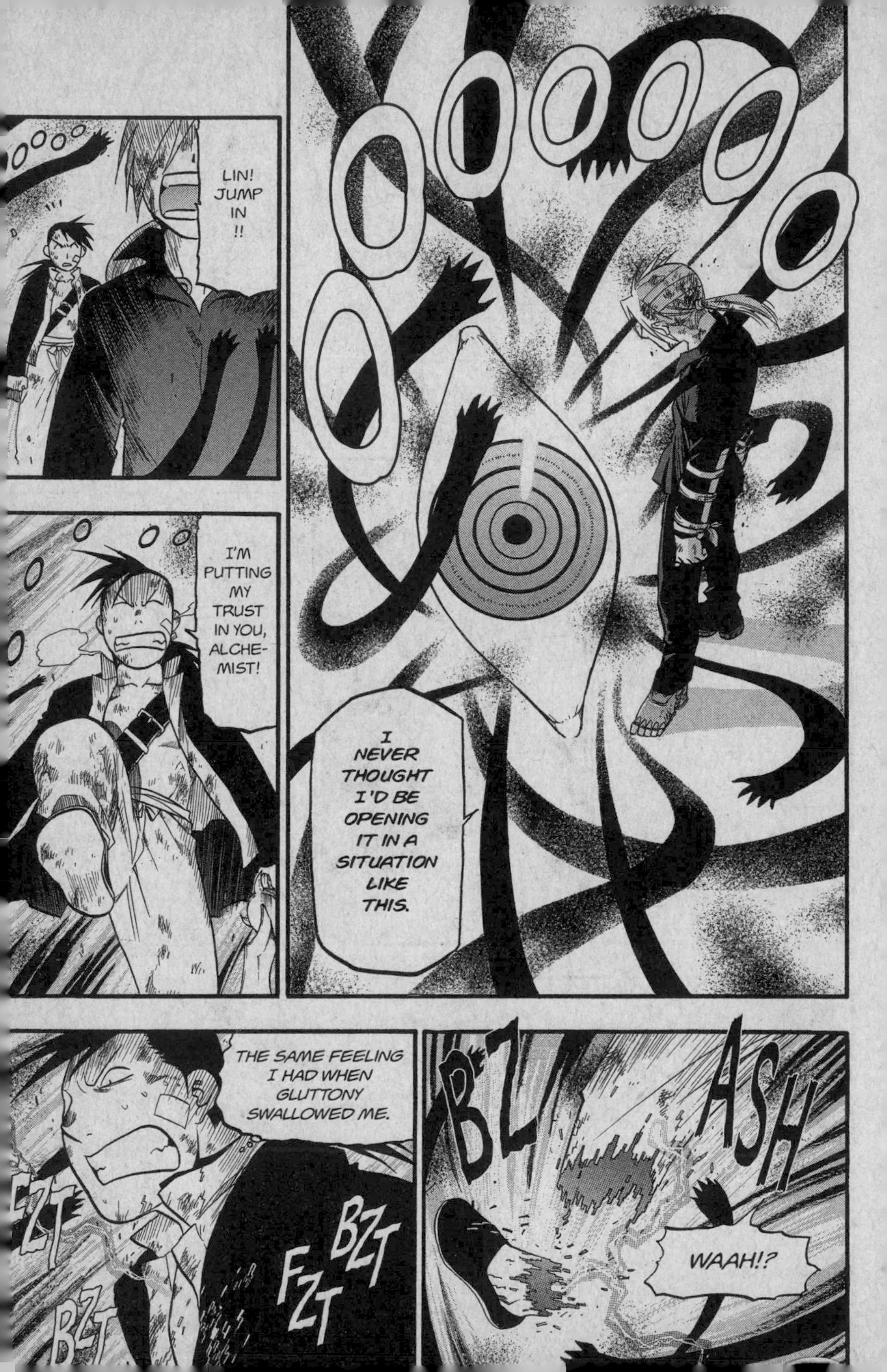
I NEVER THOUGHT I'D BE OPENING IT IN A SITUATION LIKE THIS.
LIN! JUMP IN !!
I'M PUTTING MY TRUST IN YOU, ALCHEMIST!
BZASH
WAAH!?
THE SAME FEELING I HAD WHEN GLUTTONY SWALLOWED ME.
FZT
BZT
FZT
BZT

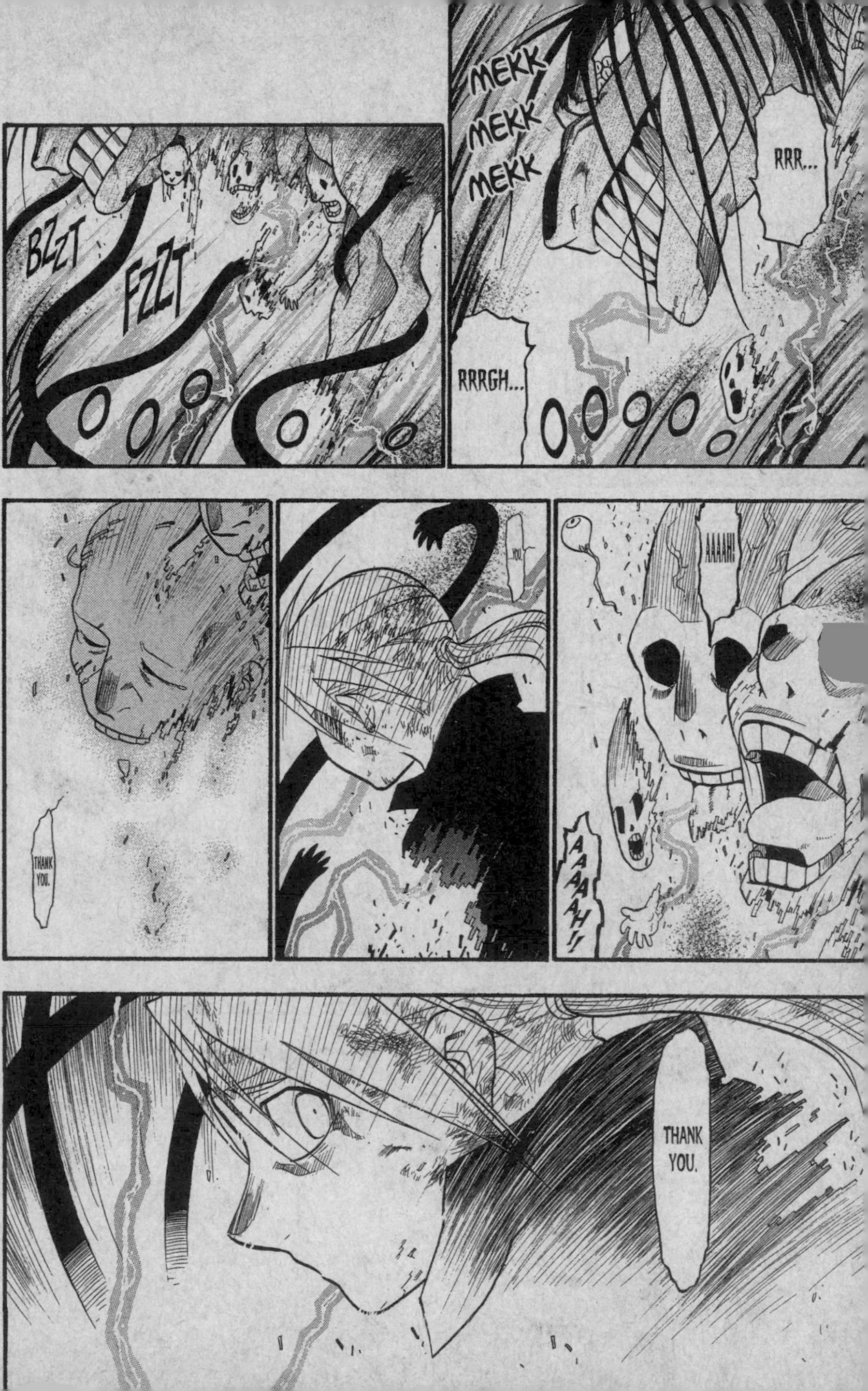
MEKK
MEKK
MEKK
RRR...
RRRGH...
BZZT
FZZT
AAAAH!
AAAAAH!!
...YOU.
THANK YOU.
THANK YOU.

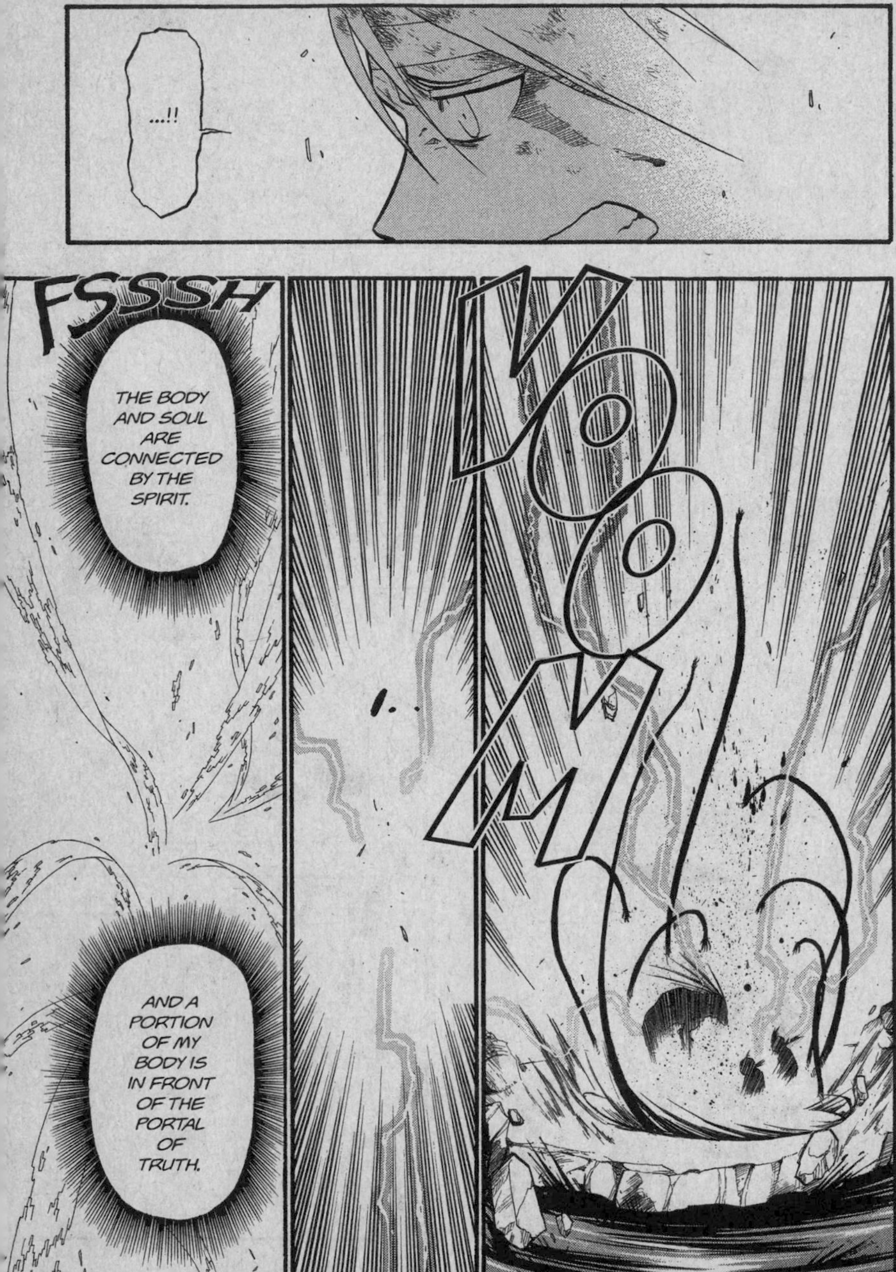
...!!
VOOOM
!..
FSSSH
THE BODY AND SOUL ARE CONNECTED BY THE SPIRIT.
AND A PORTION OF MY BODY IS IN FRONT OF THE PORTAL OF TRUTH.

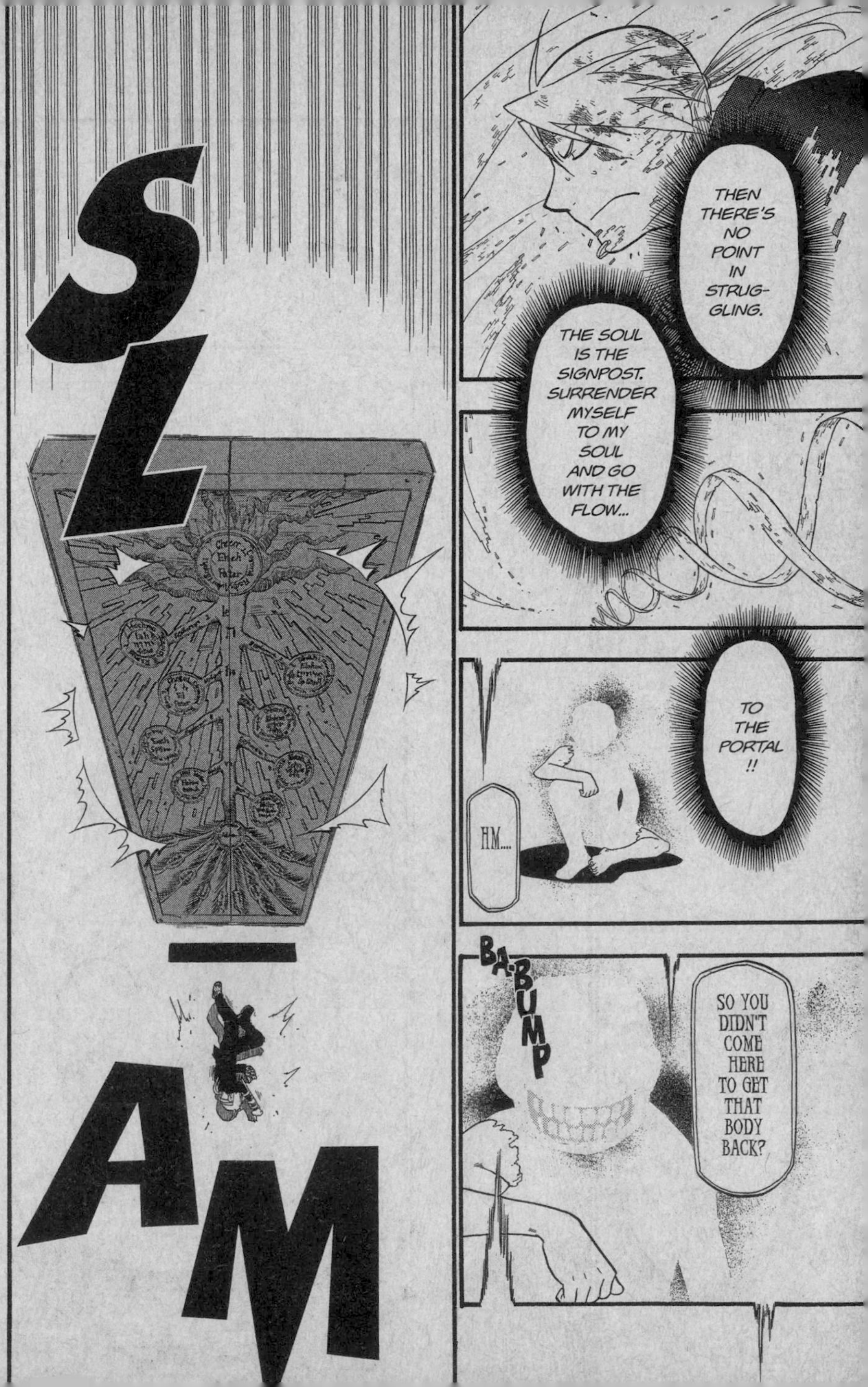
THEN THERE'S NO POINT IN STRUG-GLING.
THE SOUL IS THE SIGNPOST. SURRENDER MYSELF TO MY SOUL AND GO WITH THE FLOW...
TO THE PORTAL !!
HM....
BA-BUMP
SO YOU DIDN'T COME HERE TO GET THAT BODY BACK?
SLAM

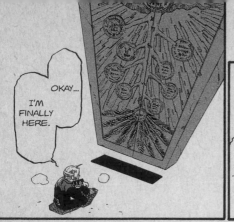

OKAY...

I'M FINALLY HERE.

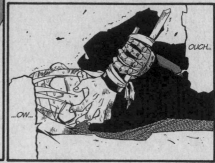

OUCH..

...OW...

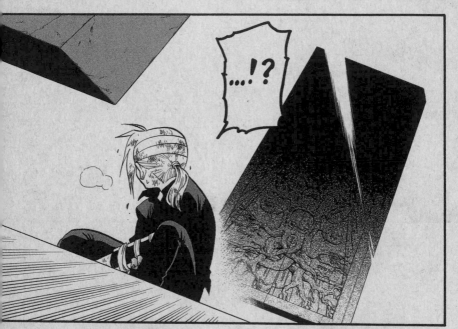

....!?

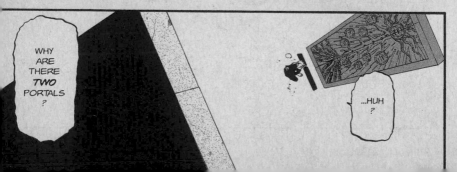

WHY ARE THERE *TWO* PORTALS ?

...HUH ?

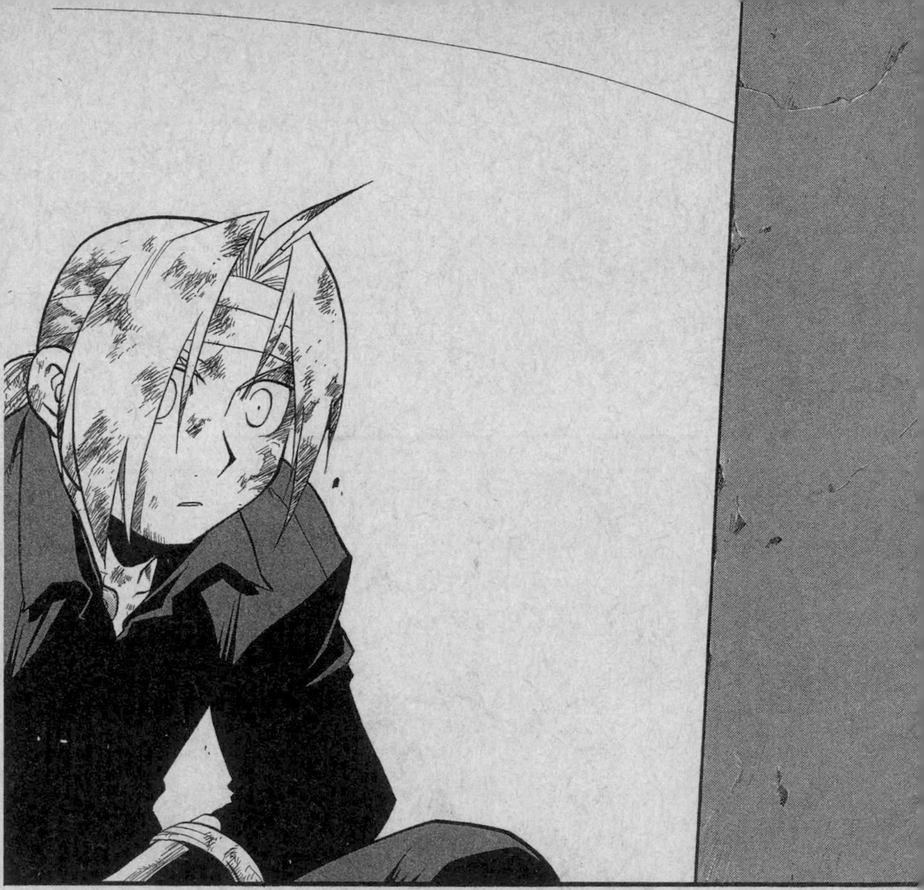
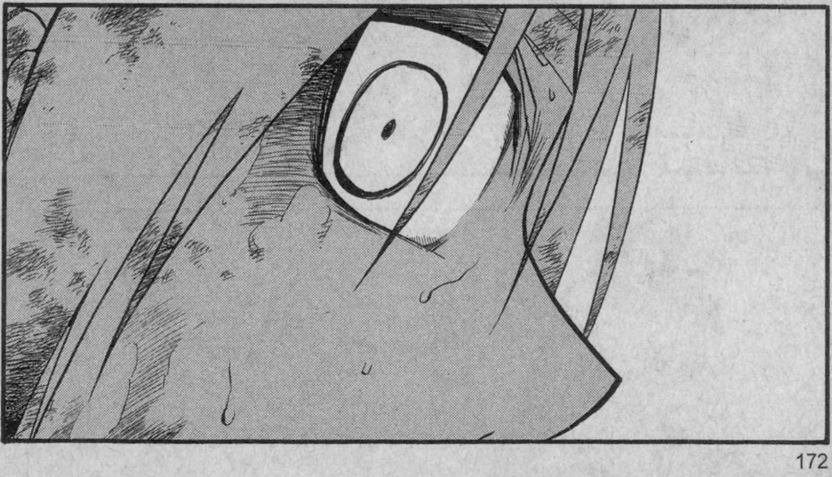

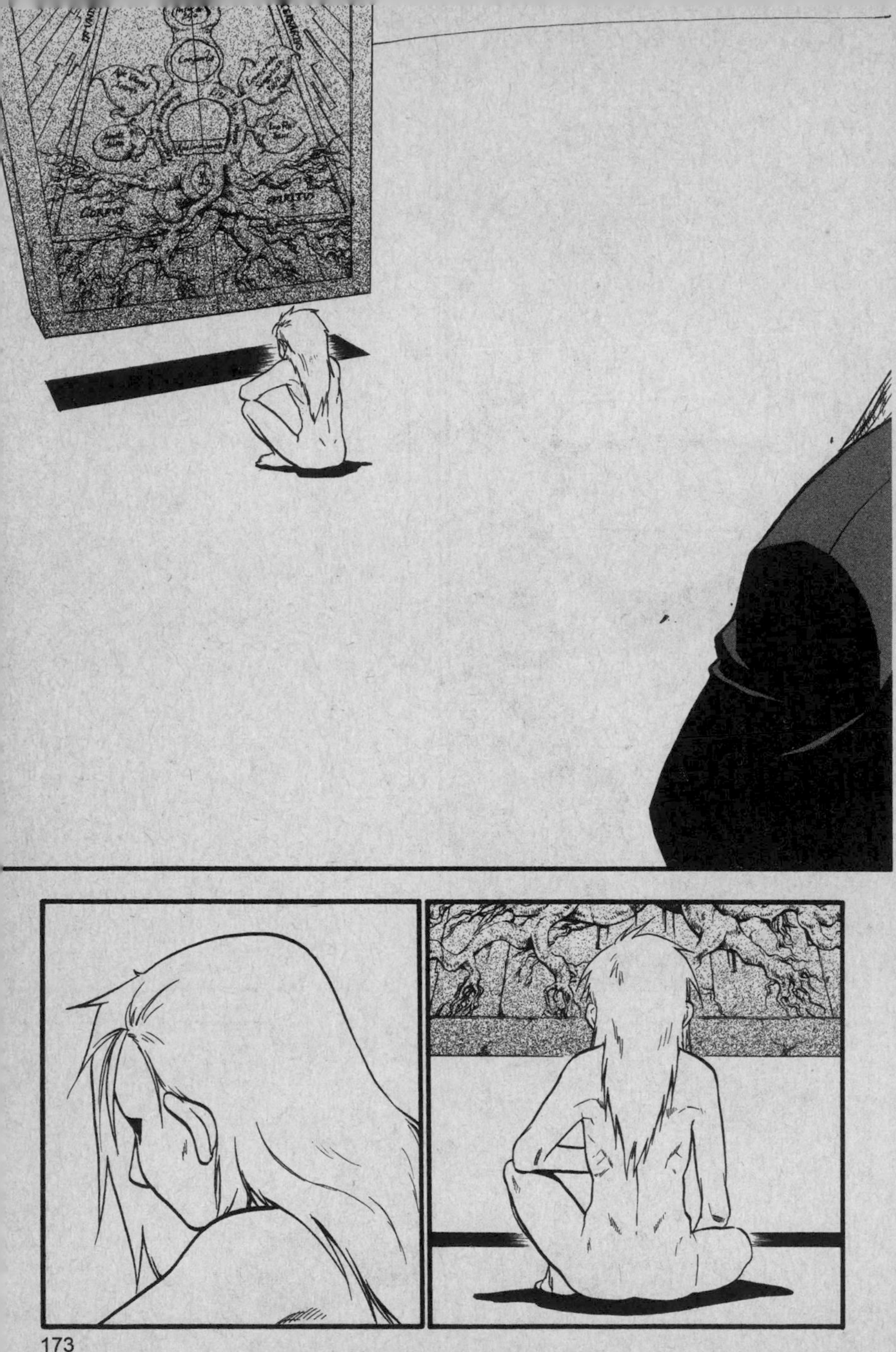

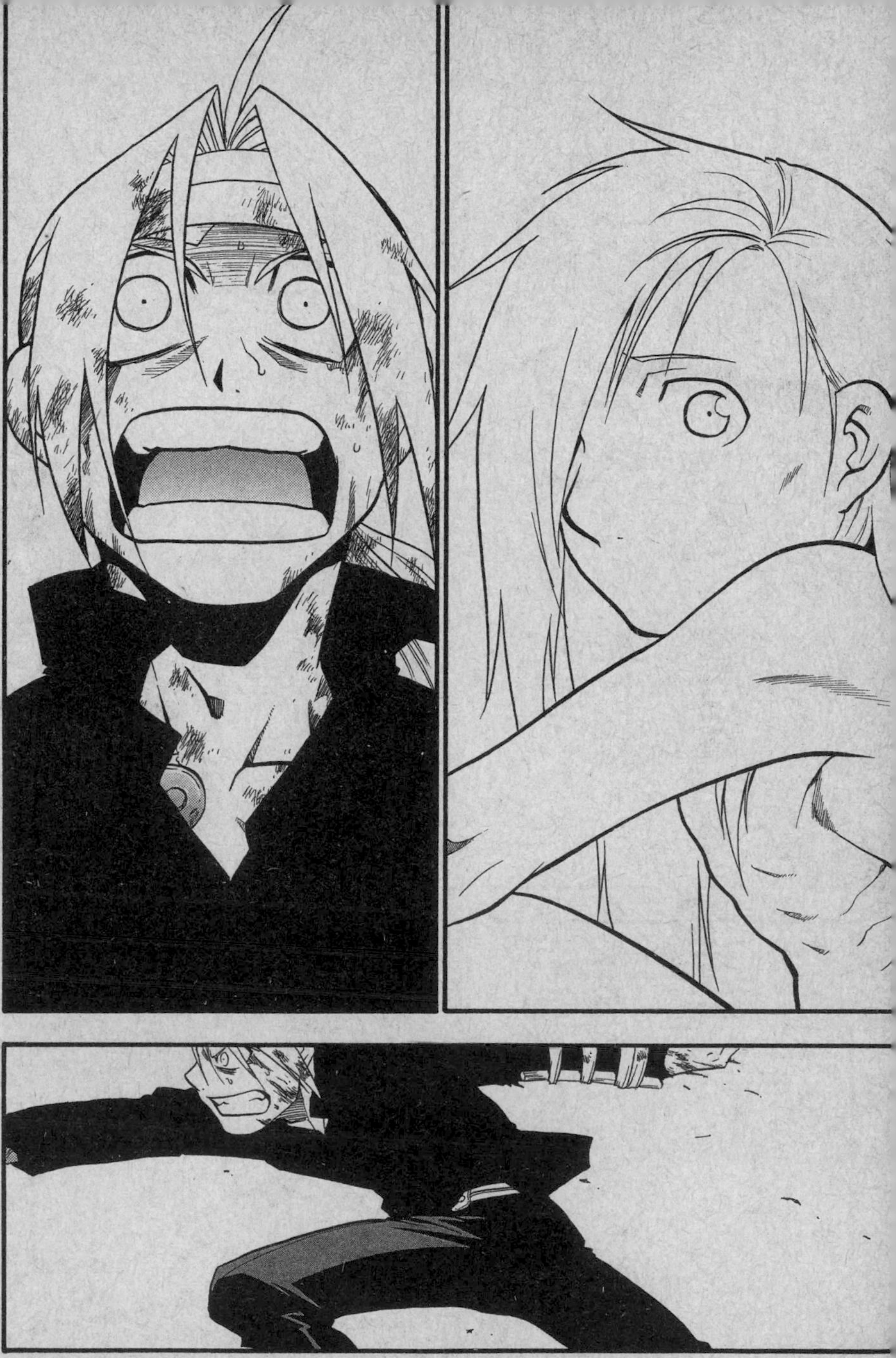

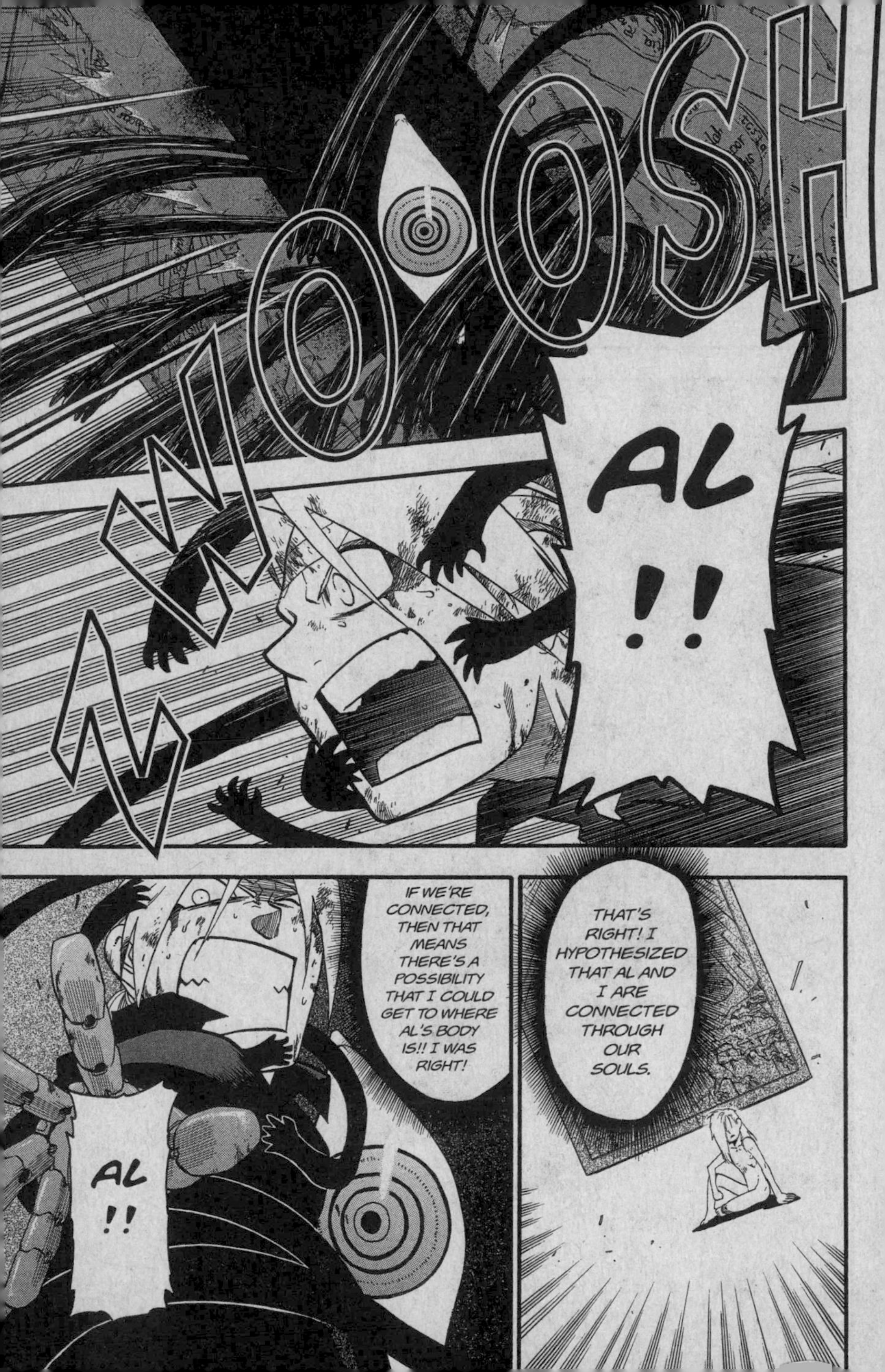
WOOOOSH
AL!!
THAT'S RIGHT! I HYPOTHESIZED THAT AL AND I ARE CONNECTED THROUGH OUR SOULS.
IF WE'RE CONNECTED, THEN THAT MEANS THERE'S A POSSIBILITY THAT I COULD GET TO WHERE AL'S BODY IS!! I WAS RIGHT!
AL!!

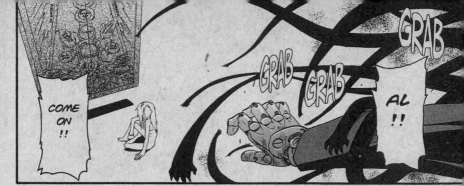

COME ON !!

GRAB

GRAB GRAB

GRAB

AL !!

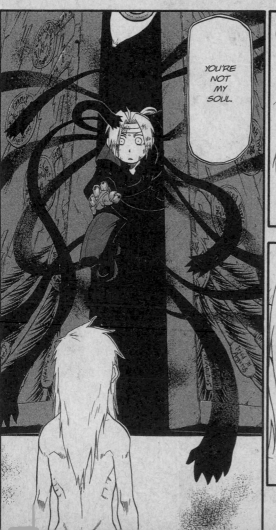

YOU'RE NOT MY SOUL.

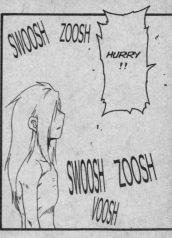

SWOOSH ZOOSH

HURRY !!

SWOOSH ZOOSH

VOOSH

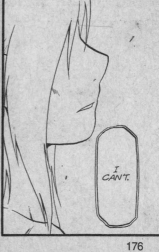

I CAN'T.

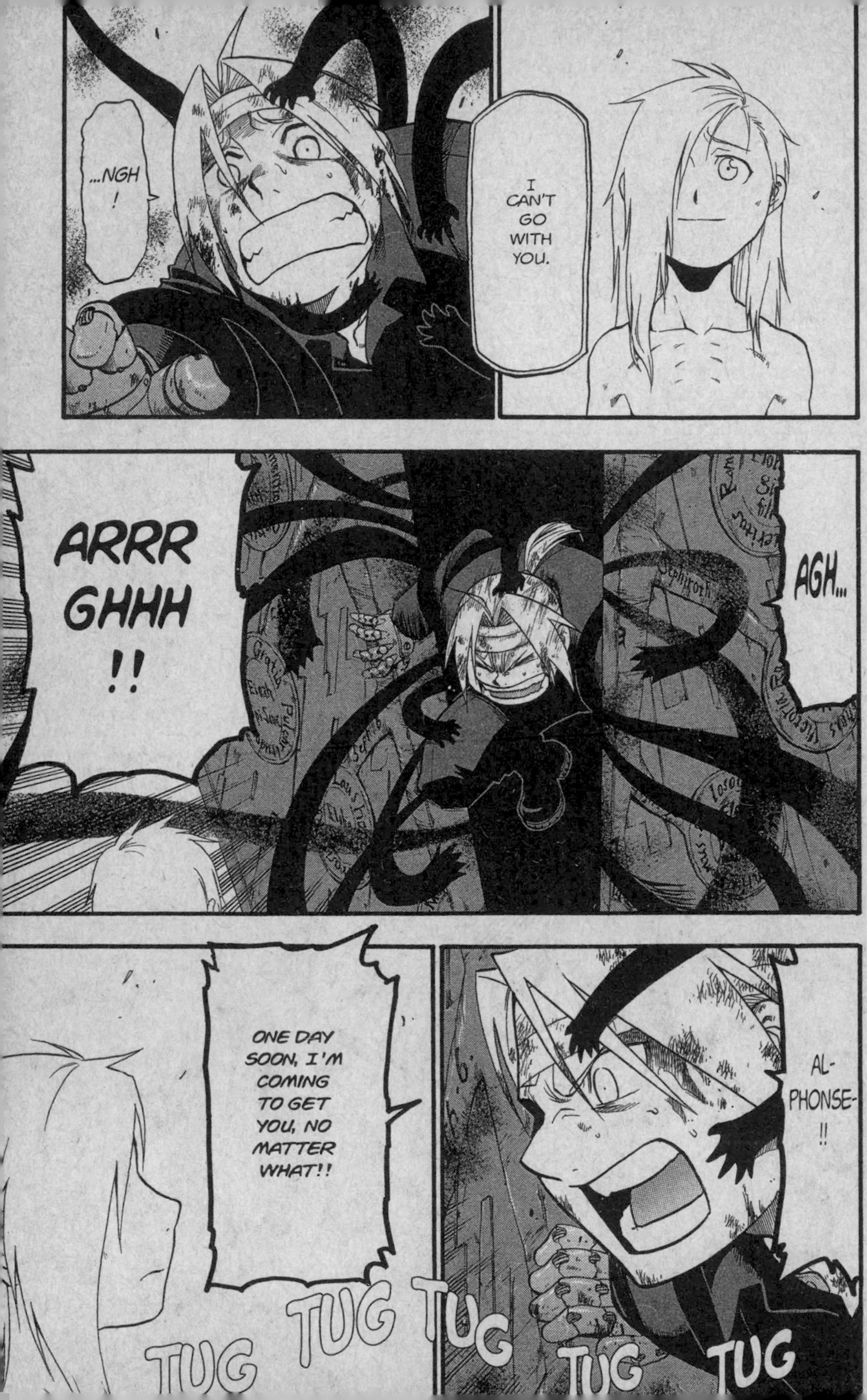
I CAN'T GO WITH YOU.
...NGH!
AGH...
ARRR GHHH!!
AL-PHONSE-!!
TUG
TUG
TUG
ONE DAY SOON, I'M COMING TO GET YOU, NO MATTER WHAT!!
TUG
TUG

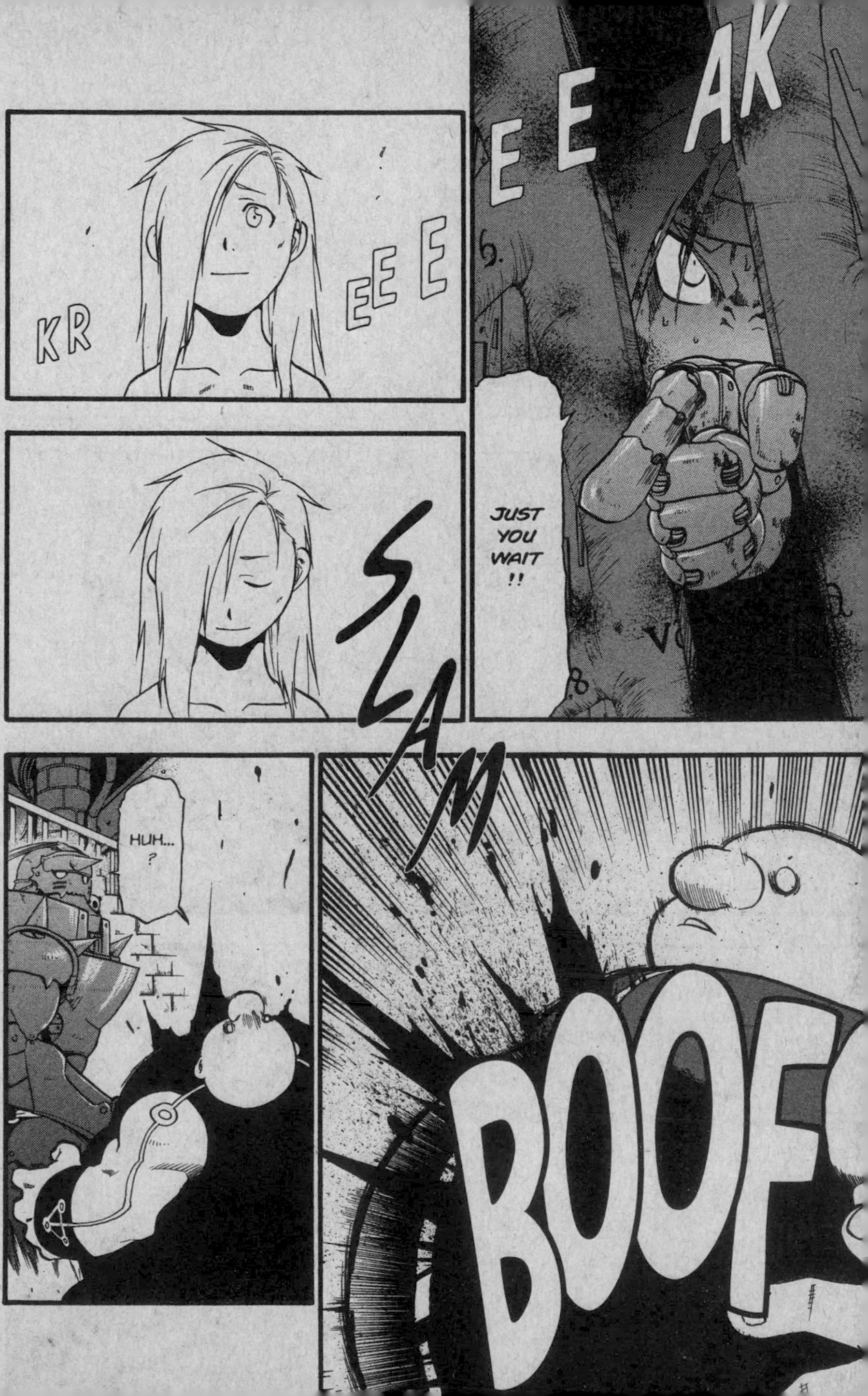E E AK
JUST YOU WAIT!!
KR
EE E
SLAM
BOOF
HUH... ?

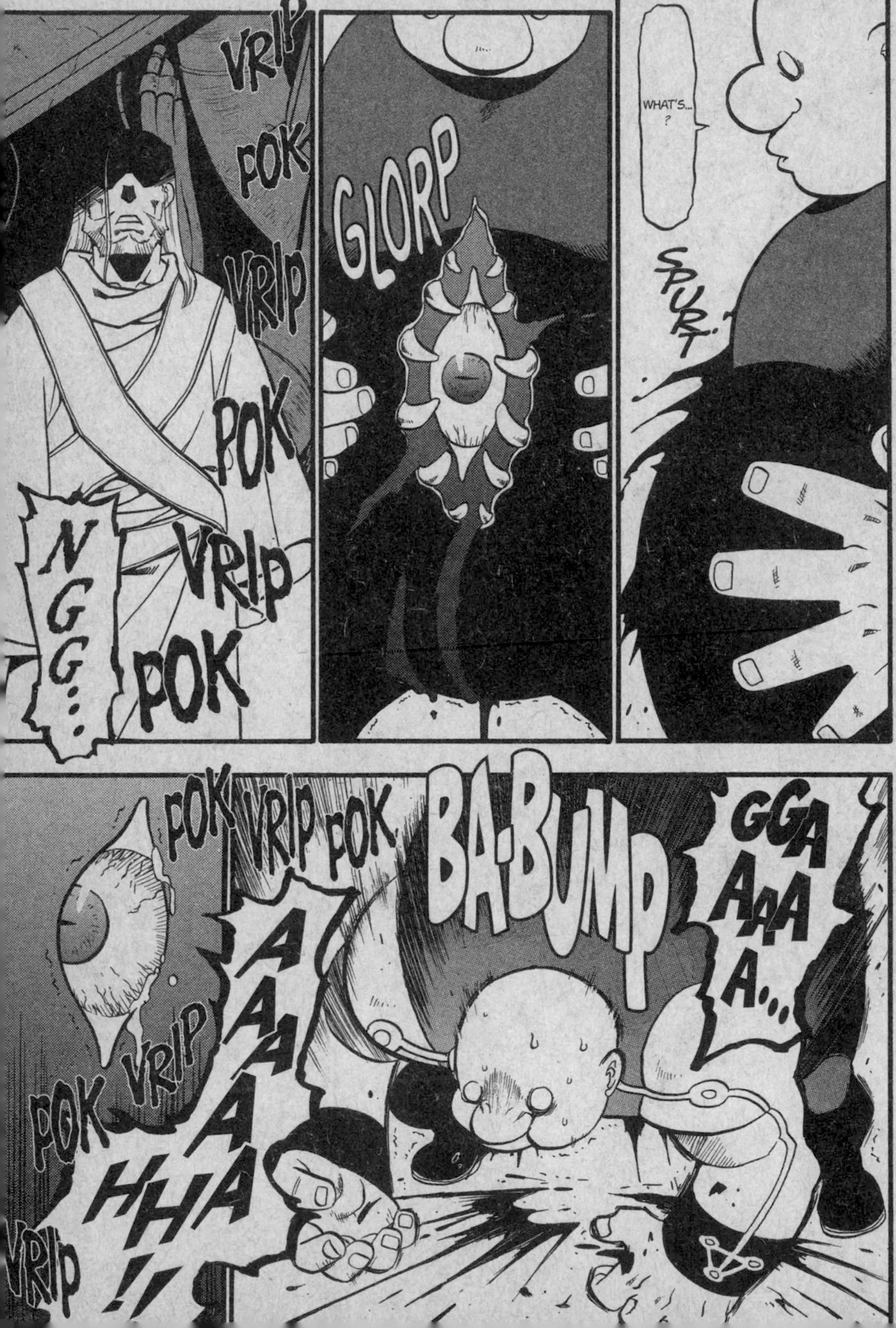
WHAT'S... ?
SPURT
GLORP
VRIP
POK
VRIP
POK
VRIP
POK
NGG...
GGAAAAAA...
BA-BUMP
POK
VRIP
POK
AAAAAHHA!!
VRIP
POK
VRIP

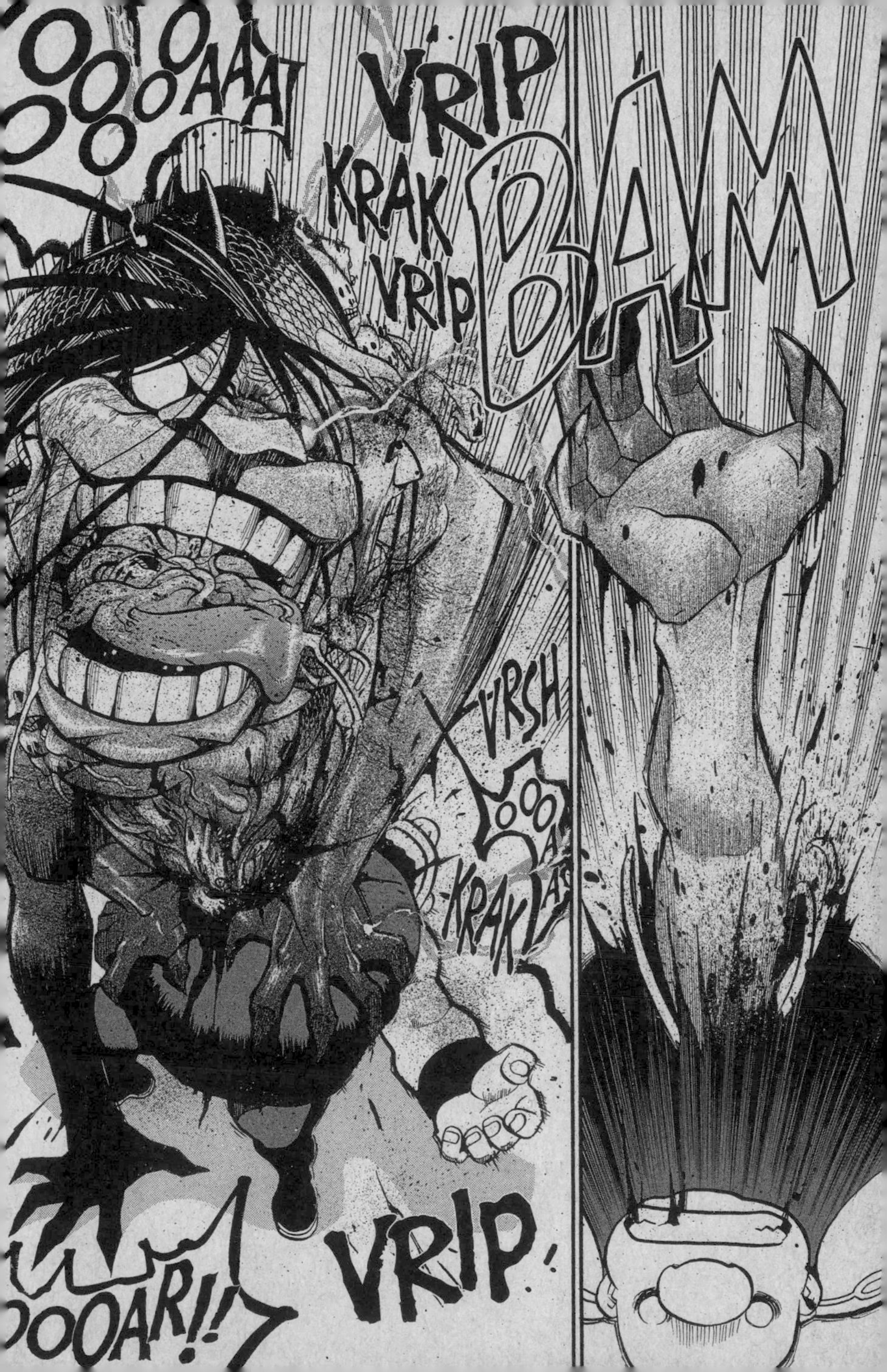
BAM
VRIP
KRAK
VRIP
OOOOOAAAT
VRSH
KRAK
VRIP
OOOAR!!

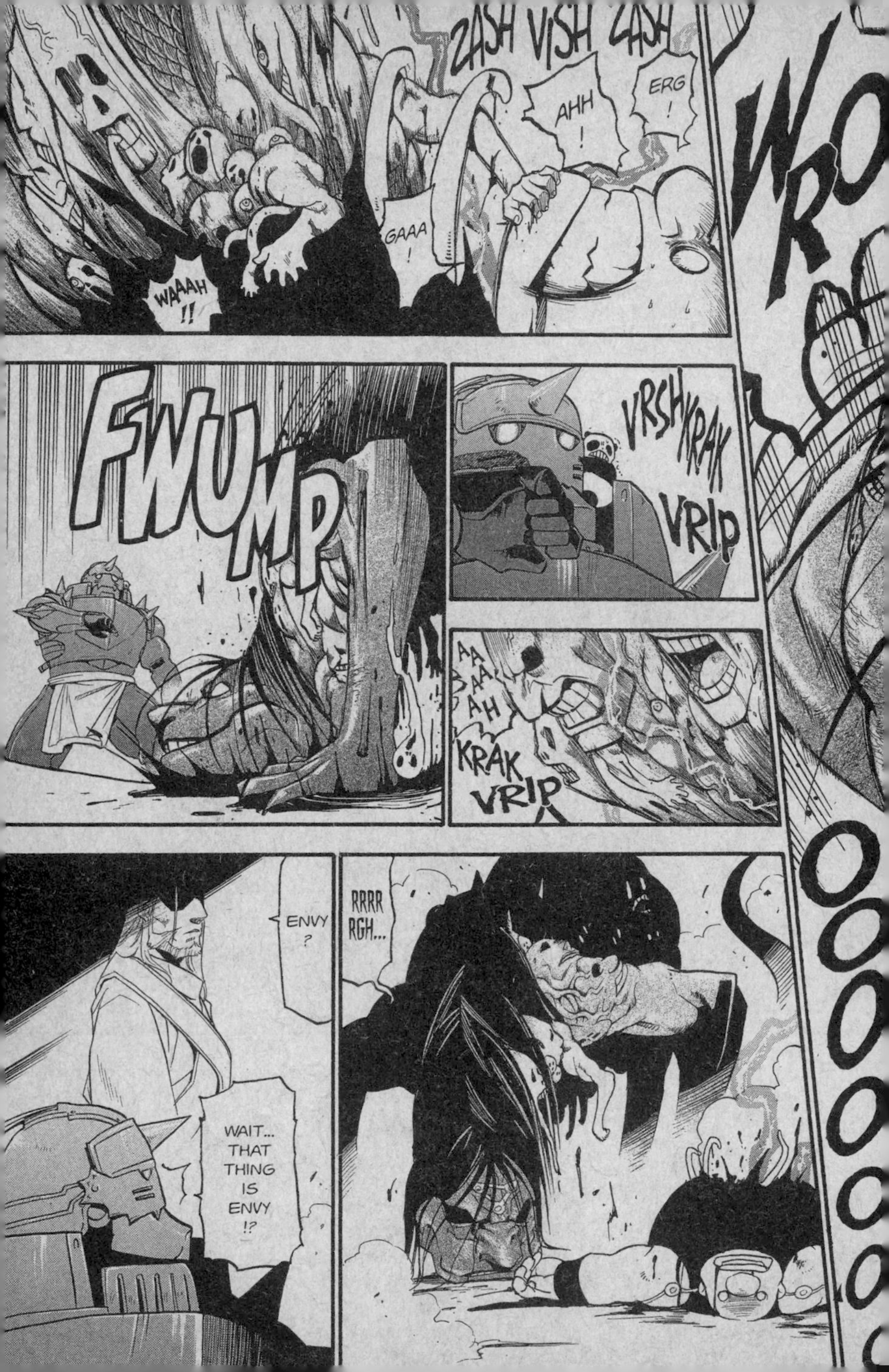

WROOOOOOO
ZASH VISH ZASH
ERG!
AHH!
GAAA!
WAAAH!!
VRSH KRAK
VRIP
AAAAAH
KRAK
VRIP
FWUMP
RRRR RGH...
ENVY?
WAIT... THAT THING IS ENVY!?

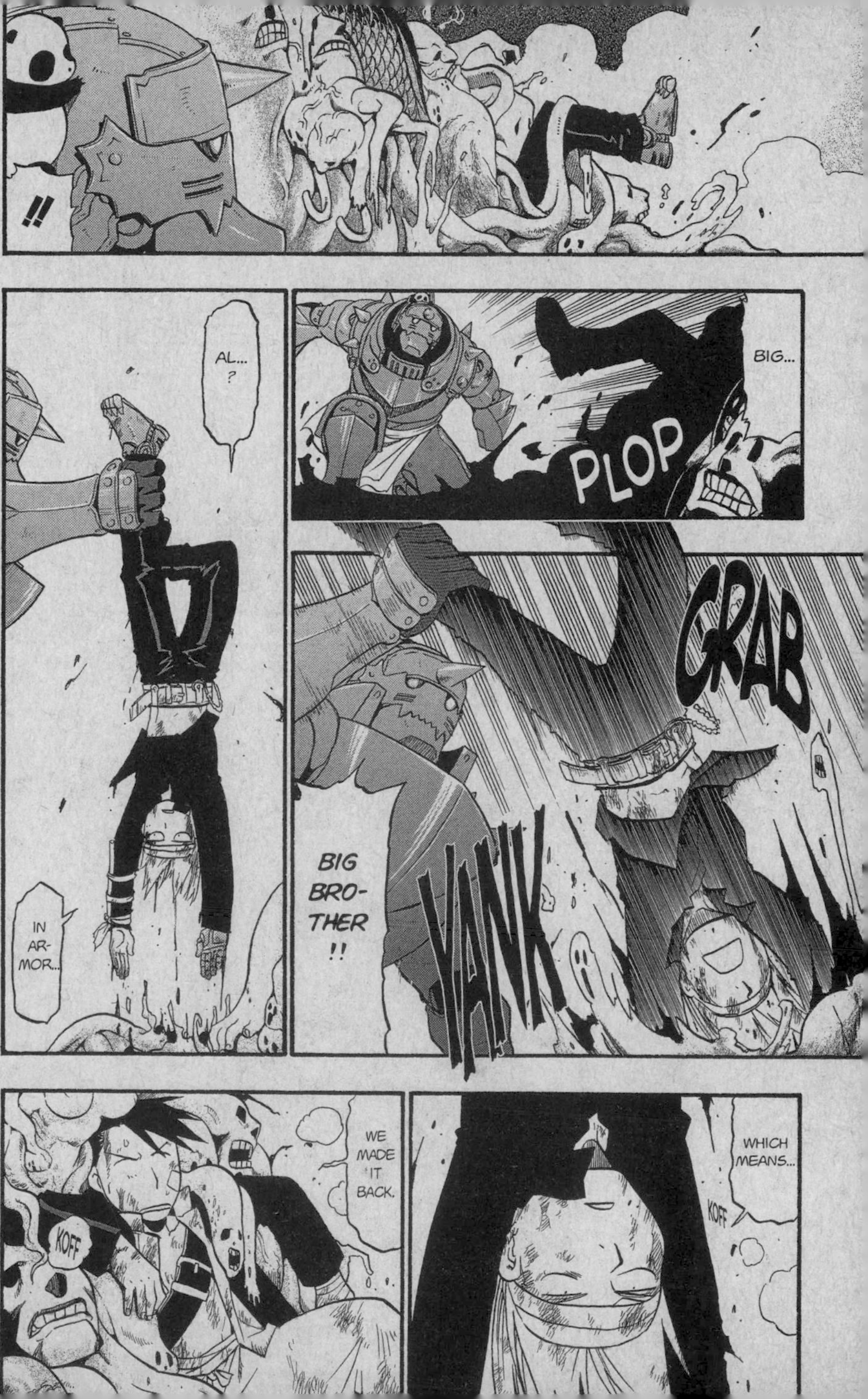
!!
BIG...
PLOP
GRAB
BIG BROTHER!!
YANK
AL...?
IN ARMOR...
WHICH MEANS...
KOFF
WE MADE IT BACK.
KOFF

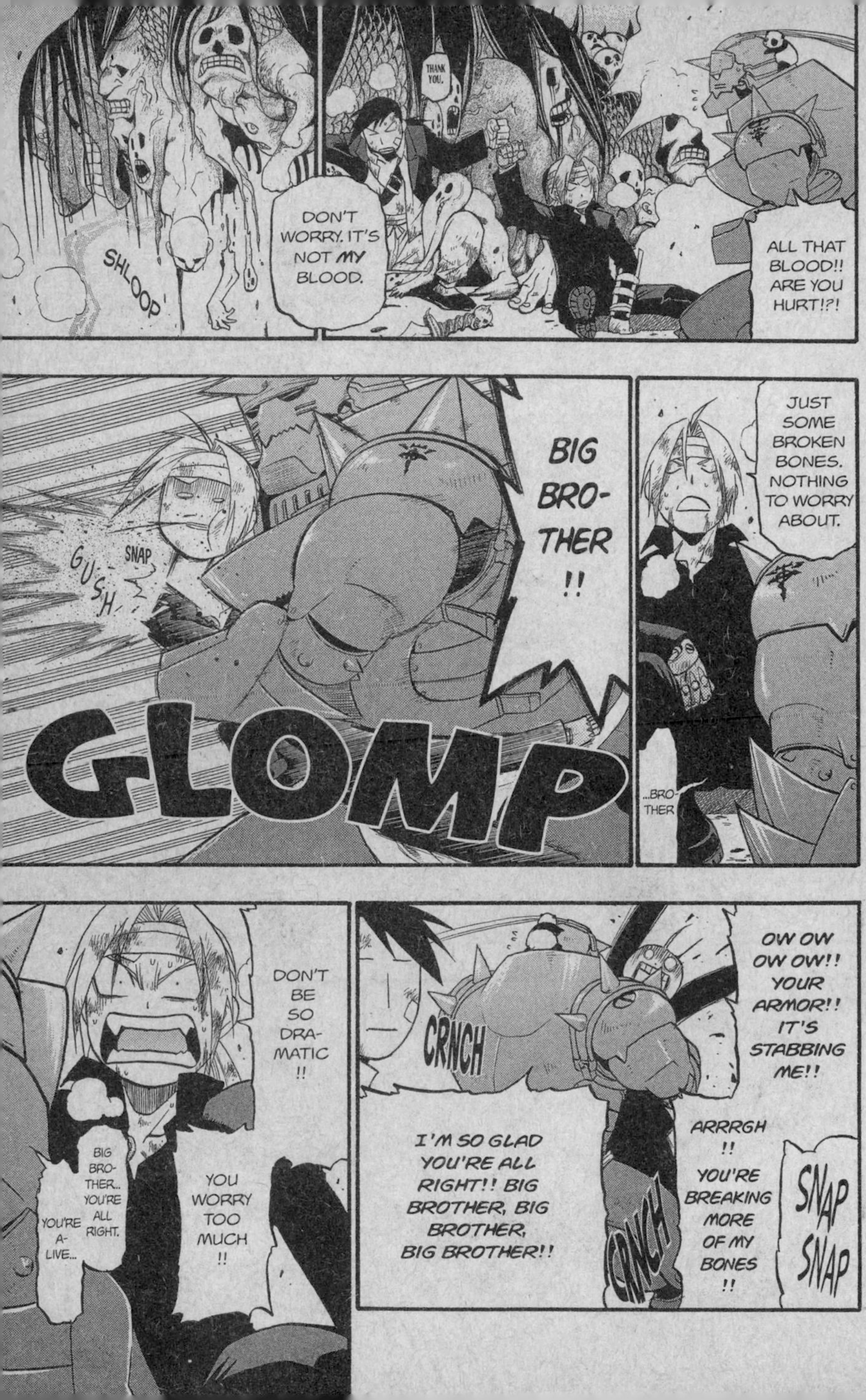
ALL THAT BLOOD!! ARE YOU HURT!?!
THANK YOU.
DON'T WORRY. IT'S NOT MY BLOOD.
SHLOOP
JUST SOME BROKEN BONES. NOTHING TO WORRY ABOUT.
...BROTHER
BIG BROTHER!!
SNAP
GUSH
GLOMP
OW OW OW OW!! YOUR ARMOR!! IT'S STABBING ME!!
CRNCH
SNAP SNAP
ARRRGH!! YOU'RE BREAKING MORE OF MY BONES!!
I'M SO GLAD YOU'RE ALL RIGHT!! BIG BROTHER, BIG BROTHER, BIG BROTHER!!
CRNCH
DON'T BE SO DRAMATIC!!
YOU WORRY TOO MUCH!!
BIG BROTHER... YOU'RE ALL RIGHT.
YOU'RE A-LIVE...

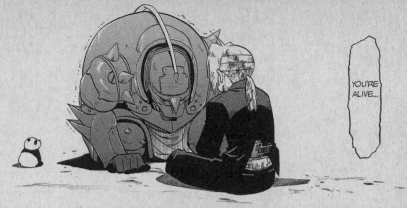

YOU'RE ALIVE...
AL!
AL...
AL-PHONSE!!
HELP... SOMEBODY...
MOM...
THAT'S RIGHT...
I SHOULD KNOW ABOUT THE TERROR AND DESPAIR OF LOSING YOUR ENTIRE FAMILY AND BEING LEFT ALL ALONE.
WIPE
RUB
SOR-RY...
...FOR MAKING YOU WORRY.

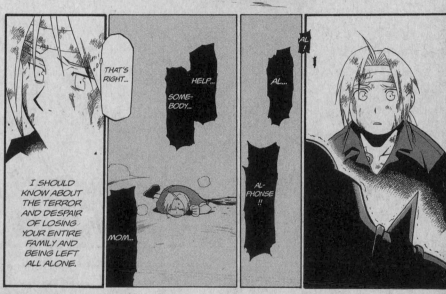

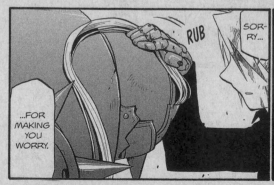

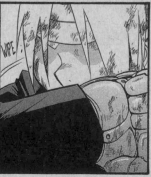

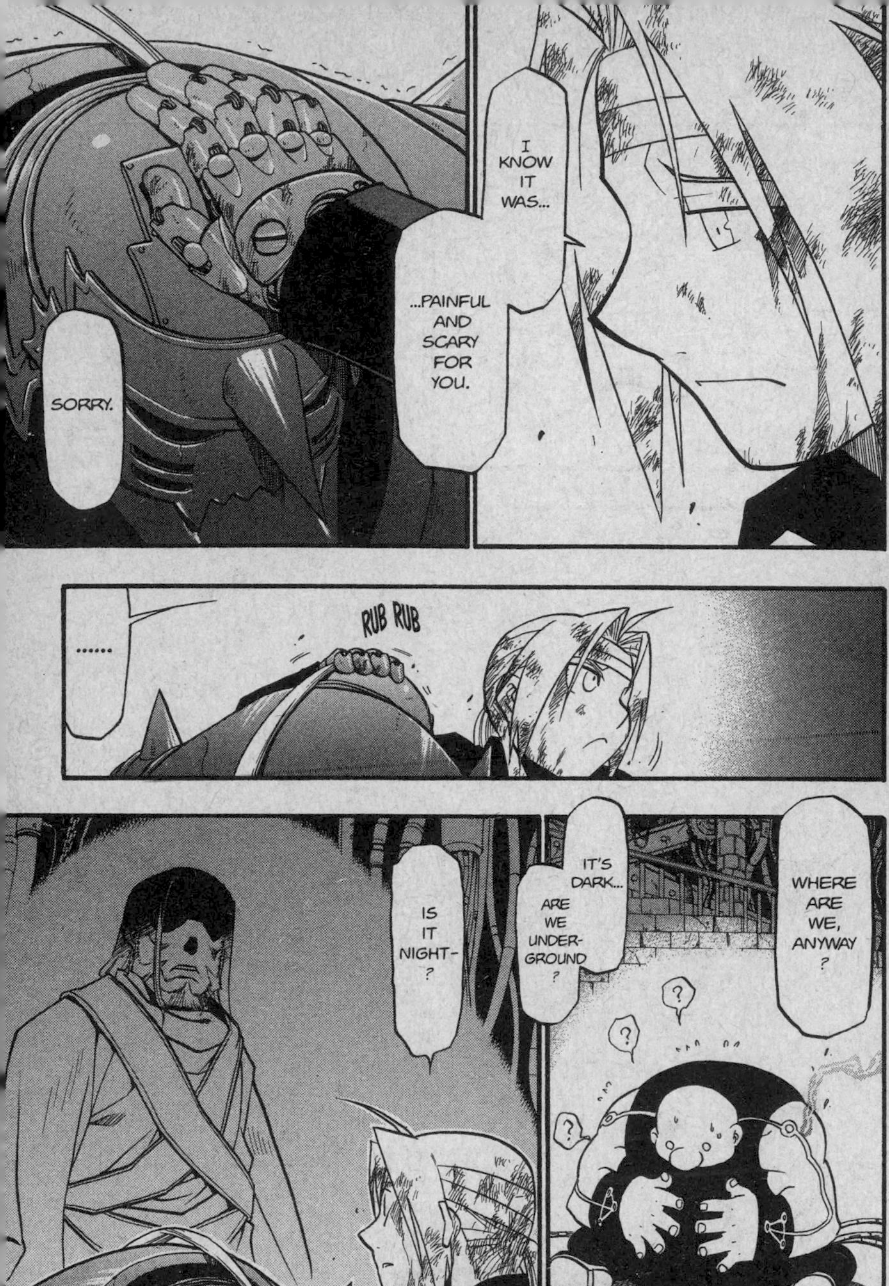
I KNOW IT WAS...
...PAINFUL AND SCARY FOR YOU.
SORRY.
RUB RUB
......
WHERE ARE WE, ANYWAY?
IT'S DARK...
ARE WE UNDERGROUND?
IS IT NIGHT-?

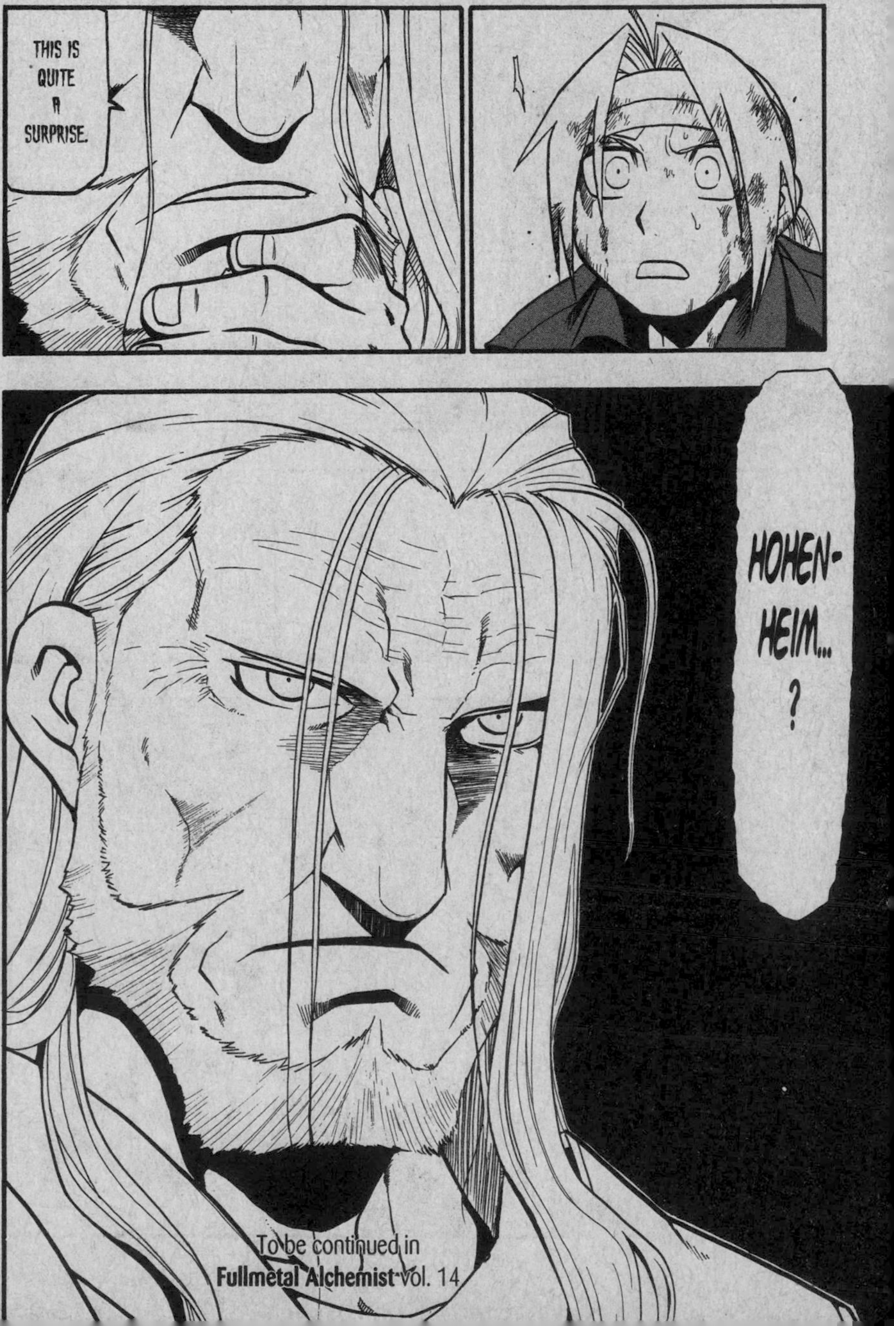
THIS IS QUITE A SURPRISE.
HOHEN-HEIM... ?

To be continued in
Fullmetal Alchemist vol. 14

The Golden Age

MY GOODNESS!! WHAT IS THAT!?!
SIMMER SIMMER
FRESHLY BOILED BOOT! THE FINEST GRADE OF LEATHER, DEAR MOTHER-IN-LAW.
GLUB GLUB
I CAN'T EAT THIS!!
ARE YOU TRYING TO STARVE ME TO DEATH!?
WHAT A CRUEL THING TO SAY! I PUT MY HEART AND SOUL INTO COOKING IT BECAUSE I WANTED YOU TO LIVE A LONG LIFE, DEAR MOTHER-IN-LAW!
HO HO
IF YOU WON'T EAT WHAT I COOKED, THEN PLEASE SLURP ON SOME SEWAGE!!
HERE!!
SOB.. WHAT A CRUEL DAUGHTER-IN-LAW YOU ARE!!
HOW COULD MY SON BRING A DEVIL LIKE YOU INTO OUR FAMILY!?
HERE!!
HO HO HO HO HO
SHOVE
WHAT ARE YOU TWO DOING?
WE'RE PLAYING DAUGHTER-IN-LAW VS. MOTHER-IN-LAW.
WHERE DO YOU GET THAT STUFF FROM?
THE AFTERNOON SOAPS.

FULLMETAL ALCHEMIST 13

SPECIAL THANKS

KEISUI TAKAEDA
SANKICHI HINODEYA
JUN TOKO
AIYABALL
NONO
BIG BROTHER YOICHI KAMITONO
MASASHI MIZUTANI
YOKO ASANEGI
RIKA SUGIYAMA
EDITOR YOICHI SHIMOMURA
AND YOU!!

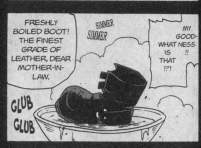

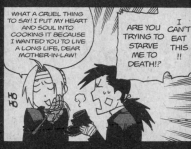

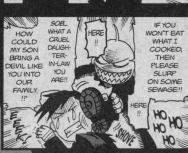

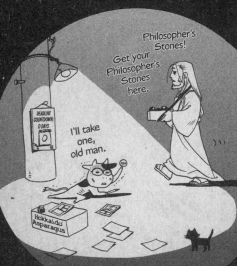

Philosopher's Stones!
Get your Philosopher's Stones here.
DEADLINE COUNTDOWN: 0 DAYS
0
I'll take one, old man.
100
Hokkaido Asparagus

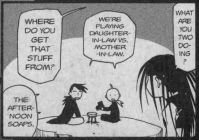

POIK
YAY!
PHUD
SPLURK

PLEASE READ THIS AFTER YOU READ CHAPTER 51 IN THIS VOLUME!
KAZAM!
ELRIC TELEPATHY!!
RECEIVE MY SIGNAL, LI'L BROTHER!!!
WAAAGH!
PING
ED?!

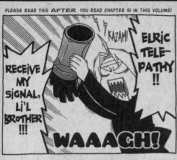

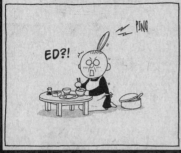

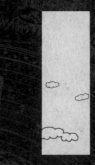

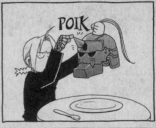

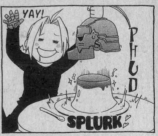

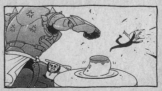

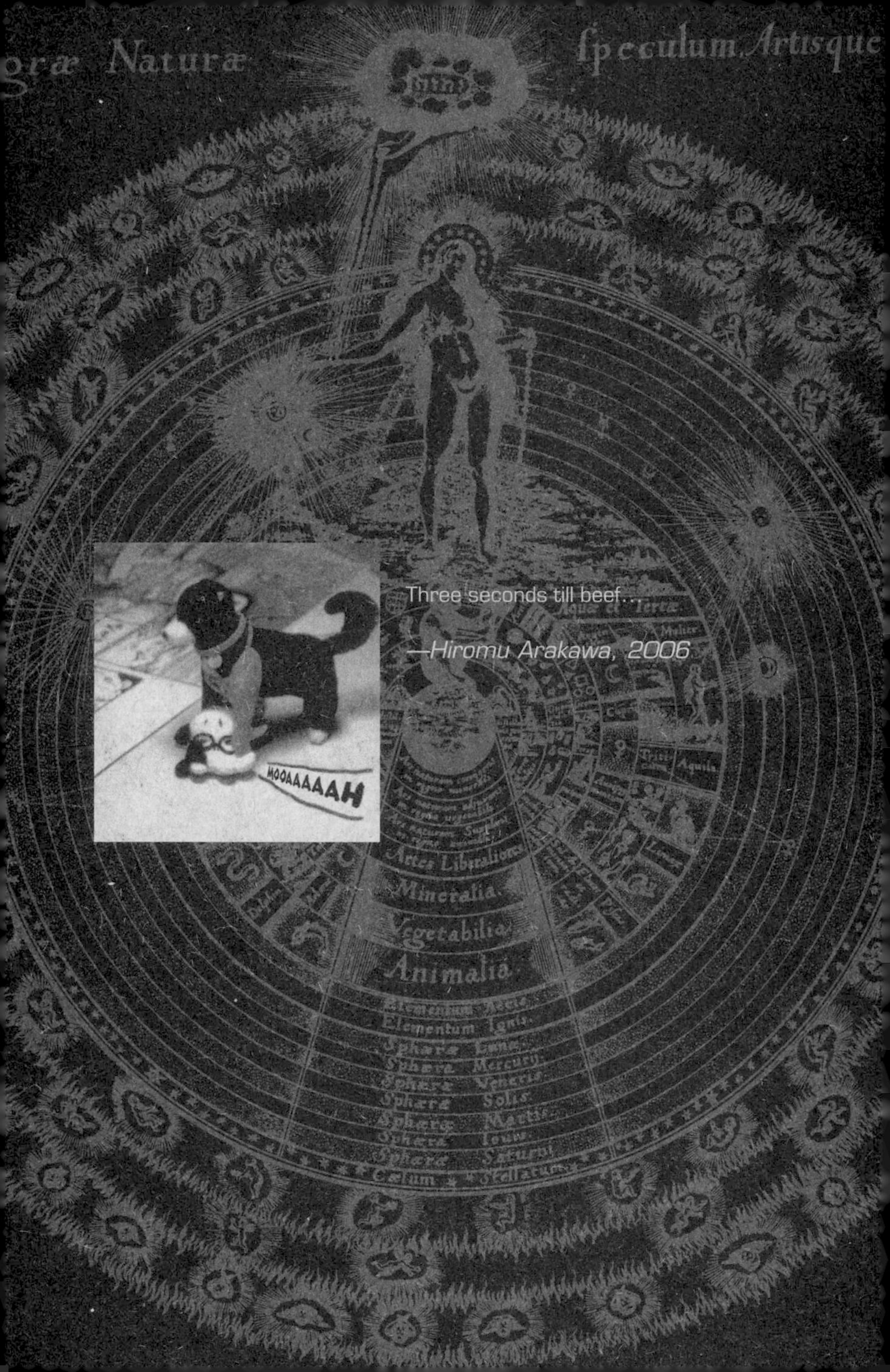
græ Naturæ
ſpeculum Artisque
Artes Liberaliores
Mineralia
Vegetabilia
Animalia
Elementum Ignis
Sphæra Lunæ
Sphæra Mercurij
Sphæra Veneris
Sphæra Solis
Sphæra Martis
Sphæra Iouis
Sphæra Saturni
Cœlum Stellatum
MOOAAAAAH

Three seconds till beef...

—Hiromu Arakawa, 2006

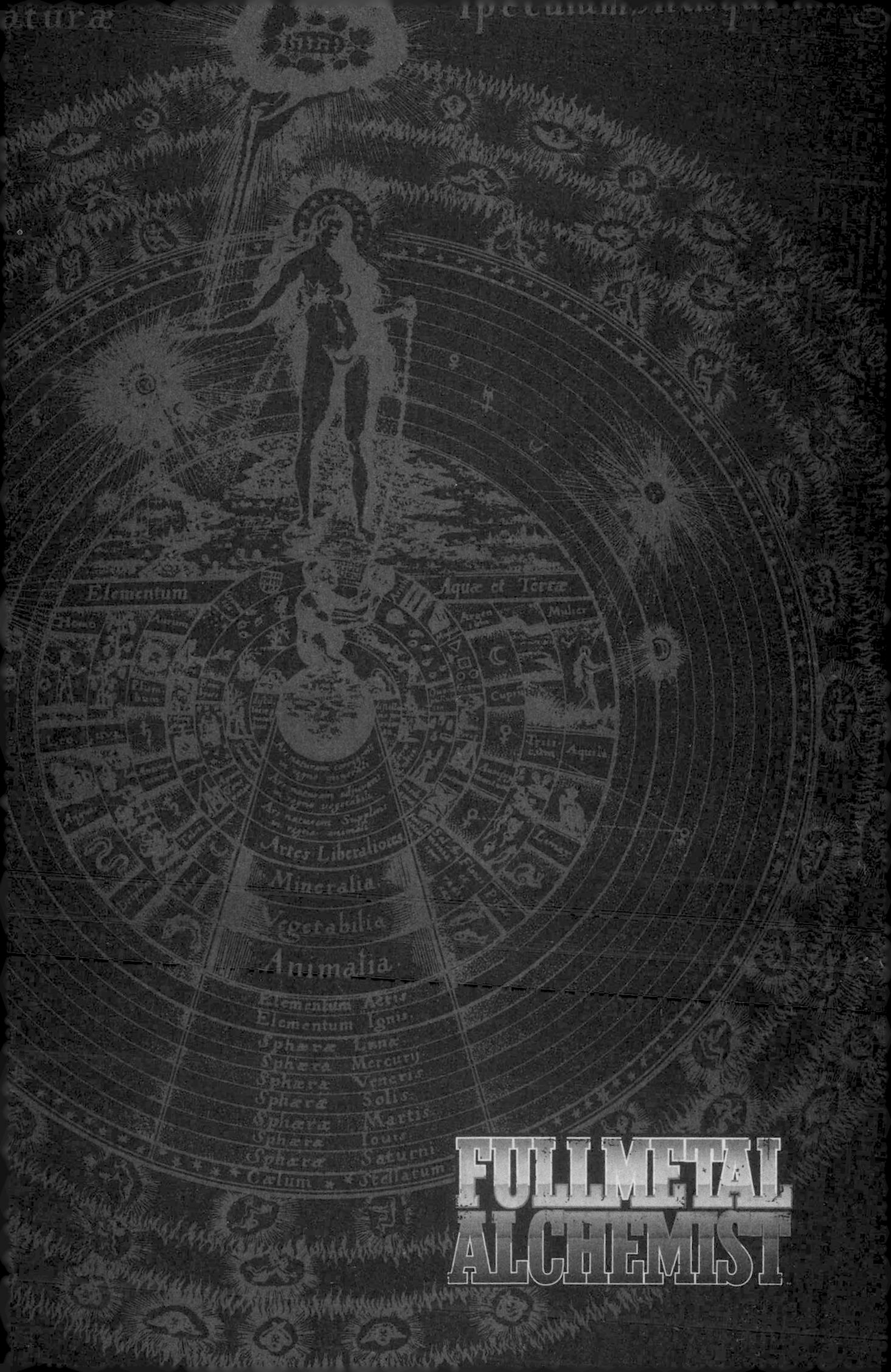
Elementum
Aquæ et Terræ
Artes Liberaliores
Mineralia
Vegetabilia
Animalia
Elementum Aeris
Elementum Ignis
Sphæra Lunæ
Sphæra Mercury
Sphæra Veneris
Sphæra Solis
Sphæra Martis
Sphæra Iouis
Sphæra Saturni
Cælum Stellatum
FULLMETAL
ALCHEMIST

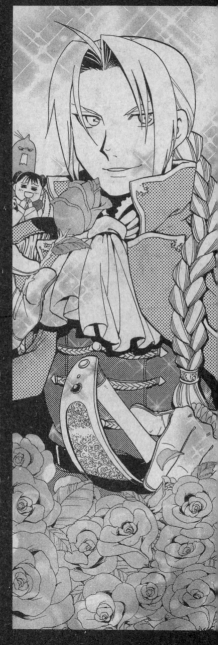

鋼の錬金術師

FULLMETAL ALCHEMIST

HIROMU ARAKAWA

荒川弘

14

FULLMETAL ALCHEMIST CHARACTER

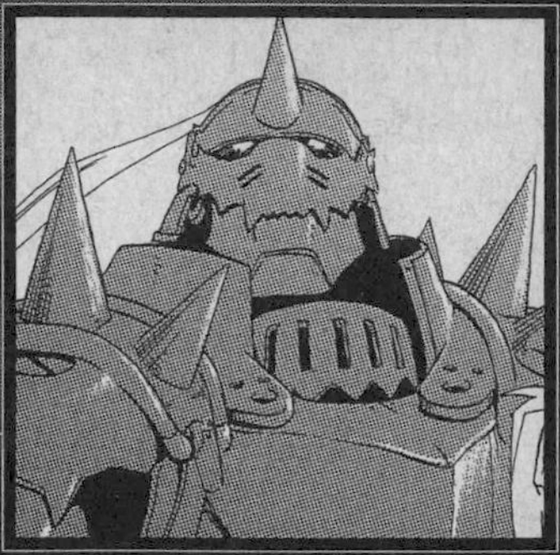

アルフォンス・エルリック

Alphonse Elric

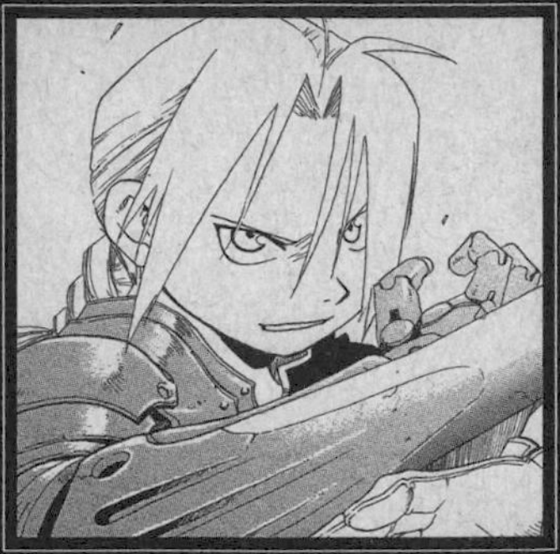

エドワード・エルリック

Edward Elric

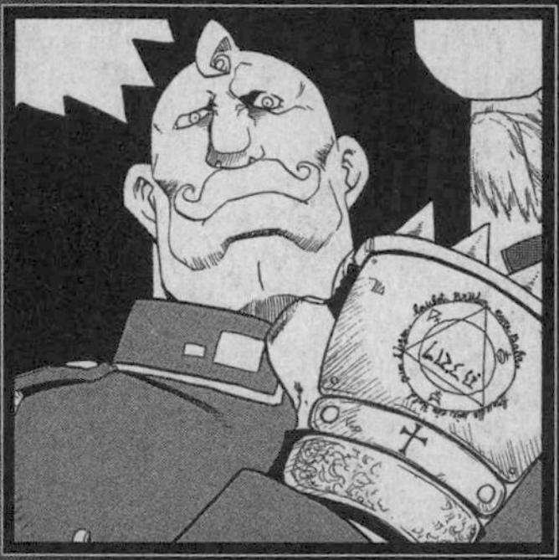

アレックス・ルイ・アームストロング

Alex Louis Armstrong

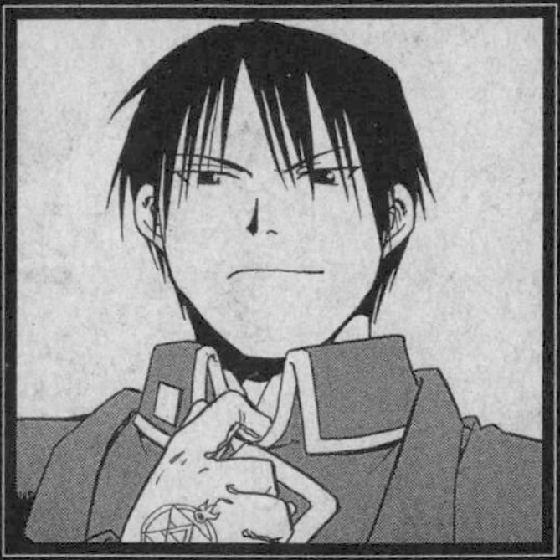

ロイ・マスタング

Roy Mustang

OUTLINE
FULLMETAL ALCHEMIST

The Elrics' plan to capture and interrogate Gluttony, one of the evil and nigh-invulnerable homunculi, goes awry when his "sibling" Envy crashes the party. Gluttony reveals his true bestial form and, in a rage, swallows Ed, Lin, and Envy, sending the three of them into a dark void eerily containing a large amount of rubble and…blood. Al, fearing his brother lost forever, demands that Gluttony take him to the mysterious "father" of the homunculi…

Meanwhile, Roy Mustang returns to Central City armed with the secret that President Bradley is actually a homunculus; however, when Mustang is summoned to meet with the top echelons of the military command, he is shocked to learn his intelligence is not as privileged as he thought. As Scar and May fight their way into the labyrinthine lair of the Homunculi which lies beneath Central, an unexpected reunion is at hand…

鋼の錬金術師
FULLMETAL ALCHEMIST

CHARACTERS
FULLMETAL ALCHEMIST

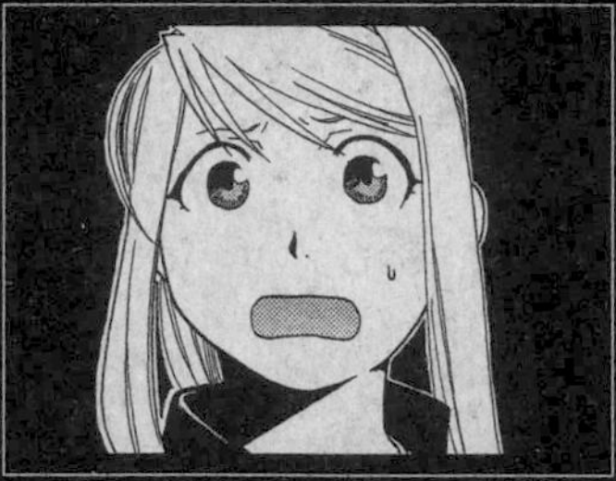

ウィンリィ・ロックベル
Winry Rockbell

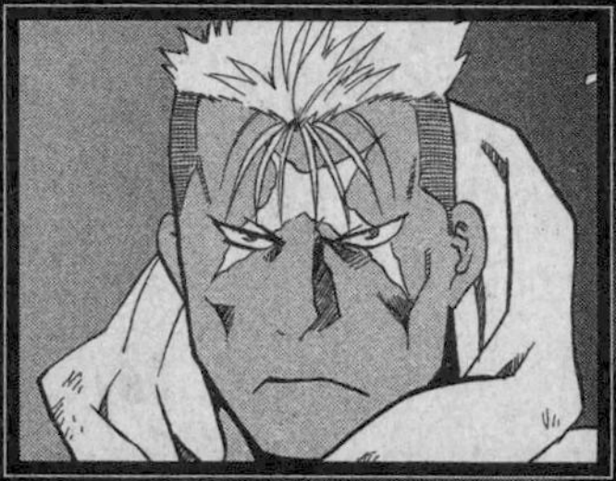

スカー
Scar

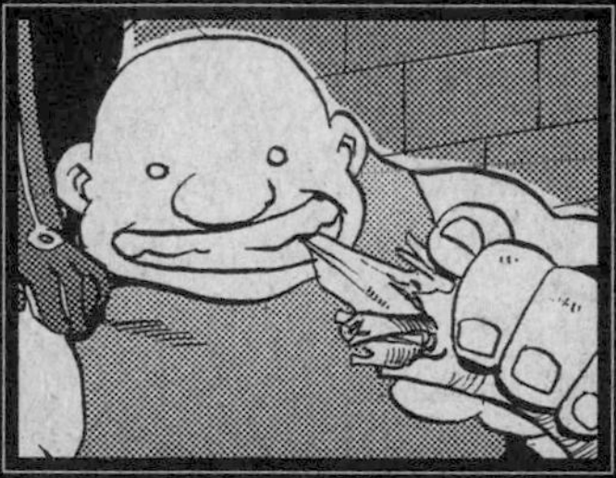

グラトニー
Gluttony

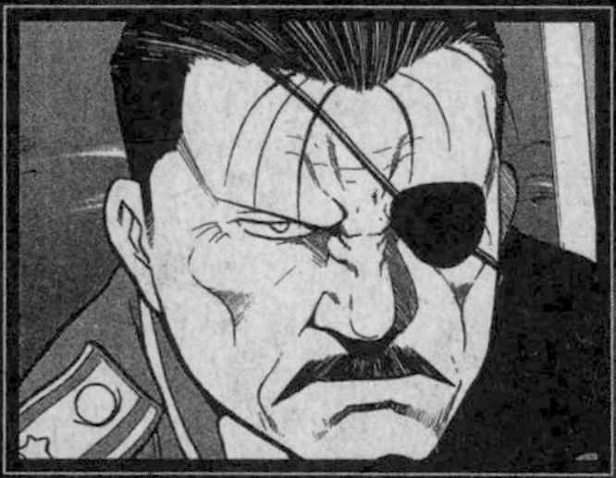

キング・ブラッドレイ
King Bradley

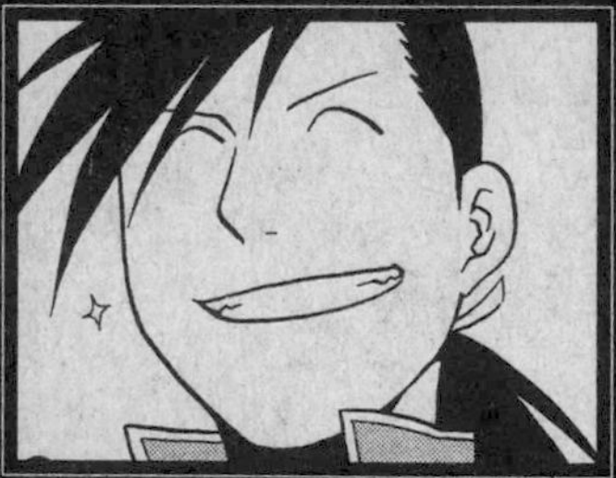

リン・ヤオ
Lin Yao

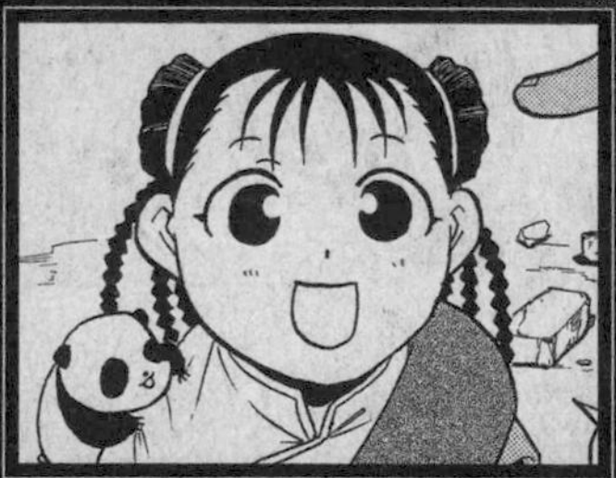

メイ・チャン
May Chang

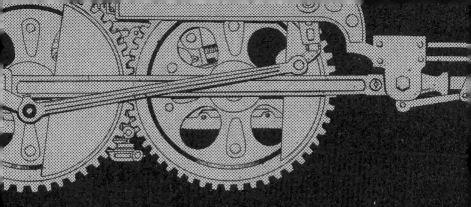

CONTENTS

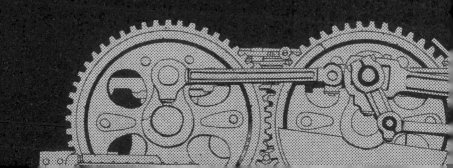

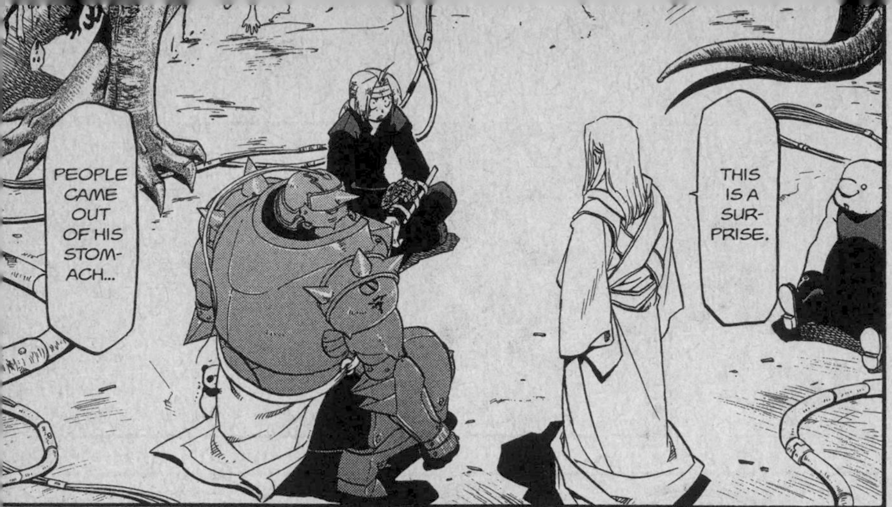
THIS IS A SURPRISE.
PEOPLE CAME OUT OF HIS STOMACH...

Chapter 54 The Fool's Struggle

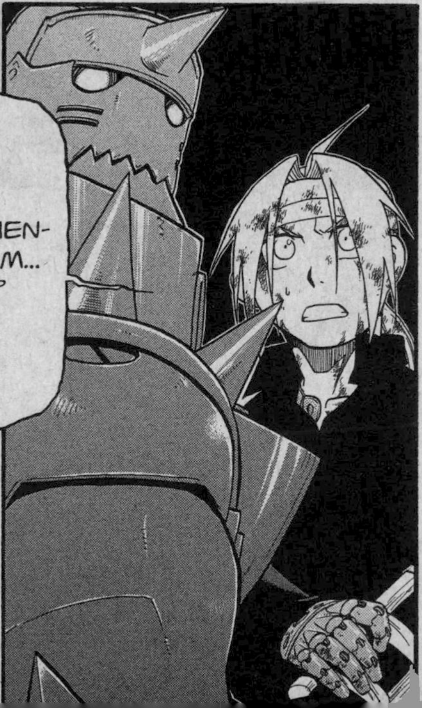
HOHENHEIM...?

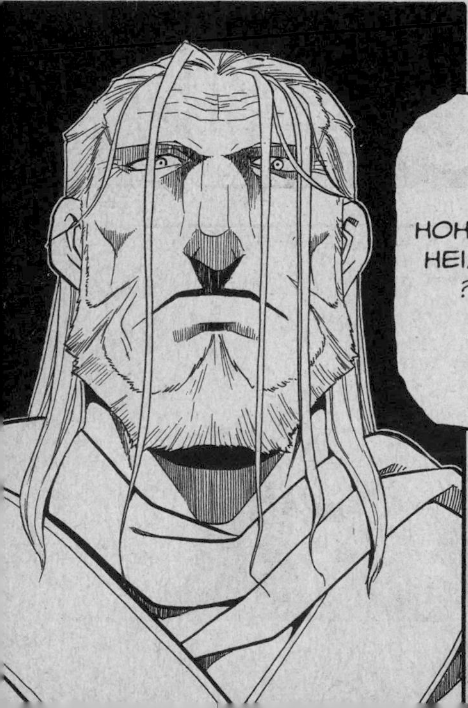

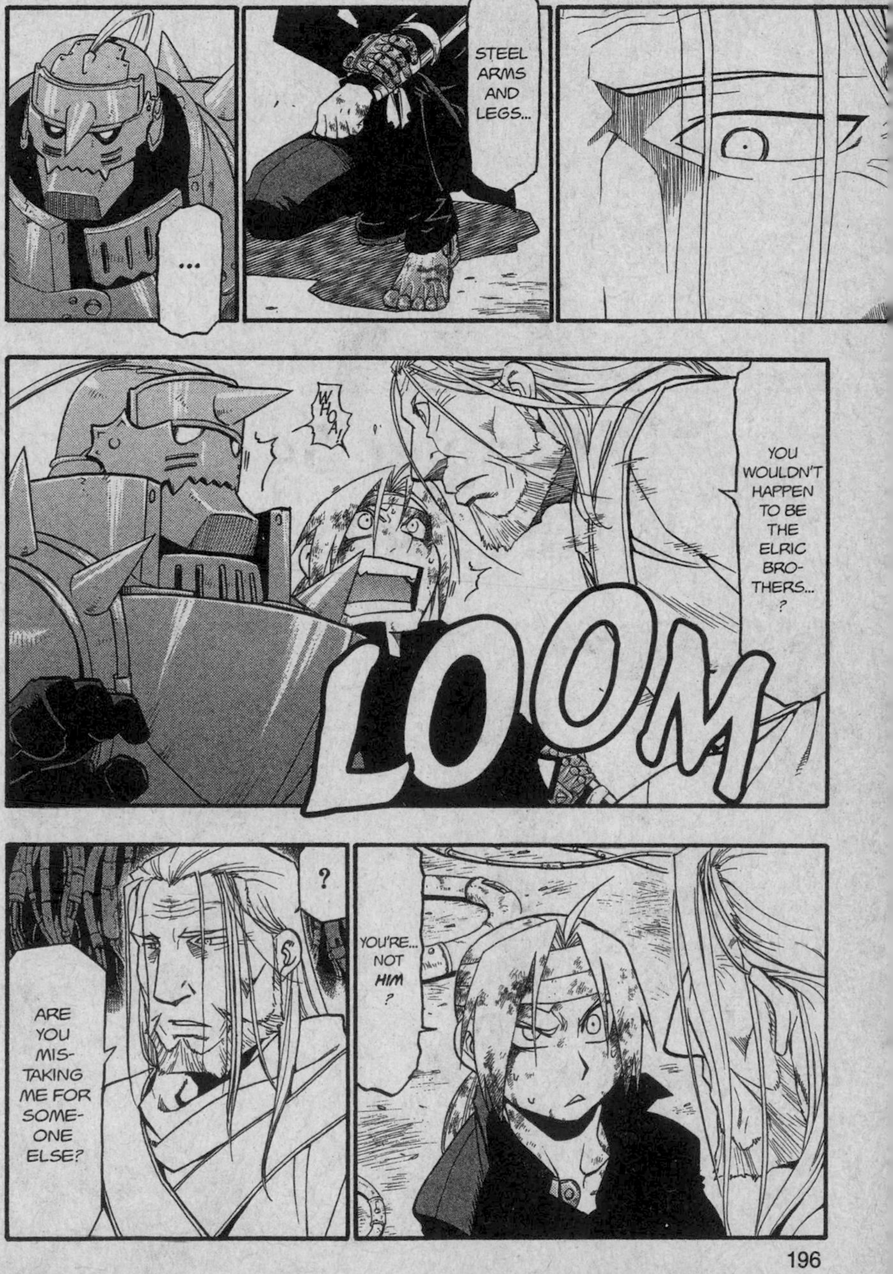
STEEL ARMS AND LEGS...
...
YOU WOULDN'T HAPPEN TO BE THE ELRIC BROTHERS...?
WHOA!!
LOOM
YOU'RE... NOT **HIM**?
?
ARE YOU MISTAKING ME FOR SOMEONE ELSE?

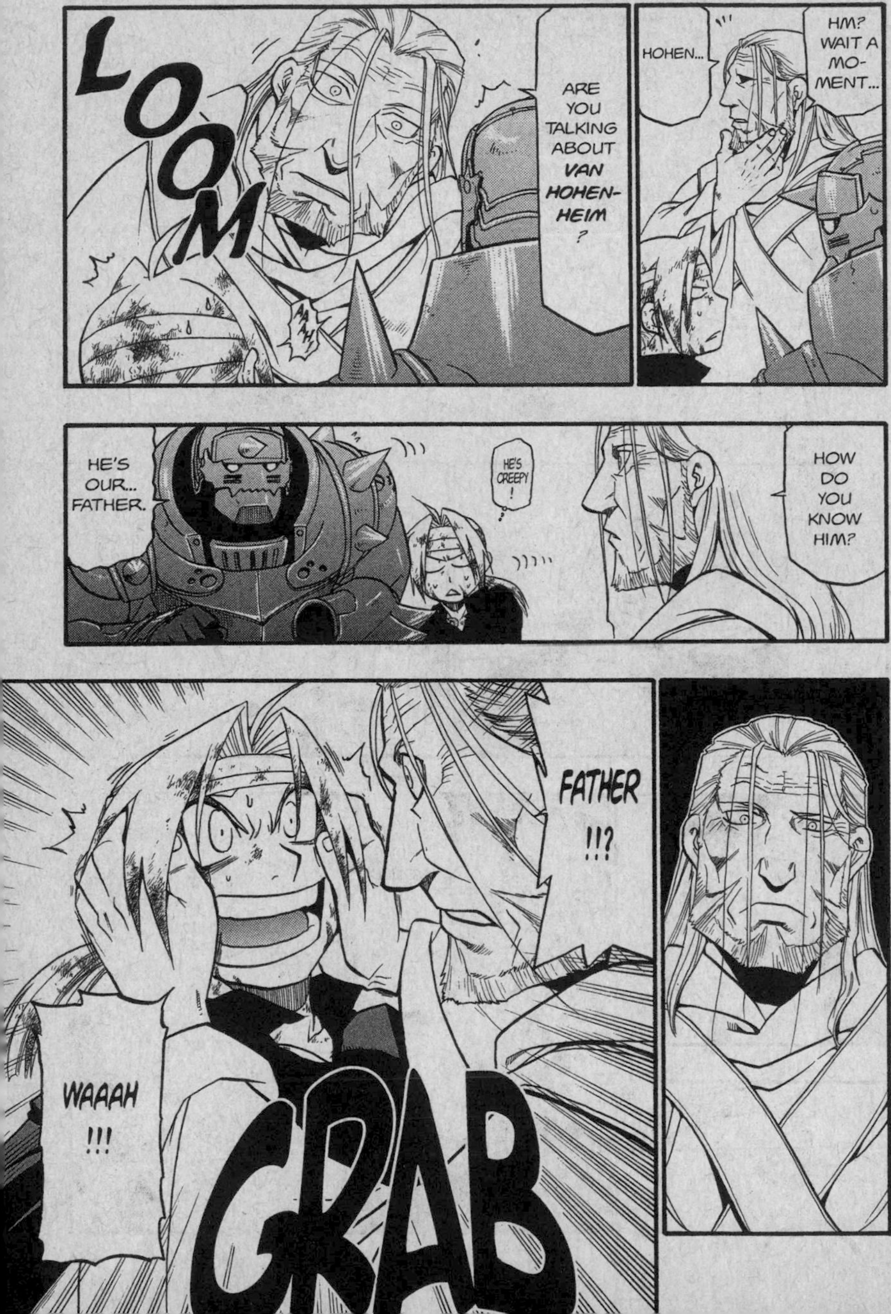
HM? WAIT A MO-MENT...
HOHEN...
ARE YOU TALKING ABOUT VAN HOHEN-HEIM ?
LOOM
HOW DO YOU KNOW HIM?
HE'S CREEPY!
HE'S OUR... FATHER.
FATHER !!?
WAAAH !!!
GRAB

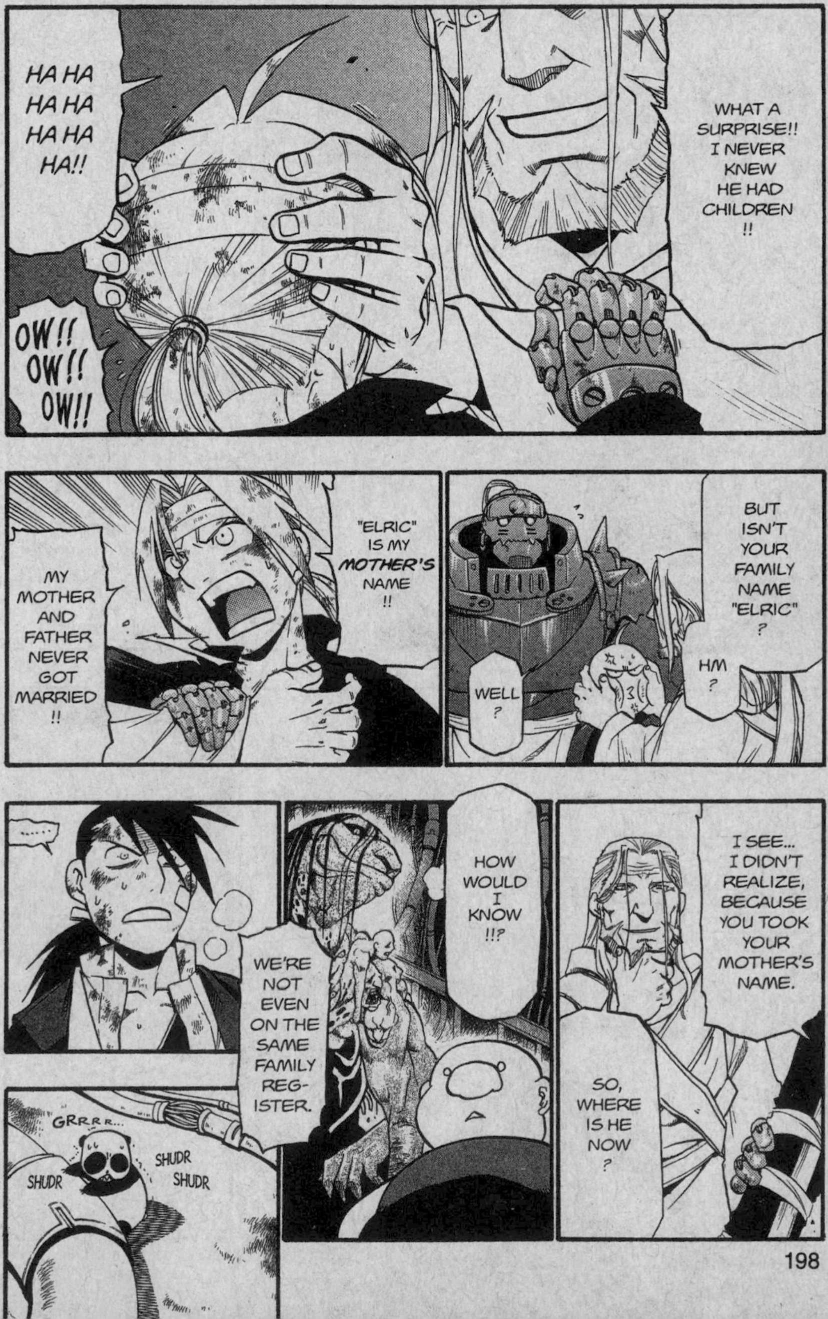
WHAT A SURPRISE!! I NEVER KNEW HE HAD CHILDREN!!
HA HA HA HA HA HA HA!!
OW!! OW!! OW!!
BUT ISN'T YOUR FAMILY NAME "ELRIC"?
HM?
WELL?
"ELRIC" IS MY MOTHER'S NAME!!
MY MOTHER AND FATHER NEVER GOT MARRIED!!
I SEE... I DIDN'T REALIZE, BECAUSE YOU TOOK YOUR MOTHER'S NAME.
SO, WHERE IS HE NOW?
HOW WOULD I KNOW!!?
WE'RE NOT EVEN ON THE SAME FAMILY REG-ISTER.
GRRRR...
SHUDR
SHUDR
SHUDR

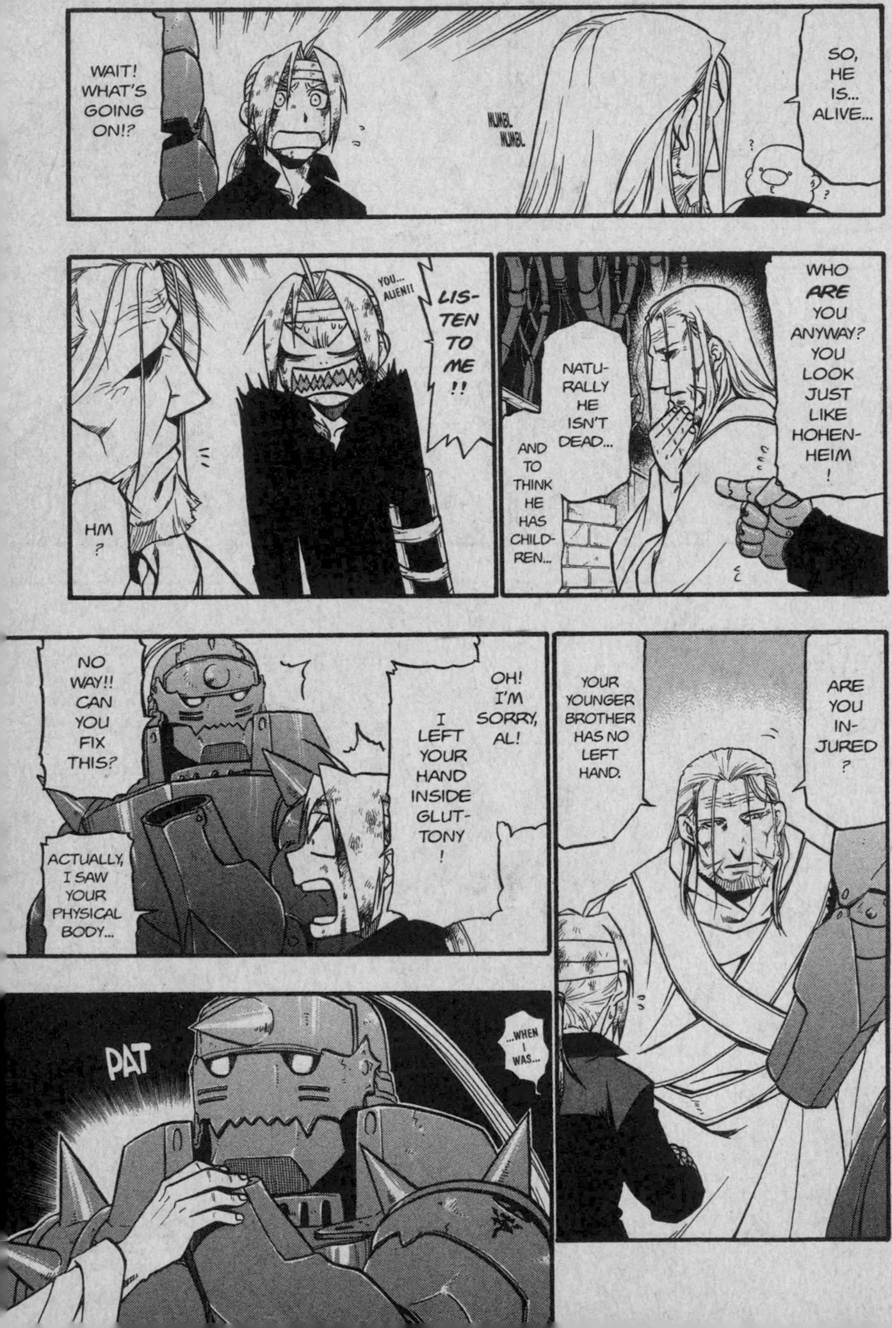
SO, HE IS... ALIVE...
MUMBL MUMBL
WAIT! WHAT'S GOING ON!?
WHO ARE YOU ANYWAY? YOU LOOK JUST LIKE HOHENHEIM!
NATURALLY HE ISN'T DEAD...
AND TO THINK HE HAS CHILDREN...
LISTEN TO ME!!
YOU... ALIEN!!
HM?
ARE YOU INJURED?
YOUR YOUNGER BROTHER HAS NO LEFT HAND.
OH! I'M SORRY, AL!
I LEFT YOUR HAND INSIDE GLUTTONY!
NO WAY!! CAN YOU FIX THIS?
ACTUALLY, I SAW YOUR PHYSICAL BODY...
...WHEN I WAS...
PAT

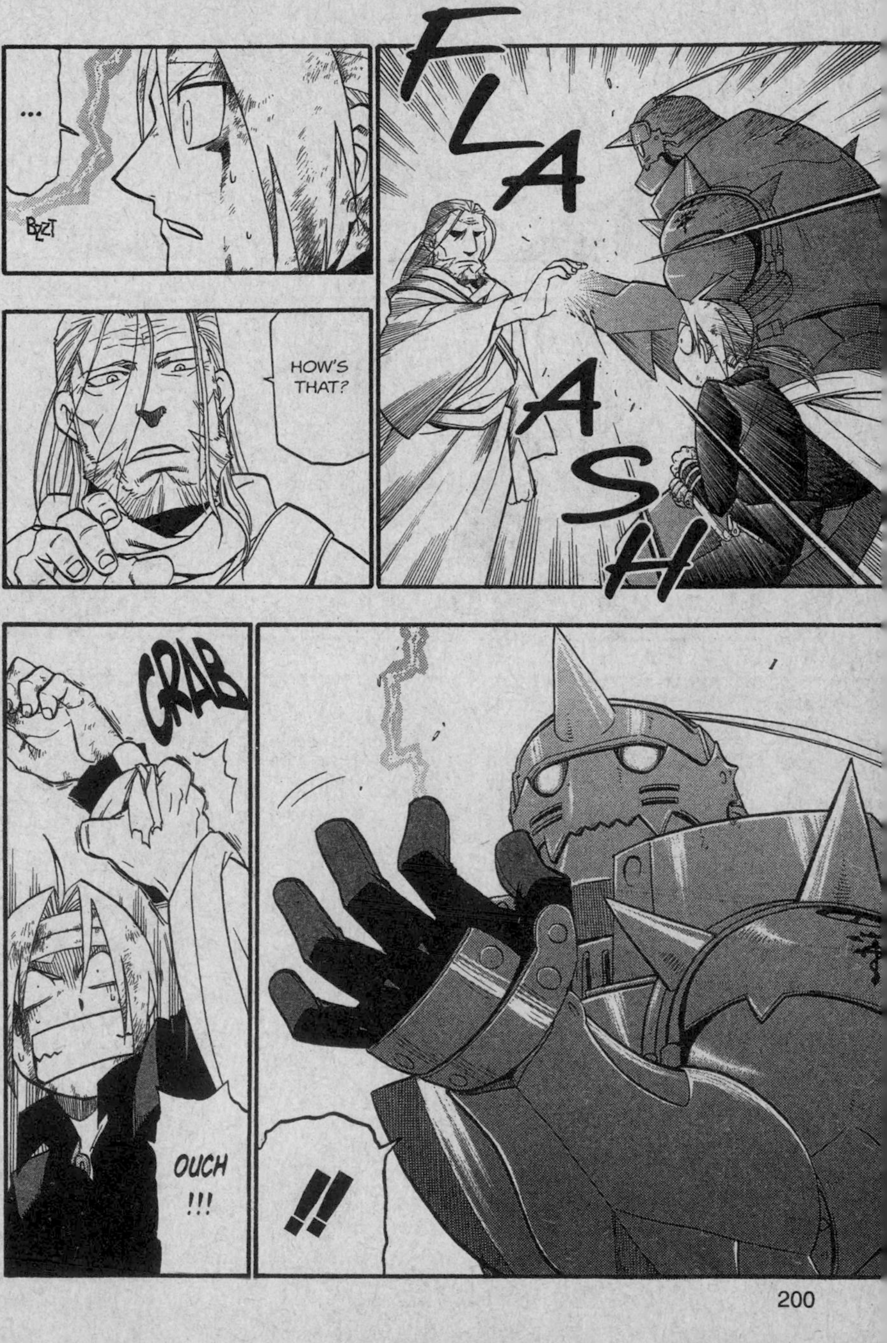
FLASH
...
BZZT
HOW'S THAT?
!!
GRAB
OUCH !!!

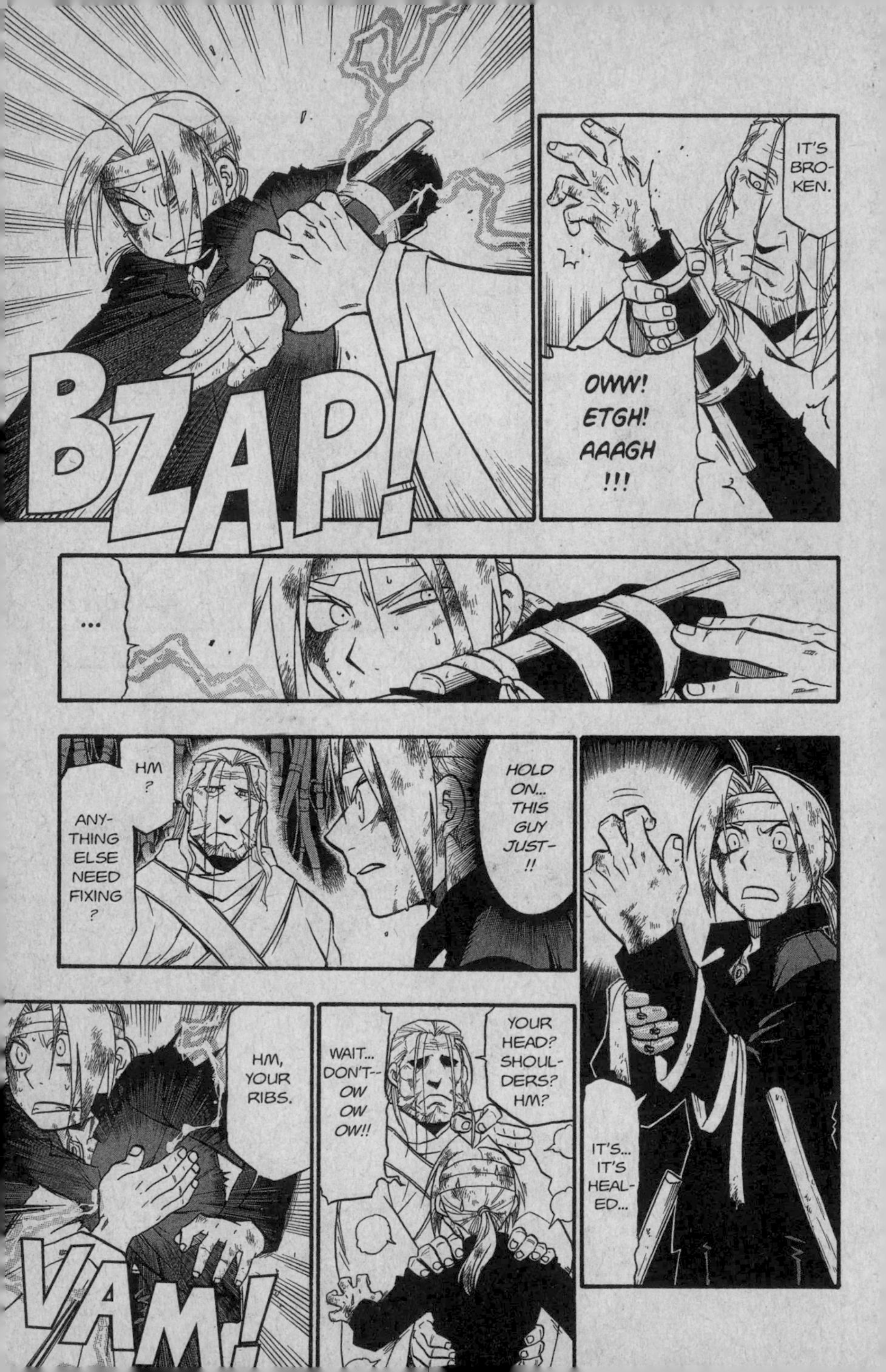
IT'S BRO-KEN.
OWW! ETGH! AAAGH!!!
BZAP!
...
IT'S... IT'S HEAL-ED...
HOLD ON... THIS GUY JUST-!!
HM?
ANY-THING ELSE NEED FIXING?
YOUR HEAD? SHOUL-DERS? HM?
WAIT... DON'T-- OW OW OW!!
HM, YOUR RIBS.
VAM!

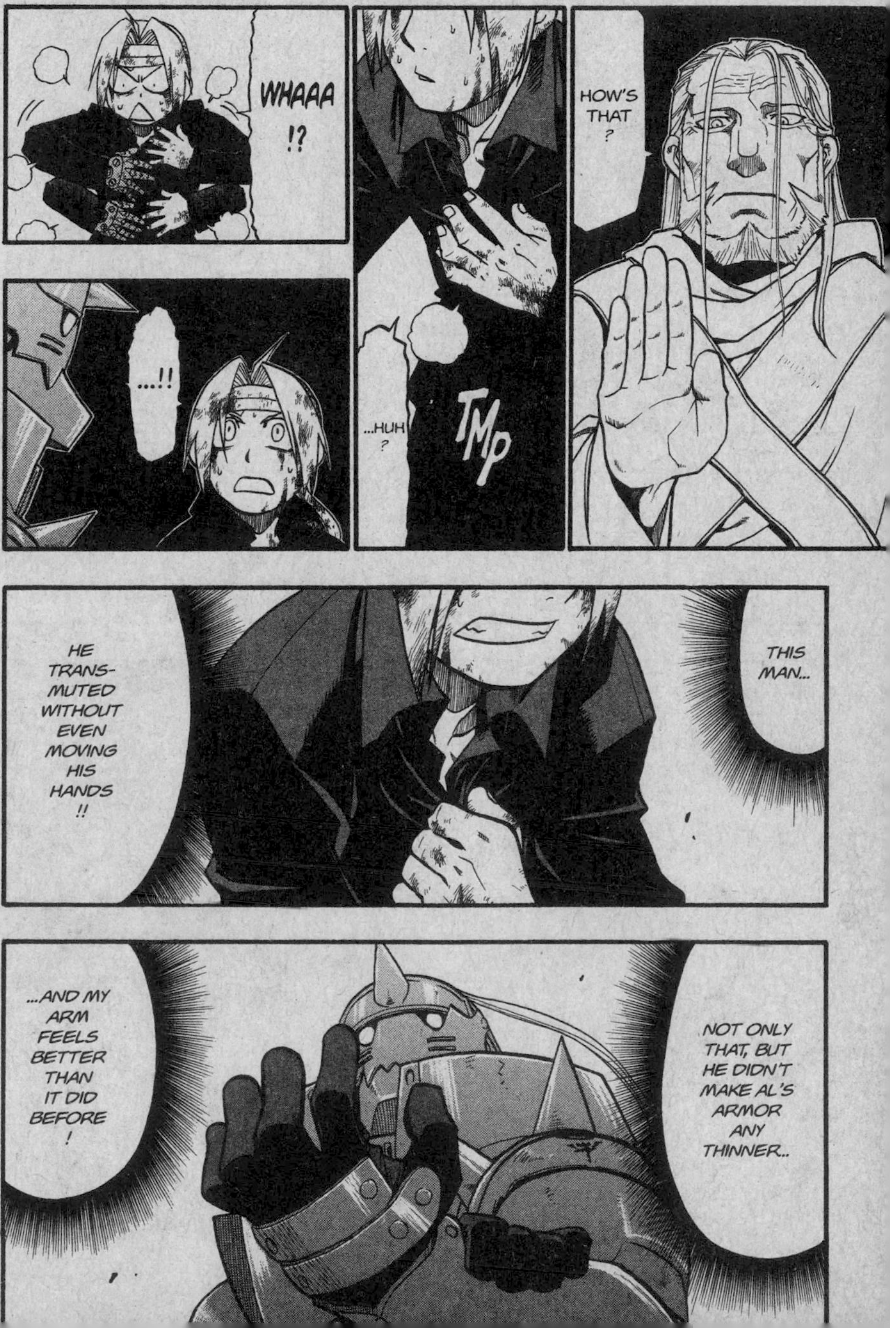
HOW'S THAT?
...HUH?
TMP
WHAAA!?
...!!
THIS MAN...
HE TRANSMUTED WITHOUT EVEN MOVING HIS HANDS!!
NOT ONLY THAT, BUT HE DIDN'T MAKE AL'S ARMOR ANY THINNER...
...AND MY ARM FEELS BETTER THAN IT DID BEFORE!

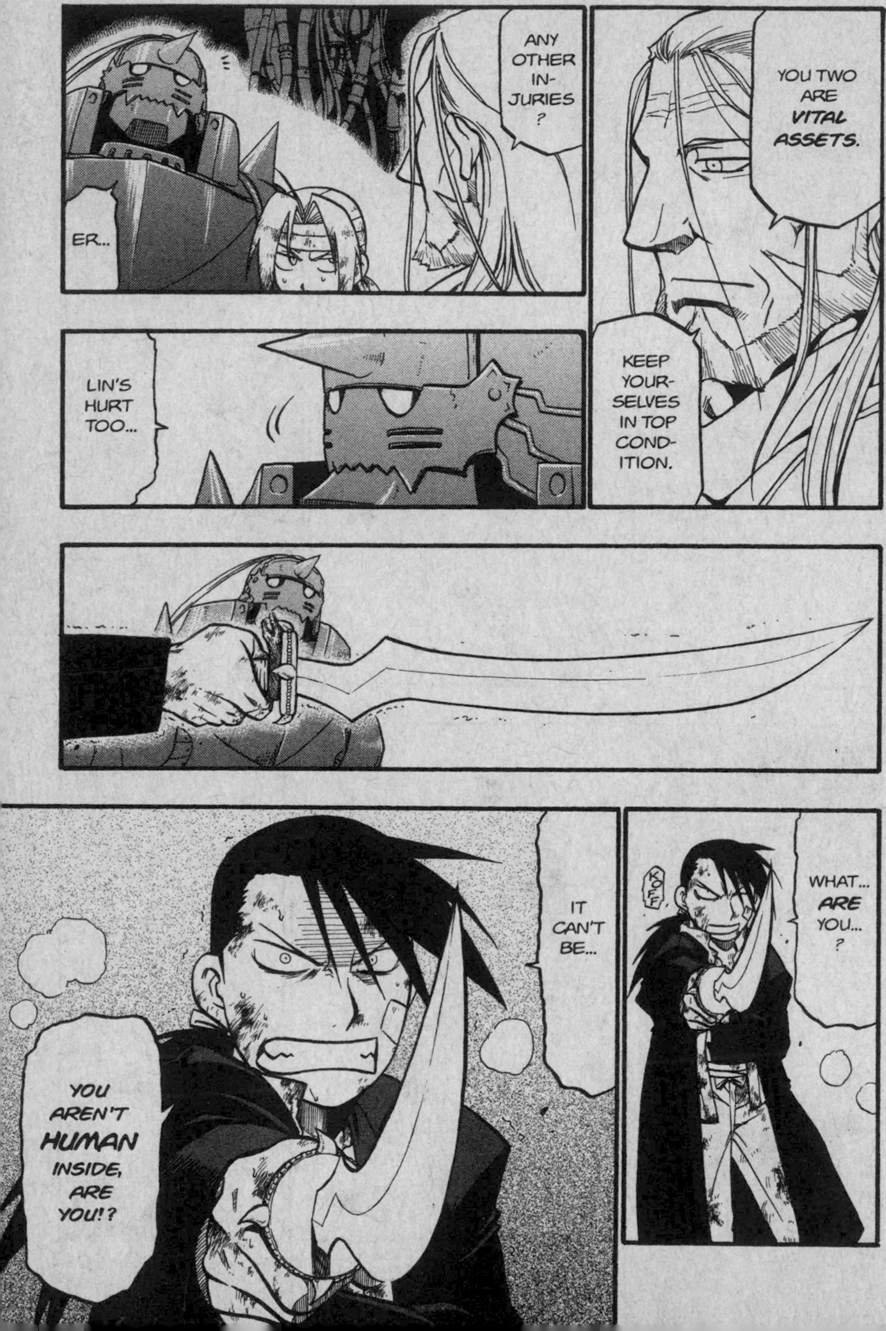
YOU TWO ARE VITAL ASSETS.
KEEP YOURSELVES IN TOP CONDITION.
ANY OTHER INJURIES?
ER...
LIN'S HURT TOO...
KOFF
WHAT... ARE YOU...?
IT CAN'T BE...
YOU AREN'T HUMAN INSIDE, ARE YOU!?

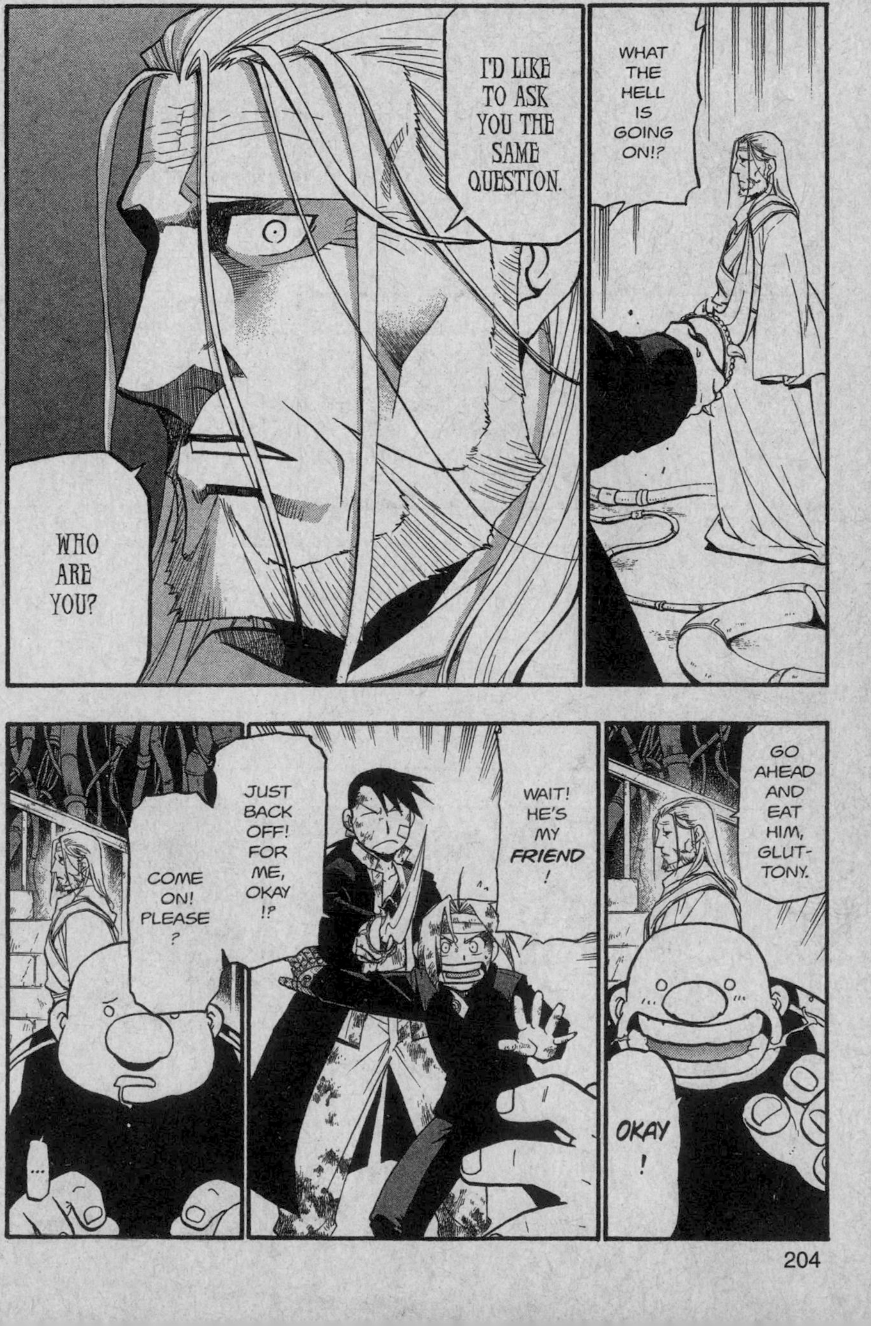
WHAT THE HELL IS GOING ON!?
I'D LIKE TO ASK YOU THE SAME QUESTION.
WHO ARE YOU?
GO AHEAD AND EAT HIM, GLUTTONY.
OKAY!
WAIT! HE'S MY *FRIEND*!
JUST BACK OFF! FOR ME, OKAY!?
COME ON! PLEASE?
...

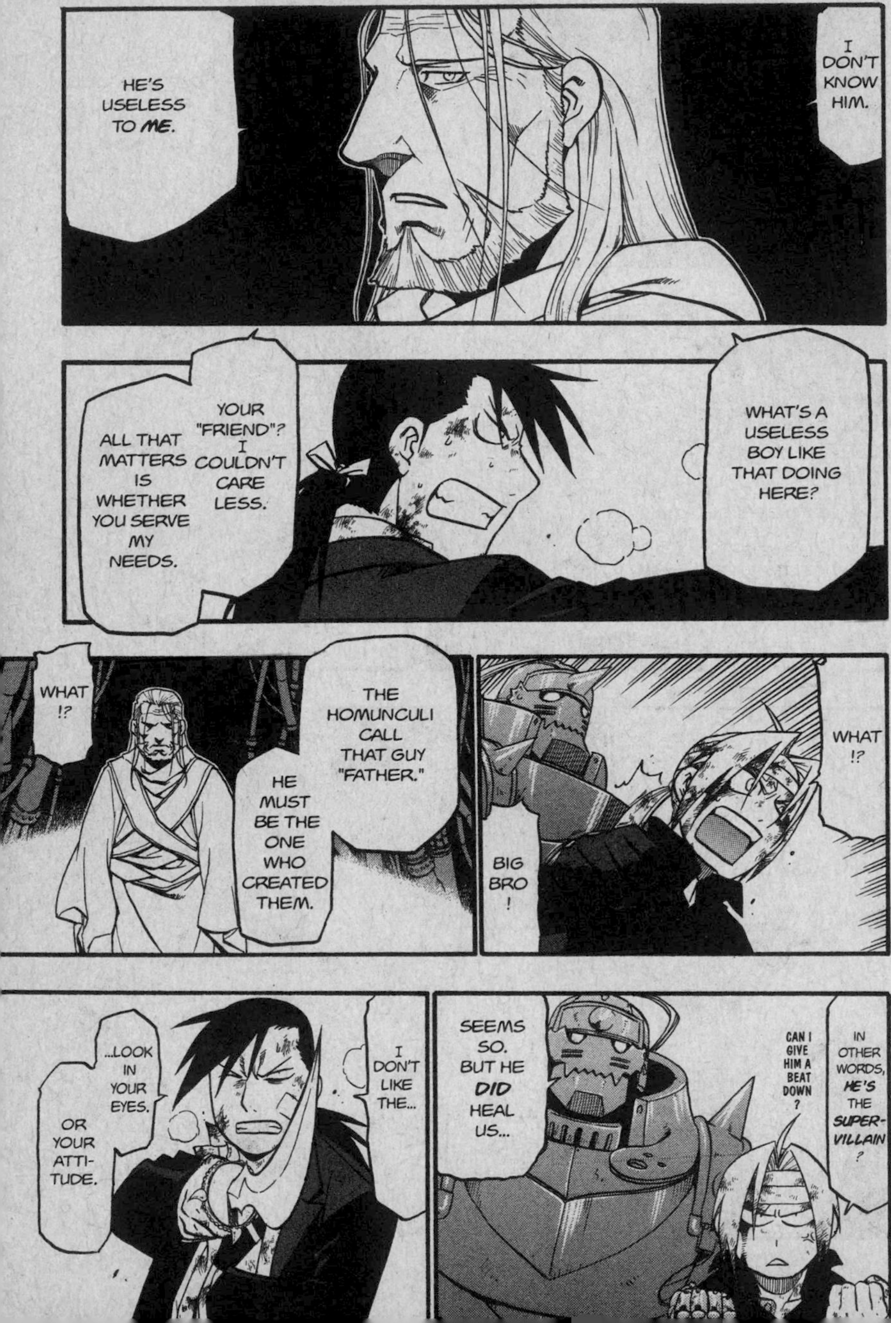
I DON'T KNOW HIM.
HE'S USELESS TO **ME**.
WHAT'S A USELESS BOY LIKE THAT DOING HERE?
YOUR "FRIEND"? I COULDN'T CARE LESS.
ALL THAT MATTERS IS WHETHER YOU SERVE MY NEEDS.
WHAT!?
BIG BRO!
THE HOMUNCULI CALL THAT GUY "FATHER."
HE MUST BE THE ONE WHO CREATED THEM.
WHAT!?
IN OTHER WORDS, **HE'S** THE **SUPER-VILLAIN**?
CAN I GIVE HIM A BEAT DOWN?
SEEMS SO. BUT HE **DID** HEAL US...
I DON'T LIKE THE...
...LOOK IN YOUR EYES.
OR YOUR ATTITUDE.

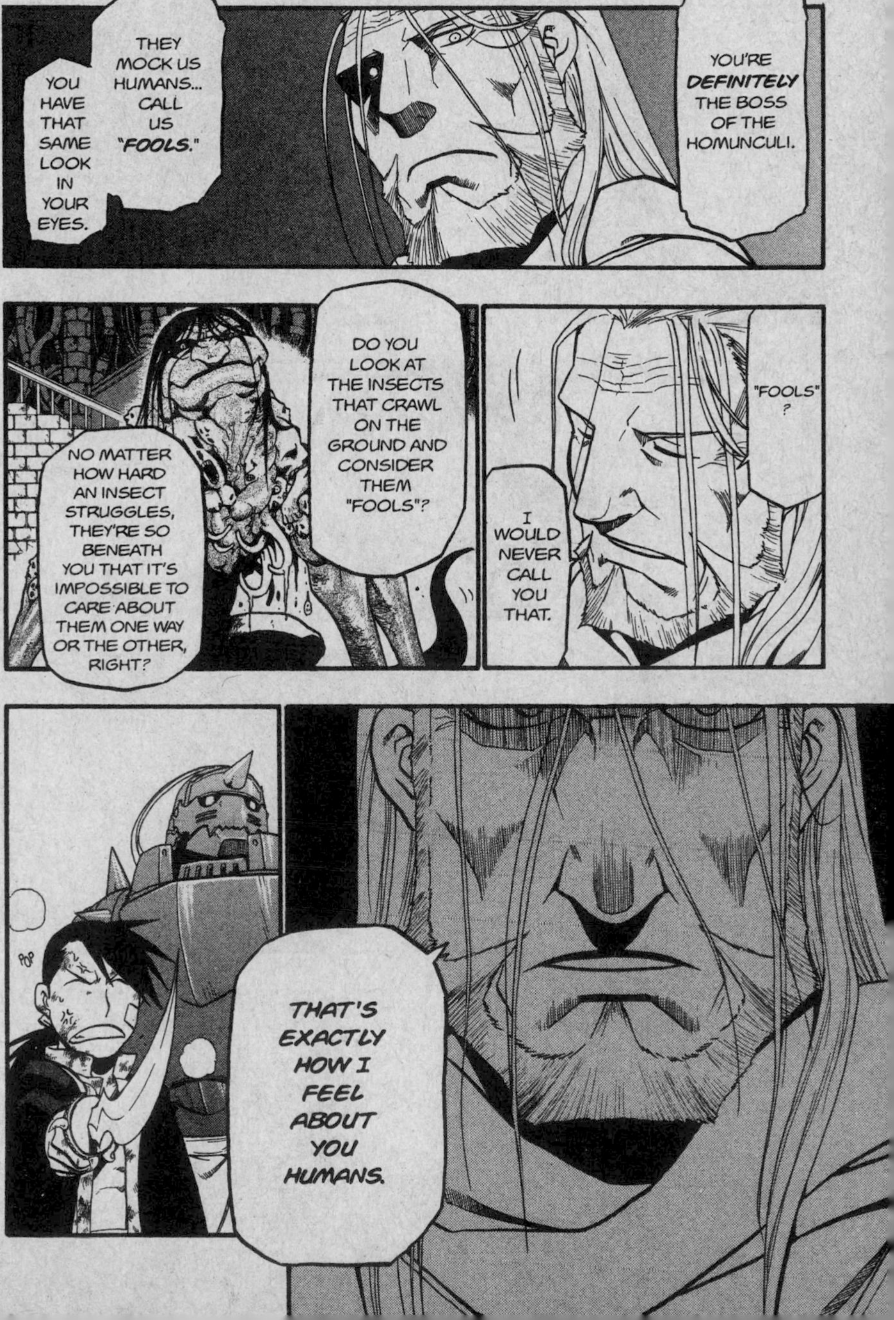
YOU'RE DEFINITELY THE BOSS OF THE HOMUNCULI.
THEY MOCK US HUMANS... CALL US "FOOLS."
YOU HAVE THAT SAME LOOK IN YOUR EYES.
"FOOLS"?
I WOULD NEVER CALL YOU THAT.
DO YOU LOOK AT THE INSECTS THAT CRAWL ON THE GROUND AND CONSIDER THEM "FOOLS"?
NO MATTER HOW HARD AN INSECT STRUGGLES, THEY'RE SO BENEATH YOU THAT IT'S IMPOSSIBLE TO CARE ABOUT THEM ONE WAY OR THE OTHER, RIGHT?
THAT'S EXACTLY HOW I FEEL ABOUT YOU HUMANS.
POP

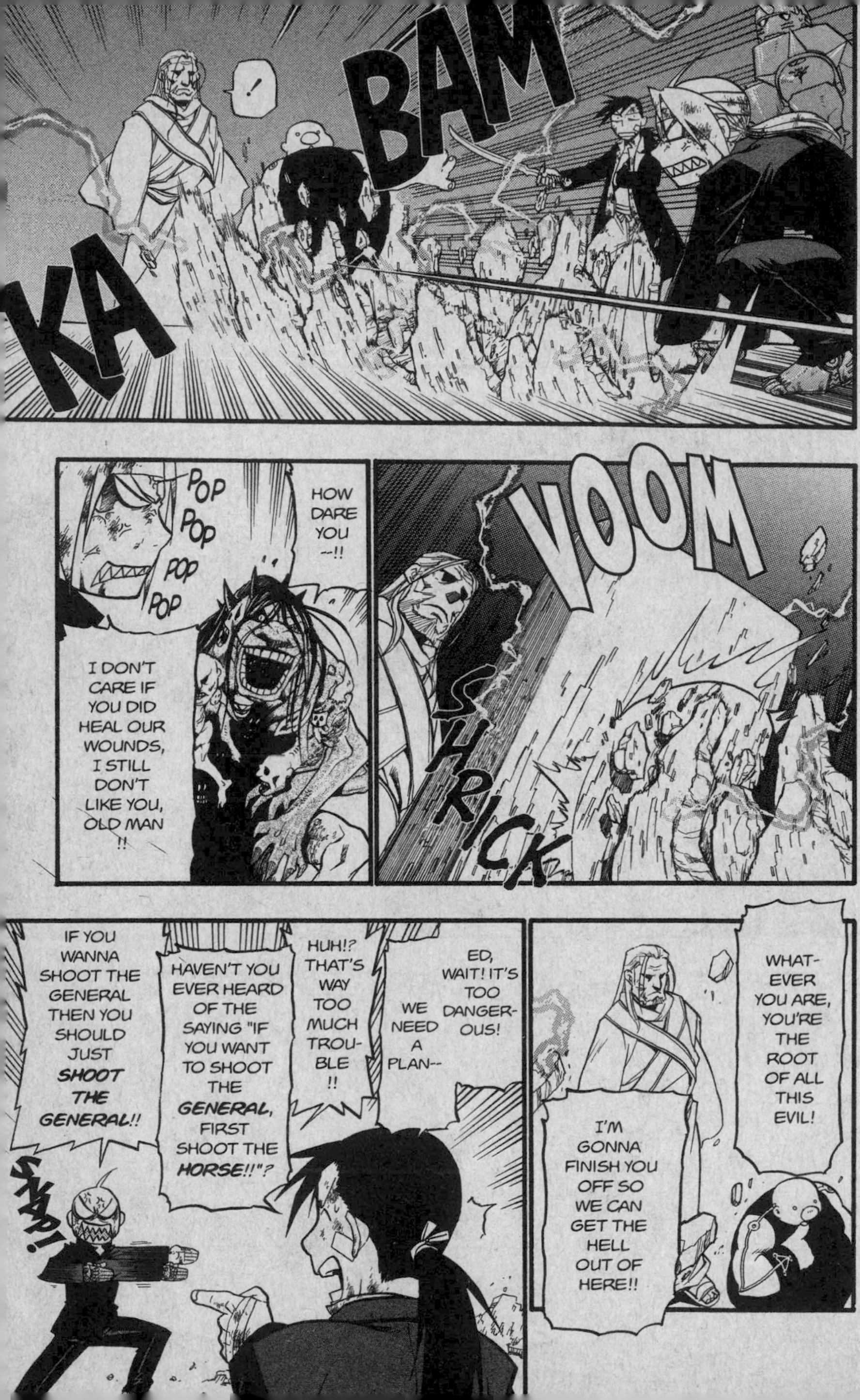
BAM
!
KA
VOOM
SHRICK
HOW DARE YOU--!!
POP POP POP POP
I DON'T CARE IF YOU DID HEAL OUR WOUNDS, I STILL DON'T LIKE YOU, OLD MAN!!
WHATEVER YOU ARE, YOU'RE THE ROOT OF ALL THIS EVIL!
I'M GONNA FINISH YOU OFF SO WE CAN GET THE HELL OUT OF HERE!!
ED, WAIT! IT'S TOO DANGEROUS!
WE NEED A PLAN--
HUH!? THAT'S WAY TOO MUCH TROUBLE!!
HAVEN'T YOU EVER HEARD OF THE SAYING "IF YOU WANT TO SHOOT THE GENERAL, FIRST SHOOT THE HORSE!!"?
IF YOU WANNA SHOOT THE GENERAL THEN YOU SHOULD JUST SHOOT THE GENERAL!!
SNAP!

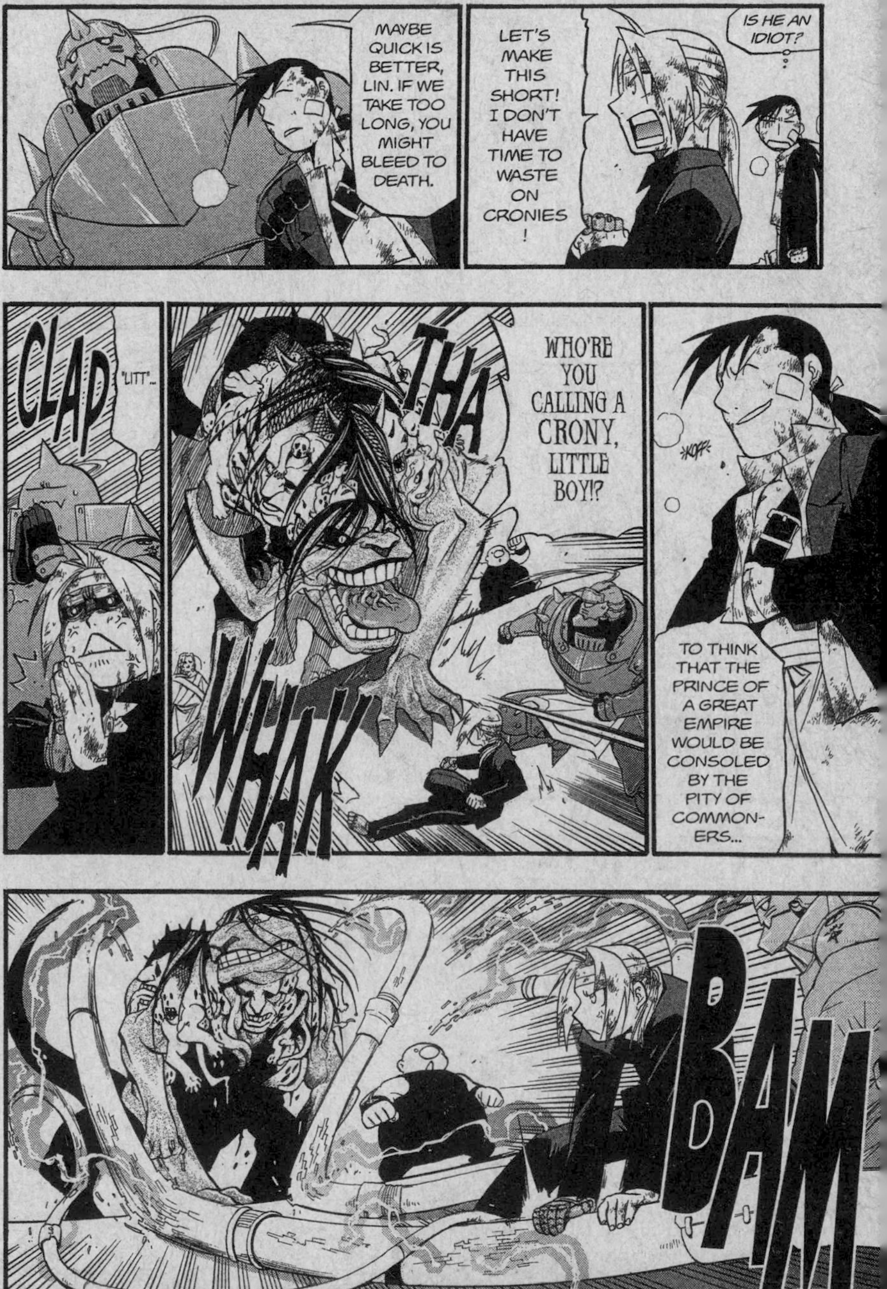
LET'S MAKE THIS SHORT! I DON'T HAVE TIME TO WASTE ON CRONIES!
IS HE AN IDIOT?
MAYBE QUICK IS BETTER, LIN. IF WE TAKE TOO LONG, YOU MIGHT BLEED TO DEATH.
KOFF
TO THINK THAT THE PRINCE OF A GREAT EMPIRE WOULD BE CONSOLED BY THE PITY OF COMMONERS...
WHO'RE YOU CALLING A CRONY, LITTLE BOY!?
THA
WHAK
CLAP
"LITT"...
BAM

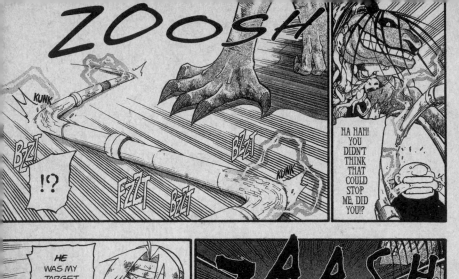

ZOOSH

KUNK

BZZT

!?

BZZT BZZT

BZZT

KUNK

HA HAH! YOU DIDN'T THINK THAT COULD STOP ME, DID YOU!?

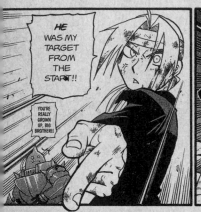

HE WAS MY TARGET FROM THE START!!

YOU'RE REALLY GROWN UP, BIG BROTHER!!

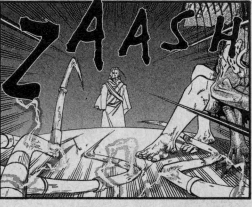

ZAASH

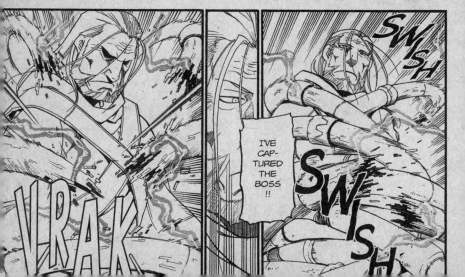

VRAK

I'VE CAP-TURED THE BOSS!!

SWISH

SWISH

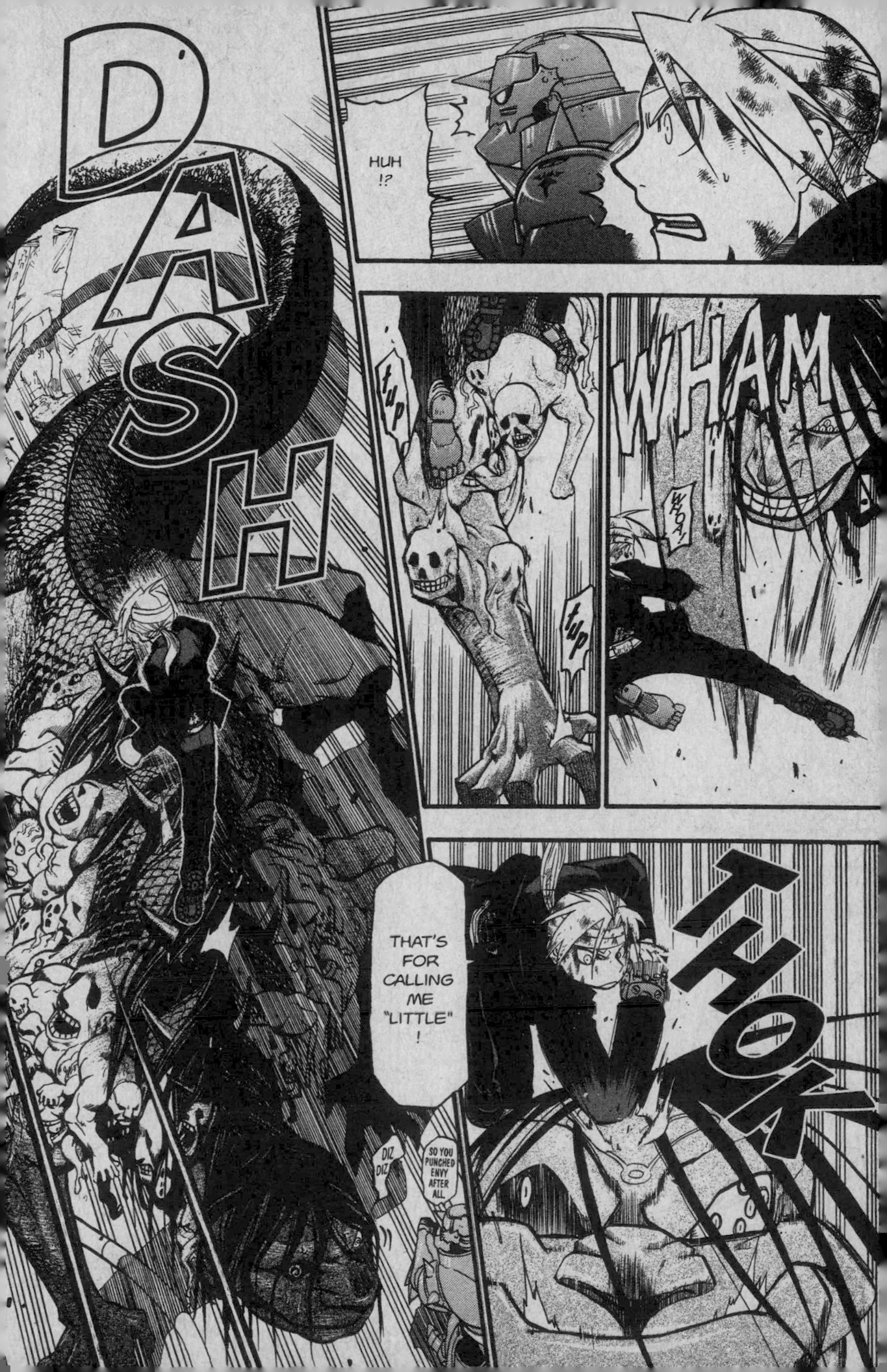
HUH !?
WHAM
WHOA!
tup
tup
THOK
THAT'S FOR CALLING ME "LITTLE" !
SO YOU PUNCHED ENVY AFTER ALL
DIZ DIZ
DASH

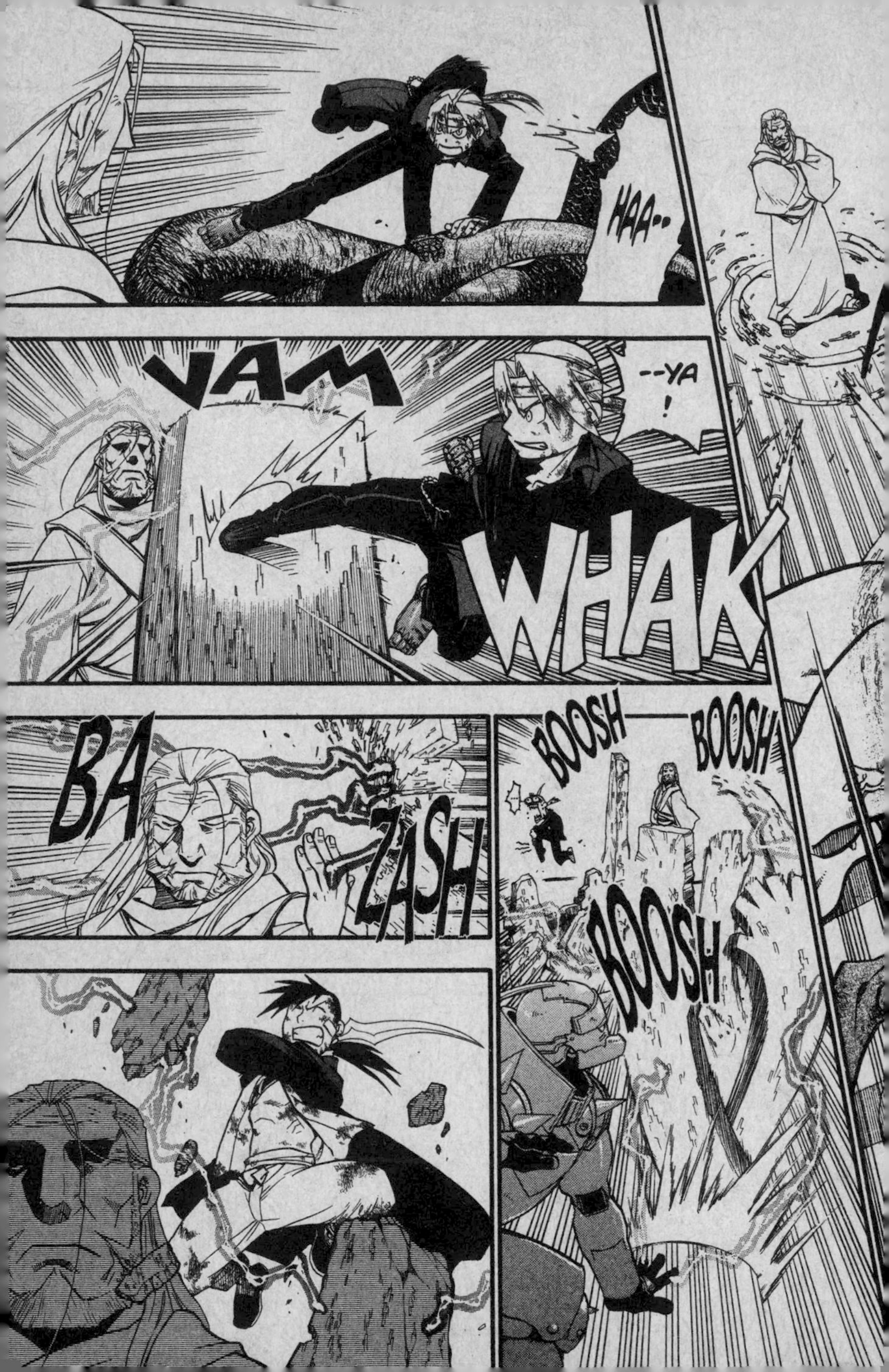
HAA..
--YA!
VAM
WHAK
BOOSH
BOOSH
BOOSH
BA
ZASH

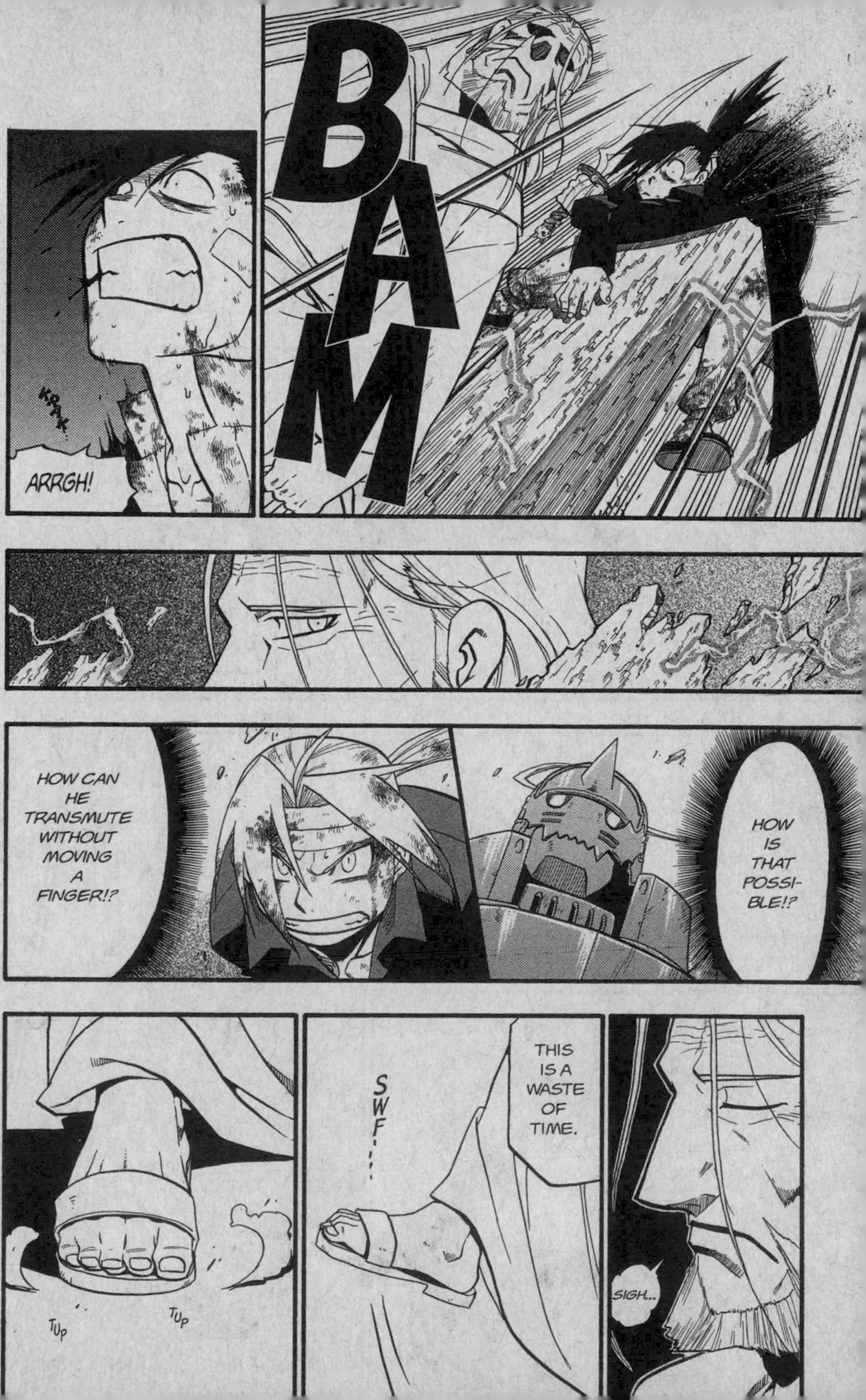
BAM
KRAK
ARRGH!
HOW IS THAT POSSIBLE!?
HOW CAN HE TRANSMUTE WITHOUT MOVING A FINGER!?
SIGH...
SWF...
THIS IS A WASTE OF TIME.
TUP
TUP

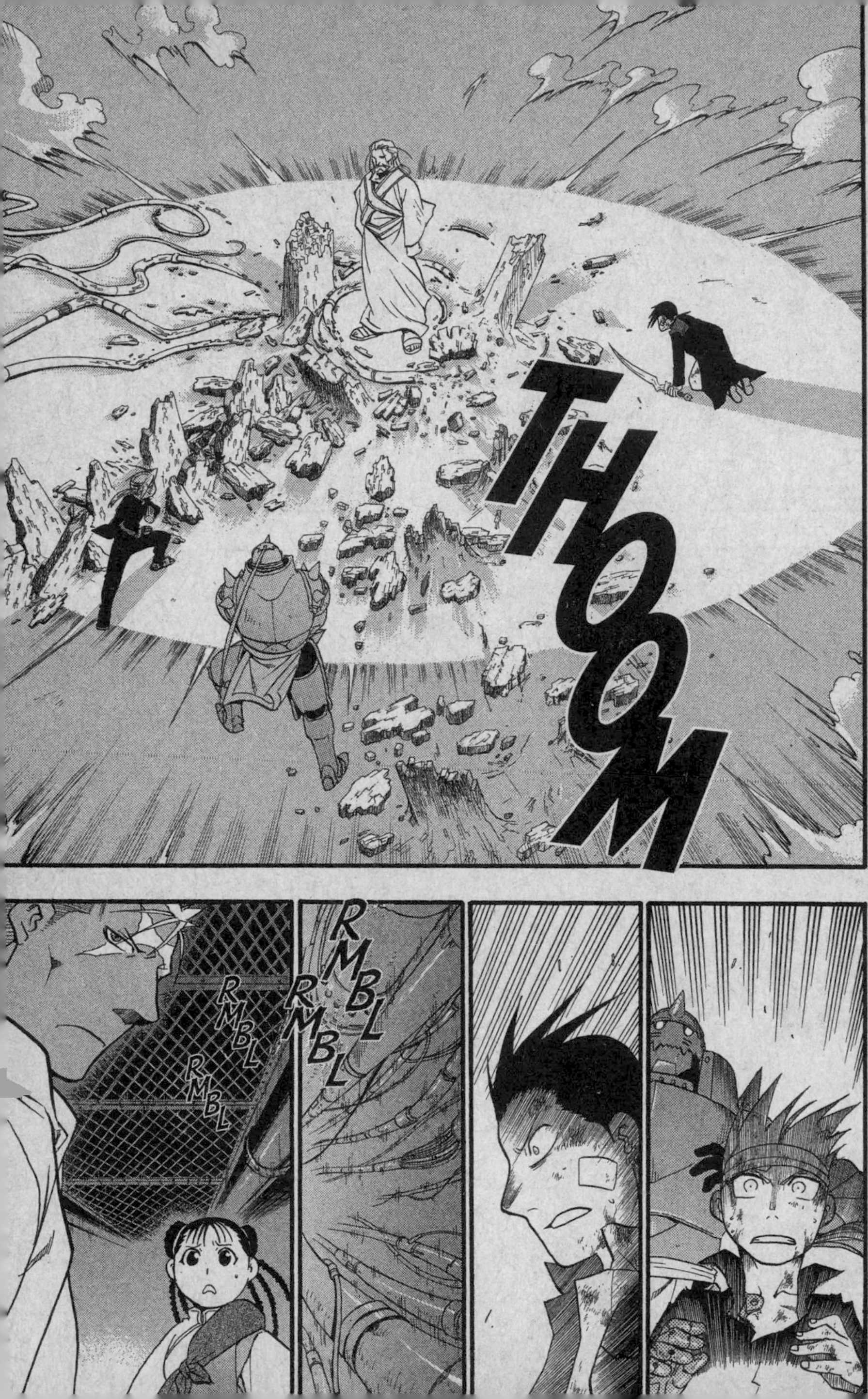
THOOM
RMBL
RMBL
RMBL
RMBL

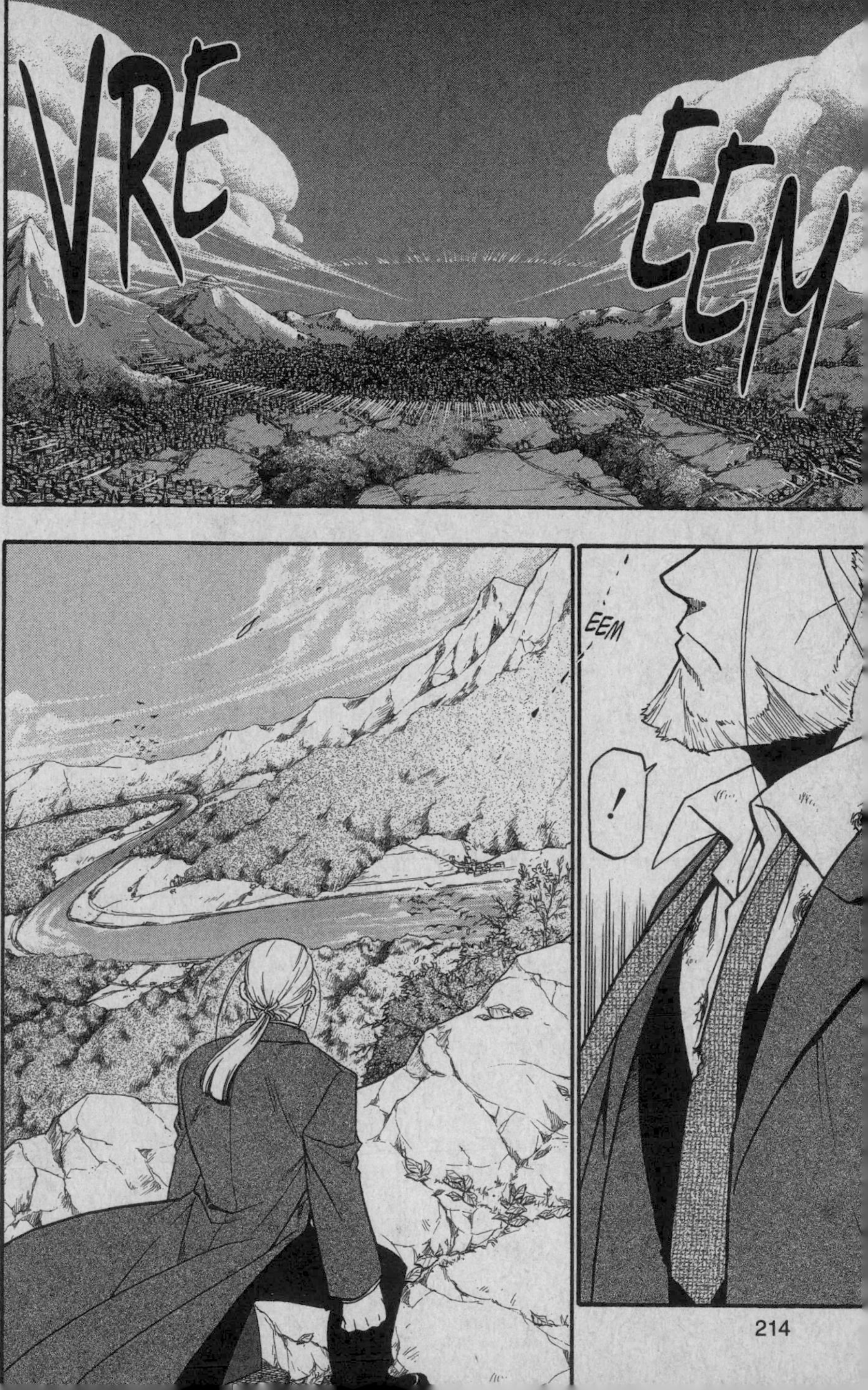
VRE
EEM
EEM
!

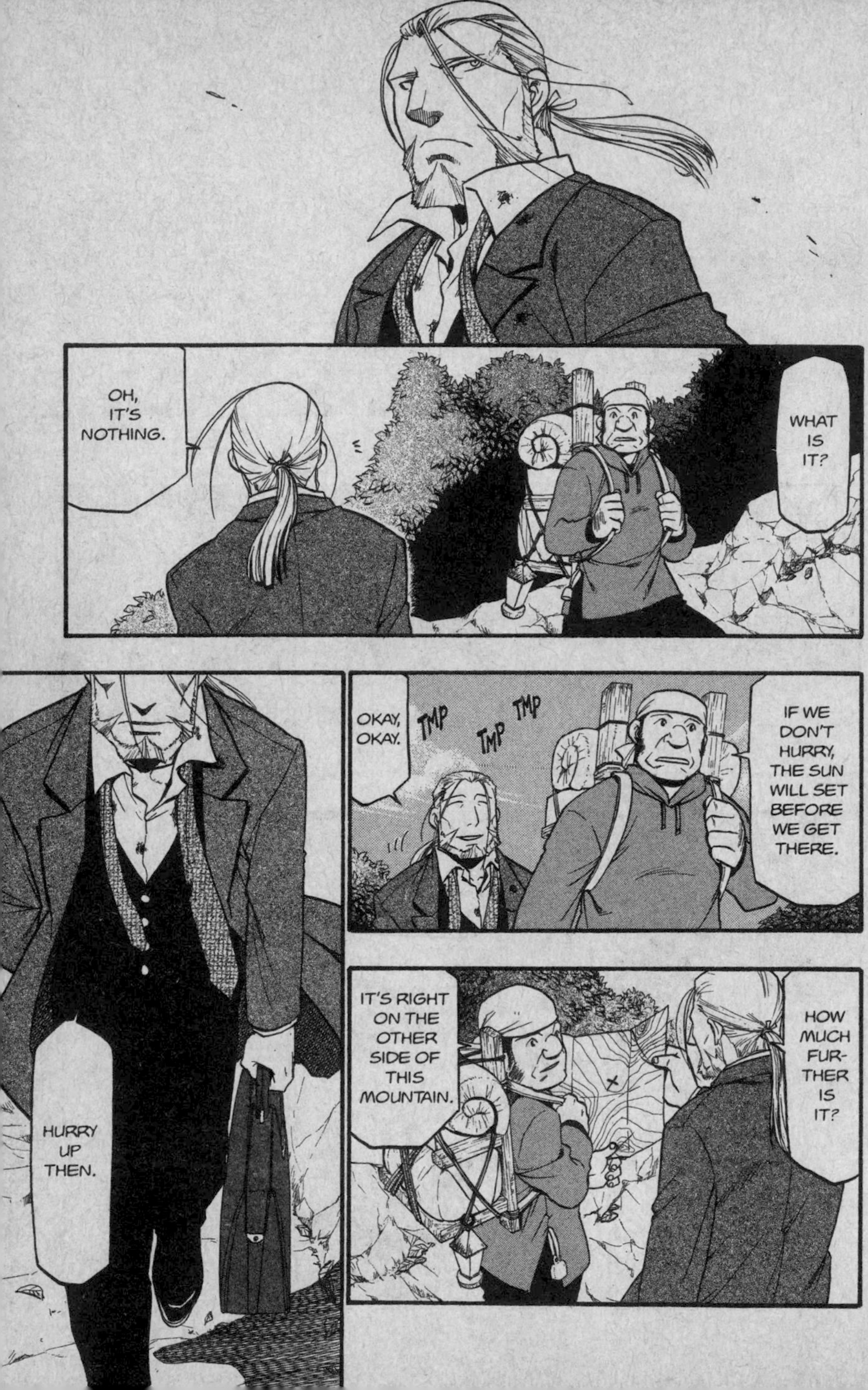
WHAT IS IT?
OH, IT'S NOTHING.
IF WE DON'T HURRY, THE SUN WILL SET BEFORE WE GET THERE.
TMP
TMP
TMP
OKAY, OKAY.
HOW MUCH FUR-THER IS IT?
IT'S RIGHT ON THE OTHER SIDE OF THIS MOUNTAIN.
HURRY UP THEN.

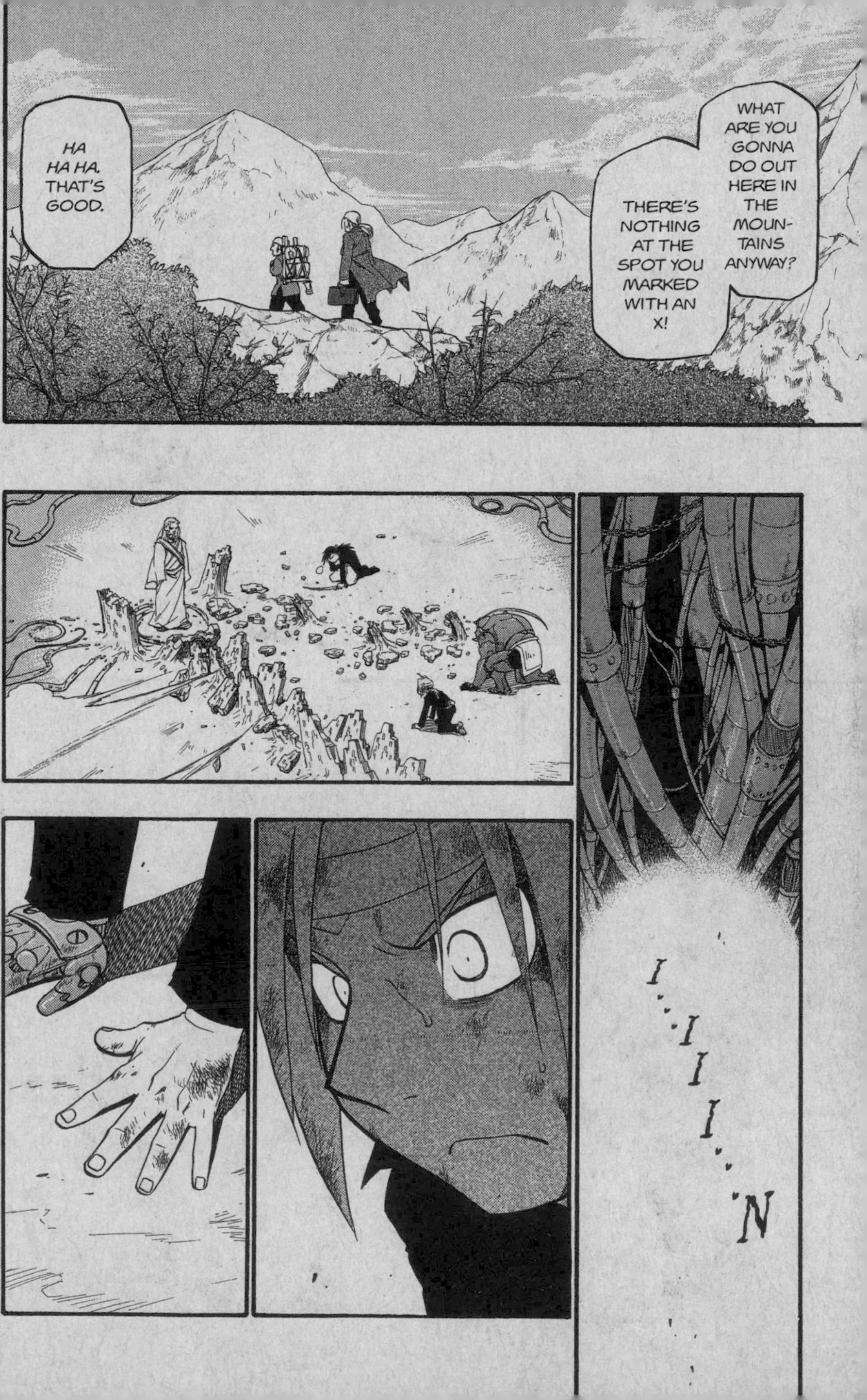
WHAT ARE YOU GONNA DO OUT HERE IN THE MOUNTAINS ANYWAY?
THERE'S NOTHING AT THE SPOT YOU MARKED WITH AN X!
HA HA HA. THAT'S GOOD.
I..IIII..N

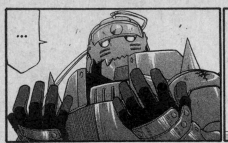

...

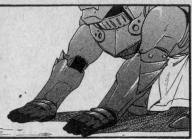

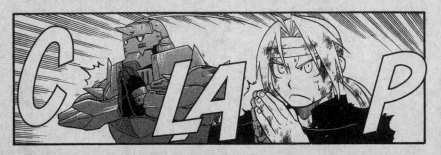

CLAP

SILENCE...

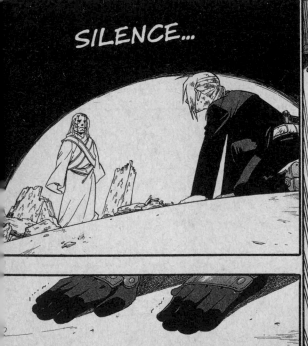

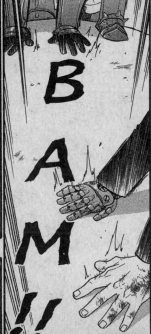

BAM!!

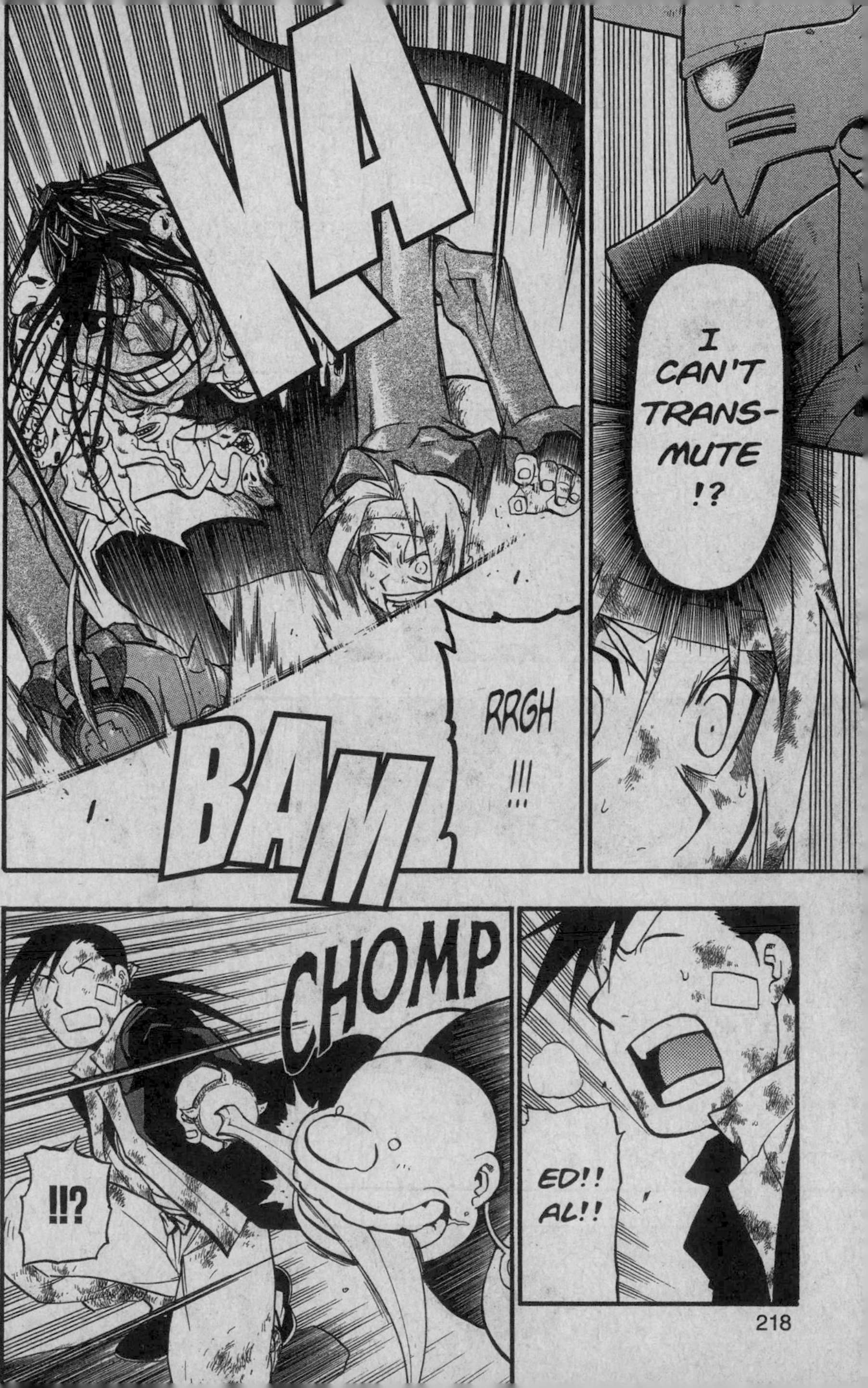
I CAN'T TRANSMUTE !?
KA
RRGH !!!
BAM
ED!! AL!!
CHOMP
!!?

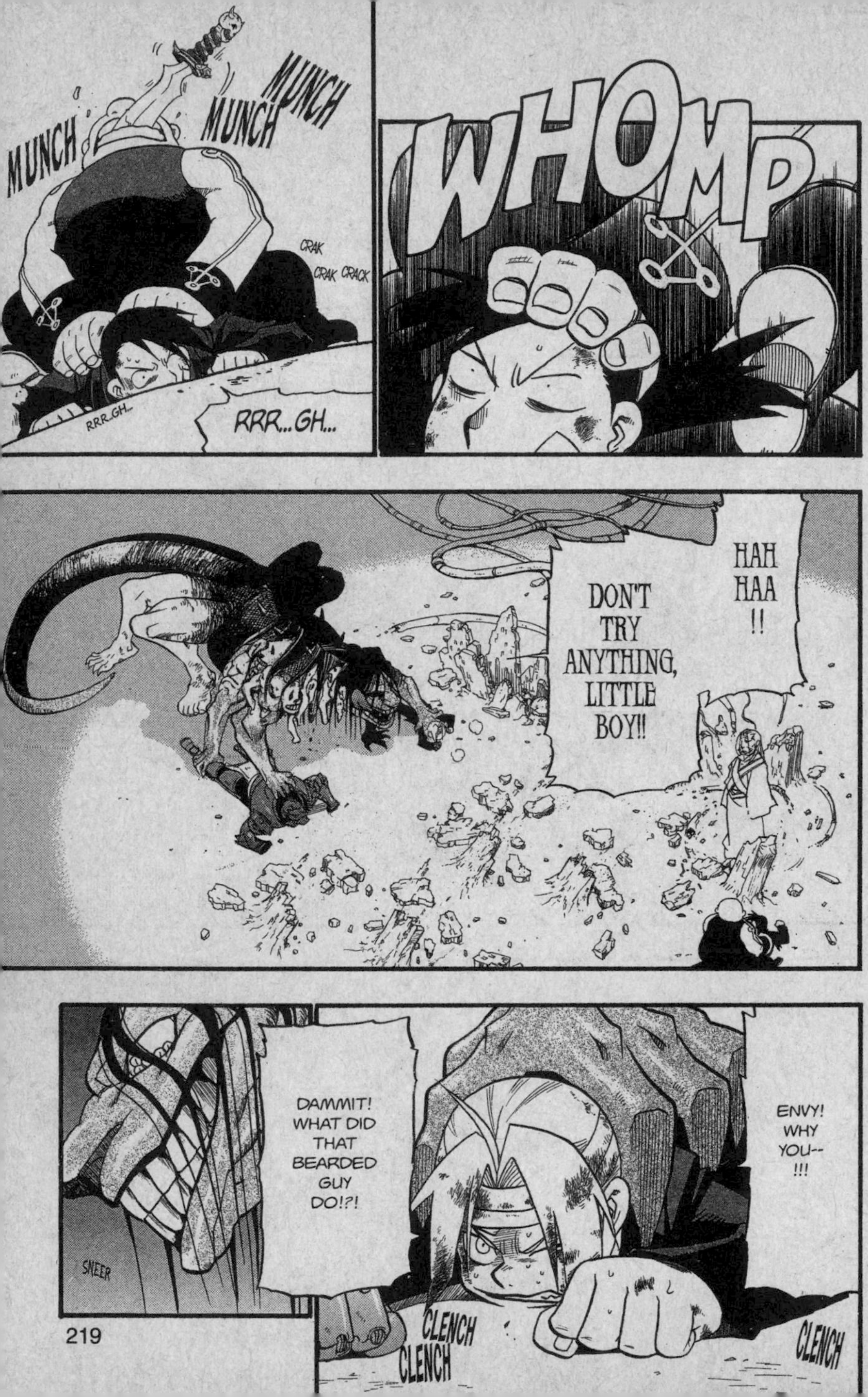
WHOMP
MUNCH
MUNCH
MUNCH
CRAK
CRAK CRACK
RRR...GH...
RRR...GH...
HAH HAA!!
DON'T TRY ANYTHING, LITTLE BOY!!
ENVY! WHY YOU--!!!
DAMMIT! WHAT DID THAT BEARDED GUY DO!?!
CLENCH
CLENCH
CLENCH
SNEER

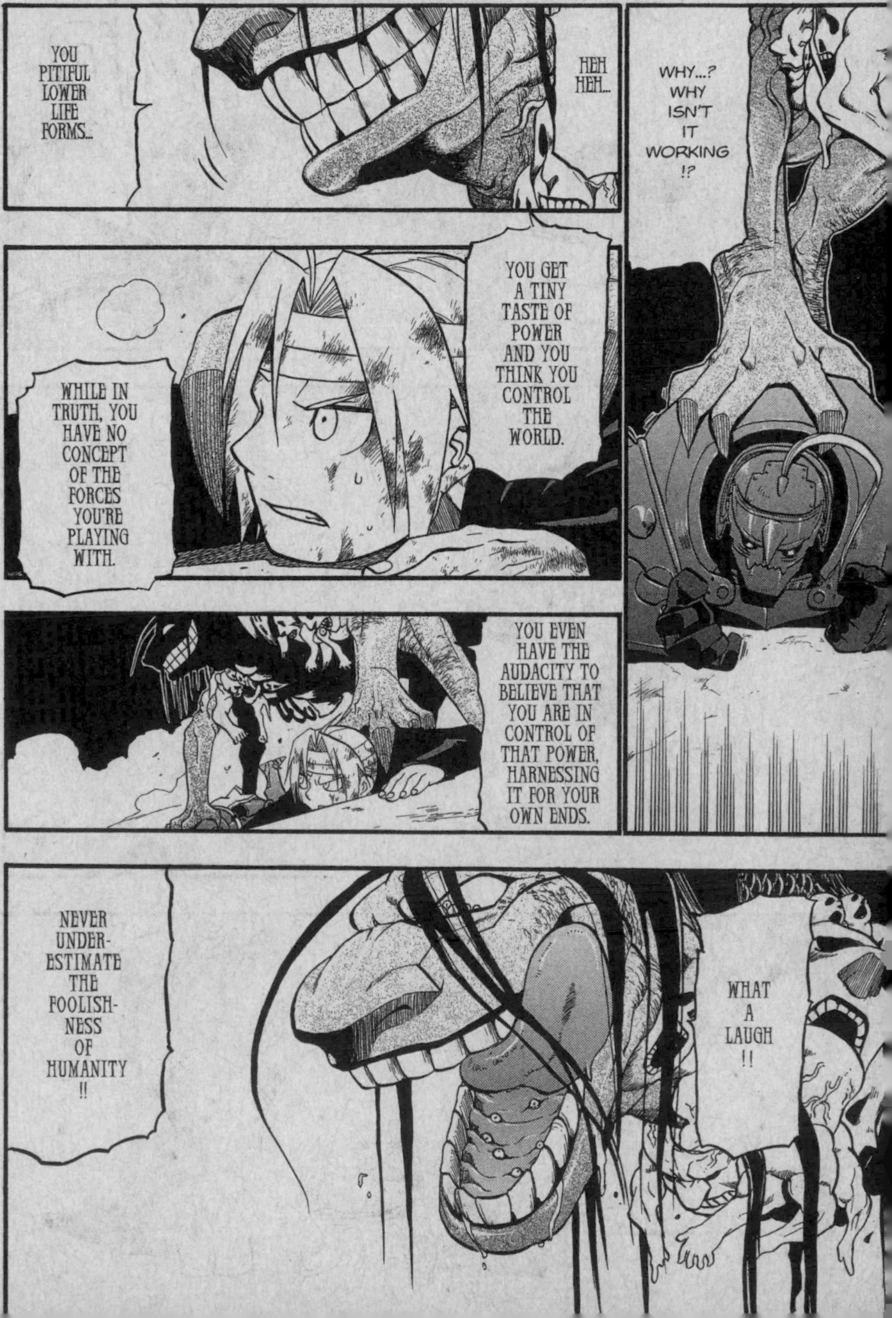
WHY...? WHY ISN'T IT WORKING !?
HEH HEH...
YOU PITIFUL LOWER LIFE FORMS...
YOU GET A TINY TASTE OF POWER AND YOU THINK YOU CONTROL THE WORLD.
WHILE IN TRUTH, YOU HAVE NO CONCEPT OF THE FORCES YOU'RE PLAYING WITH.
YOU EVEN HAVE THE AUDACITY TO BELIEVE THAT YOU ARE IN CONTROL OF THAT POWER, HARNESSING IT FOR YOUR OWN ENDS.
WHAT A LAUGH !!
NEVER UNDER-ESTIMATE THE FOOLISH-NESS OF HUMANITY !!

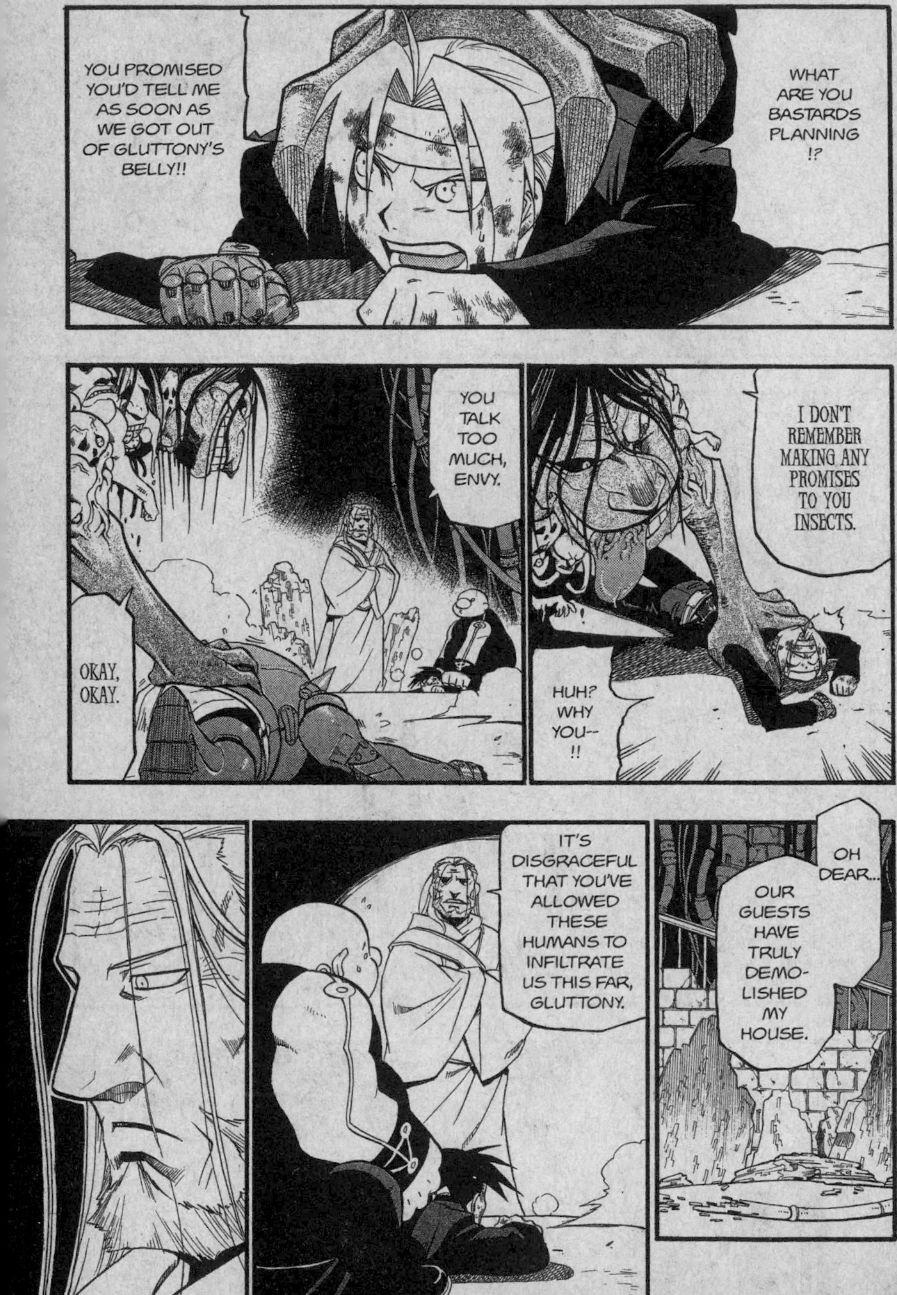
WHAT ARE YOU BASTARDS PLANNING !?
YOU PROMISED YOU'D TELL ME AS SOON AS WE GOT OUT OF GLUTTONY'S BELLY!!
I DON'T REMEMBER MAKING ANY PROMISES TO YOU INSECTS.
HUH? WHY YOU-- !!
YOU TALK TOO MUCH, ENVY.
OKAY, OKAY.
OH DEAR...
OUR GUESTS HAVE TRULY DEMOLISHED MY HOUSE.
IT'S DISGRACEFUL THAT YOU'VE ALLOWED THESE HUMANS TO INFILTRATE US THIS FAR, GLUTTONY.

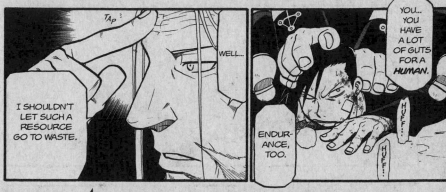

YOU... YOU HAVE A LOT OF GUTS FOR A HUMAN.
HUFF...
HUFF!!...
ENDURANCE, TOO.
TAP
WELL...
I SHOULDN'T LET SUCH A RESOURCE GO TO WASTE.
YOU'D MAKE A GOOD PAWN.
BA
GAH
GLUB
GLUB
GLUB
GLUB
GLUB

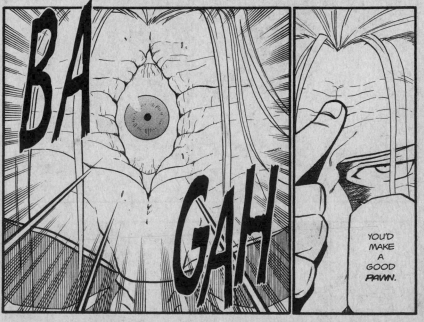

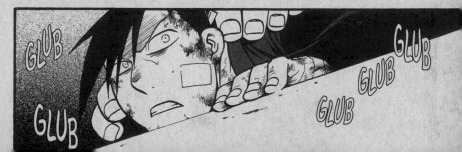

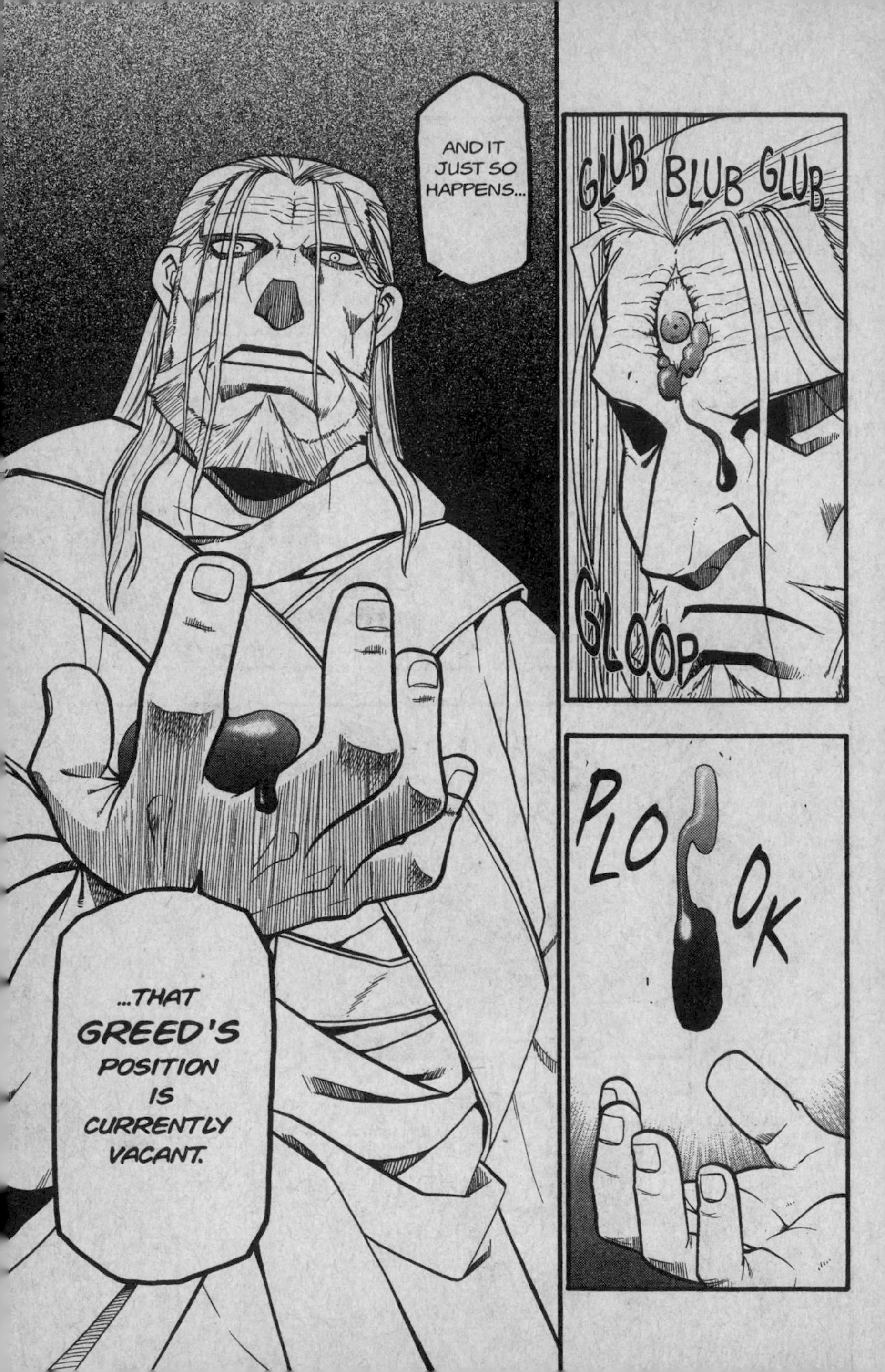
GLUB BLUB GLUB
GLOOP
PLOOK
AND IT JUST SO HAPPENS...
...THAT GREED'S POSITION IS CURRENTLY VACANT.

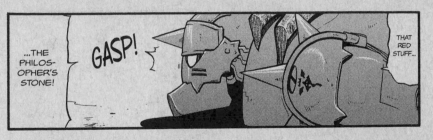

...THE PHILOSOPHER'S STONE!

GASP!

THAT RED STUFF...

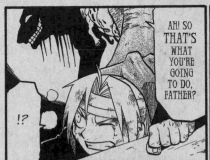

AH! SO THAT'S WHAT YOU'RE GOING TO DO, FATHER?

!?

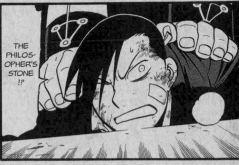

THE PHILOSOPHER'S STONE !?

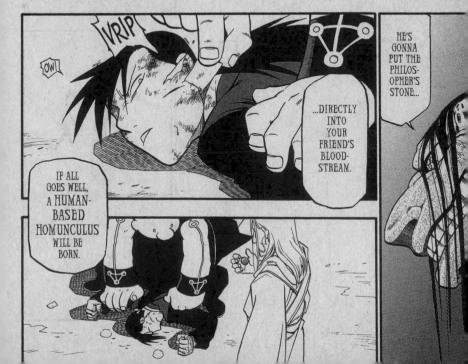

VRIP

OW!

HE'S GONNA PUT THE PHILOSOPHER'S STONE...

...DIRECTLY INTO YOUR FRIEND'S BLOODSTREAM.

IF ALL GOES WELL, A HUMAN-BASED HOMUNCULUS WILL BE BORN.

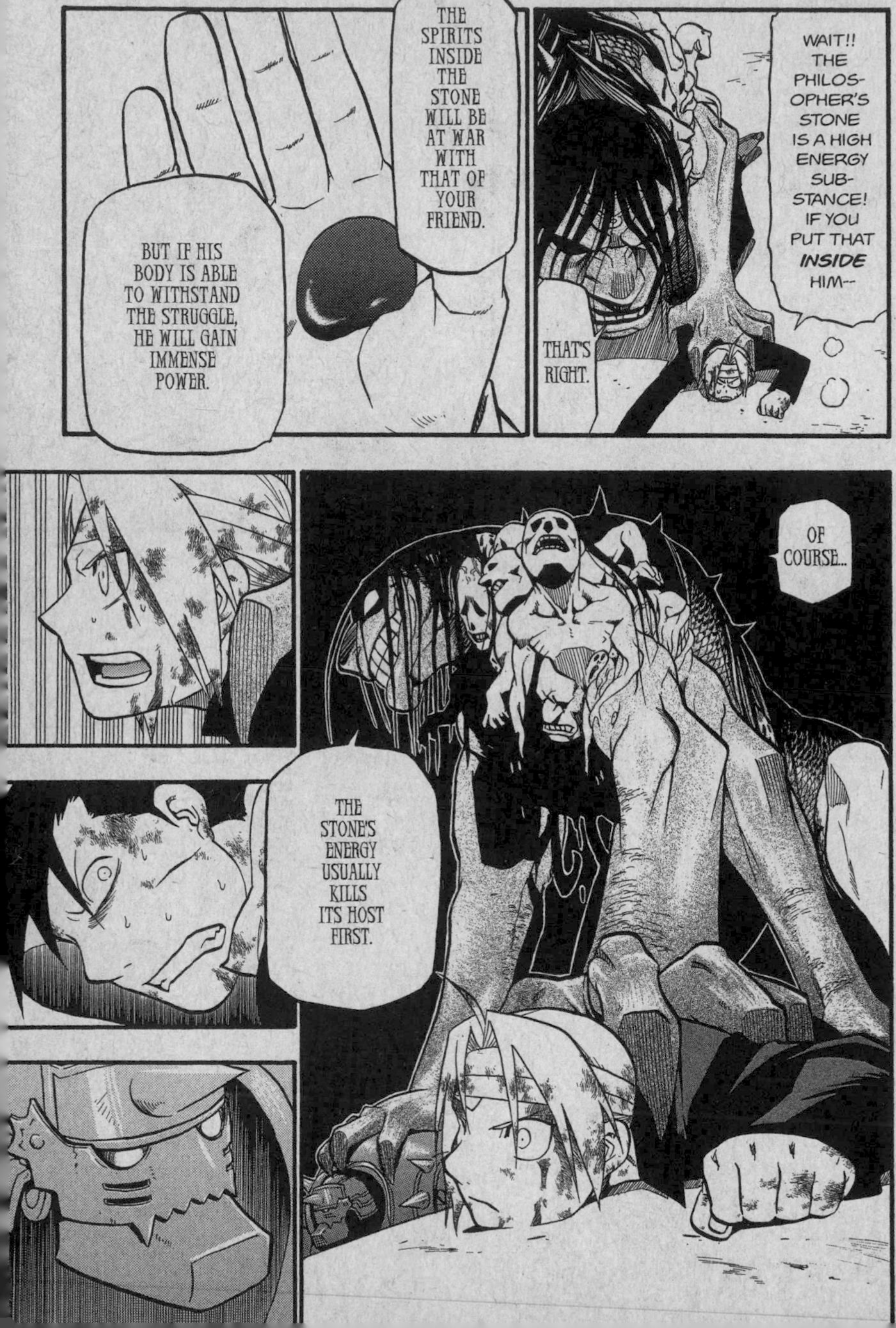
WAIT!! THE PHILOSOPHER'S STONE IS A HIGH ENERGY SUBSTANCE! IF YOU PUT THAT INSIDE HIM--
THAT'S RIGHT.
THE SPIRITS INSIDE THE STONE WILL BE AT WAR WITH THAT OF YOUR FRIEND.
BUT IF HIS BODY IS ABLE TO WITHSTAND THE STRUGGLE, HE WILL GAIN IMMENSE POWER.
OF COURSE...
THE STONE'S ENERGY USUALLY KILLS ITS HOST FIRST.

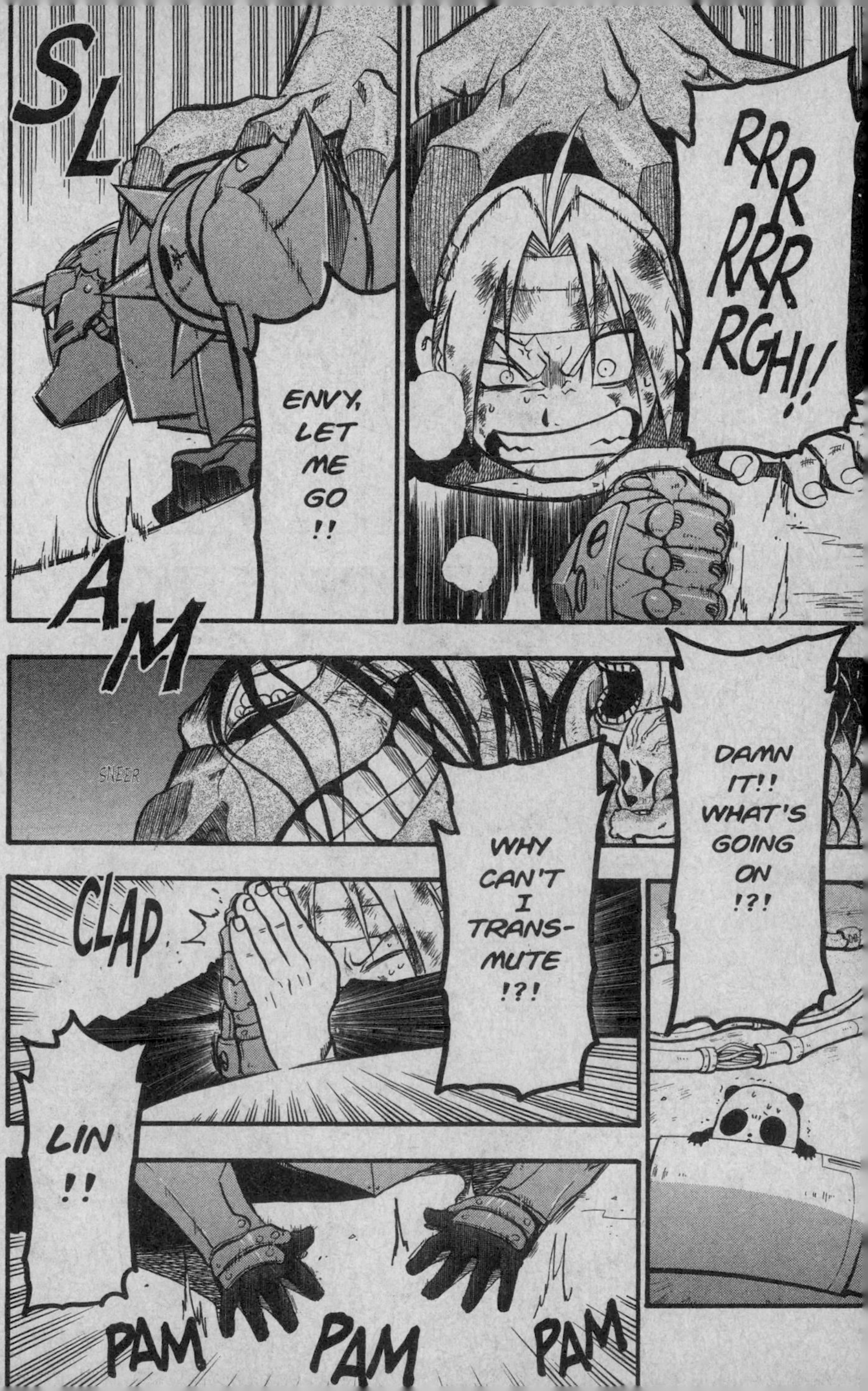
RRRRRRRRRRGH!!
ENVY, LET ME GO!!
SLAM
DAMN IT!! WHAT'S GOING ON!?!
SNEER
WHY CAN'T I TRANSMUTE!?!
CLAP
LIN!!
PAM
PAM
PAM

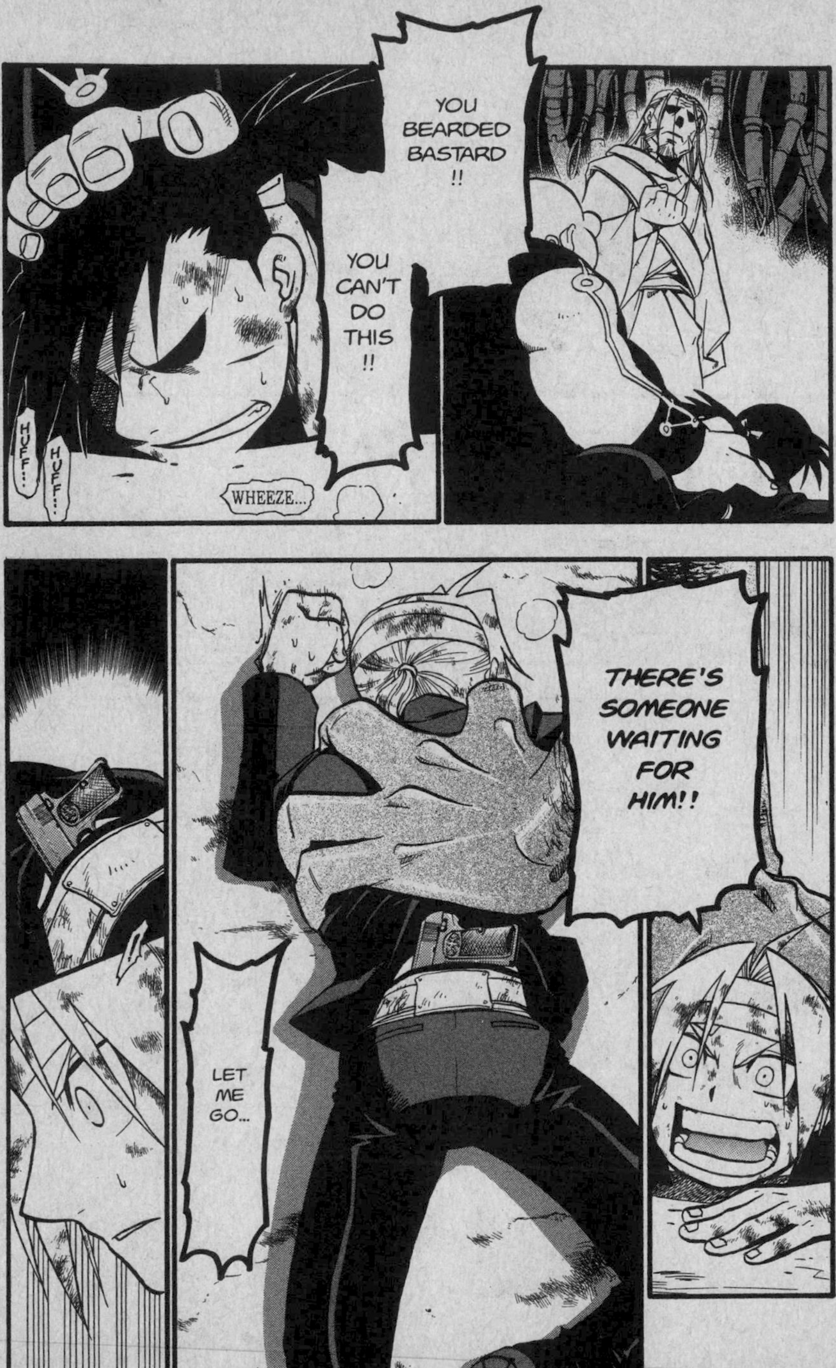
YOU BEARDED BASTARD !!
YOU CAN'T DO THIS !!
WHEEZE...
HUFF... HUFF...
THERE'S SOMEONE WAITING FOR HIM!!
LET ME GO...

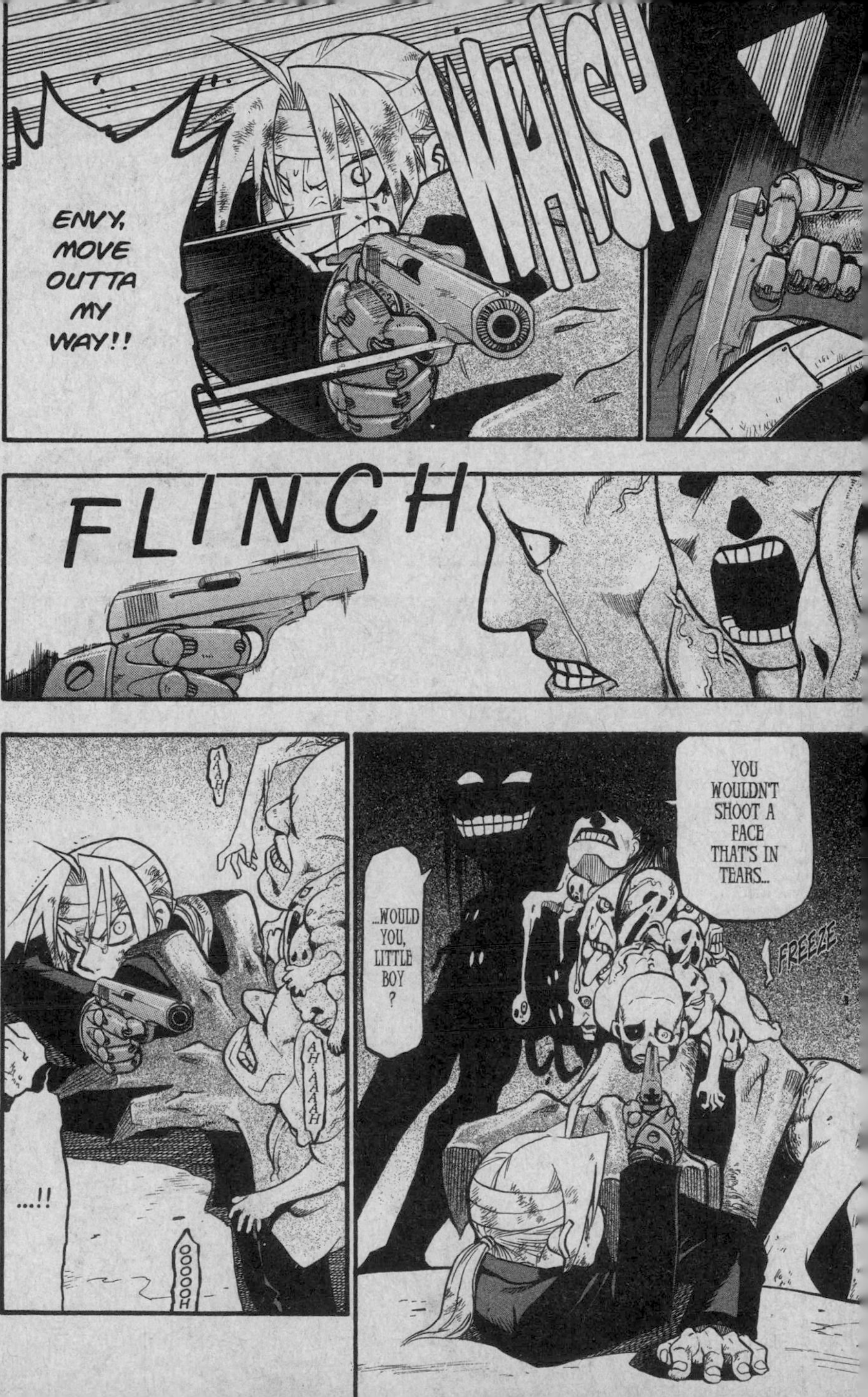
WHISH
ENVY, MOVE OUTTA MY WAY!!
FLINCH
YOU WOULDN'T SHOOT A FACE THAT'S IN TEARS...
FREEZE
...WOULD YOU, LITTLE BOY?
AAAH
AH...AAAAAH
...!!
OOOOOH

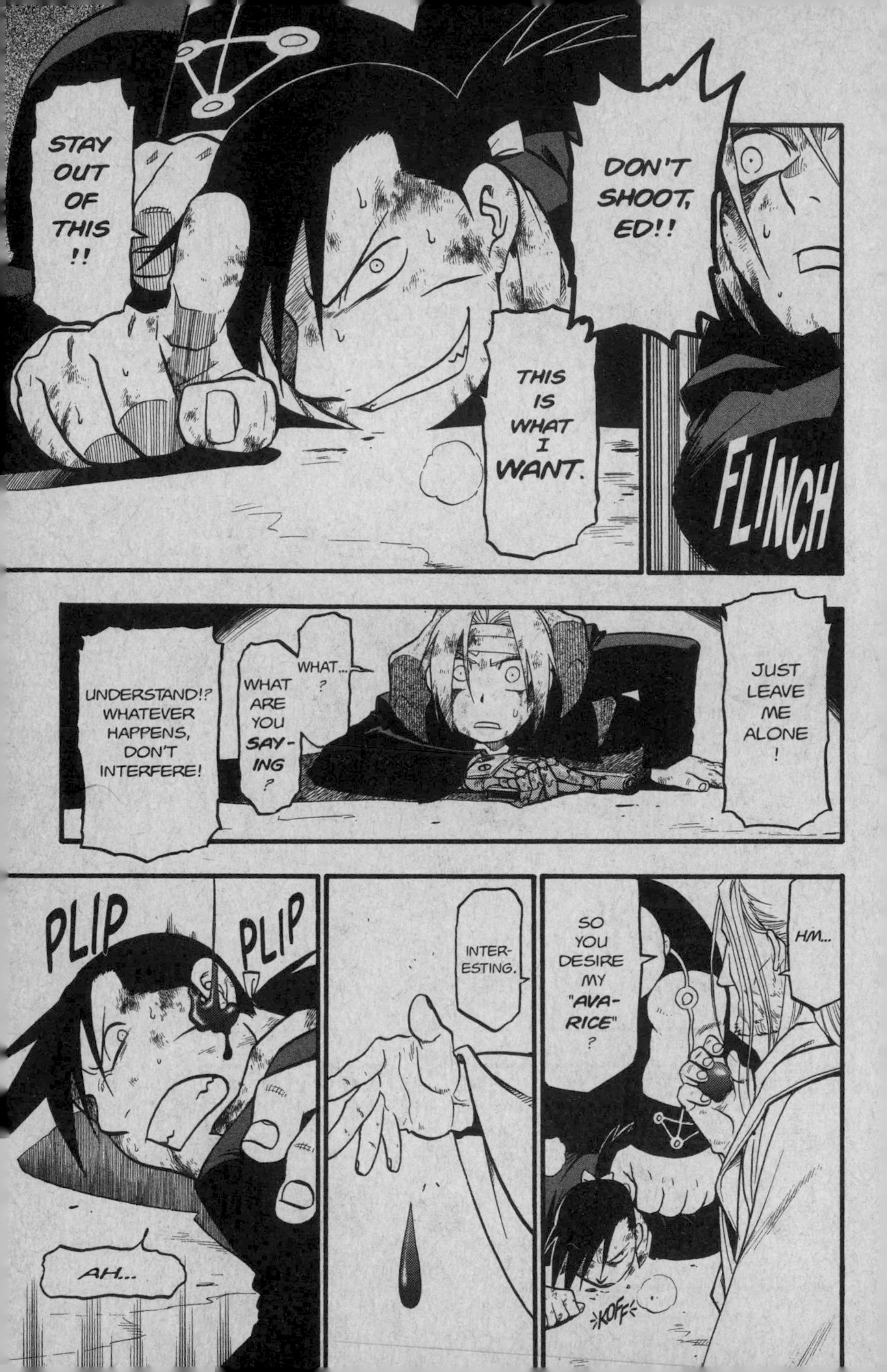
DON'T SHOOT, ED!!
FLINCH
STAY OUT OF THIS!!
THIS IS WHAT I WANT.
JUST LEAVE ME ALONE!
WHAT...?
WHAT ARE YOU SAYING?
UNDERSTAND!? WHATEVER HAPPENS, DON'T INTERFERE!
HM...
SO YOU DESIRE MY "AVARICE"?
KOFF
INTERESTING.
PLIP
PLIP
AH...

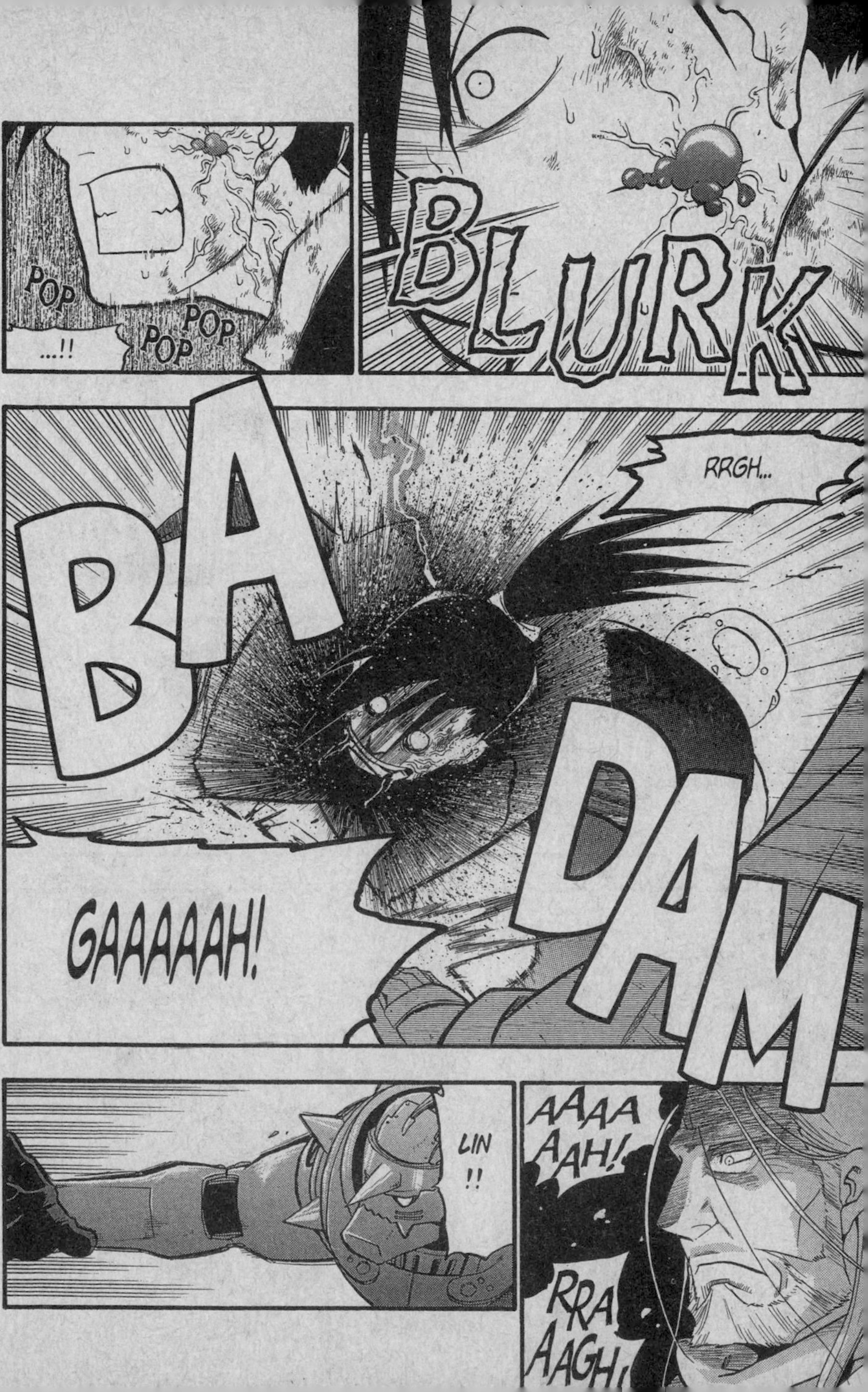
BLURK
POP
POP
POP
...!!
RRGH...
BADAM
GAAAAAH!
AAAAAAH!
RRRAAGH!
LIN !!

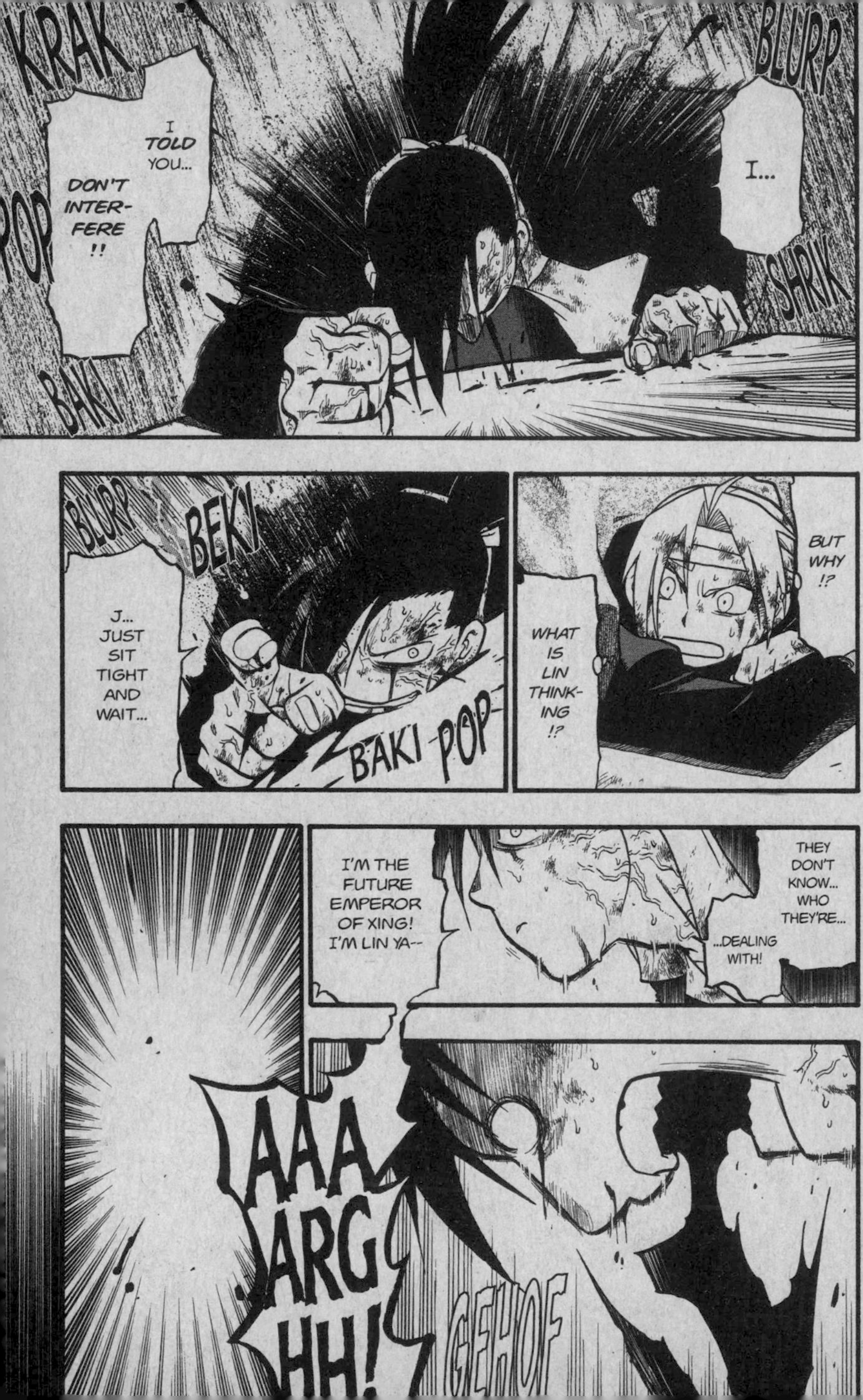
BLURP
I...
SHRIK
KRAK
I TOLD YOU...
DON'T INTERFERE!!
POP
BAKI
BUT WHY!?
WHAT IS LIN THINKING!?
BLURP
BEKI
J... JUST SIT TIGHT AND WAIT...
BAKI POP
THEY DON'T KNOW... WHO THEY'RE...
...DEALING WITH!
I'M THE FUTURE EMPEROR OF XING! I'M LIN YA--
AAAARGHH!
GEHOF

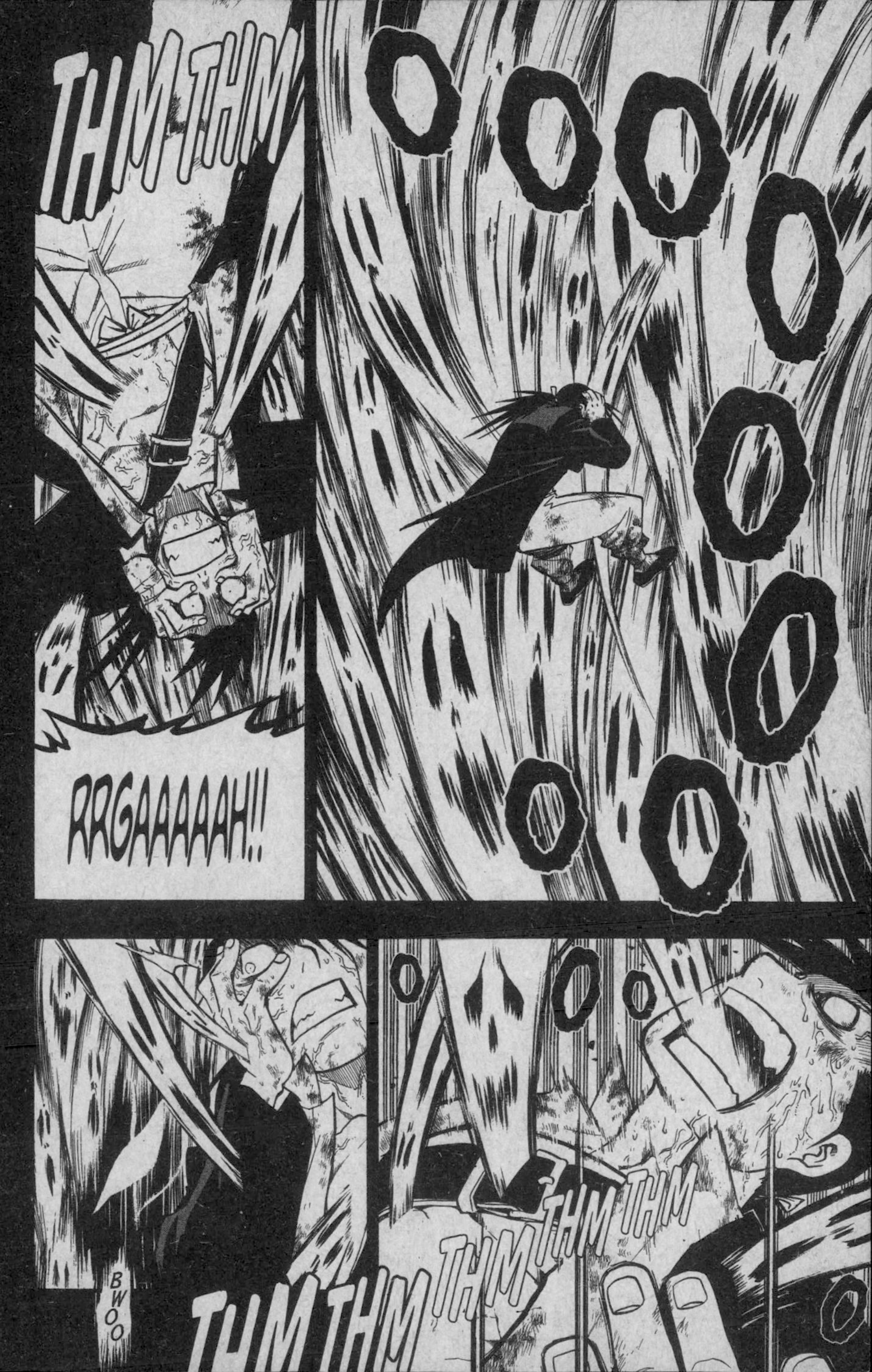
THM THM
RRGAAAAAH!!
THM THM THM
BWOO
THM THM

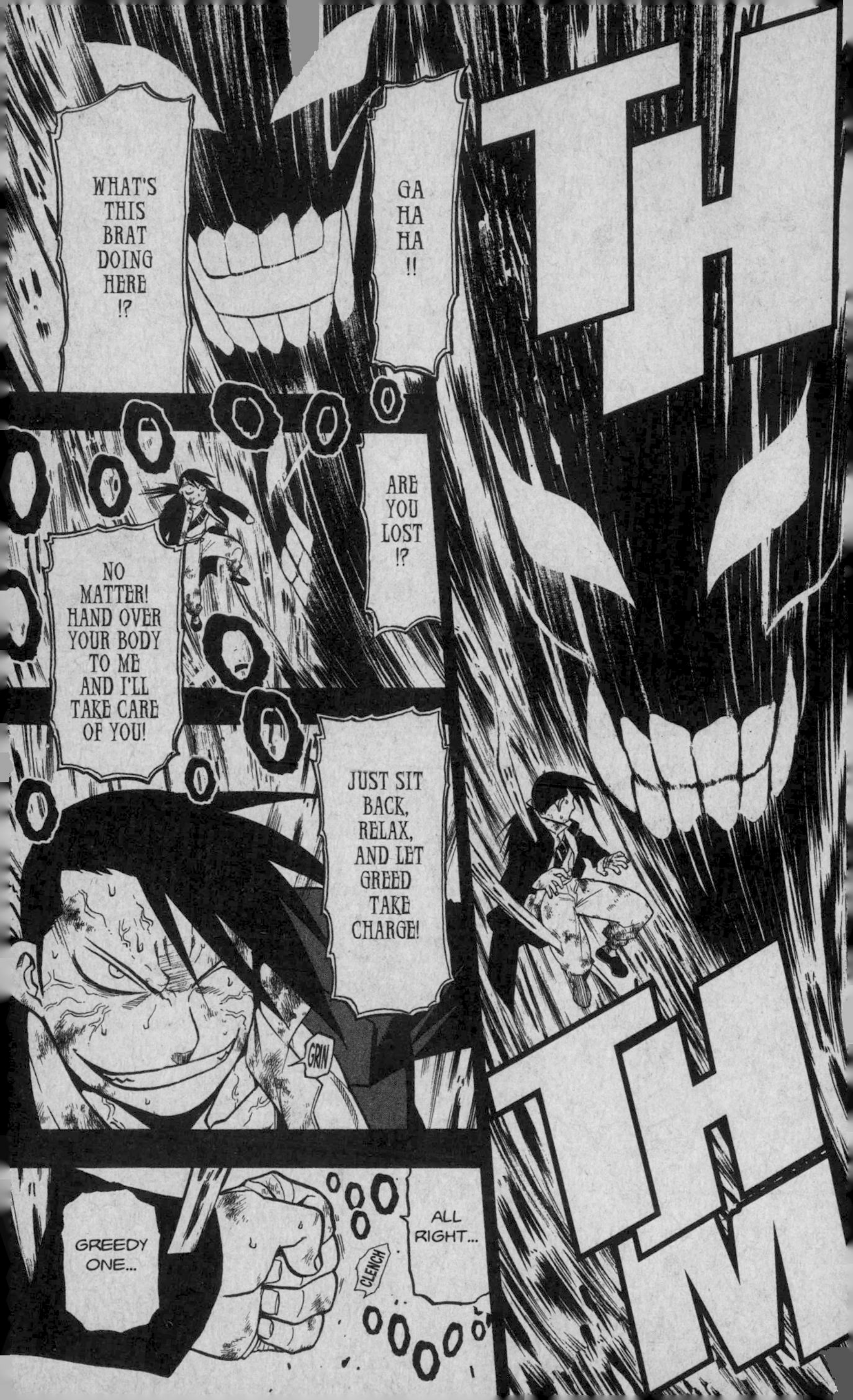
TH
THM
GA HA HA!!
WHAT'S THIS BRAT DOING HERE!?
ARE YOU LOST!?
NO MATTER! HAND OVER YOUR BODY TO ME AND I'LL TAKE CARE OF YOU!
JUST SIT BACK, RELAX, AND LET GREED TAKE CHARGE!
GRIN
ALL RIGHT...
CLENCH
GREEDY ONE...

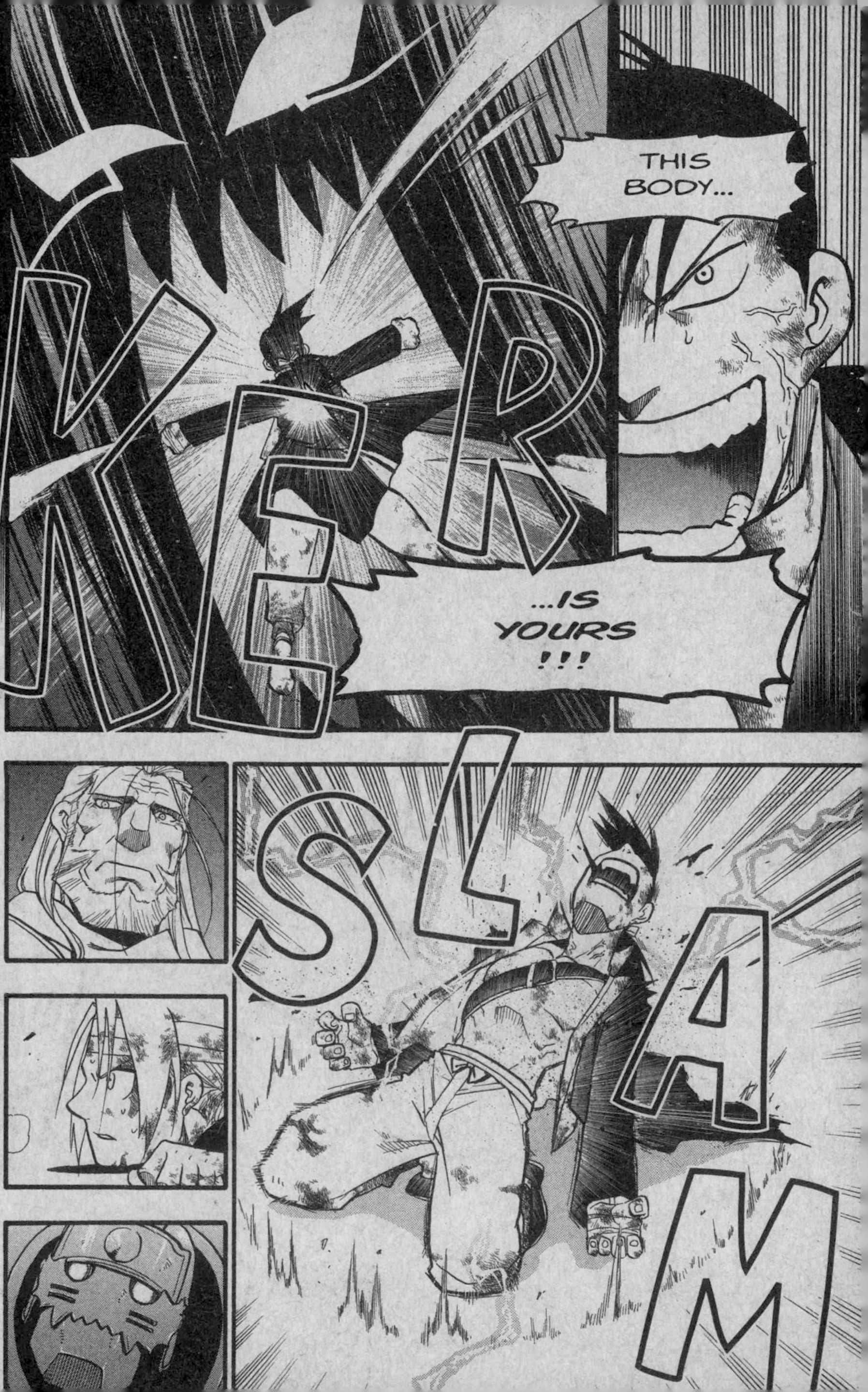

THIS BODY...
...IS YOURS !!!
KERR
SLAM

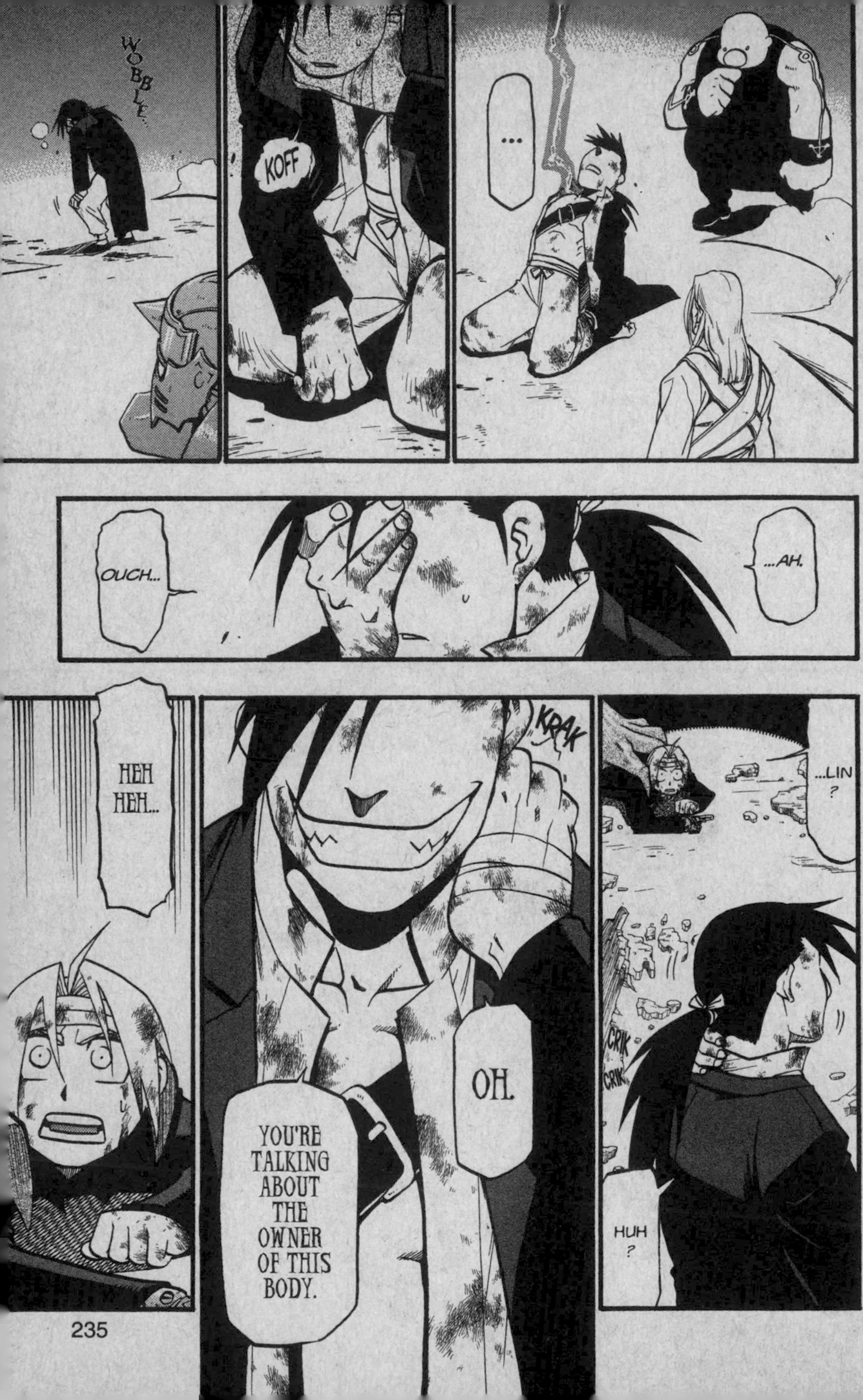
...
KOFF
WOBBLE...
...AH.
OUCH...
...LIN?
CRIK CRIK
HUH?
KRAK
OH.
YOU'RE TALKING ABOUT THE OWNER OF THIS BODY.
HEH HEH...

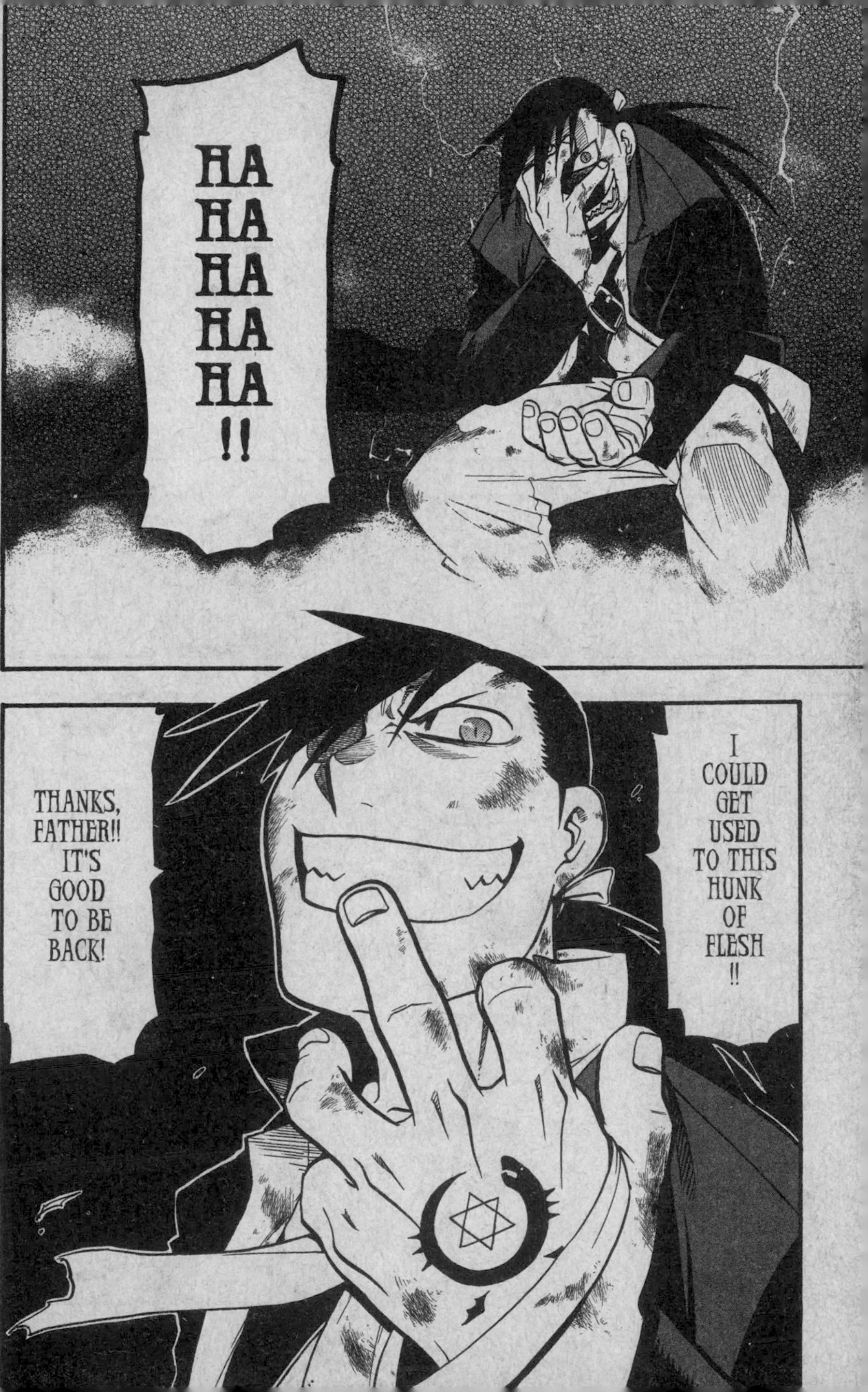
HA HA HA HA HA !!
I COULD GET USED TO THIS HUNK OF FLESH !!
THANKS, FATHER!! IT'S GOOD TO BE BACK!

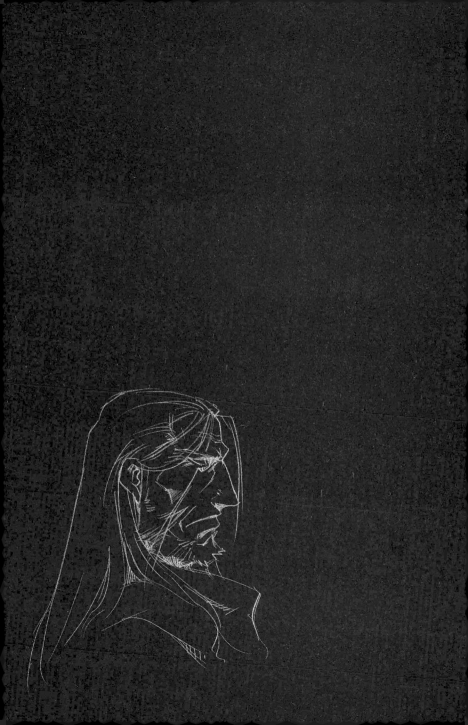

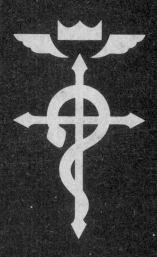

FULLMETAL
ALCHEMIST

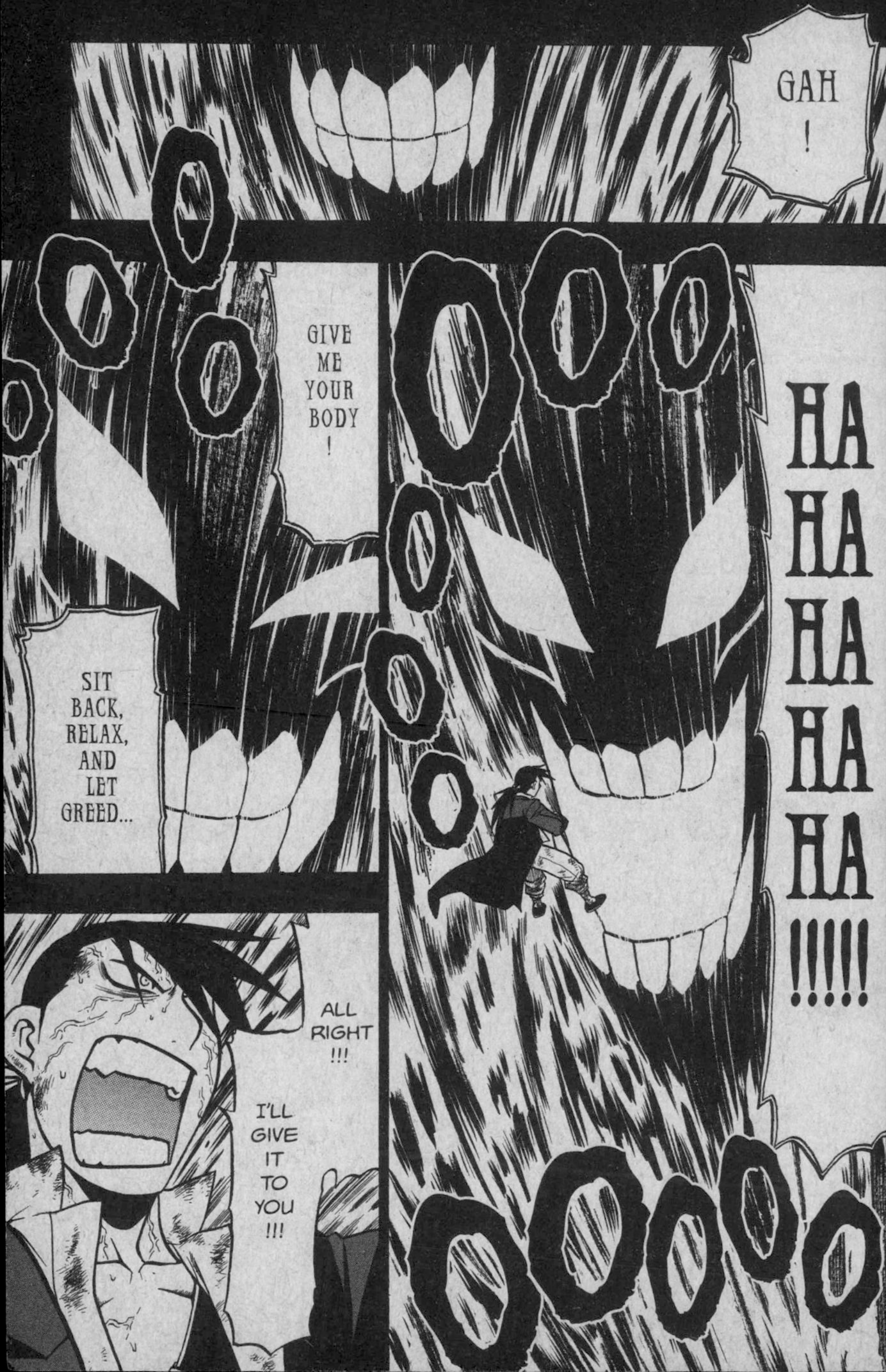
GAH!
HA HA HA HA HA HA!!!!!
GIVE ME YOUR BODY!
SIT BACK, RELAX, AND LET GREED...
ALL RIGHT!!!
I'LL GIVE IT TO YOU!!!

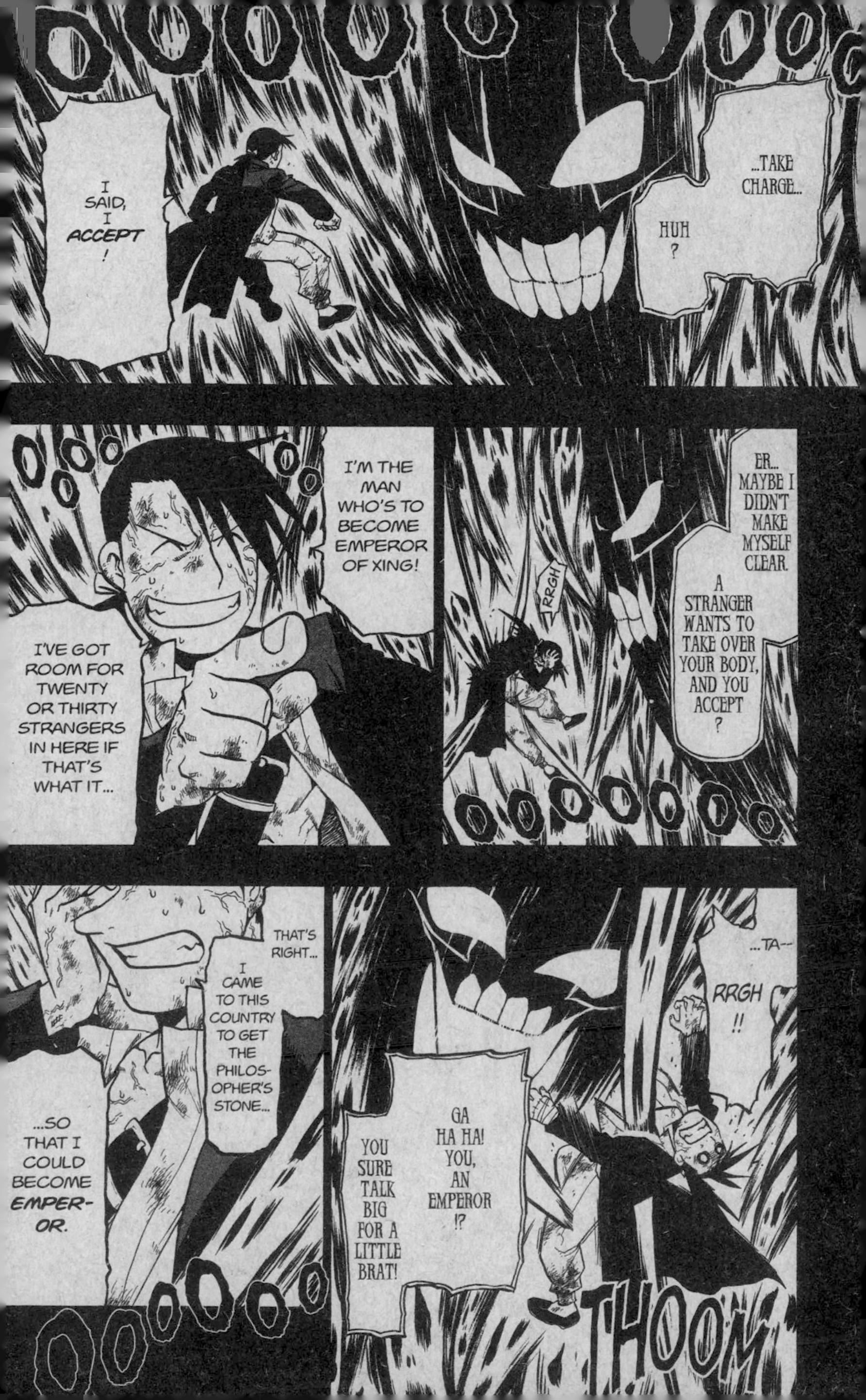
...TAKE CHARGE...
HUH?
I SAID, I ACCEPT!
ER... MAYBE I DIDN'T MAKE MYSELF CLEAR.
RRGH
A STRANGER WANTS TO TAKE OVER YOUR BODY, AND YOU ACCEPT?
I'M THE MAN WHO'S TO BECOME EMPEROR OF XING!
I'VE GOT ROOM FOR TWENTY OR THIRTY STRANGERS IN HERE IF THAT'S WHAT IT...
...TA--
RRGH!!
GA HA HA! YOU, AN EMPEROR!?
YOU SURE TALK BIG FOR A LITTLE BRAT!
THOOM
THAT'S RIGHT...
I CAME TO THIS COUNTRY TO GET THE PHILOSOPHER'S STONE...
...SO THAT I COULD BECOME EMPEROR.

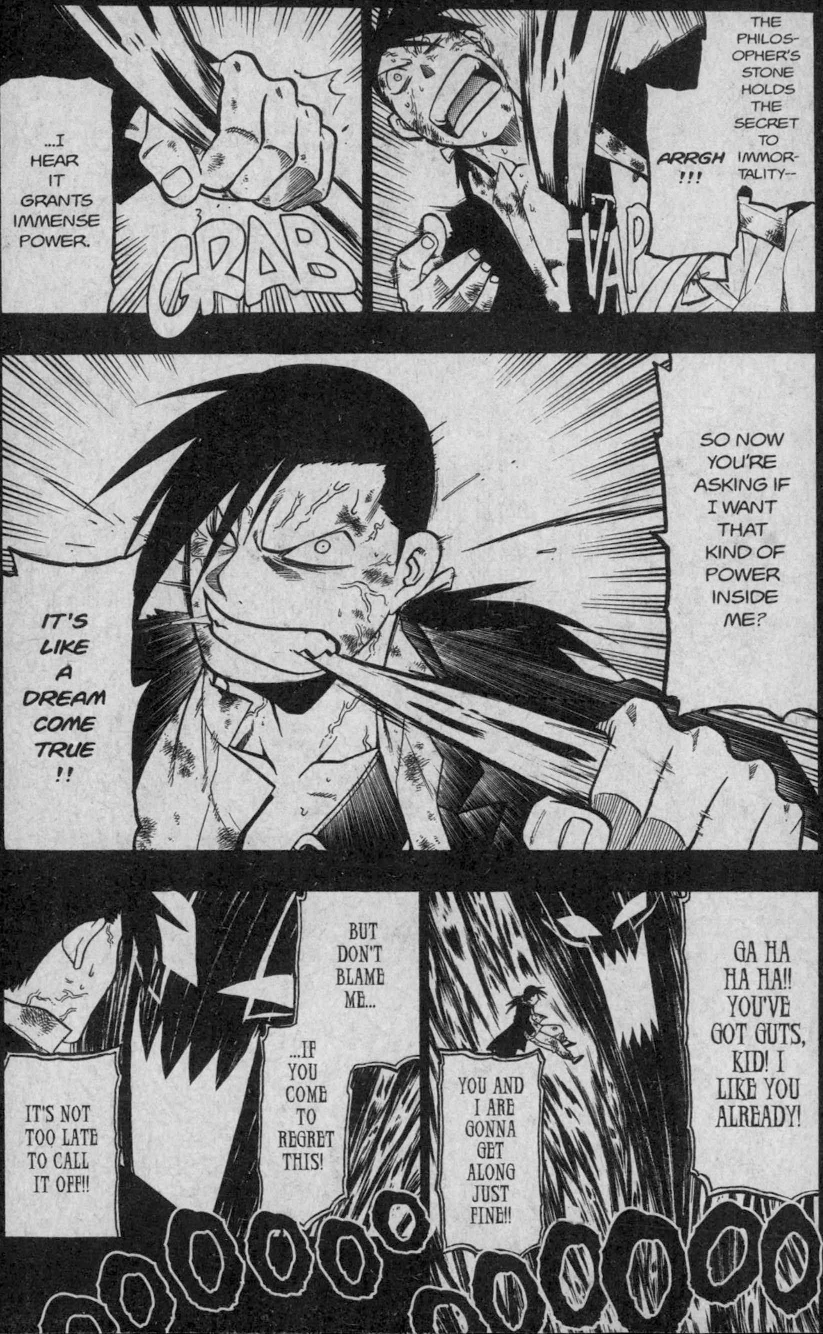
THE PHILOSOPHER'S STONE HOLDS THE SECRET TO IMMORTALITY--
ARRGH!!!
VAP
...I HEAR IT GRANTS IMMENSE POWER.
GRAB
SO NOW YOU'RE ASKING IF I WANT THAT KIND OF POWER INSIDE ME?
IT'S LIKE A DREAM COME TRUE!!
GA HA HA HA!! YOU'VE GOT GUTS, KID! I LIKE YOU ALREADY!
YOU AND I ARE GONNA GET ALONG JUST FINE!!
BUT DON'T BLAME ME...
...IF YOU COME TO REGRET THIS!
IT'S NOT TOO LATE TO CALL IT OFF!!

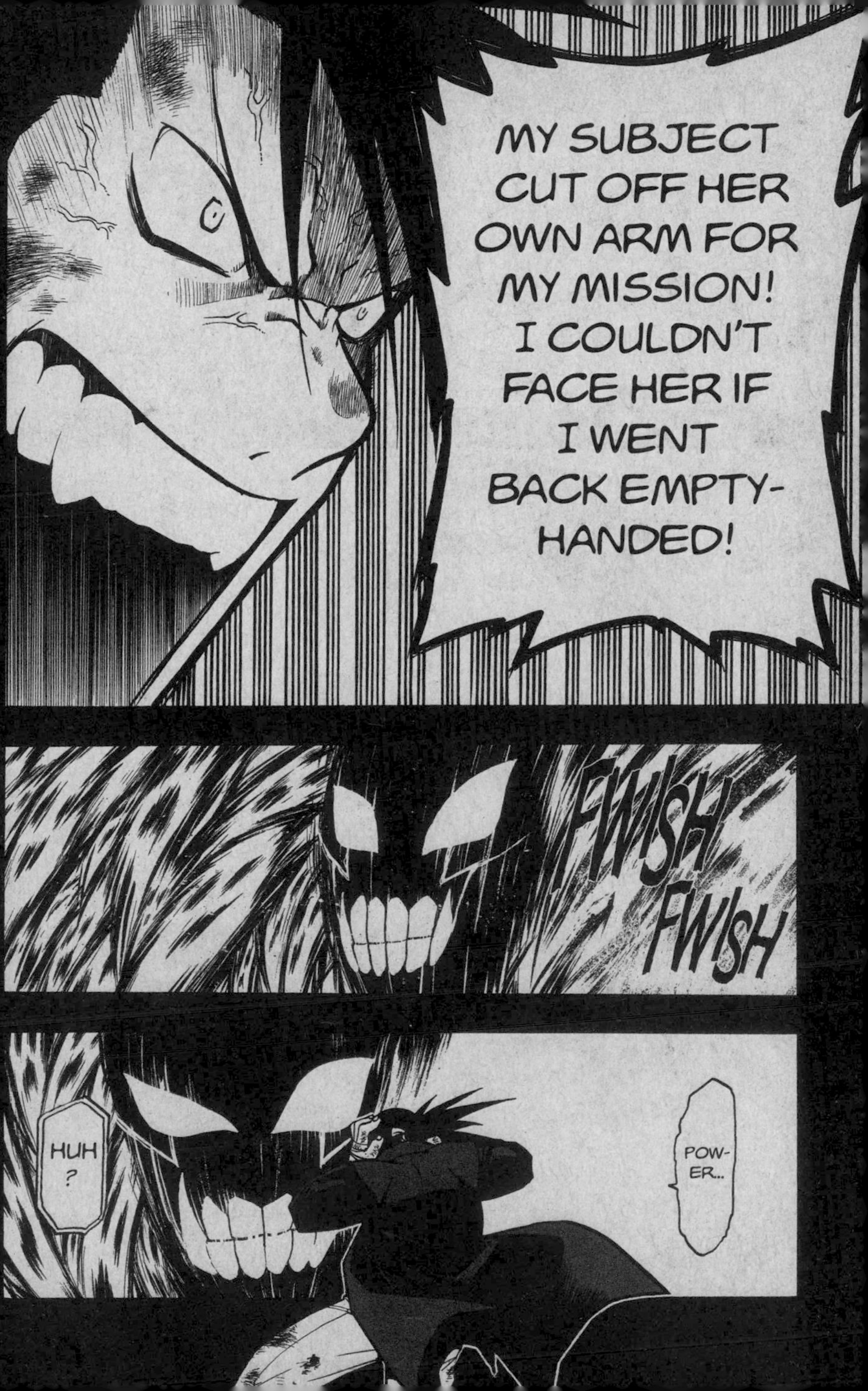
MY SUBJECT CUT OFF HER OWN ARM FOR MY MISSION! I COULDN'T FACE HER IF I WENT BACK EMPTY-HANDED!
FWISH FWISH
POW-ER...
HUH?

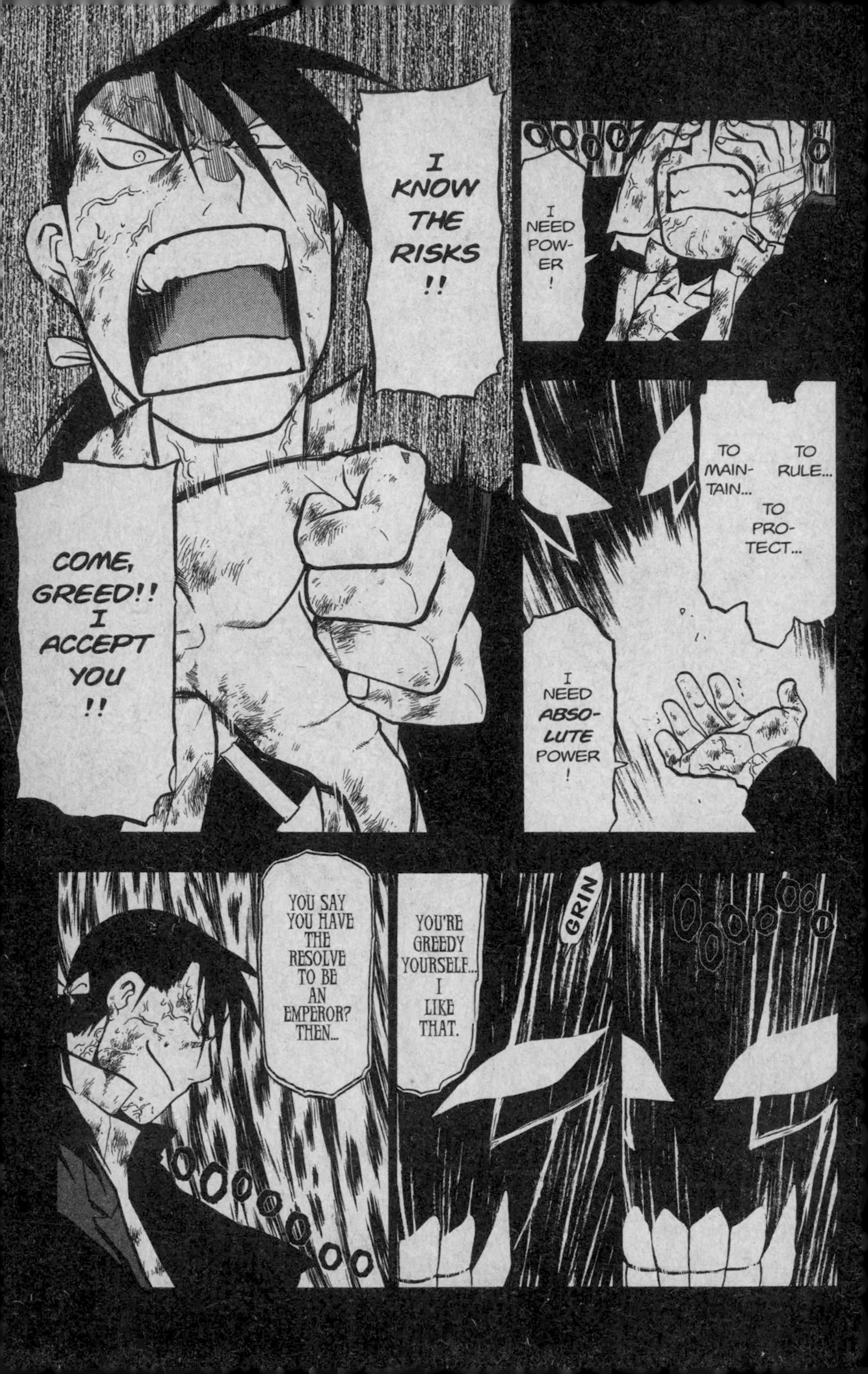
I NEED POW-ER!
TO RULE...
TO MAIN-TAIN...
TO PRO-TECT...
I NEED ABSO-LUTE POWER!
I KNOW THE RISKS!!
COME, GREED!! I ACCEPT YOU!!
GRIN
YOU'RE GREEDY YOURSELF... I LIKE THAT.
YOU SAY YOU HAVE THE RESOLVE TO BE AN EMPEROR? THEN...

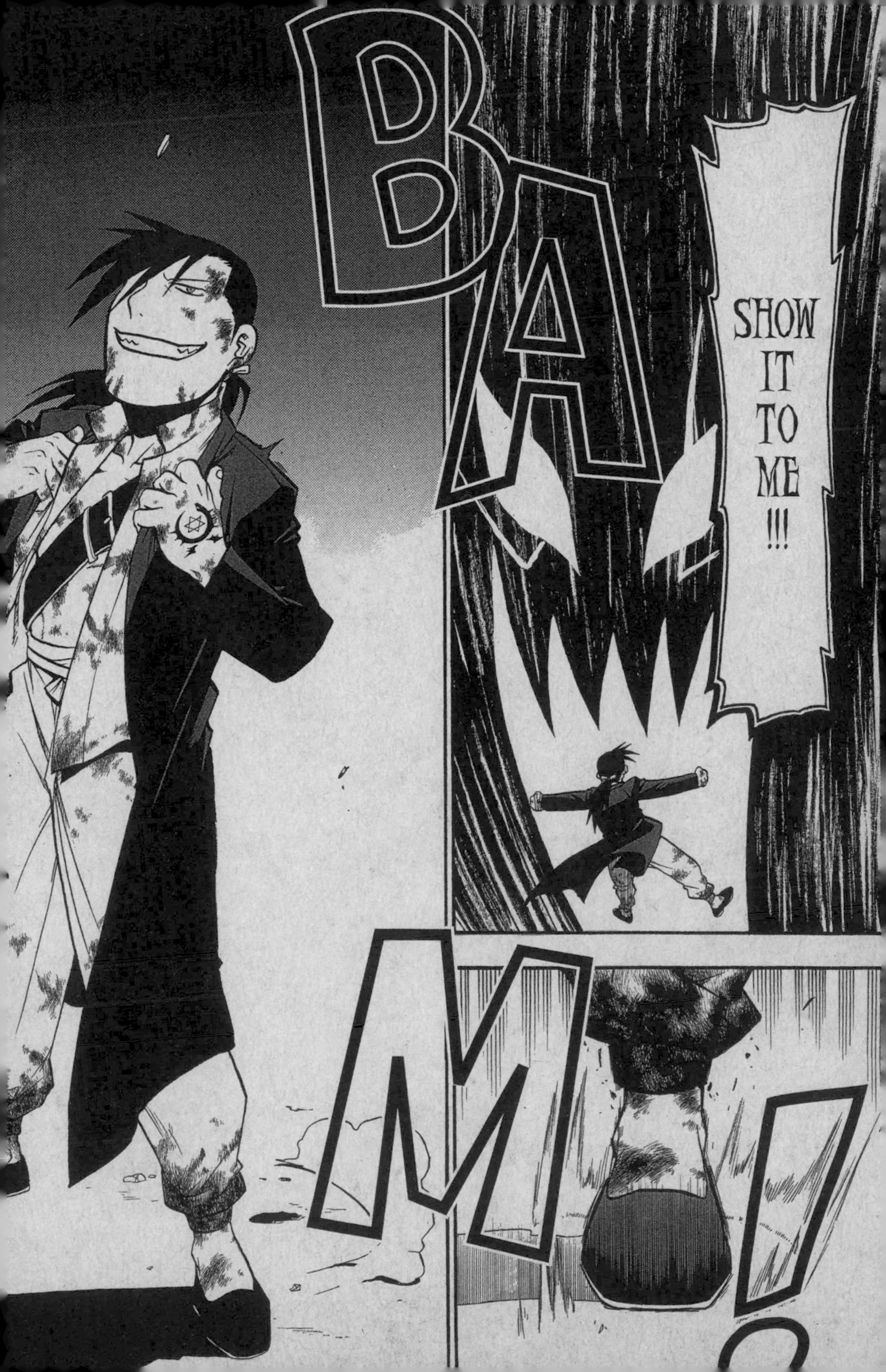
SHOW IT TO ME!!!
BAM!

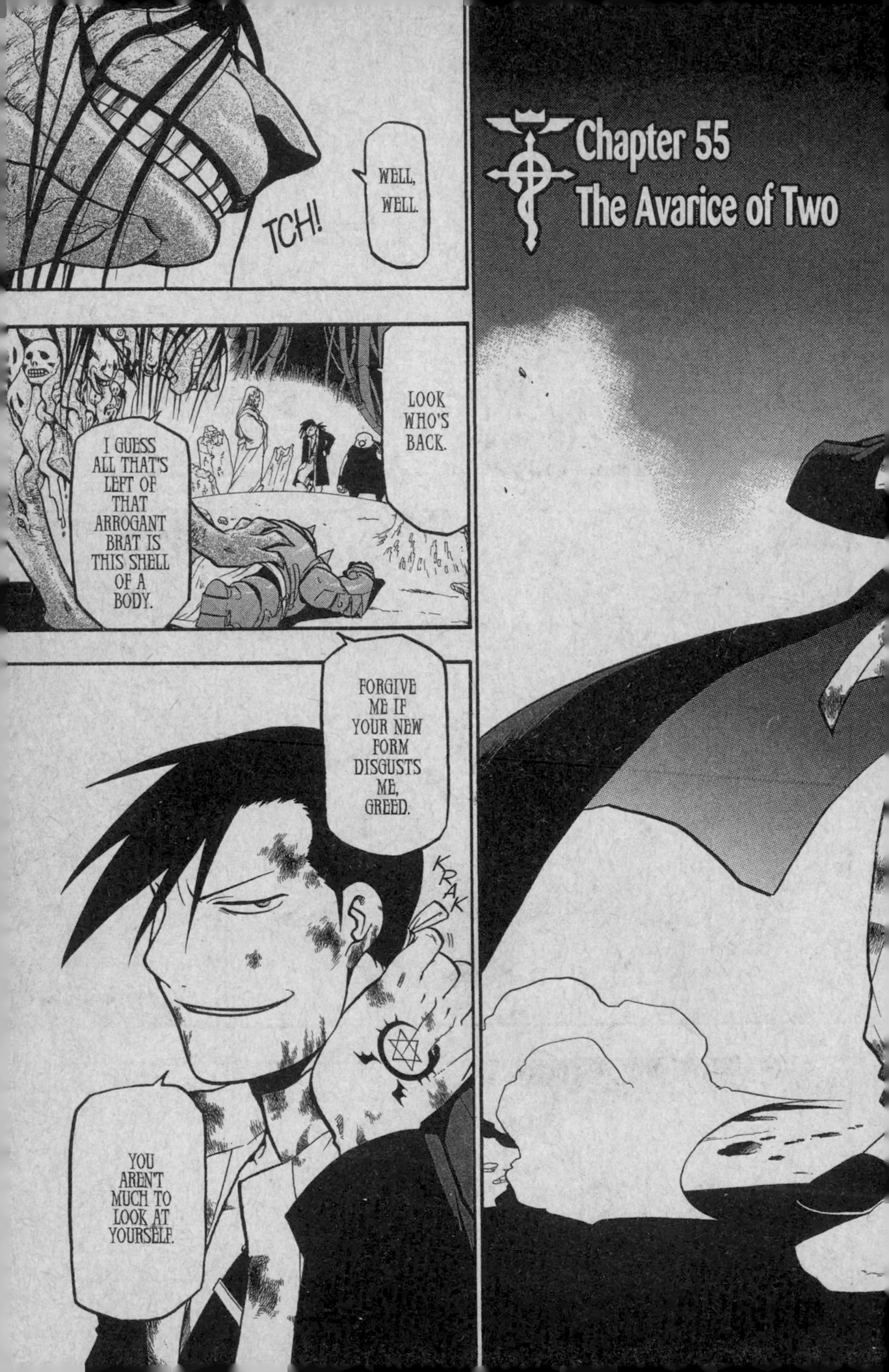
Chapter 55
The Avarice of Two
WELL, WELL.
TCH!
LOOK WHO'S BACK.
I GUESS ALL THAT'S LEFT OF THAT ARROGANT BRAT IS THIS SHELL OF A BODY.
FORGIVE ME IF YOUR NEW FORM DISGUSTS ME, GREED.
KRAK
YOU AREN'T MUCH TO LOOK AT YOURSELF.

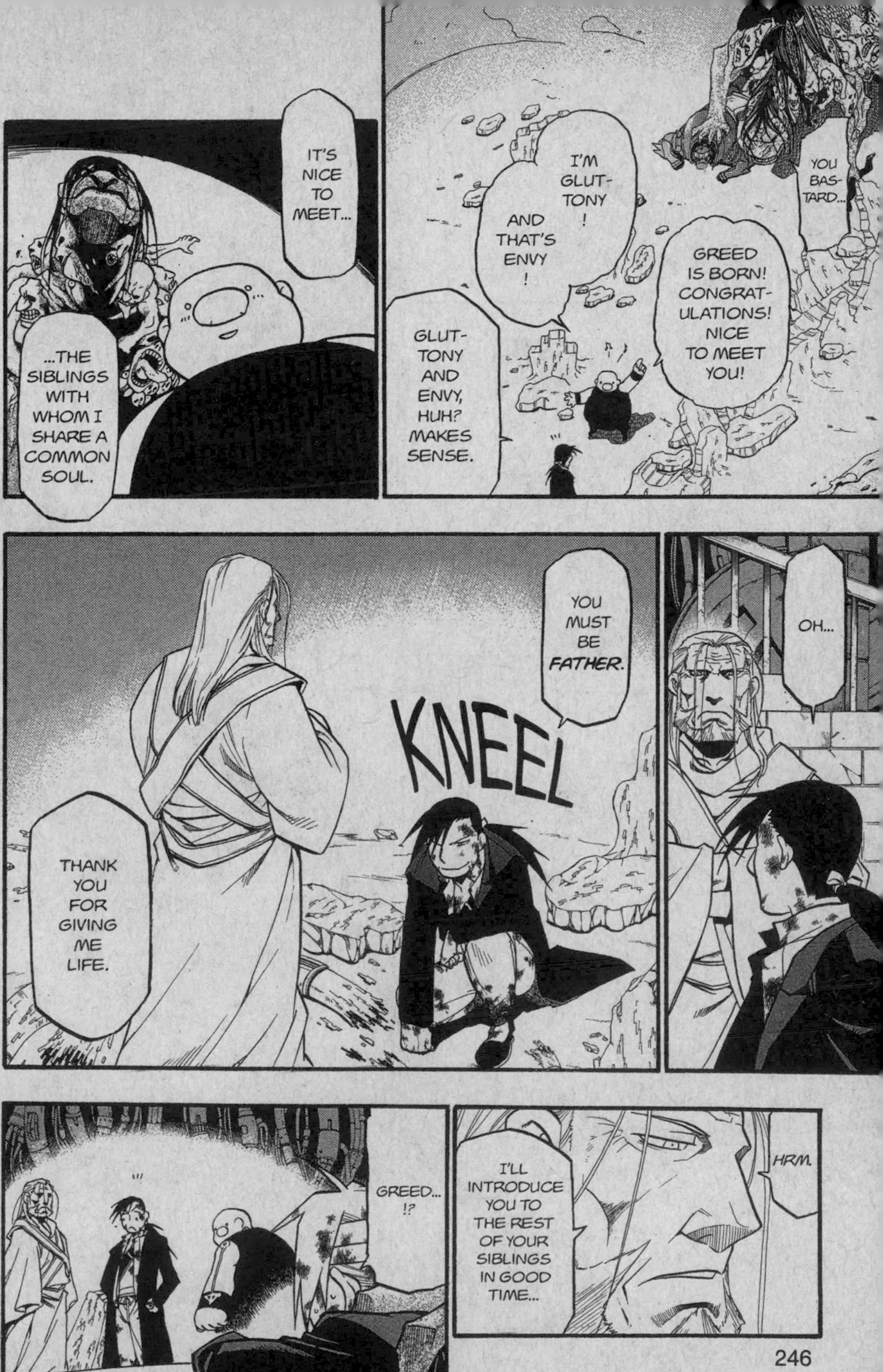
YOU BASTARD...
GREED IS BORN! CONGRATULATIONS! NICE TO MEET YOU!
I'M GLUTTONY!
AND THAT'S ENVY!
GLUTTONY AND ENVY, HUH? MAKES SENSE.
IT'S NICE TO MEET...
...THE SIBLINGS WITH WHOM I SHARE A COMMON SOUL.
OH...
YOU MUST BE *FATHER*.
KNEEL
THANK YOU FOR GIVING ME LIFE.
HRM.
I'LL INTRODUCE YOU TO THE REST OF YOUR SIBLINGS IN GOOD TIME...
GREED...!?

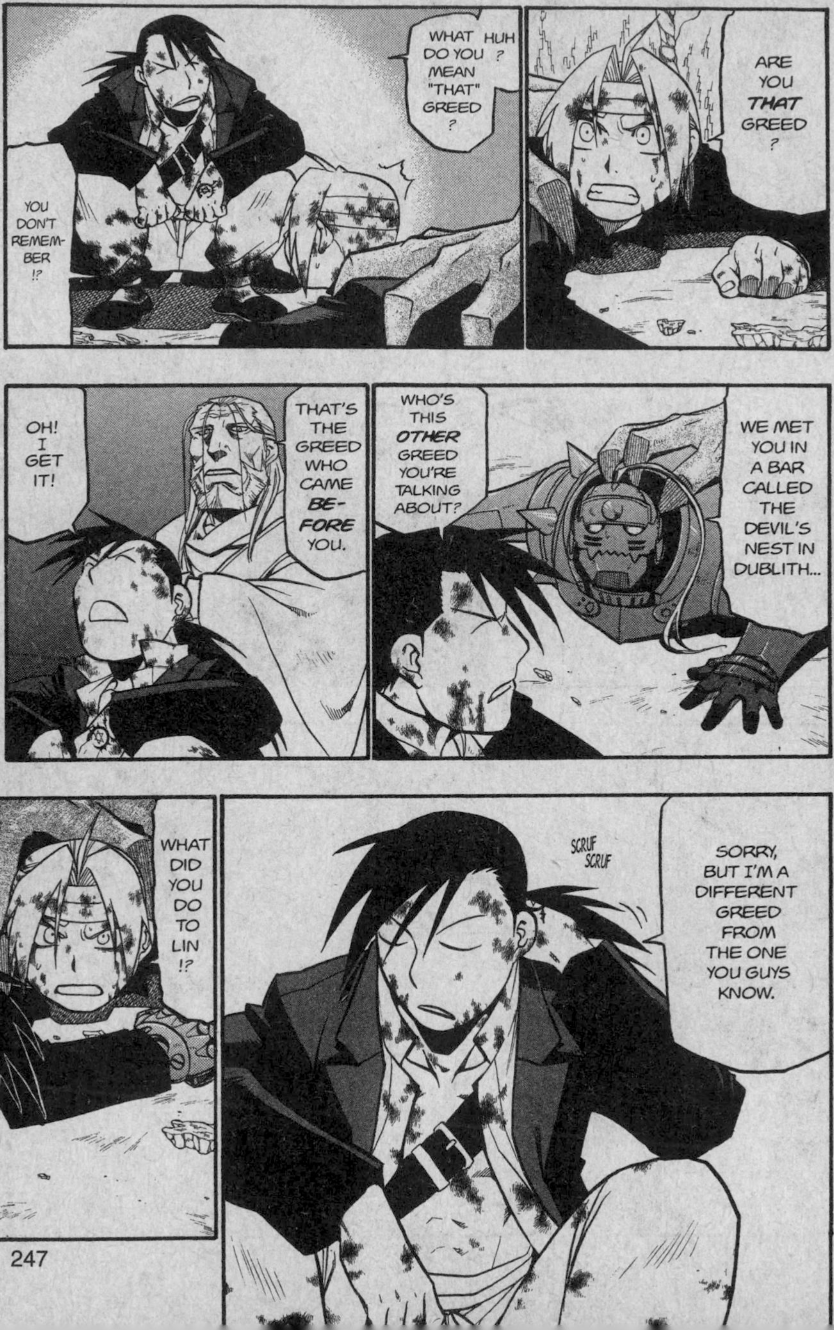
ARE YOU THAT GREED?
HUH?
WHAT DO YOU MEAN "THAT" GREED?
YOU DON'T REMEMBER!?
WE MET YOU IN A BAR CALLED THE DEVIL'S NEST IN DUBLITH...
WHO'S THIS OTHER GREED YOU'RE TALKING ABOUT?
THAT'S THE GREED WHO CAME BEFORE YOU.
OH! I GET IT!
SORRY, BUT I'M A DIFFERENT GREED FROM THE ONE YOU GUYS KNOW.
SCRUF SCRUF
WHAT DID YOU DO TO LIN!?

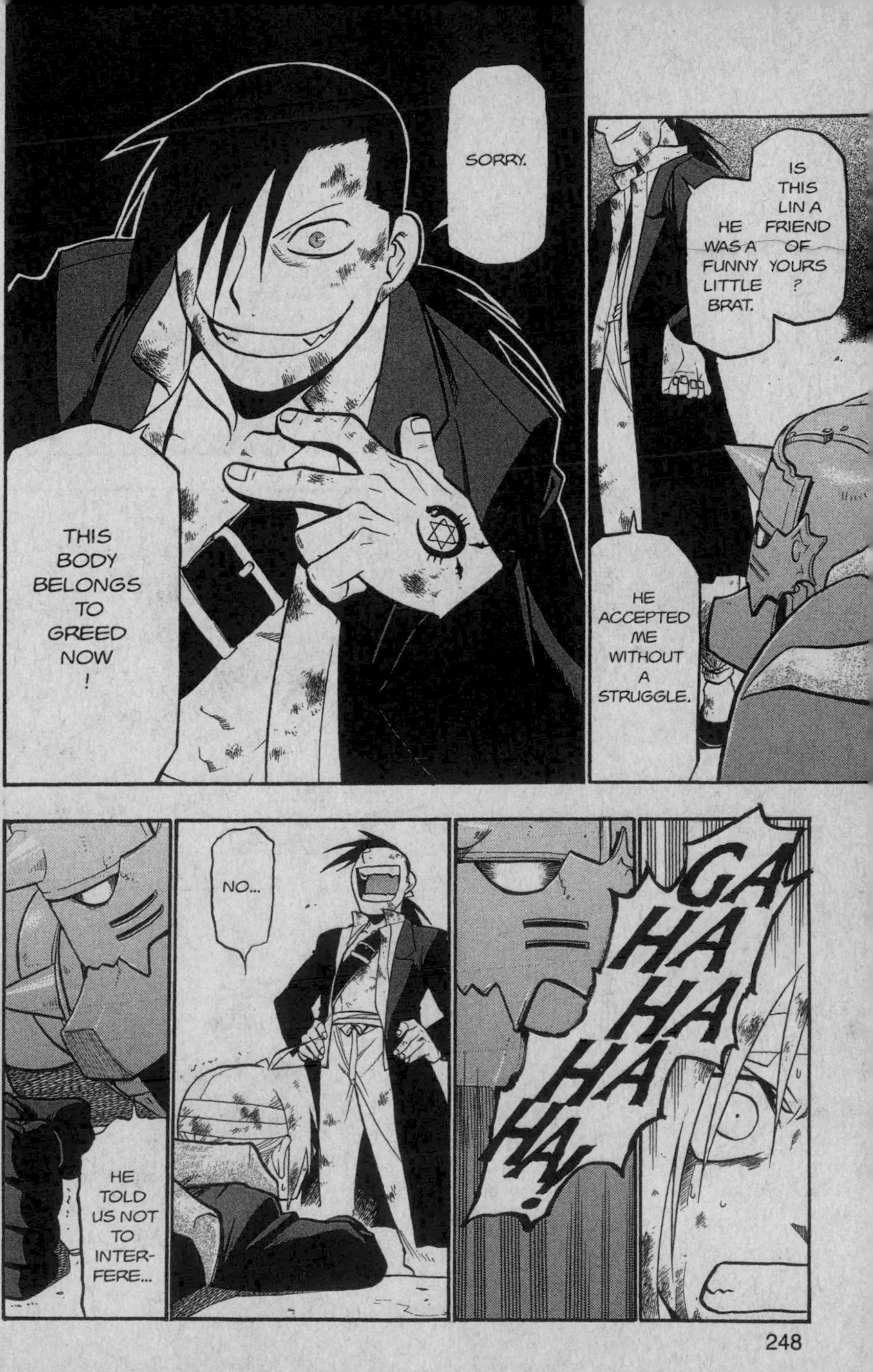
IS THIS LIN A FRIEND OF YOURS?
HE WAS A FUNNY LITTLE BRAT.
HE ACCEPTED ME WITHOUT A STRUGGLE.
SORRY.
THIS BODY BELONGS TO GREED NOW!
GAHAHAHAHAHAHA!
NO...
HE TOLD US NOT TO INTERFERE...

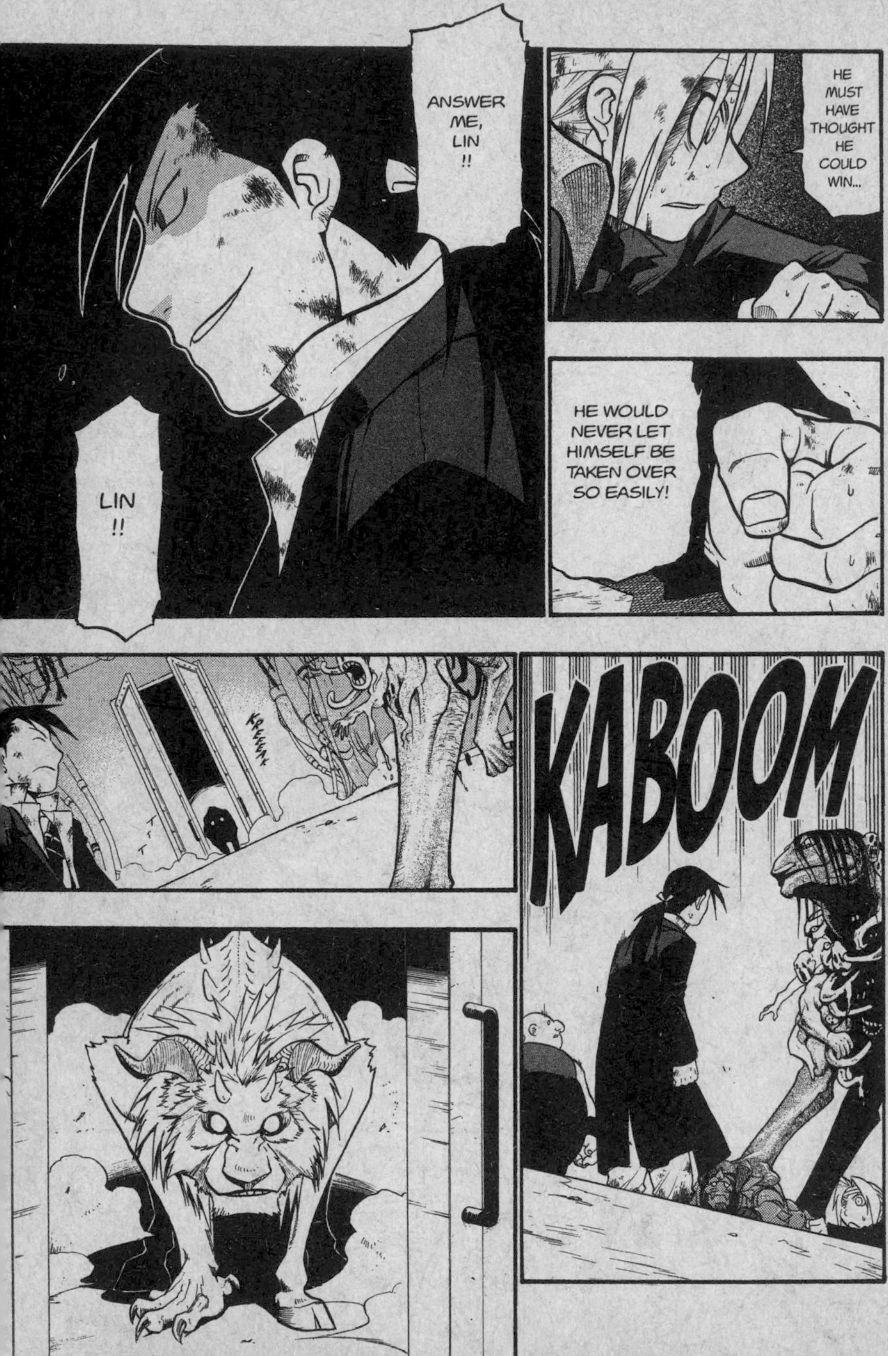
HE MUST HAVE THOUGHT HE COULD WIN...
HE WOULD NEVER LET HIMSELF BE TAKEN OVER SO EASILY!
ANSWER ME, LIN !!
LIN !!
KABOOM
KREEEAK

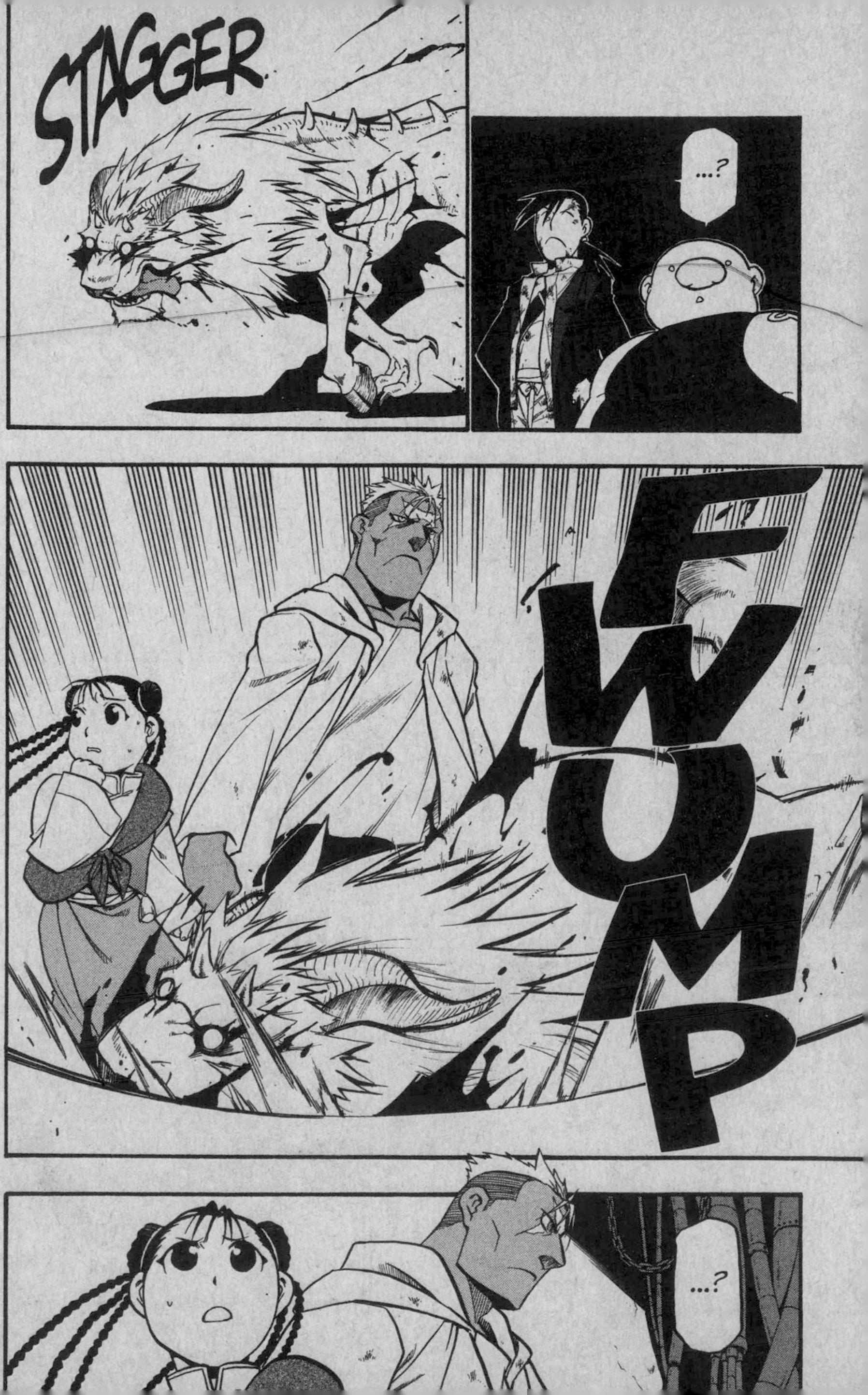
...?
STAGGER
FWUMP
...?

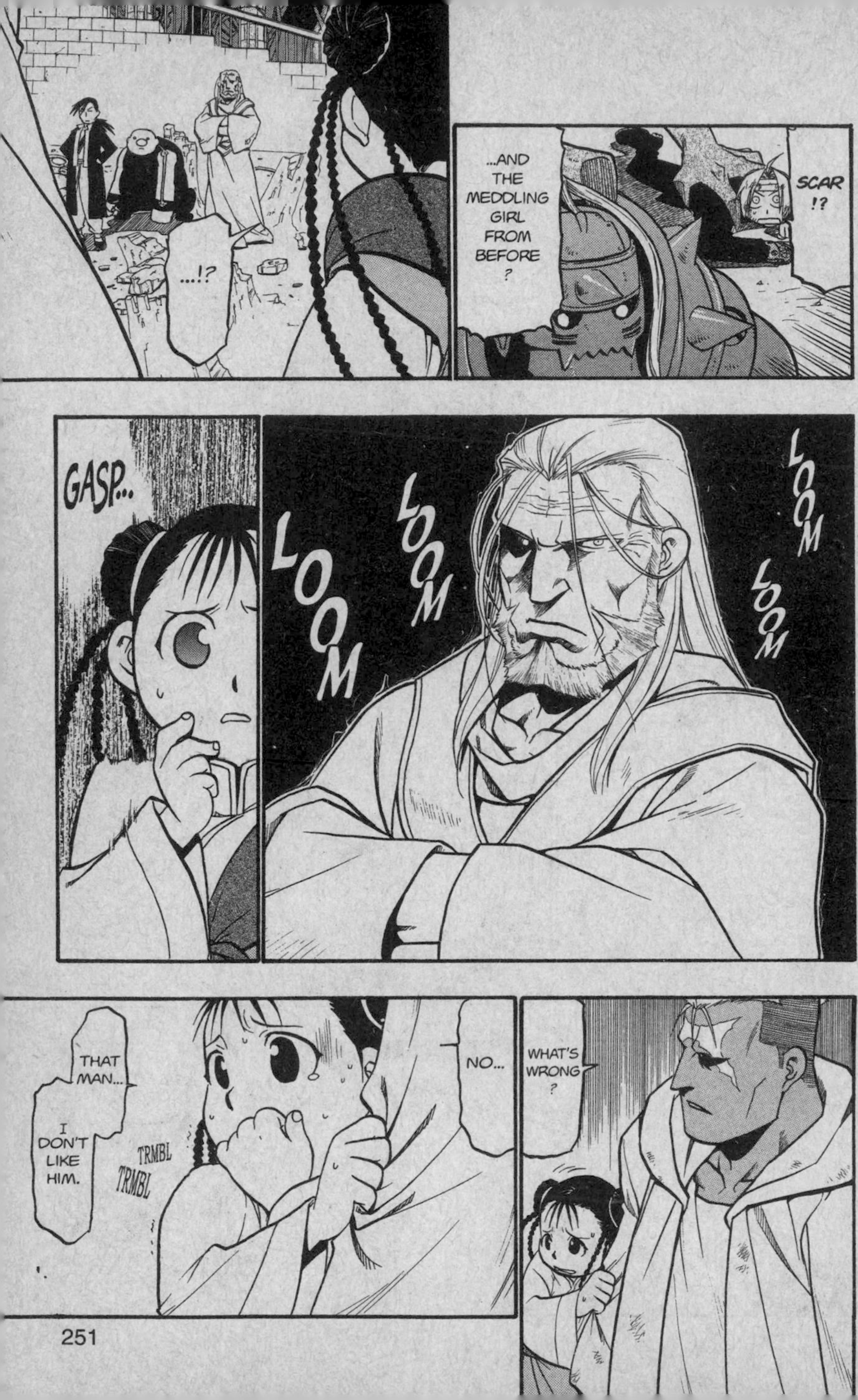
SCAR!?
...AND THE MEDDLING GIRL FROM BEFORE?
...!?
LOOM LOOM
LOOM LOOM
GASP...
WHAT'S WRONG?
NO...
THAT MAN...
I DON'T LIKE HIM.
TRMBL TRMBL

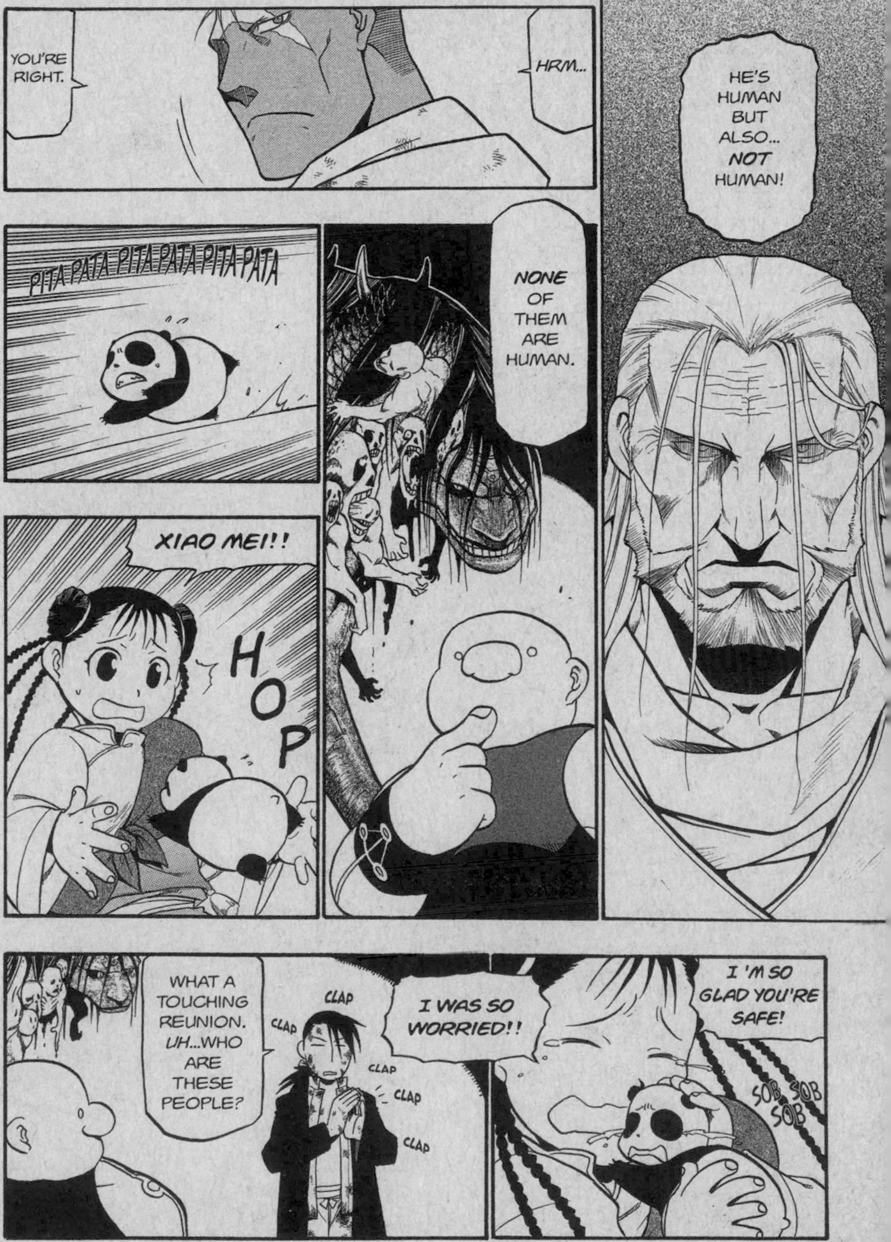
HE'S HUMAN BUT ALSO... NOT HUMAN!
HRM...
YOU'RE RIGHT.
NONE OF THEM ARE HUMAN.
PITA PATA PITA PATA PITA PATA
XIAO MEI!!
HOP
I'M SO GLAD YOU'RE SAFE!
SOB SOB SOB
I WAS SO WORRIED!!
WHAT A TOUCHING REUNION. UH...WHO ARE THESE PEOPLE?
CLAP CLAP CLAP CLAP CLAP

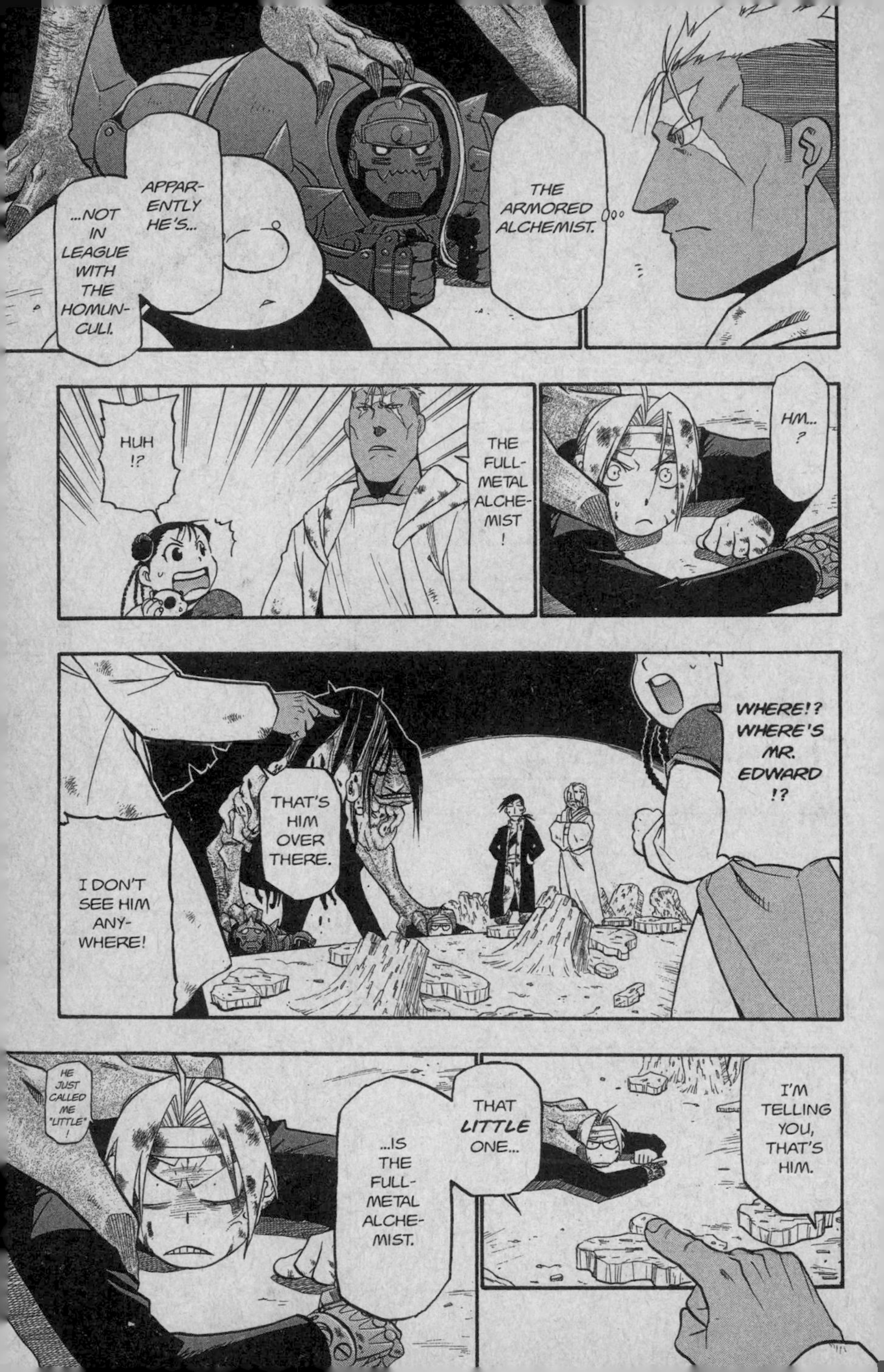
THE ARMORED ALCHEMIST.
APPARENTLY HE'S...
...NOT IN LEAGUE WITH THE HOMUNCULI.
HM...?
THE FULLMETAL ALCHEMIST!
HUH!?
WHERE!? WHERE'S MR. EDWARD!?
THAT'S HIM OVER THERE.
I DON'T SEE HIM ANYWHERE!
I'M TELLING YOU, THAT'S HIM.
THAT *LITTLE* ONE...
...IS THE FULLMETAL ALCHEMIST.
HE JUST CALLED ME "LITTLE"!

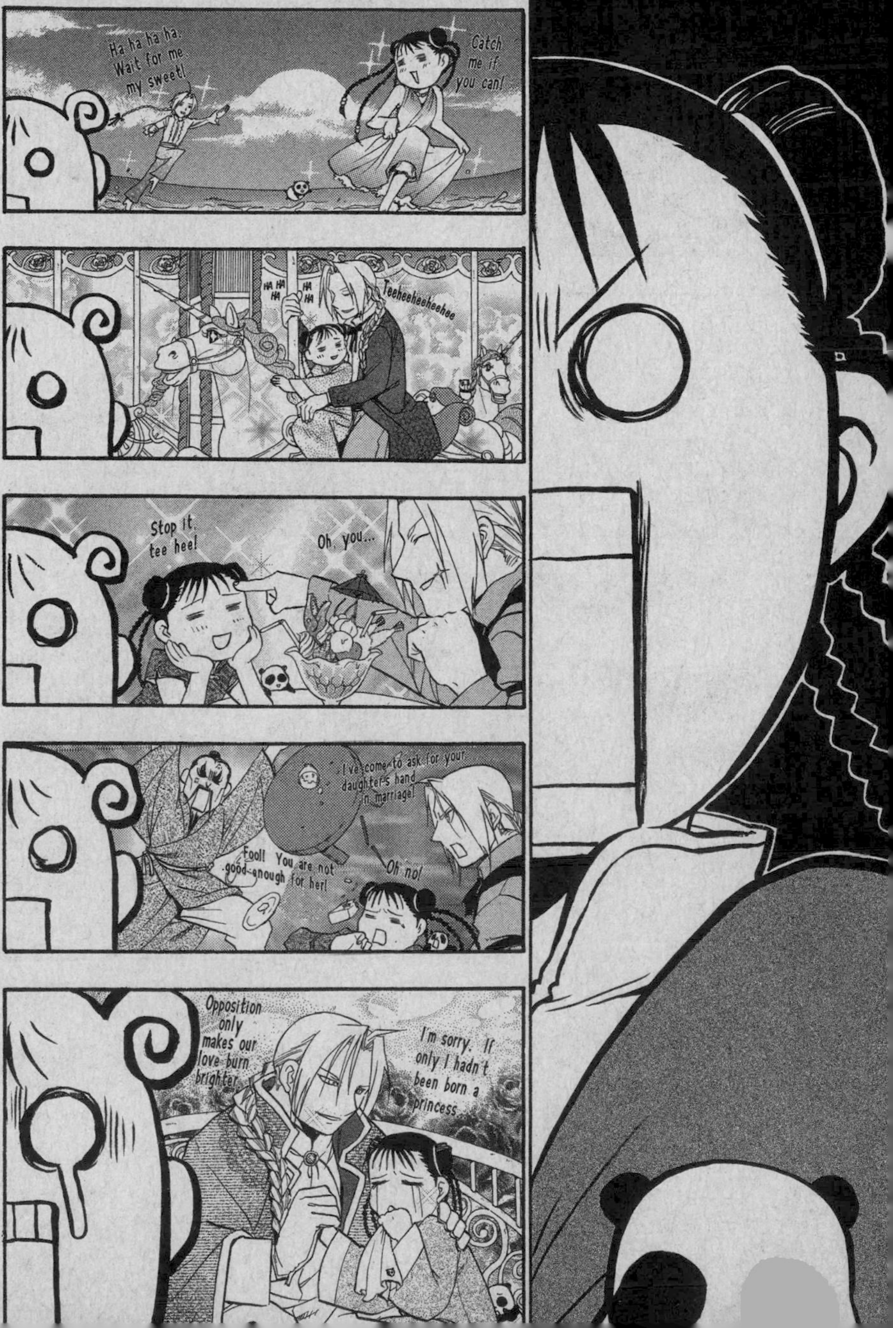

Catch me if you can!
Ha ha ha ha. Wait for me my sweet!
Teeheeheeheeheehee
HA HA
HA HA HA
Oh you...
Stop it, tee hee!
I've come to ask for your daughter's hand in marriage!
Oh no!
Fool! You are not good enough for her!
I'm sorry. If only I hadn't been born a princess.
Opposition only makes our love burn brighter.

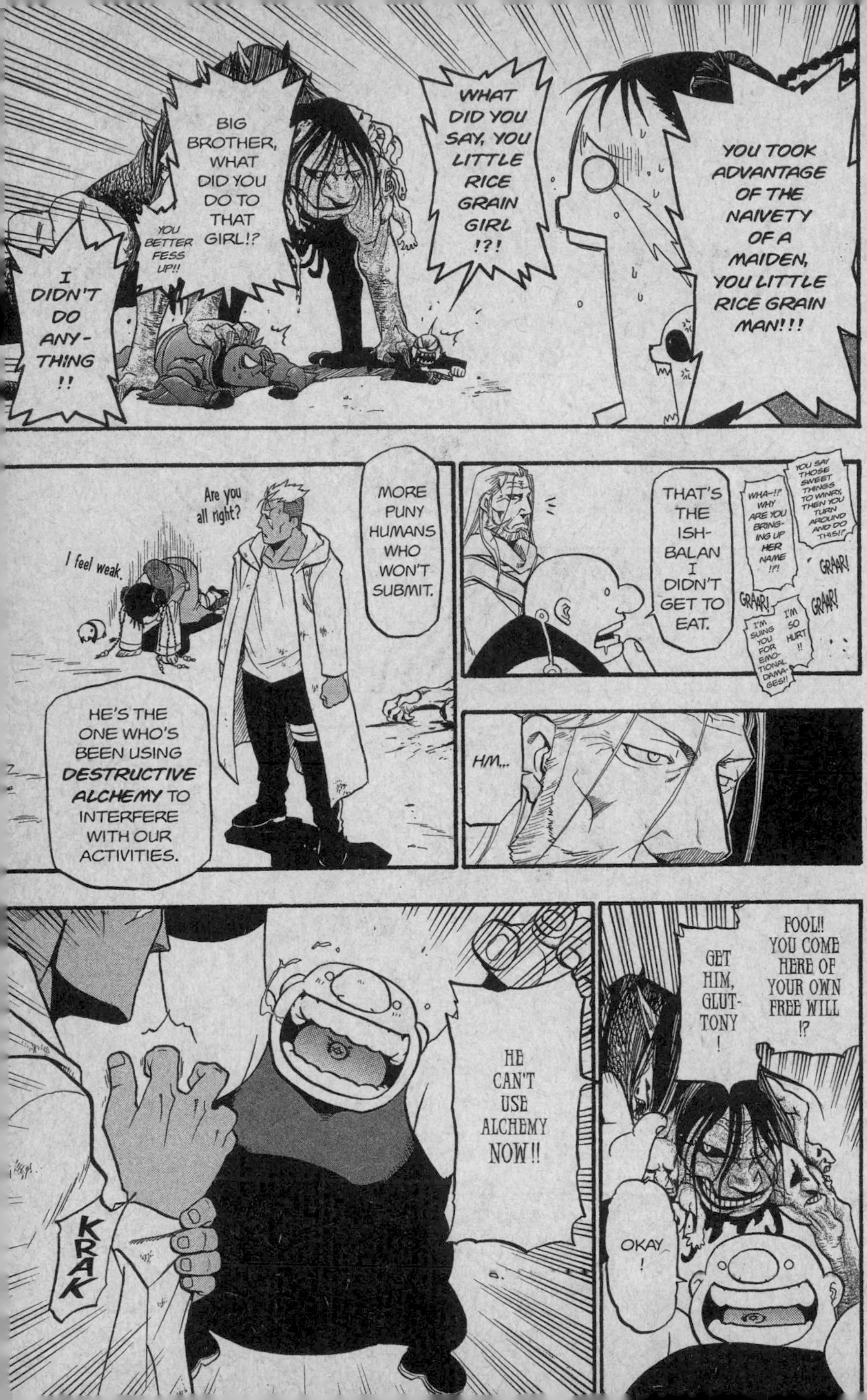

YOU TOOK ADVANTAGE OF THE NAIVETY OF A MAIDEN, YOU LITTLE RICE GRAIN MAN!!!
WHAT DID YOU SAY, YOU LITTLE RICE GRAIN GIRL!?!
BIG BROTHER, WHAT DID YOU DO TO THAT GIRL!?
YOU BETTER FESS UP!!
I DIDN'T DO ANY-THING!!
THAT'S THE ISH-BALAN I DIDN'T GET TO EAT.
YOU SAY THOSE SWEET THINGS TO WINRY, THEN YOU TURN AROUND AND DO THIS!?
WHA--!? WHY ARE YOU BRING-ING UP HER NAME!?!
GRAAR!
GRAAR!
GRAAR!
I'M SO HURT!!
I'M SUING YOU FOR EMO-TIONAL DAMA-GES!!
HM...
MORE PUNY HUMANS WHO WON'T SUBMIT.
Are you all right?
I feel weak.
HE'S THE ONE WHO'S BEEN USING DESTRUCTIVE ALCHEMY TO INTERFERE WITH OUR ACTIVITIES.
FOOL!! YOU COME HERE OF YOUR OWN FREE WILL!?
GET HIM, GLUT-TONY!
OKAY!
HE CAN'T USE ALCHEMY NOW!!
KRAK

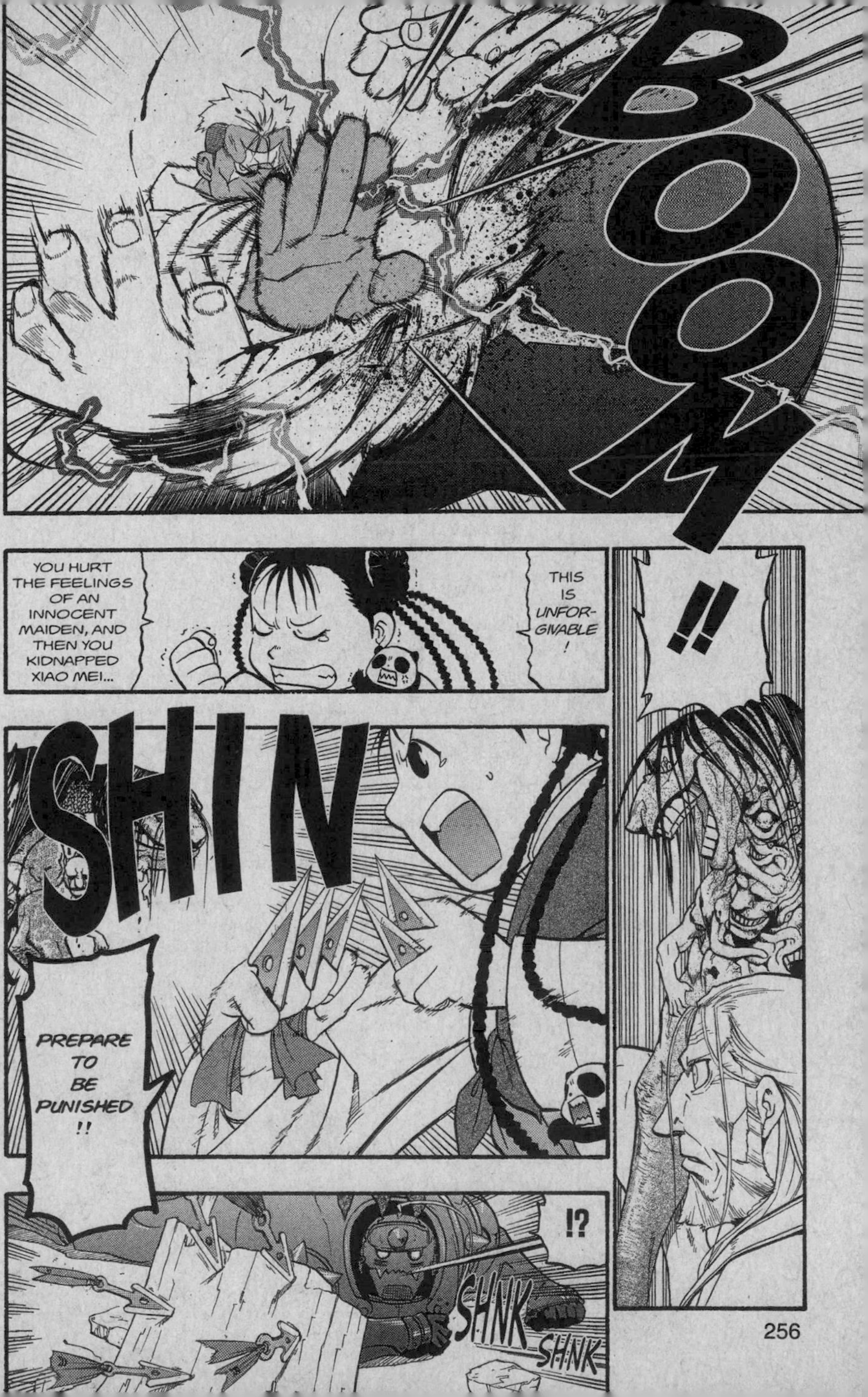
BOOM!!
THIS IS UNFORGIVABLE!
YOU HURT THE FEELINGS OF AN INNOCENT MAIDEN, AND THEN YOU KIDNAPPED XIAO MEI...
SHIN
PREPARE TO BE PUNISHED!!
!?
SHNK
SHNK

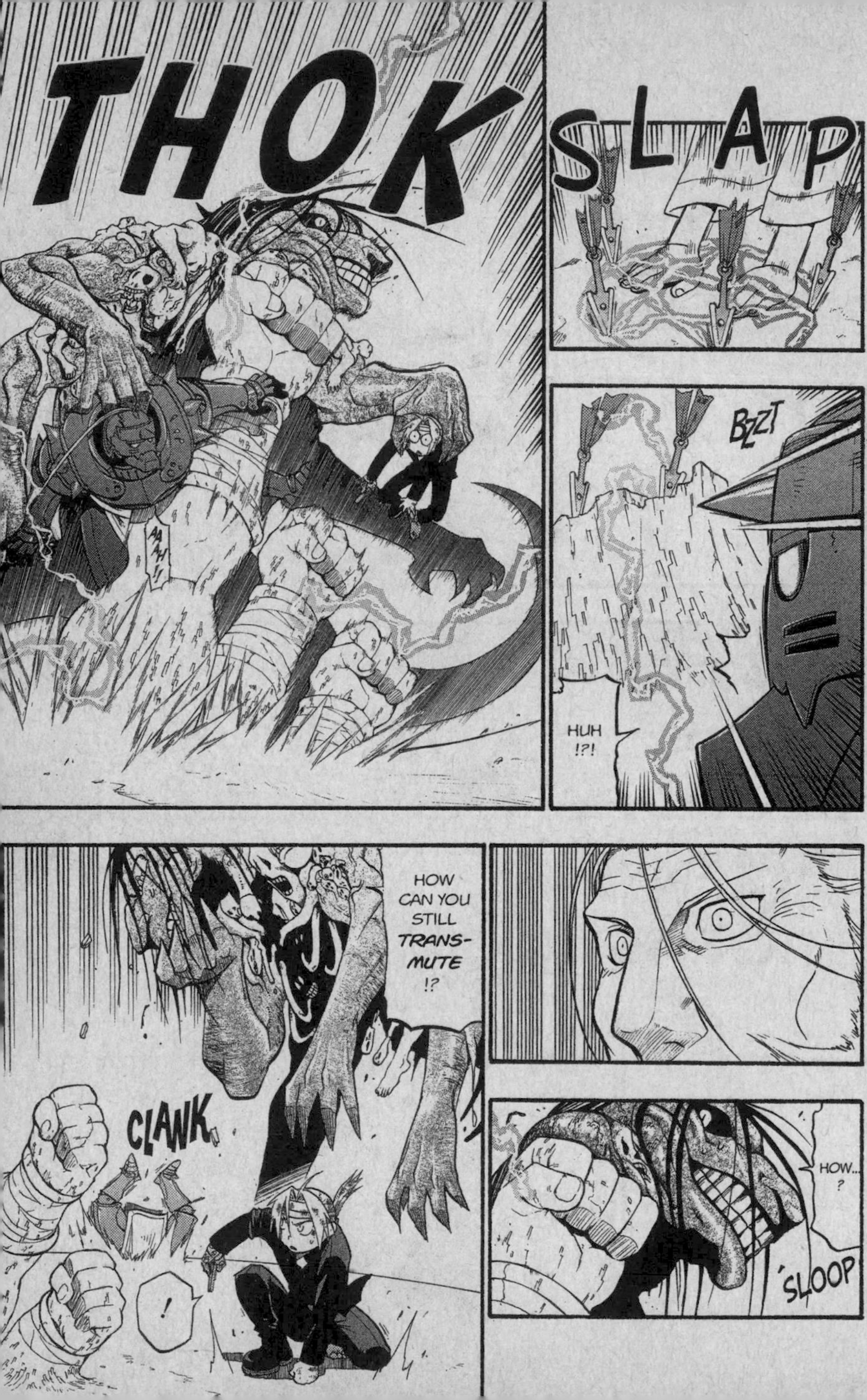
SLAP
BZZT
HUH!?!
THOK
AAAH!!
HOW...?
SLOOP
HOW CAN YOU STILL TRANSMUTE!?
CLANK
!

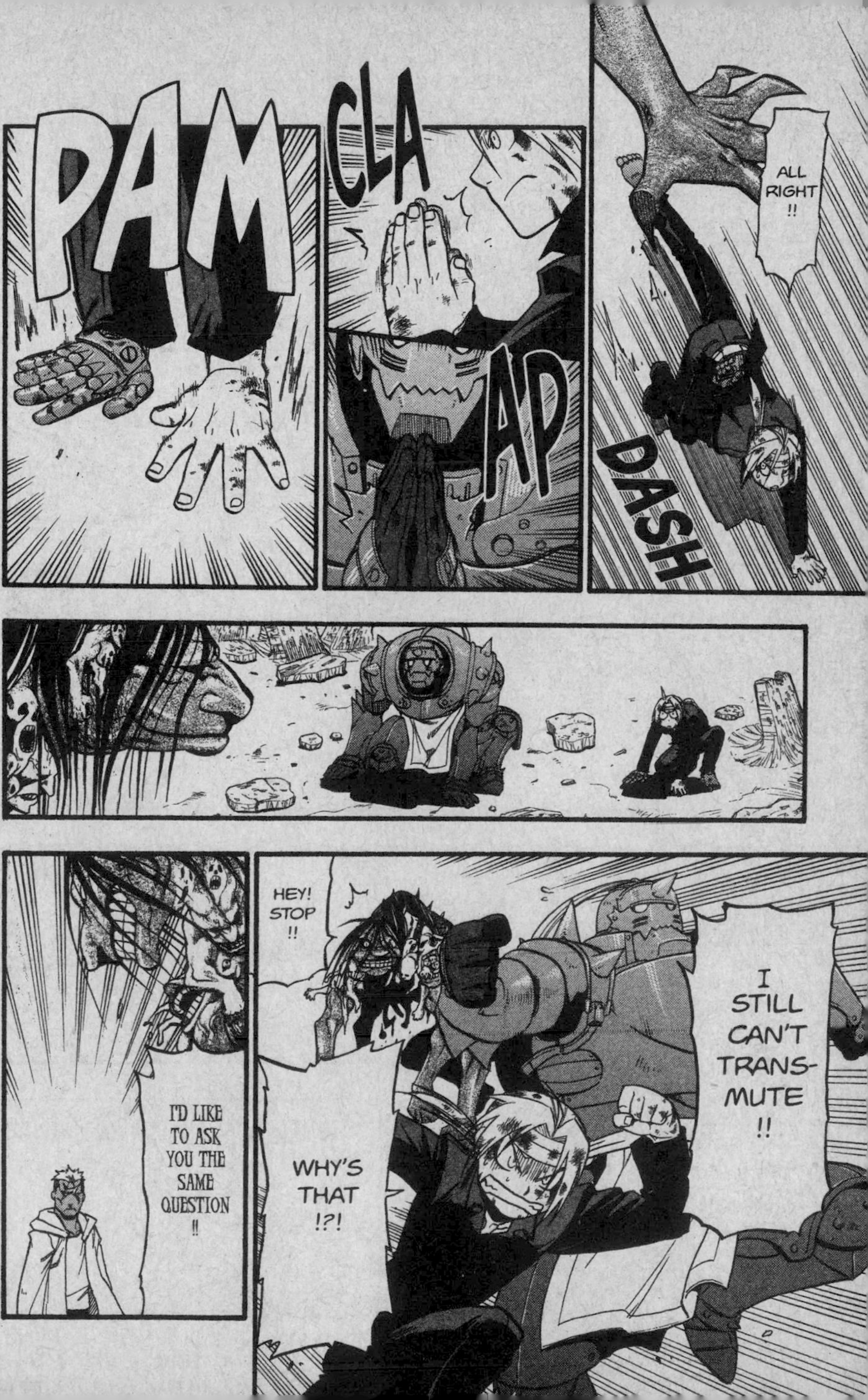
ALL RIGHT !!
DASH
CLA
AP
PAM
I STILL CAN'T TRANS-MUTE !!
HEY! STOP !!
WHY'S THAT !?!
I'D LIKE TO ASK YOU THE SAME QUESTION !!

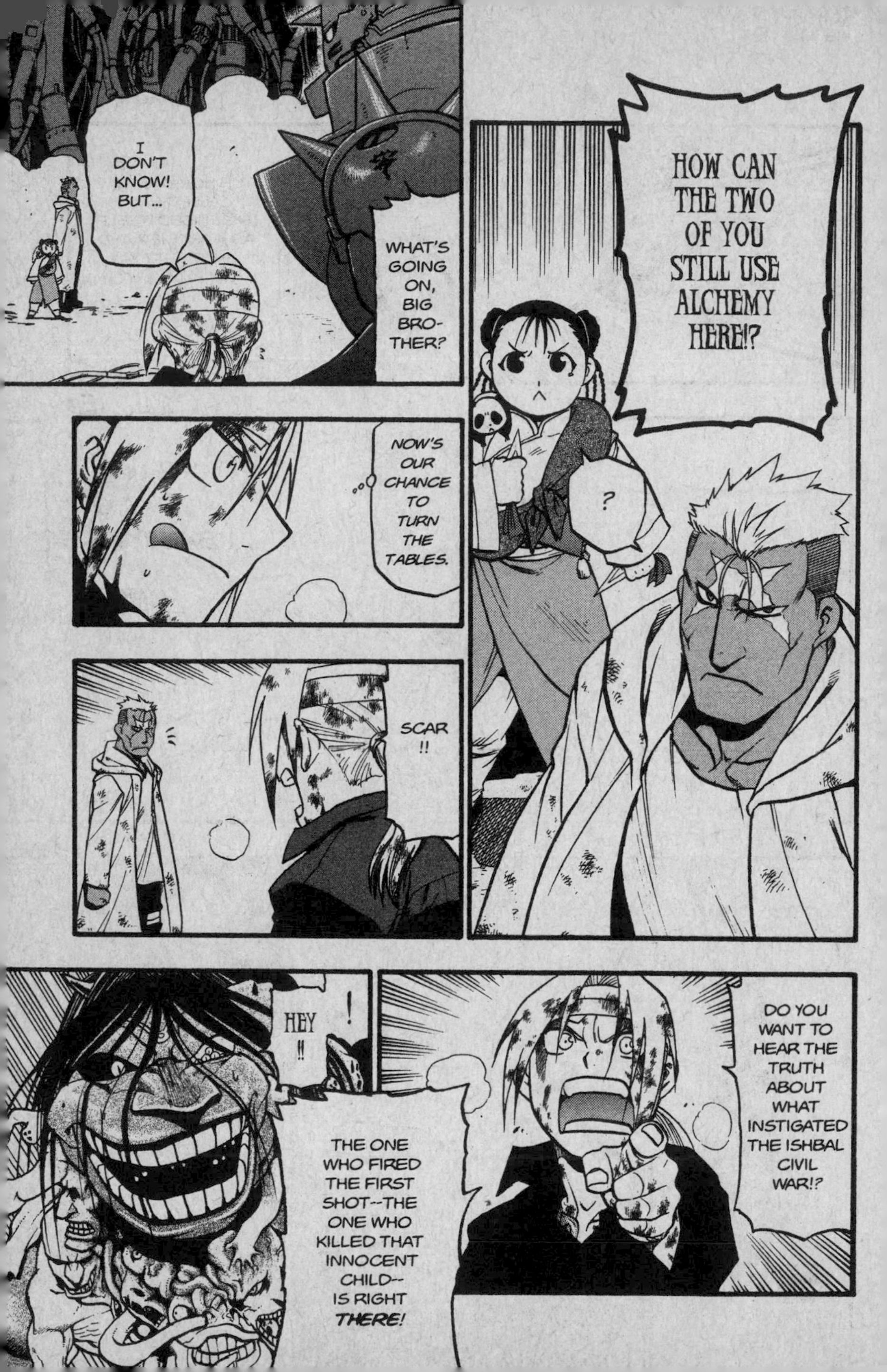
WHAT'S GOING ON, BIG BRO-THER?
I DON'T KNOW! BUT...
HOW CAN THE TWO OF YOU STILL USE ALCHEMY HERE!?
?
NOW'S OUR CHANCE TO TURN THE TABLES.
SCAR !!
DO YOU WANT TO HEAR THE TRUTH ABOUT WHAT INSTIGATED THE ISHBAL CIVIL WAR!?
THE ONE WHO FIRED THE FIRST SHOT--THE ONE WHO KILLED THAT INNOCENT CHILD-- IS RIGHT *THERE!*
!
HEY !!

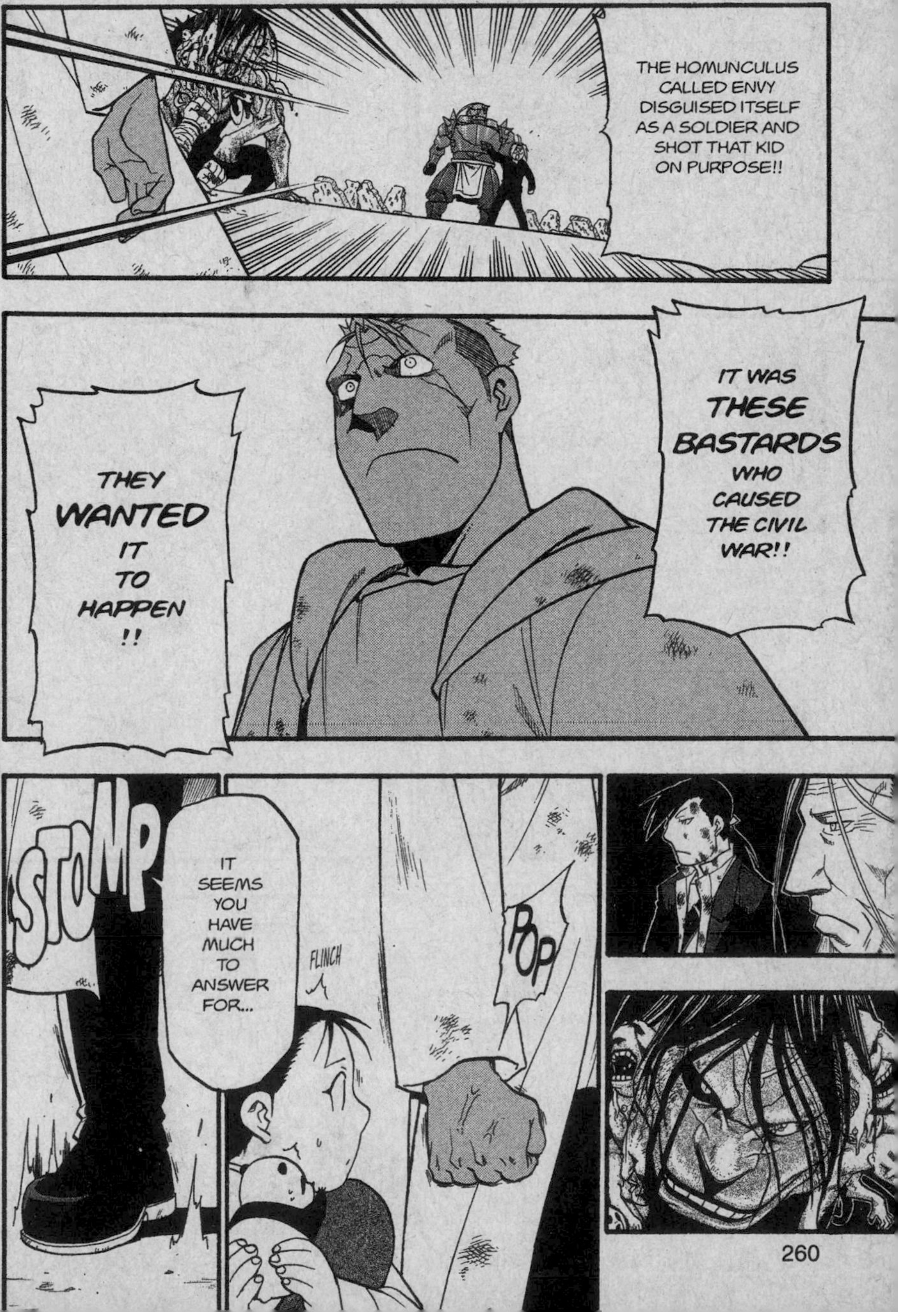
THE HOMUNCULUS CALLED ENVY DISGUISED ITSELF AS A SOLDIER AND SHOT THAT KID ON PURPOSE!!
IT WAS THESE BASTARDS WHO CAUSED THE CIVIL WAR!!
THEY WANTED IT TO HAPPEN!!
POP
STOMP
IT SEEMS YOU HAVE MUCH TO ANSWER FOR...
FLINCH

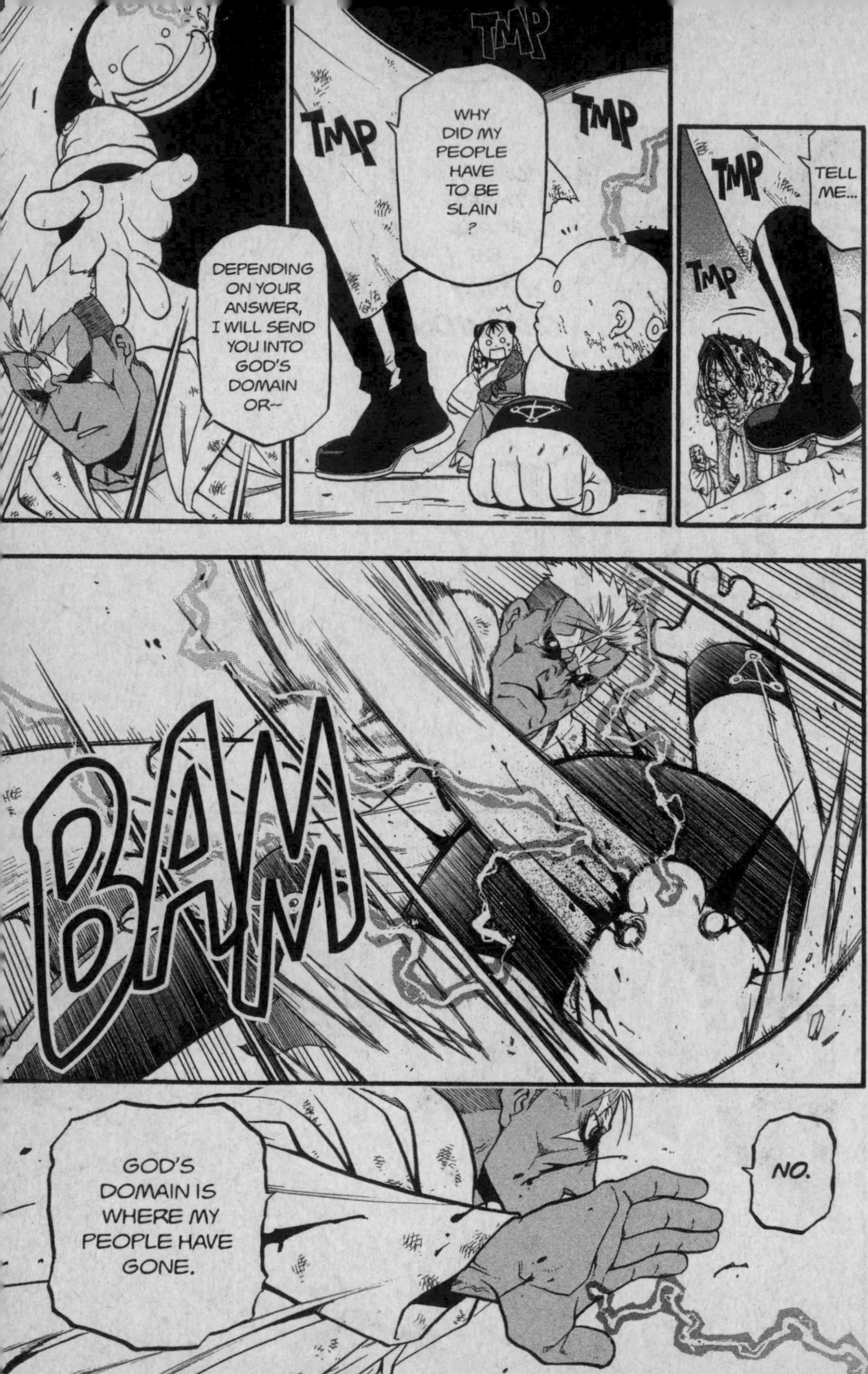
TMP
TMP
TELL ME...
TMP
WHY DID MY PEOPLE HAVE TO BE SLAIN?
TMP
TMP
DEPENDING ON YOUR ANSWER, I WILL SEND YOU INTO GOD'S DOMAIN OR--
BAM
NO.
GOD'S DOMAIN IS WHERE MY PEOPLE HAVE GONE.

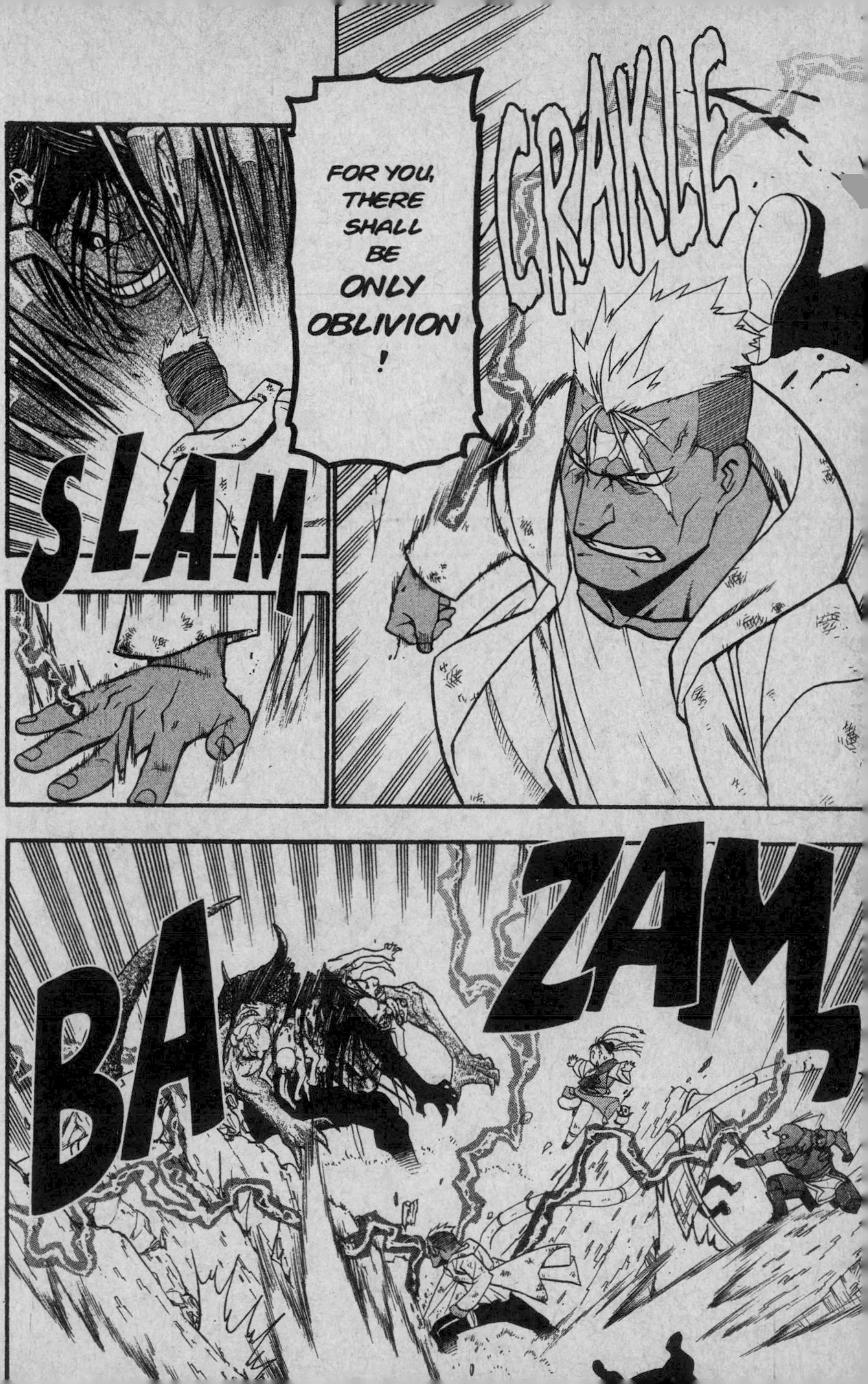
CRAKLE
FOR YOU, THERE SHALL BE ONLY OBLIVION!
SLAM
ZAM
BA

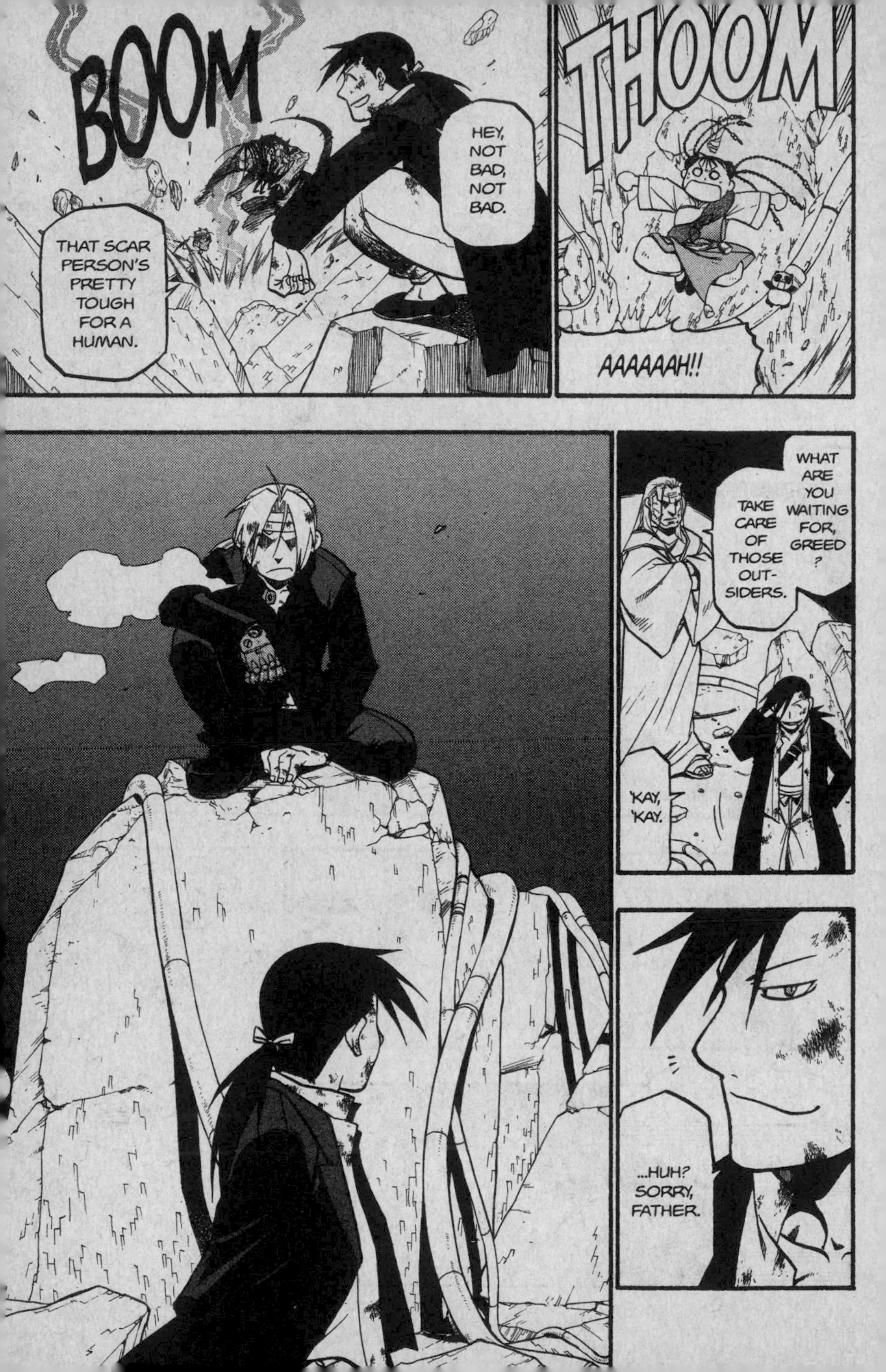
THOOM
AAAAAAH!!
HEY, NOT BAD, NOT BAD.
BOOM
THAT SCAR PERSON'S PRETTY TOUGH FOR A HUMAN.
WHAT ARE YOU WAITING FOR, GREED?
TAKE CARE OF THOSE OUT-SIDERS.
'KAY, 'KAY.
...HUH? SORRY, FATHER.

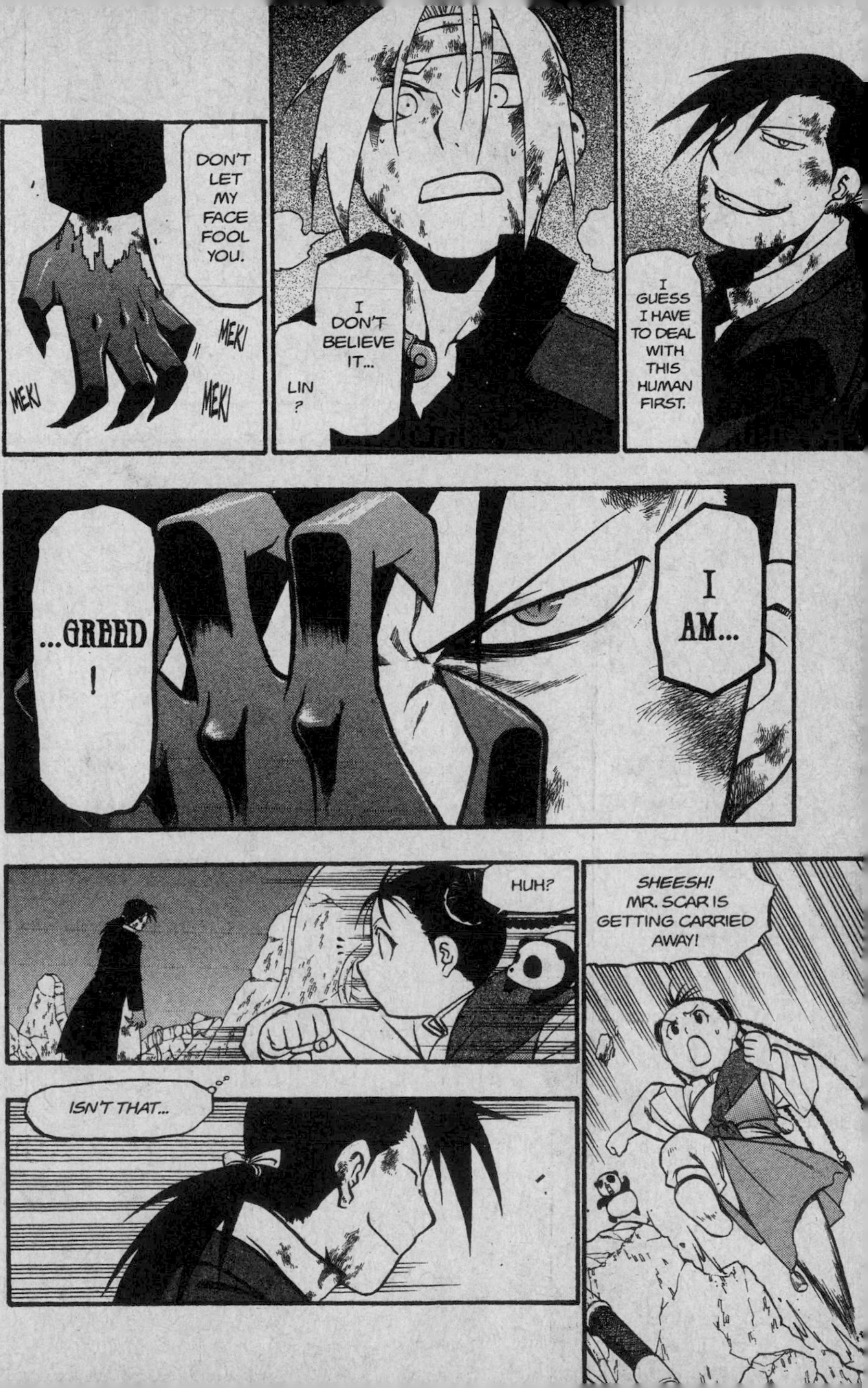
I GUESS I HAVE TO DEAL WITH THIS HUMAN FIRST.
I DON'T BELIEVE IT...
LIN ?
DON'T LET MY FACE FOOL YOU.
MEKI
MEKI
MEKI
I AM...
...GREED !
SHEESH! MR. SCAR IS GETTING CARRIED AWAY!
HUH?
ISN'T THAT...

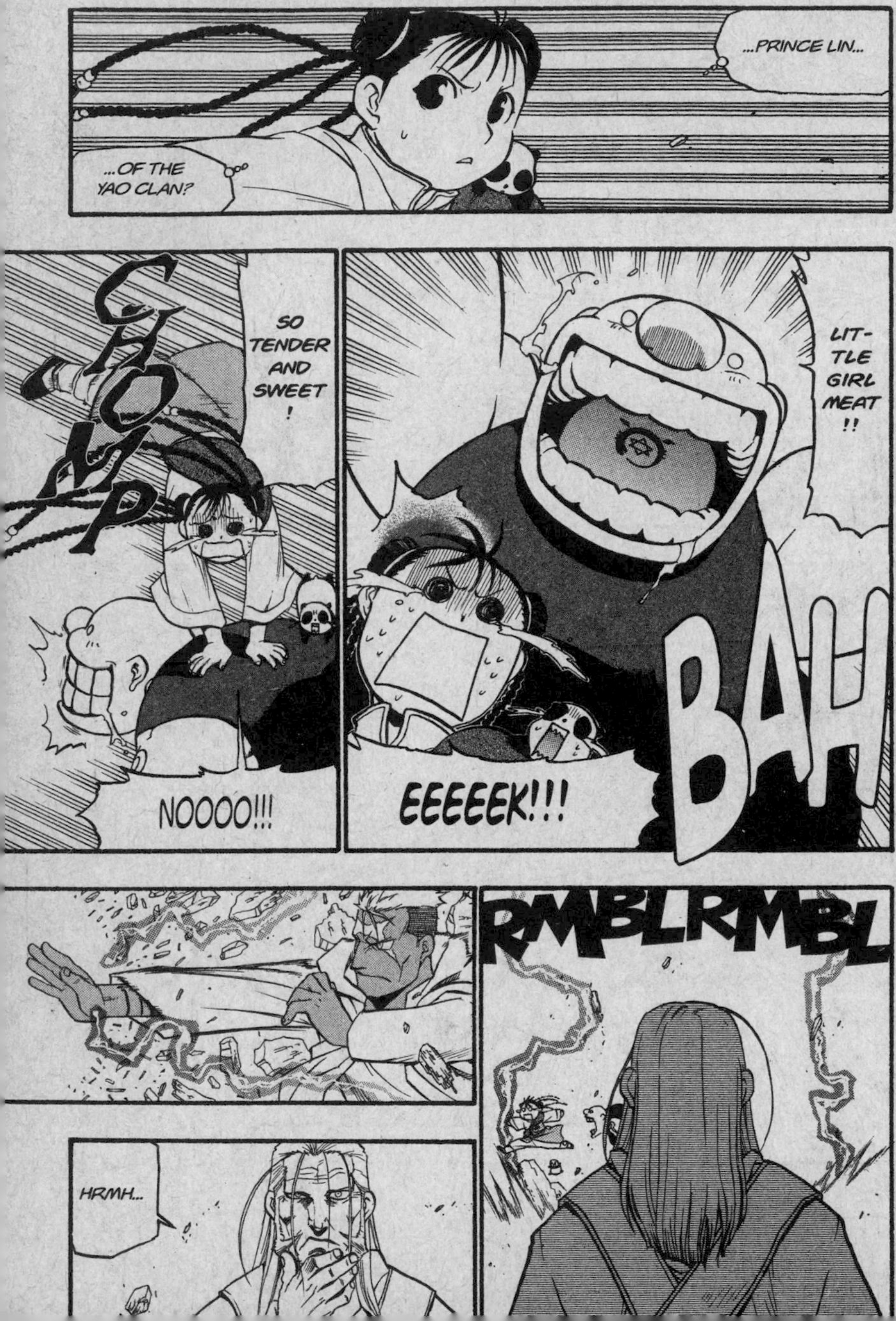
...PRINCE LIN...
...OF THE YAO CLAN?
LIT-TLE GIRL MEAT!!
BAH
EEEEEK!!!
SO TENDER AND SWEET!
CHOMP
NOOOO!!!
RMBLRMBL
HRMH...

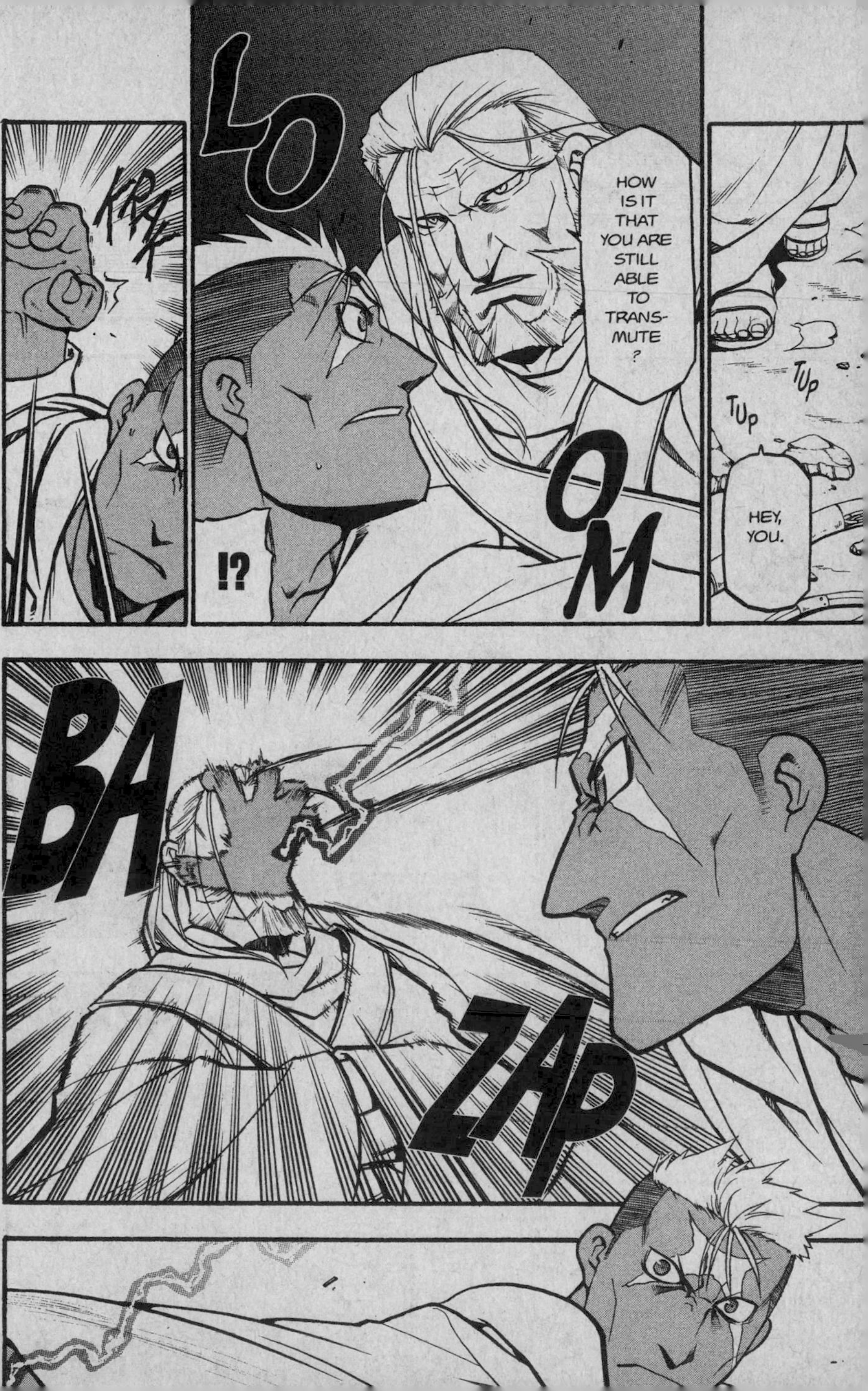

TUP
TUP
HEY, YOU.
LOOM
HOW IS IT THAT YOU ARE STILL ABLE TO TRANSMUTE?
!?
KRAK
BA
ZAP

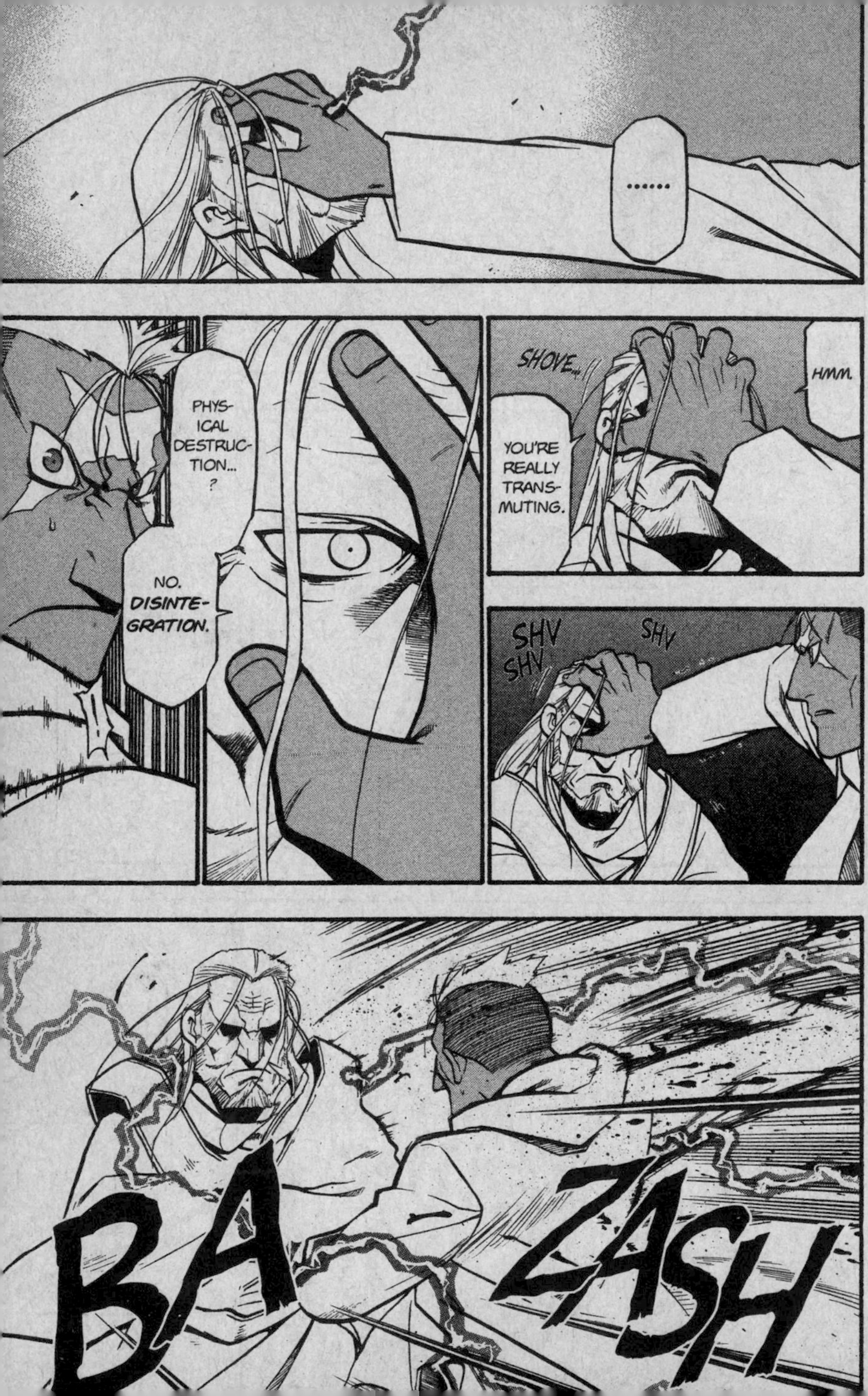
......
HMM.
SHOVE...
YOU'RE REALLY TRANSMUTING.
SHV
SHV
SHV
PHYSICAL DESTRUCTION... ?
NO. DISINTEGRATION.
BA-ZASH

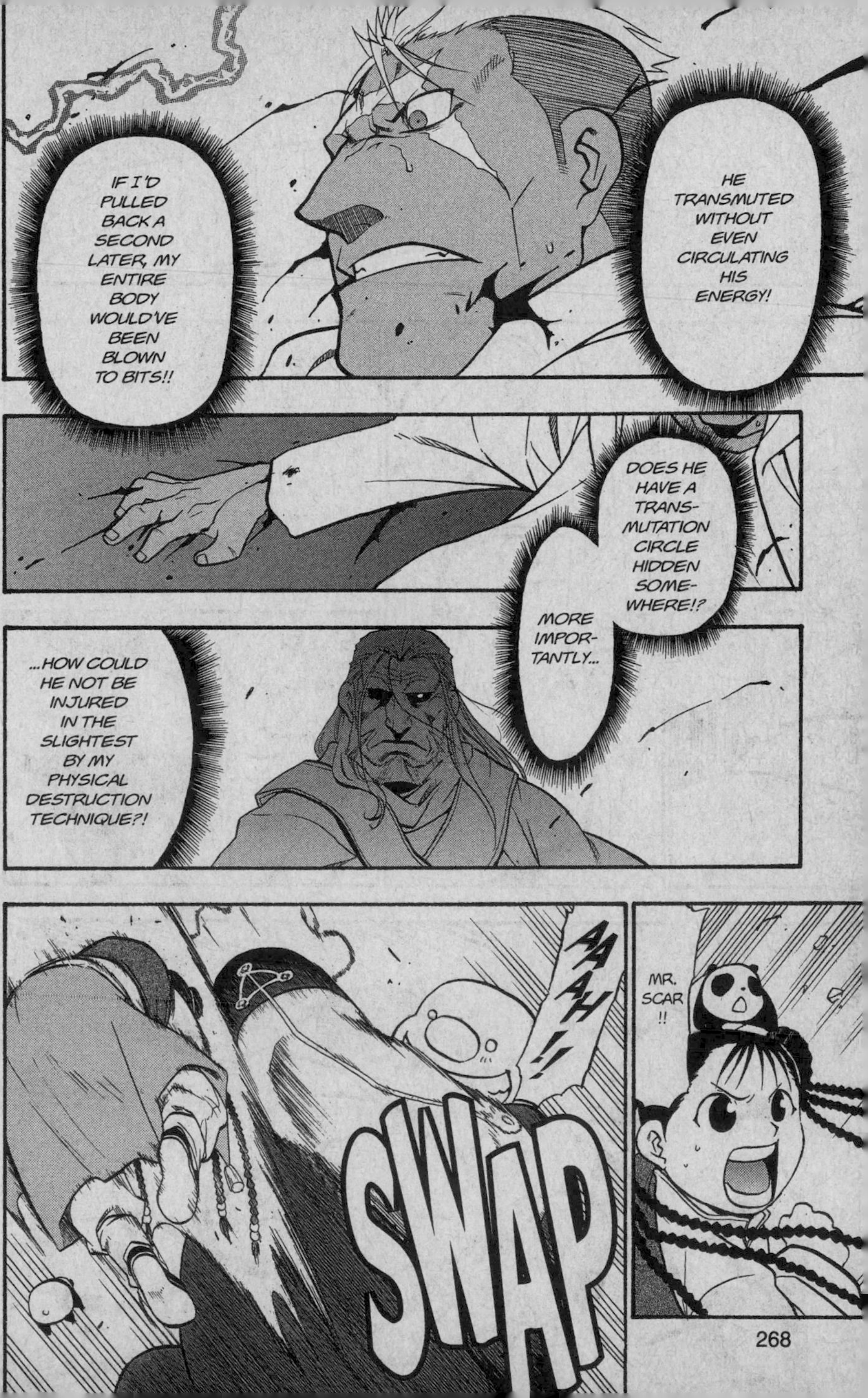
HE TRANSMUTED WITHOUT EVEN CIRCULATING HIS ENERGY!
IF I'D PULLED BACK A SECOND LATER, MY ENTIRE BODY WOULD'VE BEEN BLOWN TO BITS!!
DOES HE HAVE A TRANS-MUTATION CIRCLE HIDDEN SOME-WHERE!?
MORE IMPOR-TANTLY...
...HOW COULD HE NOT BE INJURED IN THE SLIGHTEST BY MY PHYSICAL DESTRUCTION TECHNIQUE?!
MR. SCAR !!
AAAH!!
SWAP

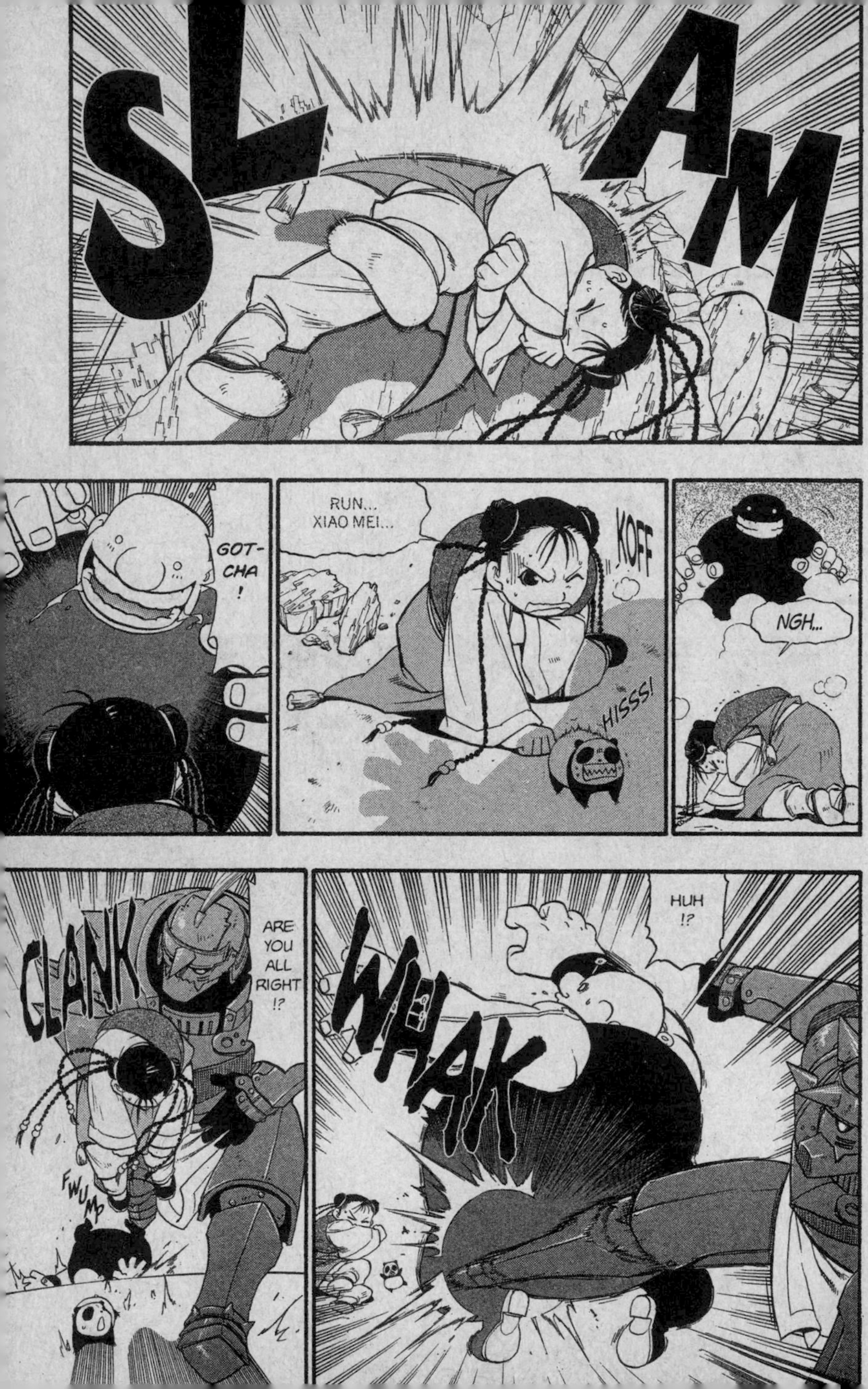
SLAM
NGH...
RUN... XIAO MEI...
KOFF
HISSS!
GOT-CHA!
HUH!?
WHAK
ARE YOU ALL RIGHT!?
CLANK
FWUMP

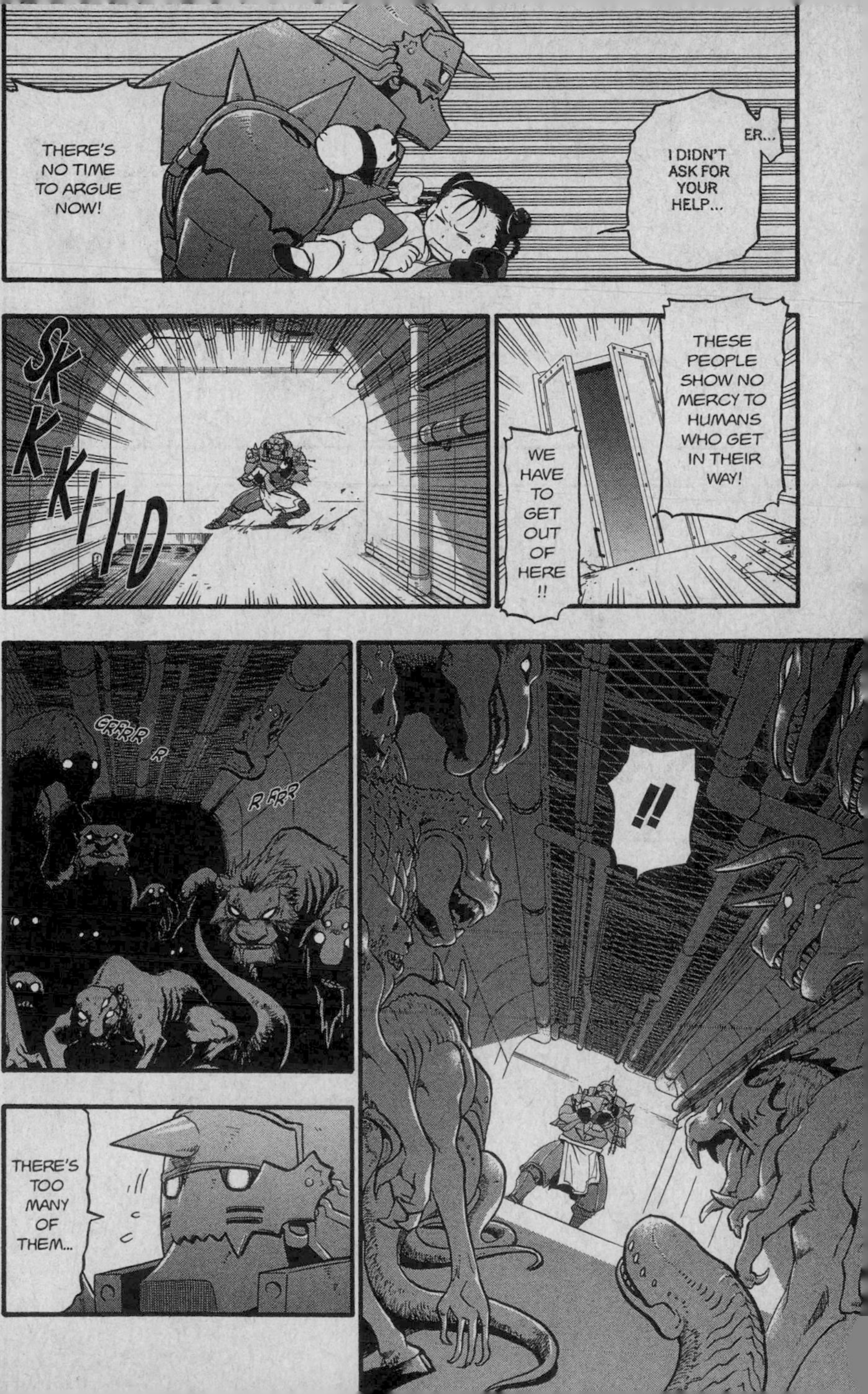
ER...
I DIDN'T ASK FOR YOUR HELP...
THERE'S NO TIME TO ARGUE NOW!
THESE PEOPLE SHOW NO MERCY TO HUMANS WHO GET IN THEIR WAY!
WE HAVE TO GET OUT OF HERE !!
SKKKIID
!!
GRRRR R
R RRR
THERE'S TOO MANY OF THEM...

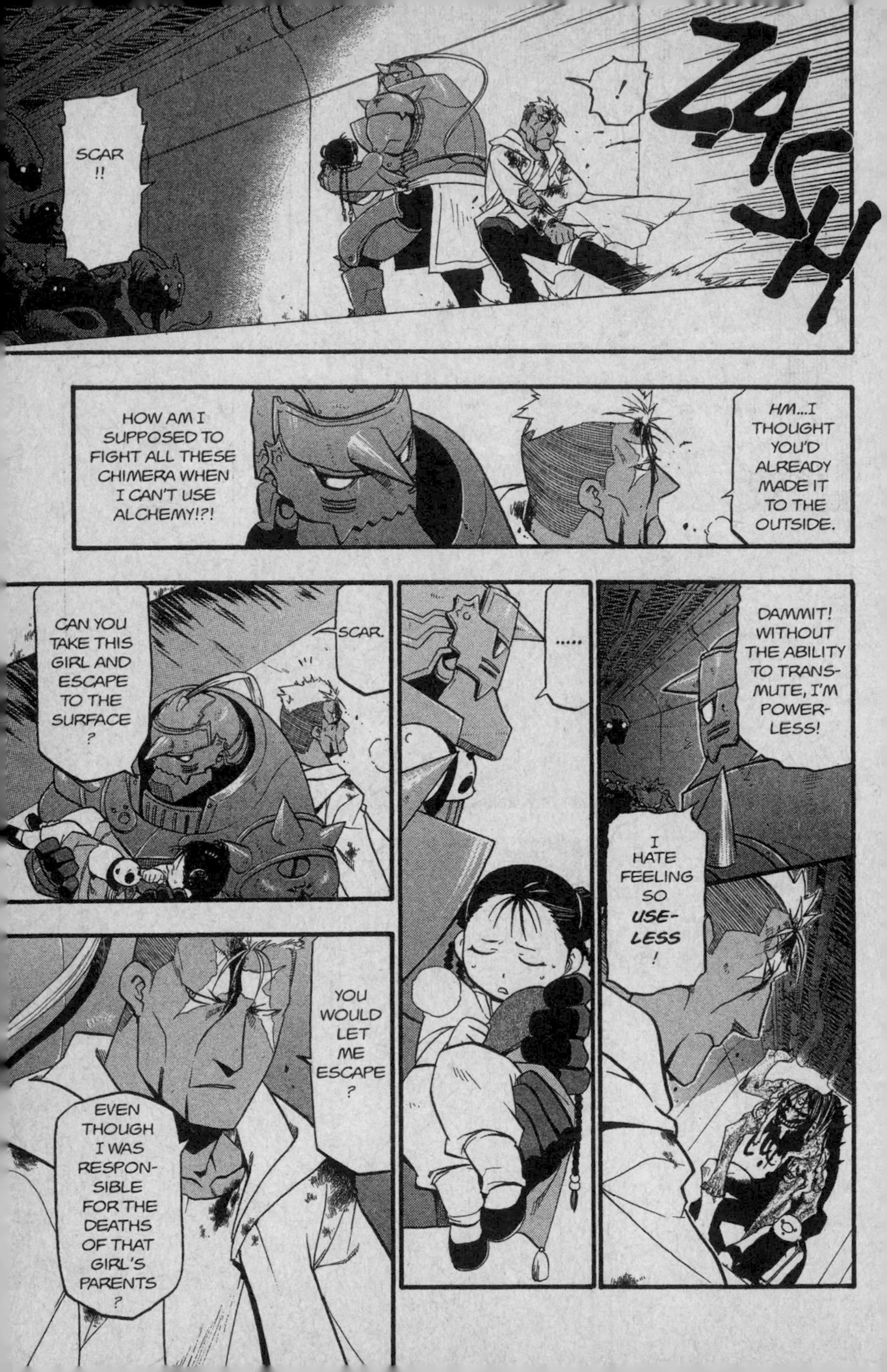
ZASH
!
SCAR !!
HM...I THOUGHT YOU'D ALREADY MADE IT TO THE OUTSIDE.
HOW AM I SUPPOSED TO FIGHT ALL THESE CHIMERA WHEN I CAN'T USE ALCHEMY!?!
DAMMIT! WITHOUT THE ABILITY TO TRANSMUTE, I'M POWERLESS!
I HATE FEELING SO USELESS!
.....
SCAR.
CAN YOU TAKE THIS GIRL AND ESCAPE TO THE SURFACE?
YOU WOULD LET ME ESCAPE?
EVEN THOUGH I WAS RESPONSIBLE FOR THE DEATHS OF THAT GIRL'S PARENTS?

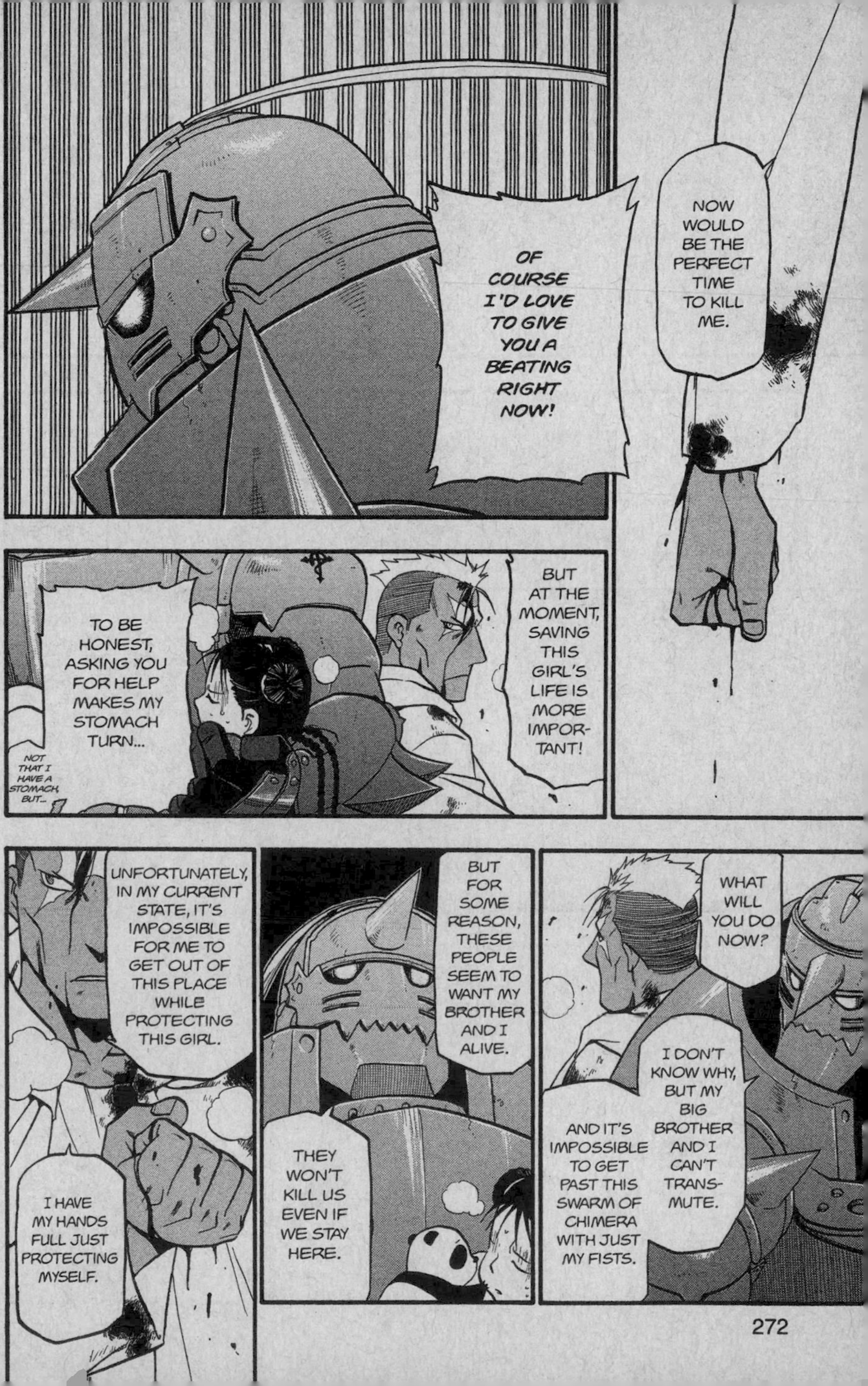
NOW WOULD BE THE PERFECT TIME TO KILL ME.
OF COURSE I'D LOVE TO GIVE YOU A BEATING RIGHT NOW!
TO BE HONEST, ASKING YOU FOR HELP MAKES MY STOMACH TURN...
NOT THAT I HAVE A STOMACH, BUT...
BUT AT THE MOMENT, SAVING THIS GIRL'S LIFE IS MORE IMPOR-TANT!
WHAT WILL YOU DO NOW?
I DON'T KNOW WHY, BUT MY BIG BROTHER AND I CAN'T TRANS-MUTE.
AND IT'S IMPOSSIBLE TO GET PAST THIS SWARM OF CHIMERA WITH JUST MY FISTS.
BUT FOR SOME REASON, THESE PEOPLE SEEM TO WANT MY BROTHER AND I ALIVE.
THEY WON'T KILL US EVEN IF WE STAY HERE.
UNFORTUNATELY, IN MY CURRENT STATE, IT'S IMPOSSIBLE FOR ME TO GET OUT OF THIS PLACE WHILE PROTECTING THIS GIRL.
I HAVE MY HANDS FULL JUST PROTECTING MYSELF.

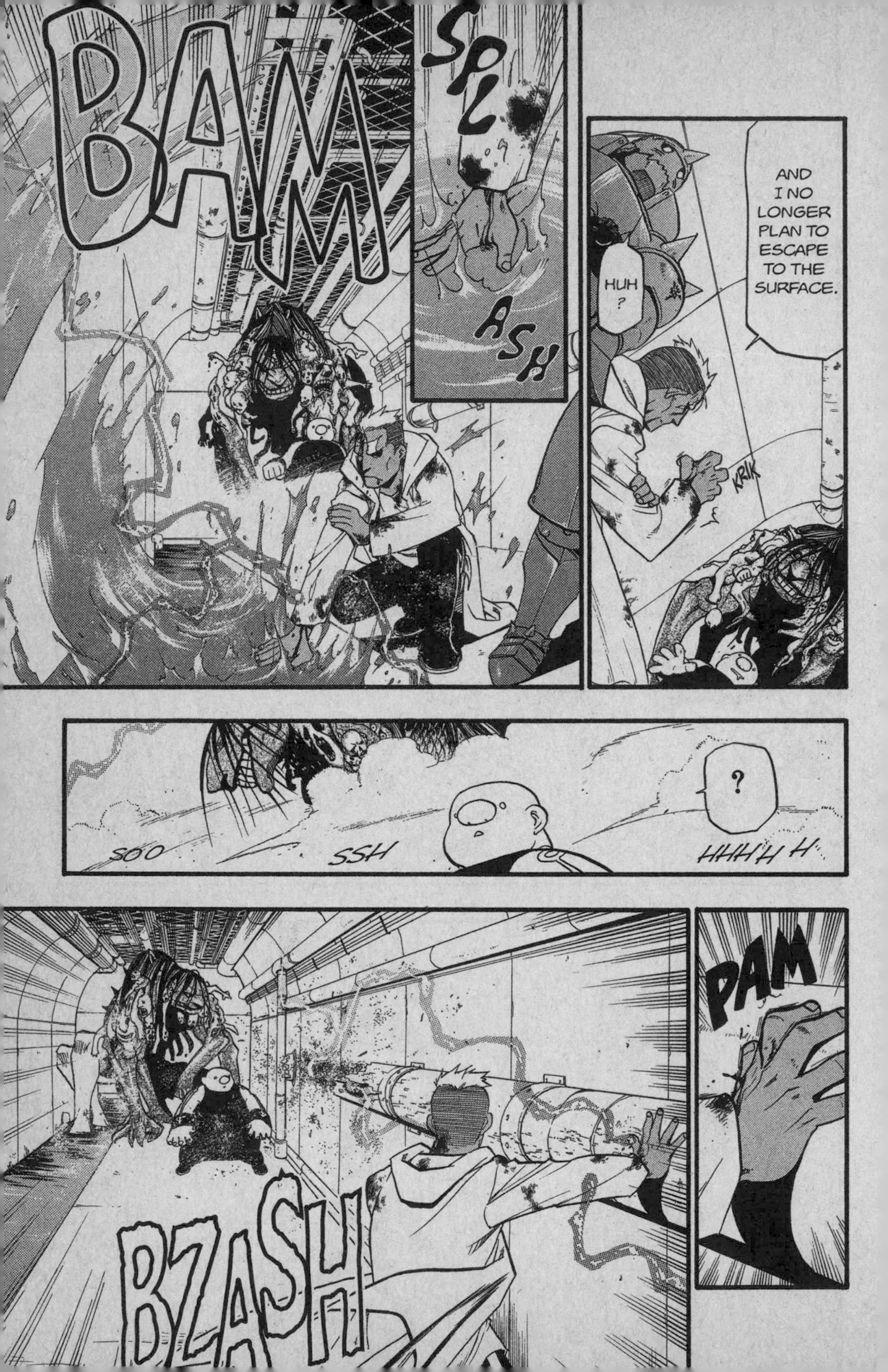
AND I NO LONGER PLAN TO ESCAPE TO THE SURFACE.
HUH ?
KRIK
SPLASH
BAM
?
HHHH H
SSH
SOO
PAM
BZASH

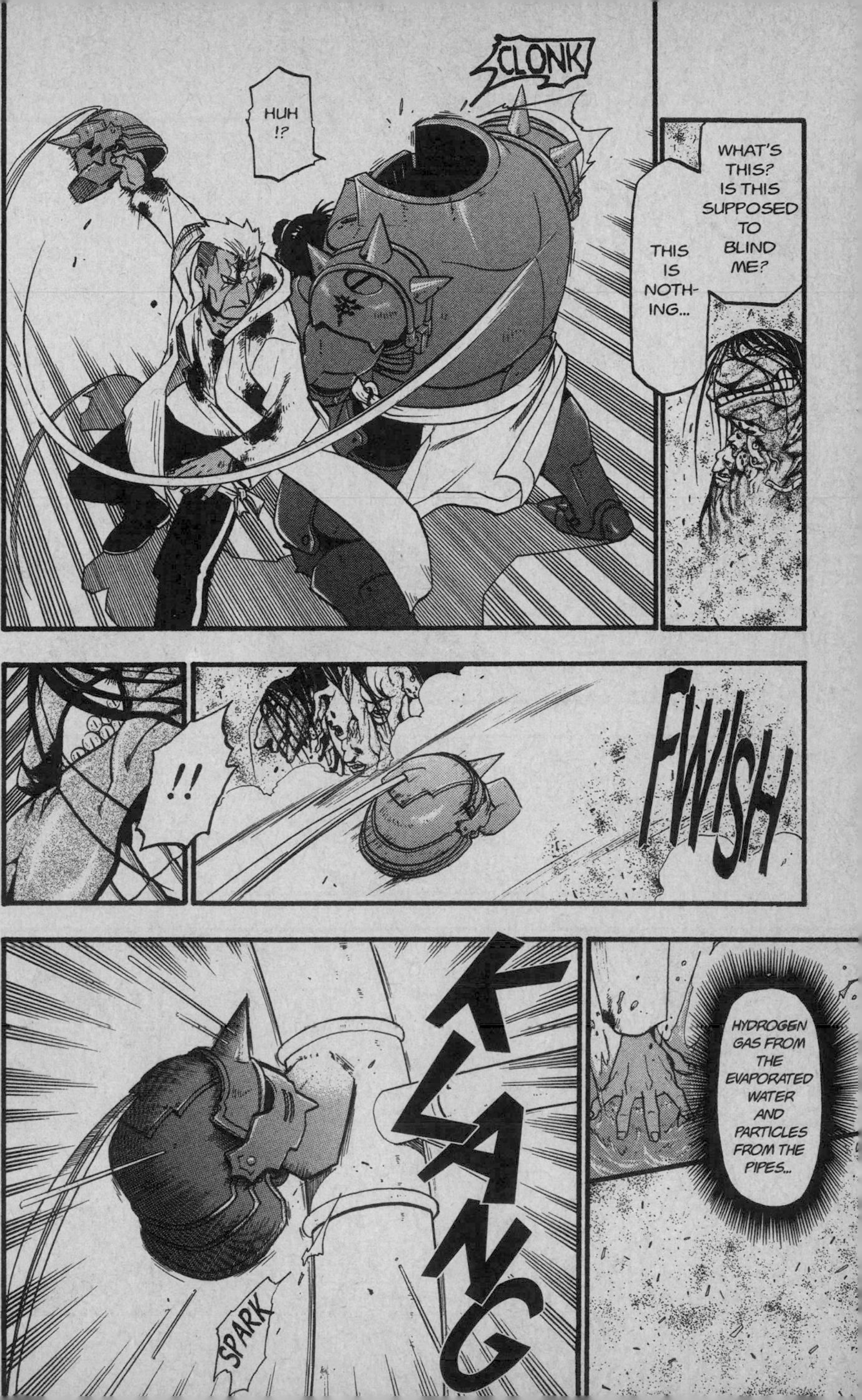
WHAT'S THIS? IS THIS SUPPOSED TO BLIND ME?
THIS IS NOTHING...
CLONK
HUH!?
FWISH
!!
HYDROGEN GAS FROM THE EVAPORATED WATER AND PARTICLES FROM THE PIPES...
KLANG
SPARK

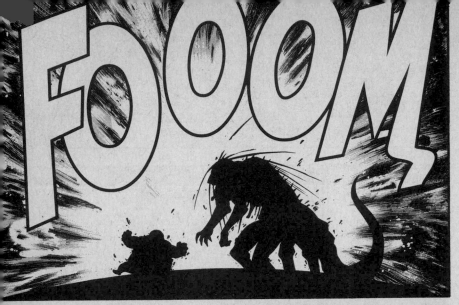

FOOOM

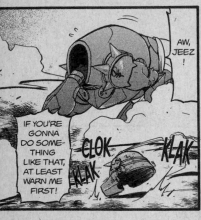

AW, JEEZ!

IF YOU'RE GONNA DO SOMETHING LIKE THAT, AT LEAST WARN ME FIRST!

CLOK
KLAK
KLAK

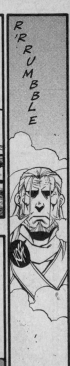

R'R'RUMBLE

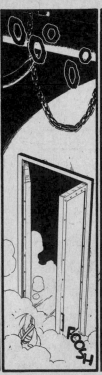

FOOSH

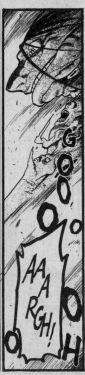

GOOOOOH

AAAARGH!

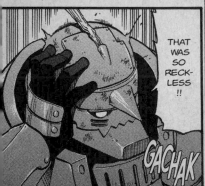

THAT WAS SO RECKLESS!!

GACHAK

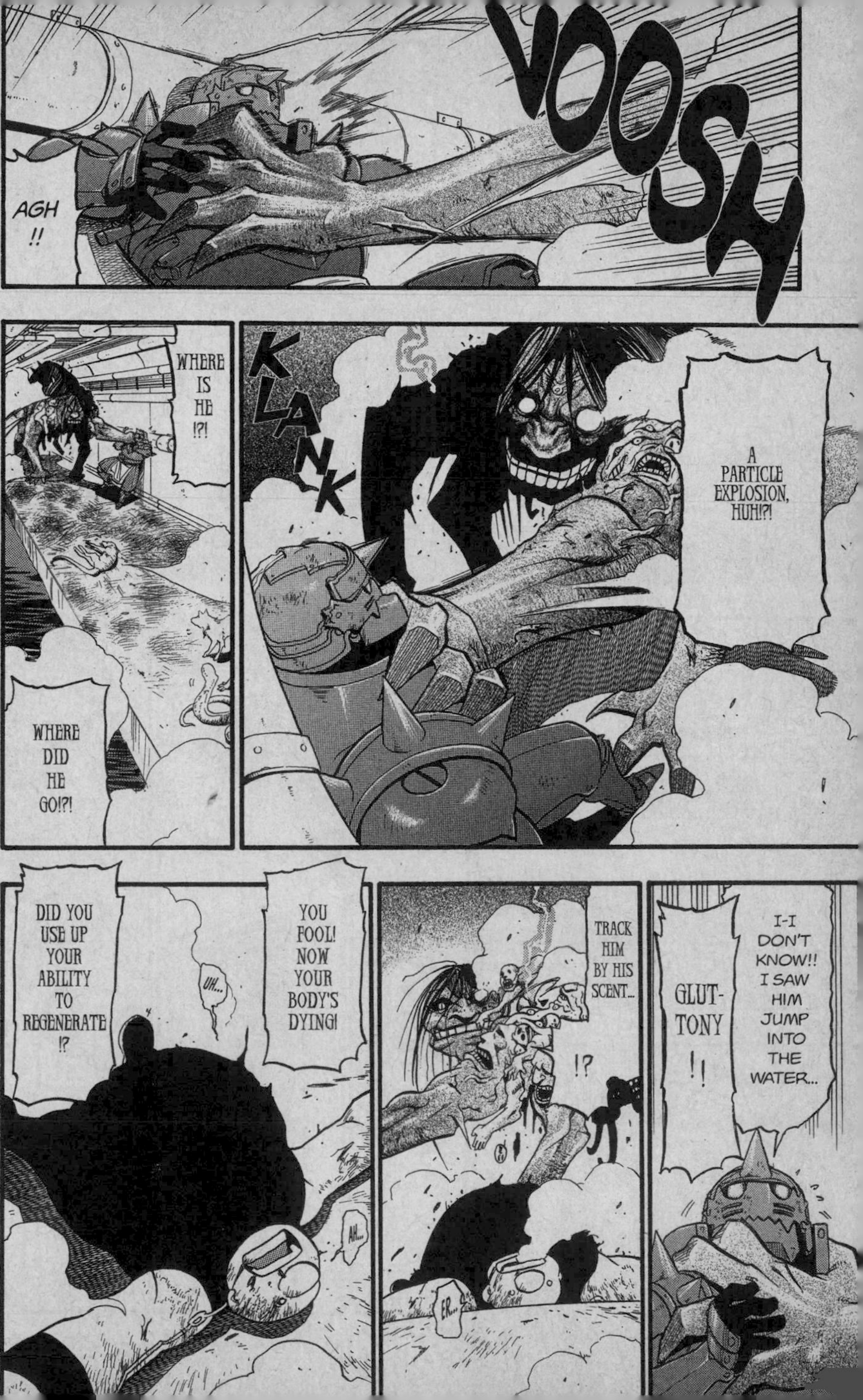
VOOSH
AGH!!
KLANK
A PARTICLE EXPLOSION, HUH!?!
WHERE IS HE!?!
WHERE DID HE GO!?!
I-I DON'T KNOW!! I SAW HIM JUMP INTO THE WATER...
GLUTTONY!!
TRACK HIM BY HIS SCENT...
!?
ER...
YOU FOOL! NOW YOUR BODY'S DYING!
DID YOU USE UP YOUR ABILITY TO REGENERATE!?
UH...
AH...

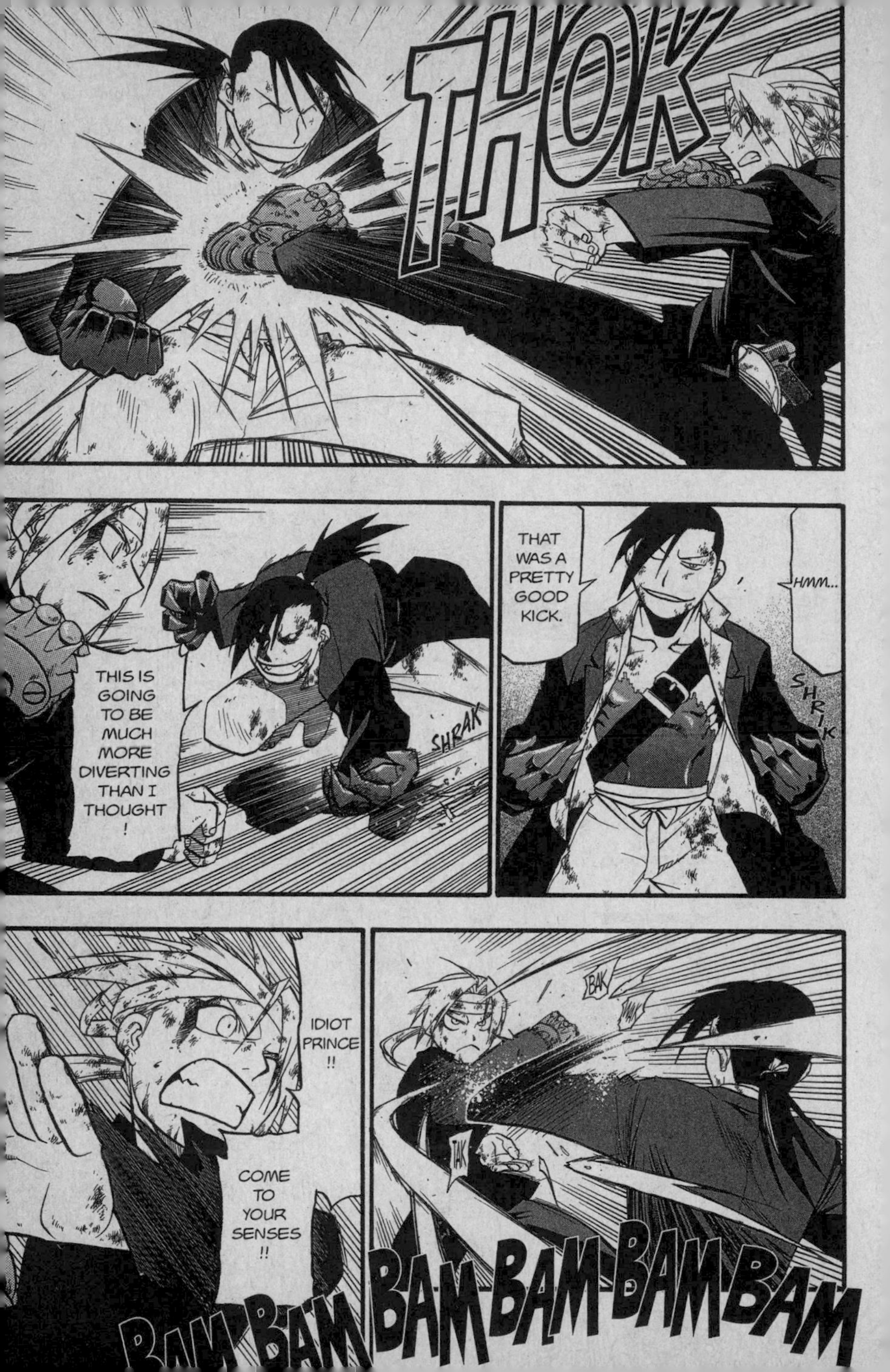
THOK
HMM...
THAT WAS A PRETTY GOOD KICK.
SHRIK
SHRAK
THIS IS GOING TO BE MUCH MORE DIVERTING THAN I THOUGHT!
BAK
TAK
IDIOT PRINCE!!
COME TO YOUR SENSES!!
BAM BAM BAM BAM BAM BAM BAM

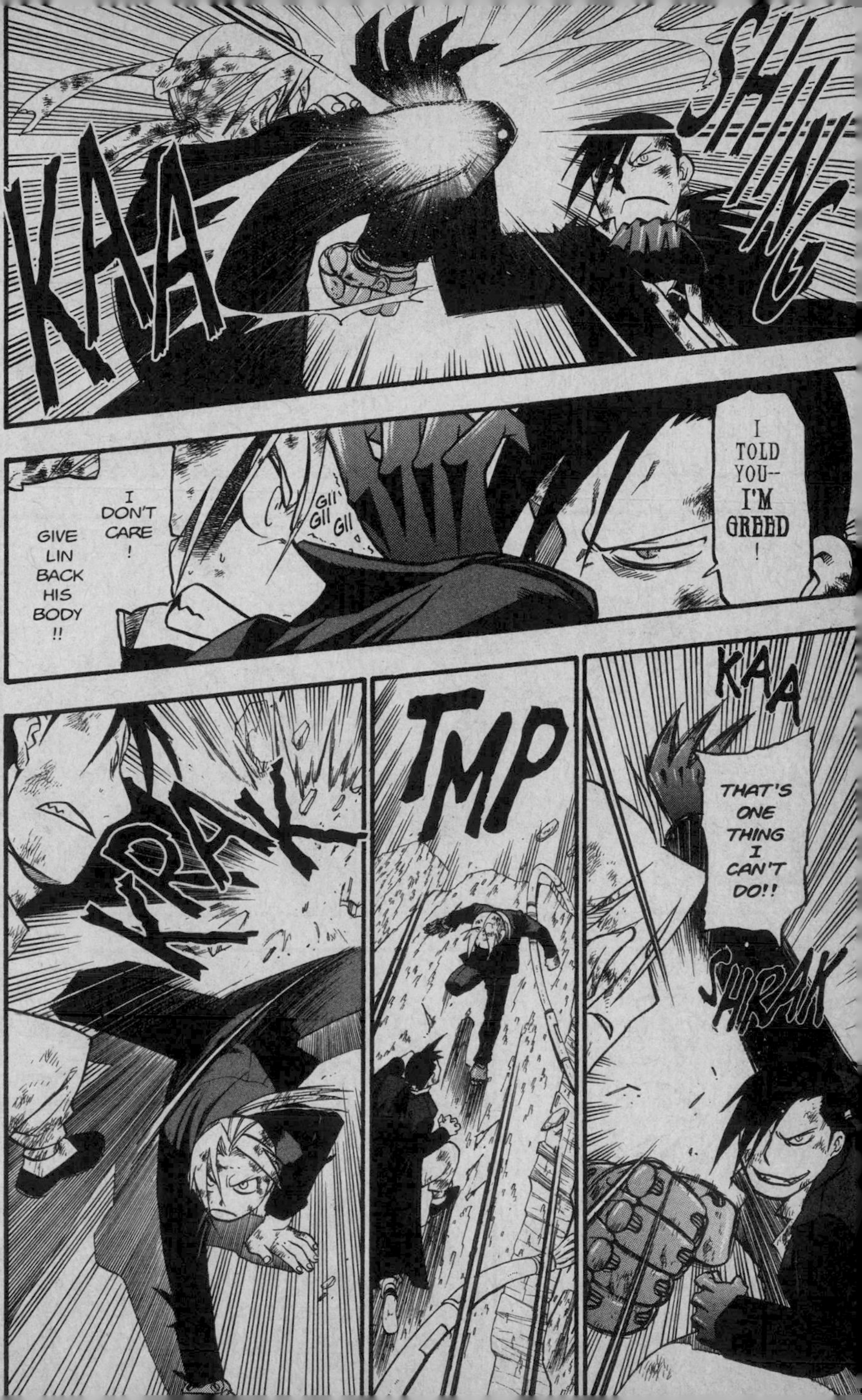
SHING
KAA
I TOLD YOU-- I'M GREED!
GII GII GII
I DON'T CARE!
GIVE LIN BACK HIS BODY!!
KAA
THAT'S ONE THING I CAN'T DO!!
SHRAK
TMP
KRAK

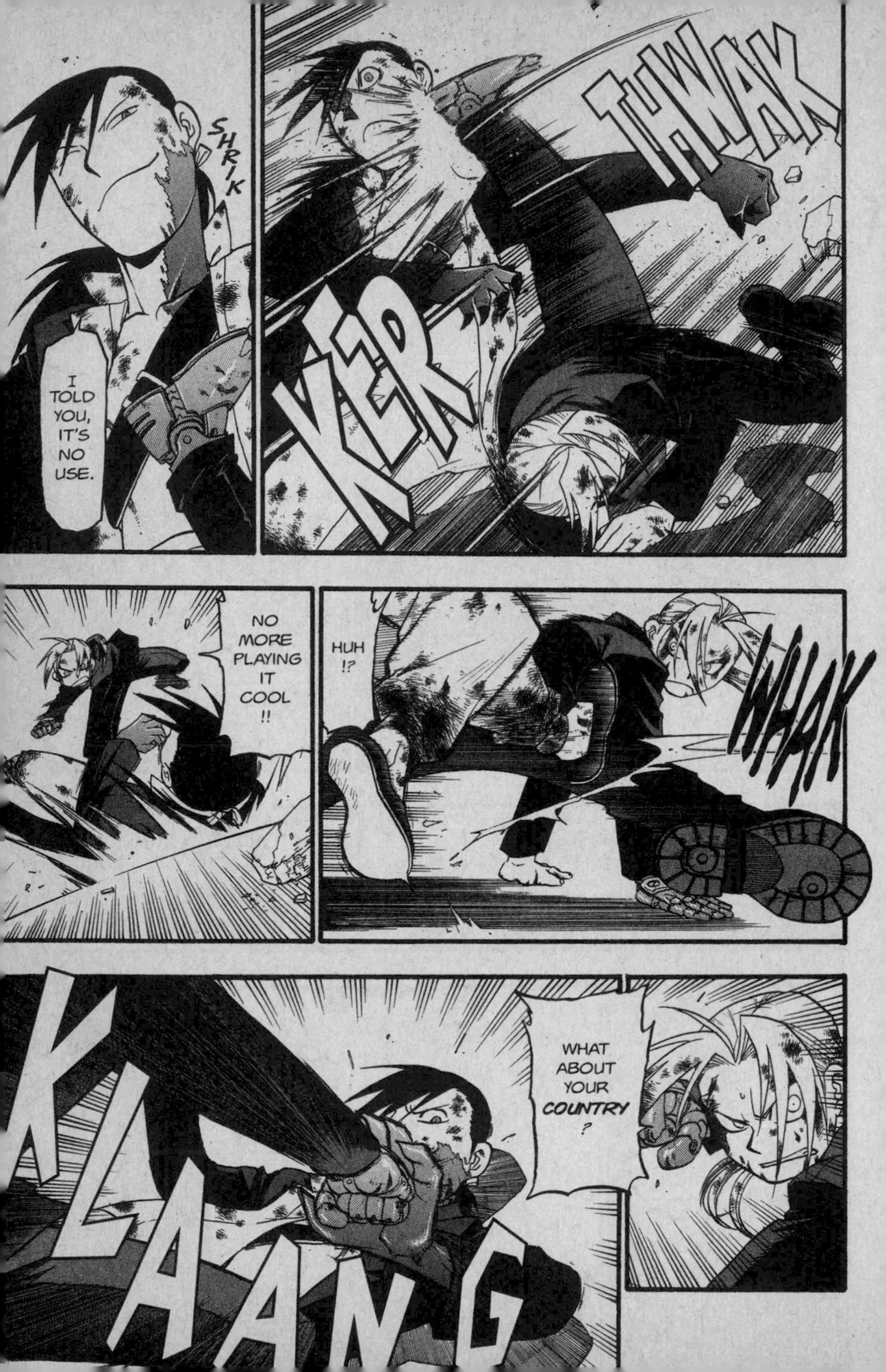
THWAK
KER
SHRIK
I TOLD YOU, IT'S NO USE.
HUH!?
WHAK
NO MORE PLAYING IT COOL!!
WHAT ABOUT YOUR COUNTRY?
KLAANG

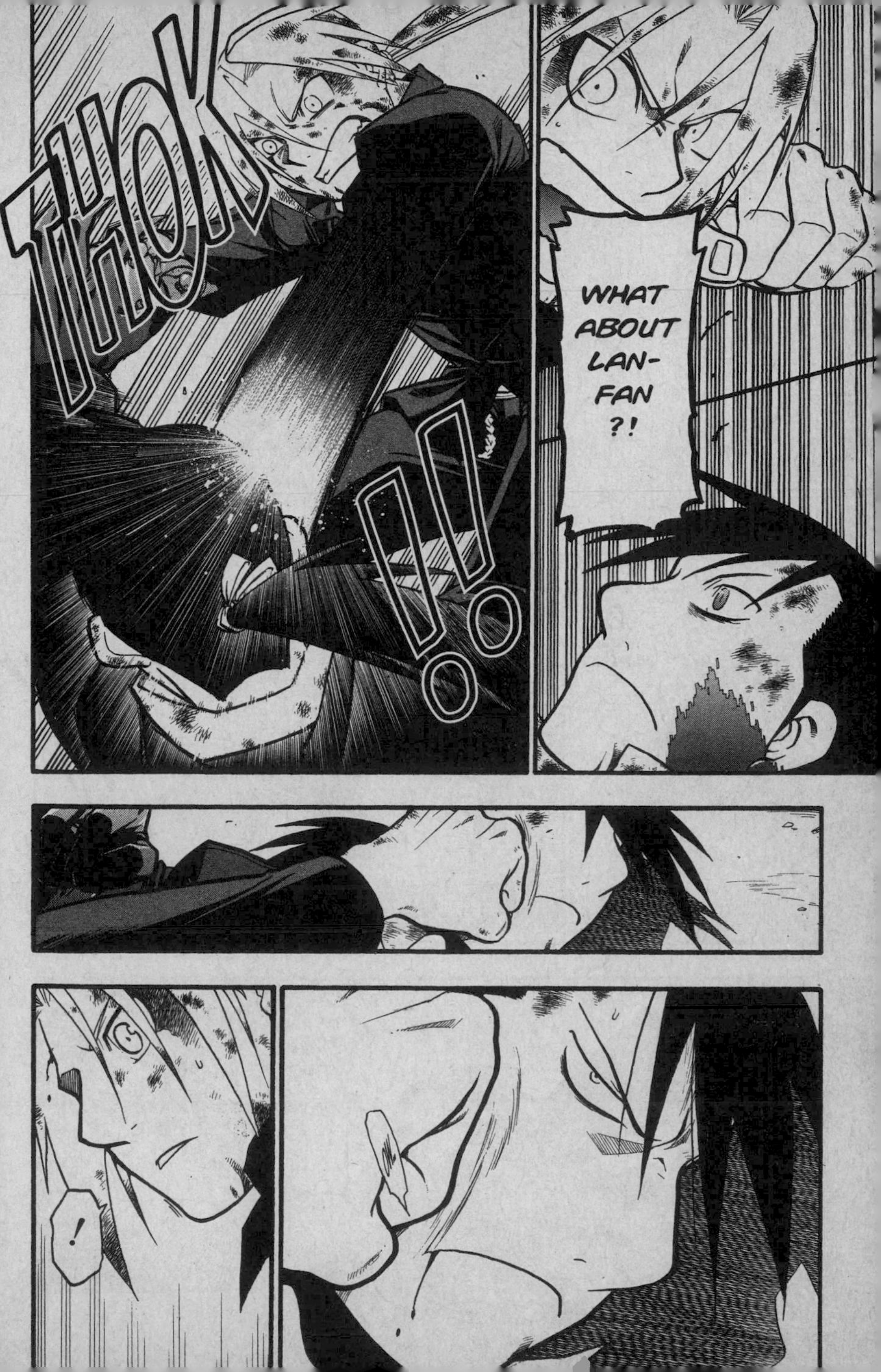
THOK
!!
WHAT ABOUT LAN-FAN?!
!

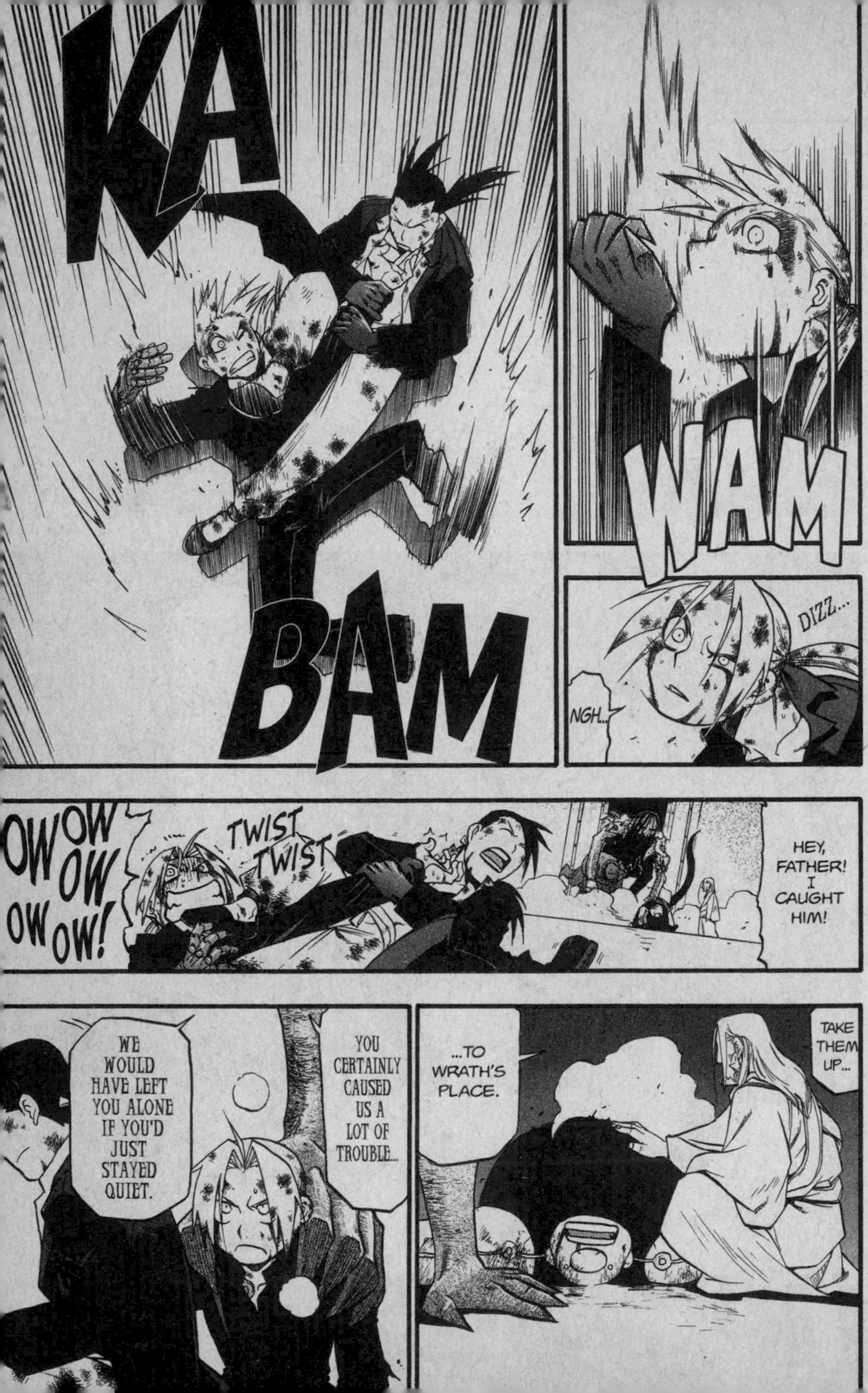
WAM
DIZZ...
NGH...
KA
BAM
HEY, FATHER! I CAUGHT HIM!
TWIST TWIST
OW OW OW OW OW OW!
TAKE THEM UP...
...TO WRATH'S PLACE.
YOU CERTAINLY CAUSED US A LOT OF TROUBLE...
WE WOULD HAVE LEFT YOU ALONE IF YOU'D JUST STAYED QUIET.

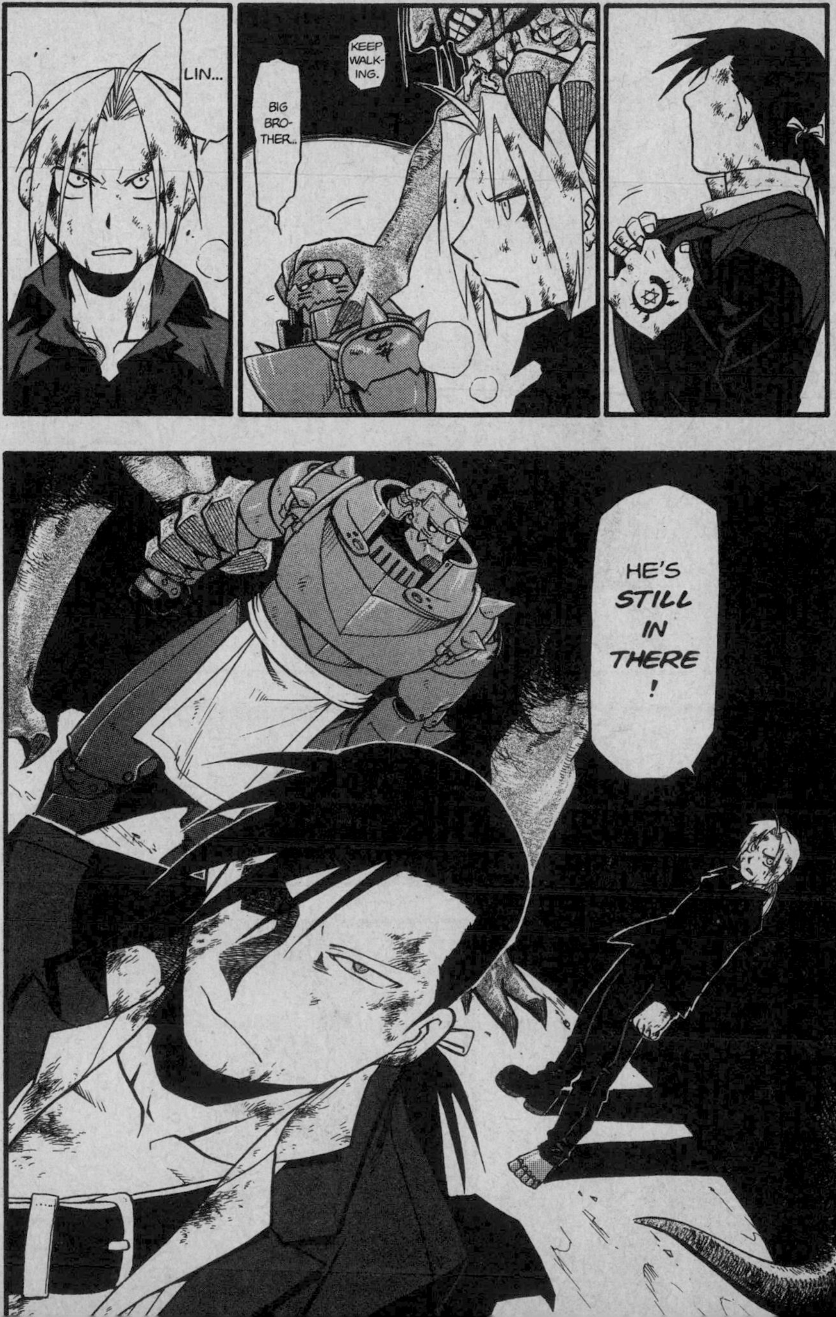
KEEP WALKING.
BIG BROTHER...
LIN...
HE'S STILL IN THERE!

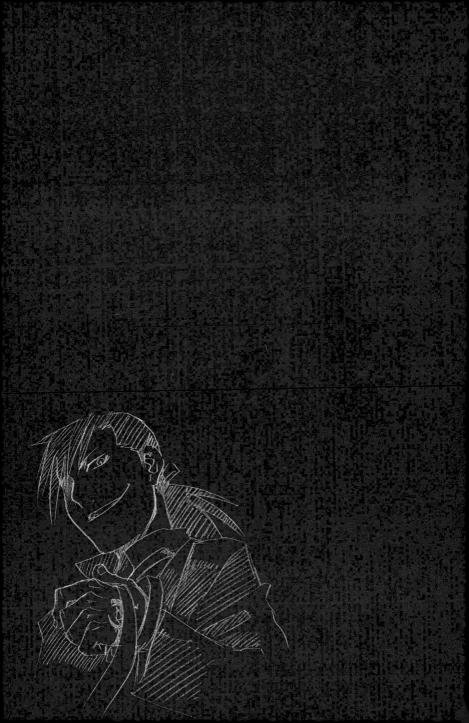

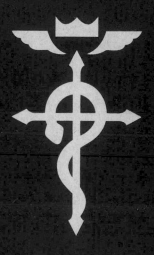

FULLMETAL
ALCHEMIST

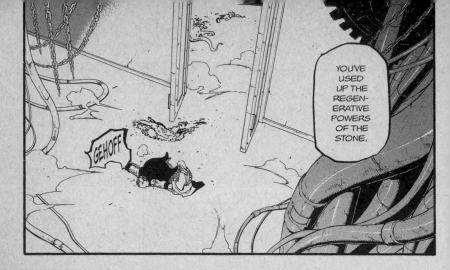

YOU'VE USED UP THE REGEN- ERATIVE POWERS OF THE STONE.

GEHOFF

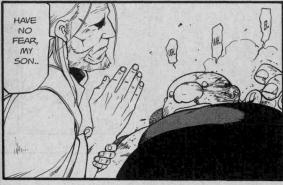

HAVE NO FEAR, MY SON..

FZZT

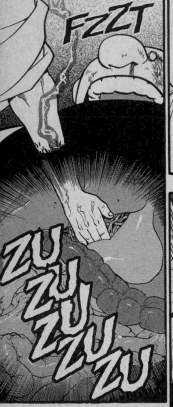

ZU ZU ZU ZU ZU

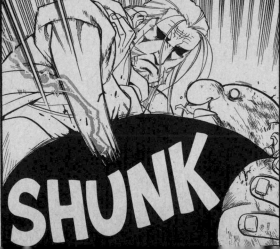

SHUNK

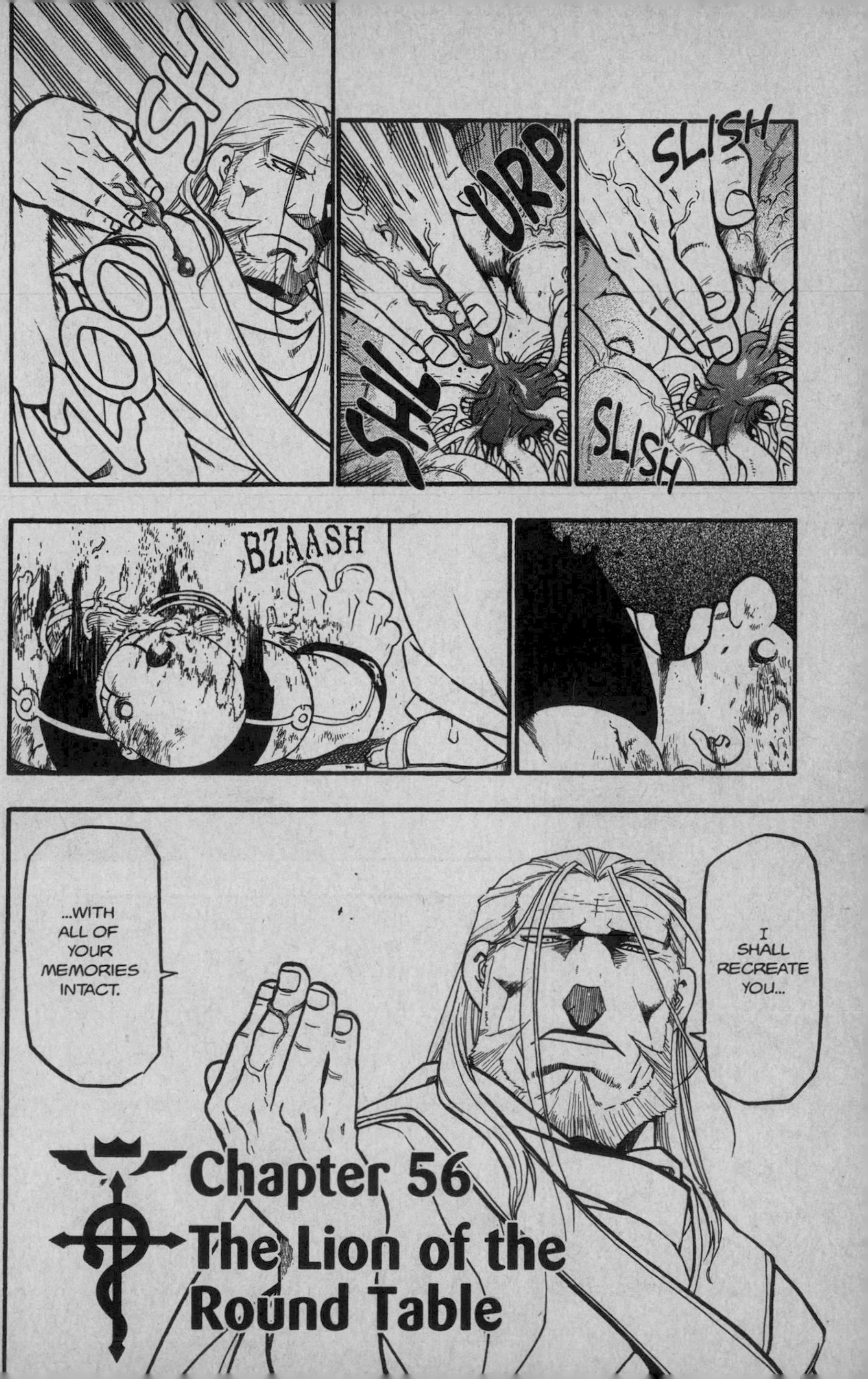
SLISH
SLISH
SHL
URP
ZOOO
SH
BZAASH
I SHALL RECREATE YOU...
...WITH ALL OF YOUR MEMORIES INTACT.

Chapter 56 The Lion of the Round Table

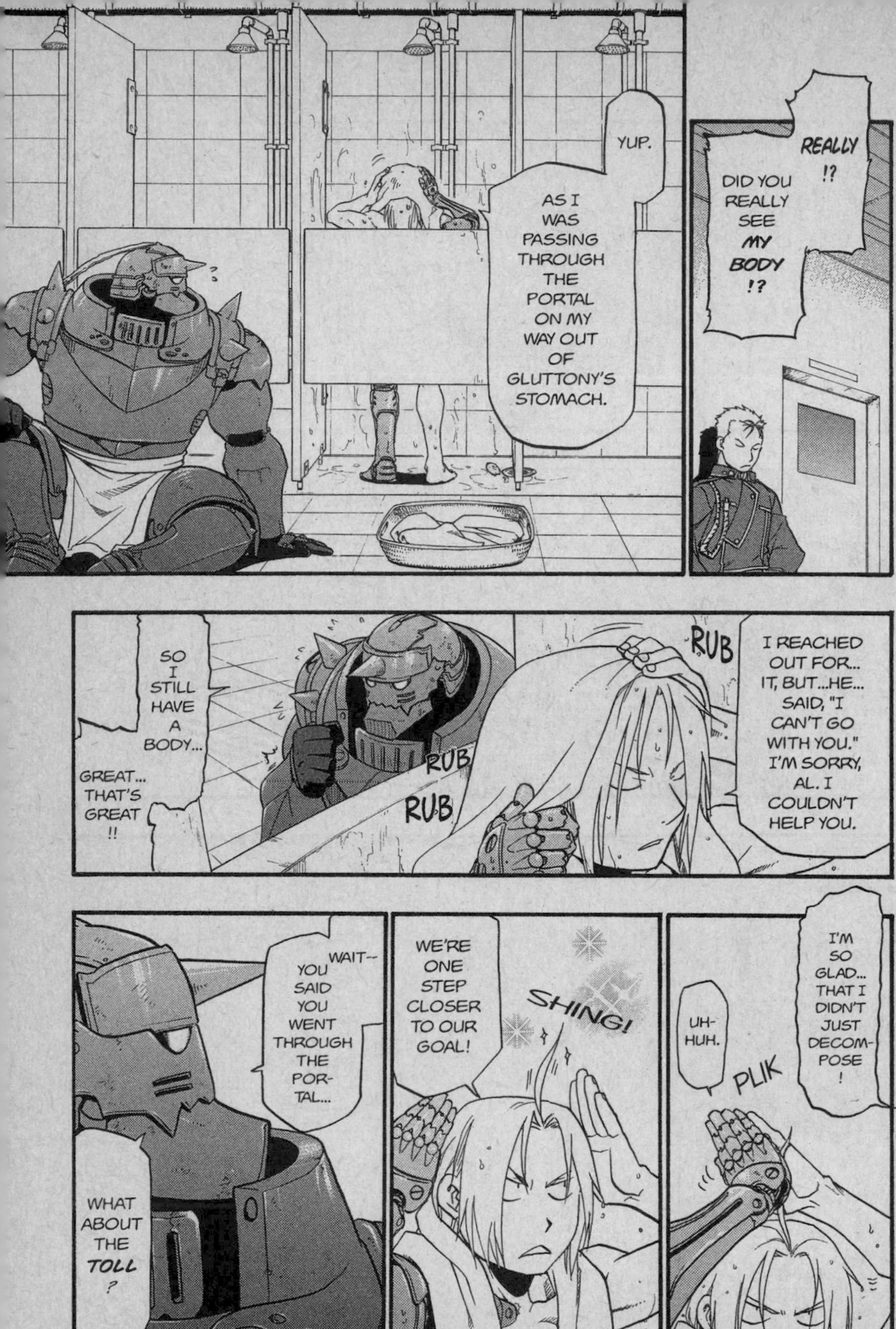
REALLY !? DID YOU REALLY SEE MY BODY !?
YUP.
AS I WAS PASSING THROUGH THE PORTAL ON MY WAY OUT OF GLUTTONY'S STOMACH.
RUB
I REACHED OUT FOR... IT, BUT...HE... SAID, "I CAN'T GO WITH YOU." I'M SORRY, AL. I COULDN'T HELP YOU.
RUB
RUB
SO I STILL HAVE A BODY...
GREAT... THAT'S GREAT !!
I'M SO GLAD... THAT I DIDN'T JUST DECOMPOSE !
UH-HUH.
PLIK
SHING!
WE'RE ONE STEP CLOSER TO OUR GOAL!
WAIT-- YOU SAID YOU WENT THROUGH THE PORTAL...
WHAT ABOUT THE TOLL ?

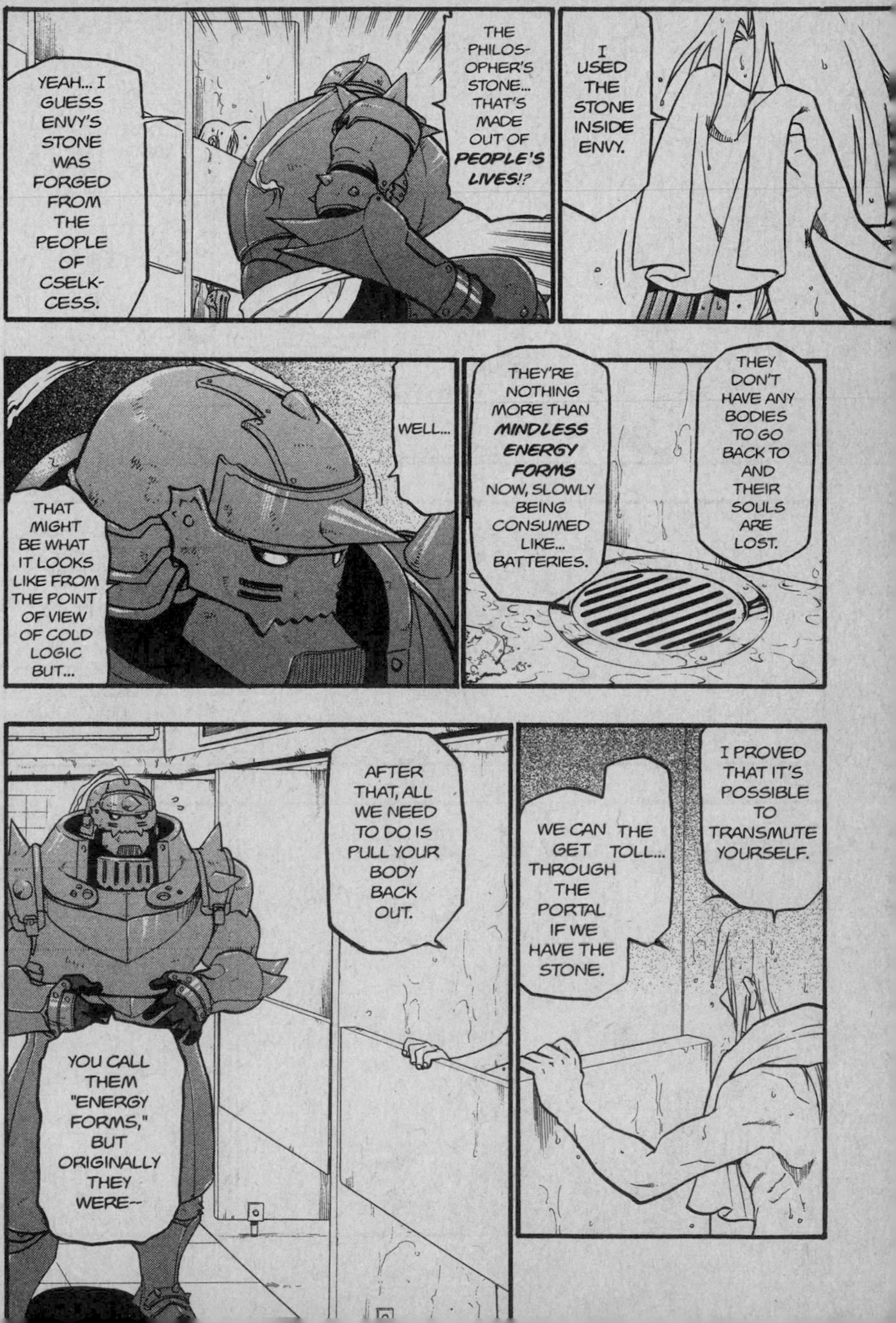
I USED THE STONE INSIDE ENVY.
THE PHILOSOPHER'S STONE... THAT'S MADE OUT OF *PEOPLE'S LIVES!?*
YEAH... I GUESS ENVY'S STONE WAS FORGED FROM THE PEOPLE OF CSELKCESS.
THEY DON'T HAVE ANY BODIES TO GO BACK TO AND THEIR SOULS ARE LOST.
THEY'RE NOTHING MORE THAN *MINDLESS ENERGY FORMS* NOW, SLOWLY BEING CONSUMED LIKE... BATTERIES.
WELL...
THAT MIGHT BE WHAT IT LOOKS LIKE FROM THE POINT OF VIEW OF COLD LOGIC BUT...
I PROVED THAT IT'S POSSIBLE TO TRANSMUTE YOURSELF.
THE TOLL...
WE CAN GET THROUGH THE PORTAL IF WE HAVE THE STONE.
AFTER THAT, ALL WE NEED TO DO IS PULL YOUR BODY BACK OUT.
YOU CALL THEM "ENERGY FORMS," BUT ORIGINALLY THEY WERE--

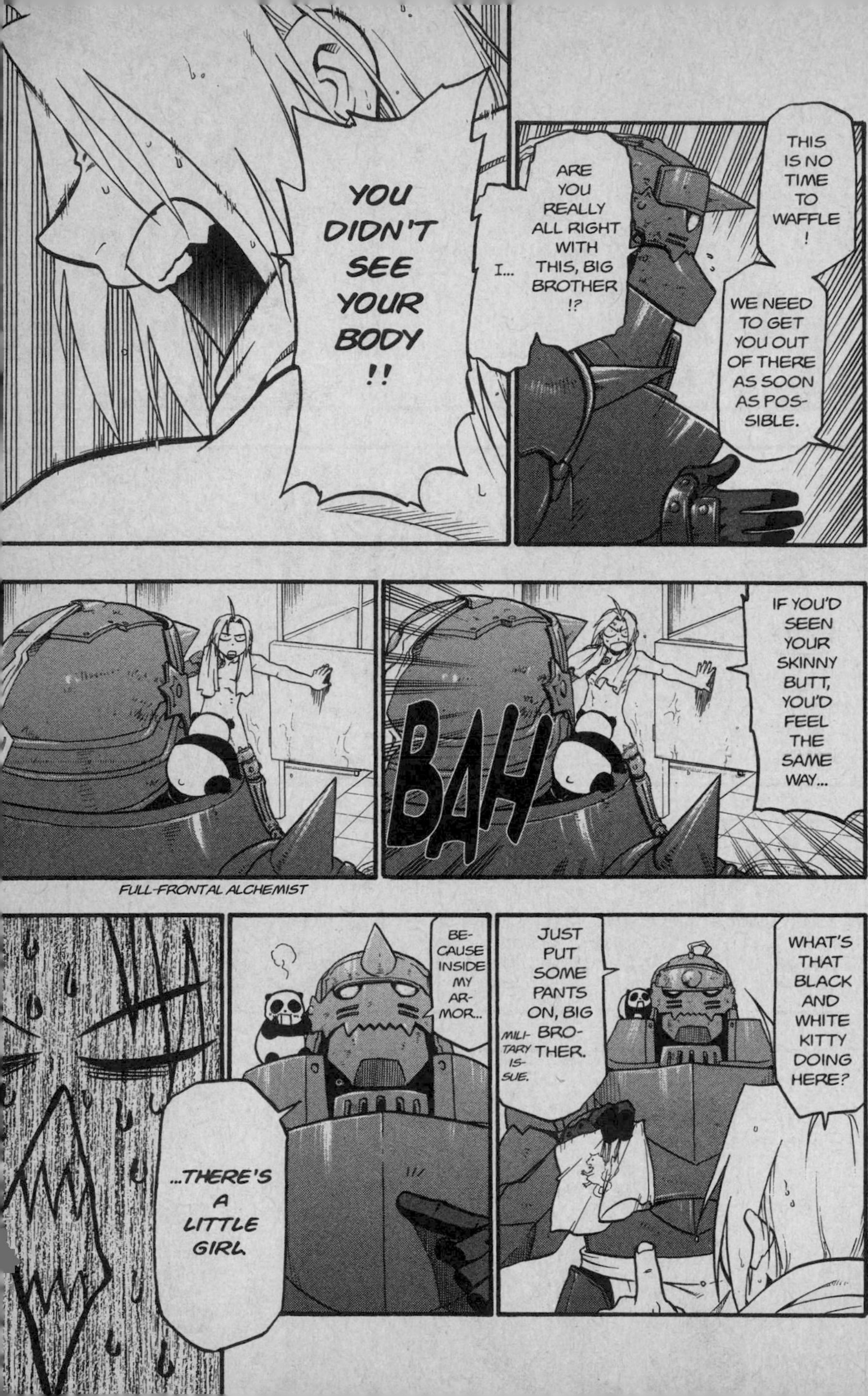
THIS IS NO TIME TO WAFFLE!
WE NEED TO GET YOU OUT OF THERE AS SOON AS POS-SIBLE.
ARE YOU REALLY ALL RIGHT WITH THIS, BIG BROTHER!?
I...
YOU DIDN'T SEE YOUR BODY!!
IF YOU'D SEEN YOUR SKINNY BUTT, YOU'D FEEL THE SAME WAY...
BAH
FULL-FRONTAL ALCHEMIST
WHAT'S THAT BLACK AND WHITE KITTY DOING HERE?
JUST PUT SOME PANTS ON, BIG BRO-THER.
MILI-TARY IS-SUE.
BE-CAUSE INSIDE MY AR-MOR...
...THERE'S A LITTLE GIRL.

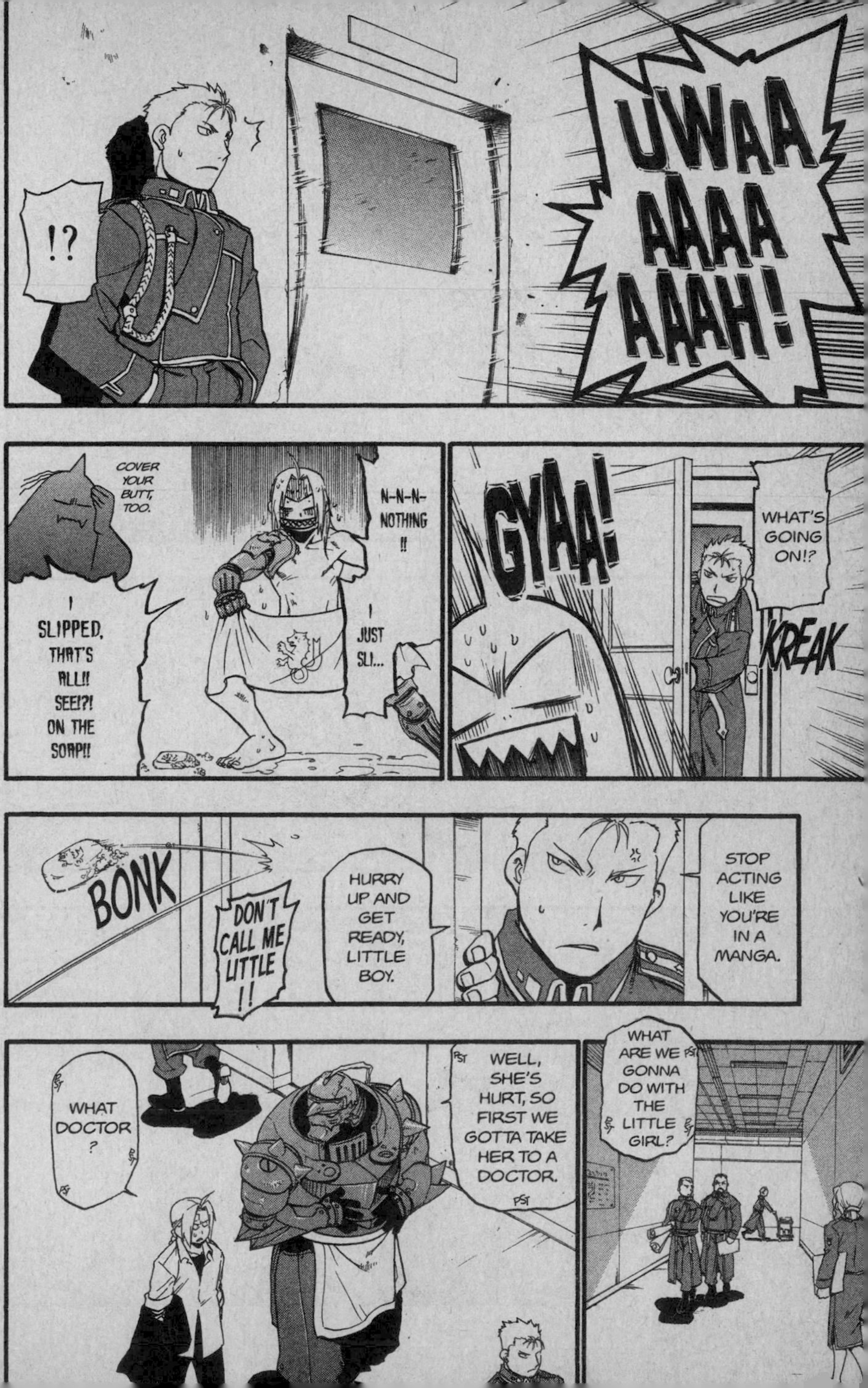
UWAA AAAA AAAH!
!?
WHAT'S GOING ON!?
KREAK
GYAA!
N-N-N-NOTHING!!
I JUST SLI...
COVER YOUR BUTT, TOO.
I SLIPPED, THAT'S ALL!! SEE!?! ON THE SOAP!!
STOP ACTING LIKE YOU'RE IN A MANGA.
HURRY UP AND GET READY, LITTLE BOY.
DON'T CALL ME LITTLE!!
BONK
WHAT ARE WE GONNA DO WITH THE LITTLE GIRL?
WELL, SHE'S HURT, SO FIRST WE GOTTA TAKE HER TO A DOCTOR.
WHAT DOCTOR?

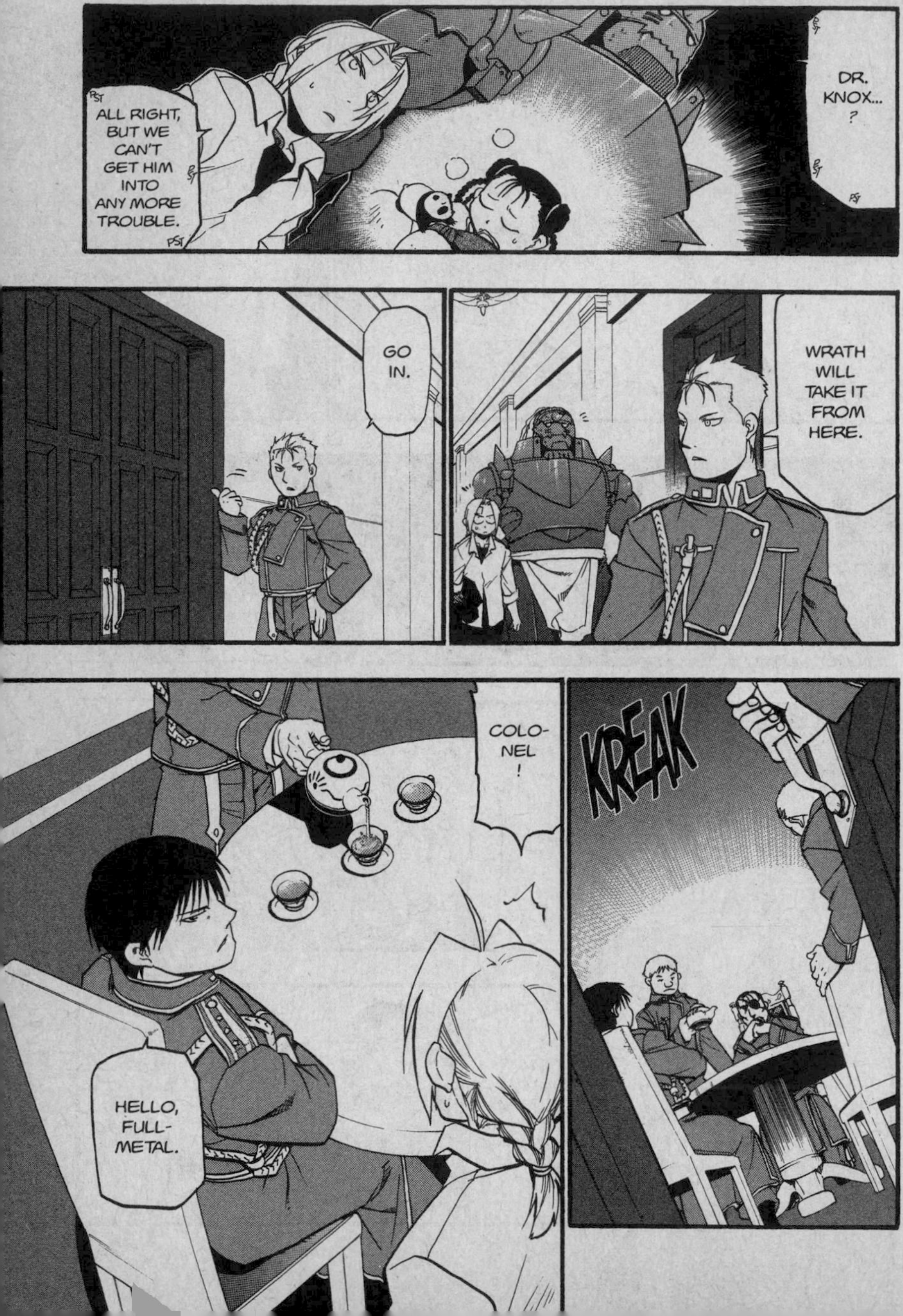
DR. KNOX... ?
ALL RIGHT, BUT WE CAN'T GET HIM INTO ANY MORE TROUBLE.
WRATH WILL TAKE IT FROM HERE.
GO IN.
KREAK
COLO- NEL !
HELLO, FULL- METAL.

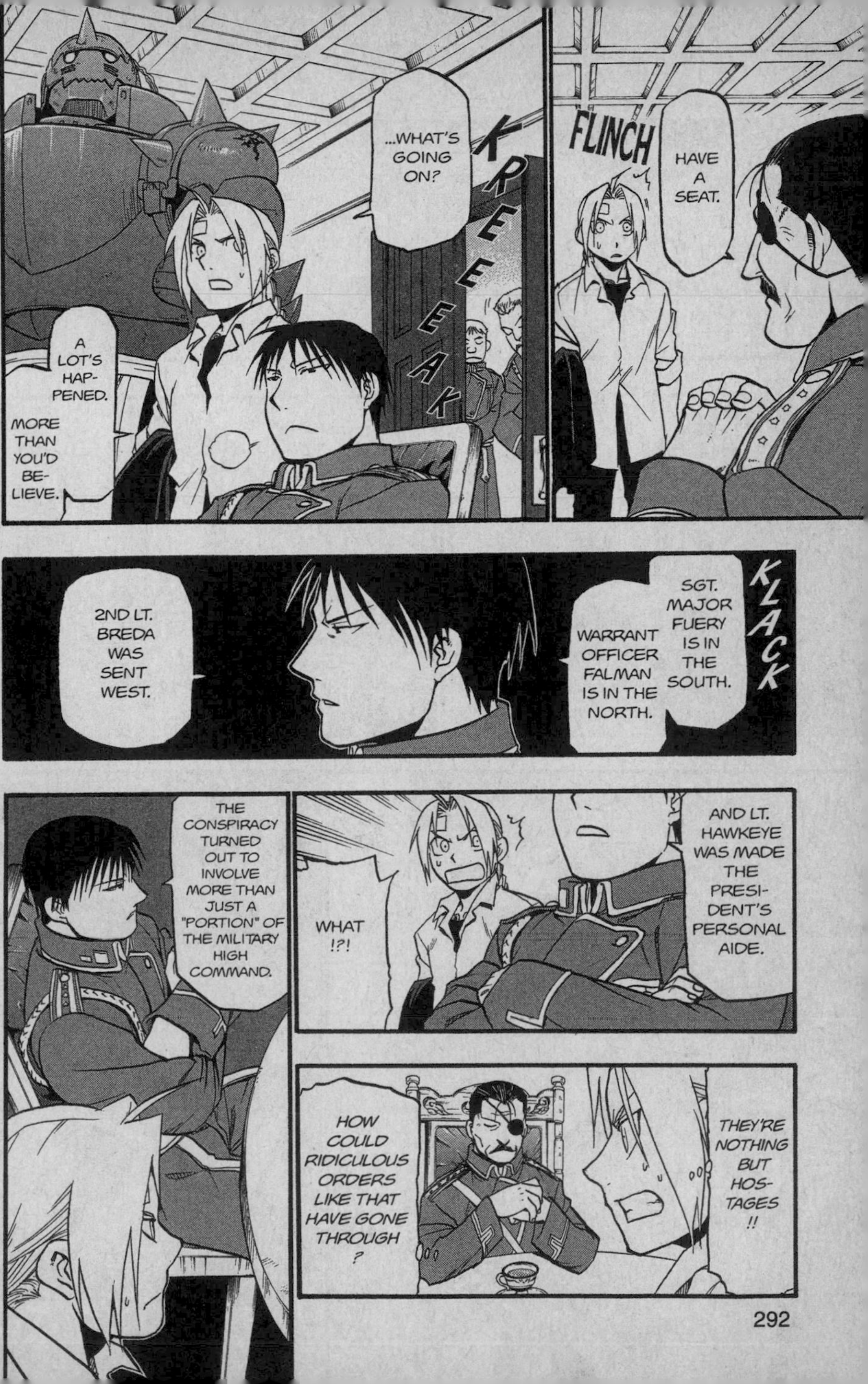
FLINCH
HAVE A SEAT.
KREEEAK
...WHAT'S GOING ON?
A LOT'S HAPPENED.
MORE THAN YOU'D BELIEVE.
KLACK
SGT. MAJOR FUERY IS IN THE SOUTH.
WARRANT OFFICER FALMAN IS IN THE NORTH.
2ND LT. BREDA WAS SENT WEST.
AND LT. HAWKEYE WAS MADE THE PRESIDENT'S PERSONAL AIDE.
WHAT !?!
THEY'RE NOTHING BUT HOSTAGES !!
HOW COULD RIDICULOUS ORDERS LIKE THAT HAVE GONE THROUGH ?
THE CONSPIRACY TURNED OUT TO INVOLVE MORE THAN JUST A "PORTION" OF THE MILITARY HIGH COMMAND.

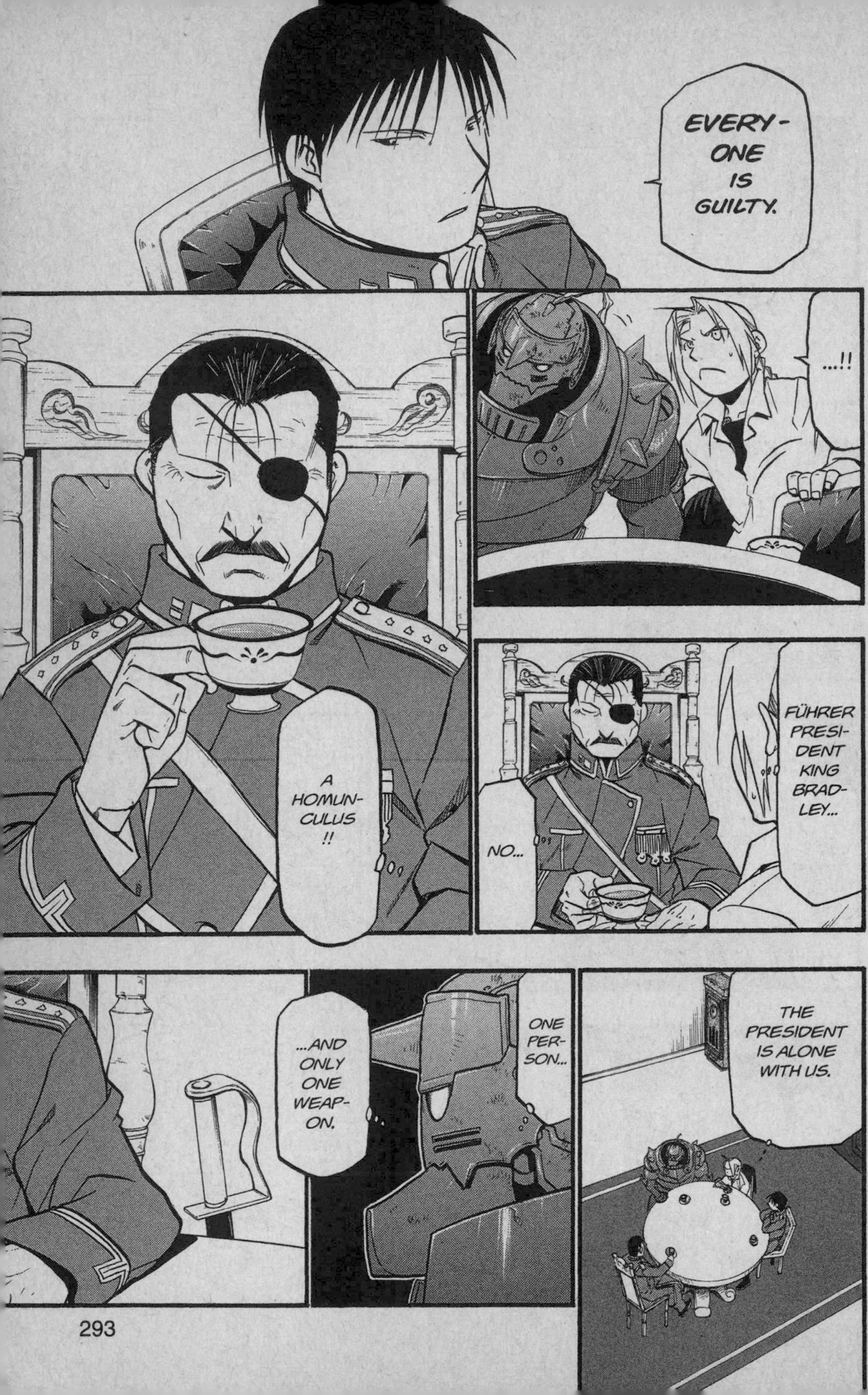
EVERY-ONE IS GUILTY.
...!!
FÜHRER PRESIDENT KING BRADLEY...
NO...
A HOMUNCULUS!!
THE PRESIDENT IS ALONE WITH US.
ONE PERSON...
...AND ONLY ONE WEAPON.

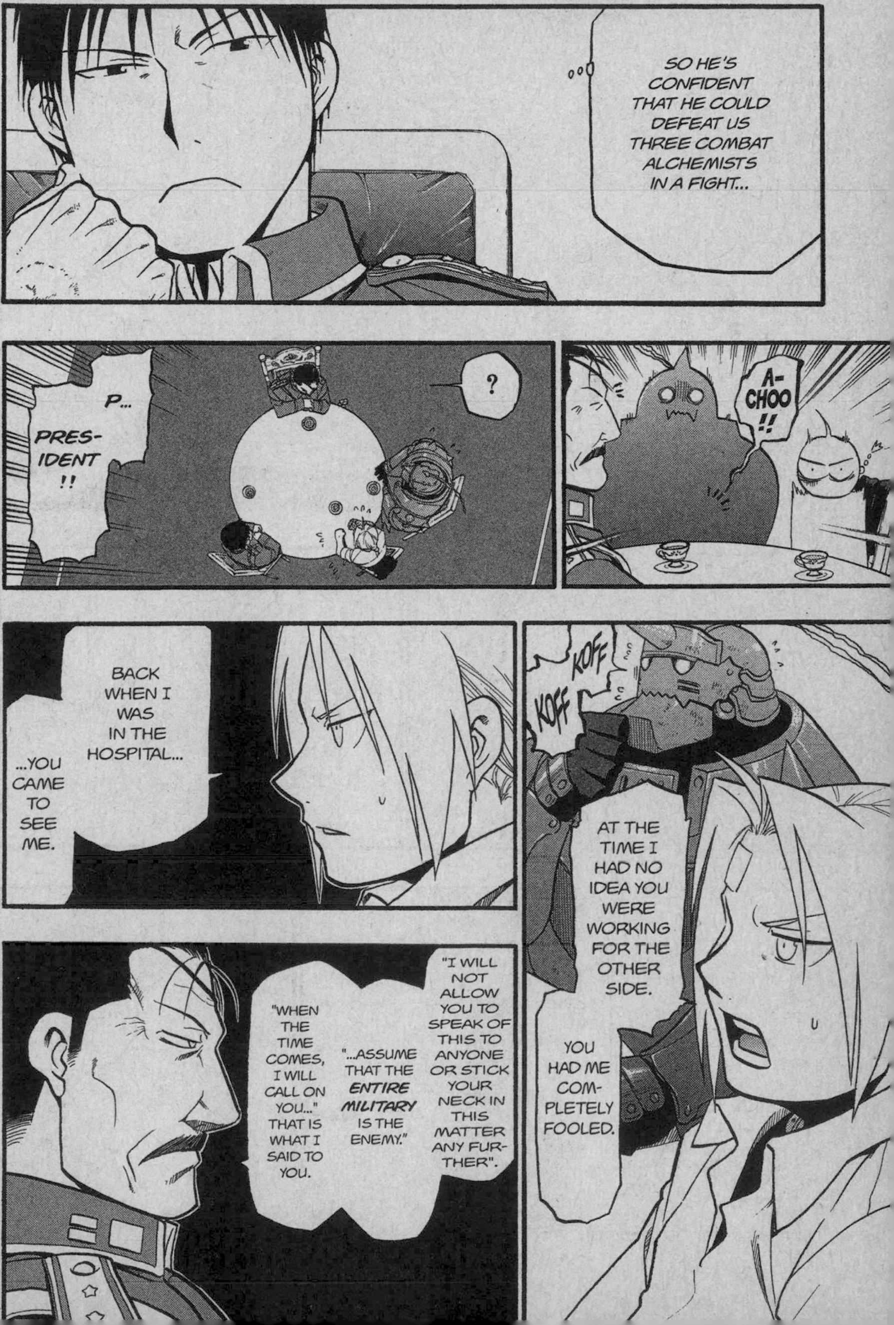
...
SO HE'S CONFIDENT THAT HE COULD DEFEAT US THREE COMBAT ALCHEMISTS IN A FIGHT...
A-CHOO!!
?
P... PRESIDENT!!
KOFF KOFF
AT THE TIME I HAD NO IDEA YOU WERE WORKING FOR THE OTHER SIDE.
YOU HAD ME COMPLETELY FOOLED.
BACK WHEN I WAS IN THE HOSPITAL...
...YOU CAME TO SEE ME.
"I WILL NOT ALLOW YOU TO SPEAK OF THIS TO ANYONE OR STICK YOUR NECK IN THIS MATTER ANY FURTHER".
"...ASSUME THAT THE ENTIRE MILITARY IS THE ENEMY."
"WHEN THE TIME COMES, I WILL CALL ON YOU..." THAT IS WHAT I SAID TO YOU.

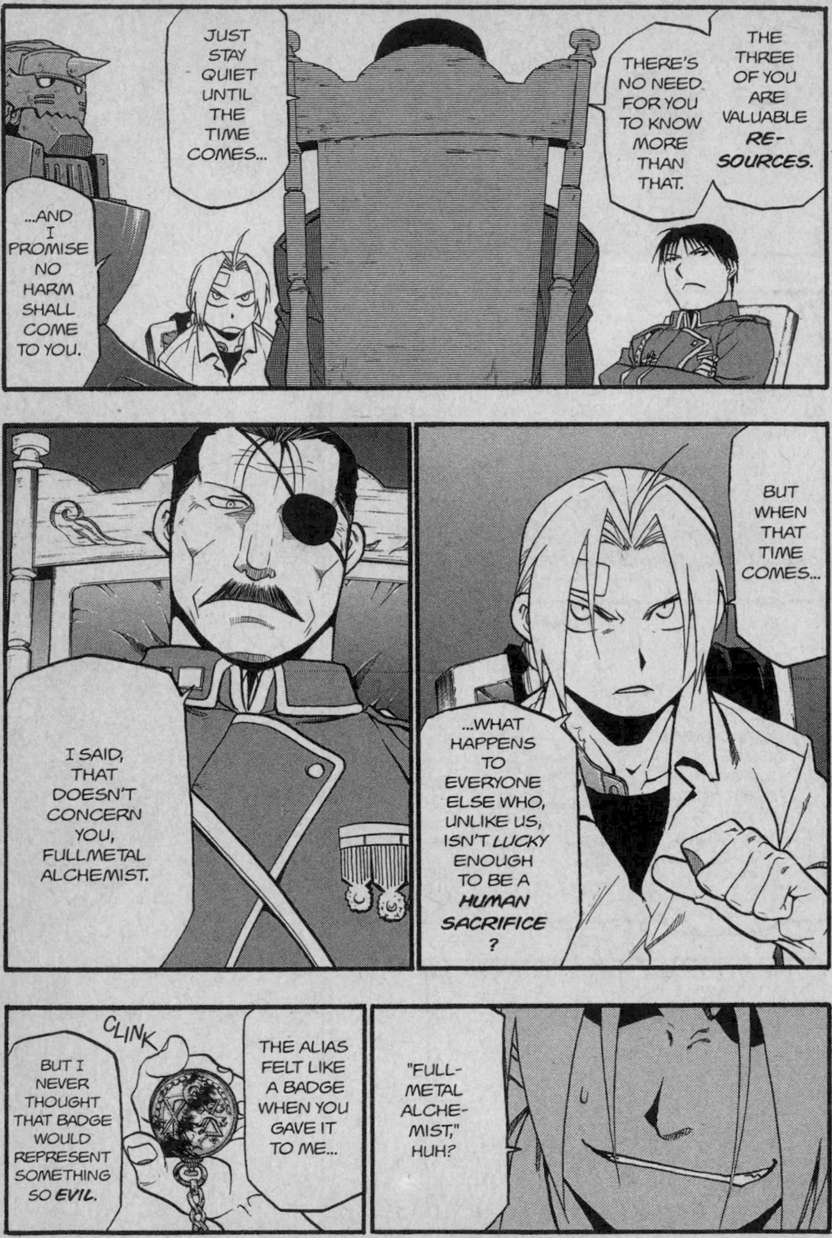
THE THREE OF YOU ARE VALUABLE RESOURCES.
THERE'S NO NEED FOR YOU TO KNOW MORE THAN THAT.
JUST STAY QUIET UNTIL THE TIME COMES...
...AND I PROMISE NO HARM SHALL COME TO YOU.
BUT WHEN THAT TIME COMES...
...WHAT HAPPENS TO EVERYONE ELSE WHO, UNLIKE US, ISN'T LUCKY ENOUGH TO BE A HUMAN SACRIFICE?
I SAID, THAT DOESN'T CONCERN YOU, FULLMETAL ALCHEMIST.
"FULL-METAL ALCHE-MIST," HUH?
THE ALIAS FELT LIKE A BADGE WHEN YOU GAVE IT TO ME...
CLINK
BUT I NEVER THOUGHT THAT BADGE WOULD REPRESENT SOMETHING SO EVIL.

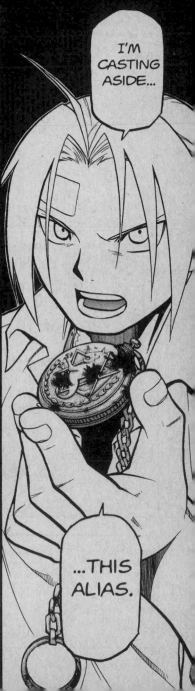

I'M CASTING ASIDE...

...THIS ALIAS.

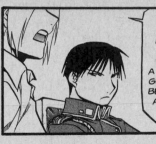

I SIGNED UP TO BE THE MILITARY'S DOG BECAUSE IT WAS THE ONLY WAY A KID LIKE ME COULD GET ACCESS TO THE BEST RESOURCES IN ALCHEMY STUDIES!

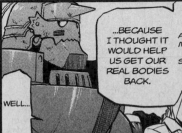

I SUFFERED THE *SHAME* OF USING ALCHEMY FOR MILITARY ENDS WHEN IT'S SUPPOSED TO BE USED TO BENEFIT SOCIETY...

...BECAUSE I THOUGHT IT WOULD HELP US GET OUR REAL BODIES BACK.

WELL...

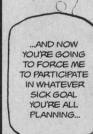

IF THE STATE ALCHEMIST PROGRAM IS JUST YOUR SYSTEM FOR SELECTING HUMAN SACRIFICES...

...AND NOW YOU'RE GOING TO FORCE ME TO PARTICIPATE IN WHATEVER SICK GOAL YOU'RE ALL PLANNING...

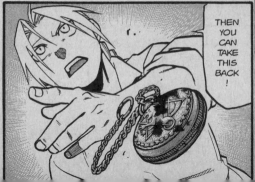

THEN YOU CAN TAKE THIS BACK!

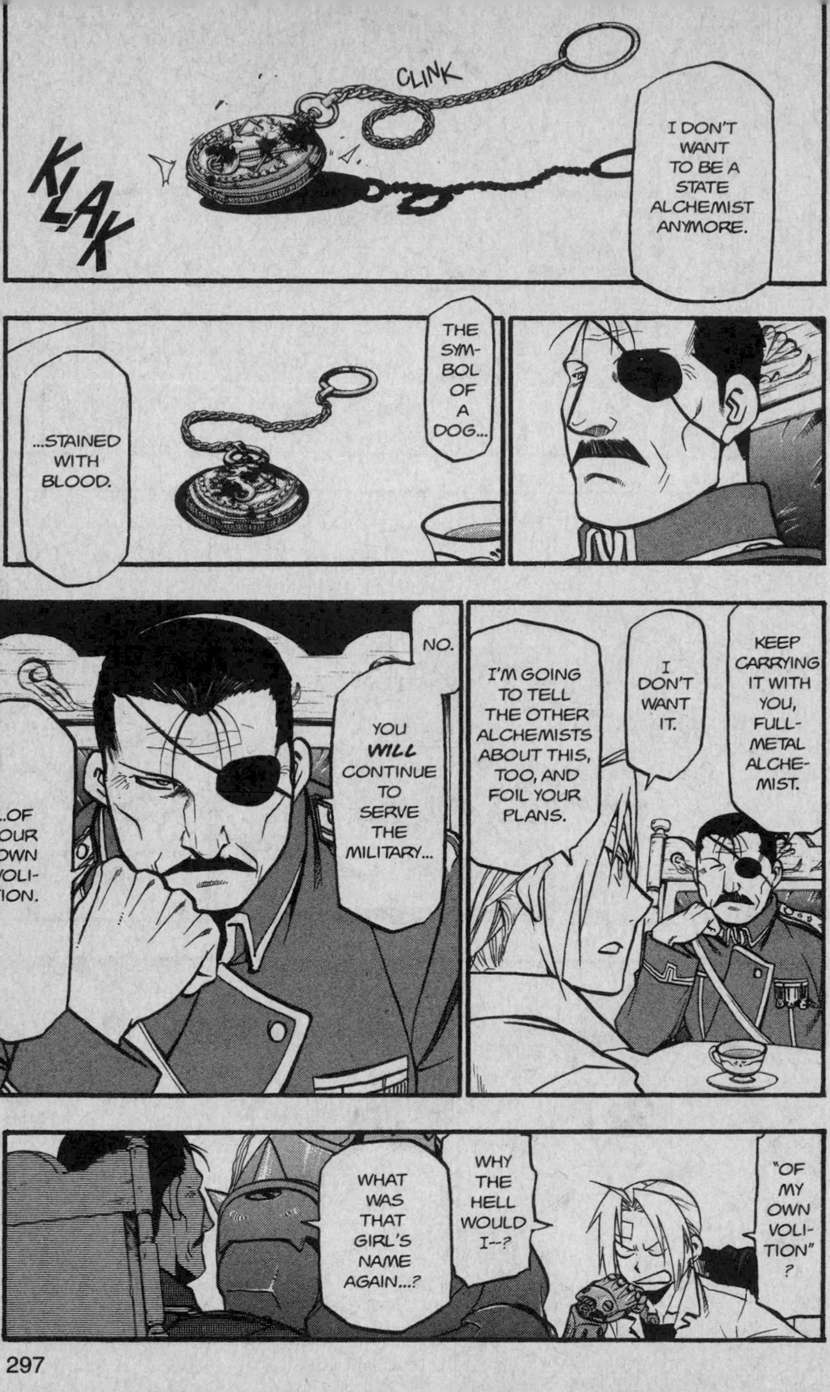
I DON'T WANT TO BE A STATE ALCHEMIST ANYMORE.
CLINK
KLAK
THE SYMBOL OF A DOG...
...STAINED WITH BLOOD.
KEEP CARRYING IT WITH YOU, FULLMETAL ALCHEMIST.
I DON'T WANT IT.
I'M GOING TO TELL THE OTHER ALCHEMISTS ABOUT THIS, TOO, AND FOIL YOUR PLANS.
NO.
YOU *WILL* CONTINUE TO SERVE THE MILITARY...
...OF YOUR OWN VOLITION.
"OF MY OWN VOLITION"?
WHY THE HELL WOULD I--?
WHAT WAS THAT GIRL'S NAME AGAIN...?

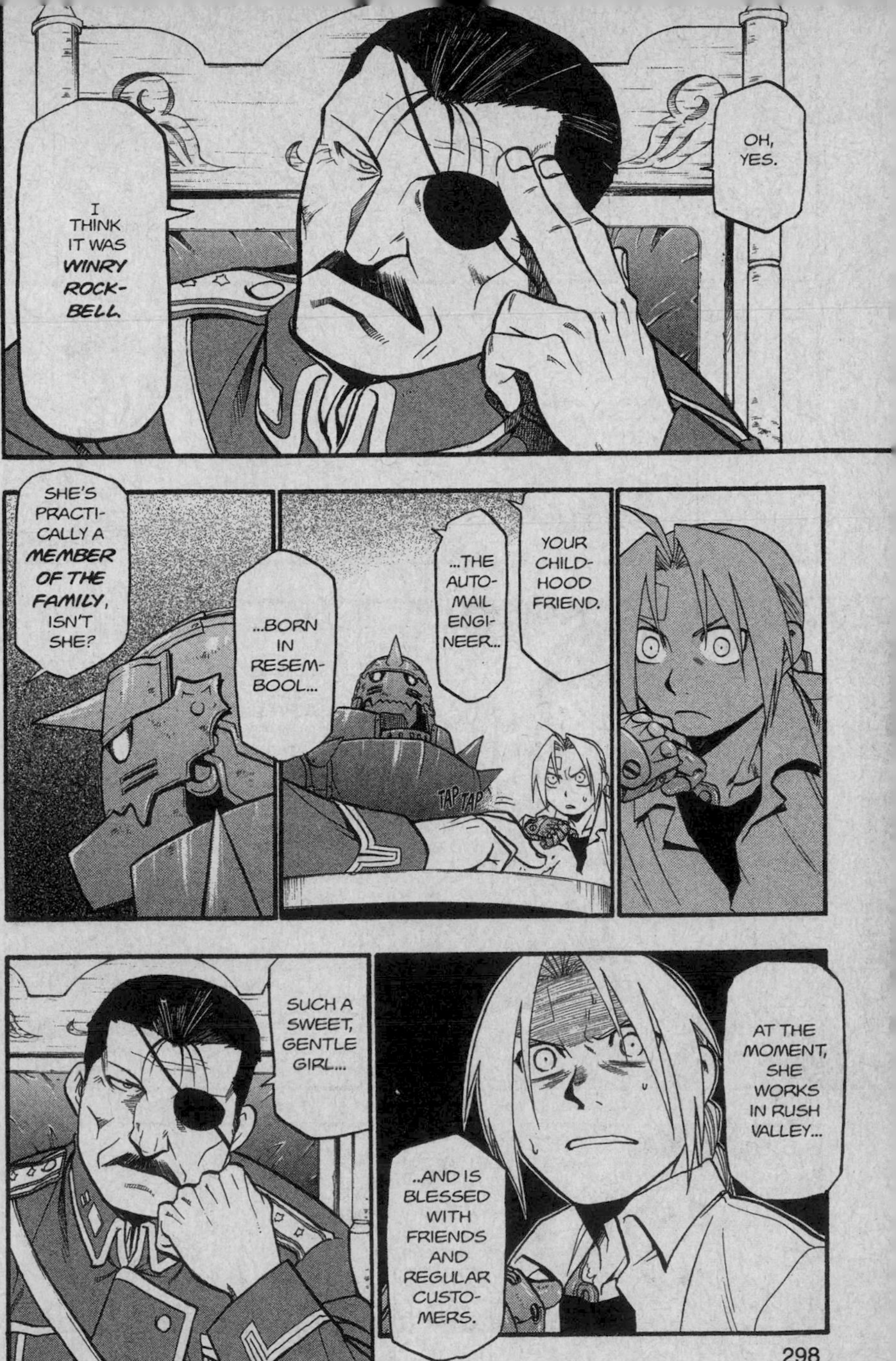
OH, YES.
I THINK IT WAS WINRY ROCKBELL.
YOUR CHILDHOOD FRIEND.
...THE AUTOMAIL ENGINEER...
TAP TAP
...BORN IN RESEMBOOL...
SHE'S PRACTICALLY A MEMBER OF THE FAMILY, ISN'T SHE?
AT THE MOMENT, SHE WORKS IN RUSH VALLEY...
..AND IS BLESSED WITH FRIENDS AND REGULAR CUSTOMERS.
SUCH A SWEET, GENTLE GIRL...

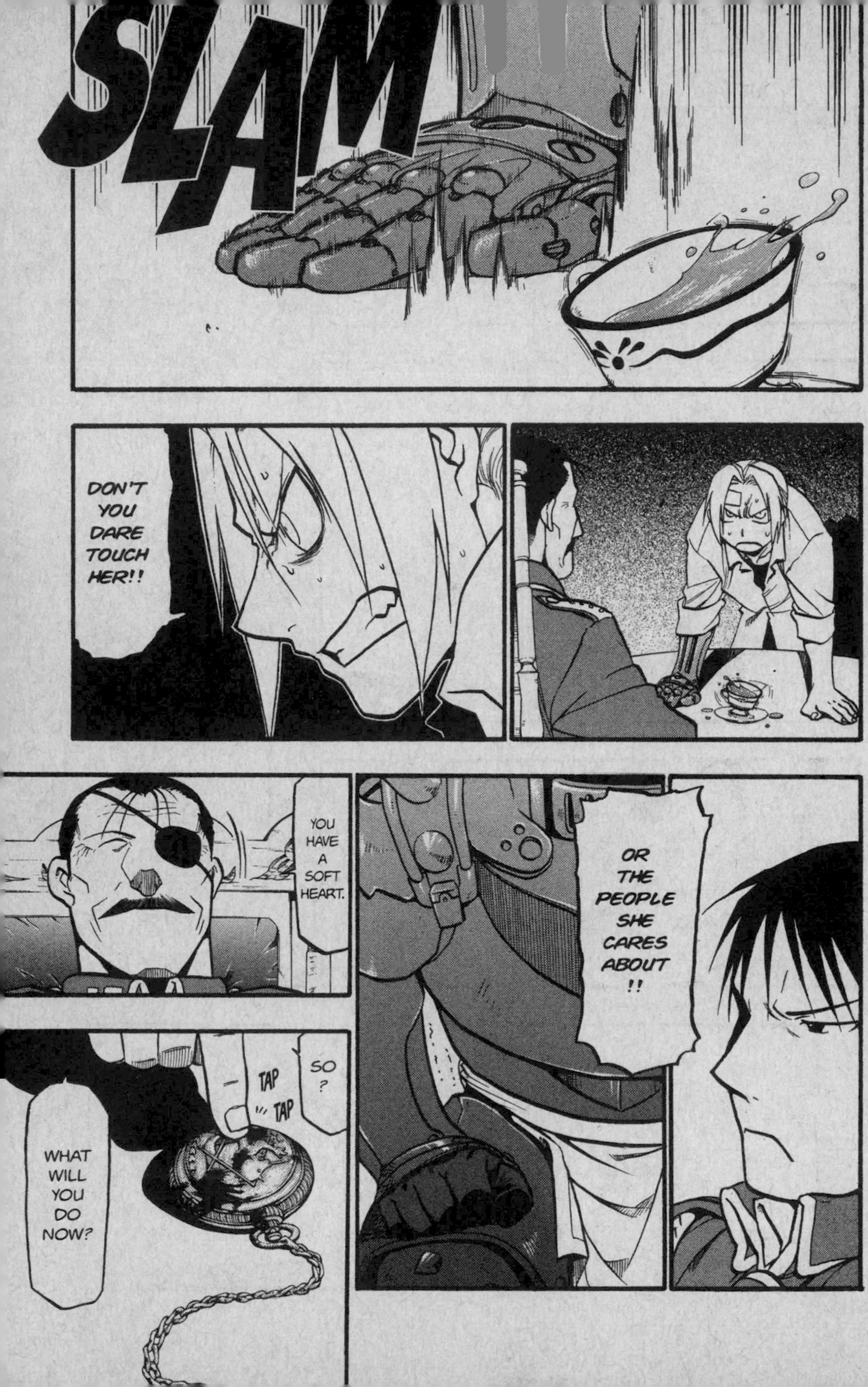
SLAM
DON'T YOU DARE TOUCH HER!!
OR THE PEOPLE SHE CARES ABOUT!!
YOU HAVE A SOFT HEART.
SO?
TAP TAP
WHAT WILL YOU DO NOW?

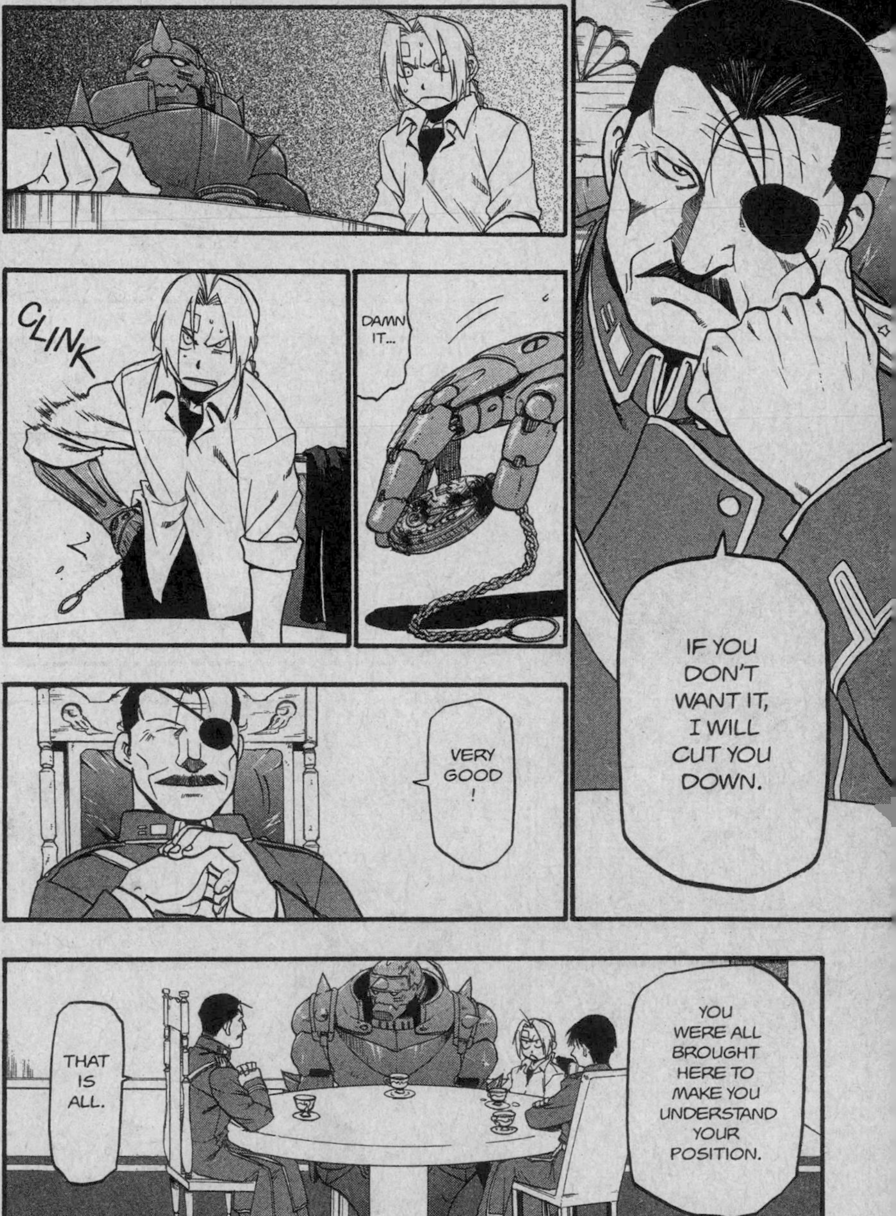
IF YOU DON'T WANT IT, I WILL CUT YOU DOWN.
DAMN IT...
CLINK
VERY GOOD!
YOU WERE ALL BROUGHT HERE TO MAKE YOU UNDERSTAND YOUR POSITION.
THAT IS ALL.

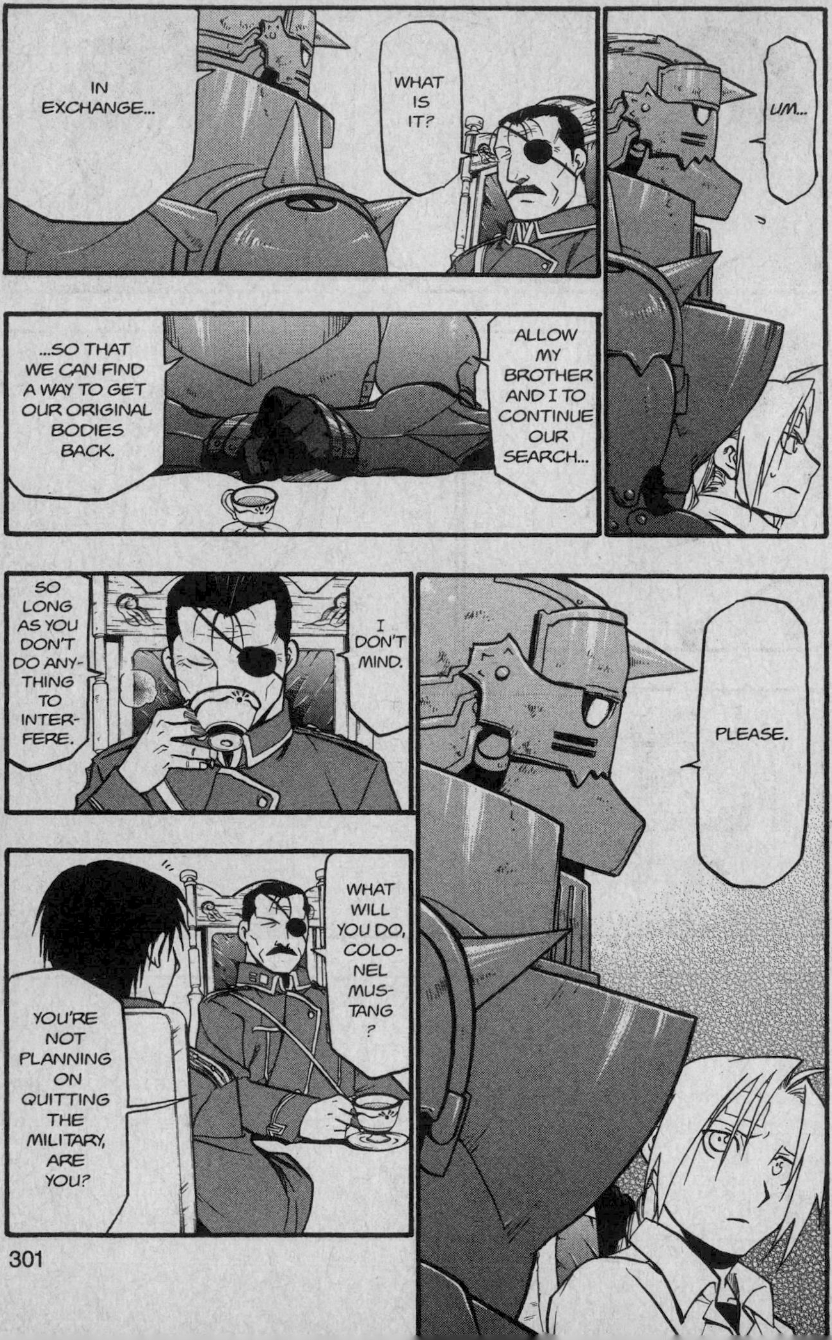
UM...
WHAT IS IT?
IN EXCHANGE...
ALLOW MY BROTHER AND I TO CONTINUE OUR SEARCH...
...SO THAT WE CAN FIND A WAY TO GET OUR ORIGINAL BODIES BACK.
PLEASE.
I DON'T MIND.
SO LONG AS YOU DON'T DO ANY-THING TO INTER-FERE.
WHAT WILL YOU DO, COLO-NEL MUS-TANG?
YOU'RE NOT PLANNING ON QUITTING THE MILITARY, ARE YOU?

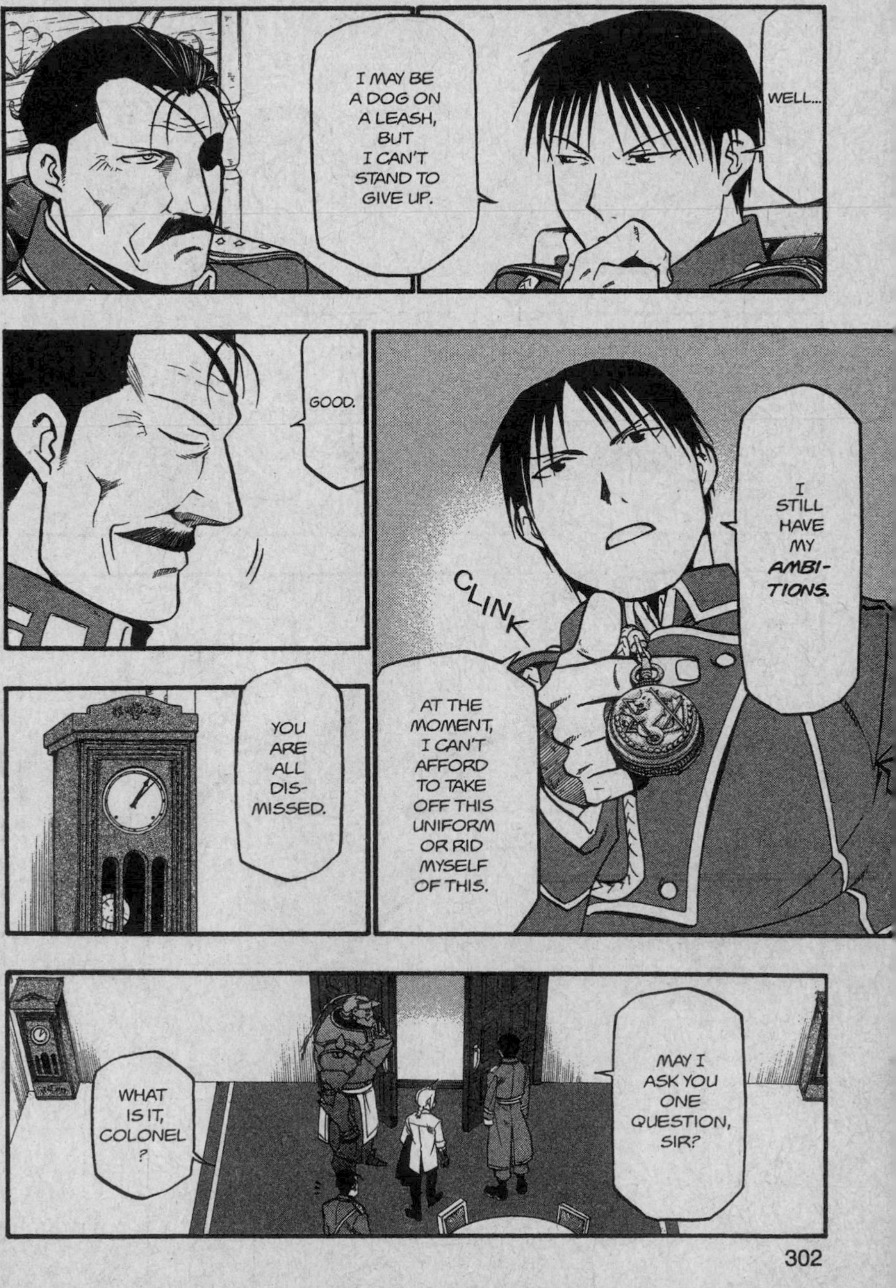
WELL...
I MAY BE A DOG ON A LEASH, BUT I CAN'T STAND TO GIVE UP.
I STILL HAVE MY AMBITIONS.
CLINK
AT THE MOMENT, I CAN'T AFFORD TO TAKE OFF THIS UNIFORM OR RID MYSELF OF THIS.
GOOD.
YOU ARE ALL DISMISSED.
MAY I ASK YOU ONE QUESTION, SIR?
WHAT IS IT, COLONEL?

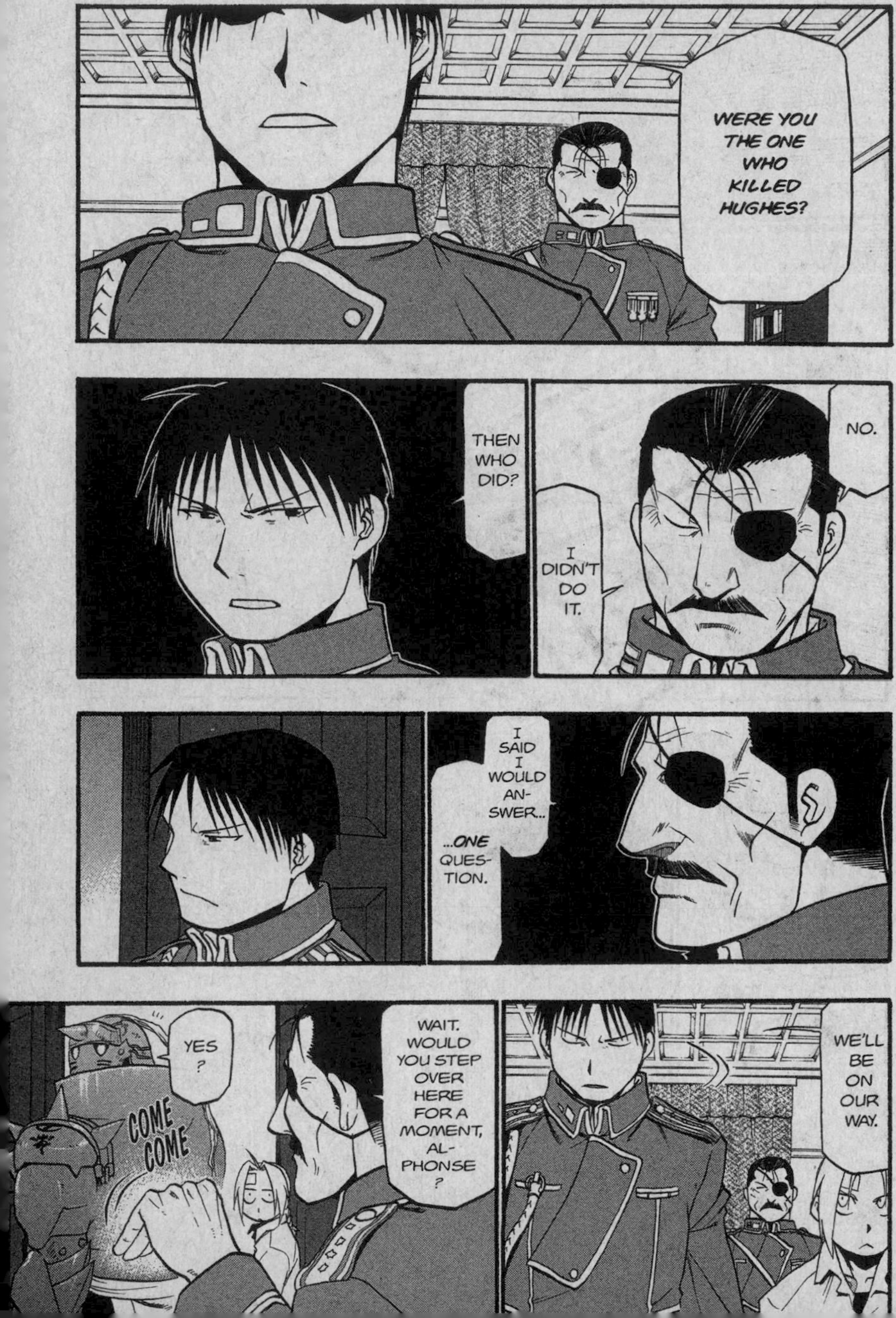
WERE YOU THE ONE WHO KILLED HUGHES?
NO.
I DIDN'T DO IT.
THEN WHO DID?
I SAID I WOULD AN-SWER...
...ONE QUES-TION.
WE'LL BE ON OUR WAY.
WAIT. WOULD YOU STEP OVER HERE FOR A MOMENT, AL-PHONSE?
YES?
COME COME

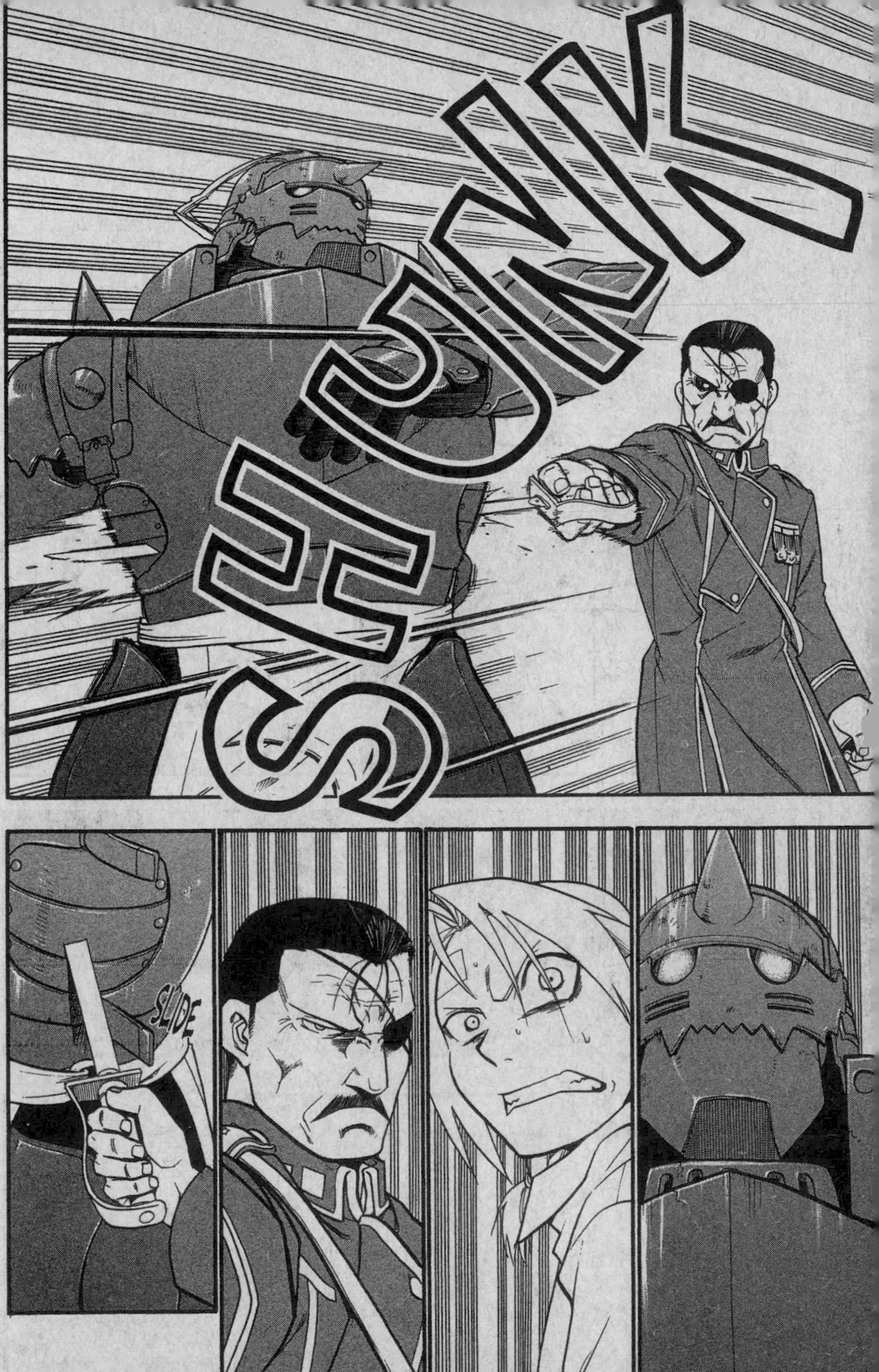
SHUNK
SLIDE

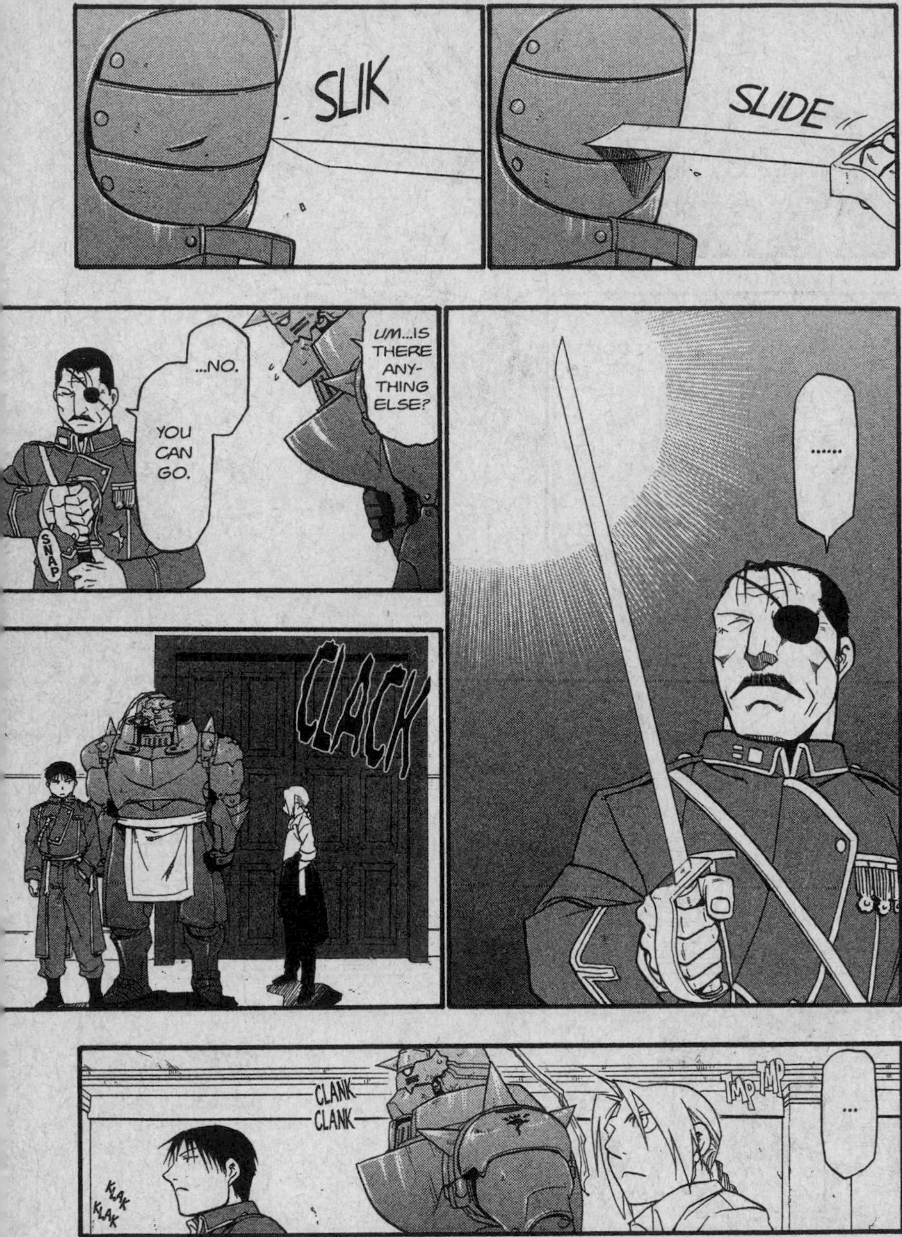
SLIDE
SLIK
......
UM...IS THERE ANY-THING ELSE?
...NO.
YOU CAN GO.
SNAP
CLACK
...
TMP TMP
CLANK CLANK
KLAK KLAK

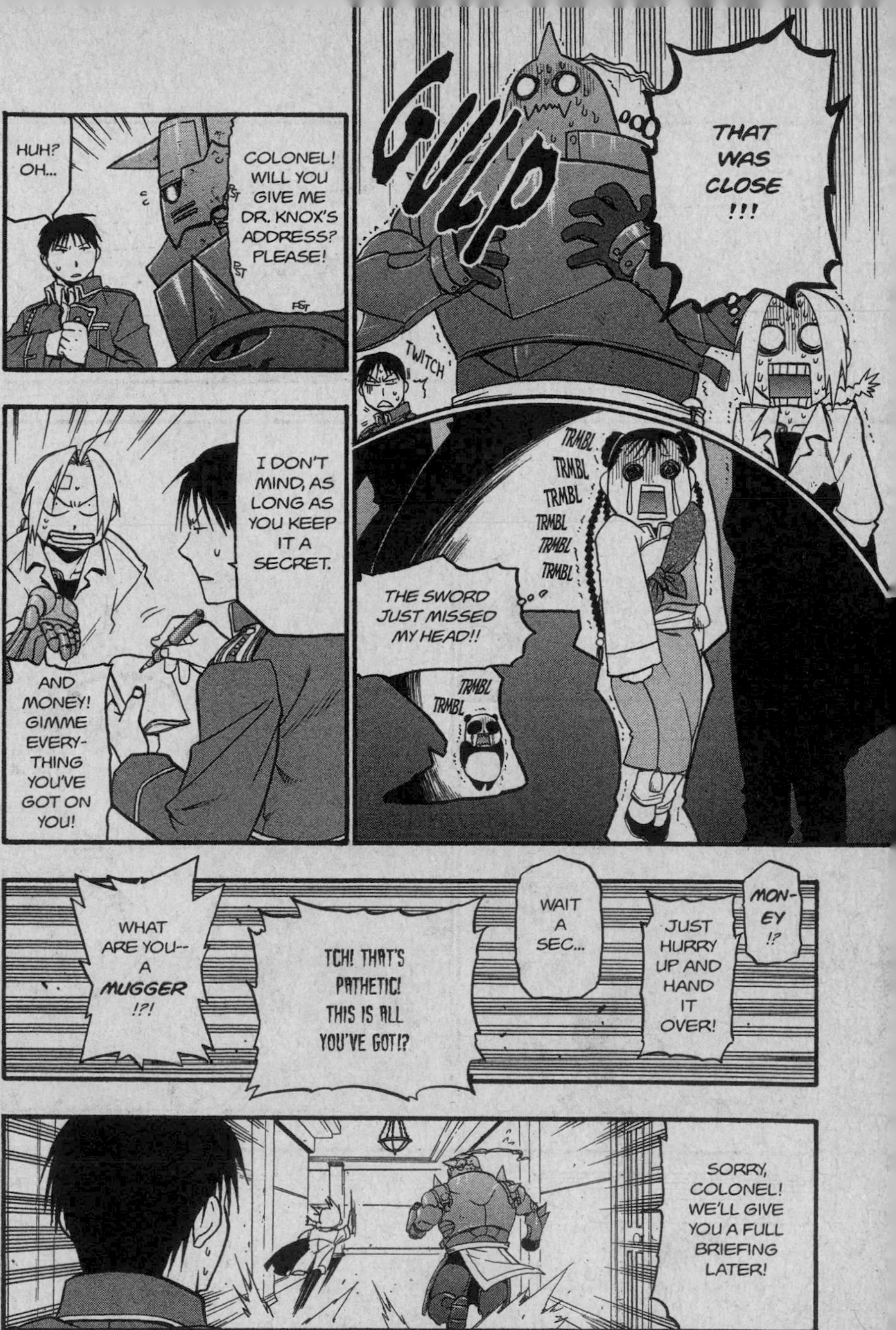
GULP
THAT WAS CLOSE!!!
TWITCH
TRMBL TRMBL TRMBL TRMBL TRMBL TRMBL
THE SWORD JUST MISSED MY HEAD!!
TRMBL TRMBL
COLONEL! WILL YOU GIVE ME DR. KNOX'S ADDRESS? PLEASE!
FST FST FST
HUH? OH...
I DON'T MIND, AS LONG AS YOU KEEP IT A SECRET.
AND MONEY! GIMME EVERYTHING YOU'VE GOT ON YOU!
MON-EY!?
JUST HURRY UP AND HAND IT OVER!
WAIT A SEC...
TCH! THAT'S PATHETIC! THIS IS ALL YOU'VE GOT!?
WHAT ARE YOU-- A MUGGER!?!
SORRY, COLONEL! WE'LL GIVE YOU A FULL BRIEFING LATER!

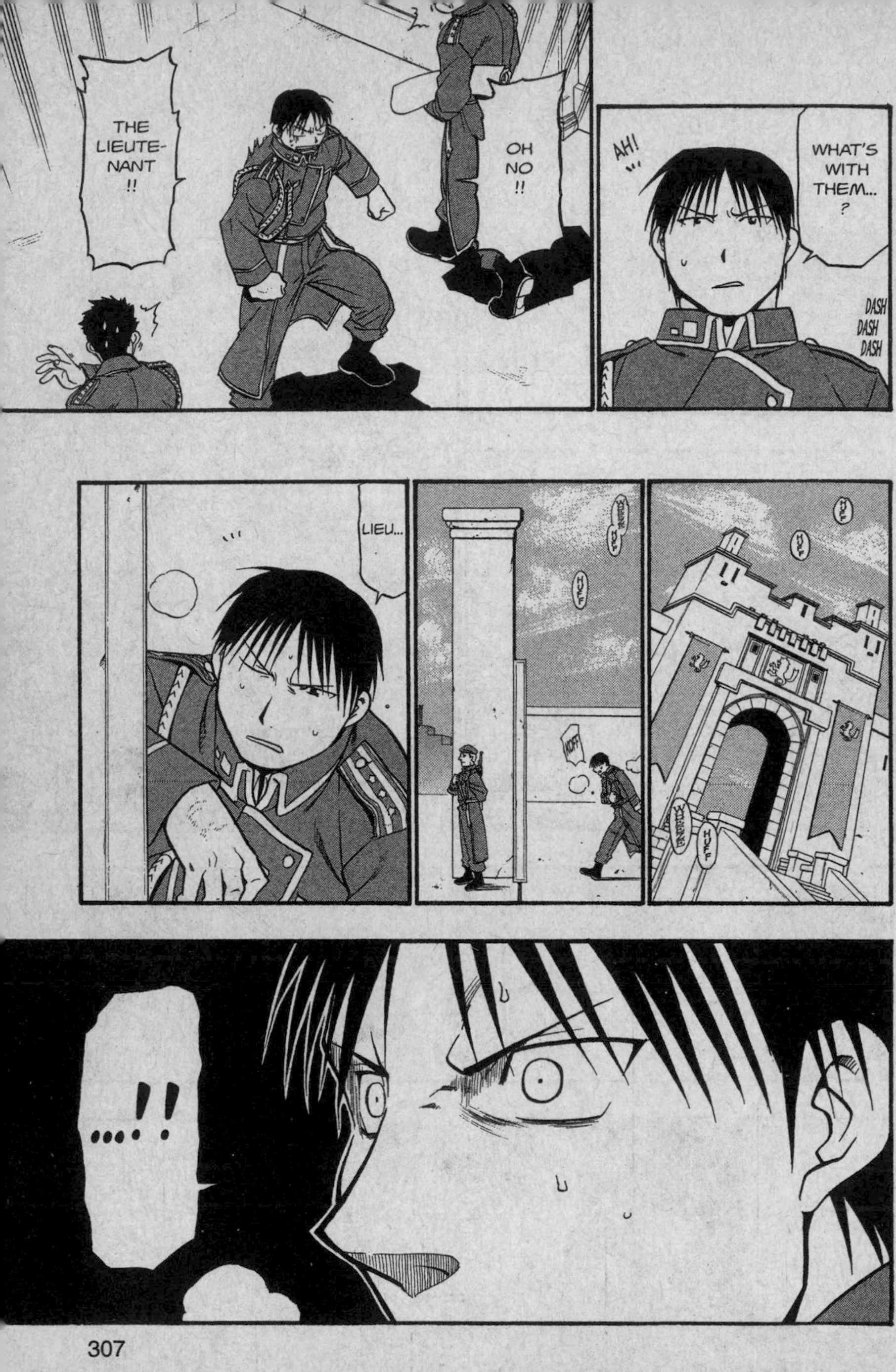
WHAT'S WITH THEM...?
AH!
DASH DASH DASH
OH NO!!
THE LIEUTENANT!!
HUFF
HUFF
HUFF
HUFF
HUFF
KOFF
LIEU...
...!!

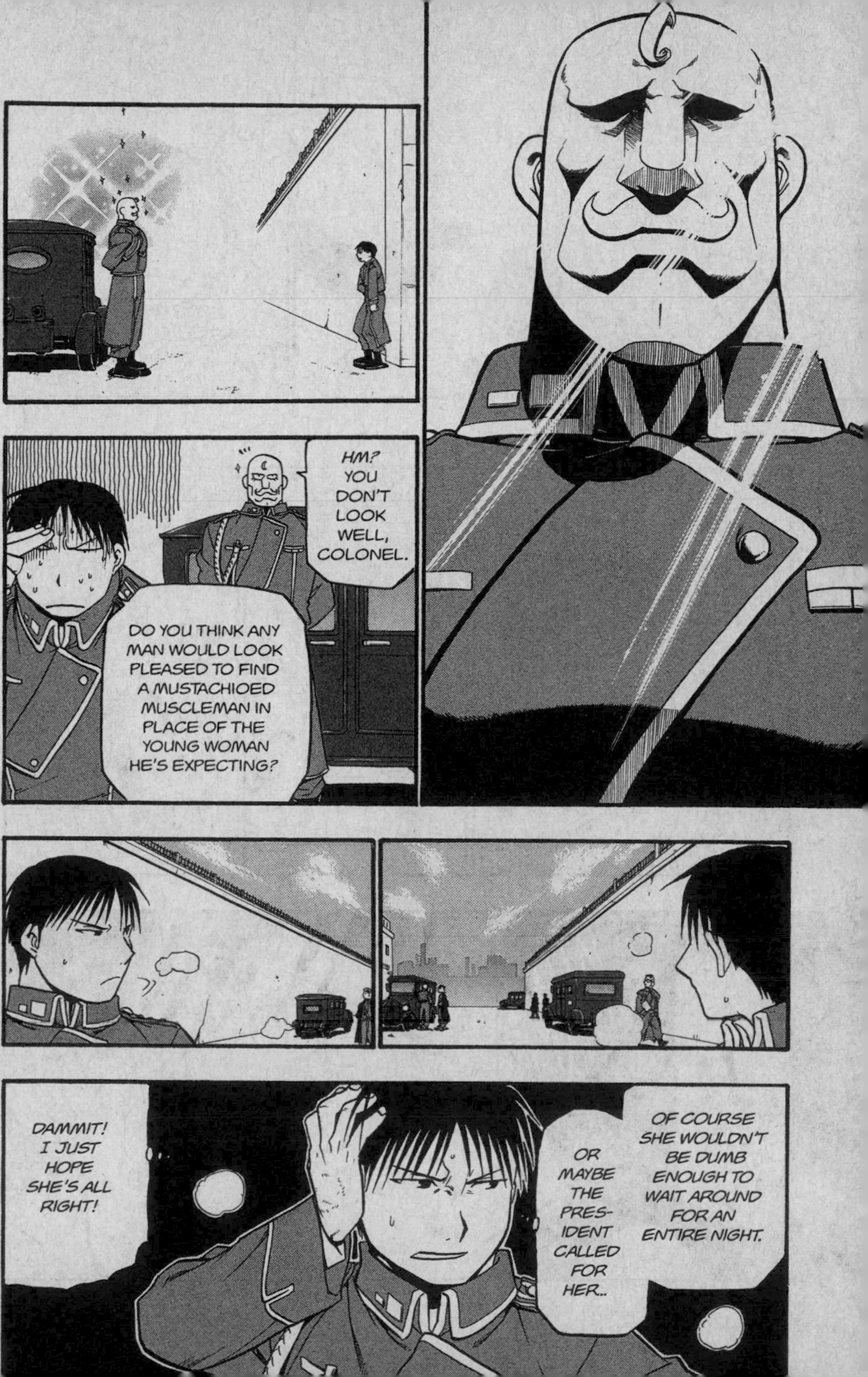
HM? YOU DON'T LOOK WELL, COLONEL.
DO YOU THINK ANY MAN WOULD LOOK PLEASED TO FIND A MUSTACHIOED MUSCLEMAN IN PLACE OF THE YOUNG WOMAN HE'S EXPECTING?
OF COURSE SHE WOULDN'T BE DUMB ENOUGH TO WAIT AROUND FOR AN ENTIRE NIGHT.
OR MAYBE THE PRES-IDENT CALLED FOR HER...
DAMMIT! I JUST HOPE SHE'S ALL RIGHT!

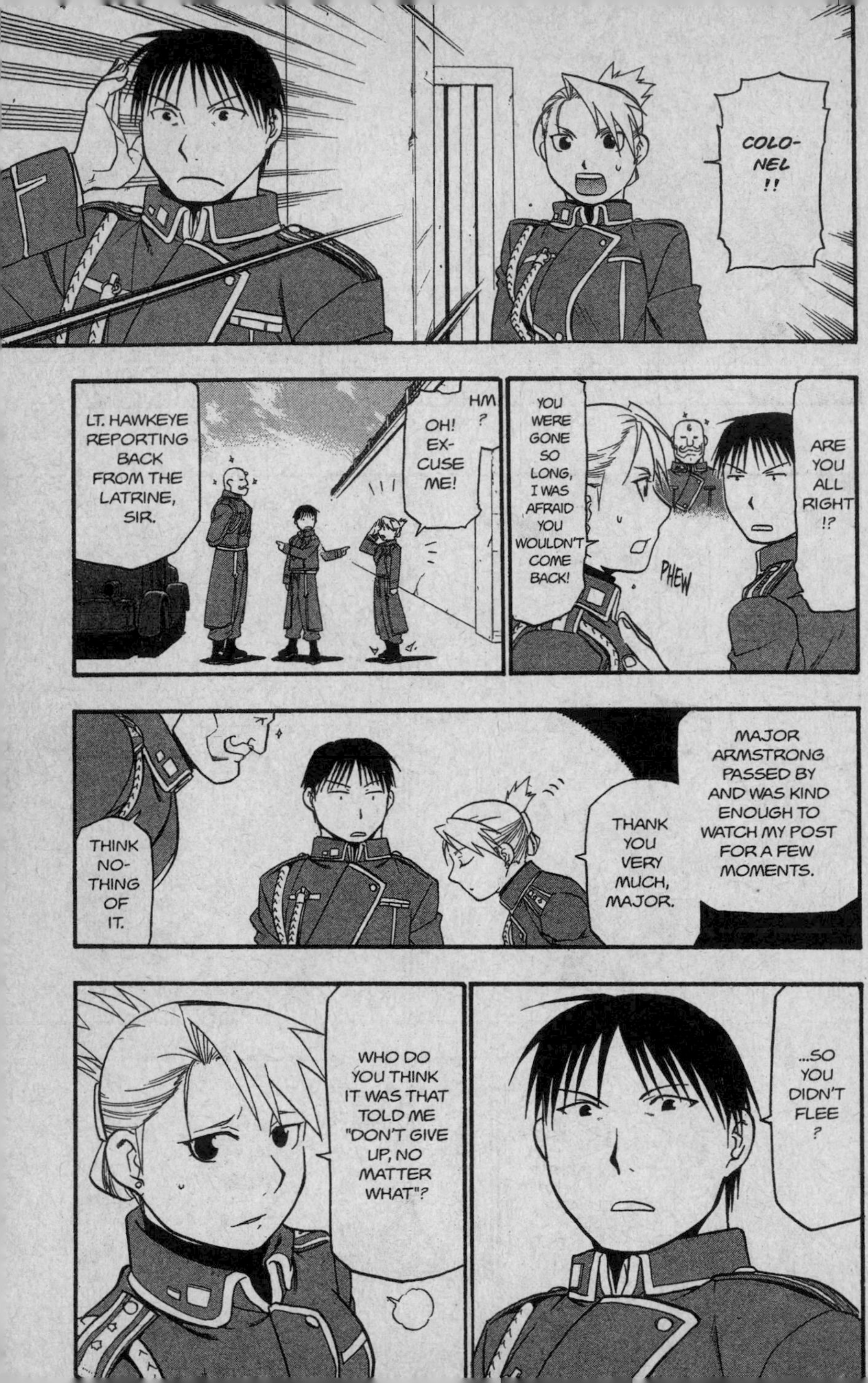
COLO-NEL !!
ARE YOU ALL RIGHT !?
YOU WERE GONE SO LONG, I WAS AFRAID YOU WOULDN'T COME BACK!
PHEW
HM ?
OH! EX-CUSE ME!
LT. HAWKEYE REPORTING BACK FROM THE LATRINE, SIR.
MAJOR ARMSTRONG PASSED BY AND WAS KIND ENOUGH TO WATCH MY POST FOR A FEW MOMENTS.
THANK YOU VERY MUCH, MAJOR.
THINK NO-THING OF IT.
...SO YOU DIDN'T FLEE ?
WHO DO YOU THINK IT WAS THAT TOLD ME "DON'T GIVE UP, NO MATTER WHAT"?

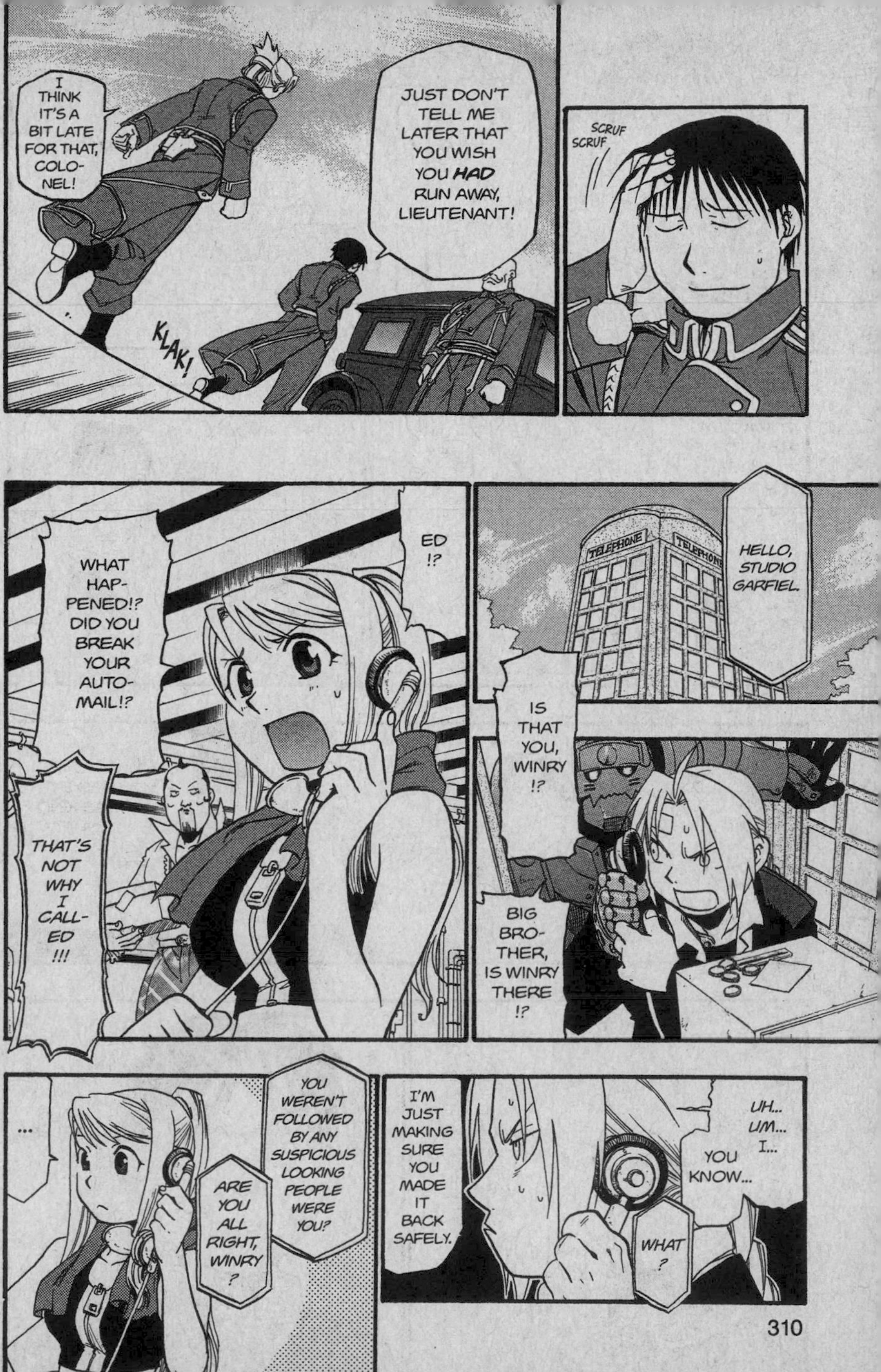
SCRUF SCRUF
JUST DON'T TELL ME LATER THAT YOU WISH YOU **HAD** RUN AWAY, LIEUTENANT!
I THINK IT'S A BIT LATE FOR THAT, COLONEL!
KLAK!
HELLO, STUDIO GARFIEL.
TELEPHONE
IS THAT YOU, WINRY!?
BIG BROTHER, IS WINRY THERE!?
ED!?
WHAT HAPPENED!? DID YOU BREAK YOUR AUTOMAIL!?
THAT'S NOT WHY I CALLED ED!!!
UH... UM... I...
YOU KNOW...
I'M JUST MAKING SURE YOU MADE IT BACK SAFELY.
WHAT?
YOU WEREN'T FOLLOWED BY ANY SUSPICIOUS LOOKING PEOPLE WERE YOU?
ARE YOU ALL RIGHT, WINRY?
...

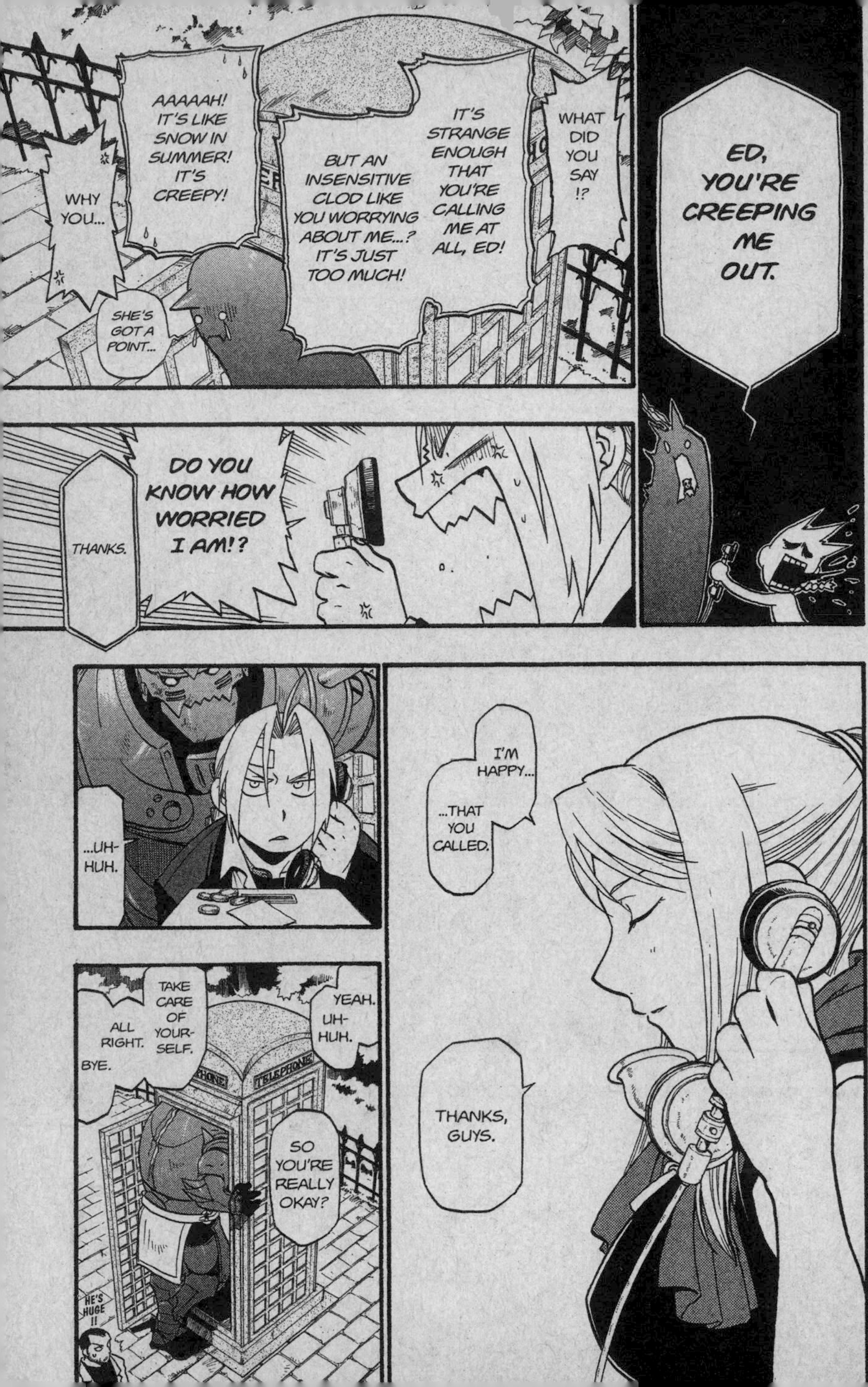

ED, YOU'RE CREEPING ME OUT.
WHAT DID YOU SAY!?
IT'S STRANGE ENOUGH THAT YOU'RE CALLING ME AT ALL, ED!
BUT AN INSENSITIVE CLOD LIKE YOU WORRYING ABOUT ME...? IT'S JUST TOO MUCH!
AAAAAH! IT'S LIKE SNOW IN SUMMER! IT'S CREEPY!
WHY YOU...
SHE'S GOT A POINT...
DO YOU KNOW HOW WORRIED I AM!?
THANKS.
I'M HAPPY...
...THAT YOU CALLED.
THANKS, GUYS.
...UH-HUH.
YEAH. UH-HUH.
TAKE CARE OF YOURSELF.
ALL RIGHT.
BYE.
SO YOU'RE REALLY OKAY?
HE'S HUGE!!

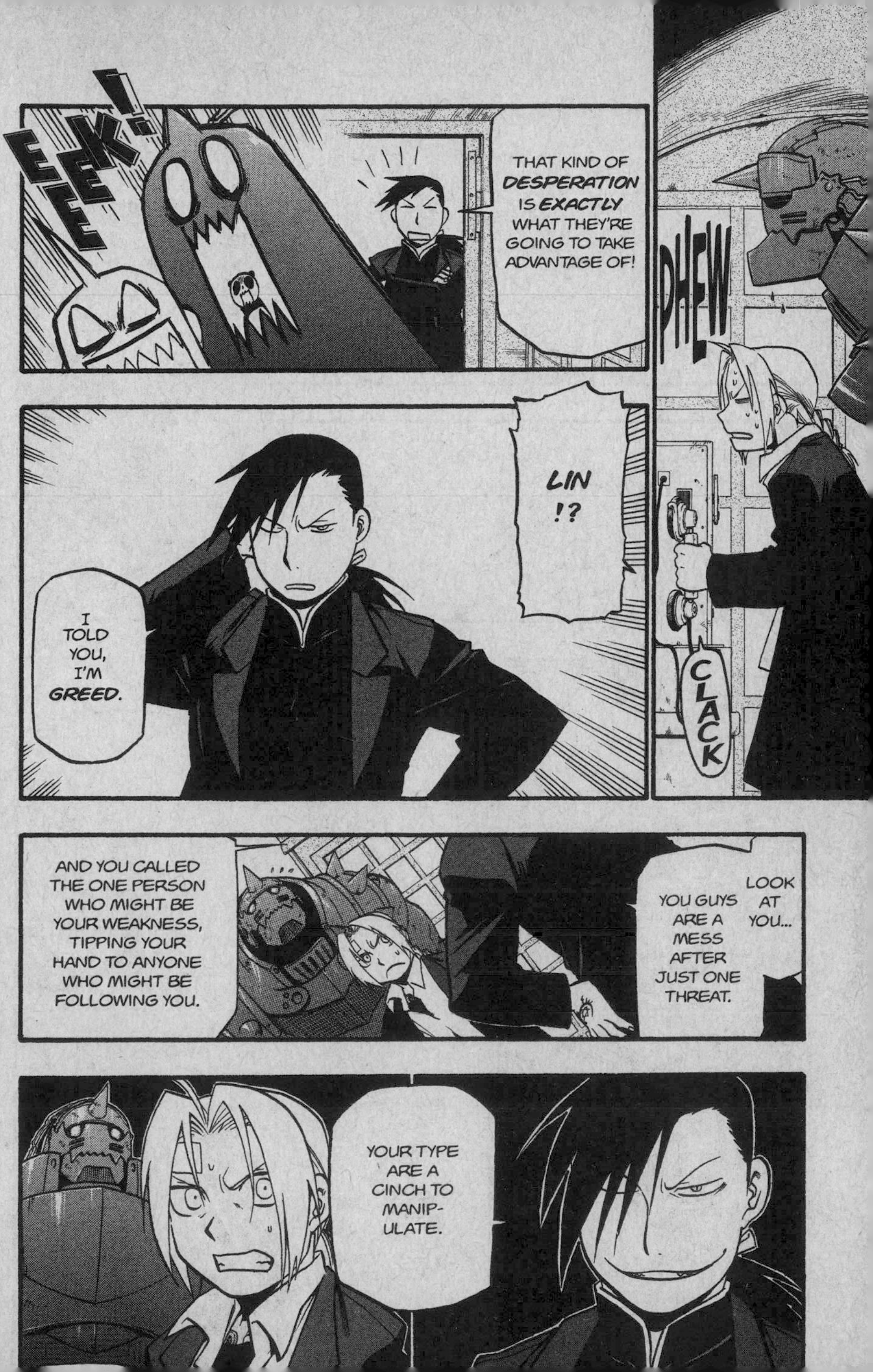
PHEW
CLACK
THAT KIND OF DESPERATION IS EXACTLY WHAT THEY'RE GOING TO TAKE ADVANTAGE OF!
EEEK!!
LIN !?
I TOLD YOU, I'M GREED.
LOOK AT YOU...
YOU GUYS ARE A MESS AFTER JUST ONE THREAT.
AND YOU CALLED THE ONE PERSON WHO MIGHT BE YOUR WEAKNESS, TIPPING YOUR HAND TO ANYONE WHO MIGHT BE FOLLOWING YOU.
YOUR TYPE ARE A CINCH TO MANIPULATE.

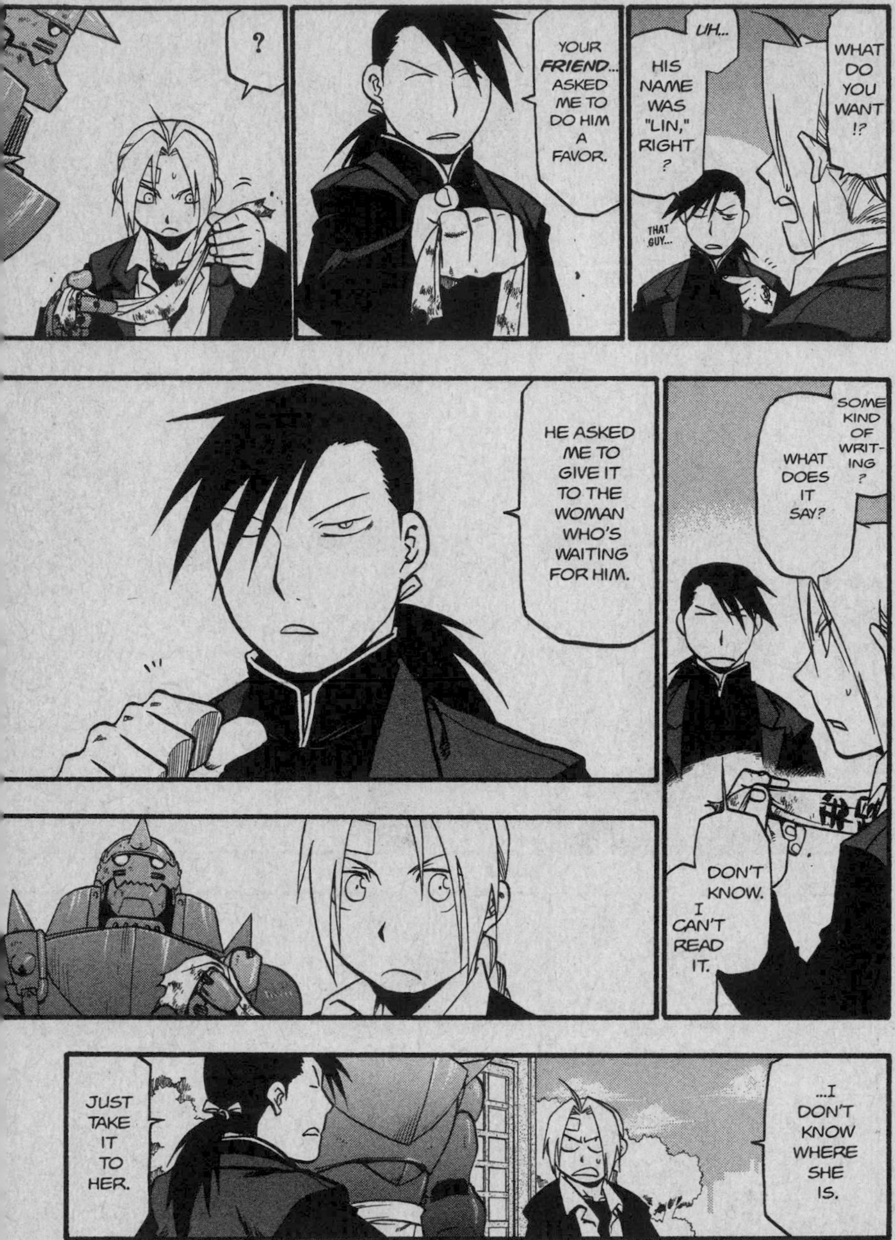
WHAT DO YOU WANT !?
UH...
HIS NAME WAS "LIN," RIGHT ?
THAT GUY...
YOUR *FRIEND*... ASKED ME TO DO HIM A FAVOR.
?
SOME KIND OF WRIT-ING ?
WHAT DOES IT SAY?
DON'T KNOW. I CAN'T READ IT.
HE ASKED ME TO GIVE IT TO THE WOMAN WHO'S WAITING FOR HIM.
...I DON'T KNOW WHERE SHE IS.
JUST TAKE IT TO HER.

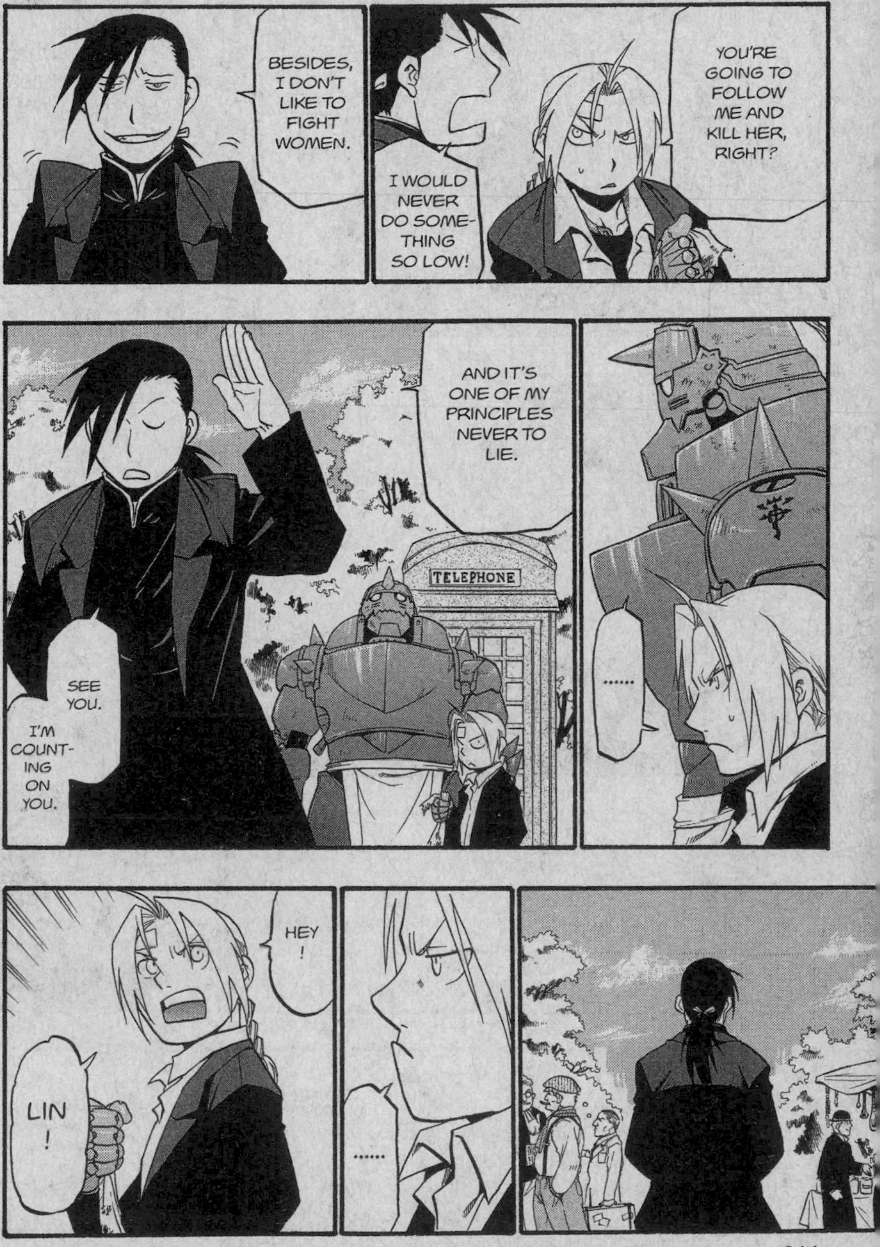
YOU'RE GOING TO FOLLOW ME AND KILL HER, RIGHT?
I WOULD NEVER DO SOME-THING SO LOW!
BESIDES, I DON'T LIKE TO FIGHT WOMEN.
......
AND IT'S ONE OF MY PRINCIPLES NEVER TO LIE.
TELEPHONE
SEE YOU.
I'M COUNT-ING ON YOU.
......
HEY!
LIN!

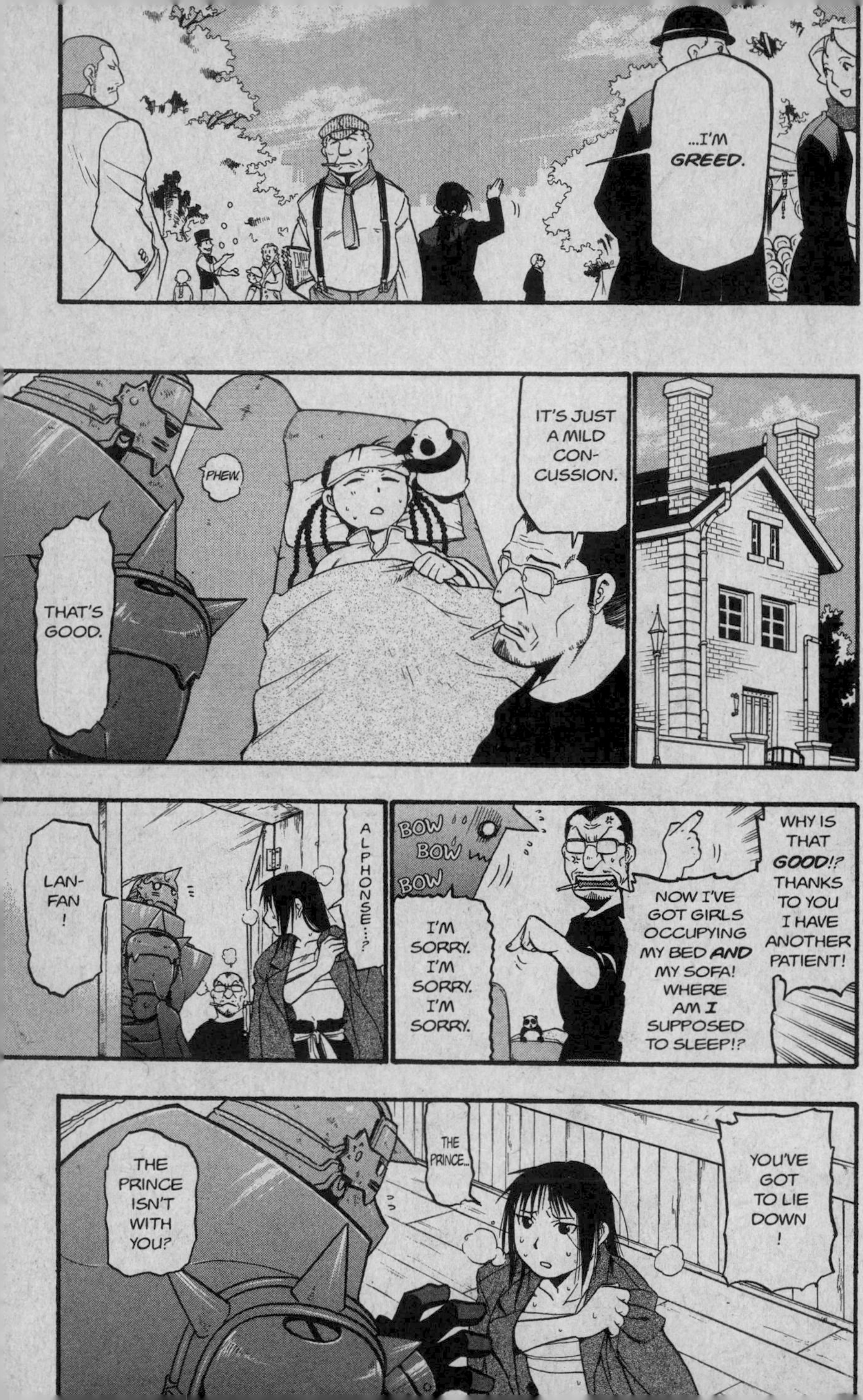
...I'M GREED.
IT'S JUST A MILD CONCUSSION.
PHEW.
THAT'S GOOD.
WHY IS THAT GOOD!? THANKS TO YOU I HAVE ANOTHER PATIENT!
NOW I'VE GOT GIRLS OCCUPYING MY BED AND MY SOFA! WHERE AM I SUPPOSED TO SLEEP!?
BOW BOW BOW
I'M SORRY. I'M SORRY. I'M SORRY.
ALPHONSE...?
LAN-FAN!
YOU'VE GOT TO LIE DOWN!
THE PRINCE...
THE PRINCE ISN'T WITH YOU?

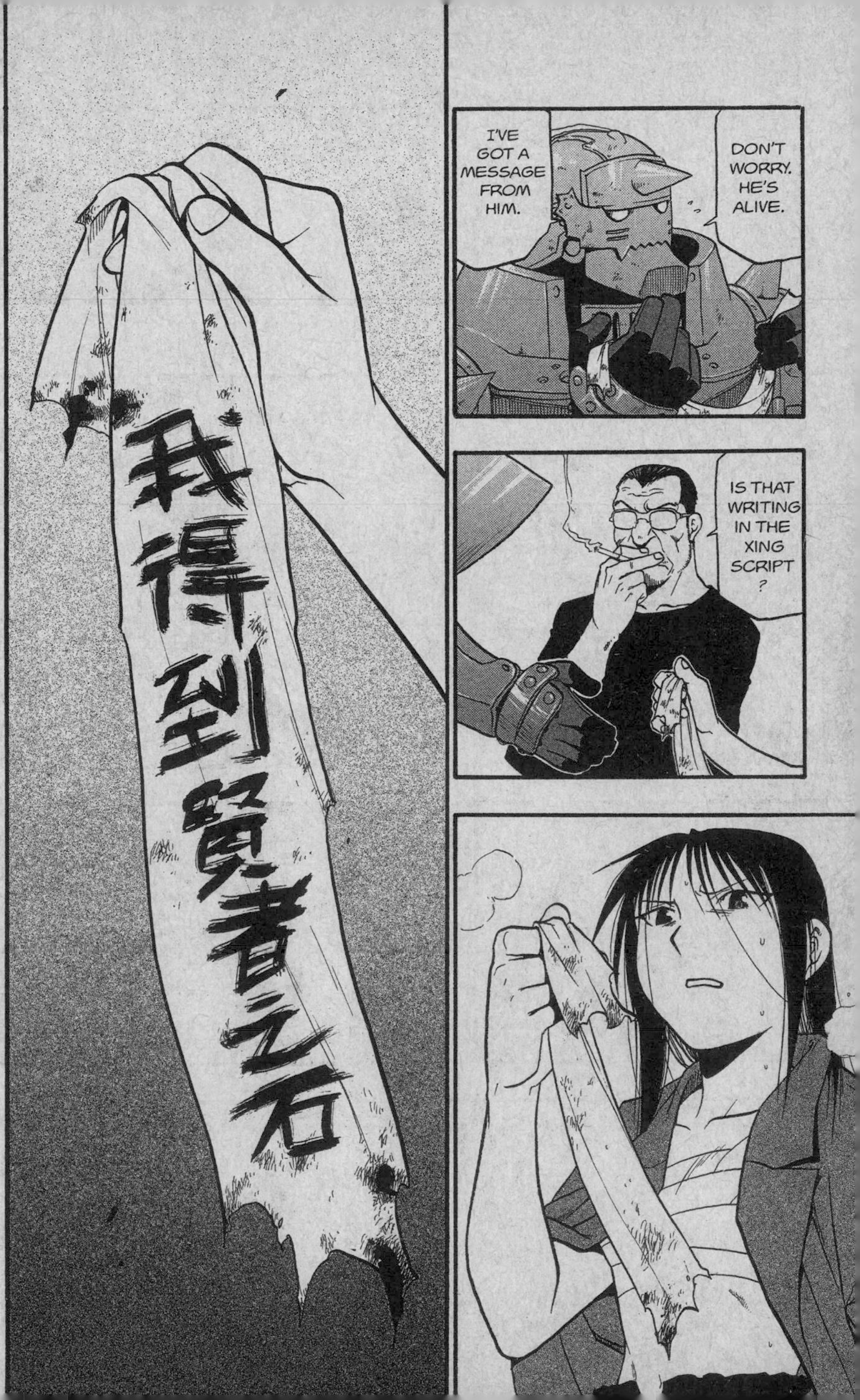
DON'T WORRY. HE'S ALIVE.
I'VE GOT A MESSAGE FROM HIM.
IS THAT WRITING IN THE XING SCRIPT?
我得到賢者之石

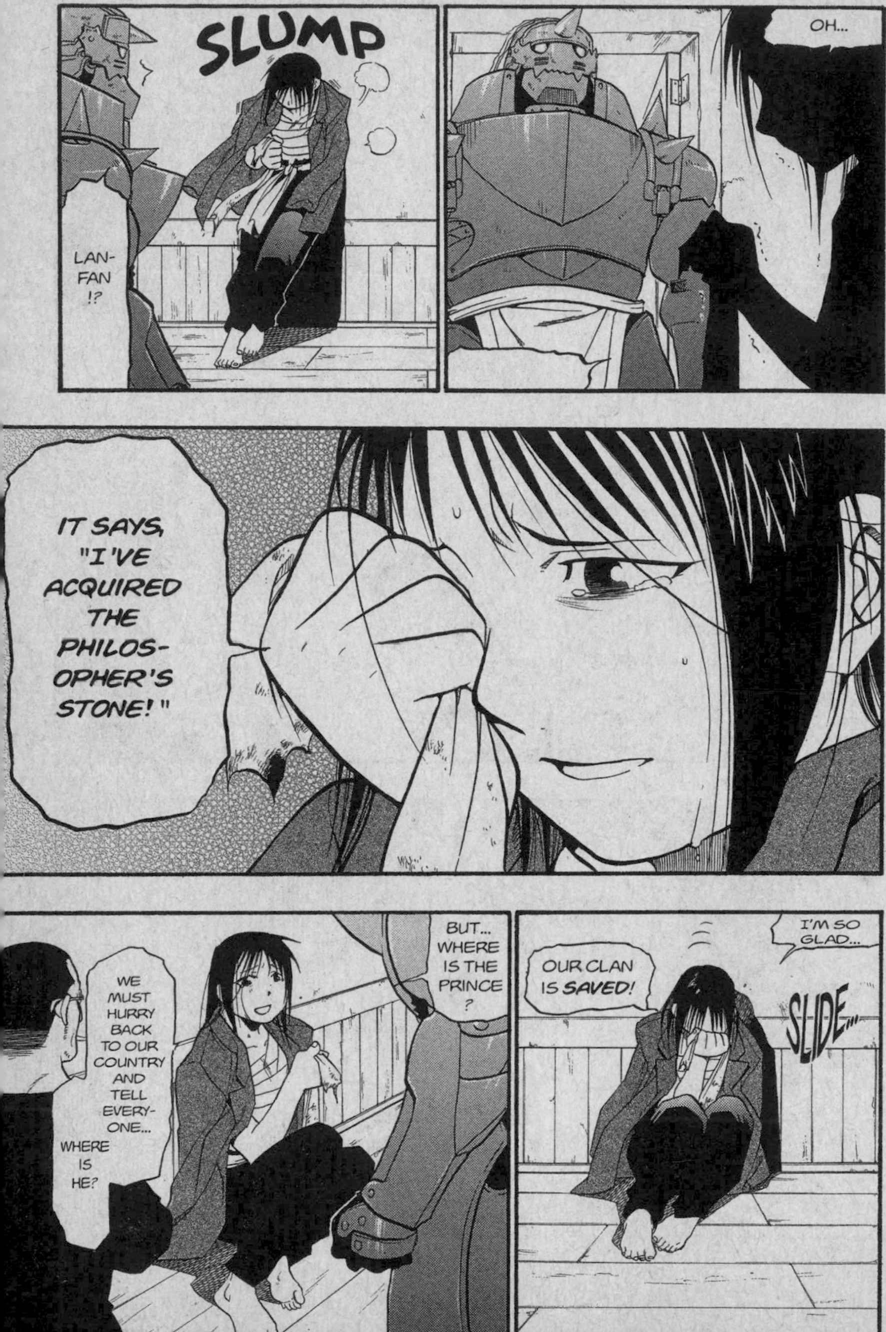
OH...
SLUMP
LAN-FAN !?
IT SAYS, "I'VE ACQUIRED THE PHILOSOPHER'S STONE!"
I'M SO GLAD...
OUR CLAN IS SAVED!
SLIDE...
BUT... WHERE IS THE PRINCE?
WE MUST HURRY BACK TO OUR COUNTRY AND TELL EVERYONE...
WHERE IS HE?

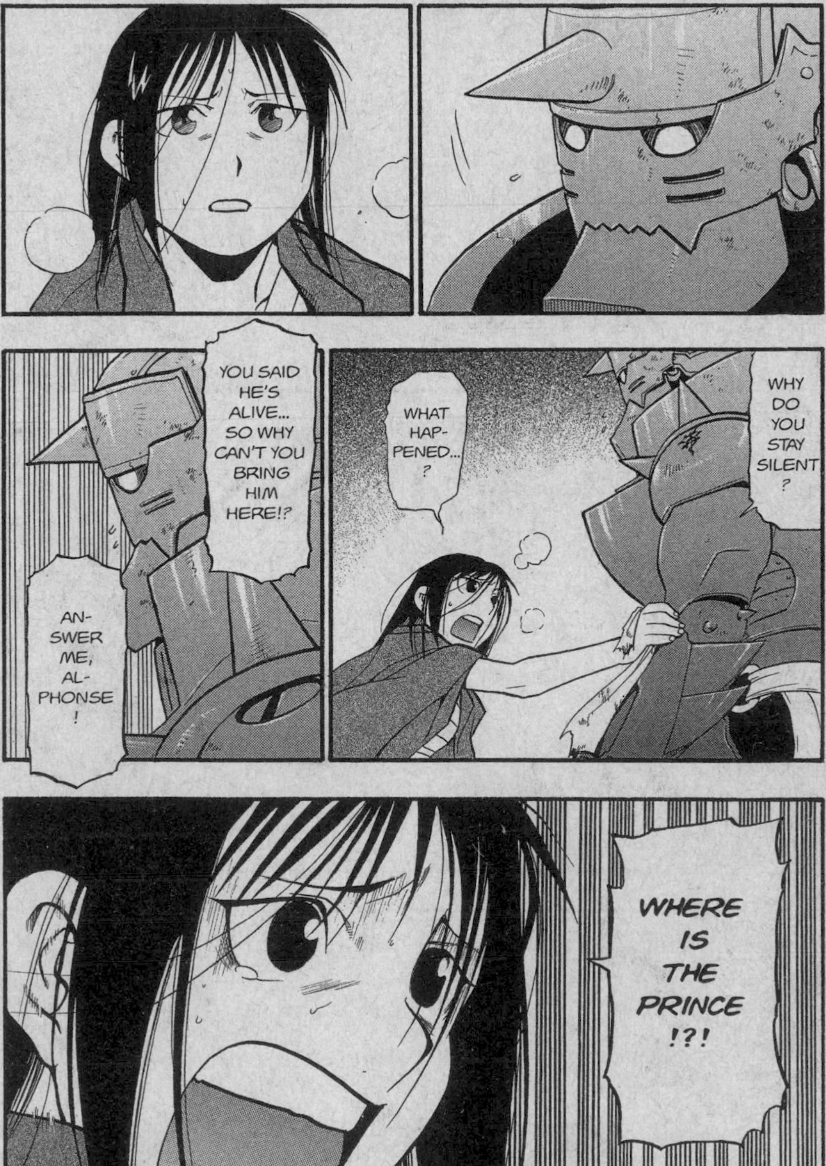
WHY DO YOU STAY SILENT?
WHAT HAPPENED...?
YOU SAID HE'S ALIVE... SO WHY CAN'T YOU BRING HIM HERE!?
ANSWER ME, ALPHONSE!
WHERE IS THE PRINCE!?!

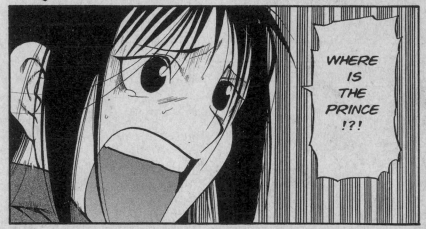

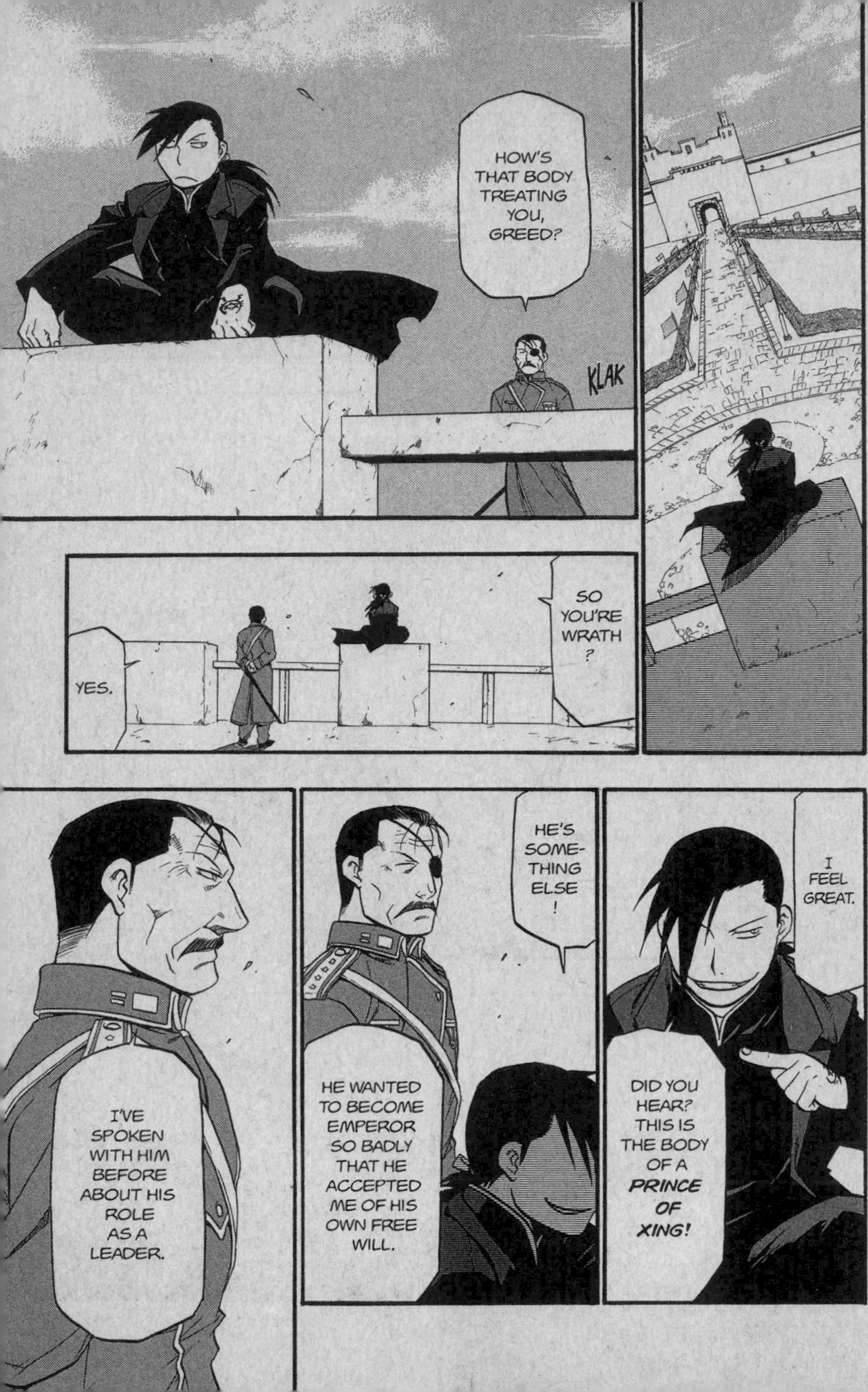
HOW'S THAT BODY TREATING YOU, GREED?
KLAK
SO YOU'RE WRATH?
YES.
I FEEL GREAT.
DID YOU HEAR? THIS IS THE BODY OF A *PRINCE OF XING!*
HE'S SOME-THING ELSE!
HE WANTED TO BECOME EMPEROR SO BADLY THAT HE ACCEPTED ME OF HIS OWN FREE WILL.
I'VE SPOKEN WITH HIM BEFORE ABOUT HIS ROLE AS A LEADER.

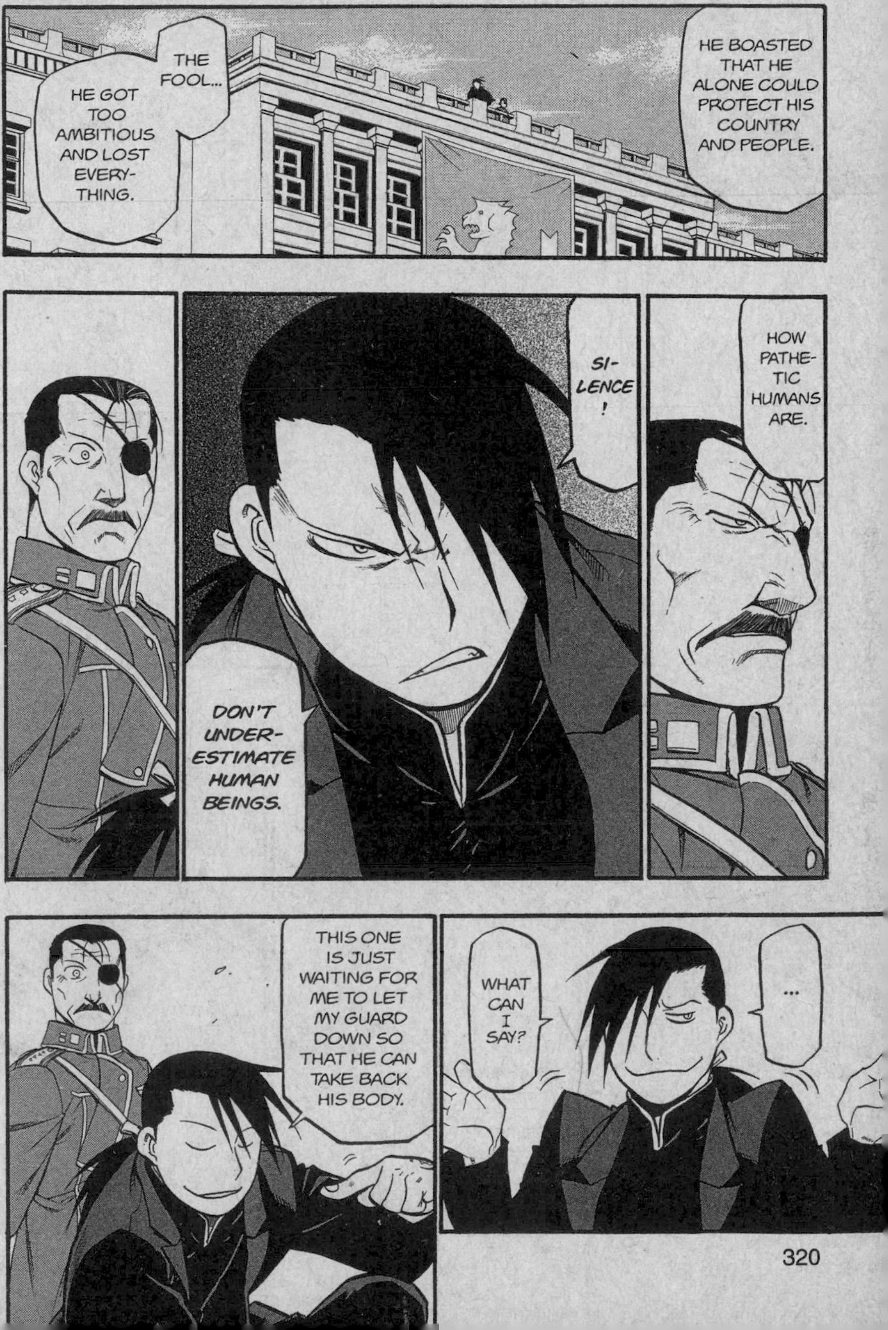
HE BOASTED THAT HE ALONE COULD PROTECT HIS COUNTRY AND PEOPLE.
THE FOOL...
HE GOT TOO AMBITIOUS AND LOST EVERY-THING.
HOW PATHE-TIC HUMANS ARE.
SI-LENCE!
DON'T UNDER-ESTIMATE HUMAN BEINGS.
...
WHAT CAN I SAY?
THIS ONE IS JUST WAITING FOR ME TO LET MY GUARD DOWN SO THAT HE CAN TAKE BACK HIS BODY.

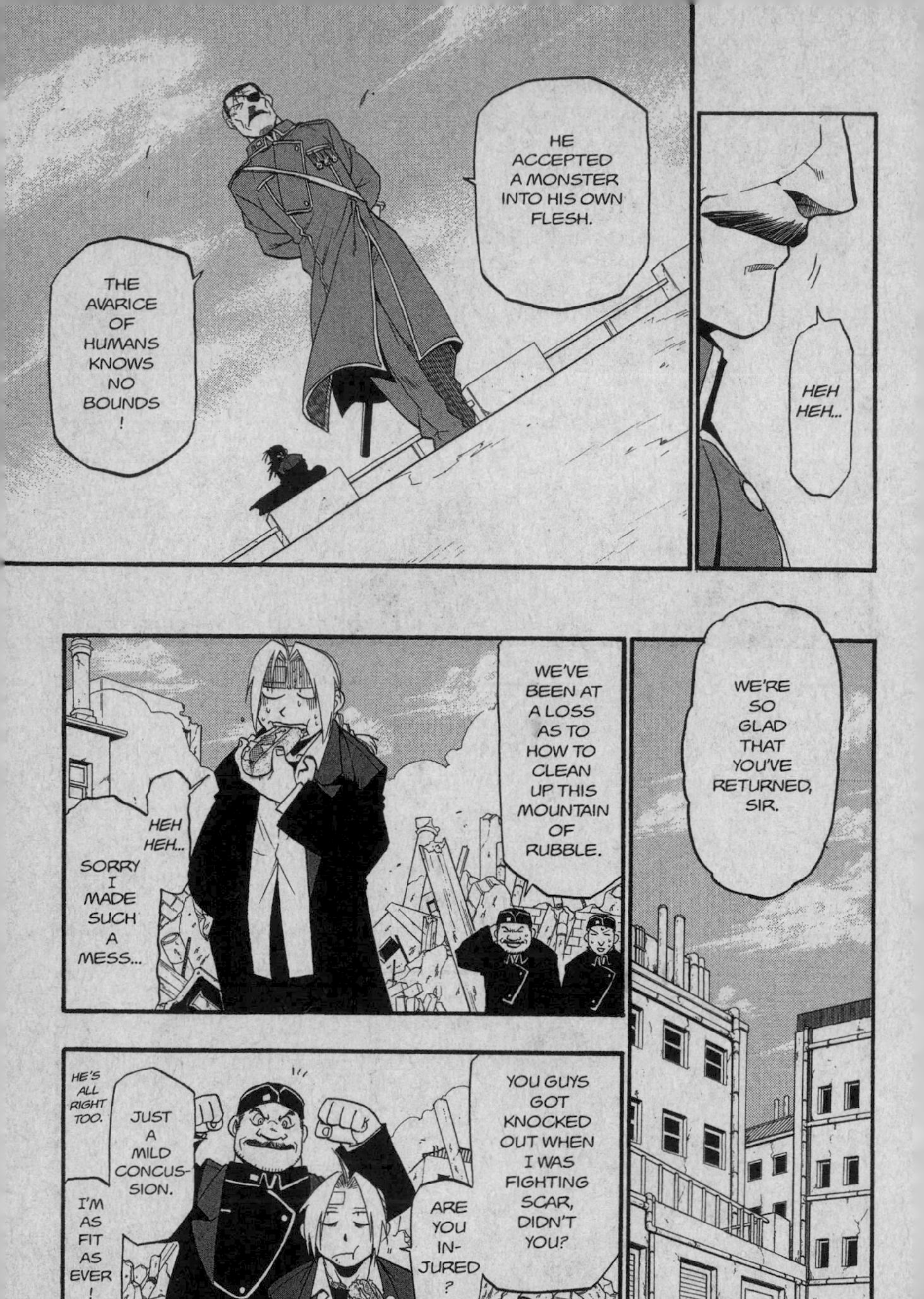
HEH HEH...
HE ACCEPTED A MONSTER INTO HIS OWN FLESH.
THE AVARICE OF HUMANS KNOWS NO BOUNDS!
WE'RE SO GLAD THAT YOU'VE RETURNED, SIR.
WE'VE BEEN AT A LOSS AS TO HOW TO CLEAN UP THIS MOUNTAIN OF RUBBLE.
HEH HEH...
SORRY I MADE SUCH A MESS...
YOU GUYS GOT KNOCKED OUT WHEN I WAS FIGHTING SCAR, DIDN'T YOU?
ARE YOU IN-JURED?
JUST A MILD CONCUS-SION.
HE'S ALL RIGHT TOO.
I'M AS FIT AS EVER!

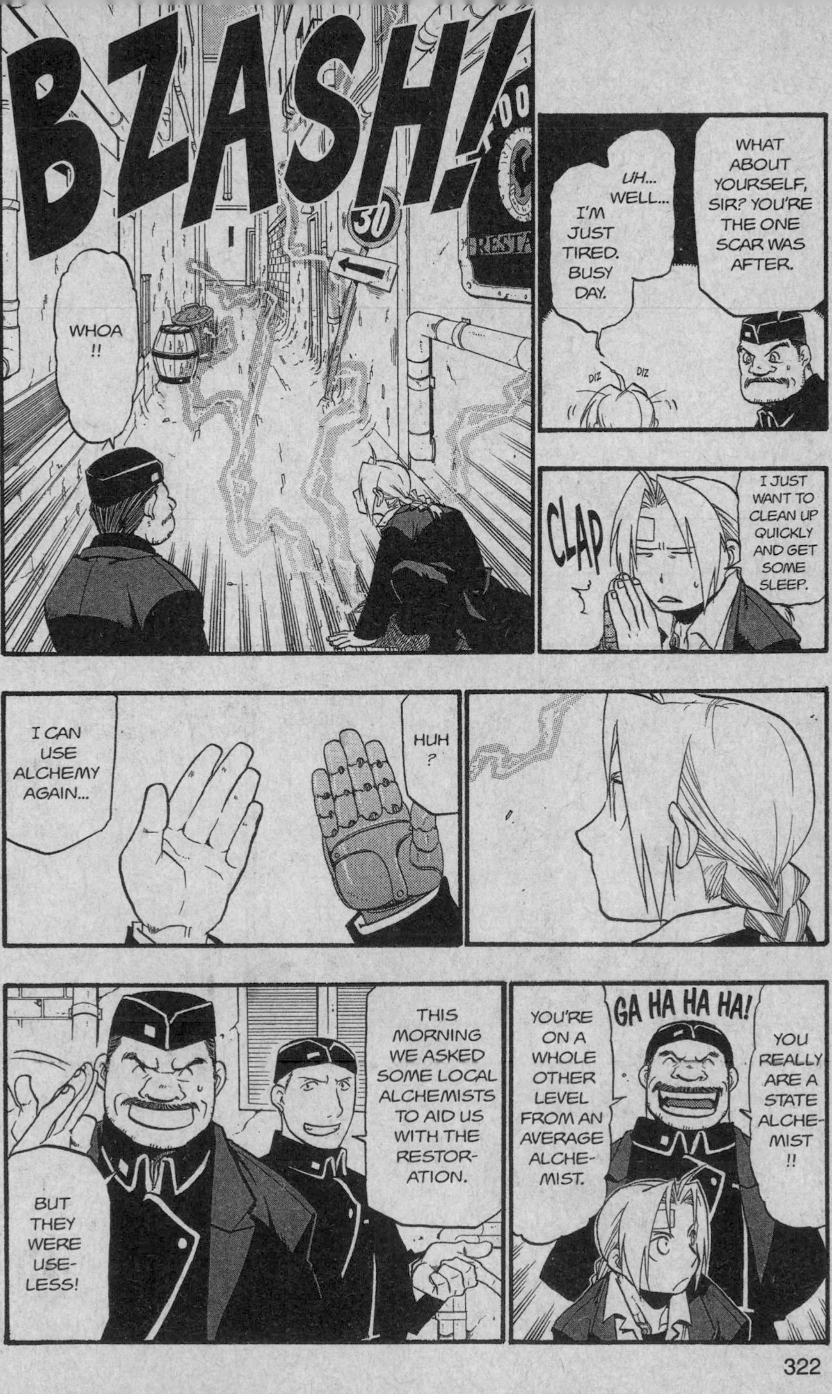
WHAT ABOUT YOURSELF, SIR? YOU'RE THE ONE SCAR WAS AFTER.
UH... WELL... I'M JUST TIRED. BUSY DAY.
DIZ DIZ
I JUST WANT TO CLEAN UP QUICKLY AND GET SOME SLEEP.
CLAP
BZASH!
30
WHOA !!
HUH ?
I CAN USE ALCHEMY AGAIN...
GA HA HA HA!
YOU REALLY ARE A STATE ALCHE-MIST !!
YOU'RE ON A WHOLE OTHER LEVEL FROM AN AVERAGE ALCHE-MIST.
THIS MORNING WE ASKED SOME LOCAL ALCHEMISTS TO AID US WITH THE RESTOR-ATION.
BUT THEY WERE USE-LESS!

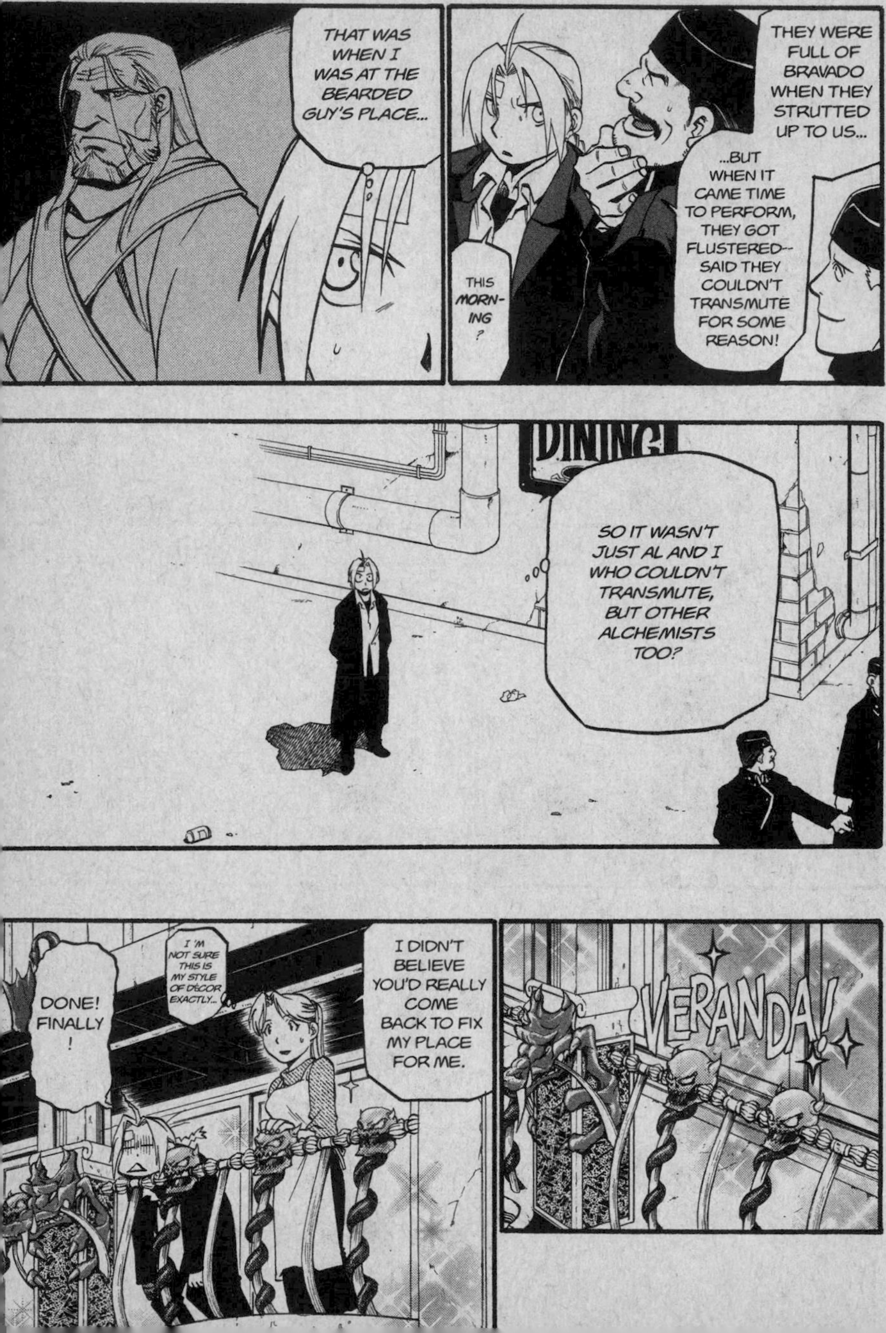
THEY WERE FULL OF BRAVADO WHEN THEY STRUTTED UP TO US...
...BUT WHEN IT CAME TIME TO PERFORM, THEY GOT FLUSTERED-- SAID THEY COULDN'T TRANSMUTE FOR SOME REASON!
THIS MORNING?
THAT WAS WHEN I WAS AT THE BEARDED GUY'S PLACE...
DINING
SO IT WASN'T JUST AL AND I WHO COULDN'T TRANSMUTE, BUT OTHER ALCHEMISTS TOO?
VERANDA!
I DIDN'T BELIEVE YOU'D REALLY COME BACK TO FIX MY PLACE FOR ME.
I'M NOT SURE THIS IS MY STYLE OF DÉCOR EXACTLY...
DONE! FINALLY!

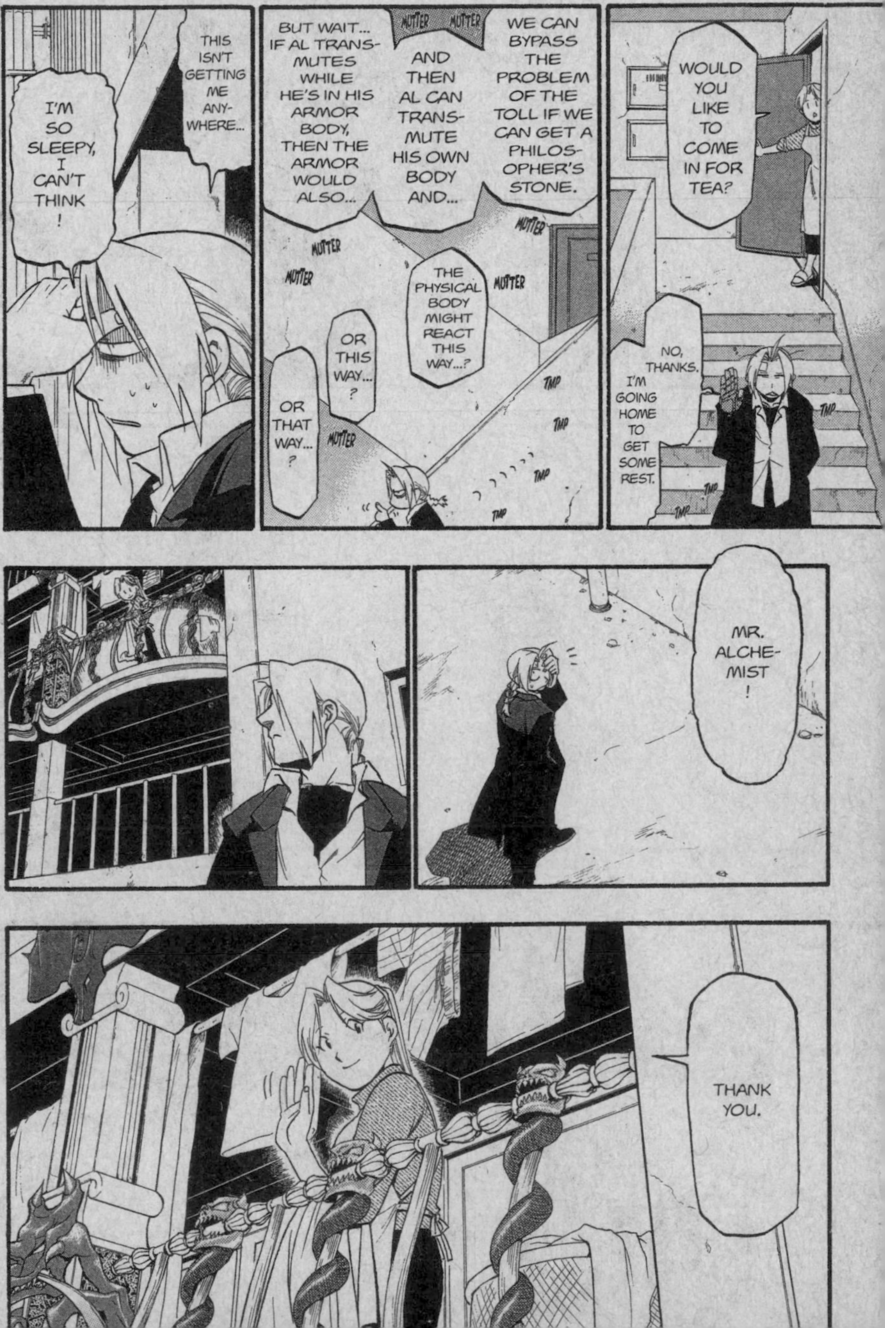
WOULD YOU LIKE TO COME IN FOR TEA?
NO, THANKS. I'M GOING HOME TO GET SOME REST.
TMP
TMP
TMP
WE CAN BYPASS THE PROBLEM OF THE TOLL IF WE CAN GET A PHILOSOPHER'S STONE.
MUTTER MUTTER
AND THEN AL CAN TRANSMUTE HIS OWN BODY AND...
BUT WAIT... IF AL TRANSMUTES WHILE HE'S IN HIS ARMOR BODY, THEN THE ARMOR WOULD ALSO...
MUTTER
MUTTER
MUTTER
MUTTER
THE PHYSICAL BODY MIGHT REACT THIS WAY...?
OR THIS WAY...?
OR THAT WAY...?
MUTTER
TMP
TMP
TMP
TMP
THIS ISN'T GETTING ME ANYWHERE...
I'M SO SLEEPY, I CAN'T THINK!
MR. ALCHEMIST!
THANK YOU.

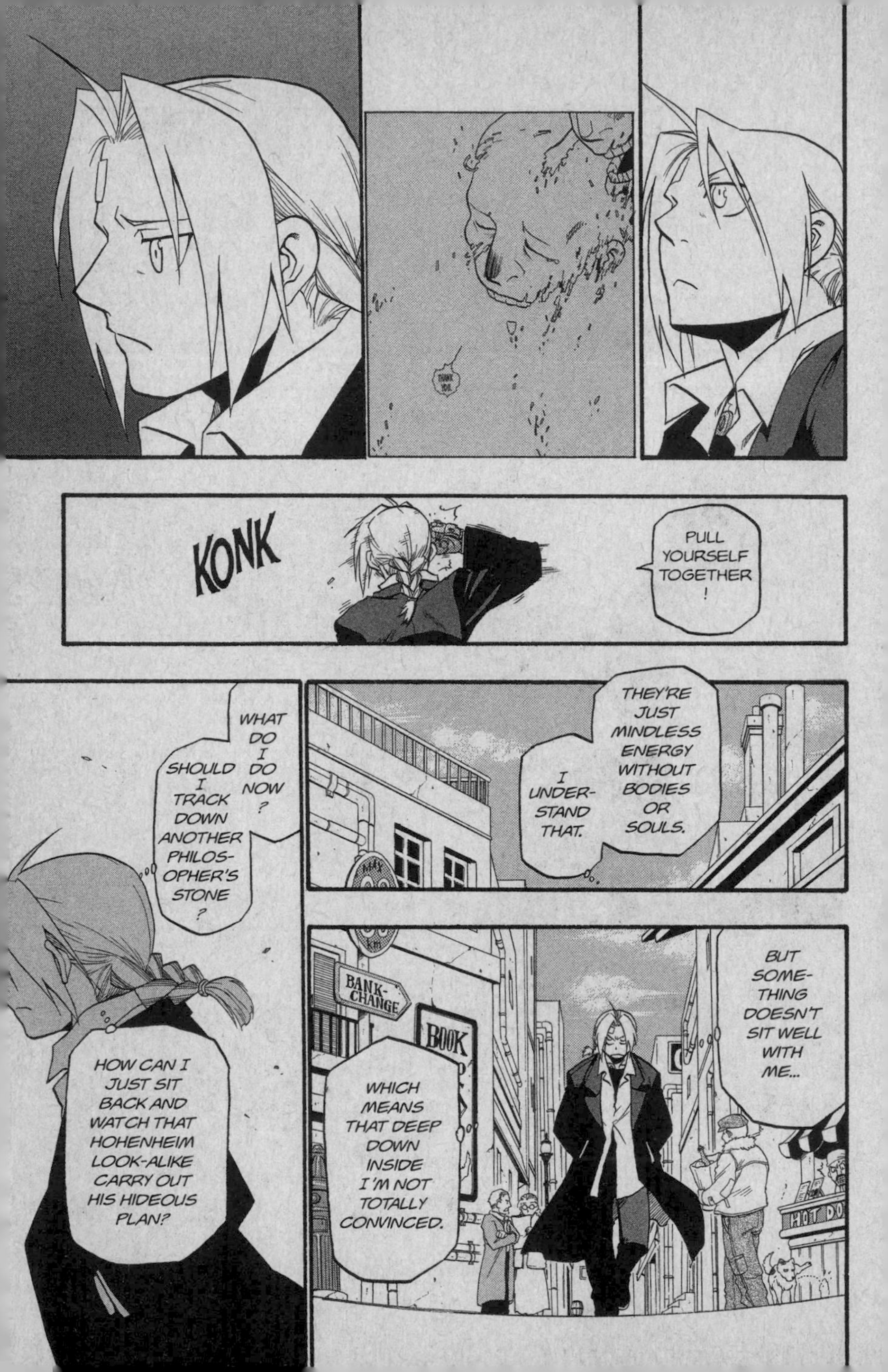
THANK YOU.
PULL YOURSELF TOGETHER!
KONK
THEY'RE JUST MINDLESS ENERGY WITHOUT BODIES OR SOULS.
I UNDERSTAND THAT.
BUT SOMETHING DOESN'T SIT WELL WITH ME...
WHICH MEANS THAT DEEP DOWN INSIDE I'M NOT TOTALLY CONVINCED.
BANK-CHANGE
BOOK
WHAT DO I DO NOW?
SHOULD I TRACK DOWN ANOTHER PHILOSOPHER'S STONE?
HOW CAN I JUST SIT BACK AND WATCH THAT HOHENHEIM LOOK-ALIKE CARRY OUT HIS HIDEOUS PLAN?

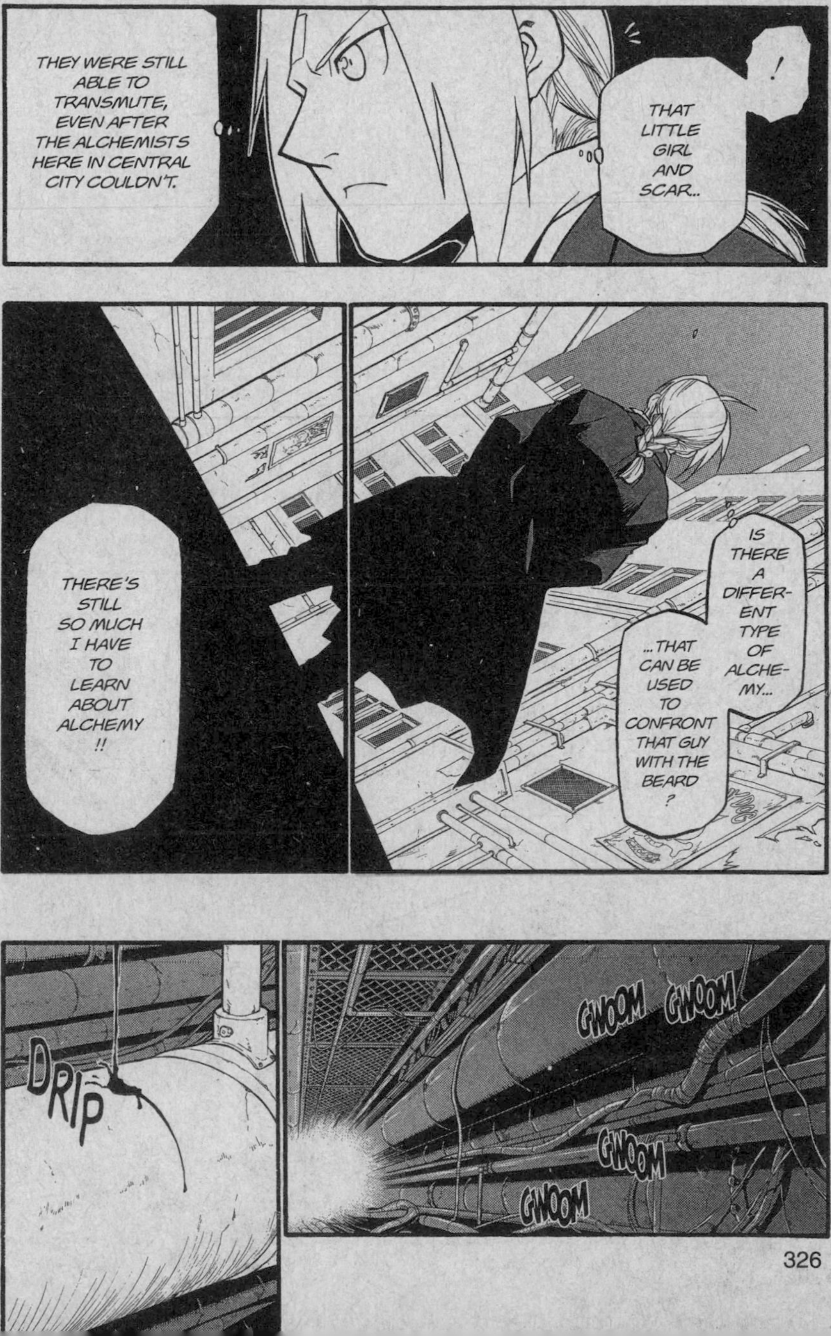
!
THAT LITTLE GIRL AND SCAR...
THEY WERE STILL ABLE TO TRANSMUTE, EVEN AFTER THE ALCHEMISTS HERE IN CENTRAL CITY COULDN'T.
IS THERE A DIFFER-ENT TYPE OF ALCHE-MY...
...THAT CAN BE USED TO CONFRONT THAT GUY WITH THE BEARD?
THERE'S STILL SO MUCH I HAVE TO LEARN ABOUT ALCHEMY!!
GWOOM GWOOM
GWOOM
GWOOM
DRIP

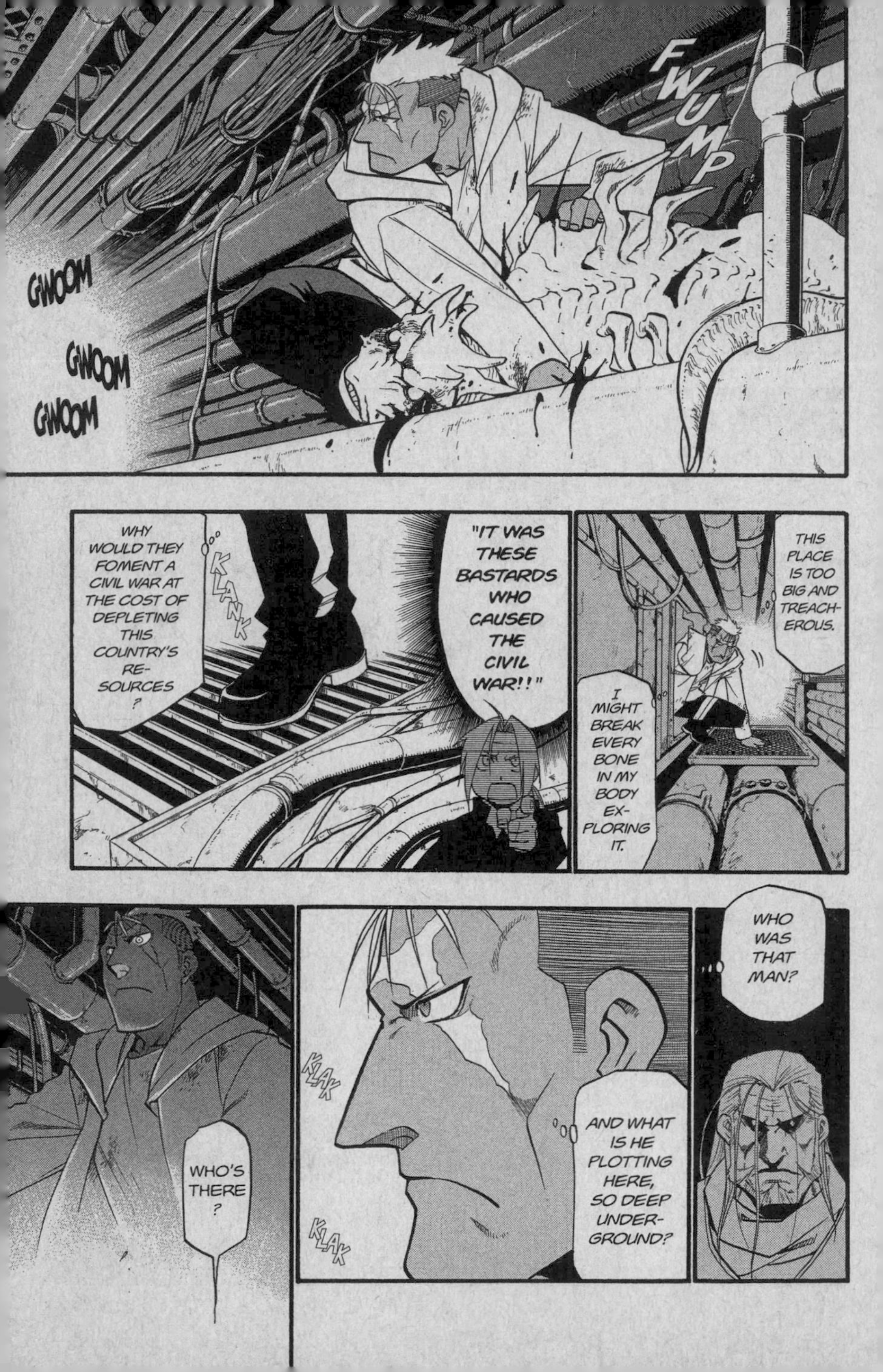
FWUMP
GWOOM
GWOOM
GWOOM
THIS PLACE IS TOO BIG AND TREACHEROUS.
I MIGHT BREAK EVERY BONE IN MY BODY EXPLORING IT.
"IT WAS THESE BASTARDS WHO CAUSED THE CIVIL WAR!!"
KLANK
WHY WOULD THEY FOMENT A CIVIL WAR AT THE COST OF DEPLETING THIS COUNTRY'S RESOURCES?
WHO WAS THAT MAN?
AND WHAT IS HE PLOTTING HERE, SO DEEP UNDERGROUND?
KLAK
KLAK
WHO'S THERE?

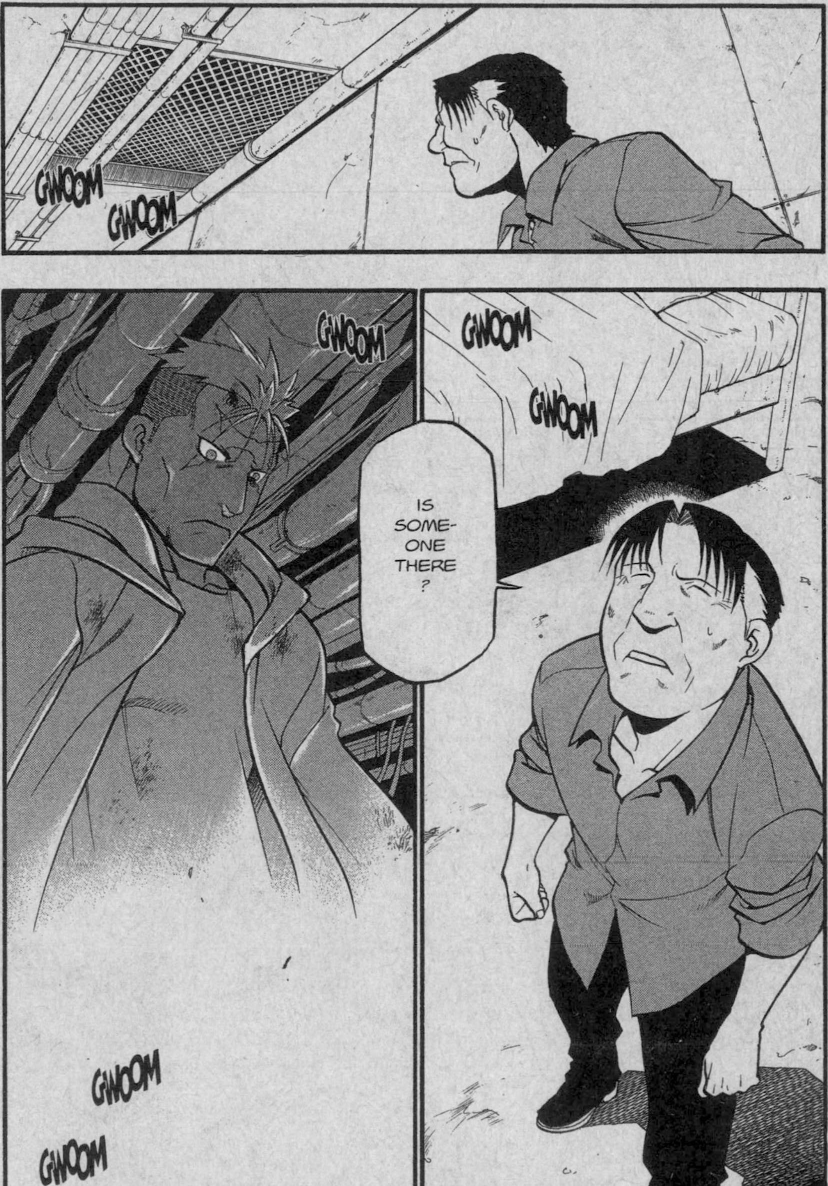
GWOOM
GWOOM
GWOOM
GWOOM
IS SOME-ONE THERE?
GWOOM
GWOOM
GWOOM

Chapter 57
Scars of Ishbal

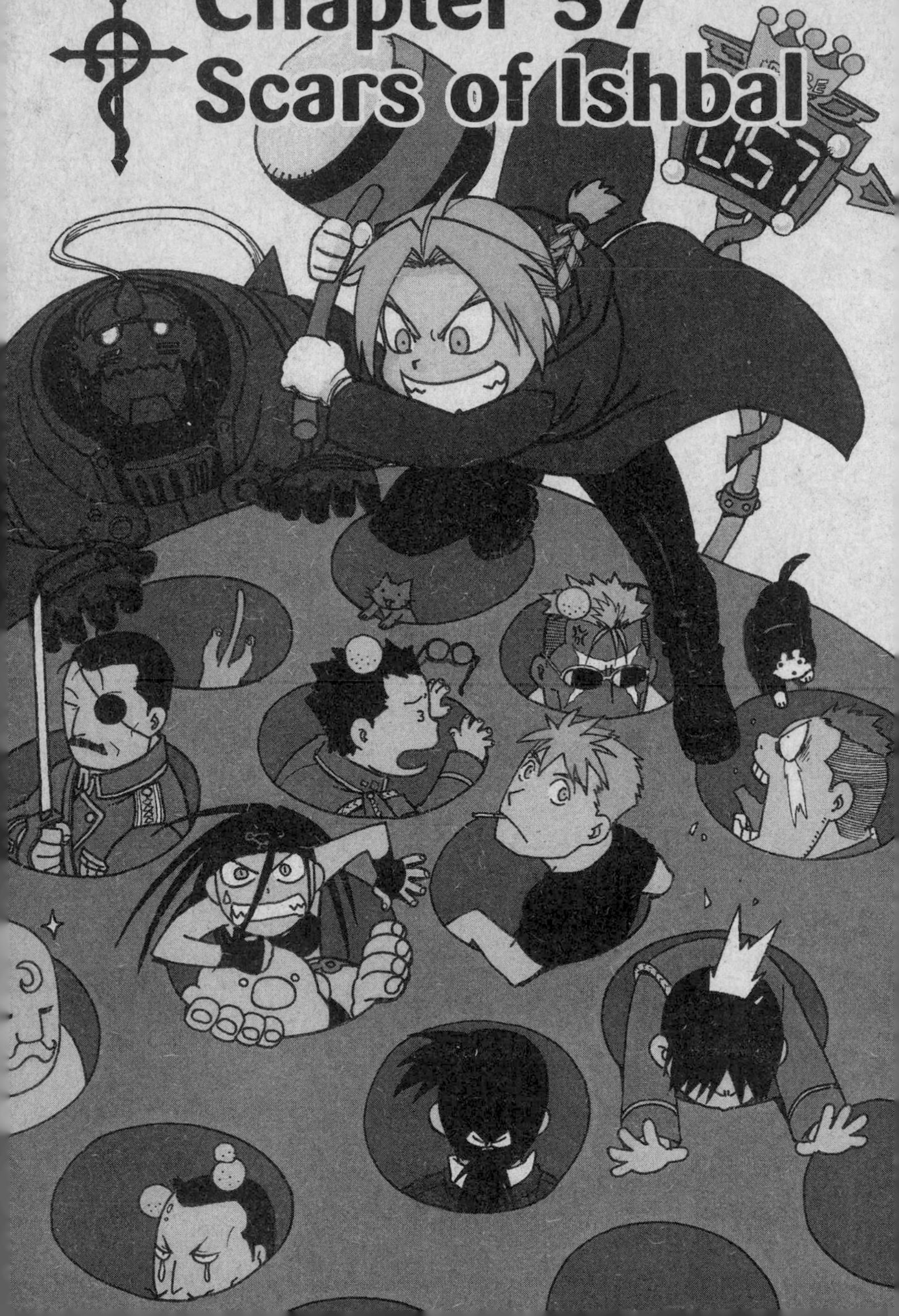

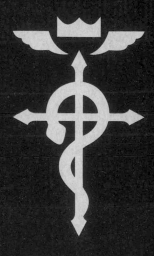

FULLMETAL
ALCHEMIST

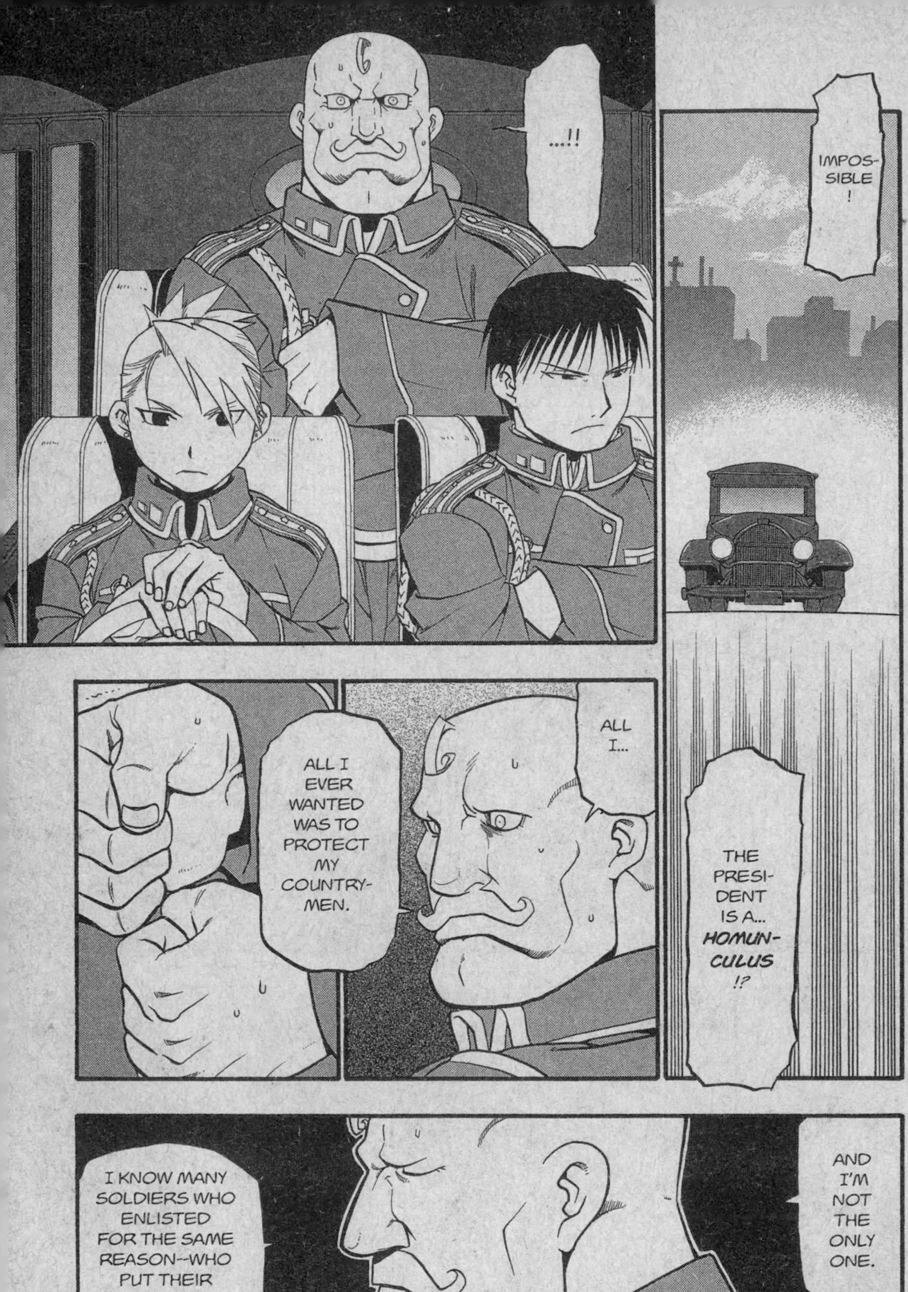
IMPOSSIBLE!
...!!
THE PRESIDENT IS A... ***HOMUNCULUS*** !?
ALL I...
ALL I EVER WANTED WAS TO PROTECT MY COUNTRYMEN.
AND I'M NOT THE ONLY ONE.
I KNOW MANY SOLDIERS WHO ENLISTED FOR THE SAME REASON--WHO PUT THEIR ***TRUST*** IN THE MILITARY.

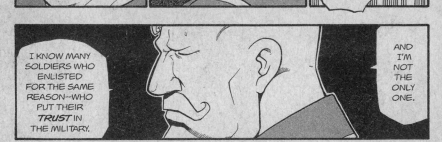

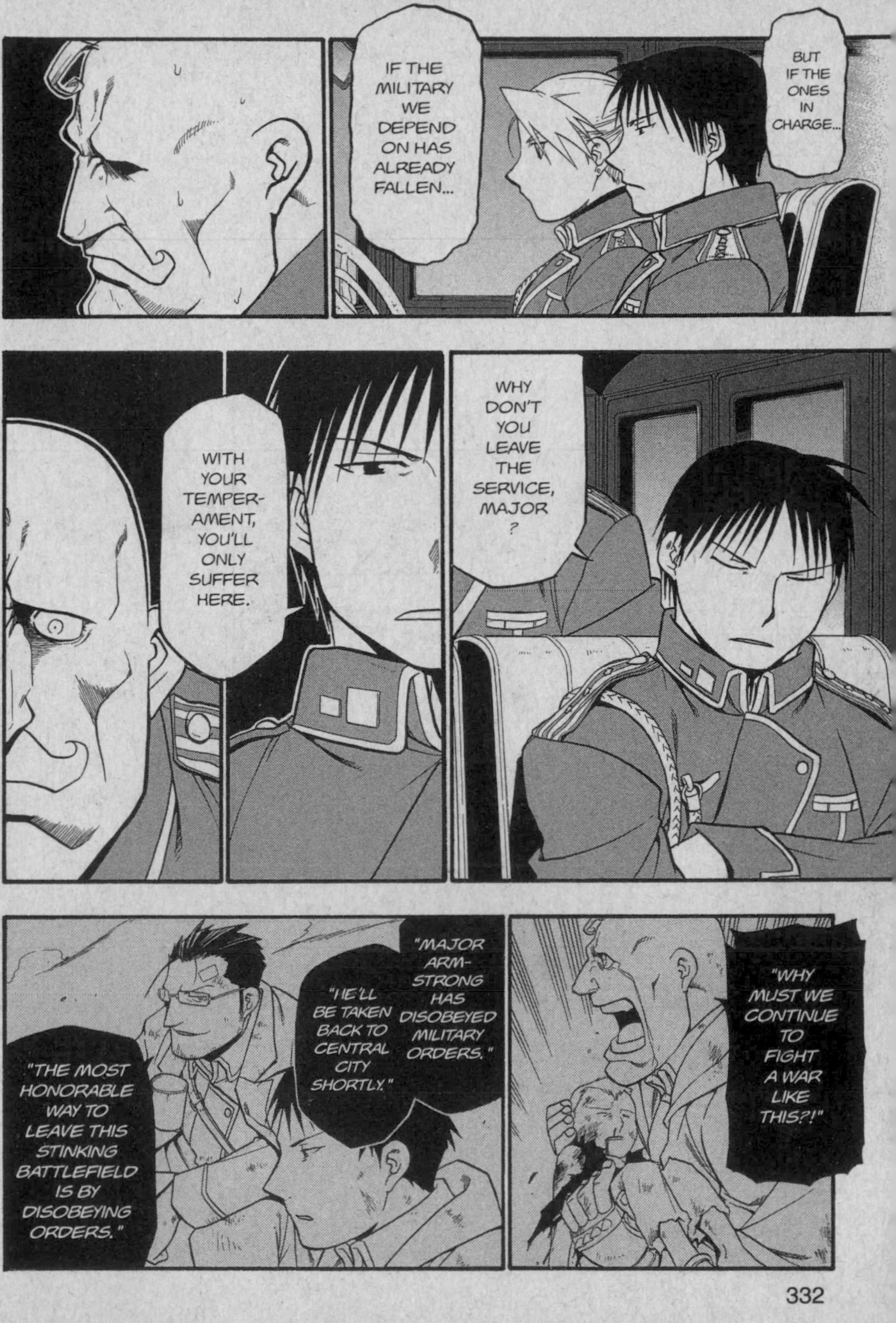
BUT IF THE ONES IN CHARGE...
IF THE MILITARY WE DEPEND ON HAS ALREADY FALLEN...
WHY DON'T YOU LEAVE THE SERVICE, MAJOR?
WITH YOUR TEMPER-AMENT, YOU'LL ONLY SUFFER HERE.
"WHY MUST WE CONTINUE TO FIGHT A WAR LIKE THIS?!"
"MAJOR ARM-STRONG HAS DISOBEYED MILITARY ORDERS."
"HE'LL BE TAKEN BACK TO CENTRAL CITY SHORTLY."
"THE MOST HONORABLE WAY TO LEAVE THIS STINKING BATTLEFIELD IS BY DISOBEYING ORDERS."

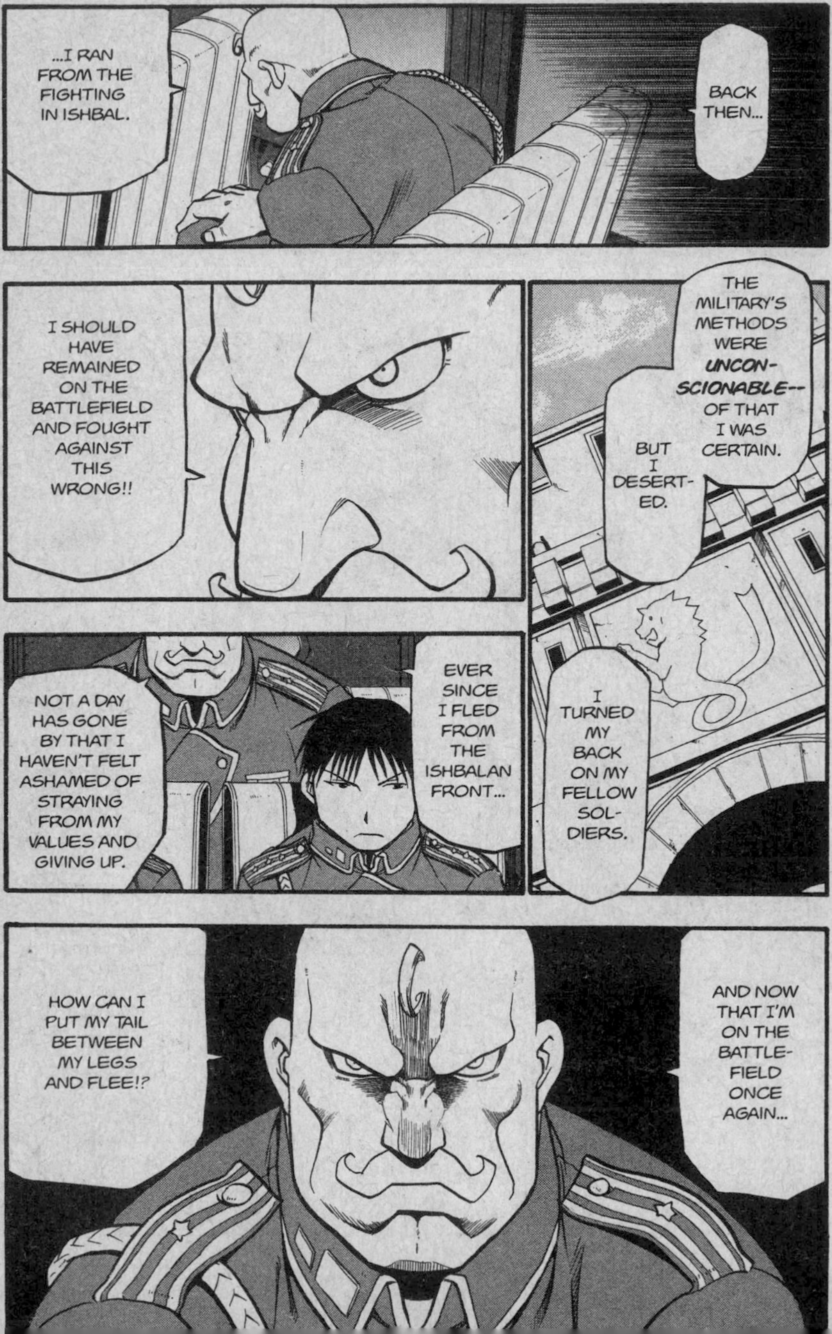
BACK THEN...
...I RAN FROM THE FIGHTING IN ISHBAL.
THE MILITARY'S METHODS WERE UNCONSCIONABLE-- OF THAT I WAS CERTAIN.
BUT I DESERTED.
I TURNED MY BACK ON MY FELLOW SOLDIERS.
I SHOULD HAVE REMAINED ON THE BATTLEFIELD AND FOUGHT AGAINST THIS WRONG!!
EVER SINCE I FLED FROM THE ISHBALAN FRONT...
NOT A DAY HAS GONE BY THAT I HAVEN'T FELT ASHAMED OF STRAYING FROM MY VALUES AND GIVING UP.
AND NOW THAT I'M ON THE BATTLEFIELD ONCE AGAIN...
HOW CAN I PUT MY TAIL BETWEEN MY LEGS AND FLEE!?

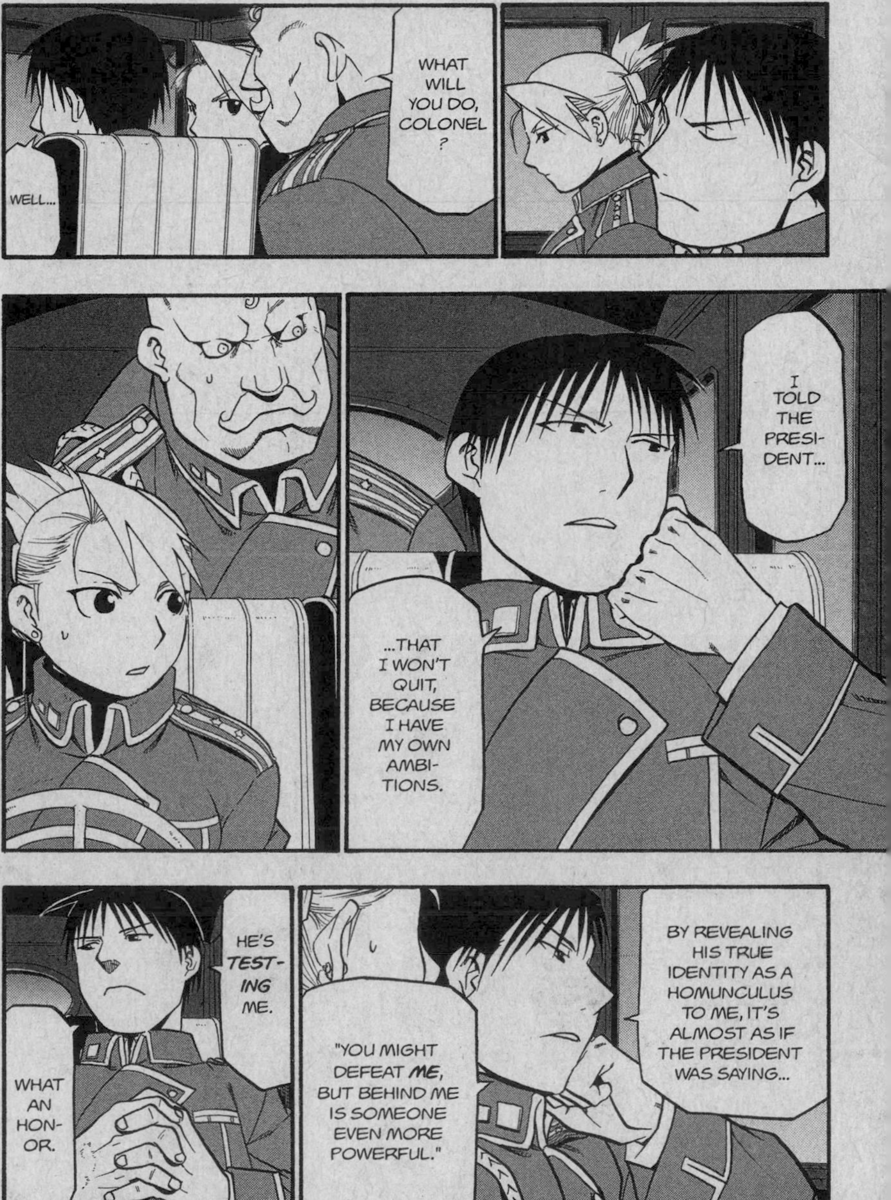
WHAT WILL YOU DO, COLONEL?
WELL...
I TOLD THE PRESIDENT...
...THAT I WON'T QUIT, BECAUSE I HAVE MY OWN AMBITIONS.
BY REVEALING HIS TRUE IDENTITY AS A HOMUNCULUS TO ME, IT'S ALMOST AS IF THE PRESIDENT WAS SAYING...
"YOU MIGHT DEFEAT *ME*, BUT BEHIND ME IS SOMEONE EVEN MORE POWERFUL."
HE'S *TESTING* ME.
WHAT AN HONOR.

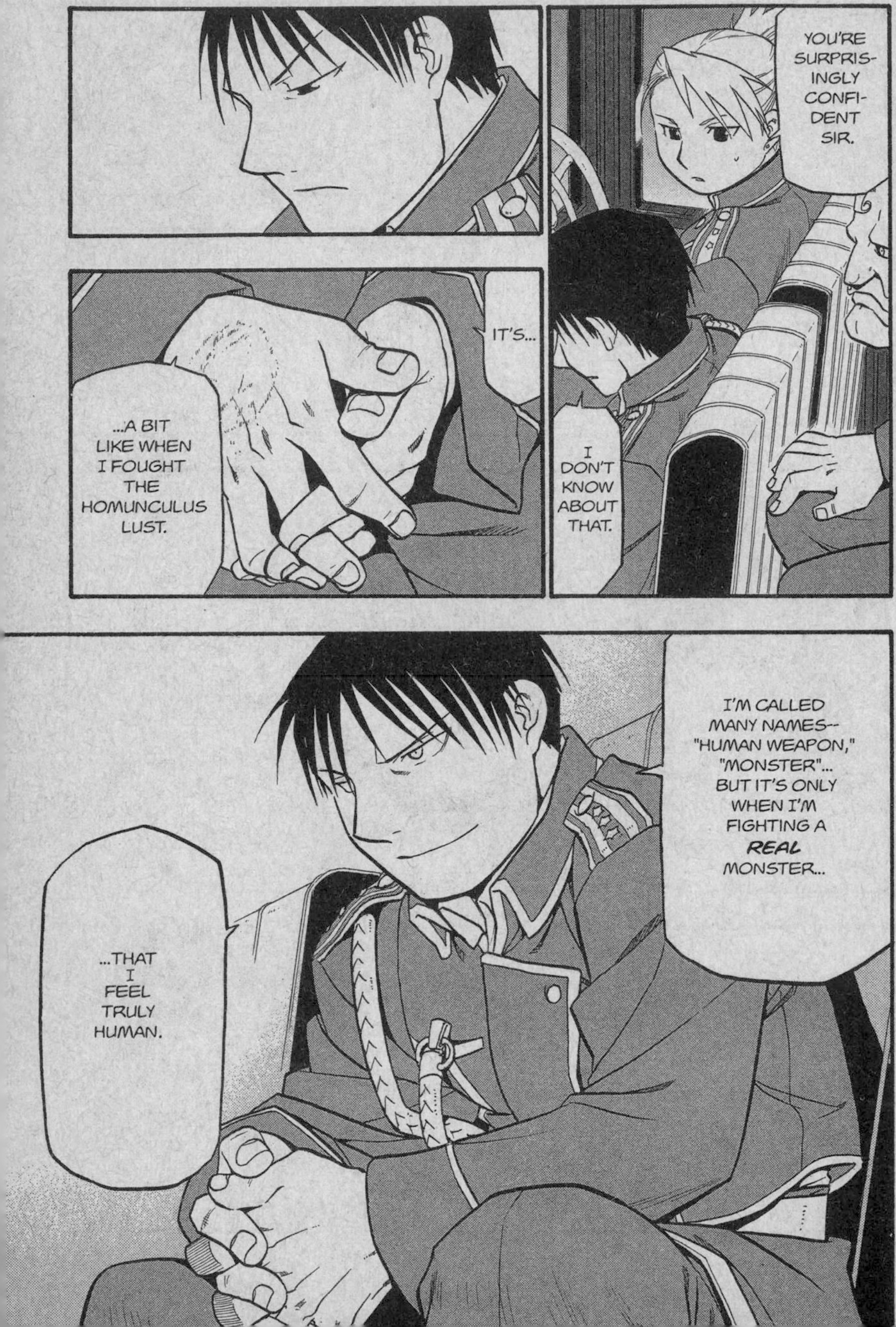
YOU'RE SURPRISINGLY CONFIDENT SIR.
I DON'T KNOW ABOUT THAT.
IT'S...
...A BIT LIKE WHEN I FOUGHT THE HOMUNCULUS LUST.
I'M CALLED MANY NAMES-- "HUMAN WEAPON," "MONSTER"... BUT IT'S ONLY WHEN I'M FIGHTING A REAL MONSTER...
...THAT I FEEL TRULY HUMAN.

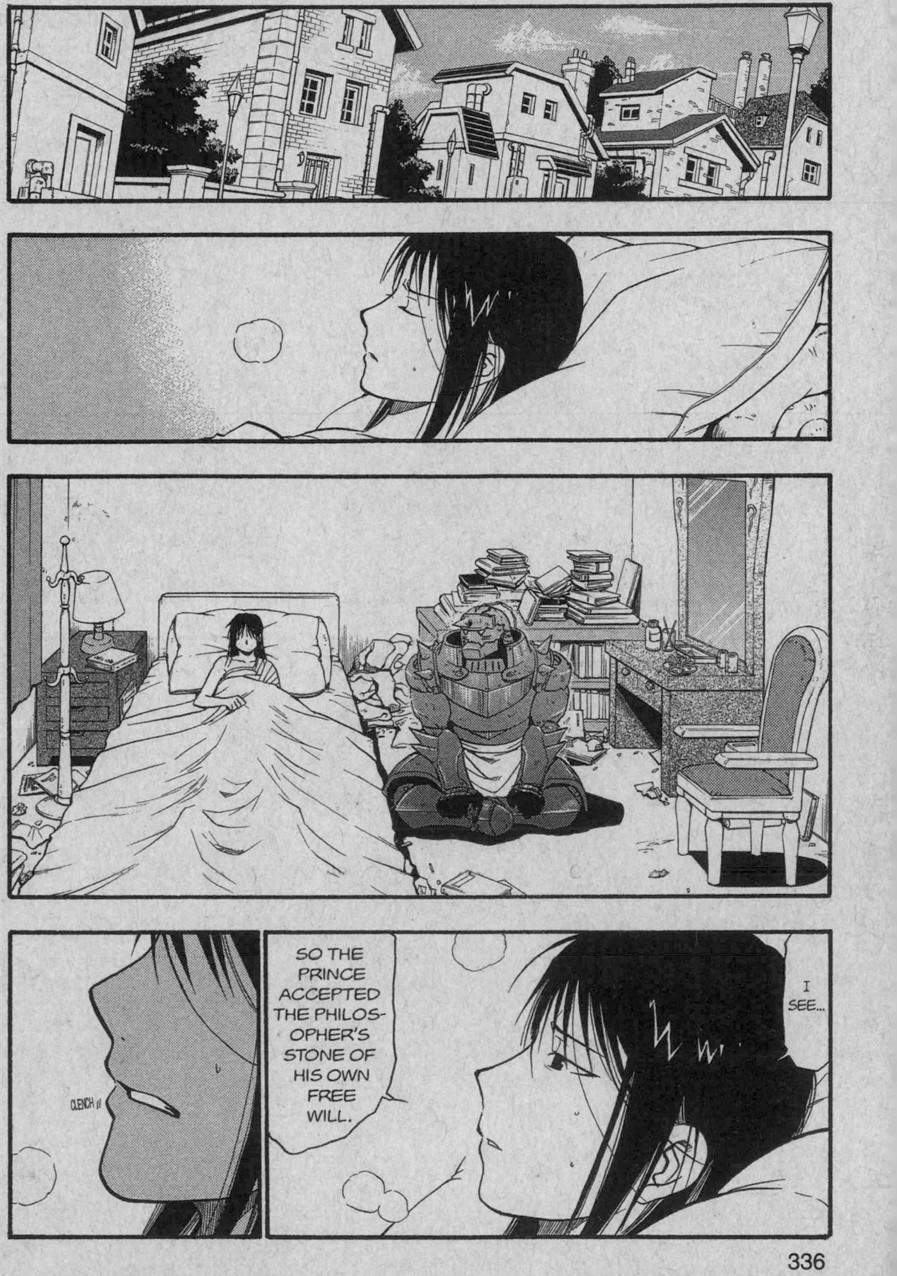
I SEE...
SO THE PRINCE ACCEPTED THE PHILOSOPHER'S STONE OF HIS OWN FREE WILL.
CLENCH

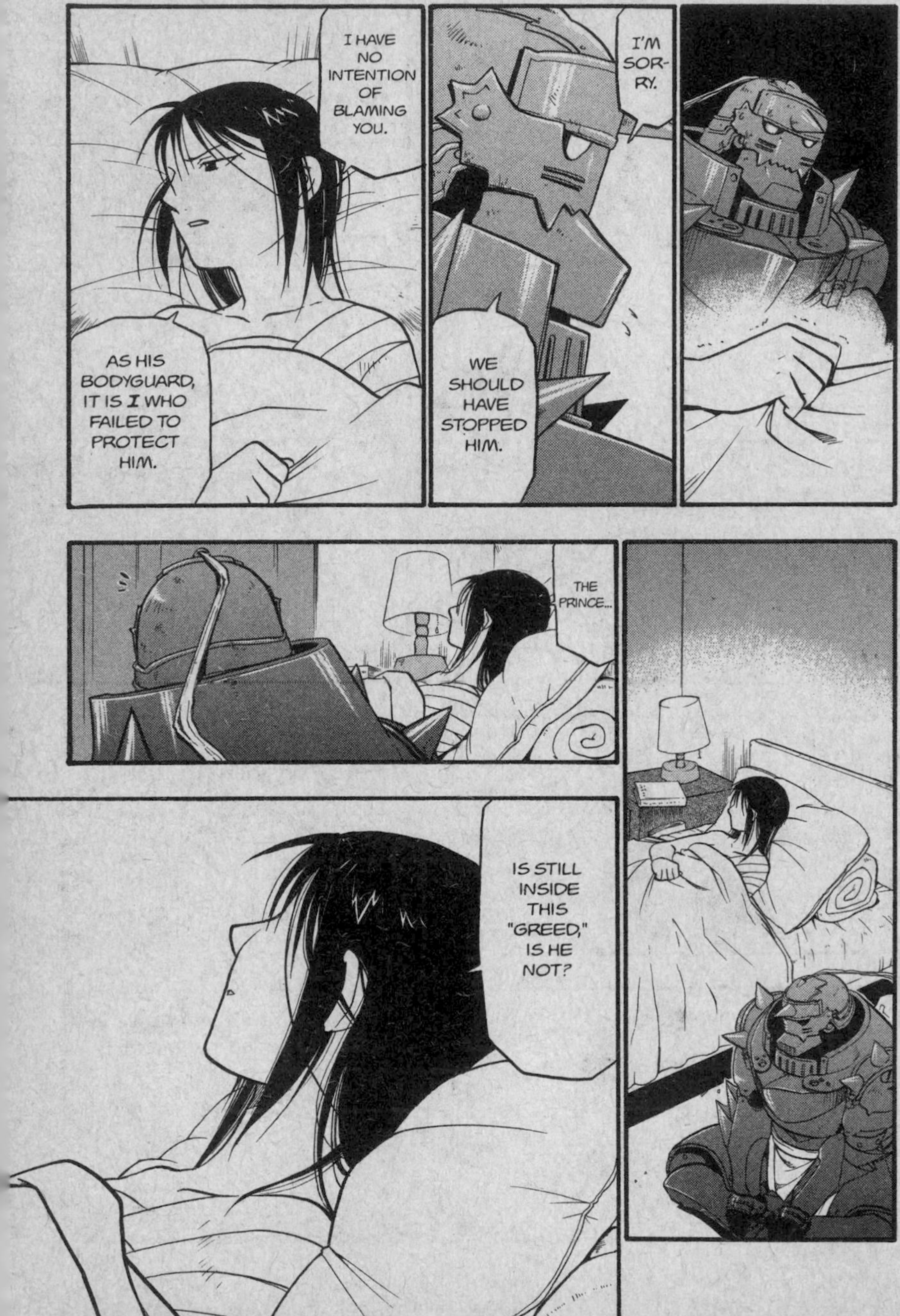
I'M SORRY.
WE SHOULD HAVE STOPPED HIM.
I HAVE NO INTENTION OF BLAMING YOU.
AS HIS BODYGUARD, IT IS I WHO FAILED TO PROTECT HIM.
THE PRINCE...
IS STILL INSIDE THIS "GREED," IS HE NOT?

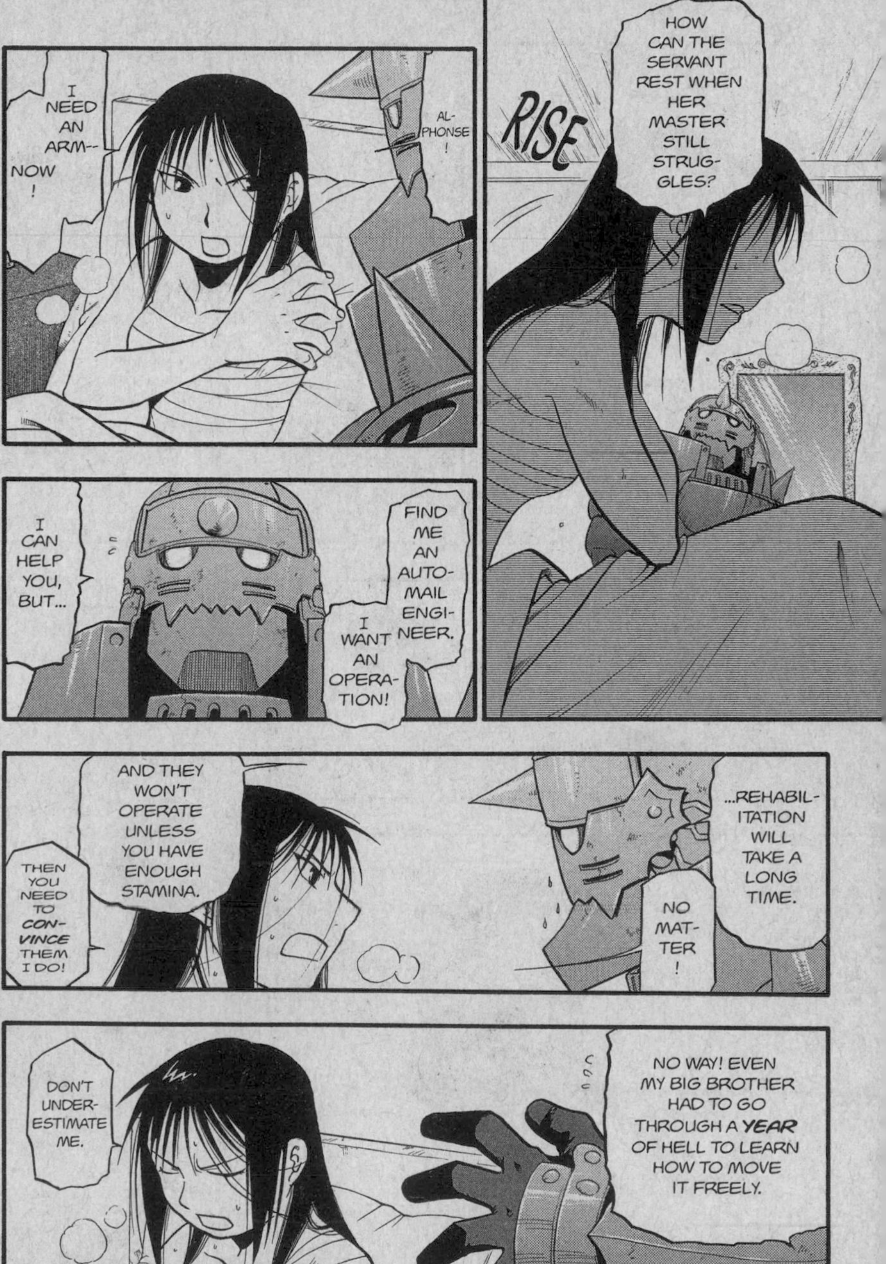
RISE
HOW CAN THE SERVANT REST WHEN HER MASTER STILL STRUGGLES?
ALPHONSE!
I NEED AN ARM-- NOW!
FIND ME AN AUTOMAIL ENGINEER.
I WANT AN OPERATION!
I CAN HELP YOU, BUT...
...REHABILITATION WILL TAKE A LONG TIME.
NO MATTER!
AND THEY WON'T OPERATE UNLESS YOU HAVE ENOUGH STAMINA.
THEN YOU NEED TO CONVINCE THEM I DO!
NO WAY! EVEN MY BIG BROTHER HAD TO GO THROUGH A YEAR OF HELL TO LEARN HOW TO MOVE IT FREELY.
DON'T UNDERESTIMATE ME.

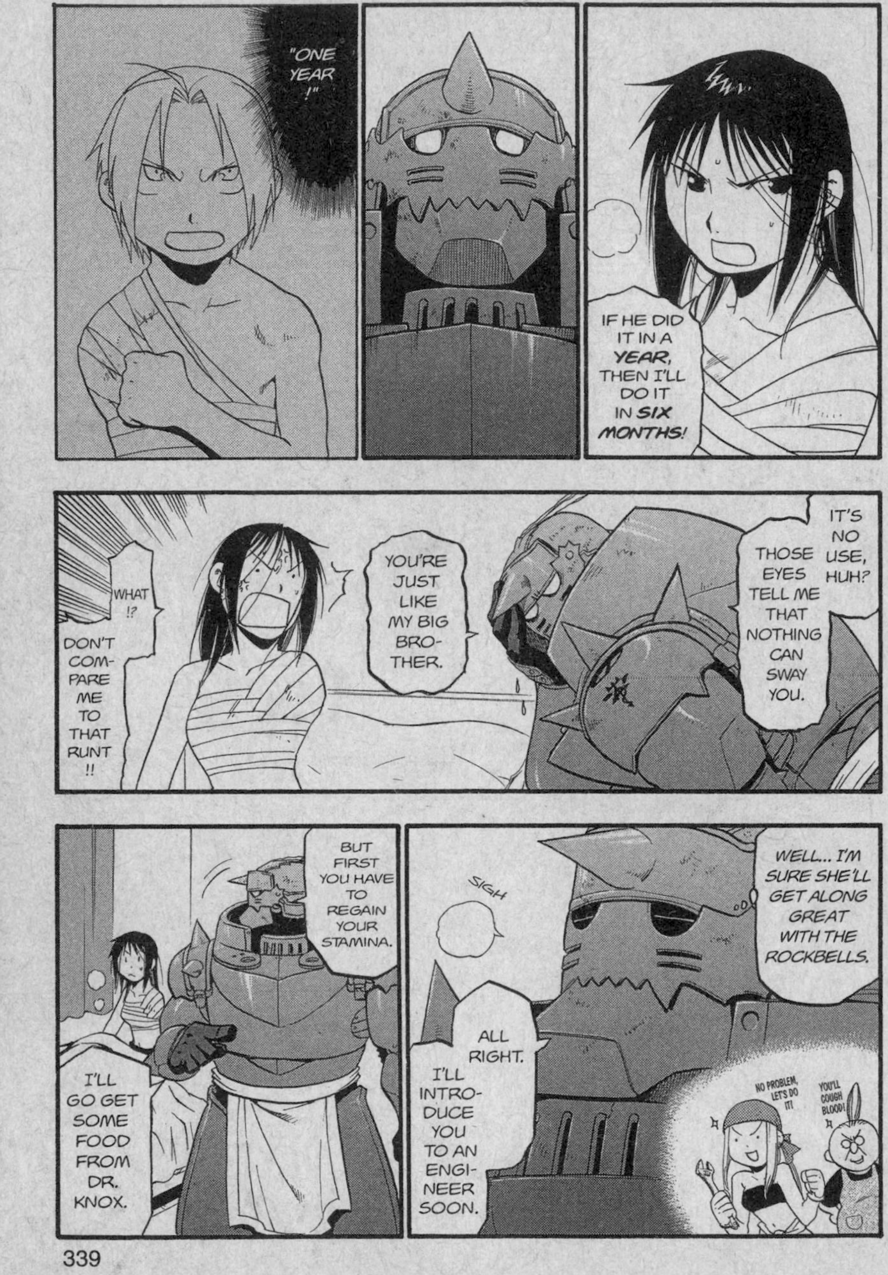
IF HE DID IT IN A YEAR, THEN I'LL DO IT IN SIX MONTHS!
"ONE YEAR!"
IT'S NO USE, HUH?
THOSE EYES TELL ME THAT NOTHING CAN SWAY YOU.
YOU'RE JUST LIKE MY BIG BROTHER.
WHAT!?
DON'T COMPARE ME TO THAT RUNT!!
WELL... I'M SURE SHE'LL GET ALONG GREAT WITH THE ROCKBELLS.
SIGH
ALL RIGHT.
I'LL INTRODUCE YOU TO AN ENGINEER SOON.
YOU'LL COUGH BLOOD!
NO PROBLEM, LET'S DO IT!
BUT FIRST YOU HAVE TO REGAIN YOUR STAMINA.
I'LL GO GET SOME FOOD FROM DR. KNOX.

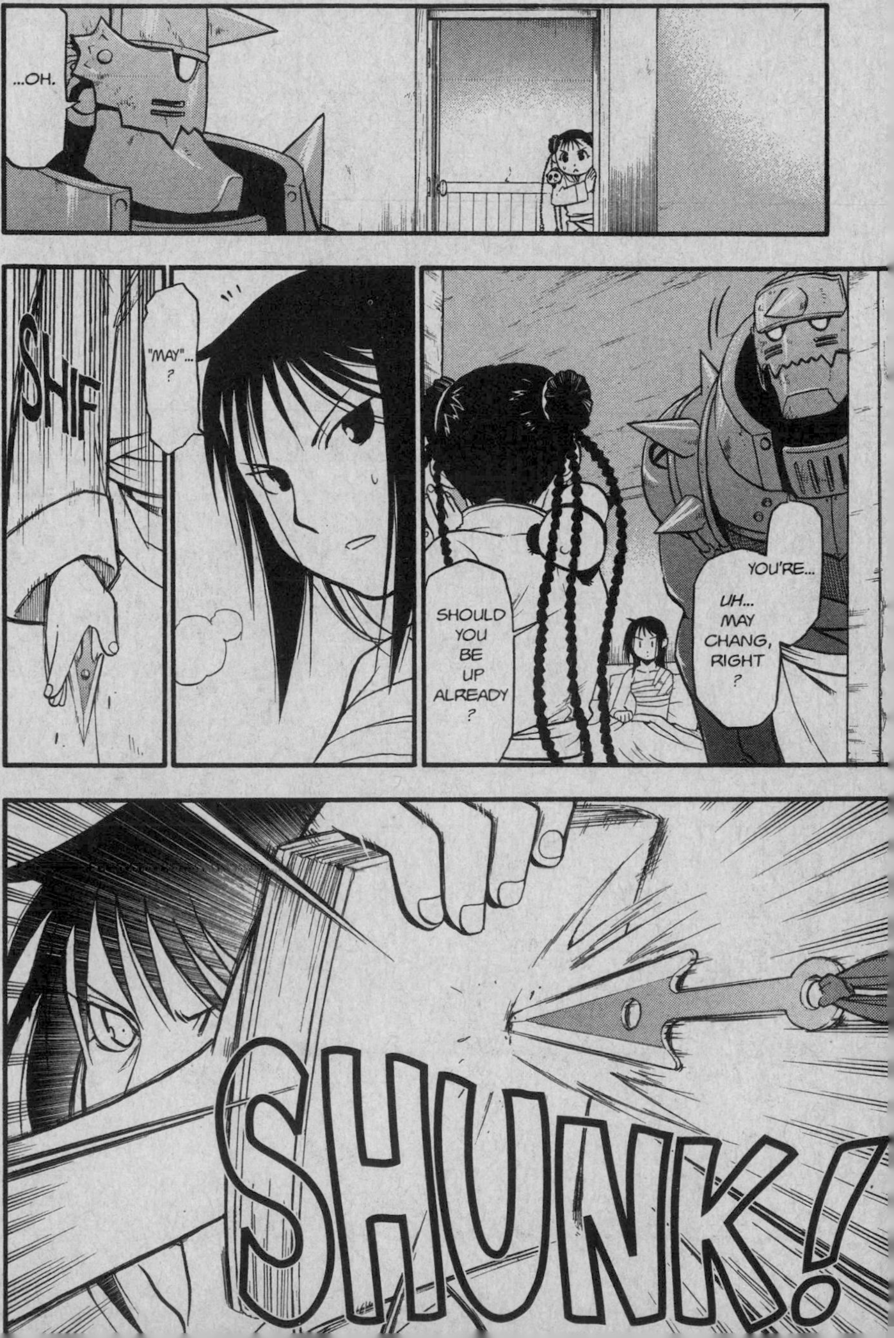
...OH.
YOU'RE... UH... MAY CHANG, RIGHT?
SHOULD YOU BE UP ALREADY?
"MAY"...?
SHIF
SHUNK!

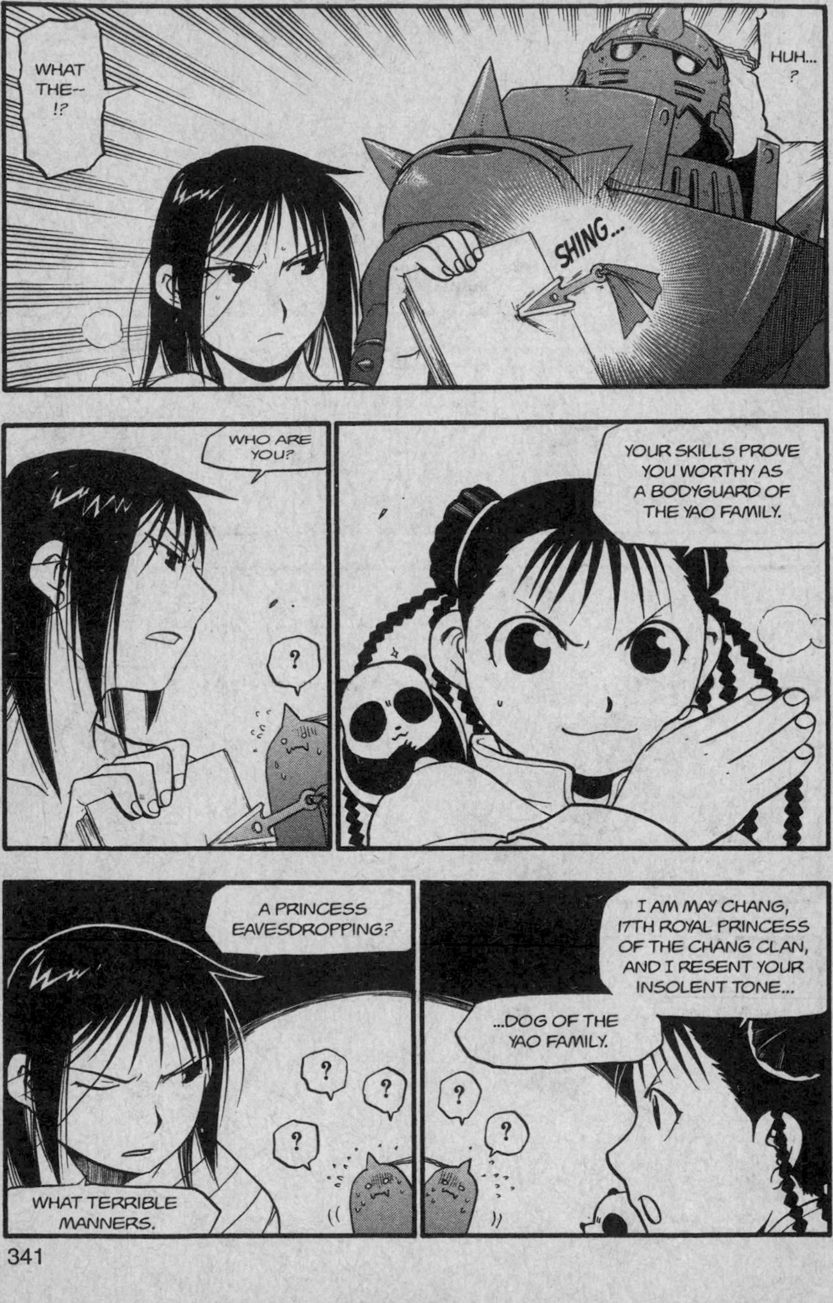
HUH... ?
WHAT THE-- !?
SHING...
YOUR SKILLS PROVE YOU WORTHY AS A BODYGUARD OF THE YAO FAMILY.
WHO ARE YOU?
?
I AM MAY CHANG, 17TH ROYAL PRINCESS OF THE CHANG CLAN, AND I RESENT YOUR INSOLENT TONE...
...DOG OF THE YAO FAMILY.
?
?
A PRINCESS EAVESDROPPING?
?
?
?
WHAT TERRIBLE MANNERS.

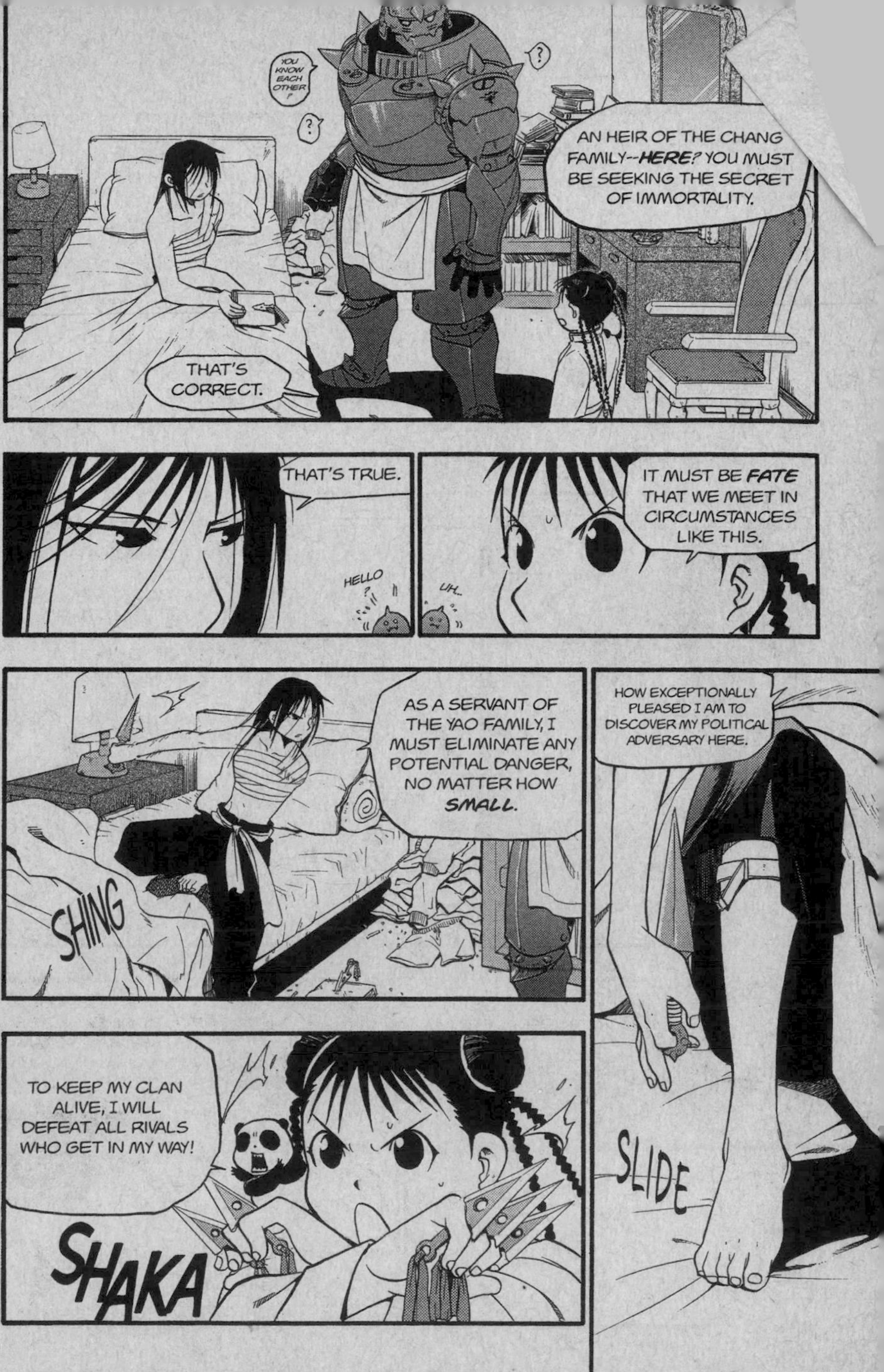
AN HEIR OF THE CHANG FAMILY--HERE? YOU MUST BE SEEKING THE SECRET OF IMMORTALITY.
?
YOU KNOW EACH OTHER?
?
THAT'S CORRECT.
IT MUST BE FATE THAT WE MEET IN CIRCUMSTANCES LIKE THIS.
UH..
THAT'S TRUE.
HELLO?
HOW EXCEPTIONALLY PLEASED I AM TO DISCOVER MY POLITICAL ADVERSARY HERE.
SLIDE
AS A SERVANT OF THE YAO FAMILY, I MUST ELIMINATE ANY POTENTIAL DANGER, NO MATTER HOW SMALL.
SHING
TO KEEP MY CLAN ALIVE, I WILL DEFEAT ALL RIVALS WHO GET IN MY WAY!
SHAKA

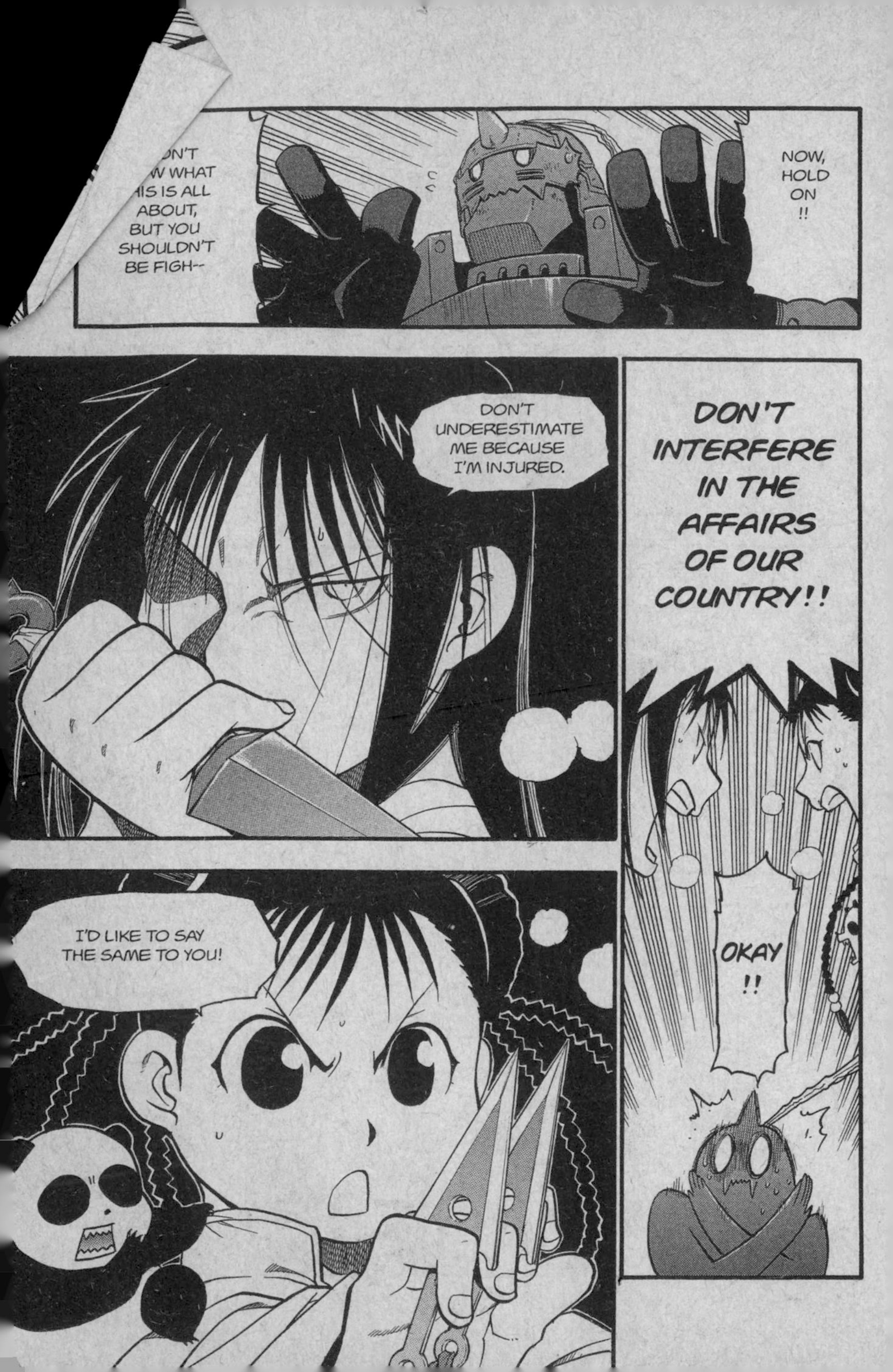
NOW, HOLD ON !!
ON'T W WHAT HIS IS ALL ABOUT, BUT YOU SHOULDN'T BE FIGH--
DON'T INTERFERE IN THE AFFAIRS OF OUR COUNTRY!!
OKAY !!
DON'T UNDERESTIMATE ME BECAUSE I'M INJURED.
I'D LIKE TO SAY THE SAME TO YOU!

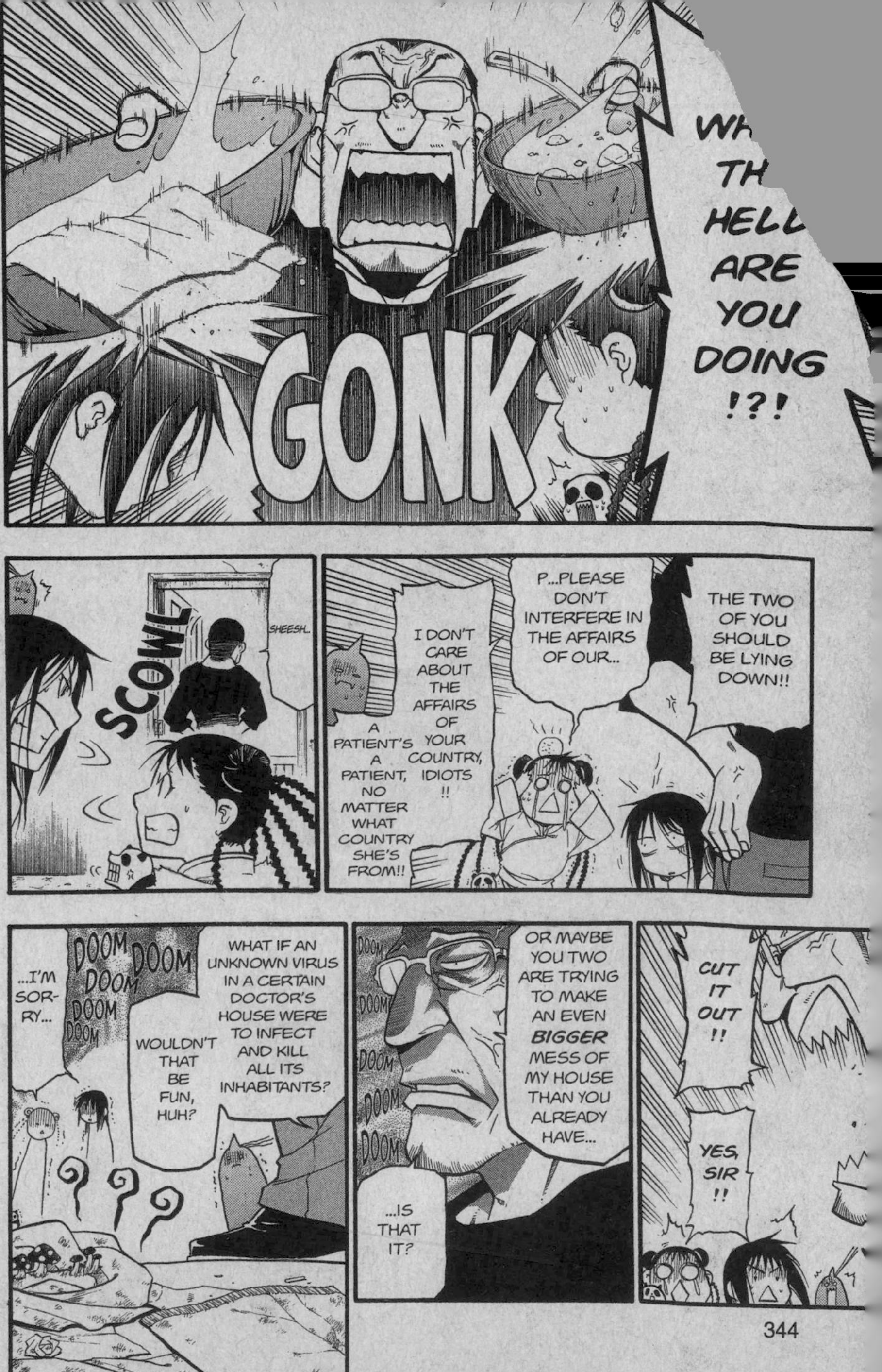
HELL ARE YOU DOING !?!
GONK
THE TWO OF YOU SHOULD BE LYING DOWN!!
P...PLEASE DON'T INTERFERE IN THE AFFAIRS OF OUR...
I DON'T CARE ABOUT THE AFFAIRS OF YOUR COUNTRY, IDIOTS!!
A PATIENT'S A PATIENT, NO MATTER WHAT COUNTRY SHE'S FROM!!
SHEESH..
SCOWL
CUT IT OUT!!
YES, SIR!!
OR MAYBE YOU TWO ARE TRYING TO MAKE AN EVEN BIGGER MESS OF MY HOUSE THAN YOU ALREADY HAVE...
...IS THAT IT?
DOOM DOOM DOOM DOOM DOOM
WHAT IF AN UNKNOWN VIRUS IN A CERTAIN DOCTOR'S HOUSE WERE TO INFECT AND KILL ALL ITS INHABITANTS?
WOULDN'T THAT BE FUN, HUH?
DOOM DOOM DOOM DOOM DOOM
...I'M SORRY...

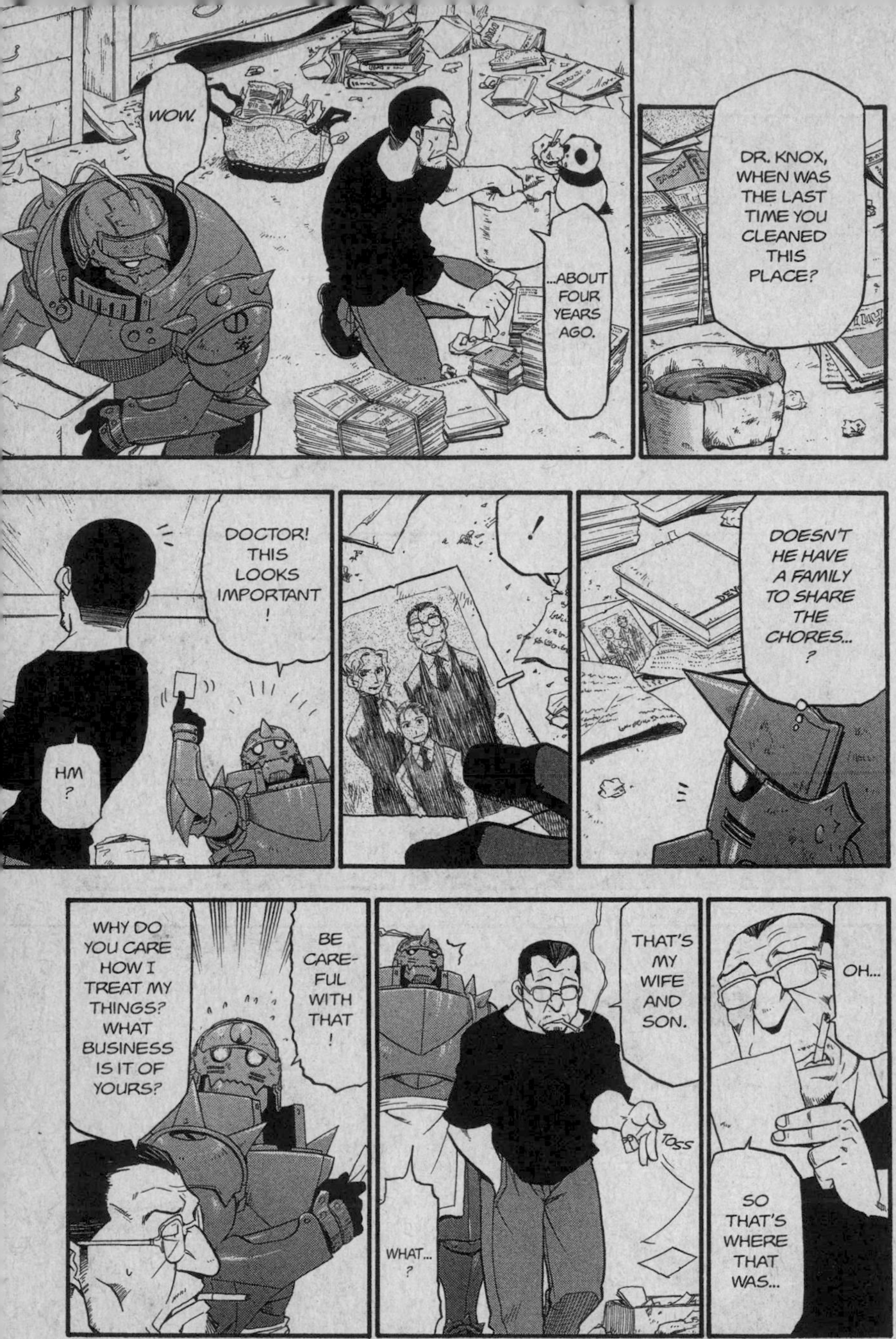
DR. KNOX, WHEN WAS THE LAST TIME YOU CLEANED THIS PLACE?
...ABOUT FOUR YEARS AGO.
WOW.
DOESN'T HE HAVE A FAMILY TO SHARE THE CHORES...?
!
DOCTOR! THIS LOOKS IMPORTANT!
HM?
OH...
SO THAT'S WHERE THAT WAS...
THAT'S MY WIFE AND SON.
TOSS
WHAT...?
BE CAREFUL WITH THAT!
WHY DO YOU CARE HOW I TREAT MY THINGS? WHAT BUSINESS IS IT OF YOURS?

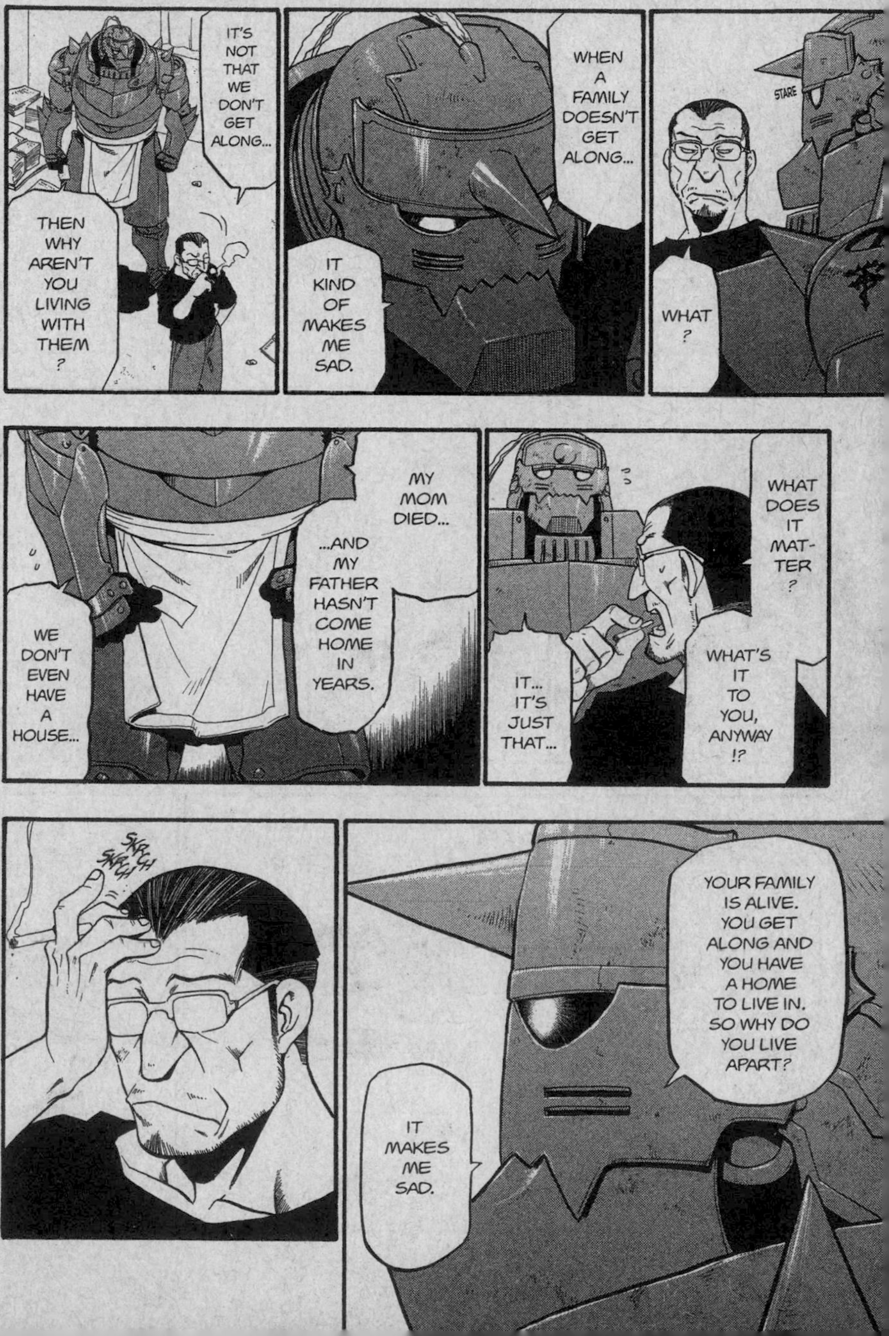
STARE
WHAT?
WHEN A FAMILY DOESN'T GET ALONG...
IT KIND OF MAKES ME SAD.
IT'S NOT THAT WE DON'T GET ALONG...
THEN WHY AREN'T YOU LIVING WITH THEM?
WHAT DOES IT MAT-TER?
WHAT'S IT TO YOU, ANYWAY!?
IT... IT'S JUST THAT...
MY MOM DIED...
...AND MY FATHER HASN'T COME HOME IN YEARS.
WE DON'T EVEN HAVE A HOUSE...
YOUR FAMILY IS ALIVE. YOU GET ALONG AND YOU HAVE A HOME TO LIVE IN. SO WHY DO YOU LIVE APART?
IT MAKES ME SAD.
SKRCH SKRCH

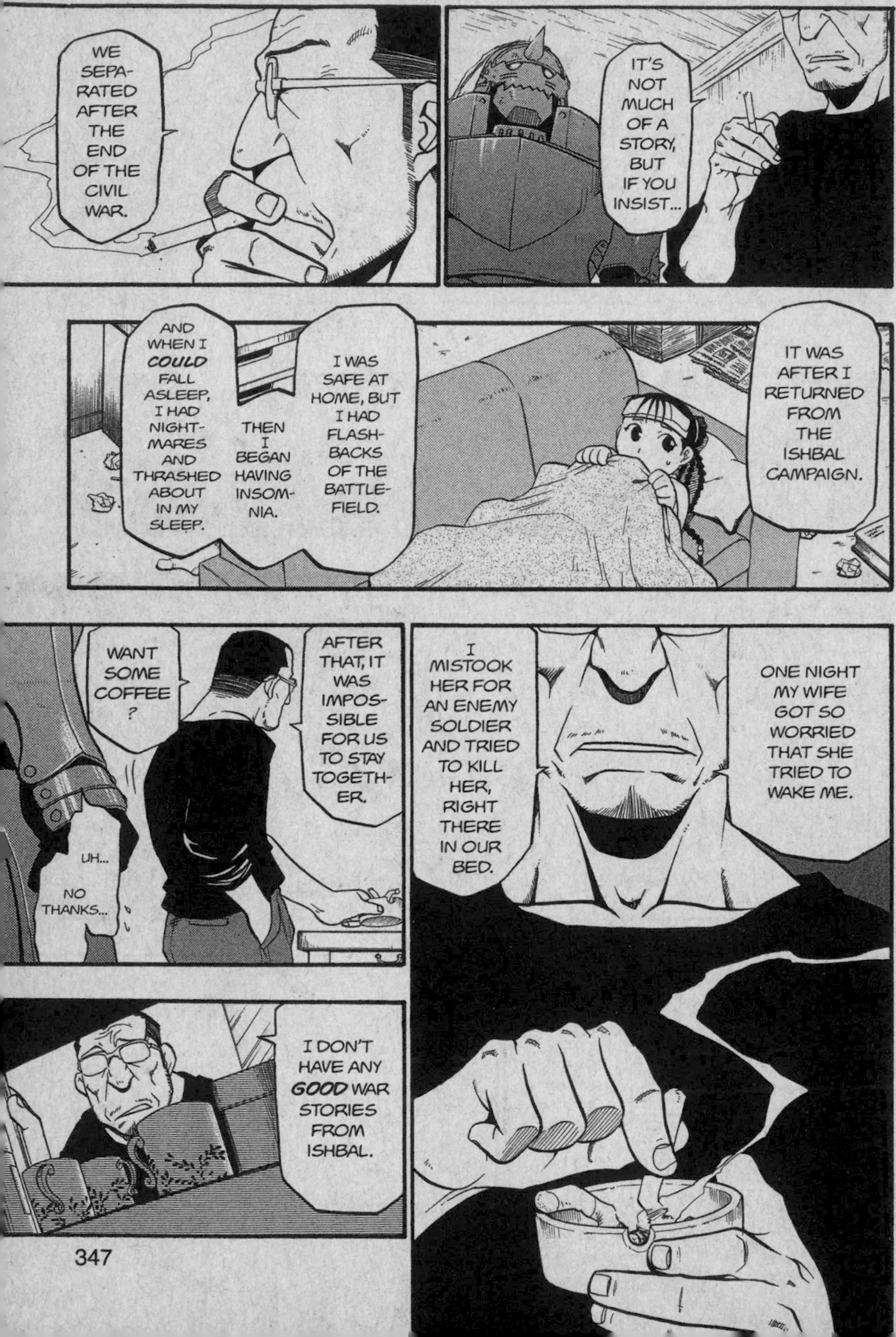
IT'S NOT MUCH OF A STORY, BUT IF YOU INSIST...
WE SEPARATED AFTER THE END OF THE CIVIL WAR.
IT WAS AFTER I RETURNED FROM THE ISHBAL CAMPAIGN.
I WAS SAFE AT HOME, BUT I HAD FLASHBACKS OF THE BATTLEFIELD.
THEN I BEGAN HAVING INSOMNIA.
AND WHEN I ***COULD*** FALL ASLEEP, I HAD NIGHTMARES AND THRASHED ABOUT IN MY SLEEP.
ONE NIGHT MY WIFE GOT SO WORRIED THAT SHE TRIED TO WAKE ME.
I MISTOOK HER FOR AN ENEMY SOLDIER AND TRIED TO KILL HER, RIGHT THERE IN OUR BED.
AFTER THAT, IT WAS IMPOSSIBLE FOR US TO STAY TOGETHER.
WANT SOME COFFEE?
UH...
NO THANKS...
I DON'T HAVE ANY ***GOOD*** WAR STORIES FROM ISHBAL.

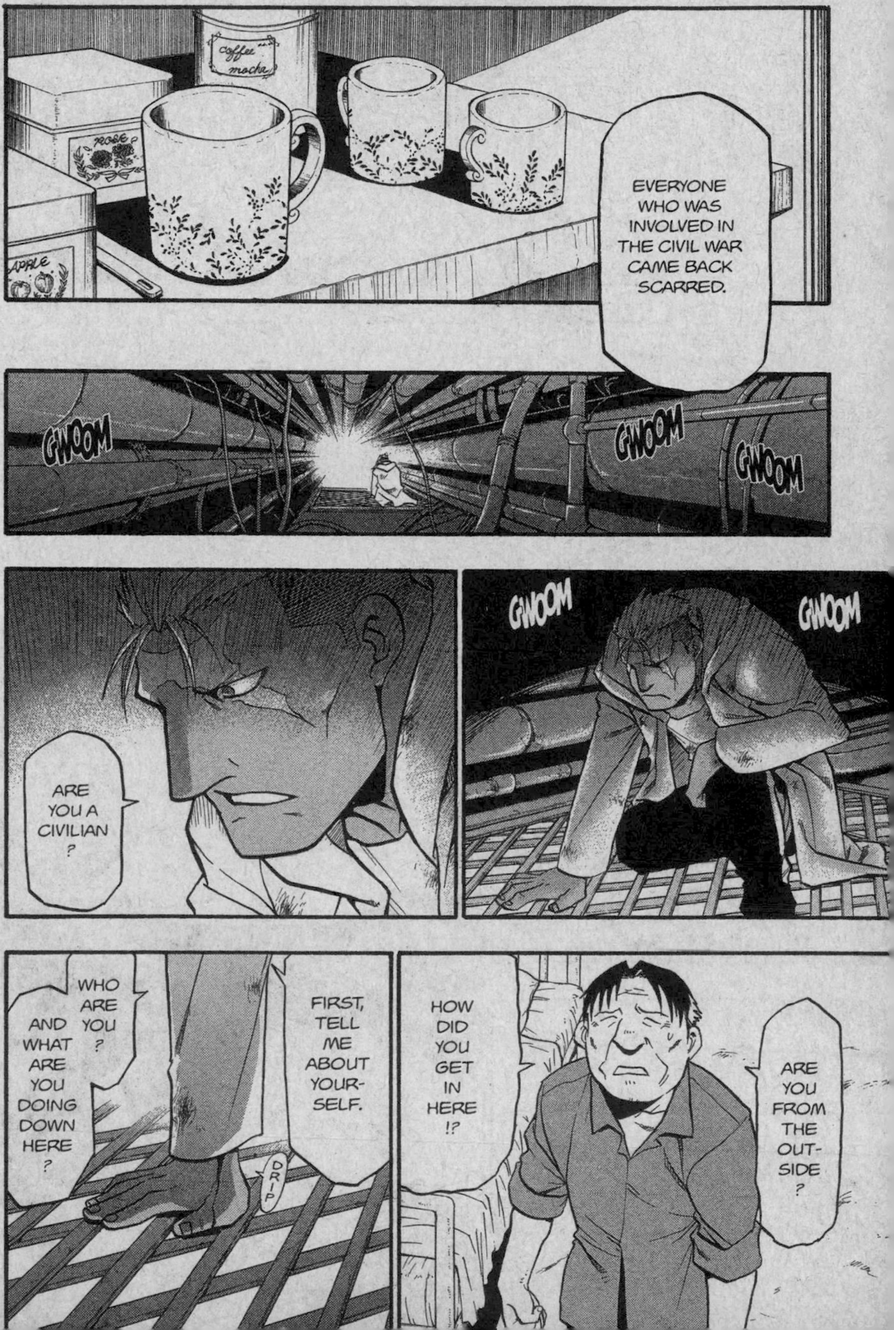
coffee mocha
ROSE
APPLE
EVERYONE WHO WAS INVOLVED IN THE CIVIL WAR CAME BACK SCARRED.
GWOOM
GWOOM
GWOOM
GWOOM
GWOOM
ARE YOU A CIVILIAN?
ARE YOU FROM THE OUT-SIDE?
HOW DID YOU GET IN HERE!?
FIRST, TELL ME ABOUT YOUR-SELF.
WHO ARE YOU?
AND WHAT ARE YOU DOING DOWN HERE?
DRIP

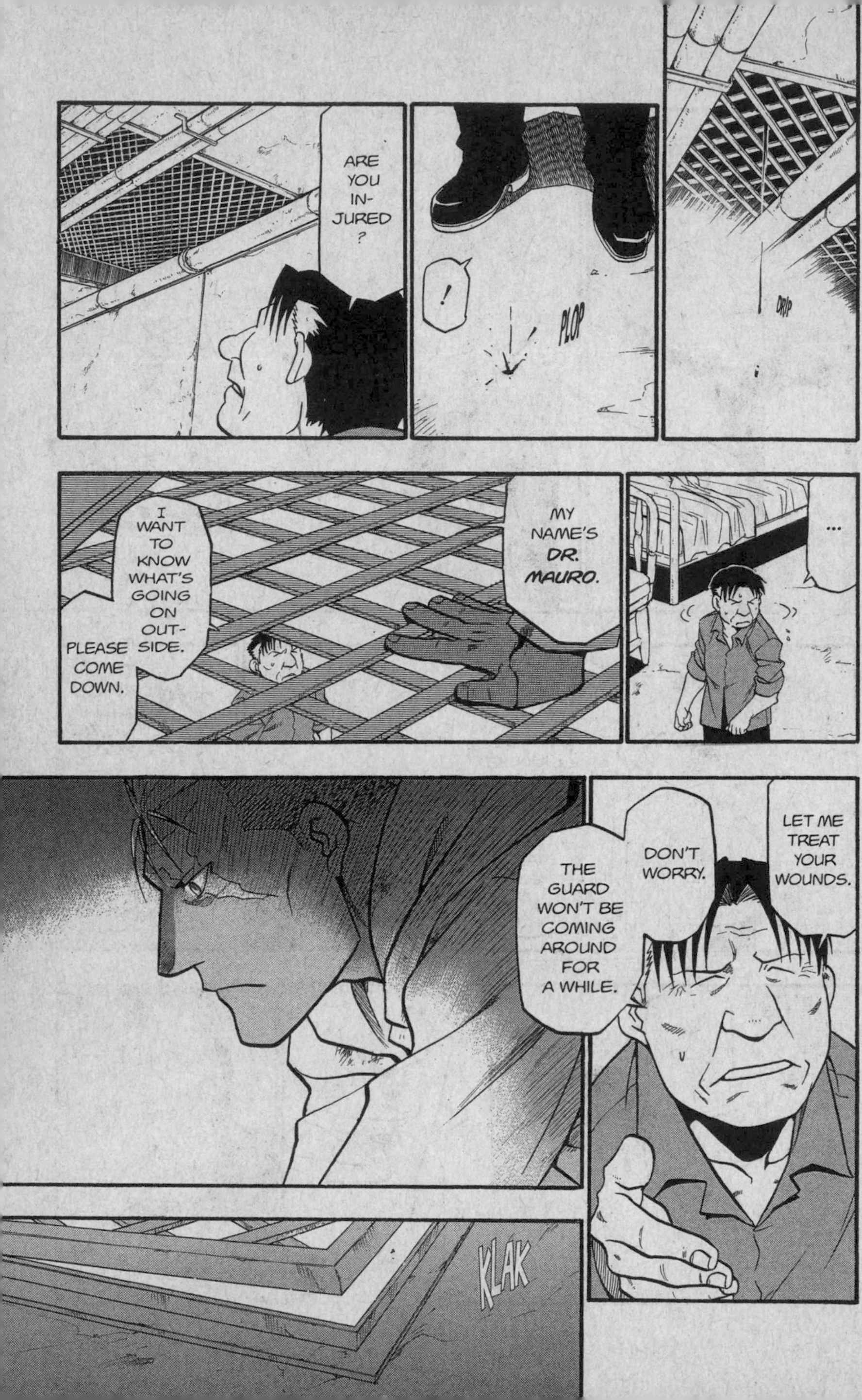
DRIP
PLOP
!
ARE YOU INJURED?
...
MY NAME'S DR. MAURO.
I WANT TO KNOW WHAT'S GOING ON OUTSIDE.
PLEASE COME DOWN.
LET ME TREAT YOUR WOUNDS.
DON'T WORRY.
THE GUARD WON'T BE COMING AROUND FOR A WHILE.
KLAK

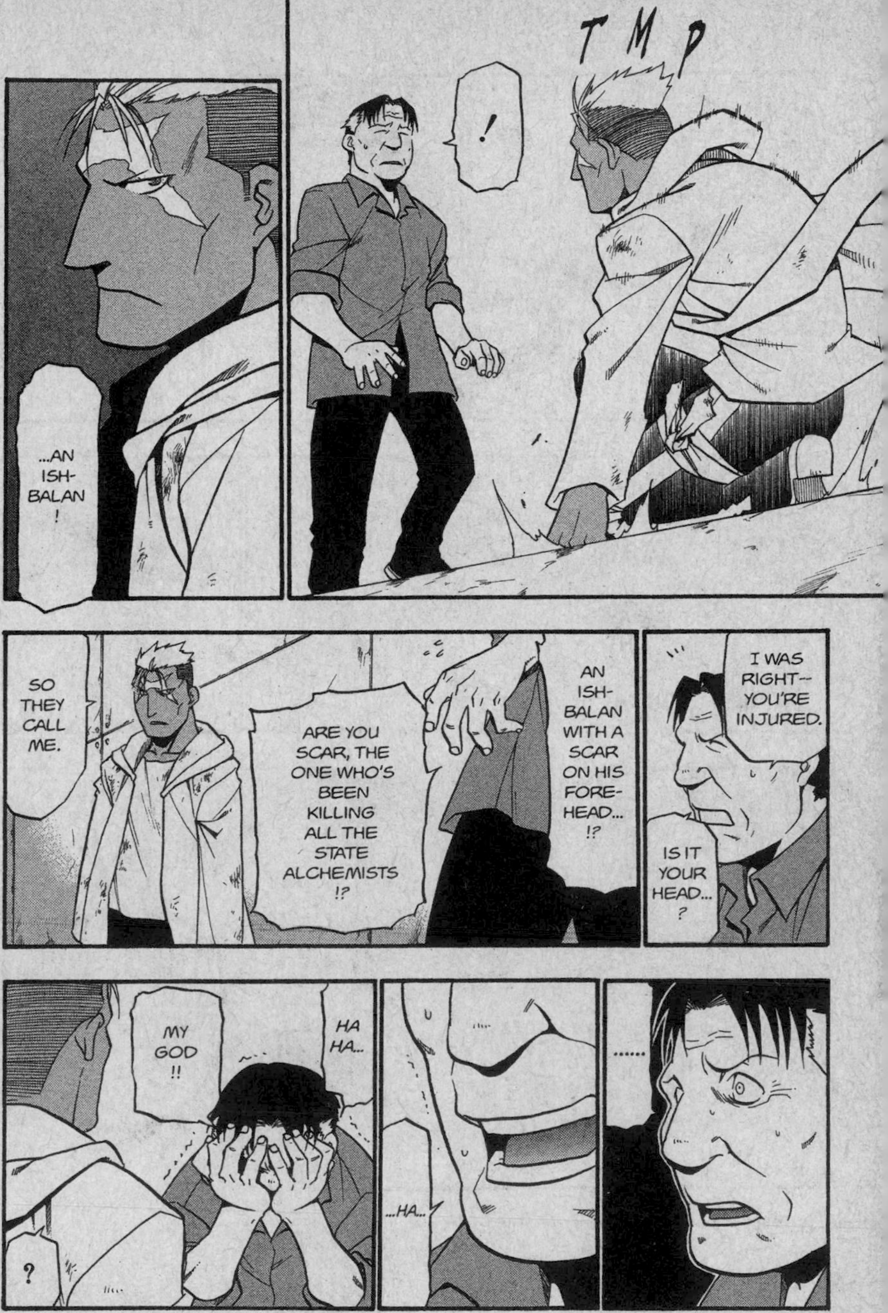
TMP
!
...AN ISH-BALAN!
I WAS RIGHT--YOU'RE INJURED.
IS IT YOUR HEAD...?
AN ISH-BALAN WITH A SCAR ON HIS FORE-HEAD...!?
ARE YOU SCAR, THE ONE WHO'S BEEN KILLING ALL THE STATE ALCHEMISTS!?
SO THEY CALL ME.
......
...HA...
HA HA...
MY GOD!!
?

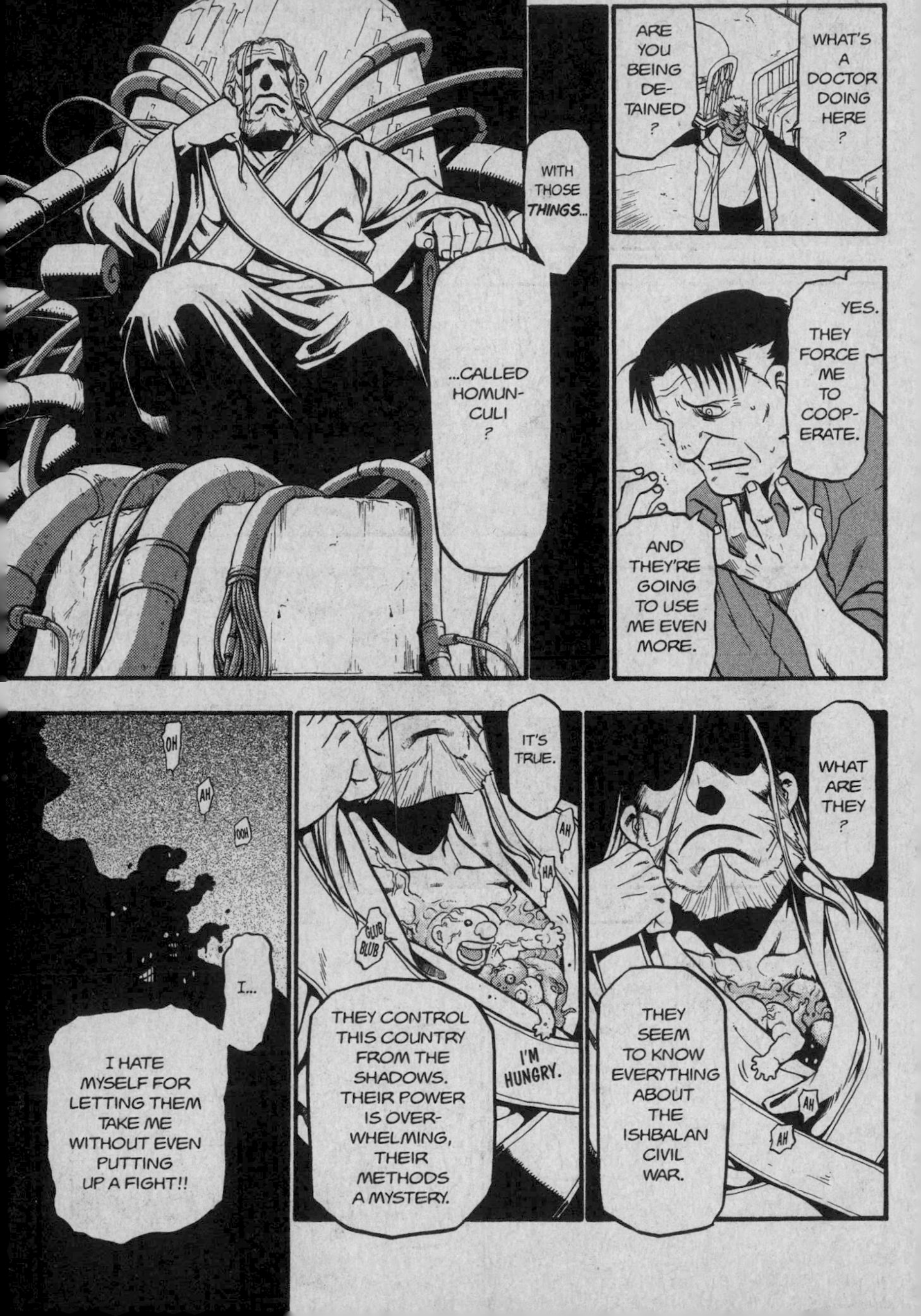
WHAT'S A DOCTOR DOING HERE?
ARE YOU BEING DE-TAINED?
YES. THEY FORCE ME TO COOP-ERATE.
AND THEY'RE GOING TO USE ME EVEN MORE.
WITH THOSE THINGS...
...CALLED HOMUN-CULI?
WHAT ARE THEY?
THEY SEEM TO KNOW EVERYTHING ABOUT THE ISHBALAN CIVIL WAR.
AH
AH
IT'S TRUE.
AH
HA
GLUB BLUB
THEY CONTROL THIS COUNTRY FROM THE SHADOWS. THEIR POWER IS OVER-WHELMING, THEIR METHODS A MYSTERY.
I'M HUNGRY.
OH
AH
OOH
I...
I HATE MYSELF FOR LETTING THEM TAKE ME WITHOUT EVEN PUTTING UP A FIGHT!!

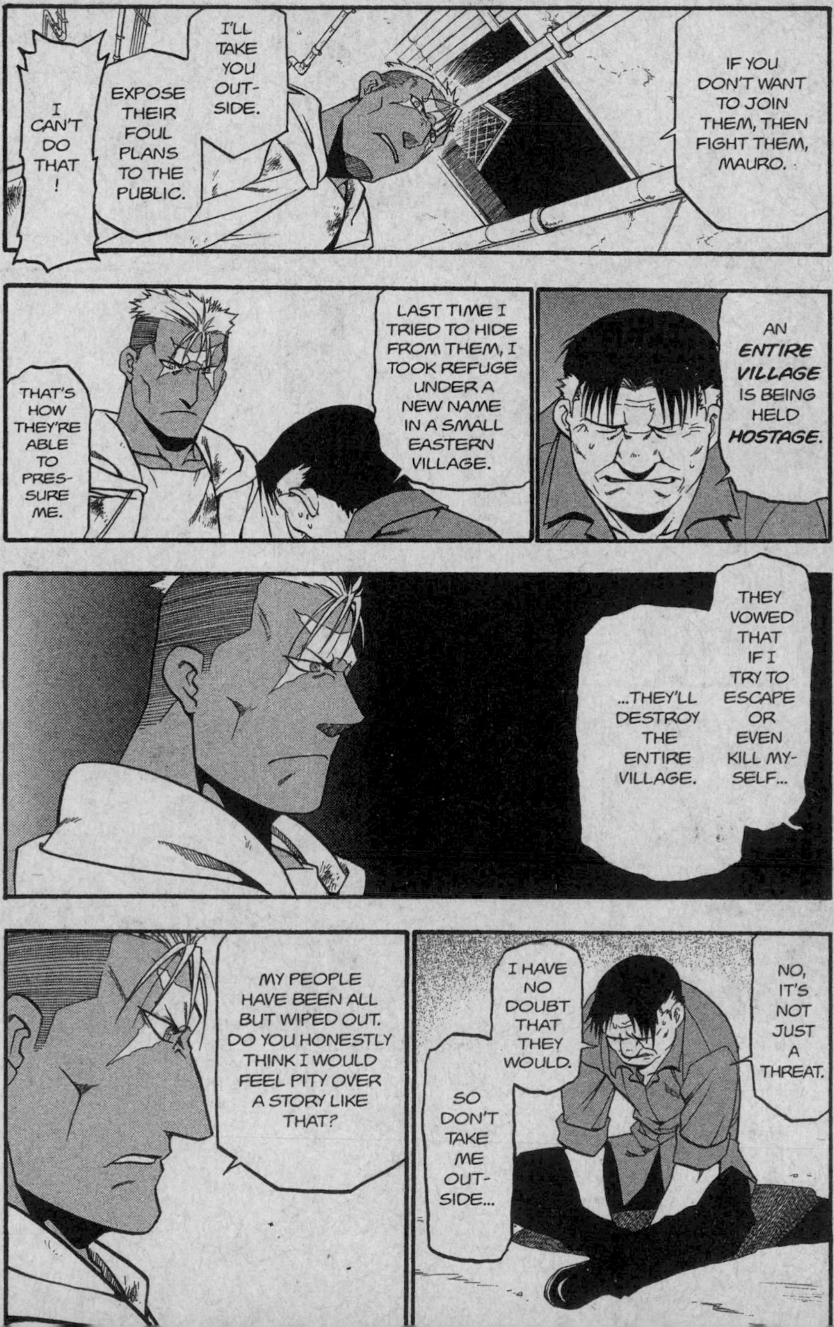
IF YOU DON'T WANT TO JOIN THEM, THEN FIGHT THEM, MAURO.
I'LL TAKE YOU OUT-SIDE.
EXPOSE THEIR FOUL PLANS TO THE PUBLIC.
I CAN'T DO THAT!
AN *ENTIRE VILLAGE* IS BEING HELD *HOSTAGE*.
LAST TIME I TRIED TO HIDE FROM THEM, I TOOK REFUGE UNDER A NEW NAME IN A SMALL EASTERN VILLAGE.
THAT'S HOW THEY'RE ABLE TO PRES-SURE ME.
THEY VOWED THAT IF I TRY TO ESCAPE OR EVEN KILL MY-SELF...
...THEY'LL DESTROY THE ENTIRE VILLAGE.
NO, IT'S NOT JUST A THREAT.
I HAVE NO DOUBT THAT THEY WOULD.
SO DON'T TAKE ME OUT-SIDE...
MY PEOPLE HAVE BEEN ALL BUT WIPED OUT. DO YOU HONESTLY THINK I WOULD FEEL PITY OVER A STORY LIKE THAT?

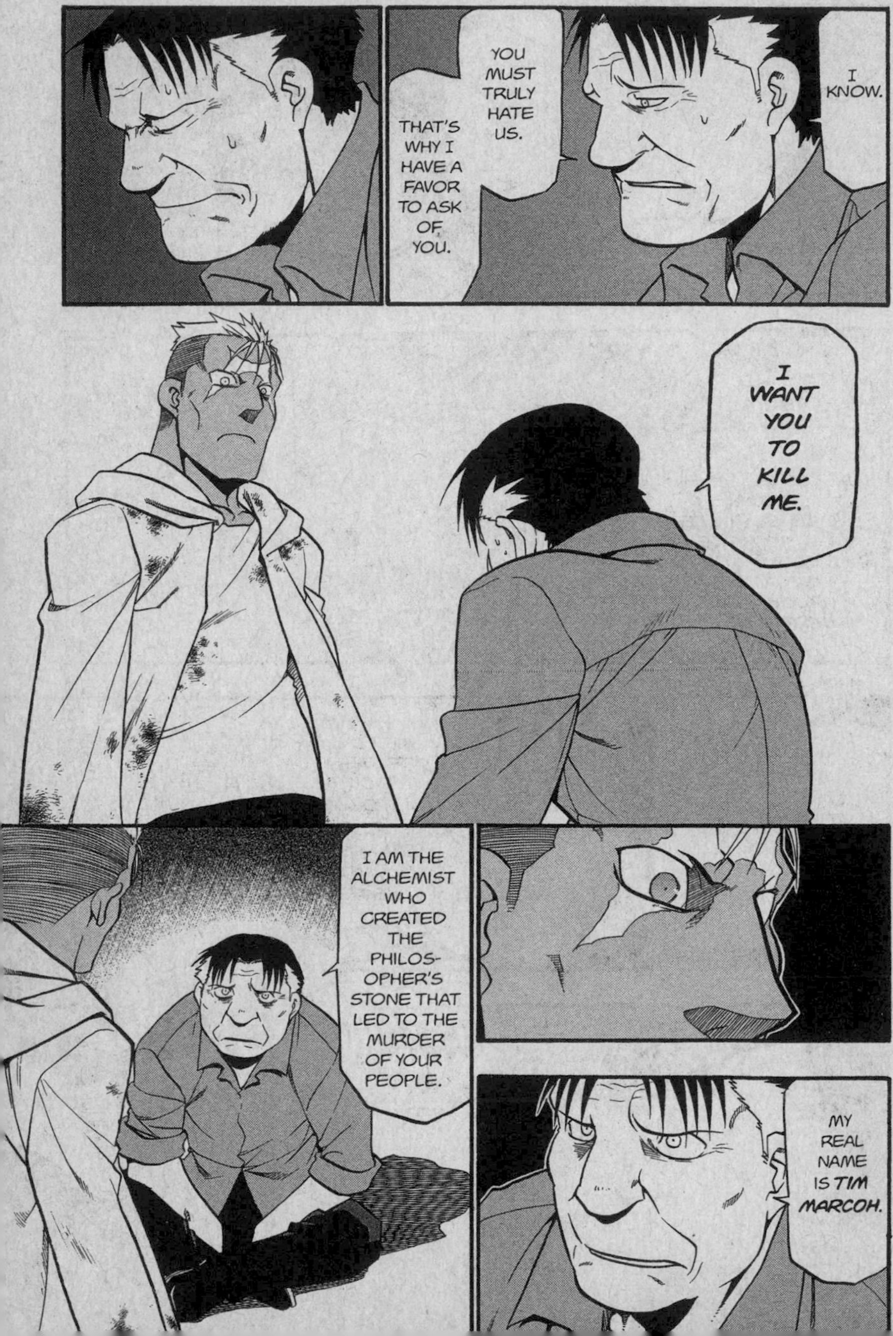
I KNOW.
YOU MUST TRULY HATE US.
THAT'S WHY I HAVE A FAVOR TO ASK OF YOU.
I WANT YOU TO KILL ME.
MY REAL NAME IS TIM MARCOH.
I AM THE ALCHEMIST WHO CREATED THE PHILOSOPHER'S STONE THAT LED TO THE MURDER OF YOUR PEOPLE.

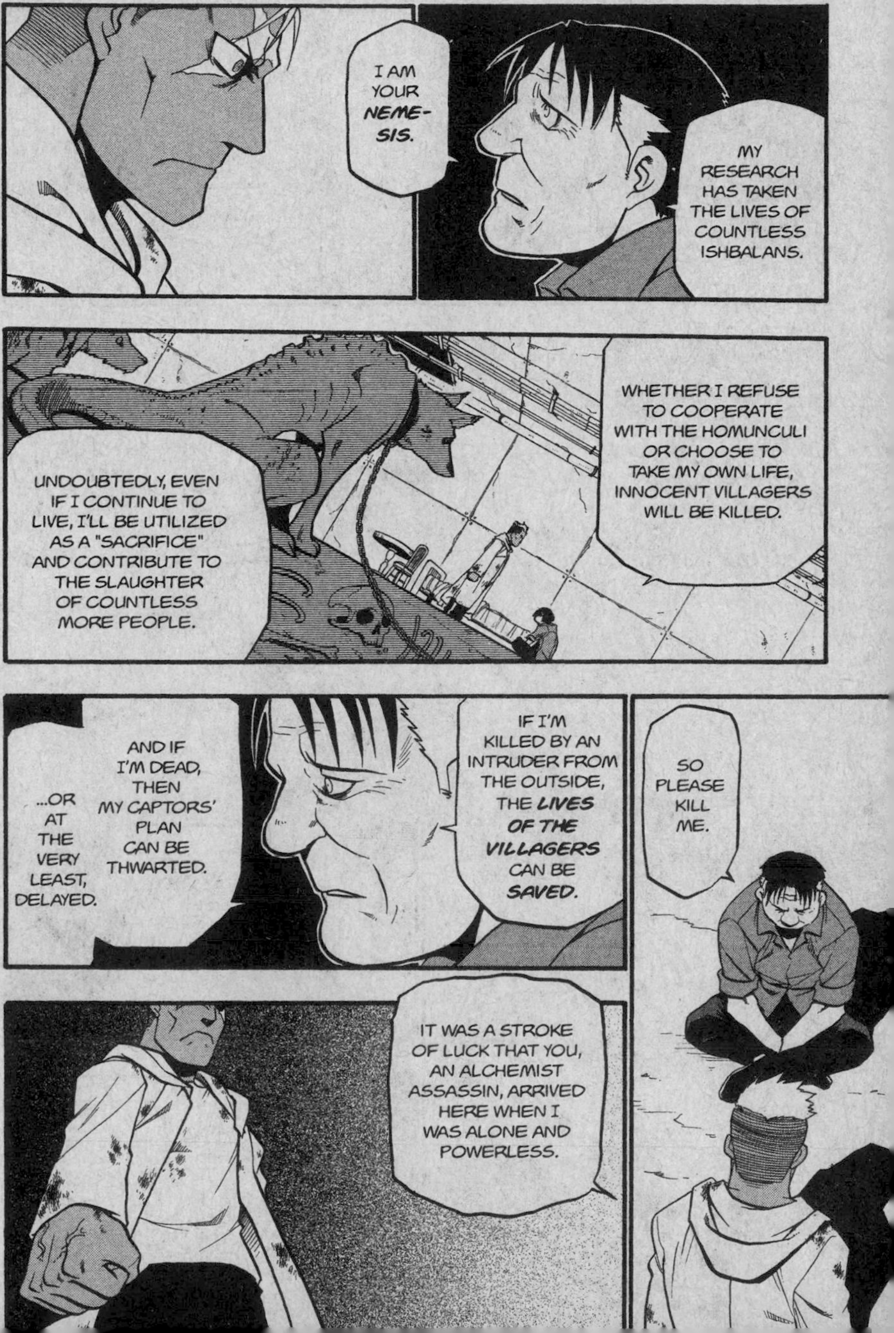
MY RESEARCH HAS TAKEN THE LIVES OF COUNTLESS ISHBALANS.
I AM YOUR ***NEMESIS.***
WHETHER I REFUSE TO COOPERATE WITH THE HOMUNCULI OR CHOOSE TO TAKE MY OWN LIFE, INNOCENT VILLAGERS WILL BE KILLED.
UNDOUBTEDLY, EVEN IF I CONTINUE TO LIVE, I'LL BE UTILIZED AS A "SACRIFICE" AND CONTRIBUTE TO THE SLAUGHTER OF COUNTLESS MORE PEOPLE.
SO PLEASE KILL ME.
IF I'M KILLED BY AN INTRUDER FROM THE OUTSIDE, THE ***LIVES OF THE VILLAGERS*** CAN BE ***SAVED.***
AND IF I'M DEAD, THEN MY CAPTORS' PLAN CAN BE THWARTED.
...OR AT THE VERY LEAST, DELAYED.
IT WAS A STROKE OF LUCK THAT YOU, AN ALCHEMIST ASSASSIN, ARRIVED HERE WHEN I WAS ALONE AND POWERLESS.

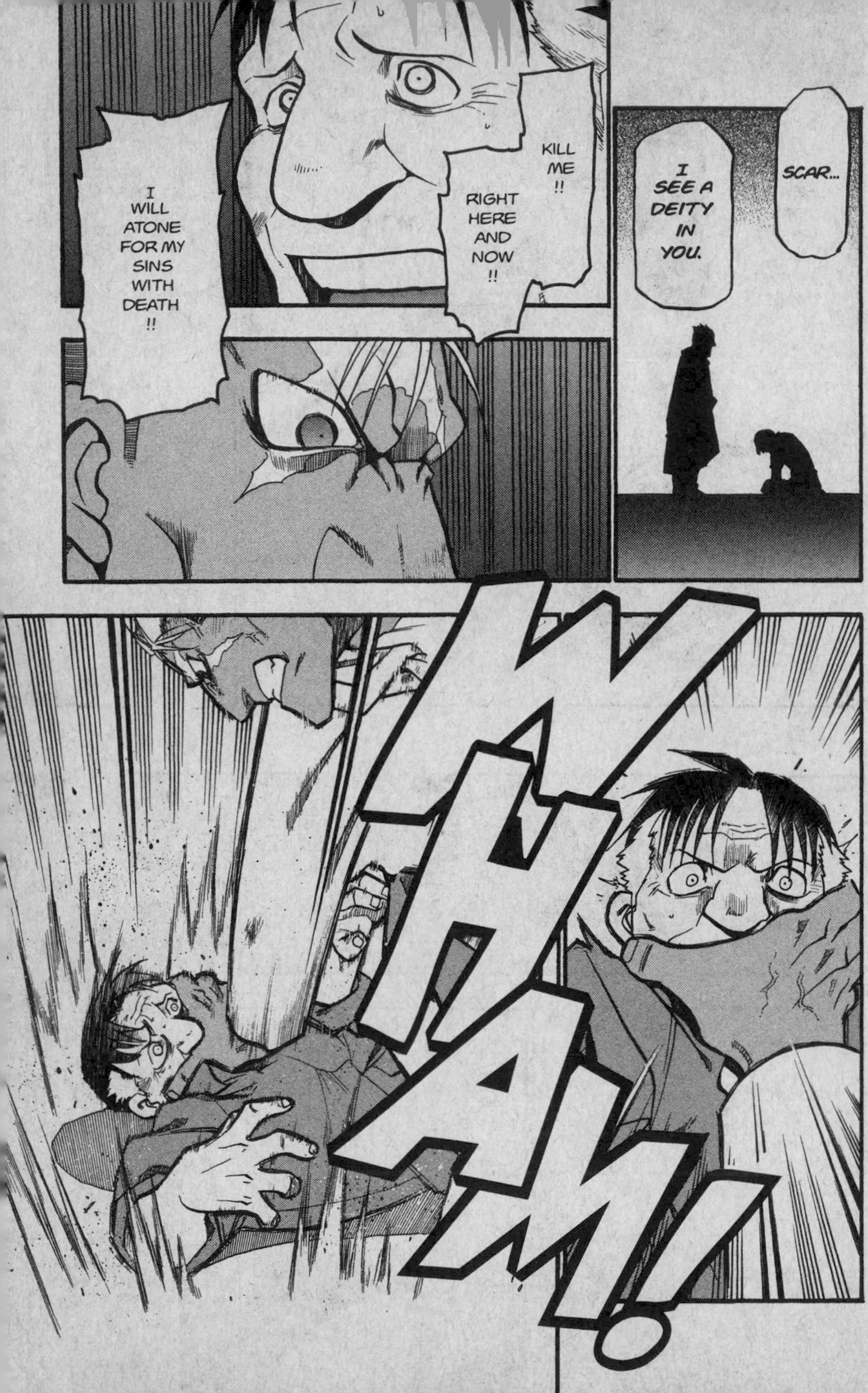

SCAR...
I SEE A DEITY IN YOU.
KILL ME!!
RIGHT HERE AND NOW!!
I WILL ATONE FOR MY SINS WITH DEATH!!
WHAM!

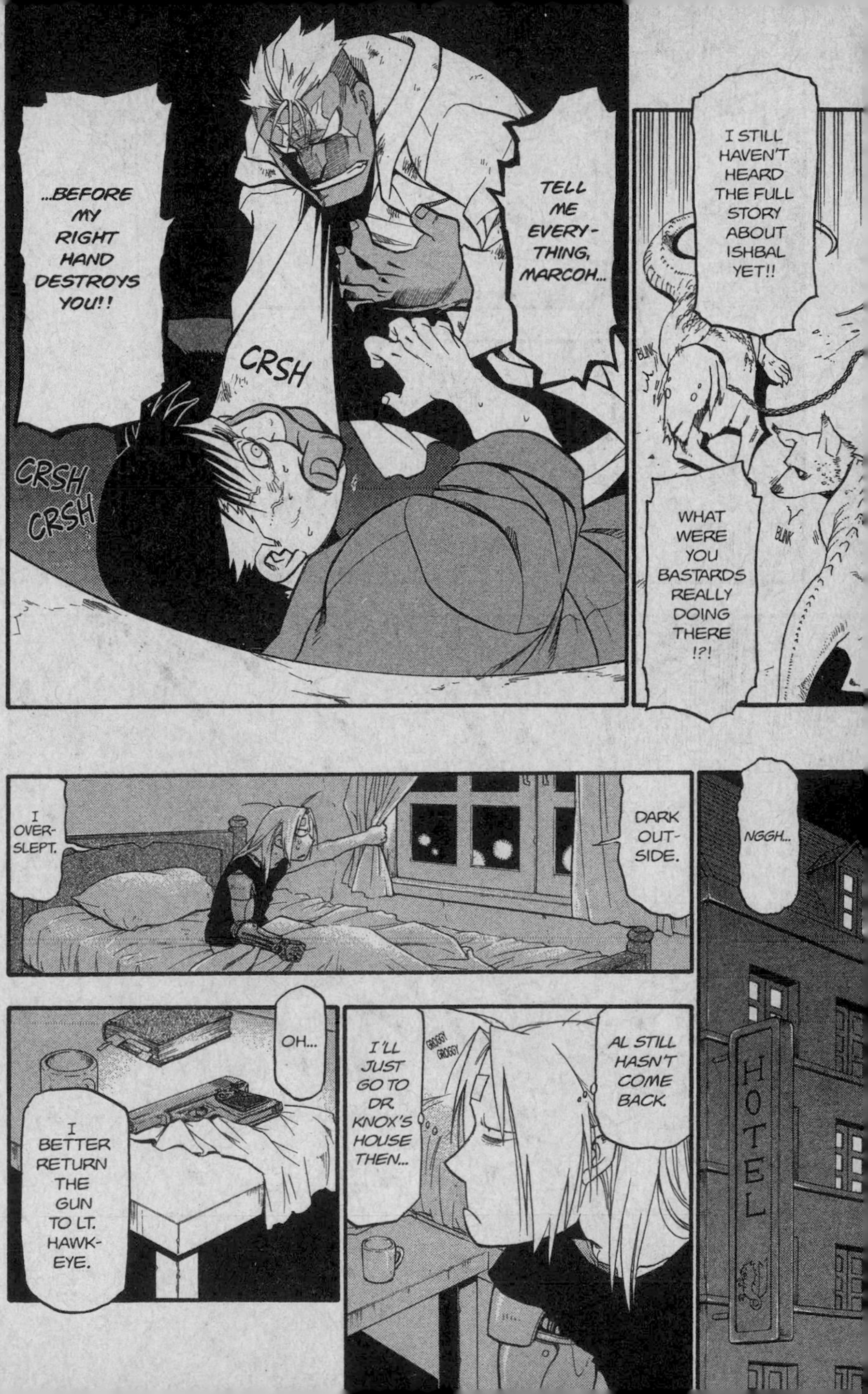
I STILL HAVEN'T HEARD THE FULL STORY ABOUT ISHBAL YET!!
BLINK
WHAT WERE YOU BASTARDS REALLY DOING THERE !?!
BLINK
TELL ME EVERY-THING, MARCOH...
...BEFORE MY RIGHT HAND DESTROYS YOU!!
CRSH
CRSH CRSH
NGGH...
HOTEL
DARK OUT-SIDE.
I OVER-SLEPT.
AL STILL HASN'T COME BACK.
GROGGY GROGGY
I'LL JUST GO TO DR. KNOX'S HOUSE THEN...
OH...
I BETTER RETURN THE GUN TO LT. HAWK-EYE.

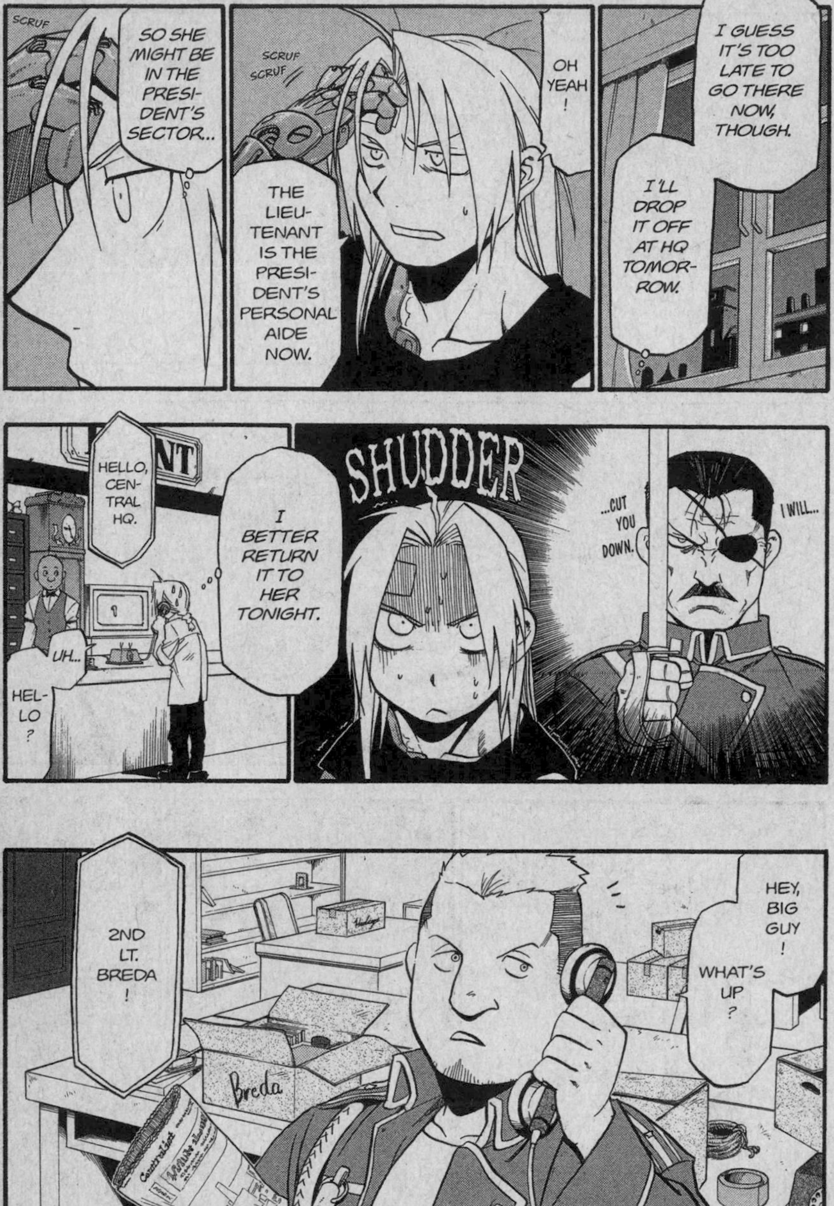
I GUESS IT'S TOO LATE TO GO THERE NOW, THOUGH.
I'LL DROP IT OFF AT HQ TOMORROW.
OH YEAH!
SCRUF SCRUF
THE LIEUTENANT IS THE PRESIDENT'S PERSONAL AIDE NOW.
SCRUF
SO SHE MIGHT BE IN THE PRESIDENT'S SECTOR...
I BETTER RETURN IT TO HER TONIGHT.
SHUDDER
I WILL...
...CUT YOU DOWN.
HELLO, CENTRAL HQ.
UH...
HELLO?
HEY, BIG GUY!
WHAT'S UP?
2ND LT. BREDA!
Breda

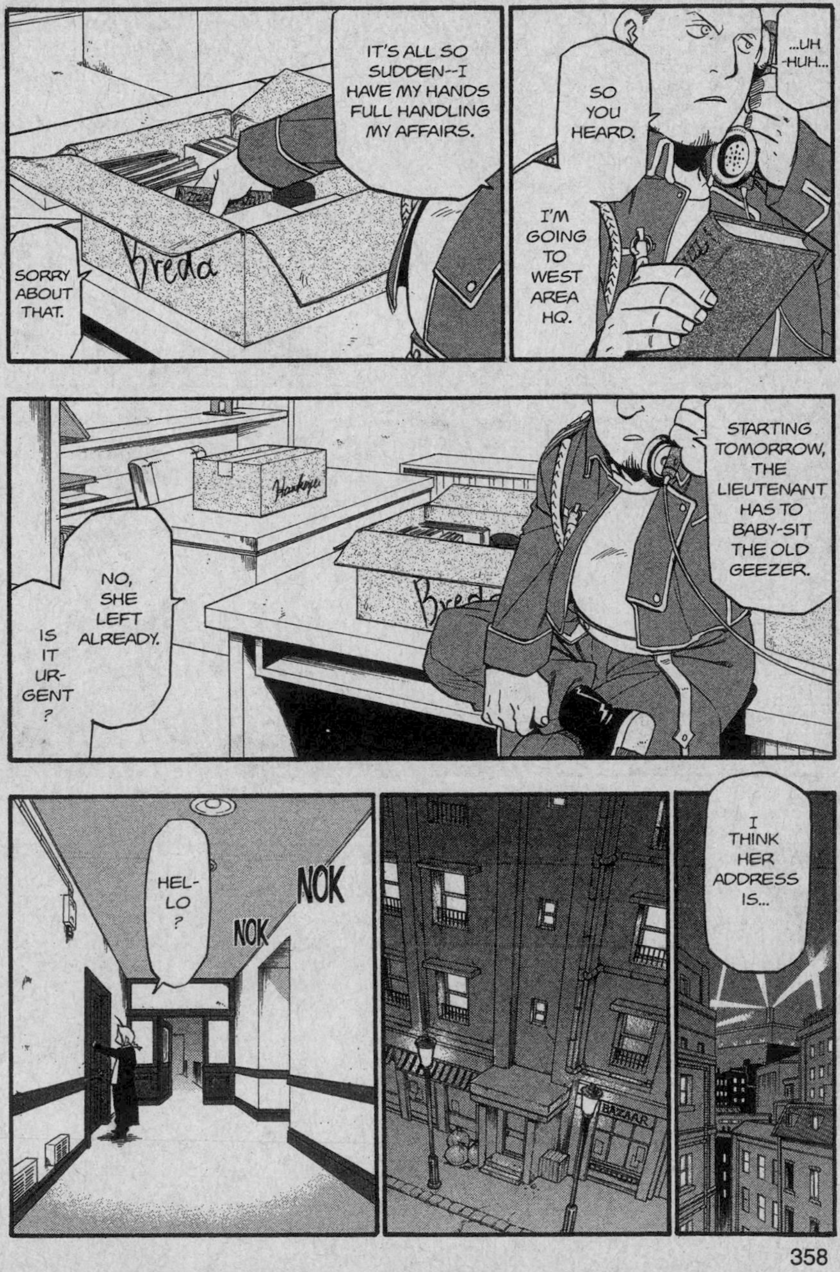
...UH -HUH...
SO YOU HEARD.
I'M GOING TO WEST AREA HQ.
IT'S ALL SO SUDDEN--I HAVE MY HANDS FULL HANDLING MY AFFAIRS.
Breda
SORRY ABOUT THAT.
STARTING TOMORROW, THE LIEUTENANT HAS TO BABY-SIT THE OLD GEEZER.
Hawkeye
NO, SHE LEFT ALREADY.
IS IT URGENT?
I THINK HER ADDRESS IS...
BAZAAR
NOK
NOK
HELLO?

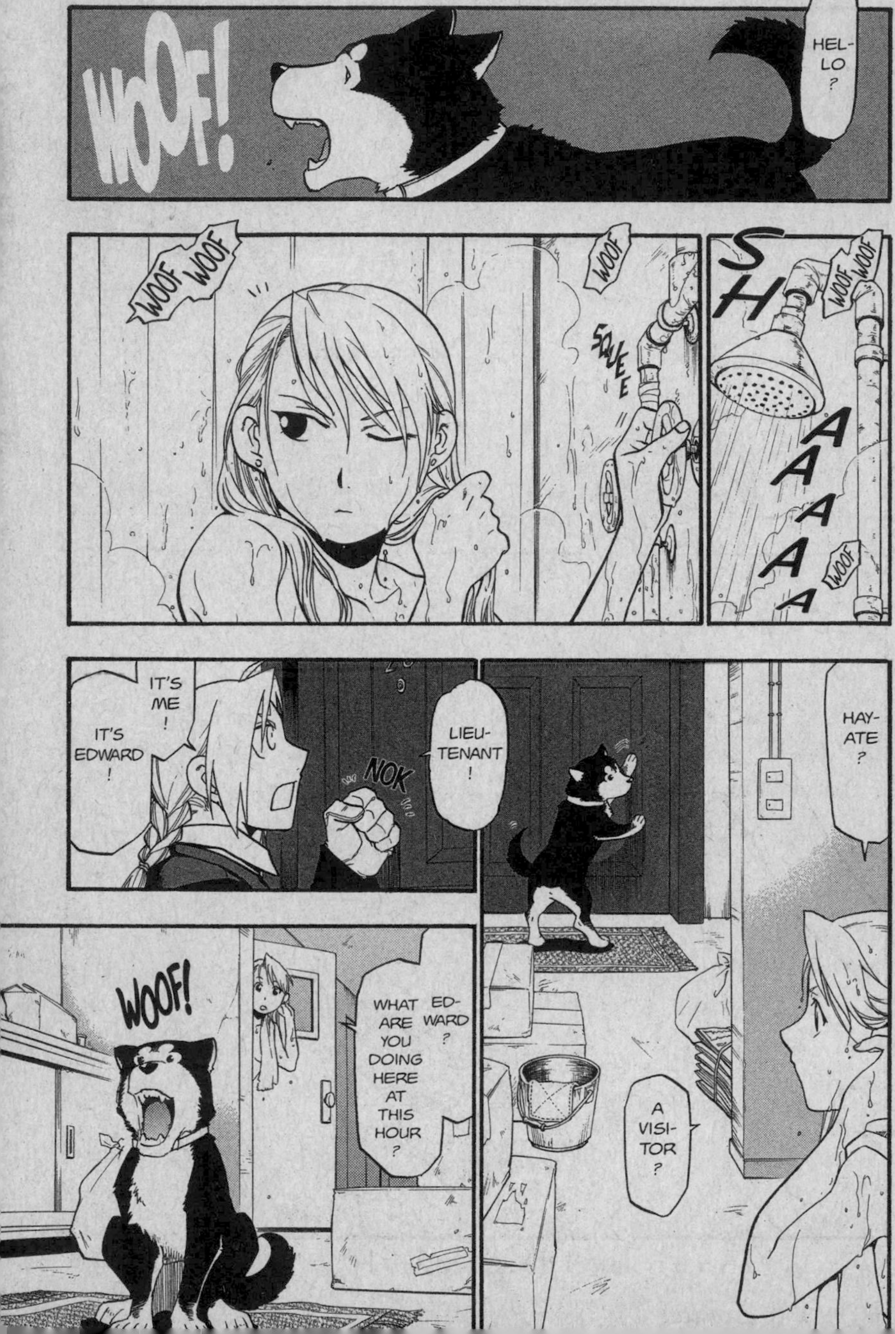
HEL-LO?
WOOF!
SHAAAAAA
WOOF WOOF
WOOF
WOOF
SQUEEE
WOOF WOOF
HAY-ATE?
A VISI-TOR?
LIEU-TENANT!
NOK
IT'S ME!
IT'S EDWARD!
ED-WARD?
WHAT ARE YOU DOING HERE AT THIS HOUR?
WOOF!

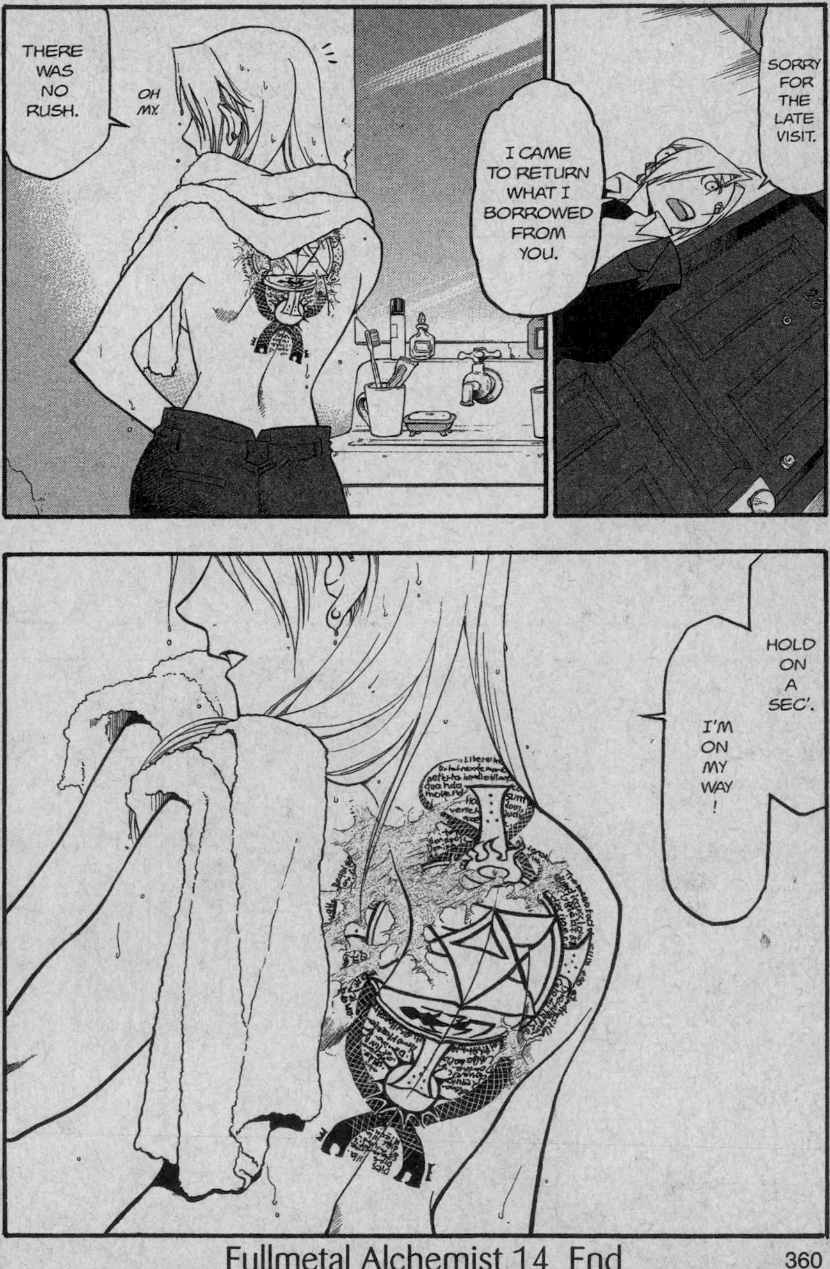
SORRY FOR THE LATE VISIT.
I CAME TO RETURN WHAT I BORROWED FROM YOU.
OH MY.
THERE WAS NO RUSH.
HOLD ON A SEC'.
I'M ON MY WAY!

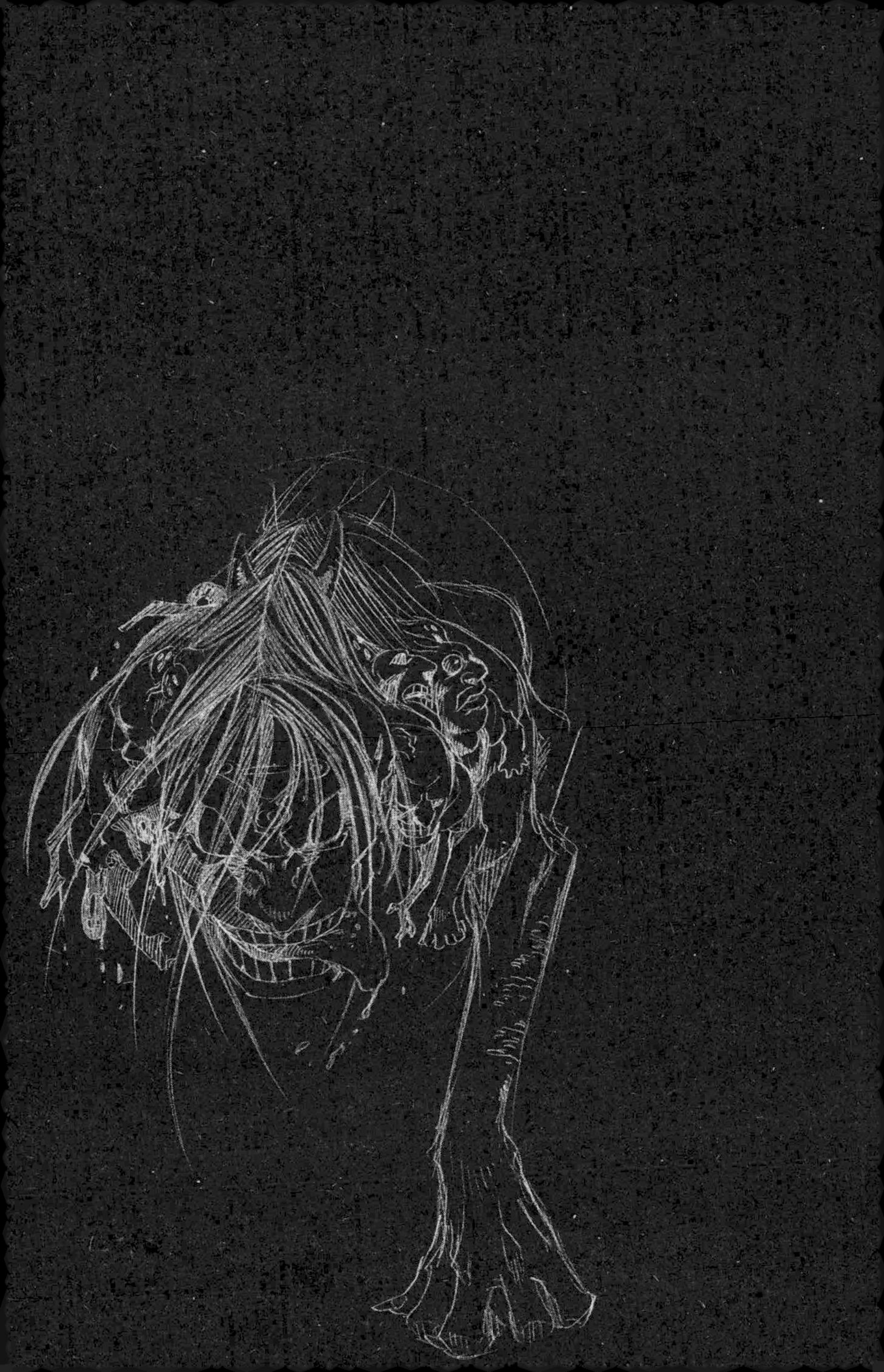

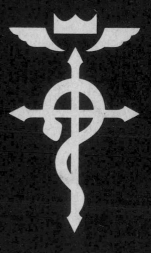

FULLMETAL
ALCHEMIST

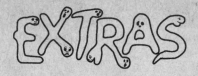

EXTRAS

Chapter 54   Change one sound effect and it's a disaster.

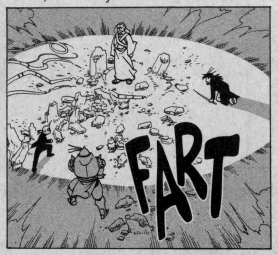

What a huge fart.

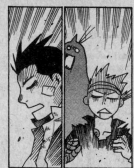

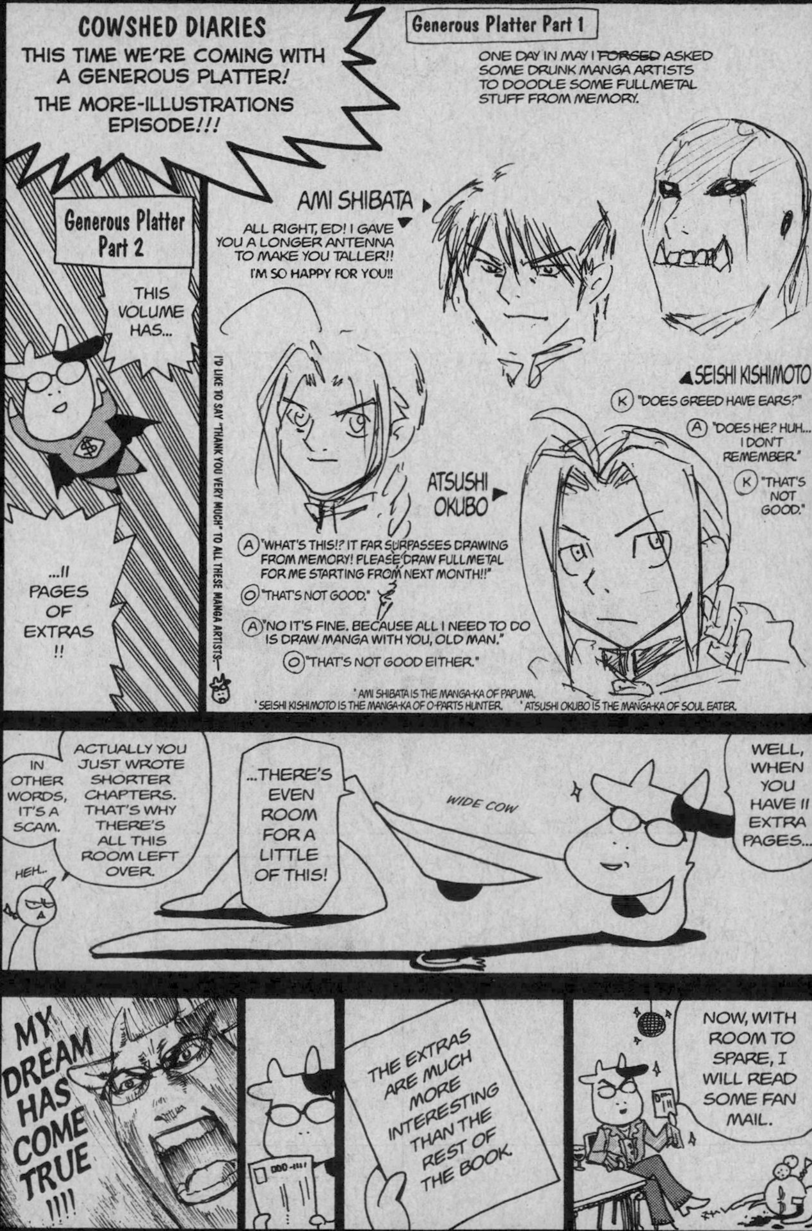
Generous Platter Part 1
ONE DAY IN MAY I ~~FORCED~~ ASKED SOME DRUNK MANGA ARTISTS TO DOODLE SOME FULLMETAL STUFF FROM MEMORY.
AMI SHIBATA
ALL RIGHT, ED! I GAVE YOU A LONGER ANTENNA TO MAKE YOU TALLER!! I'M SO HAPPY FOR YOU!!
SEISHI KISHIMOTO
(K) "DOES GREED HAVE EARS?"
(A) "DOES HE? HUH... I DON'T REMEMBER."
(K) "THAT'S NOT GOOD."
ATSUSHI OKUBO
(A) "WHAT'S THIS!? IT FAR SURPASSES DRAWING FROM MEMORY! PLEASE DRAW FULLMETAL FOR ME STARTING FROM NEXT MONTH!!"
(O) "THAT'S NOT GOOD."
(A) "NO IT'S FINE. BECAUSE ALL I NEED TO DO IS DRAW MANGA WITH YOU, OLD MAN."
(O) "THAT'S NOT GOOD EITHER."
I'D LIKE TO SAY "THANK YOU VERY MUCH" TO ALL THESE MANGA ARTISTS—
* AMI SHIBATA IS THE MANGA-KA OF PAPUWA.
* SEISHI KISHIMOTO IS THE MANGA-KA OF O-PARTS HUNTER.
* ATSUSHI OKUBO IS THE MANGA-KA OF SOUL EATER.
COWSHED DIARIES
THIS TIME WE'RE COMING WITH A GENEROUS PLATTER!
THE MORE-ILLUSTRATIONS EPISODE!!!
Generous Platter Part 2
THIS VOLUME HAS...
...11 PAGES OF EXTRAS !!
WELL, WHEN YOU HAVE 11 EXTRA PAGES...
WIDE COW
...THERE'S EVEN ROOM FOR A LITTLE OF THIS!
ACTUALLY YOU JUST WROTE SHORTER CHAPTERS. THAT'S WHY THERE'S ALL THIS ROOM LEFT OVER.
IN OTHER WORDS, IT'S A SCAM.
HEH..
NOW, WITH ROOM TO SPARE, I WILL READ SOME FAN MAIL.
THE EXTRAS ARE MUCH MORE INTERESTING THAN THE REST OF THE BOOK.
MY DREAM HAS COME TRUE !!!!

My Brother 60 Years Younger

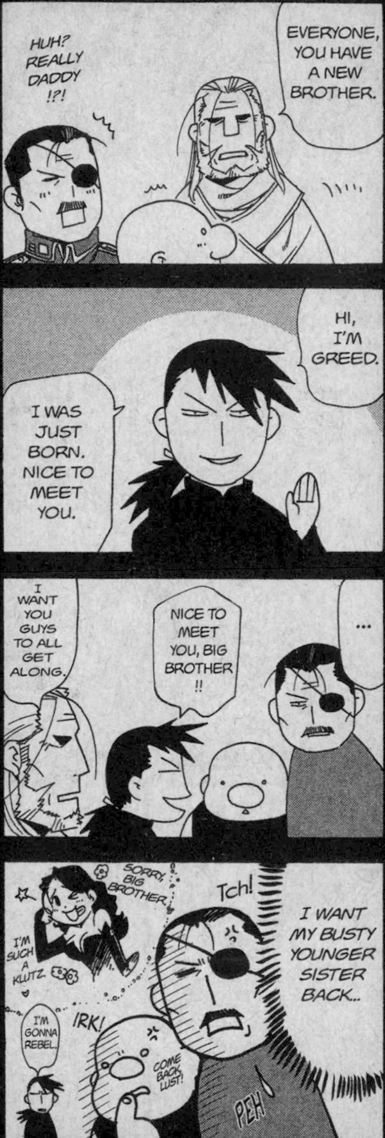
EVERYONE, YOU HAVE A NEW BROTHER.
HUH? REALLY DADDY !?!
HI, I'M GREED.
I WAS JUST BORN. NICE TO MEET YOU.
...
NICE TO MEET YOU, BIG BROTHER !!
I WANT YOU GUYS TO ALL GET ALONG.
I WANT MY BUSTY YOUNGER SISTER BACK...
Tch!
SORRY, BIG BROTHER.
I'M SUCH A KLUTZ.
COME BACK LUST!
IRK!
I'M GONNA REBEL.
PEH

Do They Still Sell Shower Caps?

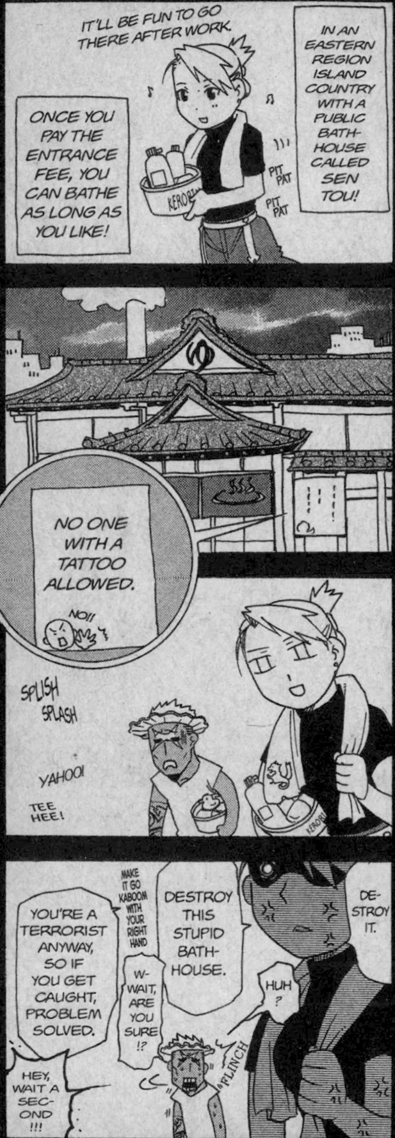
IN AN EASTERN REGION ISLAND COUNTRY WITH A PUBLIC BATH-HOUSE CALLED SEN TOU!
IT'LL BE FUN TO GO THERE AFTER WORK.
ONCE YOU PAY THE ENTRANCE FEE, YOU CAN BATHE AS LONG AS YOU LIKE!
PIT PAT
PIT PAT
KERORI
NO ONE WITH A TATTOO ALLOWED.
NO!!
SPLISH
SPLASH
YAHOO!
TEE HEE!
KERORI
DE-STROY IT.
DESTROY THIS STUPID BATH-HOUSE.
MAKE IT GO KABOOM WITH YOUR RIGHT HAND
YOU'RE A TERRORIST ANYWAY, SO IF YOU GET CAUGHT, PROBLEM SOLVED.
HUH?
W-WAIT, ARE YOU SURE !?
FLINCH
HEY, WAIT A SEC-OND !!!

SHORT STORY

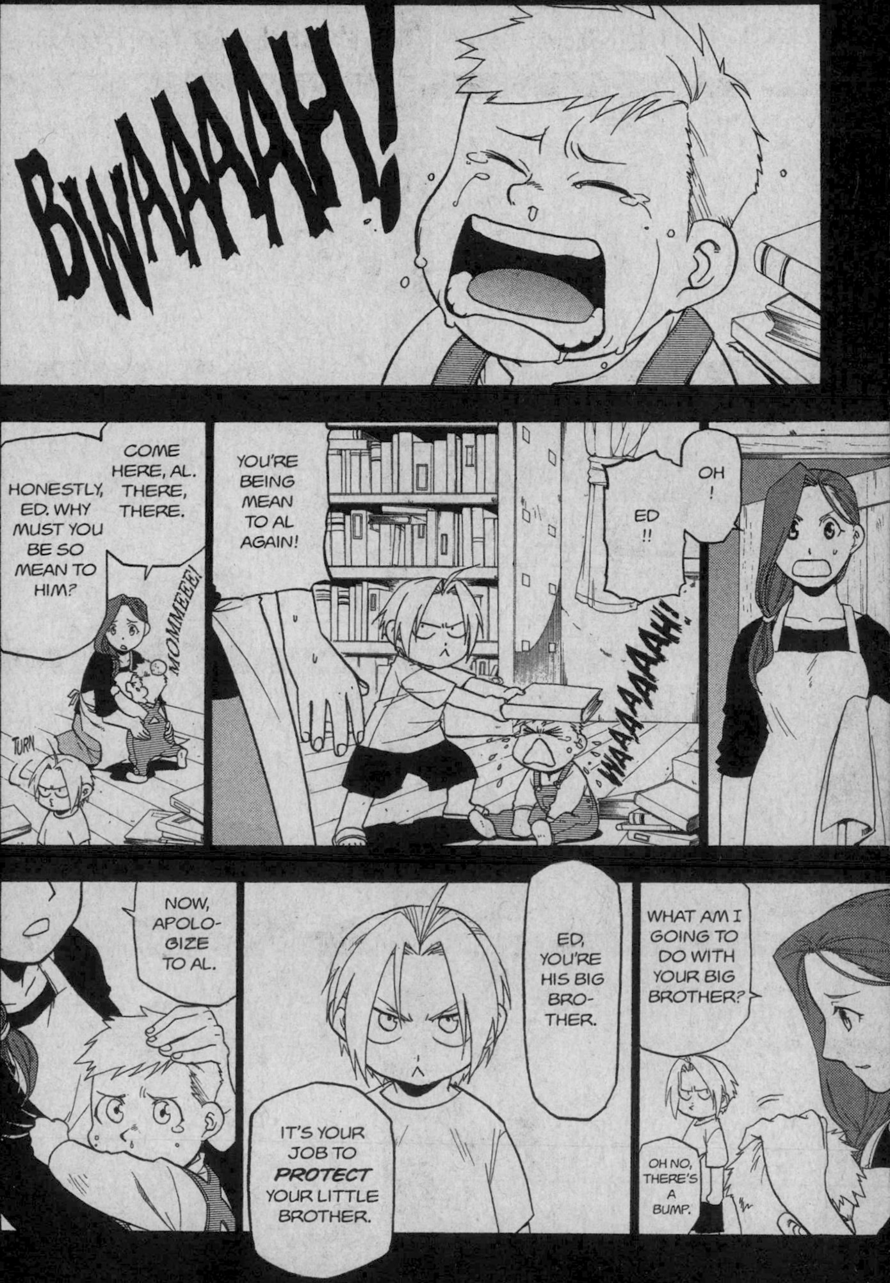
BWAAAAH!
OH! ED!!
YOU'RE BEING MEAN TO AL AGAIN!
WAAAAAAAH!
COME HERE, AL. THERE, THERE.
HONESTLY, ED. WHY MUST YOU BE SO MEAN TO HIM?
MOMMEEE!
TURN
WHAT AM I GOING TO DO WITH YOUR BIG BROTHER?
OH NO, THERE'S A BUMP.
ED, YOU'RE HIS BIG BROTHER.
IT'S YOUR JOB TO ***PROTECT*** YOUR LITTLE BROTHER.
NOW, APOLOGIZE TO AL.

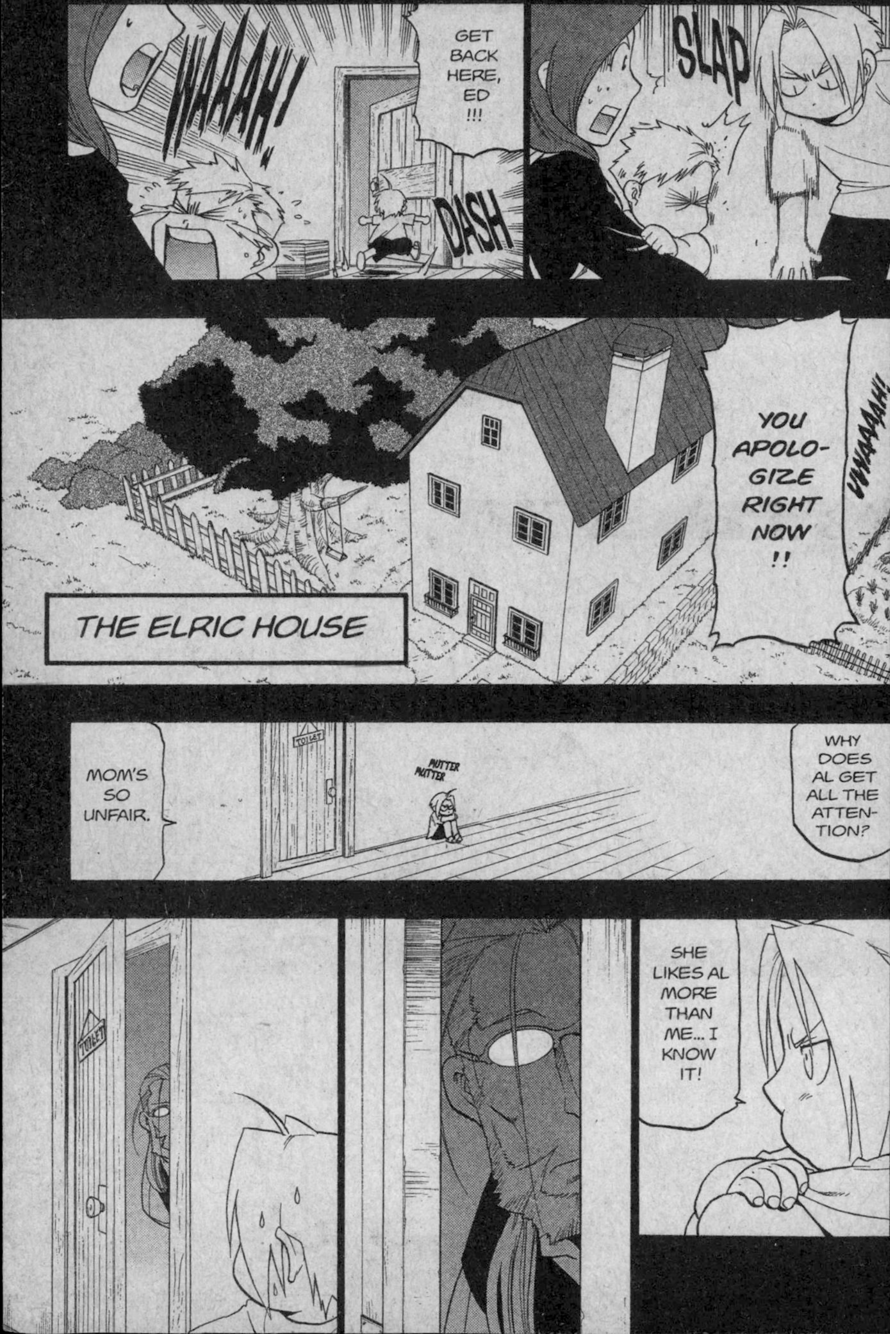
SLAP
GET BACK HERE, ED!!!
WAAAH!
DASH
UWAAAAAH!
YOU APOLOGIZE RIGHT NOW!!
THE ELRIC HOUSE
WHY DOES AL GET ALL THE ATTENTION?
MUTTER MUTTER
TOILET
MOM'S SO UNFAIR.
SHE LIKES AL MORE THAN ME... I KNOW IT!
TOILET

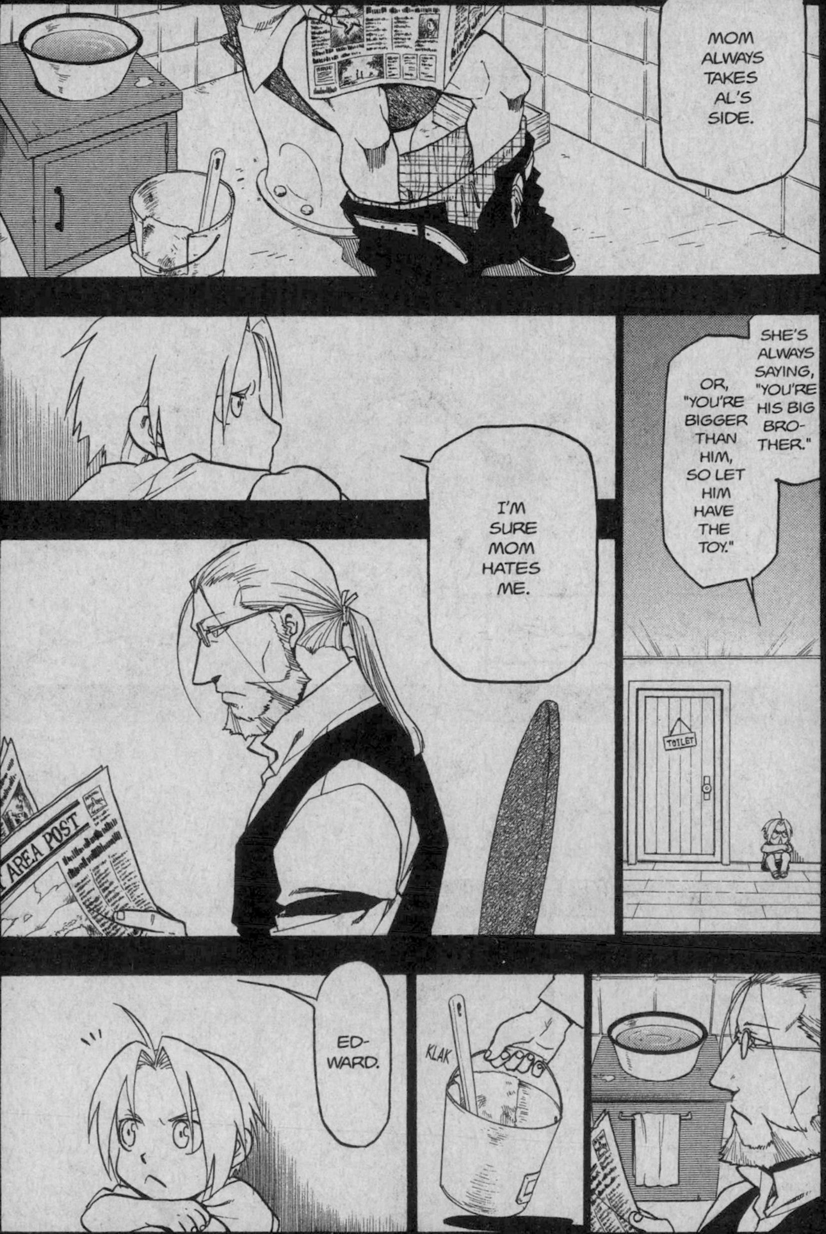
MOM ALWAYS TAKES AL'S SIDE.
SHE'S ALWAYS SAYING, "YOU'RE HIS BIG BRO-THER."
OR, "YOU'RE BIGGER THAN HIM, SO LET HIM HAVE THE TOY."
TOILET
I'M SURE MOM HATES ME.
AREA POST
KLAK
ED-WARD.

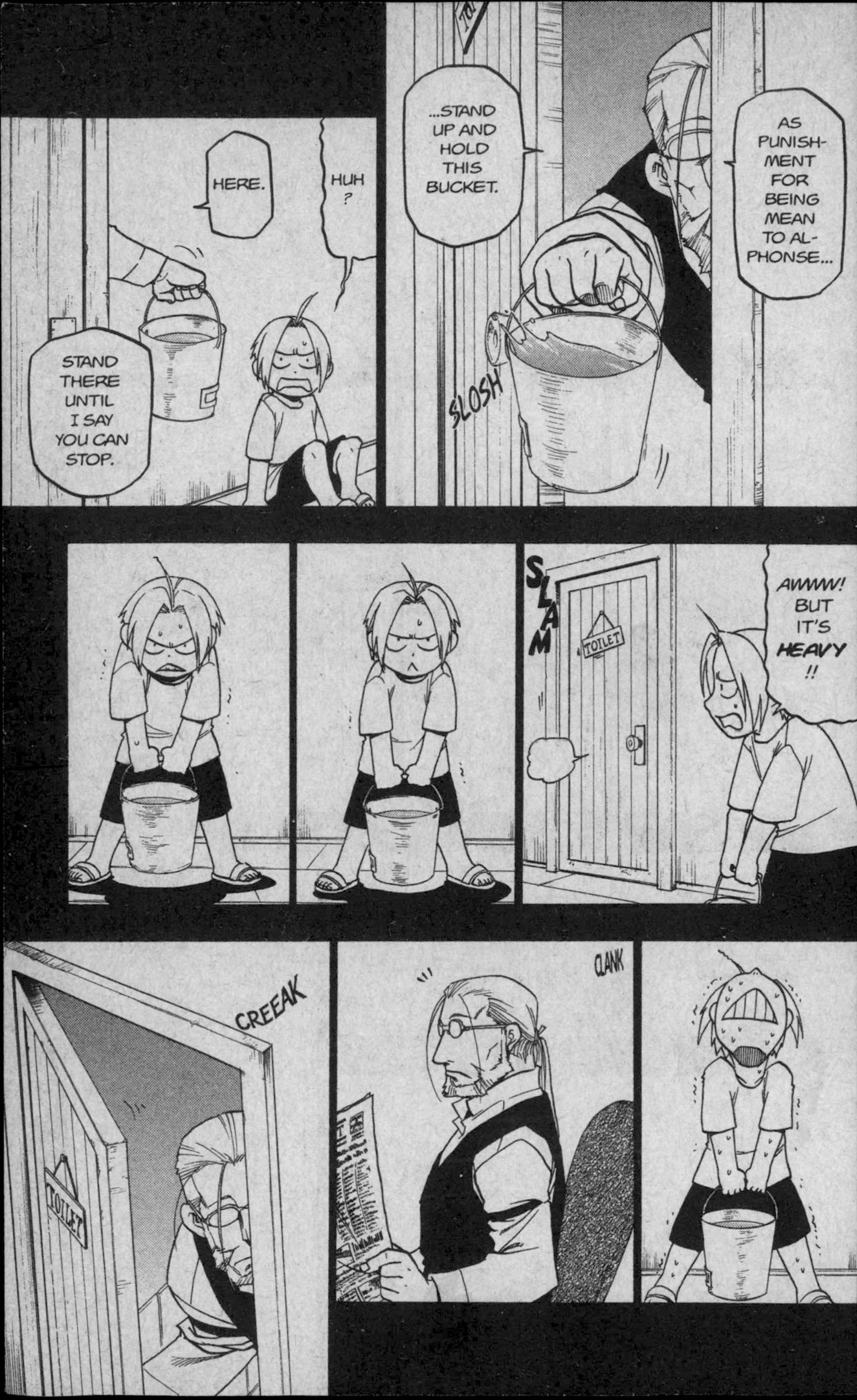
AS PUNISHMENT FOR BEING MEAN TO ALPHONSE...
...STAND UP AND HOLD THIS BUCKET.
SLOSH
HUH?
HERE.
STAND THERE UNTIL I SAY YOU CAN STOP.
AWWW! BUT IT'S HEAVY!!
TOILET
SLAM
CLANK
CREEAK
TOILET

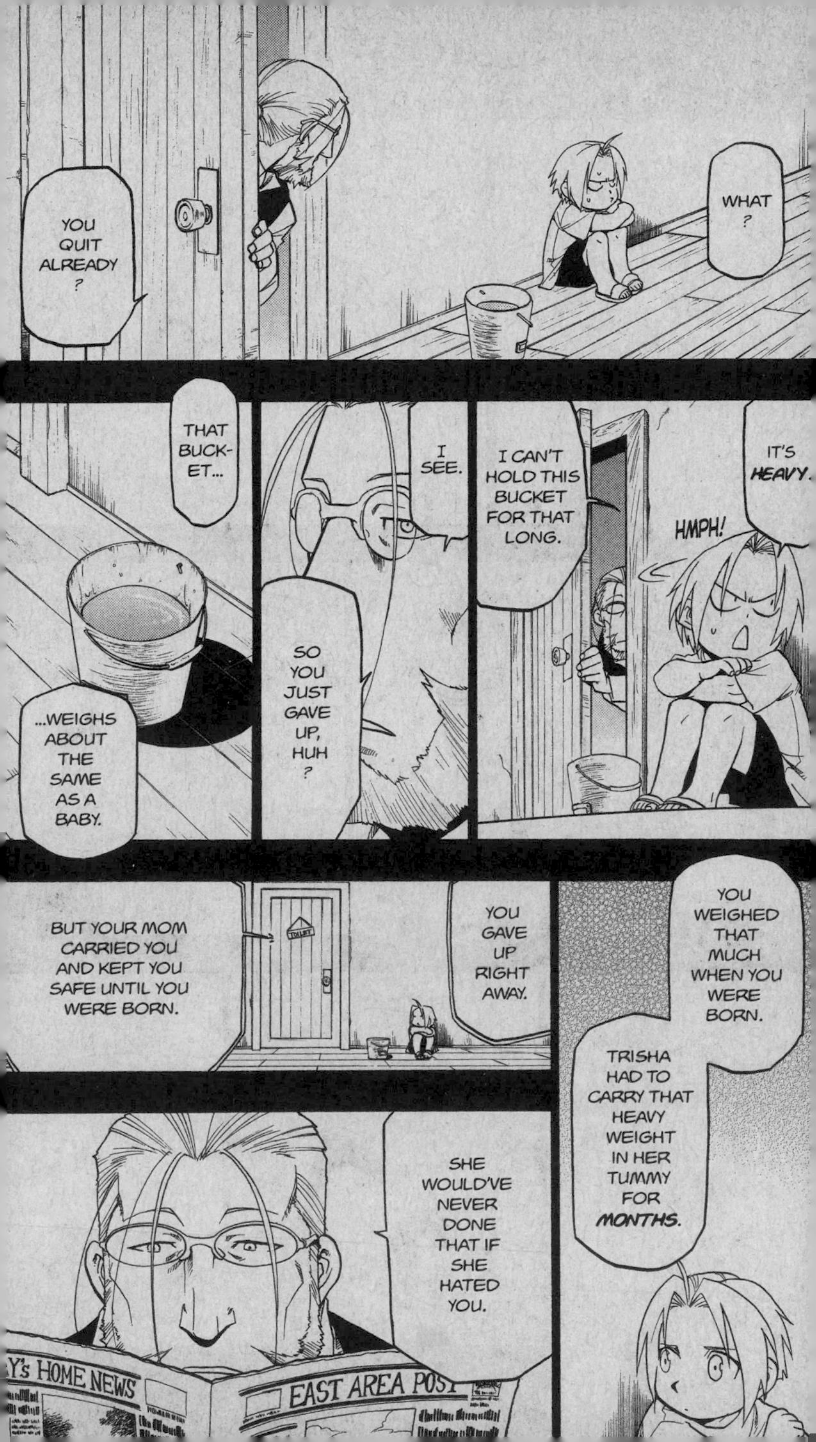
WHAT?
YOU QUIT ALREADY?
IT'S *HEAVY*.
HMPH!
I CAN'T HOLD THIS BUCKET FOR THAT LONG.
I SEE.
SO YOU JUST GAVE UP, HUH?
THAT BUCKET...
...WEIGHS ABOUT THE SAME AS A BABY.
YOU WEIGHED THAT MUCH WHEN YOU WERE BORN.
TRISHA HAD TO CARRY THAT HEAVY WEIGHT IN HER TUMMY FOR *MONTHS*.
YOU GAVE UP RIGHT AWAY.
BUT YOUR MOM CARRIED YOU AND KEPT YOU SAFE UNTIL YOU WERE BORN.
SHE WOULD'VE NEVER DONE THAT IF SHE HATED YOU.
Y's HOME NEWS
EAST AREA POST

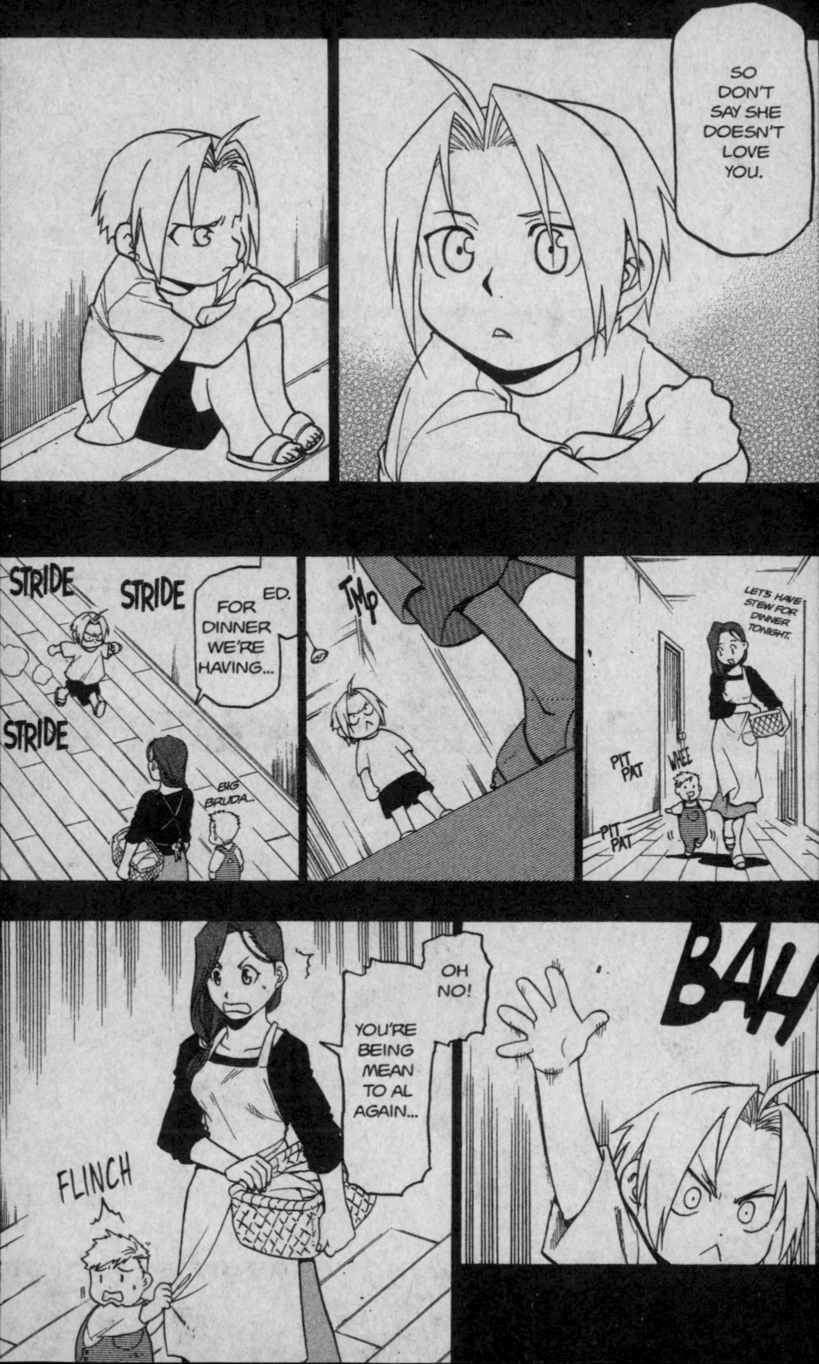
SO DON'T SAY SHE DOESN'T LOVE YOU.
LET'S HAVE STEW FOR DINNER TONIGHT.
WHEE
PIT PAT
PIT PAT
TMP
STRIDE
STRIDE
ED. FOR DINNER WE'RE HAVING...
STRIDE
BIG BRUDA...
BAH
OH NO!
YOU'RE BEING MEAN TO AL AGAIN...
FLINCH

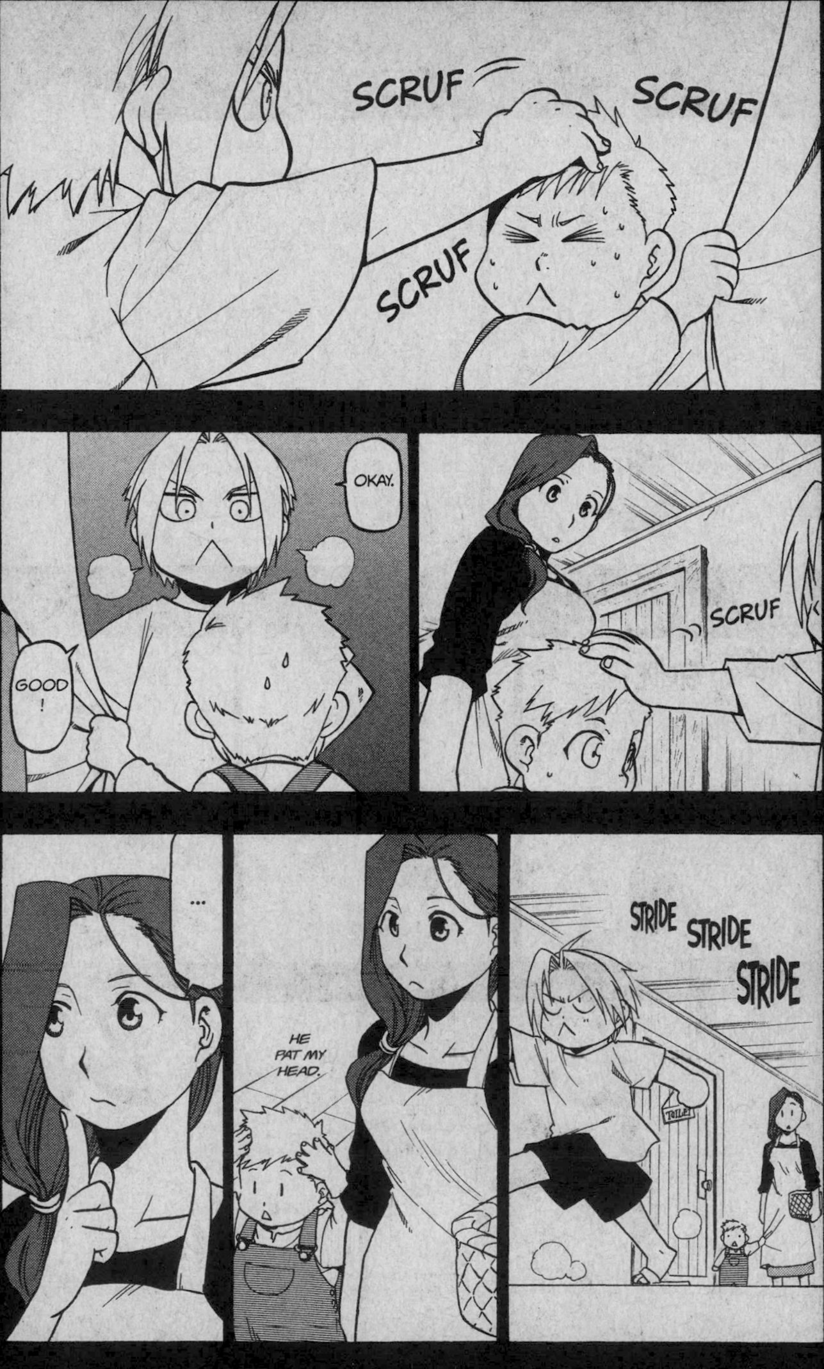
SCRUF
SCRUF
SCRUF
SCRUF
OKAY.
GOOD!
STRIDE
STRIDE
STRIDE
HE PAT MY HEAD.
...

...HONEY, YOU SAID SOMETHING TO ED, DIDN'T YOU?
TOILET
NO, I DIDN'T...
OH, THAT'S RIGHT.
I FORGOT TO ASK ED—
CAN YOU GET ME SOME TOILET PAPER... ...TRISHA?
YES, DEAR.
PIT PAT
PIT PAT
END

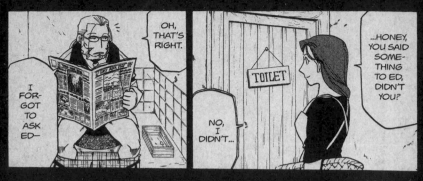

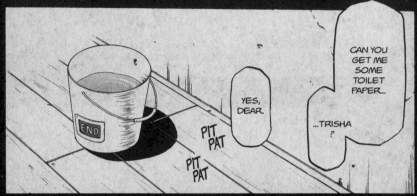

FULLMETAL ALCHEMIST 14

SPECIAL THANKS

CONTRIBUTING ARTISTS ON MEMORY DOODLES
ATSUSHI OKUBO
SEICHI KISHIMOTO
AMI SHIBATA
KEISUI TAKAEDA
SANKICHI HINODEYA
JUN TOKO
AIYABALL
NONO
BIG BROTHER YOICHI KAMITONO
MASASHI MIZUTANI

EDITOR YOICHI SHIMOMURA

DEN'S STUFFED ANIMAL ON COVER INSIDE FLAP CREATED BY
HISAE IWAOKA

AND YOU!!

Being Envy has its advantages...

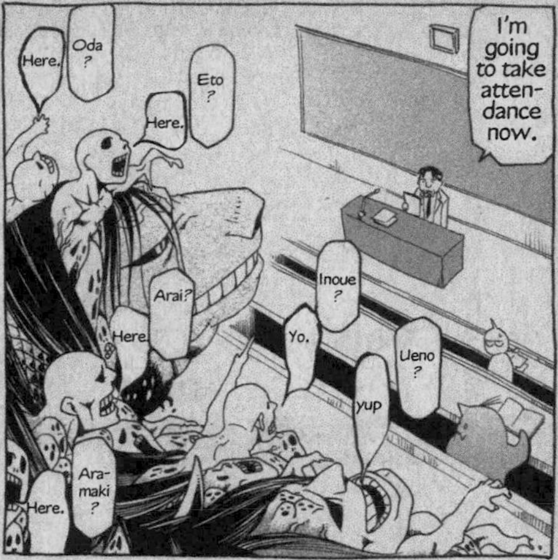
I'm going to take atten-dance now.
Eto ?
Here.
Oda ?
Here.
Ueno ?
Inoue ?
yup
Yo.
Arai?
Here.
Ara-maki ?
Here.

...like covering for people playing hooky when the teacher takes roll.

Volume 10, Chapter 43

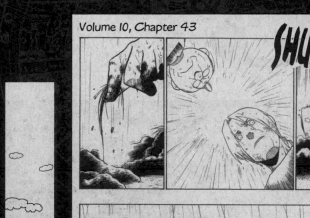

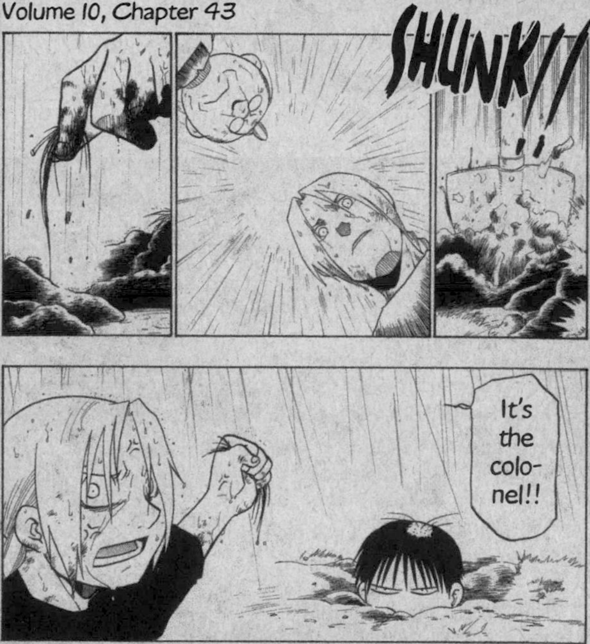
SHUNK!!
It's the colo-nel!!

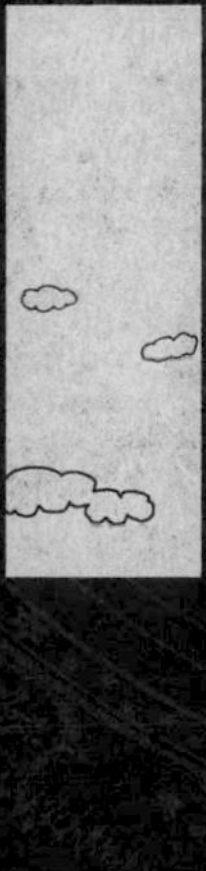

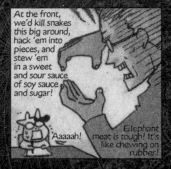

At the front, we'd kill snakes this big around, hack 'em into pieces, and stew 'em in a sweet and sour sauce of soy sauce and sugar!

Aaaaah!

Elephant meat is tough! It's like chewing on rubber!

In researching this volume, I interviewed veterans who had been at the front during World War II. I read countless books, examined film footage, and listened to many detailed and intense stories firsthand, but the one comment that affected me the most came from a former soldier who lowered his gaze to the tabletop and said, "I never watch war movies."

—*Hiromu Arakawa, 2006*

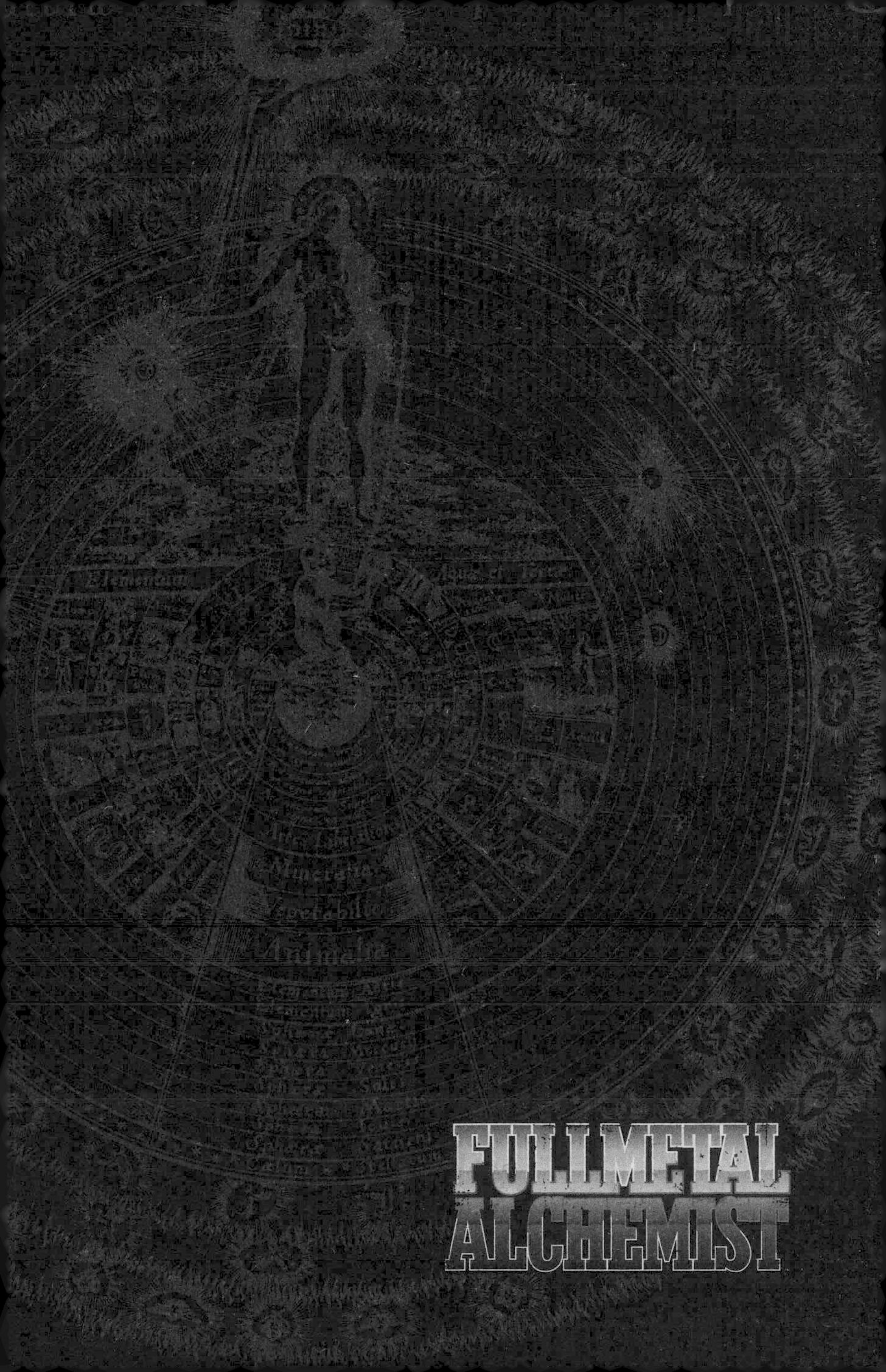
FULLMETAL
ALCHEMIST

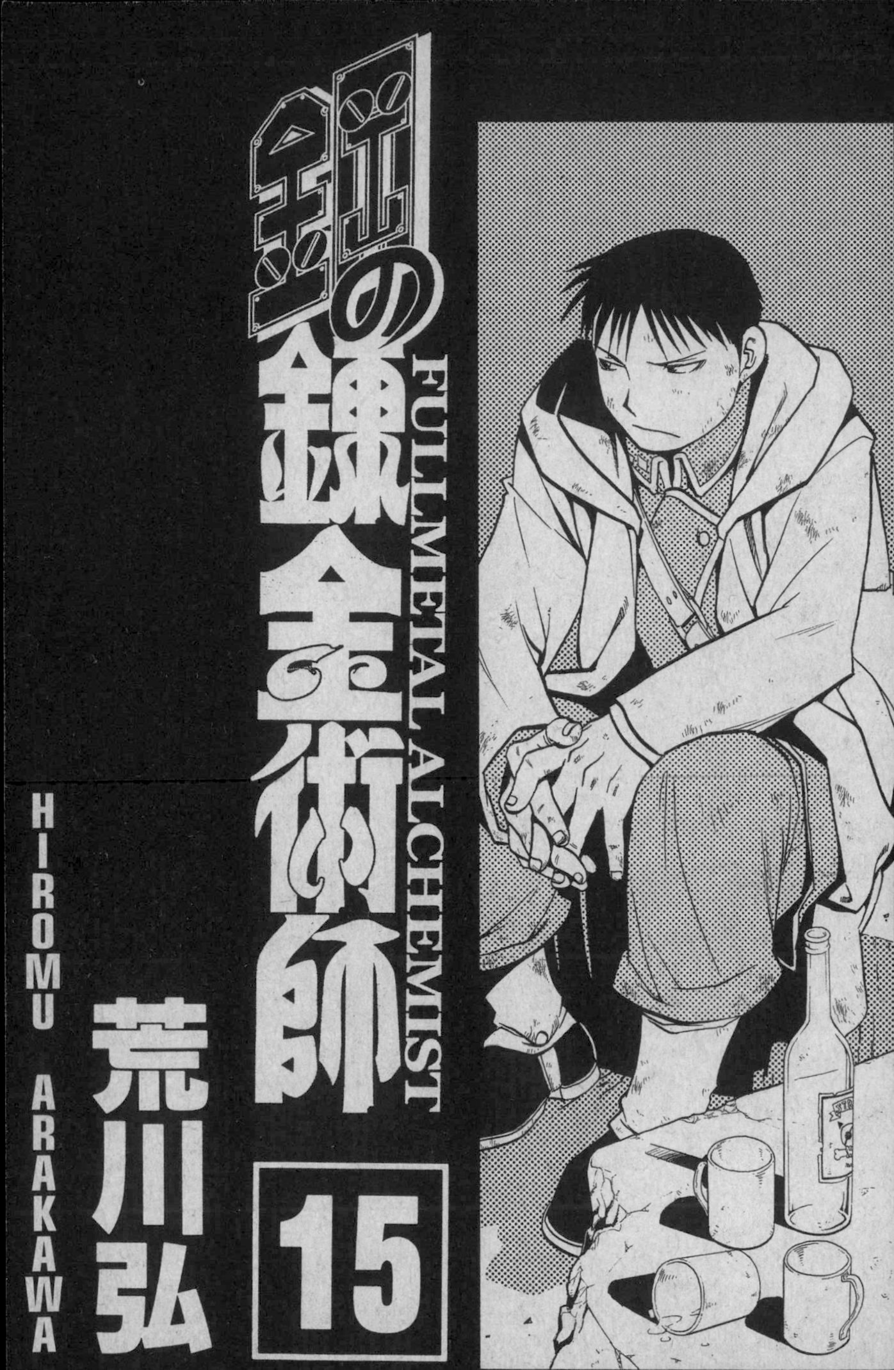

鋼の錬金術師

FULLMETAL ALCHEMIST

15

荒川弘

HIROMU ARAKAWA

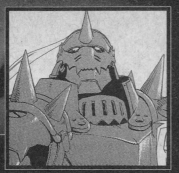
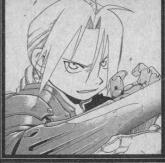

■ アルフォンス・エルリック
Alphonse Elric

■ エドワード・エルリック
Edward Elric

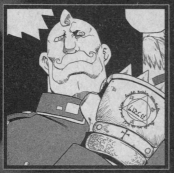
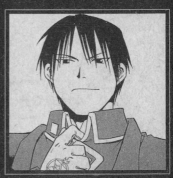

■ アレックス・ルイ・アームストロング
Alex Louis Armstrong

■ ロイ・マスタング
Roy Mustang

OUTLINE
FULLMETAL ALCHEMIST

The Elrics' plan to capture and interrogate Gluttony, one of the evil and nigh-invulnerable homunculi, goes awry when his "sibling" Envy crashes the party. Gluttony reveals his true bestial form and, in a rage, swallows Ed, Lin, and Envy, sending the three of them into a dark void eerily containing a large amount of rubble and…blood. Al, fearing his brother lost forever, demands that Gluttony take him to the mysterious "father" of the homunculi…

The Elric Brothers have made a shocking discovery—the Amestris President, King Bradley, is a Homunculus—an artificial human born of the Philosopher's Stone. Even more shocking, Bradley's rise to power was orchestrated by the military, and his master, the mysterious "Father," wants the Elrics alive for some nefarious purpose. Meanwhile, Lin, in his quest to discover the secret to immortality, has done the unthinkable—surrendered his body to "Greed," giving new life to the fallen Homunculus.

鋼の錬金術師
FULLMETAL ALCHEMIST

CHARACTERS
FULLMETAL ALCHEMIST

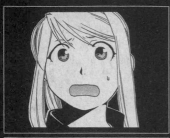

◻ ウィンリィ・ロックベル

Winry Rockbell

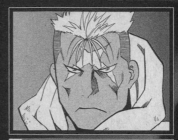

◻ スカー

Scar

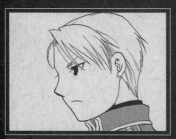

◻ リザ・ホークアイ

Riza Hawkeye

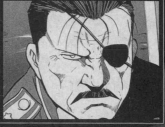

◻ キング・ブラッドレイ

King Bradley

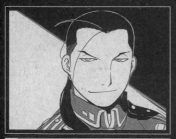

◻ ゾルフ・J・キンブリー

Solf J. Kimblee

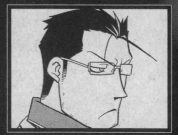

◻ マース・ヒューズ

Maes Hughes

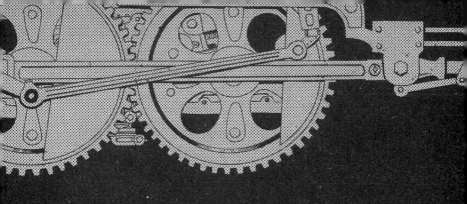

CONTENTS

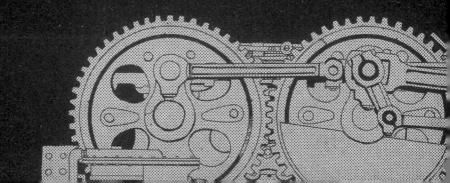

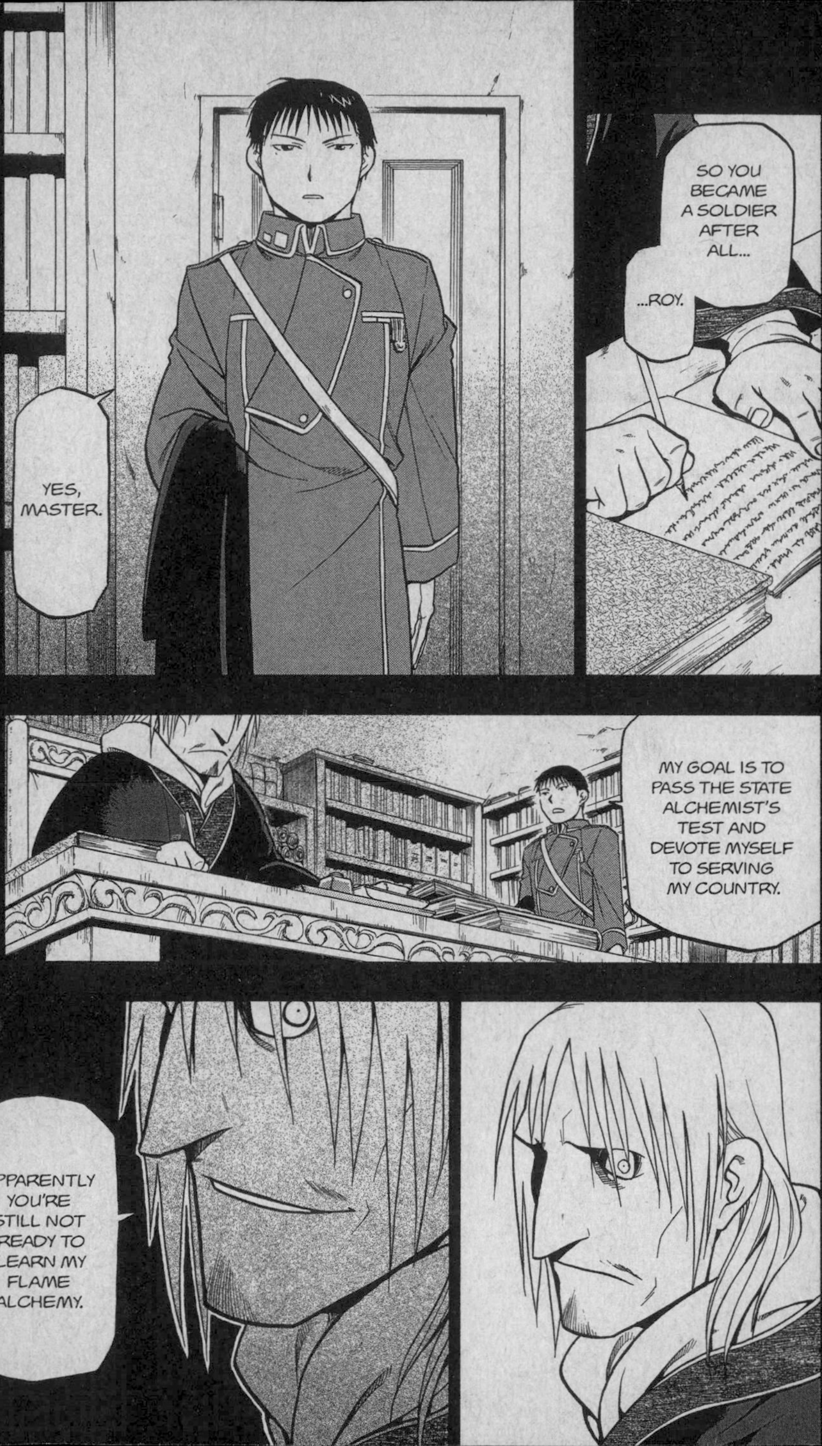
SO YOU BECAME A SOLDIER AFTER ALL...
...ROY.
YES, MASTER.
MY GOAL IS TO PASS THE STATE ALCHEMIST'S TEST AND DEVOTE MYSELF TO SERVING MY COUNTRY.
APPARENTLY YOU'RE STILL NOT READY TO LEARN MY FLAME ALCHEMY.

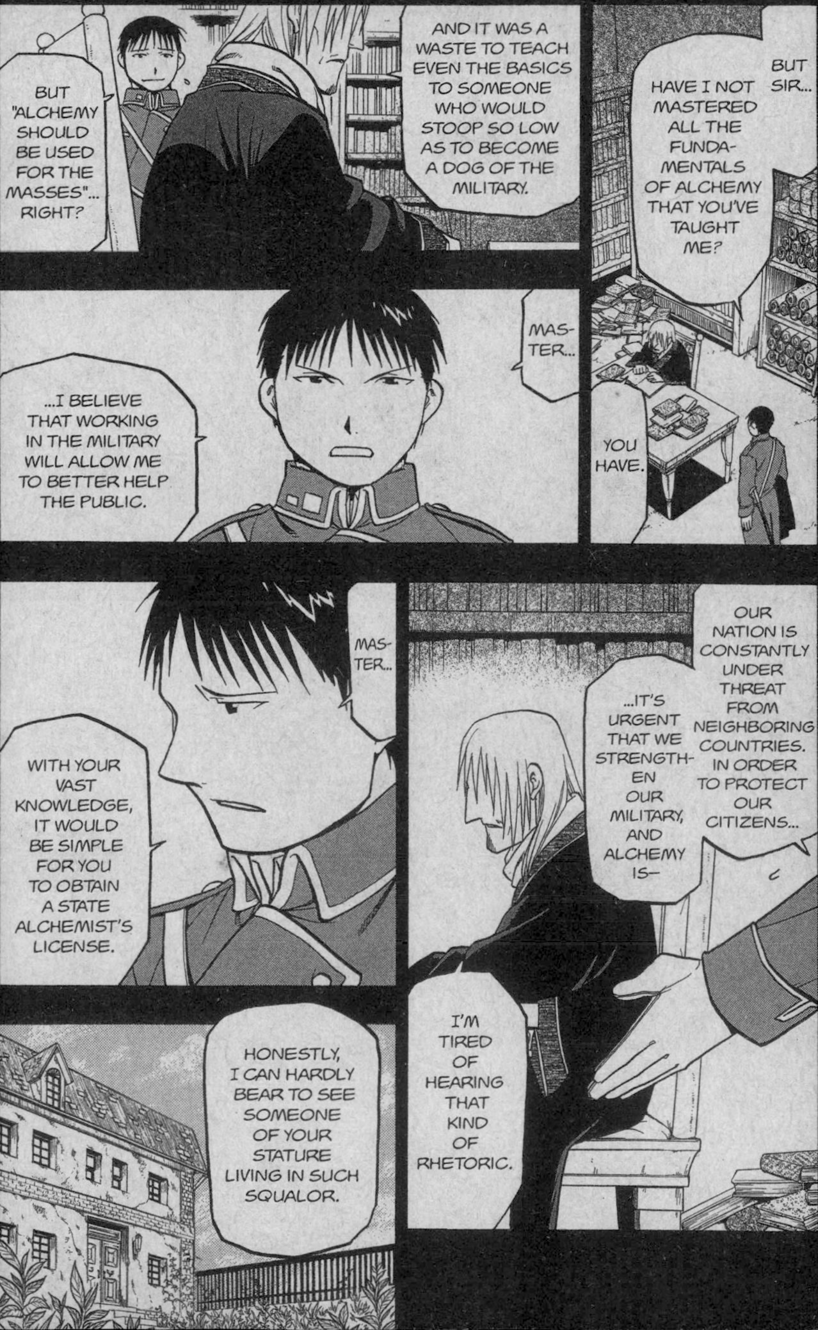
BUT SIR...
HAVE I NOT MASTERED ALL THE FUNDAMENTALS OF ALCHEMY THAT YOU'VE TAUGHT ME?
YOU HAVE.
AND IT WAS A WASTE TO TEACH EVEN THE BASICS TO SOMEONE WHO WOULD STOOP SO LOW AS TO BECOME A DOG OF THE MILITARY.
BUT "ALCHEMY SHOULD BE USED FOR THE MASSES"... RIGHT?
MASTER...
...I BELIEVE THAT WORKING IN THE MILITARY WILL ALLOW ME TO BETTER HELP THE PUBLIC.
OUR NATION IS CONSTANTLY UNDER THREAT FROM NEIGHBORING COUNTRIES. IN ORDER TO PROTECT OUR CITIZENS...
...IT'S URGENT THAT WE STRENGTHEN OUR MILITARY, AND ALCHEMY IS—
I'M TIRED OF HEARING THAT KIND OF RHETORIC.
MASTER...
WITH YOUR VAST KNOWLEDGE, IT WOULD BE SIMPLE FOR YOU TO OBTAIN A STATE ALCHEMIST'S LICENSE.
HONESTLY, I CAN HARDLY BEAR TO SEE SOMEONE OF YOUR STATURE LIVING IN SUCH SQUALOR.

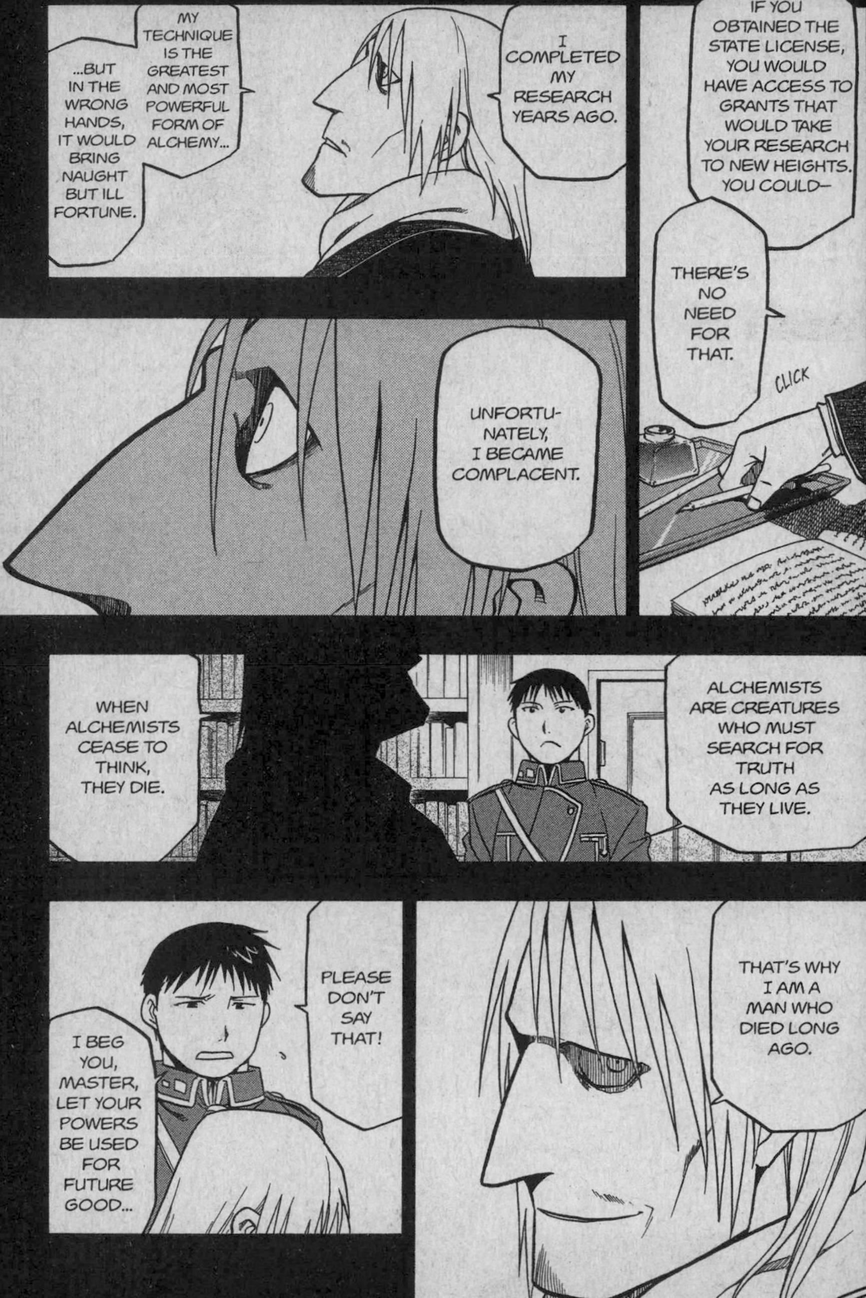
IF YOU OBTAINED THE STATE LICENSE, YOU WOULD HAVE ACCESS TO GRANTS THAT WOULD TAKE YOUR RESEARCH TO NEW HEIGHTS. YOU COULD—
THERE'S NO NEED FOR THAT.
CLICK
I COMPLETED MY RESEARCH YEARS AGO.
MY TECHNIQUE IS THE GREATEST AND MOST POWERFUL FORM OF ALCHEMY...
...BUT IN THE WRONG HANDS, IT WOULD BRING NAUGHT BUT ILL FORTUNE.
UNFORTUNATELY, I BECAME COMPLACENT.
ALCHEMISTS ARE CREATURES WHO MUST SEARCH FOR TRUTH AS LONG AS THEY LIVE.
WHEN ALCHEMISTS CEASE TO THINK, THEY DIE.
THAT'S WHY I AM A MAN WHO DIED LONG AGO.
PLEASE DON'T SAY THAT!
I BEG YOU, MASTER, LET YOUR POWERS BE USED FOR FUTURE GOOD...

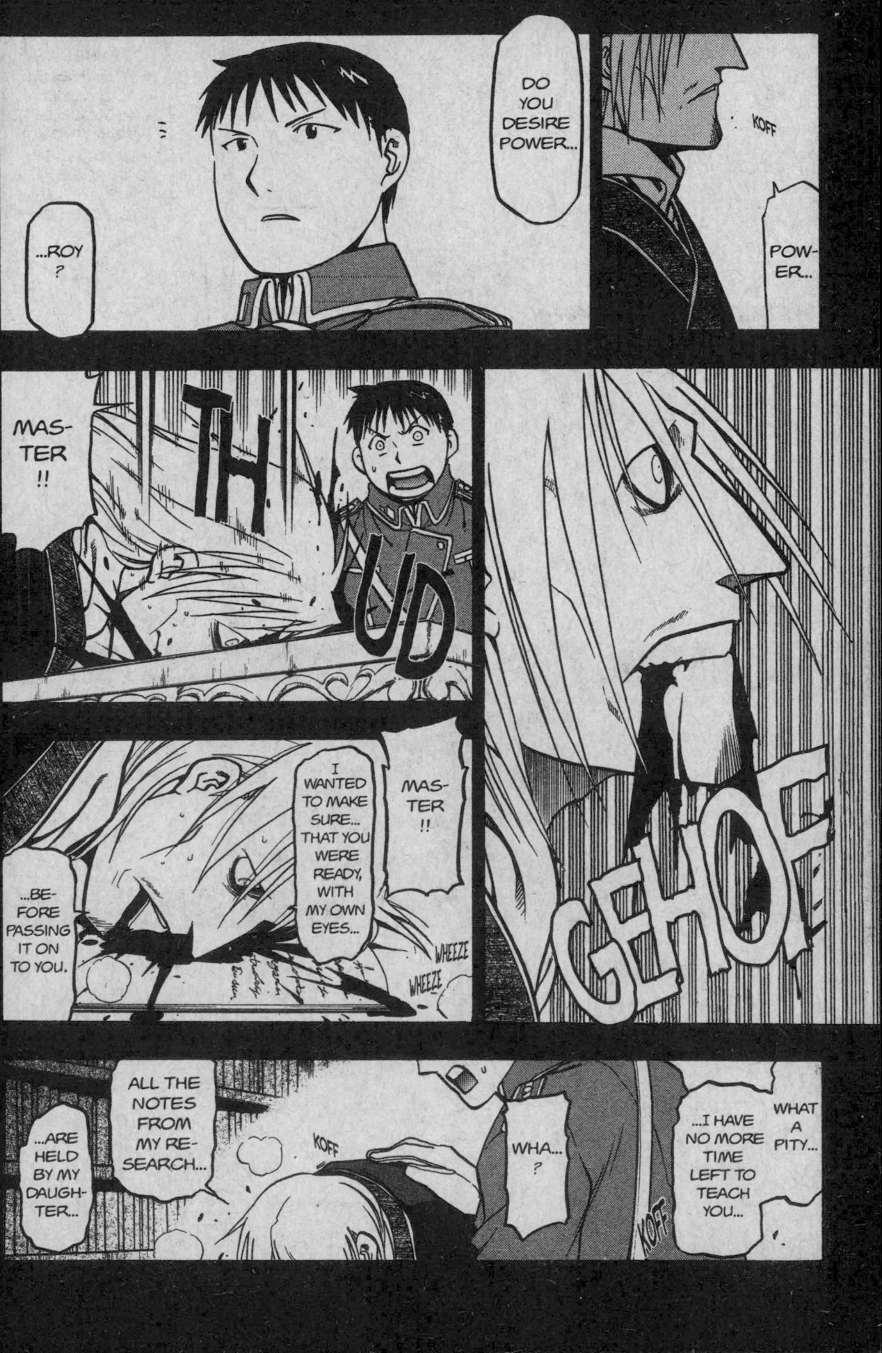

KOFF
POW-ER...
DO YOU DESIRE POWER...
...ROY ?
GEHOF
THUD
MAS-TER !!
MAS-TER !!
I WANTED TO MAKE SURE... THAT YOU WERE READY, WITH MY OWN EYES...
...BE-FORE PASSING IT ON TO YOU.
WHEEZE
WHEEZE
WHAT A PITY...
...I HAVE NO MORE TIME LEFT TO TEACH YOU...
KOFF
WHA... ?
ALL THE NOTES FROM MY RE-SEARCH...
KOFF
...ARE HELD BY MY DAUGHTER...

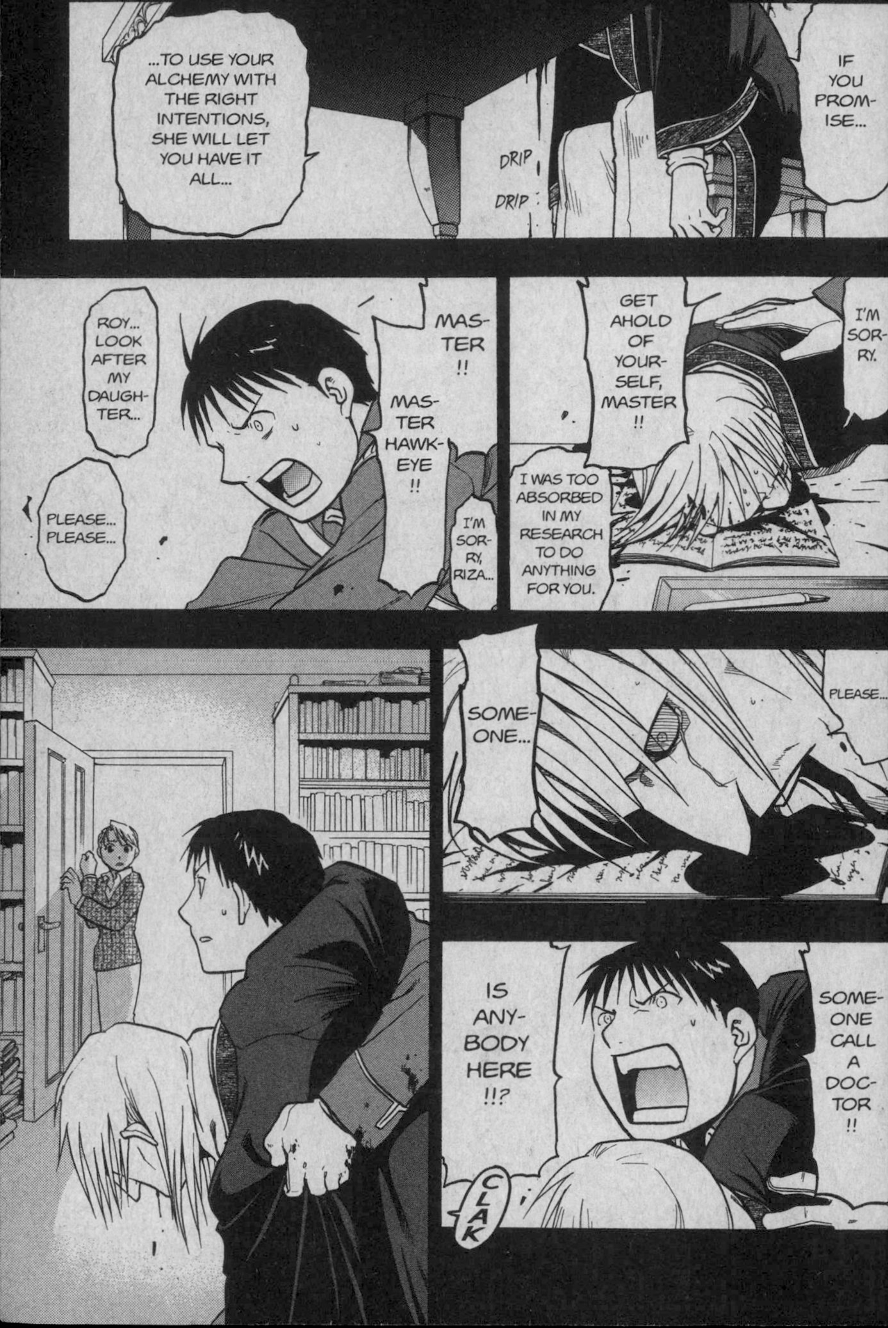
IF YOU PROMISE...
DRIP
DRIP
...TO USE YOUR ALCHEMY WITH THE RIGHT INTENTIONS, SHE WILL LET YOU HAVE IT ALL...
I'M SORRY.
GET AHOLD OF YOURSELF, MASTER!!
I WAS TOO ABSORBED IN MY RESEARCH TO DO ANYTHING FOR YOU.
MASTER!!
MASTER HAWKEYE!!
I'M SORRY, RIZA...
ROY... LOOK AFTER MY DAUGHTER...
PLEASE... PLEASE...
PLEASE...
SOMEONE...
SOMEONE CALL A DOCTOR!!
IS ANYBODY HERE!!?
CLAK

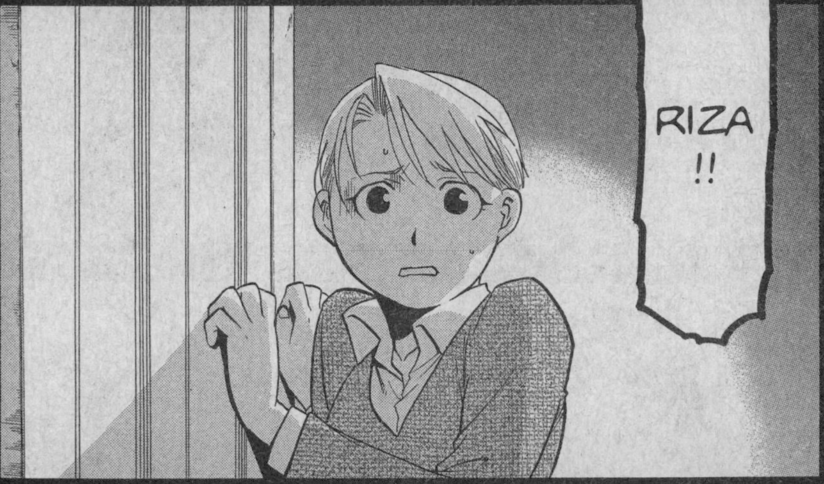
RIZA
!!

Chapter 58
The Footsteps of Ruin

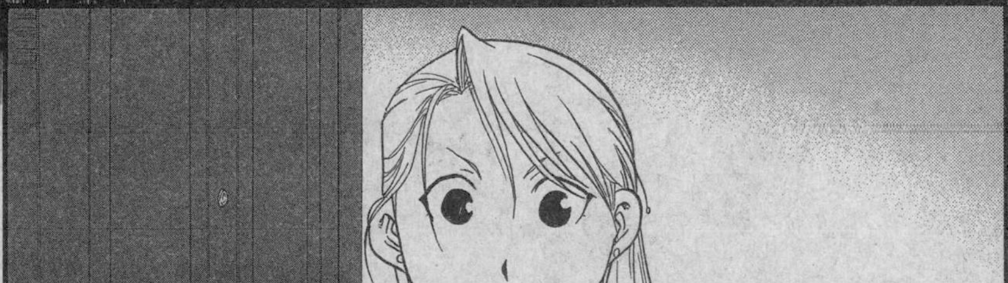

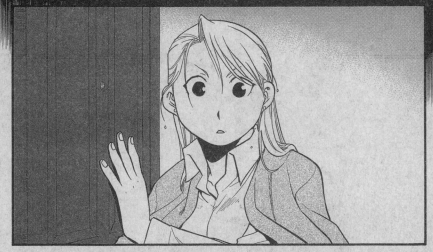

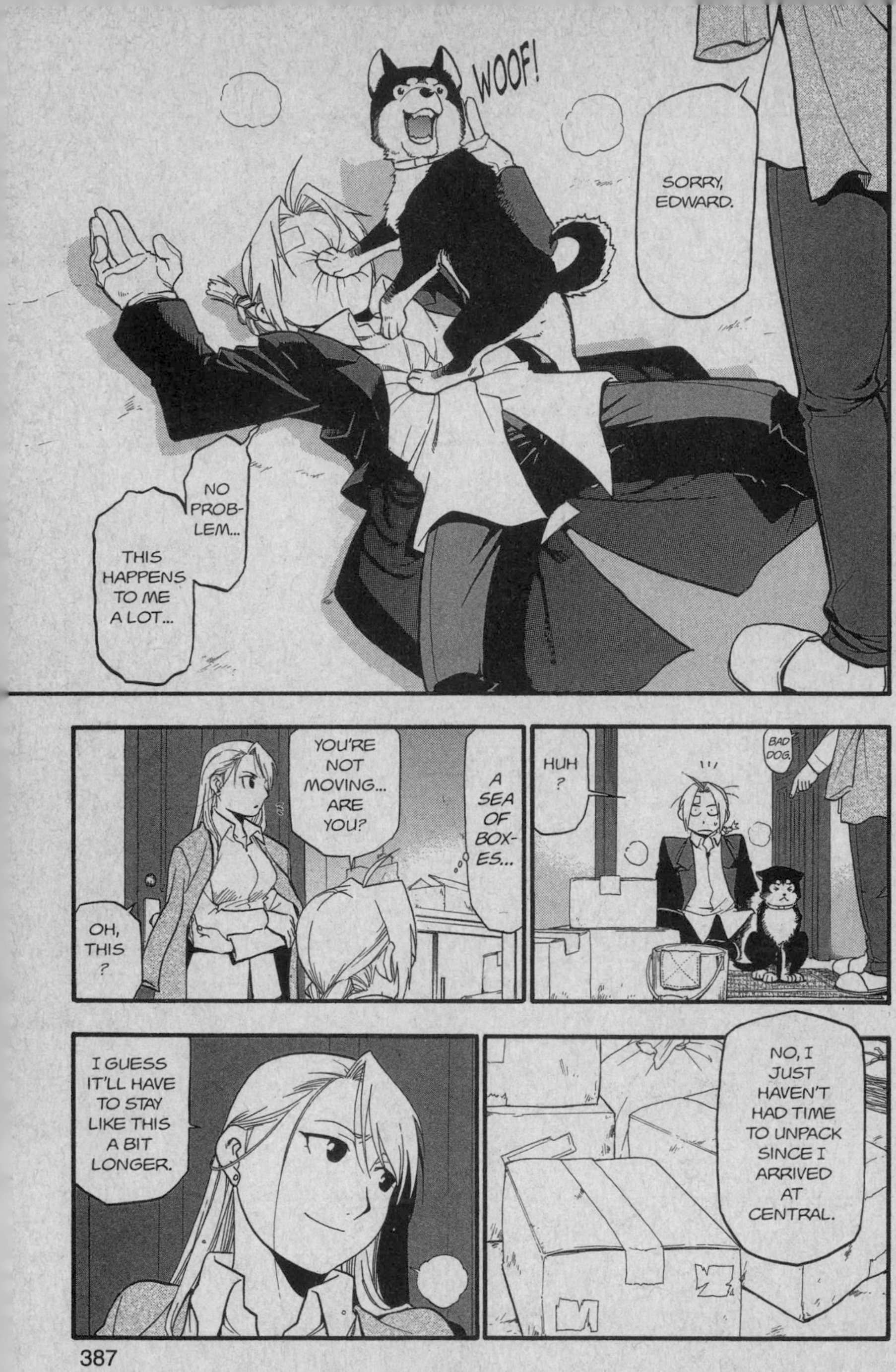
WOOF!
SORRY, EDWARD.
NO PROB-LEM...
THIS HAPPENS TO ME A LOT...
BAD DOG.
HUH?
A SEA OF BOX-ES...
YOU'RE NOT MOVING... ARE YOU?
OH, THIS?
NO, I JUST HAVEN'T HAD TIME TO UNPACK SINCE I ARRIVED AT CENTRAL.
I GUESS IT'LL HAVE TO STAY LIKE THIS A BIT LONGER.

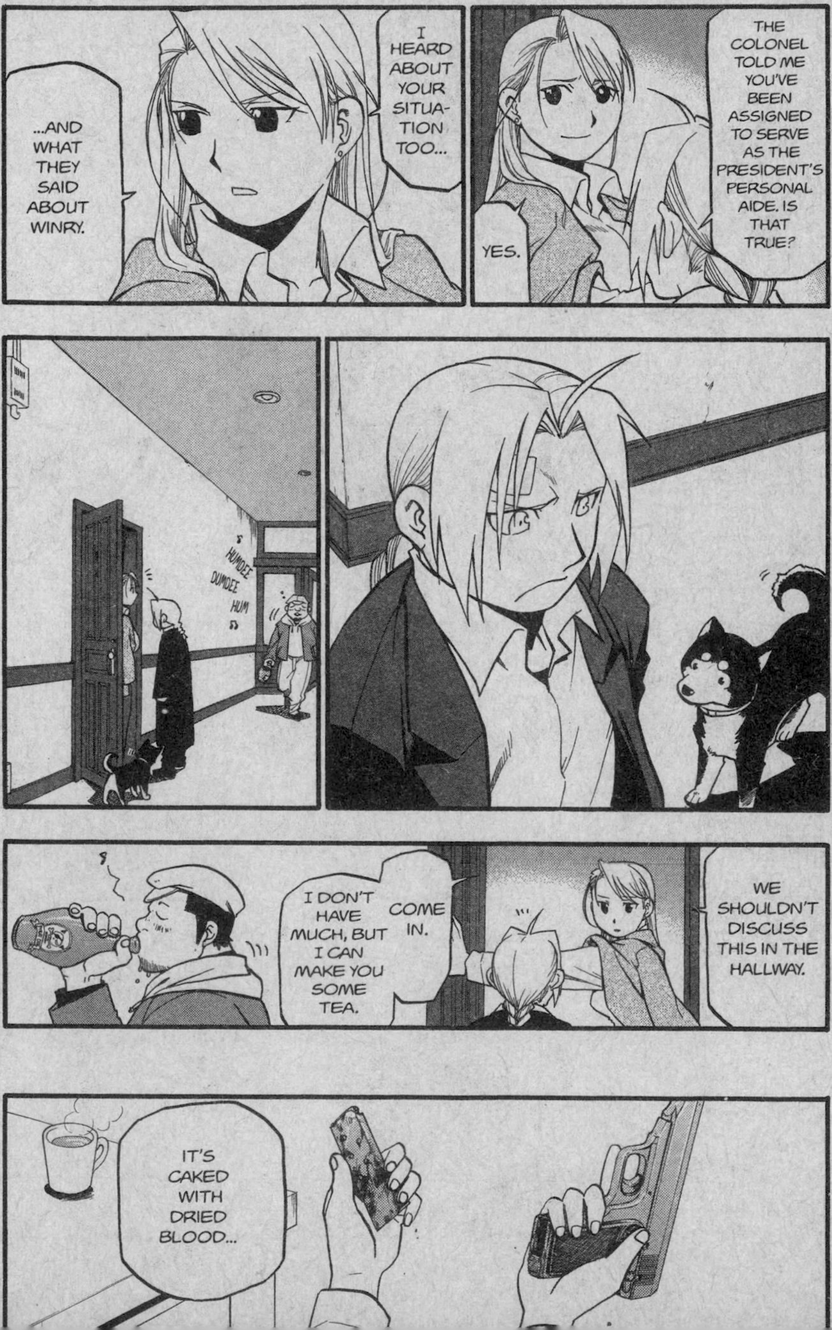
THE COLONEL TOLD ME YOU'VE BEEN ASSIGNED TO SERVE AS THE PRESIDENT'S PERSONAL AIDE. IS THAT TRUE?
YES.
I HEARD ABOUT YOUR SITUATION TOO...
...AND WHAT THEY SAID ABOUT WINRY.
HUMDEE DUMDEE HUM
WE SHOULDN'T DISCUSS THIS IN THE HALLWAY.
COME IN.
I DON'T HAVE MUCH, BUT I CAN MAKE YOU SOME TEA.
IT'S CAKED WITH DRIED BLOOD...

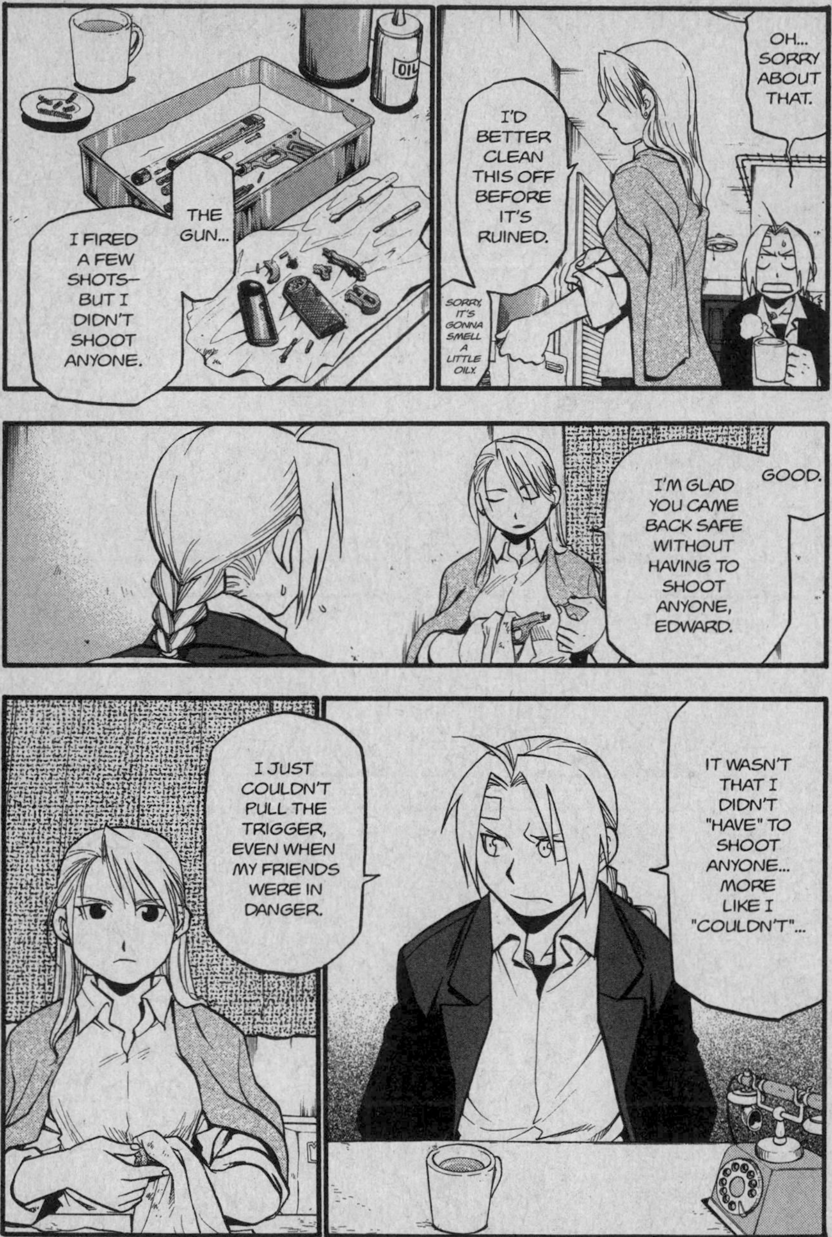
OH... SORRY ABOUT THAT.
I'D BETTER CLEAN THIS OFF BEFORE IT'S RUINED.
SORRY, IT'S GONNA SMELL A LITTLE OILY.
THE GUN...
I FIRED A FEW SHOTS— BUT I DIDN'T SHOOT ANYONE.
GOOD.
I'M GLAD YOU CAME BACK SAFE WITHOUT HAVING TO SHOOT ANYONE, EDWARD.
IT WASN'T THAT I DIDN'T "HAVE" TO SHOOT ANYONE... MORE LIKE I "COULDN'T"...
I JUST COULDN'T PULL THE TRIGGER, EVEN WHEN MY FRIENDS WERE IN DANGER.

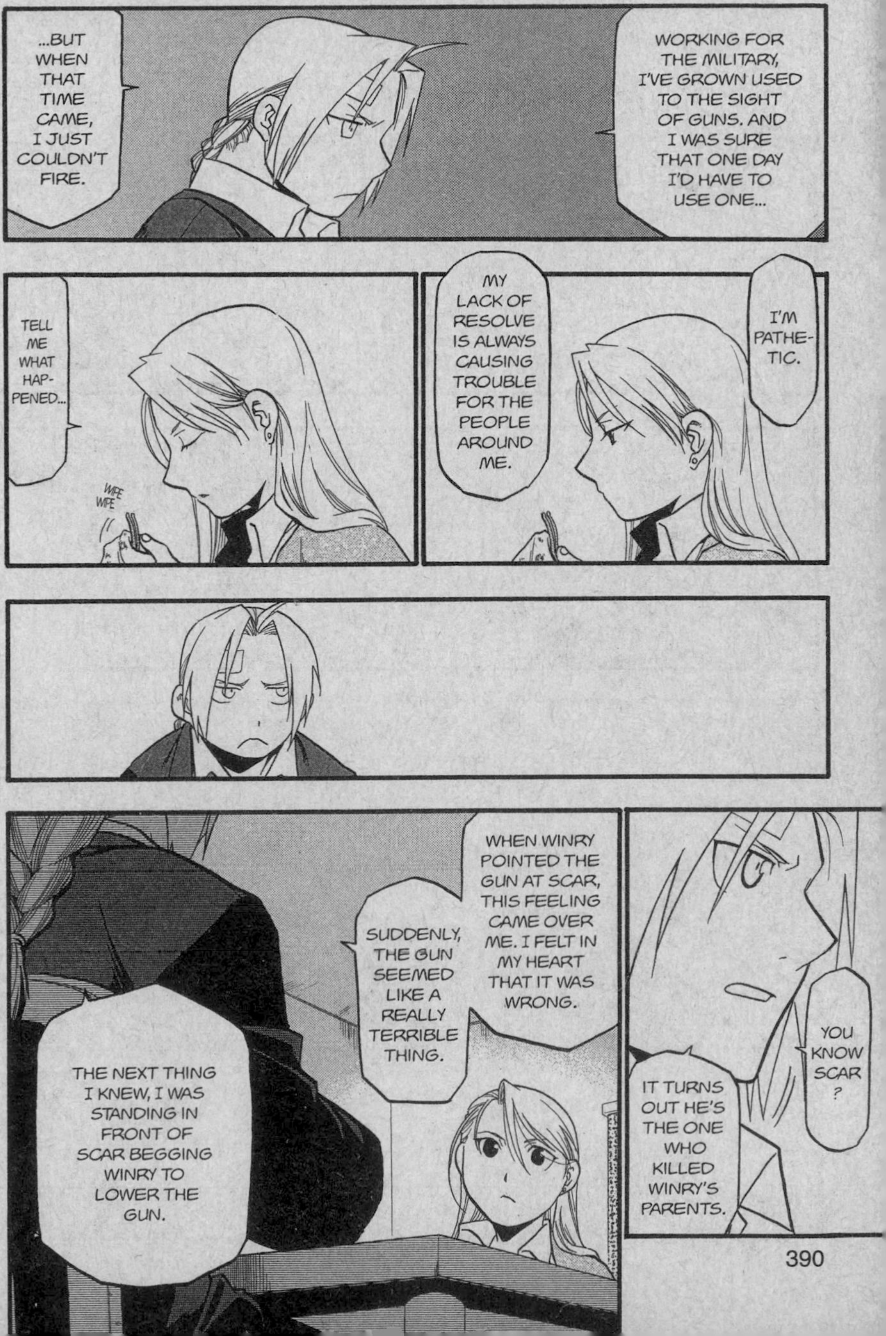
WORKING FOR THE MILITARY, I'VE GROWN USED TO THE SIGHT OF GUNS. AND I WAS SURE THAT ONE DAY I'D HAVE TO USE ONE...
...BUT WHEN THAT TIME CAME, I JUST COULDN'T FIRE.
I'M PATHETIC.
MY LACK OF RESOLVE IS ALWAYS CAUSING TROUBLE FOR THE PEOPLE AROUND ME.
WIPE WIPE
TELL ME WHAT HAPPENED...
YOU KNOW SCAR?
IT TURNS OUT HE'S THE ONE WHO KILLED WINRY'S PARENTS.
WHEN WINRY POINTED THE GUN AT SCAR, THIS FEELING CAME OVER ME. I FELT IN MY HEART THAT IT WAS WRONG.
SUDDENLY, THE GUN SEEMED LIKE A REALLY TERRIBLE THING.
THE NEXT THING I KNEW, I WAS STANDING IN FRONT OF SCAR BEGGING WINRY TO LOWER THE GUN.

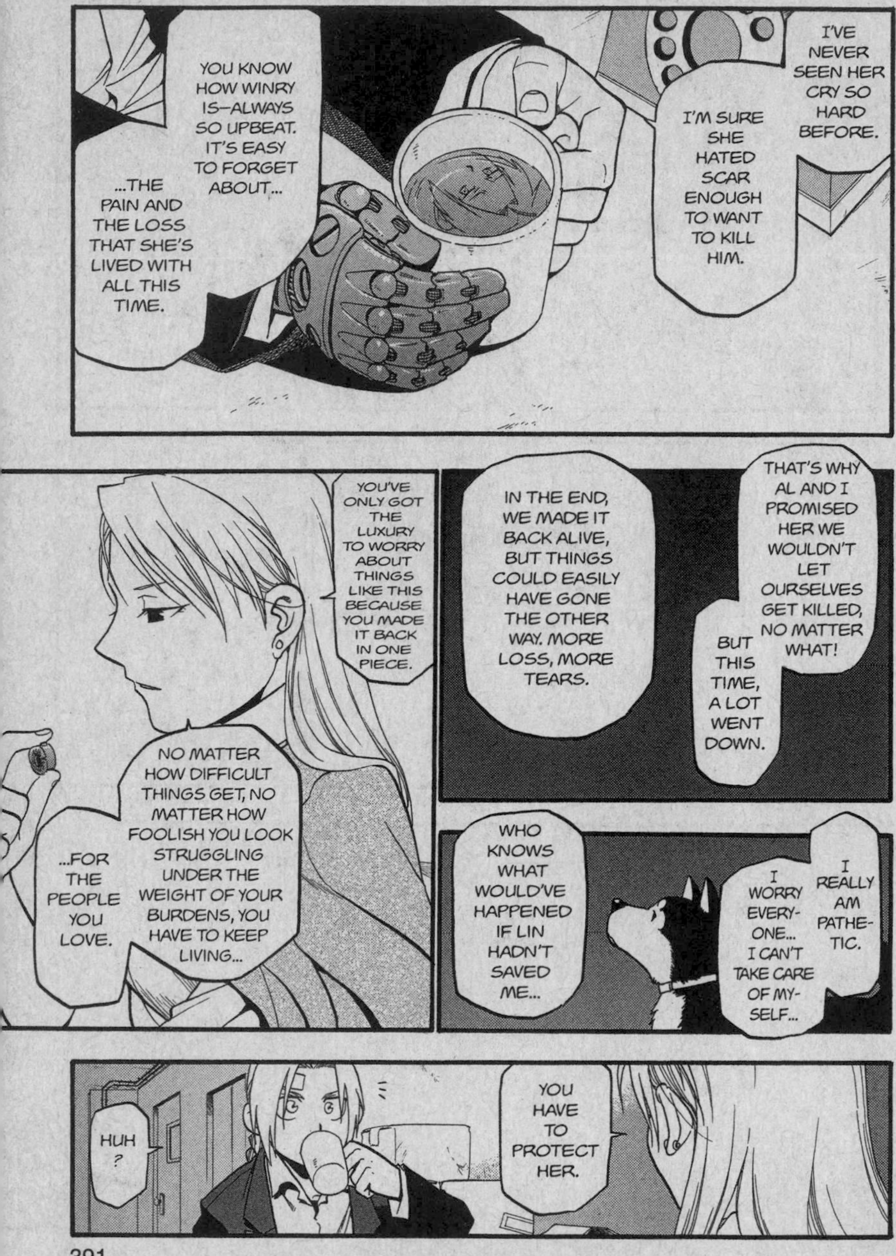
I'VE NEVER SEEN HER CRY SO HARD BEFORE.
I'M SURE SHE HATED SCAR ENOUGH TO WANT TO KILL HIM.
YOU KNOW HOW WINRY IS—ALWAYS SO UPBEAT. IT'S EASY TO FORGET ABOUT...
...THE PAIN AND THE LOSS THAT SHE'S LIVED WITH ALL THIS TIME.
THAT'S WHY AL AND I PROMISED HER WE WOULDN'T LET OURSELVES GET KILLED, NO MATTER WHAT!
BUT THIS TIME, A LOT WENT DOWN.
IN THE END, WE MADE IT BACK ALIVE, BUT THINGS COULD EASILY HAVE GONE THE OTHER WAY. MORE LOSS, MORE TEARS.
I REALLY AM PATHETIC.
I WORRY EVERY-ONE... I CAN'T TAKE CARE OF MY-SELF...
WHO KNOWS WHAT WOULD'VE HAPPENED IF LIN HADN'T SAVED ME...
YOU'VE ONLY GOT THE LUXURY TO WORRY ABOUT THINGS LIKE THIS BECAUSE YOU MADE IT BACK IN ONE PIECE.
NO MATTER HOW DIFFICULT THINGS GET, NO MATTER HOW FOOLISH YOU LOOK STRUGGLING UNDER THE WEIGHT OF YOUR BURDENS, YOU HAVE TO KEEP LIVING...
...FOR THE PEOPLE YOU LOVE.
YOU HAVE TO PROTECT HER.
HUH?

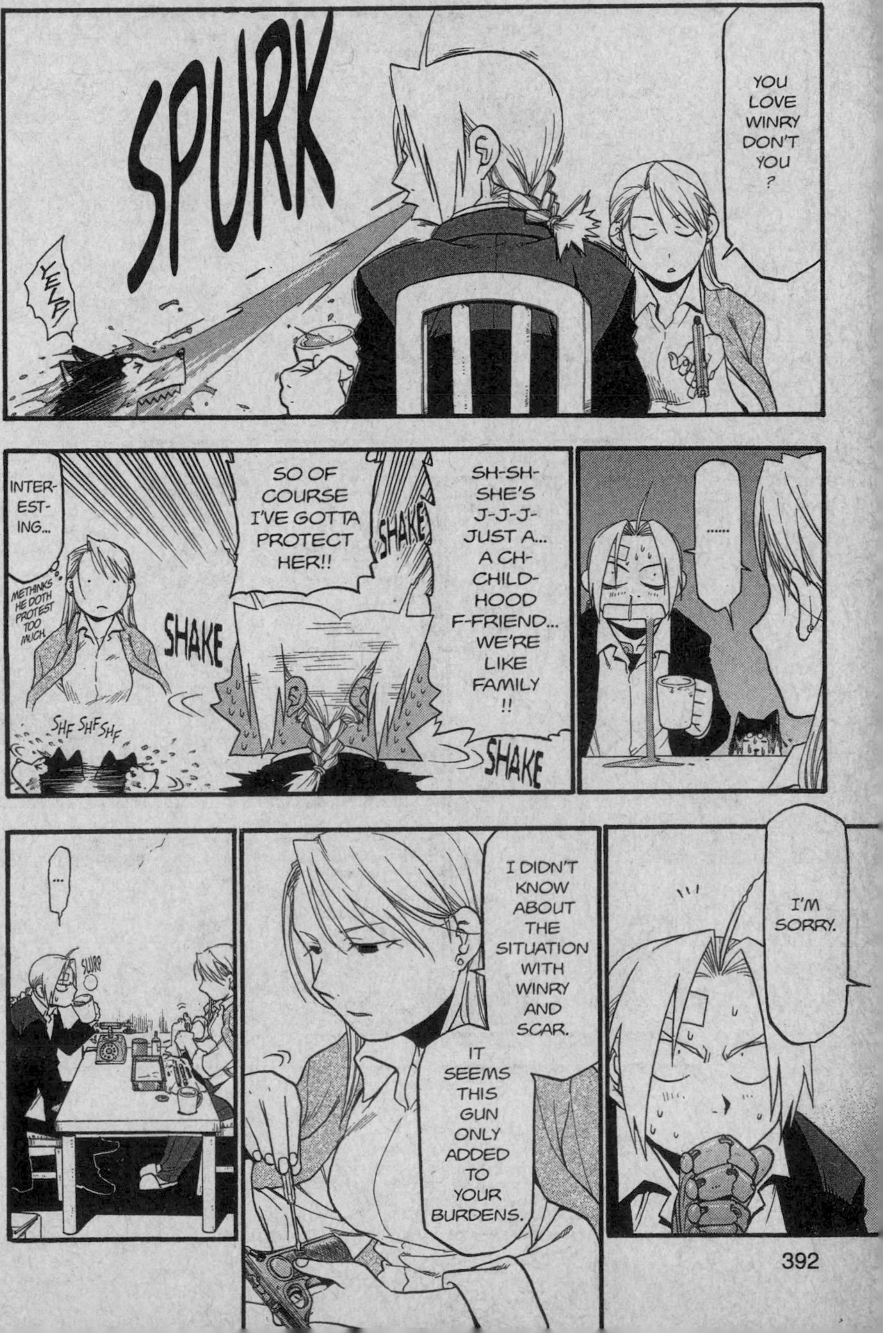
YOU LOVE WINRY DON'T YOU?
SPURK
YELP!
......
SH-SH-SHE'S J-J-J-JUST A... A CH-CHILDHOOD F-FRIEND... WE'RE LIKE FAMILY!!
SHAKE
SHAKE
SO OF COURSE I'VE GOTTA PROTECT HER!!
SHAKE
INTERESTING...
METHINKS HE DOTH PROTEST TOO MUCH.
SHF SHF SHF
I'M SORRY.
I DIDN'T KNOW ABOUT THE SITUATION WITH WINRY AND SCAR.
IT SEEMS THIS GUN ONLY ADDED TO YOUR BURDENS.
...
SLURP

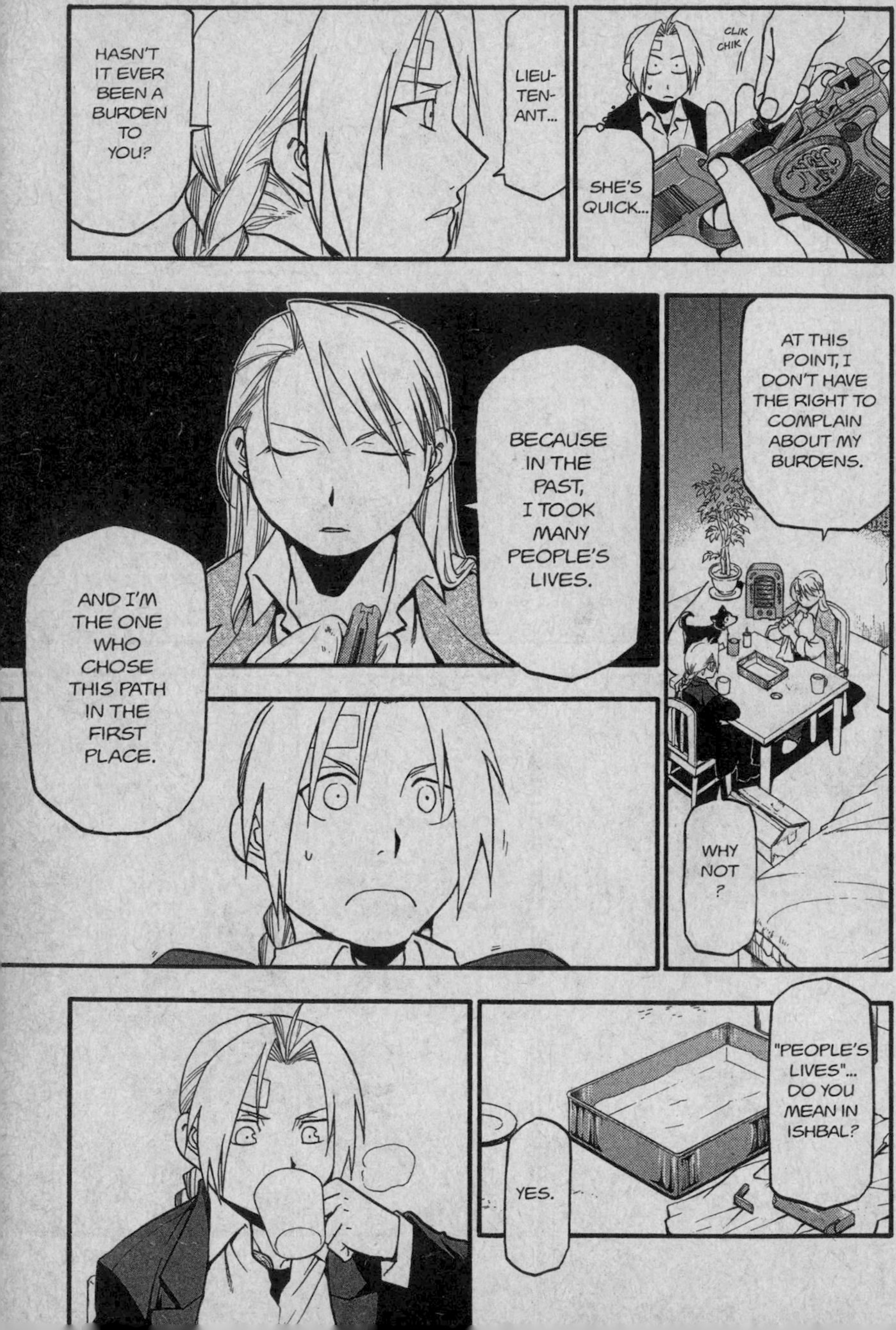
CLIK CHIK
SHE'S QUICK...
LIEU-TENANT...
HASN'T IT EVER BEEN A BURDEN TO YOU?
AT THIS POINT, I DON'T HAVE THE RIGHT TO COMPLAIN ABOUT MY BURDENS.
WHY NOT?
BECAUSE IN THE PAST, I TOOK MANY PEOPLE'S LIVES.
AND I'M THE ONE WHO CHOSE THIS PATH IN THE FIRST PLACE.
"PEOPLE'S LIVES"... DO YOU MEAN IN ISHBAL?
YES.

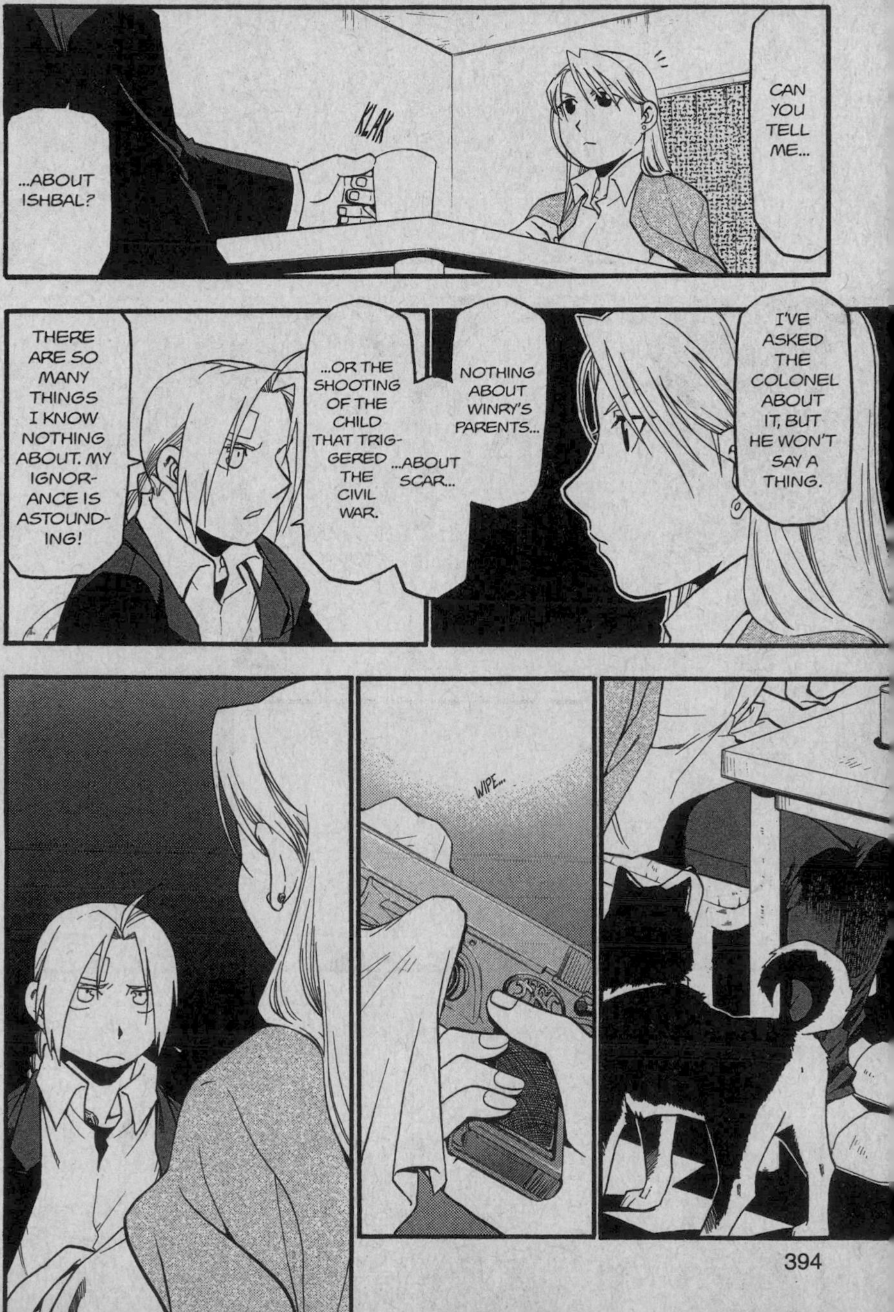
CAN YOU TELL ME...
KLAK
...ABOUT ISHBAL?
I'VE ASKED THE COLONEL ABOUT IT, BUT HE WON'T SAY A THING.
NOTHING ABOUT WINRY'S PARENTS...
...ABOUT SCAR...
...OR THE SHOOTING OF THE CHILD THAT TRIG-GERED THE CIVIL WAR.
THERE ARE SO MANY THINGS I KNOW NOTHING ABOUT. MY IGNOR-ANCE IS ASTOUND-ING!
WIPE...

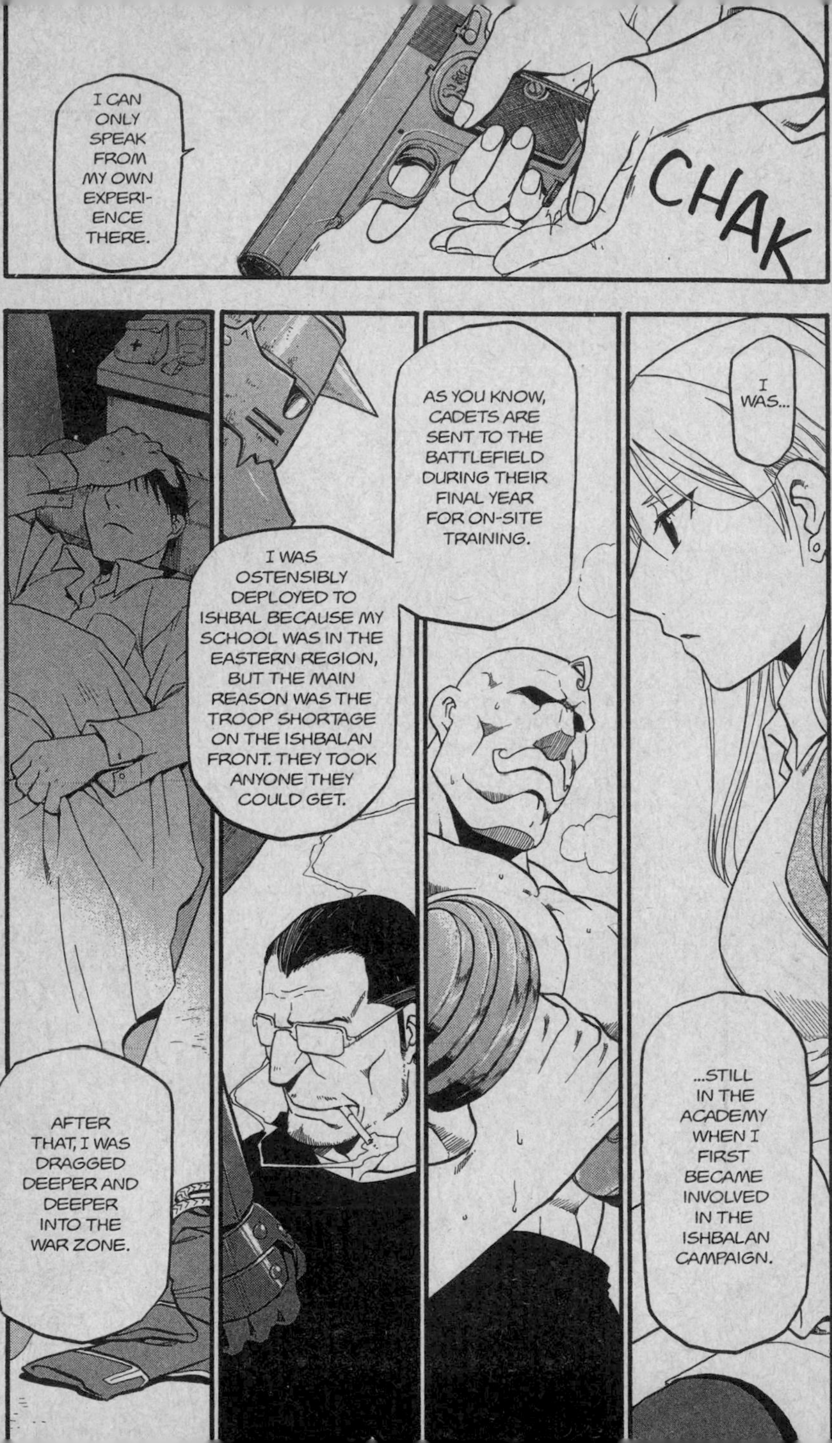
I CAN ONLY SPEAK FROM MY OWN EXPERIENCE THERE.
CHAK
I WAS...
...STILL IN THE ACADEMY WHEN I FIRST BECAME INVOLVED IN THE ISHBALAN CAMPAIGN.
AS YOU KNOW, CADETS ARE SENT TO THE BATTLEFIELD DURING THEIR FINAL YEAR FOR ON-SITE TRAINING.
I WAS OSTENSIBLY DEPLOYED TO ISHBAL BECAUSE MY SCHOOL WAS IN THE EASTERN REGION, BUT THE MAIN REASON WAS THE TROOP SHORTAGE ON THE ISHBALAN FRONT. THEY TOOK ANYONE THEY COULD GET.
AFTER THAT, I WAS DRAGGED DEEPER AND DEEPER INTO THE WAR ZONE.

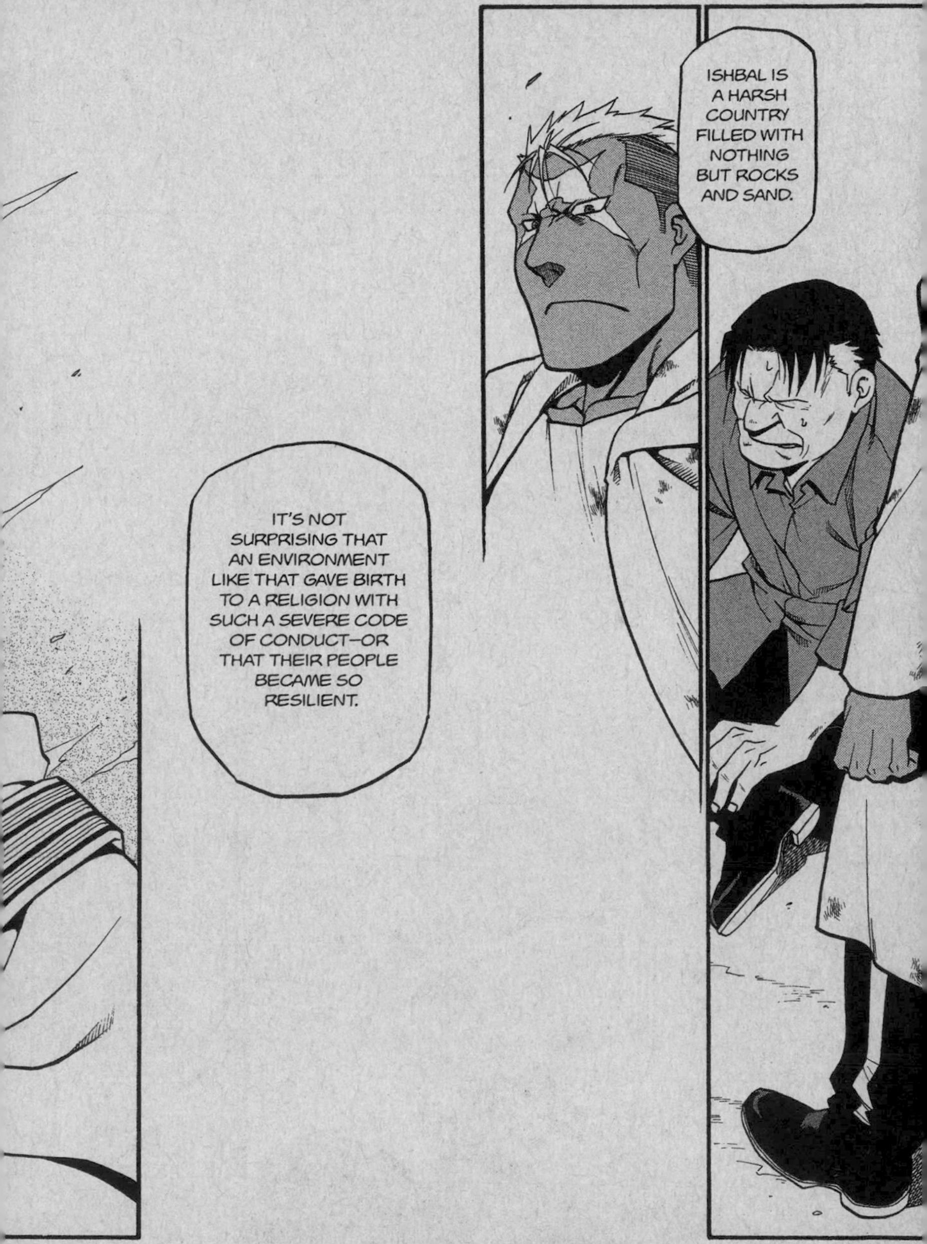
ISHBAL IS A HARSH COUNTRY FILLED WITH NOTHING BUT ROCKS AND SAND.
IT'S NOT SURPRISING THAT AN ENVIRONMENT LIKE THAT GAVE BIRTH TO A RELIGION WITH SUCH A SEVERE CODE OF CONDUCT—OR THAT THEIR PEOPLE BECAME SO RESILIENT.

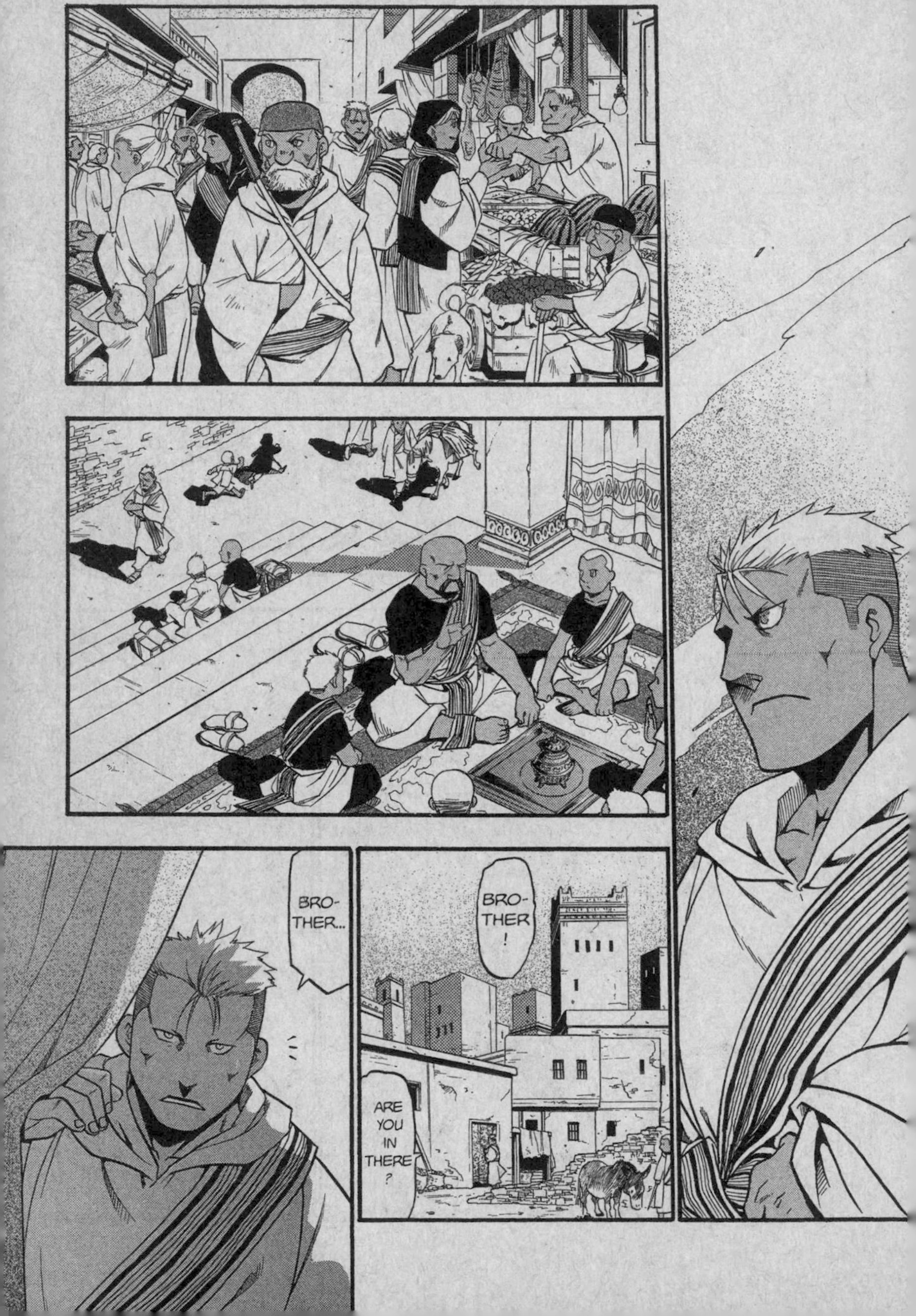
BRO-THER!
ARE YOU IN THERE?
BRO-THER...

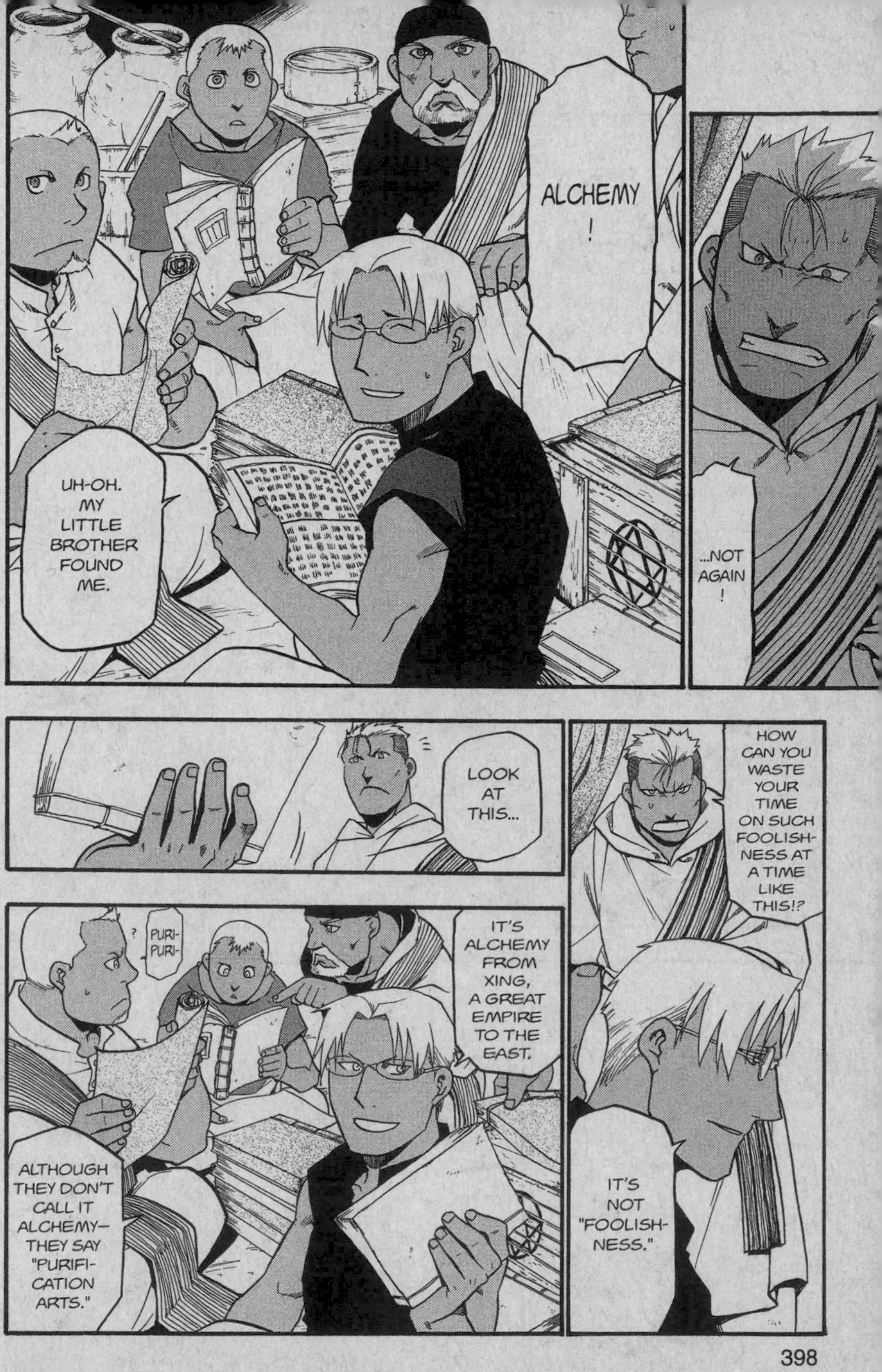
...NOT AGAIN!
ALCHEMY!
UH-OH. MY LITTLE BROTHER FOUND ME.
HOW CAN YOU WASTE YOUR TIME ON SUCH FOOLISHNESS AT A TIME LIKE THIS!?
IT'S NOT "FOOLISHNESS."
LOOK AT THIS...
IT'S ALCHEMY FROM XING, A GREAT EMPIRE TO THE EAST.
PURI-PURI-
?
ALTHOUGH THEY DON'T CALL IT ALCHEMY— THEY SAY "PURIFICATION ARTS."

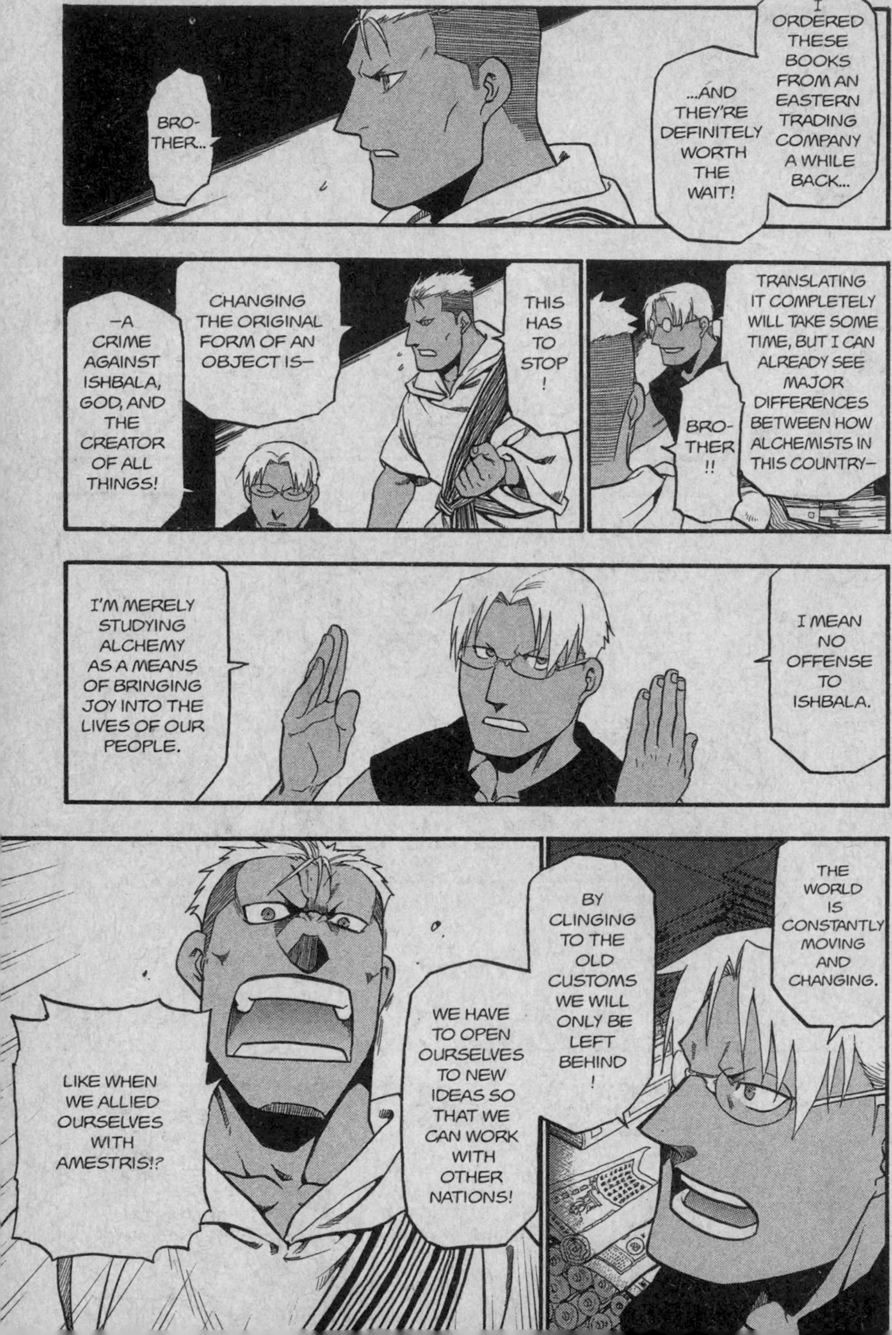
I ORDERED THESE BOOKS FROM AN EASTERN TRADING COMPANY A WHILE BACK...
...AND THEY'RE DEFINITELY WORTH THE WAIT!
BROTHER...
TRANSLATING IT COMPLETELY WILL TAKE SOME TIME, BUT I CAN ALREADY SEE MAJOR DIFFERENCES BETWEEN HOW ALCHEMISTS IN THIS COUNTRY—
BROTHER!!
THIS HAS TO STOP!
CHANGING THE ORIGINAL FORM OF AN OBJECT IS—
—A CRIME AGAINST ISHBALA, GOD, AND THE CREATOR OF ALL THINGS!
I MEAN NO OFFENSE TO ISHBALA.
I'M MERELY STUDYING ALCHEMY AS A MEANS OF BRINGING JOY INTO THE LIVES OF OUR PEOPLE.
THE WORLD IS CONSTANTLY MOVING AND CHANGING.
BY CLINGING TO THE OLD CUSTOMS WE WILL ONLY BE LEFT BEHIND!
WE HAVE TO OPEN OURSELVES TO NEW IDEAS SO THAT WE CAN WORK WITH OTHER NATIONS!
LIKE WHEN WE ALLIED OURSELVES WITH AMESTRIS!?

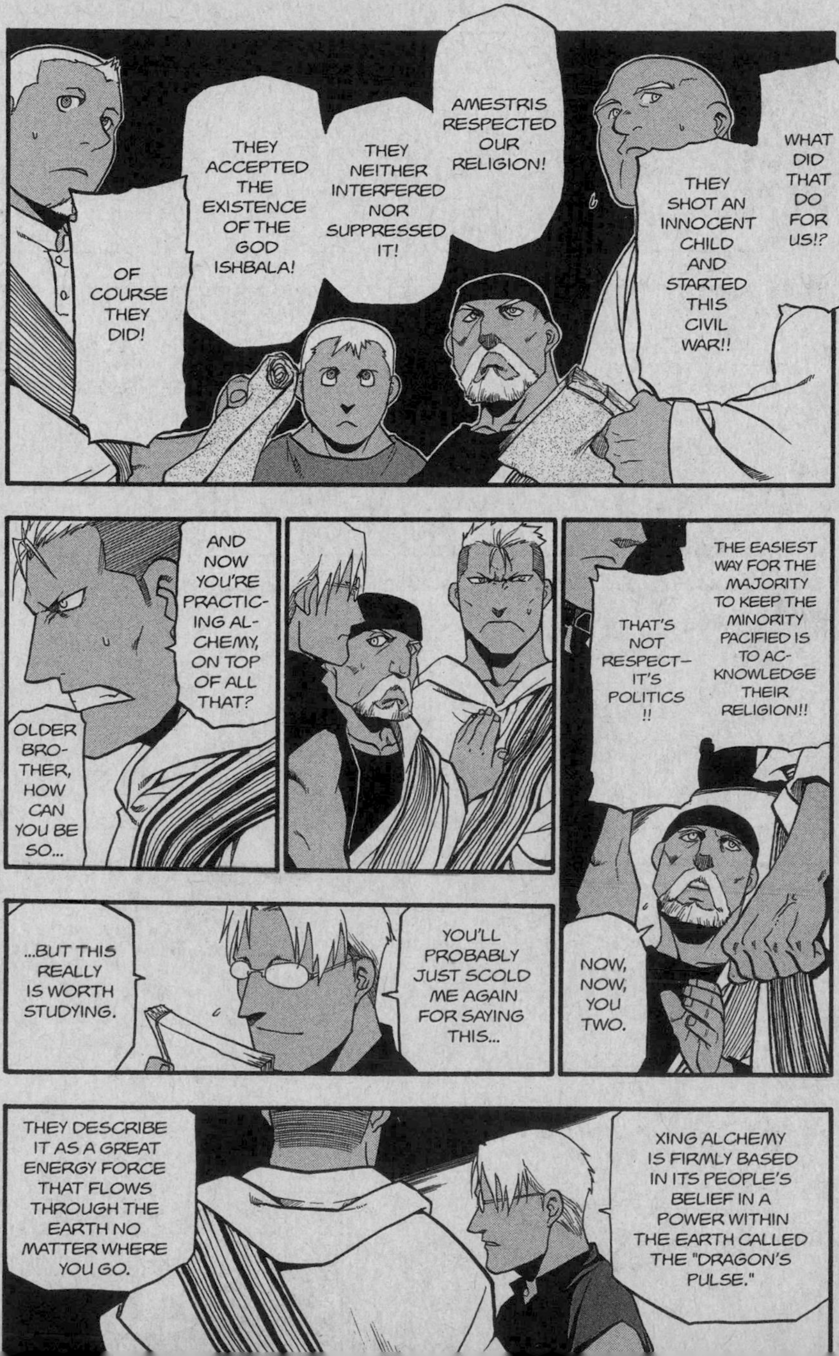
WHAT DID THAT DO FOR US!?
THEY SHOT AN INNOCENT CHILD AND STARTED THIS CIVIL WAR!!
AMESTRIS RESPECTED OUR RELIGION!
THEY NEITHER INTERFERED NOR SUPPRESSED IT!
THEY ACCEPTED THE EXISTENCE OF THE GOD ISHBALA!
OF COURSE THEY DID!
THE EASIEST WAY FOR THE MAJORITY TO KEEP THE MINORITY PACIFIED IS TO ACKNOWLEDGE THEIR RELIGION!!
THAT'S NOT RESPECT— IT'S POLITICS!!
NOW, NOW, YOU TWO.
AND NOW YOU'RE PRACTICING ALCHEMY, ON TOP OF ALL THAT?
OLDER BROTHER, HOW CAN YOU BE SO...
YOU'LL PROBABLY JUST SCOLD ME AGAIN FOR SAYING THIS...
...BUT THIS REALLY IS WORTH STUDYING.
XING ALCHEMY IS FIRMLY BASED IN ITS PEOPLE'S BELIEF IN A POWER WITHIN THE EARTH CALLED THE "DRAGON'S PULSE."
THEY DESCRIBE IT AS A GREAT ENERGY FORCE THAT FLOWS THROUGH THE EARTH NO MATTER WHERE YOU GO.

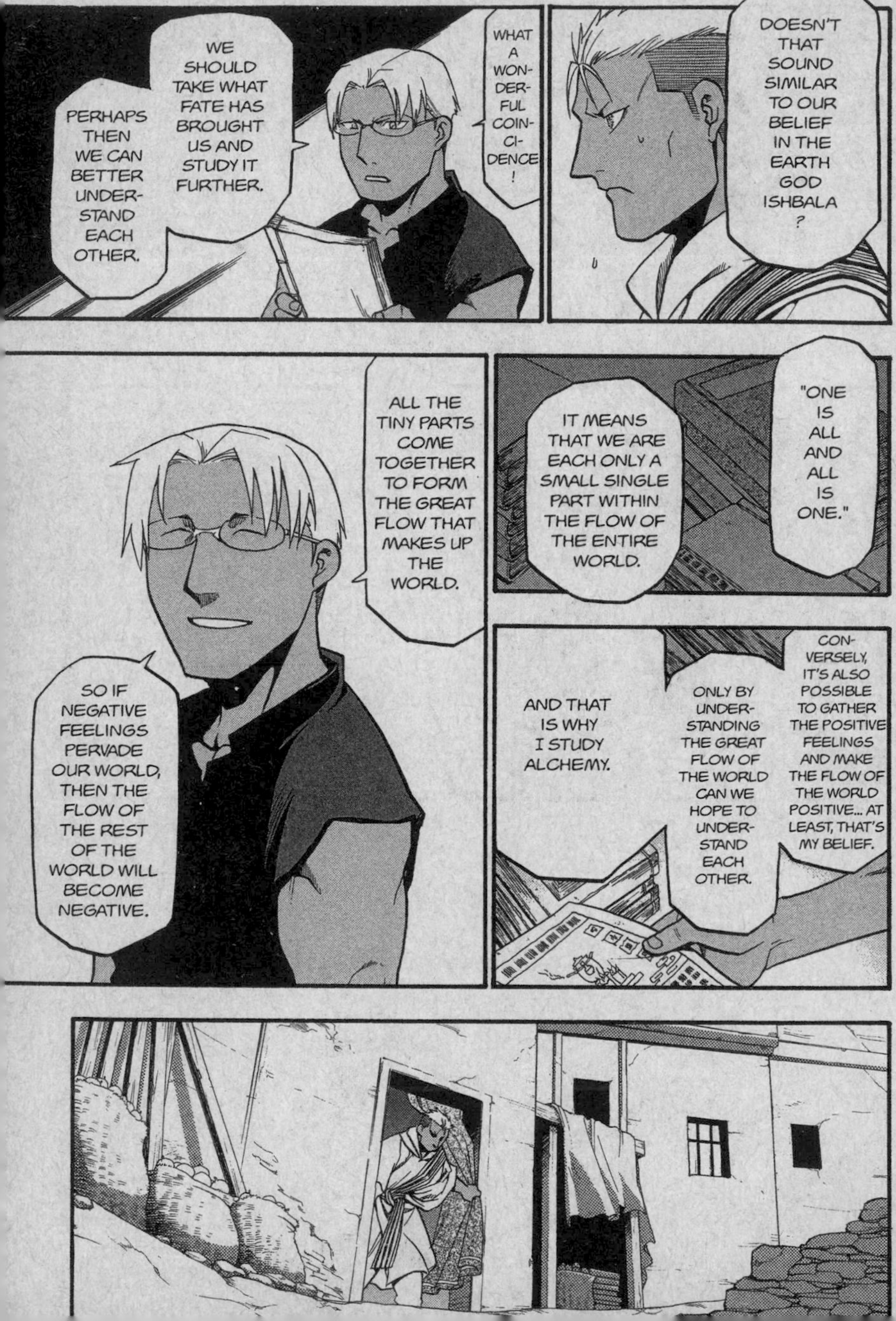
DOESN'T THAT SOUND SIMILAR TO OUR BELIEF IN THE EARTH GOD ISHBALA?
WHAT A WONDERFUL COINCIDENCE!
WE SHOULD TAKE WHAT FATE HAS BROUGHT US AND STUDY IT FURTHER.
PERHAPS THEN WE CAN BETTER UNDERSTAND EACH OTHER.
"ONE IS ALL AND ALL IS ONE."
IT MEANS THAT WE ARE EACH ONLY A SMALL SINGLE PART WITHIN THE FLOW OF THE ENTIRE WORLD.
CONVERSELY, IT'S ALSO POSSIBLE TO GATHER THE POSITIVE FEELINGS AND MAKE THE FLOW OF THE WORLD POSITIVE... AT LEAST, THAT'S MY BELIEF.
ONLY BY UNDERSTANDING THE GREAT FLOW OF THE WORLD CAN WE HOPE TO UNDERSTAND EACH OTHER.
AND THAT IS WHY I STUDY ALCHEMY.
ALL THE TINY PARTS COME TOGETHER TO FORM THE GREAT FLOW THAT MAKES UP THE WORLD.
SO IF NEGATIVE FEELINGS PERVADE OUR WORLD, THEN THE FLOW OF THE REST OF THE WORLD WILL BECOME NEGATIVE.

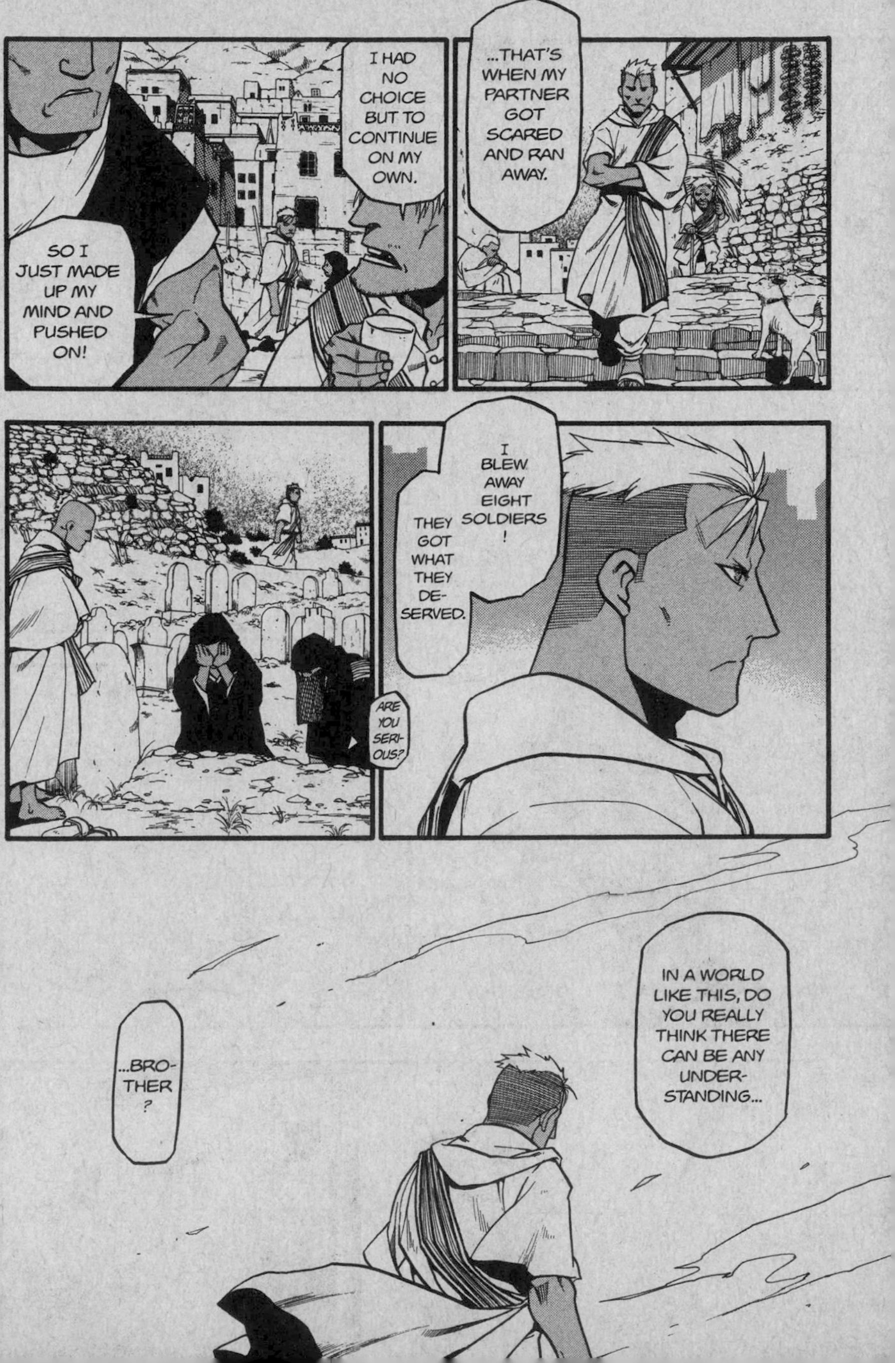
...THAT'S WHEN MY PARTNER GOT SCARED AND RAN AWAY.
I HAD NO CHOICE BUT TO CONTINUE ON MY OWN.
SO I JUST MADE UP MY MIND AND PUSHED ON!
I BLEW AWAY EIGHT SOLDIERS!
THEY GOT WHAT THEY DESERVED.
ARE YOU SERIOUS?
IN A WORLD LIKE THIS, DO YOU REALLY THINK THERE CAN BE ANY UNDERSTANDING...
...BROTHER?

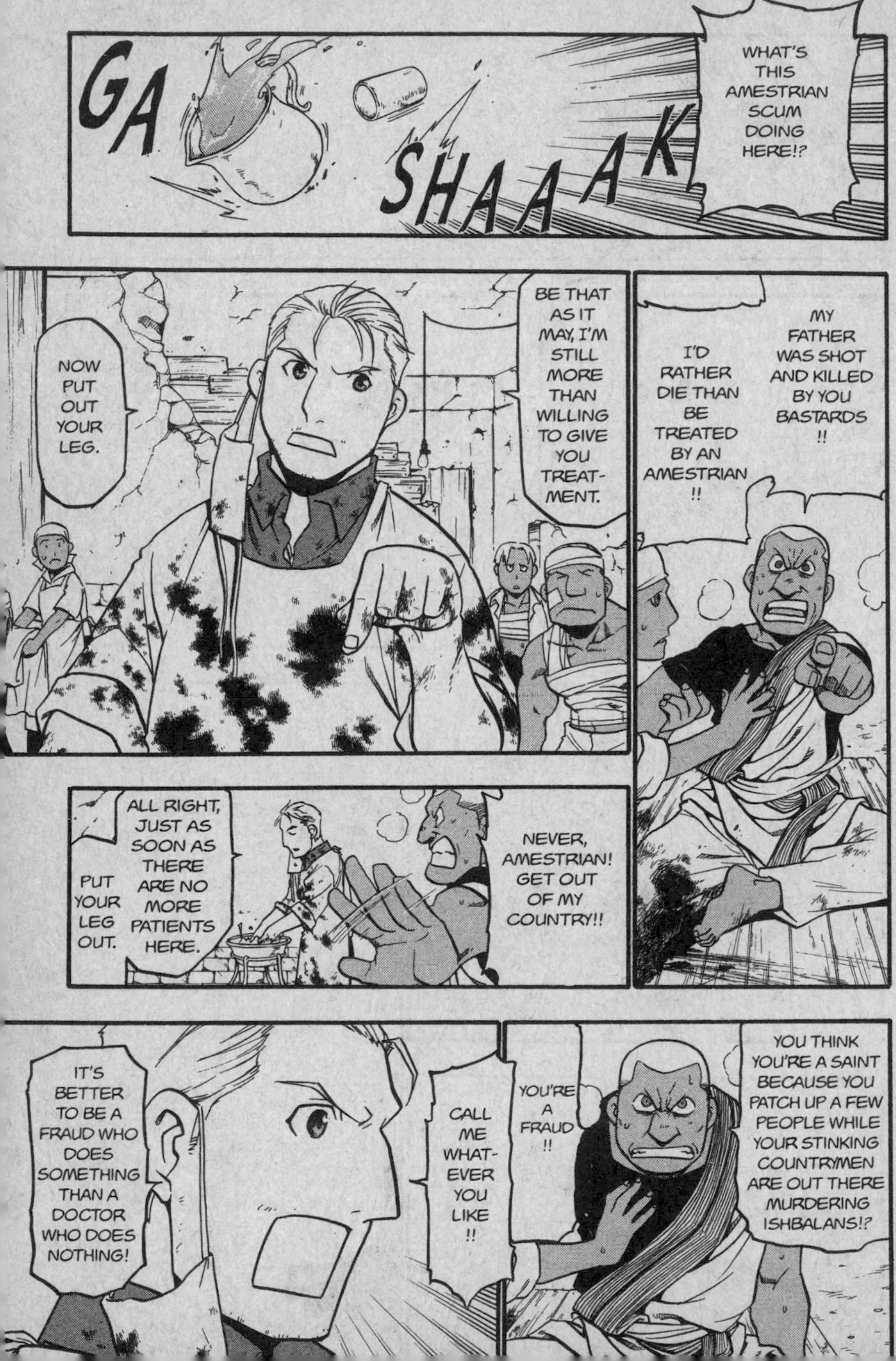
WHAT'S THIS AMESTRIAN SCUM DOING HERE!?
GA SHAAAK
MY FATHER WAS SHOT AND KILLED BY YOU BASTARDS!!
I'D RATHER DIE THAN BE TREATED BY AN AMESTRIAN!!
BE THAT AS IT MAY, I'M STILL MORE THAN WILLING TO GIVE YOU TREATMENT.
NOW PUT OUT YOUR LEG.
NEVER, AMESTRIAN! GET OUT OF MY COUNTRY!!
ALL RIGHT, JUST AS SOON AS THERE ARE NO MORE PATIENTS HERE.
PUT YOUR LEG OUT.
YOU THINK YOU'RE A SAINT BECAUSE YOU PATCH UP A FEW PEOPLE WHILE YOUR STINKING COUNTRYMEN ARE OUT THERE MURDERING ISHBALANS!?
YOU'RE A FRAUD!!
CALL ME WHATEVER YOU LIKE!!
IT'S BETTER TO BE A FRAUD WHO DOES SOMETHING THAN A DOCTOR WHO DOES NOTHING!

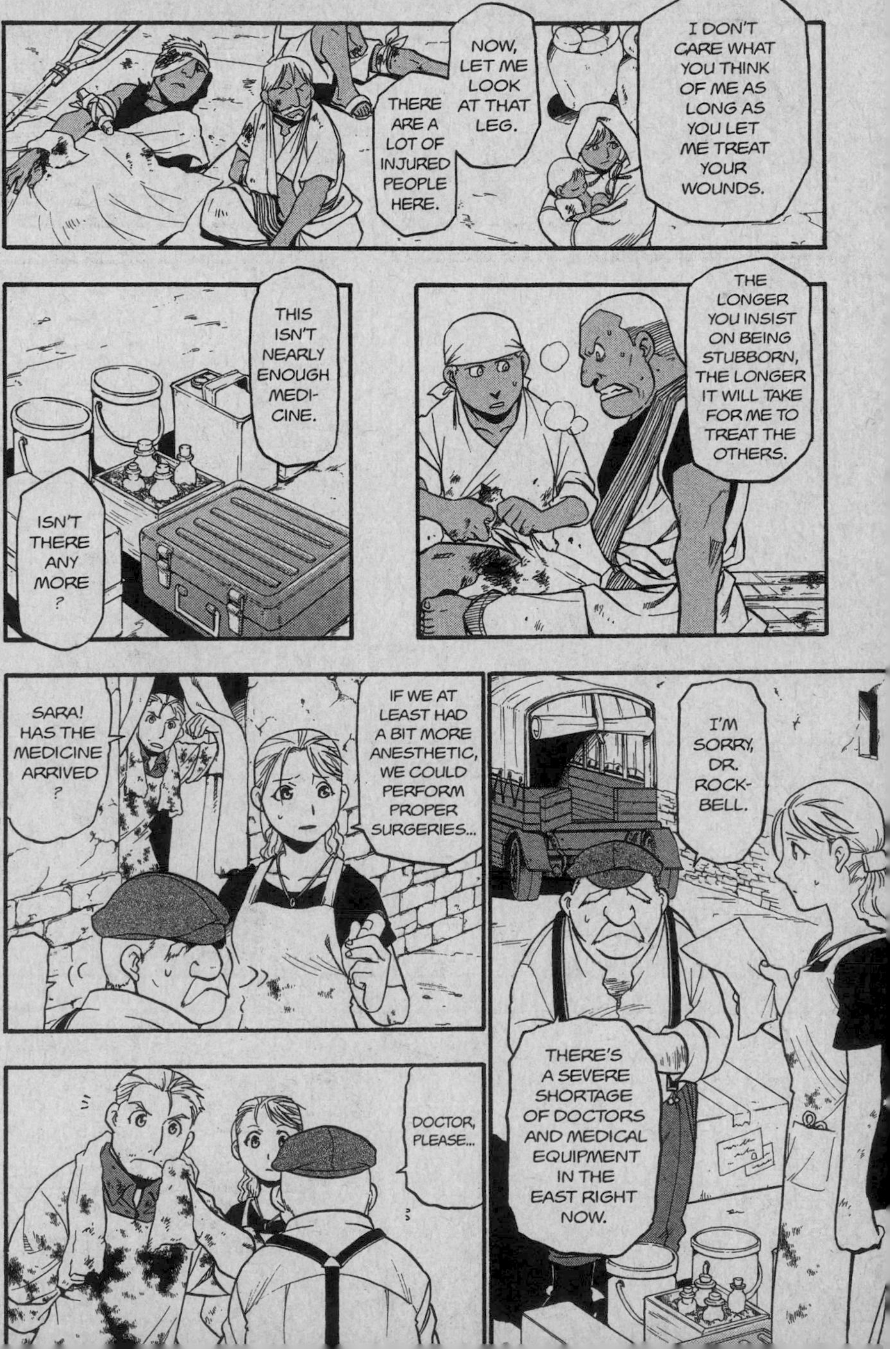
I DON'T CARE WHAT YOU THINK OF ME AS LONG AS YOU LET ME TREAT YOUR WOUNDS.
NOW, LET ME LOOK AT THAT LEG.
THERE ARE A LOT OF INJURED PEOPLE HERE.
THE LONGER YOU INSIST ON BEING STUBBORN, THE LONGER IT WILL TAKE FOR ME TO TREAT THE OTHERS.
THIS ISN'T NEARLY ENOUGH MEDI-CINE.
ISN'T THERE ANY MORE?
I'M SORRY, DR. ROCK-BELL.
THERE'S A SEVERE SHORTAGE OF DOCTORS AND MEDICAL EQUIPMENT IN THE EAST RIGHT NOW.
IF WE AT LEAST HAD A BIT MORE ANESTHETIC, WE COULD PERFORM PROPER SURGERIES...
SARA! HAS THE MEDICINE ARRIVED?
DOCTOR, PLEASE...

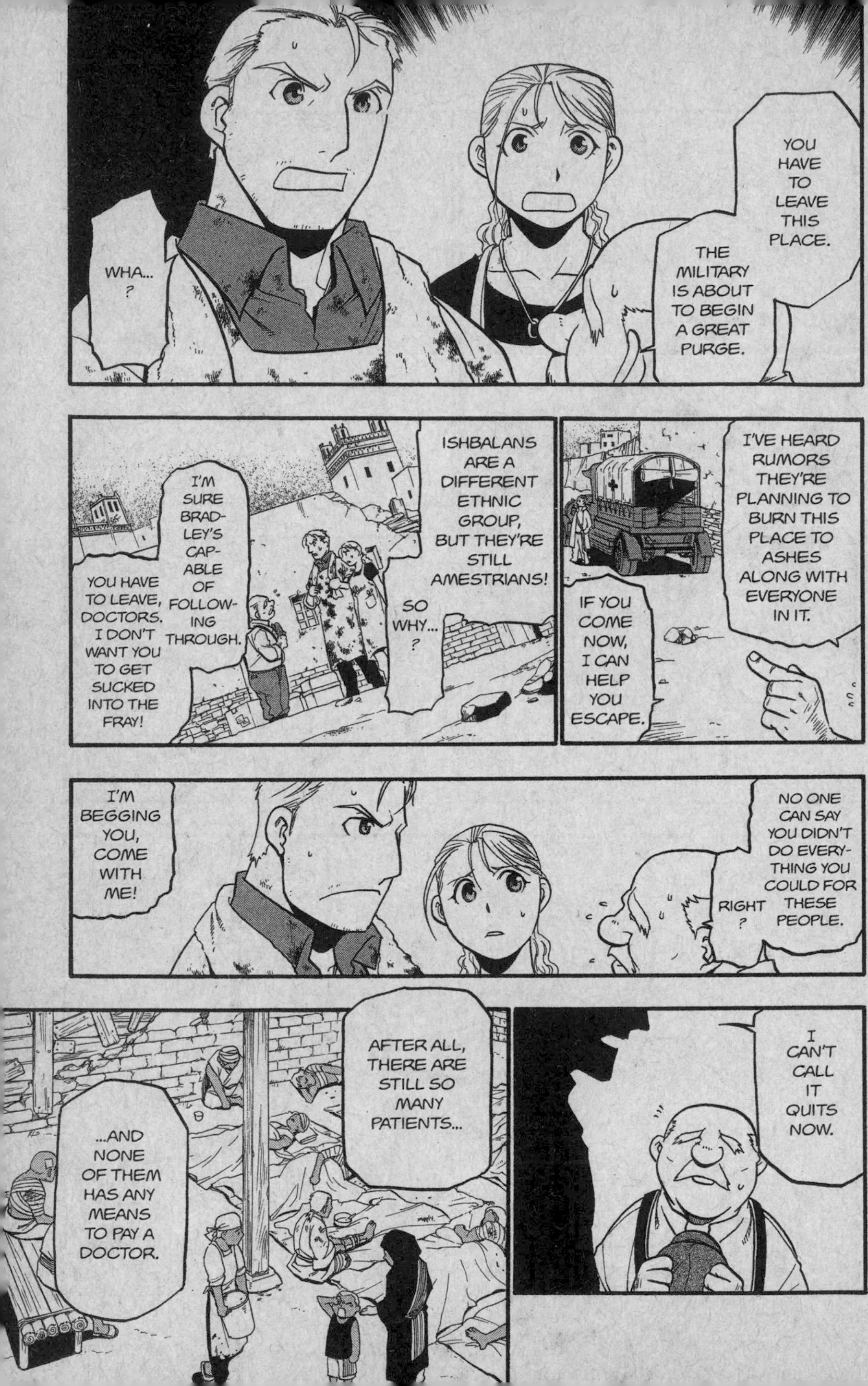
YOU HAVE TO LEAVE THIS PLACE.
THE MILITARY IS ABOUT TO BEGIN A GREAT PURGE.
WHA...?
I'VE HEARD RUMORS THEY'RE PLANNING TO BURN THIS PLACE TO ASHES ALONG WITH EVERYONE IN IT.
IF YOU COME NOW, I CAN HELP YOU ESCAPE.
ISHBALANS ARE A DIFFERENT ETHNIC GROUP, BUT THEY'RE STILL AMESTRIANS!
SO WHY...?
I'M SURE BRADLEY'S CAPABLE OF FOLLOWING THROUGH.
YOU HAVE TO LEAVE, DOCTORS. I DON'T WANT YOU TO GET SUCKED INTO THE FRAY!
NO ONE CAN SAY YOU DIDN'T DO EVERYTHING YOU COULD FOR THESE PEOPLE.
RIGHT?
I'M BEGGING YOU, COME WITH ME!
I CAN'T CALL IT QUITS NOW.
AFTER ALL, THERE ARE STILL SO MANY PATIENTS...
...AND NONE OF THEM HAS ANY MEANS TO PAY A DOCTOR.

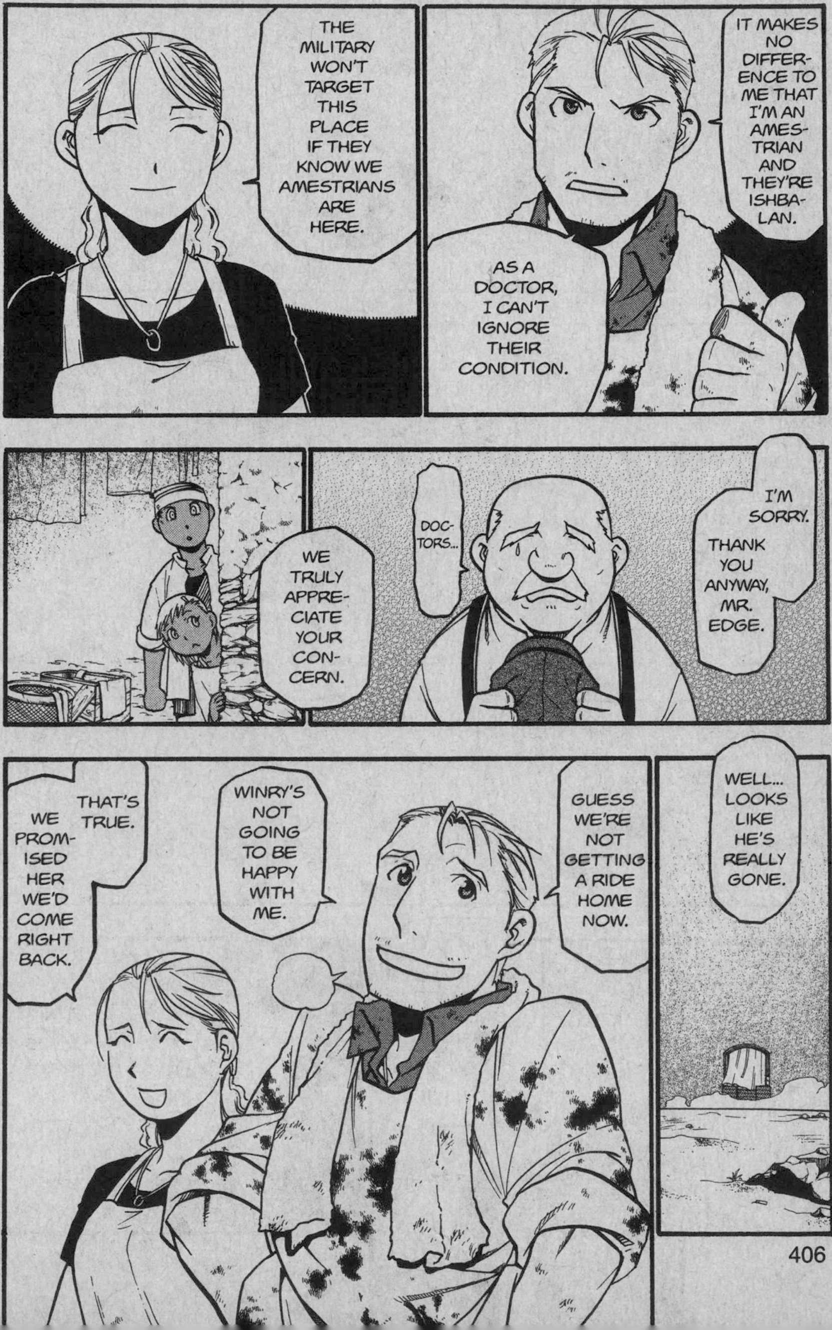
IT MAKES NO DIFFERENCE TO ME THAT I'M AN AMESTRIAN AND THEY'RE ISHBALAN.
AS A DOCTOR, I CAN'T IGNORE THEIR CONDITION.
THE MILITARY WON'T TARGET THIS PLACE IF THEY KNOW WE AMESTRIANS ARE HERE.
I'M SORRY.
THANK YOU ANYWAY, MR. EDGE.
DOCTORS...
WE TRULY APPRECIATE YOUR CONCERN.
WELL... LOOKS LIKE HE'S REALLY GONE.
GUESS WE'RE NOT GETTING A RIDE HOME NOW.
WINRY'S NOT GOING TO BE HAPPY WITH ME.
THAT'S TRUE.
WE PROMISED HER WE'D COME RIGHT BACK.

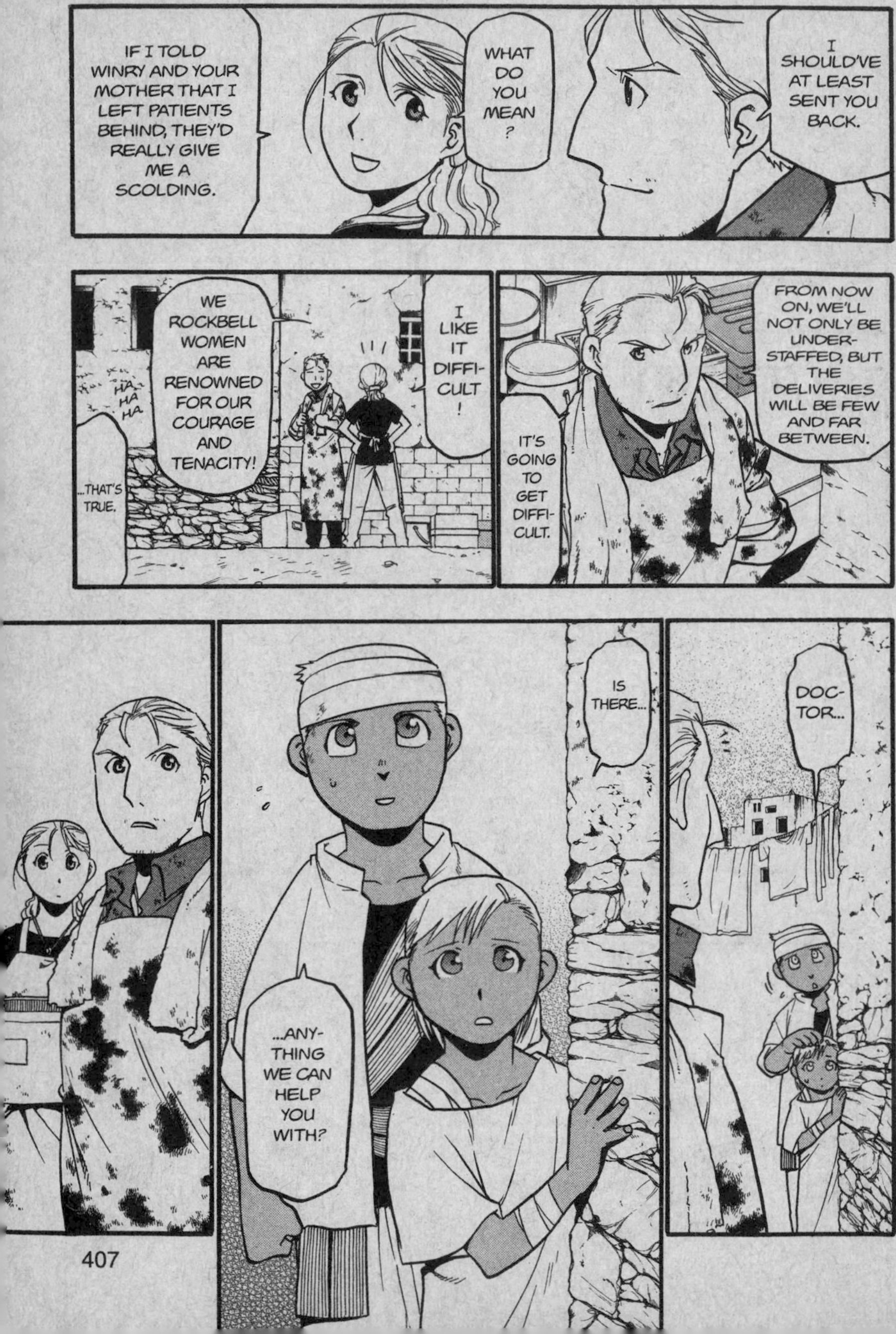
I SHOULD'VE AT LEAST SENT YOU BACK.
WHAT DO YOU MEAN?
IF I TOLD WINRY AND YOUR MOTHER THAT I LEFT PATIENTS BEHIND, THEY'D REALLY GIVE ME A SCOLDING.
FROM NOW ON, WE'LL NOT ONLY BE UNDER-STAFFED, BUT THE DELIVERIES WILL BE FEW AND FAR BETWEEN.
IT'S GOING TO GET DIFFI-CULT.
I LIKE IT DIFFI-CULT!
WE ROCKBELL WOMEN ARE RENOWNED FOR OUR COURAGE AND TENACITY!
HA HA HA
...THAT'S TRUE.
DOC-TOR...
IS THERE...
...ANY-THING WE CAN HELP YOU WITH?

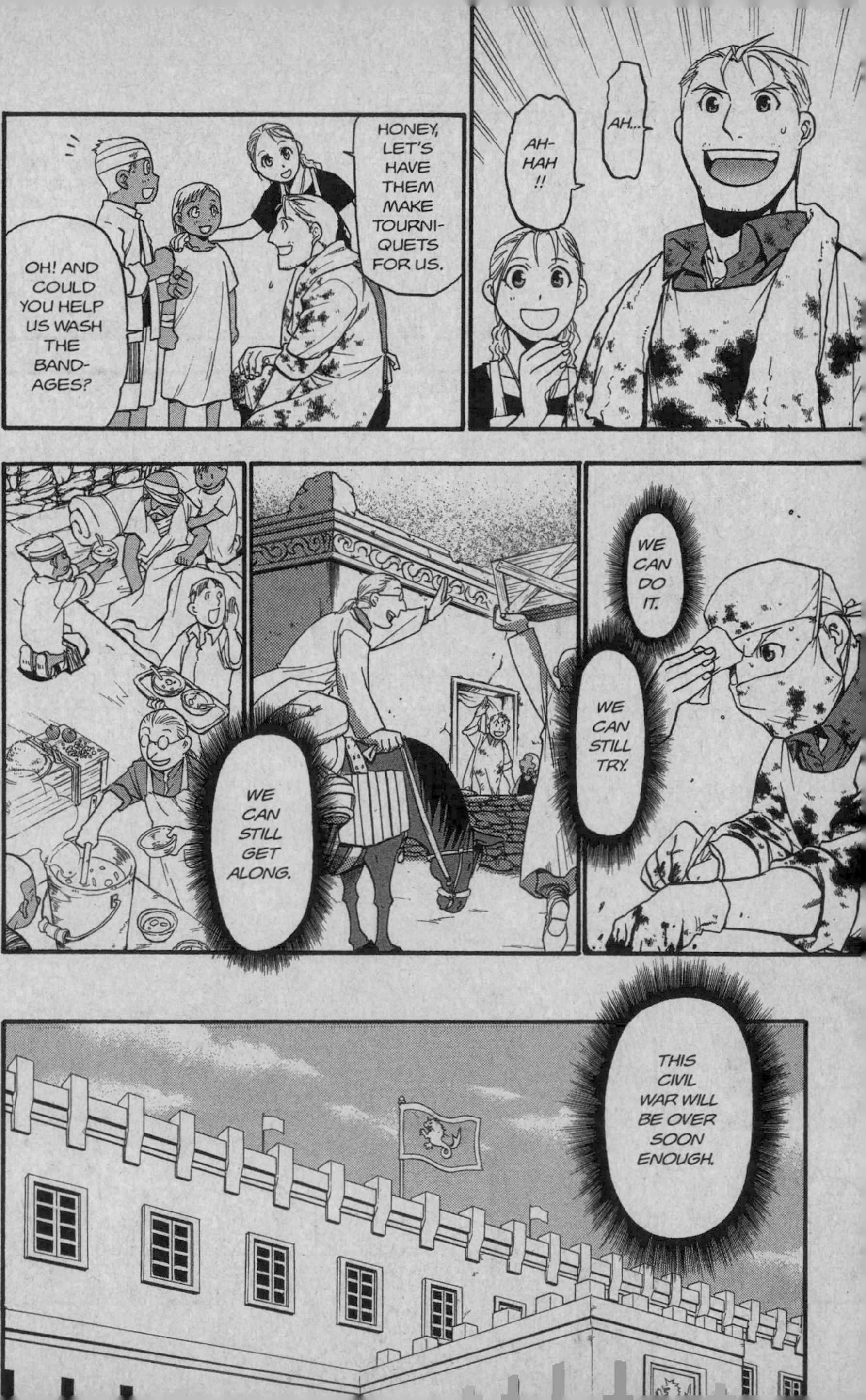
AH...
AH-HAH !!
HONEY, LET'S HAVE THEM MAKE TOURNIQUETS FOR US.
OH! AND COULD YOU HELP US WASH THE BANDAGES?
WE CAN DO IT.
WE CAN STILL TRY.
WE CAN STILL GET ALONG.
THIS CIVIL WAR WILL BE OVER SOON ENOUGH.

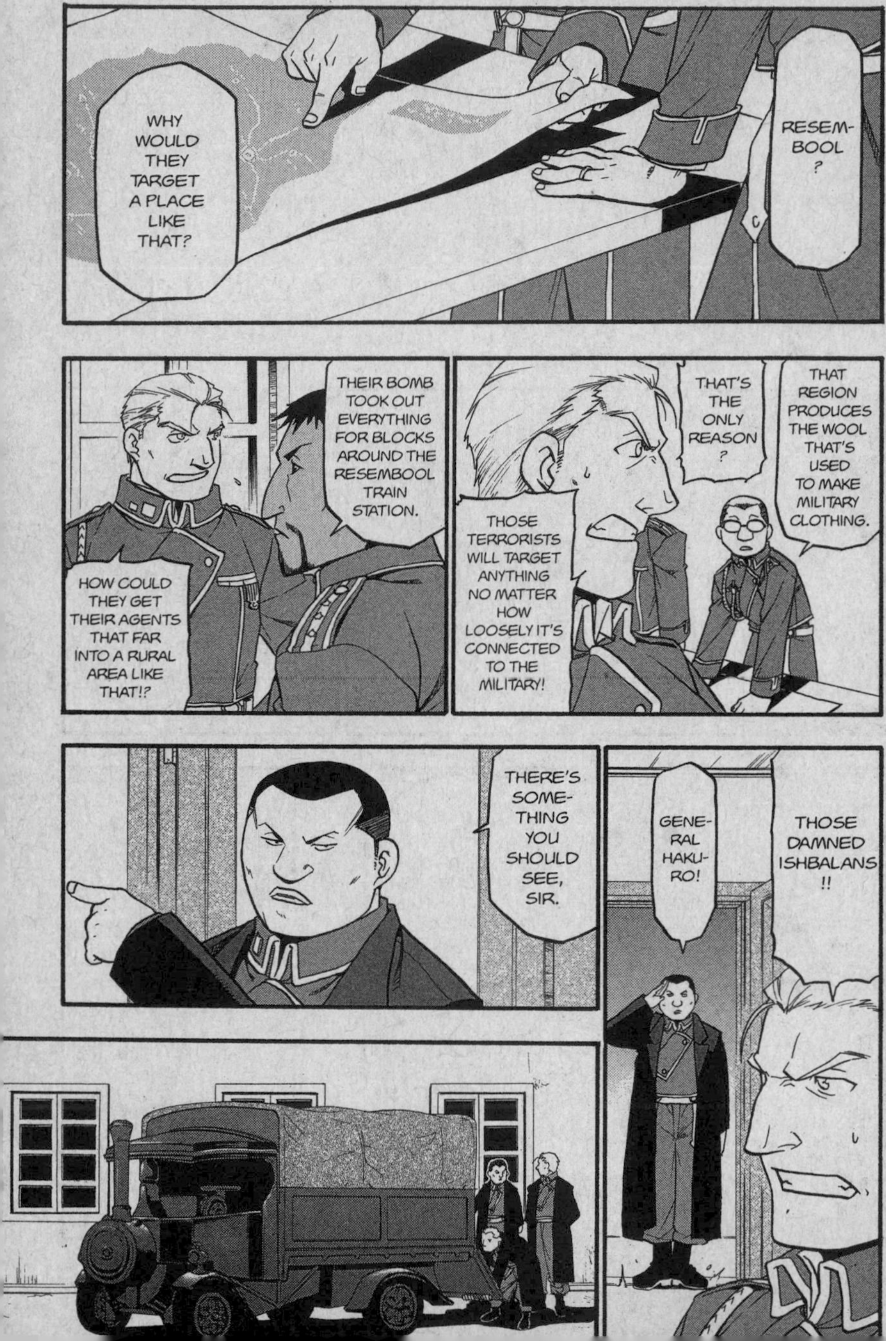
RESEMBOOL?
WHY WOULD THEY TARGET A PLACE LIKE THAT?
THAT REGION PRODUCES THE WOOL THAT'S USED TO MAKE MILITARY CLOTHING.
THAT'S THE ONLY REASON?
THOSE TERRORISTS WILL TARGET ANYTHING NO MATTER HOW LOOSELY IT'S CONNECTED TO THE MILITARY!
THEIR BOMB TOOK OUT EVERYTHING FOR BLOCKS AROUND THE RESEMBOOL TRAIN STATION.
HOW COULD THEY GET THEIR AGENTS THAT FAR INTO A RURAL AREA LIKE THAT!?
THOSE DAMNED ISHBALANS!!
GENERAL HAKURO!
THERE'S SOMETHING YOU SHOULD SEE, SIR.

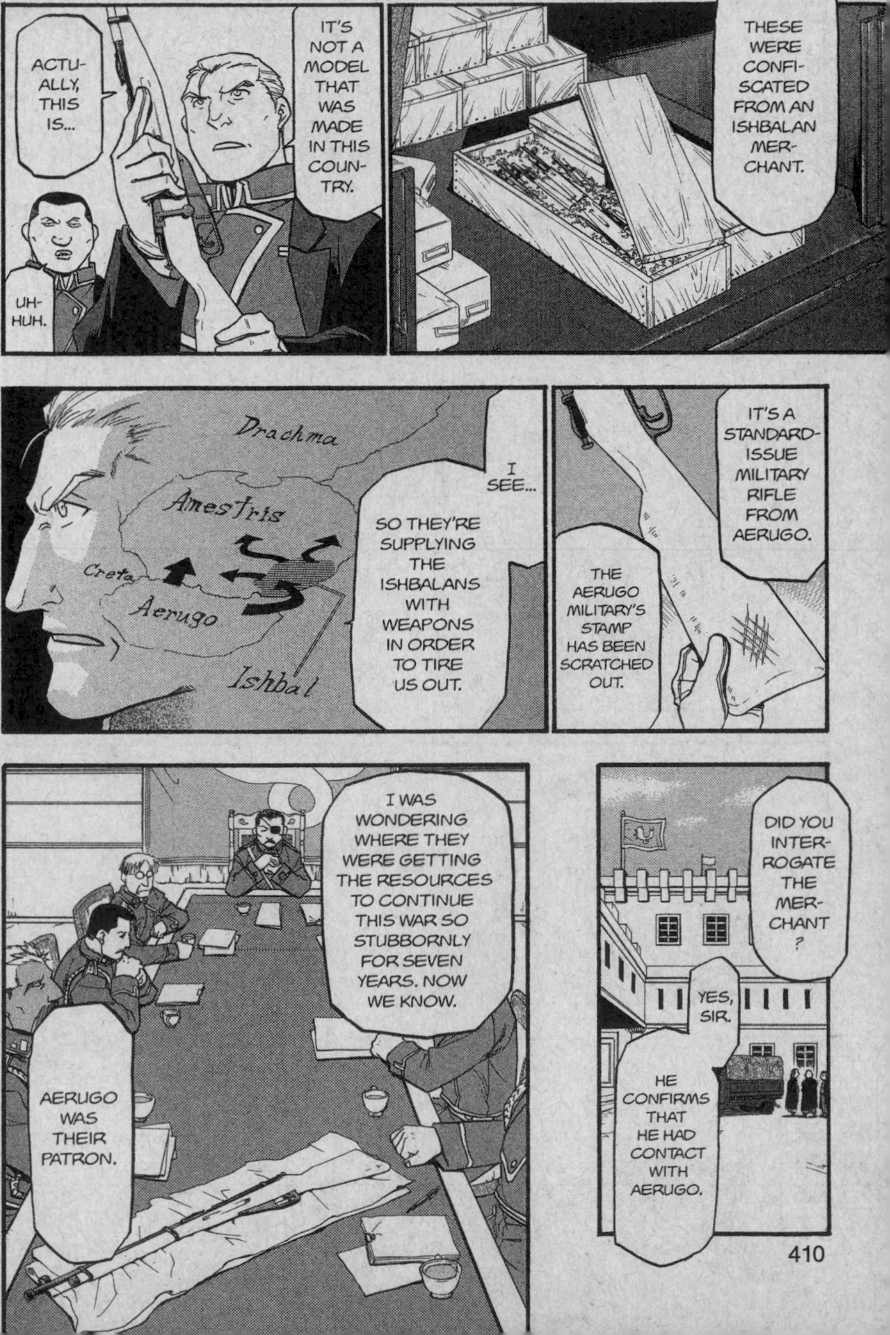
THESE WERE CONFISCATED FROM AN ISHBALAN MERCHANT.
IT'S NOT A MODEL THAT WAS MADE IN THIS COUNTRY.
ACTUALLY, THIS IS...
UH-HUH.
IT'S A STANDARD-ISSUE MILITARY RIFLE FROM AERUGO.
THE AERUGO MILITARY'S STAMP HAS BEEN SCRATCHED OUT.
I SEE...
SO THEY'RE SUPPLYING THE ISHBALANS WITH WEAPONS IN ORDER TO TIRE US OUT.
Drachma
Amestris
Creta
Aerugo
Ishbal
DID YOU INTERROGATE THE MERCHANT?
YES, SIR.
HE CONFIRMS THAT HE HAD CONTACT WITH AERUGO.
I WAS WONDERING WHERE THEY WERE GETTING THE RESOURCES TO CONTINUE THIS WAR SO STUBBORNLY FOR SEVEN YEARS. NOW WE KNOW.
AERUGO WAS THEIR PATRON.

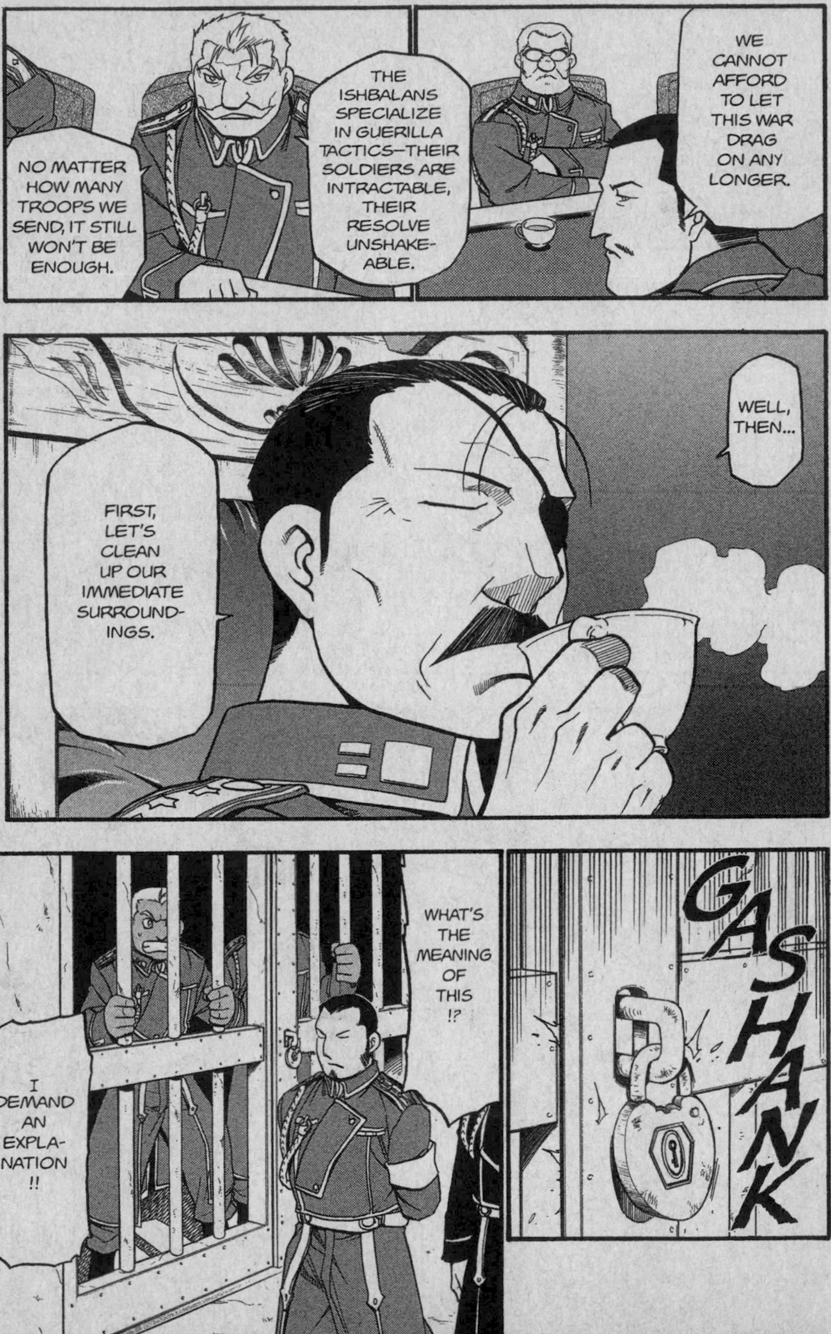
WE CANNOT AFFORD TO LET THIS WAR DRAG ON ANY LONGER.
THE ISHBALANS SPECIALIZE IN GUERILLA TACTICS—THEIR SOLDIERS ARE INTRACTABLE, THEIR RESOLVE UNSHAKE-ABLE.
NO MATTER HOW MANY TROOPS WE SEND, IT STILL WON'T BE ENOUGH.
WELL, THEN...
FIRST, LET'S CLEAN UP OUR IMMEDIATE SURROUND-INGS.
GASHANK
WHAT'S THE MEANING OF THIS !?
I DEMAND AN EXPLA-NATION !!

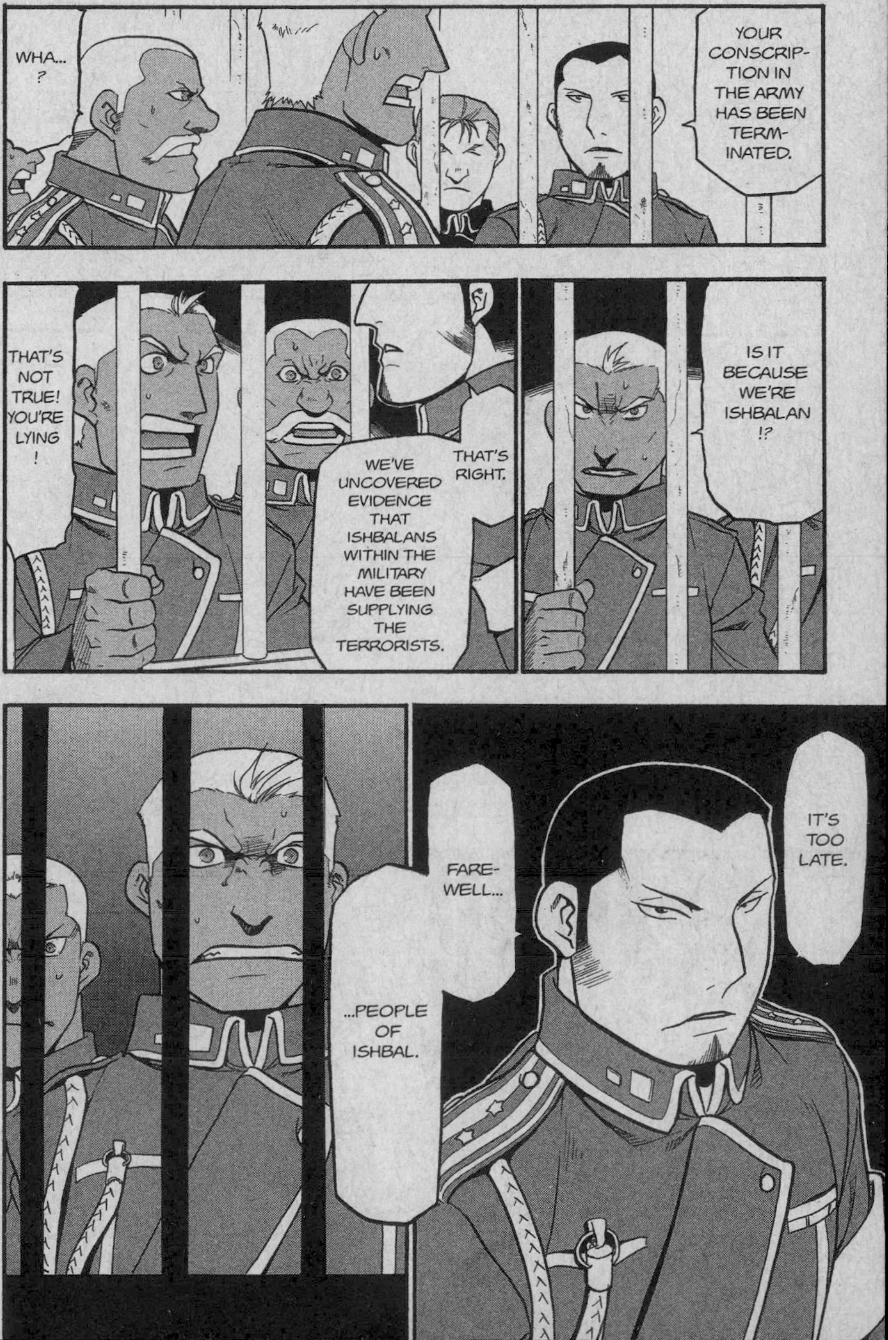
YOUR CONSCRIPTION IN THE ARMY HAS BEEN TERMINATED.
WHA...?
IS IT BECAUSE WE'RE ISHBALAN!?
THAT'S RIGHT.
WE'VE UNCOVERED EVIDENCE THAT ISHBALANS WITHIN THE MILITARY HAVE BEEN SUPPLYING THE TERRORISTS.
THAT'S NOT TRUE! YOU'RE LYING!
IT'S TOO LATE.
FAREWELL...
...PEOPLE OF ISHBAL.

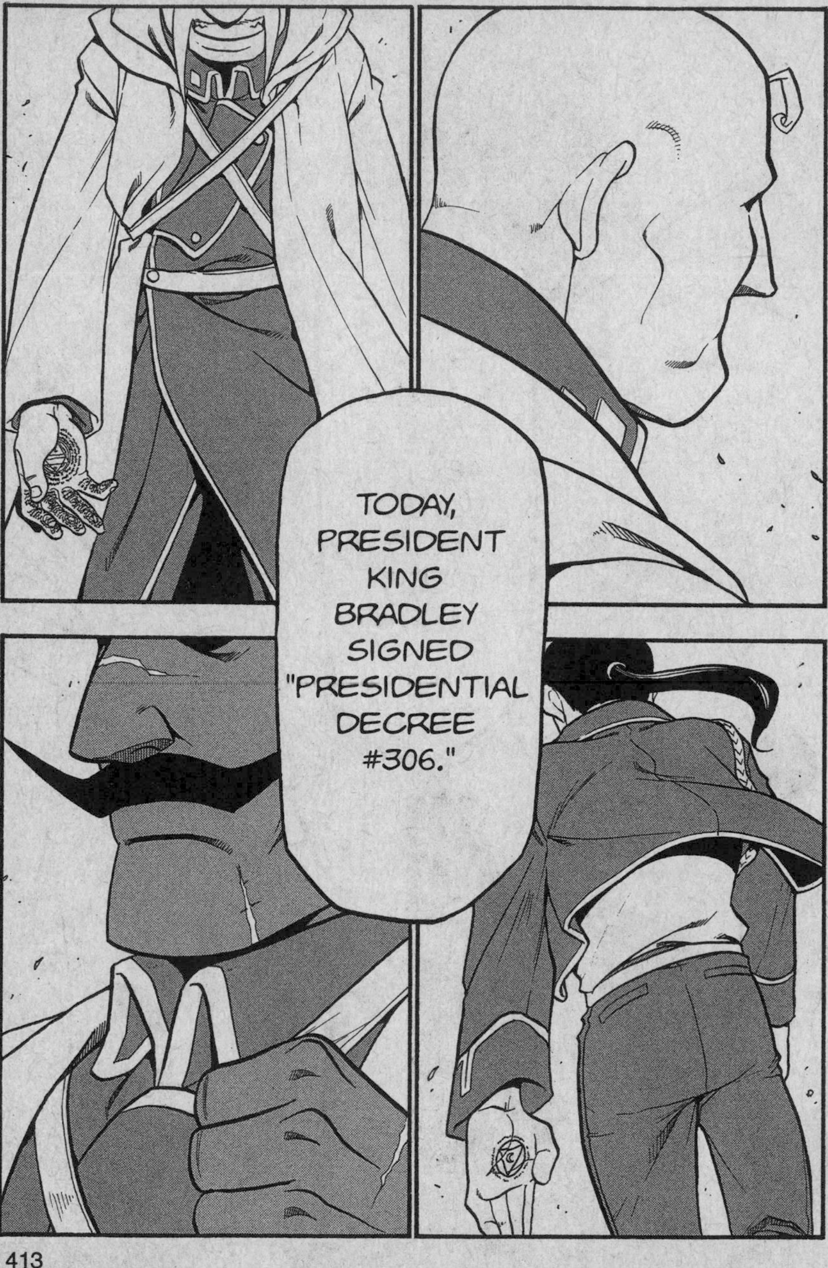
TODAY, PRESIDENT KING BRADLEY SIGNED "PRESIDENTIAL DECREE #306."

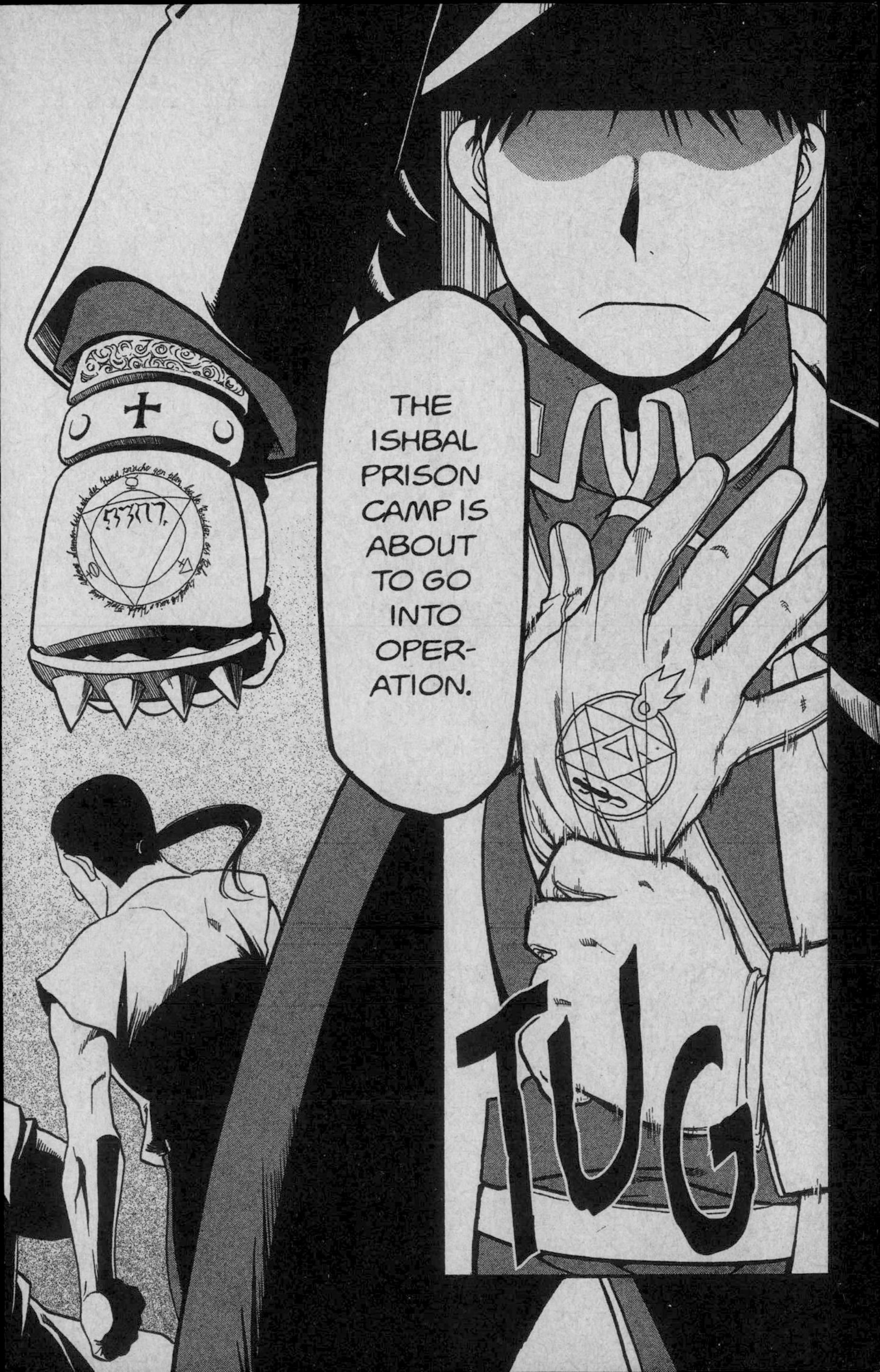
THE ISHBAL PRISON CAMP IS ABOUT TO GO INTO OPER-ATION.
TUG

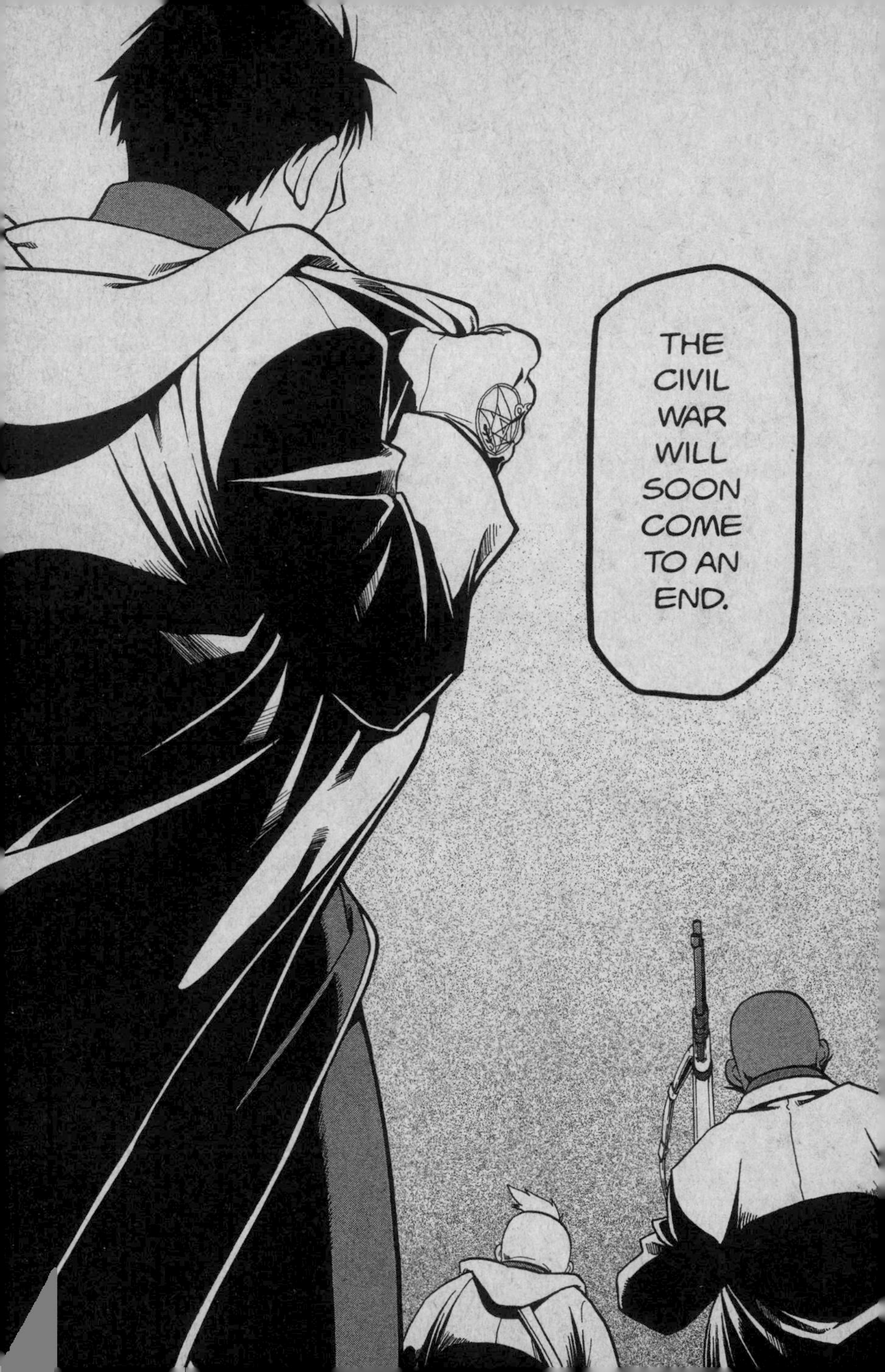
THE CIVIL WAR WILL SOON COME TO AN END.

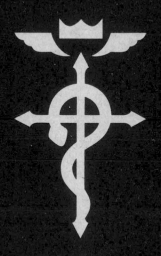

FULLMETAL
ALCHEMIST

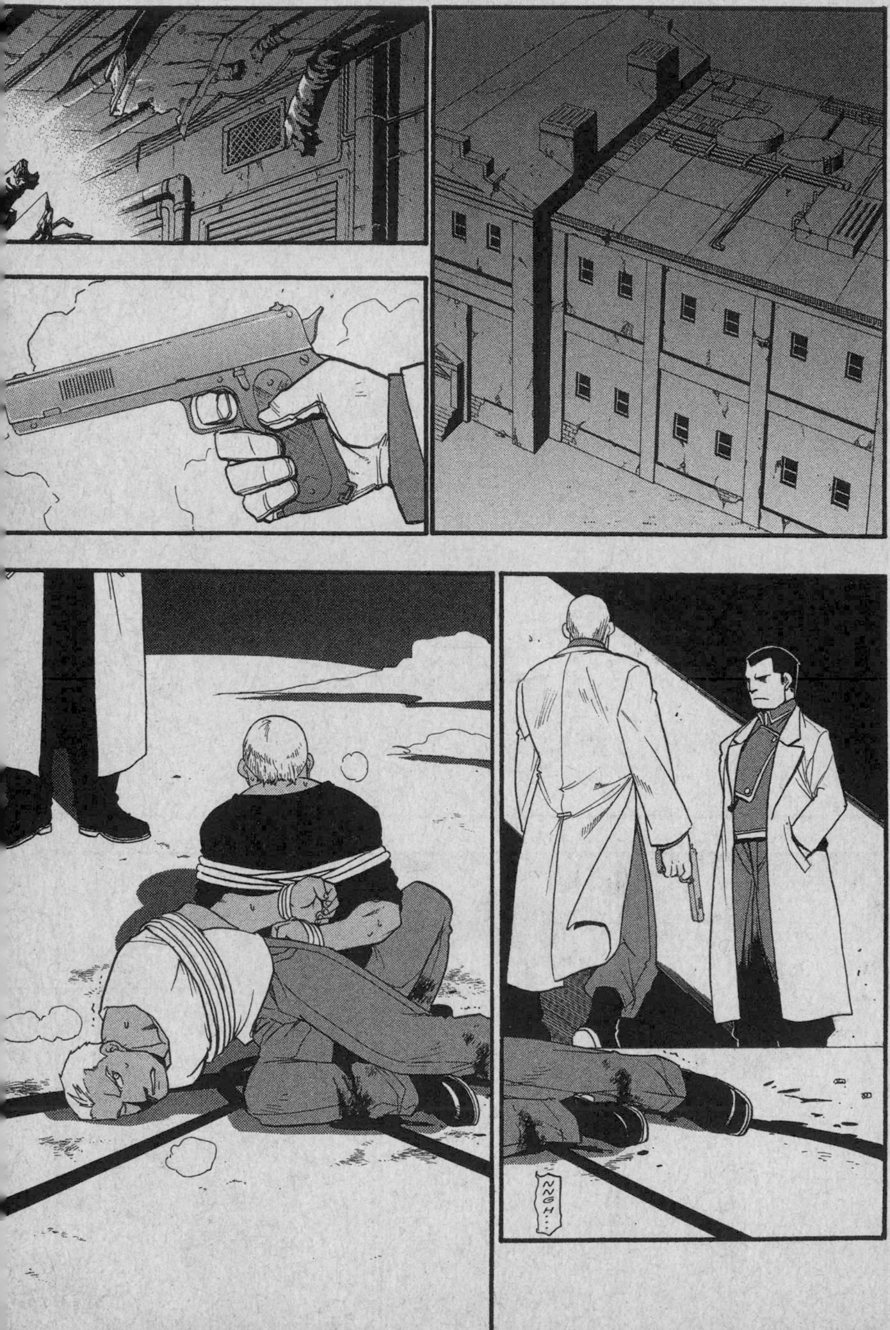
NNGH…

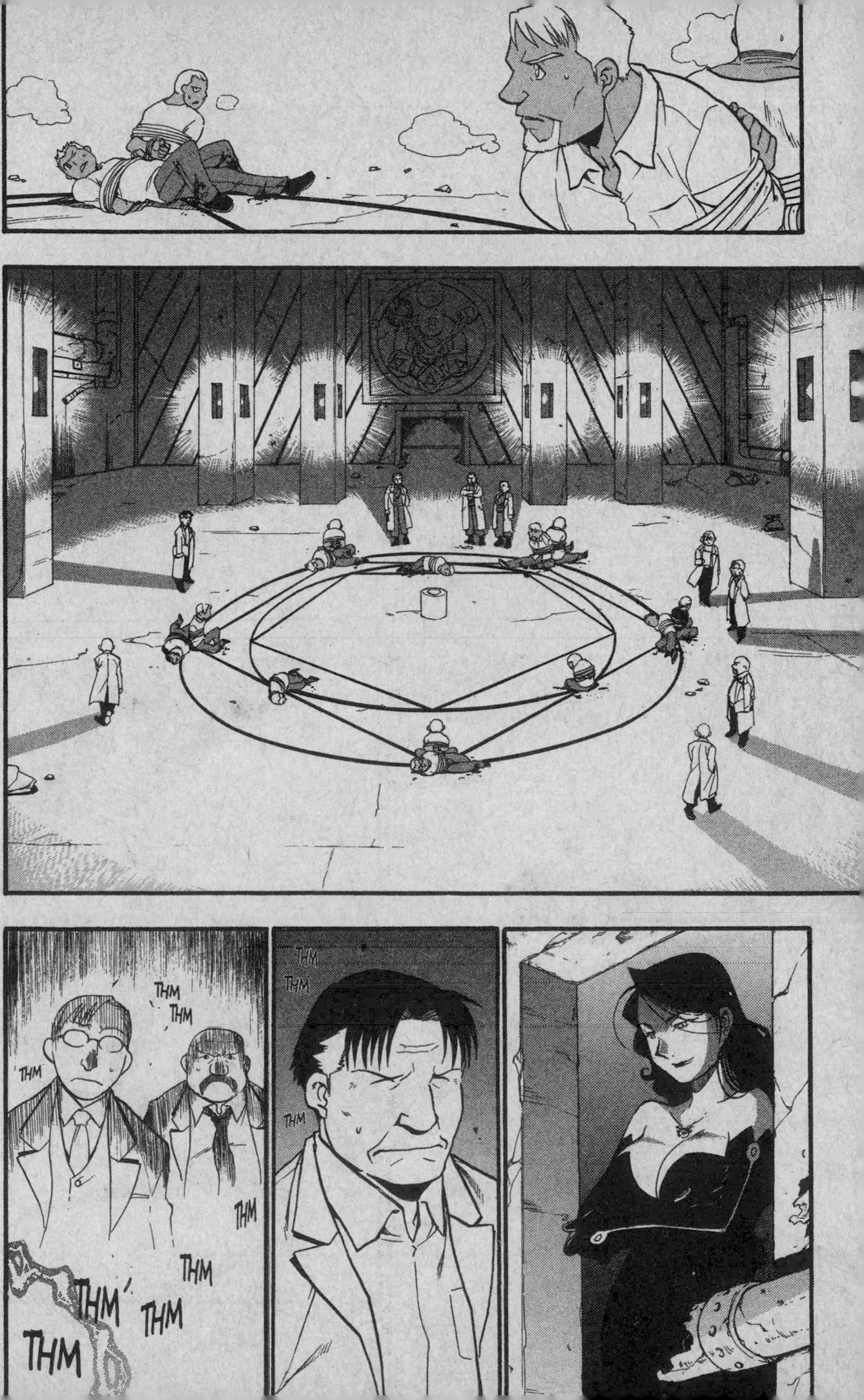
THM
THM
THM
THM
THM
THM
THM
THM
THM
THM
THM

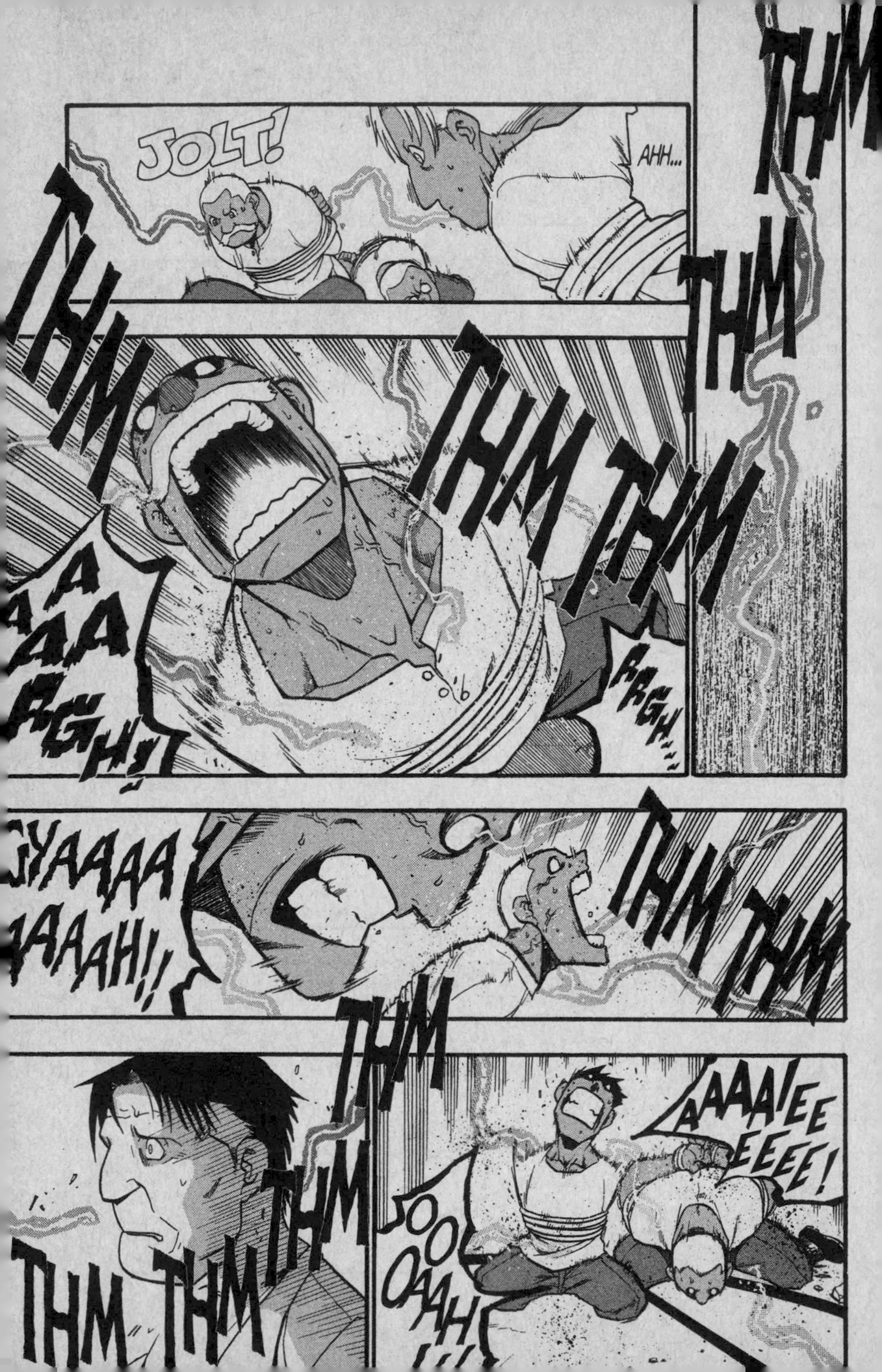
THM
THM
THM
AHH...
JOLT!
THM
THM
THM
RRGH...
AAAARGH!!
THM
THM
GYAAAAAAAAH!!
AAAAIEEEEEEE!
OOOOAAAH!!!
THM
THM
THM
THM

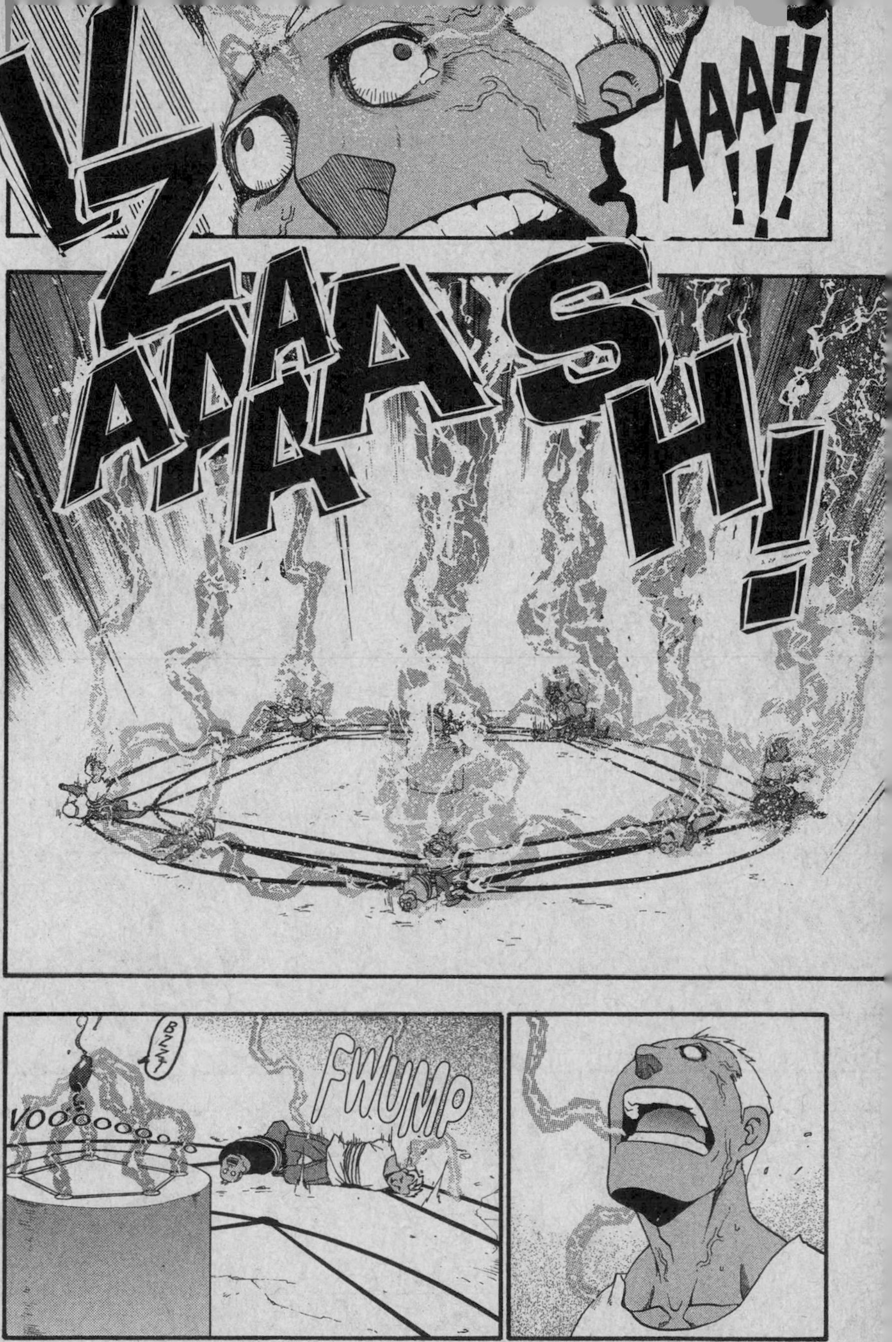
AAAH!!!
LZAAAAASH!
BZZT
VOOOOOOOO...
FWUMP

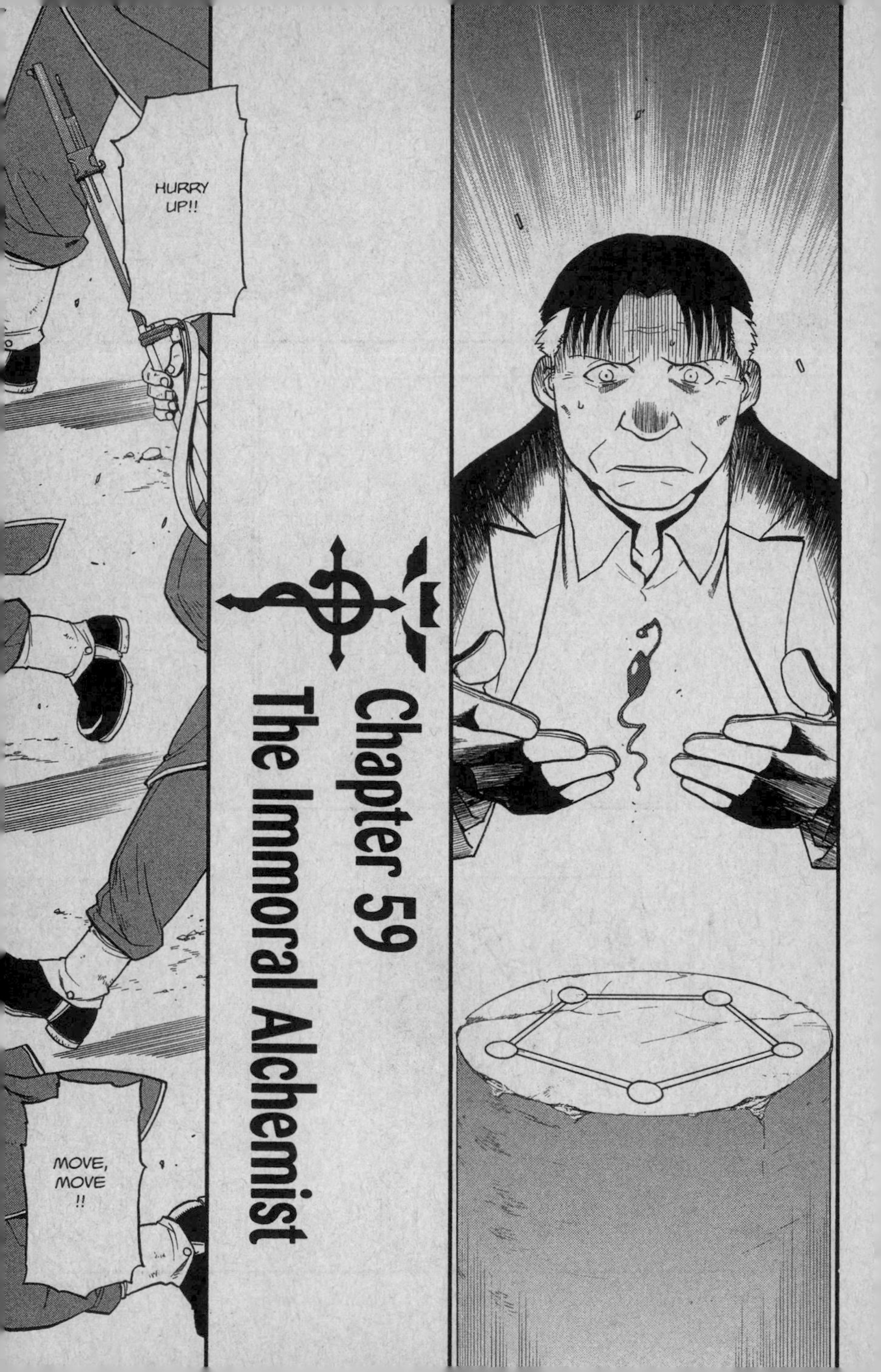
Chapter 59
The Immoral Alchemist
HURRY UP!!
MOVE, MOVE !!

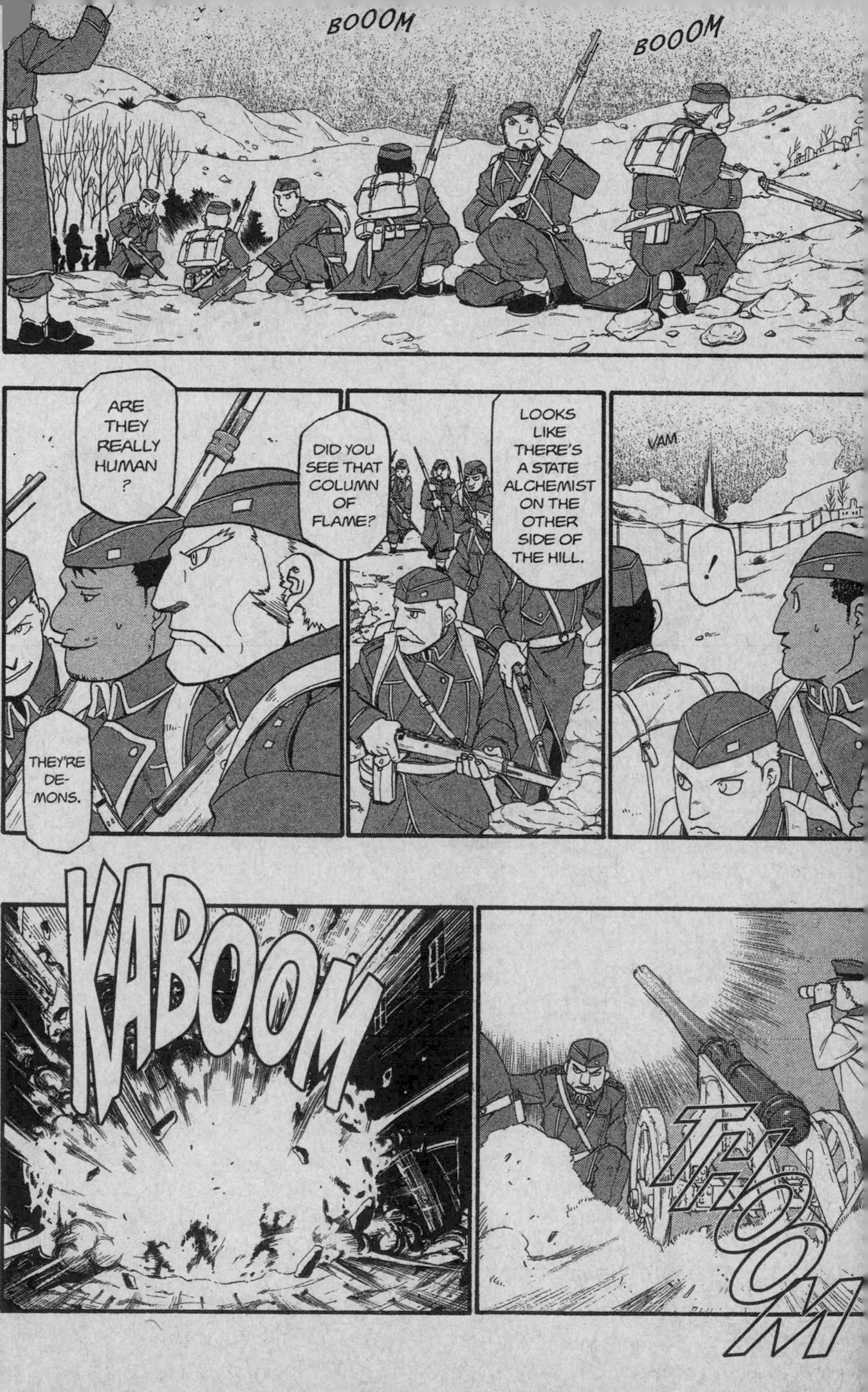
BOOOM
BOOOM
VAM
!
LOOKS LIKE THERE'S A STATE ALCHEMIST ON THE OTHER SIDE OF THE HILL.
DID YOU SEE THAT COLUMN OF FLAME?
ARE THEY REALLY HUMAN?
THEY'RE DE-MONS.
THOOM
KABOOM

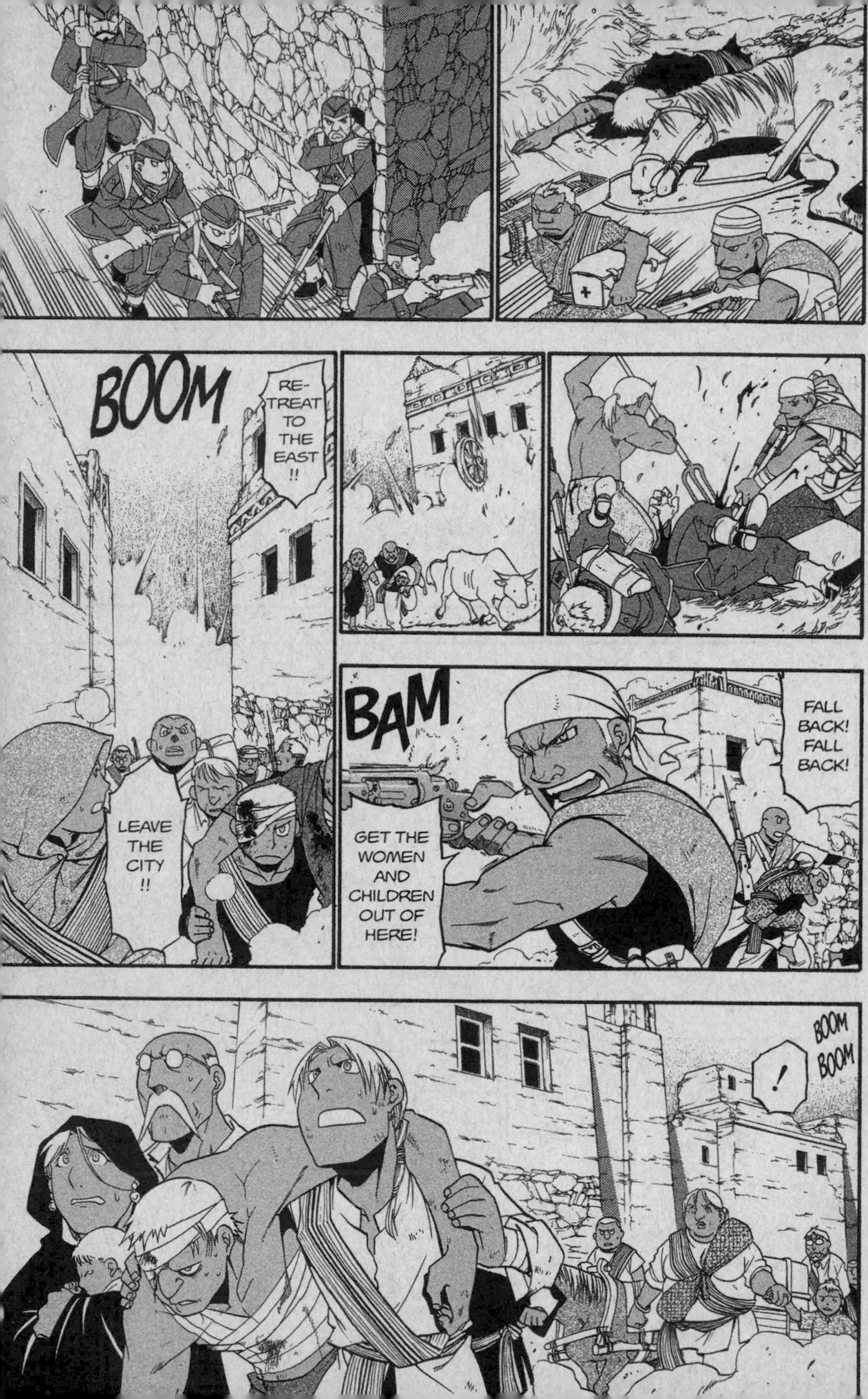
FALL BACK! FALL BACK!
BAM
GET THE WOMEN AND CHILDREN OUT OF HERE!
RE-TREAT TO THE EAST !!
BOOM
LEAVE THE CITY !!
BOOM BOOM
!

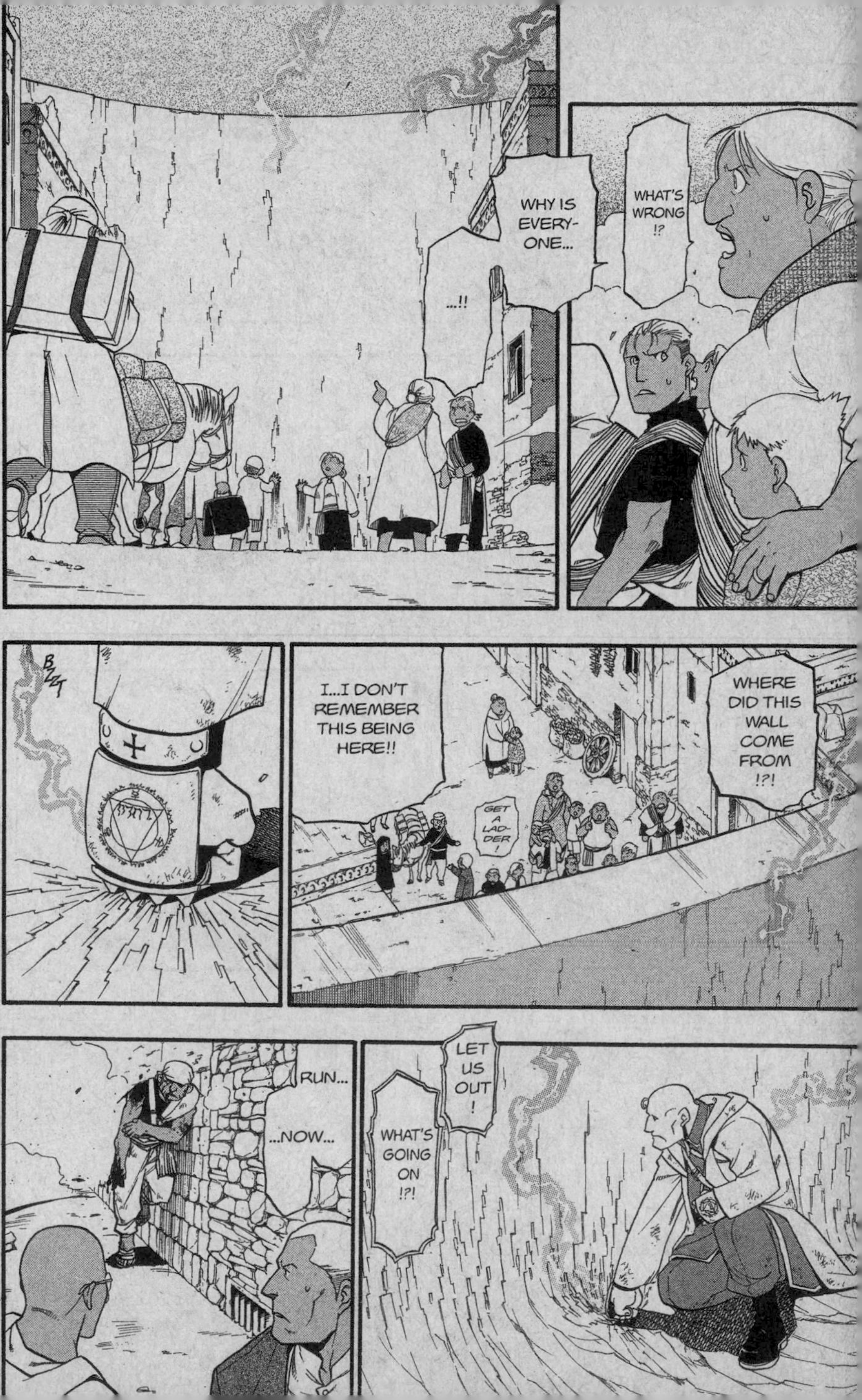
WHAT'S WRONG !?
WHY IS EVERY-ONE...
...!!
WHERE DID THIS WALL COME FROM !?!
GET A LAD-DER!
I...I DON'T REMEMBER THIS BEING HERE!!
BZZT
LET US OUT!
WHAT'S GOING ON !?!
RUN...
...NOW...

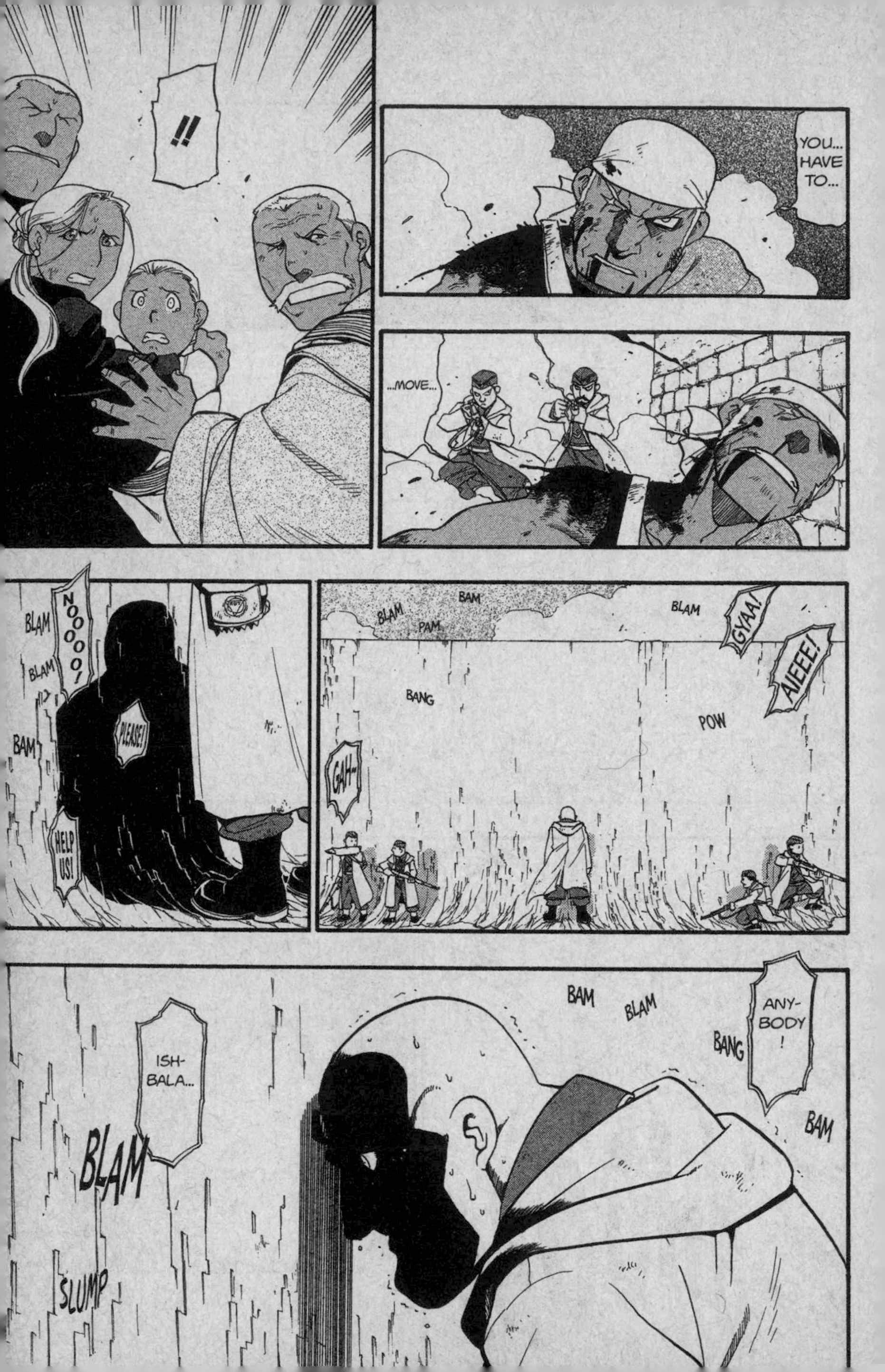
YOU... HAVE TO...
...MOVE...
!!
GYAA!
AIEEE!
BLAM
BAM
BLAM
PAM
POW
BANG
GAH-
NOOOOO!
PLEASE!
HELP US!
BLAM
BLAM
BAM
ANY-BODY!
BAM
BLAM
BANG
BAM
ISH-BALA...
BLAM
SLUMP

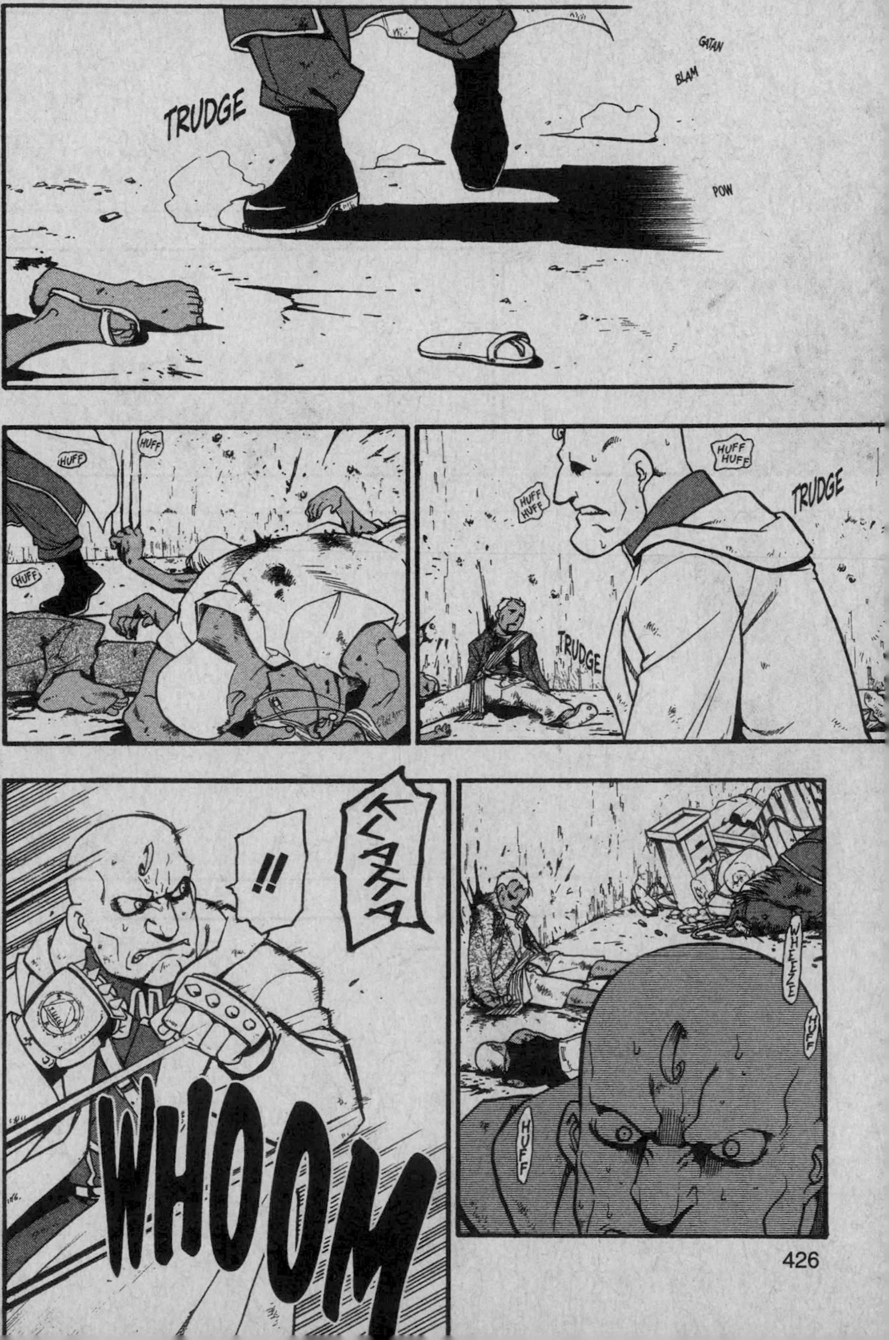
GATAN
BLAM
POW
TRUDGE
HUFF HUFF
TRUDGE
HUFF HUFF
TRUDGE
HUFF
HUFF
HUFF
WHEEZE
HUFF
HUFF
KLATTA
!!
WHOOM

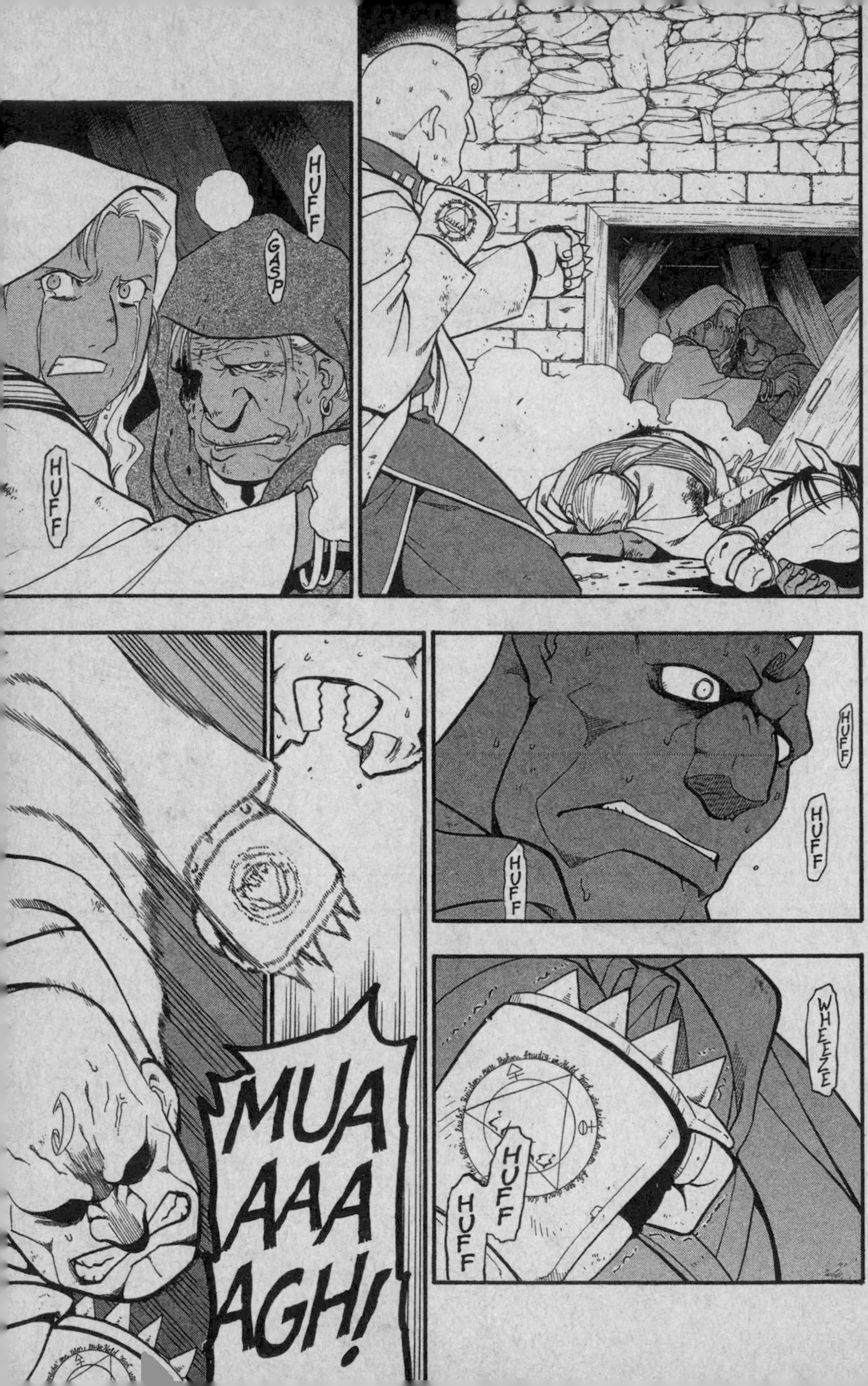
HUFF
GASP
HUFF
HUFF
HUFF
HUFF
WHEEZE
HUFF
HUFF
MUAAAAAGH!

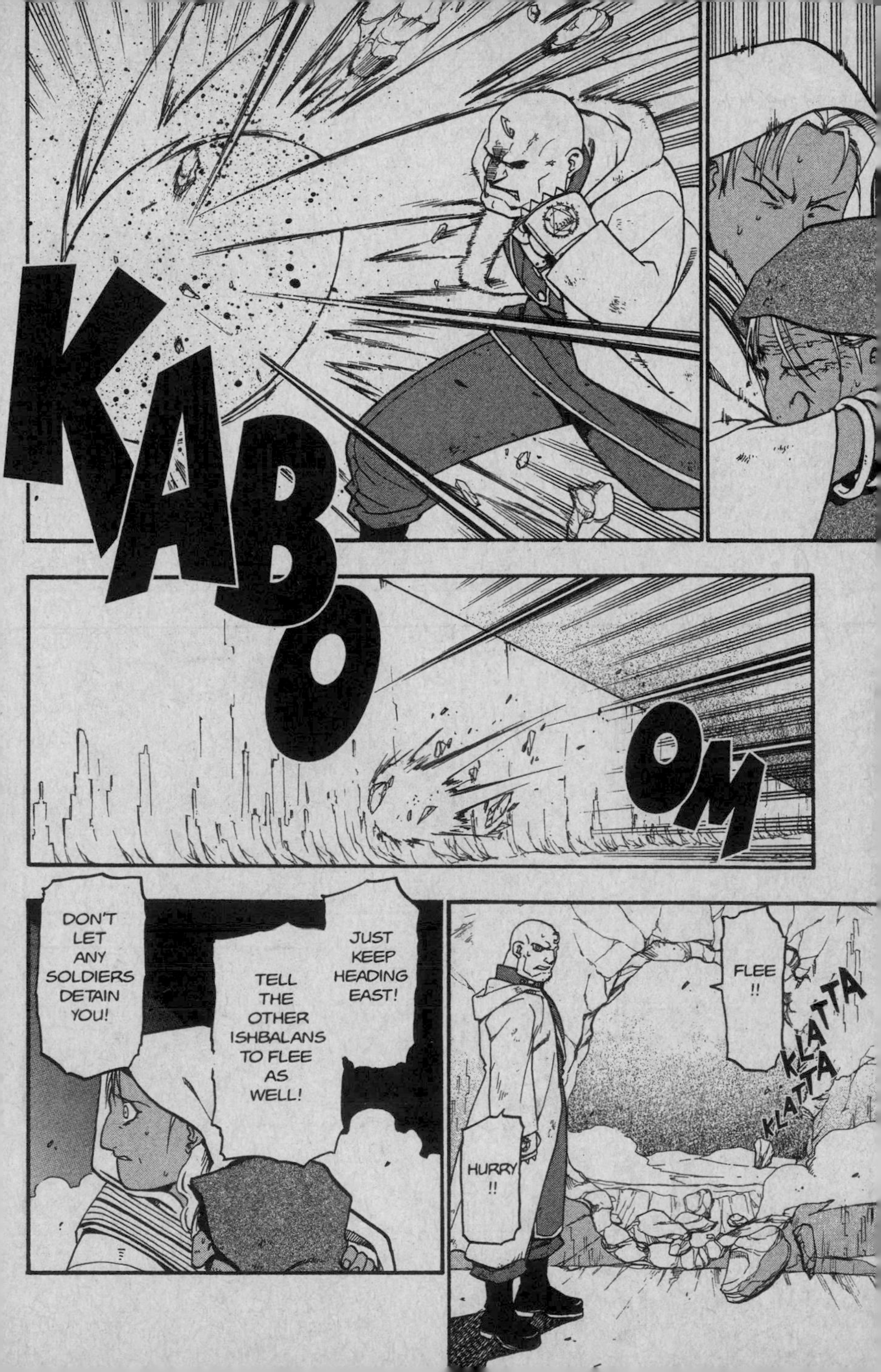
KABOOM
FLEE!!
KLATTA KLATTA
HURRY!!
JUST KEEP HEADING EAST!
TELL THE OTHER ISHBALANS TO FLEE AS WELL!
DON'T LET ANY SOLDIERS DETAIN YOU!

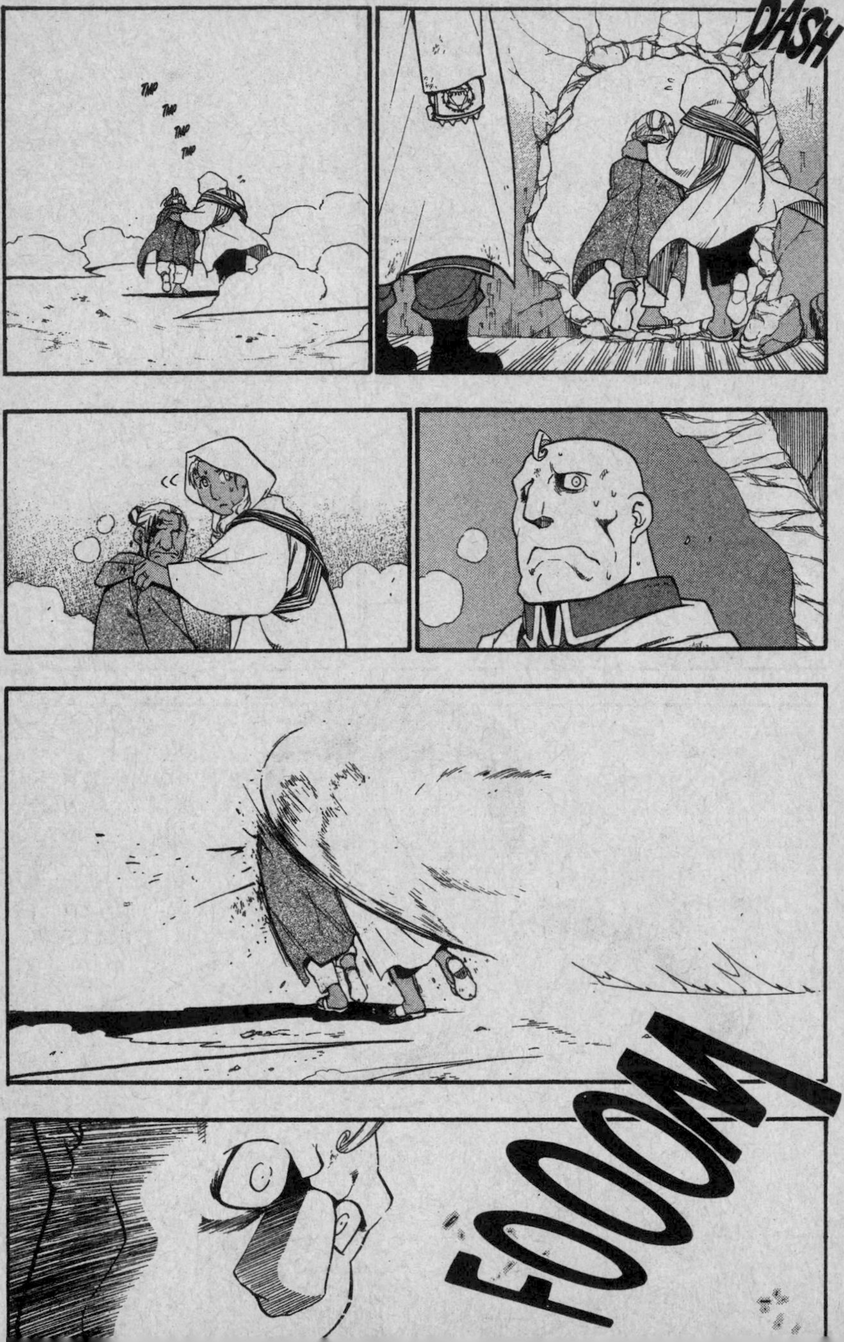
DASH
TMP
TMP
TMP
TMP
FOOOM

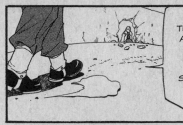

THAT WAS A CLOSE CALL, MAJOR ARM-STRONG.

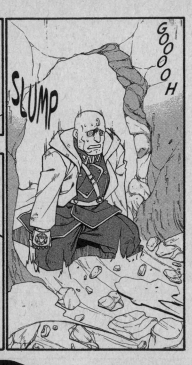

GOOOOH

SLUMP

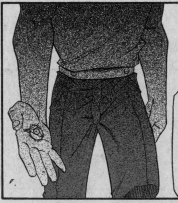

YOU ALLOWED THE ENEMY TO ESCAPE.

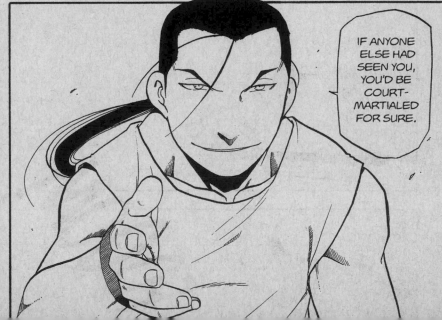

IF ANYONE ELSE HAD SEEN YOU, YOU'D BE COURT-MARTIALED FOR SURE.

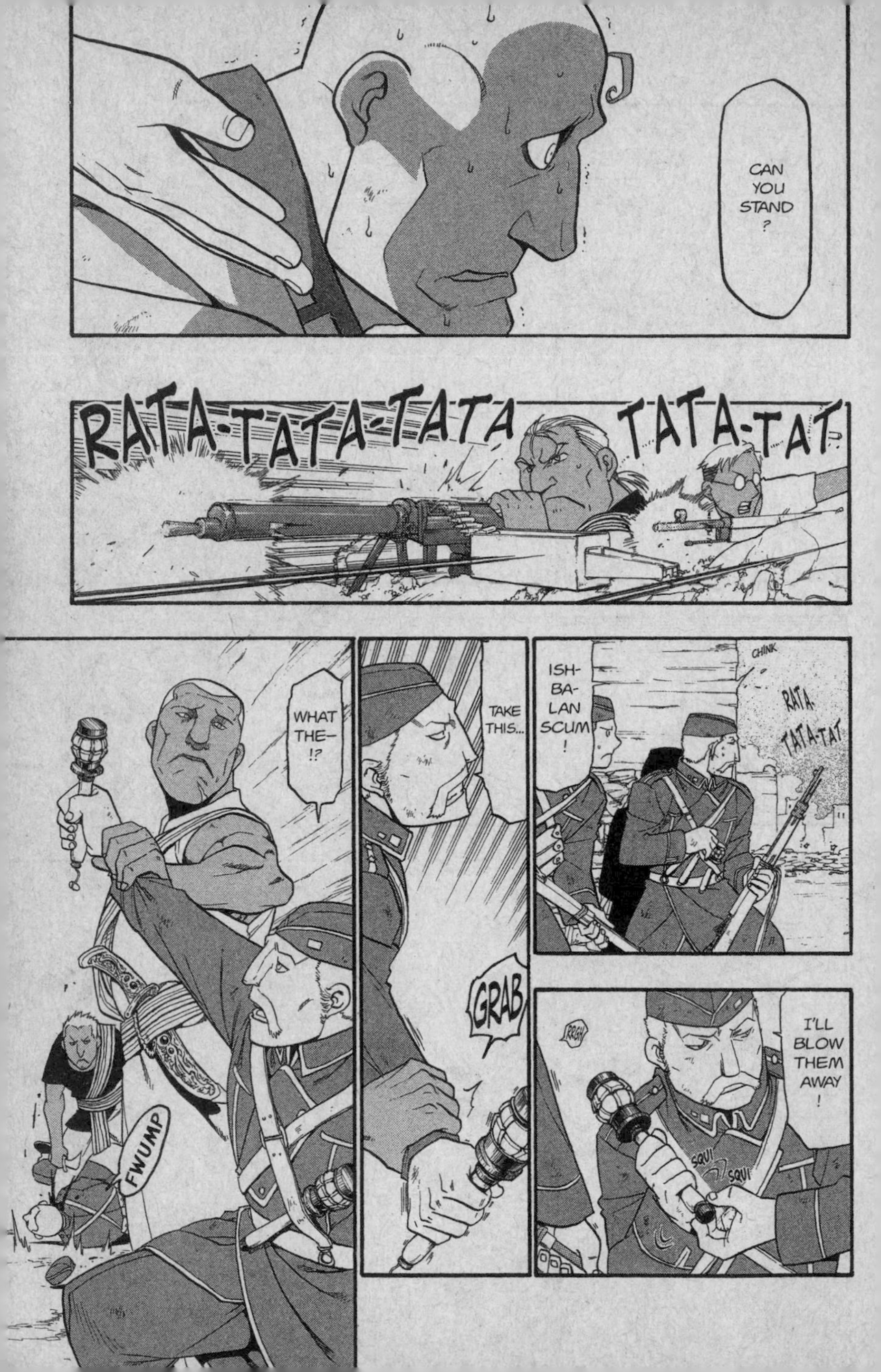
CAN YOU STAND ?
TATA-TAT
RATA-TATA-TATA
CHINK
RATA-TATA-TAT
ISH-BA-LAN SCUM !
I'LL BLOW THEM AWAY !
RRGH
SQUI SQUI
TAKE THIS...
GRAB
WHAT THE-!?
FWUMP

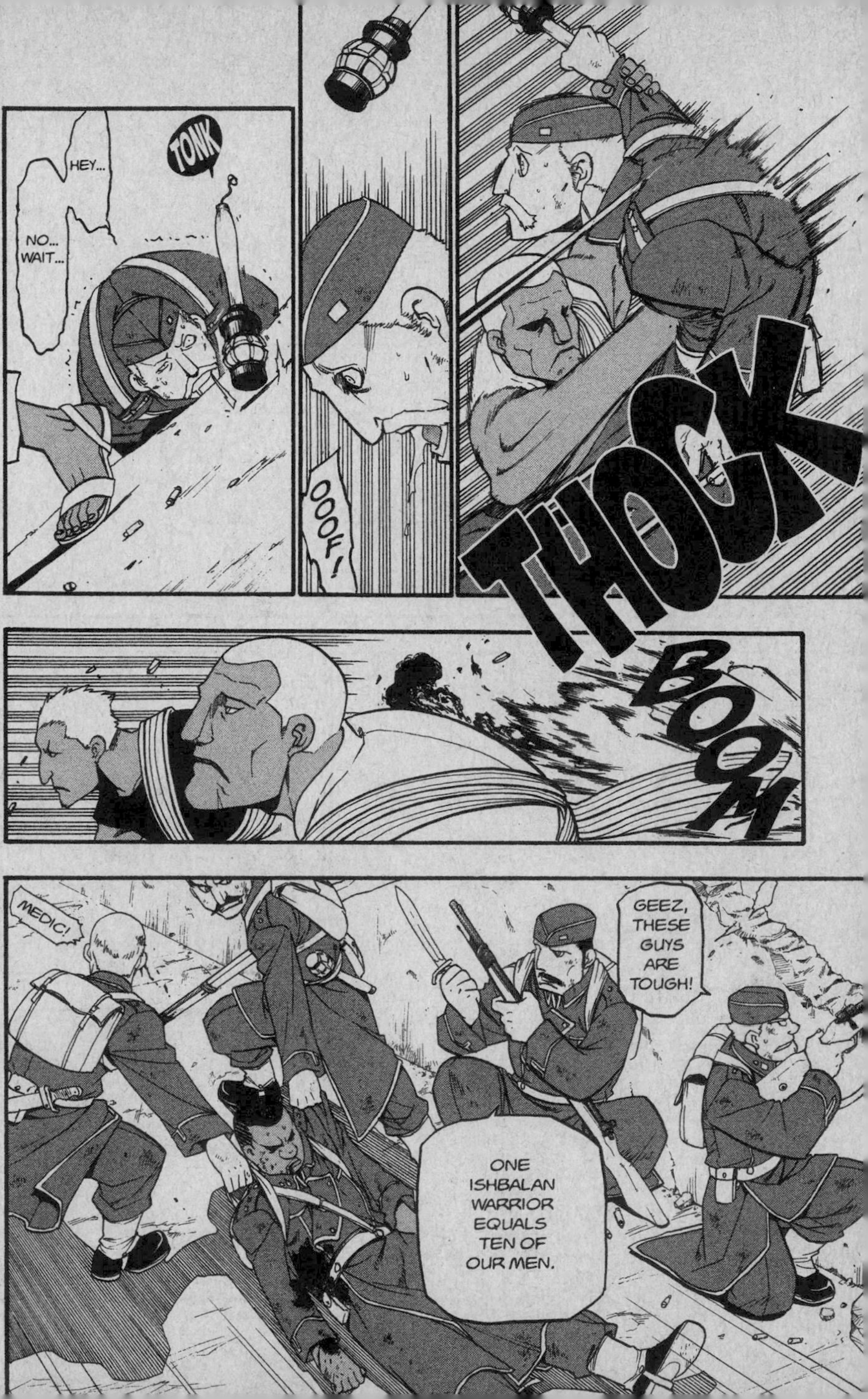
THOCK
OOOF!
TONK
HEY...
NO... WAIT...
BOOM
GEEZ, THESE GUYS ARE TOUGH!
ONE ISHBALAN WARRIOR EQUALS TEN OF OUR MEN.
MEDIC!

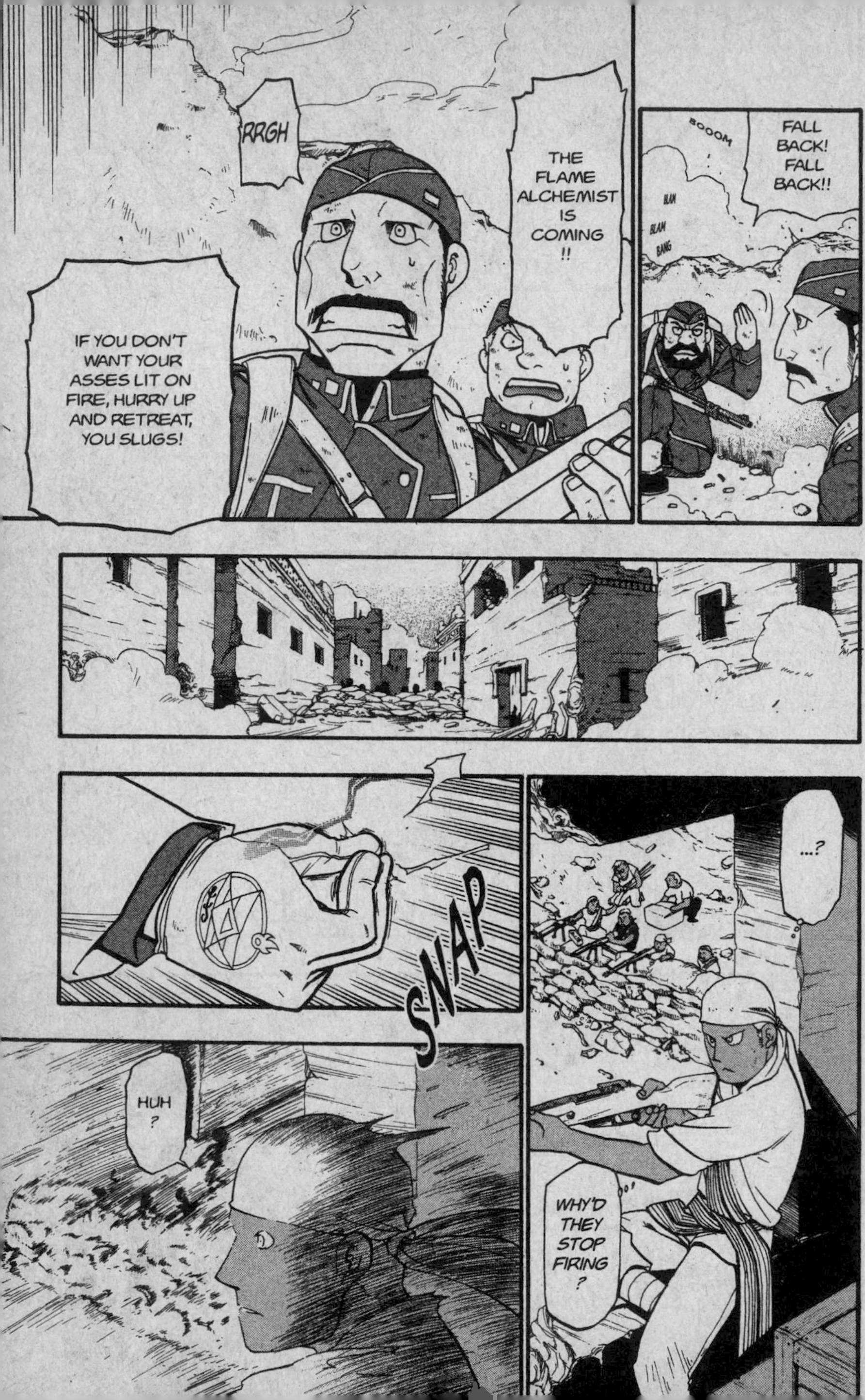
FALL BACK! FALL BACK!!
BOOOM
BLAM
BLAM
BANG
THE FLAME ALCHEMIST IS COMING!!
RRGH
IF YOU DON'T WANT YOUR ASSES LIT ON FIRE, HURRY UP AND RETREAT, YOU SLUGS!
...?
WHY'D THEY STOP FIRING?
SNAP
HUH?

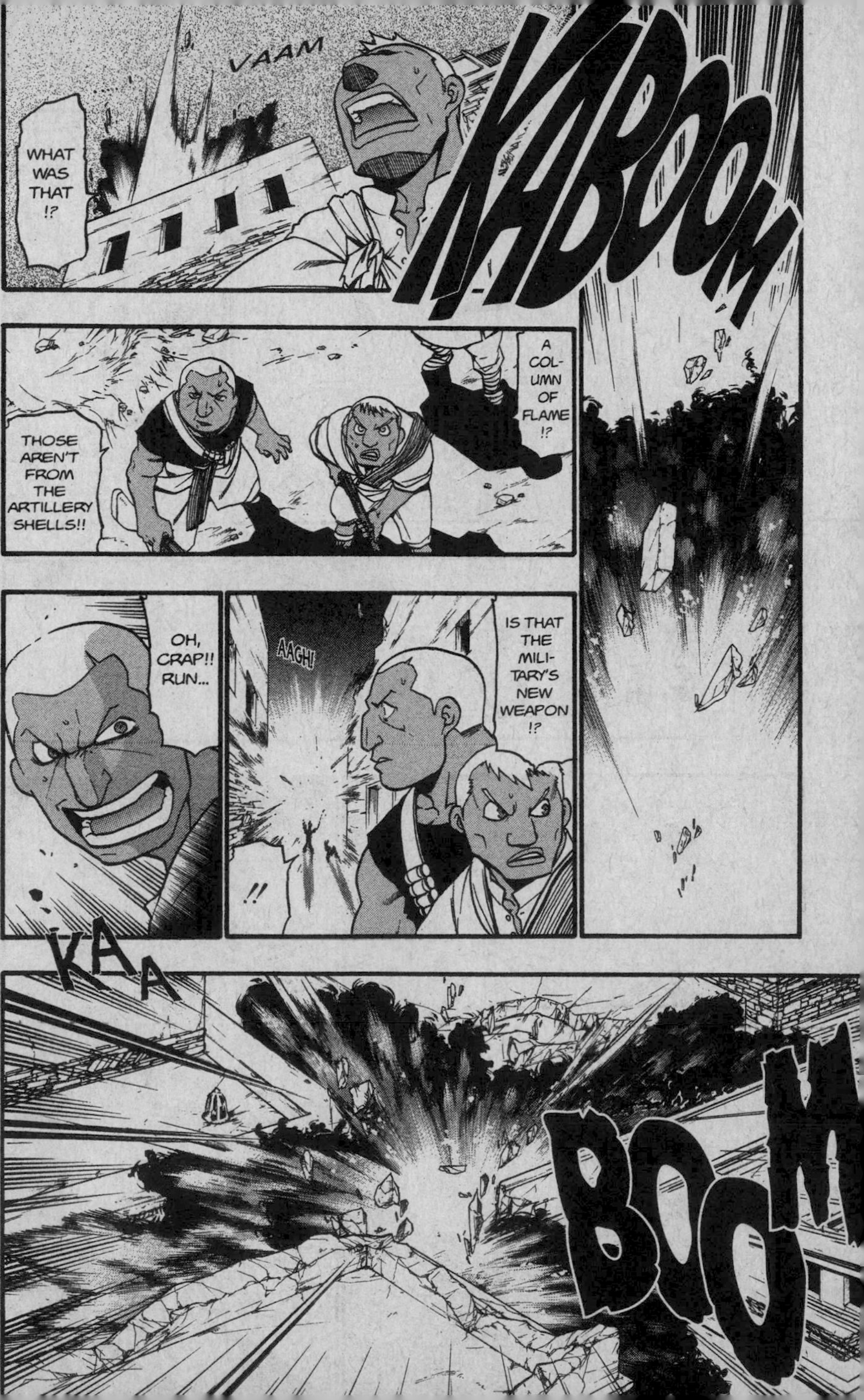
KABOOM
VAAM
WHAT WAS THAT!?
A COLUMN OF FLAME!?
THOSE AREN'T FROM THE ARTILLERY SHELLS!!
IS THAT THE MILITARY'S NEW WEAPON!?
AAGH!
!!
OH, CRAP!! RUN...
KAA
BOOM

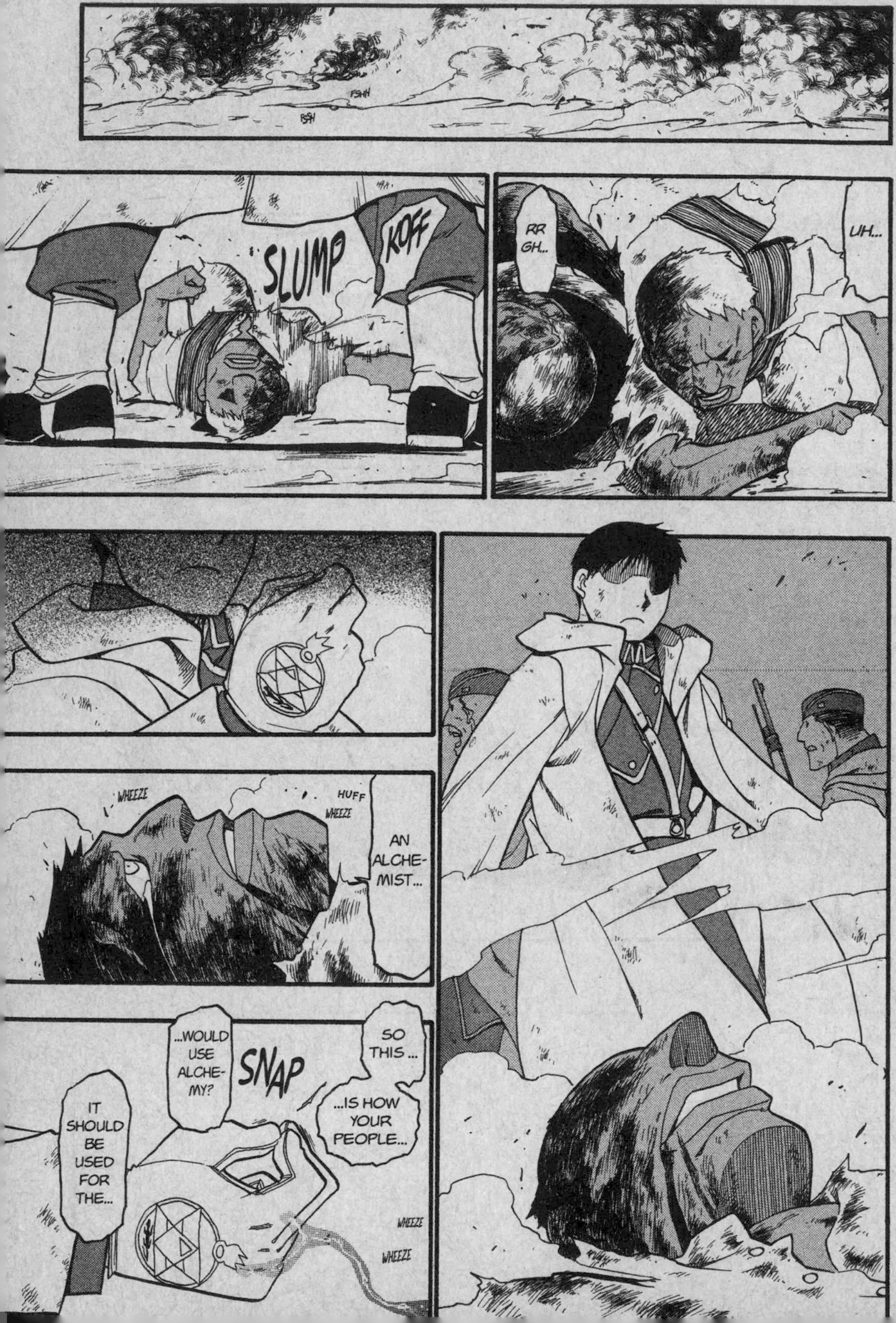
FSHH
UH...
RRGH...
KOFF
SLUMP
HUFF
WHEEZE
WHEEZE
AN ALCHEMIST...
SO THIS...
...IS HOW YOUR PEOPLE...
...WOULD USE ALCHEMY?
SNAP
IT SHOULD BE USED FOR THE...
WHEEZE
WHEEZE

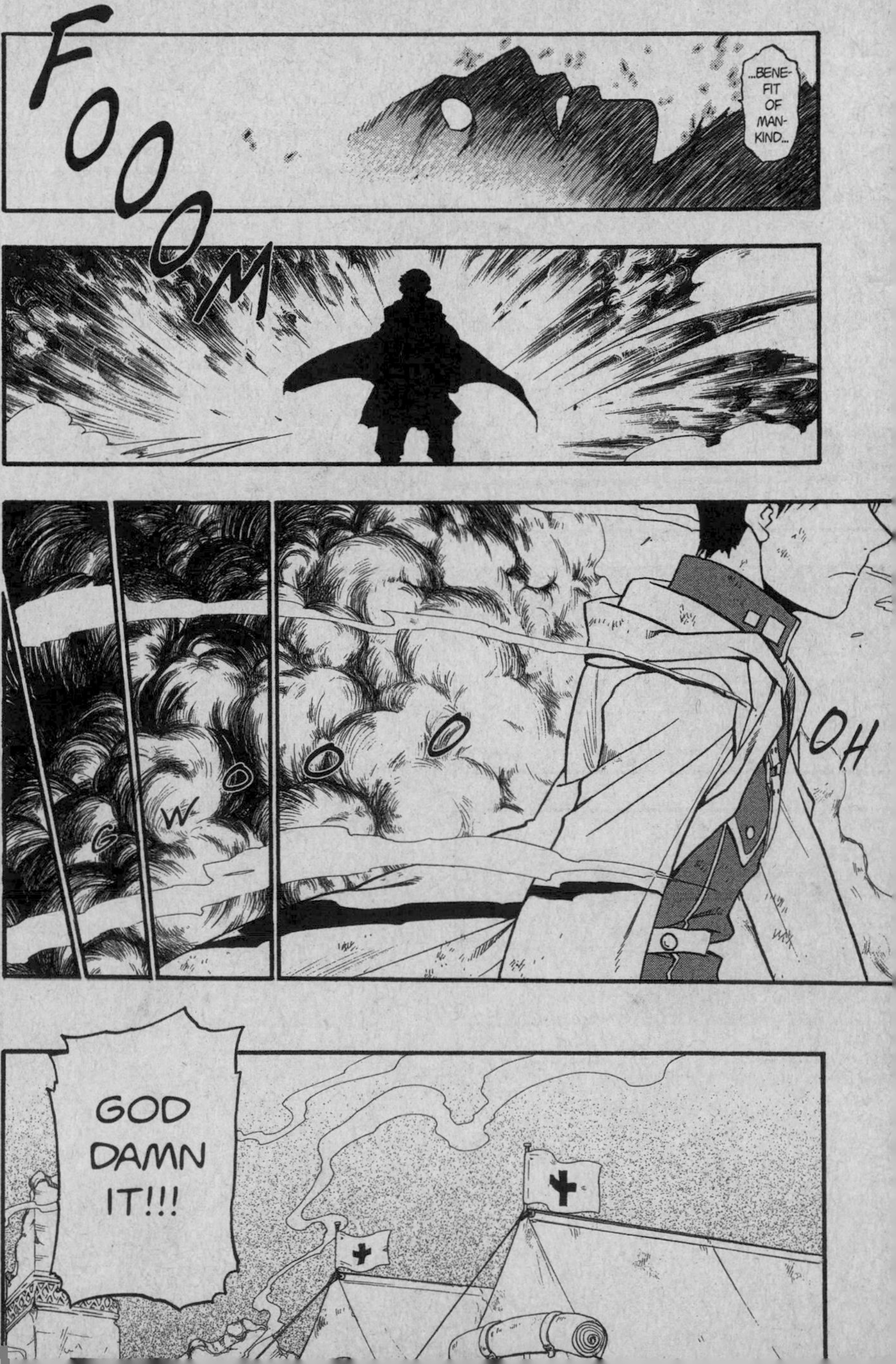
...BENE-FIT OF MAN-KIND...
FOOOM
OH
GWOOO
GOD DAMN IT!!!

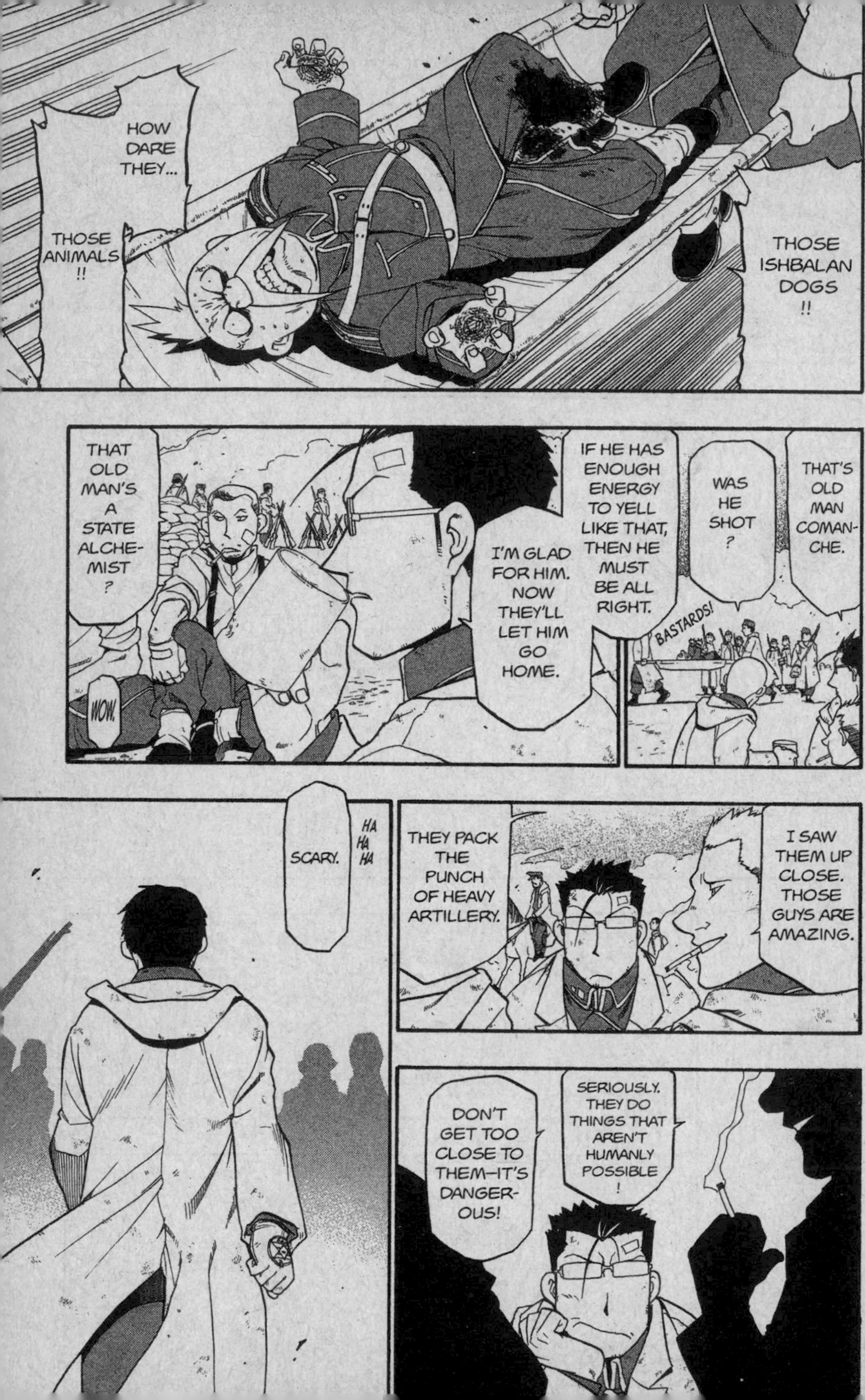
THOSE ISHBALAN DOGS!!
HOW DARE THEY...
THOSE ANIMALS!!
THAT'S OLD MAN COMANCHE.
WAS HE SHOT?
BASTARDS!
IF HE HAS ENOUGH ENERGY TO YELL LIKE THAT, THEN HE MUST BE ALL RIGHT.
I'M GLAD FOR HIM. NOW THEY'LL LET HIM GO HOME.
THAT OLD MAN'S A STATE ALCHEMIST?
WOW.
I SAW THEM UP CLOSE. THOSE GUYS ARE AMAZING.
THEY PACK THE PUNCH OF HEAVY ARTILLERY.
SERIOUSLY. THEY DO THINGS THAT AREN'T HUMANLY POSSIBLE!
DON'T GET TOO CLOSE TO THEM—IT'S DANGEROUS!
HA HA HA
SCARY.

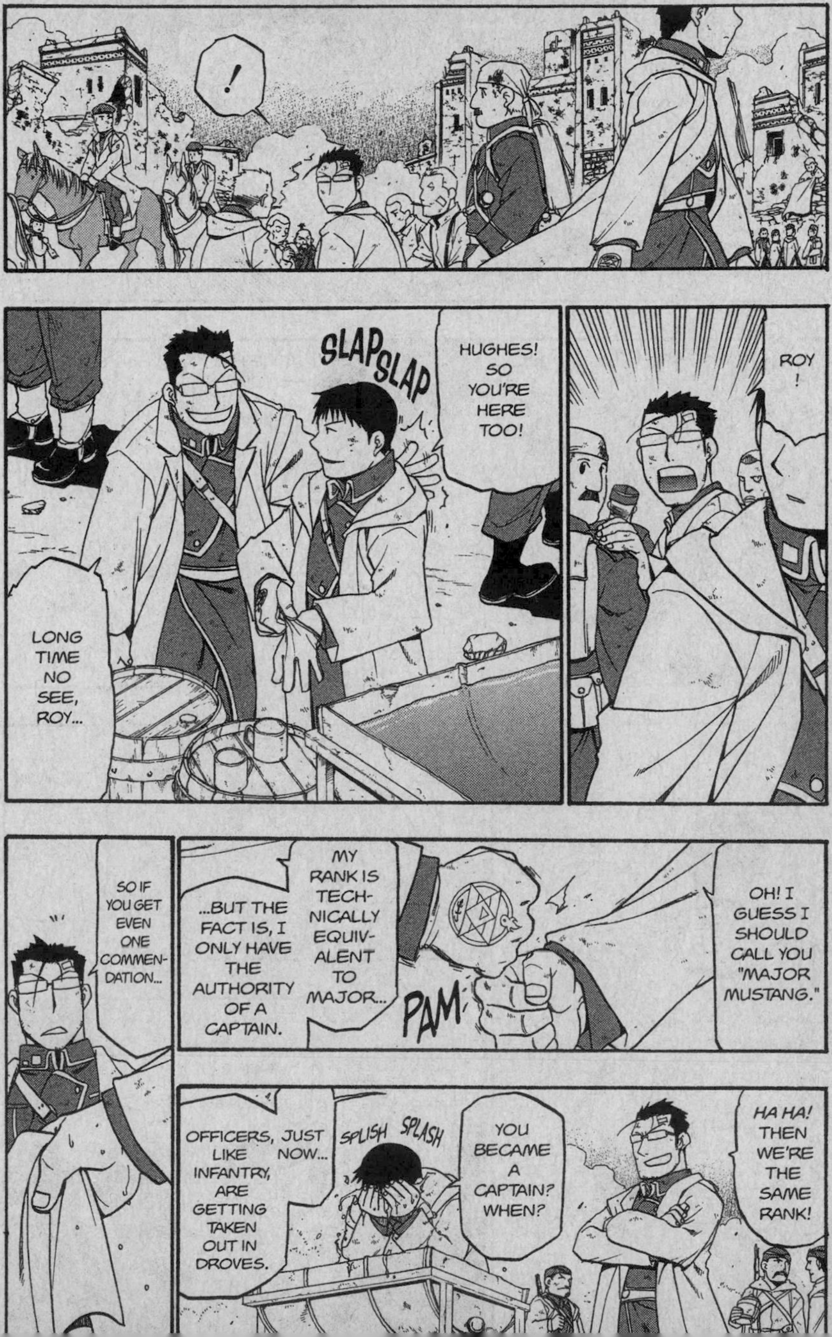
!
ROY!
HUGHES! SO YOU'RE HERE TOO!
SLAP SLAP
LONG TIME NO SEE, ROY...
OH! I GUESS I SHOULD CALL YOU "MAJOR MUSTANG."
PAM
MY RANK IS TECHNICALLY EQUIVALENT TO MAJOR...
...BUT THE FACT IS, I ONLY HAVE THE AUTHORITY OF A CAPTAIN.
HA HA! THEN WE'RE THE SAME RANK!
YOU BECAME A CAPTAIN? WHEN?
SPLASH
SPLISH
OFFICERS, JUST LIKE INFANTRY, ARE GETTING TAKEN OUT IN DROVES.
SO IF YOU GET EVEN ONE COMMENDATION...

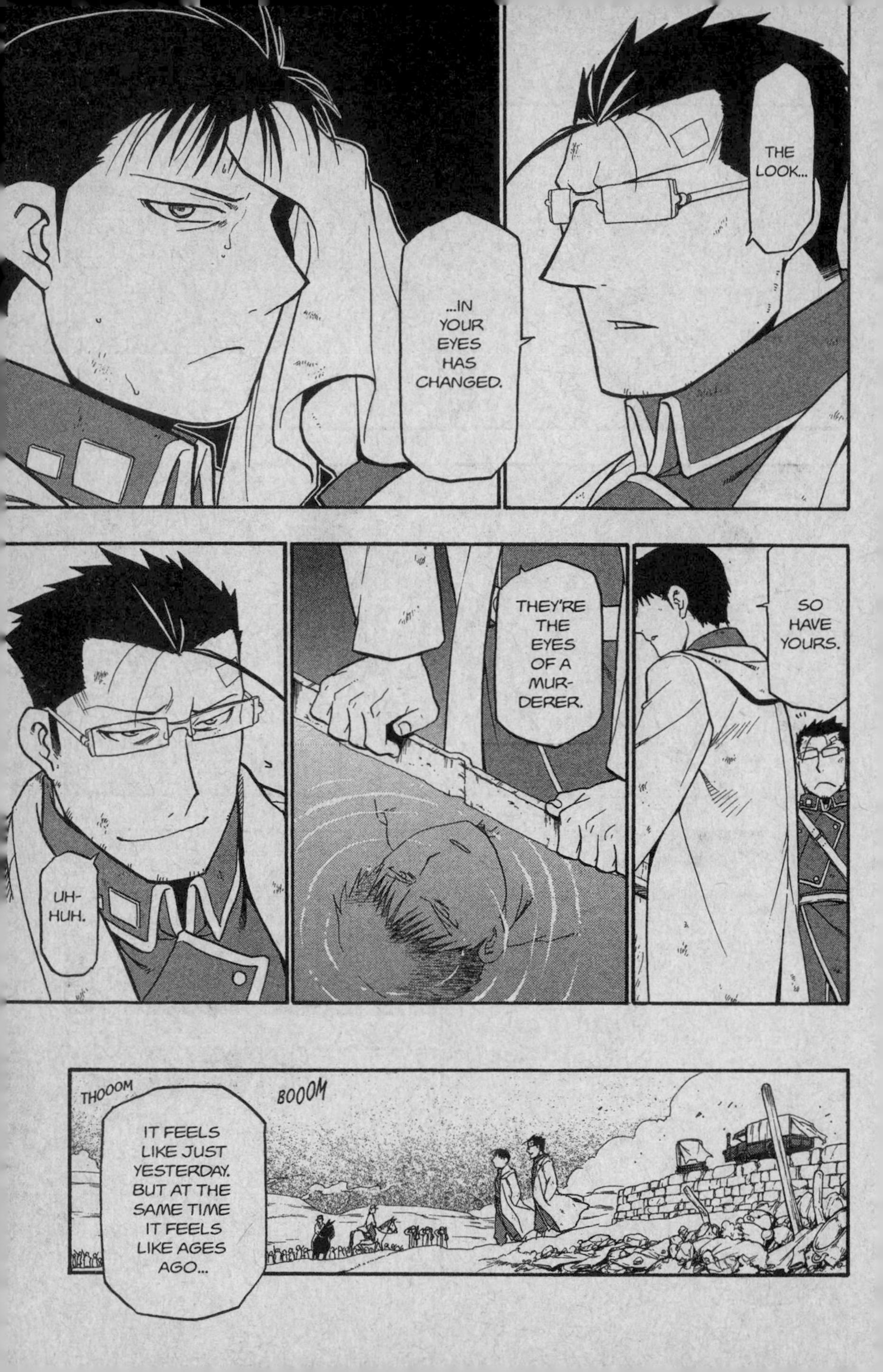
THE LOOK...
...IN YOUR EYES HAS CHANGED.
SO HAVE YOURS.
THEY'RE THE EYES OF A MURDERER.
UH-HUH.
BOOOM
THOOOM
IT FEELS LIKE JUST YESTERDAY. BUT AT THE SAME TIME IT FEELS LIKE AGES AGO...

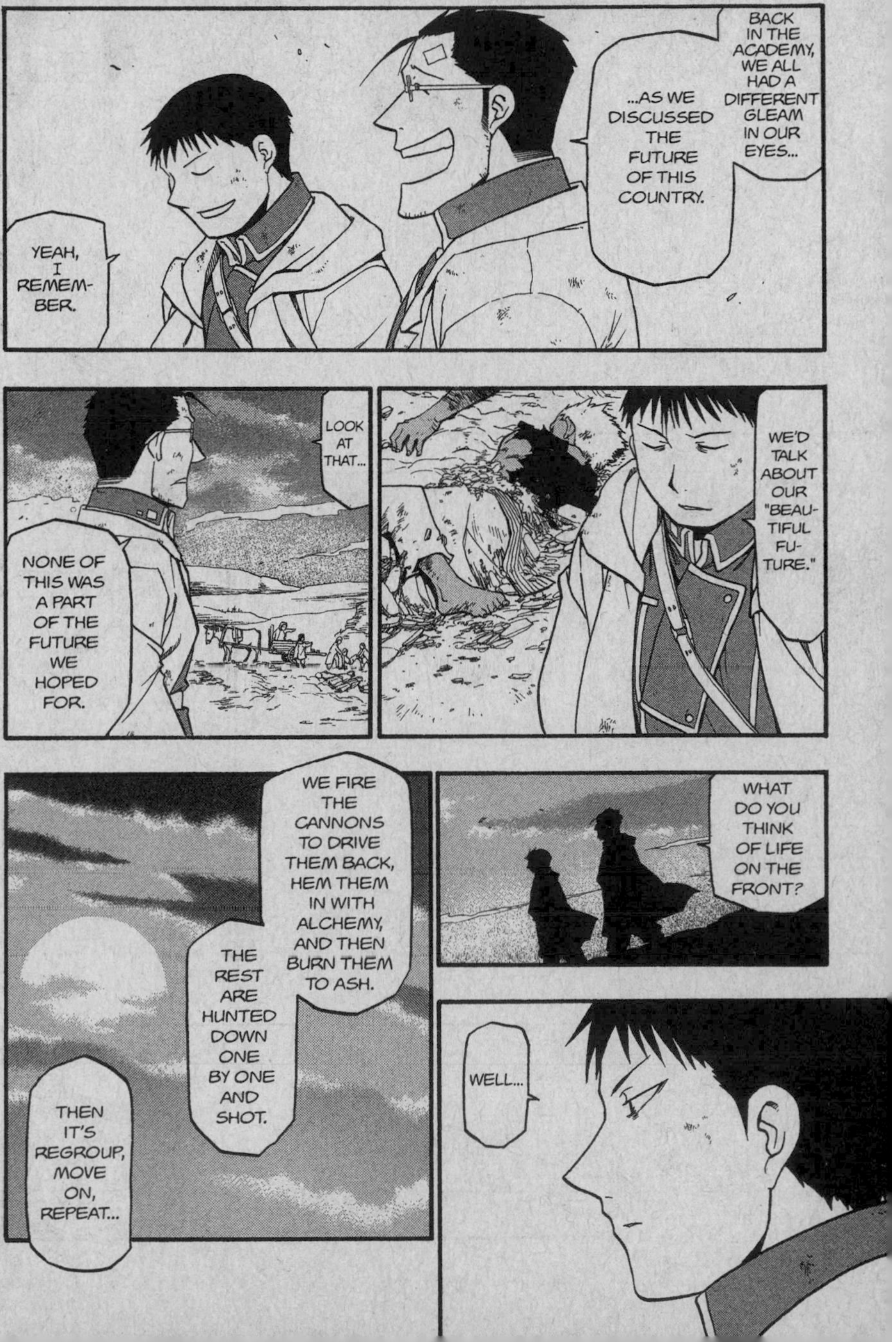
BACK IN THE ACADEMY, WE ALL HAD A DIFFERENT GLEAM IN OUR EYES...
...AS WE DISCUSSED THE FUTURE OF THIS COUNTRY.
YEAH, I REMEMBER.
WE'D TALK ABOUT OUR "BEAUTIFUL FUTURE."
LOOK AT THAT...
NONE OF THIS WAS A PART OF THE FUTURE WE HOPED FOR.
WHAT DO YOU THINK OF LIFE ON THE FRONT?
WELL...
WE FIRE THE CANNONS TO DRIVE THEM BACK, HEM THEM IN WITH ALCHEMY, AND THEN BURN THEM TO ASH.
THE REST ARE HUNTED DOWN ONE BY ONE AND SHOT.
THEN IT'S REGROUP, MOVE ON, REPEAT...

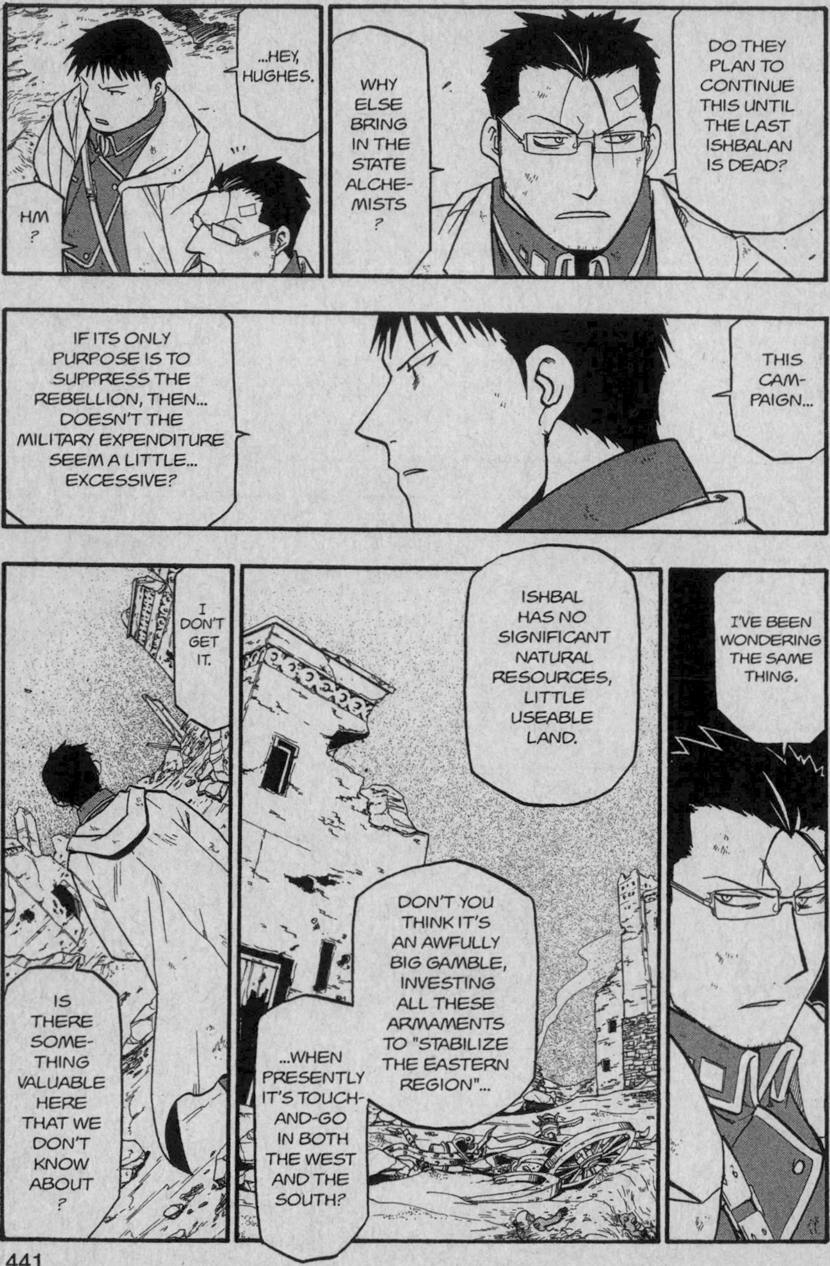
...HEY, HUGHES.
HM?
DO THEY PLAN TO CONTINUE THIS UNTIL THE LAST ISHBALAN IS DEAD?
WHY ELSE BRING IN THE STATE ALCHEMISTS?
IF ITS ONLY PURPOSE IS TO SUPPRESS THE REBELLION, THEN... DOESN'T THE MILITARY EXPENDITURE SEEM A LITTLE... EXCESSIVE?
THIS CAMPAIGN...
I DON'T GET IT.
IS THERE SOMETHING VALUABLE HERE THAT WE DON'T KNOW ABOUT?
ISHBAL HAS NO SIGNIFICANT NATURAL RESOURCES, LITTLE USEABLE LAND.
DON'T YOU THINK IT'S AN AWFULLY BIG GAMBLE, INVESTING ALL THESE ARMAMENTS TO "STABILIZE THE EASTERN REGION"...
...WHEN PRESENTLY IT'S TOUCH-AND-GO IN BOTH THE WEST AND THE SOUTH?
I'VE BEEN WONDERING THE SAME THING.

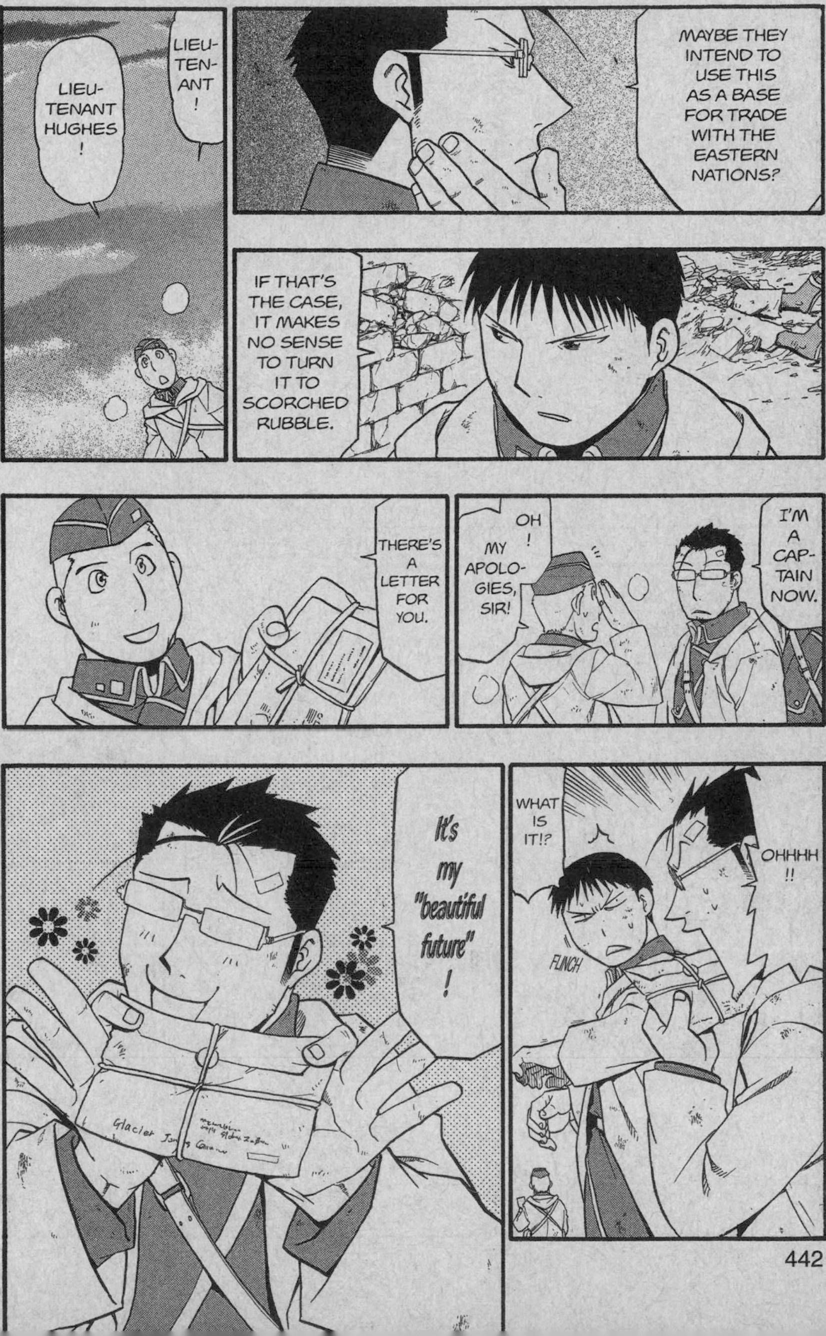
MAYBE THEY INTEND TO USE THIS AS A BASE FOR TRADE WITH THE EASTERN NATIONS?
IF THAT'S THE CASE, IT MAKES NO SENSE TO TURN IT TO SCORCHED RUBBLE.
LIEU-TENANT!
LIEU-TENANT HUGHES!
I'M A CAP-TAIN NOW.
OH!
MY APOLO-GIES, SIR!
THERE'S A LETTER FOR YOU.
OHHHH!!
WHAT IS IT!?
FLINCH
It's my "beautiful future"!

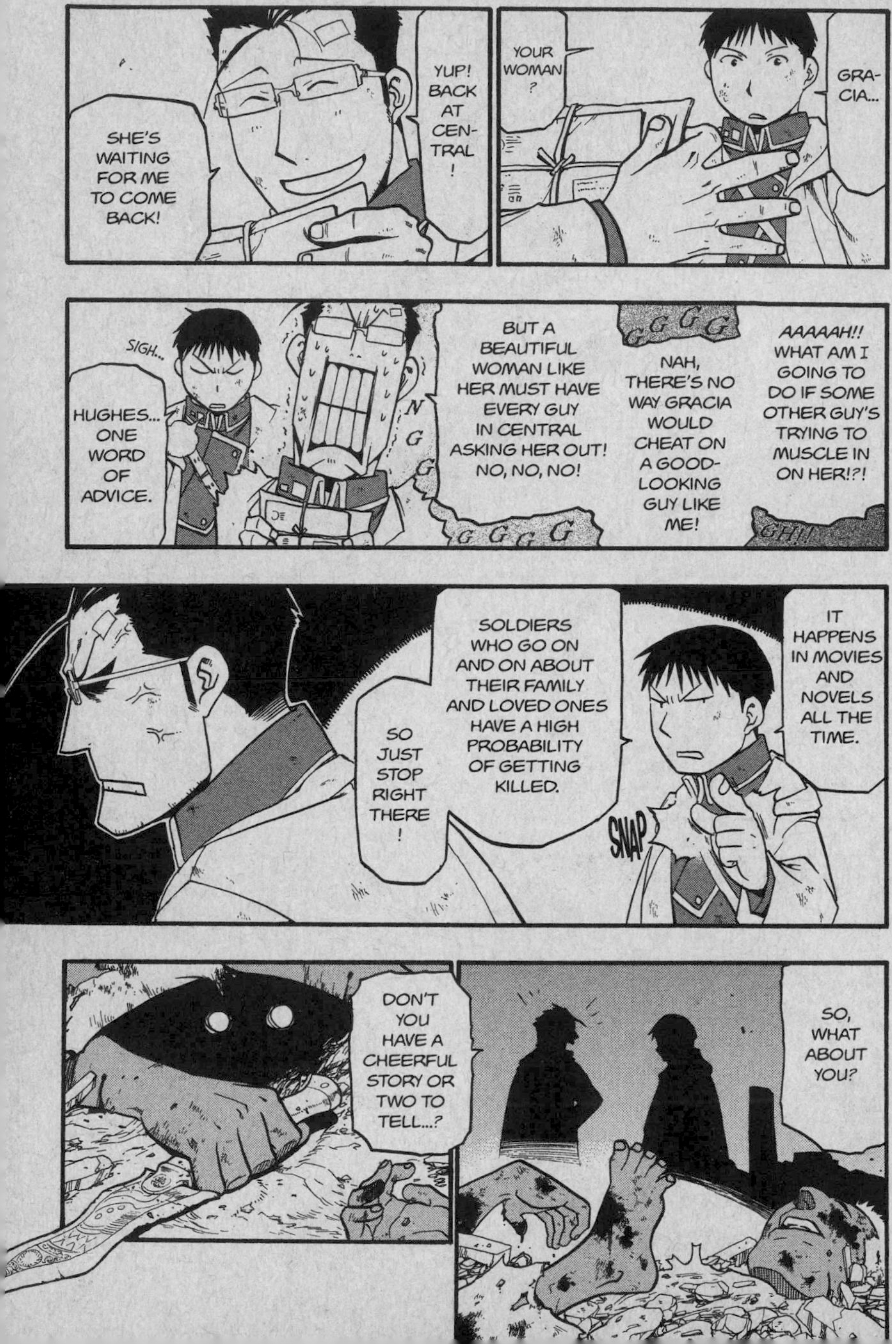
GRACIA...
YOUR WOMAN?
YUP! BACK AT CENTRAL!
SHE'S WAITING FOR ME TO COME BACK!
AAAAAH!! WHAT AM I GOING TO DO IF SOME OTHER GUY'S TRYING TO MUSCLE IN ON HER!?!
GHI!!
GGGG
NAH, THERE'S NO WAY GRACIA WOULD CHEAT ON A GOOD-LOOKING GUY LIKE ME!
BUT A BEAUTIFUL WOMAN LIKE HER MUST HAVE EVERY GUY IN CENTRAL ASKING HER OUT! NO, NO, NO!
NGG
GGGG
SIGH...
HUGHES... ONE WORD OF ADVICE.
IT HAPPENS IN MOVIES AND NOVELS ALL THE TIME.
SNAP
SOLDIERS WHO GO ON AND ON ABOUT THEIR FAMILY AND LOVED ONES HAVE A HIGH PROBABILITY OF GETTING KILLED.
SO JUST STOP RIGHT THERE!
SO, WHAT ABOUT YOU?
DON'T YOU HAVE A CHEERFUL STORY OR TWO TO TELL...?

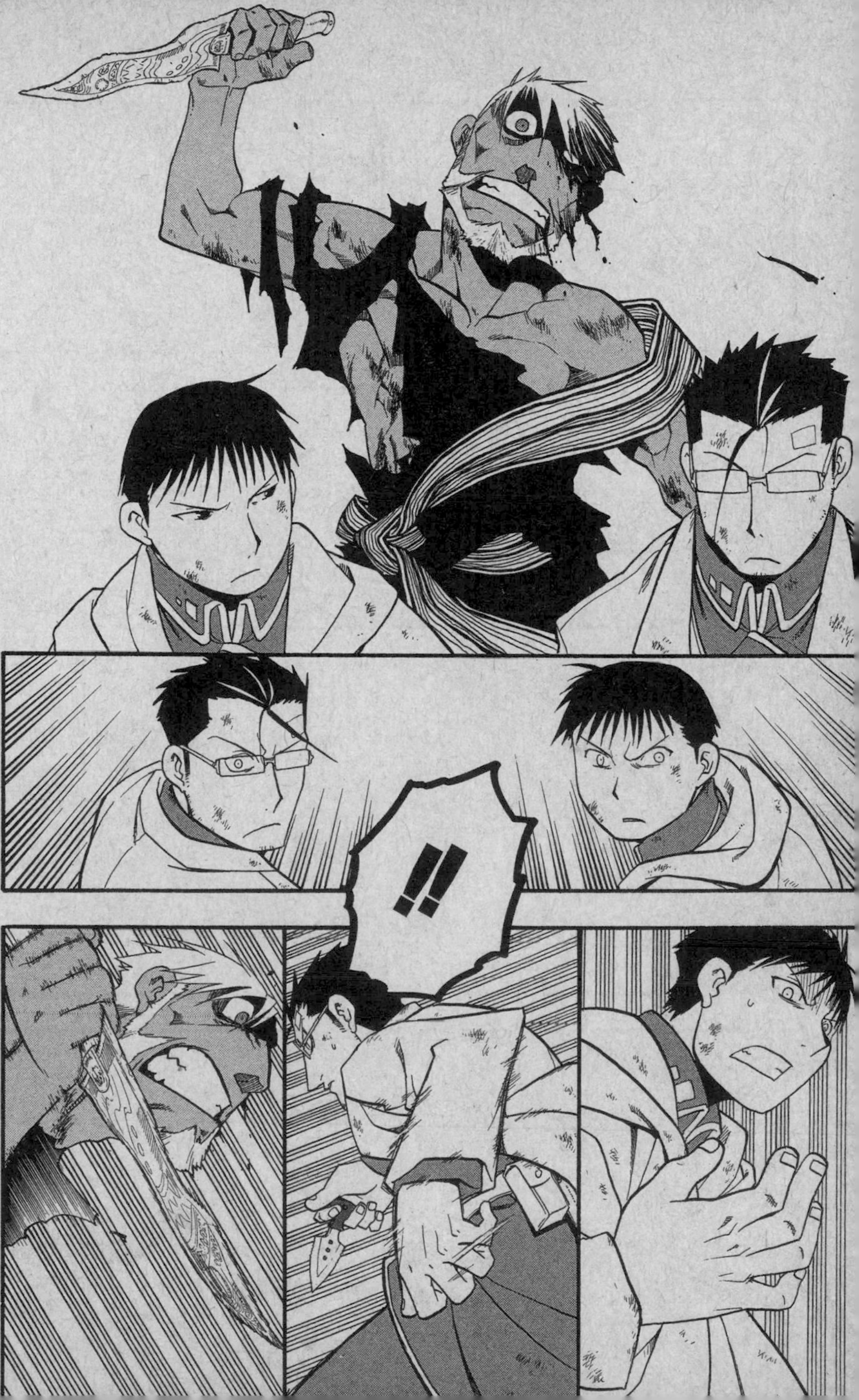
!!

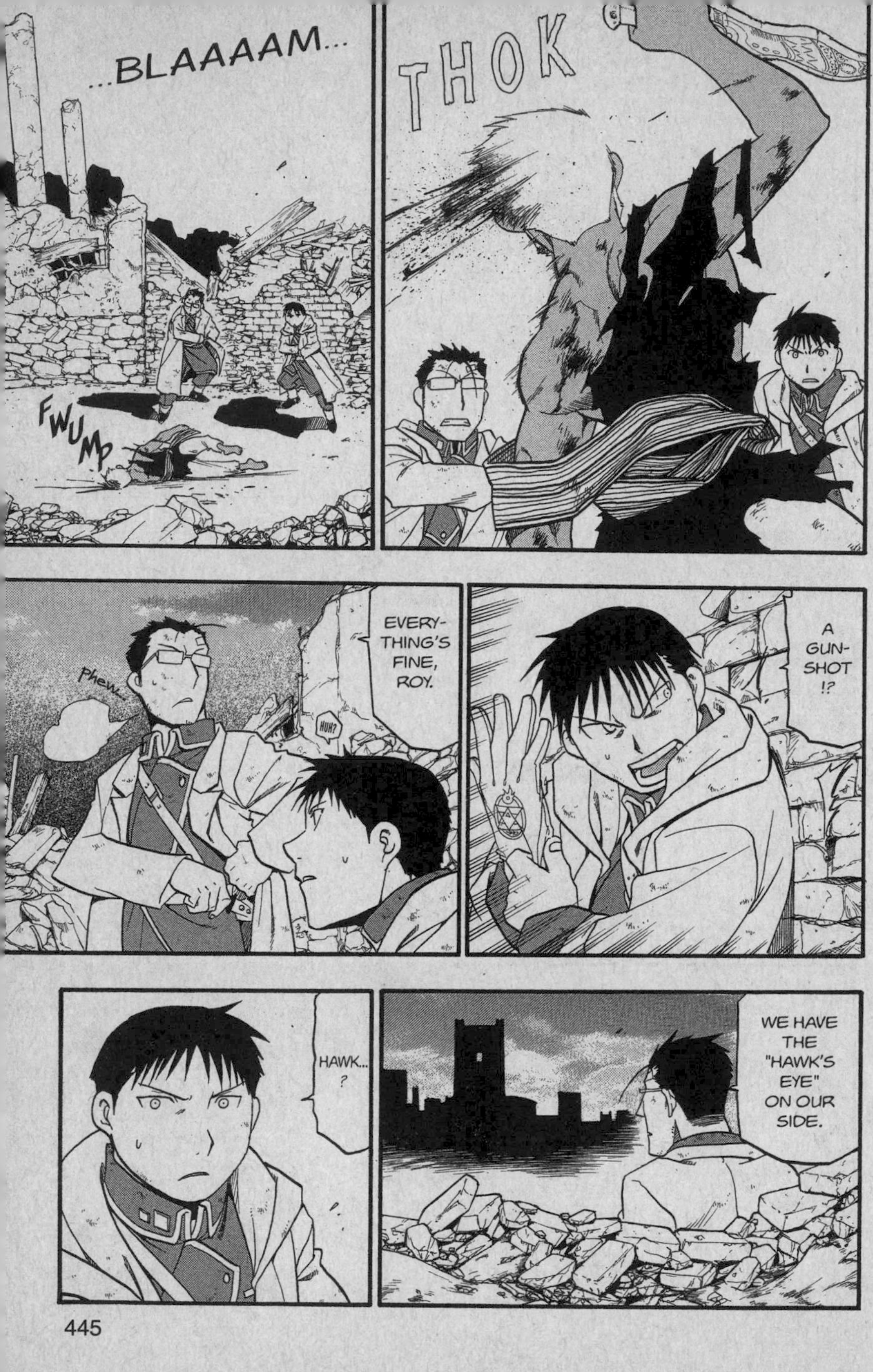
THOK
...BLAAAAM...
FWUMP
A GUN-SHOT !?
EVERY-THING'S FINE, ROY.
HUH?
Phew...
WE HAVE THE "HAWK'S EYE" ON OUR SIDE.
HAWK... ?

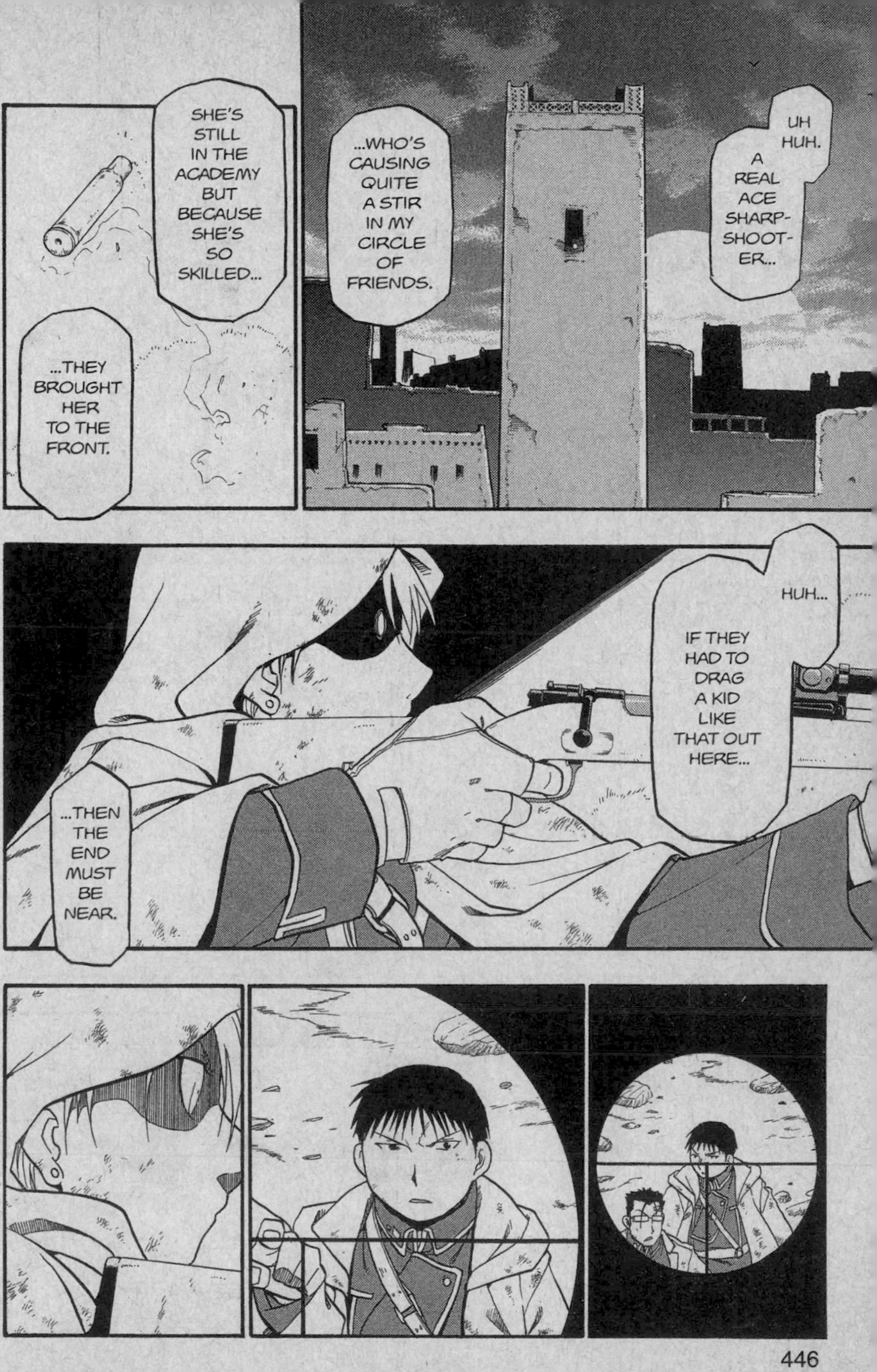
UH HUH. A REAL ACE SHARP-SHOOT-ER...
...WHO'S CAUSING QUITE A STIR IN MY CIRCLE OF FRIENDS.
SHE'S STILL IN THE ACADEMY BUT BECAUSE SHE'S SO SKILLED...
...THEY BROUGHT HER TO THE FRONT.
HUH...
IF THEY HAD TO DRAG A KID LIKE THAT OUT HERE...
...THEN THE END MUST BE NEAR.

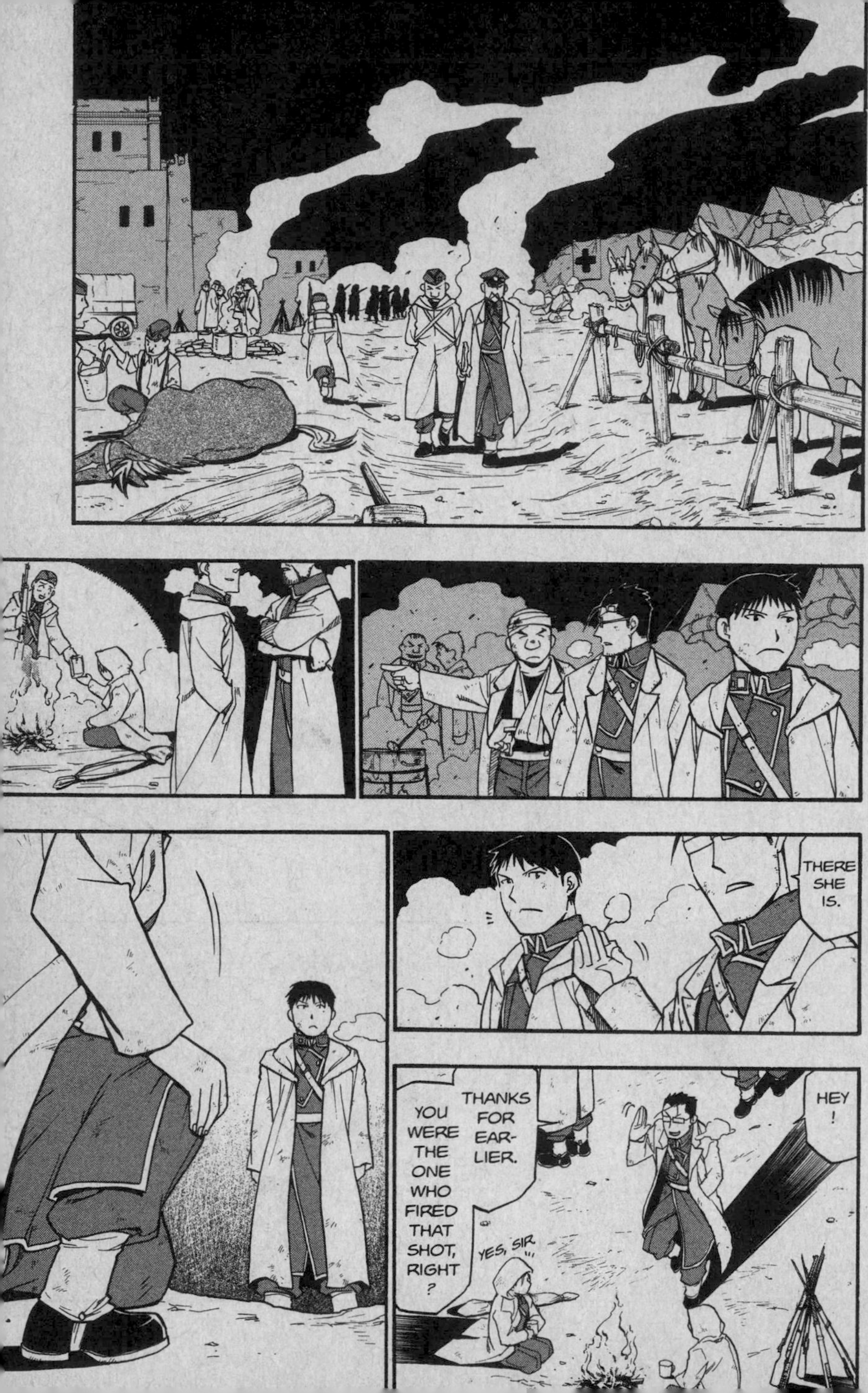
THERE SHE IS.
HEY!
THANKS FOR EAR-LIER.
YOU WERE THE ONE WHO FIRED THAT SHOT, RIGHT?
YES, SIR.

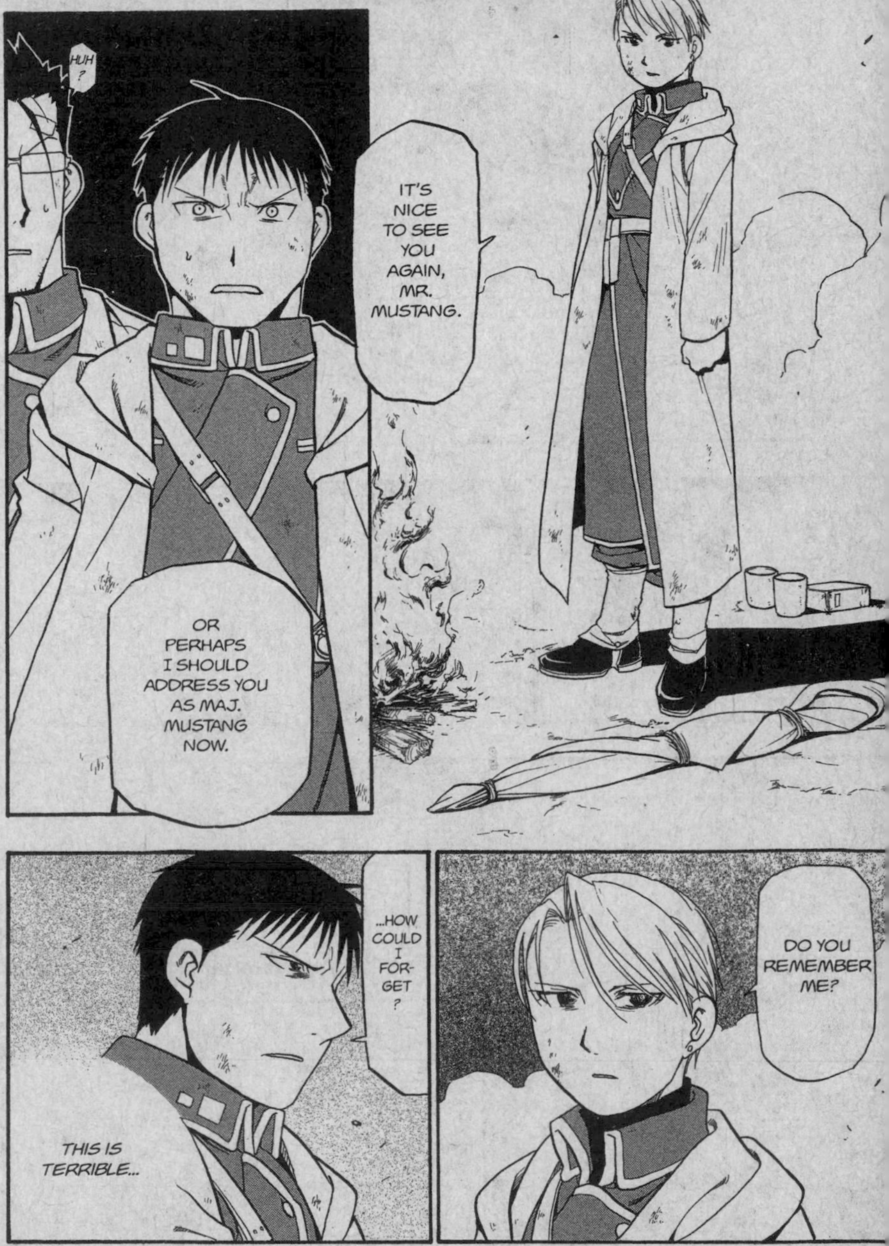
IT'S NICE TO SEE YOU AGAIN, MR. MUSTANG.
HUH?
OR PERHAPS I SHOULD ADDRESS YOU AS MAJ. MUSTANG NOW.
DO YOU REMEMBER ME?
...HOW COULD I FORGET?
THIS IS TERRIBLE...

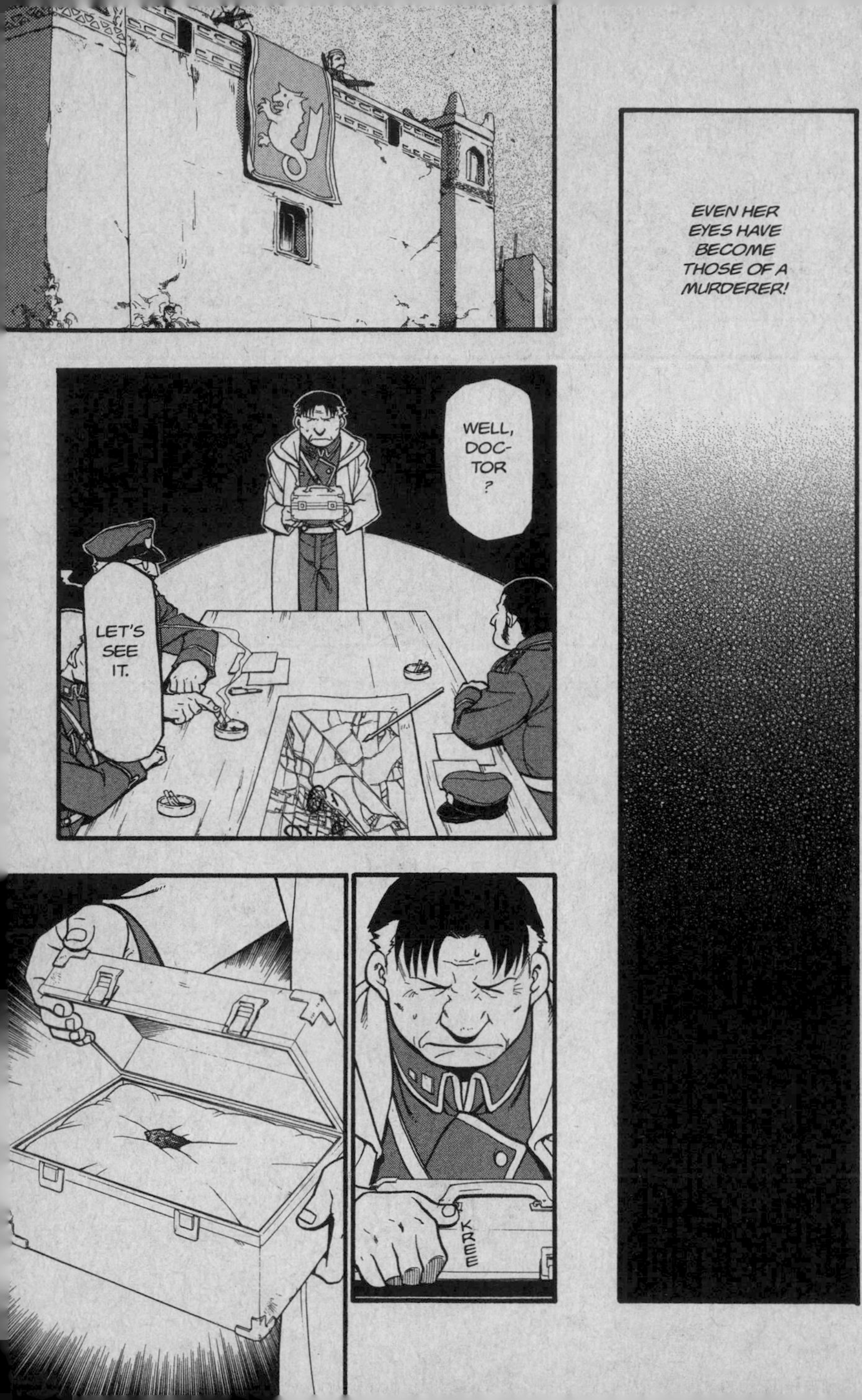
EVEN HER EYES HAVE BECOME THOSE OF A MURDERER!
WELL, DOCTOR?
LET'S SEE IT.
KREE

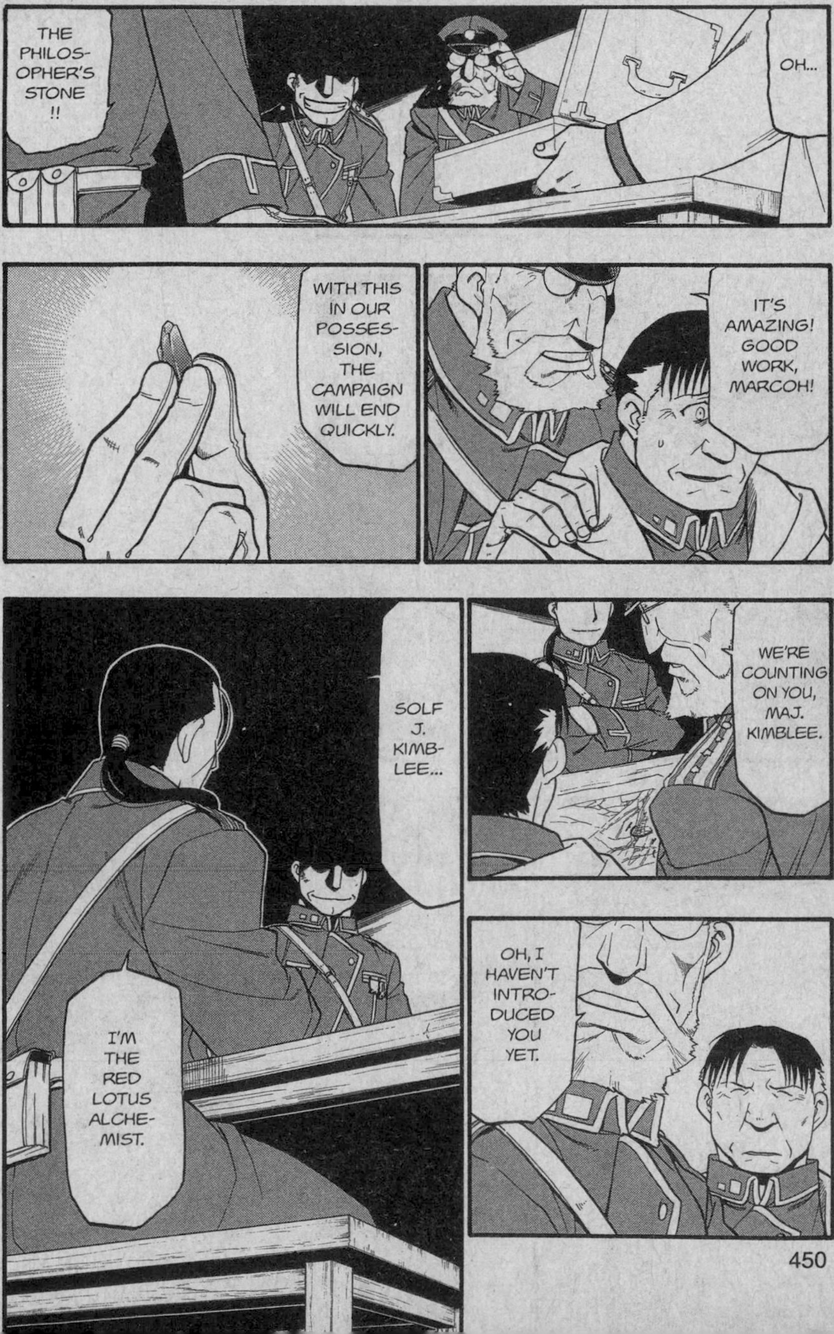
OH...
THE PHILOSOPHER'S STONE!!
IT'S AMAZING! GOOD WORK, MARCOH!
WITH THIS IN OUR POSSESSION, THE CAMPAIGN WILL END QUICKLY.
WE'RE COUNTING ON YOU, MAJ. KIMBLEE.
OH, I HAVEN'T INTRODUCED YOU YET.
SOLF J. KIMBLEE...
I'M THE RED LOTUS ALCHEMIST.

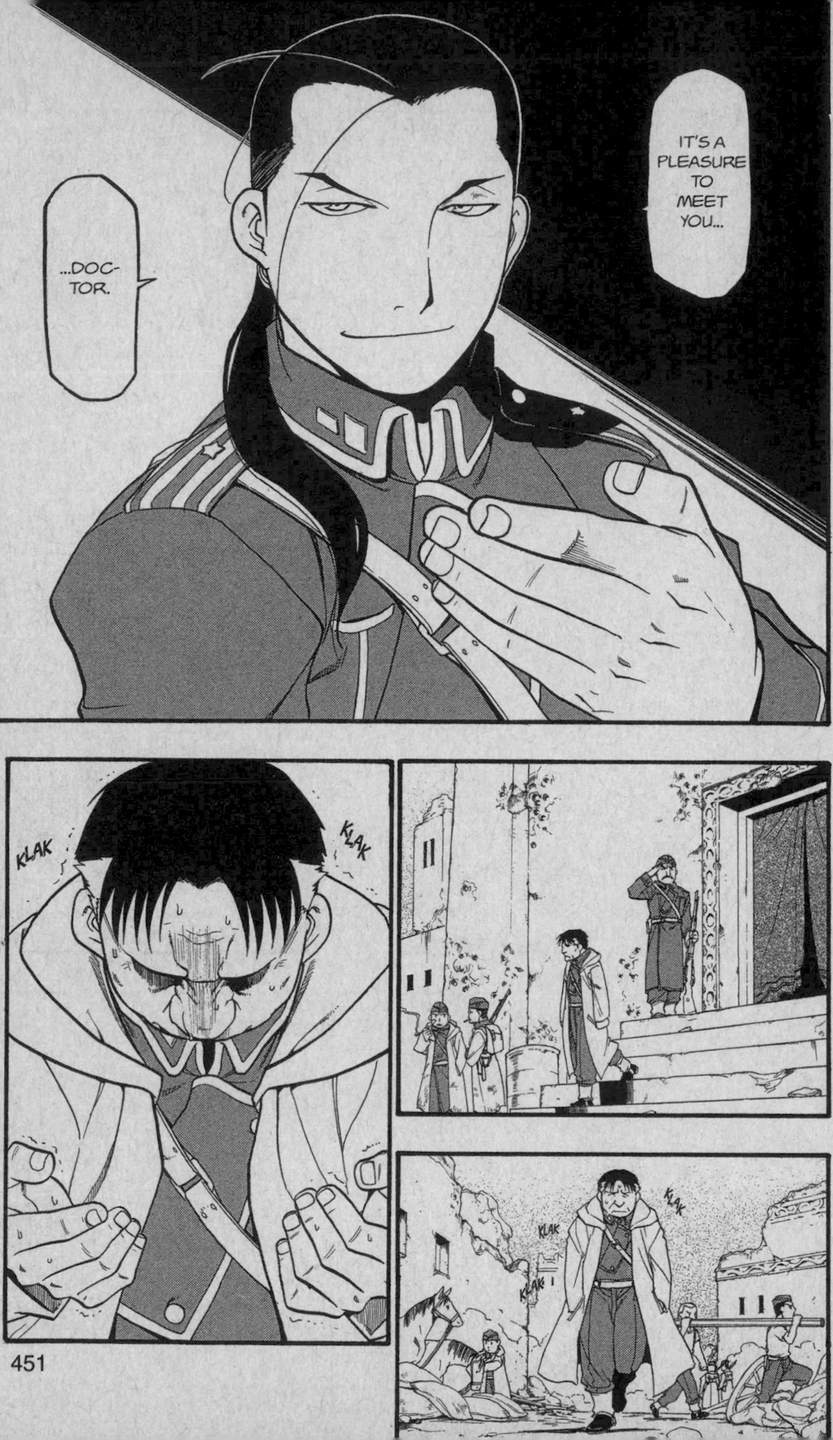
IT'S A PLEASURE TO MEET YOU...
...DOCTOR.
KLAK
KLAK
KLAK
KLAK
KLAK

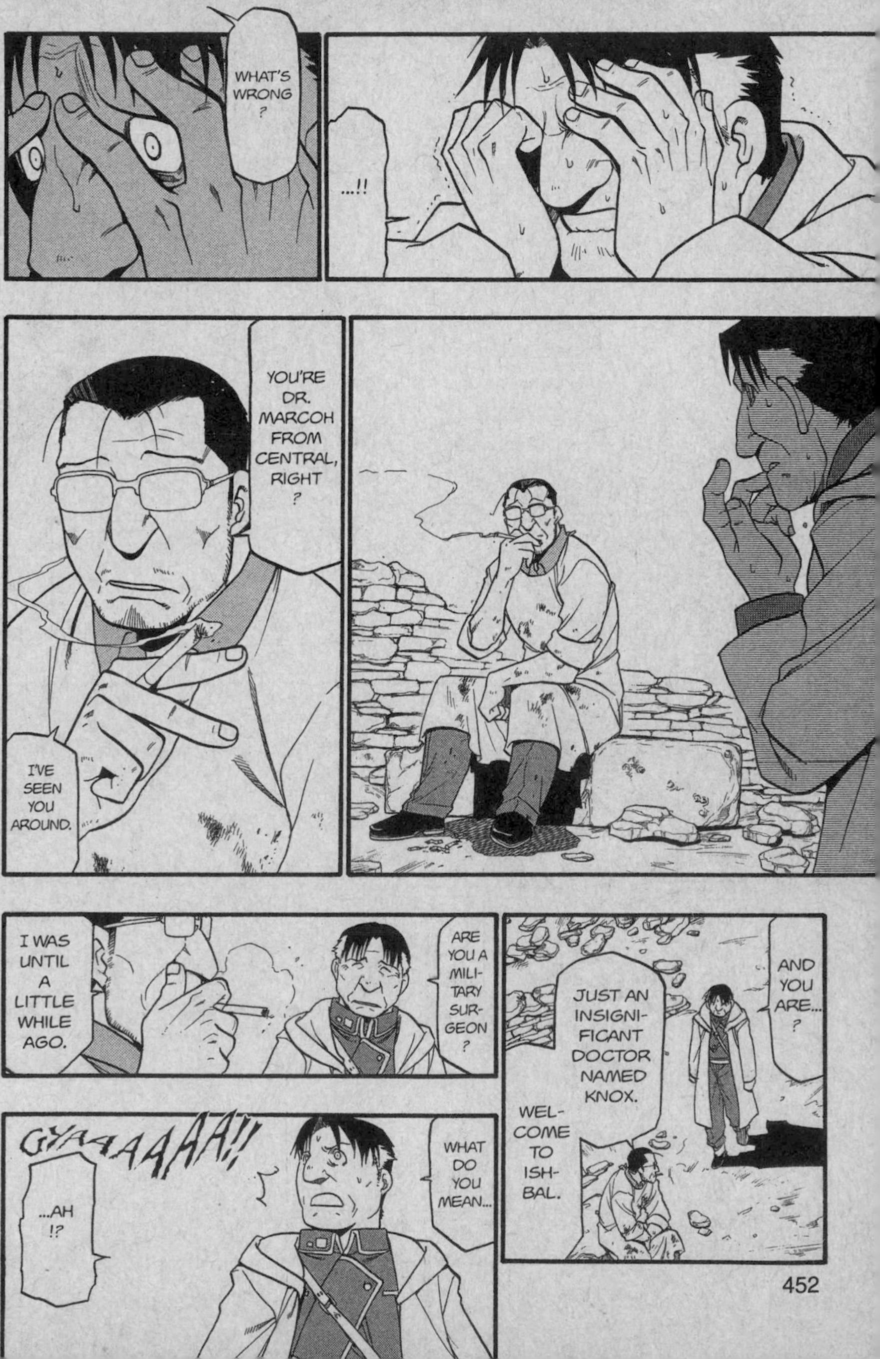
...!!
WHAT'S WRONG?
YOU'RE DR. MARCOH FROM CENTRAL, RIGHT?
I'VE SEEN YOU AROUND.
AND YOU ARE...?
JUST AN INSIGNIFICANT DOCTOR NAMED KNOX.
WELCOME TO ISHBAL.
ARE YOU A MILITARY SURGEON?
I WAS UNTIL A LITTLE WHILE AGO.
WHAT DO YOU MEAN...
GYAAAAAAH!!
...AH!?

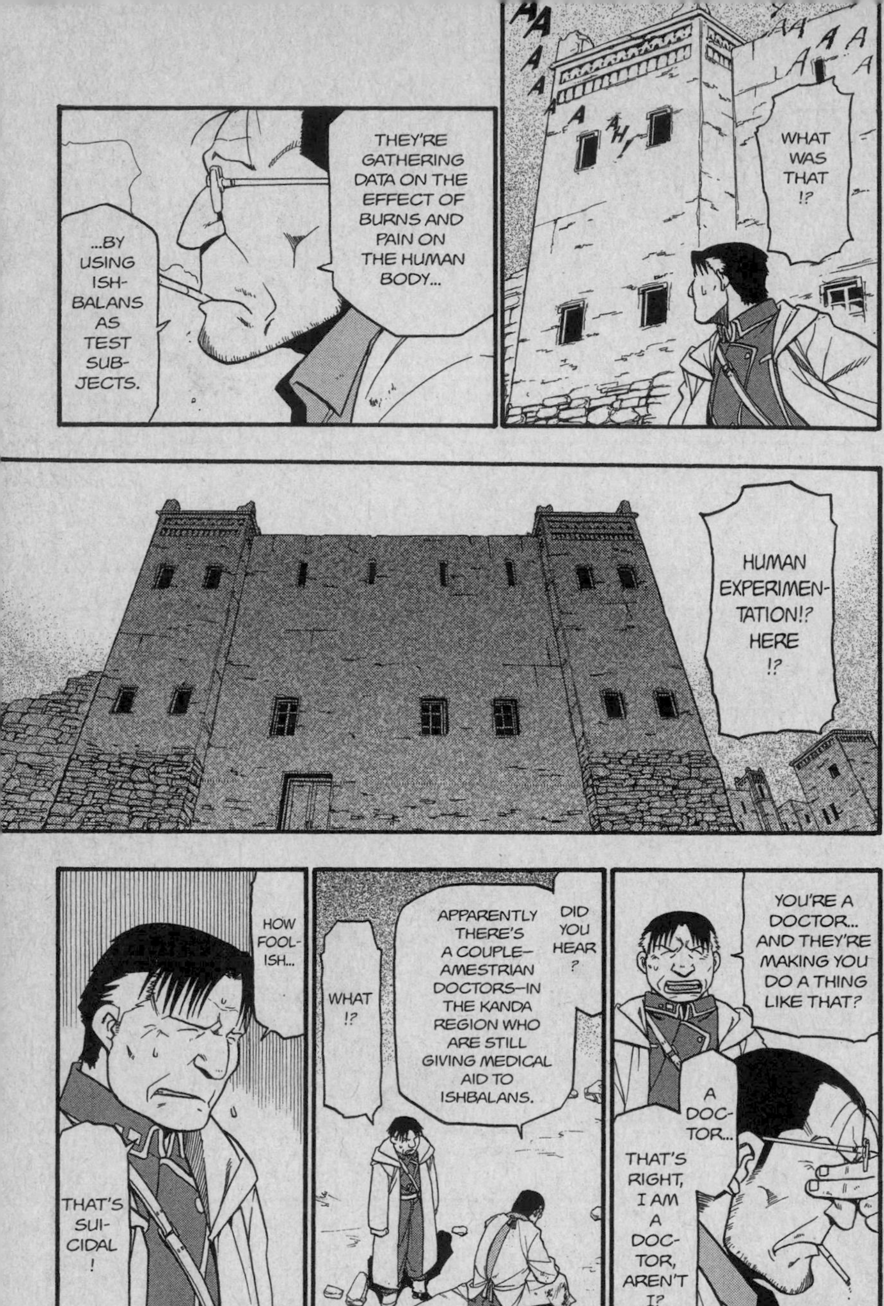
AAAAAAH!
WHAT WAS THAT!?
THEY'RE GATHERING DATA ON THE EFFECT OF BURNS AND PAIN ON THE HUMAN BODY...
...BY USING ISH-BALANS AS TEST SUB-JECTS.
HUMAN EXPERIMEN-TATION!? HERE!?
YOU'RE A DOCTOR... AND THEY'RE MAKING YOU DO A THING LIKE THAT?
A DOC-TOR...
THAT'S RIGHT, I AM A DOC-TOR, AREN'T I?
DID YOU HEAR?
APPARENTLY THERE'S A COUPLE—AMESTRIAN DOCTORS—IN THE KANDA REGION WHO ARE STILL GIVING MEDICAL AID TO ISHBALANS.
WHAT!?
HOW FOOL-ISH...
THAT'S SUI-CIDAL!

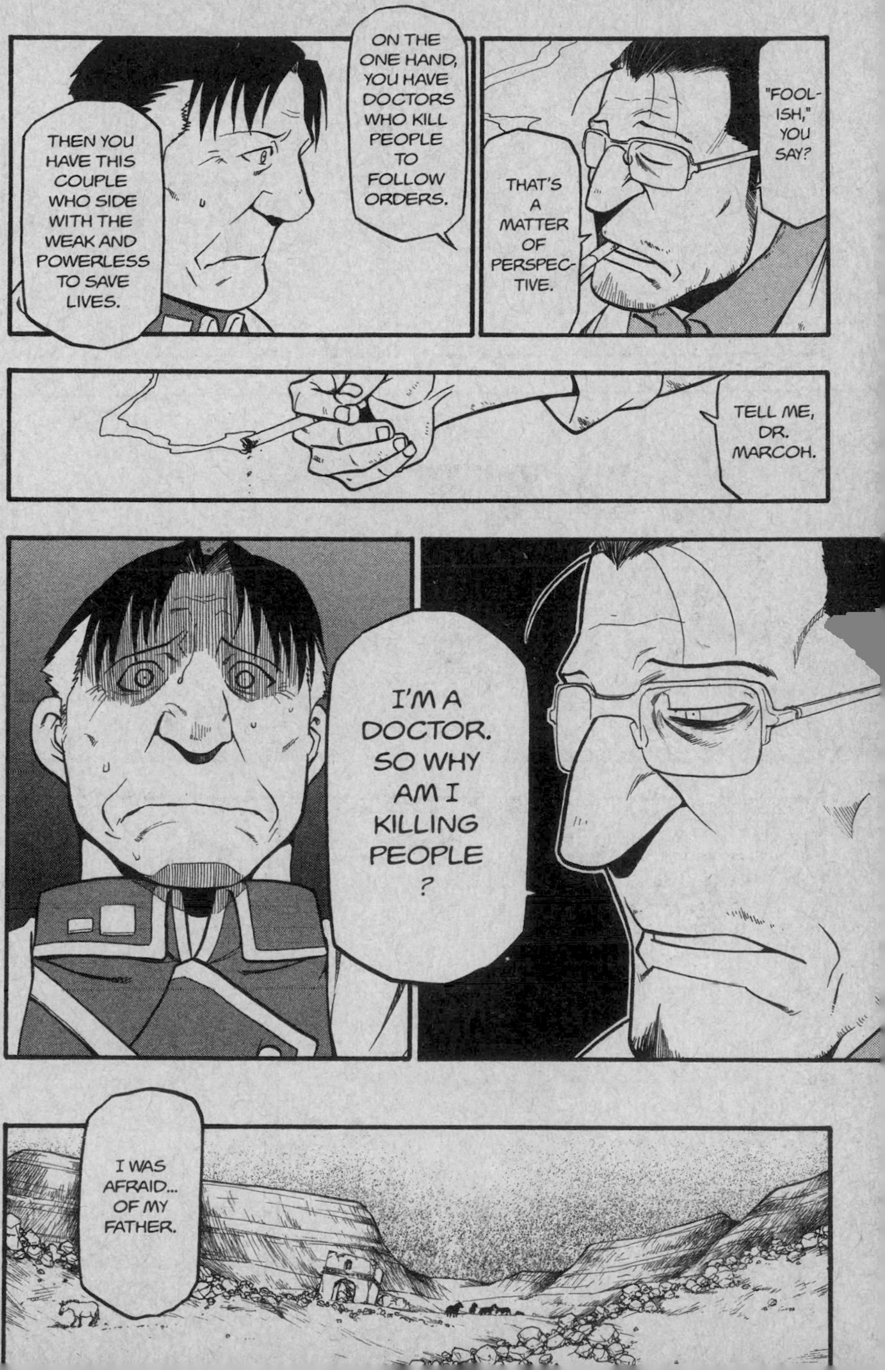
"FOOLISH," YOU SAY?
THAT'S A MATTER OF PERSPECTIVE.
ON THE ONE HAND, YOU HAVE DOCTORS WHO KILL PEOPLE TO FOLLOW ORDERS.
THEN YOU HAVE THIS COUPLE WHO SIDE WITH THE WEAK AND POWERLESS TO SAVE LIVES.
TELL ME, DR. MARCOH.
I'M A DOCTOR. SO WHY AM I KILLING PEOPLE?
I WAS AFRAID... OF MY FATHER.

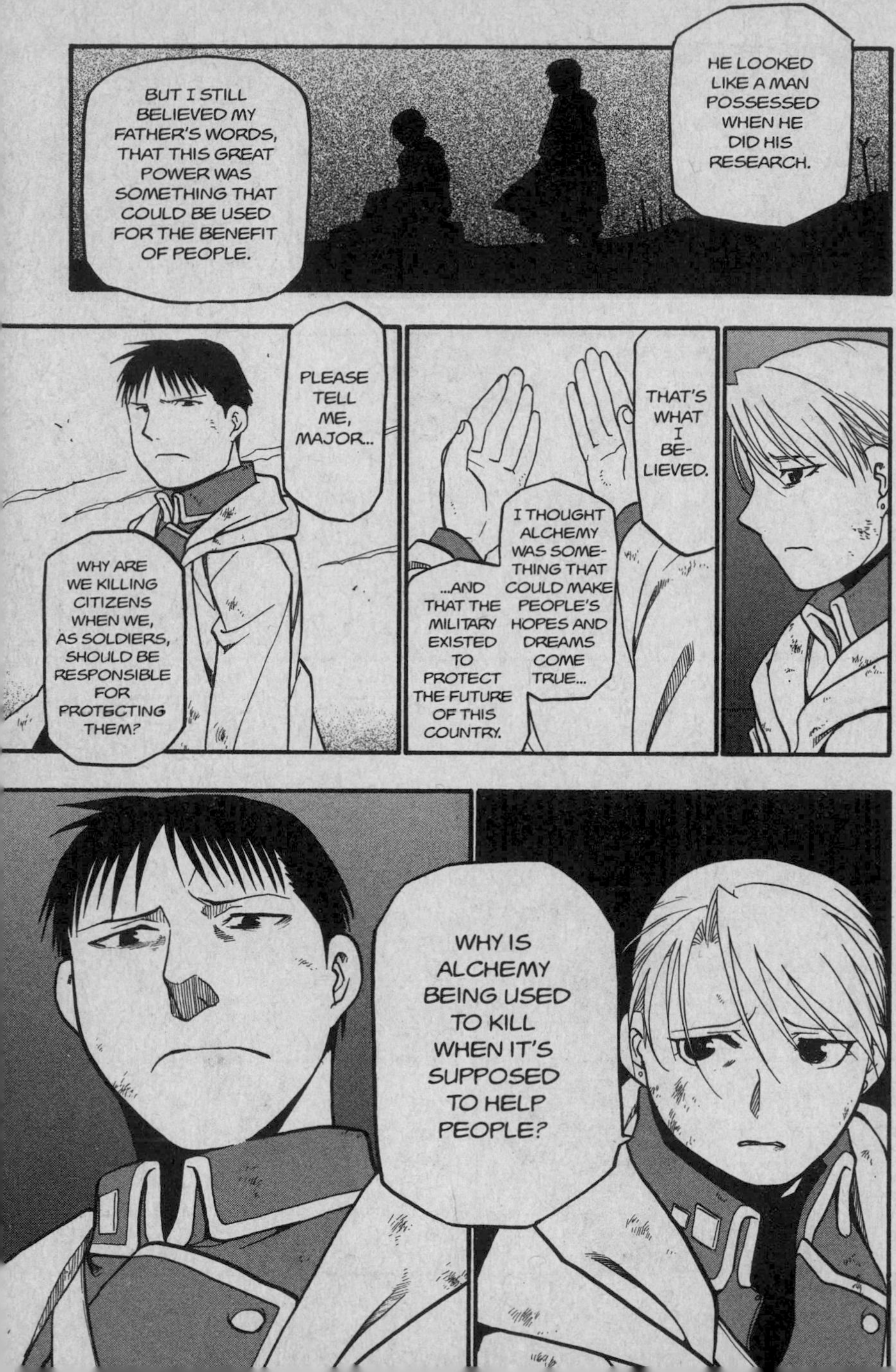
HE LOOKED LIKE A MAN POSSESSED WHEN HE DID HIS RESEARCH.
BUT I STILL BELIEVED MY FATHER'S WORDS, THAT THIS GREAT POWER WAS SOMETHING THAT COULD BE USED FOR THE BENEFIT OF PEOPLE.
THAT'S WHAT I BE-LIEVED.
I THOUGHT ALCHEMY WAS SOME-THING THAT COULD MAKE PEOPLE'S HOPES AND DREAMS COME TRUE...
...AND THAT THE MILITARY EXISTED TO PROTECT THE FUTURE OF THIS COUNTRY.
PLEASE TELL ME, MAJOR...
WHY ARE WE KILLING CITIZENS WHEN WE, AS SOLDIERS, SHOULD BE RESPONSIBLE FOR PROTECTING THEM?
WHY IS ALCHEMY BEING USED TO KILL WHEN IT'S SUPPOSED TO HELP PEOPLE?

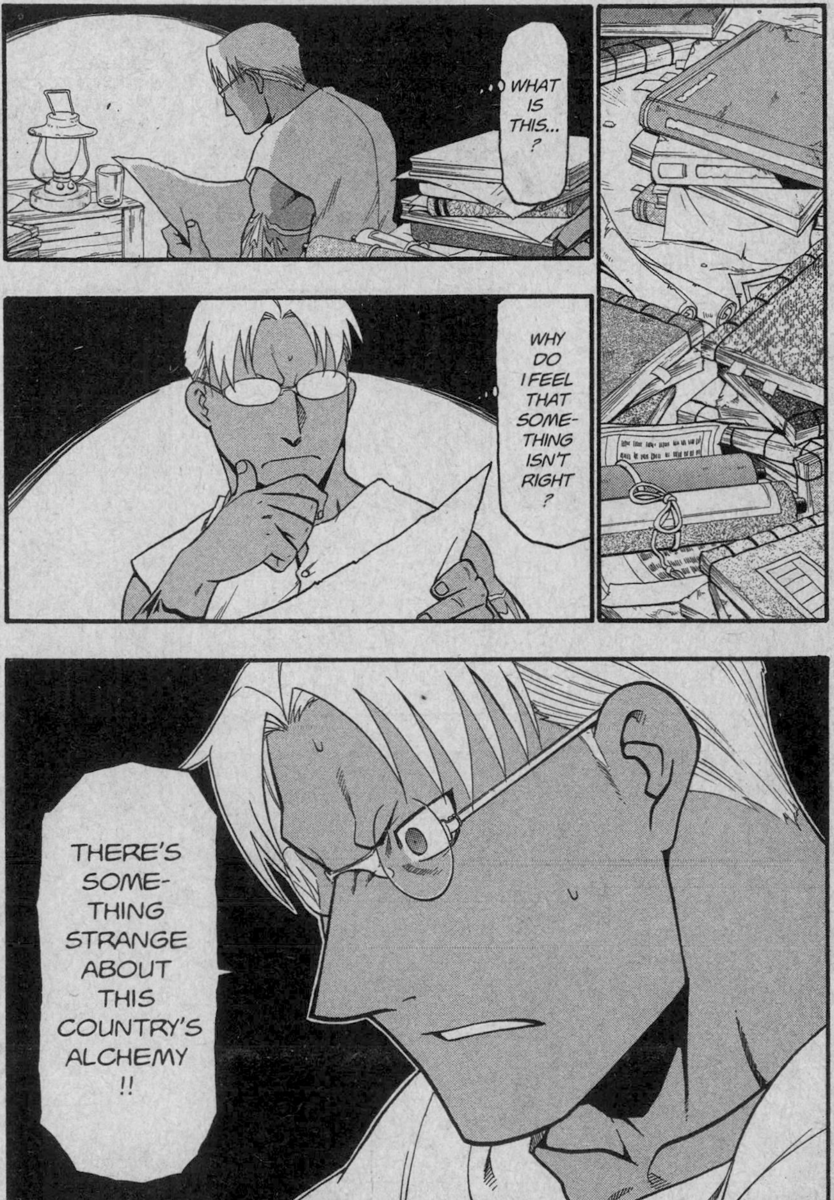
...WHAT IS THIS...?
WHY DO I FEEL THAT SOMETHING ISN'T RIGHT?
THERE'S SOMETHING STRANGE ABOUT THIS COUNTRY'S ALCHEMY!!

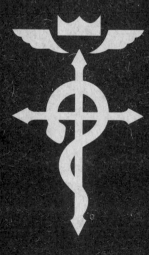

FULLMETAL
ALCHEMIST

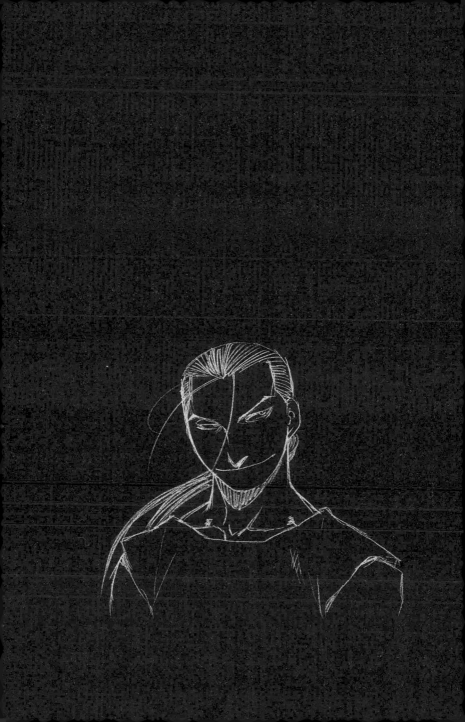

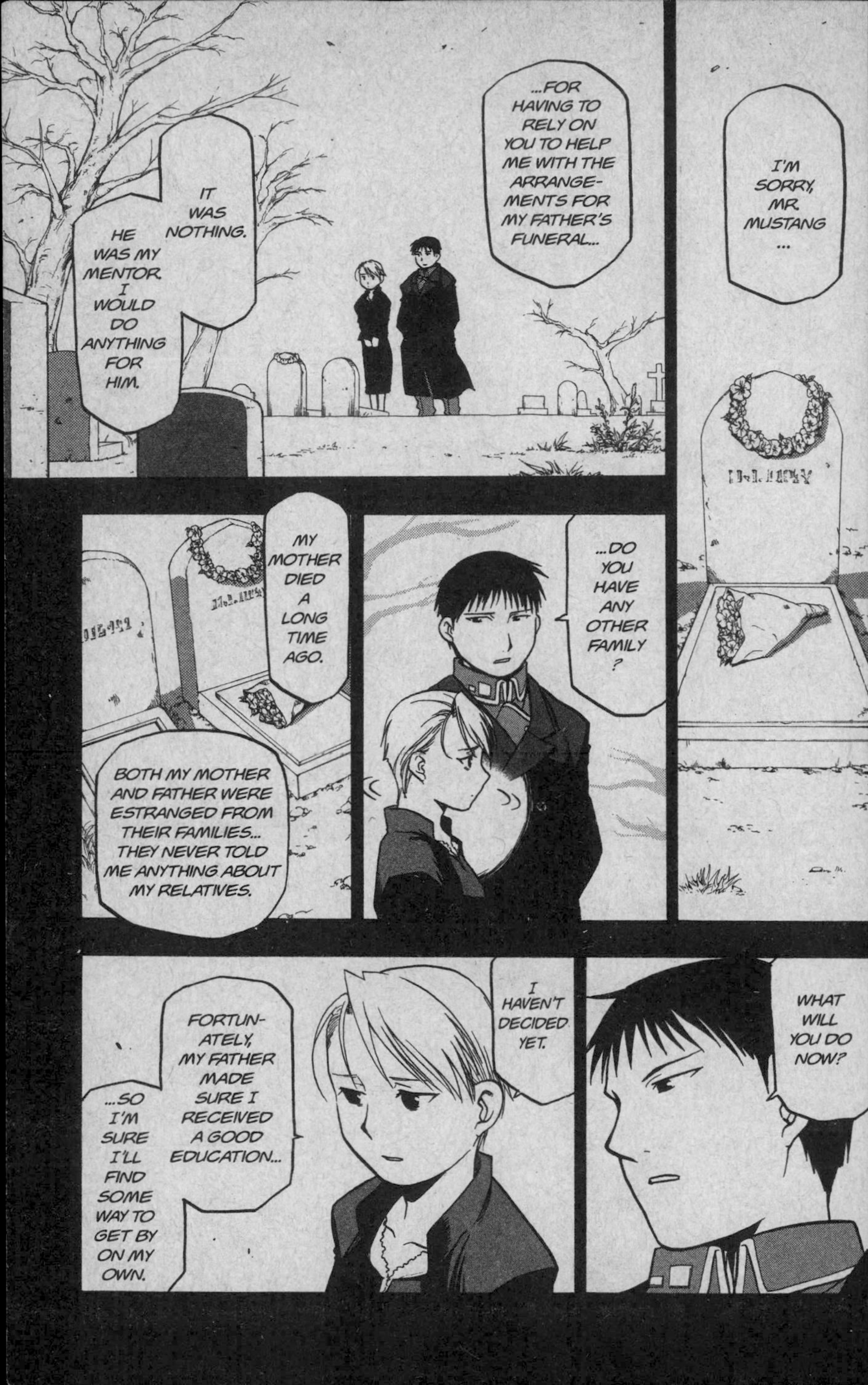
I'M SORRY, MR. MUSTANG...
...FOR HAVING TO RELY ON YOU TO HELP ME WITH THE ARRANGEMENTS FOR MY FATHER'S FUNERAL...
IT WAS NOTHING.
HE WAS MY MENTOR. I WOULD DO ANYTHING FOR HIM.
...DO YOU HAVE ANY OTHER FAMILY?
MY MOTHER DIED A LONG TIME AGO.
BOTH MY MOTHER AND FATHER WERE ESTRANGED FROM THEIR FAMILIES... THEY NEVER TOLD ME ANYTHING ABOUT MY RELATIVES.
WHAT WILL YOU DO NOW?
I HAVEN'T DECIDED YET.
FORTUNATELY, MY FATHER MADE SURE I RECEIVED A GOOD EDUCATION...
...SO I'M SURE I'LL FIND SOME WAY TO GET BY ON MY OWN.

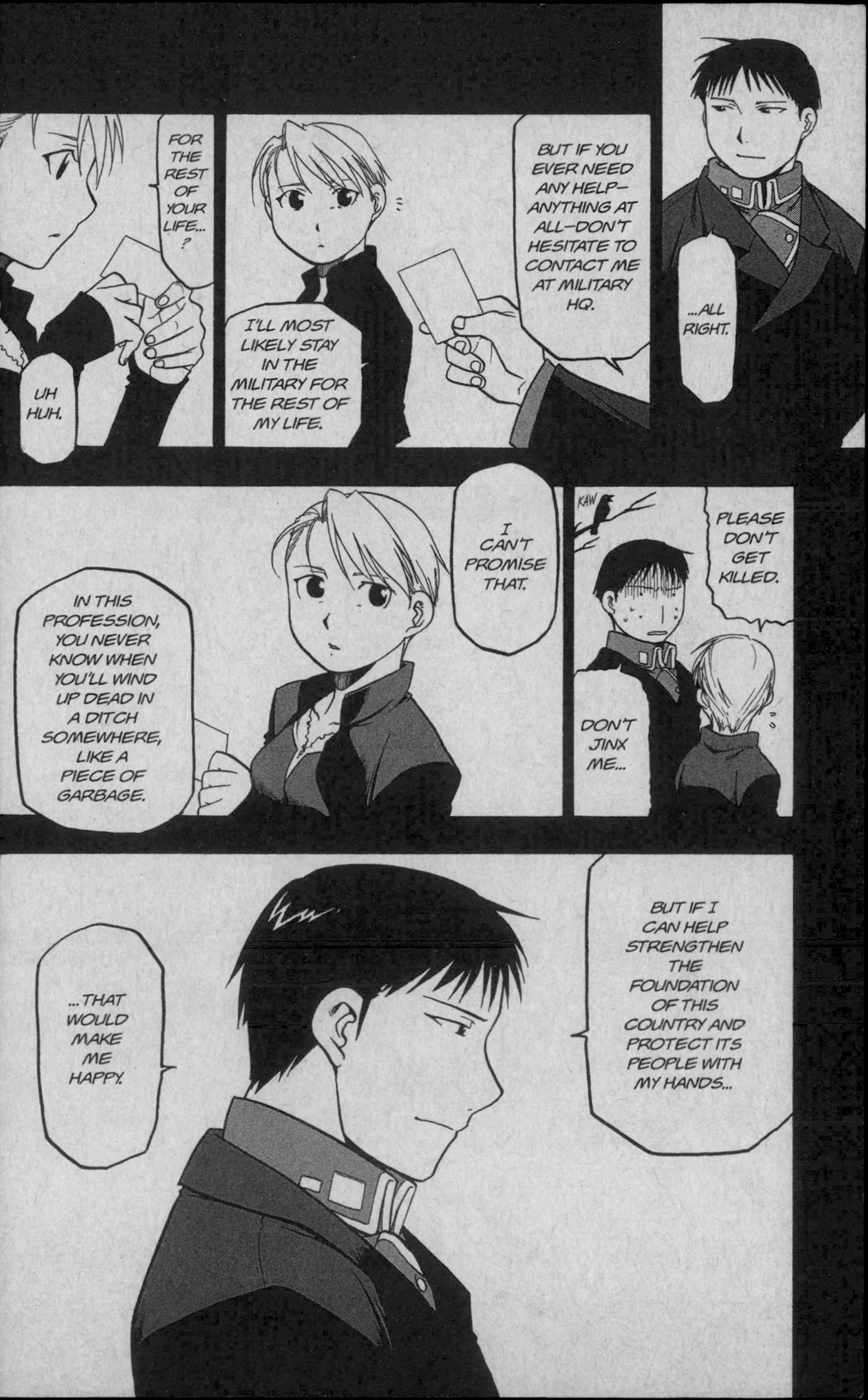
...ALL RIGHT.
BUT IF YOU EVER NEED ANY HELP—ANYTHING AT ALL—DON'T HESITATE TO CONTACT ME AT MILITARY HQ.
I'LL MOST LIKELY STAY IN THE MILITARY FOR THE REST OF MY LIFE.
FOR THE REST OF YOUR LIFE...?
UH HUH.
PLEASE DON'T GET KILLED.
KAW
DON'T JINX ME...
I CAN'T PROMISE THAT.
IN THIS PROFESSION, YOU NEVER KNOW WHEN YOU'LL WIND UP DEAD IN A DITCH SOMEWHERE, LIKE A PIECE OF GARBAGE.
BUT IF I CAN HELP STRENGTHEN THE FOUNDATION OF THIS COUNTRY AND PROTECT ITS PEOPLE WITH MY HANDS...
...THAT WOULD MAKE ME HAPPY.

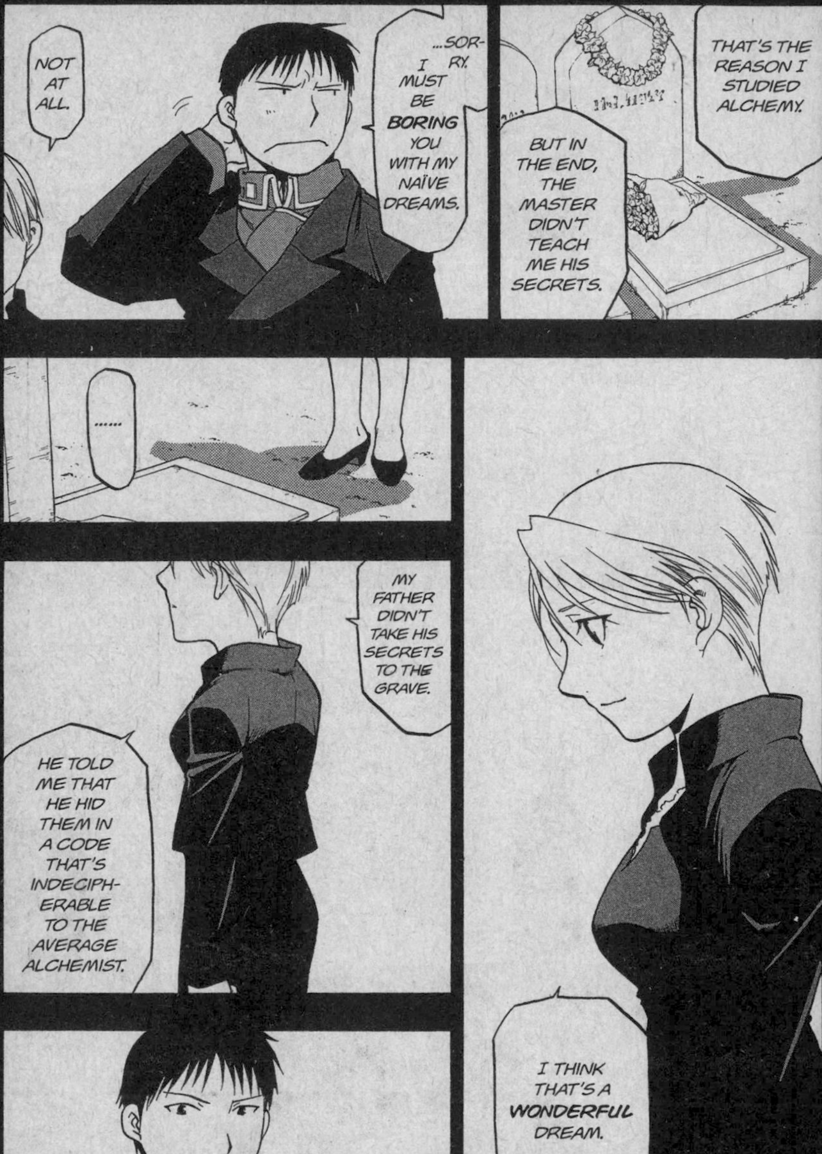
THAT'S THE REASON I STUDIED ALCHEMY.
BUT IN THE END, THE MASTER DIDN'T TEACH ME HIS SECRETS.
...SORRY. I MUST BE **BORING** YOU WITH MY NAÏVE DREAMS.
NOT AT ALL.
I THINK THAT'S A **WONDERFUL** DREAM.
......
MY FATHER DIDN'T TAKE HIS SECRETS TO THE GRAVE.
HE TOLD ME THAT HE HID THEM IN A CODE THAT'S INDECIPHERABLE TO THE AVERAGE ALCHEMIST.

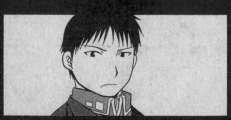

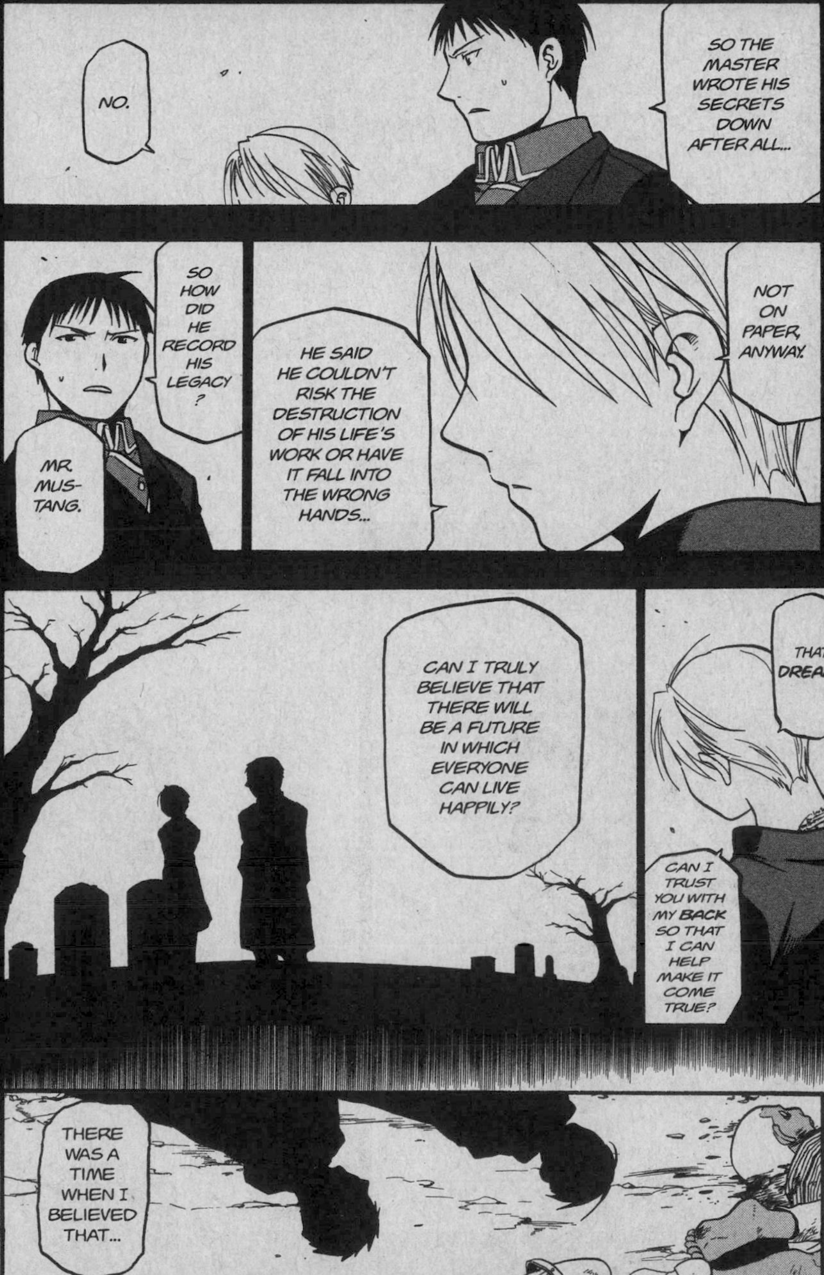
SO THE MASTER WROTE HIS SECRETS DOWN AFTER ALL...
NO.
NOT ON PAPER, ANYWAY.
HE SAID HE COULDN'T RISK THE DESTRUCTION OF HIS LIFE'S WORK OR HAVE IT FALL INTO THE WRONG HANDS...
SO HOW DID HE RECORD HIS LEGACY?
MR. MUSTANG.
THAT DREAM..
CAN I TRUST YOU WITH MY BACK SO THAT I CAN HELP MAKE IT COME TRUE?
CAN I TRULY BELIEVE THAT THERE WILL BE A FUTURE IN WHICH EVERYONE CAN LIVE HAPPILY?
THERE WAS A TIME WHEN I BELIEVED THAT...

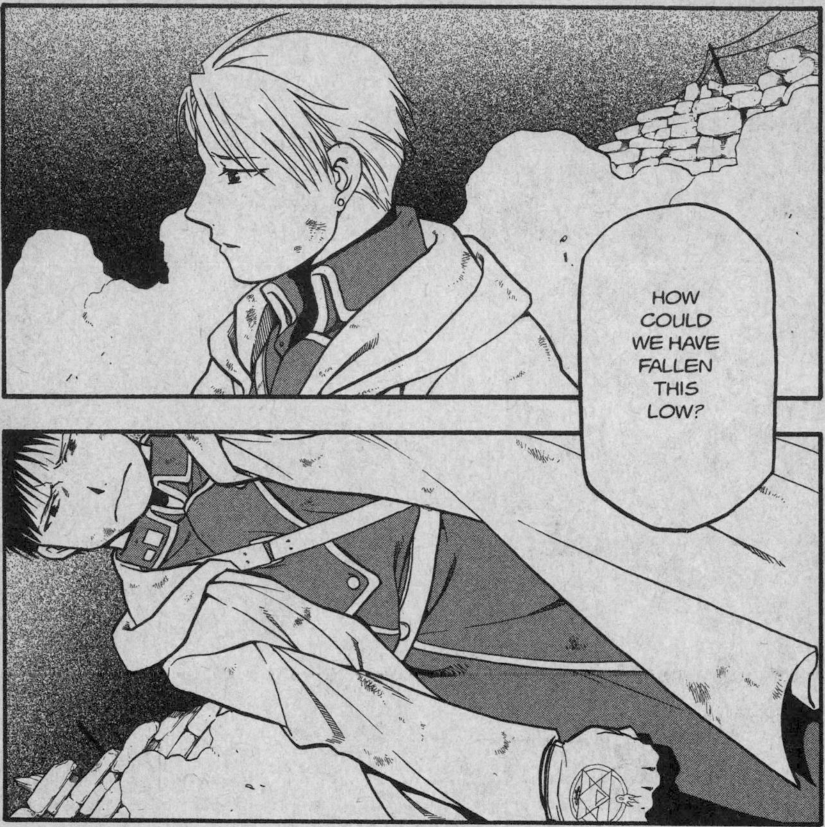
HOW COULD WE HAVE FALLEN THIS LOW?

Chapter 60
In the Absence Of God

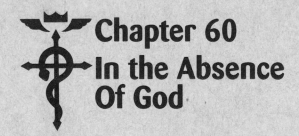

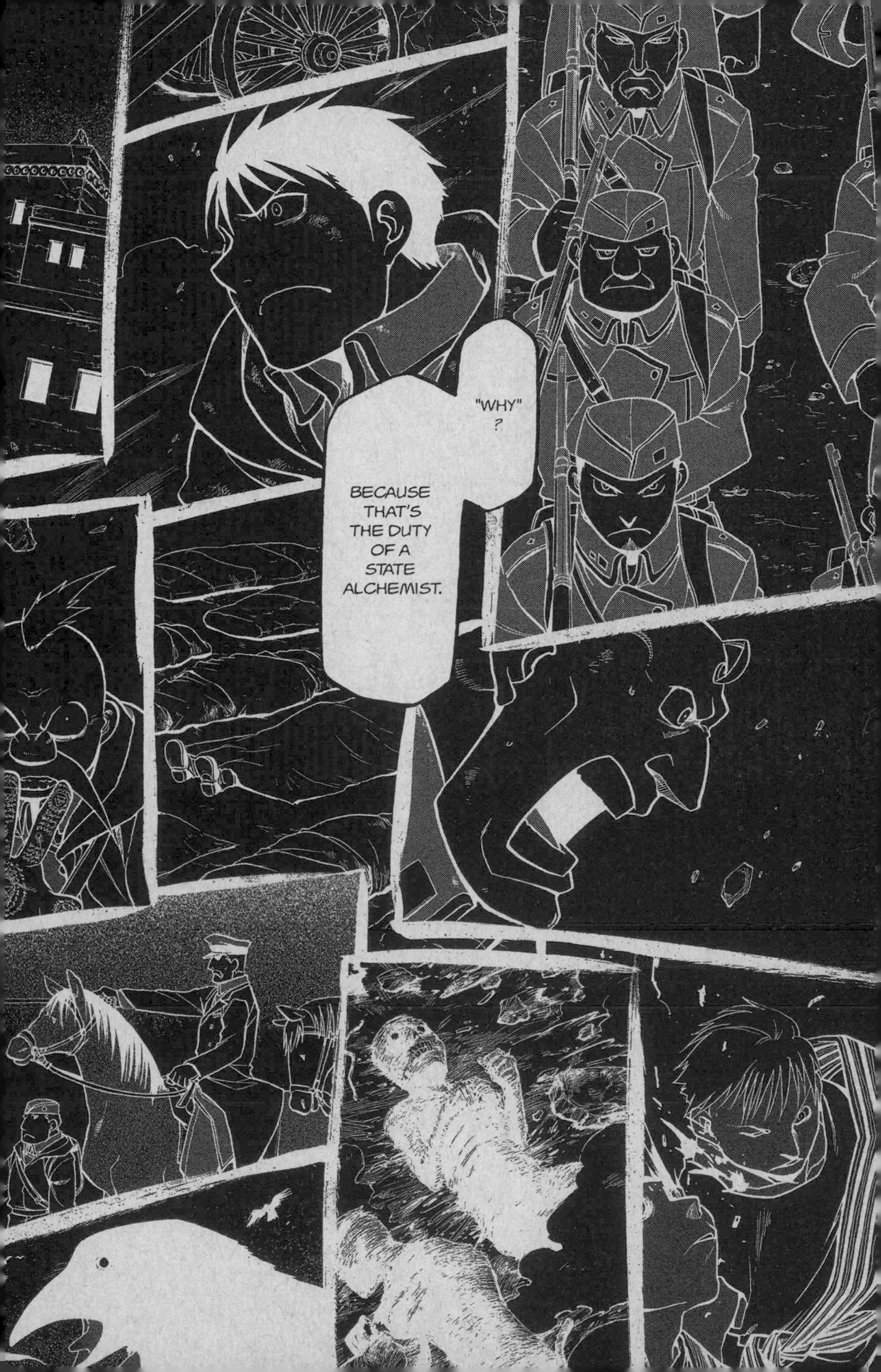
"WHY"
?
BECAUSE THAT'S THE DUTY OF A STATE ALCHEMIST.

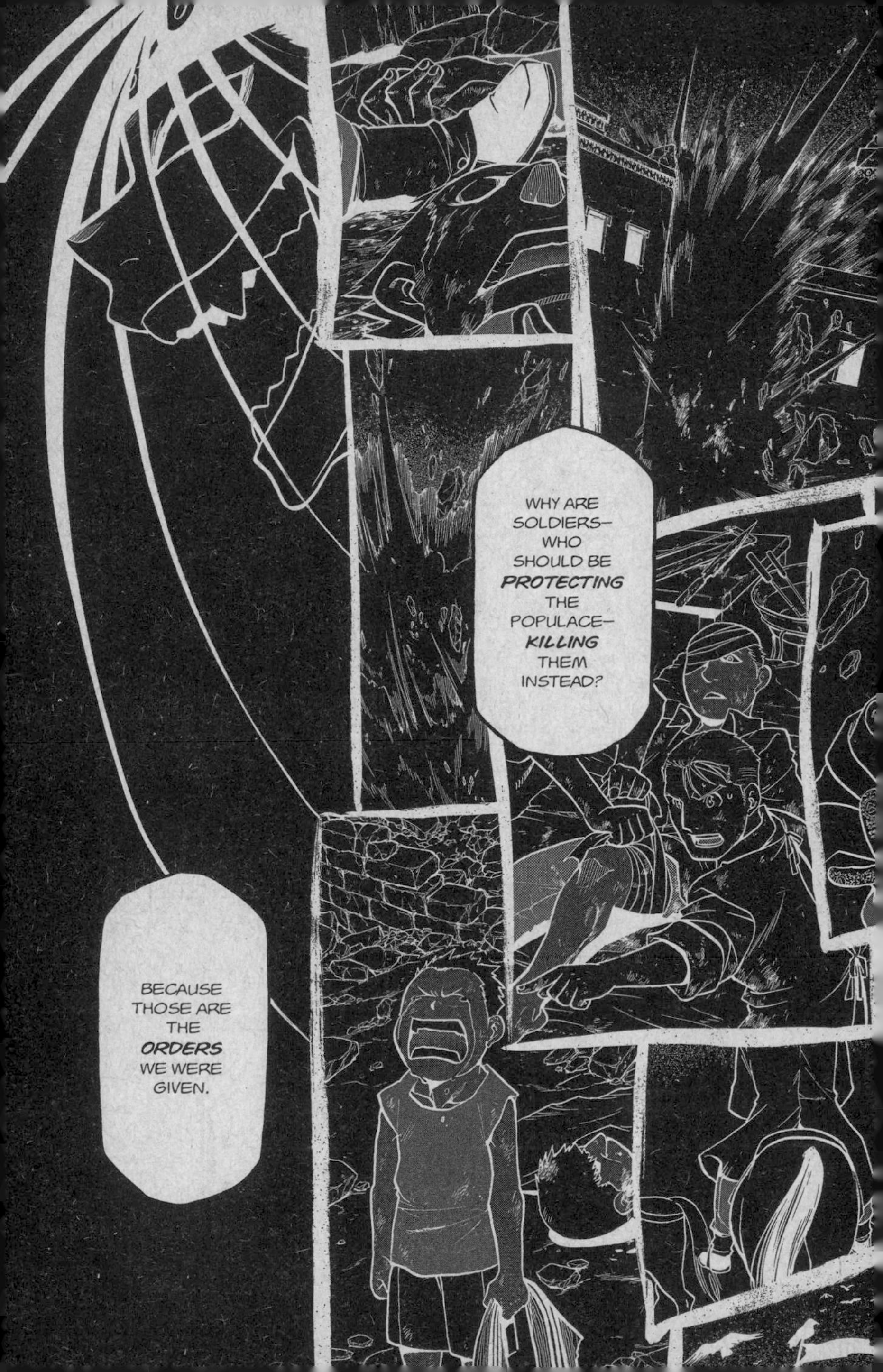
WHY ARE SOLDIERS—WHO SHOULD BE PROTECTING THE POPULACE—KILLING THEM INSTEAD?
BECAUSE THOSE ARE THE ORDERS WE WERE GIVEN.

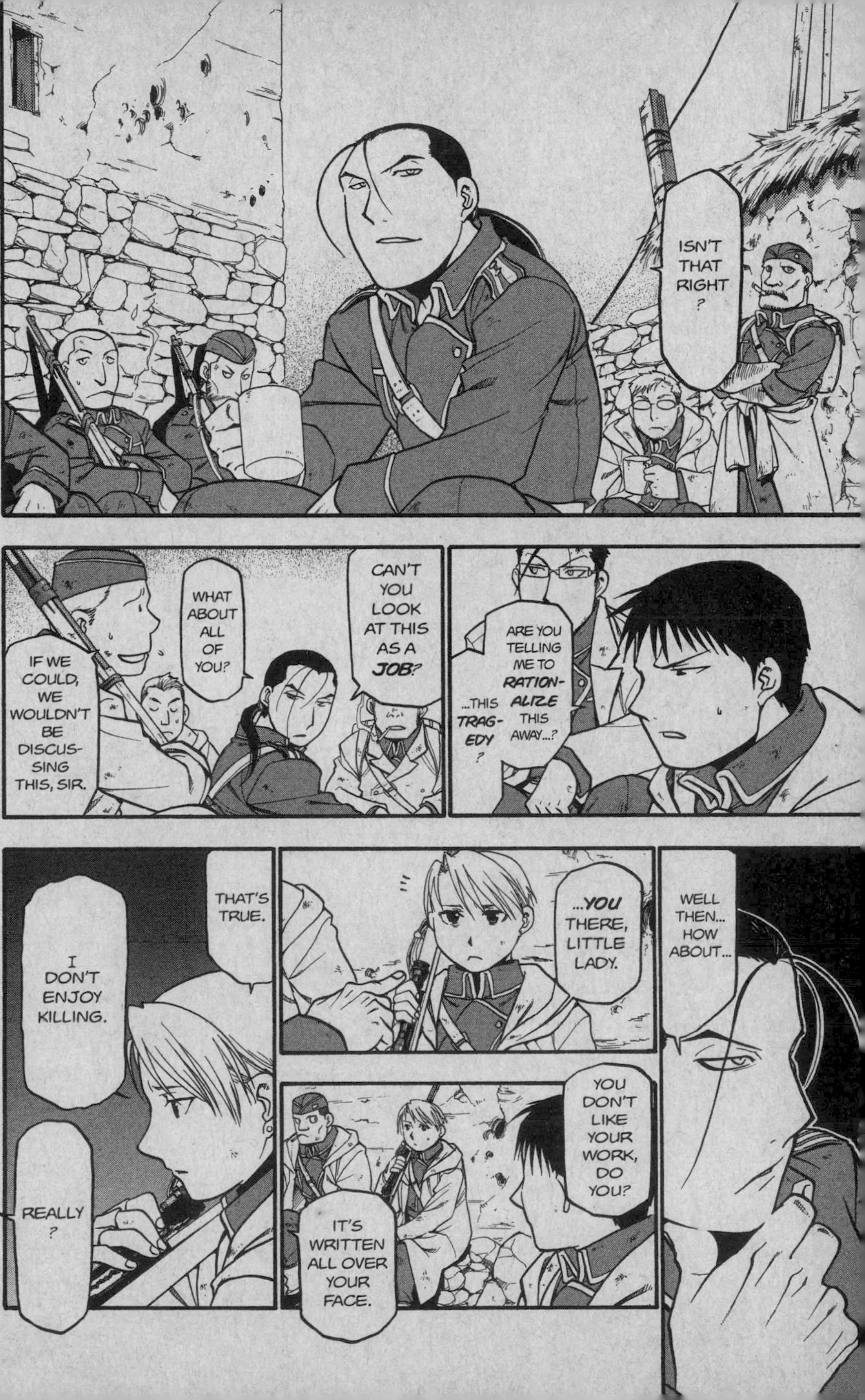
ISN'T THAT RIGHT?
ARE YOU TELLING ME TO RATIONALIZE THIS AWAY...?
...THIS TRAGEDY?
CAN'T YOU LOOK AT THIS AS A JOB?
WHAT ABOUT ALL OF YOU?
IF WE COULD, WE WOULDN'T BE DISCUSSING THIS, SIR.
WELL THEN... HOW ABOUT...
...YOU THERE, LITTLE LADY.
YOU DON'T LIKE YOUR WORK, DO YOU?
IT'S WRITTEN ALL OVER YOUR FACE.
THAT'S TRUE.
I DON'T ENJOY KILLING.
REALLY?

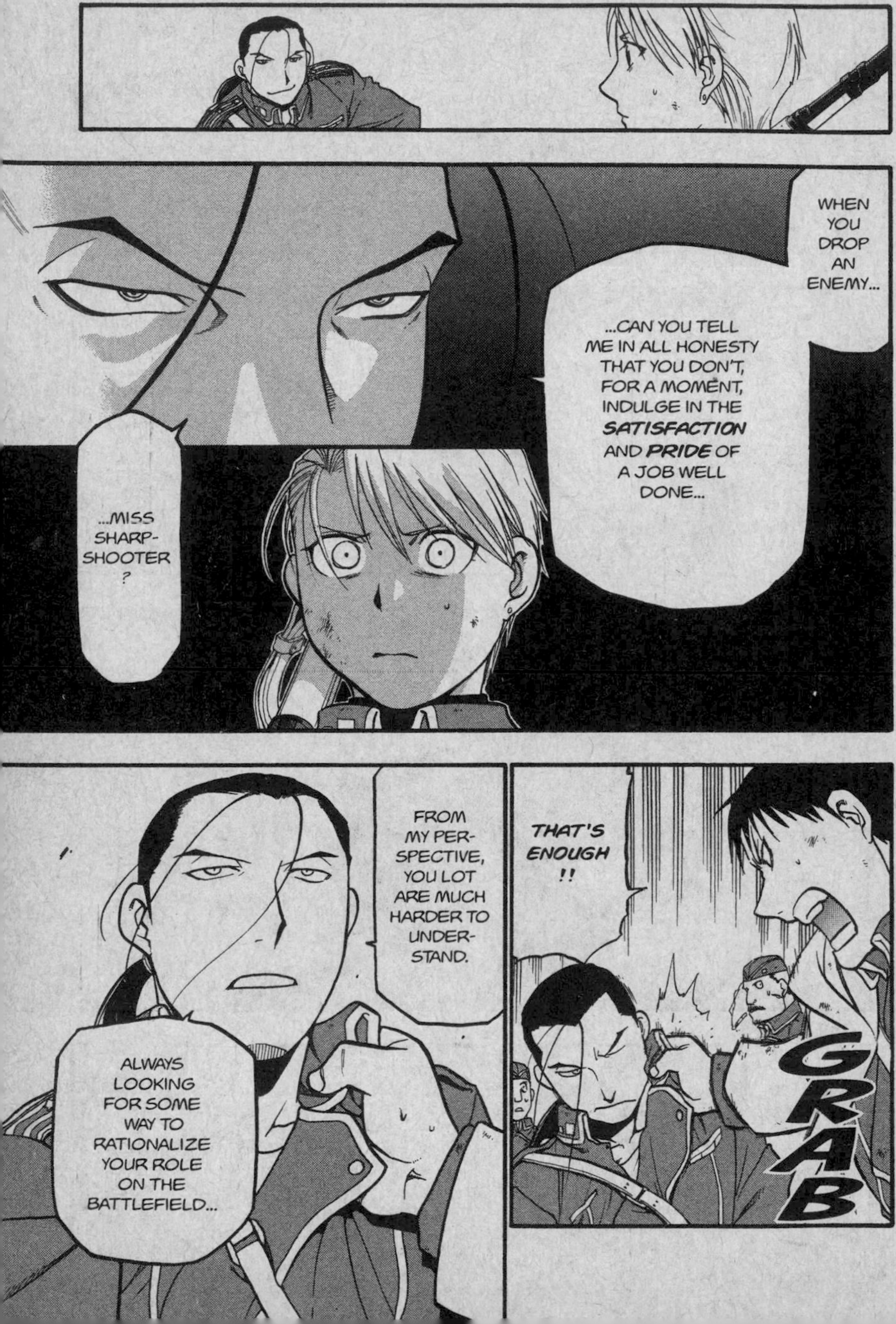
WHEN YOU DROP AN ENEMY...
...CAN YOU TELL ME IN ALL HONESTY THAT YOU DON'T, FOR A MOMENT, INDULGE IN THE SATISFACTION AND PRIDE OF A JOB WELL DONE...
...MISS SHARP-SHOOTER?
THAT'S ENOUGH!!
GRAB
FROM MY PER-SPECTIVE, YOU LOT ARE MUCH HARDER TO UNDER-STAND.
ALWAYS LOOKING FOR SOME WAY TO RATIONALIZE YOUR ROLE ON THE BATTLEFIELD...

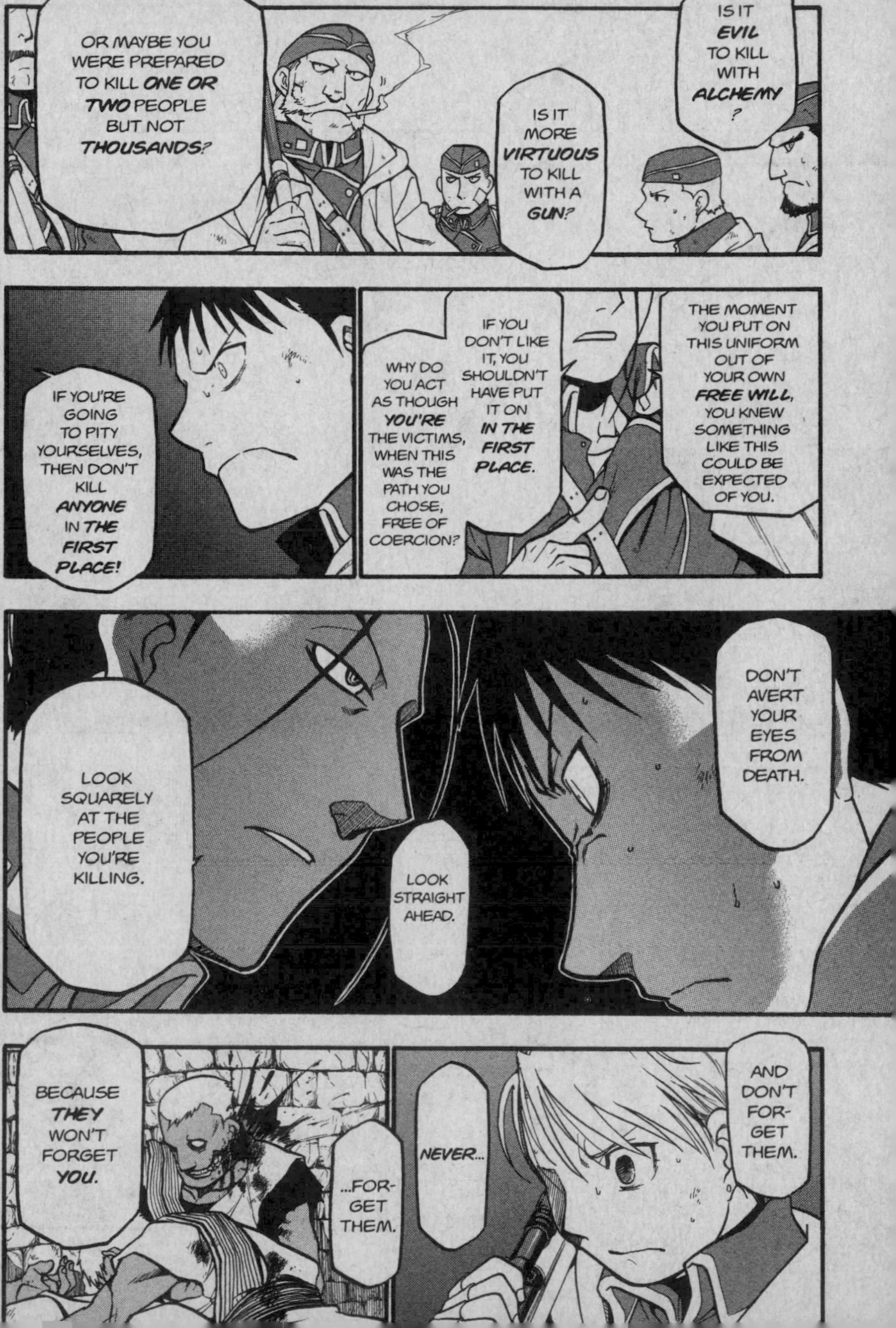
IS IT EVIL TO KILL WITH ALCHEMY?
IS IT MORE VIRTUOUS TO KILL WITH A GUN?
OR MAYBE YOU WERE PREPARED TO KILL ONE OR TWO PEOPLE BUT NOT THOUSANDS?
THE MOMENT YOU PUT ON THIS UNIFORM OUT OF YOUR OWN FREE WILL, YOU KNEW SOMETHING LIKE THIS COULD BE EXPECTED OF YOU.
IF YOU DON'T LIKE IT, YOU SHOULDN'T HAVE PUT IT ON IN THE FIRST PLACE.
WHY DO YOU ACT AS THOUGH YOU'RE THE VICTIMS, WHEN THIS WAS THE PATH YOU CHOSE, FREE OF COERCION?
IF YOU'RE GOING TO PITY YOURSELVES, THEN DON'T KILL ANYONE IN THE FIRST PLACE!
DON'T AVERT YOUR EYES FROM DEATH.
LOOK STRAIGHT AHEAD.
LOOK SQUARELY AT THE PEOPLE YOU'RE KILLING.
AND DON'T FOR-GET THEM.
NEVER...
...FOR-GET THEM.
BECAUSE THEY WON'T FORGET YOU.

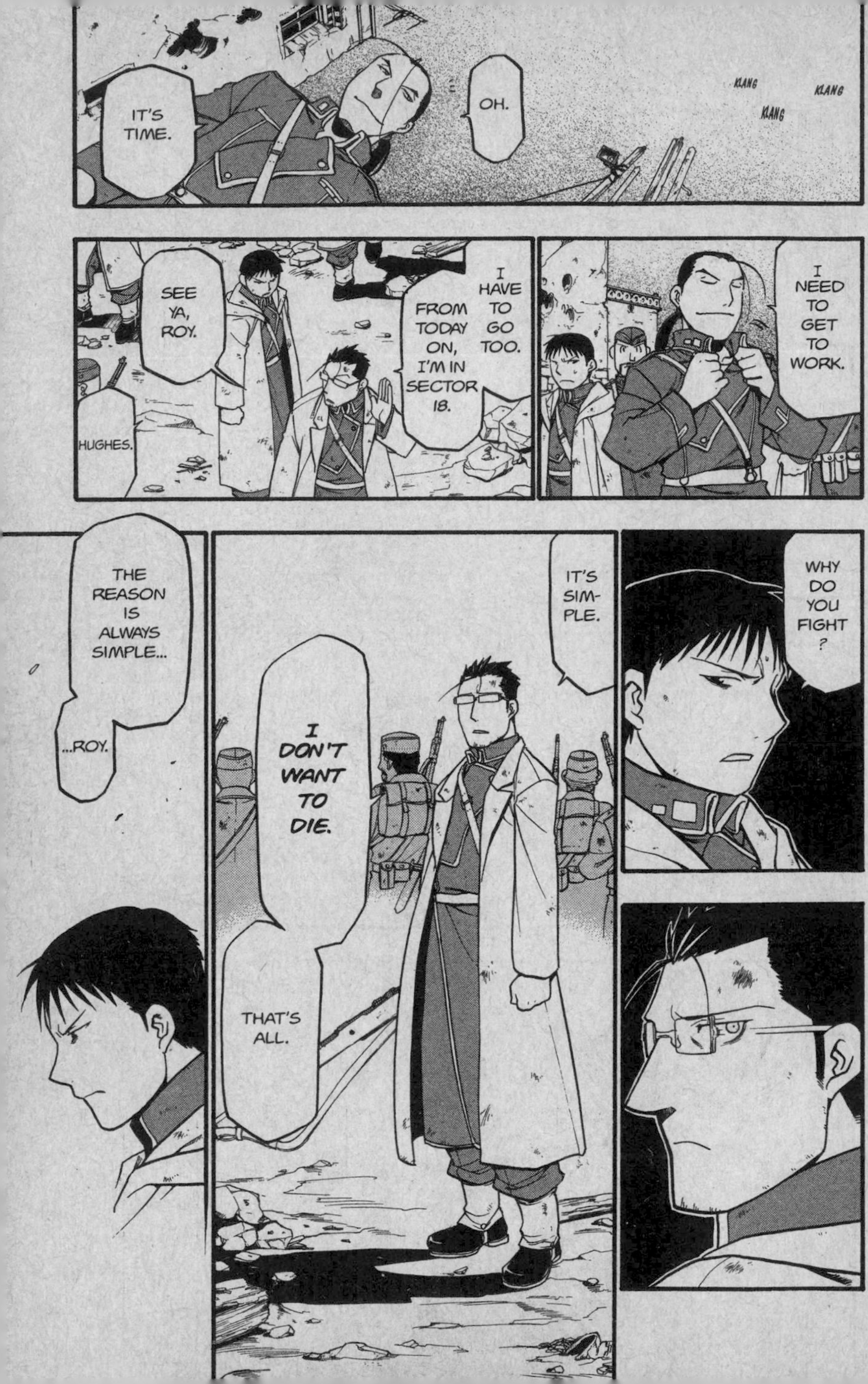
KLANG KLANG KLANG
OH.
IT'S TIME.
I NEED TO GET TO WORK.
I HAVE TO GO TOO.
FROM TODAY ON, I'M IN SECTOR 18.
SEE YA, ROY.
HUGHES.
WHY DO YOU FIGHT?
IT'S SIM-PLE.
I DON'T WANT TO DIE.
THAT'S ALL.
THE REASON IS ALWAYS SIMPLE...
...ROY.

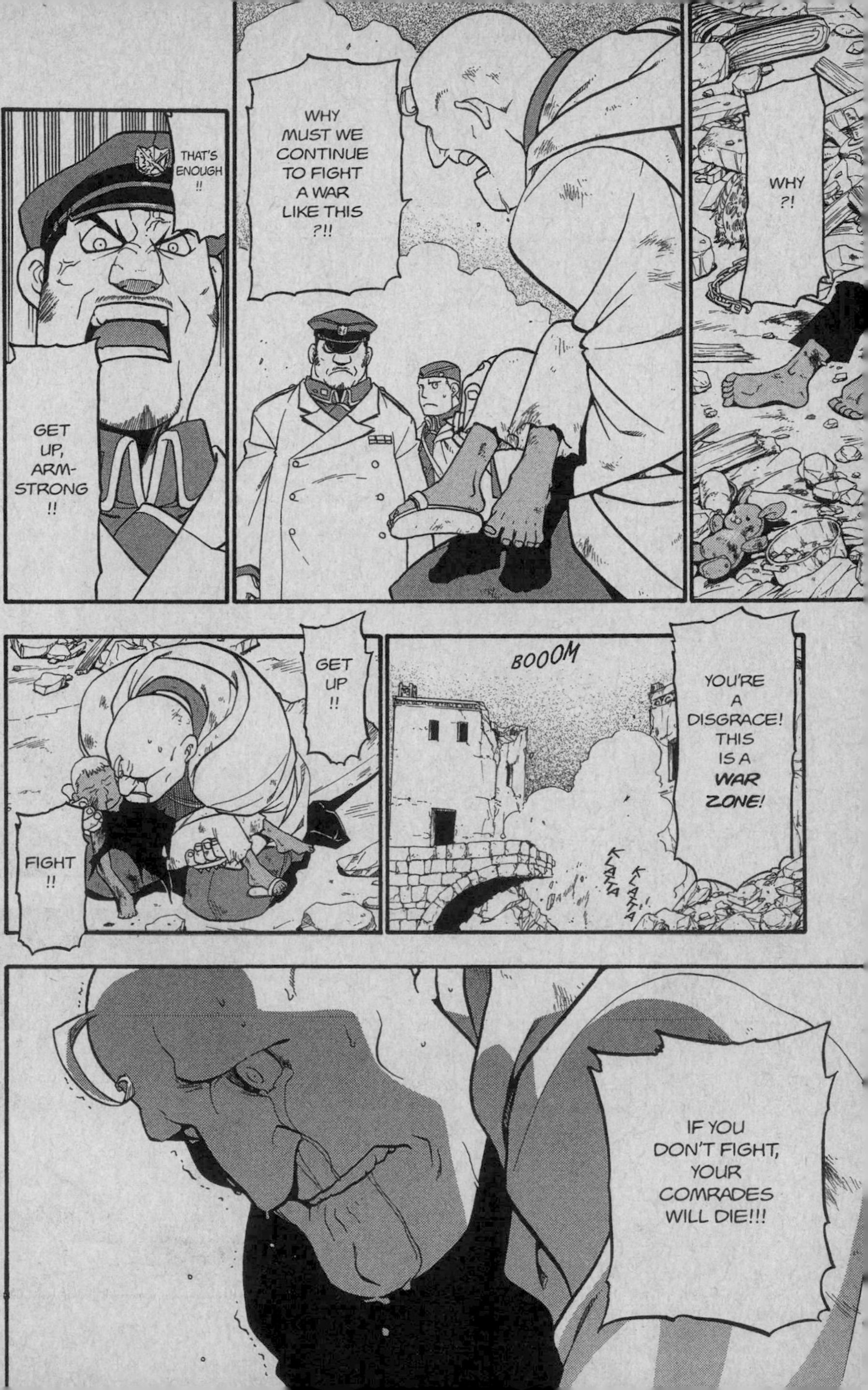
WHY ?!
WHY MUST WE CONTINUE TO FIGHT A WAR LIKE THIS ?!!
THAT'S ENOUGH !!
GET UP, ARM-STRONG !!
YOU'RE A DISGRACE! THIS IS A WAR ZONE!
BOOOM
KLATTA KLATTA
KLATTA
GET UP !!
FIGHT !!
IF YOU DON'T FIGHT, YOUR COMRADES WILL DIE!!!

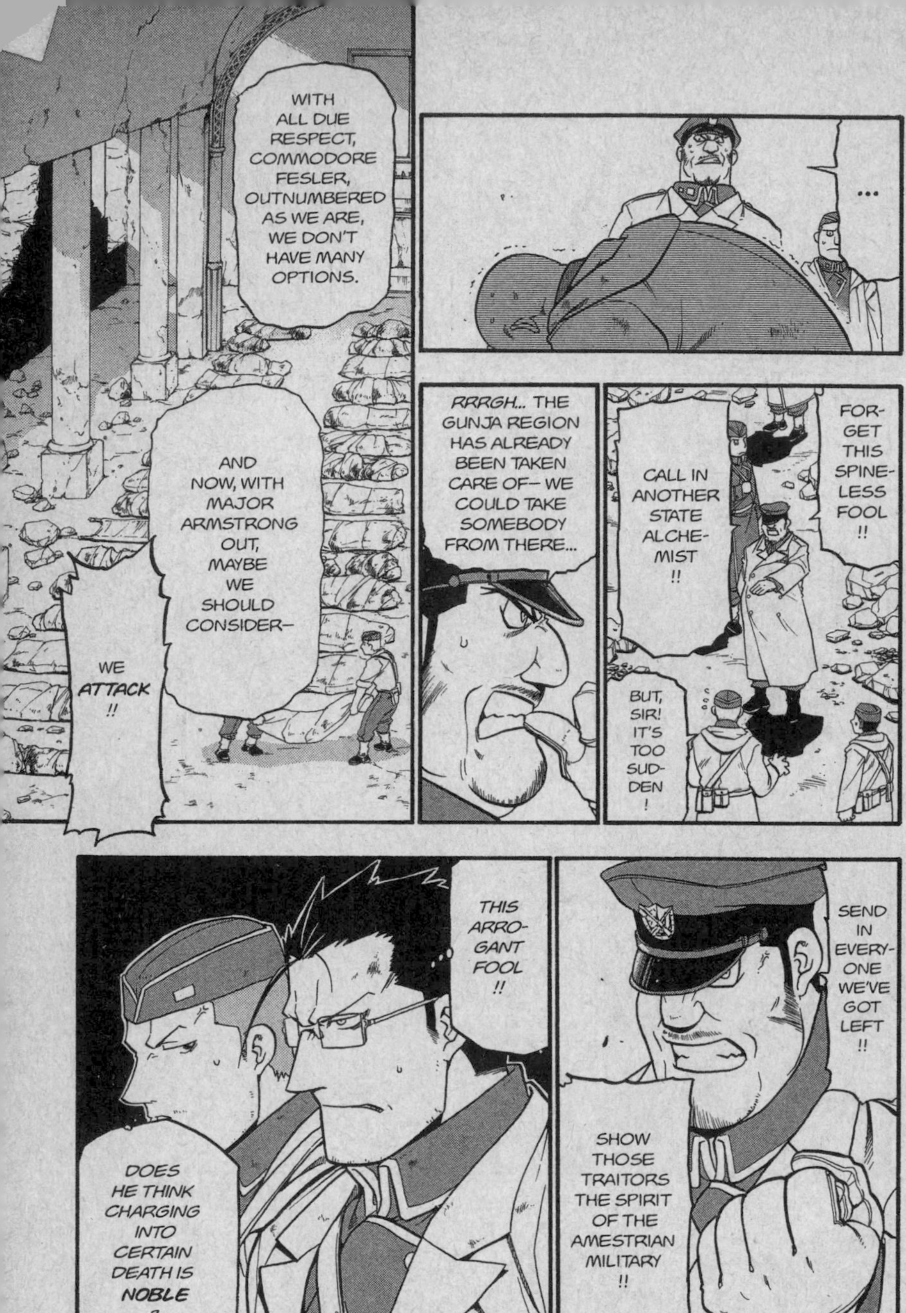
...
FORGET THIS SPINELESS FOOL!!
CALL IN ANOTHER STATE ALCHEMIST!!
BUT, SIR! IT'S TOO SUDDEN!
RRRGH... THE GUNJA REGION HAS ALREADY BEEN TAKEN CARE OF— WE COULD TAKE SOMEBODY FROM THERE...
WITH ALL DUE RESPECT, COMMODORE FESLER, OUTNUMBERED AS WE ARE, WE DON'T HAVE MANY OPTIONS.
AND NOW, WITH MAJOR ARMSTRONG OUT, MAYBE WE SHOULD CONSIDER—
WE ATTACK!!
SEND IN EVERYONE WE'VE GOT LEFT!!
SHOW THOSE TRAITORS THE SPIRIT OF THE AMESTRIAN MILITARY!!
THIS ARROGANT FOOL!!
DOES HE THINK CHARGING INTO CERTAIN DEATH IS NOBLE?

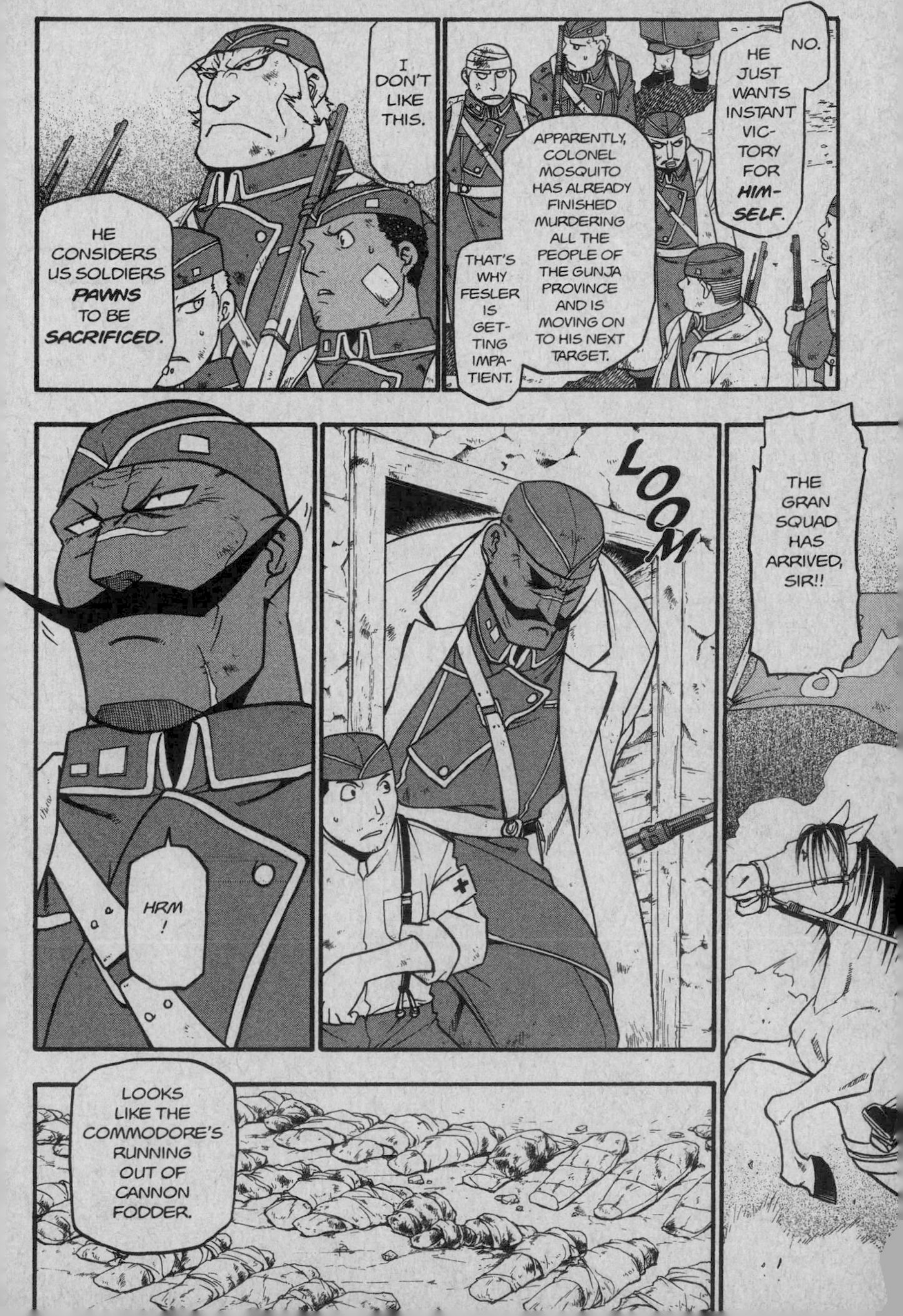
NO.
HE JUST WANTS INSTANT VICTORY FOR HIMSELF.
APPARENTLY, COLONEL MOSQUITO HAS ALREADY FINISHED MURDERING ALL THE PEOPLE OF THE GUNJA PROVINCE AND IS MOVING ON TO HIS NEXT TARGET.
THAT'S WHY FESLER IS GETTING IMPATIENT.
I DON'T LIKE THIS.
HE CONSIDERS US SOLDIERS PAWNS TO BE SACRIFICED.
THE GRAN SQUAD HAS ARRIVED, SIR!!
LOOM
HRM!
LOOKS LIKE THE COMMODORE'S RUNNING OUT OF CANNON FODDER.

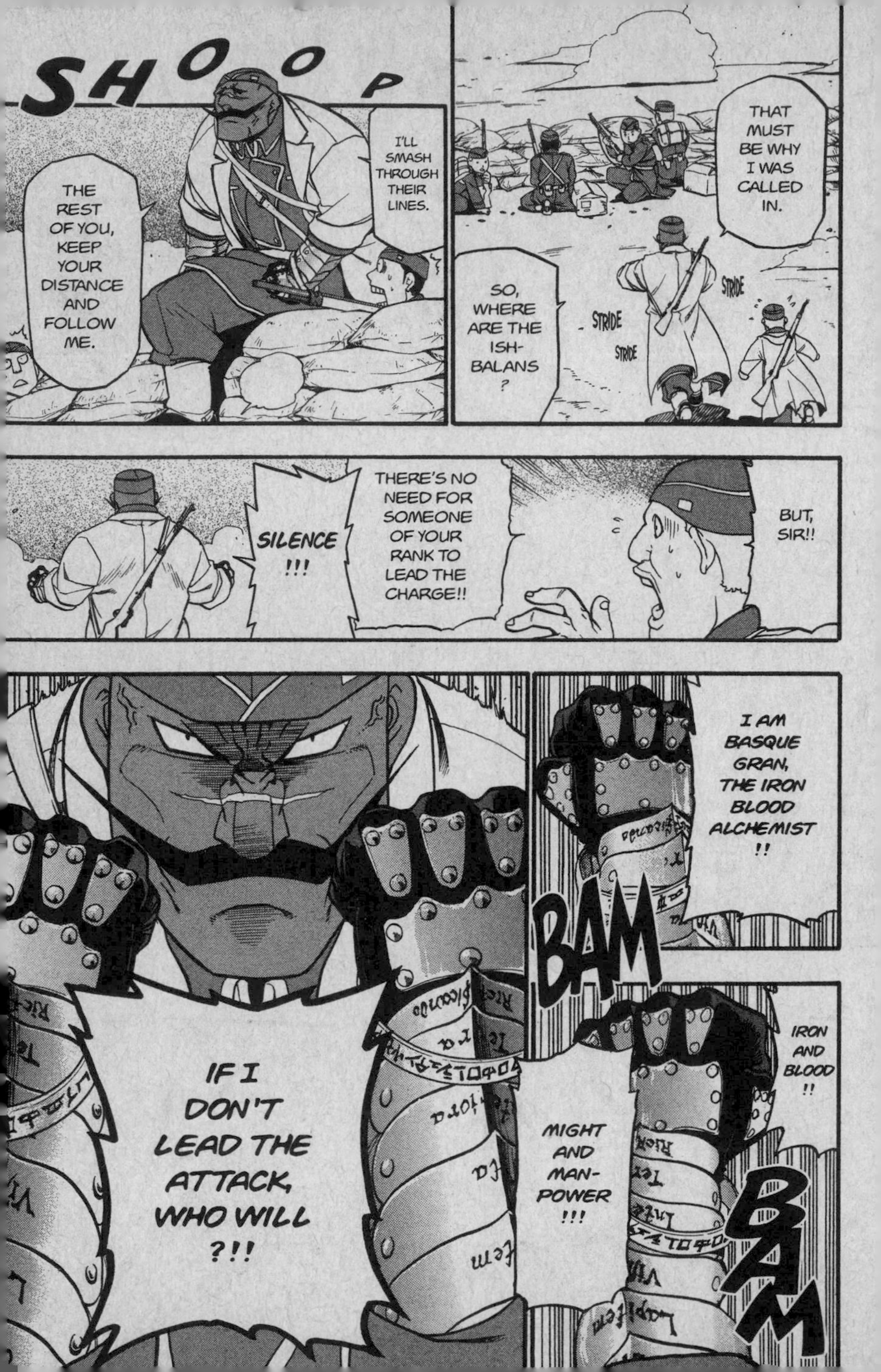
THAT MUST BE WHY I WAS CALLED IN.
SO, WHERE ARE THE ISH-BALANS?
STRIDE
STRIDE
STRIDE
SHOOP
I'LL SMASH THROUGH THEIR LINES.
THE REST OF YOU, KEEP YOUR DISTANCE AND FOLLOW ME.
BUT, SIR!!
THERE'S NO NEED FOR SOMEONE OF YOUR RANK TO LEAD THE CHARGE!!
SILENCE!!!
I AM BASQUE GRAN, THE IRON BLOOD ALCHEMIST!!
BAM
IRON AND BLOOD!!
MIGHT AND MAN-POWER!!!
BAM
IF I DON'T LEAD THE ATTACK, WHO WILL?!!

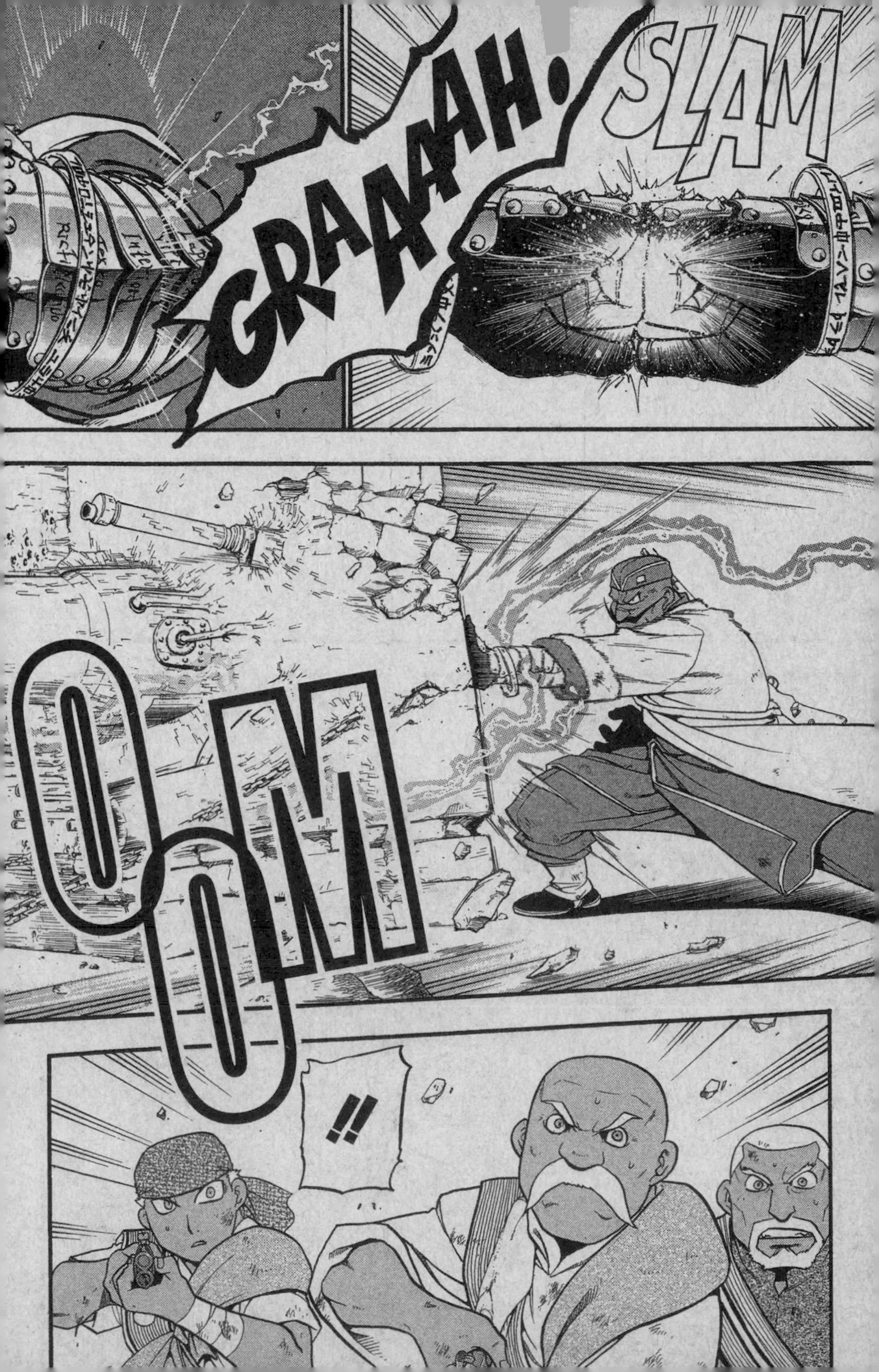
SLAM
GRAAAAH
OOM
!!

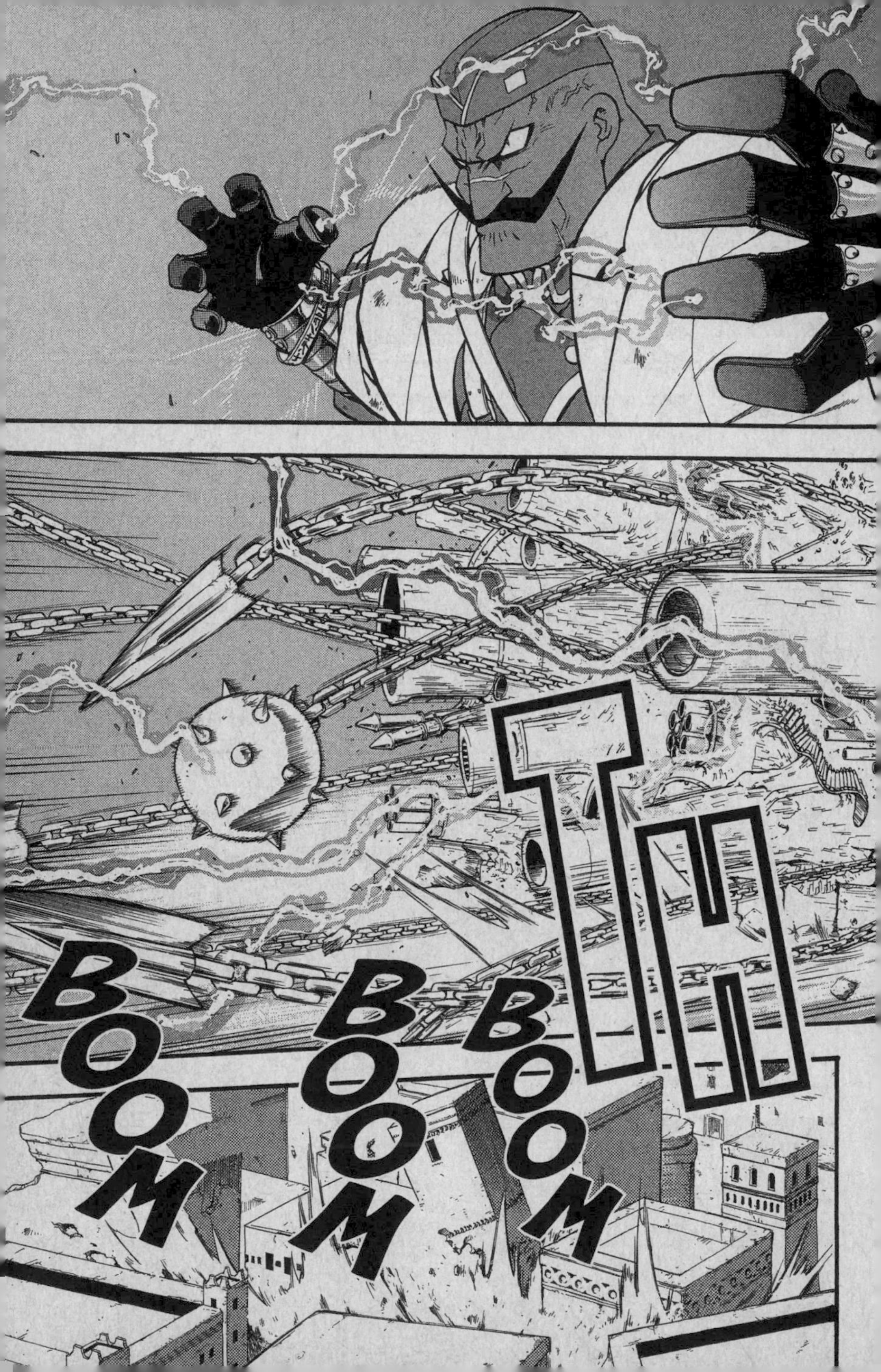
BOOM
BOOM
BOOM

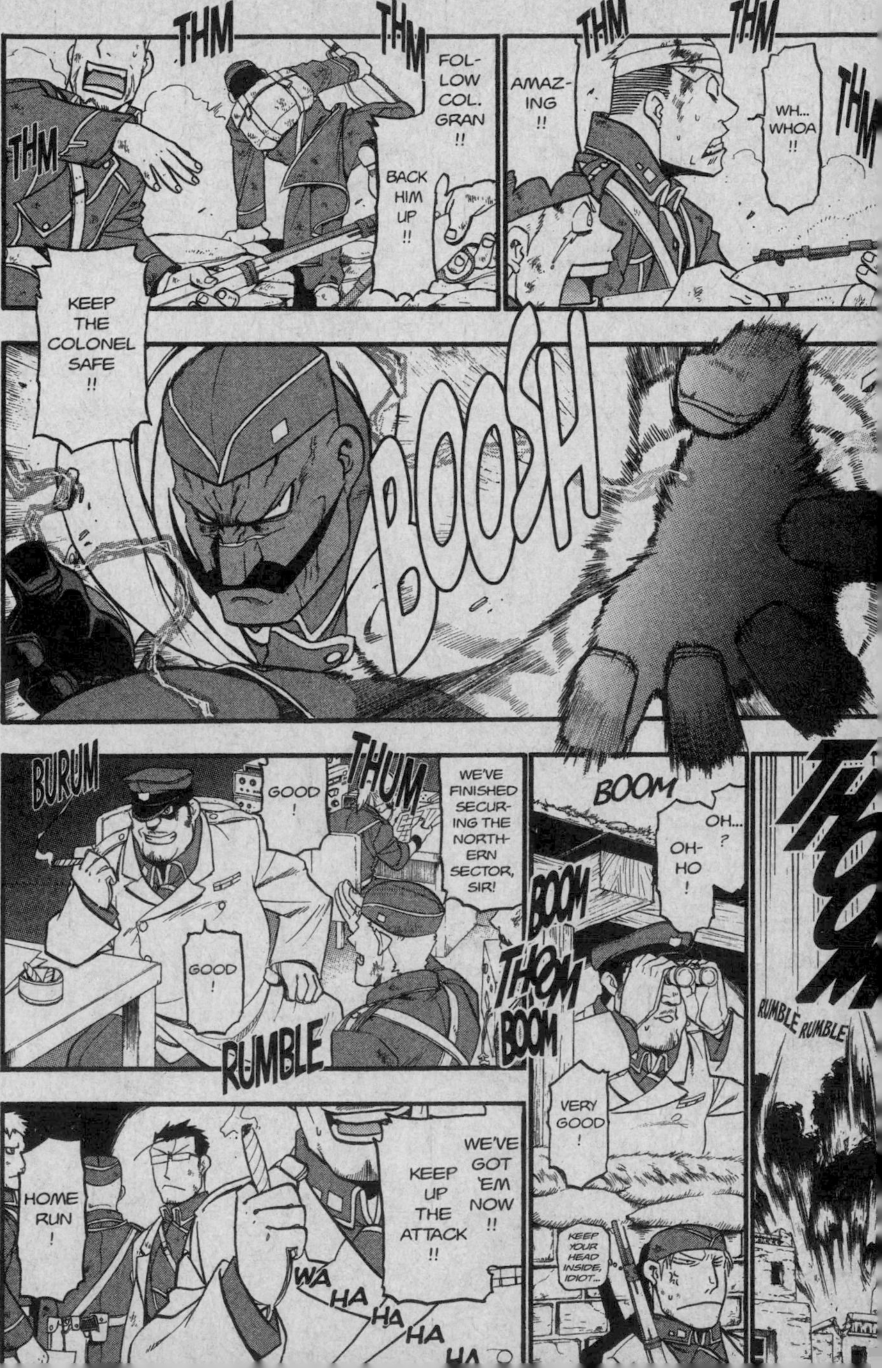

THM
THM
WH... WHOA !!
THM
AMAZ-ING !!
THM
THM
FOL-LOW COL. GRAN !!
BACK HIM UP !!
THM
KEEP THE COLONEL SAFE !!
BOOSH
THOOM
RUMBLE RUMBLE
BOOM
OH... ?
OH-HO !
BOOM
THOM
BOOM
VERY GOOD !
KEEP YOUR HEAD INSIDE, IDIOT...
BURUM
THUM
WE'VE FINISHED SECUR-ING THE NORTH-ERN SECTOR, SIR!
GOOD !
GOOD !
RUMBLE
WE'VE GOT 'EM NOW !!
KEEP UP THE ATTACK !!
HOME RUN !
WA HA HA HA HA

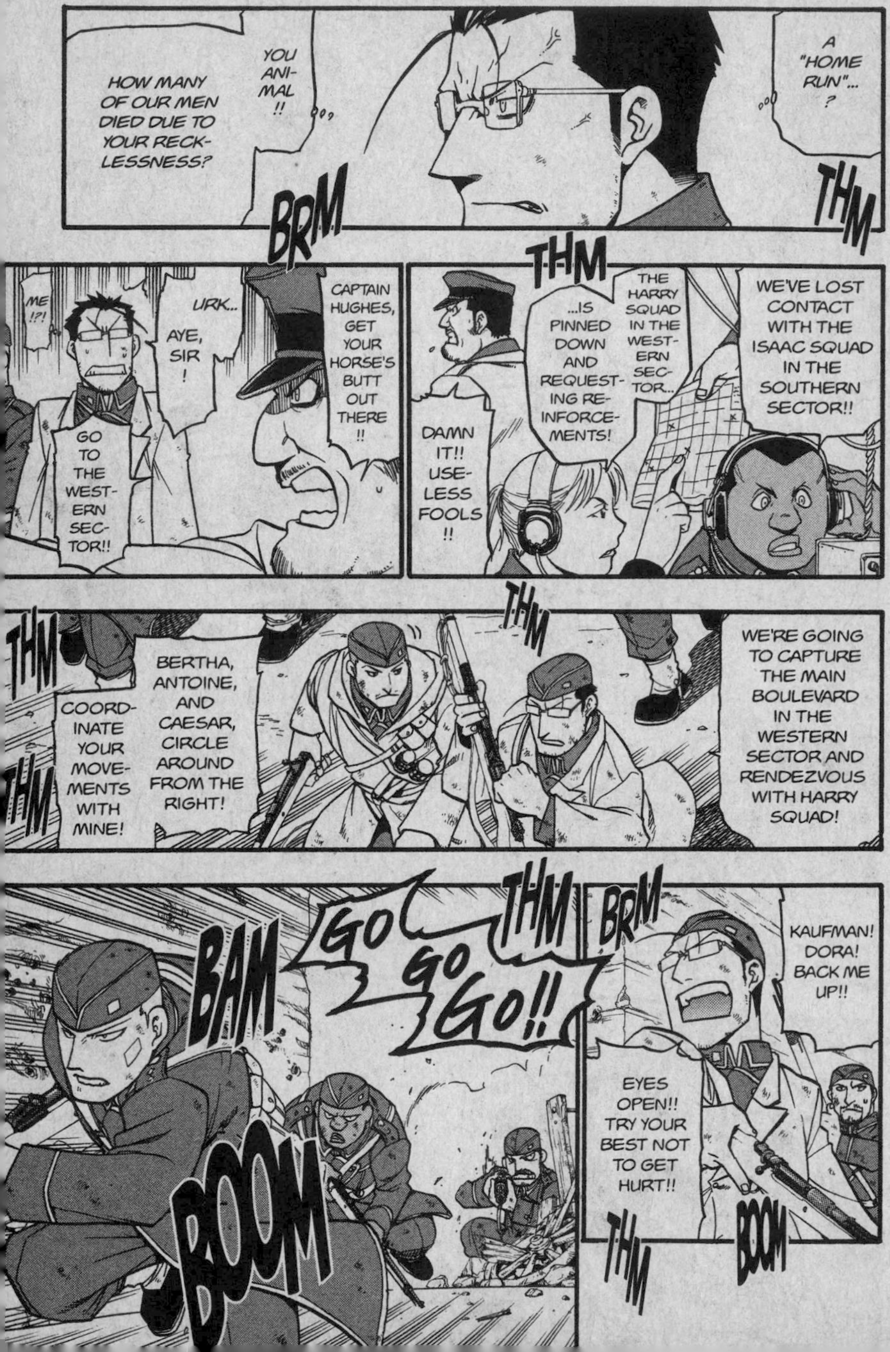
A "HOME RUN"... ?
THM
YOU ANIMAL!!
HOW MANY OF OUR MEN DIED DUE TO YOUR RECKLESSNESS?
BRM
WE'VE LOST CONTACT WITH THE ISAAC SQUAD IN THE SOUTHERN SECTOR!!
THE HARRY SQUAD IN THE WESTERN SECTOR...
...IS PINNED DOWN AND REQUESTING REINFORCEMENTS!
THM
DAMN IT!! USELESS FOOLS!!
CAPTAIN HUGHES, GET YOUR HORSE'S BUTT OUT THERE!!
URK...
AYE, SIR!
ME!?!
GO TO THE WESTERN SECTOR!!
WE'RE GOING TO CAPTURE THE MAIN BOULEVARD IN THE WESTERN SECTOR AND RENDEZVOUS WITH HARRY SQUAD!
THM
BERTHA, ANTOINE, AND CAESAR, CIRCLE AROUND FROM THE RIGHT!
COORDINATE YOUR MOVEMENTS WITH MINE!
THM
THM
BRM
KAUFMAN! DORA! BACK ME UP!!
EYES OPEN!! TRY YOUR BEST NOT TO GET HURT!!
BOOM
THM
THM
GO GO GO!!
BAM
BOOM

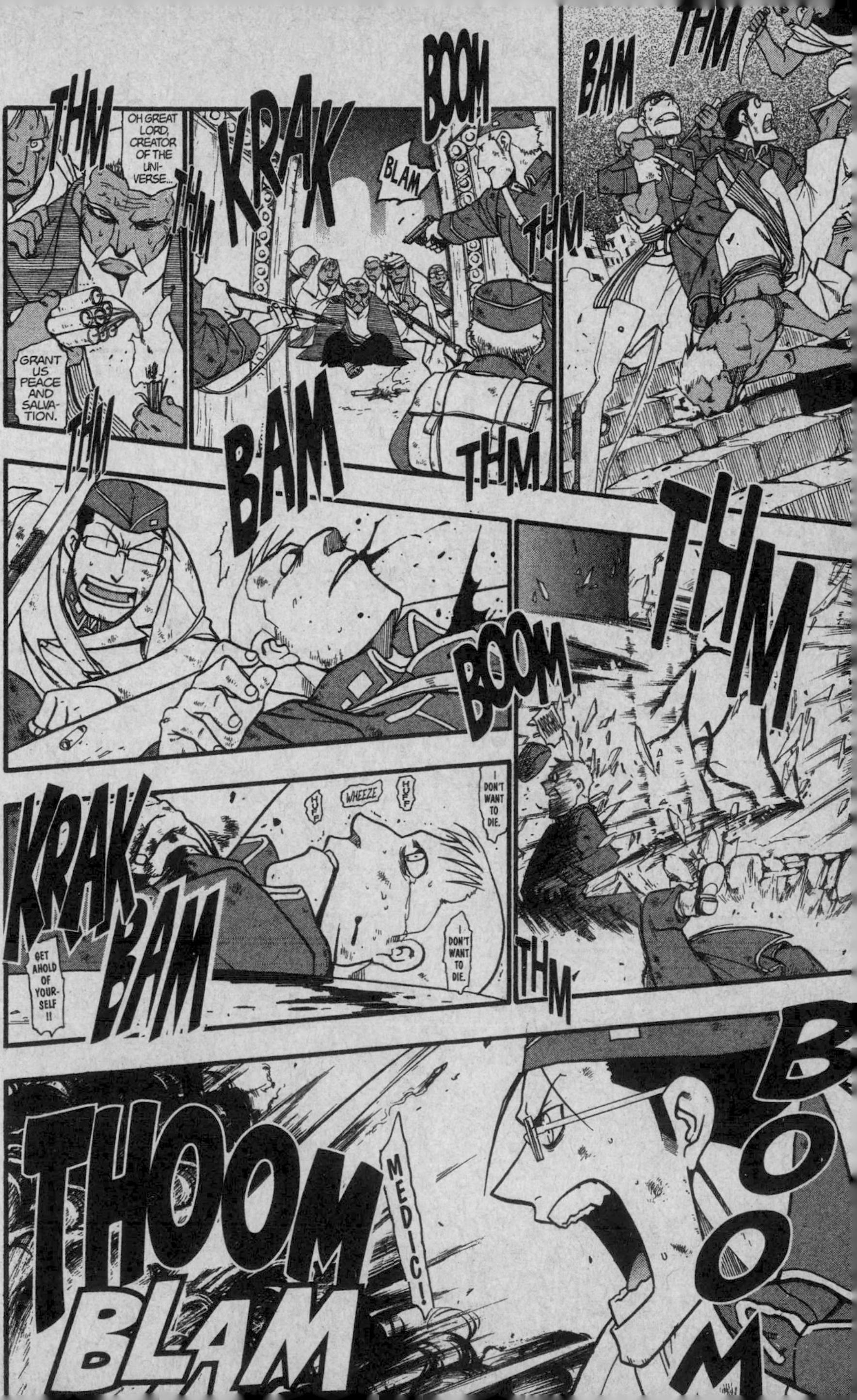

BAM
THM
THM
BOOM
BLAM
KRAK
THM
THM
OH GREAT LORD, CREATOR OF THE UNIVERSE...
THM
GRANT US PEACE AND SALVATION.
THM
BOOM
THM
BAM
THM
I DON'T WANT TO DIE.
HUFF
WHEEZE
HUFF
I DON'T WANT TO DIE.
KRAK
BAM
GET AHOLD OF YOURSELF!!
BOOM
MEDIC!
THOOM
BLAM

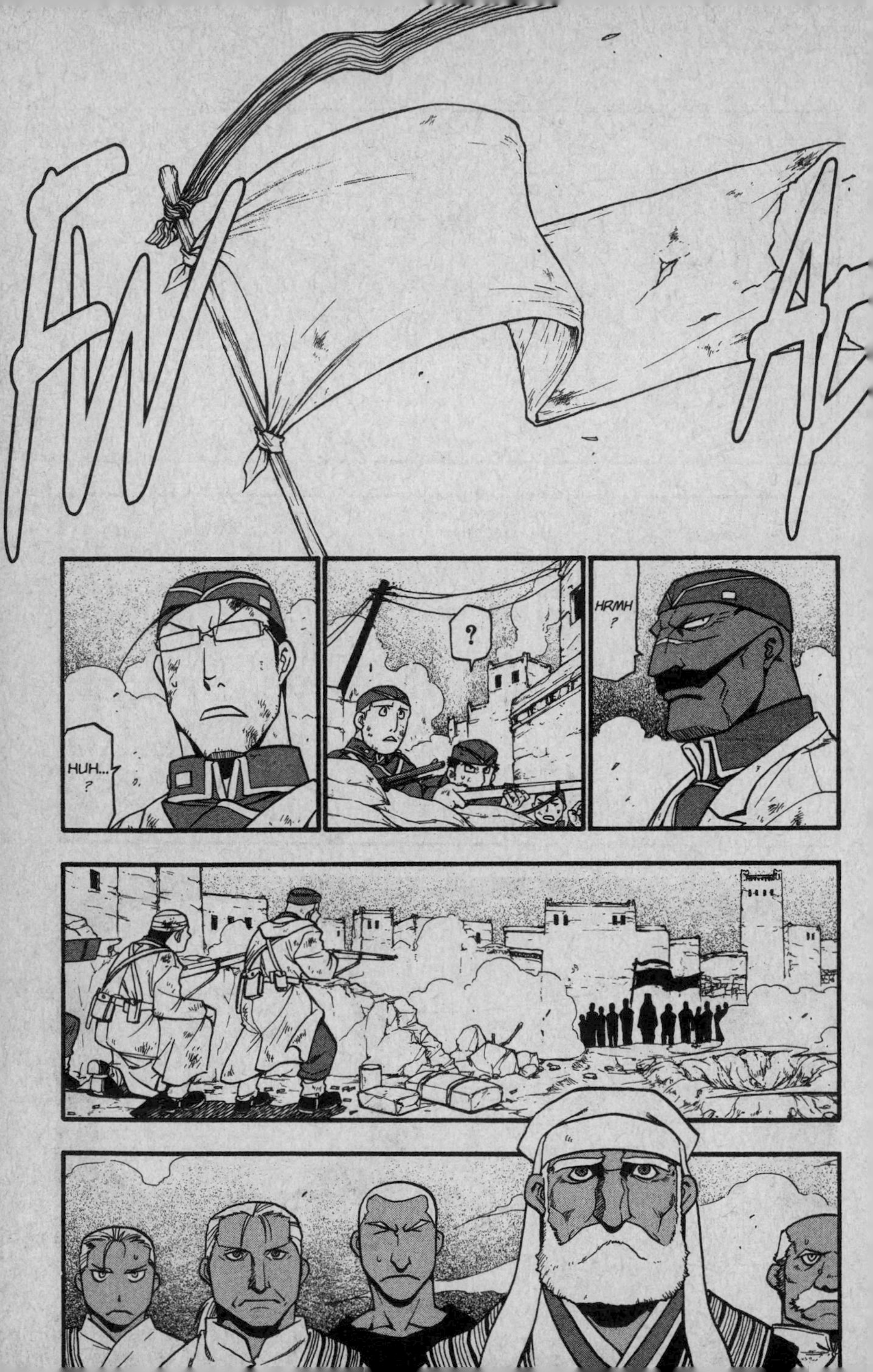
FW A
HRMH ?
?
HUH... ?

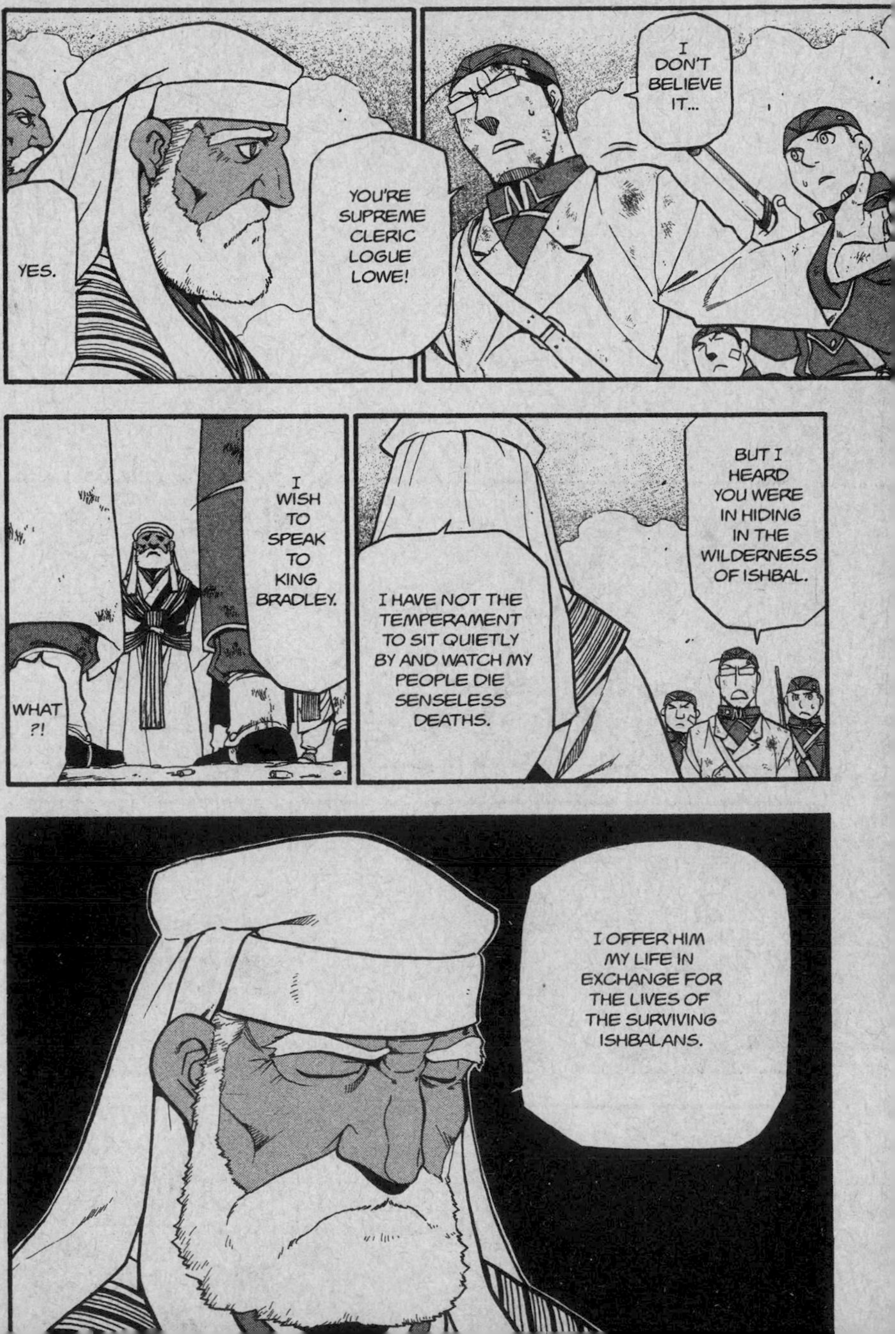
I DON'T BELIEVE IT...
YOU'RE SUPREME CLERIC LOGUE LOWE!
YES.
BUT I HEARD YOU WERE IN HIDING IN THE WILDERNESS OF ISHBAL.
I HAVE NOT THE TEMPERAMENT TO SIT QUIETLY BY AND WATCH MY PEOPLE DIE SENSELESS DEATHS.
I WISH TO SPEAK TO KING BRADLEY.
WHAT ?!
I OFFER HIM MY LIFE IN EXCHANGE FOR THE LIVES OF THE SURVIVING ISHBALANS.

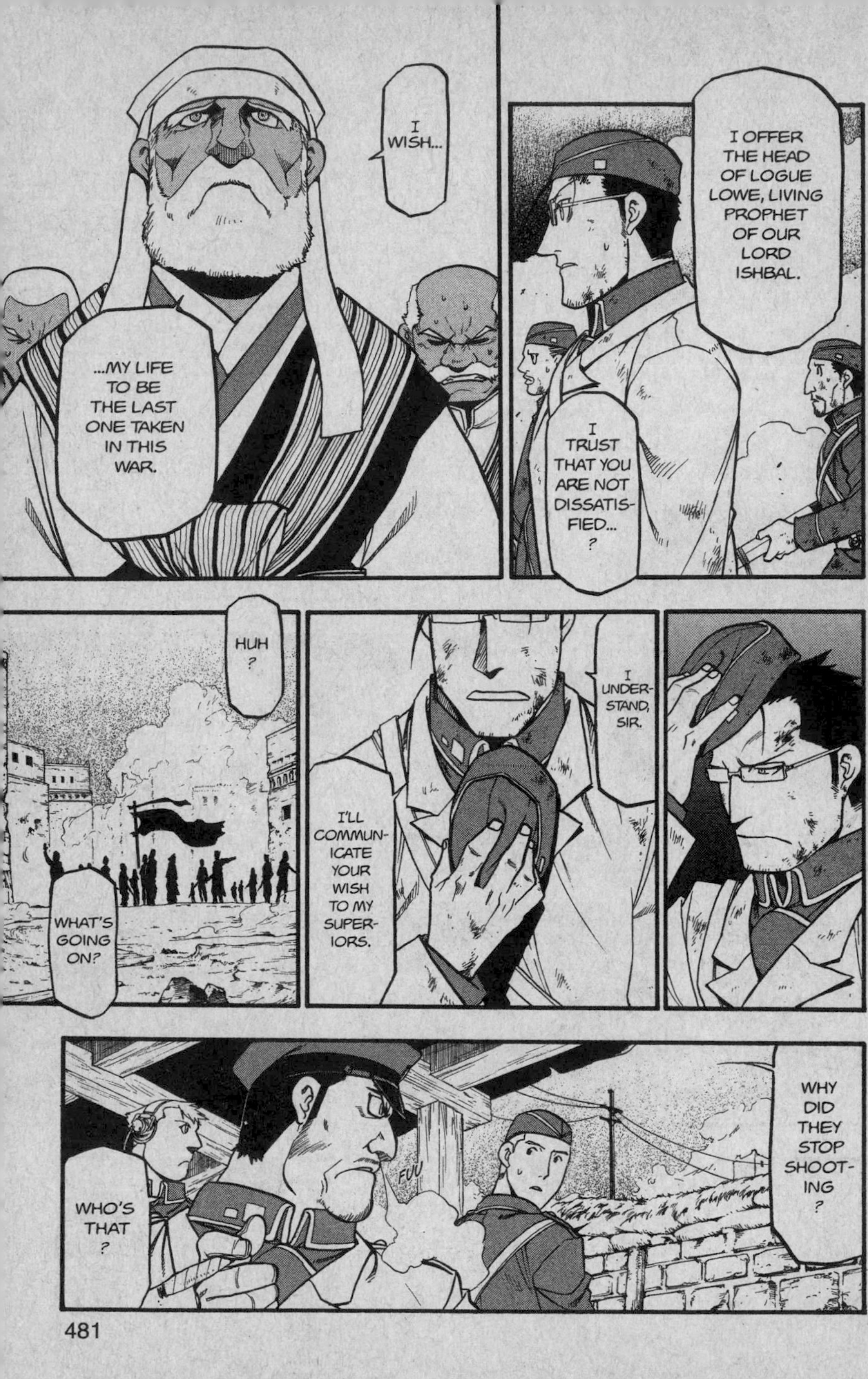
I OFFER THE HEAD OF LOGUE LOWE, LIVING PROPHET OF OUR LORD ISHBAL.
I TRUST THAT YOU ARE NOT DISSATISFIED...?
I WISH...
...MY LIFE TO BE THE LAST ONE TAKEN IN THIS WAR.
I UNDERSTAND, SIR.
I'LL COMMUNICATE YOUR WISH TO MY SUPERIORS.
HUH?
WHAT'S GOING ON?
WHY DID THEY STOP SHOOTING?
FUU
WHO'S THAT?

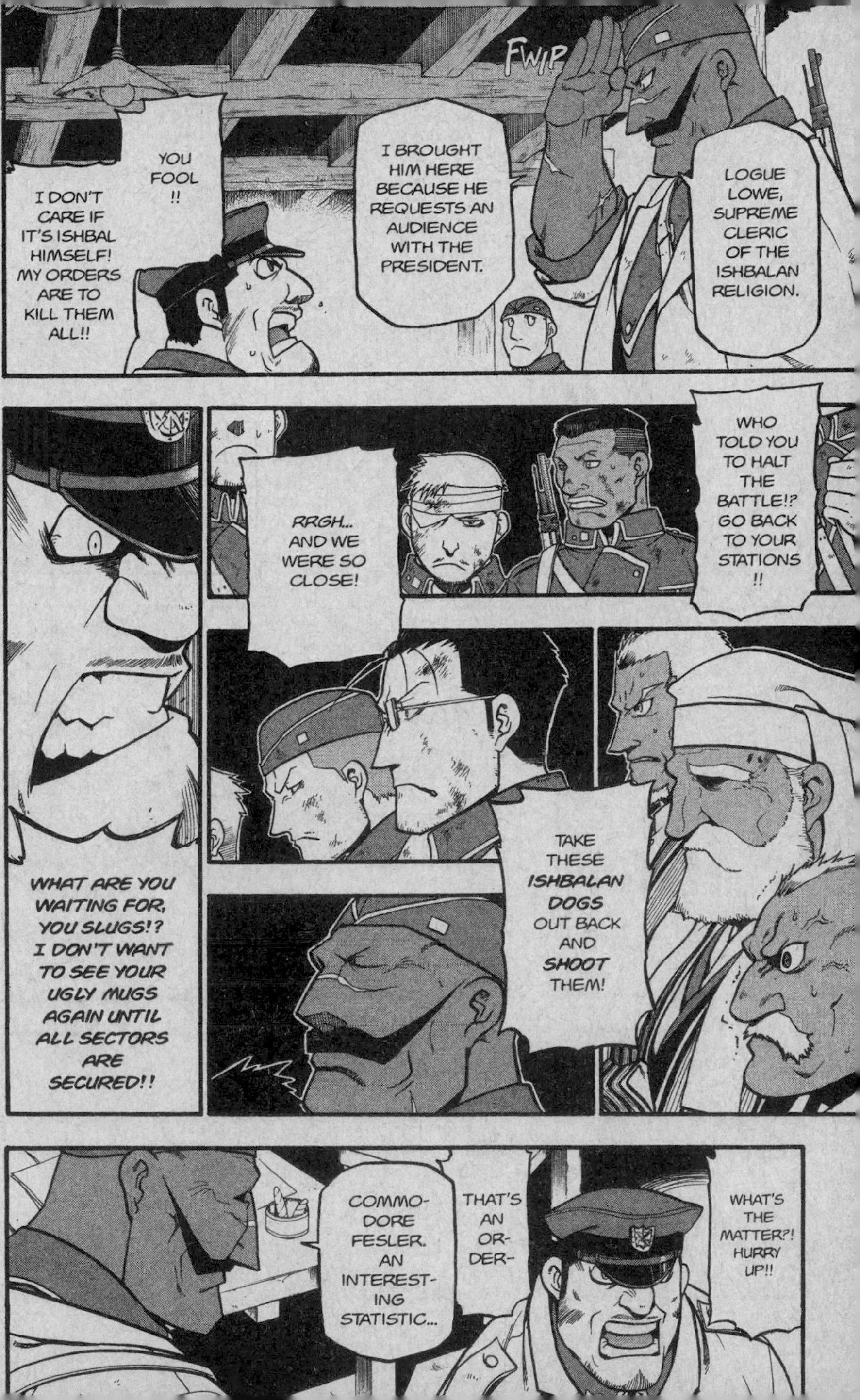
FWIP
LOGUE LOWE, SUPREME CLERIC OF THE ISHBALAN RELIGION.
I BROUGHT HIM HERE BECAUSE HE REQUESTS AN AUDIENCE WITH THE PRESIDENT.
YOU FOOL!!
I DON'T CARE IF IT'S ISHBAL HIMSELF! MY ORDERS ARE TO KILL THEM ALL!!
WHO TOLD YOU TO HALT THE BATTLE!? GO BACK TO YOUR STATIONS!!
RRGH... AND WE WERE SO CLOSE!
TAKE THESE ISHBALAN DOGS OUT BACK AND SHOOT THEM!
WHAT ARE YOU WAITING FOR, YOU SLUGS!? I DON'T WANT TO SEE YOUR UGLY MUGS AGAIN UNTIL ALL SECTORS ARE SECURED!!
WHAT'S THE MATTER?! HURRY UP!!
THAT'S AN ORDER-
COMMODORE FESLER. AN INTERESTING STATISTIC...

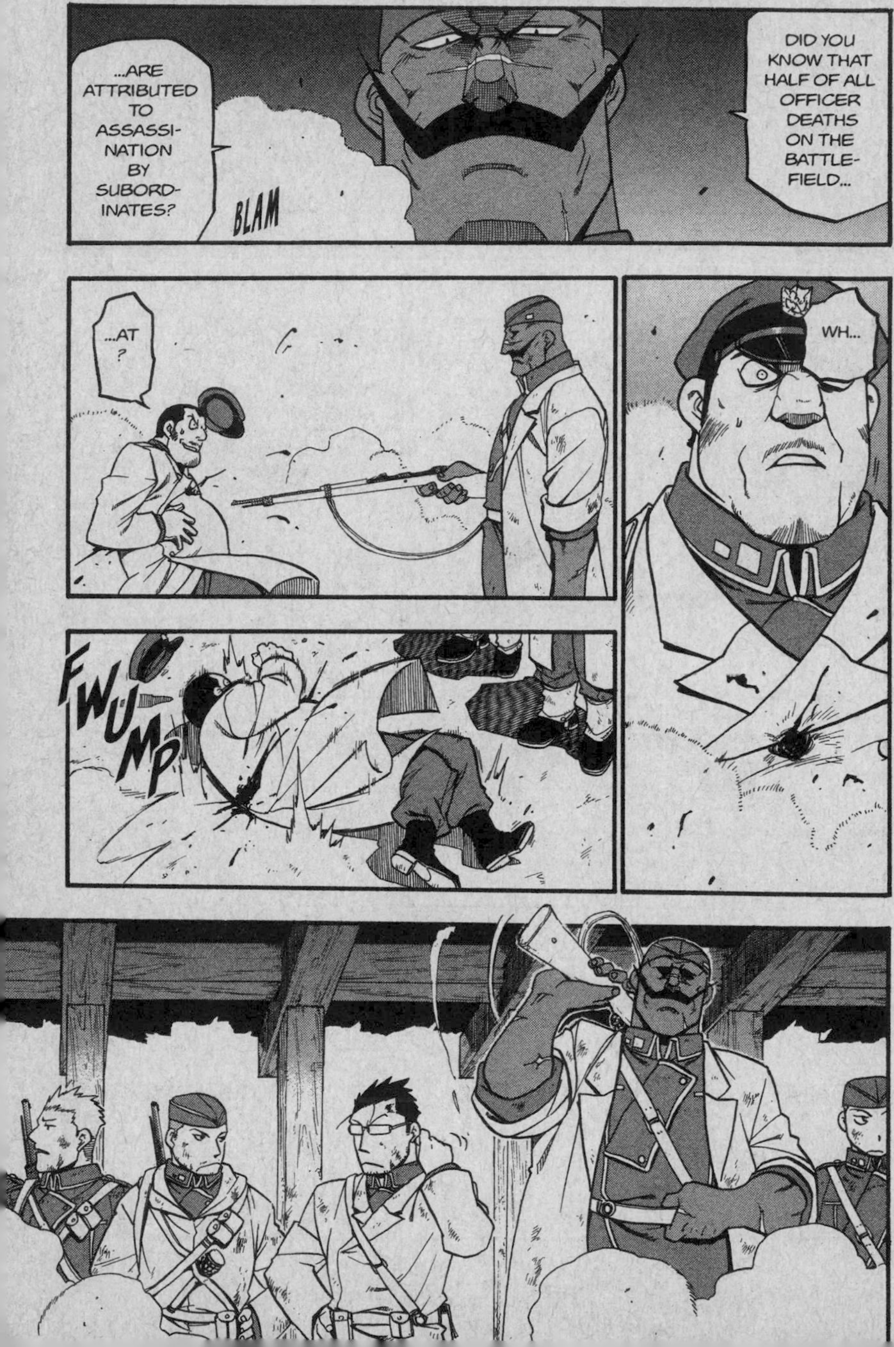
DID YOU KNOW THAT HALF OF ALL OFFICER DEATHS ON THE BATTLE-FIELD...
...ARE ATTRIBUTED TO ASSASSI-NATION BY SUBORD-INATES?
BLAM
WH...
...AT ?
FWUMP

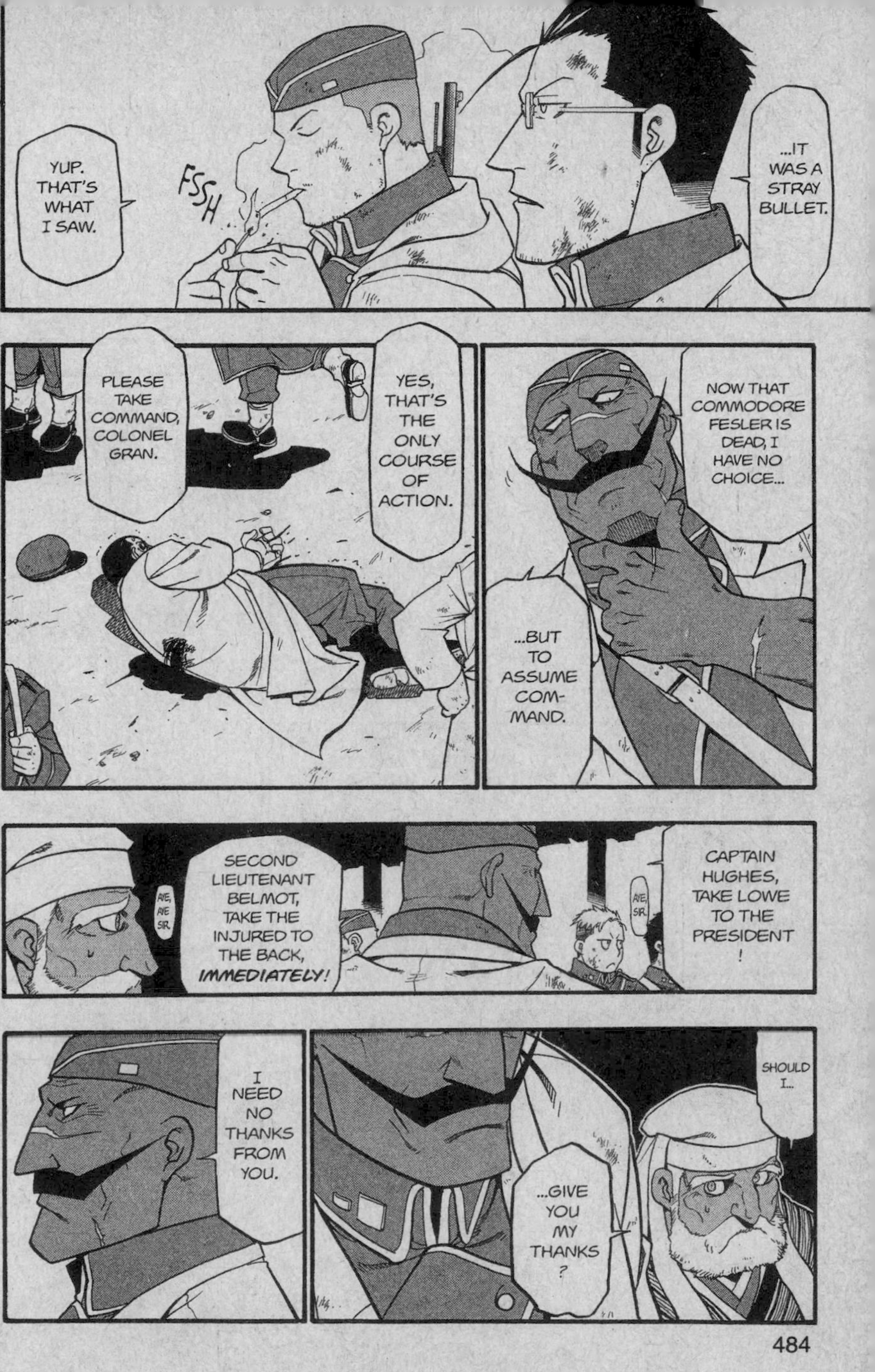
...IT WAS A STRAY BULLET.
FSSH
YUP. THAT'S WHAT I SAW.
NOW THAT COMMODORE FESLER IS DEAD, I HAVE NO CHOICE...
...BUT TO ASSUME COM-MAND.
YES, THAT'S THE ONLY COURSE OF ACTION.
PLEASE TAKE COMMAND, COLONEL GRAN.
CAPTAIN HUGHES, TAKE LOWE TO THE PRESIDENT!
AYE, SIR.
SECOND LIEUTENANT BELMOT, TAKE THE INJURED TO THE BACK, *IMMEDIATELY!*
AYE, AYE SIR.
SHOULD I...
...GIVE YOU MY THANKS?
I NEED NO THANKS FROM YOU.

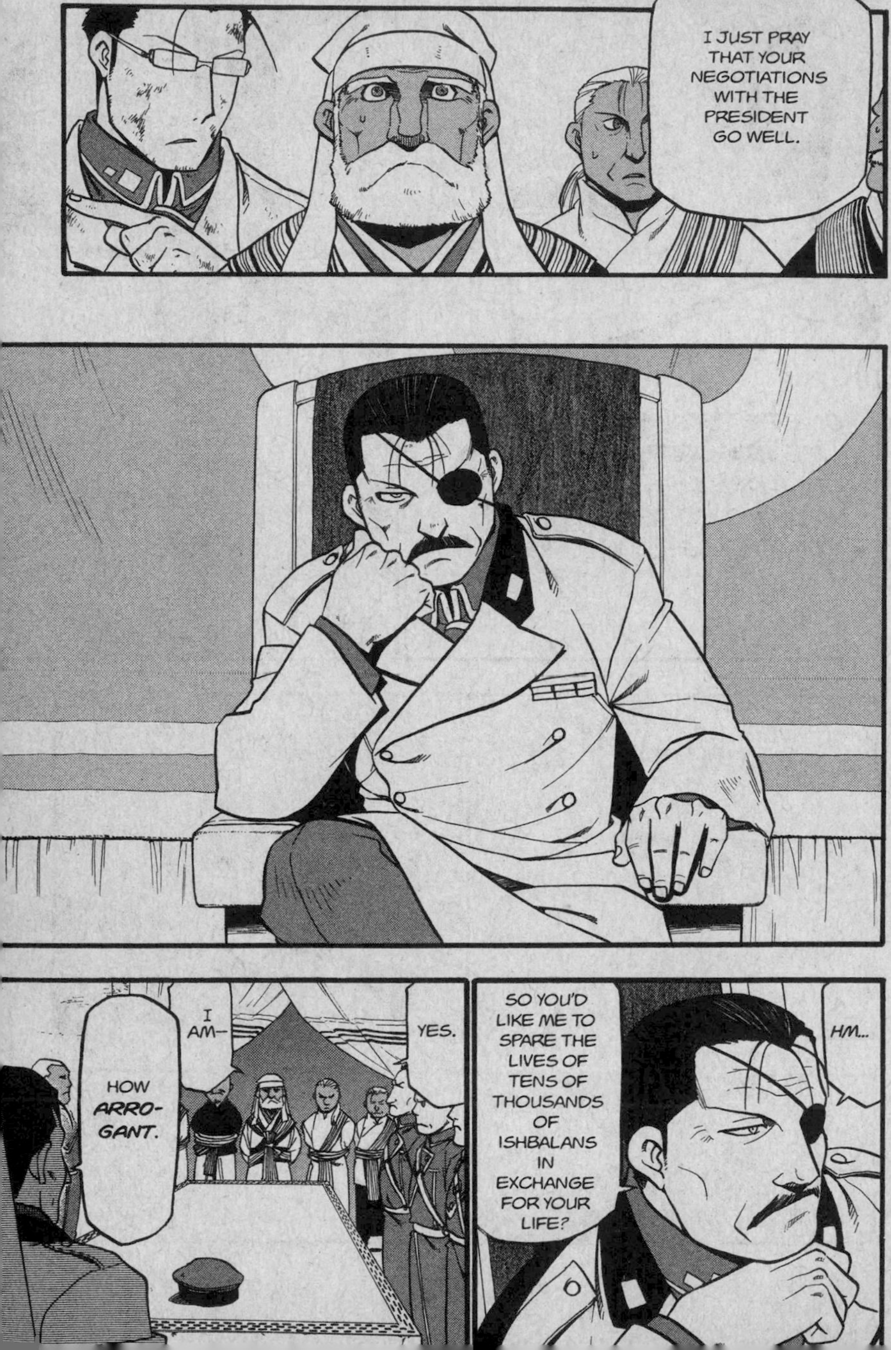
I JUST PRAY THAT YOUR NEGOTIATIONS WITH THE PRESIDENT GO WELL.
HM...
SO YOU'D LIKE ME TO SPARE THE LIVES OF TENS OF THOUSANDS OF ISHBALANS IN EXCHANGE FOR YOUR LIFE?
YES.
I AM—
HOW ARROGANT.

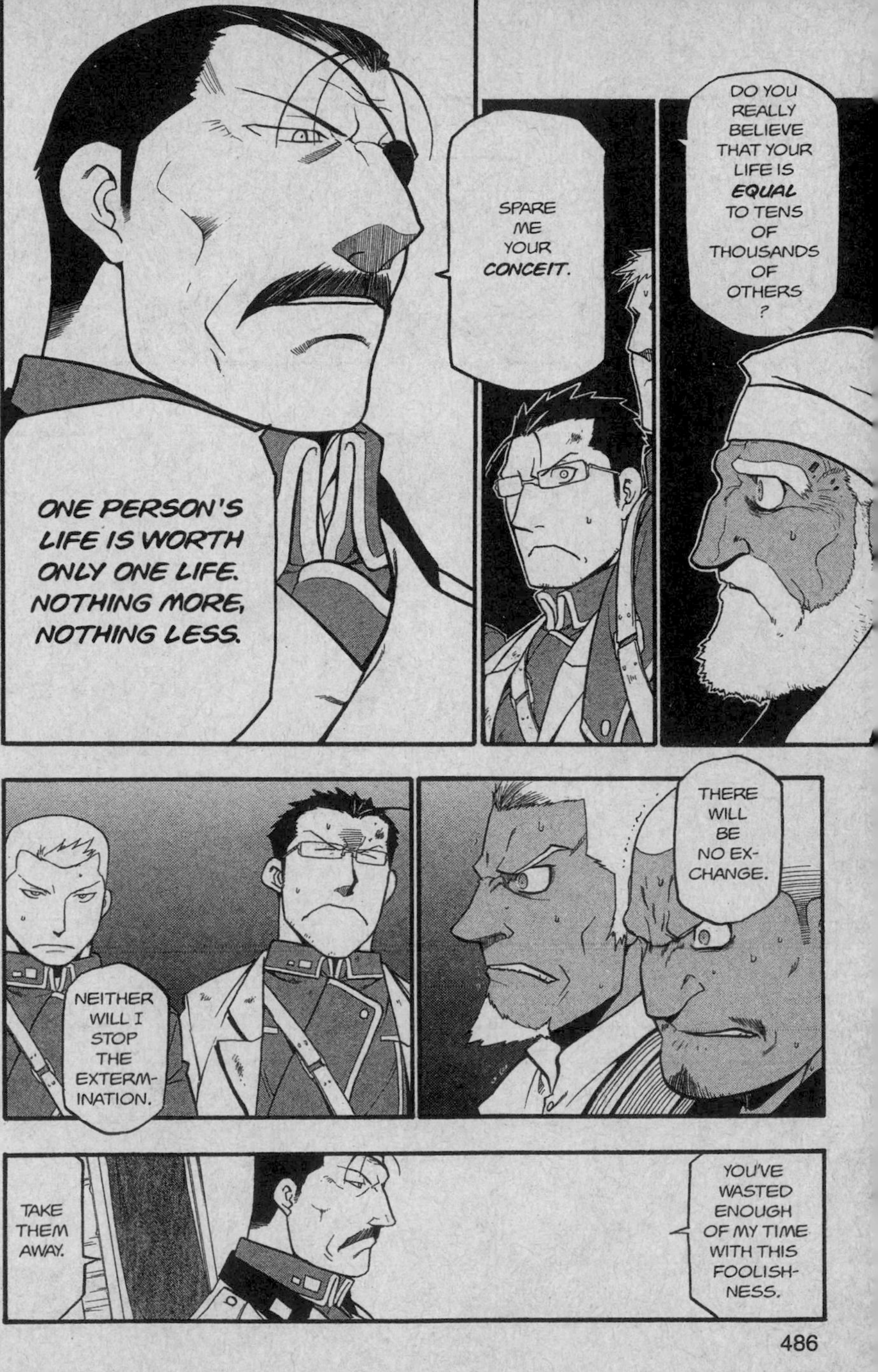
DO YOU REALLY BELIEVE THAT YOUR LIFE IS **EQUAL** TO TENS OF THOUSANDS OF OTHERS?
SPARE ME YOUR **CONCEIT**.
ONE PERSON'S LIFE IS WORTH ONLY ONE LIFE. NOTHING MORE, NOTHING LESS.
THERE WILL BE NO EX-CHANGE.
NEITHER WILL I STOP THE EXTERM-INATION.
YOU'VE WASTED ENOUGH OF MY TIME WITH THIS FOOLISH-NESS.
TAKE THEM AWAY.

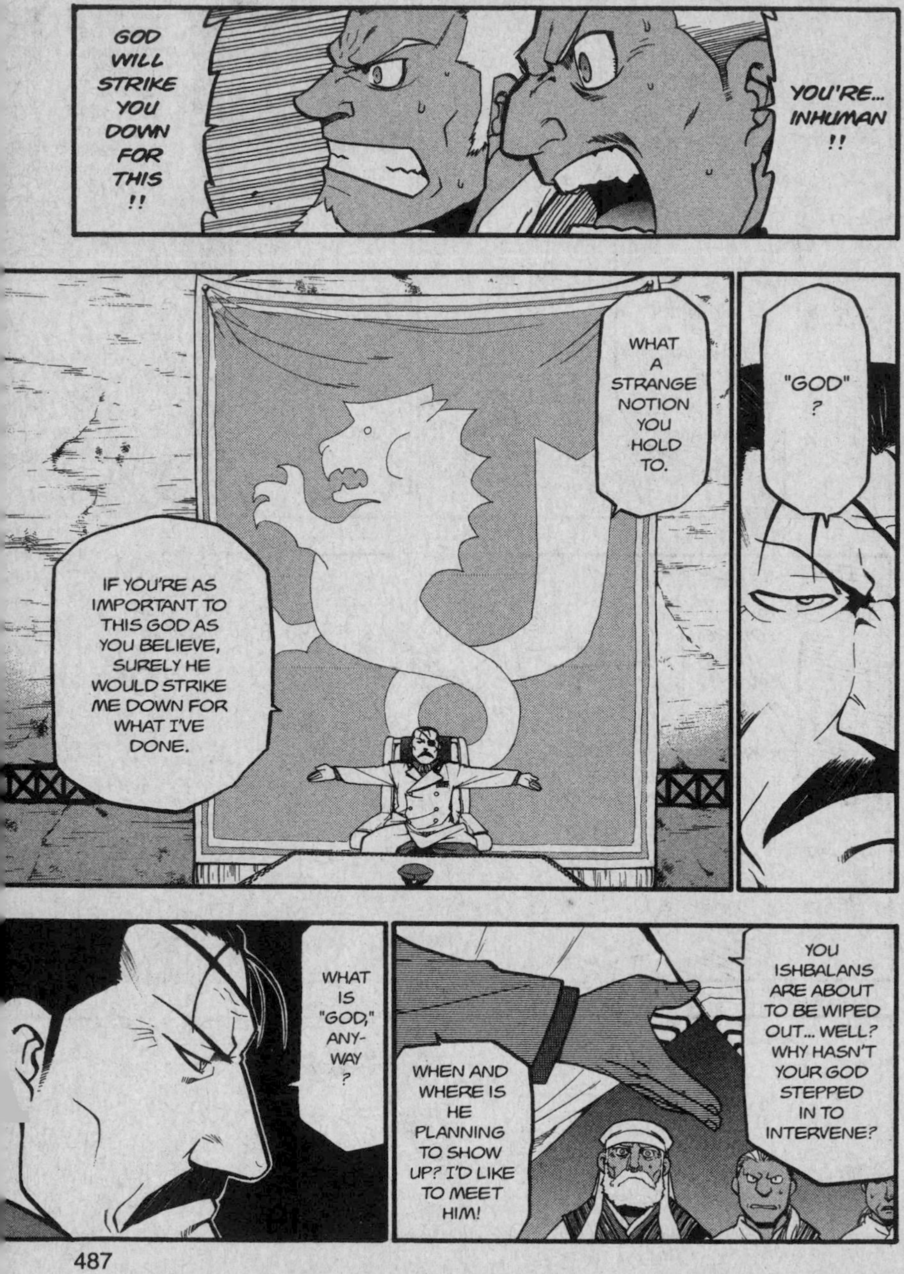
YOU'RE... INHUMAN !!
GOD WILL STRIKE YOU DOWN FOR THIS !!
"GOD" ?
WHAT A STRANGE NOTION YOU HOLD TO.
IF YOU'RE AS IMPORTANT TO THIS GOD AS YOU BELIEVE, SURELY HE WOULD STRIKE ME DOWN FOR WHAT I'VE DONE.
YOU ISHBALANS ARE ABOUT TO BE WIPED OUT... WELL? WHY HASN'T YOUR GOD STEPPED IN TO INTERVENE?
WHEN AND WHERE IS HE PLANNING TO SHOW UP? I'D LIKE TO MEET HIM!
WHAT IS "GOD," ANY-WAY ?

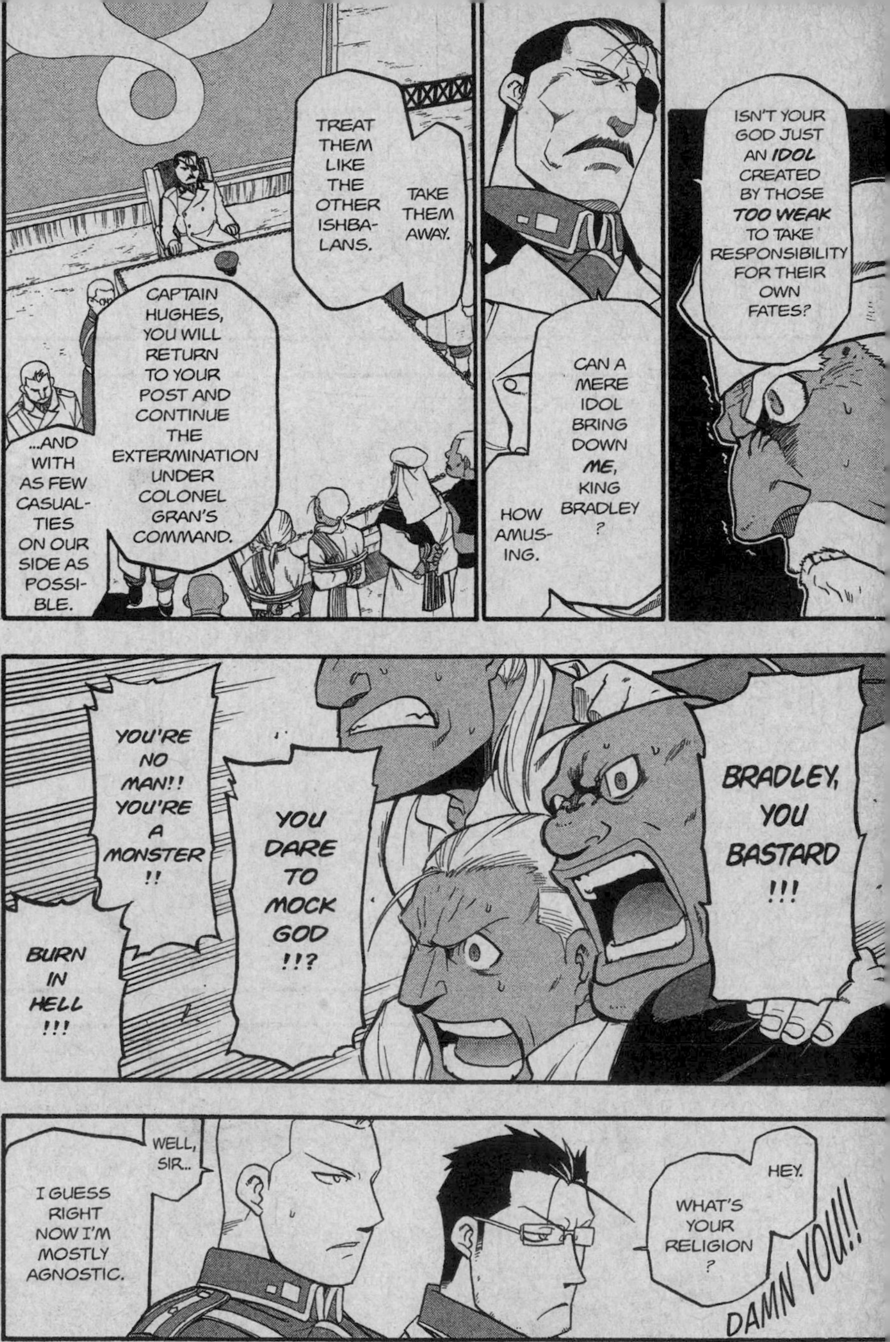
ISN'T YOUR GOD JUST AN IDOL CREATED BY THOSE TOO WEAK TO TAKE RESPONSIBILITY FOR THEIR OWN FATES?
CAN A MERE IDOL BRING DOWN ME, KING BRADLEY?
HOW AMUSING.
TAKE THEM AWAY.
TREAT THEM LIKE THE OTHER ISHBALANS.
CAPTAIN HUGHES, YOU WILL RETURN TO YOUR POST AND CONTINUE THE EXTERMINATION UNDER COLONEL GRAN'S COMMAND.
...AND WITH AS FEW CASUALTIES ON OUR SIDE AS POSSIBLE.
BRADLEY, YOU BASTARD!!!
YOU DARE TO MOCK GOD!!?
YOU'RE NO MAN!! YOU'RE A MONSTER!!
BURN IN HELL!!!
DAMN YOU!!
HEY.
WHAT'S YOUR RELIGION?
WELL, SIR...
I GUESS RIGHT NOW I'M MOSTLY AGNOSTIC.

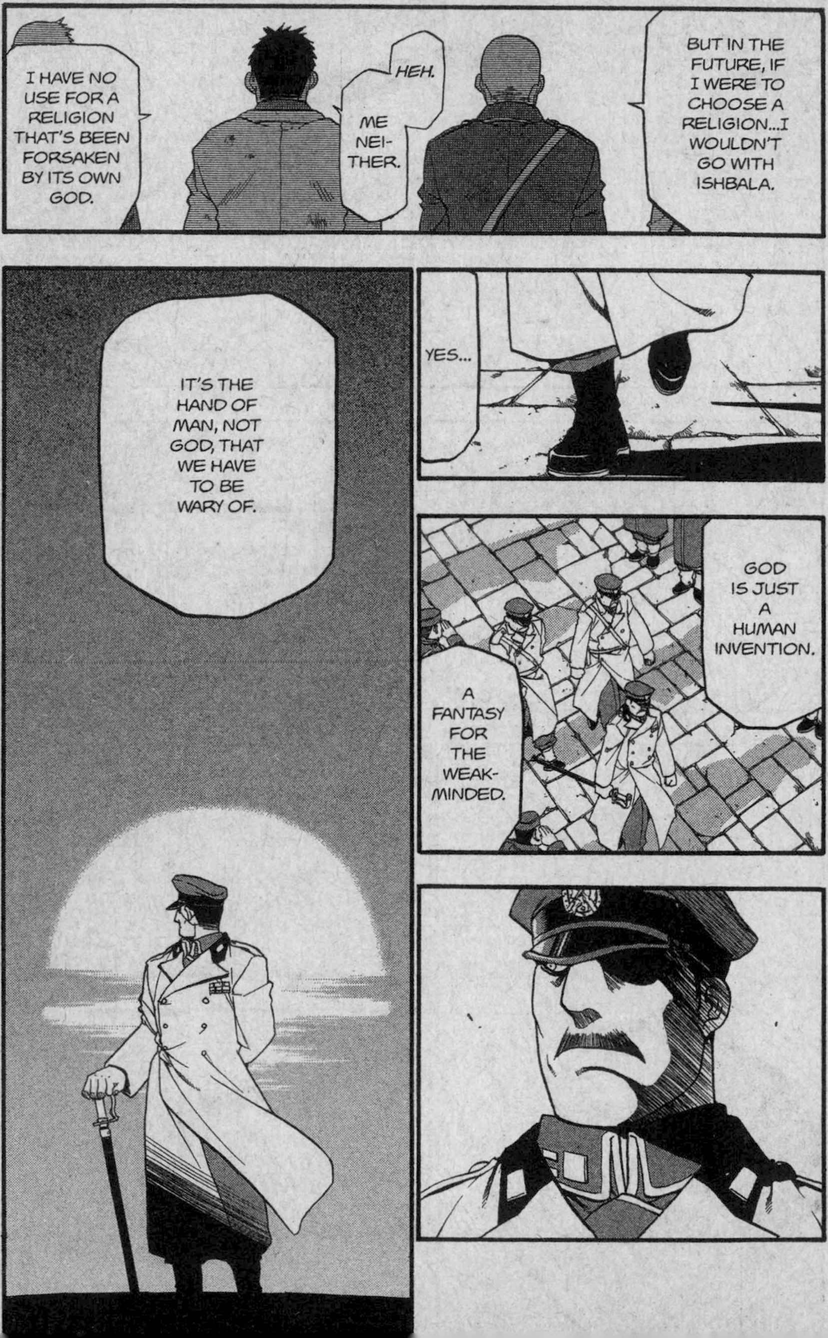
BUT IN THE FUTURE, IF I WERE TO CHOOSE A RELIGION...I WOULDN'T GO WITH ISHBALA.
HEH.
ME NEI-THER.
I HAVE NO USE FOR A RELIGION THAT'S BEEN FORSAKEN BY ITS OWN GOD.
YES...
GOD IS JUST A HUMAN INVENTION.
A FANTASY FOR THE WEAK-MINDED.
IT'S THE HAND OF MAN, NOT GOD, THAT WE HAVE TO BE WARY OF.

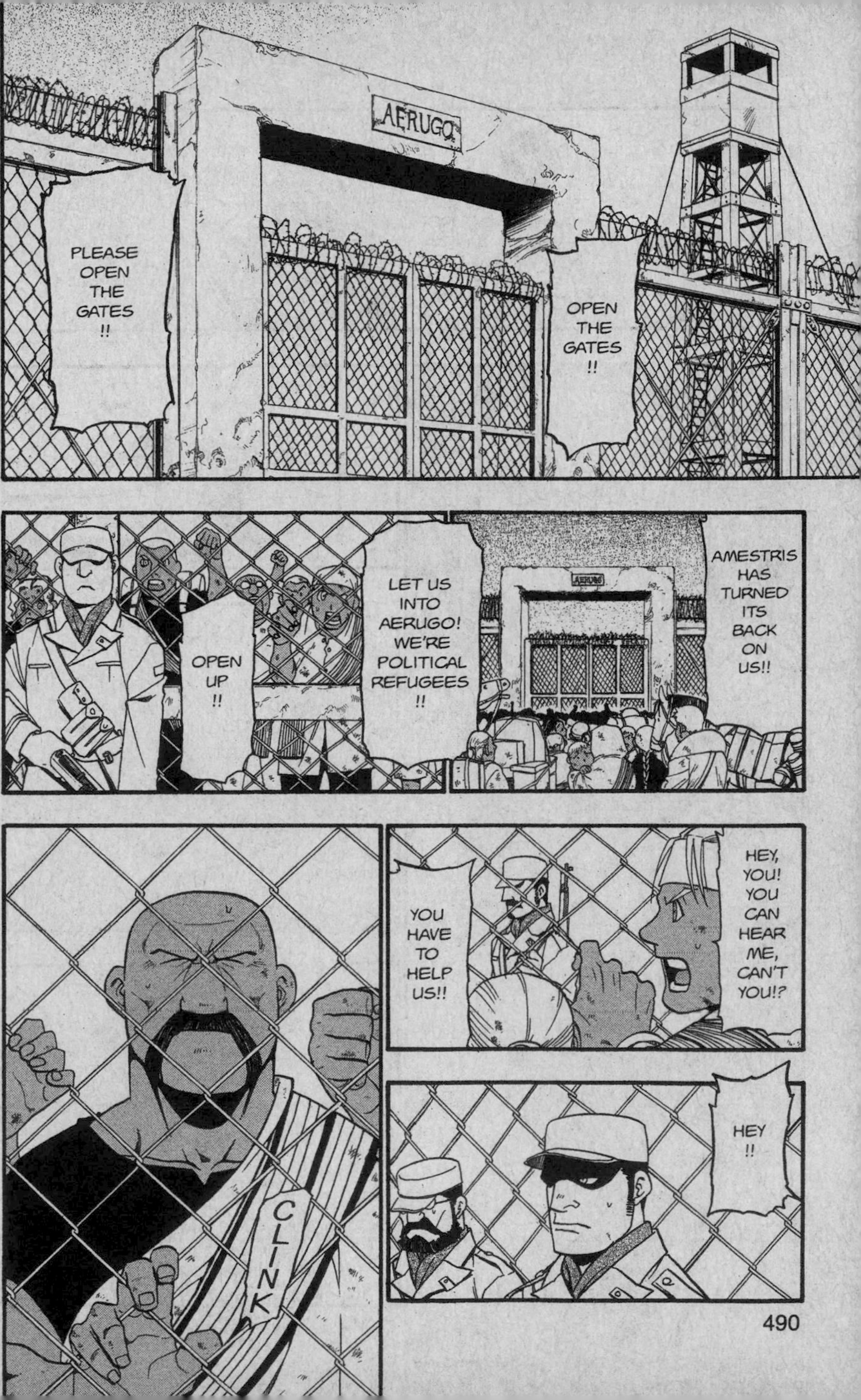
AERUGO
OPEN THE GATES!!
PLEASE OPEN THE GATES!!
AMESTRIS HAS TURNED ITS BACK ON US!!
LET US INTO AERUGO! WE'RE POLITICAL REFUGEES!!
OPEN UP!!
HEY, YOU! YOU CAN HEAR ME, CAN'T YOU!?
YOU HAVE TO HELP US!!
HEY!!
CLINK

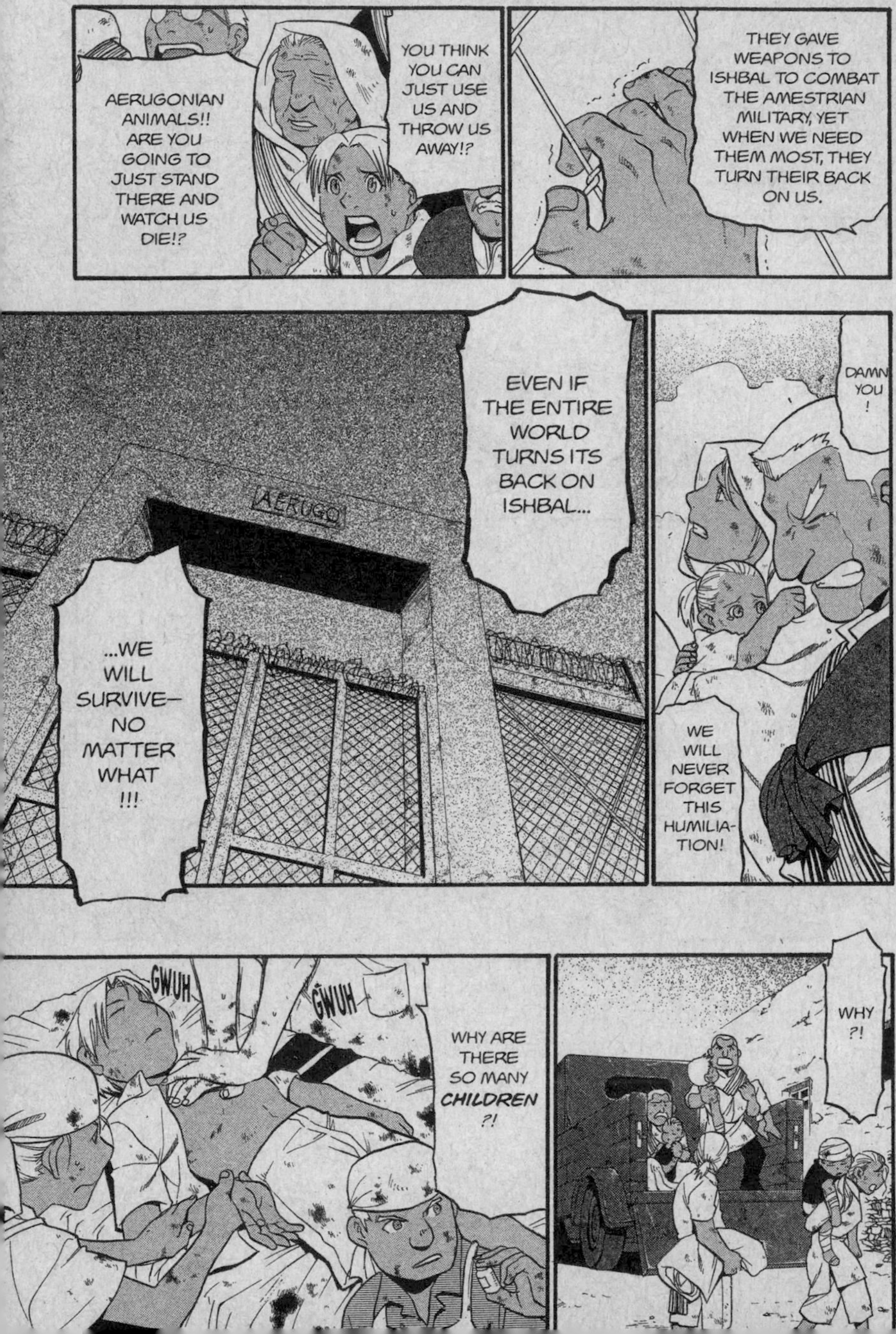
THEY GAVE WEAPONS TO ISHBAL TO COMBAT THE AMESTRIAN MILITARY, YET WHEN WE NEED THEM MOST, THEY TURN THEIR BACK ON US.
YOU THINK YOU CAN JUST USE US AND THROW US AWAY!?
AERUGONIAN ANIMALS!! ARE YOU GOING TO JUST STAND THERE AND WATCH US DIE!?
DAMN YOU!
WE WILL NEVER FORGET THIS HUMILIATION!
EVEN IF THE ENTIRE WORLD TURNS ITS BACK ON ISHBAL...
AERUGO
...WE WILL SURVIVE—NO MATTER WHAT!!!
WHY?!
WHY ARE THERE SO MANY CHILDREN?!
GWUH
GWUH

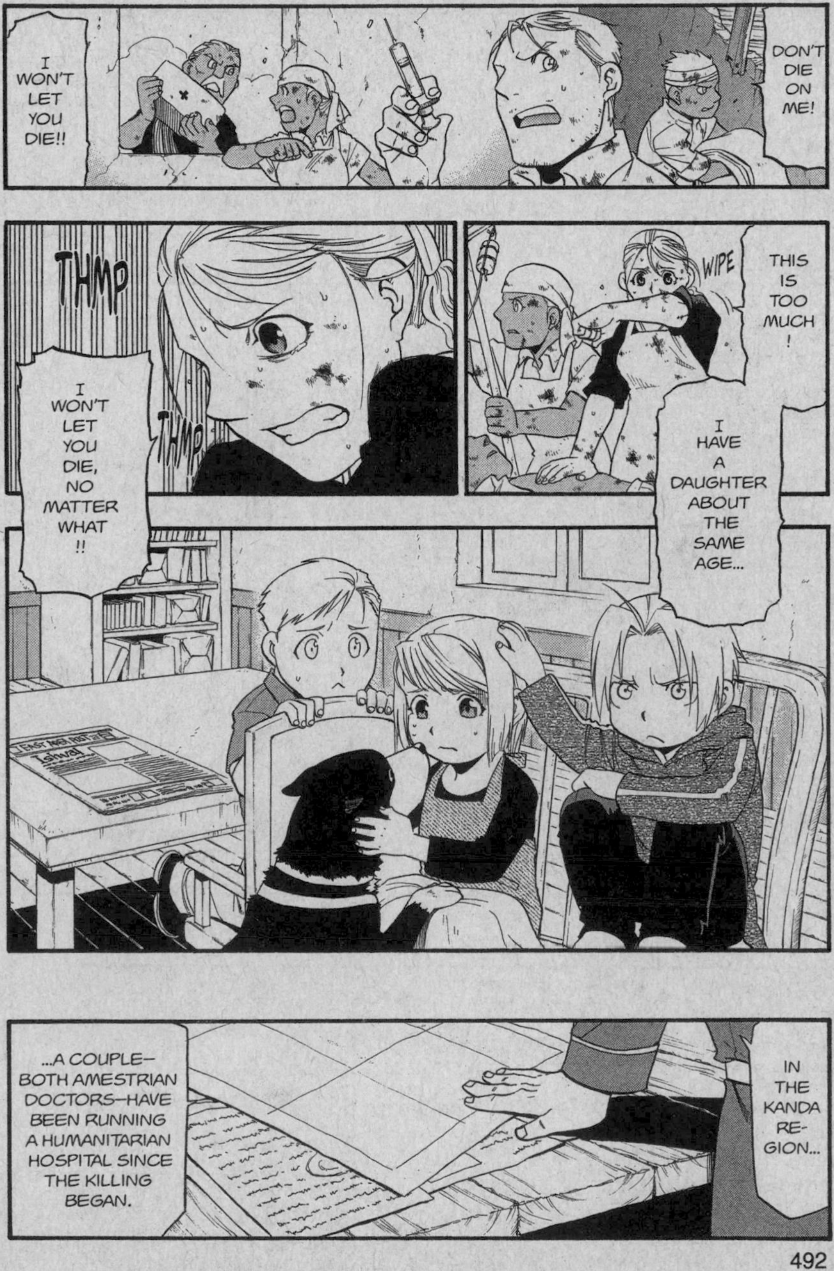
DON'T DIE ON ME!
I WON'T LET YOU DIE!!
WIPE
THIS IS TOO MUCH!
I HAVE A DAUGHTER ABOUT THE SAME AGE...
THMP
THMP
I WON'T LET YOU DIE, NO MATTER WHAT!!
Ishval
IN THE KANDA REGION...
...A COUPLE—BOTH AMESTRIAN DOCTORS—HAVE BEEN RUNNING A HUMANITARIAN HOSPITAL SINCE THE KILLING BEGAN.

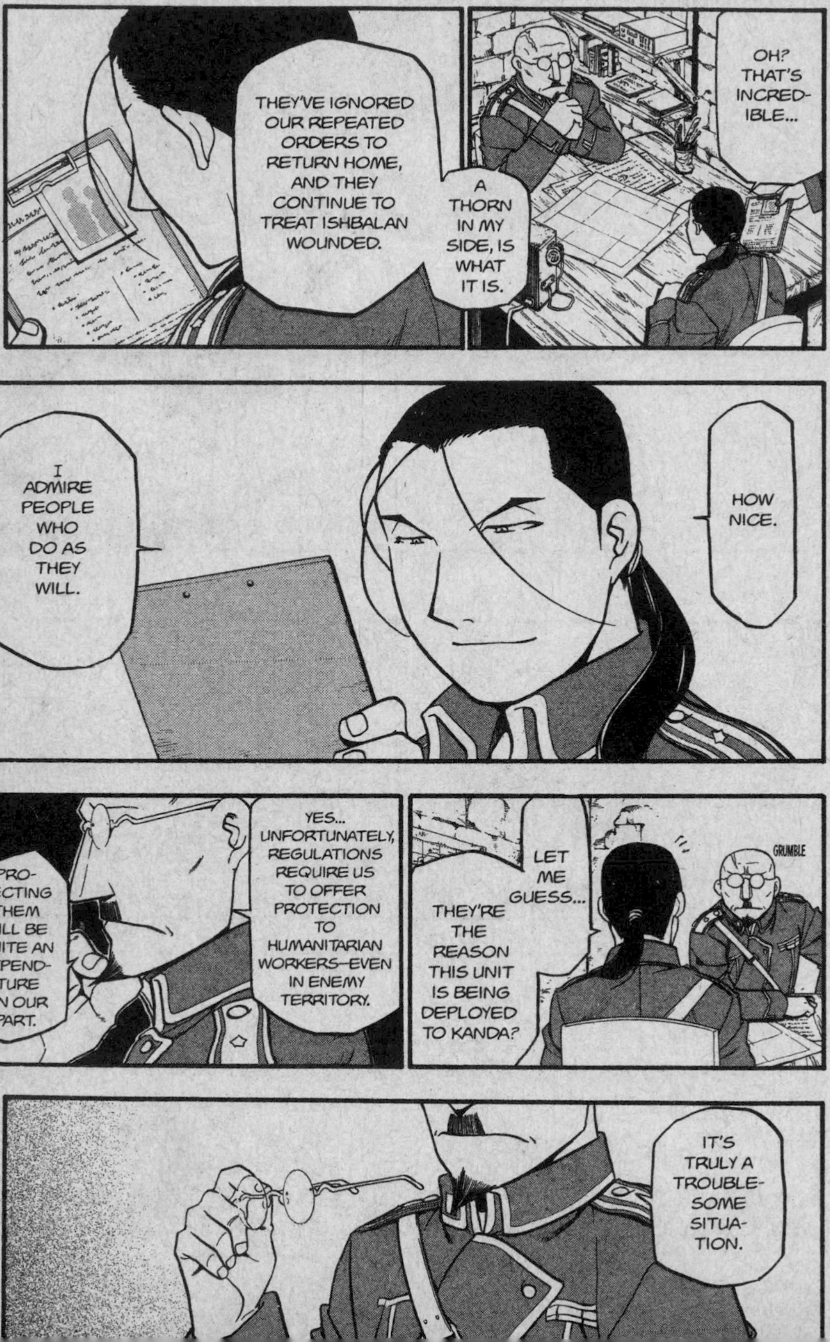
OH? THAT'S INCRED-IBLE...
A THORN IN MY SIDE, IS WHAT IT IS.
THEY'VE IGNORED OUR REPEATED ORDERS TO RETURN HOME, AND THEY CONTINUE TO TREAT ISHBALAN WOUNDED.
HOW NICE.
I ADMIRE PEOPLE WHO DO AS THEY WILL.
GRUMBLE
LET ME GUESS...
THEY'RE THE REASON THIS UNIT IS BEING DEPLOYED TO KANDA?
YES... UNFORTUNATELY, REGULATIONS REQUIRE US TO OFFER PROTECTION TO HUMANITARIAN WORKERS—EVEN IN ENEMY TERRITORY.
PRO-TECTING THEM WILL BE QUITE AN EXPEND-ITURE ON OUR PART.
IT'S TRULY A TROUBLE-SOME SITUA-TION.

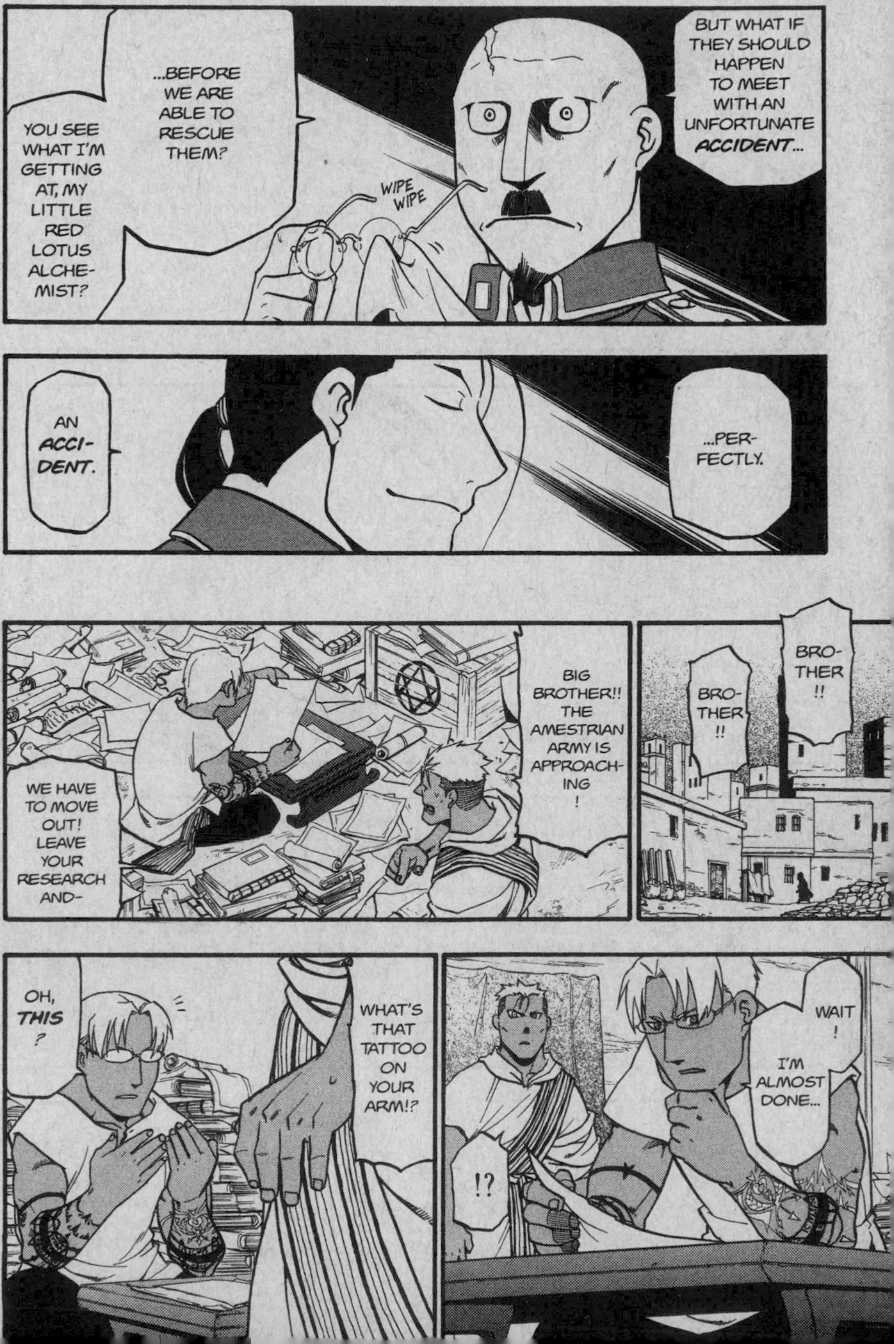
BUT WHAT IF THEY SHOULD HAPPEN TO MEET WITH AN UNFORTUNATE ACCIDENT...
...BEFORE WE ARE ABLE TO RESCUE THEM?
WIPE WIPE
YOU SEE WHAT I'M GETTING AT, MY LITTLE RED LOTUS ALCHEMIST?
...PERFECTLY.
AN ACCIDENT.
BROTHER!!
BROTHER!!
BIG BROTHER!! THE AMESTRIAN ARMY IS APPROACHING!
WE HAVE TO MOVE OUT! LEAVE YOUR RESEARCH AND-
WAIT!
I'M ALMOST DONE...
!?
WHAT'S THAT TATTOO ON YOUR ARM!?
OH, THIS?

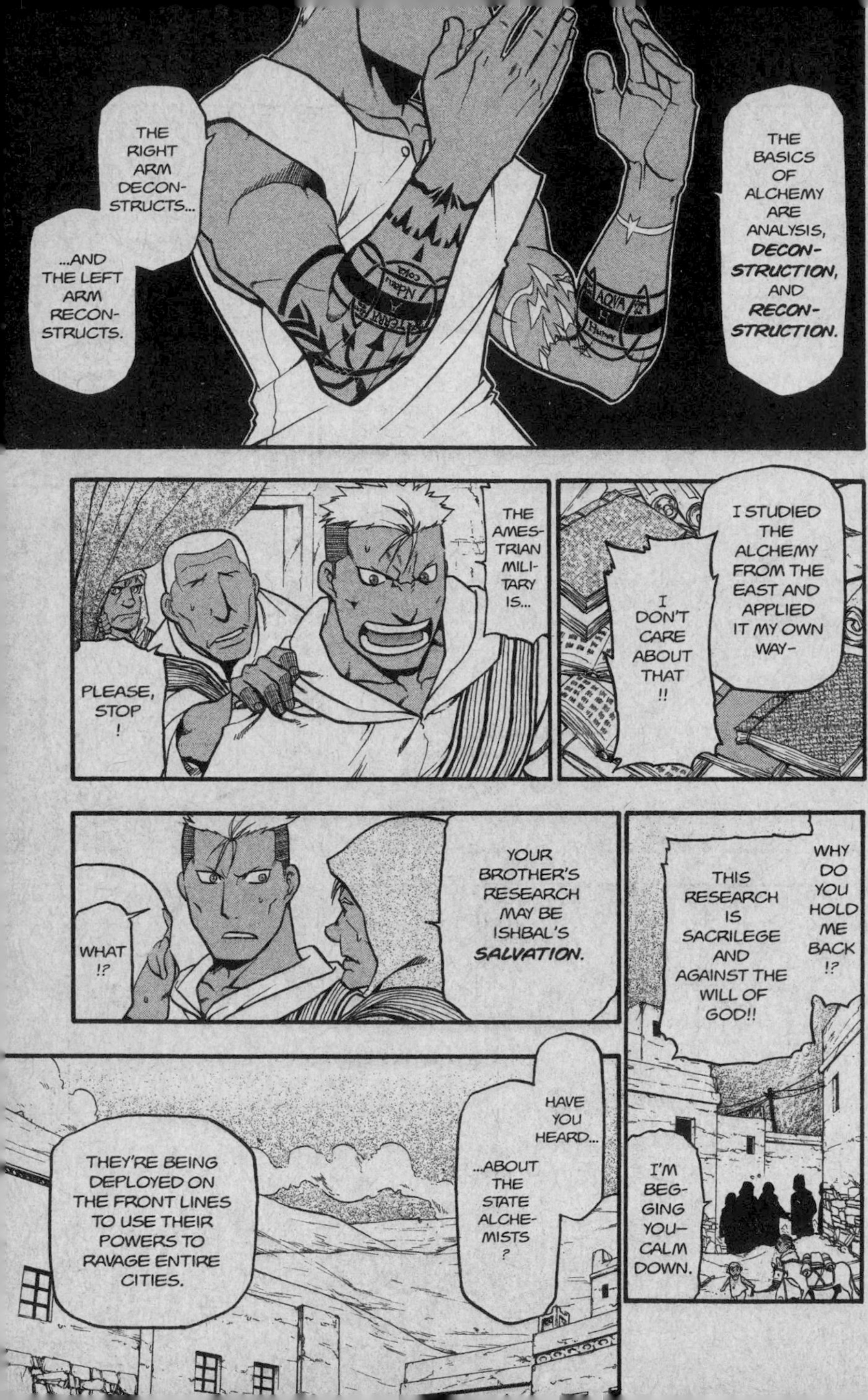
THE BASICS OF ALCHEMY ARE ANALYSIS, DECONSTRUCTION, AND RECONSTRUCTION.
THE RIGHT ARM DECONSTRUCTS...
...AND THE LEFT ARM RECONSTRUCTS.
I STUDIED THE ALCHEMY FROM THE EAST AND APPLIED IT MY OWN WAY-
I DON'T CARE ABOUT THAT!!
THE AMESTRIAN MILITARY IS...
PLEASE, STOP!
WHY DO YOU HOLD ME BACK!?
THIS RESEARCH IS SACRILEGE AND AGAINST THE WILL OF GOD!!
I'M BEGGING YOU—CALM DOWN.
YOUR BROTHER'S RESEARCH MAY BE ISHBAL'S SALVATION.
WHAT!?
HAVE YOU HEARD...
...ABOUT THE STATE ALCHEMISTS?
THEY'RE BEING DEPLOYED ON THE FRONT LINES TO USE THEIR POWERS TO RAVAGE ENTIRE CITIES.

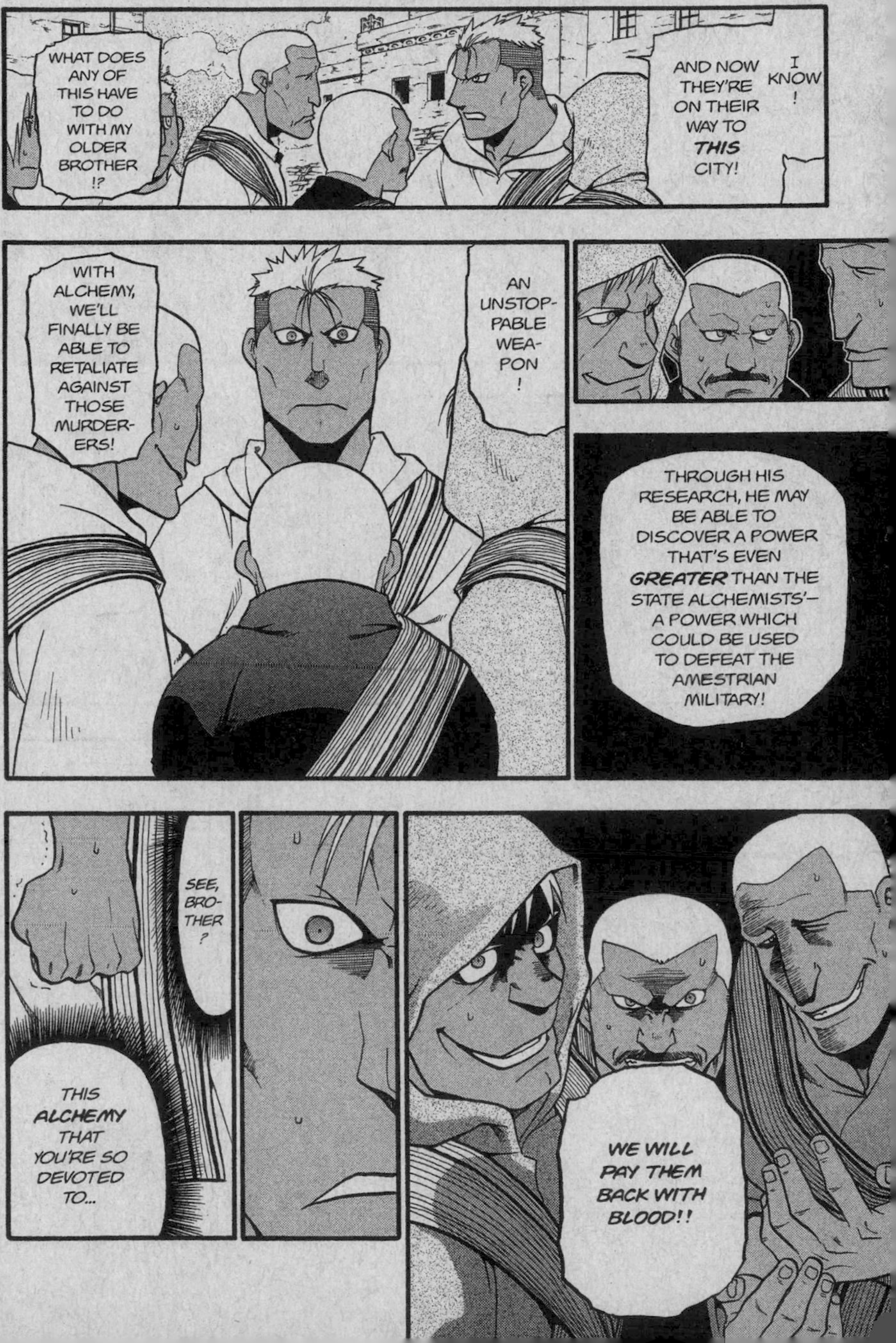
I KNOW!
AND NOW THEY'RE ON THEIR WAY TO **THIS** CITY!
WHAT DOES ANY OF THIS HAVE TO DO WITH MY OLDER BROTHER!?
THROUGH HIS RESEARCH, HE MAY BE ABLE TO DISCOVER A POWER THAT'S EVEN **GREATER** THAN THE STATE ALCHEMISTS'—A POWER WHICH COULD BE USED TO DEFEAT THE AMESTRIAN MILITARY!
AN UNSTOPPABLE WEAPON!
WITH ALCHEMY, WE'LL FINALLY BE ABLE TO RETALIATE AGAINST THOSE MURDERERS!
WE WILL PAY THEM BACK WITH BLOOD!!
SEE, BROTHER?
THIS **ALCHEMY** THAT YOU'RE SO DEVOTED TO...

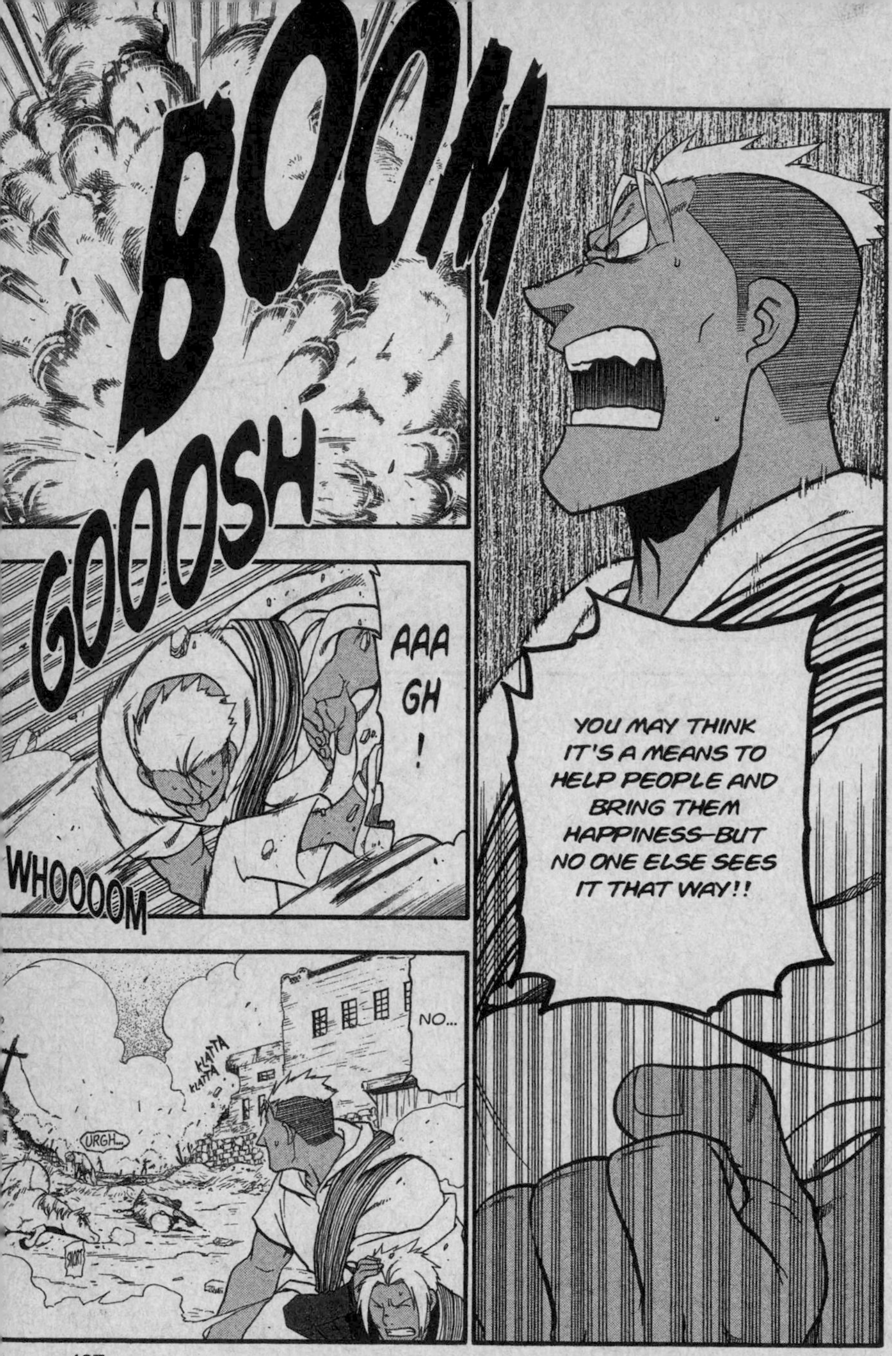
YOU MAY THINK IT'S A MEANS TO HELP PEOPLE AND BRING THEM HAPPINESS—BUT NO ONE ELSE SEES IT THAT WAY!!
BOOM
GOOOSH
AAAGH!
WHOOOOM
NO...
KLATTA KLATTA
URGH...

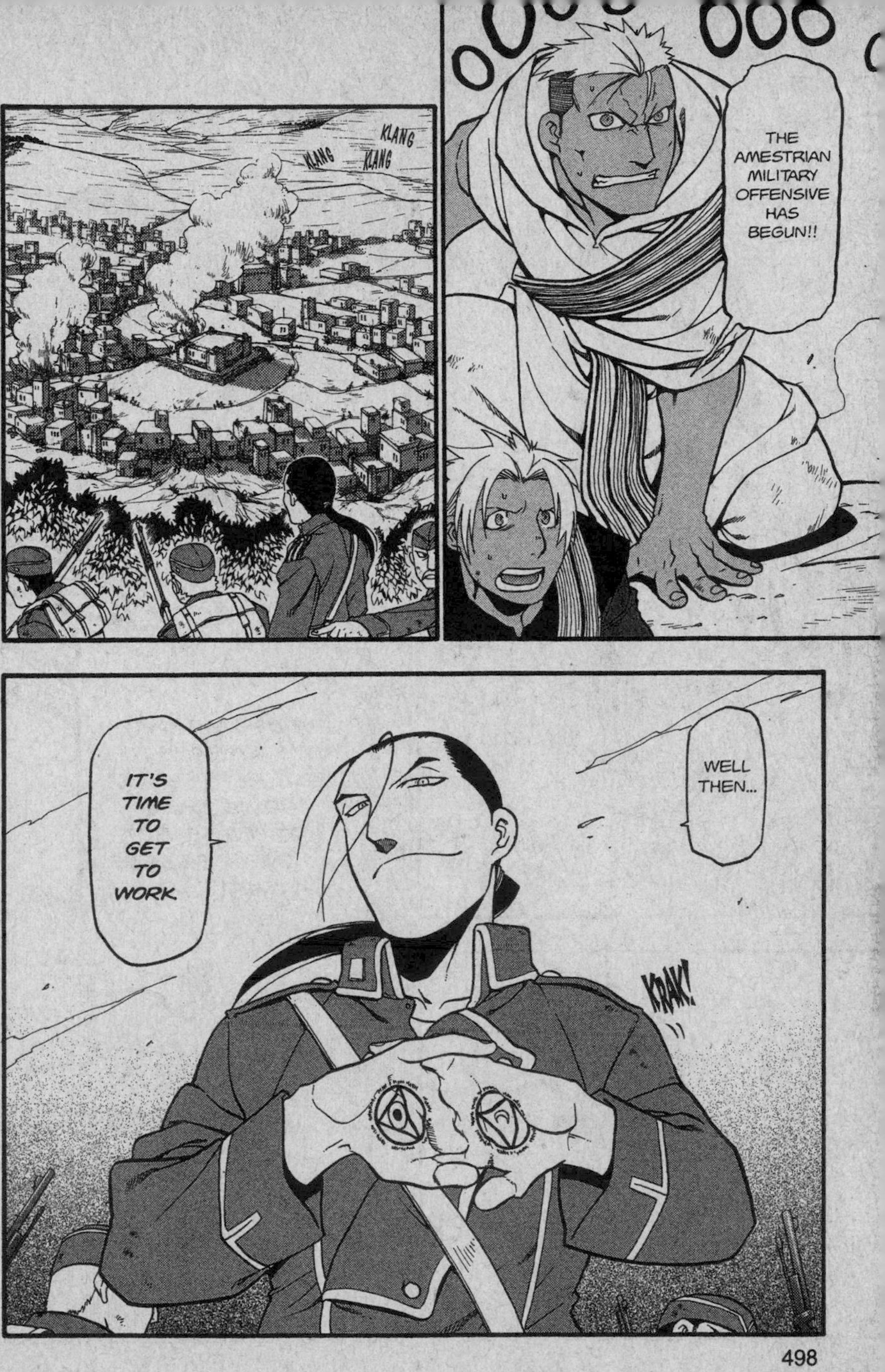
THE AMESTRIAN MILITARY OFFENSIVE HAS BEGUN!!
KLANG
KLANG
KLANG
WELL THEN...
IT'S TIME TO GET TO WORK.
KRAK!

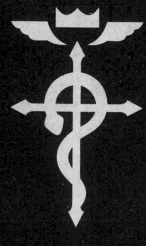

FULLMETAL
ALCHEMIST

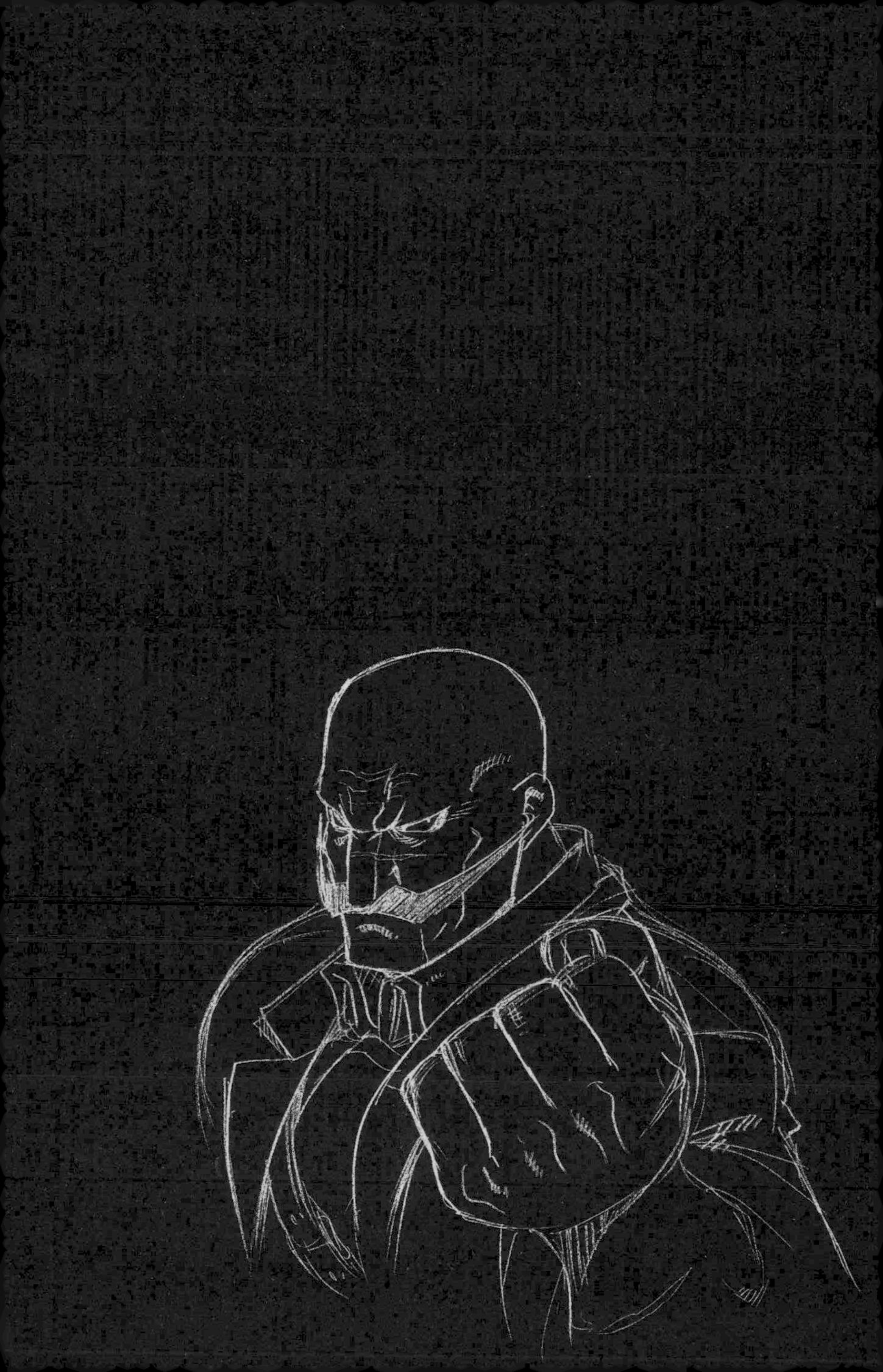

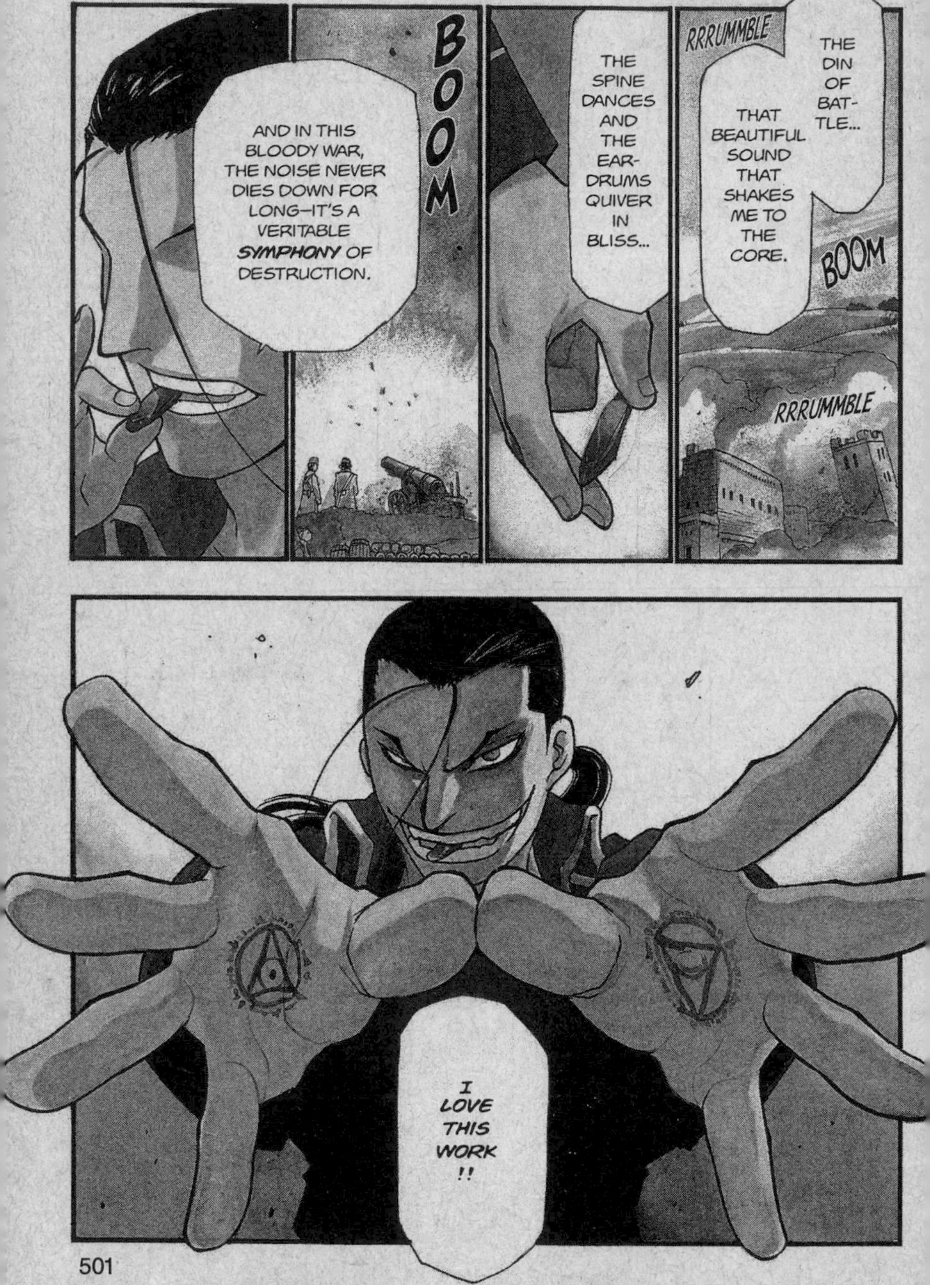
THE DIN OF BATTLE...
RRRUMMBLE
THAT BEAUTIFUL SOUND THAT SHAKES ME TO THE CORE.
BOOM
RRRUMMBLE
THE SPINE DANCES AND THE EAR-DRUMS QUIVER IN BLISS...
BOOM
AND IN THIS BLOODY WAR, THE NOISE NEVER DIES DOWN FOR LONG—IT'S A VERITABLE *SYMPHONY* OF DESTRUCTION.
I LOVE THIS WORK!!

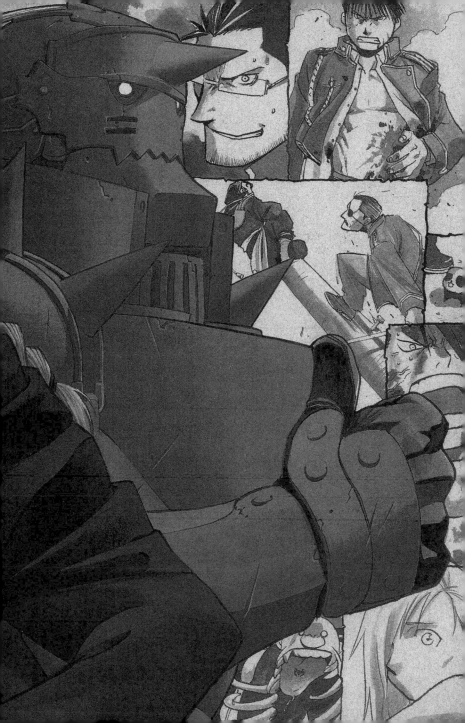

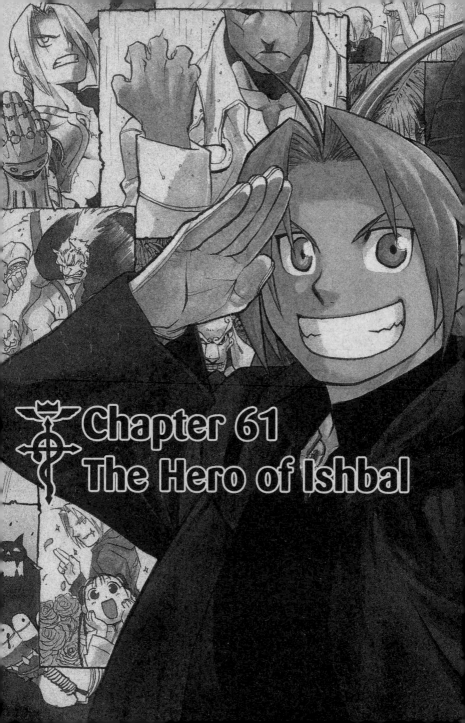

Chapter 61
The Hero of Ishbal

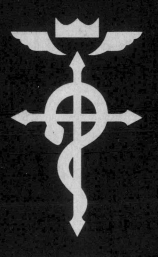

FULLMETAL
ALCHEMIST

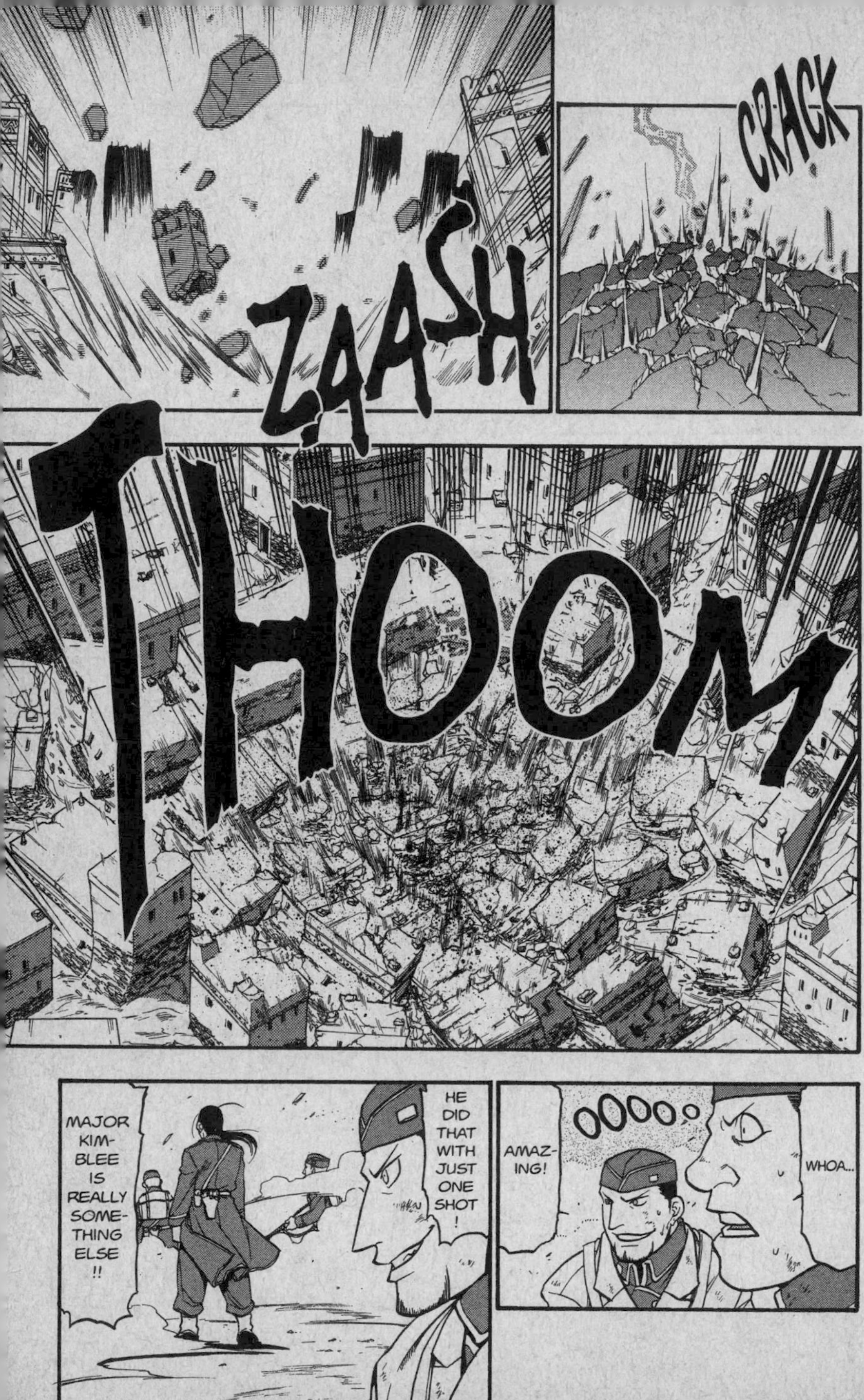
CRACK
ZAASH
THOOM
OOOOo
WHOA...
AMAZ-ING!
HE DID THAT WITH JUST ONE SHOT!
MAJOR KIM-BLEE IS REALLY SOME-THING ELSE!!

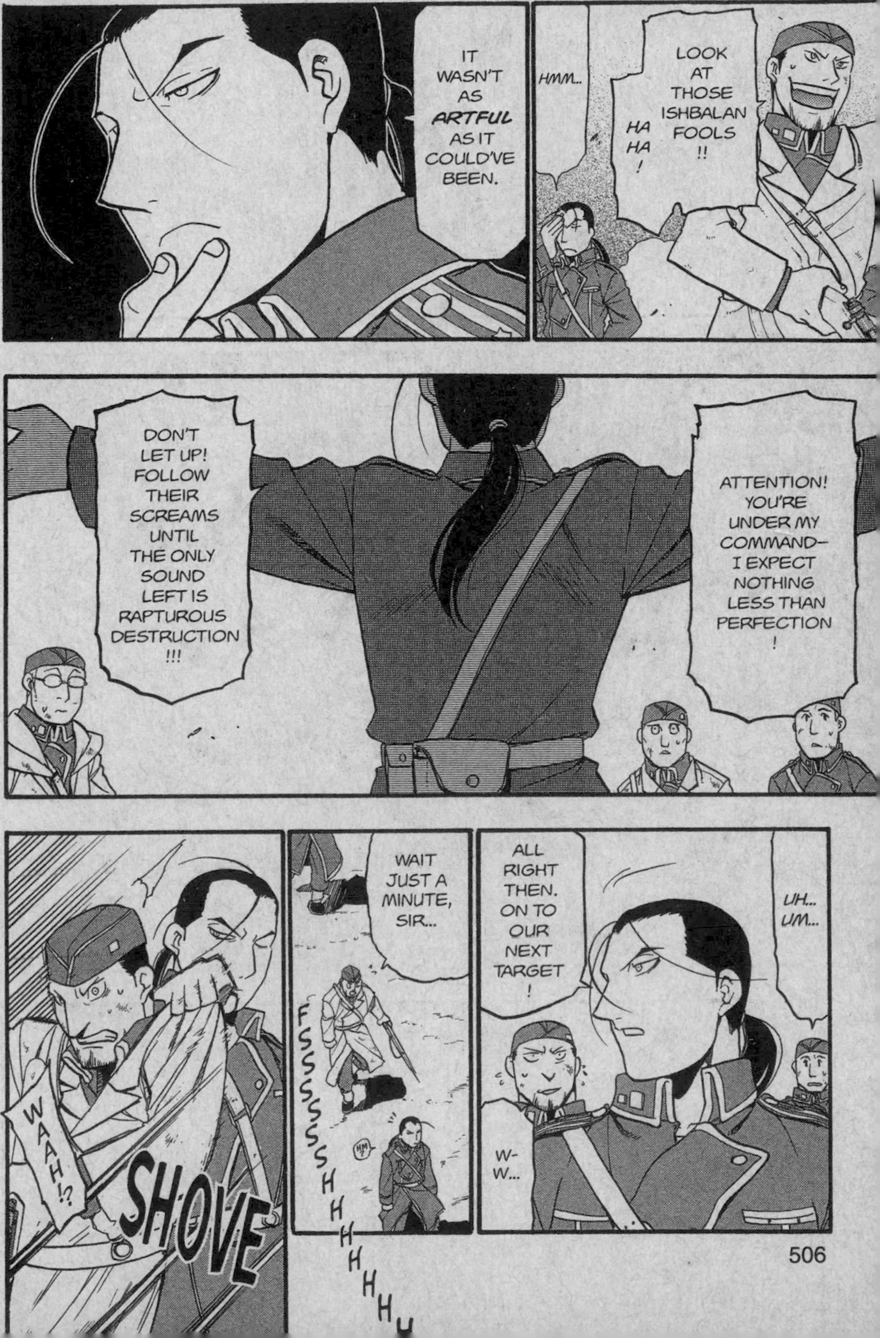

LOOK AT THOSE ISHBALAN FOOLS!!
HA HA!
HMM..
IT WASN'T AS ARTFUL AS IT COULD'VE BEEN.
ATTENTION! YOU'RE UNDER MY COMMAND— I EXPECT NOTHING LESS THAN PERFECTION!
DON'T LET UP! FOLLOW THEIR SCREAMS UNTIL THE ONLY SOUND LEFT IS RAPTUROUS DESTRUCTION!!!
UH... UM...
ALL RIGHT THEN. ON TO OUR NEXT TARGET!
W-W...
WAIT JUST A MINUTE, SIR...
FSSSSSHHHHHHU
HM?
WAAH!?
SHOVE

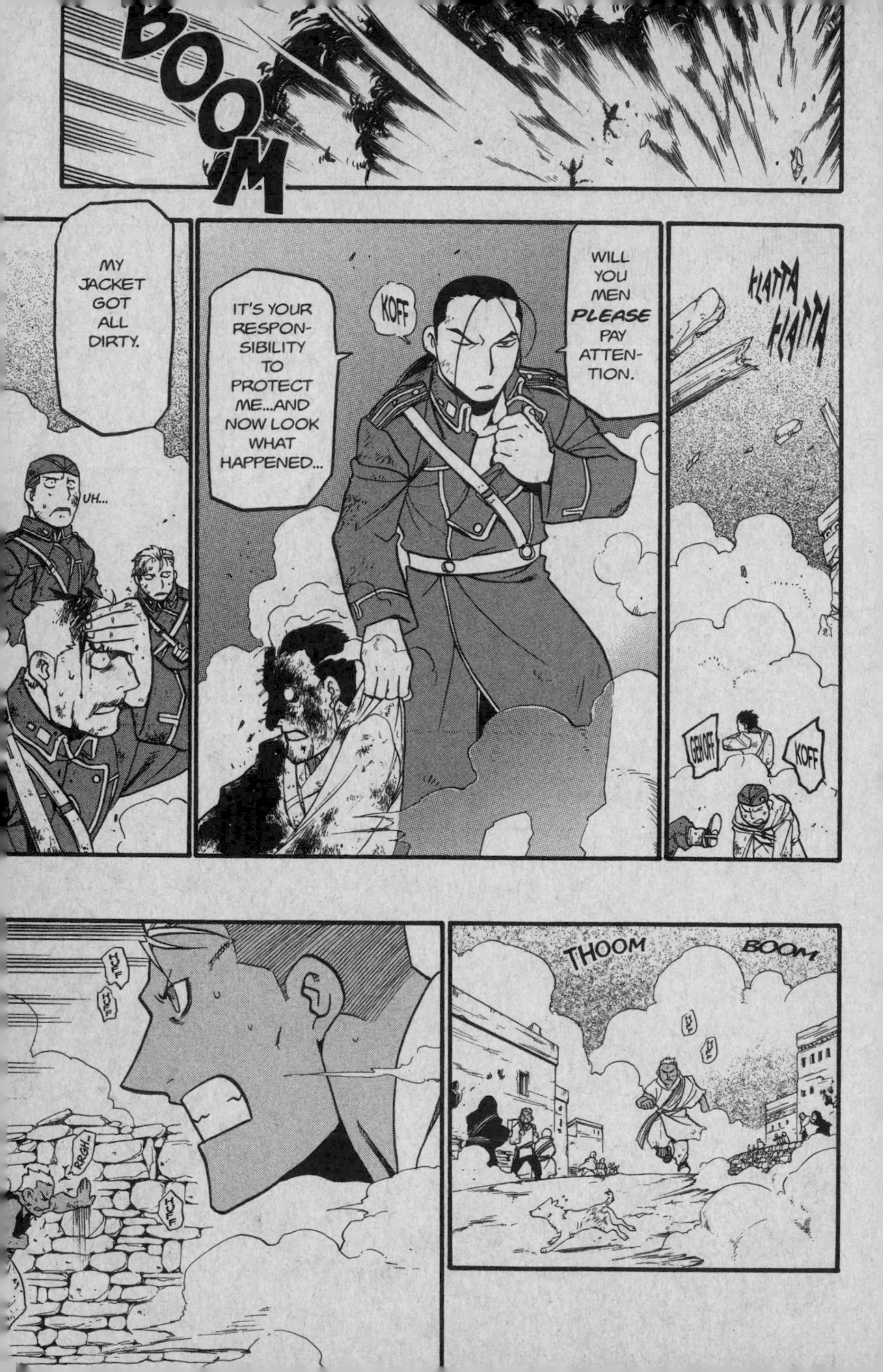
BOOM
KLATTA KLATTA
KOFF
GEHOFF
WILL YOU MEN PLEASE PAY ATTEN-TION.
KOFF
IT'S YOUR RESPON-SIBILITY TO PROTECT ME...AND NOW LOOK WHAT HAPPENED...
MY JACKET GOT ALL DIRTY.
UH...
THOOM
BOOM
HUFF
HUFF
HUFF
HUFF
RRGH...
HUFF

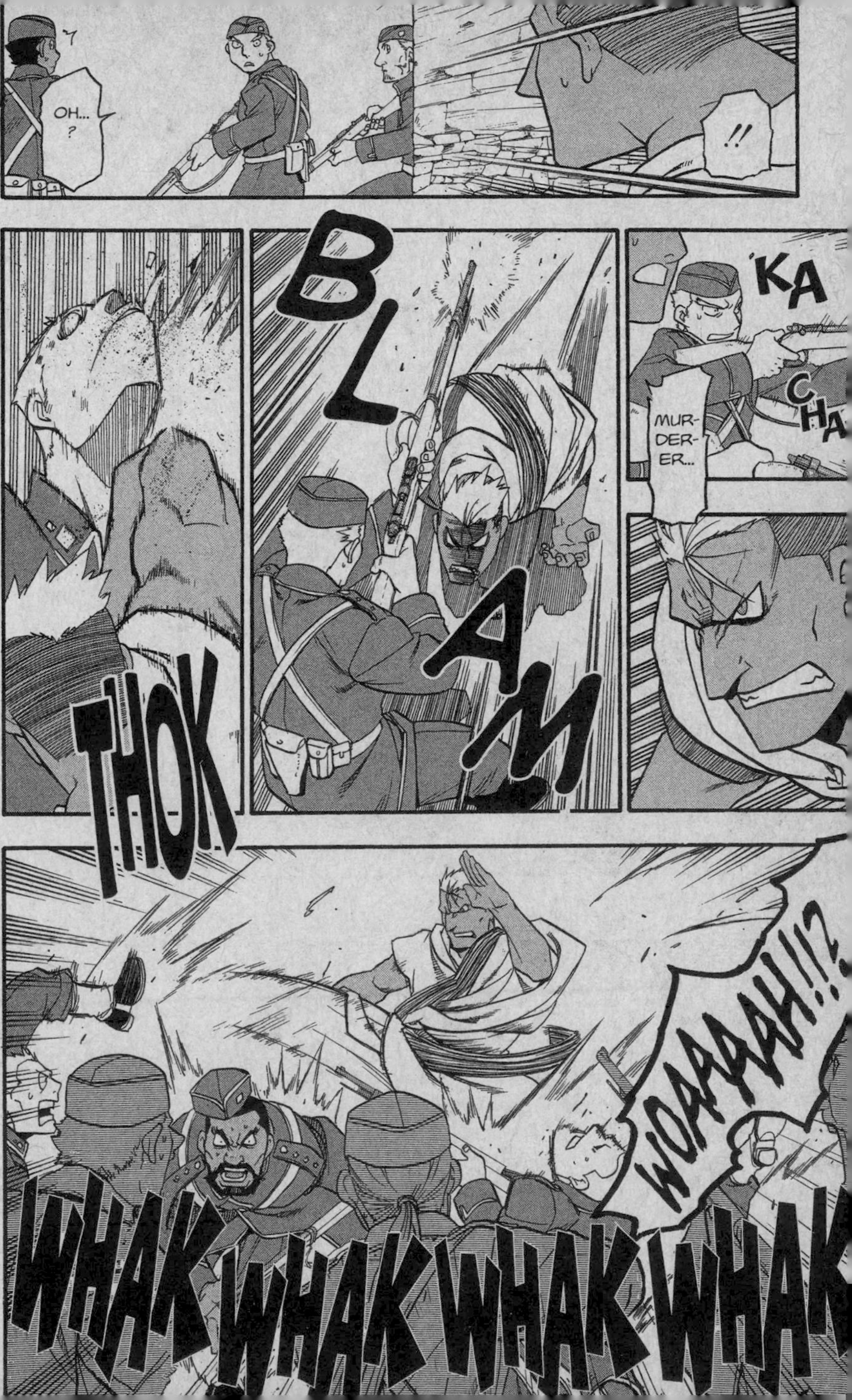
!!
OH... ?
KA CHA
MURDER-ER...
BLAM
THOK
WOAAAAH!!?
WHAK WHAK WHAK WHAK

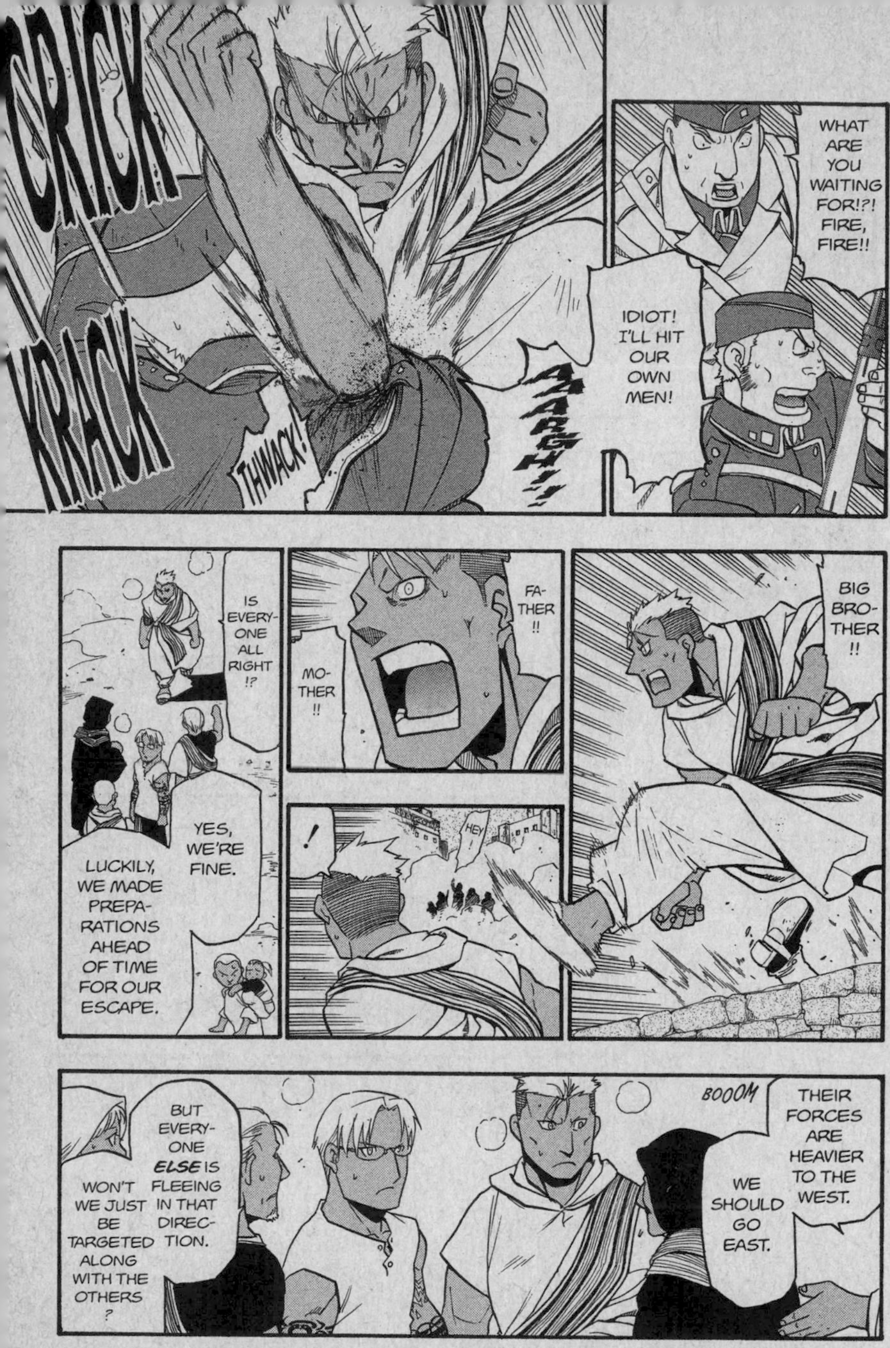

WHAT ARE YOU WAITING FOR!?! FIRE, FIRE!!
IDIOT! I'LL HIT OUR OWN MEN!
AAARGH!!
THWACK!
CRICK
KRACK
BIG BROTHER!!
FATHER!!
MOTHER!!
!
HEY
IS EVERYONE ALL RIGHT!?
YES, WE'RE FINE.
LUCKILY, WE MADE PREPARATIONS AHEAD OF TIME FOR OUR ESCAPE.
BOOOM
THEIR FORCES ARE HEAVIER TO THE WEST.
WE SHOULD GO EAST.
BUT EVERYONE ELSE IS FLEEING IN THAT DIRECTION.
WON'T WE JUST BE TARGETED ALONG WITH THE OTHERS?

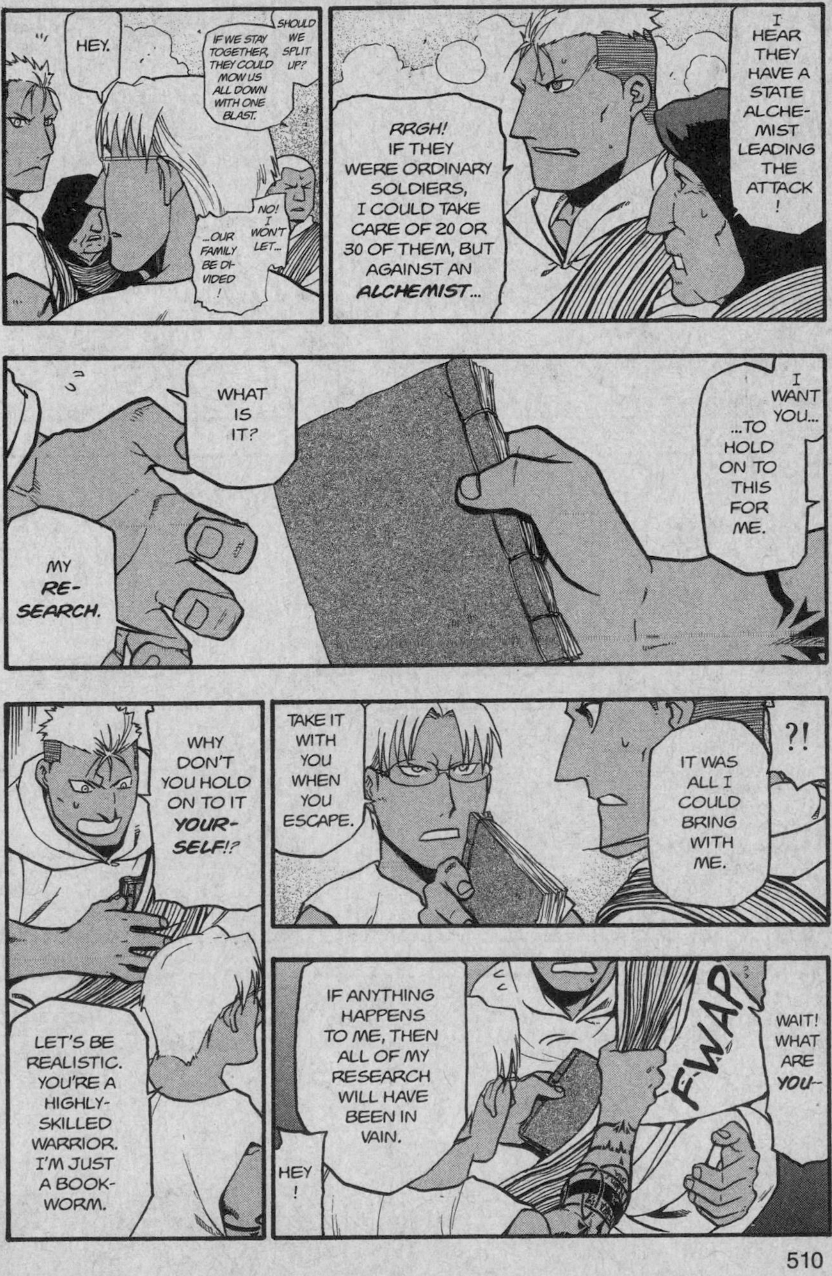
I HEAR THEY HAVE A STATE ALCHEMIST LEADING THE ATTACK!
RRGH! IF THEY WERE ORDINARY SOLDIERS, I COULD TAKE CARE OF 20 OR 30 OF THEM, BUT AGAINST AN ALCHEMIST...
SHOULD WE SPLIT UP?
IF WE STAY TOGETHER, THEY COULD MOW US ALL DOWN WITH ONE BLAST.
HEY.
NO! I WON'T LET...
...OUR FAMILY BE DIVIDED!
I WANT YOU...
...TO HOLD ON TO THIS FOR ME.
WHAT IS IT?
MY RESEARCH.
?!
IT WAS ALL I COULD BRING WITH ME.
TAKE IT WITH YOU WHEN YOU ESCAPE.
WAIT! WHAT ARE YOU-
FWAP
IF ANYTHING HAPPENS TO ME, THEN ALL OF MY RESEARCH WILL HAVE BEEN IN VAIN.
HEY!
WHY DON'T YOU HOLD ON TO IT YOURSELF!?
LET'S BE REALISTIC. YOU'RE A HIGHLY-SKILLED WARRIOR. I'M JUST A BOOKWORM.

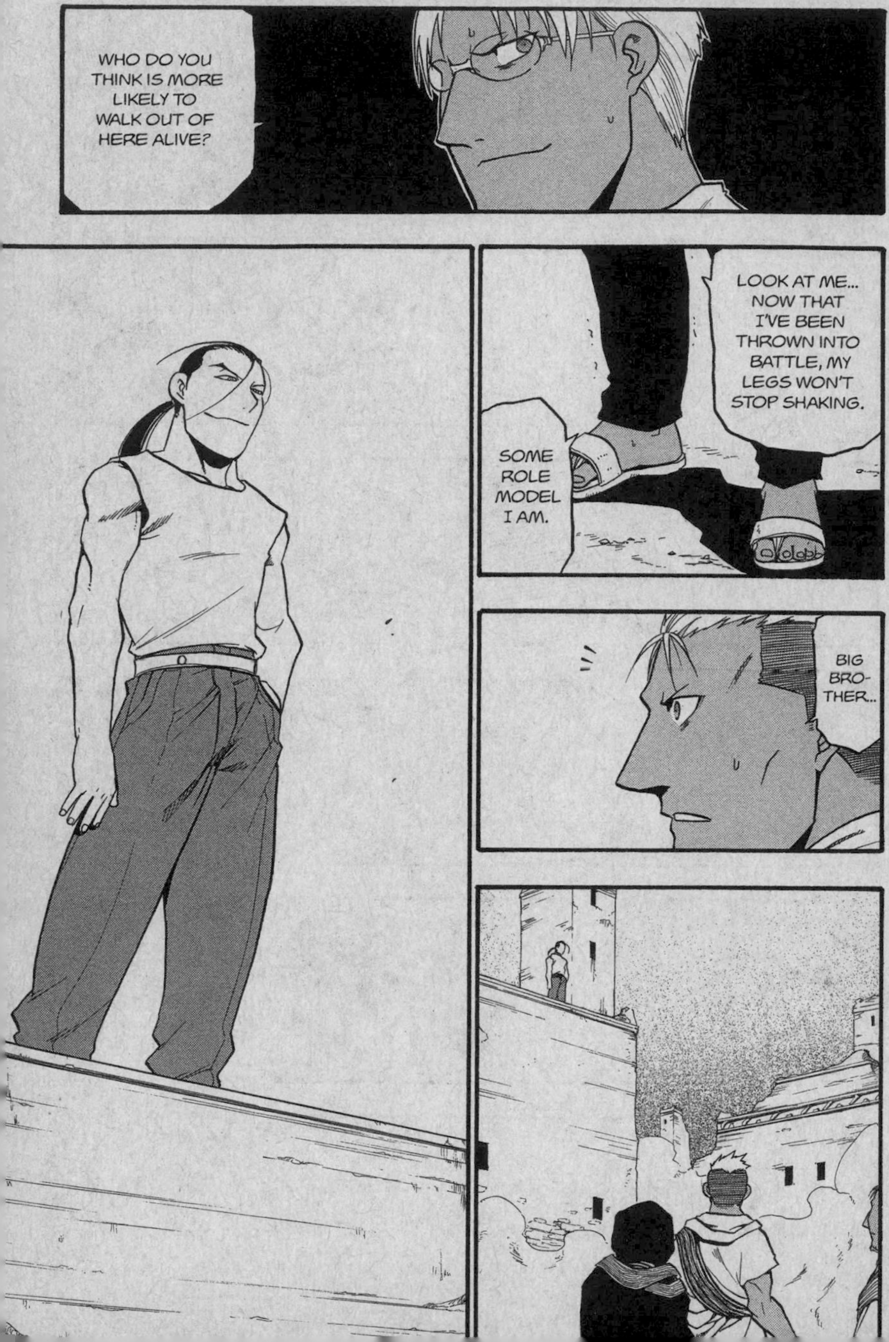
WHO DO YOU THINK IS MORE LIKELY TO WALK OUT OF HERE ALIVE?
LOOK AT ME... NOW THAT I'VE BEEN THROWN INTO BATTLE, MY LEGS WON'T STOP SHAKING.
SOME ROLE MODEL I AM.
BIG BRO-THER...

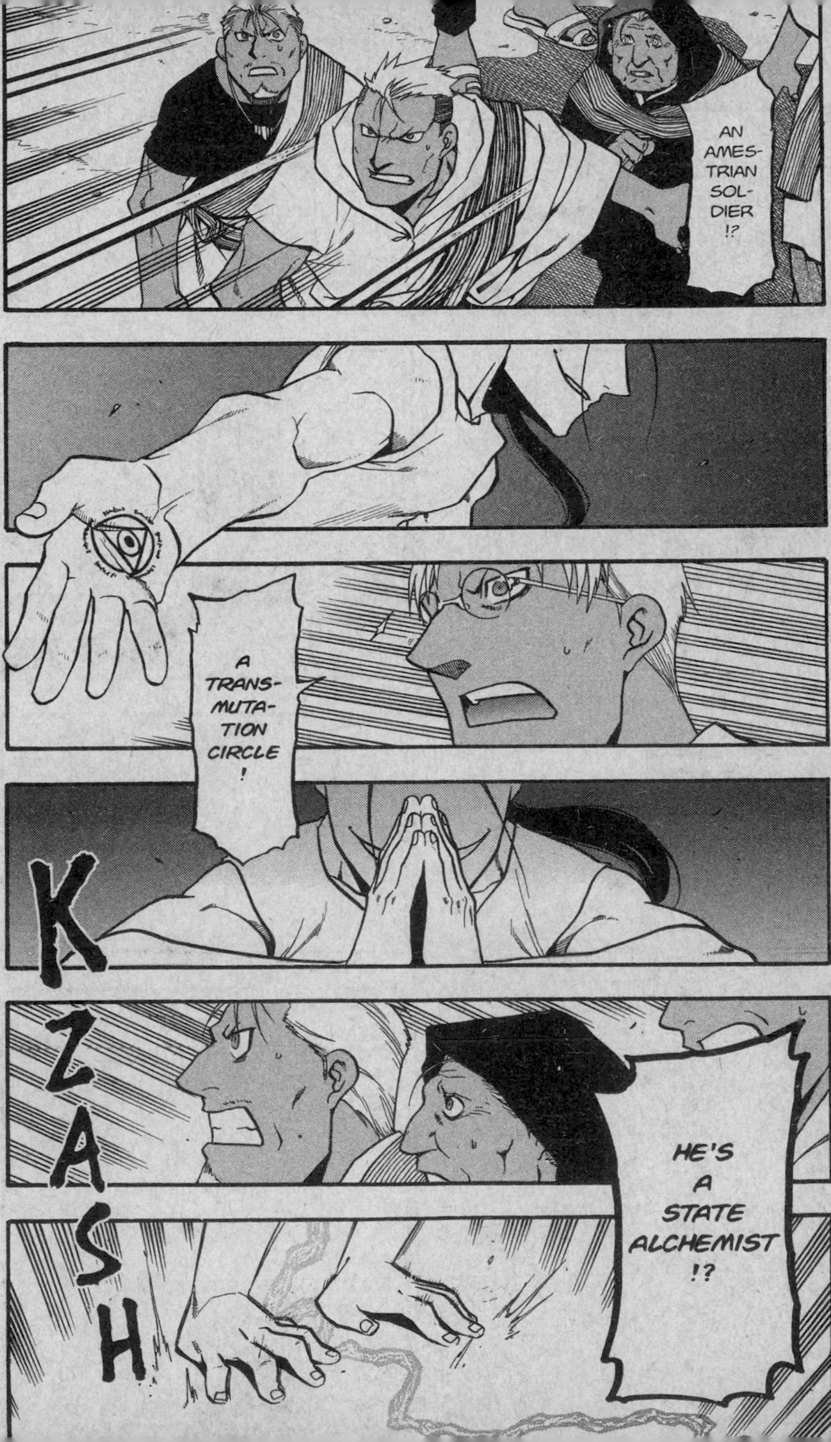
AN AMESTRIAN SOLDIER!?
A TRANSMUTATION CIRCLE!
KZASH
HE'S A STATE ALCHEMIST!?

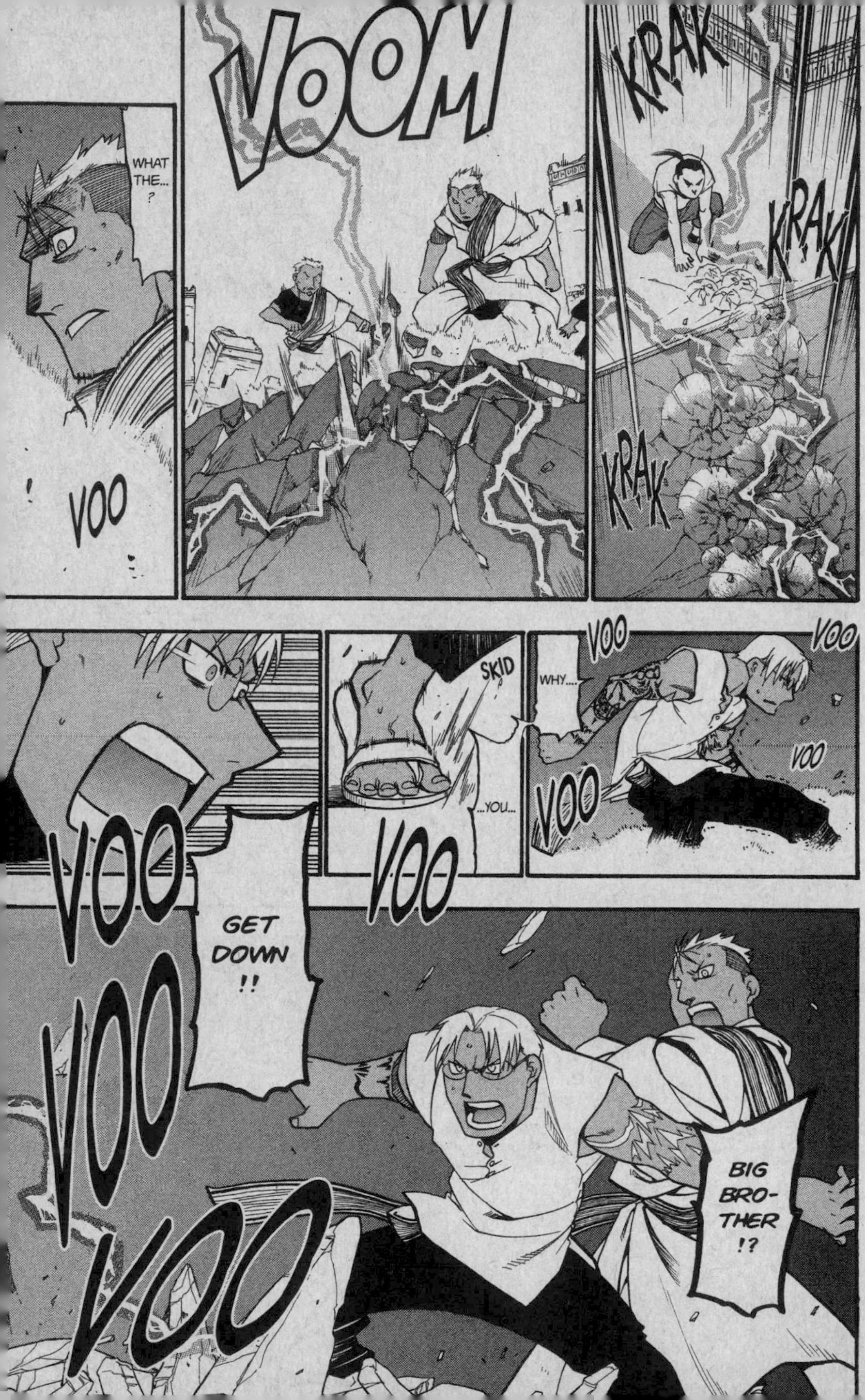
KRAK
KRAK
KRAK
VOOM
WHAT THE... ?
VOO
VOO
VOO
WHY....
VOO
VOO
SKID
...YOU...
VOO
VOO
GET DOWN !!
BIG BRO-THER !?
VOO
VOO
VOO

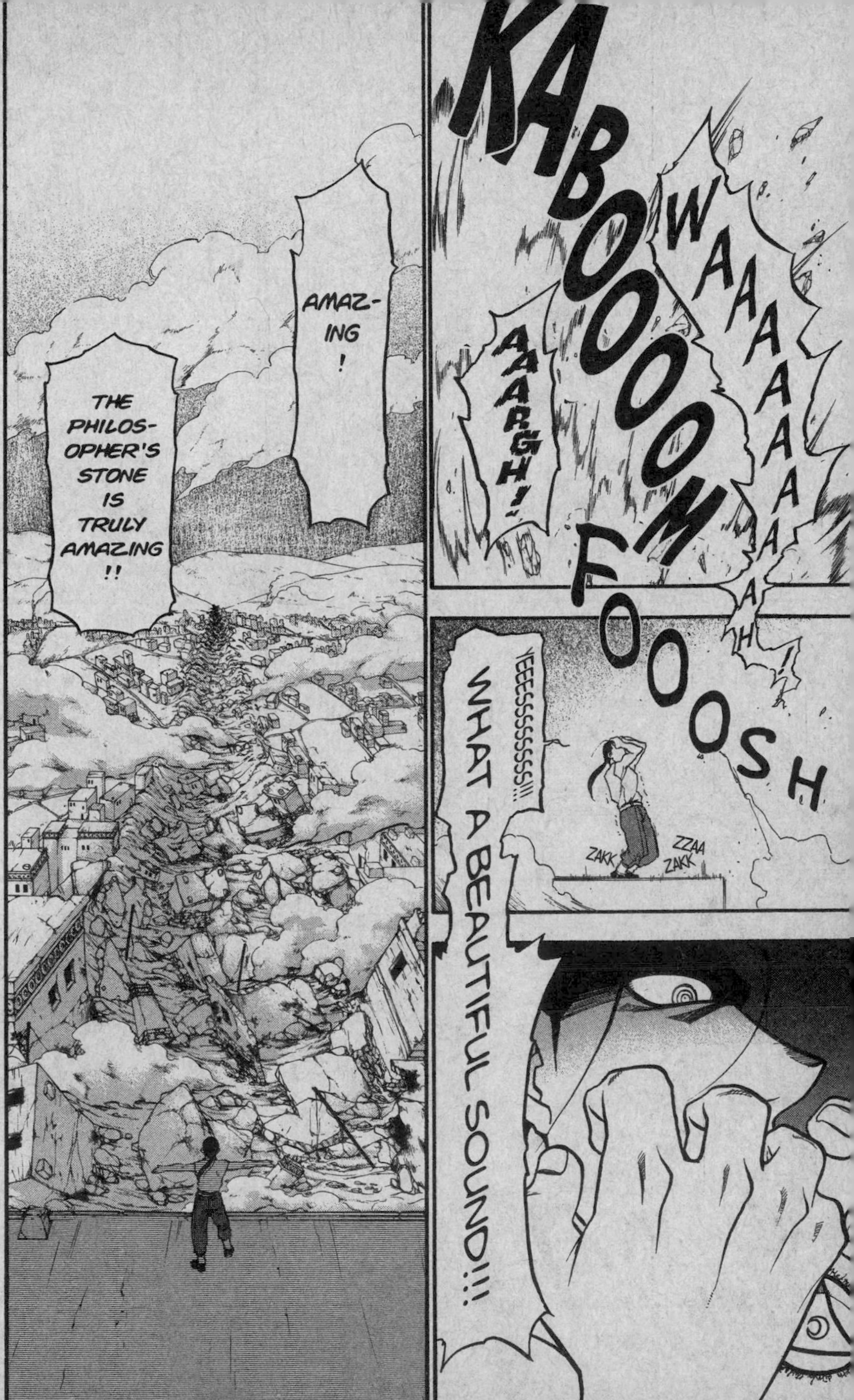
WAAAAAAAAAAH!
KABOOOOOM
AAARGH!!
FOOOOSH
YEEESSSSSSSS!!!
ZZAA
ZAKK
ZAKK
WHAT A BEAUTIFUL SOUND!!!
AMAZING!
THE PHILOSOPHER'S STONE IS TRULY AMAZING!!

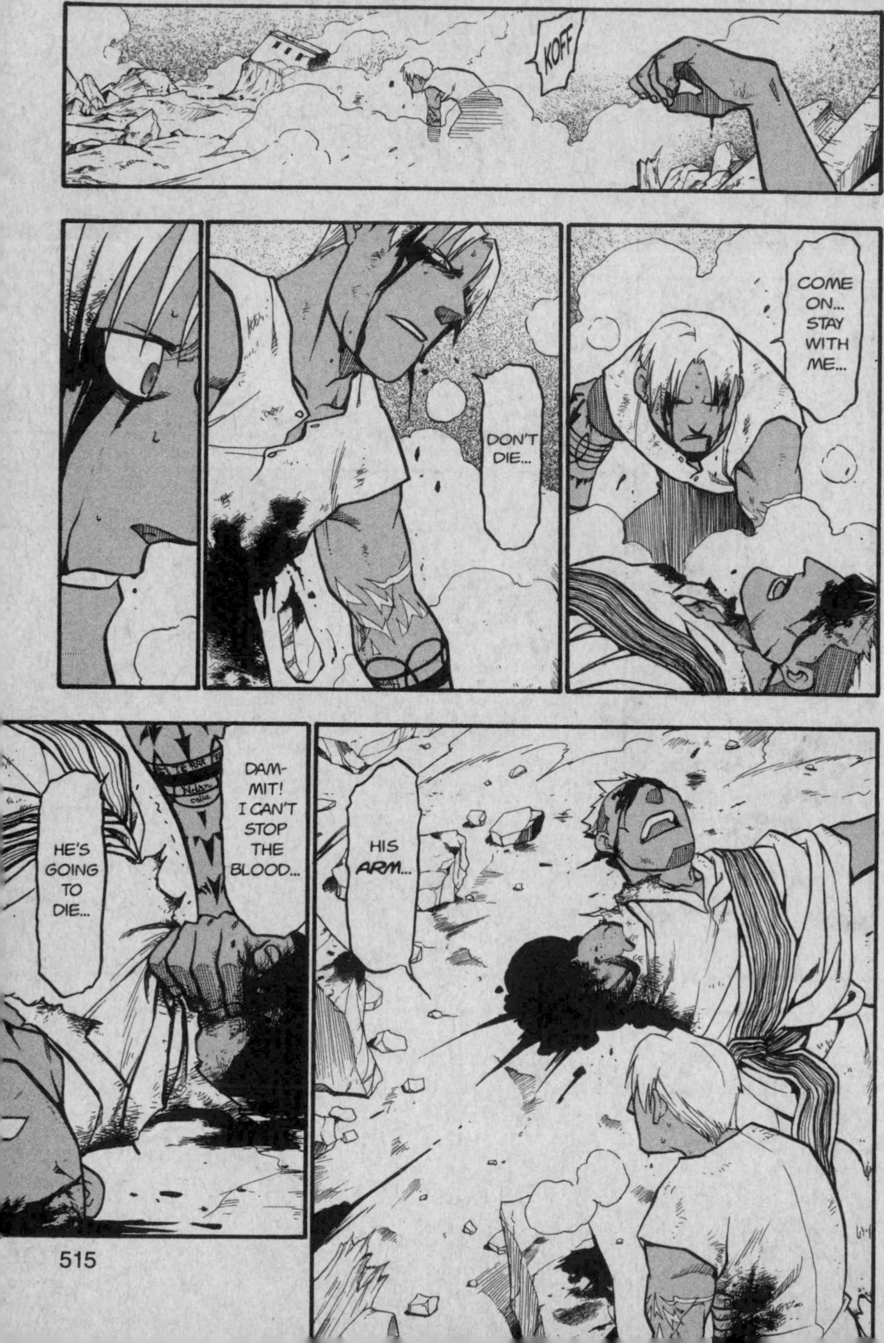
KOFF
COME ON... STAY WITH ME...
DON'T DIE...
HIS ARM...
DAM-MIT! I CAN'T STOP THE BLOOD...
HE'S GOING TO DIE...

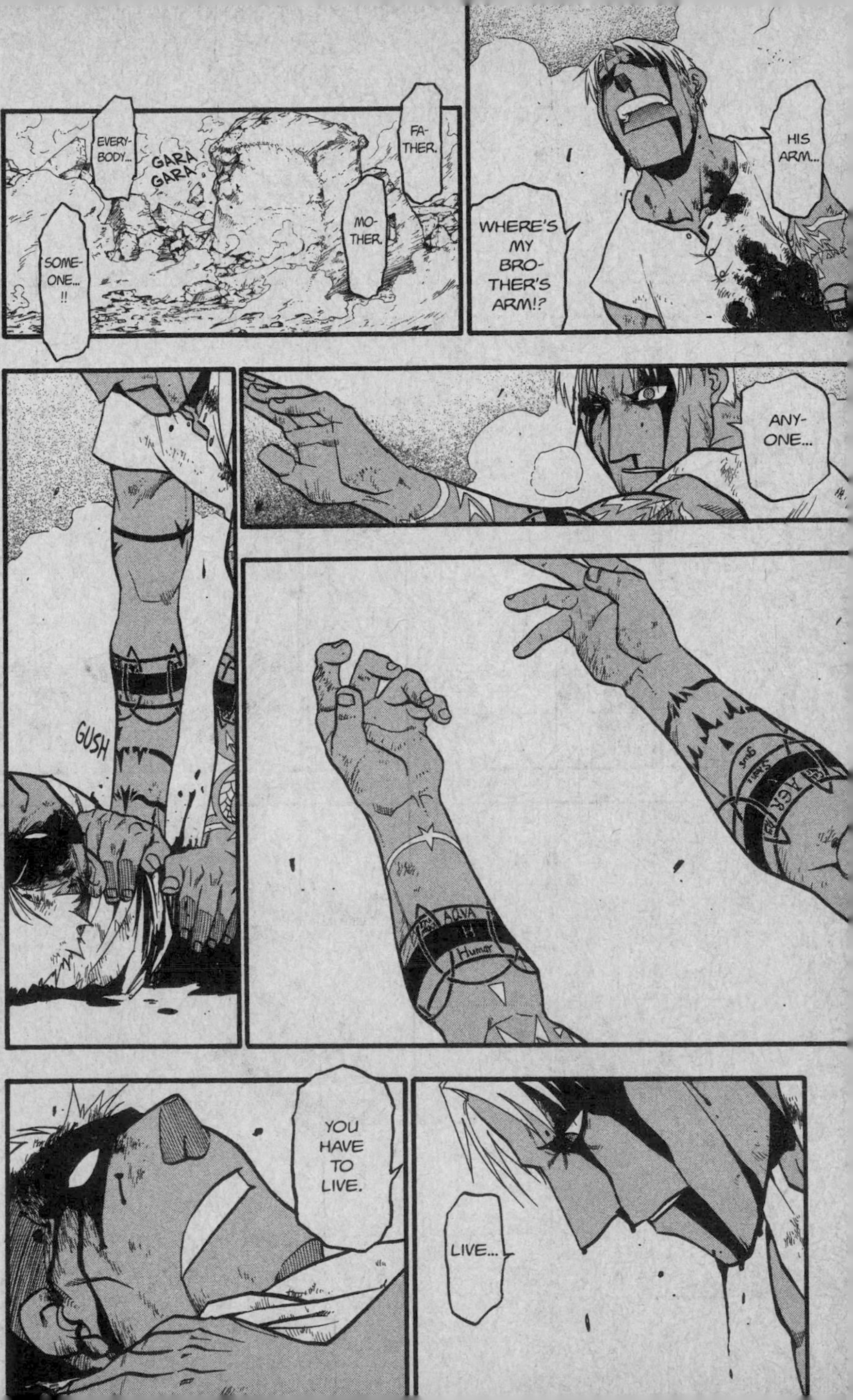
HIS ARM...
WHERE'S MY BROTHER'S ARM!?
FATHER.
MOTHER.
EVERYBODY...
GARA GARA
SOMEONE...!!
ANYONE...
GUSH
LIVE...
YOU HAVE TO LIVE.

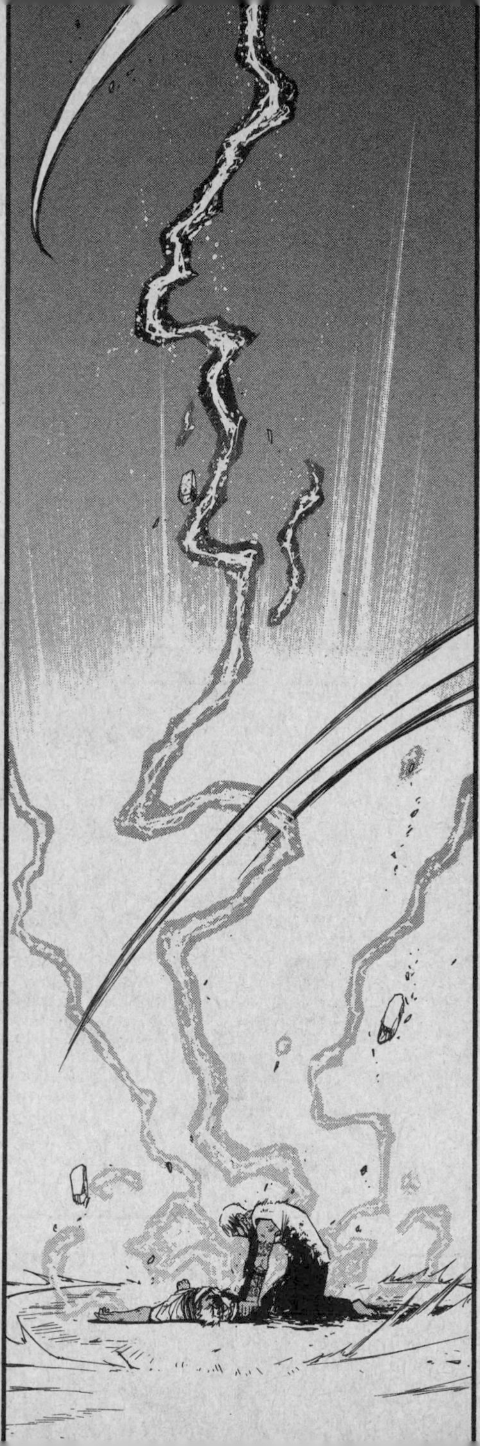

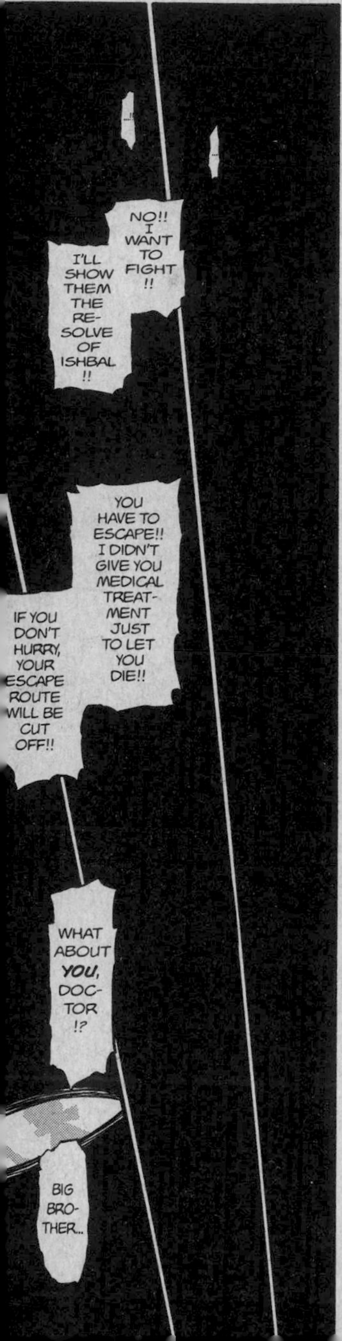
...
...!!
NO!! I WANT TO FIGHT!!
I'LL SHOW THEM THE RE-SOLVE OF ISHBAL!!
YOU HAVE TO ESCAPE!! I DIDN'T GIVE YOU MEDICAL TREAT-MENT JUST TO LET YOU DIE!!
IF YOU DON'T HURRY, YOUR ESCAPE ROUTE WILL BE CUT OFF!!
WHAT ABOUT YOU, DOCTOR!?
BIG BRO-THER...

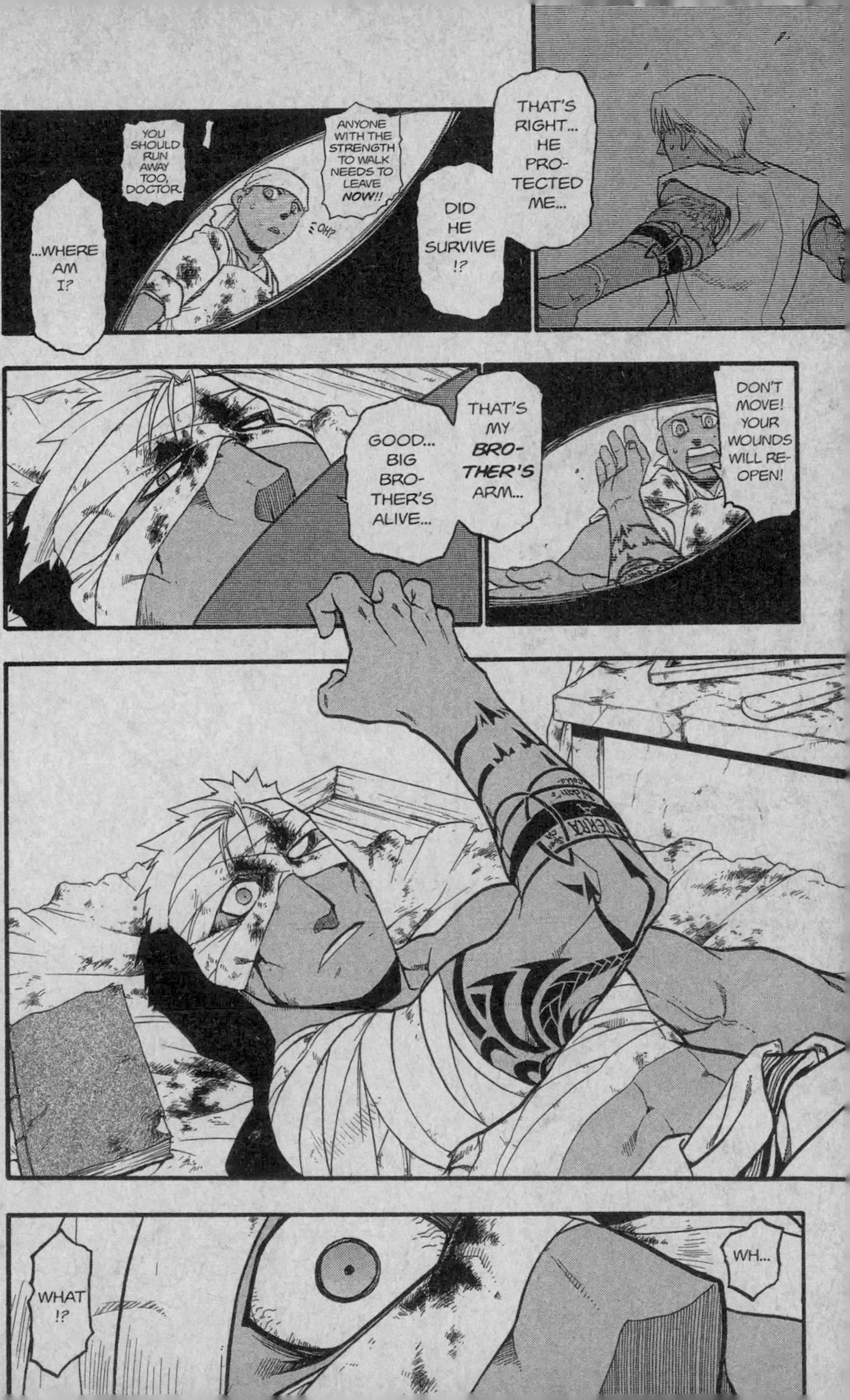
THAT'S RIGHT... HE PROTECTED ME...
DID HE SURVIVE !?
ANYONE WITH THE STRENGTH TO WALK NEEDS TO LEAVE *NOW*!!
YOU SHOULD RUN AWAY TOO, DOCTOR.
OH?
...WHERE AM I?
DON'T MOVE! YOUR WOUNDS WILL RE-OPEN!
THAT'S MY *BROTHER'S* ARM...
GOOD... BIG BROTHER'S ALIVE...
WH...
WHAT !?

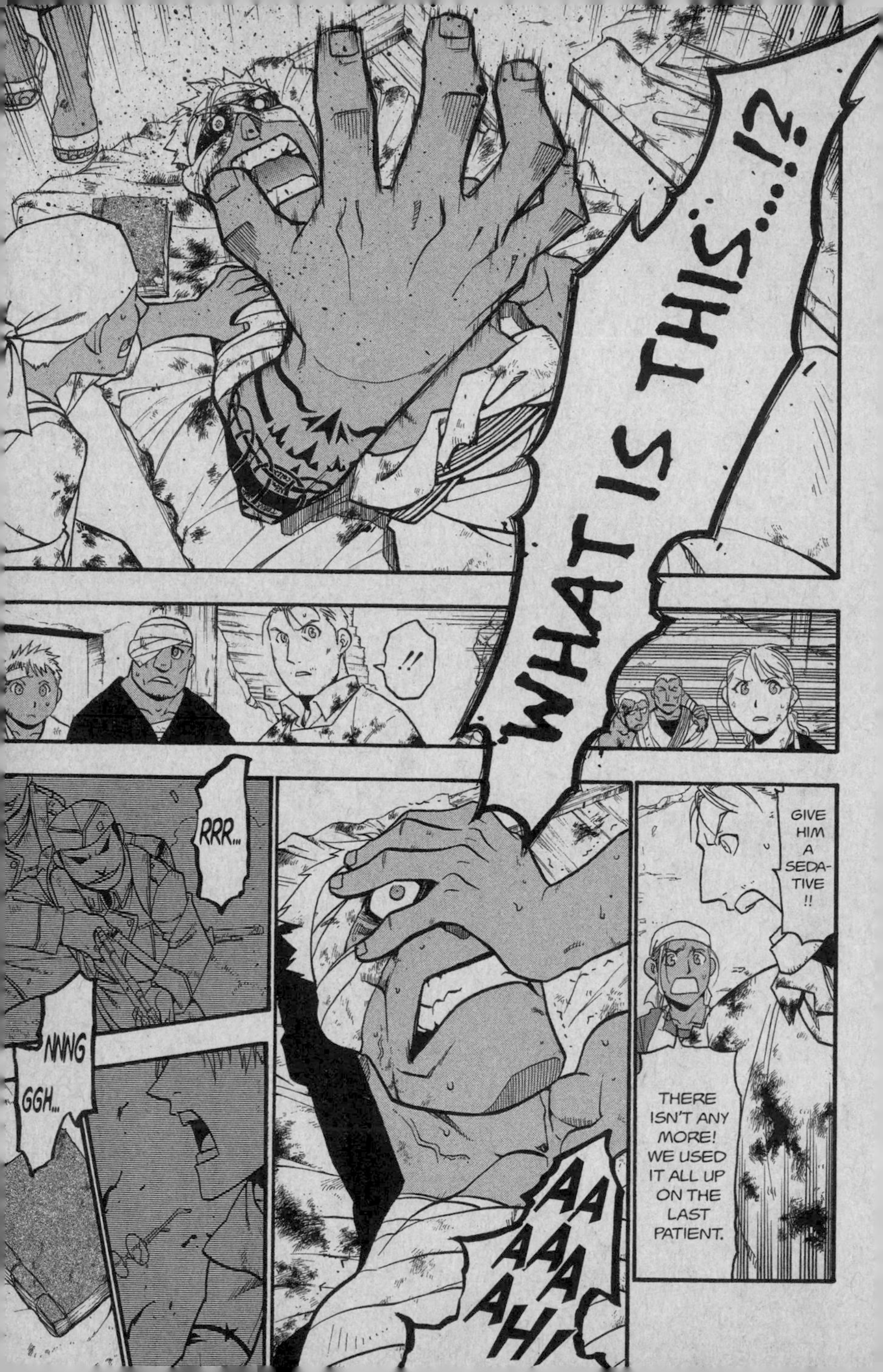
WHAT IS THIS...!?
!!
GIVE HIM A SEDATIVE!!
THERE ISN'T ANY MORE! WE USED IT ALL UP ON THE LAST PATIENT.
AAAAAAH!
RRR...
NNNGGGH...

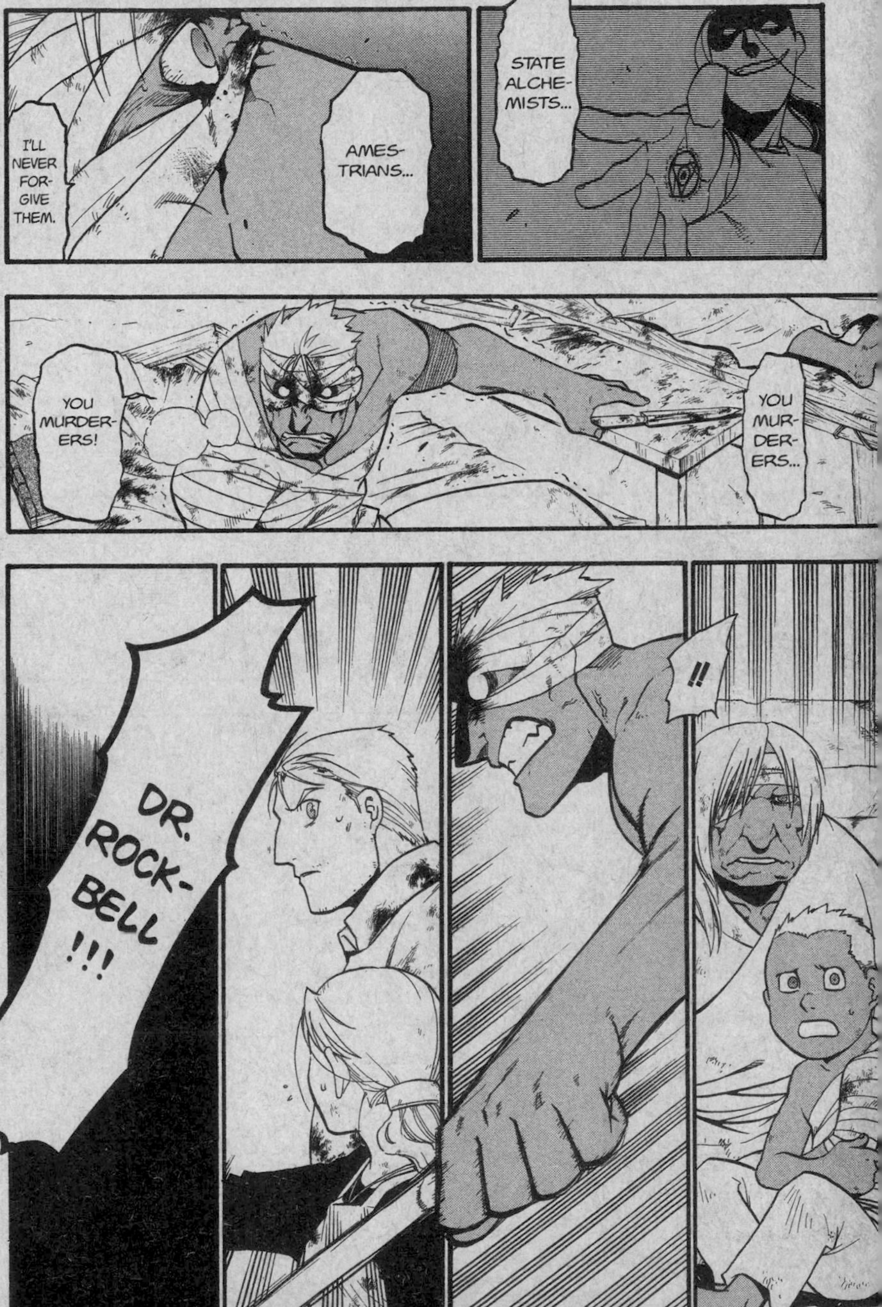
STATE ALCHE-MISTS...
AMES-TRIANS...
I'LL NEVER FOR-GIVE THEM.
YOU MUR-DER-ERS...
YOU MURDER-ERS!
!!
DR. ROCK-BELL!!!

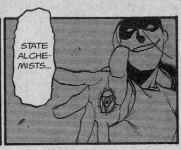

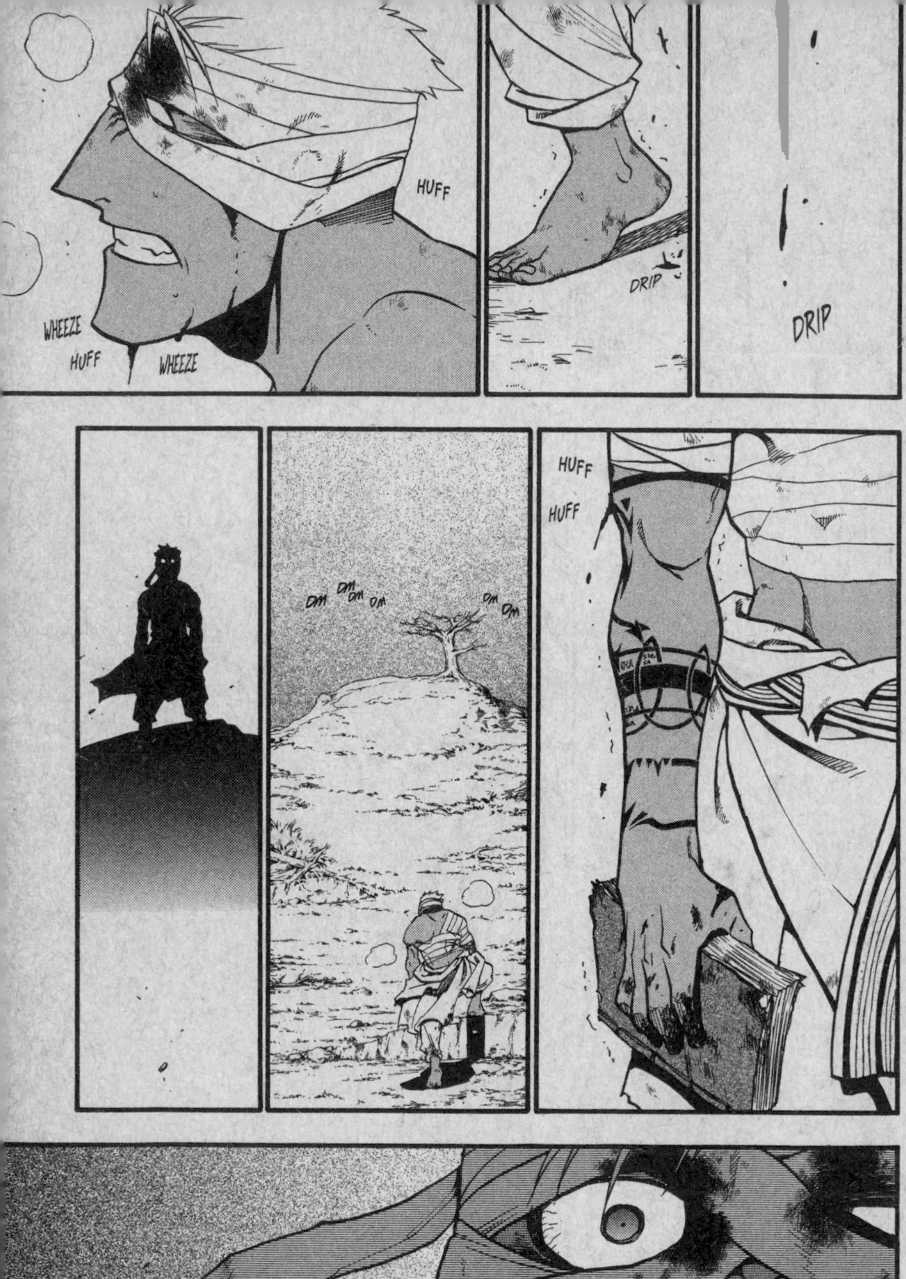
DRIP
DRIP
HUFF
WHEEZE
HUFF
WHEEZE
HUFF
HUFF
DM
DM
DM
DM
DM
DM

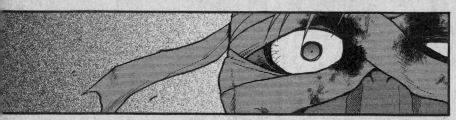

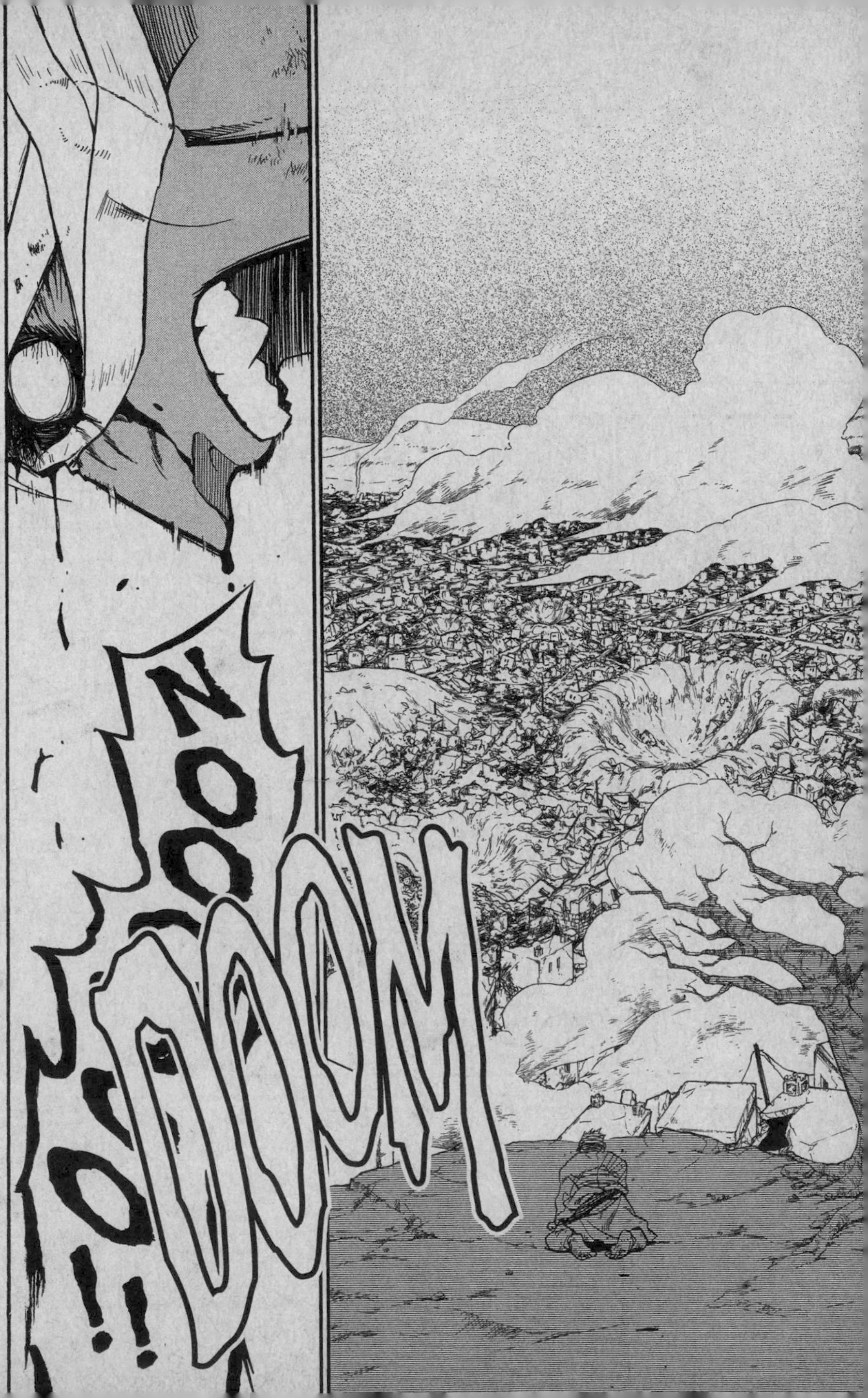
DOOOM
NOOO!!

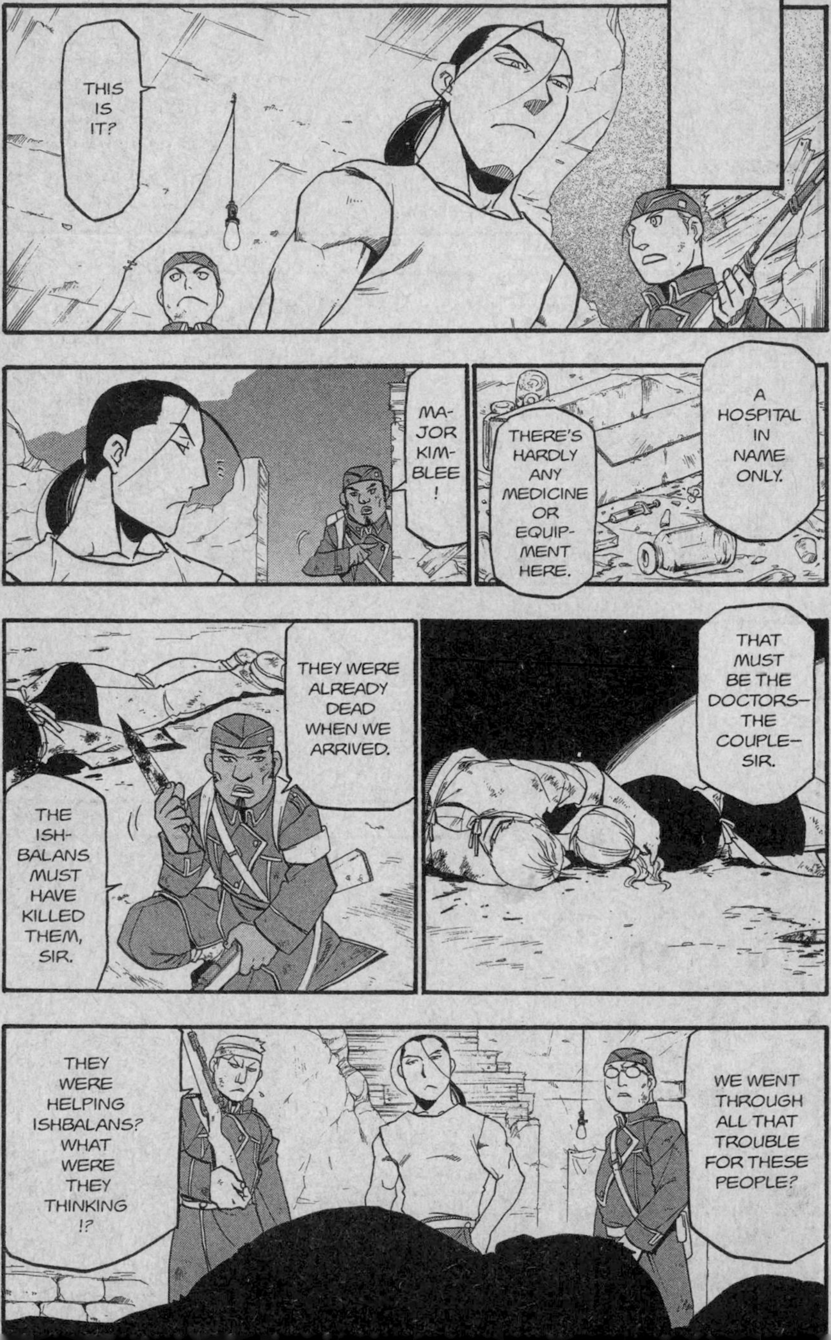
THIS IS IT?
A HOSPITAL IN NAME ONLY.
THERE'S HARDLY ANY MEDICINE OR EQUIPMENT HERE.
MAJOR KIMBLEE!
THAT MUST BE THE DOCTORS—THE COUPLE—SIR.
THEY WERE ALREADY DEAD WHEN WE ARRIVED.
THE ISHBALANS MUST HAVE KILLED THEM, SIR.
WE WENT THROUGH ALL THAT TROUBLE FOR THESE PEOPLE?
THEY WERE HELPING ISHBALANS? WHAT WERE THEY THINKING!?

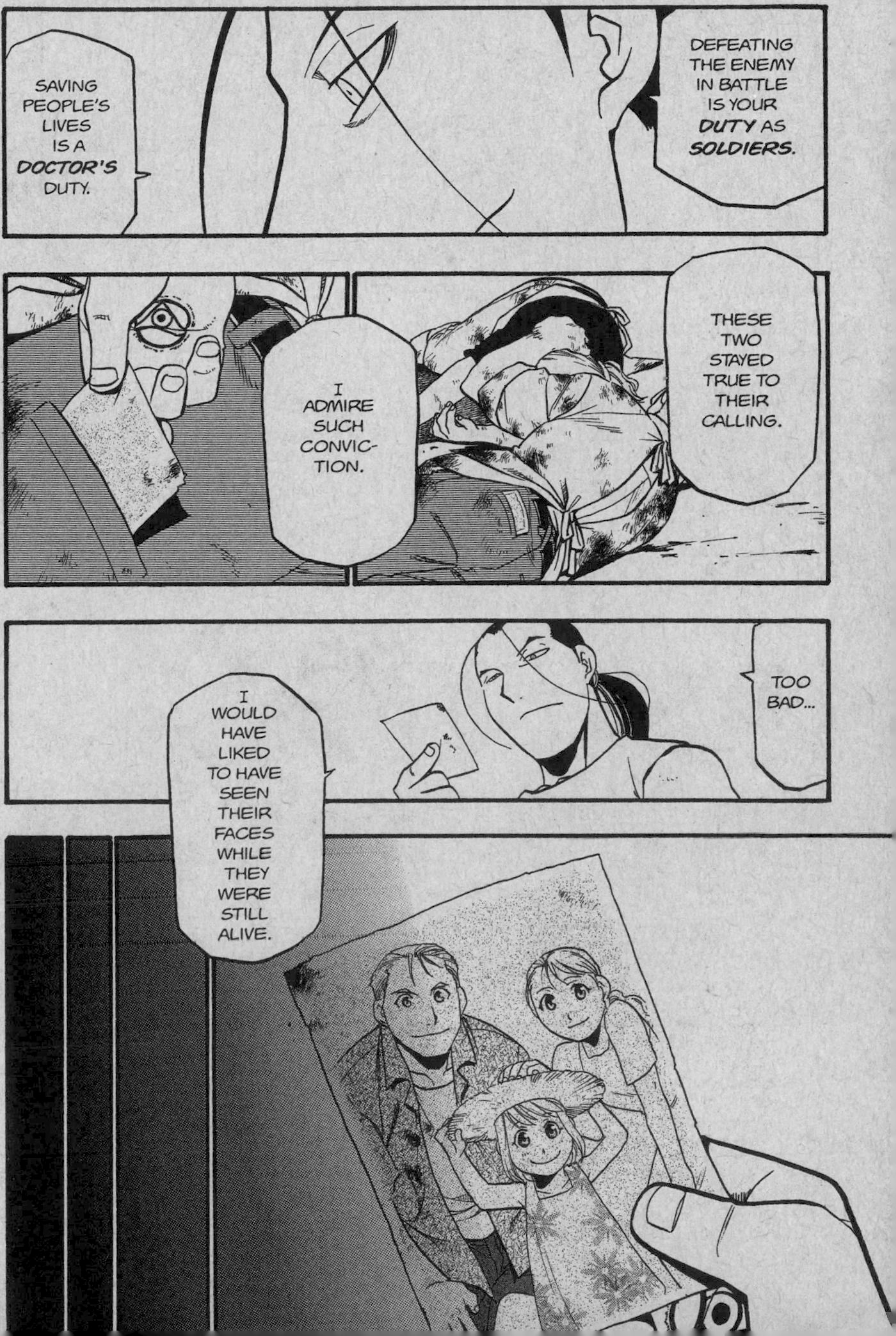
DEFEATING THE ENEMY IN BATTLE IS YOUR DUTY AS SOLDIERS.
SAVING PEOPLE'S LIVES IS A DOCTOR'S DUTY.
THESE TWO STAYED TRUE TO THEIR CALLING.
I ADMIRE SUCH CONVICTION.
TOO BAD...
I WOULD HAVE LIKED TO HAVE SEEN THEIR FACES WHILE THEY WERE STILL ALIVE.

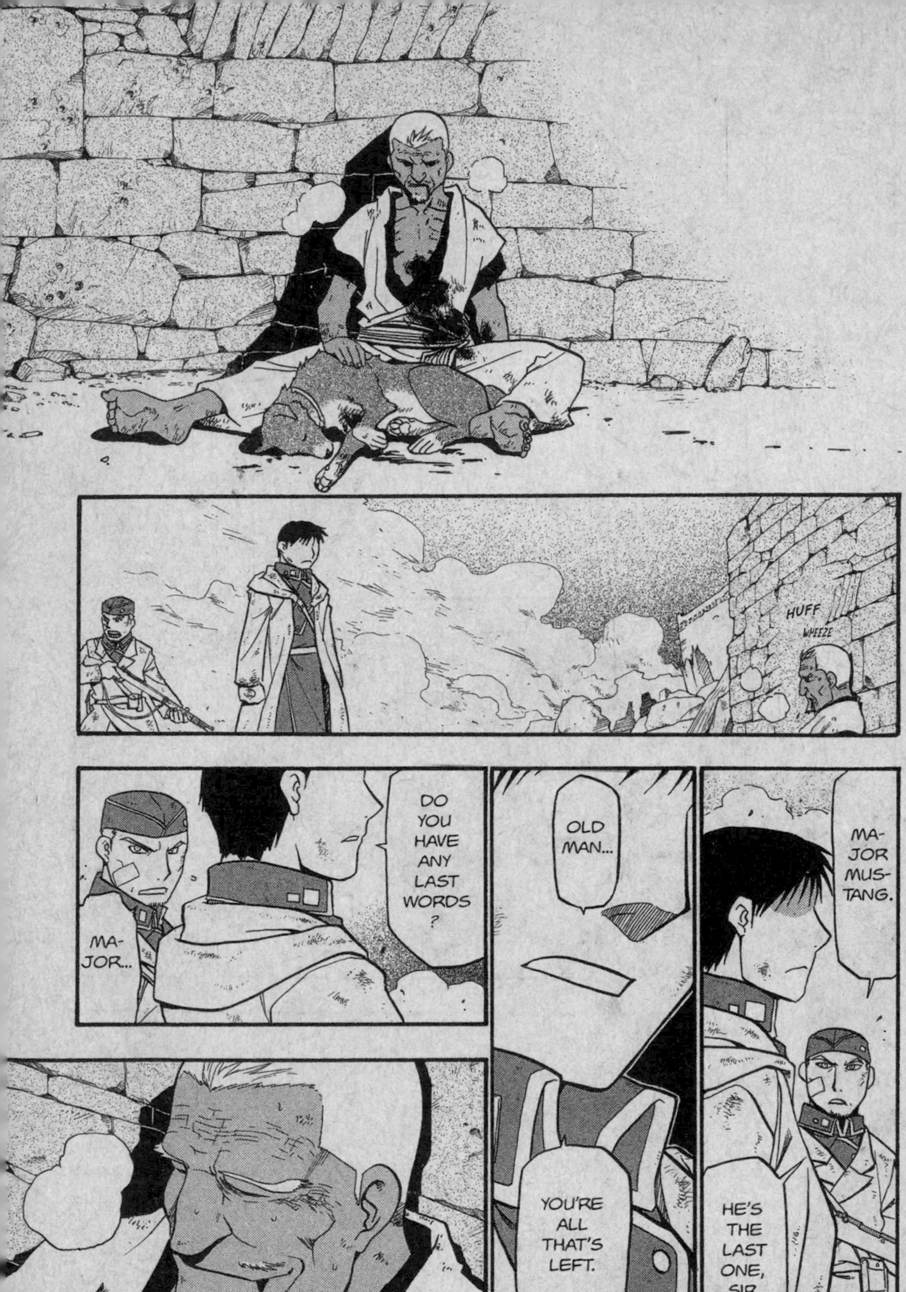
HUFF
WHEEZE
MAJOR MUSTANG.
HE'S THE LAST ONE, SIR.
OLD MAN...
YOU'RE ALL THAT'S LEFT.
DO YOU HAVE ANY LAST WORDS?
MAJOR...

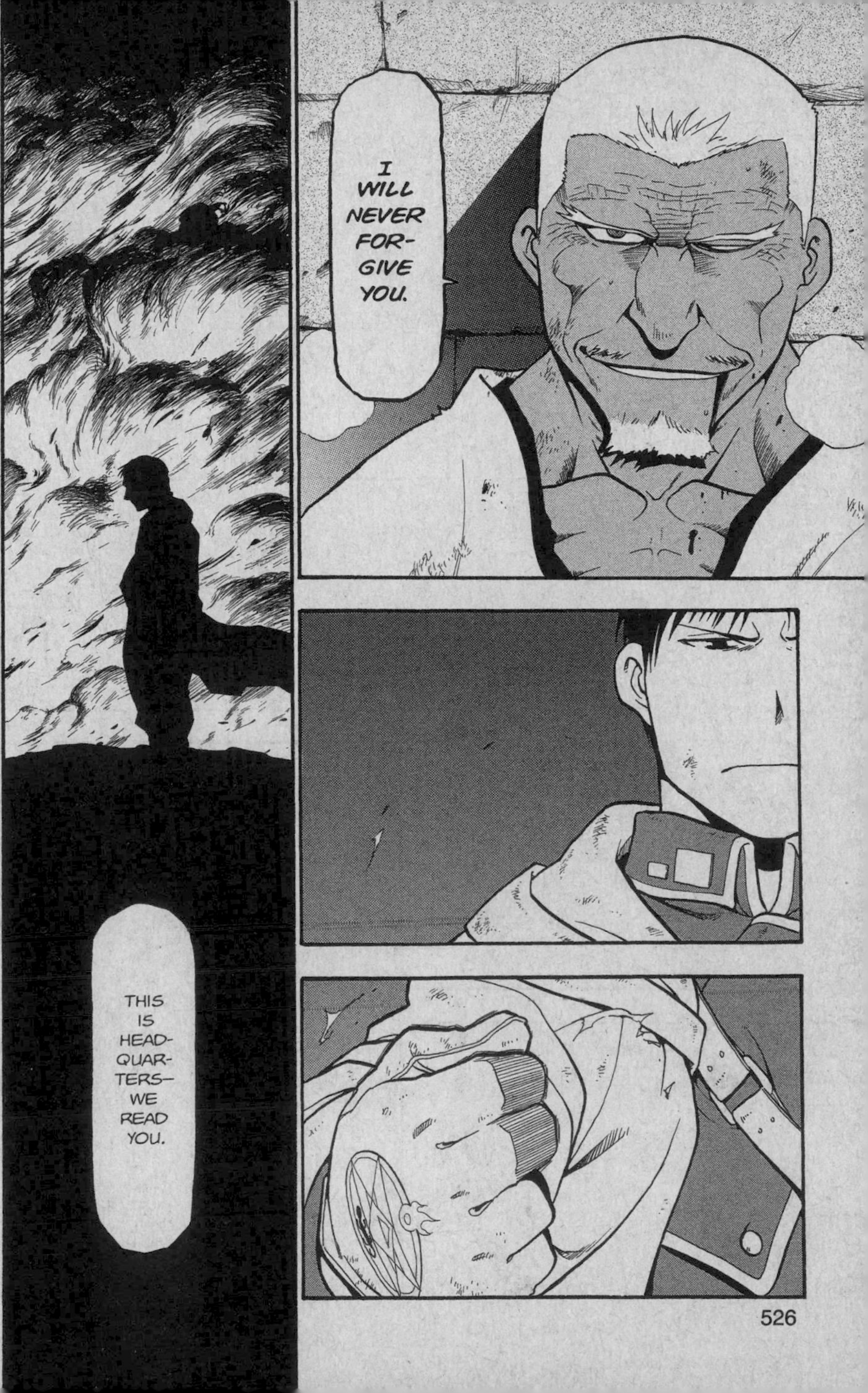
I WILL NEVER FOR-GIVE YOU.
THIS IS HEAD-QUARTERS—WE READ YOU.

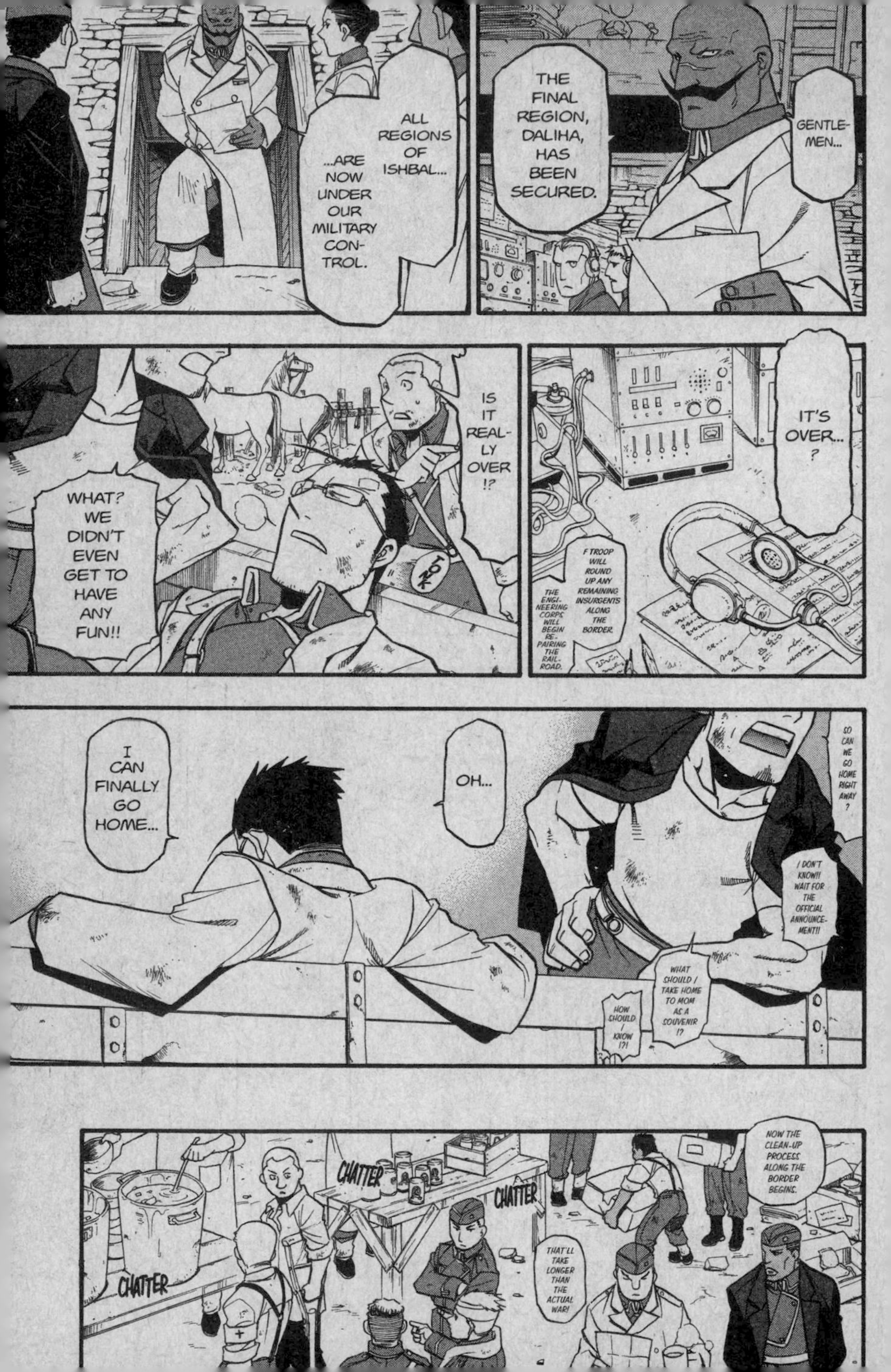
GENTLE-MEN...
THE FINAL REGION, DALIHA, HAS BEEN SECURED.
ALL REGIONS OF ISHBAL...
...ARE NOW UNDER OUR MILITARY CON-TROL.
IT'S OVER...?
F TROOP WILL ROUND UP ANY REMAINING INSURGENTS ALONG THE BORDER.
THE ENGI-NEERING CORPS WILL BEGIN RE-PAIRING THE RAIL-ROAD.
IS IT REAL-LY OVER!?
WHAT? WE DIDN'T EVEN GET TO HAVE ANY FUN!!
TONK
SO CAN WE GO HOME RIGHT AWAY?
I DON'T KNOW!! WAIT FOR THE OFFICIAL ANNOUNCE-MENT!!
WHAT SHOULD I TAKE HOME TO MOM AS A SOUVENIR!?
HOW SHOULD I KNOW!?!
OH...
I CAN FINALLY GO HOME...
NOW THE CLEAN-UP PROCESS ALONG THE BORDER BEGINS.
THAT'LL TAKE LONGER THAN THE ACTUAL WAR!
CHATTER
CHATTER
CHATTER

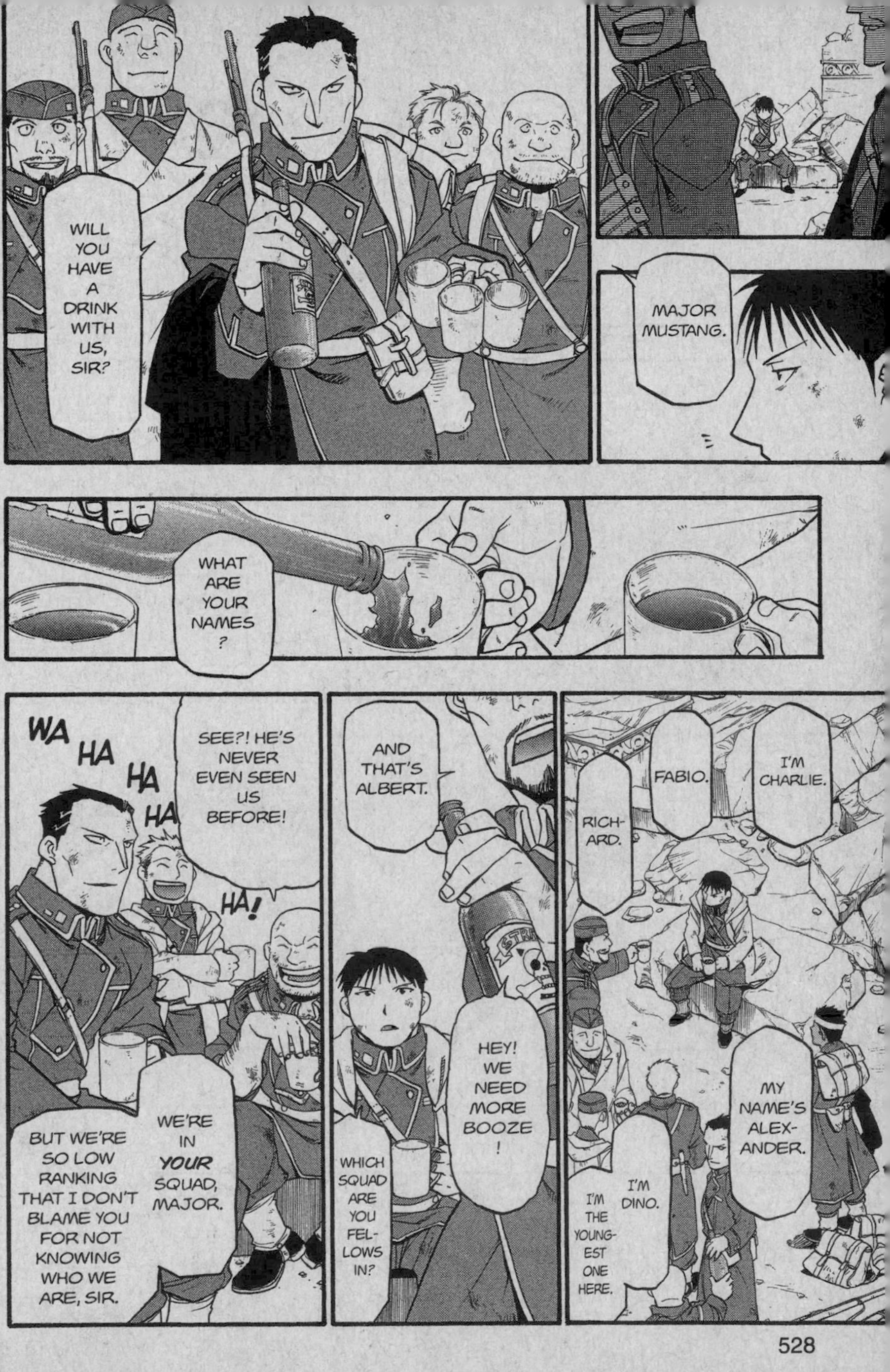
MAJOR MUSTANG.
WILL YOU HAVE A DRINK WITH US, SIR?
WHAT ARE YOUR NAMES?
I'M CHARLIE.
FABIO.
RICHARD.
MY NAME'S ALEXANDER.
I'M DINO.
I'M THE YOUNGEST ONE HERE.
AND THAT'S ALBERT.
HEY! WE NEED MORE BOOZE!
WHICH SQUAD ARE YOU FELLOWS IN?
SEE?! HE'S NEVER EVEN SEEN US BEFORE!
WA HA HA HA HA!
WE'RE IN *YOUR* SQUAD, MAJOR.
BUT WE'RE SO LOW RANKING THAT I DON'T BLAME YOU FOR NOT KNOWING WHO WE ARE, SIR.

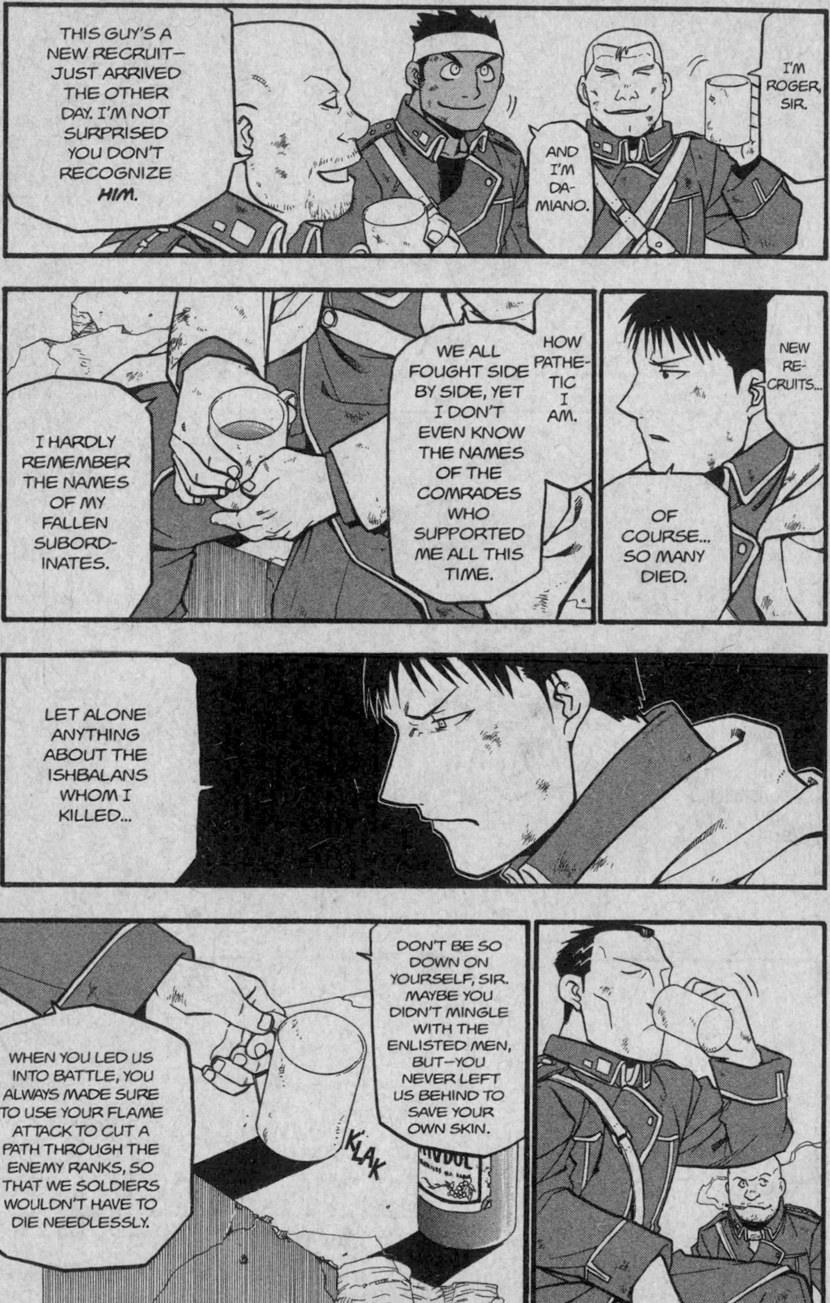
I'M ROGER, SIR.
AND I'M DAMIANO.
THIS GUY'S A NEW RECRUIT—JUST ARRIVED THE OTHER DAY. I'M NOT SURPRISED YOU DON'T RECOGNIZE *HIM.*
NEW RECRUITS...
OF COURSE... SO MANY DIED.
HOW PATHETIC I AM.
WE ALL FOUGHT SIDE BY SIDE, YET I DON'T EVEN KNOW THE NAMES OF THE COMRADES WHO SUPPORTED ME ALL THIS TIME.
I HARDLY REMEMBER THE NAMES OF MY FALLEN SUBORDINATES.
LET ALONE ANYTHING ABOUT THE ISHBALANS WHOM I KILLED...
DON'T BE SO DOWN ON YOURSELF, SIR. MAYBE YOU DIDN'T MINGLE WITH THE ENLISTED MEN, BUT—YOU NEVER LEFT US BEHIND TO SAVE YOUR OWN SKIN.
KLAK
WHEN YOU LED US INTO BATTLE, YOU ALWAYS MADE SURE TO USE YOUR FLAME ATTACK TO CUT A PATH THROUGH THE ENEMY RANKS, SO THAT WE SOLDIERS WOULDN'T HAVE TO DIE NEEDLESSLY.

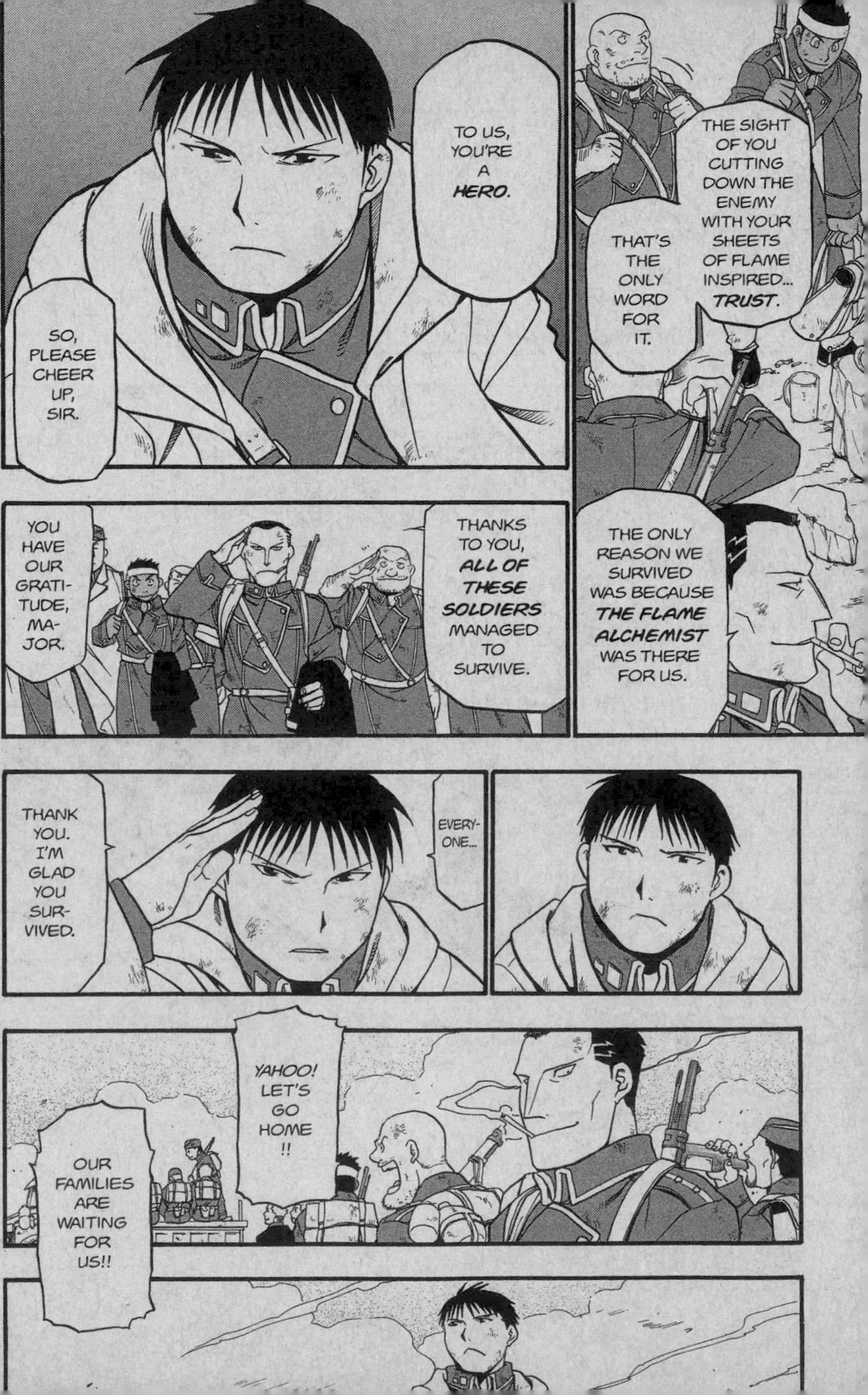
THE SIGHT OF YOU CUTTING DOWN THE ENEMY WITH YOUR SHEETS OF FLAME INSPIRED... TRUST.
THAT'S THE ONLY WORD FOR IT.
TO US, YOU'RE A HERO.
SO, PLEASE CHEER UP, SIR.
THE ONLY REASON WE SURVIVED WAS BECAUSE THE FLAME ALCHEMIST WAS THERE FOR US.
THANKS TO YOU, ALL OF THESE SOLDIERS MANAGED TO SURVIVE.
YOU HAVE OUR GRATITUDE, MAJOR.
EVERYONE...
THANK YOU. I'M GLAD YOU SURVIVED.
YAHOO! LET'S GO HOME!!
OUR FAMILIES ARE WAITING FOR US!!

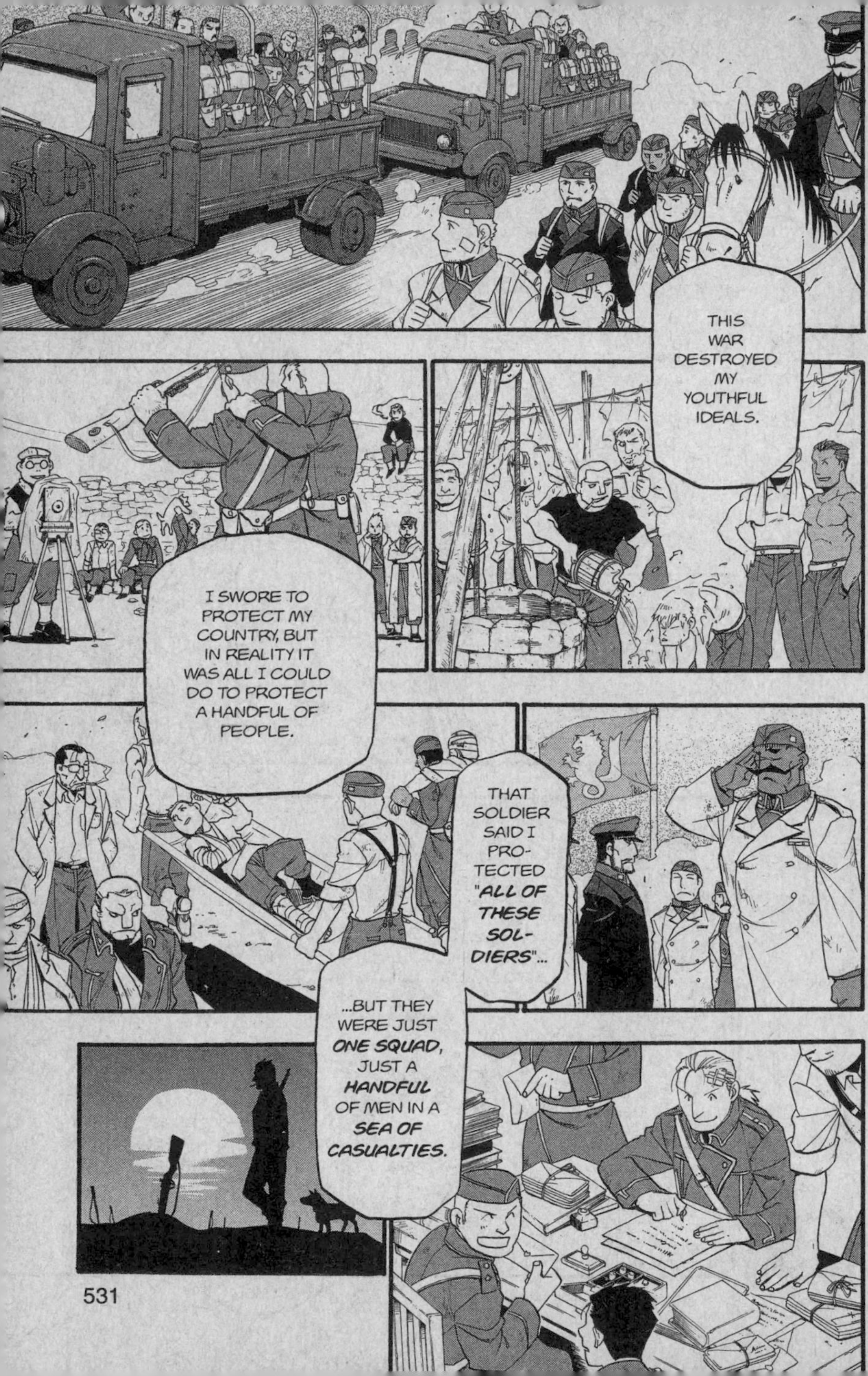
THIS WAR DESTROYED MY YOUTHFUL IDEALS.
I SWORE TO PROTECT MY COUNTRY, BUT IN REALITY IT WAS ALL I COULD DO TO PROTECT A HANDFUL OF PEOPLE.
THAT SOLDIER SAID I PRO-TECTED "ALL OF THESE SOL-DIERS"...
...BUT THEY WERE JUST ONE SQUAD, JUST A HANDFUL OF MEN IN A SEA OF CASUALTIES.

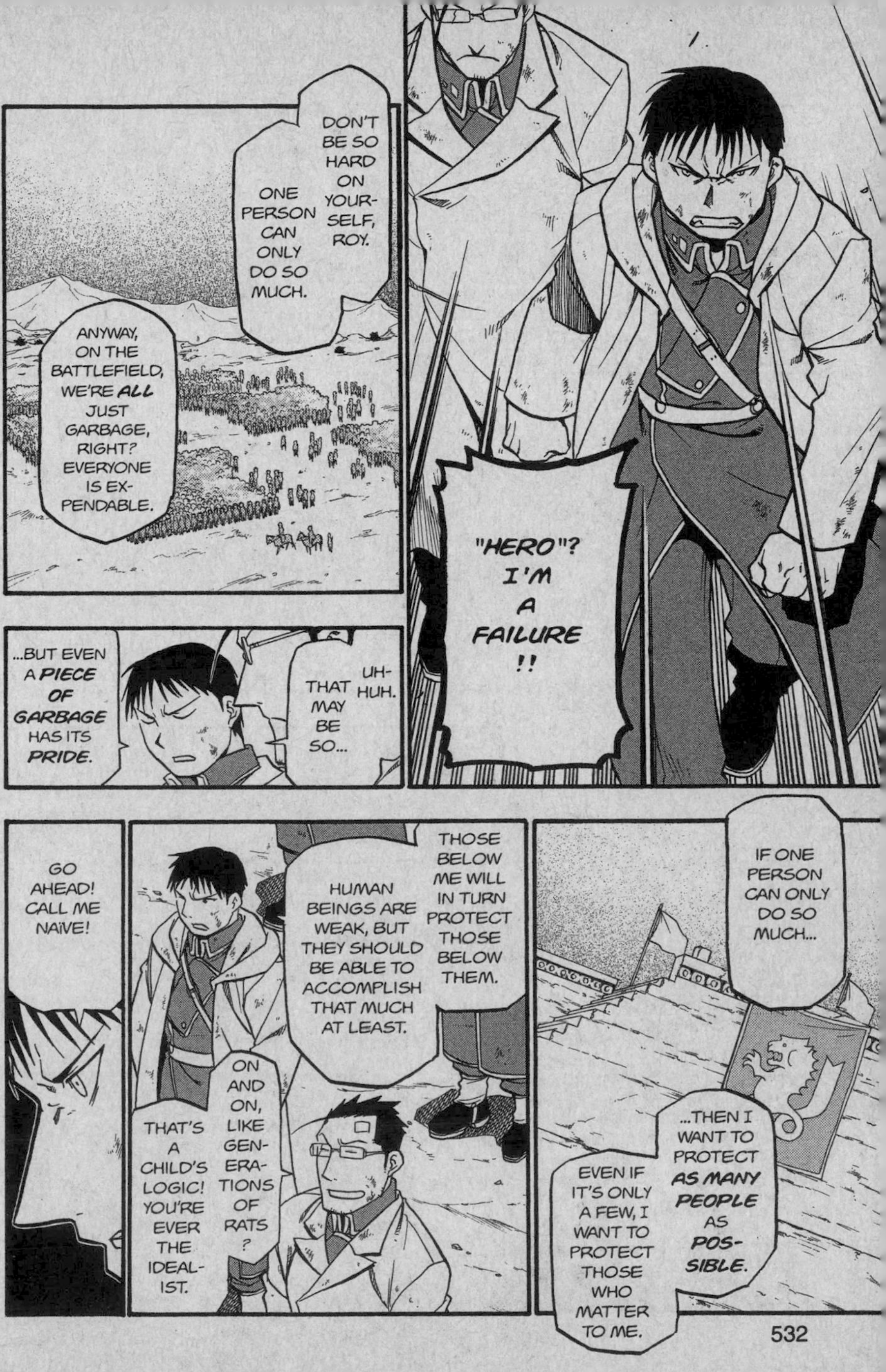
"HERO"? I'M A FAILURE!!
DON'T BE SO HARD ON YOURSELF, ROY.
ONE PERSON CAN ONLY DO SO MUCH.
ANYWAY, ON THE BATTLEFIELD, WE'RE ALL JUST GARBAGE, RIGHT? EVERYONE IS EXPENDABLE.
UH-HUH.
THAT MAY BE SO...
...BUT EVEN A PIECE OF GARBAGE HAS ITS PRIDE.
IF ONE PERSON CAN ONLY DO SO MUCH...
...THEN I WANT TO PROTECT AS MANY PEOPLE AS POSSIBLE.
EVEN IF IT'S ONLY A FEW, I WANT TO PROTECT THOSE WHO MATTER TO ME.
THOSE BELOW ME WILL IN TURN PROTECT THOSE BELOW THEM.
HUMAN BEINGS ARE WEAK, BUT THEY SHOULD BE ABLE TO ACCOMPLISH THAT MUCH AT LEAST.
ON AND ON, LIKE GENERATIONS OF RATS?
THAT'S A CHILD'S LOGIC! YOU'RE EVER THE IDEALIST.
GO AHEAD! CALL ME NAÏVE!

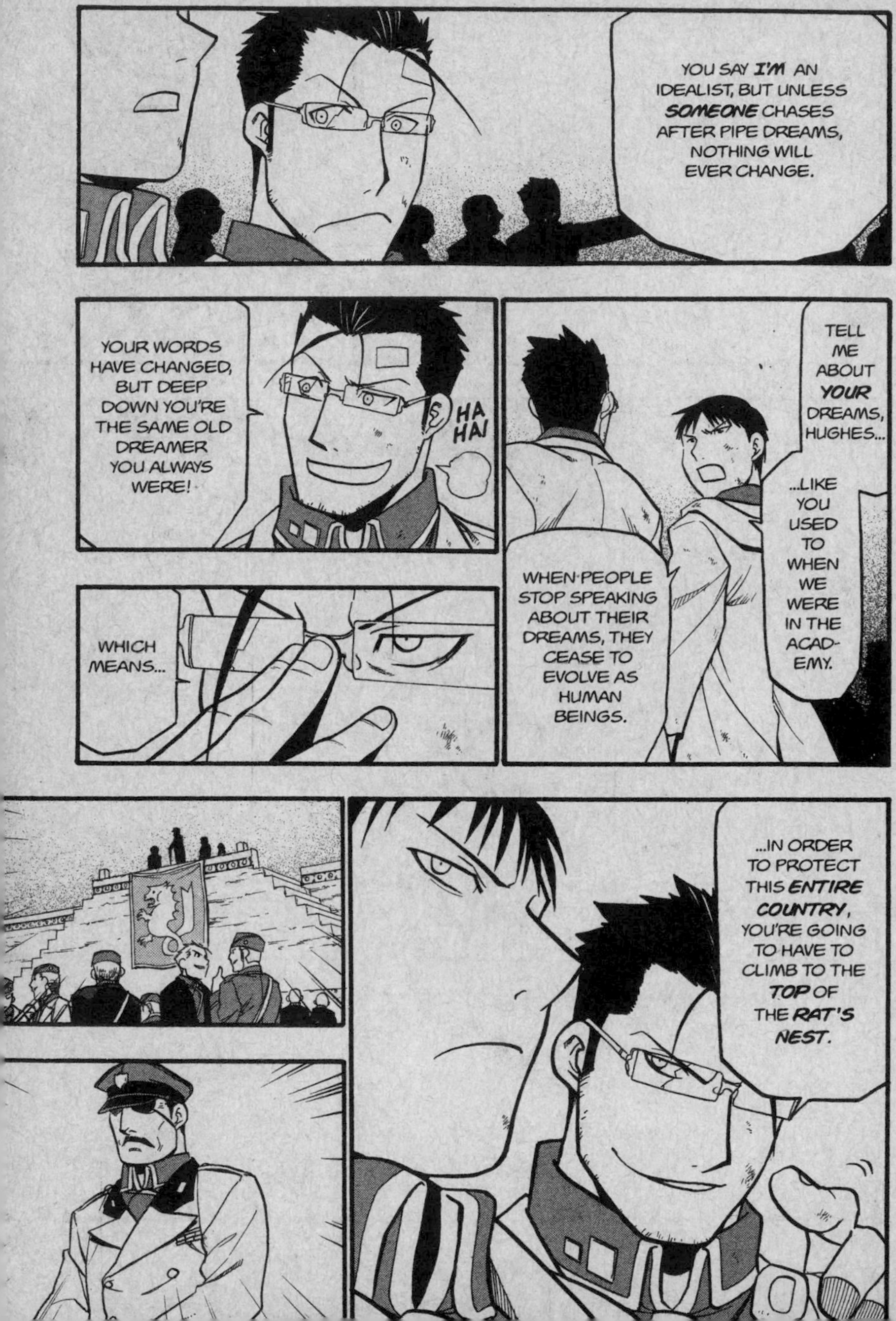
YOU SAY I'M AN IDEALIST, BUT UNLESS SOMEONE CHASES AFTER PIPE DREAMS, NOTHING WILL EVER CHANGE.
TELL ME ABOUT YOUR DREAMS, HUGHES...
...LIKE YOU USED TO WHEN WE WERE IN THE ACAD-EMY.
WHEN PEOPLE STOP SPEAKING ABOUT THEIR DREAMS, THEY CEASE TO EVOLVE AS HUMAN BEINGS.
YOUR WORDS HAVE CHANGED, BUT DEEP DOWN YOU'RE THE SAME OLD DREAMER YOU ALWAYS WERE!
HA HA!
WHICH MEANS...
...IN ORDER TO PROTECT THIS ENTIRE COUNTRY, YOU'RE GOING TO HAVE TO CLIMB TO THE TOP OF THE RAT'S NEST.

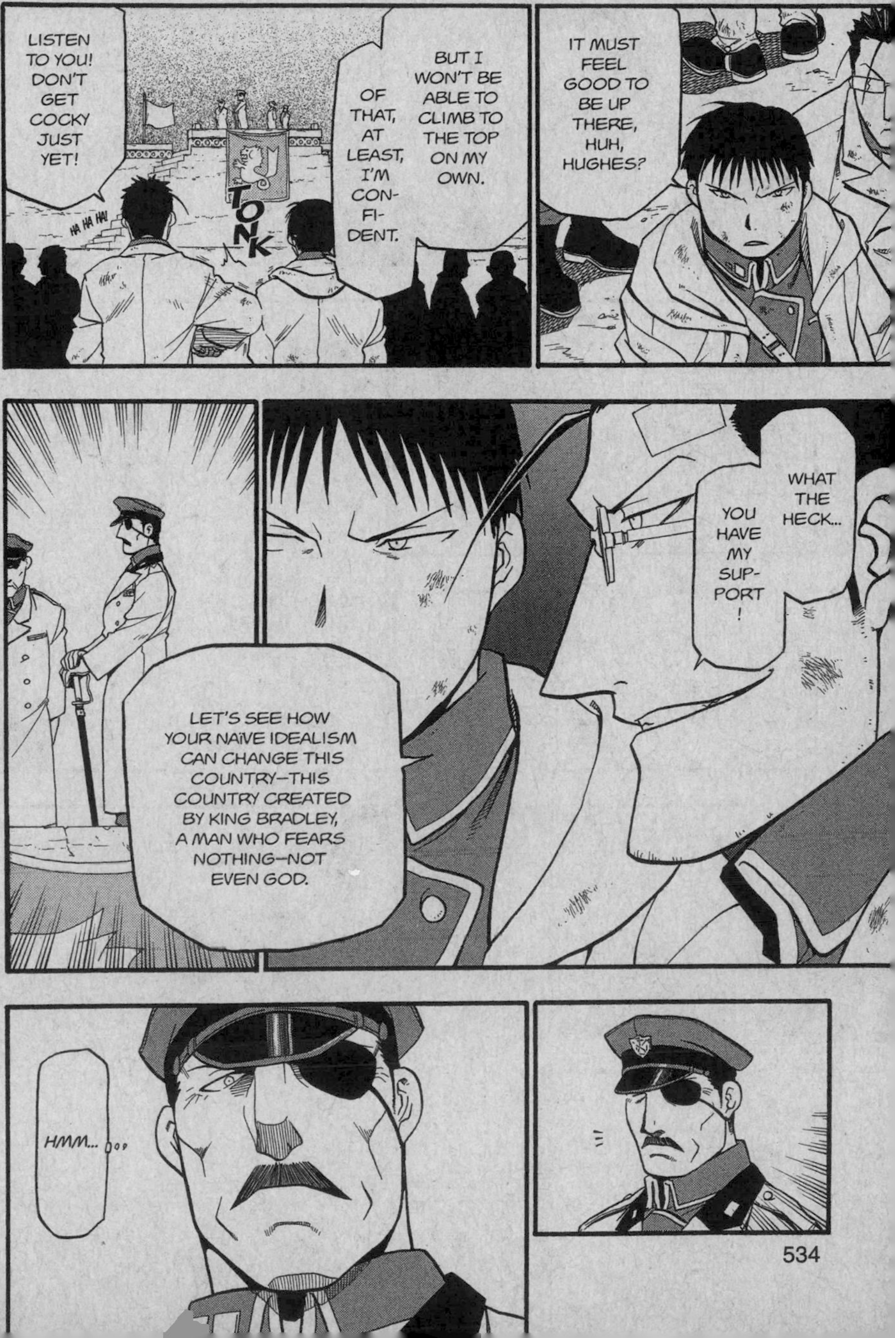
IT MUST FEEL GOOD TO BE UP THERE, HUH, HUGHES?
BUT I WON'T BE ABLE TO CLIMB TO THE TOP ON MY OWN.
OF THAT, AT LEAST, I'M CON-FI-DENT.
TONK
LISTEN TO YOU! DON'T GET COCKY JUST YET!
HA HA HA!
WHAT THE HECK...
YOU HAVE MY SUP-PORT!
LET'S SEE HOW YOUR NAïVE IDEALISM CAN CHANGE THIS COUNTRY—THIS COUNTRY CREATED BY KING BRADLEY, A MAN WHO FEARS NOTHING—NOT EVEN GOD.
HMM...

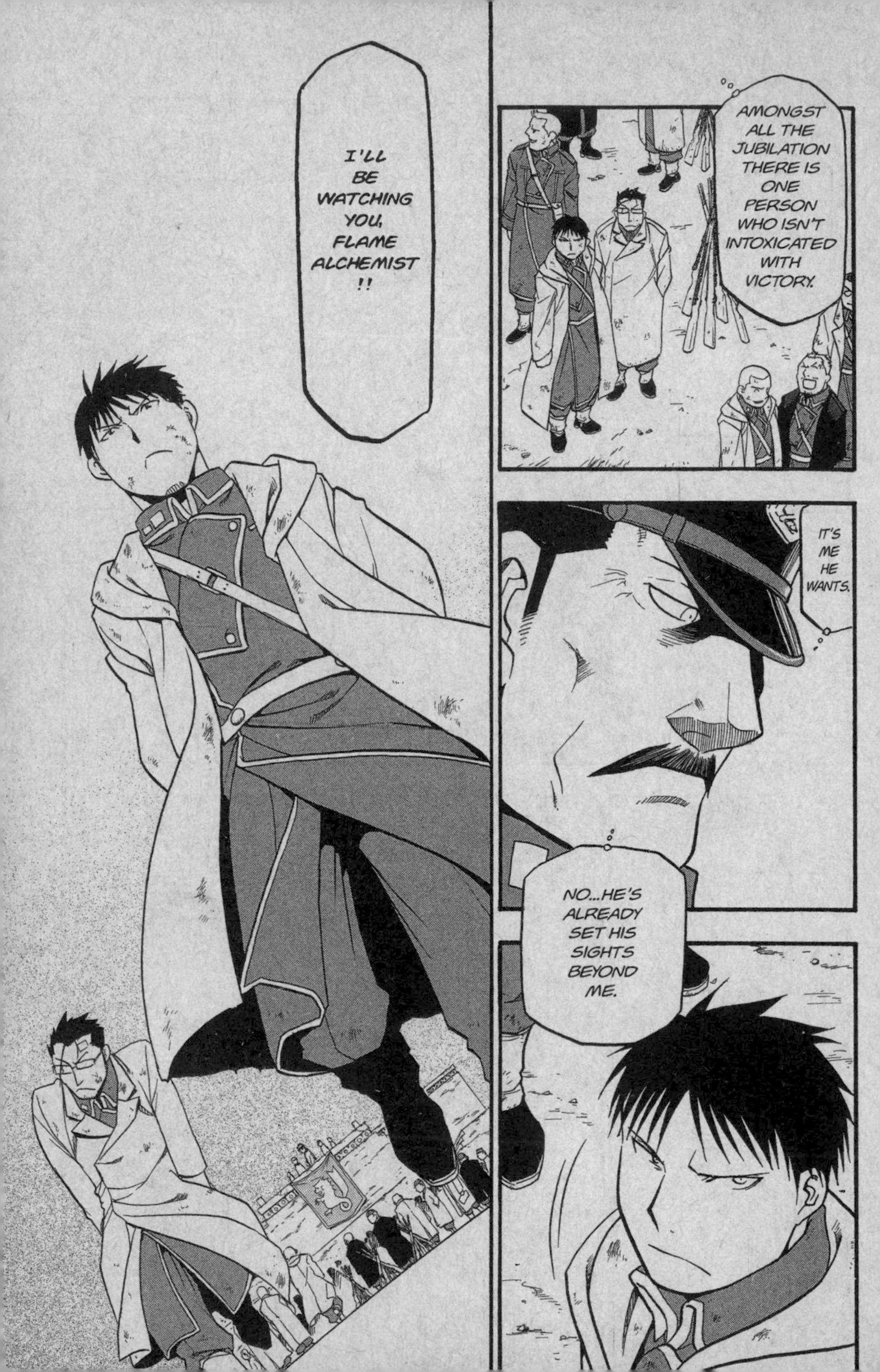
AMONGST ALL THE JUBILATION THERE IS ONE PERSON WHO ISN'T INTOXICATED WITH VICTORY.
IT'S ME HE WANTS.
NO...HE'S ALREADY SET HIS SIGHTS BEYOND ME.
I'LL BE WATCHING YOU, FLAME ALCHEMIST !!

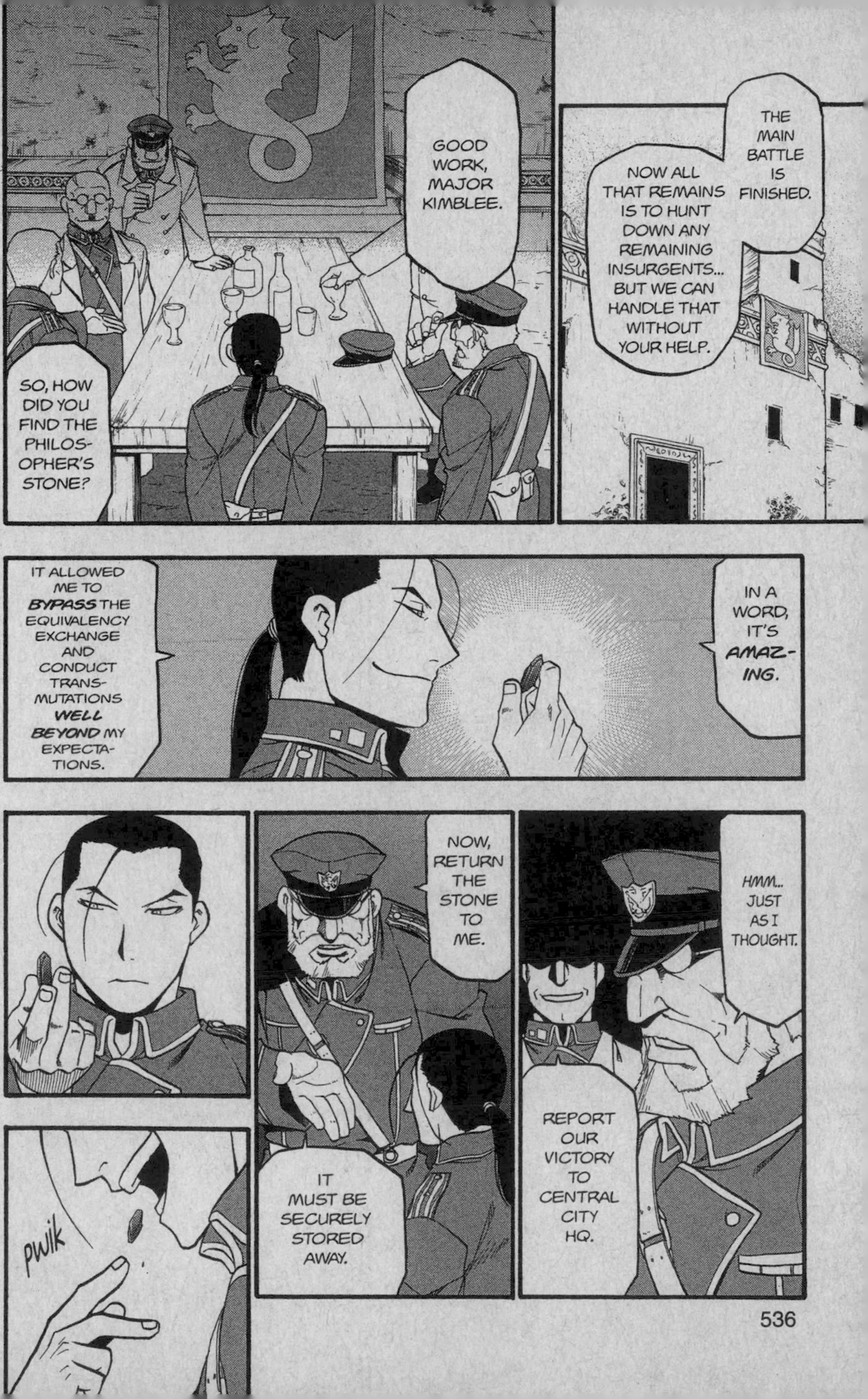
THE MAIN BATTLE IS FINISHED.
NOW ALL THAT REMAINS IS TO HUNT DOWN ANY REMAINING INSURGENTS... BUT WE CAN HANDLE THAT WITHOUT YOUR HELP.
GOOD WORK, MAJOR KIMBLEE.
SO, HOW DID YOU FIND THE PHILOS-OPHER'S STONE?
IN A WORD, IT'S AMAZ-ING.
IT ALLOWED ME TO BYPASS THE EQUIVALENCY EXCHANGE AND CONDUCT TRANS-MUTATIONS WELL BEYOND MY EXPECTA-TIONS.
HMM... JUST AS I THOUGHT.
REPORT OUR VICTORY TO CENTRAL CITY HQ.
NOW, RETURN THE STONE TO ME.
IT MUST BE SECURELY STORED AWAY.
pwik

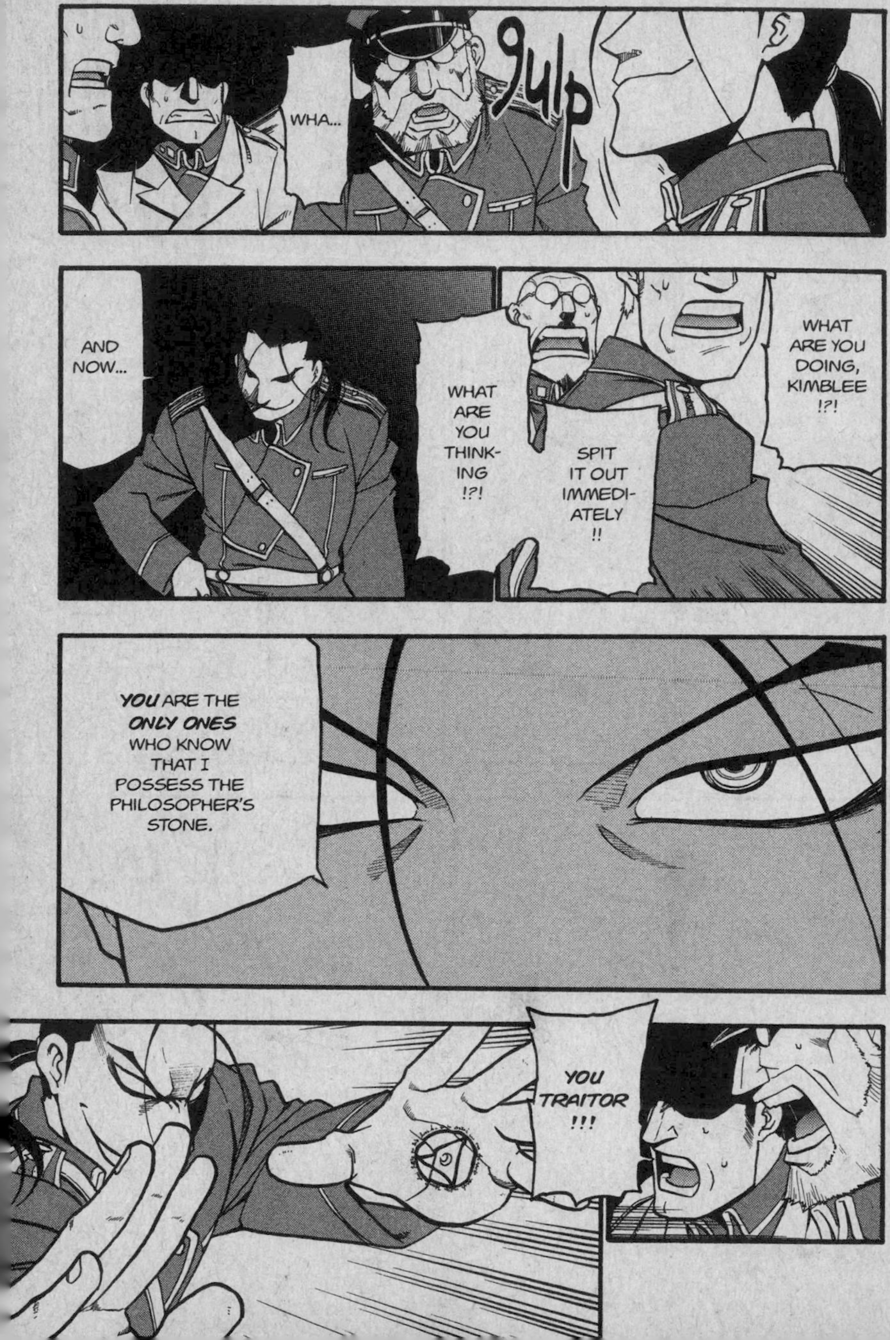
gulp
WHA...
WHAT ARE YOU DOING, KIMBLEE !?!
WHAT ARE YOU THINKING !?!
SPIT IT OUT IMMEDIATELY !!
AND NOW...
YOU ARE THE ONLY ONES WHO KNOW THAT I POSSESS THE PHILOSOPHER'S STONE.
YOU TRAITOR !!!

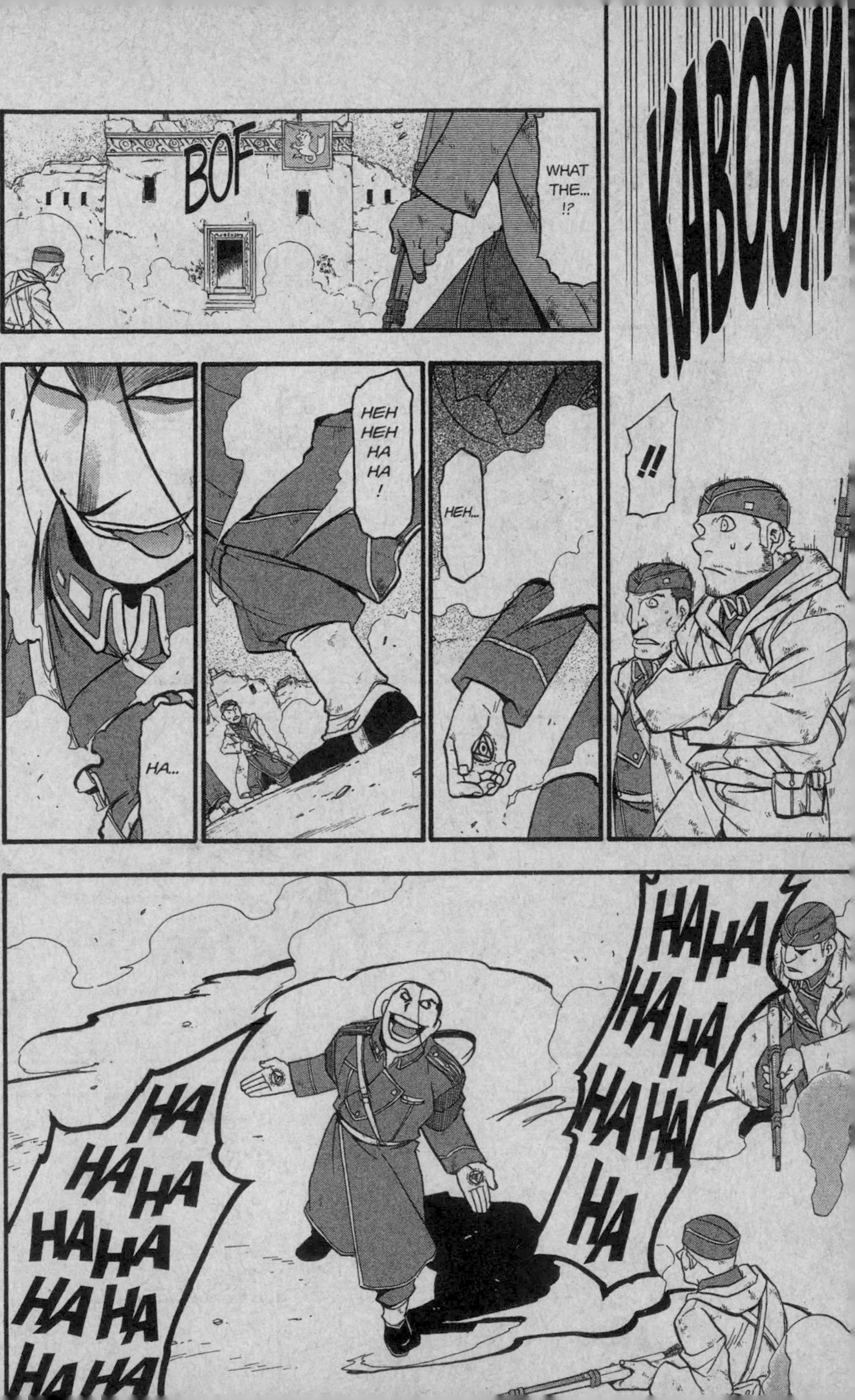
KABOOM
!!
BOF
WHAT THE... !?
HEH...
HEH HEH HA HA !
HA...
HA HA HA HA HA HA HA HA HA HA HA
HA HA HA HA HA HA HA HA HA HA HA

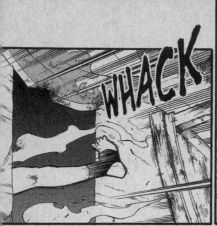

WHACK

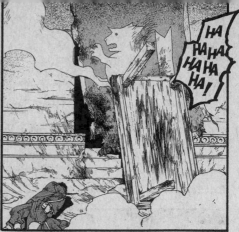

HA HA HA HA HA HA HA!

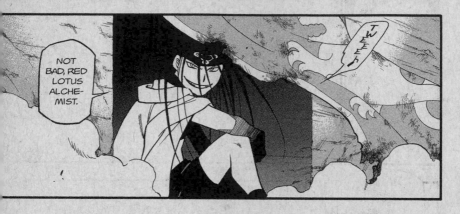

NOT BAD, RED LOTUS ALCHEMIST.

TWEEE

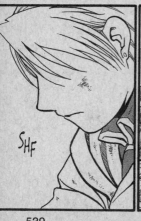

SHF

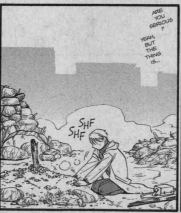

ARE YOU SERIOUS?

YEAH, BUT THE THING IS...

SHF SHF

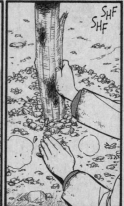

SHF SHF

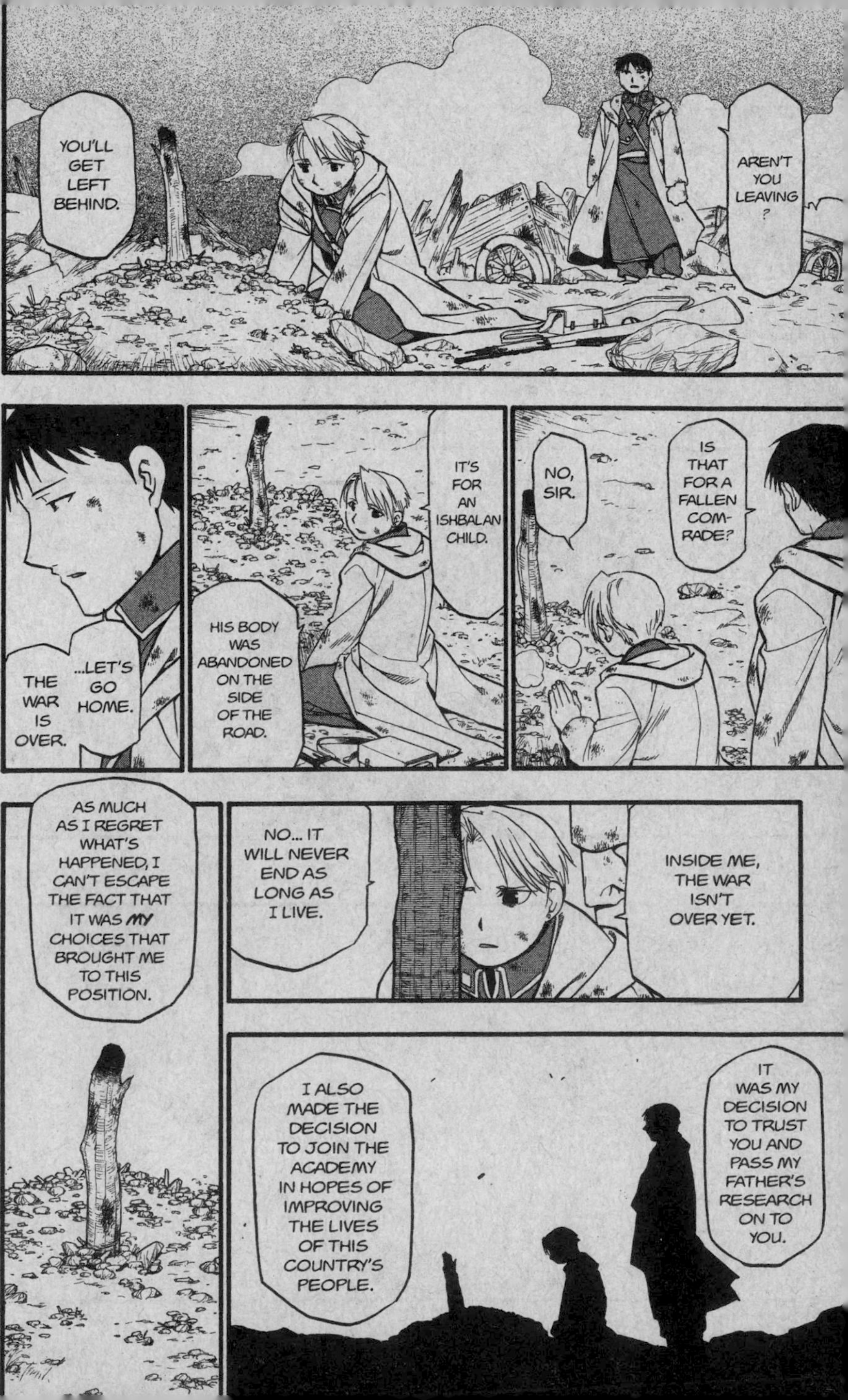
AREN'T YOU LEAVING?
YOU'LL GET LEFT BEHIND.
IS THAT FOR A FALLEN COMRADE?
NO, SIR.
IT'S FOR AN ISHBALAN CHILD.
HIS BODY WAS ABANDONED ON THE SIDE OF THE ROAD.
...LET'S GO HOME.
THE WAR IS OVER.
INSIDE ME, THE WAR ISN'T OVER YET.
NO... IT WILL NEVER END AS LONG AS I LIVE.
IT WAS MY DECISION TO TRUST YOU AND PASS MY FATHER'S RESEARCH ON TO YOU.
I ALSO MADE THE DECISION TO JOIN THE ACADEMY IN HOPES OF IMPROVING THE LIVES OF THIS COUNTRY'S PEOPLE.
AS MUCH AS I REGRET WHAT'S HAPPENED, I CAN'T ESCAPE THE FACT THAT IT WAS *MY* CHOICES THAT BROUGHT ME TO THIS POSITION.

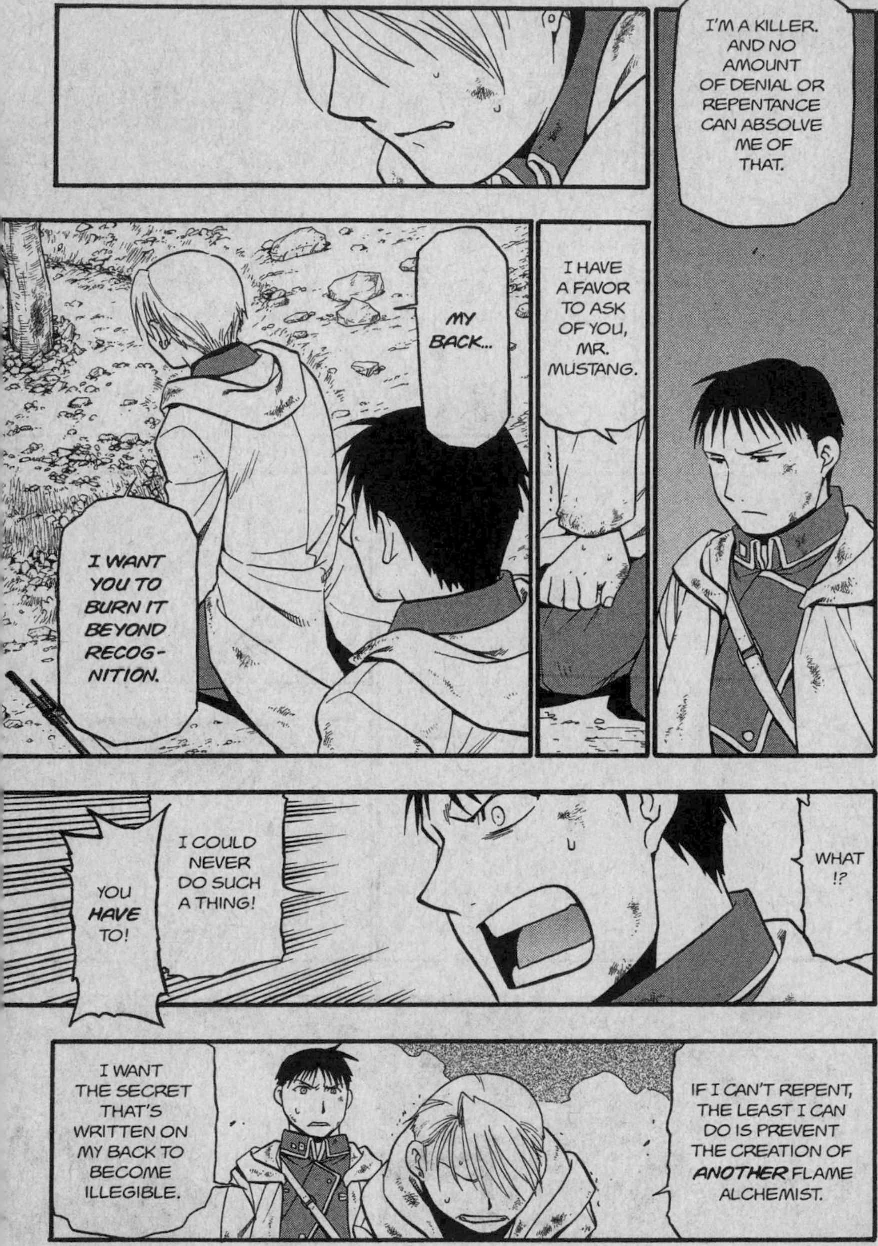
I'M A KILLER. AND NO AMOUNT OF DENIAL OR REPENTANCE CAN ABSOLVE ME OF THAT.
I HAVE A FAVOR TO ASK OF YOU, MR. MUSTANG.
MY BACK...
I WANT YOU TO BURN IT BEYOND RECOG-NITION.
WHAT !?
I COULD NEVER DO SUCH A THING!
YOU HAVE TO!
IF I CAN'T REPENT, THE LEAST I CAN DO IS PREVENT THE CREATION OF ANOTHER FLAME ALCHEMIST.
I WANT THE SECRET THAT'S WRITTEN ON MY BACK TO BECOME ILLEGIBLE.

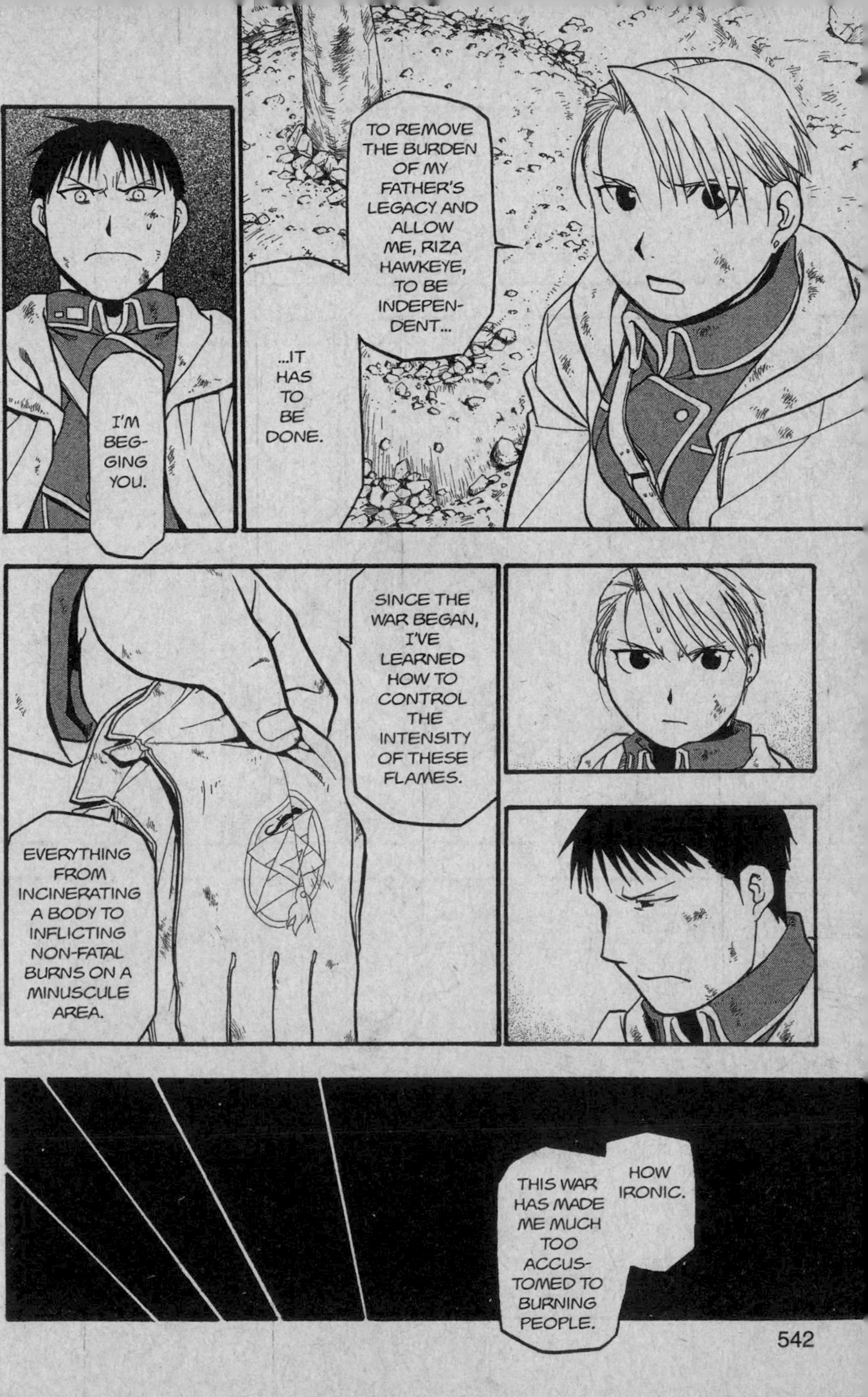
TO REMOVE THE BURDEN OF MY FATHER'S LEGACY AND ALLOW ME, RIZA HAWKEYE, TO BE INDEPENDENT...
...IT HAS TO BE DONE.
I'M BEGGING YOU.
SINCE THE WAR BEGAN, I'VE LEARNED HOW TO CONTROL THE INTENSITY OF THESE FLAMES.
EVERYTHING FROM INCINERATING A BODY TO INFLICTING NON-FATAL BURNS ON A MINUSCULE AREA.
HOW IRONIC.
THIS WAR HAS MADE ME MUCH TOO ACCUSTOMED TO BURNING PEOPLE.

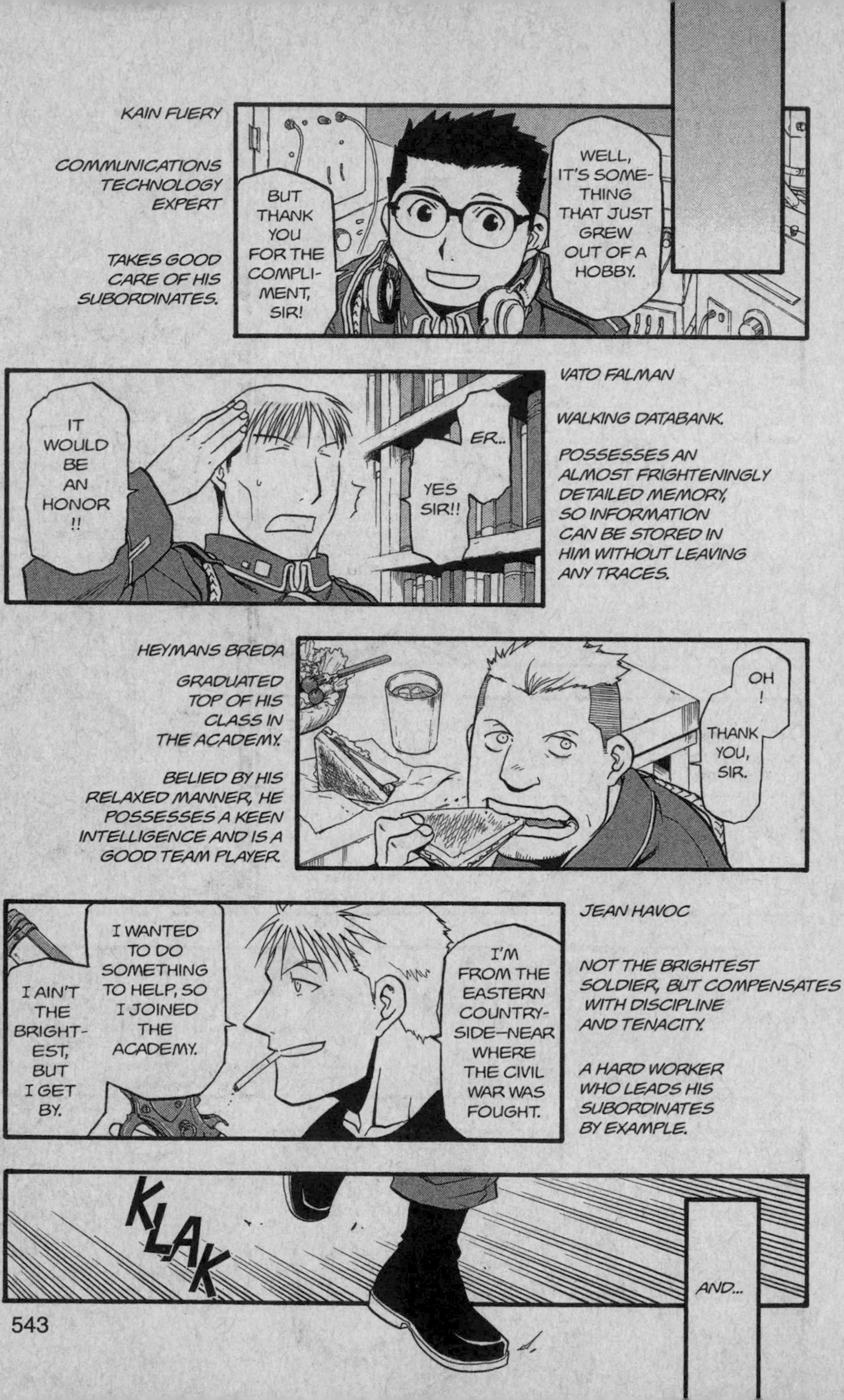
WELL, IT'S SOME-THING THAT JUST GREW OUT OF A HOBBY.
BUT THANK YOU FOR THE COMPLI-MENT, SIR!
KAIN FUERY
COMMUNICATIONS TECHNOLOGY EXPERT
TAKES GOOD CARE OF HIS SUBORDINATES.
VATO FALMAN
WALKING DATABANK.
POSSESSES AN ALMOST FRIGHTENINGLY DETAILED MEMORY, SO INFORMATION CAN BE STORED IN HIM WITHOUT LEAVING ANY TRACES.
ER...
YES SIR!!
IT WOULD BE AN HONOR!!
OH! THANK YOU, SIR.
HEYMANS BREDA
GRADUATED TOP OF HIS CLASS IN THE ACADEMY.
BELIED BY HIS RELAXED MANNER, HE POSSESSES A KEEN INTELLIGENCE AND IS A GOOD TEAM PLAYER.
JEAN HAVOC
NOT THE BRIGHTEST SOLDIER, BUT COMPENSATES WITH DISCIPLINE AND TENACITY.
A HARD WORKER WHO LEADS HIS SUBORDINATES BY EXAMPLE.
I'M FROM THE EASTERN COUNTRY-SIDE—NEAR WHERE THE CIVIL WAR WAS FOUGHT.
I WANTED TO DO SOMETHING TO HELP, SO I JOINED THE ACADEMY.
I AIN'T THE BRIGHT-EST, BUT I GET BY.
AND...
KLAK

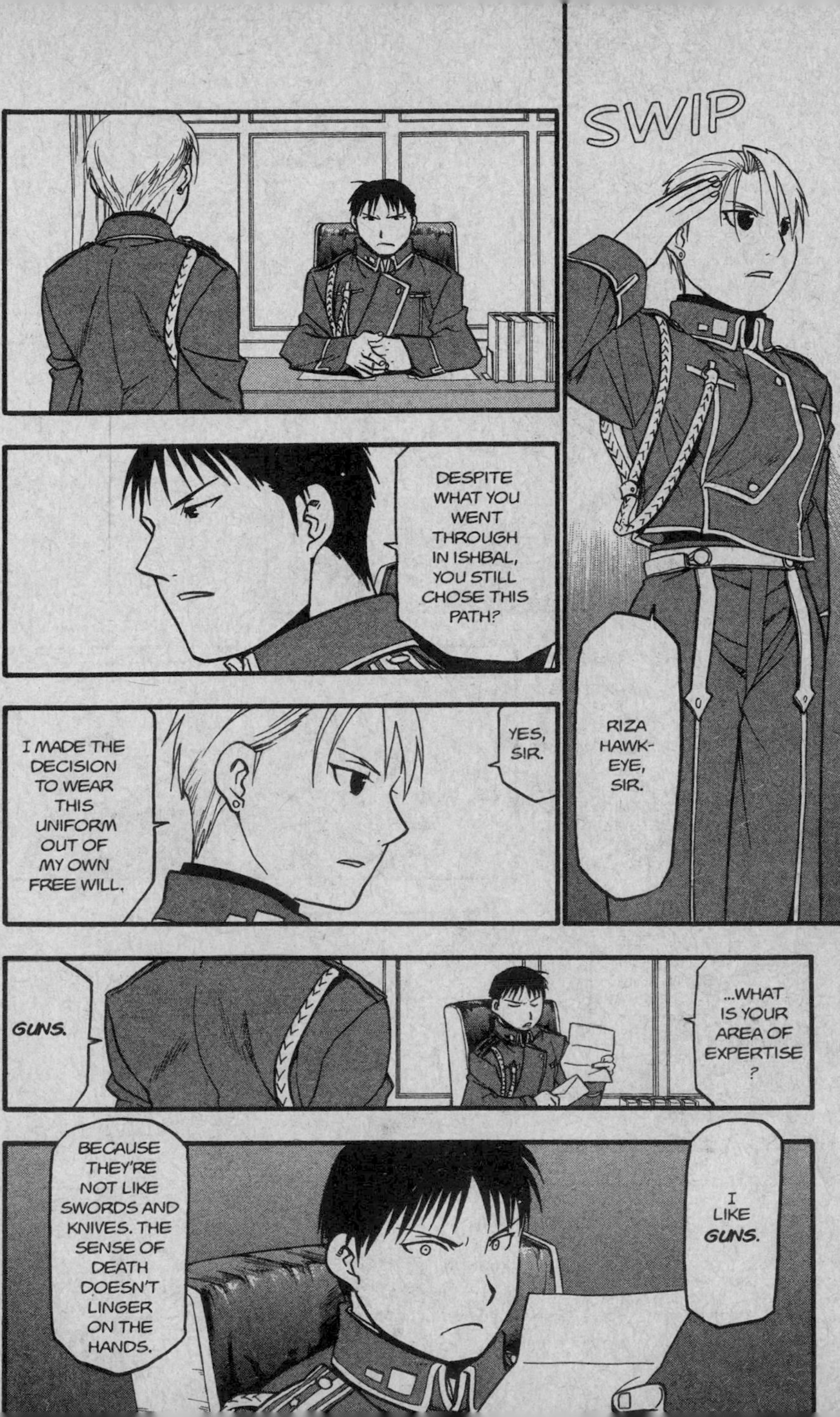
SWIP
RIZA HAWKEYE, SIR.
DESPITE WHAT YOU WENT THROUGH IN ISHBAL, YOU STILL CHOSE THIS PATH?
YES, SIR.
I MADE THE DECISION TO WEAR THIS UNIFORM OUT OF MY OWN FREE WILL.
...WHAT IS YOUR AREA OF EXPERTISE?
GUNS.
I LIKE GUNS.
BECAUSE THEY'RE NOT LIKE SWORDS AND KNIVES. THE SENSE OF DEATH DOESN'T LINGER ON THE HANDS.

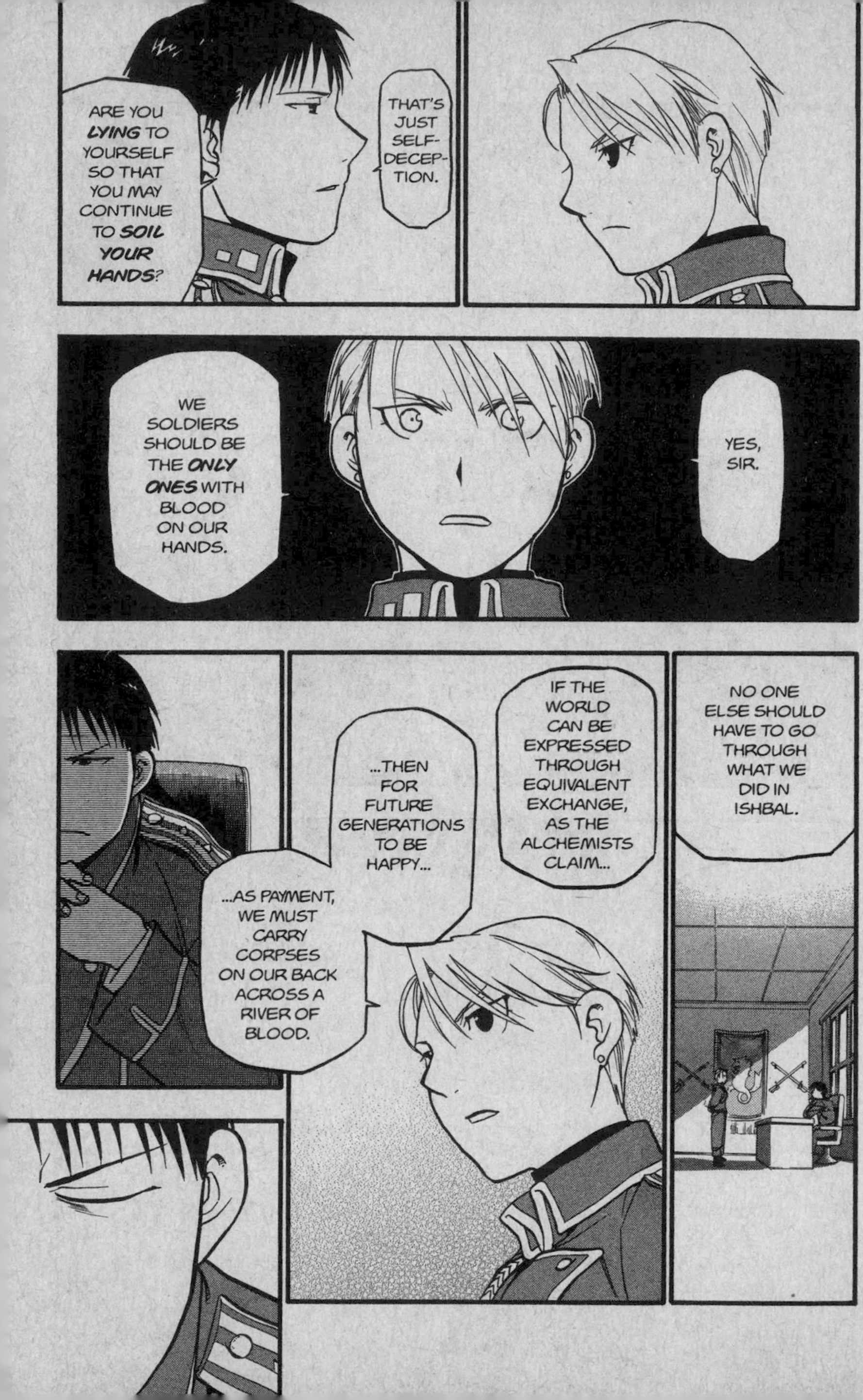
THAT'S JUST SELF-DECEPTION.
ARE YOU **LYING** TO YOURSELF SO THAT YOU MAY CONTINUE TO **SOIL YOUR HANDS**?
YES, SIR.
WE SOLDIERS SHOULD BE THE **ONLY ONES** WITH BLOOD ON OUR HANDS.
NO ONE ELSE SHOULD HAVE TO GO THROUGH WHAT WE DID IN ISHBAL.
IF THE WORLD CAN BE EXPRESSED THROUGH EQUIVALENT EXCHANGE, AS THE ALCHEMISTS CLAIM...
...THEN FOR FUTURE GENERATIONS TO BE HAPPY...
...AS PAYMENT, WE MUST CARRY CORPSES ON OUR BACK ACROSS A RIVER OF BLOOD.

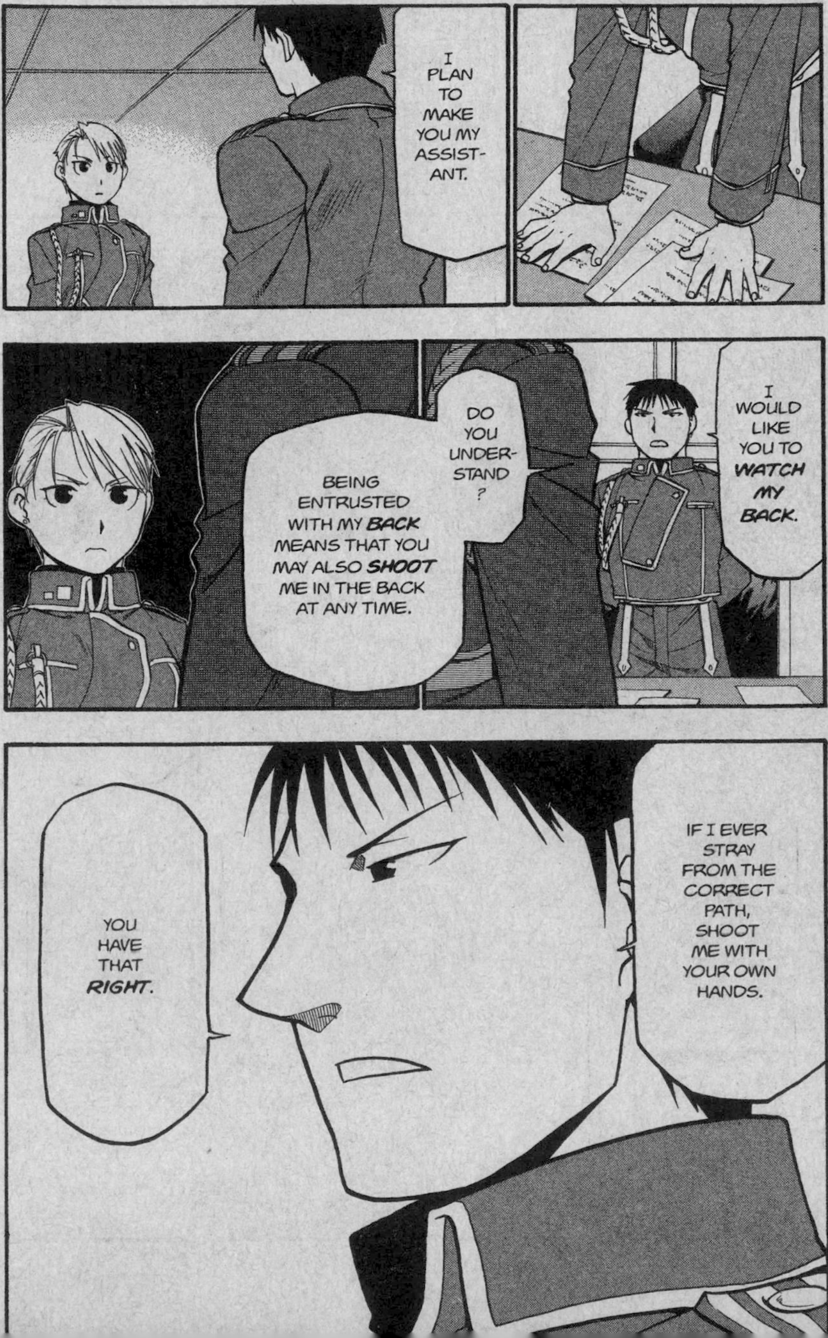

I PLAN TO MAKE YOU MY ASSISTANT.
I WOULD LIKE YOU TO WATCH MY BACK.
DO YOU UNDERSTAND?
BEING ENTRUSTED WITH MY BACK MEANS THAT YOU MAY ALSO SHOOT ME IN THE BACK AT ANY TIME.
IF I EVER STRAY FROM THE CORRECT PATH, SHOOT ME WITH YOUR OWN HANDS.
YOU HAVE THAT RIGHT.

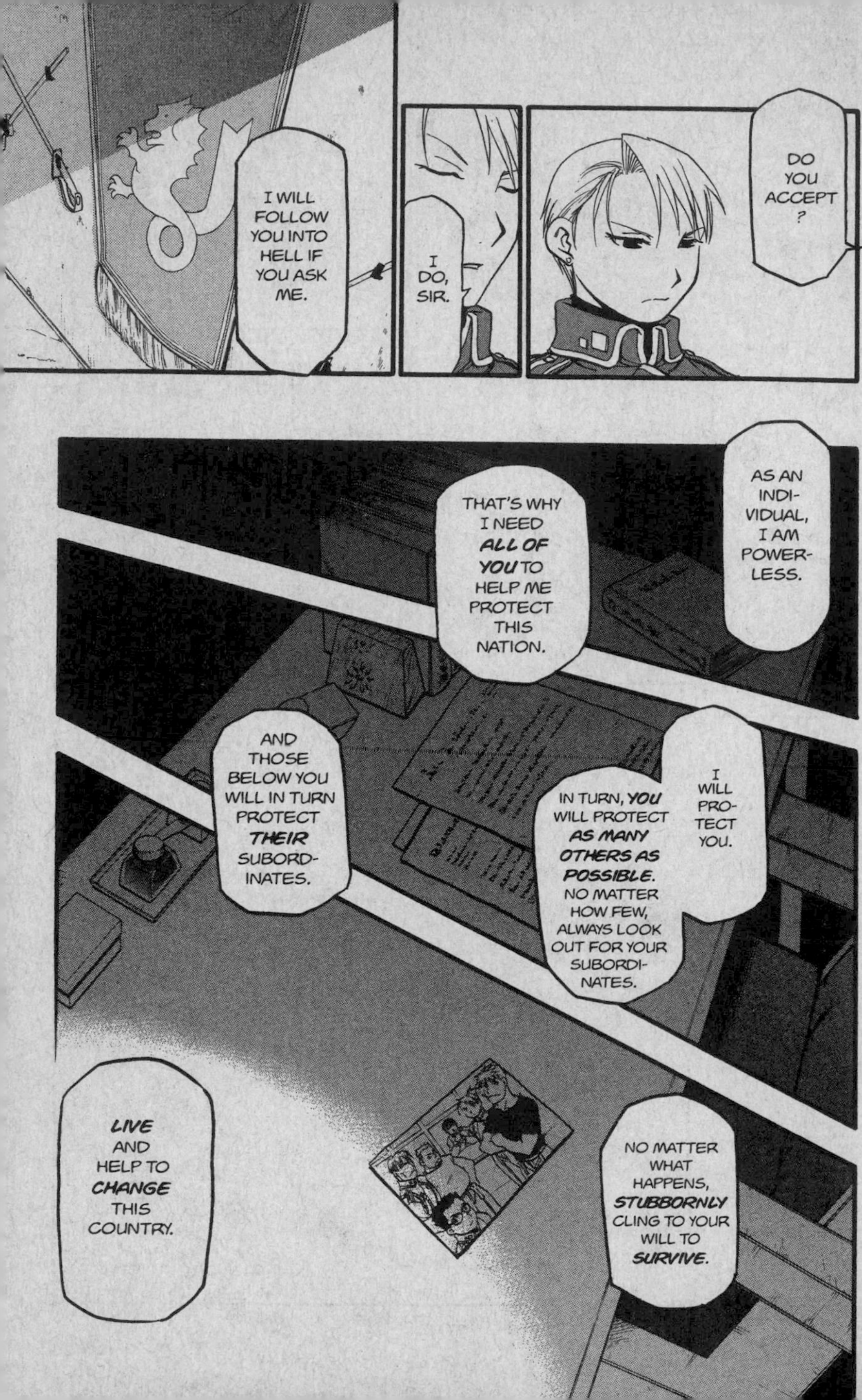
DO YOU ACCEPT?
I DO, SIR.
I WILL FOLLOW YOU INTO HELL IF YOU ASK ME.
AS AN INDI-VIDUAL, I AM POWER-LESS.
THAT'S WHY I NEED **ALL OF YOU** TO HELP ME PROTECT THIS NATION.
I WILL PRO-TECT YOU.
IN TURN, **YOU** WILL PROTECT **AS MANY OTHERS AS POSSIBLE.** NO MATTER HOW FEW, ALWAYS LOOK OUT FOR YOUR SUBORDI-NATES.
AND THOSE BELOW YOU WILL IN TURN PROTECT **THEIR** SUBORD-INATES.
NO MATTER WHAT HAPPENS, **STUBBORNLY** CLING TO YOUR WILL TO **SURVIVE**.
LIVE AND HELP TO **CHANGE** THIS COUNTRY.

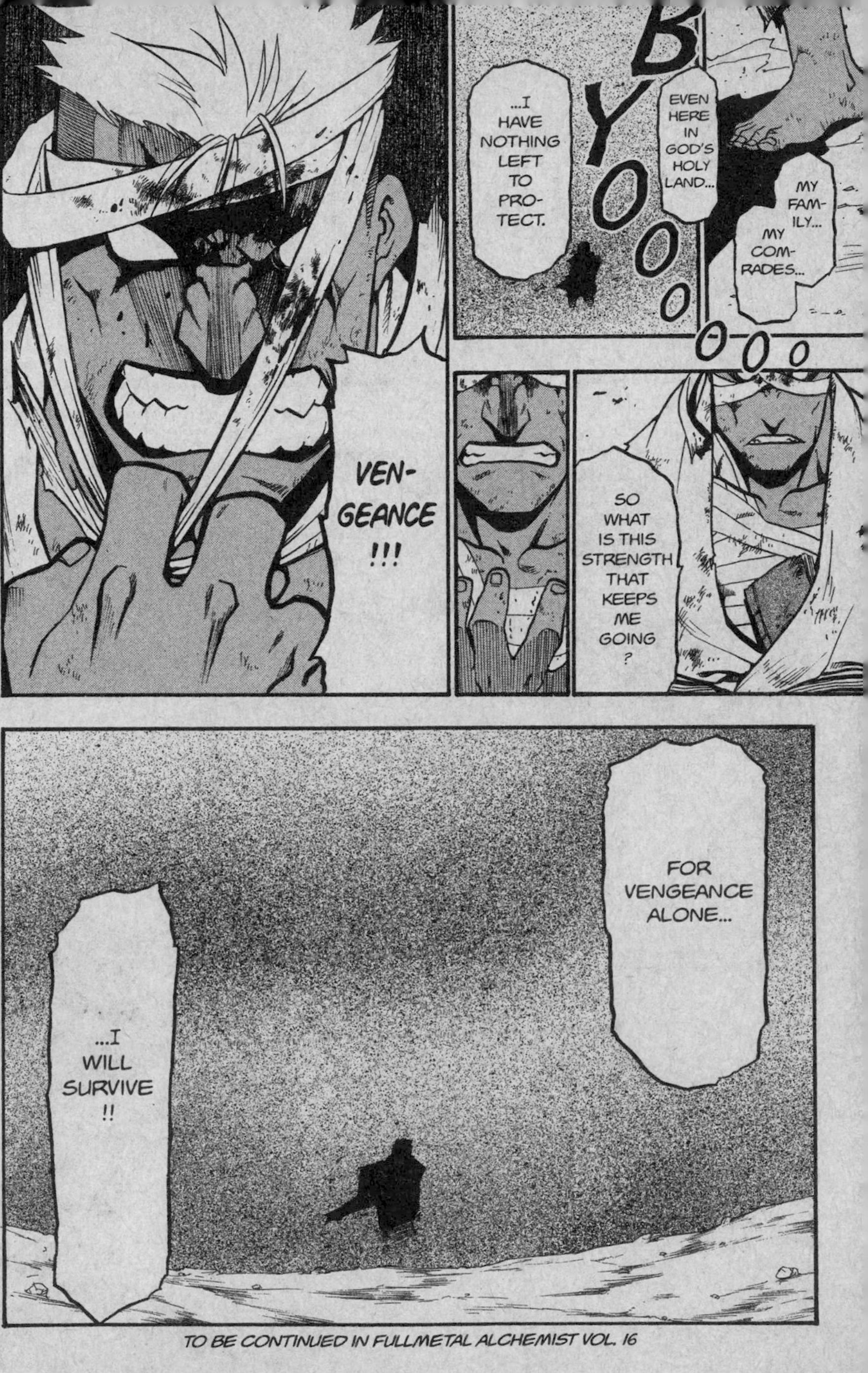
BYOOOOOOOO
EVEN HERE IN GOD'S HOLY LAND...
MY FAMILY... MY COMRADES...
...I HAVE NOTHING LEFT TO PROTECT.
SO WHAT IS THIS STRENGTH THAT KEEPS ME GOING?
VENGEANCE!!!
FOR VENGEANCE ALONE...
...I WILL SURVIVE!!

TO BE CONTINUED IN FULLMETAL ALCHEMIST VOL. 16

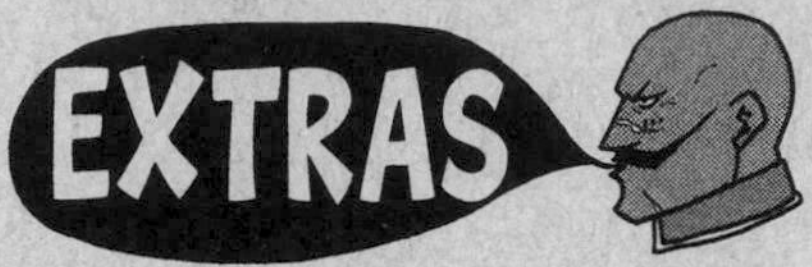
EXTRAS

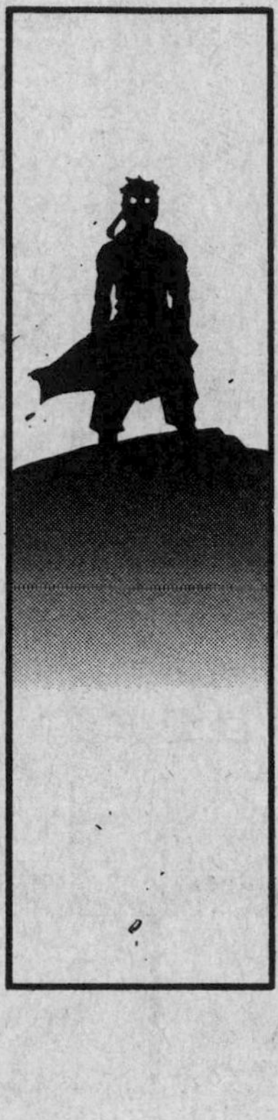
SCAR FROM CHAPTER 61

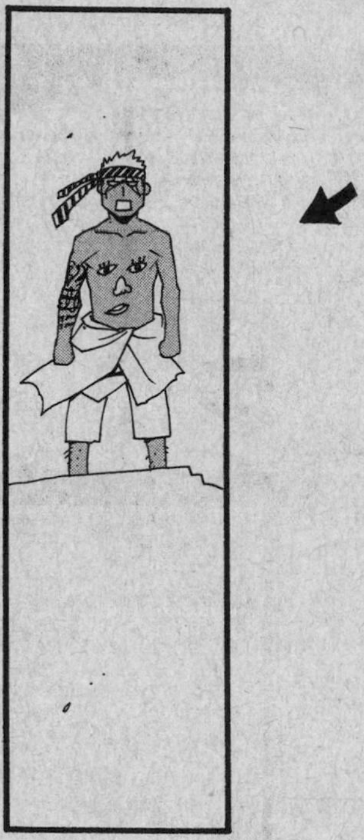
THIS IS WHY YOU SHOULD NEVER FALL ASLEEP AROUND YOUR SO-CALLED "FRIENDS."

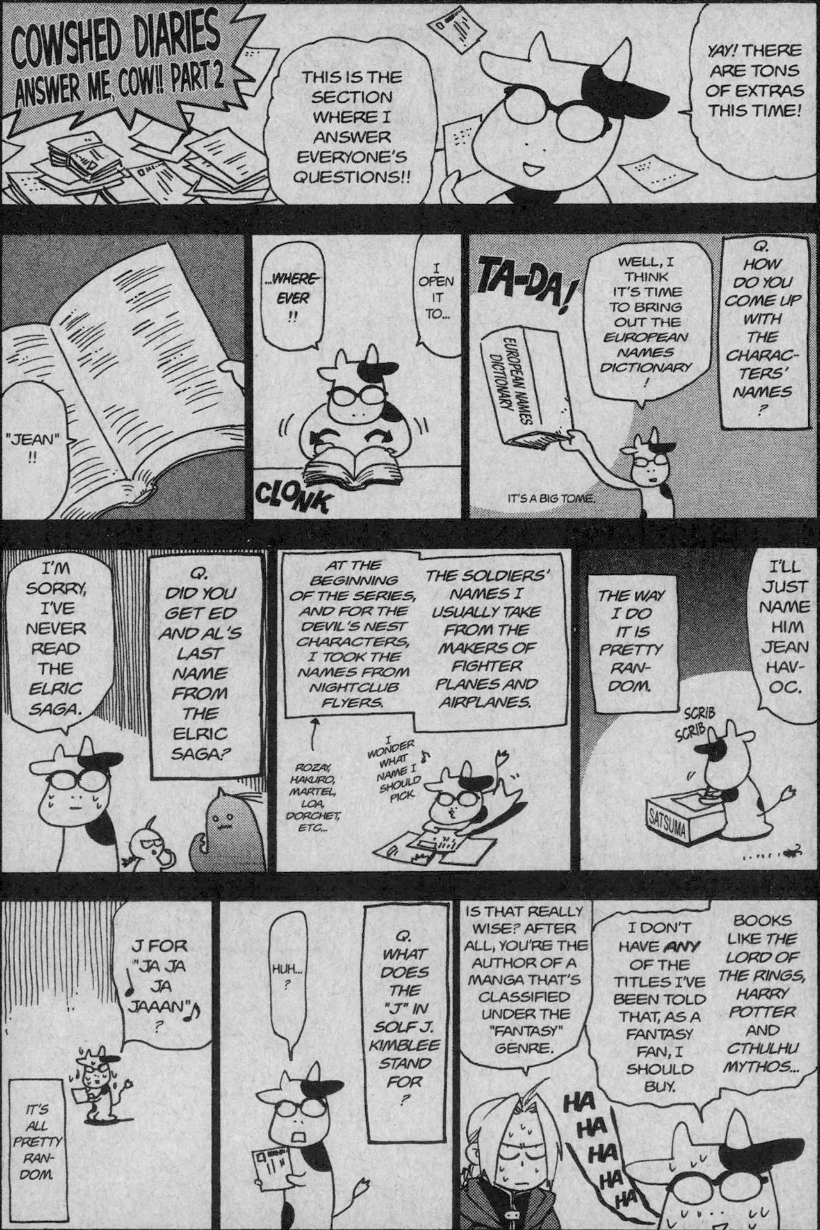
COWSHED DIARIES
ANSWER ME, COW!! PART 2
YAY! THERE ARE TONS OF EXTRAS THIS TIME!
THIS IS THE SECTION WHERE I ANSWER EVERYONE'S QUESTIONS!!
Q. HOW DO YOU COME UP WITH THE CHARACTERS' NAMES?
WELL, I THINK IT'S TIME TO BRING OUT THE EUROPEAN NAMES DICTIONARY!
TA-DA!
EUROPEAN NAMES DICTIONARY
IT'S A BIG TOME.
I OPEN IT TO...
...WHEREEVER!!
CLONK
"JEAN"!!
I'LL JUST NAME HIM JEAN HAVOC.
THE WAY I DO IT IS PRETTY RANDOM.
SCRIB SCRIB
SATSUMA
THE SOLDIERS' NAMES I USUALLY TAKE FROM THE MAKERS OF FIGHTER PLANES AND AIRPLANES.
AT THE BEGINNING OF THE SERIES, AND FOR THE DEVIL'S NEST CHARACTERS, I TOOK THE NAMES FROM NIGHTCLUB FLYERS.
I WONDER WHAT NAME I SHOULD PICK
ROZAY, HAKURO, MARTEL, LOA, DORCHET, ETC...
Q. DID YOU GET ED AND AL'S LAST NAME FROM THE ELRIC SAGA?
I'M SORRY, I'VE NEVER READ THE ELRIC SAGA.
BOOKS LIKE THE LORD OF THE RINGS, HARRY POTTER AND CTHULHU MYTHOS...
I DON'T HAVE ANY OF THE TITLES I'VE BEEN TOLD THAT, AS A FANTASY FAN, I SHOULD BUY.
IS THAT REALLY WISE? AFTER ALL, YOU'RE THE AUTHOR OF A MANGA THAT'S CLASSIFIED UNDER THE "FANTASY" GENRE.
HA HA HA HA HA
Q. WHAT DOES THE "J" IN SOLF J. KIMBLEE STAND FOR?
HUH...?
J FOR "JA JA JA JAAAN"?
IT'S ALL PRETTY RANDOM.

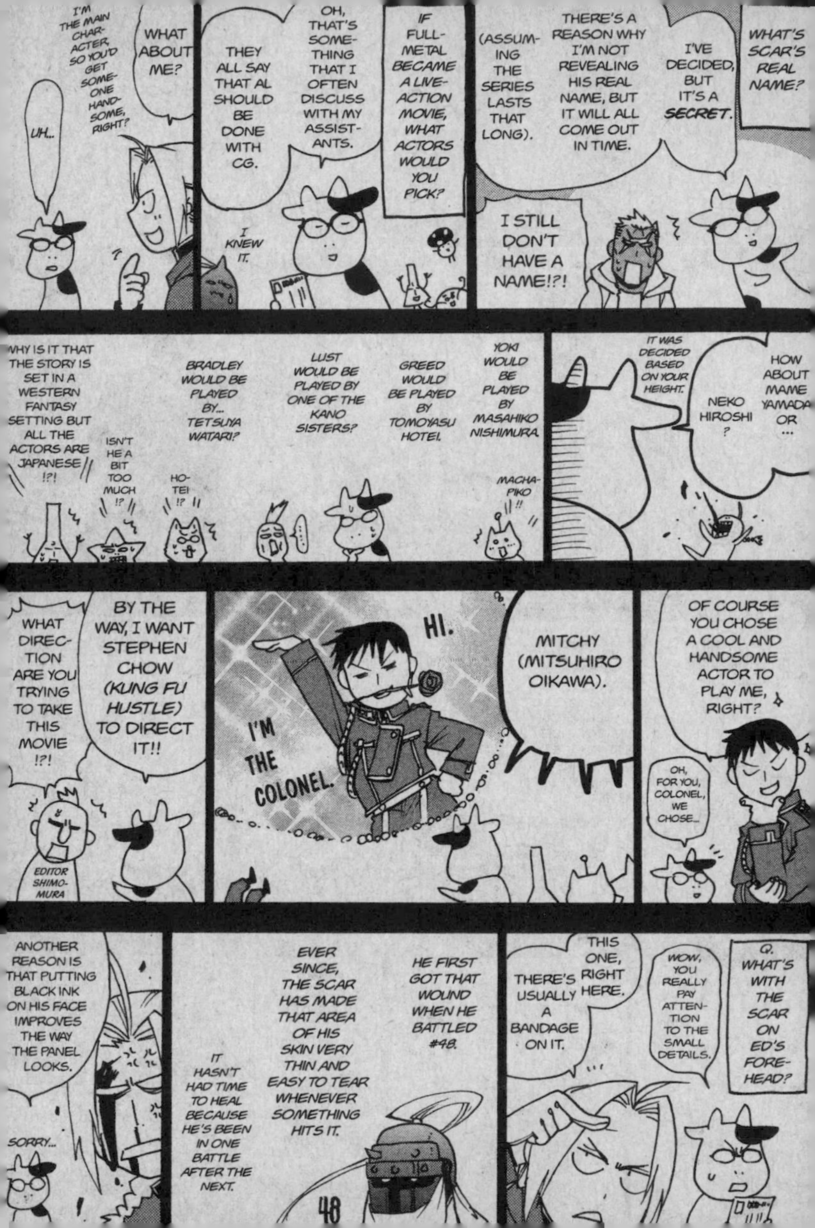
WHAT'S SCAR'S REAL NAME?
I'VE DECIDED, BUT IT'S A SECRET.
THERE'S A REASON WHY I'M NOT REVEALING HIS REAL NAME, BUT IT WILL ALL COME OUT IN TIME.
(ASSUMING THE SERIES LASTS THAT LONG).
I STILL DON'T HAVE A NAME!?!
IF FULLMETAL BECAME A LIVE-ACTION MOVIE, WHAT ACTORS WOULD YOU PICK?
OH, THAT'S SOMETHING THAT I OFTEN DISCUSS WITH MY ASSISTANTS.
THEY ALL SAY THAT AL SHOULD BE DONE WITH CG.
I KNEW IT.
WHAT ABOUT ME?
I'M THE MAIN CHARACTER, SO YOU'D GET SOMEONE HANDSOME, RIGHT?
UH...
HOW ABOUT MAME YAMADA OR ...
NEKO HIROSHI?
IT WAS DECIDED BASED ON YOUR HEIGHT.
YOKI WOULD BE PLAYED BY MASAHIKO NISHIMURA.
MACHAPIKO!!
GREED WOULD BE PLAYED BY TOMOYASU HOTEI.
LUST WOULD BE PLAYED BY ONE OF THE KANO SISTERS?
BRADLEY WOULD BE PLAYED BY... TETSUYA WATARI?
HOTEI!?
ISN'T HE A BIT TOO MUCH!?
WHY IS IT THAT THE STORY IS SET IN A WESTERN FANTASY SETTING BUT ALL THE ACTORS ARE JAPANESE!?!
OF COURSE YOU CHOSE A COOL AND HANDSOME ACTOR TO PLAY ME, RIGHT?
OH, FOR YOU, COLONEL, WE CHOSE...
MITCHY (MITSUHIRO OIKAWA).
HI.
I'M THE COLONEL.
BY THE WAY, I WANT STEPHEN CHOW (KUNG FU HUSTLE) TO DIRECT IT!!
WHAT DIRECTION ARE YOU TRYING TO TAKE THIS MOVIE!?!
EDITOR SHIMOMURA
Q. WHAT'S WITH THE SCAR ON ED'S FOREHEAD?
WOW, YOU REALLY PAY ATTENTION TO THE SMALL DETAILS.
THIS ONE, RIGHT HERE.
THERE'S USUALLY A BANDAGE ON IT.
...
HE FIRST GOT THAT WOUND WHEN HE BATTLED #48.
EVER SINCE, THE SCAR HAS MADE THAT AREA OF HIS SKIN VERY THIN AND EASY TO TEAR WHENEVER SOMETHING HITS IT.
IT HASN'T HAD TIME TO HEAL BECAUSE HE'S BEEN IN ONE BATTLE AFTER THE NEXT.
ANOTHER REASON IS THAT PUTTING BLACK INK ON HIS FACE IMPROVES THE WAY THE PANEL LOOKS.
SORRY...

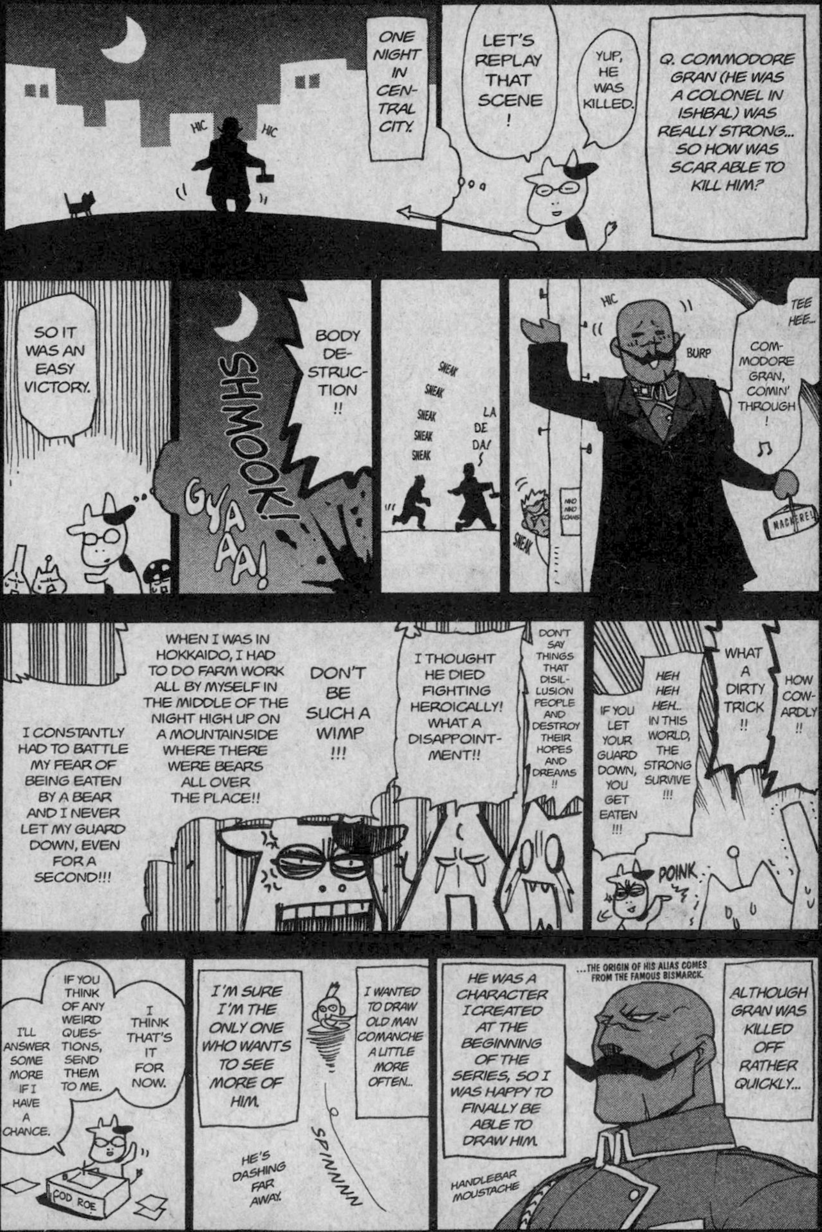
Q. COMMODORE GRAN (HE WAS A COLONEL IN ISHBAL) WAS REALLY STRONG... SO HOW WAS SCAR ABLE TO KILL HIM?
YUP, HE WAS KILLED.
LET'S REPLAY THAT SCENE!
ONE NIGHT IN CENTRAL CITY.
HIC
HIC
TEE HEE...
COMMODORE GRAN, COMIN' THROUGH!
HIC
BURP
MACKEREL
SNEAK
SNEAK
SNEAK
SNEAK
SNEAK
SNEAK
LA DE DA!
BODY DESTRUCTION!!
SHMOOK!
GYAAA!
SO IT WAS AN EASY VICTORY.
HOW COWARDLY!!
WHAT A DIRTY TRICK!!
HEH HEH HEH.. IN THIS WORLD, THE STRONG SURVIVE!!!
IF YOU LET YOUR GUARD DOWN, YOU GET EATEN!!!
POINK
DON'T SAY THINGS THAT DISILLUSION PEOPLE AND DESTROY THEIR HOPES AND DREAMS!!
I THOUGHT HE DIED FIGHTING HEROICALLY! WHAT A DISAPPOINTMENT!!
DON'T BE SUCH A WIMP!!!
WHEN I WAS IN HOKKAIDO, I HAD TO DO FARM WORK ALL BY MYSELF IN THE MIDDLE OF THE NIGHT HIGH UP ON A MOUNTAINSIDE WHERE THERE WERE BEARS ALL OVER THE PLACE!!
I CONSTANTLY HAD TO BATTLE MY FEAR OF BEING EATEN BY A BEAR AND I NEVER LET MY GUARD DOWN, EVEN FOR A SECOND!!!
ALTHOUGH GRAN WAS KILLED OFF RATHER QUICKLY...
...THE ORIGIN OF HIS ALIAS COMES FROM THE FAMOUS BISMARCK.
HE WAS A CHARACTER I CREATED AT THE BEGINNING OF THE SERIES, SO I WAS HAPPY TO FINALLY BE ABLE TO DRAW HIM.
HANDLEBAR MOUSTACHE
I WANTED TO DRAW OLD MAN COMANCHE A LITTLE MORE OFTEN...
I'M SURE I'M THE ONLY ONE WHO WANTS TO SEE MORE OF HIM.
HE'S DASHING FAR AWAY.
SPINNNN
I THINK THAT'S IT FOR NOW.
IF YOU THINK OF ANY WEIRD QUESTIONS, SEND THEM TO ME.
I'LL ANSWER SOME MORE IF I HAVE A CHANCE.
COD ROE

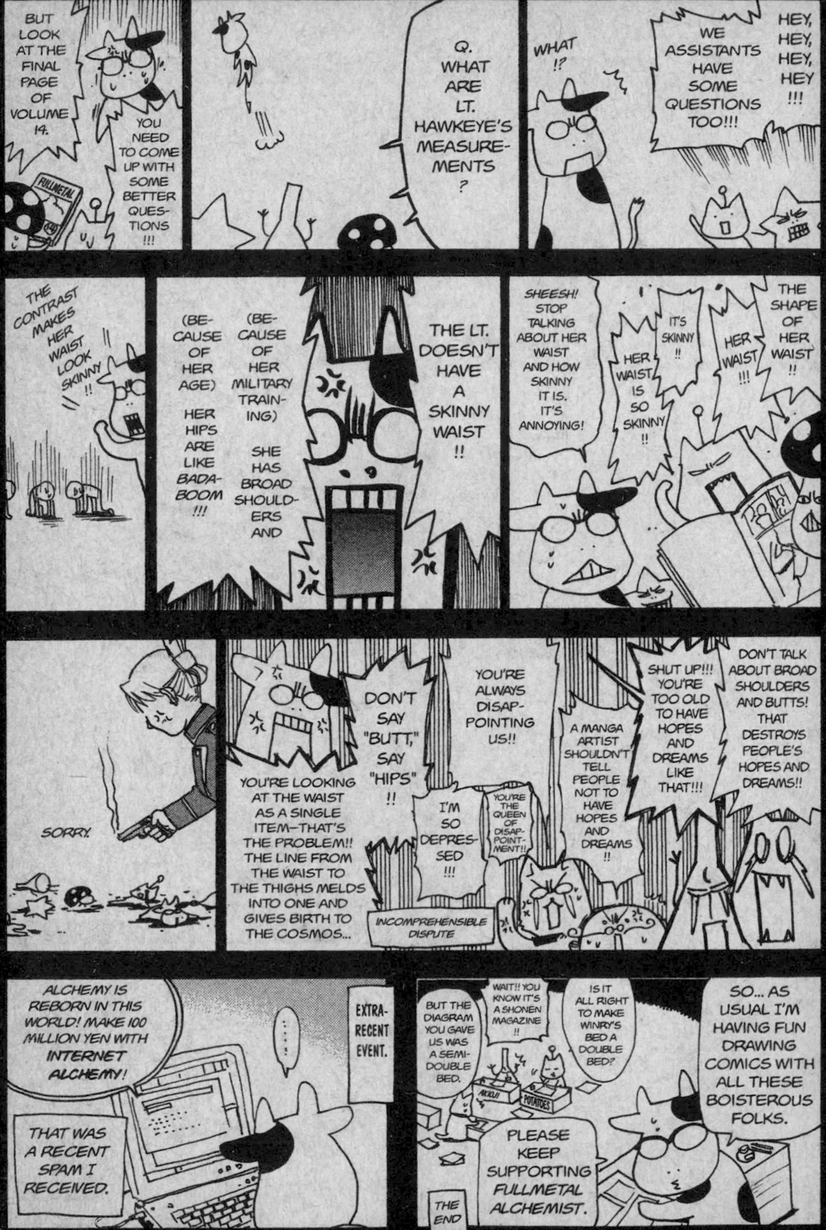
HEY, HEY, HEY, HEY!!!
WE ASSISTANTS HAVE SOME QUESTIONS TOO!!!
WHAT!?
Q. WHAT ARE LT. HAWKEYE'S MEASUREMENTS?
BUT LOOK AT THE FINAL PAGE OF VOLUME 14.
YOU NEED TO COME UP WITH SOME BETTER QUESTIONS!!!
FULLMETAL
THE SHAPE OF HER WAIST!!
HER WAIST!!!
IT'S SKINNY!!
HER WAIST IS SO SKINNY!!
SHEESH! STOP TALKING ABOUT HER WAIST AND HOW SKINNY IT IS. IT'S ANNOYING!
THE LT. DOESN'T HAVE A SKINNY WAIST!!
(BECAUSE OF HER MILITARY TRAINING) SHE HAS BROAD SHOULDERS AND
(BECAUSE OF HER AGE) HER HIPS ARE LIKE BADA-BOOM!!!
THE CONTRAST MAKES HER WAIST LOOK SKINNY!!
DON'T TALK ABOUT BROAD SHOULDERS AND BUTTS! THAT DESTROYS PEOPLE'S HOPES AND DREAMS!!
SHUT UP!!! YOU'RE TOO OLD TO HAVE HOPES AND DREAMS LIKE THAT!!!
A MANGA ARTIST SHOULDN'T TELL PEOPLE NOT TO HAVE HOPES AND DREAMS!!
YOU'RE ALWAYS DISAPPOINTING US!!
YOU'RE THE QUEEN OF DISAPPOINTMENT!!
I'M SO DEPRESSED!!!
DON'T SAY "BUTT," SAY "HIPS"!!
YOU'RE LOOKING AT THE WAIST AS A SINGLE ITEM—THAT'S THE PROBLEM!! THE LINE FROM THE WAIST TO THE THIGHS MELDS INTO ONE AND GIVES BIRTH TO THE COSMOS...
INCOMPREHENSIBLE DISPUTE
SORRY.
SO... AS USUAL I'M HAVING FUN DRAWING COMICS WITH ALL THESE BOISTEROUS FOLKS.
IS IT ALL RIGHT TO MAKE WINRY'S BED A DOUBLE BED?
WAIT!! YOU KNOW IT'S A SHONEN MAGAZINE!!
BUT THE DIAGRAM YOU GAVE US WAS A SEMI-DOUBLE BED.
POTATOES
PLEASE KEEP SUPPORTING FULLMETAL ALCHEMIST.
THE END
EXTRA-RECENT EVENT.
ALCHEMY IS REBORN IN THIS WORLD! MAKE 100 MILLION YEN WITH INTERNET ALCHEMY!
......
THAT WAS A RECENT SPAM I RECEIVED.

EDWARD AND THE MAGIC LAMP

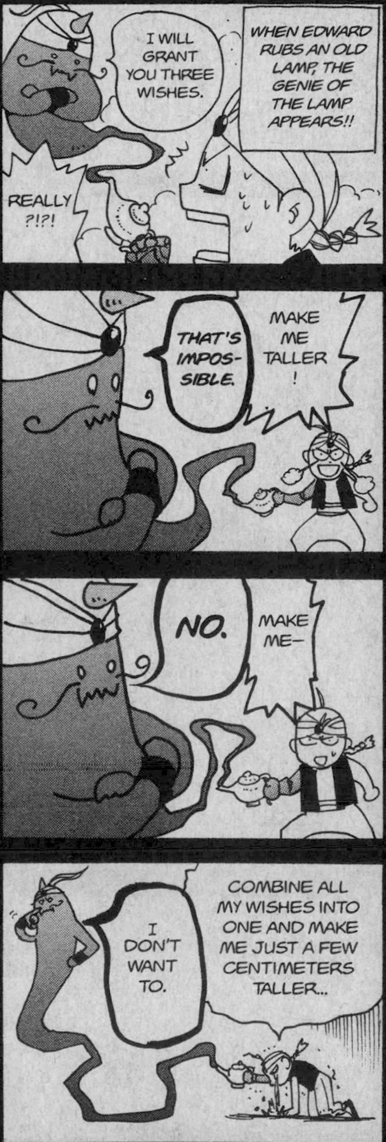
WHEN EDWARD RUBS AN OLD LAMP, THE GENIE OF THE LAMP APPEARS!!
I WILL GRANT YOU THREE WISHES.
REALLY ?!?!
MAKE ME TALLER !
THAT'S IMPOSSIBLE.
MAKE ME—
NO.
COMBINE ALL MY WISHES INTO ONE AND MAKE ME JUST A FEW CENTIMETERS TALLER...
I DON'T WANT TO.

FOR YOUR EYES...

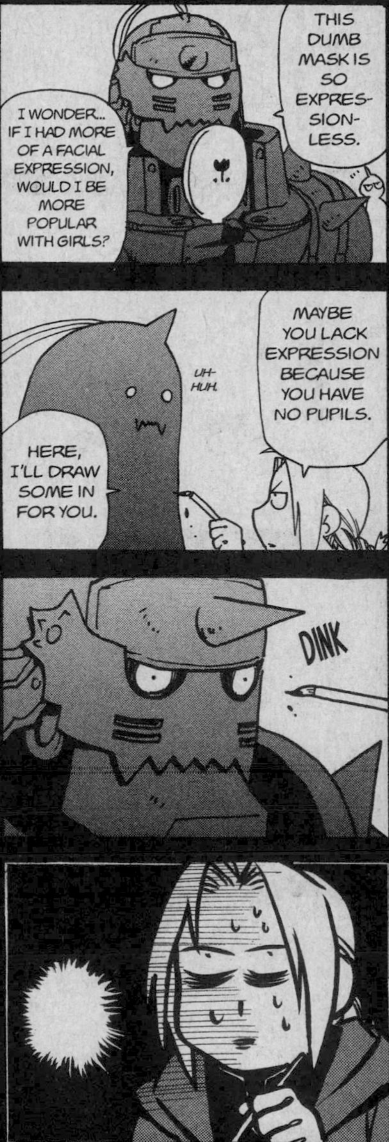
THIS DUMB MASK IS SO EXPRESSIONLESS.
I WONDER... IF I HAD MORE OF A FACIAL EXPRESSION, WOULD I BE MORE POPULAR WITH GIRLS?
MAYBE YOU LACK EXPRESSION BECAUSE YOU HAVE NO PUPILS.
UH-HUH.
HERE, I'LL DRAW SOME IN FOR YOU.
DINK

OLDER BROTHER'S WISH

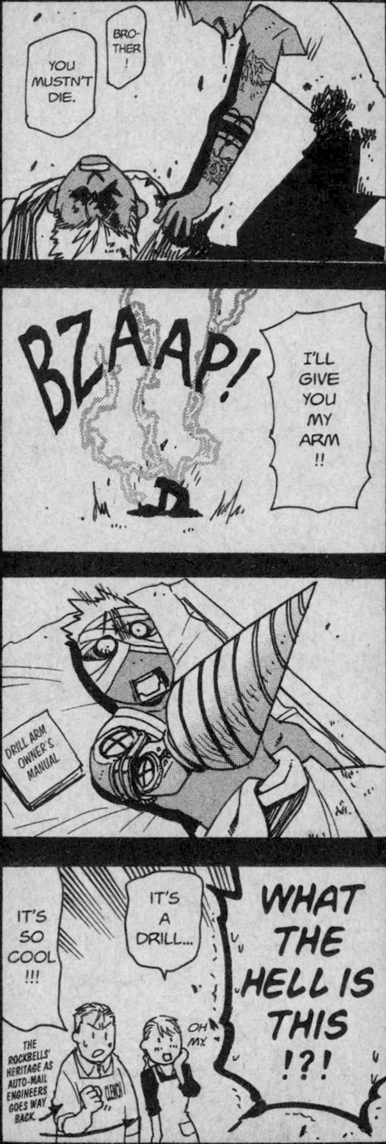
BROTHER!
YOU MUSTN'T DIE.
I'LL GIVE YOU MY ARM!!
BZAAP!
DRILL ARM OWNER'S MANUAL
WHAT THE HELL IS THIS!?!
IT'S A DRILL...
IT'S SO COOL!!!
OH MY.
CLENCH
THE ROCKBELLS' HERITAGE AS AUTO-MAIL ENGINEERS GOES WAY BACK.

PLEASE LET ME USE YOUR RESTROOM!

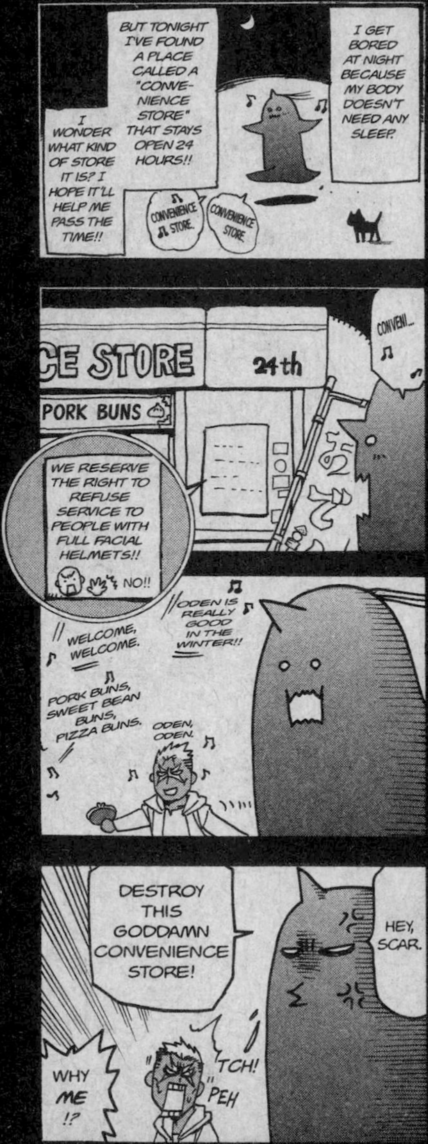
I GET BORED AT NIGHT BECAUSE MY BODY DOESN'T NEED ANY SLEEP.
BUT TONIGHT I'VE FOUND A PLACE CALLED A "CONVENIENCE STORE" THAT STAYS OPEN 24 HOURS!!
I WONDER WHAT KIND OF STORE IT IS? I HOPE IT'LL HELP ME PASS THE TIME!!
CONVENIENCE STORE
CONVENIENCE STORE.
CONVENI...
24th
CE STORE
PORK BUNS
WE RESERVE THE RIGHT TO REFUSE SERVICE TO PEOPLE WITH FULL FACIAL HELMETS!!
NO!!
ODEN IS REALLY GOOD IN THE WINTER!!
WELCOME, WELCOME.
PORK BUNS, SWEET BEAN BUNS, PIZZA BUNS.
ODEN, ODEN.
HEY, SCAR.
DESTROY THIS GODDAMN CONVENIENCE STORE!
TCH!
PEH
WHY ME!?

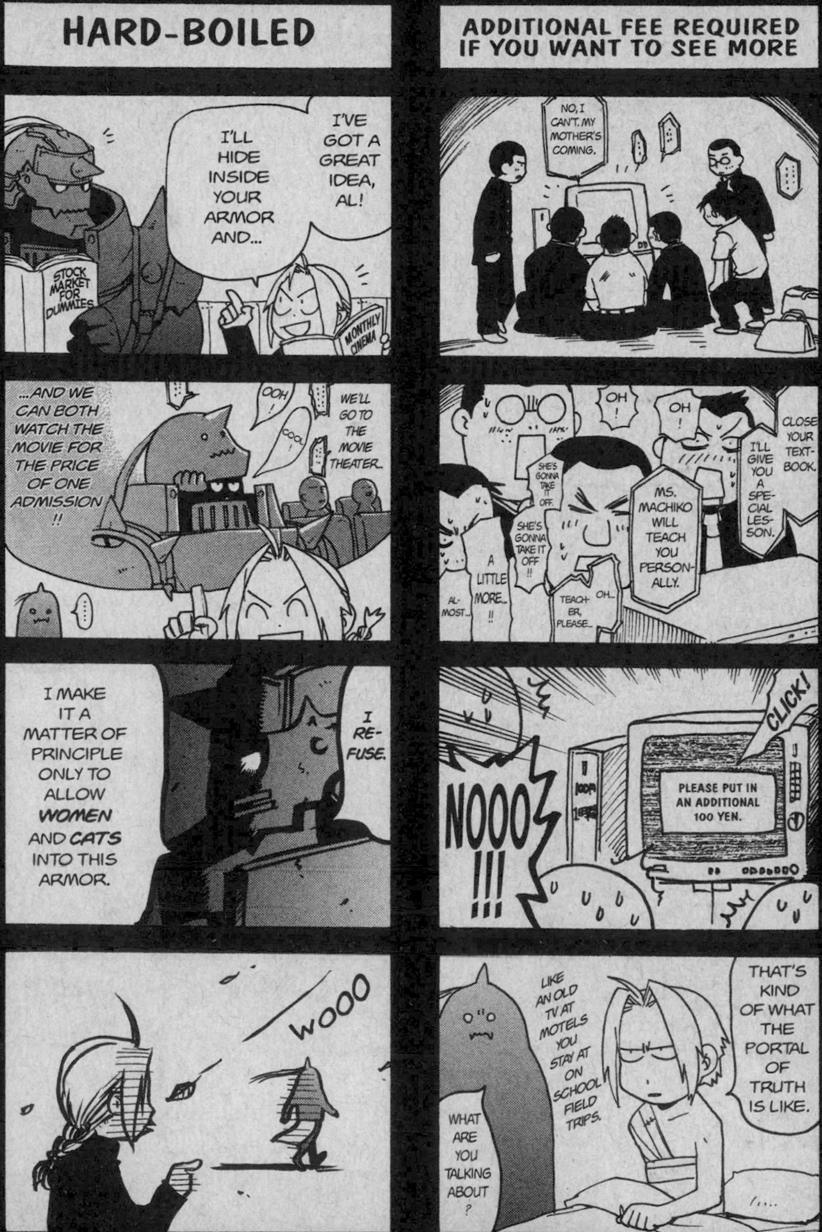
ADDITIONAL FEE REQUIRED IF YOU WANT TO SEE MORE
NO, I CAN'T. MY MOTHER'S COMING.
CLOSE YOUR TEXTBOOK.
I'LL GIVE YOU A SPECIAL LESSON.
OH !
OH !
MS. MACHIKO WILL TEACH YOU PERSONALLY.
SHE'S GONNA TAKE IT OFF.
SHE'S GONNA TAKE IT OFF !!
OH...
TEACHER, PLEASE...
A LITTLE MORE... !!
ALMOST...
CLICK!
PLEASE PUT IN AN ADDITIONAL 100 YEN.
NOOO !!!
THAT'S KIND OF WHAT THE PORTAL OF TRUTH IS LIKE.
LIKE AN OLD TV AT MOTELS YOU STAY AT ON SCHOOL FIELD TRIPS.
WHAT ARE YOU TALKING ABOUT ?
HARD-BOILED
I'VE GOT A GREAT IDEA, AL!
I'LL HIDE INSIDE YOUR ARMOR AND...
MONTHLY CINEMA
STOCK MARKET FOR DUMMIES
WE'LL GO TO THE MOVIE THEATER...
OOH !
COOL !
...AND WE CAN BOTH WATCH THE MOVIE FOR THE PRICE OF ONE ADMISSION !!
I REFUSE.
I MAKE IT A MATTER OF PRINCIPLE ONLY TO ALLOW WOMEN AND CATS INTO THIS ARMOR.
WOOO

HUMAN VS. ARTIFICIAL HUMAN

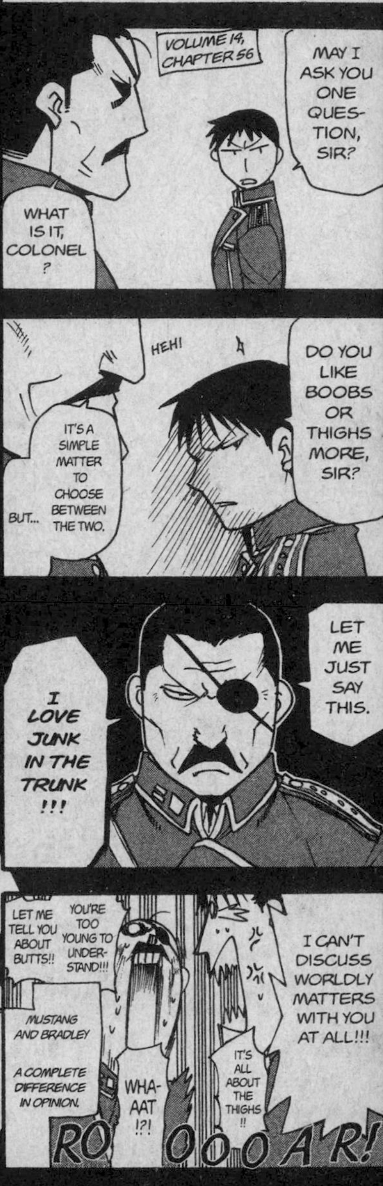
VOLUME 14, CHAPTER 56
MAY I ASK YOU ONE QUESTION, SIR?
WHAT IS IT, COLONEL?
DO YOU LIKE BOOBS OR THIGHS MORE, SIR?
HEH!
IT'S A SIMPLE MATTER TO CHOOSE BETWEEN THE TWO.
BUT...
LET ME JUST SAY THIS.
I LOVE JUNK IN THE TRUNK!!!
I CAN'T DISCUSS WORLDLY MATTERS WITH YOU AT ALL!!!
IT'S ALL ABOUT THE THIGHS!!
WHA-AAT!?!
YOU'RE TOO YOUNG TO UNDERSTAND!!!
LET ME TELL YOU ABOUT BUTTS!!
MUSTANG AND BRADLEY
A COMPLETE DIFFERENCE IN OPINION.
RO OOOAR!

FULLMETAL ALCHEMIST 15

SPECIAL THANKS to:

KEISUI TAKAEDA
SANKICHI HINODEYA
JUN TOKO
AIYABALL
NONO
BIG BROTHER YOICHI KAMITONO
MASASHI MIZUTANI
SAKAMAKI
COUPON
SAORI TAKAGI
MASANARI YUZUKA, sensei
EDITOR YOICHI SHIMOMURA

AND YOU!!

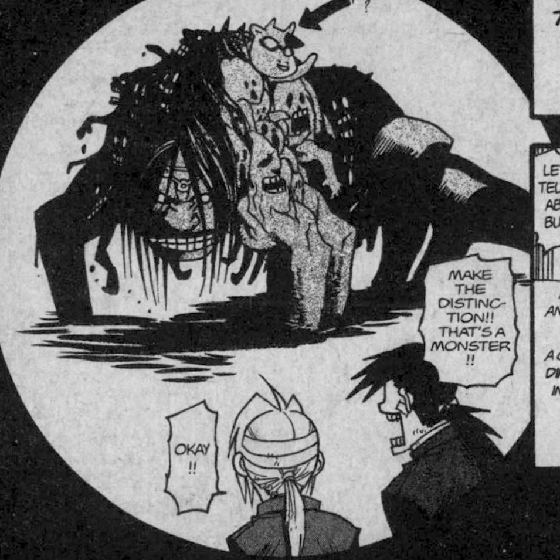
HUH?
MAKE THE DISTINCTION!! THAT'S A MONSTER!!
OKAY!!

NOW THE STORY CONTINUES...

THANK YOU FOR TELLING ME ABOUT ISHBAL.
EVERYONE CONTINUES ON THEIR PATH...
YOU WERE CHOSEN BY THIS WORN-OUT OLD MAN.
SMILE
THIS IS JUST MY WAY OF SHOWING THANKS.
...ALTHOUGH EACH IS SEARCHING FOR SOMETHING DIFFERENT.
WE WILL RETURN.

SCAR'S OLDER BROTHER DECLARED, **"THERE'S SOMETHING STRANGE ABOUT THIS COUNTRY'S ALCHEMY!!"** WHAT IS THE MEANING BEHIND HIS WORDS?! AS THE ACTION HEADS NORTH, THE CHARACTERS CONVERGE FOR A NEW CONFLICT. KIMBLEE IS RELEASED FROM INCARCERATION, AND A **NEW CHARACTER** MAKES AN APPEARANCE! WHO IS GENERAL ARMSTRONG?!

FULLMETAL ALCHEMIST 16 ON SALE NOW!

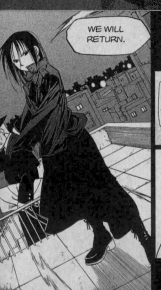

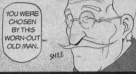

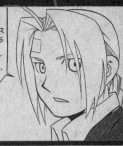

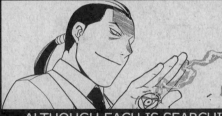

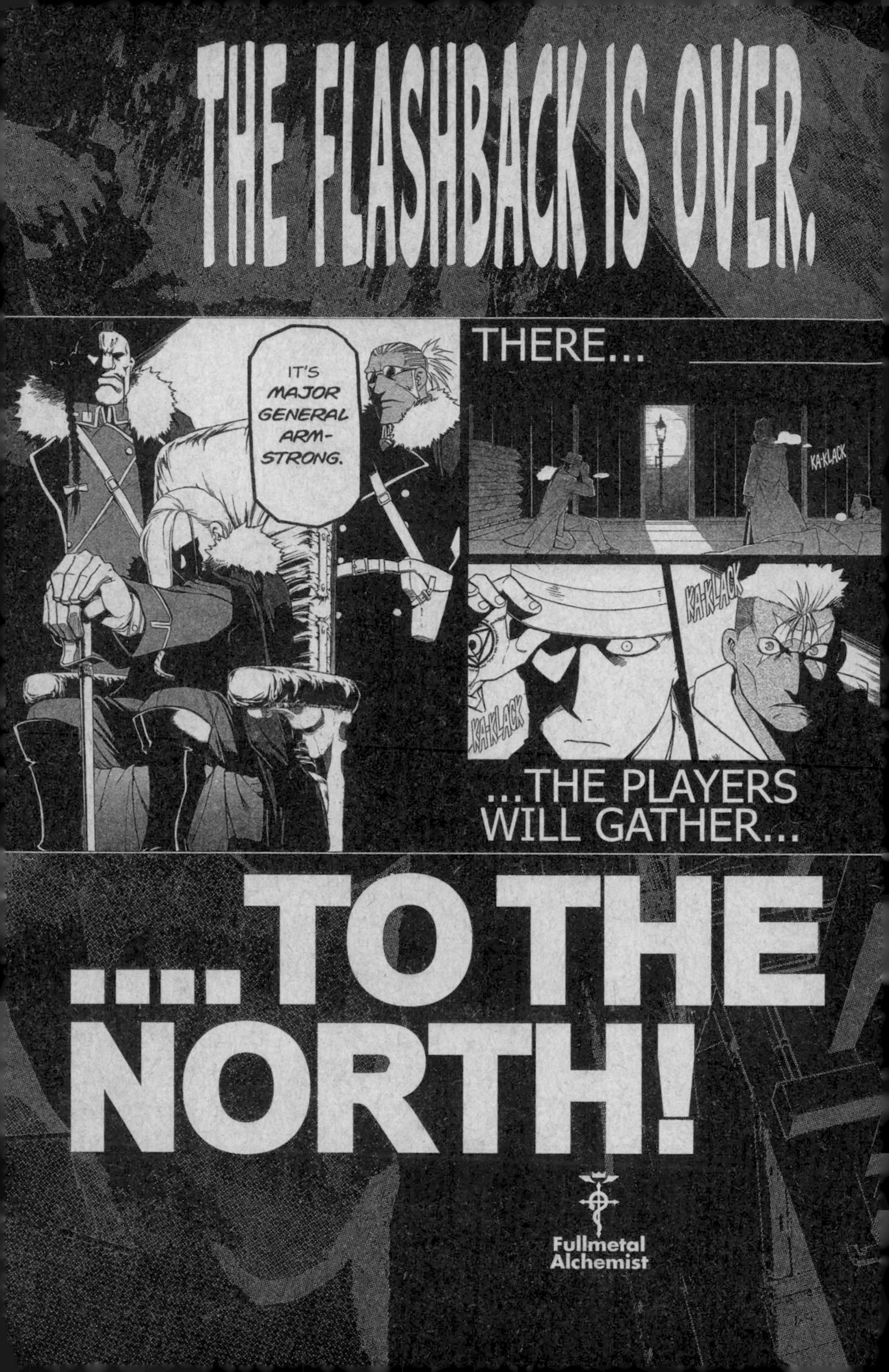
THE FLASHBACK IS OVER.
THERE...
KA-KLACK
KA-KLACK
KA-KLACK
...THE PLAYERS WILL GATHER...
IT'S MAJOR GENERAL ARM-STRONG.
...TO THE NORTH!
Fullmetal Alchemist

Whoa!!

Once again, some Elric Telepathy!!

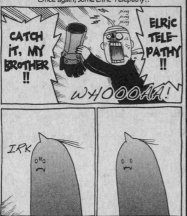

ELRIC TELEPATHY!!
ping ping ping
CATCH IT, MY BROTHER!!
WHOOOAA!
IRK

Apparently, something did reach him.

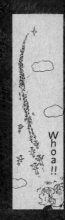

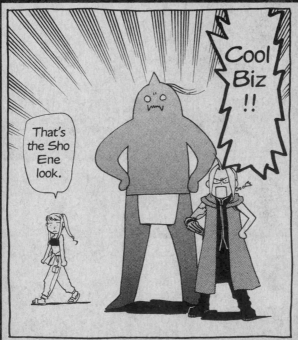

Cool Biz!!
That's the Sho Ene look.

"Cool Biz" is a Japanese fashion term coined in 2005 for dressing down in cooler/lighter business attire in order to cut down on air conditioning. "Sho Ene" was a similar attempt at energy-saving fashion from the '70s that bombed with consumers.

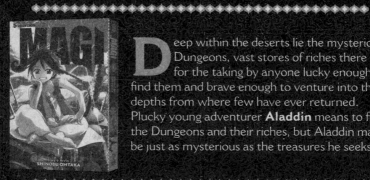

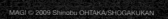

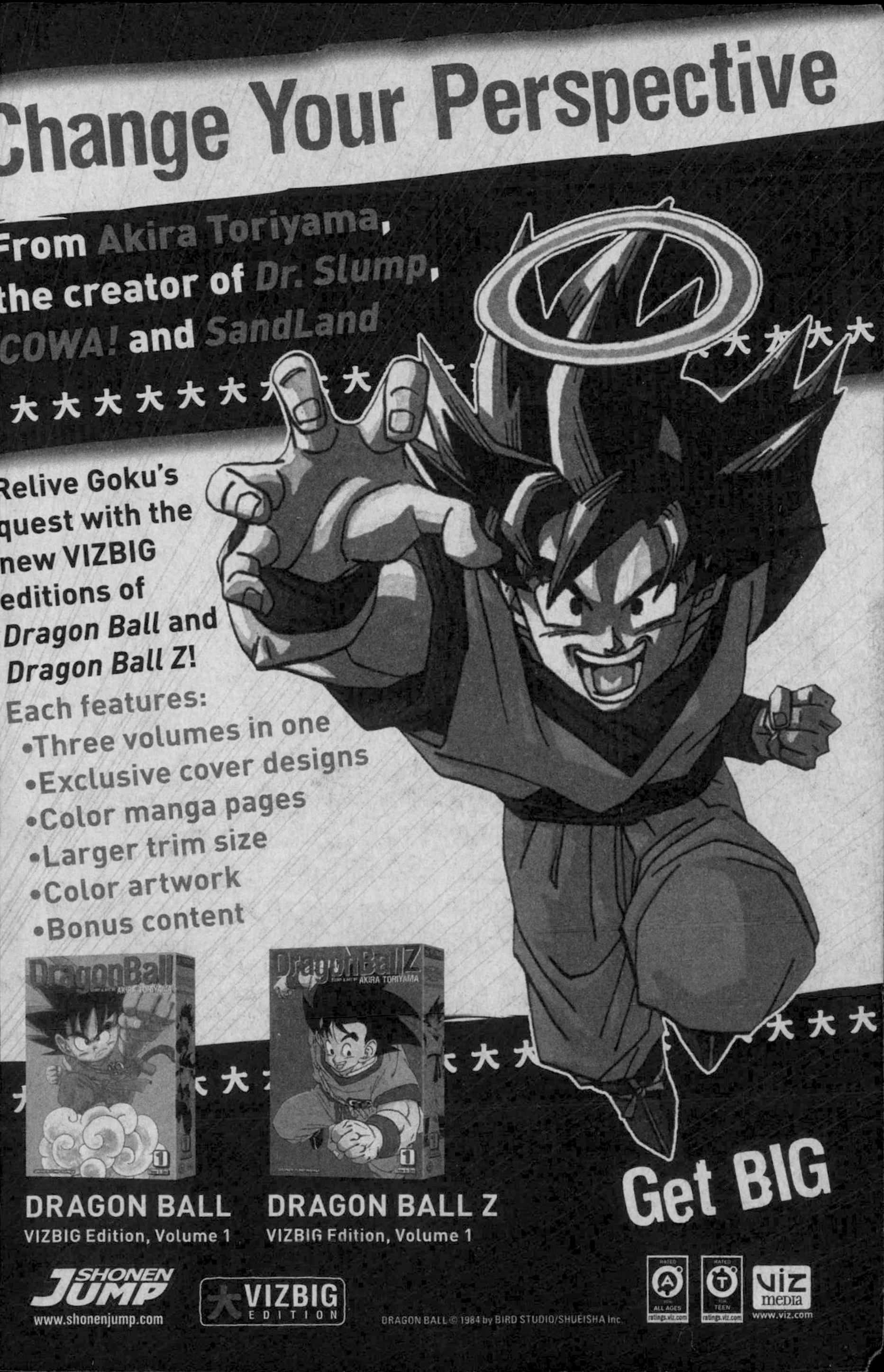
Change Your Perspective
From Akira Toriyama, the creator of Dr. Slump, COWA! and SandLand
Relive Goku's quest with the new VIZBIG editions of Dragon Ball and Dragon Ball Z!
Each features:
•Three volumes in one
•Exclusive cover designs
•Color manga pages
•Larger trim size
•Color artwork
•Bonus content
DRAGON BALL
VIZBIG Edition, Volume 1
DRAGON BALL Z
VIZBIG Edition, Volume 1
Get BIG
SHONEN JUMP
www.shonenjump.com
VIZBIG EDITION
DRAGON BALL © 1984 by BIRD STUDIO/SHUEISHA Inc.
RATED A ALL AGES ratings.viz.com
RATED T TEEN ratings.viz.com
viz media
www.viz.com

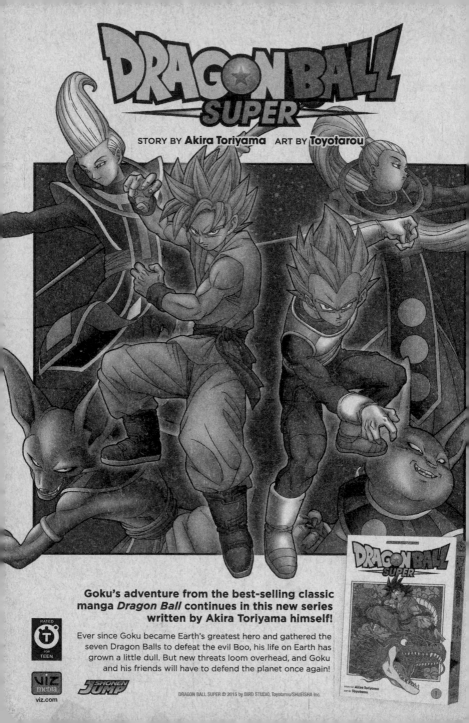

EAST BLUE
ONE PIECE
SHONEN JUMP MANGA
Eiichiro Oda

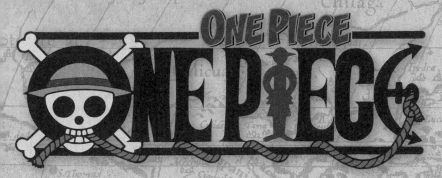

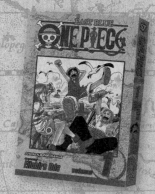

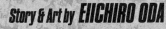

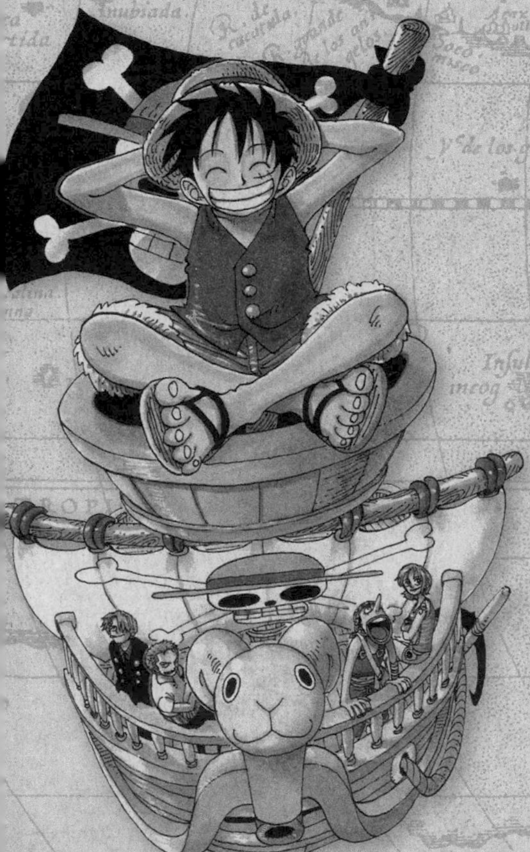

A PREMIUM BOX SET OF THE FIRST TWO STORY ARCS OF ONE PIECE!

A PIRATE'S TREASURE FOR ANY MANGA FAN!

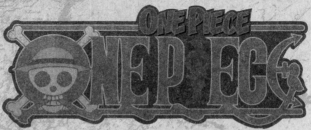

STORY AND ART BY EIICHIRO ODA

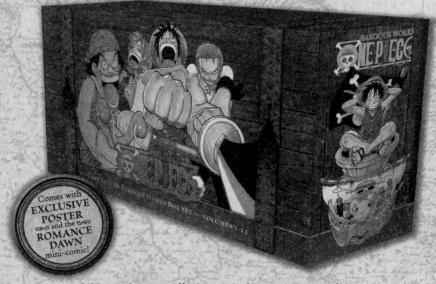

Comes with EXCLUSIVE POSTER and the ROMANCE DAWN mini-comic!

As a child, Monkey D. Luffy dreamed of becoming King of the Pirates. But his life changed when he accidentally gained the power to stretch like rubber...at the cost of never being able to swim again! Years later, Luffy sets off in search of the "One Piece," said to be the greatest treasure in the world...

This box set includes VOLUMES 1-23, which comprise the EAST BLUE and BAROQUE WORKS story arcs.

EXCLUSIVE PREMIUMS and GREAT SAVINGS over buying the individual volumes!

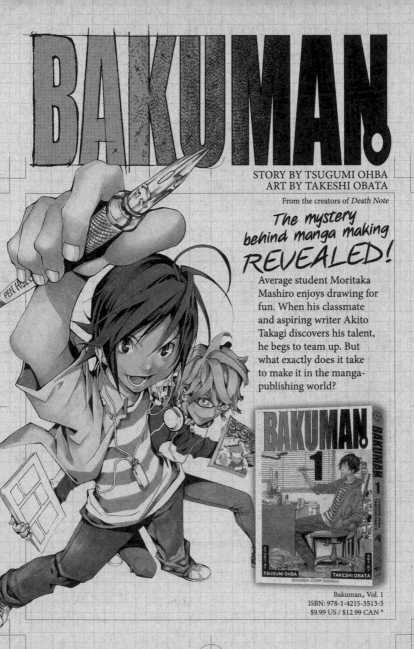

BAKUMAN.

STORY BY TSUGUMI OHBA
ART BY TAKESHI OBATA

From the creators of *Death Note*

The mystery behind manga making REVEALED!

Average student Moritaka Mashiro enjoys drawing for fun. When his classmate and aspiring writer Akito Takagi discovers his talent, he begs to team up. But what exactly does it take to make it in the manga-publishing world?

Bakuman. Vol. 1
ISBN: 978-1-4215-3513-5
$9.99 US / $12.99 CAN *

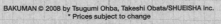

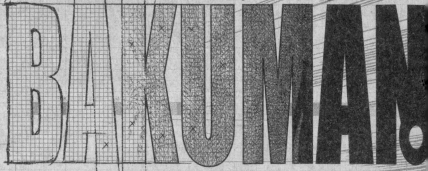
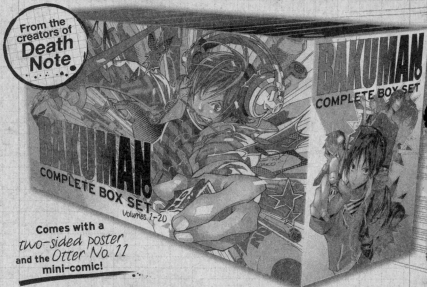
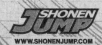

Hey! You're Reading in the Wrong Direction!

This is the **end** of this graphic novel!

To properly enjoy this VIZ graphic novel, please turn it around and begin reading from **right to left.** Unlike English, Japanese is read right to left, so Japanese comics are read in reverse order from the way English comics are typically read.

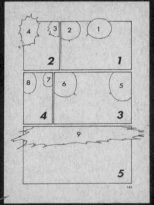

Follow the action this way

This book has been printed in the original Japanese format in order to preserve the orientation of the original artwork. Have fun with it!